THE OXFORD HANDB

EIGHTEENTH-CENTURY SATIRE

Eighteenth-century Britain thought of itself as a polite, sentimental, enlightened place, but often its literature belied that self-image. This was an age of satire, and the century's novels, poems, plays, and prints resound with mockery and laughter, with cruelty and wit. The streetlevel invective of Grub Street pamphleteers is full of satire, and the same accents of raillery echo through the high scepticism of the period's philosophers and poets, many of whom were part-time pamphleteers themselves. The novel, a genre that emerged during the eighteenth century, was from the beginning shot through with satirical colours borrowed from popular romances and scandal sheets. This *Handbook* is a guide to the different kinds of satire written in English during the 'long' eighteenth century. It focuses on texts that appeared between the restoration of the Stuart monarchy in 1660 and the outbreak of the French Revolution in 1789. Outlier chapters extend the story back to first decade of the seventeenth century, and forward to the second decade of the nineteenth. The scope of the volume is not confined by genre, however. So prevalent was the satirical mode in writing of the age that this book serves as a broad and characteristic survey of its literature. *The Oxford Handbook of Eighteenth-Century Satire* reflects developments in historical criticism of eighteenth-century writing over the last two decades, and provides a forum in which the widening diversity of literary, intellectual, and socio-historical approaches to the period's texts can come together.

THE OXFORD HANDBOOK OF

EIGHTEENTH-
CENTURY
SATIRE

Edited by
PADDY BULLARD

OXFORD
UNIVERSITY PRESS

OXFORD

UNIVERSITY PRESS

Great Clarendon Street, Oxford, OX2 6DP,
United Kingdom

Oxford University Press is a department of the University of Oxford.
It furthers the University's objective of excellence in research, scholarship,
and education by publishing worldwide. Oxford is a registered trade mark of
Oxford University Press in the UK and in certain other countries

Published in the United States of America by Oxford University Press
198 Madison Avenue, New York, NY 10016, United States of America

British Library Cataloguing in Publication Data
Data available

Library of Congress Cataloging in Publication Data
Data available

ISBN 978-0-19-872783-5 (Hbk.)
ISBN 978-0-19-285911-2 (Pbk.)

ACKNOWLEDGEMENTS

THE plan for this handbook first took shape from conversations with Tom Keymer, and the volume has continued to grow with his support. At Oxford University Press Jacqueline Norton has been the most generous and go-ahead of editors, and I have received endless help from her colleagues Aimee Wright, Lowri Ribbons, and Zackery Cuevas. Three anonymous readers of the original proposal showed how the volume could be more catholic in its coverage than I had imagined at first—my thanks to them for their careful scrutiny. The editors of four distinguished *Oxford Handbooks* gave encouragement and wise precautions at the start of the project: they were Matthew Bevis, James Harris, Peter Robinson, and David Francis Taylor. At key points I benefited from valuable advice given by James McLaverty, Isabel Rivers, Valerie Rumbold, Marcus Walsh, and Abigail Williams. I was lucky to have the help of Krissie West as copy editor during the summer of 2017, when her experience and professionalism saw the volume to the verge of completion. Most special thanks, as always, go to Rebecca Bullard.

Contents

PART I SATIRICAL ALIGNMENTS

PART II SATIRICAL INHERITANCES

PART III SATIRICAL MODES

PART IV SATIRICAL OBJECTS

PART V SATIRICAL ACTIONS

PART VI SATIRICAL TRANSITIONS

LIST OF FIGURES

LIST OF ABBREVIATIONS

For pre-1900 works the place of publication is London, unless otherwise stated. All biblical references are to the Authorized Version, unless otherwise stated. Full references are given within each individual chapter, other than for the texts whose abbreviations are listed below.

Addison and Steele

Spectator	*The Spectator*, ed. Donald F. Bond, 5 vols. (Oxford: Clarendon Press, 1965).
Tatler	*The Tatler*, ed. Donald F. Bond, 3 vols. (Oxford: Clarendon Press, 1987).

Dryden

Dryden, 'Discourse'	John Dryden, *Discourse Concerning the Original and Progress of Satire*, in Dryden, *Works*, volume 4.
Dryden, *Poems* (Longman)	*The Poems of John Dryden*, ed. Paul Hammond and David Hopkins, 5 vols. (London and New York: Longman, 1995–2005).
Dryden, *Works*	*The Works of John Dryden*, ed. H. T. Swedenberg, Jr, et al., 20 vols. (Berkeley and Los Angeles: University of California Press, 1956–2000).

Gay

Gay, *Dramatic Works*	John Gay, *Dramatic Works*, ed. John Fuller, 2 vols. (Oxford: Clarendon Press, 1983).
Gay, *Letters*	*The Letters of John Gay*, ed. C. F. Burgess (Oxford: Clarendon Press, 1966).
Gay, *Poetry and Prose*	John Gay, *Poetry and Prose*, ed. Vinton A. Dearing and Charles E. Beckwith, 2 vols. (Oxford: Clarendon Press, 1974).

Pope

Pope, *Corr.* (Sherburn)	*The Correspondence of Alexander Pope*, ed. George Sherburn, 5 vols. (Oxford: Clarendon Press, 1956).
Pope, *Dunciad Four Books*	Alexander Pope, *The Dunciad in Four Books*, ed. Valerie Rumbold (Harlow: Longman 1999).

Pope, *Poems* (Longman)	*The Poems of Alexander Pope*, ed. Julian Ferraro et al. (Harlow: Longman, 2007–).
—, iii.	*The Dunciad (1728) & The Dunciad Variorum (1729)*, ed. Valerie Rumbold (2007).
Pope, *Poems* (Twickenham)	*The Twickenham Edition of the Poems of Alexander Pope*, ed. John Butt et al., 11 vols. in 12 (London: Methuen, 1939–69).
—, i.	*Pastoral Poetry and An Essay on Criticism*, ed. E. Audra and Aubrey Williams (1961).
—, ii.	*The Rape of the Lock and Other Poems*, ed. Geoffrey Tillotson, 3rd edn. (1962).
—, iii.1	*An Essay on Man*, ed. Maynard Mack (1951).
—, iii.2	*Epistles to Several Persons* (Moral Essays), ed. F. W. Bateson, 2nd edn. (1961).
—, iv.	*Imitations of Horace with An Epistle to Dr Arbuthnot and The Epilogue to the Satires*, ed. John Butt, 2nd edn. (1953).
—, v.	*The Dunciad*, ed. James Sutherland (1943).
—, vi.	*Minor Poems*, ed. Norman Ault and John Butt, 2nd edn. (1964).
—, vii–viii.	*The Iliad of Homer*, ed. Maynard Mack et al. (1967).
—, ix–x.	*The Odyssey of Homer*, ed. Maynard Mack et al. (1967).
—, xi.	*Index* (1969).
Pope, *Prose*	*The Prose Works of Alexander Pope*
—, i.	*The Earlier Works, 1711–1720*, ed. Norman Ault (Oxford: Blackwell, 1936).
—, ii.	*The Major Works, 1725–1744*, ed. Rosemary Cowler, (Hamden, CT: Archon, 1986).

Swift

Swift, *Corr.* (Woolley)	*The Correspondence of Jonathan Swift, D.D.*, ed. David Woolley, 5 vols. (Frankfurt am Main: Lang, 1999–2014).
Swift, *Poems* (Williams)	*The Poems of Jonathan Swift*, ed. Harold Williams, 3 vols., 2nd edn. (Oxford: Clarendon Press, 1966).
Swift, *PW*	*The Prose Writings of Jonathan Swift*, ed. Herbert Davis et al., 14 vols. (Oxford: Basil Blackwell, 1939–74).
—, i.	*A Tale of a Tub and other Early Works 1696–1707*, ed. Herbert Davis (1939).
—, ii.	*Bickerstaff Papers and Pamphlets on the Church*, ed. Herbert Davis (1940).
—, iii.	*Examiner and Other Pieces Written in 1710–11*, ed. Herbert Davis (1941).
—, iv.	*A Proposal for Correcting the English Tongue, Polite Conversation, Etc.*, ed. Herbert Davis (1957).

—, v.	*Miscellaneous and Autobiographical Pieces, Fragments, and Marginalia*, ed. Herbert Davis (1962).
—, vi.	*Political Tracts 1711–13*, ed. Herbert Davis (1951).
—, vii.	*History of the Four Last Years of the Queen*, ed. Herbert Davis and Harold Williams (1951).
—, viii.	*Political Tracts 1713–1719*, ed. Herbert Davis and Irvin Ehrenpreis (1953).
—, ix.	*1720–1723 Tracts relating to England. Letters to Clergyman and Poet. Sermons*, ed. Herbert Davis; intro. to the sermons by Louis A. Landa (1948).
—. x.	*Drapier's Letters and other Works 1724–1725*, ed. Herbert Davis (1941).
—. xi.	*Gulliver's Travels*, ed. Herbert Davis (1941).
—, xii.	*Irish Tracts 1728–1733*, ed. Herbert Davis (1955).
—, xiii.	*Directions to Servants and Miscellaneous Pieces 1733–1742*, ed. Herbert Davis (1959).
—. xiv.	*Index*, compiled by Irvin Ehrenpreis (1968).
Swift, *Works* (Cambridge)	*The Cambridge Edition of the Works of Jonathan Swift* (Cambridge: Cambridge University Press, 2008–).
—, i.	*A Tale of a Tub and Other Works*, ed. Marcus Walsh (2010).
—, ii.	*Parodies, Hoaxes, Mock Treatises: Polite Conversation, Directions to Servants and Other Works*, ed. Valerie Rumbold (2013).
—, viii.	*English Political Writings, 1711–1714: The Conduct of the Allies and Other Works*, ed. Bertrand A. Goldgar and Ian Gadd (2008).
—, ix.	*Journal to Stella: Letters to Esther Johnson and Rebecca Dingley, 1710–1713*, ed. Abigail Williams (2013).
—, xvi.	*Gulliver's Travels*, ed. David Womersley (2012).

Notes on Contributors

Matthew C. Augustine teaches literature at the University of St Andrews. His main interests include poetry, politics, and cultures of reading from roughly Milton to Swift. He is the co-editor of two volumes of essays: *Lord Rochester in the Restoration World* (with Steven N. Zwicker) and *Texts and Readers in the Age of Marvell* (with Christopher D'Addario). He is also the author of *Aesthetics of Contingency: Writing, Politics, and Culture in England 1639–89*, a study of political instability and imaginative writing from the Bishops' Wars to the Glorious Revolution and beyond.

Paul Baines is Professor of English Literature in the Department of English, University of Liverpool, where he specializes in eighteenth-century literature, crime writing, book history, and satire. He is the author of *The House of Forgery in Eighteenth-Century Britain* (2000), *The Complete Critical Guide to Alexander Pope* (2000), *The Long Eighteenth Century* (2004), and, with Pat Rogers, *Edmund Curll, Bookseller* (2007). With Edward Burns he edited *Five Romantic Plays, 1768–1821* (2001). He is editor of *The Collected Writings of Edward Rushton* (2014), co-editor with Julian Ferraro of the *Longman Annotated Edition of the Poems of Alexander Pope*, volumes 1 and 2, and, with Greg Lynall, of volume 3 of the *Oxford Edition of the Writings of Alexander Pope* (*Early Prose*).

Ros Ballaster is Professor of Eighteenth-Century Studies in the Faculty of English, Oxford University at Mansfield College. Her research interests are in oriental fiction, women's writing, drama and performance. She is author of two monographs: *Seductive Forms: Women's Amatory Fiction 1684–1740* (1992) and *Fabulous Orients: Fictions of the East in England 1662–1785* (2005) and a further is forthcoming entitled *Being There: Theatre and Novel in Eighteenth-Century England*.

Jennie Batchelor is Professor of Eighteenth-Century Studies at the University of Kent. Her most recent books include the co-edited collections (with Manushag N. Powell) *Women's Periodicals and Print Culture in Britain, 1690–1820s* (2018) and (with Gillian Dow) *Women's Writing, 1660–1830* (2017), and a monograph, *Women's Work: Labour, Gender, Authorship, 1750–1830* (2014).

Clare Bucknell is an Examination Fellow in English at All Souls College, Oxford. She works on eighteenth-century poetry, primarily satire, and the history of critical reception. She has published recent articles on eighteenth-century country house poetry, the idea of poverty in Charles Churchill's poetry, and the early satires of Byron. She writes for the *London Review of Books* on eighteenth-century subjects.

Paddy Bullard is Associate Professor of English Literature and Book History at the University of Reading. He is the author of *Edmund Burke and the Art of Rhetoric* (2011). With James McLaverty he co-edited *Jonathan Swift and the Eighteenth-Century Book* (2013) and, with Alexis Tadié, *Ancients and Moderns in Europe* (2016). With Timothy Michael he is co-editor of volume 15 (*Later Prose*) of *The Oxford Edition of the Works of Alexander Pope*.

Jill Campbell is Professor of English at Yale University. She is the author of *Natural Masques: Gender and Identity in Fielding's Plays and Novels* and articles on Lord Hervey, Lady Mary Wortley Montagu, Horace Walpole, Maria Edgeworth, Mary Wollstonecraft, and others. Her essay on "The Scriblerian Project" appears in *The History of British Women Writers, 1690–1750*, vol. 4. She has recently completed a series of essays on adaptations of *Robinson Crusoe* for children, from the eighteenth century to *Lord of the Flies*.

Daniel Carey is Director of the Moore Institute for Research in the Humanities and Social Studies at the National University of Ireland, Galway. He is author of *Locke, Shaftesbury, and Hutcheson: Contesting Diversity in the Enlightenment and Beyond* (2006) and editor of *Richard Hakluyt and Travel Writing in Early Modern Europe* (with Claire Jowitt, 2012); *The Postcolonial Enlightenment: Eighteenth-Century Colonialism and Postcolonial Theory* (with Lynn Festa, 2012); *Asian Travel in the Renaissance* (2004); and *Les voyages de Gulliver: mondes lointains ou mondes proches* (with François Boulaire, 2002). With Claire Jowitt he is General Editor of the first critical edition of Richard Hakluyt's *Principal Navigations, Voyages, Traffiques, and Discoveries of the English Nation*, under preparation for OUP in 14 volumes.

Louise Curran is a Lecturer in Eighteenth-Century English Literature at the University of Birmingham. She is the author of *Samuel Richardson and the Art of Letter-Writing* (2016) and a co-editor of a forthcoming volume of *Correspondence Primarily on 'Pamela' and 'Clarissa'* for the *The Cambridge Edition of the Works and Correspondence of Samuel Richardson*. Her current research project is a book about the epistolary imagination and its links to authorial character in a range of writers from Alexander Pope to Frances Burney.

Helen Deutsch, Professor of English and Director of the Center for Seventeenth- and Eighteenth-Century Studies and William Andrews Clark Memorial Library at UCLA, is the author of *Resemblance and Disgrace: Alexander Pope and the Deformation of Culture* (1996), and *Loving Dr. Johnson* (2005), as well as co-editor of *"Defects": Engendering the Modern Body* (2000), and *Vital Matters: Eighteenth-Century Views of Conception, Life and Death* (2012). She researches and teaches at the crossroads of eighteenth-century studies and disability studies. She is currently finishing a book, tentatively titled *The Last Amateur*, about the unfinished conversation between Jonathan Swift and Edward Said.

Lynn Festa is Associate Professor of English at Rutgers University. She is the author of *Sentimental Figures of Empire in Eighteenth-Century Britain and France* (2006) and co-editor, with Daniel Carey, of *The Postcolonial Enlightenment: Eighteenth-Century Colonialism and Postcolonial Theory* (2009). Her new book, *Fiction Without Humanity: Person, Animal, Thing in Early Enlightenment Literature and Culture*, will be published by the University of Pennsylvania Press in 2019.

James Fowler is Senior Lecturer at the School of European Culture and Languages of the University of Kent. His publications include: *Richardson and the philosophes* (2014); *New Essays on Diderot* (2013), and *The Libertine's Nemesis: The Prude in 'Clarissa' and the 'roman libertin'* (2011). His research interests span European thought and literature of the period 1660–1800, with an emphasis on 'cross-Channel' influence. He is currently preparing a study of notions of virtue and merit in the long eighteenth century, to include chapters on Shaftesbury, Diderot, and Franklin. He is Associate Editor of *Eighteenth-Century Fiction*.

Sophie Gee is Associate Professor and Director of Undergraduate Studies in the Department of English at Princeton University. She is author of *Making Waste: Leftovers and the Eighteenth-Century Imagination* (2009), and of a novel, *The Scandal of the Season* (2008), which is a comedy of manners set in eighteenth-century London. She has published essays on Milton, Pope, Swift, and others, and has written for the *TLS*, the *New York Times Book Review*, the *Washington Post*, and the *Financial Times*.

Kristine Louise Haugen is Professor of English Literature at Caltech. She has long explored the connections between England and Europe and between poetry and humanism, publishing *Richard Bentley: Poetry and Enlightenment* in 2011. She is currently completing a book on ideas of poetic sound and rhythm in England before the Romantics. Professor Haugen has also published extensively on European humanism, including debates over whether the Greek tragedy was sung, visions of the nature of Hebrew poetry, and Julius Caesar Scaliger's attempt to recreate the love poetry of Aristotle.

Judith Hawley is Professor of Eighteenth-Century Literature in the Department of English, Royal Holloway, University of London. As well as publishing essays on Laurence Sterne, encyclopaedias, Siamese twins, Grub Street, and the history of the amateur performance, she has edited various eighteenth-century texts, including Jane Collier, *The Art of Ingeniously Tormenting*, Henry Fielding, *Joseph Andrews* and *Shamela*, Laurence Sterne, *Tristram Shandy*, and works by the Bluestocking, Elizabeth Carter. With Mary Isbell, she co-directs RAPPT: Researchers in Amateur Performance and Private Theatricals, a research network which aims to increase understanding and raise the profile of non-professional performance. Currently she is writing a group biography of Pope, Swift, and the Scriblerus Club.

Claudine van Hensbergen is Senior Lecturer in Eighteenth-Century English Literature at Northumbria University. She is volume editor (Vol. 3, *The Late Plays*) of *The Plays and Poetry of Nicholas Rowe* (2017) and has co-edited two special journal issues on Queen Anne and British Culture (2014) and the eighteenth-century letter (2011).

Claudine has published a range of articles and essays on topics including Aphra Behn, the Earl of Rochester, miscellany culture, public sculpture, satire, secret history, and drama.

Joseph Hone is the Lumley Research Fellow in English at Magdalene College, Cambridge. He is the author of *Literature and Party Politics at the Accession of Queen Anne* (2017) and one of the editors of *The Oxford Edition of the Writings of Alexander Pope*. His research centres on literature and political culture in the early eighteenth century, on which he has published articles in *The Review of English Studies, English Literary History, Studies in Philology, Philological Quarterly*, and elsewhere. He is currently writing a book about Alexander Pope.

Robert W. Jones is Professor of Eighteenth-Century Studies at the University of Leeds. His most recent book, *Literature, Gender and Politics in Britain during the War for America 1770–1785*, was published by Cambridge University Press in 2011. He is the author of several essays and articles on the political and literary culture of Georgian Britain and he is currently working a book entitled, *The Theatre of Richard Brinsley Sheridan: Drury Lane, Politics and Performance 1775–1787*. Together with Martyn J. Powell, he is editing *The Political Works of Richard Brinsley Sheridan* in four volumes for Oxford University Press.

Lawrence E. Klein taught in the History Faculty of the University of Cambridge and is currently an Emeritus Fellow of Emmanuel College, Cambridge, and an Associate Fellow of the History Department at the University of Warwick. He has published widely on aspects of eighteenth-century thought and culture, specializing in the theory and practice of politeness. He is the author of *Shaftesbury and the Culture of Politeness* (1994) and the editor of Shaftesbury's *Characteristics of Men, Manners, Opinions, Times* (1999), both for Cambridge University Press.

Jonathan Lamb has taught English Literature at Auckland, Princeton and (most recently) Vanderbilt, where he holds the Andrew W. Mellon Chair of the Humanities. His recent books are *The Evolution of Sympathy* (2009), *Settler and Creole Reenactment* (2009, co-edited with Vanessa Agnew), and *The Things Things Say* (2011). His latest is called *Scurvy: The Disease of Discovery*, published 2017. It deals with the unevenness both of the epidemiological history of the disease and of its effects on what Thomas Trotter called 'the nervous temperament'. Currently he is speculating on the narrative and pictorial exploitation of the ellipse, defined by Marx as 'two contrary motions reconciled in a single figure'.

Bonnie Latimer is an Associate Professor at Plymouth University, where she is Associate Head (English and Creative Writing) of the School of Humanities. She is the author of *Making Gender, Culture and the Self in the Fiction of Samuel Richardson: The Novel Individual* (2013). Her articles have appeared in *Review of English Studies, Year's Work in English Studies, The Eighteenth-Century Novel*, and *The Journal for Eighteenth-Century Studies*.

Kate Loveman is an Associate Professor in English at the University of Leicester. She works on seventeenth- and eighteenth-century literature and history, with particular interests in reading habits, collecting, and information networks. Her publications include *Samuel Pepys and his Books: Reading, Newsgathering, and Sociability, 1660–1703* (2015) and *Reading Fictions, 1660–1740: Deception in English Literary and Political Culture* (2008).

Gregory Lynall is Reader in English at the University of Liverpool. His publications include *Swift and Science: The Satire, Politics, and Theology of Natural Knowledge, 1690–1730* (2012). His essay 'Swift's "Poetical Chymistry": Alchemy and Allusion in the Verse' (*Review of English Studies*, 2012) was winner of the 2013 Richard H. Rodino Prize. He is currently writing a cultural history of solar energy and a biography of Dr John Arbuthnot.

Nicholas McDowell is Professor of Early Modern Literature and Thought at the University of Exeter. He is the author of *The English Radical Imagination: Culture, Religion, and Revolution, 1630–1660* (2003) and *Poetry and Allegiance in the English Civil Wars: Marvell and the Cause of Wit* (2008), and the co-editor of *The Oxford Handbook of Milton* (2009) and *The Complete Works of John Milton, Volume VI: Vernacular Regicide and Republican Writings* (2013). He is currently completing a study of the reception and translation of Rabelais in seventeenth- and eighteenth-century Britain and editing, with Henry Power, *The Oxford Handbook of English Prose, 1640–1714*.

John McTague is Lecturer in English at the University of Bristol, co-editor (with Rebecca Bullard) of *The Plays and Poems of Nicholas Rowe, Volume 1: The Early Plays* (2016), and the author of articles on Jonathan Swift, Delarivier Manley, popularity and censorship in poetic miscellanies, hoaxes, bites, shams, and conspiracies. His monograph, *Things that Didn't Happen*, is under contract with Boydell and Brewer.

Ashley Marshall is Professor of English at the University of Nevada, Reno. She is the author of *The Practice of Satire in England, 1658–1770* (2013) and *Swift and History: Politics and the English Past* (2015), and has published essays in *The Review of English Studies, Huntington Library Quarterly, Swift Studies, Eighteenth-Century Life, Modern Philology*, and elsewhere. She is currently completing a book on political journalism in London, 1695–1720.

Jon Mee is Professor of Eighteenth-Century Studies at the University of York. He is the author of various books and articles on literature and politics in the period, most recently *Print, Publicity, and Popular Radicalism in the 1790s: The Laurel of Liberty* (2016). He also wrote the essay 'Treason, Seditious Libel, and Literature in the Romantic Period' for *Oxford Handbooks Online*.

Jesse Molesworth is an Associate Professor of English at Indiana University. His book *Chance and the Eighteenth-Century Novel: Realism, Probability, Magic* (2010) was awarded Honorable Mention for the Barbara Perkins and George Perkins Prize, recognizing the year's best book on narrative. He has published widely on eighteenth-century British literature, visual culture, and contemporary comics, in such publications as *ELH, Criticism, MLQ, ImageText, Eighteenth-Century Studies, The Eighteenth Century: Theory and Interpretation*, and *Eighteenth-Century Fiction*.

David O'Shaughnessy is Associate Professor for Eighteenth-Century Studies in the School of English, Trinity College Dublin. He is the author of *William Godwin and the Theatre* (2010), editor of *The Plays of William Godwin* (2010), and has written many essays on Godwin and on Georgian theatrical culture. He edited *Networks of Aspiration: The London Irish in the Long Eighteenth Century*, a special issue of *Eighteenth-Century Life* (2015). He is co-editor of *The Cambridge Edition of the Letters of Oliver Goldsmith* (2018) and is a general editor of the *Cambridge Edition of the Collected Works of Oliver Goldsmith* (in progress).

Melinda Alliker Rabb is Professor of English at Brown University. She is author of *Satire and Secrecy in English Literature 1650–1750* (2007) and *Miniature and the English Imagination: Literature, Cognition, and Small-Scale Culture, 1650–1765* (2019), as well as chapters and articles on Swift, Pope, Defoe, Johnson, Fielding, Manley, Sterne, Collier, Scott, and Godwin. She has edited *Lucius: The First Christian King of England* for *The Broadview Anthology of Restoration and Early Eighteenth-Century Drama*, ed. Douglas Canfield (2000). Her current project is *Parting Shots: Displacements of Civil War Trauma in Eighteenth-Century Literature*.

Peter Robinson is Professor of English and American Literature at the University of Reading, and poetry editor for Two Rivers Press. He has been awarded the Cheltenham Prize, the John Florio Prize, and two Poetry Book Society Recommendations for his poetry and translations from the Italian. His most recent publications include a novel, *September in the Rain* (2016), his *Collected Poems 1976–2016* (2017), and a critical monograph, *The Sound Sense of Poetry* (2018). He is also the editor of *The Oxford Handbook of Contemporary British & Irish Poetry* (2013), which came out in paperback in 2016.

Adam Rounce is Associate Professor in English Literature at the University of Nottingham. He has written extensively on various seventeenth- and eighteenth-century writers, including Dryden, Pope, Churchill, and Johnson. He is co-editing two volumes for the ongoing Cambridge University Press edition of the writings of Jonathan Swift, as well as writing a separately published Chronology. He is the author of *Fame and Failure, 1720–1800: The Unfulfilled Literary Life* (2013).

Matthew Scott lectures, inter alia, on the Romantic Period in the Department of English Literature at the University of Reading, and has contributed elsewhere to the Oxford Handbooks project with several essays on Coleridge and Wordsworth.

Sean Silver is Associate Professor of Literature at the University of Michigan. His last project, entitled *The Mind Is a Collection* (2015), is the exhibit catalogue for a virtual museum tracing the development of empirical cognitive models through their material environments (visit at www.mindisacollection.org). He is currently at work on the origins of the complexity concept in the arts, sciences, and craft practices of seventeenth- and eighteenth-century Britain.

George Southcombe is Director of the Sarah Lawrence Programme, Wadham College, Oxford. He is the editor of *English Nonconformist Poetry* (2012), and co-author (with Grant Tapsell) of *Restoration Politics, Religion, and Culture: Britain and Ireland, 1660–1714* (2010). He is also the co-editor (with Almut Suerbaum and Benjamin Thompson) of *Polemic: Language as Violence in Medieval and Early Modern Discourse* (2015), and (with Grant Tapsell) of *Revolutionary England, c.1630–c.1660: Essays for Clive Holmes* (2017).

Carolyn Steedman is Emeritus Professor of History at the University of Warwick. Among her books are *Dust* (2001), *Master and Servant: Love and Labour in the English Industrial Age* (2007), *Labours Lost: Domestic Service and the Making of Modern England* (2009), *An Everyday Life of the English Working Class* (2013), and *Poetry for Historians; or, W. H. Auden and History* (2018). She is currently writing *History and the Law: A Love Story*.

Alexis Tadié is Professor of English Literature at Sorbonne Université, Paris. He is the author of monographs on Bacon, Locke, and Sterne, as well as of editions of *Tristram Shandy* (2012) and of *Gulliver's Travels* (1998). He edited a special issue of the journal *Paragraph* on the Theory of Quarrels (2017) and co-edited *Ancients and Moderns in Europe* (2016) with Paddy Bullard, and *Sporting Cultures 1650–1850* (2018) with Daniel O'Quinn.

David Francis Taylor is Associate Professor and Reader in Eighteenth-Century Literature at the University of Warwick. He is co-editor of *The Oxford Handbook of the Georgian Theatre, 1737–1832* (2014) and author of *Theatres of Opposition: Empire, Revolution, and Richard Brinsley Sheridan* (2012) and *The Politics of Parody: A Literary History of Caricature, 1760–1830* (2018).

Marcus Walsh is Emeritus Professor of English Literature at the University of Liverpool. He has edited Smart's *Hymns and Spiritual Songs* and *A Song to David* for Oxford (1983, 1987), and Swift's *Tale of a Tub and other Works* for Cambridge (2010). His monograph on eighteenth-century editing of Shakespeare and Milton appeared in 1997. He is a General Editor of the new *Writings of Alexander Pope*, to be published by Oxford University Press, and is currently working (with Dr Hazel Wilkinson) on the volume including Pope's *Ethic Epistles*.

Gillian Wright is a Reader in English and Irish Literature at the University of Birmingham. Her publications include *Early Modern Women's Manuscript Poetry*, co-edited with Jill Seal Millman (2005), *Producing Women's Poetry, 1600–1730: Text and Paratext, Manuscript and Print* (2013), and *Katherine Philips: Form, Reception and Literary Contexts*, co-edited with Marie-Louise Coolahan (2018). Her new monograph, *The Restoration Transposed: Poetry, Place and History, 1660-1700*, will be published by Cambridge University Press in 2020, and she is a general editor on the new Cambridge Edition of the Works of Aphra Behn, for which she is also editing Behn's verse.

CHAPTER 1

···

DESCRIBING
EIGHTEENTH-CENTURY
BRITISH SATIRE

···

PADDY BULLARD

THE eighteenth century was an age of description. With their encyclopaedias, handbooks, and gazetteers, their global voyages of discovery, their political economies and sciences of humanity, eighteenth-century writers set out to specify the world around them as comprehensively as they could.[1] It was also an age of satire. These two generalizations sit uncomfortably with one another. Satire distorts rather than describing things accurately: it shrinks human grandeur and it blows up blemishes; it sees hooves under the petticoat, and horns beneath the periwig.[2] Moreover, satire is itself a phenomenon that resists definition and description. We think of it as a literary genre, but a glance through this volume suggests that it works more like cultural virus, a 'mental position' that infects different sorts of art and literature, different kinds of speech and action, in many different ways.[3]

With a view to anticipating these hazards, this introductory chapter looks at some ways of describing satire, and of placing it in the British eighteenth century. It gathers a handful of extracts and anecdotes from the period, crossing-points at which different discussions of satire intersect with larger ideas about culture and society. Each extract

---

[1] See John B. Bender and Michael Marrinan, eds., *Regimes of Description: In the Archive of the Eighteenth Century* (Stanford: Stanford University Press, 2005); Cynthia Wall, *The Prose of Things: Transformations of Description in the Eighteenth Century* (Chicago: University of Chicago Press, 2006); Joanna Stalnaker, *The Unfinished Enlightenment: Description in the Age of the Encyclopedia* (Ithaca: Cornell University Press, 2010).

[2] John Brown, in *An Essay on Satire* (1744), 12–13, combined these effects: satire 'Displays the cloven hoof, or lengthen'd ear; / Bids vice and folly take unborrow'd shapes...'; for contrary claims for the realism of satire cf. P. K. Elkin, *The Augustan Defense of Satire* (Oxford: Clarendon Press, 1973), 14, 82–3.

[3] Charles A. Knight, *The Literature of Satire* (Cambridge: Cambridge University Press, 2004), 4; see also Dustin Griffin, *Satire: A Critical Reintroduction* (Lexington: University Press of Kentucky, 1994), especially 95–114.

has themes and contexts that need unpacking, and references to trace. Each represents a small shift in the way that satire was practised or perceived.

The evidence collected here is anecdotal and fragmentary, so I have given it structure by arranging it in three sections. The first looks at some satirical commonalities. It considers the location of satire amongst scenes of associational life; it considers the body of commonplace critical opinion that grew up around its practice; and it traces a connection with emerging constructions of British nationhood. The second turns to literary satire's material forms, looking across the bibliographical record to find patterns in the way it was consumed by readers of printed books. The third moves on from these generalized contexts to examine some of satire's personal, particular implications. The question of whether satire should always be general, whether it could avoid referring to individuals, preoccupied eighteenth-century commentators.[4] Across the century there was an increasing focus on the ethical integrity of satirical writers, and much anxious discussion of what it meant to have a satirical 'humour'. By looking in turn across these three intersecting perspectives—communal, material, personal—we can form a general impression of what eighteenth-century satire was, and how it developed.

Satirical Commonalities

Despite the unreliability of its descriptions, there were plenty of enlightened, scientific people who embraced the century's spirit of ridicule. Richard Lovell Edgeworth, the educational reformer and gentleman-engineer, belonged to a London club that met weekly at Slaughter's Coffee House in the early 1780s. Its members were writers, explorers, and natural scientists, including the surgeon John Hunter, Joseph Banks (recently elected President of the Royal Society), Nevil Maskelyne (the Astronomer Royal), and Captain Cook himself.[5] Getting into the club was hard. New members endured a sort of trial by satire, as Edgeworth recalled in his memoirs:

> ...we practised every means in our power, except personal insult, to try the temper and understanding of each candidate for admission. Every prejudice, which his pro-fession or situation in life might have led him to cherish, was attacked, exposed to argument and ridicule. The argument was always ingenious, and the ridicule some-times coarse. This ordeal prevented for some time the aspiration of too numerous

---

[4] See, in this volume, Marshall, 'Thinking about Satire', Chapter 28; Tadié, 'Quarrelling', Chapter 32; Mee, 'Satire in the Age of the French Revolution', Chapter 39; Bucknell, 'Satire, Morality, and Criticism', Chapter 41.

[5] For another account of the club and its connection with the Lunar Society of Birmingham, see Eric Robinson, 'R. E. Raspe, Franklin's "Club of Thirteen", and the Lunar Society', *Annals of Science* 11 (1955), 142–4.

candidates; but private attachments at length softened the rigour of probation, the society became too numerous, and too noble, and was insensibly dissolved.[6]

The self-consciousness with which the club at Slaughter's Coffee House created a ritual out of ridicule is itself distinctive. It is hard to think of another age or place in which a culture of satire could be so generally, and to some extent tacitly, understood. Edgeworth touches on several themes that crop up repeatedly in the pages of this handbook. First, he recalls how the club's tests focused on people's 'profession or situation in life'. Eighteenth-century satire often lingered over social descriptions and occupational identities, worrying about the individual in the group. 'I have ever hated all nations, professions, and communities', wrote the satirist Jonathan Swift in a famous letter, '...but principally I hate and detest that animal called man, although I heartily love John, Peter, Thomas, and so forth'.[7] Satire's interest in groups and individuals was complicated by the tendency of satirists to set themselves amid scenes of associational life, like the one painted here.[8] Second, Edgeworth balances 'ingenious' argument against 'coarse' ridicule. Again, that simple combination evokes a century of debates about polite wit and pedantry, about philosophers using ridicule as a test for truth, about whether it is appropriate for satirists to smile or to snarl.[9] Above all Edgeworth is describing a practice of satire here. Hugh Kenner once argued that satire is parasitic on literary technologies and genres, and on them alone: 'It requires that the language by which we recount events be externalized for inspection, the way only writing externalizes.'[10] The mere talker can mock, in other words, but cannot satirize. But the club at Slaughter's Coffee House shows how satire could manifest itself through social codes as well as literary ones. Third, Edgeworth describes a specific instrument of exclusion—the trial that puts off crowds and unwanted noblemen—that is embedded within a larger public system of exclusions. As Maria Edgeworth will have noticed while she transcribed her father's reminiscences, women do not qualify even as candidates for this scientific club. But women had other ways to participate in the age's rituals of ridicule, as her satirical novels, among many other texts by women discussed in this handbook, had so often proved.[11] Ultimately, the club dissolves when the rigours of its initiation ceremony are softened. Here once again the club's story corresponds with a familiar narrative about satire in the eighteenth

---

[6] *Memoirs of Richard Lovel Edgeworth, Begun by Himself and Concluded by his Daughter, Maria Edgeworth*, 2 vols. (1820), i. 189.

[7] Swift to Pope, 29 September 1725, Swift, *Corr.* (Woolley), ii. 606–7.

[8] See, in this volume, Hawley, 'Corporate Acts of Satire', Chapter 2; Rounce, 'Churchill and his Circle', Chapter 7; Jones, 'Foxite Satire', Chapter 8.

[9] See, in this volume, Loveman, 'Epigram and Spontaneous Wit', Chapter 29; Klein, 'Ridicule as a Tool for Discovering Truth', Chapter 34.

[10] Hugh Kenner, 'Wyndham Lewis: The Satirist as Barbarian', in *English Satire and the Satiric Tradition*, ed. Claude Rawson (London: Blackwell, 1984), 264–75, at 265.

[11] See David Francis Taylor, 'Edgeworth's Belinda and the Gendering of Caricature', *Eighteenth-Century Fiction* 26 (2014), 593–624; for different experiences of women as satirists see, in this volume, Hensbergen, 'The Female Wits', Chapter 5; Wright, 'Fable and Allegory', Chapter 16; Curran, 'Self-portraiture', Chapter 26; Rabb, 'Satire and Domesticity', Chapter 27; Campbell, 'Sexing Satire', Chapter 33; Batchelor, 'Pamela and the Satirists', Chapter 36.

century, one that needs much qualification: that it slowly fell out of fashion in an age of science and sensibility.[12]

The century's spirit of ridicule took polite and sentimental forms, as well as forms that externalized and excluded. While the variety of these forms created problems of definition—which in turn prompted many careful essays on the differences between satire, raillery, libel, and burlesque—eighteenth-century people generally knew what to think about them.[13] Horace, Persius, and Juvenal remained staples of schoolroom and academy, and a tradition of humanistic scholarship and debate about the classical canon of satire was readily accessible, digested, for example, in John Dryden's 'Discourse on Satire' (1693).[14] In the vernacular realm, opinions had settled in part because satire's moral ambivalence made it such a good topic for the conventionalized discourse of the periodicals and, at a personal level, for commonplace books.[15] Samuel Richardson seems to have turned to his as he drafted Clarissa Harlowe's sixty-ninth letter, where she taxes her friend Anna Howe with a satirical (albeit perfectly tactful) mind:

> What patient shall be afraid of a probe in so delicate a hand? – I say I am almost afraid to pray to you to give way to it, for fear you should, for that very reason, restrain it. For the edge may be taken off, if it does not make the subject of its raillery wince a little. *Permitted* and *desired* satire may be apt, in a generous satirist, mending as it rallies, to turn too soon into panegyric. Yours is intended to instruct; and though it bites, it pleases at the same time: no fear of a wound's rankling or festering by so delicate a point as you carry; not envenomed by *personality*, not intending to expose, or ridicule, or exasperate. The most admired of our moderns know nothing of this art. Why? Because it must be founded in good nature, and directed by a right heart. The *man*, not the *fault*, is generally the subject of *their* satire: and were it to be *just*, how should it be *useful*? How should it answer any good purpose? When every gash (for their weapon is the broadsword, not a lancet) lets in the air of public ridicule, and exasperates where it should heal.[16]

---

[12] See, in this volume, Lynall, 'Science and Satire', Chapter 23; Festa, 'Satire to Sentiment', Chapter 38.

[13] See, in this volume, Latimer, 'Burlesque and Travesty', Chapter 17; Taylor, 'The Practice of Parody', Chapter 21; Tadié, 'Quarrelling', Chapter 32; for libel and satire see Jones, 'Foxite Satire', Chapter 8; Hone, 'Legal Constraints, Libellous Evasions', Chapter 31; Mee, 'Satire in the Age of the French Revolution', Chapter 39. For an eighteenth-century taxonomy of satire and its varieties see Corbyn Morris, *Essay on Wit and Humour* (1744), 50–1; for a modern taxonomy see Ashley Marshall, *The Practice of Satire in England, 1658–1770* (Baltimore: Johns Hopkins University Press, 2013).

[14] For discussion see, in this volume, Augustine, 'The Invention of Dryden as Satirist', Chapter 10; Haugen, 'Alexander Pope and the Philosophical Horace', Chapter 11; Fowler, 'Moralizing Satire', Chapter 35; cf. William Kupersmith, *English Versions of Roman Satire in the Earlier Eighteenth Century* (Newark: University of Delaware Press, 2007), and *Roman Satirists in Seventeenth-Century England* (Lincoln: University of Nebraska Press, 1985).

[15] See, in this volume, Baines, 'Satire in the Miscellanies', Chapter 15; Marshall, 'Thinking about Satire', Chapter 28.

[16] Samuel Richardson, *Clarissa: or, The History of a Young Lady*, ed. Angus Ross, 2 vols. (Aylesbury: BPCC Hazell Books, 1991), i. 280.

Several of these thoughts would be filleted out as commonplaces in the 'Collection of Moral and Instructive Sentences' that Richardson prepared for readers of *Clarissa* in 1751.[17] Others had been worn smooth by tradition. For example, Clarissa's main theme is classical. The Roman poet Persius had railed admiringly at his predecessor Horace for performing a sort of secret moral surgery with his satires: 'While his friend is laughing, the rascal Horace touches every fault in him and, once he's got in, he frolics around his heart.'[18] The delicately 'probing' hand of Anna Howe is imagined following the Horatian example, albeit with less laughter going around. Clarissa's worry about the wound from satire 'rankling or festering' owes something to Joseph Addison's warning that 'lampoons and satires, that are written with wit and spirit, are like poisoned darts, which not only inflict a wound, but make it incurable', issued in *Spectator* no. 23 (27 March 1711).[19] Periodicals are also the source for her hopeful insistence that satire should be 'founded in good nature'. Richard Steele complained in *Tatler* no. 242 about 'Smart Satirical Fellows' about town who are 'by no means qualified for the Characters they pretend to…because they want Good-nature'.[20] Addison and Steele were the century's great reformers of raillery, and Clarissa is entirely of their party, but she draws on writers who were less scrupulous about the collateral effects of satire as well. Her image of the 'edge' of satire working like a lancet (or broadsword) belongs to a well-known passage in John Dryden's 'Discourse Concerning Satire' that contrasts 'the slovenly butchering of a man, and the fineness of a stroke that separates the head from the body and leaves it standing in its place'.[21] It was Jonathan Swift who appropriated the idea of satire as a surgical instrument most often to his own writing.[22] This body of commonplace imagery and opinion concerning satire could serve as a resource and as a provocation for eighteenth-century writers, even where definitions of satire did not keep up with contemporary practice.

If satirists often positioned themselves at tea-tables, clubs, and coffee-houses, and if the companies they found there shared a body of opinion about what ridicule was and what it did, is it possible to place these commonalities in any larger setting? It seemed natural for eighteenth-century Britons to think about satire as a national habit, bound

---

[17] *A Collection of the Moral and Instructive Sentiments…Contained in the Histories of Pamela, Clarissa…*(1755), in *Samuel Richardson's Published Commentary on Clarissa, 1747–65*, ed. O. M. Brack et al., 3 vols. (London: Pickering & Chatto), iii. 200–1.

[18] Persius, *Satires*, in *Juvenal and Persius*, ed. Susanna Morton Braund (Cambridge, MA: Harvard University Press, 2004), 58 [1.116–17]; the line had been a favourite of British commonplacers since Sir Philip Sidney used it in *An Apology for Poetry* (1595): see Brian Vickers, ed., *English Renaissance Literary Criticism* (Oxford: Oxford University Press, 1994), 361–2; for the Horatian inheritance see, in this volume, Haugen, 'Alexander Pope and the Philosophical Horace', Chapter 11; Scott, 'Augustan Romantics', Chapter 14.

[19] *Spectator*, i. 97.   [20] *Tatler*, iii. 241.

[21] 'Discourse Concerning Satire', Dryden, *Poems* (Longman), iii. 423.

[22] See, in this volume, Robinson, 'The Edge of Satire', Chapter 37; also see Paddy Bullard, 'Swift's Razor', *Modern Philology* 113 (2016), 353–72.

up with their weather, with their constitution, and with the humour of the people.[23] In his last sermon Archbishop Tillotson regretted that he had lived to see an age in which satire and evil speech had become a national entertainment: "'Tis the *Sawce* of Conversation, and all Discourse is counted but flat and dull which hath not something of *piquancy* and sharpness in it against some body."[24] His contemporary the diplomat and essayist Sir William Temple worried about the nation's 'Vein of Ridiculing' in 1690: "'Tis the Itch of our Age and Clymat, and has over-run both the Court and the Stage, [...] and I have known in my Life, more than one or two Ministers of State, that would rather have said a Witty thing, than done a Wise one."[25] Perhaps as he wrote this, Temple was thinking about the court of Charles II rather than that of William III—the echo of Rochester's satire on the former king, who 'never said a foolish thing, / Nor ever did a wise one', is a giveaway.[26] In any case, the British climate, in its very instability, is a constant factor. Lawrence Sterne attributed to climate the ascendancy of English character satire over that of France: 'this strange irregularity in our climate, producing so strange an irregularity in our characters,—doth thereby, in some sort, make us amends, by giving us somewhat to make us merry with when the weather will not suffer us to go out of doors'.[27] But Sterne's daughter Lydia, returning from residence on the continent after her father's death in January 1769, made a darker comparison between the two nations. Her correspondent Elizabeth Montagu, doyenne of the Bluestockings, asked Lydia whether she had inherited her father's wit, which the daughter denied rather hotly:

> — I look upon satire with detestation and I must own when we returned from france we were much hurt with the satirical things we heard in every company we went into, having lived six Years amongst people who know not what it is to be satirical.[28]

It may be that satire was associated particularly with the British eighteenth century because the national character seemed to blend Shandean humorousness with the more melancholy, aggressive satirical turn experienced by Lydia Sterne. 'The English have greatly changed within this century', wrote the traveller Gebhard Wendeborn in 1791; 'they have grown more gay... it, therefore, cannot be said, as I have frequently heard

---

[23] See, in this volume, O'Shaughnessy, 'National Identity', Chapter 6; see also Thomas R. Preston, *Not in Timon's Manner: Feeling, Misanthropy, and Satire in Eighteenth-Century England* (Tuscaloosa: University of Alabama Press, 1975), 14–19; Knight, *Literature of Satire*, 50–80.

[24] John Tillotson, *The Last Sermon of his Grace John late Lord Archbishop of* (1695), 13; Tillotson borrows from his fellow latitudinarian divine Isaac Barrow, as he often did: see Barrow, *Several Sermons Against Evil Speaking* (1678), 56: 'this Age, wherein plain Reason is deemed a dull and heavy thing... cannot relish any food without some piquant sawce...'.

[25] William Temple, 'Upon Ancient and Modern Learning', in *Miscellanea. The Second Part* (1690), 74.

[26] Rochester, *Works*, 292–4.

[27] Laurence Sterne, *The Life and Opinions of Tristram Shandy*, ed. Melvyn New and Joan New, 3 vols. (Gainesville: University Press of Florida, 1978), i. 71.

[28] Lydia Sterne to Elizabeth Montagu, January 1769, in Laurence Sterne, *The Letters, Part 2: 1765–1768*, ed. Melvyn New and Peter de Voogd (Gainesville: University Press of Florida, 2009), 733.

abroad, that their blood, by nature, is blacker and thicker than that of other nations'.[29] But the black blood was perhaps more persistent than he thought.

Satirical Materials

Thinking about the commonalities of eighteenth-century British society in which satire came to prominence helps us begin to place it in this period. These commonalities included, as we have seen, those of associational life, of literary culture, and of national identity. But looking at satire's material forms can also give a general sense of its significance to the age. Satire appeared in an extraordinary variety of shapes and manifestations, spilling out across the media. Its impact as a mode for graphic art was especially important.[30] Several essays in this volume look at satire's trajectories still further from the purely literary, the way it overflowed into oral expressions, into personal enactments and dramatic performances.[31] It added its distinctive codes to the representation of human bodies, and it even refracted the period's descriptions of things themselves.[32] Looking at the range of media in which satire appeared also makes us reconsider the materiality of its literary forms. Satire's significance to late seventeenth-century manuscript culture is well known, but (at the risk of stating the obvious) it was in the form of printed books, pamphlets, and broadsides that it found its way into all libraries, and into every reader's hand.[33] One great advantage of printed literary media to this survey is that eighteenth-century books are minutely catalogued on the ESTC electronic database, which means that books of satire can be counted and categorized by automatic mechanisms. This allows us to identify some general historical trends in the production of printed satire.

One way of measuring satire's impact on the eighteenth-century book trade is to look at the number of imprints booksellers were able to sell of early editions, and the frequency with which texts were reprinted.[34] These are yardsticks that show how a handful of satires established themselves among the most popular and long-lived publications of

---

[29] Gebhard Wendeborn, *A View of England towards the Close of the Eighteenth Century* (1791), 404.

[30] See, in this volume, Molesworth, 'Graphic Satire', Chapter 18; Taylor, 'The Practice of Parody', Chapter 21.

[31] For performances and enactments see Loveman, 'Epigram and Spontaneous Wit', Chapter 29; McTague, 'Satire as Event', Chapter 30; for satire's pervasive presence in drama see Hensbergen, 'The Female Wits', Chapter 5; Latimer, 'Burlesque and Travesty', Chapter 17; Ballaster 'Dramatic Satire', Chapter 20.

[32] For bodies see Deutsch, 'Misanthropy and Violence', Chapter 25 in this volume; Batchelor, 'Pamela and the Satirists', Chapter 36; for things see Lamb, 'Romance, Satire, and the Exploitation of Disorder', Chapter 19; Silver, 'Satirical Objects', Chapter 22; Rabb, 'Satire and Domesticity', Chapter 27.

[33] Harold Love, *English Clandestine Satire, 1660–1702* (Oxford: Oxford University Press, 2004); for satire and print culture see, in this volume, Jones, 'Foxite Satire', Chapter 8; Baines, 'Satire in the Miscellanies', Chapter 15; Hone, 'Legal Constraints, Libellous Evasions', Chapter 31.

[34] For the reprint trade see T. F. Bonnell, *The Most Disreputable Trade: Publishing the Classics of English Poetry, 1765–1810* (Oxford: Oxford University Press, 2008).

the century. The best-known satires sold strongly as single-title publications, and then continued to be read as anthology pieces. John Dryden's *Absalom and Achitophel* (1681) went through seven editions within a year of publication, two of them styled 'second', and had reached a 'tenth' by 1701. But it was its prominent position as the second poem in the continuously reprinted Dryden–Tonson *Miscellany Poems* (1685) that consolidated its place in the canon.[35] Jonathan Swift's difficult satire on modern learning and religion, *A Tale of a Tub*, is an unlikely candidate for popularity.[36] But it was much reprinted after its publication in 1704, often in tiny, cheap formats, with four distinct 'small duodecimo' editions appearing in 1711 alone. The *Tub*'s longevity as a stand-alone publication—Charles Barthurst issued a 'fifteenth' edition in 1766—was due in part to Swift's reluctance to acknowledge authorship by including it in his *Miscellany* collections during his lifetime (although it did appear in editions of his works after 1743). Alexander Pope's *The Rape of the Lock* (1714) was a phenomenon of the trade: a year after publication Pope boasted of 'the uncommon Sale of this Book (for above 6000 of 'em have been already vended).'[37] These are 'surprisingly large figures' for the print run of a poem, writes David Foxon: 'the nearest I know is the 2000 and 250 fine copies of [John] Gay's *Trivia* printed in January 1716'.[38] What makes them more surprising is that the *Rape* had appeared already in the Pope-edited *Miscellaneous Poems and Translations* of 1712. Notwithstanding its frequent inclusion in anthologies and collected editions, the *Rape* reached a 'sixth' stand-alone edition in 1726. The canonical status that these works retain to this day is underlined by their lucrative history as bookseller's copy.

Stories of prodigious popularity can be told about the other very well-known satires written by Swift, Pope, and their 'Scriblerian' circle. John Arbuthnot's *History of John Bull* was a series of satires on European politics during the War of Spanish Succession. The first pamphlet in the sequence, *The Law is a Bottomless-Pit*, ran to nine impressions in 1712, but their initial popularity was short-lived. Rescued from oblivion in 1727 by inclusion in the Pope–Swift *Miscellanies*, however, they appeared, unattributed to Arbuthnot, in collections of Swift's works into the nineteenth century. It is less easy to sum up the complicated publication histories and vast popularity of the three most famous 'Scriblerian' satires of the late 1720s, Swift's *Gulliver's Travels* (1726), John Gay's *Beggar's Opera* (1728), and Pope's original *Dunciad* (1728). Swift for one imagined them occupying successively the same high-ground of success: 'The Beggars Opera hath knockt down Gulliver', he told Gay in 1728, 'I hope to see Popes Dullness knock down the Beggars Opera, but not till it hath fully done its Jobb'.[39] Tales of astonishingly rapid early sales circulated. Ten days after *Gulliver* appeared, Gay and Pope assured Swift that it 'hath been the conversation of the whole town ever since: The whole impression sold

---

[35] See, in this volume, Baines, 'Satire in the Miscellanies', Chapter 15.

[36] See, in this volume, Walsh, 'Against Hypocrisy and Dissent', Chapter 3.

[37] See Latimer, 'Burlesque and Travesty', Chapter 17 in this volume; Alexander Pope, *A Key to the Lock* [...] *by Esdras Barnivelt, apoth* (1715), 'Epistle Dedicatory', iv.

[38] David Foxon, *Pope and the Early Eighteenth-Century Book Trade*, ed. James McLaverty (Oxford: Clarendon Press, 1991), 42.

[39] Swift, *Corr.* (Woolley), iii. 171; cf. iii. 181.

in a week.'[40] There was gratifying chaos when *The Dunciad* first appeared: 'a crowd of authors besieged [Anne Dodd's] shop', as Richard Savage recalled, '...to hinder the coming-out of *The Dunciad*: on the other side, the booksellers and hawkers made as great efforts to procure it. What could a few poor authors do against so great a majority as the publick? There was no stopping a torrent with a finger, so out it came.'[41] For Swift, the fact of popular success gave a peculiar moral weight to his satires: drawn to comment on Swift's works in verse and prose, his imagined eulogist in *Verses on the Death of Dr Swift* declines to adjudicate: 'Nor, can I tell what Criticks thought 'em; / But, this I know, all People bought 'em.'[42] There is little in the bibliographical record to challenge all this excitement and self-congratulation.

An indication of the reach that eighteenth-century satires could have is that Daniel Defoe achieved the greatest success of his career, not with the *Review* or *Robinson Crusoe*, but with a verse satire, *The True-Born Englishman* (1701).[43] Like *John Bull* it was a work of its time, written in response to an anti-Williamite lampoon by John Tutchin called *The Foreigners* (1700), and yet it continued to appear in edition after edition through the century. A 'twenty-fifth' was issued in 1777, and the ESTC lists seven more up to 1795. It was also one of the period's most pirated works, so even these numbers tell only part of the story. In 1705 Defoe claimed that, beside the nine one-shilling 'official' editions that had appeared by that date, *The True-Born Englishman* 'has been Twelve Times printed by other Hands...80000 of the Small Ones have been sold in the Streets for 2d. or at a Penny'—an over-enthusiastic compositor perhaps adding an extra zero to that extraordinary figure.[44] Other satires that enjoyed enduring popularity as stand-alone publications included Sir Samuel Garth's *The Dispensary* (1699), which reached a 'ninth' edition in 1726 and an 'eleventh' in 1768. Lady Mary Wortley Montagu's *Verses Address'd to the Imitator of the First Satire of the Second Book of Horace* (1733), written collaboratively with John, Baron Hervey, reached a 'sixth' edition in 1735. That tally includes neither the 1733 Dublin edition nor a rival first edition (titled *To the Imitator of the Satire*) apparently issued by Hervey himself.[45] Its target, Pope's *First Satire of the Second Book of Horace, Imitated*, was perhaps a shade less popular, appearing in several different formats and six impressions (plus two Dublin printings and an Edinburgh false imprint) in 1733–4. Slightly later in the century, Christopher Anstey's jolly social satire *The New Bath Guide* was very widely read from 1766, prompting dozens of imitators to

---

[40] Swift, *Corr.* (Woolley), iii. 47; for *Gulliver's Travels* see Carey, 'Swift, Gulliver, and Travel Satire', Chapter 12 in this volume.

[41] Richard Savage, *A Collection of Pieces in Verse and Prose* (1732), vi; Johnson attributed this to Pope, presumably on Savage's authority: Samuel Johnson, *Lives of the Most Eminent English Poets*, ed. Roger Lonsdale, 4 vols. (Oxford: Clarendon Press, 2006), iv. 32.

[42] Swift, *Poems* (Williams), ii. 565.

[43] See, in this volume, Southcombe, 'The Satire of Dissent', Chapter 4; Marshall, 'Thinking about Satire', Chapter 28.

[44] See P. N. Furbank and W. R. Owens, *A Critical Bibliography of Daniel Defoe* (London: Pickering & Chatto, 1998), 3–6.

[45] D. F. Foxon, *English Verse 1701–1750: A Catalogue of Separately Printed Poems*, 2 vols. (Cambridge: Cambridge University Press, 1975), i. 838–9.

adopt its galloping anapestic style. The Dodsleys issued a 'fourteenth' edition in 1791, with four more editions before end of century. It is worth mentioning here that satire set up the Dodsley publishing business in the first place. In 1735 Robert Dodsley had combined the profits from his after-piece *The Toy-Shop: A Dramatick Satire* with a contribution of £100 from Alexander Pope, allowing him to establish his famous premises in Pall Mall. *The Toy-Shop* continued to sell well, sixteen editions appearing with the Dodsley imprint before the end of the century.

There is evidence that this handful of very well-known satires sold rapidly on their publication and remained popular over several years. But this is not to imply that the market remained level: both supply and demand for printed satire fluctuated significantly throughout the eighteenth century. The British Library's electronic edition of the ESTC allows us to make a rough sketch of the shifting market for satire between 1650 and 1800.[46] Figure 1.1 plots year-by-year figures generated by the widest possible searches of the ESTC for individual publications that feature words with the roots 'satir-' or 'saytr-' in their long titles, or that have had those words applied to them by modern

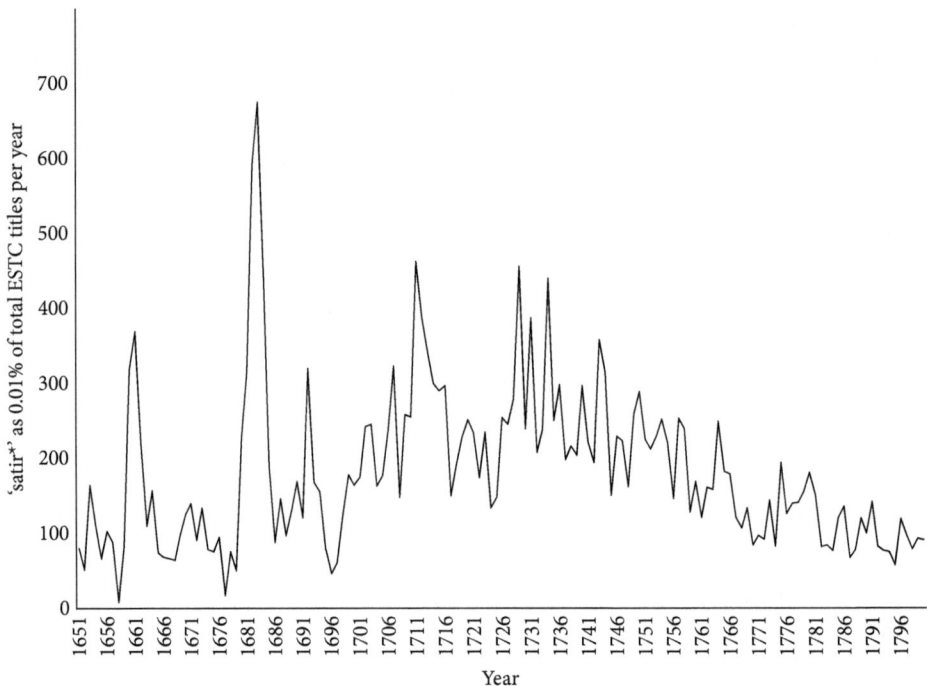

FIGURE 1.1 Occurrences of keyword 'satir*' in ESTC database records per year

[46] http://estc.bl.uk, site accessed 8 September 2017; for the ESTC in period context see Paddy Bullard, 'Digital Humanities and Electronic Resources in the Long Eighteenth Century', *Literature Compass* 10 (2013), 748–60.

cataloguers. Bibliometric analyses of databases are best done by sampling—by examining records for single years at ten-year intervals, for example—so that the analyst has a chance to screen their data in a series of reduced sets.[47] But the number of satire-related publications fluctuated unpredictably from one year to the next: a selective method will not work here. Still, the raw data needs to be contextualized. The production and sale of printed books was affected across the period by volatility in financial markets (bookselling was a highly capitalized trade), by costs of raw materials (especially imported ones like paper), and by expanding or contracting capacity in the trade more generally, among other dynamic factors.[48] In order at least to register these factors I have divided the annual figures for my word-search on 'satir-' by the total number of titles on the ESTC for each year. At the same time I have added records for a few well-known texts that did not come up on my initial word-search. It never occurred to the ESTC's cataloguers to note, for example, that many people (if not everyone) describe *The Rape of the Lock* and *Gulliver's Travels* as satires. The resulting sets of figures constitute rather 'noisy' data, but across a century and a half they allow us to recognize distinct correlations and patterns.

In terms of publication patterns for satire the graph indicates a contrast between the first and second halves of the period 1650–1800. Before *c.*1725 the proportion of published titles identified as satires was apt to fluctuate suddenly, with particular years (1660, 1682, 1710) showing dramatic, short-lived increases.[49] After *c.*1725 one can see a stronger medium-term correlation amid annual variations, with the market share of 'satir-' titles declining steadily across the decades to the century's end. The relatively distinct trend that emerges in the second half of the period can be explained in part by the growing capacity of the book trade.[50] The total number of titles published annually increases across the century, and larger samples absorb local fluctuations in the numbers. But it is only from the 1770s that annual increases in overall book production begin rising steeply, and the correlation is established during the preceding half-century of more steady growth.

If we look for peaks in satire production, the graph shows spikes at the points we would expect it to on the evidence of received literary history. The most dramatic spike occurs in 1681–2, years of extraordinary political ferment that saw the Exclusion Crisis and the publication of John Dryden's satire *Absalom and Achitophel*. We should not assume, of course, that the 277 titles returned by a search for 'satir-' over these years are all, like Dryden's quarto, recognizable as 'literary' productions. The ESTC lists 169 of

---

[47] Sampling methods are discussed by Michael Suarez, 'Towards a Bibliometric Analysis of the Surviving Record, 1701–1800', in *The Cambridge History of the Book in Britain, Volume V: 1695–1830*, ed. Michael Suarez and Michael L. Turner (Cambridge: Cambridge University Press, 2010), 37–65, at 41–3.

[48] See James Raven, *Publishing Business in Eighteenth-Century England* (Woodbridge: Boydell Press, 2014), 33–51.

[49] General spikes in numbers of surviving titles for these years can be seen in the graph for book production illustrated in James Raven, *The Business of Books: Booksellers and the English Book Trade* (New Haven: Yale University Press, 2007), 8, to which 'satir-' titles made a significant contribution.

[50] For context see Raven, *Business of Books*, 131–4, and Suarez, 'Bibliometric Analysis', 43–5.

those titles as single-sheet ballad-style publications, and a similar proportion (49 out of 117) of 'satir-' titles take broadside formats in 1660. By 1728 these proportions have fallen, with a quarter of the 88 'satir-' titles returned being single-sheet productions, whereas half of them are now octavo books or pamphlets.

More generally, the graph indicates that consistently larger proportions of 'satir-' titles were published during periods of heightened political activity and excitement. There are distinct 'shoulders' to peaks seen in 1710–14, the turbulent four last years of Queen Anne's reign and of the Tory 'paper wars'. There is another peak in c.1726–30, when Bolingbroke was reviving those paper wars with *The Craftsman*, and when *Gulliver's Travels*, *The Beggars Opera*, and *The Dunciad* were enjoying the first flush of their success. Other shouldered peaks are identifiable with the period between Walpole's Excise Bill of 1733 and the Licensing Act of 1737, when his ministry was especially hard pressed; with the years around his fall from office in 1742; and later with the Earl of Bute's controversial ministry, c.1762. The graph does not reflect the turbulent political culture of the late 1760s, the period of John Wilkes's Middlesex Election dispute and of *The Letters of Junius*, as one might expect it to, but there is another predictable set of shouldered peaks after 1774, corresponding with the American revolutionary wars.

So the noisy data from these ESTC searches allows us to make a few tentative, though broad-ranging conclusions about the material production of satire in the long eighteenth century. First, the publication rates of satirical titles, be they popular, polemical, or literary, correlate noticeably with periods of turbulence and excitement in high politics, and they recede again in periods of relative socio-political stability, such as the first decades of the reigns of William III (acc. 1689) and George I (acc. 1714). Second, the exceptionally popular single-title satires discussed above tend to appear during these years of political restlessness. Third, after about 1750 satire lost a capacity to make sudden increases in its share of the book trade: it no longer passed dramatically in and out of fashion as it had in 1681–2, 1710–14, or 1727–30. In the later century, satire occupied a settled place in the cultural landscape, but never again made such a distinctive feature in the scene.

Satirical Personalities

So far we have looked at anecdotes that reflect some commonalities of eighteenth-century satire—in associational life, in a tradition of commonplace, in national identity—and we have made a general survey of the period's printed satire by searching for patterns in the bibliographical record. It often suits satirists, as well as historians of satire, to rise above the level of the particular like this: 'Come on then Satire!' urges Pope in the *Epilogue to the Satires*, 'gen'ral, unconfin'd / Spread thy broad wing, and sowze on all the Kind'.[51] Sooner or later, however, the personal and the individual

---

[51] Pope, *Poems* (Twickenham), iv. 314; for general satire see Marshall, 'Thinking about Satire', Chapter 28 in this volume; Wright, 'Fable and Allegory', Chapter 16; Bullard, 'Against the Experts', Chapter 24.

reassert themselves.[52] Pope was as willing as any of his contemporaries to acknowledge the virtue of general satire, but he was impatient with its lack of force: 'People have ceas'd to be ashamed of [general satire] when so many are joined with them', he complained to Arbuthnot; 'and tis only by hunting One or two from the Herd that an Example can be made'.[53] Satires may paint composite or group portraits, but they will be consumed ultimately by readers as individuals, and satirists found irony in this as well. 'I am not conscious of the least malevolence to any particular person thro' all the Characters', claimed Edward Young in the preface to his *Love of Fame* satires; 'tho' some persons may be so selfish, as to engross a general application to themselves'.[54] Henry Fielding insisted that *Joseph Andrews* is a novel that describes 'not Men, but Manners; not an Individual, but a Species': as such its satire is 'calculated for much more general and noble Purposes, than to expose one pitiful Wretch, to the small Circle of his Acquaintance; but to hold the Glass to thousands in their Closets, that they may contemplate their Deformity'.[55] The important point here is that the deformed thousands have no corporate body.[56] Satire is experienced by particular readers, shut up alone in their closets. The movements that satire made between the general and the personal, the public and the private, were understood to cut more deeply than mere fiction into the personal sphere.[57] This may be why there is such a strong line of eighteenth-century satire that plays with experiences of lying, credulity, and private faith.[58] There were implications for the moral claims that satirists made, as well as for the experience of individual readers.

There is a striking example of the pressure that the debate about general satire could put on the moral characterization of an individual satirist in Samuel Johnson's *Dictionary of the English Language* (1755). Johnson chose three literary examples to illustrate his definition for the word 'SÁTRIST. *n.f.* [from *satire*]. One who writes satires'. Arranged as a group, it is clear that the reader is expected to spot a link between the quotations, which are laid out in this order:

> Wycherly, in his writing, is the sharpest *satirist* of his time; but, in his nature, he has all the softness of the tenderest disposition: in his writings, he is severe, bold, undertaking; in his nature gentle, modest, inoffensive. *Granville.*

---

[52] See, in this volume, Scott, 'Augustan Romantics', Chapter 14; Tadié, 'Quarrelling', Chapter 32; Curran, 'Self-portraiture', Chapter 26.

[53] Pope to Arbuthnot, published version, dated 26 July 1734, Alexander Pope, *Selected Letters*, ed. Howard Erskine-Hill (Oxford: Oxford University Press, 2000), 248; for a conspectus of eighteenth-century statements on general vs. personal satire see Elkin, *Augustan Defense*, 118–45.

[54] Young, *Love of Fame*, A2^r.

[55] Fielding, *The History of the Adventures of Joseph Andrews*, 2 vols. (1742), ii. 5–6.

[56] See, in this volume, Deutsch, 'Misanthropy and Violence', Chapter 25.

[57] For public–private see, in this volume, Tadié, 'Quarrelling', Chapter 32; Curran, 'Self-portraiture', Chapter 26; Rabb, 'Satire and Domesticity', Chapter 27; see also Michael McKeon, *The Secret History of Domesticity: Public, Private and the Division of Knowledge* (Baltimore: Johns Hopkins University Press, 2005), 83–5, 95–9.

[58] See, in this volume, Walsh, 'Against Hypocrisy and Dissent', Chapter 3; McDowell, 'The Double Personality of Lucianic Satire', Chapter 9; Carey, 'Swift, Gulliver, and Travel Satire I', Chapter 12; Gee, 'Believing and Unbelieving in *The Dunciad*', Chapter 13.

All vain pretenders have been constantly the topicks of the most candid *satyrists*, from the Codrus of Juvenal to the Damon of Boileau. *Letter to the Publisher of the Dunciad.*

> Yet soft his nature, though severe his lay;
> His anger moral, and his wisdom gay:
> Blest *satirist,* who touch'd the mean so true,
> As show'd vice had his hate and pity too.
>
> *Pope.*[59]

The first quotation comes from a 'Character' of William Wycherley written by his fellow dramatist George Granville, Lord Lansdown, to whom Pope dedicated *Windsor Forest.*[60] The second and third are both by Alexander Pope: one is from *The Dunciad*'s prefatory material, the other from an epitaph for Charles, Earl of Dorset, published in 1735. In the criticism of Pope's epitaphs that Johnson wrote in 1756 for *The Universal Visitor*, later republished in his life of Pope, the line 'Yet soft his nature, though severe his lay', is described as 'a high compliment, but was not first bestowed on Dorset by Pope'.[61] Johnson makes no specific attribution. In terms of general sense, an obvious precedent is the Earl of Rochester's famous lines in 'An Allusion to Horace', where Dorset is singled out as supreme contemporary satirist, 'The best good Man, with the worst-natur'd Muse'.[62] But the sequence of quotations that Johnson selected for the *Dictionary* indicates that Pope has borrowed from Granville—the 'Character' of Wycherley does indeed anticipate Pope's opposition of 'soft' and 'severe'.[63]

The attribution is so obscure that Johnson preferred, perhaps, not to make an open claim. But the second of the *Dictionary*'s three quotations shows there was a more important point that he wanted to add. In the 'Letter to the Publisher of the *Dunciad*' Pope rehearsed a commonplace argument about affectation and hypocrisy ('all vain pretenders') being the most proper subjects for satire.[64] Johnson takes him absolutely at his word, implying that anyone who writes harsh satire when his nature is reticent is a sort of hypocrite, and that Pope is dishonest twice over to publish a paradox that is both morally frivolous and stolen. Paul Fussell has described the 'dualistic vision' that the earlier generation of Scriblerian satirists had of human nature, 'a surface of contempt, disparagement, and ridicule masking something quite different, namely, an implicit faith in

---

[59] Samuel Johnson, *A Dictionary of the English Language*, 2 vols. (1755), ii. 'Satirist'.

[60] George Granville, 'Character of Mr. Wycherley', in Charles Gildon, *Memoirs of the Life of William Wycherley* (1718), 23–6. Pope, whose earliest writings are praised by Granville in the 'Character', quotes that praise in the 1736 *Works*, vol. 1 (Pope, *Poems* (Twickenham), i. 59): see Joseph Spence, *Observations, Anecdotes, and Characters of Books and Men*, ed. James M. Osborn, 2 vols. (Oxford: Clarendon Press, 1966), no. 165, and appendix on ii. 625, for context.

[61] Johnson, *Lives*, iv. 82–3.

[62] *Works of John Wilmot, Earl of Rochester*, ed. Harold Love (Oxford: Oxford University Press, 1999), 72; its fame confirmed by Steele's quotation in no. 242 of *The Tatler*, iii. 242.

[63] Lonsdale (Johnson, *Lives*, iv. 352) points out that 'P's editors do not note the borrowing SJ has in mind', referring to Pope, *Poems* (Twickenham), vi. 334–6.

[64] Pope, *Poems* (Longman), iii. 132; see Elkin, *Augustan Defense*, 173, for the commonplace.

man's capacity for redemption'.[65] They were often contented, moreover, to let that doubleness cast a fog of irony over their own ethical positions.[66] In his 'Epistle to Bolingbroke' Pope wrote of the 'Man divine whom Wisdom calls her own' as an immortal thing, half angelic, '– except (what's mighty odd) / A Fit of Vapours clouds this Demi-God'. Bolingbroke himself identified Swift as a 'hypocrite reversed', so determined to preserve his integrity that he dissembled his piety and virtue under a false display of irreverence.[67] By 1755 Samuel Johnson seems to have felt that these ironic, doubled ethical positions were at best affectations, and at worst dishonest. In the *Dictionary* he leaves them to create their own impression of unsound sophistication, fundamentally at odds with the strenuous virtue to which Swift and Pope also laid claim.

Examples like these support the received idea that there was a shift in literary opinion around 1750 against satire, a shift that coincided with a new 'Age of Sensibility', with an emerging urban commercial class that was self-consciously sentimental and polite, and eventually with Romantic constructions of the self.[68] This vision of the British eighteenth century is settled, but historians have begun recently to qualify it. Graphic satire and popular fiction provide the principal evidence that the British nation continued to wallow in cruelty, coarseness, and hilarity, even while the philosophers and novelists insisted on its growing refinement.[69]

Looking at the complex picture we now have of the mid-century, one theme that emerges from contemporary commentary is the increasing dissatisfaction of writers with the instrumental emphasis of earlier accounts of satire—the abiding concern of the Scriblerian generation, that is, with satire's capacity (or failure) to instruct, to chastise, to vex, or to forewarn.[70] The Enlightenment 'science of man' directed the attention of philosophers towards 'moral causes', as David Hume termed them, the full range of circumstances 'which are fitted to work on the mind as motives or reason, and which render a

---

[65] Paul Fussell, *The Rhetorical World of Augustan Humanism: Ethics and Imagery from Swift to Burke* (Oxford: Oxford University Press, 1965), 112; Fussell's mention of 'redemption' fudges the problem posed by deistic and irreligious strands in eighteenth-century satire, often passed down through the Lucianic tradition, and discussed in this volume by McDowell, 'The Double Personality of Lucianic Satire', Chapter 9; Haugen, 'Alexander Pope and the Philosophical Horace', Chapter 11; and Gee, 'Believing and Unbelieving in *The Dunciad*', Chapter 13.

[66] For irony and satire see especially Lamb, 'Romance, Satire, and the Exploitation of Disorder', Chapter 19 in this volume; Tadié, 'Quarrelling', Chapter 32.

[67] Pope, Poems (Twickenham), iv. 293. Thomas Sheridan, *The Life of the Rev. Dr Jonathan Swift* (1784), A2ᵛ.

[68] See, in this volume, Scott, 'Augustan Romantics', Chapter 14; Lamb, 'Romance, Satire, and the Exploitation of Disorder', Chapter 19; Rabb, 'Satire and Domesticity', Chapter 27; Batchelor, 'Pamela and the Satirists', Chapter 36; Festa, 'Satire to Sentiment', Chapter 38.

[69] See Jones, 'Foxite Satire', Chapter 8 in this volume; Deutsch, 'Misanthropy and Violence', Chapter 25; Steedman, 'Satire in Metropolis and Province', Chapter 40; Vic Gatrell, *City of Laughter: Sex and Satire in Eighteenth-Century London* (London: Atlantic Books, 2006); Simon Dickie, *Cruelty and Laughter: Forgotten Comic Literature and the Unsentimental Eighteenth Century* (Chicago: University of Chicago Press, 2011).

[70] See, in this volume, Deutsch, 'Misanthropy and Violence', Chapter 25; Klein, 'Ridicule as a Tool for Discovering Truth', Chapter 34; Robinson, 'The Edge of Satire', Chapter 37.

peculiar set of manners habitual to us'.[71] But non-philosophers also wanted more complete accounts of the dynamics of social exchange. In 1765 Lord Chesterfield wrote a letter to his son against satire, basing his case on some acute psychological observations:

> Wit is so shining a quality, that everybody admires it, most people aim at it, all people fear it, and few love it unless in themselves. A man must have a good share of wit himself to endure a great share of it in another. When wit exerts itself in satire it is a most malignant distemper; wit it is true may be shown in satire, but satire does not constitute wit, as most fools imagine it does. A man of real wit will find a thousand better occasions of showing it. Abstain therefore most carefully from satire, which though it fall upon no particular person in company, and momentarily from the malignity of the human heart, pleases all; upon reflection, it frightens all too, they think it may be their turn next [...] Fear and hatred are next door neighbours. The more wit you have the more good nature and politeness you must show, to induce people to pardon your superiority, for that is no easy matter.[72]

The outlines of the old defence of satire are still visible here, particularly Dryden's design for the reception of 'fine raillery'—'a witty man is tickled when he is hurt in this manner, and fool feels it not'.[73] There are also shades of the highly qualified defence of satire that Addison made in *The Freeholder* no. 45: that while 'Detraction and Obloquy' always gets an eager response, the pleasure they give lasts only a moment, and the satirist 'must be a very ill Man, if by such a Proceeding he could please himself'.[74] The difference is that Chesterfield's thinking is focused not on the satirist but on the rest of the company, and beyond them on the full range of Humean moral causes in which acts of satire are set. For all his worldliness, Chesterfield shows both the moral acuity and, more unexpectedly, the suspicion of cynicism that characterize contemporary Scottish philosophers. As David Hume asked in his second *Enquiry* (1751), 'why rake into those corners of nature which spread a nuisance all around? Why dig up the pestilence from the pit in which it is buried? The ingenuity of your researches may be admired; but your systems will be detested'.[75] Chesterfield understands the delicate adjustments people must make to their sentiments if they are to avoid jeopardizing the sympathy of others—Adam Smith, for example, made similar calculations in the *Theory of Moral Sentiments* (1759).[76] He understands, as Lord Kames put it in *The Elements of Criticism* (1762), that the 'irregular use made of a talent for wit or ridicule, cannot long impose on mankind. It cannot

[71] David Hume, *Essays Moral, Political and Literary*, ed. Eugene F. Miller (Indianapolis: Liberty Fund, 1985), 198.

[72] *Lord Chesterfield's Letters*, ed. David Roberts (Oxford: Oxford University Press, 1992), 345.

[73] Dryden, 'Discourse', 423, echoing Persius 1.116–7, cited above.

[74] Joseph Addison, *The Freeholder*, ed. James Leheny (Oxford: Clarendon Press, 1979), 237.

[75] David Hume, *Enquiries Concerning Human Understanding and the Principles of Morals*, ed. P. H. Nidditch, 3rd edn. (Oxford: Clarendon Press, 1975), 279.

[76] See Adam Smith, *The Theory of Moral Sentiments*, ed. D. D. Raphael and A. L. Macfie (Oxford: Clarendon Press, 1976), 43–50.

stand the test of correct or delicate taste.'[77] Chesterfield's letter shows once again how hard it was by the mid-eighteenth century to maintain the postures of satiric heroism that had served Pope and Swift so well only a few decades earlier.

The positions taken by Johnson and Chesterfield in these comments and quotations stand as examples of the moral pressure that was placed on satirists from mid-century.[78] One way of easing this pressure was to take a step back from the ethical dilemmas, and to fictionalize both the individuals who face them and the people that they satirize. Chesterfield's comment about the momentary malignity of humanity assumes that everyone—author, victim, and audience—is implicated in the satirical event.[79] Isaac Barrow had come to the same conclusion in 1678: 'satyrical taunts do owe their seeming piquancy, not to the speaker, or his words, but to the subject, and the hearers; the matter conspiring with the bad nature, or the vanity of men.'[80] Fiction provides a frame in which implicated audience, victim, and satirist can be individualized without involving the author directly.

Accordingly, satirists became stock characters in eighteenth-century novels and plays: examples include Mr Spatter in *David Simple* (1744), *Roderick Random*'s (1748) Miss Snapper, and Mr Tinsel in Lennox's *Female Quixote* (1752). But none creates more doubt and confusion among her fellow characters than Mrs Selwyn in Frances Burney's novel *Evelina* (1778). Evelina's unwanted suitor Sir Clement Willoughby—himself a wit and practical joker—is excited by Mrs Selwyn's banter, but is no match for her aggressive energy: 'she keeps alive a perpetual expectation of satire,' he complains, 'that spreads a general uneasiness among all who are in her presence; and she talks so much, that even the best things she says weary the attention.'[81] Mr Villars, Evelina's angelic but distant mentor, diagnoses gender trouble: 'for, in studying to acquire the knowledge of the other sex, she has lost all the softness of her own'. It is Evelina herself, however, who has the best understanding of how Mrs Selwyn exemplifies the moral limitations of the satirist's role:

> It is true, Mrs. Selwyn is very obliging, and, in every respect, treats me as an equal; but she is contented with behaving well herself, and does not, with a distinguishing politeness, raise and support me with others. Yet I mean not to blame her, for I know she is sincerely my friend; but the fact is, she is herself so much occupied in conversation, when in company, that she has neither leisure nor thought to attend to the silent.[82]

---

[77] Henry Home, Lord Kames, *Elements of Criticism*, ed. Peter Jones, 2 vols. (Indianapolis: Liberty Fund, 2005), i. 262–3.

[78] See, in this volume, Rounce, 'Churchill and his Circle', Chapter 7; Fowler, 'Moralizing Satire', Chapter 35; Batchelor, 'Pamela and the Satirists', Chapter 36; Robinson, 'The Edge of Satire', Chapter 37.

[79] See, in this volume, Curran, 'Self-Portraiture', Chapter 26.

[80] Barrow, *Several Sermons*, 74.

[81] Frances Burney, *Evelina*, ed. Edward A. Bloom (London: Oxford University Press, 1968), 343.

[82] Burney, *Evelina*, 294.

Evelina sees that Mrs Selwyn's self-directed motives for ridicule correspond with her obsessive focus on the satirical object before her. Both are ungenerously narrow, and both mean that she cannot do her common duty within the larger social group. This narrowness is understood by Evelina as a failure to think and to distinguish, that rather compromises Mrs Selwyn's claim to intellectual distinction. But it is significant that a more polite and rational manner is assumed to be within her power. Mrs Selwyn is much more than a humour character, for all her narrowness. When Lady Mary Wortley Montagu had fought back against Pope's attacks on her, she represented her opponent as a sort of vicious animal, and his aggression as a bodily compulsion.[83] Of course she did not neglect to mention his physical deformity in this context: it 'shows the Uniformity of Fate, / That one so odious should be born to hate'.[84] She told Joseph Spence that Addison had once advised her to 'leave him as soon as you can [...]; he has an appetite to satire'.[85] With Burney's Mrs Selwyn, on the other hand, we can see all the way around the satirist's psychological circumstances. We see her appetite for satire hardened by a will to dominate, yet subtilized by knowledge and observation (always of others, never of the self); we see it wielded to defend the unprotected, but we note its inflexibility. It is useless when kindness and encouragement are required.[86] Above all we see how it mortifies and discourages everyone it touches, both friend and foe. By the end of the eighteenth century satire has itself become an object for social description and moral anatomization. And this, as much as anything, marks the period of satire's ascendancy over eighteenth-century culture.

Parts of the Handbook

This handbook contains forty-one chapters, all of them concerned with satire, a kind of writing that is unusual among the literary genres and modes: it is protean and digressive; it represents a confluence of several different modes and literary traditions, some very ancient and some new; it tends to assemble itself, as Paul Baines points out in Chapter 16, in raggedy, miscellaneous collections. These disorderly tendencies need to be kept in check by a collection like this, but it would not do to rein them in too hard. A chronological or taxonomic organization would be wrong here: this handbook is divided into six thematically defined, diachronically arranged parts. Each contains chapters that

---

[83]   See, in this volume, Campbell, 'Sexing Satire', Chapter 33; Fowler, 'Moralizing Satire', Chapter 35.

[84]   Lady Mary Wortley Montagu, *Essays and Poems and Simplicity, a Comedy*, ed. Robert Halsband and Isobel Grundy (Oxford: Clarendon Press, 1977), 268.

[85]   Spence, *Observations*, no. 748; cf. Colley Cibber, *Letter from Mr Cibber to Mr Pope* (1742), 65: 'When you used to pass your Hours at *Button*'s you were even there remarkable for your satirical Itch of Provocation.'

[86]   See, in this volume, Rabb, 'Satire and Domesticity', Chapter 27; Robinson, 'The Edge of Satire', Chapter 37.

discuss books and writers ranging from the earliest to the latest years of the long eighteenth century (*c.*1660–*c.*1815).

Part I, 'Satirical Alignments', expands on the range of cultural commonalities sketched out at the start of this introductory essay. It contains chapters on the associational life that provided a background to so much eighteenth-century satirical writing, and others on alignments that were the expressions of religion, gender, nation, and political party. Part II, 'Satirical Inheritances', deals with the influence of different intellectual traditions on eighteenth-century satirists. The most significant of these are generic: the literary codes and traditions transmitted through imitation and criticism of ancient Greek and Roman satirical writings, particularly of those by Lucian, Horace, and Juvenal (the latter championed by John Dryden). But others are in play, including the lately evolved conventions of early modern travel writing, and the controversial theology of the material universe.

Part III, 'Satirical Modes', looks at some of the forms of writing that were associated conventionally with satire: fable, parody, travesty, and romance. But modes of satire also moved outward from the textual realm into dimensions that were not purely literary: they found a natural bibliographical form in the printed miscellany; graphic form in the designs of Hogarth and Gillray; and dramatic form on the mid-eighteenth-century stage. Part IV, 'Satirical Objects', continues this outward trajectory towards the things on which satire was designed to impact: its material objects, and its human and social ones, including the satirist herself.

Part V, 'Satirical Actions', considers things that eighteenth-century people did with satire. Some satirical actions were reflective, such as the deployment of ridicule as a tool of analysis, or self-reflexive, such as the theorization of satire itself; others were performative; others again were more directly instrumental, equipping satirists with the means to negotiate fields of legal, cultural, or political conflict. Part VI, 'Satirical Transitions', looks at the widening cultural arena in which satire operated during the second half of the eighteenth century and beyond: between metropolis and province; between Britain and the continent; between an age of wit and an age of sentiment.

PART I

SATIRICAL ALIGNMENTS

CHAPTER 2

··

CORPORATE ACTS
OF SATIRE

··

JUDITH HAWLEY

SATIRE is necessarily an oppositional art, depending on the existence of rival perspectives, if not rival camps. Some satirists in this period acted as lone wolves, alienated outsiders, picking off their prey. Notable in this line are Junius, Peter Pindar, and the Juvenalian Johnson, friendless and deploring the state of London. Many preferred to hunt in packs. This chapter will describe and analyse the activity of satirical clubs and groups in the period, attempting to understand the motives and impact of corporate acts of satire from the age of Dryden to that of the Scriblerians. Few of these groups had a formal club constitution with rules of membership and few lasted for long. Nonetheless, their influence on their members and the literary scene was sometimes profound. The Scriblerus Club only met regularly for a brief period in 1713–14, but it informed the thinking of its members for years to come and fostered such works as *The Dunciad*, *Gulliver's Travels*, and *The Beggar's Opera*. That is not to say that these works were actually composed during club meetings. With the exception of the Nonsense Club, few clubs actually collaborated by writing together in the same room.

Moreover, corporate acts of satire took numerous forms. To understand the sociability of eighteenth-century satire, it is necessary to conceive of collaboration more broadly. As well as joint authorship, it includes sociable forms such as the dialogue in which the satirist imagines and responds to his opponents. It also includes periodicals, many of which were attributed to figures such as the 'Craftsman' or the 'Champion' but were the work of many hands. The satirical persona could also incorporate multiple authors in different ways. Martinus Scriblerus was not only the corporate author of the works of the Scriblerus Club; writings by opponents such as Bentley were attributed to him.[1] Furthermore, later writers affiliated themselves to him: Henry Fielding wrote as Scriblerus Secundus and numerous others claimed to descend from him. Even the

---

[1] *Memoirs of the Extraordinary Life, Works, and Discoveries of Martinus Scriblerus*, ed. Charles Kerby-Miller (Oxford: Clarendon Press, 1988; 1st ed. 1950), 171.

singular Peter Pindar advertised himself as 'a distant relation of the poet of Thebes' (i.e. Pindar (*c.*522–*c.*443 BCE)). These kinds of *ex post facto* relationships demonstrate the fact that in this period satirists wished to club together, to forge affiliations in a literary and political environment which fostered both factional divisions and clubbable associations.

THE RAGE OF PARTY

To some extent, the state of politics fostered the emergence of clubs of satirists. From the unresolved tensions following the Restoration to the 'Rage of Party' which followed the Glorious Revolution (the period 1690–1715 was so fractious that it produced eleven parliaments), to the vocal opposition to Walpole in the 1730s and the political crisis triggered by the radical MP John Wilkes in the 1760s, the climate was ripe not just for satire but for the formation of factions and defensive associations. In the seventeenth century when courtiers and poets met not only socially but in the same person there was very little difference between a literary club and a political faction. Both George Villiers, Duke of Buckingham and John Wilmot, Earl of Rochester conducted politics by other means in their often scabrous satires. The poems on affairs of state—a genre popular in the later seventeenth century—were obvious political satires, but pornographic libels which might not refer to obviously ideological issues had the political aim of damaging the reputation of an opponent. More idealistically, writers frequently held up the Augustan age as a model of political-literary relations and looked for a Maecenas to provide patronage. Some politicians did foster writers; the Dukes of Buckingham and Dorset provided patronage in the form of literary encouragement and practical support. Writers who dined in Dorset's 'poet's parlour' in his house at Knole 'might well find banknotes under their plates'.[2] Some later clubs were set up with the aim of bringing together writers and powerful backers: both the Whig Kit-Kats and Tory Brothers Club were notable in this regard.[3] Despite the fact that both groups included numerous wits, they produced almost no writing of note. Their energies seemed to have been largely consumed by the business of eating and drinking. Robert Walpole, frequently criticized for failing to support the arts, could be said to have fostered a satirical club as he ran a propaganda machine by paying scores of hacks to write satire for him.[4] George, Lord

---

[2] John Harold Wilson, *The Court Wits of the Restoration: An Introduction* (Princeton: Princeton University Press, 1948), 23. For the Court Wits as patrons more generally, see *Plays, Poems, and Miscellaneous Writings associated with George Villiers, Second Duke of Buckingham*, ed. Robert D. Hume and Harold Love, 2 vols. (Oxford: Oxford University Press, 2007), i. xlix.

[3] On the Kit-Kats, see Ophelia Field, *The Kit-Cat Club: Friends who Imagined a Nation* (London: Harper Press, 2008). The only surviving account of the Brothers occurs in Swift's *Journal to Stella*; see Swift, *Works* (Cambridge), ix. 227, 231, 349.

[4] See Tone Sundt Urstad, *Sir Robert Walpole's Poets: The Use of Literature as Pro-Government Propaganda, 1721–1742* (London: Associated University Presses, 1999).

Lyttelton, too, supported writers promoting the Patriot opposition, some of whom were utopian rather than satirical.[5]

Other literary congregations and coteries flourished in the period, the most important of which are the virtuous circle which revolved around Katherine Philips in the 1650s, the network of learned ladies known as the Bluestockings, and Johnson's Club (which went through several iterations from 1764). None of these were satirical groups. Moreover, the primary purpose of Johnson's Club, although its members included writers, was conversation rather than corporate production. Three groups of satirical writers brought together by their shared literary and political values stand out as exemplary in different ways: the Court Wits, the Scriblerus Club, and the Nonsense Club. The last of these is the subject of another chapter (see Rounce, 'Churchill and his Circle', Chapter 7) so this chapter will focus on the Wits and the Scriblerians while also attending to wider and less obvious forms of corporate satire, such as periodical literature.

THE COURT WITS

Rochester ends his 'Allusion to Horace' (*c*.1675)—a lecture on the right and wrong ways to write—with an invocation of his literary saints:

> I loath the Rabble, 'tis enough for me,
> If Sydley, Shadwell, Shepheard, Wicherley,
> Godolphin, Butler, Buckhurst, Buckinghame,
> And some few more, whome I omitt to name
> Approve my sence, I count their Censure Fame.[6]

While his model is consciously antique, his references are contemporary. His satire accurately delineates the rival literary gangs that duked it out in Restoration England. On the one hand, there was what he calls the 'Rabble' or the 'poor-fed Poets of the Town': paid writers (and ardent Tories) such as Dryden, Thomas Flatman, Charles Cotton, Thomas Shipman, and Nahum Tate.[7] On the other, there were his friends and fellow Court Wits (dubbed 'the Merry Gang' by Andrew Marvell). The Court Wits were both a

---

[5] See Christine Gerrard, *The Patriot Opposition to Walpole: Politics, Poetry, and National Myth, 1725–1742* (Oxford: Clarendon Press, 1994).

[6] John Wilmot, 2nd Earl of Rochester, 'An Allusion to Horace 10 Sat: 1st Book', ll. 120–4, in Harold Love, ed., *The Works of John Wilmot Earl of Rochester* (Oxford: Oxford University Press, 1999).

[7] 'Allusion to Horace', ll. 118, 120. Love reads 'poor led Poets' but accepts that Vieth's reading: 'poor-fed' is 'equally satisfactory'. See David M. Vieth, ed., *The Complete Poems of John Wilmot, Earl of Rochester* (New Haven: Yale University Press, 1968), 126.

political coalition with shared ideological values and a literary group.[8] As courtiers, they performed services in the royal household; some were members of government or of parliament and were expected to vote as instructed or they would lose their places at court.[9] Hanging around at court gave them plenty of opportunities to cluster and cabal. Indeed, the most powerful aristocratic patron of the Court Wits, George Villiers, 2nd Duke of Buckingham (1628–87) was one of the original CABAL.[10]

Narrowly defined, the Court Wits comprised the nobles: Buckingham, Buckhurst, Butler, Carbery, Rochester, and Sheffield.[11] Conceived broadly and loosely, they also included the gentlemen: Henry Bulkeley, Sidney Godolphin, Henry Guy, Henry Killigrew, Henry Savile, Sir Carr Scroope, Sir Charles Sedley Fleetwood Shepherd, and William Wycherley; and the commoners: Samuel Butler, Martin Clifford, Abraham Cowley, and Thomas Sprat. Membership of this coterie was not entirely unified or stable. Rochester was the centre of an inner circle of wits known for their wild ways—he names them in the passage above.[12] As with any gang, there are fallings out because of clashes of personality, and allegiances change along with circumstances. Dryden at first associated himself with the Wits; he sought Rochester's patronage in 1673, dedicating his *Marriage-à-la Mode* to him, but, as a professional writer, he could never be fully accepted by the upper-class amateurs. Rochester turned against him and attacked him in 'An Allusion to Horace', and Dryden joined the group led by Mulgrave, who had himself broken with Rochester in 1669. The split between the Buckingham and Mulgrave circles hardened after 1673 when it became clear that the heir to the throne, James, Duke of York, had converted to Catholicism. Mulgrave's group supported the Stuart succession, even if some had qualms about James's religious beliefs. At some point, Sprat, Etherege, and Wycherley also threw in their lot with the Yorkist faction—a faction which eventually developed into the Tory party. Buckingham and his followers, later dubbed Whigs,

---

[8] According to Love: 'Poetry, along with sceptical philosophy and practical debauchery, was the bonding agent of a group whose ultimate rationale was political—the heterodox, Erastian wing of the Whig alliance.' Harold Love, *The Culture and Commerce of Texts: Scribal Publication in Seventeenth-Century England* (Oxford: Clarendon Press, 1993), 252–3.

[9] Wilson, *Court Wits*, 47, 60, 63–6.

[10] This term for secret clique is derived from 'Cabala'—the mystical interpretation of the Hebrew scripture, but its particular meaning might derive from the initial letters of the names of Charles II's ministers who signed a secret treaty with France in 1670: Sir Thomas Clifford, Lord Arlington, the Duke of Buckingham, Lord Ashley, and Lord Lauderdale. The group was never really unified and broke up after a year or so, but the name survived.

[11] The full names and titles of the nobles are George Villiers, 2nd Duke of Buckingham (1628–87); Charles Sackville, Lord Buckhurst, 6th Earl of Dorset and Middlesex (1643–1707); Lord John Vaughan, 3rd Earl of Carbery (1639–1713); John Wilmot, Earl of Rochester (1647–80); John Sheffield (1648–1721) (confusingly, he was also 1st Duke of Buckingham and Normanby, and later Earl of Mulgrave). 'Butler' might refer to either Lord John Butler or the poet, Samuel Butler.

[12] Love suggests that 'the inclusion of the Tory, Godolphin, and the elderly Samuel Butler (if he is the individual intended) indicates that this is rather a list of Rochester's primary readership as an author-publisher than of the Buckingham faction per se; but otherwise the fit is exact.' Love, *Culture and Commerce*, 252.

supported the constitutional monarchy established at the Restoration and promoted the succession of a Protestant monarch.

These rival coteries produced a number of jointly-authored satires. Sometimes a poem deemed to be badly written, or written on the wrong side of the political argument, would provoke responses from several of the Wits. Thus, the Hon. Edward Howard's allegorical poem about the conflict between Buckingham and Charles II, *The Duel of the Stags* (written 1667, pub. 1668) provoked obscene parodies attributed to Savile and Buckhurst. In 'The Duel' and 'The Duel of the Crabs', the mighty conflict between monarchs of the glen was reduced to a fight between venereal lice.[13] Sometimes the rival gangs maintained running battles in pamphlet form. There was a protracted exchange of fire over Elkanah Settle's tragedy *The Empress of Morocco* (1673).[14]

News that satires were in the offing provoked consternation. In 1677, Savile wrote to his friend Rochester:

> I must tell you the whole tribe are alarumed att a libell against them lately sent by the post to Will's coffe [*sic*] house. I am not happy enough to have seen it, but I heare it commended and therefore the more probably thought to be composed att Woodstock, especially considering what an assembly either is yett or att least has been there, to whom my most humble service, if they are yett with you.[15]

The 'libell' might have been the anonymous 'Advice to Apollo' (1678) which attacks Dryden, Mulgrave, Scroope, and Shepherd and praises Rochester and Dorset. Savile's letter to Rochester presents a vivid image of the collaborative nature of both the composition and the consumption of these corporate satires. Savile tells his friend Rochester that the tribe which met under their chieftain Dryden at Will's coffee-house in Covent Garden were sitting around discussing a rumour that their clan had written a libel against them. The High Lodge at Woodstock, where Rochester resided as Ranger and Keeper of the Park, became a resort for rakes, and a writing workshop. Wilson conjectures that Rochester and his associates jointly composed 'A Session of the Poets', their satire on professionals such as Settle and Dryden, 'sitting about a long table in the great hall at Woodstock, with bumpers of wine before them and a log burning in the fire-place'.[16] A lampoon which dates from 1678–9, 'A Song on Thomas Earl of Danby', attributed to Buckingham but likely to be the work of many hands, might have been composed in an after-dinner drinking and singing session at which the friends around the table improvised verses to a well-known tune. Significantly, the term 'lampoon' derives from a seventeenth-century French slang word, lampons: 'let us drink'.[17] Other verses might have been added later in response to changing events. Wilson also speculates that a

---

[13] Wilson, *Court Wits*, 180. 'The Duel of the Crabs' was published in *Poems on Affairs of State* (1697).

[14] Wilson, *Court Wits*, 181.

[15] John Harold Wilson, ed., *The Rochester–Savile Letters, 1671–1680* (Columbus: Ohio State University Press, 1941), 49.

[16] Wilson, *Court Wits*, 182.   [17] *OED*.

group of eight poems mocking the Hon. Edward Howard's narrative poem, *The Brittish Princes* (1669) might all have been written at 'a single session at the Duke of Buckingham's London residence, Wallingford House.... We can imagine Buckingham...proposing a wit contest with *The Brittish Princes* as the subject.'[18] Again, hostilities continued: Howard's protests produced more attacks from Butler and Buckhurst.

While Wilson imagines a roomful of warm bodies and heated imaginations composing a series of satires as a group, Harold Love sees a collection of texts that circulated in manuscript form, 'probably assembled during the following summer by the time-honoured method of circulating the growing file from writer to writer'.[19] The materiality of the manuscript record should contribute to our understanding of how this corpus of writings and of writers was both produced and received. It emerged from a social ideal of creation and consumption: works were written for and by an intimate group with manuscript rather than print publication in mind. Moreover, the transmission of these productions via scribal publication was also symbolically multiple. Individual lampoons might circulate as 'separates', peddled by scribal publishers such as the infamous Robert Julian, so-called 'Secretary to the Muses'.[20] Equally important were the manuscript miscellanies assembled either by individual readers or by professional 'scriptoria'. When he died, Buckingham had in his pocket a manuscript commonplace book which was probably compiled by his secretary, Martin Clifford. So, while the works of the Buckingham and Mulgrave factions might not have been composed at one sitting, they were collected so that they were physically proximate on paper. A reasonably stable corpus of works was assembled by these communities of readers. Yet identifying who wrote what is impossible, partly because writers deliberately cloaked the politically or sexually charged contents of poems in anonymity, making misattribution by distributors common.[21] The mystification of anonymity could be dangerous. On 18 December 1679, Dryden was beaten up by unknown assailants in Rose Alley, Covent Garden. It was probably a revenge attack commissioned by one of the targets of the anonymous poem 'An Essay upon Satire'. Although this satire was fathered on Dryden, Mulgrave might have been the chief author.[22] In his *Essay upon Poetry* (1682), Mulgrave noted that the laureate was 'prais'd and punish'd for another's Rimes': Dryden took a hit for the team.[23]

---

[18] Wilson, *Court Wits*, 178. Love lists the titles and ascriptions in the largest MS collection: Bodleian MS Eng. poet. 3 4 (Love, *Culture and Commerce*, 245–6). This collection of nine poems includes two that satirize a later play by Buckingham.

[19] Love, *Culture and Commerce*, 245.

[20] Rochester carried 'separates' with him. On one occasion he reached into his pocket to fish out a poem for Charles II but accidentally pulled out one *on* him rather than *for* him (Vieth, *Rochester*, xxvii; see also Love, *Culture and Commerce*, 213, 237, 247). For Robert Julian, see Love, *Culture and Commerce*, 249–50, 253–9.

[21] In 'Timon, A Satyr', Rochester comically dramatizes a case of misattribution.

[22] John Mullan, 'Dryden's Anonymity', in *The Cambridge Companion to John Dryden*, ed. Steven N. Zwicker (Cambridge: Cambridge University Press, 2004), 156.

[23] Mullan, 'Dryden's Anonymity', 157.

TROPES OF CORPORATION

Some of the works produced by these rival coteries include markers of the convivial circumstances of their production and reception. Others trope their corporate nature in different ways. The most common form is a variation on the list or litany in which one poet runs through a series of individual targets. Although the speaker and the targets are individuals, the effect is of a spokesperson itemizing the members of the opposing group. Rochester's 'An Allusion to Horace', already mentioned, is an instance of this type. Written from the opposing camp, Scroope's 'In Defence of Satire' does not name names, but his list of 'types' such as the vain Fop, the Fool who thinks he is a Wit, the back-biting railer, or his nicknames such as the Booby Sotus, Chattering Boras, and Florid Roscius were readily identified by his contemporaries.[24]

The act of group judgement is dramatized in Buckingham's *The Rehearsal*, a magnificent satire on heroic drama in which the plain-speaking observers, Johnson and Smith, criticize a rehearsal of a nonsensical heroic drama by the poet Bayes. First drafted in 1665, it mocked the whole school of heroic drama. But when it was first performed in 1671 it was more pointedly a satire on Dryden, who had made a reputation as an author and defender of heroic verse drama, and, as poet laureate since 1668, wore the bays.[25] One of the first charges it makes against Bayes is that he is not sole author of his works. He draws them from two sources: his 'book of *Drama Common places*' culled from numerous writers, and his 'Table-Book' into which he has transcribed witticisms he has overheard in coffee-houses.[26] Bayes's plagiarism is presented as a kind of corporate authorship as he recruits other writers (albeit unwittingly) to contribute to his works. Collaboration was common practice in the theatre of Shakespeare's day but, according to Paulina Kewes, it was out of fashion by the 1630s.[27] However, this charge is disingenuous—or hypocritical—as *The Rehearsal* was written by a team, which probably included Sprat, Clifford, Butler, Cowley, and Edmund Waller.

To some extent, all works are corporate productions: they are composed of intertextual traces of other works. Some might be composed collaboratively by a group, and that collaboration might be figured as a sign of strength, of a team working as a team. But it could also lead to charges of incompetence. Both Dryden and Rochester accused Shadwell of being such a bad writer that he needed help. In his brilliantly concentrated

---

[24] The Mulgrave–Dryden 'Essay upon Satire' includes both real names and nicknames; the anonymous 'Advice to Apollo' cites its targets by name.

[25] On heroic drama, see Elaine McGirr, *The Heroic Mode and Political Crisis* (Newark: University of Delaware Press, 2009). When *The Rehearsal* was revived in 1717 with Cibber in the part of Bayes, Cibber added allusions to *Three Hours After Marriage* which 'was so heinously taken by Mr. Pope, that, in the swelling of his Heart, after the Play was over, he came behind the Scenes, with his Lips pale and his Voice trembling, to call me to account for the Insult'. *A Letter from Mr Cibber, to Mr Pope* (London, 1742), 17–19.

[26] Buckingham, *The Plays*, i. 400–1 [I.i.78, 102–3].

[27] See Paulina Kewes, *Authorship and Appropriation: Writing for the Stage in England, 1660–1710* (Oxford: Clarendon Press, 1998), App. A.

satire *Mac Flecknoe* Dryden accused him of relying on Sedley 'To lard with wit thy hungry Epsom prose'.[28] This satire employs another key trope of corporate authorship: the idea of succession which compounds the pressing political issue of royal succession with the literary concern with the tension between tradition and originality. Dryden treats Shadwell as the inheritor of the dull poet Richard Flecknoe's tatty cloak: 'The mantle fell to the young prophet's part, / With double portion of his father's art'.[29] This final couplet of the poem suggests that Shadwell's inheritance is not worth a fart.

New Forms of Association

Socially the Court Wits out-ranked Dryden, and physically they may have bested him— if the stories told about the Rose Alley beating are true—but history has proved to be on the side of the professional writer and print publication. While literary coteries and scribal publication survived into the eighteenth century, new models of literary association arose towards the end of the seventeenth century in the form of the more or less formal club in which men met to pool their resources both financial and intellectual— they often 'clubbed together' to pay for their refreshments as well as sharing ideas. Crucially, these groups met in social spaces distinct from the institutions of court, church, and university. In his general survey of early modern club life, Peter Clark notes that clubs were 'umbilically linked to the arrival of coffee-houses' in Britain in the 1650s.[30] The coffee-house was a consciously modern phenomenon, largely urban, and largely sober. Most Restoration coffee-house clubs were primarily political. Writers were slower off the mark to establish literary clubs, but Will's coffee-house, on the corner of Russell and Bow Street, at the heart of London's pleasure zone, established pre-eminence. Intellectually and physically Dryden dominated 'the wits' coffee-house'. Johnson records how he presided over a kind of critical court: 'the appeal upon any literary dispute was made to him'.[31] Aspiring writers would call in at Will's in the hope of getting a seat near his table. Pope was brought to see the great man when he was perhaps no more than ten and Dryden was in his late sixties.[32]

After Dryden's death in 1700, Will's gradually lost its dominant position in London's cultural landscape. It was replaced by Button's Coffee House, which the Whig mobilizer Joseph Addison established as the headquarters of the coterie of Whig writers who

---

[28] Dryden, *Poems* (Longman), i. 329.   [29] Dryden, *Poems* (Longman), i. 336.

[30] Peter Clark, *British Clubs and Societies 1580–1800: The Origins of an Associational World* (Oxford: Oxford University Press, 2000), 40; see also John Brewer, *The Pleasures of the Imagination: English Culture in the Eighteenth Century* (London: HarperCollins, 1997), 34–50; Markman Ellis, *The Coffee-House: A Cultural History* (London: Weidenfeld & Nicolson, 2004).

[31] Samuel Johnson, *The Lives of the Most Eminent English Poets*, ed. Roger Lonsdale, 4 vols. (Oxford: Clarendon Press, 2006), ii. 118.

[32] Joseph Spence, *Observations, Anecdotes, and Characters of Books and Men Collected from Conversation*, ed. James M. Osborn (Oxford: Clarendon Press, 1966), ii. 611.

gathered around him after the success of his tragedy *Cato* (1713). The group—which included Richard Steele, Ambrose Philips, Thomas Tickell, Eustace Budgell and Samuel Garth—was dubbed 'the little Senate' because of the association between Addison and the virtuous Republican, Cato. Swift and Pope gravitated there when they first came to London in the hope of breaking into the literary scene.[33] But when personal and political animosity developed between the groups from 1713, Pope went after Ambrose Philips and Addison mobilized his deputy Tickell against Pope.[34]

The coffee-house was the home of a new kind of corporate satire: the essay periodical. Eschewing the violence of the lampoon, it proposed to correct the manners and morals of the nation by means of a gentler, more polite form of satire. The first of this new genre, *The Tatler* (1709–11) claimed to act as a literal 'magazine' collecting all the gossip from the coffee-houses. When Richard Steele found the labour of inventing the news three times a week too onerous, he recruited Addison and Swift to help. After the *The Tatler* folded, Addison and Steele together set up *The Spectator* (1712–14) which was supposedly compiled by a club of friends meeting every Tuesday and Thursday—thus creating a new kind of satirical corporation: the imaginary club. The spirit of public good and collaborative authorship which was the ideal of these publications was not as politically neutral as it sounds. They supported a Whig ideal of polite sociability.[35]

One striking feature of these periodicals and their mid-eighteenth-century imitators is that they are fronted by a singular eponymous character such as the Rambler, the Craftsman, the Hyp Doctor.[36] This figure is known as the 'eidolon', a term which suggests, according to Manushag Powell, 'a projected image, the double, phantom, or simulacrum' of the author.[37] He (or she, in the case of the Female Tatler, Female Spectator, and Midwife) might have a particular as well as a generic name. Thus, the putative author of the *Guardian* is Isaac Bickerstaffe and of *The Champion* (1739–40), an opposition paper edited by Henry Fielding, Captain Hercules Vinegar. These paper phantoms took on a life of their own and frequently spawned imitators. For example, within a fortnight of Steele discontinuing *The Tatler*, Swift and Bolingbroke set up William Harrison as his successor. Harrison continued to write as 'Isaac Bickerstaffe' for a further fifty-two issues.[38] As with Restoration satire, a periodical written by one party

[33] John Timbs, FSA, *Clubs and Club Life in London. With Anecdotes of its Famous Coffee Houses, Hostelries and Taverns, from the Seventeenth Century to the Present Time* (London: John Camden Hotton, [1866]), 331.

[34] Maynard Mack, *Alexander Pope: A Life* (New York: W. W. Norton & Co., 1985), 214–18, 275–8.

[35] On this point, see Brian Cowan, 'Mr Spectator and the Coffeehouse Public Sphere', *ECS* 37 (2004), 345–66.

[36] *The Rambler* (1750–2) was largely written by Johnson; *The Craftsman* (1726–52) was an opposition paper managed by Bolingbroke, and William Pulteney, 1st Earl of Bath; *The Hyp Doctor* (1730–9), produced by John 'Orator' Henley under various pseudonyms, was pro-Ministerial. See Michael Harris, *London Newspapers in the Age of Walpole: A Study of the Origins of the Modern English Press* (Madison, NJ; Fairleigh Dickinson University Press, 1987); Robert Harris, *A Patriot Press: National Politics and the London Press in the 1740s* (Oxford: Oxford University Press, 1993).

[37] Manushag N. Powell, *Performing Authorship in Eighteenth-Century English Periodicals* (Lewisburg: Bucknell University Press, 2012), 10, 24.

[38] See Swift, *Journal to Stella*, 118–19.

might call forth another, thus the Tory *Examiner* (1710–14) was countered by the *Whig Examiner* (1710).[39] A single eidolon might cover joint authorship, as in the case of *The Examiner*, and that figure may or may not have been surrounded by a fictional group, as in *The Spectator* and *The Female Spectator*, or 'Mr Town's helpful cousin Mr Village in the *Connoisseur*'.[40] As well as contributing the notion of a virtual club with a composite character as a figurehead, such periodicals also added a temporal dimension to corporate satire as they intervened in particular moments and unfolded over time.

THE SCRIBLERIANS

The Scriblerus Club comes out of this coffee-house periodical context both in the sense that it has its roots in it and that it set itself against it by being more exclusive and private. Its members comprised Jonathan Swift, Alexander Pope, John Gay, Thomas Parnell, and John Arbuthnot. The final member of the group, Robert Harley, Earl of Oxford was not a writer but a politician, and might be seen as the patron of the group. The venue of their original meetings in 1713–14 is symbolic: rather than assembling in a coffee-house, they met in Dr Arbuthnot's rooms in St James's Palace. Arbuthnot as a royal physician had to be on hand in case needed by the increasingly infirm Queen Anne. Harley as Lord High Treasurer, the queen's chief minister, also attended her in the Palace. To what degree were they a political club? In a broad sense, their decision to satirize the forces of modernism—science, professional scholarship, commercial publication, and so forth—was conservative with a small c and Tory with a big T. Moreover, the fact that the Club was forced to disperse when the accession of George I in 1714 produced a profound regime change, indicates how closely their fortunes were tied to those of Harley's nominally Tory ministry, even if none of them self-identified as Tories.

The principal publication of the group is *The Memoirs of Martinus Scriblerus*, which tells the story of the life of Martin in a series of adventures both obscure and absurd, from his conception as the brain-child of his pedantic antiquarian father, through his education in the principal arts and sciences, to his doomed first love affair. The plot is a peg on which to hang satires on what the friends saw as abuses and errors in learned culture. Scriblerus is both an eidolon like Isaac Bickerstaffe, and a persona like Lemuel Gulliver. As is fitting for a mock periodical, the Scriblerians submitted their eidolon to mockery rather than employing him as a spokesperson.

Although they sketched out plans for the biography of their fictional polymath, little writing survives from the brief period in which they met regularly in 1713–14, other than the rhymed invitations they jointly composed to encourage Harley to join them.[41]

---

[39] Similarly, Tobias Smollett's pro-Ministerial *Briton* (1762–3) was opposed by the *North Briton*, written by John Wilkes and Charles Churchill.

[40] Powell, *Performing Authorship*, 24.   [41] Printed in Kerby-Miller, ed., *Memoirs*, 351–9.

The fact that there was such a long gap between their last known formal meeting in June 1714 and the publication of the *Memoirs of Martinus Scriblerus* in the second volume of Pope's collected works in prose in 1741 has prompted one critic to question whether they ever existed as a club, and even whether the name Scriblerus originated with them.[42] However, while it may be agreed that Pope, Swift, and company were not always and everywhere Scriblerian, or even a formal club beyond 1714, they continued to be lumped together by their enemies, and to collaborate in various ways and combinations long after the death of Queen Anne broke up their meetings.[43] Moreover, the *Memoirs* in the form in which they were published by Pope, edited to fit his current conceptions, do not fully embody the club's original intentions. It makes sense to think of the *Memoirs* as a project rather than a product. Pope's initial proposal in 1713 was for a journal, *An Account of the Works of the Unlearned*, a parody of the monthly digest, *The History of the Works of the Learned*. Most of the surviving Scriblerian productions demonstrate them to have been engaged in something more fluid and responsive to the times than a retrospective biography. Throughout the seventeen teens, the Scriblerians continued to correspond, meet, and collaborate. As well as the two comedies on Scriblerian themes—*The What D'Ye Call It* (1715) on bad writing and *Three Hours After Marriage* (1717) on bad science—fragments of the *Memoirs* can be dated to this period, as can several minor squibs responding to what was in the cultural air.[44] They also probably whipped up a fake paper storm around publications by members of the group, including pamphlets concerning *The What D'Ye Call It*, *The Rape of the Lock*, and Pope's translation of Homer.[45] Thus they continued the Restoration tradition of literary gang battles.

Swift's visits to England in 1726 and 1727 produced spectacular progress in the Scriblerian project. When he came to England in 1726 to arrange the publication of his *Gulliver's Travels*, the surviving members of the group gathered in Pope's villa in Twickenham. It is likely that they sorted out the Scriblerian papers, deciding what to preserve, what to develop further, and what to abandon. When Swift returned to Ireland in August, he left Pope preparing a series of volumes of *Miscellanies* for the press.[46] This collection eventually contained numerous works which were not Scriblerian in origin, for such as Swift's 'Stella' poems and *A Modest Proposal*, but it reprinted or published for

---

[42] Ashley Marshall, 'The Myth of Scriblerus', *BJECS* 31 (2008), 77–99. Her argument is gaining some traction; see Dustin Griffin, *Swift and Pope: Satirists in Dialogue* (Cambridge: Cambridge University Press, 2010), 68–9.

[43] They were treated as a coalition in, e.g., J. D. Breval, *The Confederates* (1717), *Gulliver Decypher'd* (1726), Jonathan Smedley, *The Metamorphosis: A Poem. Shewing the Change of Scriblerus into Snarlerus* (1728), 'Caleb D'Anvers' [Nicholas Amhurst], *The Twickenham Hotch-Potch...Being a Sequel to the Beggars Opera* (1728), and 'Scriblerus Quartus' [Thomas Cooke], *The Petty Sessions of Poets* (1730).

[44] *Memoirs*, 57–67. Some of Kerby-Miller's claims are unsupported.

[45] *A Complete Key to the What D'Ye Call It* (1715), attributed to Lewis Theobald and Benjamin Griffin, was possibly by Pope and Gay; *A Key to the Lock*, by Esdras Barnivelt, Apoth. (1715); Thomas Parnell, 'Battle of the Frogs and Mice, with Remarks of Zoilus' (1717); *Verses on Gulliver's Travels* (1727).

[46] The publication history of these volumes is somewhat confusing: the first two volumes of *Miscellanies in Prose and Verse* appeared in 1727; a third, called 'The Last' was published in 1728, but then a fourth and final volume, called 'The Third' was issued in 1732.

the first time numerous pieces which were, including perhaps most significantly *Peri Bathous*, the first work they publicly attributed to Scriblerus.[47] This treatise on the art of writing low verse was probably published as a way of drawing the fire of hacks and dunces to justify Pope's retaliation against them in the *Dunciad*. However, it was begun much earlier. In the summer of 1714, Arbuthnot reported to Swift that 'Pope has been collecting high flights of poetry, which are very good, they are to be solemn nonsense.'[48] As it includes the works of numerous poets under the title, 'Martin Scriblerus his Treatise of the Art of Sinking in Poetry', it too can be considered a work of corporate satire. Pope certainly saw the *Miscellanies* as a significant group production; he wrote to Swift on 17 February 1727: 'I am prodigiously plead with this joint-venture, in which methinks we look like friends, side by side, serious and merry by turns, conversing interchangeably, and walking down hand in hand to posterity.'[49] However, as Alexander Pettit argues, it is unlikely that Swift was as invested in this corporate identity as Pope was.[50] He had enough singular identities of his own which he used interchangeably— 'Dean, Drapier, Bickerstaff, or Gulliver', as Pope called him in the *Dunciad Variorum* (1729).[51] Although the *Miscellanies* were perhaps the high water mark of their group activity, they were viewed by others as a sign that Pope, Swift, and Gay were all now opposition writers.[52] The reunion with his colleagues also inspired Swift once he returned to Ireland. Pat Rogers notes 'his obsessive return to English materials in his poetry, for almost a decade after his visits to the metropolis of Britain in 1726 and 1727'.[53] Rogers demonstrates that not only did he keep referring to London and his Scriblerian friends in the poetry he composed in the 1730s, but he fought Pope's literary battles, even though Grub Street was far removed from the deanery of St Patrick's.[54]

In what ways and to what extent does it make sense to think of *Gulliver's Travels*, *The Beggar's Opera*, and *The Dunciad* as products of the Scriblerus Club? The fact that the question cannot be answered in a simple way points to the complexity of corporate authorship in this period more generally. On one level, *Gulliver's Travels* is very much Swift's work and the product of his Irish experience. It is likely the *Travels* were written in Ireland between 1721 and 1724, but Swift continued to add to the text up to his

---

[47] A satire by someone who had got wind of the project called *Memoirs of the Life of Scriblerus. By D. S—t* appeared under the false imprint 'A. Moore' in 1723. See *Memoirs*, 374–85.

[48] Arbuthnot to Swift, 26 June 1714, in Swift, *Corr.* (Woolley), i. 625–6. Pope also incorporated his 'Receipt to make an Epic Poem' which had first appeared in the *Guardian* (1713).

[49] Pope, *Correspondence* (Sherburn), ii. 426.

[50] *Miscellanies in Prose and Verse by Pope, Swift and Gay*, ed. Alexander Pettit, 4 vols. (London: Pickering & Chatto, 2002), i. xvi.

[51] Pope, *Poems* (Longman), iii. 177.

[52] See, e.g. Jonathan Smedley, *Gulliveriana: or, a Fourth Volume of Miscellanies. Being a Sequel of the Three Volumes, Published by Pope and Swift* (1728). On Walpole and the opposition, see Bertrand Goldgar, *Walpole and the Wits* (Lincoln: University of Nebraska Press, 1976).

[53] Pat Rogers, 'Swift and the Poetry of Exile', in *Swift's Travels: Eighteenth-Century British Satire and Its Legacy*, ed. Nicholas Hudson and Aaron Santesso (Cambridge: Cambridge University Press, 2008), 124.

[54] Compare, for example, Swift's 'Character of Sir Robert Walpole', 'On Poetry: A Rhapsody', and Pope's *Imitations of Horace*.

departure from England in August 1726.[55] Swift achieves an extraordinary density in his text by pleating time back upon itself. He has in mind not just the Irish 1720s or his sojourn in London in the seventeen teens, but also his time with Sir William Temple in the 1690s. Walpole and Harley are folded together when, for example, Gulliver decodes 'a running Sore' as 'the Administration'.[56] *Gulliver's Travels* part III is similarly multi-layered. While it allegorizes British dominance in Ireland, it also furthers the Scriblerians' satire on natural philosophers.[57]

Aside from thematic consistency, there are other ways in which *Gulliver's Travels* is a Scriblerian work; it might have originated in the plans hatched in Arbuthnot's rooms.[58] Its publication certainly was managed by the group; Gay even wrote out a letter supposedly from Gulliver's cousin, Richard Sympson, and took charge of Swift's copy.[59] They then jumped on the bandwagon by composing verses in the voices of Swift's characters.[60] Pope invented a Lilliputian poet laureate, 'Titty Tit, Esq.' who looked up to Swift's 'Man-Mountain' and exclaimed:

> May my lays
> Swell with praise,
> Worthy thee!
> Worthy me!

Pope's tiny couplets at once evoke the miniaturism of Swift's Lilliputians and mock the inanity of the self-aggrandizing puffery written by poets laureate. The current incumbent, Laurence Eusden, was about to be mocked in *The Dunciad*, so with these lines Pope is also hitching his project to Swift's satiric vehicle.

The Dunciad had a similarly long and complex gestation. Although advertised as a direct response to very recent attacks against Pope, its origin probably predates the club's meetings. Pope might have been prompted to revive a poem on the progress of dullness by Lewis Theobald's 1726 critique of his edition of Shakespeare, but *The Dunciad* is also part of the Scriblerian project.[61] As well as sharing the themes of many Scriblerian pieces—corruption in writing, learning, and politics—Pope partly attributes responsibility for the work to Swift. Swift, he claimed, 'may be said in a sort to be Author of the Poem: For when He, together with Mr. Pope' were selecting material to include in their

---

[55] See Swift, *Works* (Cambridge), xvi. lxxxviii, 94, n. 42, 593, and 451.

[56] Swift, *Works* (Cambridge), xvi. lx–lxi; III.vi, 283, n. 39.

[57] Cf. *Gulliver's Travels*, III.vi, and *Memoirs*, xi. Arbuthnot continued to offer suggestions on the topic of natural philosophy as late as 17 October 1725 (Swift, *Works* (Cambridge), xvi. 593).

[58] Pope made this claim in conversations recorded by the man of letters, Joseph Spence in 1728 or 1729 (Spence, *Observations*, i. 56). Lady Mary Wortley Montagu thought that *Gulliver's Travels* was written by Pope, Swift, and Arbuthnot (Swift, *Works* (Cambridge), xvi. 583).

[59] See Swift, *Works* (Cambridge), xvi. 632–3.

[60] Pope was the principal author but Gay probably contributed to 'The Lamentation of Glumdalclitch' (Swift, *Works* (Cambridge), xvi. 573–86). Some of the verses were printed in Motte's 'Second Edition' of *Gulliver's Travels* in May 1727, and all included in the *Miscellanies* 'Last Volume' in 1727.

[61] For a fuller account of the origins of *The Dunciad*, see Pope, *Poems* (Longman), iii. 1–5.

Miscellanies and destroying the rest, 'the first sketch of this poem was snatch'd from the fire by Dr *Swift*, who persuaded his friend to proceed in it, and to him it was therefore Inscribed'.[62] In the 1728 *Dunciad*, Pope set himself up as a lone voice against the corporate forces of Grub Street, refusing to see commercial writers as individuals but only as a mass or as interchangeable functionaries. *The Dunciad Variorum* was more of a group work as it not only incorporated a dedication to Swift in the first book (I.17–26), but it was encrusted with the contributions 'of various people' (as the subtitle 'Variorum' implies), recruited and embellished by Martinus Scriblerus.[63]

Pope's poem adapts many of the tropes of corporation employed by Restoration satirists. It shares their concern with literary and political succession. In particular, Pope alludes extensively to the coronation of Shadwell in Dryden's *Mac Flecknoe*. While the mock-epic action of *The Dunciad* concerns the replacement of Settle with Tibbald as city laureate, the parallel with the accession of George II in 1727 is made dangerously obvious by Pope: 'Still Dunce the second reigns like Dunce the first' (1729, I.6). Pope also combines the idea of succession with that of the 'session' of the poets, and with the mock-heroic trope of rival legions of authors lined up in battle array (which is also employed by Swift in *The Battle of the Books*). In Book III, Settle presents Tibbald with a vision of the future in which the progeny of Dulness bear down in an endless onslaught: 'Down, down they larum, with impetuous whirl, / The Pindars, and the Miltons, of a Curl'.[64] In the *Battle of the Books*, the advance of the Moderns was halted by the ranks of the Ancients. In Pope's gloomier vision, the Dunces will swarm unopposed over the land like a zombie apocalypse. The idea of succession has morphed into mob rule—a new amorphous, disorderly kind of corporation.

Pope differs from the Restoration satirists in that not only does he present the danger his enemies pose to culture as massively different in scale but also qualitatively different in kind from what was at stake in a world of scribal publication. He urges that the proliferation of print and the growth of the literary marketplace has created a new kind of corporate author: the phantom poet manufactured by unscrupulous publishers such as Edmund Curll.[65] In Book II, Dulness challenges booksellers to compete for the prize of a plump poet. This form, with 'A brain of feathers, and a heart of lead' (a writer's means of production: the materials respectively of quills and type) is a mere 'copy of a Wit'.[66] When the 'shapeless shade' melts from Curll's sight as he reaches for it, he tries to seize its works and publish them but 'His papers light... the winds uplift, / And whisk 'em back to Evans, Young, and Swift'.[67] Pope recalls Restoration attacks on plagiarism, but

---

[62] Note to Preface to *Dunciad* (1729), in Pope, *Poems* (Longman), iii. 321.

[63] The fluidity of the project—and the interchangeability of modern authors—is represented in the fact that in 1743 Pope swapped Colley Cibber for Theobald as hero of the poem. For the subsequent evolution of the poem, see Pope, *Dunciad Four Books*.

[64] Pope, *Poems* (Longman), iii. 280.

[65] Pope's attitudes to print were complex, as James McLaverty demonstrates in *Pope, Print and Meaning* (Oxford: Oxford University Press, 2001).

[66] Pope, *Poems* (Longman), iii. 213.   [67] Pope, *Poems* (Longman), iii. 221–2.

his brilliant allegory outdoes them in both complexity and pessimism. The body of the phantom poet is identical with his poetic corpus but that corpus comprises nothing more than a miscellany of printed papers purloined from real poets.

Gay's *Beggar's Opera* similarly addresses Scriblerian concerns to do with corruption in literature and politics while building on Restoration techniques. It adapts the frame structure of *The Rehearsal* and incorporates a compendium of adapted songs and airs. Yet, although Gay worked on it at Twickenham while Swift, Pope, and Arbuthnot were completing their own projects, it is less obviously a group composition. Perhaps because he had suffered on account of his contributions to *Three Hours After Marriage*, Pope did not have a hand in it. Nonetheless, Swift claimed some authorial credit, and did so in a way that further complicates the notion of corporate authorship. In 1716 he sent Pope 'a hint that a sett of Quaker-pastorals might succeed, if our friend Gay could fancy it… I believe further, the pastoral ridicule is not exhausted… what think you of a Newgate pastoral, among the whores and thieves there?'[68] It took twelve years for one of these hints to ripen into *The Beggar's Opera*. The Scriblerians frequently initiated projects by proposing 'hints'; Arbuthnot was the chief hint-monger, issuing subjects that he expected others to work upon.[69] But who should claim the credit for the creation: the originator of the initial idea, or the one who wrote it up?

CONCLUSION

The concept of corporate authorship has been approached intelligently by librarians, for whom cataloguing multi-author works is a practical problem. Michael Carpenter points out that writing involves a diverse range of activities, and that we have a number of phrasal verbs to suggest the complexity of the process: 'Writing… down… up… out… in… over'.[70] So, when thinking about collaboration, we have to think not only of who wrote what, but what writing is. Rather than thinking about the finished product, it might make more sense to acknowledge the different phases of producing a text: the different activities involved in writing include brainstorming, note making, drafting, revising, cutting and pasting in bits from other people, and producing the fair copy. For the Scriblerians, it also involved writing *ex post facto*; they not only created but they adopted texts. In this sense, the Scriblerus Club can be seen as the corporate author of *Gulliver's Travels*, *The Dunciad*, and *The Beggar's Opera*. They also satirically 'vindicated' texts to Scriblerus, suggesting that Richard Bentley's nit-picking edition of Milton's *Paradise Lost* (1732), and the controversial theories of the earth published by William Whiston and John Woodward in the 1690s, were the work of a dunce. Similarly, the corpus of the

---

[68] Swift, *Corr.* (Woolley), ii. 177–8.   [69] See, e.g., Swift, *Corr.* (Woolley), i. 625–6.
[70] Michael Carpenter, *Corporate Authorship: Its Role in Library Cataloguing* (London: Greenwood Press, 1981), 135.

Court Wits and Restoration satirists was not all produced by a group sitting around a table and writing together. Hume and Love caution: 'In a context of coterie collaboration, adaptation, and scribal publication we will be wise to accept the inevitability of radically varying and frequently indeterminate degrees of agency for such authors as contemporary rumour and later scholarship have delivered to us.' An awareness of these circumstances allows us to appreciate 'What might be dubbed "contributory authorship"'.[71] That is, varying degrees of authorial agency and activity including writing and revising, adapting and inserting, parodying, responding and collaborating in numerous ways were involved in the creation of corporate satires.

SELECT BIBLIOGRAPHY

Allen, Robert J. *The Clubs of Augustan London* (Cambridge, MA: Harvard University Press, 1933).

Ezell, Margaret. *Social Authorship and the Advent of Print* (Baltimore: Johns Hopkins University Press, 1999).

Farrell, Michael P. *Collaborative Circles: Friendship Dynamics and Creative Work* (Chicago and London: University of Chicago Press, 2001).

Gerrard, Christine. 'Pope, *Peri Bathous*, and the Whig Sublime', in *'Cultures of Whiggism': New Essays on English Literature and Culture in the Long Eighteenth Century*, ed. David Womersley, assisted by Paddy Bullard and Abigail Williams (Newark: University of Delaware Press, 2005), 200–15.

Griffin, Dustin. 'The Social World of Authorship', in *The Cambridge History of English Literature, 1660-1780*, ed. John Richetti (Cambridge: Cambridge University Press, 2005).

Hume, Robert D. ' "Satire" in the Reign of Charles II', *Modern Philology* 102 (2005), 332–71.

Nokes, David. *John Gay: A Profession of Friendship* (Oxford: Oxford University Press, 1995).

Prendergast, Amy. *Literary Salons across Britain and Ireland in the Long Eighteenth Century* (Basingstoke: Palgrave Macmillan, 2015).

Schellenberg, Betty A. *Literary Coteries and the Making of Modern Print Culture 1740-1790* (Cambridge: Cambridge University Press, 2016).

Speck, W. A. *Literature and Society in Eighteenth-Century England, 1680-1820: Ideology, Politics and Culture* (London: Longman, 1998).

Trolander, Paul and Zeynep Tenger. *Sociable Criticism in England, 1625-1725* (Newark: University of Delaware Press, 2007).

---

[71] Buckingham, *Plays, Poems*, i. x.

CHAPTER 3

....

AGAINST HYPOCRISY
AND DISSENT

....

MARCUS WALSH

'THE only Source of the true Ridiculous', wrote Henry Fielding, in the early 1740s, 'is Affectation'. Affectation, Fielding tells us, arises 'from one of these two Causes, Vanity, or Hypocrisy', and of these hypocrisy is much the worse, setting us 'on an Endeavour to avoid Censure by concealing our Vices under an Appearance of their opposite Virtues'.[1] Fielding makes his familiar remark about affectation as a chief foundation for satire in a novel itself much concerned with vanity and hypocrisy, including vanity and hypocrisy in matters of belief and worship. The charge of hypocrisy could be levelled against men of different kinds of cloth (Fielding's Trulliber and Thwackum not least), but dissenters of various stripes had been a particular target for many decades before Fielding wrote. Religious satire had become a major literary mode as rival factions, civil and religious, battled for influence and power through the successive events, debates, and crises of the post-Restoration years, and the reigns of William and Anne: the Clarendon Code and Act of Uniformity, the Popish plot, the Monmouth rebellion, the Exclusion Bill, the Glorious Revolution, the Act of Toleration, the Test Act. Satire thrives, structurally and verbally, on difference, such as characterizes hypocrisy: difference between appearance and reality, profession and performance, promise and fulfilment. In their attack on sectarianism, writers of the late seventeenth and early eighteenth century made hypocrisy and its close relatives—dishonesty, deceit, simulation, and dissimulation—a central and telling theme. Many satires written against dissent employ Juvenalian anger as well as Horace's sly, polite, insinuating style; many employ the stereotypes which arise out of prejudice or polarized preferences; many employ a rhetoric which verges on, and trespasses into, the violent and the obscene. This chapter considers the pot's perspective; there are of course many books and essays, written and to be written, from the perspective of the kettle.

---

[1] Henry Fielding, *Joseph Andrews* (1741), ed. Martin C. Battestin (Oxford: Oxford University Press, 1967), Preface, 7–8.

SAMUEL BUTLER

The most developed and extended poetic satire on dissent published in the latter half of the seventeenth century is also the most original and the least typical. Samuel Butler began composing his mock-heroic, mock-romance poem *Hudibras* only two years before the Restoration. Its first Part was published by December 1662; the second Part appeared (with the revised first Part) in 1674; and the third Part in 1677. It tells the tale of Hudibras and his Squire, Ralpho; though neither can be said properly to be heroes, and no one ever read *Hudibras* for its narrative. A superannuated knight riding forth in search of adventures, Hudibras is evidently a quixotic figure. He is altogether less deluded, however, and more knowing, than Cervantes's hero.

The poem presents itself from its opening lines as historical, describing the times 'When *civil* Fury first grew high'.[2] Its targets are specific, limited, political: the two factions, Presbyterian and Independent, who vied for power through the Civil War period, but adopted and stood for two different forms of Church government. For a statement of that struggle, heavily inflected by Church of England sympathies and understanding, and broadly in line with Butler's, a modern reader might usefully turn to Jonathan Swift. Swift explains that though there were episcopally ordained Puritan bishops and preachers during the reign of James I, and at first under Charles I, there was no 'separate Species of Religion'. However:

> soon after the Rebellion broke out, the Term *Puritan* gradually dropt, and that of *Presbyterian* succeeded; which Sect was, in two or three Years, established in all its Forms...And, from this Period, the Church continued under Persecution until Monarchy was restored...

> In a Year or two after, we began to hear of a new Party risen, and growing in the Parliament, as well as the Army; under the Name of *Independent*: It spread, indeed, somewhat more in the latter; but not equal with the *Presbyterians*...until some Time before the King was murdered...[T]his *Independant* Party, upon whom all the Mischief is charged by their *Presbyterian* Brethren...during the whole Usurpation,...contended by Degrees with their Parent Sect, and...shared in Employments; and gradually, after the Restoration, mingled with the Mass of *Presbyterians*; lying ever since undistinguished in the Herd of *Dissenters*.[3]

In Butler's poem, Hudibras himself is a satiric version of a Presbyterian, Ralpho of an Independent. The action of the poem displays the ill-matched pair herding, and

---

[2] Samuel Butler, *Hudibras*, 1. 1. 1. All quotations and references are from *Hudibras*, ed. John Wilders (Oxford: Oxford University Press, 1967), except where noted as being from Zachary Grey's edition of the poem (2 vols., Cambridge, 1744).

[3] *The Presbyterian's Plea of Merit* (Dublin, 1733); *The Prose Writings of Jonathan Swift*, ed. Herbert Davis et al., 16 vols. (Oxford: Basil Blackwell, 1939–74), 12. 264–5, 267. For a much more detailed historical account, from an equally committed Church of England point of view, see *Hudibras*, ed. Grey, 1. iii–xvii.

contending, together. The details of significant arguments of Civil War and Protectorate political and religious history are set out in a series of extended dialogues between Hudibras and Ralpho.

Satires are never purely historiographical however; their business is always more current. So it is with *Hudibras*. Zachary Grey, who produced an edition of *Hudibras* in 1744 with extensive illustrative, and highly tendentious, notes, praised Butler for exposing 'the Hypocrisy and Wickedness of those, who began and carried on the Rebellion, under a Pretence of promoting Religion and Godliness'.[4] Butler did so, however, less to explore historical sins, than to warn his Restoration contemporaries of the continuing danger posed by Presbyterianism in particular, as well as by dissent in general. The first years of the Restoration saw a crucial debate about the proper status and treatment of dissenters, not least about how far Presbyterians could be trusted and tolerated in worship and governance in the new order. An extensive body of writing in the 1660s set out to demonstrate how undependable, and how dangerously opposed to monarchy, nonconformists remained. Hard-line Anglicans argued that Presbyterians should be excluded from the Church of England, and from civil power; the success of that argument rested in part on associating them with more radical dissenting sects, not least the Independents.[5] Just such an unholy nonconforming alliance is allegorized, and made discursive, by the pairing of Hudibras and his squire.[6]

The main satiric targets of *Hudibras* are what Butler considers the frank deceptions and hypocrisy of dissent. Hudibras and Ralpho conduct a series of arguments, but neither can lay claim to disinterested scholarship, reason, or honesty. Hudibras himself is presented as a logic-chopping pseudo-Aristotelian, learned always in self-justifying and self-serving ways. The Presbyterians are described from the beginning as paradoxical, contradictory, radically unsatisfied:

> More peevish, cross, and spleenatick,
> Than Dog distract, or Monky sick:
> That with more care keep holy-day
> The wrong, then others the right way.[7]

Hudibras is a knight errant, but not of a romantic kind. He is a warrior not wandering but erroneous. No seeker of disinterested truth, he is one of those who

> ... build their Faith upon
> The holy Text of *Pike* and *Gun*;
> Decide all Controversies by

---

[4] Butler, *Hudibras*, ed. Grey, 1. iv.

[5] See John Spurr, *The Restoration Church of England, 1646–1689* (New Haven: Yale University Press, 1991), 48–9.

[6] The argument has been convincingly made by Ashley Marshall, 'The Aims of Butler's Satire in *Hudibras*', *Modern Philology* 105 (2008), 637–65.

[7] Butler, *Hudibras*, 1. 1. 209–12.

> Infallible *Artillery*;
> And prove their Doctrine Orthodox
> By Apostolick *Blows* and *Knocks*.[8]

Though the Bible only was the religion of Protestants, and more especially of the Anglican Church, Hudibras's scripture is military force. His theological criteria are those notoriously attributed to Rome by Anglican controvertists, the Vatican's exercise of secular power, the Pope's claim to infallibility, the reliance not on holy writ but on apostolic tradition Rome claimed to trace back to St Peter.

Ralpho is a tradesman, as many sectarians were, but his genealogy presents him ambiguously, and mock-heroically. His working pose as a tailor is 'cross-legg'd' like that of knightly effigies; providing made-up garments on credit he is 'fam'd', like the crusaders, for his 'faith'; he pricks lice with his needle as he sews, at war 'against the bloudy Caniball'.[9] His learning is more personal and individual than his master's, deriving not from study or experience but from the saint's claimed inner light:

> Some call it *Gifts*, and some *New light*;
> A Liberal Art, that costs no pains
> Of Study, Industry, or Brains.[10]

Such solipsism, uninformed by and untestable against worldly or textual knowledge, gives unchallengeable certainty: 'Whate're men speak by this *new Light*, / Still they are sure to be i'th' right'.[11]

Hudibras trades in materialistic deceit. One of many sectarian behaviours at odds with sectarian spiritual profession is an ungodly interest in the things of this world. In Canto One of the Third Part, Hudibras is subjected to an interrogation by 'Furies and Hobgoblins' sent by the wealthy widow he has been pursuing. Asked during the course of his catechizing why he chose to set himself up in '*that cursed Sin, Hypocrisie*', he replies that it is 'the Thriving'st Calling':

> *What makes all Doctrines Plain and Clear?—*
> About two Hundred Pounds a Year.
> *And that which was prov'd true before,*
> *Prove false again?*—Two Hundred more.[12]

---

[8] Butler, *Hudibras*, 1. 1. 193–8.   [9] Butler, *Hudibras*, 1. 1. 465–7.

[10] Butler, *Hudibras*, 1. 1. 476–8.

[11] Butler, *Hudibras*, 1. 1. 497–8. Anglican theologians insisted, to take William Chillingworth as an instance, that reason is public, available 'to all mens tryall and examination'. Hence, the Anglican interpreter may credibly account for his procedures by saying, 'these & these Reasons I have to shew that this or that is true doctrine, or that this or that is the meaning of such a Scripture'. The Puritan who appeals to the Holy Spirit 'saying the Spirit of God tels me that this is the meaning of such a Text' makes a claim that cannot be validated, 'it being a secret thing' (*The Religion of Protestants* (London, 1638), 95). The Puritan's claim is therefore peculiarly liable to dissimulation.

[12] Butler, *Hudibras*, 3. 1. 1221–3, 1277–80. Zachary Grey's note points out that this parodic catechism is 'a Ridicule on the numerous Pamphlets publish'd in those Times, under the Name, and Form of Catechism'.

Tangible profit serves as motive and justification for violence and duplicity. It removes all contradictions, explains all complexities, allows all forms of dishonesty.

The abuse of plain and honest language and understanding is a regular engine and aspect of hypocrisy. Hudibras from the beginning is described as an expert in the obscure. He speaks in 'a *Babylonish* dialect, / Which learned Pedants much affect'. His vocabulary is full of new coined and counterfeit words, designed to deceive the vulgar: 'And when with hasty noise he spoke 'em, / The Ignorant for currant took 'em.'[13] Grey's note to these lines aptly cites Addison's remark that 'those Swarms of Sectaries that overran the Nation in the time of the great Rebellion, carried their Hypocrisie so high, that they had converted our whole Language into a Jargon of Enthusiasm'.[14]

Ralpho's views on the uses of language and the stability of meanings are most fully explored in his astonishing extended disquisition on the licence given to the Saints to lie and to break promises.[15] One of the most famous and most quoted lines in *Hudibras* is Ralpho's assertion that '*Oaths* are but *words*, and *words* but *wind*';[16] this is not an isolated apothegm, but an integral part of one of the poem's most significant arguments, with general ethical as well as particular political implications. Christ had instructed his first disciples to 'Swear not at all... But let your communication be, Yea, yea; Nay, nay'.[17] 'Our late *Apostles*', however, as Ralpho explains, take the view that 'W'are not commanded to forbear / Indefinitely, at all to *swear*'. Indeed, to break an oath once made is 'but a kind of *Self-denying*', and therefore 'a *Saint-like virtue*'. Ralpho provides a whole series of examples from Commonwealth history to demonstrate this 'constant *Rule* and *practice*'. Among those who 'broke *Oaths* by *Providence*' was Cromwell, who justified the Commons motion to proceed capitally against the king, in contradiction of previous parliamentary claims to be fighting 'for the KING's *safety*, and his *Right*', by arguing that '*Providence*, and Necessity had cast them upon it'.[18] The sectarian approach to vows and promises becomes the central instance of special pleading. Ralpho achieves a triumph of sophistry, arguing that oaths, like Old Testament Law, are meant to control not the enlightened Saints, but the 'Moral Cattle' of more conventional Anglican belief.[19] A Saint is 'of th'heav'nly Realm a *Peer*'; Peers swear on their honour, which is their own property, and of which they may therefore dispose as they think fit. The breaking of a sworn oath, Ralpho concludes, is logically

---

[13] Butler, *Hudibras*, 1. 1. 93, 109–14.

[14] *Spectator*, 458, 15 August 1712; *The Spectator*, ed. Donald F. Bond, 5 vols. (Oxford: Oxford University Press, 1965), 4. 117.

[15] Butler, *Hudibras*, 2. 2. 102–258. This is a licence Hudibras appeals to specifically in the breach of his oath to his Lady to castigate himself as a condition of her releasing him from the stocks ('Hudibras to his Lady', 39–88).

[16] Butler, *Hudibras*, 2. 2. 107.   [17] Matt. 5:34, 37.

[18] Butler, *Hudibras*, 2. 2. 129–40, 160; *Hudibras*, ed. Grey, note to 2. 2. 136.

[19] 1 Tim. 1:9: 'The law is not made for a righteous man, but for the lawless and disobedient, for the ungodly and for sinners'.

'no *perjury*', but 'a breach / Of nothing, but a form of speech'.[20] Nor does swearing on the Scriptures constrain:

> The *Saints* have freedom to digress,
> And vary from 'em, as they please;
> Or misinterpret them, by *private*
> *Instructions*, to all *Aims* they drive at.[21]

The Bible becomes for the sectarians not a text whose meaning might be a rule of faith, but a waxen nose, twisted to conform to their desires. Grey's note to these lines invokes Walker's *History of Independency*: 'they professed their Consciences to be the Rule and Symbol both of their Faith and Doctrine. By this…they interpret, and to this they conform the Scripture; not their Consciences to the Scriptures.' Indeed, the sectarians are accused at a number of points in Butler's poem of using the Bible as it proves most convenient to their interests. Ralpho's worldview is informed by a useful and far-fetched literalism in biblical interpretation; what the Bible does not authorize must be forbidden. He justifies the duo's attack on the bear-baiting by denouncing that recreation as 'Antichristian': 'For certainly there's no such word / In all the *Scripture* on record'.[22] (This version of Puritan literalism would find a further literary life in Swift's Jack.) Taking a different position, but equally conveniently, Hudibras explains his breaking of his oath to his Lady by professing himself a sceptic in matters of plain textual understanding: 'Oaths are not bound to bear / That *Literal Sense*, the words infer'.[23]

JOHN DRYDEN

In John Dryden's major satires of the early 1680s, sectarians, pretended sectarians, and alleged sectarians are frequently a target. Anti-dissenting satiric themes made familiar by earlier writers appear in a richer poetic context. In his poem *The Hypocrite*, John Caryll had accused the Earl of Shaftesbury of taking on a new role and appearance, the 'action, looks and garb' of Puritan hypocrisy; in *The Medall* Dryden alleges that Shaftesbury, for equally selfish purposes, 'cast himself into the Saint-like mould', and 'Groan'd, sigh'd, and pray'd, while Godliness was gain'.[24] Butler had accused the Presbyterians of choosing those sins they could construe as righteous; Dryden finds that Shaftesbury failed in his role as Saint because of his (probably falsely) alleged sexual licence:

> His open lewdness he cou'd ne'er disguise.
> There split the Saint: for Hypocritique Zeal
> Allows no Sins but those it can conceal.[25]

---

[20] Butler, *Hudibras*, 2. 2. 197–208.   [21] Butler, *Hudibras*, 2. 2. 213–16.
[22] Butler, *Hudibras*, 1. 1. 797, 801–2.   [23] Butler, *Hudibras*, 'Hudibras to his Lady', 69–70.
[24] Caryll, *Hypocrite* (1678), lines 7–20; Dryden, *Works*, ii. 44, *The Medall* (1682), lines 33–4.
[25] Dryden, *Works*, ii. 44, lines 37–9; cf. *Hudibras*, 1. 1. 197–8.

Dryden's attack on dissent and its fellow travellers has a political dimension, as Butler's has and Swift's would have, but Dryden's occasion is more immediate and more urgent. In *Absalom and Achitophel* the opportunistic and dissembling Shaftesbury/Achitophel, the tempter of Monmouth/Absalom, is an appropriate leader and provoker of the English crowd, 'a Headstrong, Moody, Murmuring race', infected with 'publick Lunacy'. This 'Solymaean Rout' are described in a telling oxymoron as 'well vers'd of old / In godly faction'. In the Civil War years, they had tried Gods 'of every shape and size', and executed a king. Now they resume 'their Cant, and with a Zealous Cry, / Pursu'd their old belov'd Theocracy'.[26] Now they would challenge the authority of Charles II himself.

Dryden was especially concerned with the sectarians' uses, and abuses, of Scripture. Before, Reformation Rome had controlled access to and interpretation of the Bible: 'Scripture was scarce, and as the Market went, / Poor Laymen took Salvation on Content'.[27] The translation of the Bible into vulgar tongues, however, had as bad a consequence. Mere tradesmen, like Ralpho the tailor, or guildsmen, might gall 'the tender Page with horney Fists'. Interpretative privilege might be appropriated by readers who, like Ralpho, had given no labour to formal scholarship and had graduated to no qualification, but claimed the authority rather of individual inspiration:

> The *Spirit* gave the *Doctoral Degree*:
> And every member of a *Company*
> Was of *his Trade*, and of the *Bible free*.
> ...
>
> *Study* and *Pains* were now no more their *Care*;
> *Texts* were explain'd by *Fasting*, and by *Prayer*.[28]

The Bible was meant for spiritual food; fly-blown, the text produces the whimsical and ephemeral maggots of the sectarian mind. Worse, Dryden accuses the sectarians of 'rack[ing] Scripture to confess their cause', torturing its sense to make it agree with their beliefs. As Ralpho had argued for the right of the Saints to misinterpret Scripture 'by private / Instructions to all aims they drive at', so Dryden accuses them of seizing 'this talking Trumpet' to their own use, to 'make it speak whatever Sense they please!' This is an exercise in subjective, uncontrolled interpretation, the operations of the spirit working only in reverse: 'the Text inspires not them; but they the Text inspire'.[29] Honest appeal to a text as a potentially stable rule of faith gives way to the personal and party motive. Scripture becomes a vehicle not of salvation but damnation: 'the Fanaticks, or Schismaticks, of the *English* Church' have used the translated Bible 'as if their business was not to be sav'd but to be damn'd by its Contents'.[30] Sectarian perversions of biblical guidance, and sectarian duplicities, are intimated elliptically in Dryden's satiric puns. In *Absalom and Achitophel*, Corah is named for Korah, who led

---

[26] Dryden, *Works*, ii. 5–26, *Absalom and Achitophel*, lines 45, 788, 513, 49, 521–2.

[27] Dryden, *Works*, ii. 120, *Religio Laici*, lines 380–1.

[28] Dryden, *Works*, ii. 121, *Religio Laici*, lines 404, 406–8, 413–14.

[29] Dryden, *Works*, ii. 48, *The Medall*, lines 162–6.   [30] Dryden, *Works*, ii. 105, 110.

a rebellion against Moses (Numbers 16:1–40). Dryden's prophetic Corah is repeatedly and emphatically referred to as a 'witness', a word with double implications. 'Witness' is used in the New Testament of those who testify to Christ's divinity, and particularly of John the Baptist, sent 'to bear witness of the Light, that all men through him might believe'.[31] At the same time Dryden's reiterated 'witness' mocks the lying evidencer Titus Oates, 'Arch-Attestor' of the Popish plot.[32] In the Bible, Shimei is the kinsman of Saul who cursed David (2 Sam. 16:5–12). In Dryden's poem, Shimei is the frugal Slingsby Bethel, leather seller and Whig Lord Mayor of London, who, though he notoriously refused to give the hospitality his office required, 'yet lov'd his wicked Neighbour as himself', thus satisfying, in his own terms, the second of Christ's great commandments (Mark 12:31). Christ had promised the apostles that 'where two or three are gathered together in my name, there am I in the midst of them' (Matt. 18:20); cursing the king, like his biblical original, Dryden's Shimei keeps Christian fellowship with a difference:

> When two or three were gather'd to declaim
> Against the monarch of *Jerusalem*,
> *Shimei* was always in the midst of them.[33]

Such allusive doubleness expresses in compressed and telling form the hypocrisy, and the blasphemy, of these two dissenting leaders.

JONATHAN SWIFT

Jonathan Swift had a strong historical sense of the importance, and to his mind the dangers, of sectarianism. His first satiric masterpiece, the *Tale of a Tub* volume which first appeared in 1704 and comprised not only the *Tale* but also *The Battel of the Books* and *The Mechanical Operation of the Spirit*, aimed at a broad range of present and past Protestant dissent. In the allegorical narrative of the *Tale*, Anglican Martin is beset by his brothers Peter, who represents the Pope and Romanism, and Jack, who represents an extremely diverse range of Protestant sects and leaders: John Calvin, John of Leyden (an Anabaptist tailor, and one of the leaders of the Münster rebellion of 1534[34]), the Family of Christ, the Sweet Singers of Israel, the Huguenots, the Quakers, the Independents, and both the English and Scottish Presbyterians: 'the little Boys in the Streets... would call Him, *Jack the Bald*; sometimes, *Jack with a Lanthorn*; sometimes, *Dutch Jack*; sometimes, *French Hugh*; sometimes, *Tom the Beggar*; and sometimes, *Knocking Jack of*

---

[31] John 1:7; cf. John 1:8, 15.
[32] Dryden, *Works*, ii. 24–5, *Absalom and Achitophel*, lines 631, 640, 642, 668, 681.
[33] Dryden, *Works*, ii. 23, *Absalom and Achitophel*, lines 600, 601–4.
[34] Butler discusses the edification of the Saints by John of Leyden's example, *Hudibras*, 3. 2. 243–60.

the North.[35] For Swift, as for Butler, the Presbyterians were a substantial target. Swift's own early clerical career in Ireland had brought him unwelcome familiarity with immigrant Scottish Presbyterians, driven from their own country by the famine years of the mid-1690s. Swift's choice of the name Jack has a particular resonance, invoking the phrase 'Jack Presbyter' as used in seventeenth-century polemic.[36]

In the *Tale* volume, Swift attacks many of what he and other Anglicans took to be the characterizing affectations of sectarian worship, the eyes rolled up as a mark of sanctity, the droning nasal tone and distorted facial features of the preacher, the 'jargon' or 'Babel' of their language of devotion. He devotes a lengthy passage of the *Tale* to sectarian biblical literalism. Scripture is for Jack 'Meat, Drink, and Cloth': 'his common Talk and Conversation, ran wholly in the Phrase of his Will'.[37] 'The Mechanical Operation of the Spirit' contains an inventive running conceit on the long-alleged connection and similarity of religious zeal and sexual licence. Swift's persona insists on the 'fundamental Point' amongst the fanatics of their belief and practice of 'the Community of Women', and observes ('with wonder', though scientifically) the attraction of 'all Females' to 'Visionary or Enthusiastick Preachers', usually supposed to be the result of 'Considerations, purely Spiritual, without any carnal Regards at all'. This much is certain, Swift's persona concludes; 'however Spiritual Intrigues begin, they generally conclude like all others; they may branch upwards towards Heaven; but the Root is in the Earth'.[38]

At the centre of Swift's satire, however, is a concerted attack, taking highly extended and developed forms, on a central theological issue: the dissenting claim to the private inspiration of individual believers by the Holy Ghost, variously labelled 'zeal' and 'enthusiasm'. Such claims, deluded and deliberately deluding in Swift's view, are reduced to mechanical fundamentals. Jack, in Swift's new religious mythology, turns out to have been the 'Author and Founder' of 'the most Illustrious and Epidemick Sect of Aeolists', who 'maintain the Original Cause of all Things to be *Wind*, from which this whole Universe was at first produced'.[39] Learning is understood by the Aeolists to be mere wind, for (and here Swift follows Butler's parodic syllogism) '*Words are but Wind; and Learning is nothing but Words; Ergo, Learning is nothing but Wind.*' The modern tub-preacher, a committed Aeolist, performs his mysteries and rites as the ancient oracles did, with equal show, deceit, and persuasive power:

> ...the Virtuoso's of former Ages, had a Contrivance for carrying and preserving *Winds* in Casks or Barrels...ascribed to *Æolus* himself....this Sect...have to this Day preserved great Numbers of those *Barrels,* whereof they fix one in each of their

---

[35] *The Cambridge Edition of the Works of Jonathan Swift* (Cambridge: Cambridge University Press, 2008–), vol. 1, *A Tale of a Tub and other Works*, ed. Marcus Walsh (2010), 94.

[36] For example, *The Disconsolate Reformado; or the sad look'd Presbyterian Jack* (1647); *Geneva & Rome: or, The Zeal of both boiling over...at a Private Conference between Jack a Presbyter and Believe-All a Papist* (1679). Roger L'Estrange, in *Observator*, 66 (29 October 1681), 'traces the History of Jack Presbyter' and finds similarity with 'Jack of Leyden'. For discussion, see *Tale of a Tub*, lxii–lxvi.

[37] Swift, *Works* (Cambridge), i. 123–4.   [38] Swift, *Works* (Cambridge), i. 185–7.

[39] Swift, *Works* (Cambridge), i. 94, 99.

Temples...into this *Barrel*;...the Priest enters;...a secret Funnel is also convey'd from his Posteriors, to the Bottom of the Barrel, which admits new Supplies of Inspiration from a *Northern* Chink or Crany....In this Posture he disembogues whole Tempests upon his Auditory, as the Spirit from beneath gives him Utterance.[40]

Northern European, British, and especially North British enthusiasm operates by insufflation, through the anus of the dissenting preacher, emerging not as sacred truth but eructation.

Swift's attack on enthusiasm reaches its satiric and poetic apogee in the 'Fragment' included with the *Tale*, 'A Discourse Concerning the Mechanical Operation of the Spirit'. The 'Discourse' parodies the 'Letters' written to the Royal Society, and published in the *Philosophical Transactions*. The scientific discovery that the persona of the 'Discourse' has to communicate is that there are not three but four different modes of inspiration. The first three are well known: 'the immediate Act of God...called, *Prophecy* or *Inspiration*'; 'the immediate Act of the Devil...termed *Possession*'; 'the Product of natural Causes, the effect of strong Imagination, violent Anger, Fear, Grief, Pain, and the like'. The fourth, however, is distinctively and purely 'an Effect of Artifice and *Mechanick Operation*'.[41] 'Mechanick' is a word that suggests the mechanical systems of the circulation of the blood, or the motions of the planets, but it calls to mind also the vulgar trades which, as Anglican satire so gleefully insisted, so many of the sectaries pursued. Mechanical enthusiasm, which has benefited from many 'Advancements and Refinements' in the modern world, is 'performed' by the dissenting preachers who are 'our *British Workmen*'.[42] The 'Discourse' treats specifically, and exclusively, of this fourth, mechanical, mode of inspiration. Swift, or his persona, acknowledges that 'It hath continued these hundred Years an even Debate, whether the Deportment and the Cant of our *English* Enthusiastick Preachers, were *Possession*, or *Inspiration*', and therefore is resolved to make clear that 'this Mystery of venting spiritual Gifts is nothing but a *Trade*, acquired by as much Instruction, and mastered by equal Practice and Application as others are'.[43] Amongst the dissenters, inspiration comes not from God or the Devil, but is the merchandise of tradesmen, whose mystery is not sacred truth but learnt craft. Religious devotion becomes a huckster's performance, governed not by the need for understanding and clear communication but by the practised jargon and patter, the hypnotic chant and cant of the salesman:

> without a competent Skill in tuning and toning each Word, and Syllable, and Letter, to their due Cadence, the whole Operation...misses entirely of its effect on the Hearers...For...in the Language of the Spirit, *Cant* and *Droning* supply the Place of *Sense* and *Reason*, in the Language of Men.[44]

---

[40] Swift, *Works* (Cambridge), i. 100.
[41] Swift, *Works* (Cambridge), i. 173. On the sources of Swift's taxonomy of inspiration, see 513–14.
[42] Swift, *Works* (Cambridge), i. 173.   [43] Swift, *Works* (Cambridge), i. 178.
[44] Swift, *Works* (Cambridge), i. 180.

No great harm might ensue, perhaps, if this exercise in dishonesty and delusion were confined to the enthusiasts themselves. Unfortunately, however, as Swift argues in his 'Digression concerning the Original, the Use, and Improvement of *Madness* in a Commonwealth', the frenzy which characterizes the Aeolists is a necessary distemper of those who propagate 'New Religions', as it is of those who establish 'New Empires by Conquest', and 'New Schemes in Philosophy'. It is an essential qualification of all those who would sponsor new systems in the intellectual, political, and religious worlds, 'For, what Man in the natural State, or Course of Thinking, did ever conceive it in his Power, to reduce the Notions of all Mankind, exactly to the same Length, and Breadth, and Heighth of his own?' The result of the sleep of reason is the eviction of common sense, of communal understanding, in the individual, and then in his sectarian followers:

> when a Man's Fancy gets *astride* on his Reason...and common Understanding, as well as common Sense, is kickt out of Doors; the first Proselyte he makes is Himself, and when that is once compass'd, the Difficulty is not so great in bringing over others.[45]

This process of proselytizing in Swift's view is characteristic of all shades of dissent, and threatens the safety of the spiritual and secular state. Swift was no advocate of thought control; we all have liberty of conscience, the right to our own private beliefs, which, 'properly speaking, is no more than the liberty of possessing our own thoughts and opinions, which every man enjoys without fear of the magistrate'.[46] If men publish their thoughts to the world, however, 'they ought to be answerable for the effects their thoughts produce upon others'.[47]

This line of reasoning has a remarkable and challenging consequence for Swift's views of hypocrisy in relation to religion. Much of his satire against the sectarians turns on the exposure of hypocritical difference, between the appearance of chastity and the indulgence of the flesh, between the claim of truly divine inspiration and the reality of mechanical operation of the dissenting spirit. A different kind of hypocrisy, however, a hypocrisy which leads to quiet, security, and peace rather than histrionics, tumescence, and violence, might be considered not only permissible but essential to Church and State. Swift's *Project for the Advancement of Religion, and the Reformation of Manners* (1709) seems at least at first sight as serious and unironic a piece as he was capable of writing. That he titled the work 'a Project', and chose to publish it under the authorial identity of 'a Person of Quality', might raise some suspicion.[48] Swift, or his persona,

---

[45] Swift, *Works* (Cambridge), i. 110.

[46] 'Thoughts on Religion', *The Prose Writings of Jonathan Swift*, ed. Herbert Davis et al., 16 vols. (Oxford: Basil Blackwell, 1939–74), ix. 263.

[47] 'Some Thoughts on Free-Thinking', Swift, *PW*, iv. 49.

[48] Contributions to the critical debate about the nature of this pamphlet include Leland D. Peterson, 'Swift's *Project*: A Religious and Political Satire', *PMLA* 82 (1967), 54–63; Phillip Harth, 'Swift's *Project*: Tract or Travesty?', *PMLA* 84 (1969), 336–43; John Kay, 'The Hypocrisy of Jonathan Swift: Swift's *Project* Reconsidered', *University of Toronto Quarterly* 44 (1975), 213–23; Judson B. Curry, 'Approaches to Swift's *An Argument Against Abolishing Christianity* and *A Project for the Advancement of Religion*', *Eighteenth-Century Life* 20 (1996), 67–78.

asserts that 'the Nation is extreamly corrupted in Religion and Morals'; 'hardly One in a Hundred among our People of Quality, or Gentry appears to act by any Principle of Religion', and the common people are almost as bad. These are credibly Swiftian complaints. The pamphlet proposes as a solution that the sovereign should take steps to make it 'every Man's Interest and Honour to cultivate Religion and Virtue', and in particular to make appointment to offices of state dependent upon virtuous behaviour and religious observance. This would have a valuable practical effect:

> There is no Quality so contrary to any Nature, which Men cannot affect, and put on upon Occasion, in order to serve an Interest, or gratify a prevailing Passion.... How ready therefore would most Men be to step into the Paths of Virtue and Piety, if they infallibly led to Favour and Fortune?[49]

The projector understands very well 'that the making Religion a necessary Step to Interest and Favour, might encrease Hypocrisy among us', but insists that the price would be worth paying 'if One in Twenty should be brought over to true Piety by this, or the like Methods, and the other Nineteen be only Hypocrites'. Hypocrisy in such a cause is a relative good: 'Hypocrisy is much more eligible than open Infidelity and Vice; it wears the Livery of Religion, it acknowledgeth her Authority, and is cautious of giving Scandal.'[50] These arguments may seem disingenuous. They are inflected at least by the shifting ironic tone of the Swiftian voice, and an almost Gulliverian optimism about the moral and practical efficacy of good examples. They are nevertheless consistent with Swift's regular argument that behaviour, not sentiment, is the key to public quiet. The Swift of the *Project*, like the Swift of the sermons, is a believer in authority, obedience, and the truth and importance to civil order of Anglican belief and the Anglican Church Established. The hypocrisy of even a feigned orthodox belief is, for him, altogether preferable to the hypocrisy of the fanaticks.

SATIRE, RECEPTION, INTERPRETATION

The public reaction to Swift's *Tale of a Tub*, following its first appearance in 1704, provides an unusually fully documented instance of the opposition and misunderstanding encountered by authors of religious satire. Strikingly, there are few responses from the ostensible targets of Swift's satire, Romanist or dissenting. Daniel Defoe attacked a key element of Swift's satire against dissenting notions of the operation of the spirit as 'a mistaken Notion of *Wind*, which... flew upward in blew Strakes of a livid Flame call'd *Blasphemy*, which burnt up all the Wit and Fancy of the Author, and left a strange *stench* behind it'.[51] Some commentators suspected the author of the *Tale* of being one of those

---

[49] Swift, *PW*, ii. 45, 47, 50.   [50] Swift, *PW*, ii. 56–7.

[51] Daniel Defoe, *The Consolidator; or, Memoirs of Sundry Transactions from the World in the Moon* (1705), 62.

'Profane and debauched Deists', who claim in their writings 'to expose the Abuses and Corruptions of Religion', but in reality 'indeavour to ridicule and banter all *Humane* as well as *Divine* Accomplishments'.[52] The most common theme amongst critics of the *Tale* was that its anonymous author consistently indulged himself in levity and indecency wholly inappropriate to his subject, and in doing so ridiculed and attempted to bring into disrepute not only his apparent Romanist and dissenting targets, but all Christianity, including the English Church. William King, in the persona of a night-soil man, spelled out the four apparent purposes of the author of the *Tale* volume: 'the...first...is, to be Prophane.... The Second is to show how great a Proficient he is... at Cursing and Swearing.... His Third is to exceed all Bounds of Modesty...His next is a great Affectation for every thing that is nasty...almost every Part has a Tincture of such Filthiness'.[53] John Dennis accused the *Tale*'s author of being 'a Priest...who mad'st thy first Appearance in the World like a...spiritual Buffoon, an Ecclesiastical *Jack Pudding*, by publishing a Piece of waggish Divinity, which was writ with a Design to banter all Christianity'.[54]

Such suspicion of indecorous and jesting expression of all kinds in relation to religion had a very long history. The Bible had itself provided ample warrant. Seventeenth- and eighteenth-century divines and homilists regularly referred to Peter's prophecy that 'there shall come in the last days scoffers' (2 Pet. 3:3), and, more especially, to Paul's warning that the saints must avoid 'filthiness', 'foolish talking', and 'jesting' (Ephes. 5:4). The issue was taken seriously, and discussed with rigour and nuance, by major theologians. Isaac Barrow devoted a long sermon to Ephesians 5:4, in which he suggested that Paul's words, like other 'seemingly formal prohibitions' should be received only as a 'sober caution'. There is a difference, Barrow insists, between mere 'foolish talking' (Paul's Greek is *mōrología*), and facetiousness used as a 'proper instrument for exposing things apparently base and vile in due contempt'. Indeed, Barrow would appear to license just the kind of parabolic invention that characterizes Swift's *Tale*:

> If it be lawfull, (as by the best authorities it plainly doth appear to be,) in using Rhetorical schemes, Poetical strains...Allegories, Fables, Parables, and Riddles, to discoast from the plain and simple way of speech; why may not Facetiousness, issuing from the same principles, directed to the same ends, serving to like purposes, be likewise used blamelessly?

Though parables, fables, and allegories are permitted in the service of virtue, however, Barrow's sermon provides no licence for Swift's jesting in matters of religion, or for his sexual and coprophilic satire, that 'filthiness' at which even William King's night-soil man would turn up his nose. Barrow insists that 'All profane Jesting, all speaking loosely

---

[52] Samuel Clarke, *A Discourse Concerning the Unchangeable Obligations of Natural Religion, and the Truth and Certainty of the Christian Revelation* (1706), 28, 29.

[53] William King, *Some Remarks upon the Tale of a Tub. In a Letter* (1704), 8–10.

[54] 'To the Examiner. Upon his Wise Paper of the Tenth of January, 1712', in *The Critical Works of John Dennis*, ed. E. N. Hooker, 2 vols. (Baltimore: Johns Hopkins University Press, 1943), ii. 397–8.

and wantonly about Holy things…making such things the matters of sport and mockery…is certainly prohibited', and indeed that on all subjects 'it is very culpable to be facetious in obscene and smutty matters'.[55]

When the *Tale* was published in its revised fifth edition, in 1710, Swift prefaced an 'Apology' which sought explicitly to answer his contemporary critics, and, less explicitly, to situate and defend his work against the long-standing Anglican suspicion of the application of the methods of satire to religious argument. He was not the first, nor would he be the last, ironizing satirist to find the need to explain himself. Daniel Defoe's *The Shortest Way with the Dissenters* (1702) responded to debate concerning the Bill 'to Prevent Occasional Conformity', which had just been passed by the Commons. Defoe's method was to make 'other Peoples thoughts speak in his words',[56] exaggerating violent and immoderate High Tory anti-dissenting rhetoric, especially that of Henry Sacheverell's 'Oxford Sermon' of June 1702. Not altogether surprisingly, Defoe's bodiless voice and barely flagged ironies upset all parties, the Dissenters who thought themselves attacked, and the High Churchmen who thought themselves travestied. Defoe promptly published *A Brief Explanation of a Late Pamphlet* ([1703]), to make a 'Declaration of his real Design', though he complained that 'If any man takes the pains seriously to reflect upon the Contents, the Nature of the Thing, and the Manner of the Stile, it seems Impossible to imagine it should pass for any thing but an Irony.'[57] A dozen years later, Francis Hare published his *Difficulties and Discouragements which attend the Study of the Scriptures* (1714), which presents itself as a letter from an older Anglican cleric, warning a 'Young Clergyman' against the 'free, serious, impartial, and laborious Study of the Scriptures', on the grounds of the difficulty of the text, the impossibly wide range of knowledge required, and the numerous and challenging languages to be learnt. Close study of the Bible is neither safe nor profitable for a clergyman, who does better 'to study the *Tradition of the Church*'.[58] Such a preference is paradoxical for a clergyman of the Anglican Church, which like other Protestant churches had insisted on the primacy of Scripture as a Rule of Faith, and urged both the clergy and the laity to 'search the Scriptures'. Hare's letter writer is in fact intended as a burlesquing personation of conservative churchmen, and their condemnation of Samuel Clarke's *Scripture Doctrine of the Trinity* (1712), which had argued that careful examination of the holy writings revealed no clear authority for orthodox Trinitarian belief. Fearing that his ironic *reductio* might be misunderstood, or misapplied, or taken seriously, Hare appends, even with his first edition, a Conclusion, in which he explicitly and formally denies allegiance to this 'strange Paradox…that Clergymen should lay aside what *ought* to be their *chief Study*'.[59]

---

[55] Barrow, 'The Second Sermon. Ephes. 5. 4. – *Nor foolish talking, nor jesting, which are not convenient*', *Several Sermons against Evil-Speaking* (1678), 39–40, 49, 58, 61, 75. Barrow's sermon is discussed at valuable length by Raymond A. Anselment, *'Betwixt Jest and Earnest': Marprelate, Milton, Marvell, Swift and the Decorum of Religious Ridicule* (Toronto: University of Toronto Press, 1979), 8–32.

[56] Defoe, *A Brief Explanation of a Late Pamphlet* [1703], 4.   [57] Defoe, *Explanation*, [1], 4.

[58] Francis Hare, *Difficulties and Discouragements*, 9, 11.

[59] Hare, *Difficulties and Discouragements*, 48.

It is striking that one of the key points Swift felt impelled to make in his 'Apology' is that 'there generally runs an Irony through the Thread of the whole Book, which the Men of Tast will observe and distinguish, and which will render some objections that have been made, very weak and insignificant'.[60] Another point, closely related and equally striking, is that 'the judicious Reader cannot but have observed, some of those Passages...which appear most liable to Objection are what they call Parodies, where the Author personates the Style and Manner of other Writers, whom he has a mind to expose'.[61] These are optimistic claims: the reception history of satire shows of course (as Swift knew and acknowledged) that not all readers may observe and distinguish irony and parody. Claiming that it is Peter who is represented in the *Tale* as repeating 'Oaths and Curses', Swift attempts to escape the accusation that he himself used 'Prophane or Immodest Speech';[62] but Peter is not the only such voice in the *Tale*, nor would the absolute prohibition of such speech by Barrow amongst others be reasonably circumvented even if he were.

It might credibly be argued therefore that, despite his protests, the Swift of *A Tale of a Tub* remains vulnerable to Anglican objections, made before or in his own time, against such rhetorical methods. Swift, however, makes more consequential claims about the substance and targets of his satire. Insisting that his book 'Celebrates the Church of *England* as the most perfect of all others in Discipline and Doctrine, it advances no Opinion they reject, nor condemns any they receive', he undertakes 'to forfeit his life, if any one Opinion can be fairly deduced from that Book which is contrary to Religion or Morality'.[63] A recent commentator has characterized Swift's challenge as 'bravado';[64] Swift's gage, however, has to do with the *meaning* of his book. It poses an *interpretative* question, which can only be answered by interpretative methods. If it were merely an act of bravado, it might be expected that Swift's challenge would have been decisively taken up and defeated. No such decisive refutation has ever appeared. It is true that such contemporaries as Richard Blackmore and Matthew Tindal, for instance, accused Swift of making himself 'pleasant with the Principles of the Christian' and 'talking ridiculously about Religion in general',[65] but no quantity of such assertions could amount to *interpretative* evidence. We know that King and Dennis, Blackmore and Tindal, and many others, charged the *Tale of a Tub* with heterodoxy; but the question is whether their charges were well-founded in any valid understanding of the words of Swift's book.

The most extended and testing contemporary examination of the *Tale*, William Wotton's 'Observations upon the *Tale of a Tub*', was published within a year of the first

---

[60] Swift, *Works* (Cambridge), i. 8.   [61] Swift, *Works* (Cambridge), i. 7.

[62] Swift, *Works* (Cambridge), i. 13.   [63] Swift, *Works* (Cambridge), i. 6.

[64] Roger Lund, 'The Trammels of Christian Wit', chapter 5 of his *Ridicule, Religion and the Politics of Wit in Augustan England* (Farnham: Ashgate, 2012), 175.

[65] Richard Blackmore, *An Essay upon Wit* (1716), 217; Matthew Tindal, *An Address to the Inhabitants of the Two Great Cities of London and Westminster* (1729), 33–4.

edition of the *Tale*.[66] Wotton stands out as a serious critic of the *Tale*. He pays detailed and sustained attention to his text. He does not, however, as a matter of method, drive home his attacks hermeneutically. Wotton alleges, for instance, amongst many allegations, that the number of the three sons, Peter, Martin, and Jack, 'looks asquint at the TRINITY' (but Wotton does not show how).[67] He denies that 'any Christian [would] compare a *Mountebank's Stage*, a *Pulpit*, and a Ladder together' (but the pulpit Swift mocks—or rather, the pulpit his hack-persona 'esteems'—is 'That made of Timber from the *Sylva Caledonia*', that is, the pulpit of Presbyterian and dissenting worship).[68] Wotton particularly objects to Swift's satire against enthusiasm, which in Wotton's eyes, though Swift's target was dissent, causes extensive collateral damage:

> all extraordinary Inspirations are the Subjects of his Scorn and Mockery, whilst the Protestant Dissenters are … the most directly levelled at … [e]nthusiasm with him is an Universal Deception which has run through all Sciences in all Kingdoms, and every thing has some *Fanatic Branch annexed to it*.[69]

Certainly Swift's attack on enthusiasm permeates the whole; but he is explicit, not only in the 'Apology' but also in the meat of his text, about the contrived and simulated kinds of enthusiasm which are the objects of his satiric derision. Wotton's 'Observations' are marked throughout by his unwillingness or refusal to engage with or recognize shifts of voice in the *Tale*, his obtuseness to irony, his hostility to coarser kinds of satiric humour, and the biases of his involvement in controversial battle with Swift during the briefly bloody Ancients and Moderns debate. His general insistence that to direct 'Scorn and Mockery' against any branch or sect of religion is to attack all religion, and his constant complaints against what he considers Swift's blasphemy and profanity, are coherent given his stated principles, and in line with Anglican writing on the proper uses of wit in controversy. Wotton's 'Observations' do not, however, at any single point, demonstrate that the *Tale* promulgates any opinion contrary to Anglican belief and observance.

Wotton's 'Observations' offer a paradigm case for the reading of religious satire. Swift hoped for, and possibly expected, readers of candour and discrimination, as he understood those qualities. Readers of parodic and ironic texts, however, have not always had the generosity to suppose good meanings, or the interpretative discernment to distinguish true meanings. Swift had reason to complain, as Defoe had done, that 'Ignorance, or Prejudice has led most Men to a hasty Censure of the Book', and to insist, as Defoe had done, on the 'Native Genuine Meaning and Design' of his work.[70] These are complaints about the misreading of satires which employ irony as a structural as well as a local tool. Satire is a genre, and irony is a mode, notoriously liable to misunderstanding. They are particularly liable to misunderstanding when their targets are deeply held, and complexly constructed, spiritual beliefs and observances.

---

[66] William Wotton, *Reflections upon Ancient and Modern Learning. To which is now added, a Defense thereof, in Answer to the Objections of Sir W. Temple, and Others. With Observations upon the Tale of a Tub* (1705).

[67] Swift, *Works* (Cambridge), i. 219.

[68] Swift, *Works* (Cambridge), i. 224; for discussion, see 348–9.

[69] Swift, *Works* (Cambridge), i. 227.   [70] Defoe, *Explanation*, [1], 2.

SELECT BIBLIOGRAPHY

Anselment, Raymond A. *'Betwixt Jest and Earnest': Marprelate, Milton, Marvell, Swift and the Decorum of Religious Ridicule* (Toronto: University of Toronto Press, 1979).

Lund, Roger. *Ridicule, Religion and the Politics of Wit in Augustan England* (Farnham: Ashgate, 2012).

Marshall, Ashley. 'The Aims of Butler's Satire in *Hudibras*', *Modern Philology* 105 (2008), 637–65.

Tadav, Alok. 'Fractured Meanings: Hudibras and the Historicity of the Literary Text', *ELH* 62 (1995), 529–49.

Terry, Richard. 'Hudibras amongst the Augustans', *Studies in Philology* 90 (1993), 426–41.

Walsh, Marcus. 'Text, "Text", and Swift's *A Tale of a Tub*', *Modern Language Review* 85 (1990), 290–303.

CHAPTER 4

···

THE SATIRE OF DISSENT

···

GEORGE SOUTHCOMBE

...yet there is still a vast difference betwixt the slovenly butchering of
a man, and the fineness of a stroke that separates the head from the body
and leaves it standing in its place. A man may be capable, as Jack Ketch's
wife said of his servant, of a plain piece of work, a bare hanging; but to
make a malefactor die sweetly was only belonging to her husband. I wish
I could apply it to myself, if the reader would be kind enough to think it
belongs to me. The character of 'Zimri' in my *Absalom* is, in my opinion,
worth the whole poem; 'tis not bloody, but 'tis ridiculous enough; and he
for whom it was intended was too witty to resent it as an injury.[1]

DRYDEN was lying, if not directly then to himself. In a period where the savagery of
capital punishment was all too familiar, and in which the common hangman, Jack
Ketch, took three attempts to cut off the Whig martyr Lord Russell's head and five to
sever the Duke of Monmouth's, to use it to stand for the sweetness and grace of ideal
satire was somewhat audacious.[2] Dryden's own reading of his *Absalom and Achitophel*,
and the place of Zimri (the Duke of Buckingham) within it is similarly misleading,
and Buckingham seethed about the way in which he had been represented.[3] In fact, at
the same time as seeking to deny it, and to set a new, politer template for future satire,
Dryden captured much of the brutality and viciousness of Restoration satire. This
observation might initially seem surprising. As Nigel Smith has remarked, 'With the
Restoration came rules. Dryden's prefaces to his major satires and his essay on satire
extract the genre from the uncertain state in which it had existed between 1640 and
1660, and ultimately claim it for High Tory neo-Catholicism.'[4] But as he, and others,

I would like to thank Grant Tapsell for commenting on an earlier draft of this chapter.

[1] John Dryden, 'Discourse Concerning Satire', in Dryden, *Poems* (Longman), iii. 423–4.
[2] Dryden, *Poems* (Longman), iii. 423–4, n.; Tim Wales, 'John Ketch', *ODNB*.
[3] Dryden, *Poems* (Longman), i. 494, n.
[4] Nigel Smith, *Literature and Revolution in England, 1640–1660* (New Haven and London: Yale
University Press, 1994), 317.

have noted these 'rules' were established late in the seventeenth century and their retrospective application to the reigns of Charles II and James II distorts the nature of satire produced at the time.[5] A further distortion has been identified by Ashley Marshall, in particular, who has pointed to the misleading effect of concentrating on a small group of prominent authors without situating them within the much larger world of satirical writing available at the time.[6] One effect of this has been to hide from view—with some notable exceptions—much work produced to engage with what was the central political issue of the age, Church and dissent.[7] This occlusion has been aided by an assumption that there would be little point in seeking such material because it should not exist. Keith Thomas encapsulates a particularly tenacious view of the Puritan tradition and its antithesis, by the late seventeenth century, to satire: 'The Puritan cult of godly sorrow may have given its adherents their revolutionary impetus, but in the long run it appears a tactical mistake.... They had no shortage of comic talent available, but they seldom chose to employ it; though to say this is rather like criticizing a conscientious objector for not using force to avoid arrest.'[8] The purpose of the current chapter is thus threefold. First, it attempts to bring into focus the nonconformist contribution to Restoration satire, most specifically through an analysis of the popular Presbyterian poet Robert Wild. Second, it highlights, within works engaged with religious controversy, the continued fascination with the 'wantonness and lubricity', the bodily and scatological, and the continued potency of blunt insult, that Dryden would later see as improper in satire.[9] Third, by locating 'major' writers—Marvell and Defoe—in relation to this work it seeks to demonstrate the significance of the nonconformist tradition to the roots of the eighteenth-century satire boom.

UNIFORMITY AND PERSECUTION

'Restoration England was a persecuting society.'[10] Early hopes that the Restoration of the monarchy in 1660 might lead to a comprehensive Church settlement were soon destroyed. In 1662 the Act of Uniformity—which required clergymen to declare their

---

[5] This case has been made with peculiar force for the reign of Charles II by Robert D. Hume, '"Satire" in the Reign of Charles II', *Modern Philology* 102 (2005), 332–71.

[6] Ashley Marshall, *The Practice of Satire in England, 1658–1770* (Baltimore: Johns Hopkins University Press, 2013).

[7] For arguments concerning the centrality of this issue see George Southcombe and Grant Tapsell, *Restoration Politics, Religion and Culture: Britain and Ireland, 1660–1714* (Basingstoke: Palgrave Macmillan, 2010), ch. 2; Tim Harris, *Politics under the Later Stuarts: Party Conflict in a Divided Society 1660–1715* (London: Longman, 1993), 65–75.

[8] Keith Thomas, 'The Place of Laughter in Tudor and Stuart England', *Times Literary Supplement*, 21 January 1977, 81.

[9] Dryden, *Poems* (Longman), iii. 370.

[10] Mark Goldie, 'The Theory of Religious Intolerance in Restoration England', in *From Persecution to Toleration: The Glorious Revolution and Religion in England*, ed. Ole Peter Grell, Jonathan I. Israel, and Nicholas Tyacke (Oxford: Clarendon Press, 1991), 331.

assent to a set of propositions that many of them found abhorrent—led to the ejection of a large number of Presbyterian ministers from the Church, and created a body of reluctant nonconformists. Further laws tightened the legal proscription against dissent, and allowed for the hounding of those who could not, for reasons of conscience, and to varying degrees, accept the doctrine and worship of the national Church.[11] The campaign to remove or alleviate the effects of this legislation developed almost conterminously with its creation. This was in part due to the recognition that while a commanding interest in parliament had pushed through this programme, there was significant desire to lessen its impact at the very centre of government. On 26 December 1662 Charles II issued a statement suggesting that parliament should 'incline their wisdom at this next approaching sessions to concur with us in the making some such Act for that purpose as may enable us to exercise with a more universal satisfaction that power of dispensing which we conceive to be inherent in us'. What was intended was an acceptance that the king, acting through his prerogative, might allow a degree of toleration for those who could not accept the strictures of Uniformity. It was not embraced by the Presbyterians—who feared both the king's use of an arbitrary power over a parliamentary decision and the alleviation of the position of Catholics—but it did indicate that the religious settlement was open to contestation.[12] This was the context for one of the first great legal controversies of Restoration nonconformity.

On 28 December 1662 the ejected minister of St Mary Aldermanbury, and leading Presbyterian, Edmund Calamy preached in his former parish. It was the second time he had done so since St Bartholomew's Day, and he was arrested on 6 January 1663. His imprisonment was brief—a warrant for his release being issued on 13 January—but it was of sufficient symbolic importance to feature at the centre of a small explosion of satire.[13] Central to the shaping of this satirical controversy was the Presbyterian poet Robert Wild. Like Calamy, Wild too was a clergyman ejected from his living in 1662. He had enjoyed some early success in the Restoration with his poem *Iter Boreale* which concerned the man whose actions had proved central to the king's return, General George Monck. In the aftermath of Uniformity he sought to harness his popularity for the Presbyterian cause.

On one level Wild's satire was addressed quite specifically to a particular Presbyterian audience. It contained an extended play on themes developed by Calamy in the final sermon he preached before his ejection. Where Calamy had spoken sensitively of the

---

[11] For discussions of this legislative landscape and its effects see George Southcombe, 'Dissent and the Restoration Church of England', in *The Later Stuart Church, 1660–1714*, ed. Grant Tapsell (Manchester: Manchester University Press, 2012), 199–200; Nicholas Tyacke, 'The "Rise of Puritanism" and the Legalizing of Dissent', in *From Persecution to Toleration*, ed. Grell, Israel, and Tyacke, 17–49.

[12] N. H. Keeble, *The Restoration: England in the 1660s* (Oxford: Blackwell, 2002), 122–3, quotation at 123.

[13] Richard L. Greaves, *Saints and Rebels: Seven Nonconformists in Stuart England* (Macon: Mercer University Press, 1985), 57–9; TNA, SP 44/9, fo. 224. The explosion has previously been noted by Sharon Achinstein, *Literature and Dissent in Milton's England* (Cambridge: Cambridge University Press, 2003), 1–2; William Poole, 'Milton and Calamy', *Notes and Queries* 50, no. 2 (June 2003), 180–3.

sweetness of suffering for God, and drawn attention to the example of the Marian martyrs, Wild produced his points in a robust comic register:

> One Sermon hath preferr'd you so much Honor
> A man could scarce have had from *Bishop Bonner*;
> Whilst We (your Brethren) poor Erraticks be,
> You are a glorious fixed Star we see,
> Hundreds of us turn out of House and Home;
> To a safe Habitation you are come.[14]

He then, towards the end of the poem, in a move typical of his verse, turned to the grossness of the human body—specifically his body (Anthony Wood would later call him 'a fat, jolly, and boon presbyterian'[15]):

> Sir, I may challenge you to pity me:
> I am the older Gaol-bird; my hard fate
> Hath kept me twenty years in *Cripple-Gate*;
> Old *Bishop Gout*, that Lordly proud disease,
> Took my fat body for his Diocess,
> Where he keeps Court, there visits every Limb,
> And makes them (*Levite*-like) conform to him.[16]

Again, on one level the satire functions as in-joke for beleaguered Presbyterians. In his ejection sermon, Calamy had drawn a distinction between suffering for conscience and the results of sin: 'Sin brings Agues and Feavours, Gout and Stone, and all manner of Diseases'.[17] Wild made the joke at his own expense, and it would have been recognized by a number in his original audience. But it is also clear that Wild's satire is not dependent on this in-joke for meaning, and that a broader, anti-prelatical satirical discourse was being developed. Bishops were figured as pluralists seeking to recreate Babel ('I envy not our Mitred men, their Places, / Their rich Preferments, nor their richer *Faces*: / To see them Steeple upon Steeple set, / As if they meant that way to Heaven to get'.[18]). The poem announced a general hostility to the episcopal bench, but the Bishop of London—in whose see Calamy was imprisoned—Gilbert Sheldon, was singled out for particular opprobrium: ''Tis prov'd, when you pray most devout / For all good men, you leave the Bishops out: / This makes Seer *Sheldon* by his powerful spell / Conjure and lay you safe in *Newgate*-hell'.[19] Presbyterians had initially accepted the case for working within a reduced episcopacy

---

[14] Robert Wild, *A Poem Upon the Imprisonment of Mr Calamy in Newgate*, in *English Nonconformist Poetry*, ed. George Southcombe, 3 vols. (London: Pickering & Chatto, 2012), i. 181.

[15] *Alumni Oxonienses 1500–1700* (Oxford, 1891), s.v. 'Wild, Robert'.

[16] Wild, *A Poem Upon the Imprisonment of Mr Calamy*, 183.

[17] Edmund Calamy, *The Fixed Saint* (1662), 7.

[18] Wild, *A Poem Upon the Imprisonment of Mr Calamy*, 181.

[19] Wild, *A Poem Upon the Imprisonment of Mr Calamy*, 182.

on the Restoration, but following Uniformity, even if anti-episcopal rhetoric was not based in a complete ideological rejection of government by bishops, it took on a potency that could only serve to harden distinctions, to create and cement binary divisions.[20] This Presbyterian use of satire was thus significant both in setting the dominant tone of the debate, and in starting to shape a distinctive Presbyterian identity against a prelatical Other.

The most vehement response to Wild's poem sought to exploit the popularity of Samuel Butler's anti-Presbyterian mock-epic, by announcing itself as by 'Hudibras'. The author emphasized anti-prelatical themes in Wild's poem while developing its bodily imagery in an expressly scatological way:

> The *Cage* is open, and the *Bird* is flown:
> That *Bird* (whom though your Lordships do despise)
> May *Shite in Paul's*, and *Pick out Sheldon's Eyes.*[21]

A further poem, satirically ventriloquizing a Presbyterian respondent to Wild, introduced a sexual edge:

> As I was *Preaching* on the *secret point*
> Of *Venery*, I did but slip a *joint*
> Too far, when straight old *Bishop Pox*, cry'd cease,
> You do encroach upon my *Dioceß.*[22]

His respondents thus harnessed the grossly corporeal in Wild's verse, but this physically-rooted comedy ran alongside a clear investigation of the political implications of the poet's Presbyterianism. Calamy's role as part of Smectymnuus—the group of clergymen who wrote for the reform of Church government and liturgy in 1641—was recalled, and this was conceptually linked to an anti-monarchical stance: 'For Non-Conformists heretofore were known / To be the most dreadful Drawers from the Crown. / Old *Smecks* proud Foot did claim the highest Seat, / Thence th' *Presbyterian* toes did swell so great.'[23] Calamy it was said was 'He who taught the *Pulpit* and the *Press* / To mask *Rebellion* in a *Gospel-dress*'.[24] This linking of political with religious Presbyterianism was central to the failure of both, and the political past of Presbyterianism in particular was seen as legitimating extreme measures: 'O may the *Gout* no more disturb thy ease, / But *Bishop Halter* take his *Diocese*'.[25] In a poem that presented itself as 'Doctor Wildes Recantation' the fantasy was not of the judicial execution of Wild but Calamy's suicide:

[20] For more on this process see Southcombe, 'Dissent and the Restoration Church', 199–204; George Southcombe, 'Presbyterians in the Restoration', in *The Oxford History of Protestant Dissenting Traditions*, ed. John Coffey (Oxford: Oxford University Press, forthcoming).
[21] *Hudibras On Calamy's Imprisonment, and Wild's Poetry* ([London], 1663]).
[22] *An Answer to Wild* ([London], 1663]).   [23] *Dr Wild's Eccho* ([London], 1663]).
[24] *Hudibras On Calamy's Imprisonment.*
[25] *Hudibras On Calamy's Imprisonment.* On Presbyterianism as a political and religious phenomenon in the Restoration, see Mark Goldie, *Roger Morrice and the Puritan Whigs* (Woodbridge: Boydell Press, 2016).

> I cann't behold you take into your *gills*
> Rebellious doses, as men swallow *pills*;
> Nor let you swim again in *Royal Blood*,
> Whilest Loyal Souls are drowned in a flood
> Of *briny tears*, which fitter deemed are
> For your *Repentance Stool* than *Peter's Chair*:
> If *Peter's chains* your fury cann't restrain,
> Let *Judas's halter* be your curbing *Rein*[26]

In such fantasies Wild's comedy of the body took on a darker edge, and this clearly unsettled some readers:

> A Satyrist may lash (no doubt)
> But not beyond his Whip Lash out;
> Thus to invade the Hangmans place
> With Sledge and Halter; foul disgrace
> Of Poets Pen to treat of these,
> Which only Reader, Rout can please.[27]

Others expressed concern that the tone adopted by 'Hudibras' lacked the decorum expected of episcopacy:

> A *Bishop's* calmly urgent, makes no stir,
> Nor Thumps the Cushion like a *Presbyter*,
> He spits no fire, nor Wildly throws about
> Hell and Damnation amongst the rout;
> Flint breaks on *Pillows*: Tis not Pulpit Thunder
> But mild perswasion melts mens hearts asunder.[28]

Such concerns may have eventually coalesced into the sense that a strongly abusive satirical tradition was to be associated with fanaticism. Some did seek to make more complex arguments about how a lack of reform had created the Presbyterian problem:

> When *States* shall breed, more learned, active Spirits,
> Then they can keep or answer to their merits;
> You must not think, they'l *starve* or *beggar* be,
> If by their Rhet'rick, they can earn a Fee.
> Whil'st *Ideots, Women, Hawkes and Hounds* devour:
> The fattest *tithes*, once the poor *Churches Dower.*
> Whil'st the *impropriate Lord,* will not consent,
> To yeild his needy vicar, *Ten per cent*;
> You must not think it strange, if *discontents,*

---

[26] *Iter Boreale, to the Presbyterian Party* (1663).
[27] *On the Answer to Dr Wilds Poem* (1663).
[28] *Your Servant Sir, or Ralpho to Hudibras* ([London, 1663]).

> Work in the Church and State such *fatall rents;*
> And that compell'd men seek *Benevolence,*
> From better *Christians* honest *Citizens.*[29]

Subtlety, though, was not the dominant feature of satire at this point, and even here the language remains one of devouring and fatness. The tone had been set by Wild's initial poem and escalated by 'Hudibras'. Even one of those who then attacked 'Hudibras' adopted his language:

> He's not prophetick, but a shitten critic,
>   not honest, true or wise,
> See how he brawles to shite in P*auls,*
>   And pull out reverend eyes.[30]

This early satirical outburst set in place a number of the features that might be traced in later works concerning the religious situation: *ad hominem* attacks; scatological and sexual humour; and concentration on the political implications of religious positions. These all resonated in a group of poems that have been much more frequently studied.

Painters, Poets, and War

Due primarily to dispute over trade, but driven also by an ideological distrust of republicanism, the English went to war with the Dutch for the second time in the seventeenth century in 1665.[31] Initial victory at the battle off Lowestoft was overseen by the Lord High Admiral, James, Duke of York, and was met by an outpouring of celebratory verse. William Smith wrote of how 'A Herd of Sheep with such a Chieftain might / Tygers subdue, and Leopards put to flight', while an anonymous author asked 'Why should the Dutch our Colliers then Desire? / They need no Coals to set their Ships afire: / Thanks to his Royal Highness *James* the Great, / And Brave Prince *Rupert* for this Grand Defeat'.[32] Where others had hyperbole, Robert Wild responded in a different register:

> GOUT! I conjure thee by the powerful Names
> Of *CHARLES* and *JAMES*, and their victorious Fames,
> On this great Day set all thy Prisoners free,
> (Triumphs command a Goal-Delivery)

---

[29] J.R., *An Answer for Mr Calamie* (1663).

[30] *Hudibras Answered by True de Case* ([S.l., 1663]).

[31] Charles Wilson, *Profit and Power: A Study of England and the Dutch Wars* (London: Longmans, Green, 1957); Steven C. A. Pincus, *Protestantism and Patriotism: Ideologies and the Making of English Foreign Policy, 1650–1668* (Cambridge: Cambridge University Press, 1995). Pincus argues for the centrality of ideological causes.

[32] William Smith, *Ingratitude Reveng'd* (1665), 7; *One Broad-Side more for the Dutch* (1665).

> Set them all free, leave not a limping Toe
> From my *Lord Chancellors* to mine below;
> Unless thou giv'st us leave this day to dance,
> Thou'rt not th'old Loyal Gout, but com'st from *France*.[33]

It is a poem that ostensibly praises the victory but does so in a way that punctures the bloated panegyric of others, moving bathetically from Wild's gout to the Lord Chancellor's (the Earl of Clarendon, Edward Hyde) to a politically loaded pun on the French pox, syphilis. What is more it contains explicit recognition of this fact. It is, Wild claimed, 'my Pens miscarriage, not a Birth', and he called upon John Denham, Edmund Waller, and Abraham Cowley to provide works written in the correct idiom.[34] It is therefore a poem that is situated between poles. It is neither panegyric nor is it vicious satire. It is easy to see why such a poem should be attractive to a Presbyterian audience that was forced to stand outside the centrally endorsed Church structure, but which had difficulty in constructing themselves in an oppositional context, and recognized that the possibility of ameliorating the situation lay with the court. Its ultimate effect though may have been paradoxical. While the poem carefully avoids strong assertion of a critical line, and indeed was licensed by the Surveyor of the Press, Roger L'Estrange, it develops a comedy that would appeal to a Presbyterian audience, and the laughter it elicited could have played a role in binding that audience together as a distinct group.

The mention of Waller links the poem to the Advice-to-a-Painter satires that responded to his *Instructions to a Painter*. Wild's poem refers to the shorter version of Waller's work, published in 1665, while the other poems responded to the longer version of 1666. It is now generally accepted that Marvell had a major part in the writing of the second and third advices, while 'The Last Instructions to a Painter' is clearly his work.[35] These poems produced a strong indictment of the conduct of the war, and in particular of Clarendon's chancellorship. Clarendon's bloated body became something considerably more sinister, his 'transcendent paunch so swells of late, / That he the rupture seems of law, and state.'[36] His gout was referenced, but again in Marvell's conception it was linked to constitutional impropriety. It was said to disappear on the prorogation of parliament, and to be desired by Clarendon to hinder his penning of a clause to summon another one.[37] This verse, for all its technical brilliance, portrayed a much darker world than Wild's, and when it engaged directly with Wild's work it did so in a way that admitted, and used creatively, the tensions—aesthetic and, to a lesser extent, ideological—between the different poetic visions.

---

[33] Robert Wild, *An Essay upon the Late Victory Obtained* (1665), in *English Nonconformist Poetry*, ed. Southcombe, i. 209.

[34] Wild, *An Essay upon the Late Victory Obtained*, 210–11.

[35] *The Poems of Marvell*, ed. Nigel Smith, rev. edn. (Harlow: Longman, 2007), 323–4.

[36] *The Second Advice to a Painter*, in Marvell, *Poems* (Longman), 336, ll. 117–18.

[37] Andrew Marvell, 'The Last Instructions to a Painter', in *Poems* (Longman), 379, ll. 335–40; 383, ll. 469–72.

The Third Advice to a Painter was written in the aftermath of the Four Days' Battle (1–4 June 1666). The command of the English fleet was divided between Monck (who had been made Duke of Albemarle in 1660) and the royalist civil-war commander Prince Rupert. Rupert's ships were sent to engage the French, leaving Monck to initiate combat against the Dutch. In the ensuing battle the English fleet suffered heavy losses.[38] The official response to this defeat was mendacious, and it was publicly presented as a victory. As Marvell remarked, the traditional modes of celebration were matched with a press campaign.[39] His poem, circulating in manuscript by early 1667, was an engagement with, and undermining of, this representation of events, but its mode of achieving its ends was complex. The main critique of the government was placed in the mouth of Monck's wife, Ann, Duchess of Albemarle, 'Half witch, half prophet' like a 'Presbyterian sibyl'.[40] Physically repulsive, she speaks robustly and vulgarly. Critics have puzzled over this representation. The critique of the government seems vigorous and intended to be treated respectfully, and yet the speaker of the critique appears herself to be the subject of satire. One suggestion has been that the very crudity of the Duchess is necessary to distance her from the duplicitous world of the court and to allow her critique to be understood as an unvarnished act of truth-telling: her 'very coarseness has a special appropriateness to her task'.[41] As Martin Dzelzainis has commented, this view has much to support it, but it does not fully resolve the tension between the presentation of the Duchess and the veracity of her speech. Dzelzainis's own suggestion, that this tension arises from her presentation as parrhesiast (a truth-teller), a category which itself was riddled with tensions, is ingenious.[42] However, Marvell's presentation of the Duchess, as both the subject and speaker of satire, was in part the result of his own debt to Wild's earlier work on Monck.

Nigel Smith has noted that Marvell drew specifically on Wild's writing in the Duchess's speech, but the *Third Advice* owes a more general debt to *Iter Boreale* that deserves further investigation.[43] Early in the poem Marvell sensitized his readers to his use of Wild, when the Dutch Admiral Ruyter 'threatens' Monck that 'though he now so proudly sail, / He shall tread back his Iter Boreale'.[44] In many ways, the poem works through inverting Wild's celebratory verse. Where Monck triumphed in Wild's *Iter Boreale*, his

[38] Pincus, *Protestantism and Patriotism*, 283–5; J. D. Davies, *Gentlemen and Tarpaulins: The Officers and Men of the Restoration Navy* (Oxford: Clarendon Press, 1991), 144–5.

[39] Andrew Marvell, *The Third Advice to a Painter*, in *Poems* (Longman), 349, ll. 163, 164.

[40] Marvell, *The Third Advice to a Painter*, 350, ll. 199–200.

[41] Annabel Patterson, *Marvell: The Writer in Public Life* (Harlow: Longman, 2000), 94. See also Steven N. Zwicker, 'Lines of Authority: Politics and Literary Culture in the Restoration', in *Politics of Discourse: The Literature and History of Seventeenth-Century England*, ed. Kevin Sharpe and Steven N. Zwicker (Berkeley and London: University of California Press, 1987), 239–42.

[42] Martin Dzelzainis, ' "Presbyterian Sibyl": Truth-Telling and Gender in Andrew Marvell's *The Third Advice to a Painter*', in *Rhetoric, Women and Politics in Early Modern England*, ed. Jennifer Richards and Alison Thorne (London: Routledge, 2007), 111–28.

[43] Nigel Smith, *Andrew Marvell: The Chameleon* (New Haven and London: Yale University Press, 2010), 195.

[44] Marvell, *Poems* (Longman), 347, ll. 48–9.

victories were reversed in the *Third Advice*, and his intimate wounding by Dutch fire became the focus of the kind of joke beloved of Wild: 'But should the Rump perceive 't, they'd say that Mars / Had now revenged them upon Aumarle's arse'.[45] Where in *Iter Boreale* Monck was represented as having saved the church bells from sectaries who would have turned them into guns or sold them to the Dutch, in the *Third Advice* the bells—in concert with the official bi-weekly newspaper the *London Gazette*—are complicit in propagating the government lie:

> Now joyful fires, and the exalted bell,
> And court-gazettes our empty triumph tell.
> Alas: the time draws near when, overturned
> The lying bells shall through the tongue be burned;
> Paper shall want to print that lie of state,
> And our false fires true fires shall expiate.[46]

When the Duchess is introduced, her starting point is the end of *Iter Boreale*. Wild's poem had looked forward to Monck being made a member of the Order of the Garter ('That *Charles* may wear His *Dieu Et Mon Droit*, / And Thou the Noble Garter'd *Honi Soit*'), and in the *Third Advice* the Duchess is found putting up wall hangings: 'With Hony pensy honestly she wrought'.[47] Her speech is thus authorized by reference to her husband's honour, won on the Restoration. But her critique continues within the pattern already set by the poem by concentrating precisely on the ways in which the vision of a Presbyterian Restoration encoded in *Iter Boreale* had been reversed:

> I told George first, as Calamy did me,
> If the King these brought over, how 'twould be:
> Men, that there picked his pocket to his face,
> To sell intelligence or buy a place,
> That their religion pawned for clothes; not care
> ('T has run so long) now to redeem't, nor dare.
> O what egregious loyalty to cheat!
> O what fidelity it was to eat!
> While Langdales, Hoptons, Glenhams starved abroad,
> And here true Roy'lists sunk beneath the load.
> Men that did there affront, defame, betray
> The King, and do so here, now who but they?[48]

The Duchess aligns herself directly with Wild's hero, Calamy, and uses this relationship to introduce a distinction between loyal royalists, including those Presbyterians who

[45] Marvell, *Poems* (Longman), 349, ll. 129–30.

[46] Marvell, *Poems* (Longman), 349–50, ll. 163–8. Cf. Robert Wild, *Iter Boreale*, in *English Nonconformist Poetry*, ed. Southcombe, i. 13.

[47] Wild, *Iter Boreale*, 15; Marvell, *Poems* (Longman), 350, l. 180.

[48] Marvell, *Poems* (Longman), 351, ll. 217–28.

remained in England, and the dilettante group who were exiles in France and now held sway. She proceeds to lament the Restoration settlement that saw the disbandment of the New Model Army, which left 'good George' with 'a gen'ral's empty name', and most particularly the religious settlement that was so destructive of the Presbyterian cause:

> The Lords' House drains the houses of the Lord,
> For bishops' voices silencing the Word.
> O Barthol'mew, saint of their calendar!
> What's worse? thy 'jection or thy massacre?[49]

The conjoining of the ejection of Presbyterian ministers on St Bartholomew's Day with the St Bartholomew's Day massacre of 1572, a coincidence rarely mentioned in the ministers' own farewell sermons, made the point powerfully.[50] The anti-prelatical edge of Wild's earlier verse resonates again here.

Ultimately, though, the poem's, and the Duchess's, animus is aimed at Clarendon:

> Curst be the man that first begot this war,
> In an ill house, under a blazing star.
> For others' sport, two nations fight a prize:
> Between them both religion wounded dies.[51]

Wild had written before of 'when the raging Dog did rule the Skies, / And with his Scorching face did tyrannize' and of 'cruel *Cromwell*, Whelp of that mad Star, / But sure more fiery than his Syre by far'.[52] He had also praised Monck's actions in suppressing sectarian fanatics who had left 'Religion panting for her life, / Like *Isaac*, bound under the bloody knife'.[53] In Marvell's poem Clarendon takes Cromwell's place, and religion—international Protestantism destroyed in the Anglo-Dutch conflict—is not reprieved. Monck's triumph in 1660 is fully undone. This explains in part the tensions between the speaker and the satire noted by previous commentators. The satirization of the Duchess, even at the same time as she produces a potent critique of the government, is a satirization of the failure of the Presbyterian vision for Church and State. Underlying it is a questioning of the Presbyterians' continued stress on their loyalism. By the time of the *Last Instructions to a Painter*, Marvell's critique of government, and his questioning of the king's own position, had developed a radicalism that was at odds with the preferred public presentation of the Presbyterians. The tensions were not simply the product of this political distinction, however. Wild's voice was clearly not Marvell's, and Marvell acknowledged and used it while, through the character of the Duchess, showing his

---

[49] Marvell, *Poems* (Longman), 351, ll. 238, 241–4.
[50] For the farewell sermons see David J. Appleby, *Black Bartholomew's Day: Preaching, Polemic and Restoration Nonconformity* (Manchester: Manchester University Press, 2007), 97.
[51] Marvell, *Poems* (Longman), 355, ll. 423–6.
[52] Robert Wild, *The Tragedy of Christopher Love at Tower-Hill*, in *English Nonconformist Poetry*, ed. Southcombe, i. 22.
[53] Wild, *Iter Boreale*, 14.

disdain for its vulgarity. Marvell thus adopted a satirical pose necessary to lambast the government and maintained an aesthetic distance from it. The Duchess was to be laughed with and at. Marvell, and not for the first time, used a poetic diction necessitated by the political context but also indicated that he wished that this were not required.

DEFOE AND DISSENTING SATIRE

It is unsurprising that this satirical mode was continued into the eighteenth century by Daniel Defoe. Defoe had been educated at Charles Morton's dissenting academy in Newington Green, and had been one of the Monmouth rebels.[54] His work was profoundly shaped by his understanding of the history of dissent in the late seventeenth century, and his satire was rooted not simply in a response to contemporary religious debates but in a consideration of how those debates related to the position of dissenters since 1660.[55] Indeed, in 1704 he sought to place himself within a tradition that, while it dated from the Restoration, was based on earlier occurrences:

> ... the Dissenters, Sir, have been guilty of more Plots against the Government than you charge them with, and more have been executed for it than you tell us of; for I assure you the Author of this wears a Mourning Ring on his Finger, given at the Funeral of Mr. *Christopher Love*, a Presbyterian Minister, Beheaded *Anno* 1653. for the horrid Phanatick Plot, contriv'd for the bringing in, *as they then call'd him*, *Charles Stuart*, and the restoring of Monarchy.[56]

The Presbyterian minister Christopher Love had been at the centre of a pro-Stuart plot in the aftermath of the regicide, and he was executed in August 1651.[57] Following the Restoration, Love was erected as a symbol of Presbyterian loyalism. An account of his trial was published in 1660, and the first publication of Robert Wild's poem on Love also dates from this year.[58] Despite misdating his death, Defoe clearly identified with Love's cause and resented the fact that his martyrdom went unrewarded on the Restoration.

---

[54] Paula R. Backscheider, 'Defoe, Daniel (1660?–1731)', *ODNB*.

[55] A similar argument, advanced at times in a more speculative way, may be found in Tom Paulin, 'Crusoe's Secret: Daniel Defoe', in his *Crusoe's Secret: The Aesthetics of Dissent* (London: Faber and Faber, 2005), 80–104.

[56] Daniel Defoe, *The Dissenters Answer to the High-Church Challenge* (1704), in W. R. Owens and P. N. Furbank, eds., *Political and Economic Writings of Daniel Defoe*, 8 vols. (London: Pickering & Chatto, 2008), iii. 180.

[57] Blair Worden, *The Rump Parliament, 1648-1653* (Cambridge: Cambridge University Press, 1974), 243–8.

[58] *The Whole Triall of Mr Christopher Love* (1660). Robert Wild, *The Tragedy of Christopher Love*, i. 17–27. For the argument concerning the date of publication of Wild's work see *English Nonconformist Poetry*, ed. Southcombe, i. 17. Wild's poem was published both separately, in a number of different editions, and as part of *The Whole Triall*.

Defoe's account of Restoration history admitted its complexities, and the problems of conscience presented to dissenters by the actions of the later Stuart kings:

> ...by several Ups and Downs, Turns and Returns, in the publick Administration of Affairs, they suffered also several Changes and Turns, as the Situation of the Politicks of those Days happened to be; to Day persecuted by illegal and arbitrary Command from the Court, to Morrow tolerated and encourag'd by like illegal Practice; in one Parliament Laws and Acts made to suppress them, and then Liberty given them by Proclamation, as an Experiment of the dispensing Power, in order to draw in the Dissenters to be Parties in the Tyranny of the Prince, because their own Interest concurr'd with it; from whence like Conclusions might be drawn in Defence of that Tyranny when it should be used against them.[59]

The declarations of indulgence had offered an alleviation from persecution, but at the expense of accepting the monarch's arbitrary power. The tension had been recognized, and discussed at the time, but Defoe, with the hindsight of one writing post-1688 was able to connect dissenters' actions to a longer history. His sardonic apology ('I am very sorry if the like clear View of, and Disinterested Concern for, the Liberty of *England*, did not appear thro' the whole *Series* of the Dissenters Behaviour') was swiftly followed by a vindication of their later actions: 'they soon repented that Sin of Ignorance, and vigorously joined in with the Church of *England* in all the Wonderful Mazes of the Revolution: Indeed I cannot say they have been gratefully treated for that Part of their Conduct, tho' without them it is manifest the Revolution could never have been attempted, much less brought to pass.'[60] From Christopher Love to the Glorious Revolution the history of nonconformity had been one of heroism overlooked by an ungrateful nation. The enemies of dissent had used the 'Power of Persecution, not of Perswasion', and the impact of this had been severe, as Defoe noted in relation to the nonconformist author Thomas Delaune: 'I am sorry to say, he is One of near 8000 Protestant Dissenters that perish't in Prison, in the Days of that Merciful Prince King *Charles* the Second.'[61]

Defoe's own sense of religious history was thus one in which 1660 marked an important turning point, and the religious conflicts of his own age were a continuation of that history. In those terms, it can be misleading to see Defoe as an eighteenth-century rather than late seventeenth-century author. His poetic satire continued in the anti-prelatical vein that had developed strongly in dissenting writing in the preceding years. In his very first poem, *A Discovery of an Old Intreague*, he wrote of his intent to describe the initial response to the coming of James II:

> How that loud Echoing Theatre the Church,
> Burlesque their God, and sacred Theams debauch,

---

[59] Daniel Defoe, *Wise as Serpents* (1712), in *Political and Economic Writings of Defoe*, iii. 286.

[60] *Political and Economic Writings of Defoe*, iii. 287.

[61] Daniel Defoe, *Preface to Delaune's Plea for the Non-Conformists* (1706), in *Political and Economic Writings of Defoe*, iii. 271.

> Loud thanks return for th' Monster they had made;
> A *Protestant* Body with a *Popish* Head;
> With humble prayers that Christ would now permit
> That *Antichrist* should take his sacred Seat;
> The Body govern, and the Members keep,
> So Wolves protect the unarm'd and easie Sheep.[62]

And in his *The True-Born Englishman*, he pithily encapsulated the dangers of clerical despotism:

> For Wise Men say 't's as dangerous a thing,
> *A Ruling Priesthood, as a Priest-rid King.*
> And of all Plagues with which Mankind are curst,
> *Ecclesiastick Tyranny's the worst.*[63]

Most famously, in his prose satire *The Shortest Way with the Dissenters* he ventriloquized an intemperate Anglican calling for the strongest penalties to be applied to nonconformists. Again his mode of explanation was historical:

> Had not King *James* the First witheld the full execution of the Laws; had he given them strict Justice, he had clear'd the Nation of them, and the Consequences had been plain; his *Son had never been murther'd by them*, nor the Monarchy overwhelm'd; 'twas *too much Mercy* shewn them, was the ruin of his Posterity, and the ruin of the Nation's Peace.[64]

When dissenters had had power in the mid-century the effects had been deleterious to say the least:

> How did they treat the Clergy of the Church of *England*, sequester'd the Ministers, devour'd the Patrimony of the Church, and divided the Spoil, by sharing the Church-Lands among their Soldiers, and turning her Clergy out to starve; just such Measure as they have mete, shou'd be measur'd to them again.[65]

The solutions were obvious, 'Heaven has made way for their Destruction', and 'if the Gallows instead of the Counter, and the Gallies instead of the Fines, were the Reward of going to a Conventicle, to preach or hear, there wou'd not be so many Sufferers.'[66]

---

[62] Defoe, *A New Discovery of an Old Intreague: A Satyr*, in W. R. Owens and P. N. Furbank, eds., *Satire, Fantasy, and Writings on the Supernatural by Daniel Defoe*, 8 vols. (London: Pickering & Chatto, 2003–5), i. 43, ll. 152–9.

[63] Daniel Defoe, *The True-Born Englishman* (1700 or 1701), in *Satire, Fantasy*, i. 105, ll. 755–8.

[64] Daniel Defoe, *The Shortest Way with the Dissenters* (1702), in *Political and Economic Writings of Defoe*, iii. 99.

[65] *Political and Economic Writings of Defoe*, iii. 99. There is a possible echo of Robert Wild here. See Wild, *Iter Boreale*, 10.

[66] *Political and Economic Writings of Defoe*, iii. 103, 105–6.

Defoe captured the tone of the persecutory Anglican so effectively that many—Anglicans and dissenters—did not initially recognize it as satire at all. The backlash against it gathered pace, and, after his authorship became known, Defoe's insistence on his ironic intent made no difference. In July 1703, he was found guilty of seditious libel and sentenced to be fined, pilloried three times, and imprisoned until he had sureties of good behaviour for seven years.[67] The public punishment of previous Puritan 'martyrs' had gone wrong, when crowds had not fulfilled their expected role, and so it was with Defoe in the pillory, when flowers replaced the more usual missiles hurled at the convicted.[68] Defoe himself sought to shape understandings of his punishment through the medium of print. In his *A Hymn to the Pillory*, published on the occasion of his first appearance in the pillory, he drew attention to the tradition within which he stood as he addressed the pillory itself:

> Tell us, *Great Engine*, how to understand,
> Or reconcile the Justice of the Land;
> How *Bastwick, Pryn, Hunt, Hollingsby* and *Pye*,
>   Men of unspotted Honesty;
>   Men that had Learning, Wit and Sence,
>   And more than most Men have had since,
>   Could equal Title to thee claim,
> With *Oats* and *Fuller*, Men of later Fame[69]

Those who should fill the pillories instead of Defoe are enumerated from generic corrupt clerics that could appear in almost any period ('the Drunken Priest, / Who turns the Gospel to a baudy Jest' and the 'Lewder Clergy' the '*Sons of God* who every day *Go in*, / Both to *the Daughters* and *the Wives* of Men'[70]) to the more specific targets of his own age:

> Those *Nimshites*, who with furious Zeal drive on,
> And build up *Rome* to pull down *Babylon*;
> The real Authors of the *Shortest Way*,
> Who for Destruction, not Conversion pray[71]

There is much that is experimental about Defoe's writing here—not least his adoption of Pindarics—but his diction and themes remain recognizably those of the tradition that

---

[67] Paula R. Backscheider, *Daniel Defoe: His Life* (Baltimore and London: Johns Hopkins University Press, 1989), 100–10; W. R. Owens, 'Introduction', in *Political and Economic Writings of Defoe*, iii. 16–18.

[68] Backscheider, *Daniel Defoe*, 117–18. For the experience of earlier 'martyrs', most specifically, William Prynne see David Cressy, *Travesties and Transgressions in Tudor and Stuart England: Tales of Discord and Dissension* (Oxford: Oxford University Press, 2000), ch. 13.

[69] Daniel Defoe, *A Hymn to the Pillory* (1703), in *Satire, Fantasy*, i. 242, ll. 39–46.

[70] Defoe, *Satire, Fantasy*, i. 246, ll. 204–5, 210, 212–13.

[71] Defoe, *Satire, Fantasy*, i. 247, ll. 240–3.

has been traced through Wild and Marvell. His was fundamentally a dissenting satire written self-consciously within a particular historical tradition.

Still in Newgate prison Defoe produced a further 'hymn' this time lambasting the Ordinary of Newgate, Paul Lorrain. Lorrain preached at executions, and tapped into a long-standing prurient interest in the events through publishing on the condemned. His sermon of 13 August 1703 on the murderer, Thomas Cook, presented the convicted man as penitent, and probably 'enjoying an honourable and happy Life in God's Glorious Kingdom'.[72] Defoe responded with mock fascination at the nature of the transformation:

> Church Discipline and Conduct shew
> In what disguise Religion may be drest,
>   The crooked Paths of *Priest-craft* Paint?
> Where lies the Secret, let us know,
>   To make a *Sheep-stealer* a *Saint*?
> Or bid me tell them that 'tis all a Jest;
>   What need they point out other ways,
> Since *Earthly Rogues* can Merrit *Holy Praise*?
> If this *Wise Precedent* the World receives,
> *Newgate* shall ne're be call'd a *Den of Thieves*:
> What Rev'rence ought to such a Place be given,
> That Ships so many Loads of *Saints* to *Heaven*?[73]

Despite there having been five monarchs and one revolution in the interim, Defoe found himself in the same position as Calamy in 1662. His poetic response also shared features with Robert Wild's. Both, alluding to Scripture, used the phrase 'Den of Thieves' in relation to Newgate in a heavily ironized sense. Where Defoe sarcastically denied the veracity of the phrase in relation to a place from which men like Cook could make the trip to Heaven, Wild used it to offer 'thanks' to those behind the imprisonment of Calamy:

> Thanks to the Bishop and his good Lord Mayor,
> Who turn'd the Den of Thieves into a House of Prayer[74]

The similarity in approach is notable, but the similarity in the circumstance of both poems is also significant. It is a clear reminder of the role dissenting satire had to play within contexts where various forms of nonconformist action—even following toleration—could be met with state coercion. The very forcefulness of dissenting satire is an indication of what was at stake.

---

[72] Quoted in Defoe, *Satire, Fantasy*, i. 498.

[73] Daniel Defoe, *A Hymn to the Funeral Sermon* (1703), in *Satire, Fantasy*, i. 257, ll. 13–24.

[74] Wild, *A Poem Upon the Imprisonment of Mr Calamy*, 182. The scriptural allusion is to Matthew 21:13; Mark 11:17; Luke 19:46.

CONCLUSIONS

When Robinson Crusoe safely lands he has a religious experience that turns—perhaps tellingly—into thoughts about condemned men:

> I believe it is impossible to express to the Life what the Extasies and Transports of the Soul are, when it is so sav'd, as I may say, out of the very Grave; and I do not wonder now at that Custom, *viz.* That when a Malefactor who has the Halter about his Neck, is tyed up, and just going to be turn'd off, and has a Reprieve brought to him: I say, I do not wonder that they bring a Surgeon with it, to let him Blood that very Moment they tell him of it, that the Surprise may not drive the Animal Spirits from the Heart, and overwhelm him:
>
> > *For sudden Joys, like Griefs, confound at first.*[75]

As has been recognized since 1998 (although the allusion would have been known to many of Defoe's original readers) Crusoe quoted Robert Wild.[76] It is an unsurprising moment. Defoe was the obvious heir to Wild, and his own satirical poetry owed much to the tradition represented by the Presbyterian. This Puritan tradition might be traced back to Marprelate, but it developed a peculiar force in the Restoration both as a result of the widening market for print and as a response to persecution.[77] It was forthright, frequently abusive, and often focused on bodies: constrained, sexual, and scatological. It is important to note that no claim is being made for this being a unique tradition—indeed the enemies of dissenters could just as easily attack them in works that included these features. However, it is also clear that this was a tradition harnessed by dissenters. This might be taken to have two further implications for the broader history of satire.

First, when Dryden came to formulate his vision of satire he did so in part to deny the power of a religious tradition that he was not only dismissive of, but which had defined itself—through its virulent anti-Catholicism—against his own. Second, in the response to Defoe's *The Shortest Way*, it may be possible to discern one reason why it is now unusual to discuss Puritan or dissenting satire. Many dissenters were horrified by Defoe's work and he was in turn, and in print, scornful of them. The features of dissenting satire emphasized in this chapter did not make for comfortable, godly reading. They were produced in styles, and with a vocabulary, that removed them from the aggressive jeremiads that might have been considered a licit way of engaging with enemies. They undoubtedly found markets, and they must have been read in dissenting communities (even the negative response to *The Shortest Way* confirms its readership). But the laughter they provoked was uneasy. The irony may be that in forging an effective dissenting satire, authors undermined its status within dissenting communities, producing not just a distaste for such works but, in certain contexts, a discomfort with laughter itself.

---

[75] Daniel Defoe, *Robinson Crusoe*, ed. Thomas Keymer and James Kelly (Oxford: Oxford University Press, 2007), 40–1.

[76] Geoffrey Sill, 'The Source of Robinson Crusoe's "sudden joys"', *Notes and Queries* 45 (1998), 67–8.

[77] On the importance of Marprelate to the tradition see Smith, *Literature and Revolution*, ch. 9.

SELECT BIBLIOGRAPHY

Achinstein, Sharon. *Literature and Dissent in Milton's England* (Cambridge: Cambridge University Press, 2003).

Appleby, David J. *Black Bartholomew's Day: Preaching, Polemic and Restoration Nonconformity* (Manchester: Manchester University Press, 2007).

Dzelzainis, Martin. ' "Presbyterian Sibyl": Truth-Telling and Gender in Andrew Marvell's *The Third Advice to a Painter*', in *Rhetoric, Women and Politics in Early Modern England*, ed. Jennifer Richards and Alison Thorne (London: Routledge, 2007), 111–28.

Grell, Ole Peter, Jonathan I. Israel, and Nicholas Tyacke, eds. *From Persecution to Toleration: The Glorious Revolution and Religion in England* (Oxford: Clarendon Press, 1991).

Harris, Tim. *Politics under the Later Stuarts: Party Conflict in a Divided Society 1660–1715* (London: Longman, 1993).

Hume, Robert D. ' "Satire" in the Reign of Charles II', *Modern Philology* 102 (2005), 332–71.

Keeble, N. H. *The Restoration: England in the 1660s* (Oxford: Blackwell, 2002).

Paulin, Tom. 'Crusoe's Secret: Daniel Defoe', in *Crusoe's Secret: The Aesthetics of Dissent* (London: Faber and Faber, 2005), 80–104.

Pincus, Steven C. A. *Protestantism and Patriotism: Ideologies and the Making of English Foreign Policy, 1650–1668* (Cambridge: Cambridge University Press, 1995).

Smith, Nigel. *Literature and Revolution in England, 1640–1660* (New Haven and London: Yale University Press, 1994).

Southcombe, George and Grant Tapsell. *Restoration Politics, Religion and Culture: Britain and Ireland, 1660–1714* (Basingstoke: Palgrave Macmillan, 2010).

Tapsell, Grant, ed. *The Later Stuart Church, 1660–1714* (Manchester: Manchester University Press, 2012).

....

CHAPTER 5

THE FEMALE WITS

Gender, Satire, and Drama

....

CLAUDINE VAN HENSBERGEN

DEDICATING her 1707 play, *The Platonick Lady*, 'To all the Generous Encouragers of Female Ingenuity', Susanna Centlivre railed against what she perceived to be widespread discriminatory attitudes to the work of female playwrights:

> My Muse chose to make this Universal Address, hoping, among the numerous Crowd, to find some Souls Great enough to protect her against the Carping Malice of the Vulgar World; who think it a proof of their Sense, to dislike every thing that is writ by Women. I was the more induc'd to this General Application, from the Usage I have met on all sides.

> A Play secretly introduc'd to the House, whilst the Author remains unknown, is approv'd by every Body: The Actor's cry it up, and are in expectation of a great Run; the Bookseller of a Second Edition, and the Scribbler of a Sixth Night: But if by chance the Plot's discover'd, and the Brat found Fatherless, immediately it flags in the Opinion of those that extoll'd it before, and the Bookseller falls in his Price, with this Reason only, *It is a Woman's*.[1]

In the dedication Centlivre relates a series of anecdotes to illustrate her claim. She tells us that William Turner, the bookseller of her 1705 play *The Gamester*, recounted an episode to her of a male customer who, having seen the play performed 'three or four times', came to purchase a copy. On discovering that its author was a woman the customer 'threw down the Book', remarking that if the town had known this, the play 'wou'd never have run ten days'. A subsequent anecdote attributes Bernard Lintot's publication of her 1703 play *Love's Contrivance* under the mistaken authorial initials of 'R. M.' as a commercial ploy, intended to obscure her authorship and thereby ensure healthy sales. By 'passing for a Man's', Centlivre notes, the comedy has been 'play'd at least a hundred Times'.

---

[1] Susanna Centlivre, *The Platonick Lady* (1707), Epistle Dedicatory.

Centlivre argues that the discriminatory attitudes women writers encountered directly affected the popularity of their work. However, as Paddy Lyons and Fidelis Morgan remind us, '[m]ore than fifty plays attributed to female playwrights appeared in print during the half-century from 1660–1710', a figure representing only those plays which publishers thought it financially viable to print.[2] *The London Stage*'s catalogue of theatrical performances staged during the early eighteenth century provides us with clear evidence of the popularity of female dramatists, especially Centlivre, whose comedy *The Busy Body* (1709) became one of the most successful plays in the eighteenth-century repertory, acted more than 450 times.[3] To what extent, then, should we take Centlivre's claims seriously? Was it indeed true that female dramatists only succeeded where they obscured authorship of their works? A brief inspection of both Centlivre's published plays and those of her contemporary dramatists, Delarivier Manley (*c.*1670–1724), Mary Pix (*c.*1666–1709), and Catharine Trotter (1674?–1749), reveals that—as with Aphra Behn before them—they openly acknowledged their gender in the title pages and prefatory materials of the majority of their published plays.[4] In light of this, Centlivre's claims in *The Platonick Lady* demand further scrutiny, and we might query whether they represent an accurate assessment of the status quo. Centlivre is certainly exaggerating when she claims that *Love's Contrivance* had been played 'at least a hundred Times', when the figure was closer to nine performances.[5] To what extent was she also exaggerating the influence of 'the Carping Malice of the Vulgar World'?

One means of thinking through this supposed discrepancy lies in an analysis of the literary form that embodies carping malice: satire. Predominantly associated with poetry of the period, satire permeated an enormous range of literary productions, not least those of the theatre.[6] In analysing the relationship of theatre and satire, critics have paid most attention to satire's uses within dramatic genre, most notably that of the social satire at the heart of the comedy of manners which flourished under Restoration and early eighteenth-century dramatists such as George Etherege, George Farquhar, John Vanbrugh, William Wycherley, William Congreve, and Centlivre, and was to find its most celebrated expression in the hands of Richard Brinsley Sheridan in the 1770s. Satire was, however, much more deeply implemented within the theatrical milieu than we might first think. Theatre criticism, a genre that emerged with the vast expansion of the

---

[2] Paddy Lyons and Fidelis Morgan, eds., *Female Playwrights of the Restoration* (London: J. M. Dent, 1991), xx.

[3] Fidelis Morgan, *The Female Wits: Women Playwrights on the London Stage 1660–1720* (London: Virago Press, 1981), 56.

[4] See Jane Milling, 'The Female Wits: Women Writers at Work', in *Theatre and Culture in Early Modern England, 1650–1737: From Leviathan to Licensing Act*, ed. Catie Gill (Farnham: Ashgate, 2010), 119–29, at 122.

[5] *The London Stage* records performances of *Love's Contrivance* on the following dates between its premiere in 1703 and 1707: 4, 5, 7, 14, 22 June 1703; 20 October 1703; 28 April 1704; 7 June 1705; 14 February 1706. The figure may have been higher, but it seems unlikely that this would approach ninety plus performances. See William van Lennep, ed., *The London Stage 1660–1800*, vol. 1: *1660–1700* (Carbondale: Southern Illinois University Press, 1965).

[6] Ashley Marshall, *The Practice of Satire in England, 1658–1770* (Baltimore: Johns Hopkins University Press, 2013), 139.

theatres and their repertoires in the eighteenth century, was, from its earliest writings, entangled with satire. Much early theatre criticism may have claimed a disinterested stance, but in the majority of cases the biases of its authors are clear, and the critiques made on plays and playwrights are levelled in a tone of acerbic personal attack rather than polite critique; such criticism aimed to destroy reputations, rather than to assess dramatic merit. Satire was also the predominant mode employed in the writing of the prologues and epilogues that accompanied plays in the period. Here, dramatists and their patrons penned verses that directly addressed the audience, commenting upon contemporary society, and in doing so critiquing it. Such satire was, overwhelmingly, comic in its tone and turned upon the audience's mutual recognition of the social faults being decried. But, as we will see, prologues and epilogues were also used to pre-empt satirical attacks, not least those levelled upon gender.

In recent years our understanding of the relationship between satire and gender has undergone much change. With the rise of feminist criticism in the 1970s and 1980s, scholars highlighted the liminal position of women in the literary marketplace, suggesting that we should pay closer attention to their voices. Many of those voices have now ceased to be marginal: the development of a wealth of scholarship on women's writing in the period has brought a recognition of the central place of writers such as Aphra Behn, Delarivier Manley, Susannah Centlivre, and Eliza Haywood, acknowledging their popularity and leading role in the extraordinary literary developments that took shape at the turn of the century.[7] A model for tracing this critical shift is found in the reception of Pope's infamous satire of Haywood in *The Dunciad* as a 'Juno of majestic size, / With cow-like udders, and with ox-like eyes'.[8] Pope's portrait of Haywood coloured critical understanding of her works for decades, leading scholars to perceive her as the ultimately unsuccessful writer Pope presents. Ros Ballaster first cautioned against an 'overestimate' of the effect of Pope's attack on Haywood's career in this 'single text which included, after all, attacks on nearly every other popular writer'.[9] Valerie Rumbold has more recently argued that the attack on Haywood is an anomaly, and that one of the most notable features of Pope's *Dunciad* is his overwhelming exclusion of women writers from the world of the poem: 'Pope's neglect of an opportunity to satirize women writers is striking, since their success and persistence in the early decades of the eighteenth century were a clear contribution to the modernizing trends in the literary marketplace.'[10] The reception of Pope's *Dunciad* reveals the importance of not accepting the claims of satire at face value, but rather of reading between its lines. To understand a satire properly, and to assess the validity of the claims it makes, we must situate it within the wider context of its production, thereby understanding the forces it was working against.

---

[7] See Laura J. Rosenthal, 'Restoration and Eighteenth-Century Drama: New Directions in the Field', *Literature Compass* 5 (2008), 174–94, at 184–6.

[8] Pope, *Poems* (Twickenham), v. 303.

[9] Ros Ballaster, *Seductive Forms: Women's Amatory Fiction from 1684 to 1740* (Oxford: Clarendon Press, 1998), 160, 166 n. 28.

[10] Valerie Rumbold, 'Cut the Caterwauling: Women Writers (Not) in Pope's Dunciads', *RES* 52, no. 208 (2001), 524–39, at 525.

THE FEMALE WITS

Taking as its focus the anonymously-written satirical play, *The Female Wits: or, the Triumvirate of Poets at Rehearsal*, first performed in 1696 yet not printed until 1704, this chapter reconstructs the satirical milieu around female dramatists at the turn of the eighteenth century at a time when women were experiencing a new prominence within the playwriting profession.[11] In doing so it aims to better situate Centlivre's claims of the discrimination female dramatists faced by questioning whether performed and printed satire, like *The Female Wits*, was a key form of the malice that these playwrights encountered, and the extent to which it denied them professional success.

The Female Wits is a farce in three acts which follows the attendance of the megalomaniacal and conceited playwright Marsilia at the rehearsal of her latest play at Drury Lane. Towards the close of the comedy, Marsilia boasts of her play's assured success, stating 'Well, sure by this Play, the Town will perceive what a woman can do.'[12] Moments after she has uttered her triumphant words, events descend into chaos when Marsilia reacts badly to the company's improvised 'Dance upon all Four' (p. 64), and she storms out of the theatre to take her script to the rival playhouse at Lincoln's Inn. In the confusing and flamboyant world of the play-within-a-play that we, its audience, have just seen performed, which involves the storming of Lord Whimsicall's castle and a projected finale set in 'the World in the Moon' (p. 63), the idea of a dance on all fours is perhaps one of its more rational elements.[13] Marsilia's triumphant claim is, then, to be interpreted through an ironic lens, with the words operating as a satirical judgement upon the play we have just seen rehearsed, and upon female-authored drama in general.

The Female Wits was written in imitation of the Duke of Buckingham's 1671 play *The Rehearsal*, a celebrated satirical attack on the heroic drama of the then poet laureate, John Dryden. Jean Marsden has pointed to the popularity of *The Rehearsal*, noting that the 'play's ridicule of overblown writing, formulaic and frequently nonsensical plotting, and novelty for the sake of novelty enabled it to retain its viability on the stage long after the specific objects of its satire had vanished'.[14] *The Female Wits* attempted to replicate this formula for success, borrowing its title from Margaret Cavendish's comedy, *The Sociable Companions; or, the Female Wits*, published in a 1668 collection that Cavendish ventured 'in spight of the Criticks, to call... Plays'.[15] This appropriation was ironic, for

---

[11] See Robert Adams Day, 'Muses in the Mud: *The Female Wits* Anthropologically Considered', *Women's Studies* 7 (1980), 61–74 , at 65.

[12] W. M., *The Female Wits: or, the Triumvirate of Poets at Rehearsal* ([1704]), 63.

[13] Milling notes that the inclusion of references to 'the World in the Moon' within Marsilia's play served as a puff for Elkannah Settle's forthcoming work, *The World in the Moon*, which was performed at Dorset Garden in late June 1697; Milling, 'The Female Wits', 128.

[14] Jean I. Marsden, 'Dramatic Satire in the Restoration and Eighteenth Century', in *A Companion to Satire Ancient and Modern*, ed. Ruben Quintero (Oxford: Blackwell, 2007), 161–75, at 166.

[15] Margaret Cavendish, Duchess of Newcastle, *Plays, Never before Printed* (1668), 'To the Readers'.

the play is a crushing satire of the individual characters and dramatic productions of three contemporary women playwrights: Manley, Pix, and Trotter.[16] Manley is satirized as Marsilia, described in the cast list as 'A Poetess, that admires her own Works, and a great Lover of Flattery'. Her vanity leads Marsilia to invite her fellow playwrights Calista and Mrs Wellfed along to the rehearsal, enabling the work's satirical net to ensnare Trotter (as 'Calista, A Lady that pretends to the learned Languages, and assumes to her self the Name of a Critick'), and Pix (as 'Mrs. Wellfed, One that represents a fat Female Author, a good sociable well-natur'd Companion, that will not suffer Martyrdom rather than take off three Bumpers in a Hand'). Manley had recently enjoyed theatrical success with her second play, *The Royal Mischief* (1696), which was performed at Lincoln's Inn, and it is a farcical parody of this work that we see rehearsed in *The Female Wits*. The play also satirizes the recent breakdown of relations between Manley and Drury Lane following the relative failure of her first play, *The Lost Lover, or The Jealous Husband* (1696). *The Female Wits* therefore vindicates Drury Lane in its dealings with a vain and controlling playwright, blaming on her character the need to take *The Royal Mischief* to Lincoln's Inn.[17]

Performed in the theatrical season of 1696–7, *The Female Wits* ran for six nights without intermission. The date of its first performance is unknown, but evidence suggests that it must have been performed between the April premiere of *The Royal Mischief* and the end of December when the actress Susanna Verbruggen, who played Marsilia, left Drury Lane temporarily.[18] What we know of the play derives from its publication, which took place some eight years later in 1704 at a time, as the preface informs us, by which its anonymous author (solely identified as 'W. M.') was deceased, and 'when the Town has almost lost the Remembrance of it'. *The Female Wits*, then, seems to have belonged to a specific moment of theatre history, and embodied a satirical attack that spoke to its immediate context rather than more lasting concerns. In its satire, the play enables us to recover a pressure point at which the value and rights of female participation in professional playwriting were challenged, albeit to questionable effect.

FAIR TARGETS?

In her 1984 analysis of *The Female Wits*, Laurie Finke understood its satire as a successful misogynistic silencing:

> The play does not merely satirize women playwrights: it seeks to deny them the authority to write. At the end of *The Female Wits*, Marsilia's voice has been effectively silenced when she angrily withdraws her play from rehearsal... *The Female Wits*

---

[16]   George Villiers, Duke of Buckingham, *The Rehearsal* (1672).
[17]   Fidelis Morgan has detailed this episode; Morgan, *The Female Wits*, 39.
[18]   See van Lennep, *The London Stage*, 467.

achieves its ends—laughing women from the stage—by reasserting the masculinity of art and of language...Women, the play implies, can make noise, but can have nothing to say.[19]

Laura Rosenthal's 1996 analysis of the play likewise concluded that whilst the satire's existence is a testimony to how important its female targets had become, its tone was so vituperative that it 'may have had real [negative] effects on the careers of these women'.[20] Whilst the play's content allows for such analysis, other factors complicate a reading of its satire as purely motivated by a desire to contain female playwrights. More recently, Jane Milling has provided a reassessment of the work, arguing that 'there are compelling reasons for thinking that the play was not necessarily designed predominantly to satirise the female writers', citing as evidence its relatively successful run of six nights, and the ways in which it played to the strengths of the acting company at Drury Lane.[21] Such a view is supported by Rachel Carnell's suggestion that the play was 'probably written by a group of actors and actor-writers', who would best have known how to serve those strengths.[22] Milling goes as far as to claim that the satire ultimately promoted the careers of the women it critiqued, serving as 'advertisement' and a 'sophisticated legitimization' of the objects of its satire.[23] These varied analyses of the play reveal a shift in methodology: where Finke reads the satire at face value, Milling's analysis extends to consider issues of theatrical production and other writings by the satire's targets. These methodologies are founded upon each critic's differing interpretations of the primary motivation behind the play's composition: for Finke and Rosenthal, the satire's central goal is ideological, and to promote a negative view of women playwrights; for Milling the play's key purpose is commercial, and to offer a play to the Drury Lane company that would be successful in the competitive theatrical climate of the 1690s. This chapter attempts to advance these conflicting readings by paying closer attention both to the form of satire employed in the play and to the extent of its influence. If we consider these ideas in light of the wider dramatic milieu at the turn of the century, we can better understand the extent to which *The Female Wits* was either a representative or a unique satire of female dramatists, and thereby query the extent to which it reflected more broadly-held views.

The Female Wits is a burlesque satire, which lampoons real people through the presentation of caricatures that make them appear ridiculous. Caricature is at the heart of the play, with the figures of Marsilia, Calista, and Mrs Wellfed exaggerating and distorting their subject's distinctive physical features and personality traits to comic effect. In the long term, the caricatures of these women have had a more damaging effect than that

---

[19] Laurie A. Finke, 'The Satire of Women Writers in *The Female Wits*', *Restoration: Studies in English Literary Culture, 1660–1700* 8 (1984), 64–71, at 66.

[20] Laura J. Rosenthal, *Playwrights and Plagiarists in Early Modern England: Gender, Authorship, Literary Property* (Ithaca: Cornell University Press, 1996), 173.

[21] Milling, 'The Female Wits', 128.

[22] See Rachel Carnell, *A Political Biography of Delarivier Manley* (London: Pickering & Chatto, 2008), 84; Anon., *The Female Wits*, ed. Lucyle Hook (Los Angeles: William Andrews Clark Memorial Library, 1967), xii–xiii.

[23] Milling, 'The Female Wits', 129.

drawn of Dryden in *The Rehearsal*, since comparatively little biographical detail survives about Manley, Pix, or Trotter; as with Haywood's description in *The Dunciad*, their caricature in *The Female Wits* has been used as evidence in recovering ideas about their appearance and character.[24] For example, we know that Pix must have been overweight, since a repetitive feature of the play's humour derives from the multiple jokes that played upon this: Calista remarks that Mrs Wellfed is 'big enough to be the Mother of the Muses' (p. 5); *Praiseall* comments on her late arrival at the theatre with the phrase, 'Mrs. *Wellfed*, tho' last, not least' (p. 8); and Wellfed herself explains that her weight is the reason behind her intention to walk rather than be carried in a chair:

> MRS. WELLF.   I have no Inclination to break poor Mens Backs; I thank you, Madam, I'll go a Foot.
> CALIST.   A Foot!
> MRS. WELLF.   Ay, a Foot, 'tis not far, 'twill make me leaner.   (p. 11)

The comedic effect of the lampoons of Manley, Pix, and Trotter turned upon an audience's familiarity with their physical appearance and character traits since, to respond to caricature, audiences needed to recognize the gap between the portrayal being staged and the real woman. The success of the satire in *The Female Wits* therefore rested upon the public visibility of these women, confirming their professional success and celebrity in the very act of attacking them.

As the aforementioned descriptions of Marsilia, Calista, and Mrs Wellfed in the play's list of *dramatis personæ* suggests, it is the exaggeration of their characters that provides the main force of the comedy. For Rosenthal the extremely personal nature of this caricature makes it impossible to laugh at the play's content: 'Writers, of course, pilloried each other all the time during these years, but the actual impersonation and public performance of an author's intimate vulnerabilities, produced by the company for which these women wrote, expresses a particular vehemence.'[25] Rosenthal's analysis encourages us to read the play's satire as Juvenalian in its tone, vindictively attacking its female targets. However, caricature is a form generally employed to promote laughter, and the play-within-a-play we see performed is so ridiculous both in its use of caricature and in its imitation of its source play that we might argue that it is hard to take its satire seriously. Indeed, Milling reminds us that 'there is little negative in the portrayal of Marsilia that Manley has not already presaged herself', since the characterization of Marsilia is indebted to Manley's own portrayal of an affected poetess, Orinda, in *The Lost Lover*; furthermore, in her later writings Manley promoted an image of herself as a woman surrounded by male admirers just as Marsilia is in the play.[26]

The play's closing lines enforce the idea that this is no Juvenalian attack, but rather a satire that has served the purposes of entertainment. Awdwell, described in the *dramatis*

---

[24] See Jacqueline Pearson, *The Prostituted Muse* (London: Harvester Wheatsheaf, 1988), 170, 181, 187, 191, 196–7.

[25] Rosenthal, *Playwrights and Plagiarists*, 173.   [26] Milling, 'The Female Wits', 127.

personæ as 'a Gentleman of Sense and Education', reflects on Marsilia's rejection of his romantic advances, noting:

> *I'll leave the Scribler to her Fops, and Fate;*
> *I find she's neither worth my Love or Hate.*
>
> (67)

His words suggest an indifference that deflates the force of the satire and encourages the audience to leave Marsilia, like Awdwell, at the theatre door. The play's epilogue goes on to comment directly upon the nature of its satire, claiming that its attack was not one made to promote a misogynistic ideology:

> *What here he writes to quash the Womens Pride,*
> *May to the Men with Justice be apply'd.*
> *Each Sex is now so self-conceited grown,*
> *None can digest a Treat that's not their own […]*
> *But Manners might have hinder'd him, you'll say,*
> *From Ridiculing Women in his Play,*
> *When his own Sex so very open lay.*
> *Troth so he might, but as I said before,*
> *Wits do themselves, as Beaux, themselves adore;*
> *Your Man of Dress, your Dressing Female Apes,*
> *And doats upon their several Aires and Shapes:*
> *Fearful that what upon the Sex is cast,*
> *May on themselves stick scandalously fast.*
>
> ('Epilogue', ll. 13–16, 21–9)

The play's author claims that its satire is not gender specific: if male targets had been selected, the satire would have hit too close to home. The figure of the female dramatist here offers a means of satirizing all playwright 'Wits' at a comfortable distance, in turn suggesting the even greater vanity of those male dramatists who can only accept such critique at a remove. This includes the author himself who acknowledges that pride has overridden his manners in determining his choice of female targets. The epilogue suggests, then, that the play is not as misogynistic in its ideology as Finke argues. *The Female Wits* is not so much a silencing of female voices as a ventriloquism used to expose the vanity of all playwrights, irrespective of gender. We should not forget the play's indebtedness to Buckingham's *The Rehearsal*, a work that satirizes a male playwright, as did Charles Gildon's later approximation of this source in his 1714 satire of Nicholas Rowe.[27] Even after his death, Dryden—a figure at the heart of the literary establishment—continued to undergo similar attacks to that made upon Manley, Pix, and Trotter in *The Female Wits*. For example, in *A Comparison Between The Two Stages* (1702) Dryden's play *Amphitryon* is described as a 'Hodge-Podge', mirroring the representation of Manley's play in *The Female Wits* as 'a farcical generic hodgepodge' (p. 65).[28] Such parallels

[27] [Charles Gildon], *A New Rehearsal, or Bays the Younger* (1714).
[28] [Charles Gildon?], *A Comparison Between the Two Stages* (1702), 148.

remind us that satires of playwrights cut across gender boundaries in their subject and critique, an approach that the epilogue to *The Female Wits* upholds. Whilst Derek Hughes concludes his brief analysis of *The Female Wits* by claiming that the satire proves that the 'woman writer still had many battles to fight', we might argue that this was equally true of the many male playwrights condemned by contemporary satires.[29]

The satire found in *The Female Wits* goes beyond a caricature of its female protagonists, extending to an attack made on the broader theatrical establishment of which women playwrights were but a part. As Lucyle Hook points out, the play's satire extended to 'an entire gallery of burlesqued portraits of the famous actors [including Elizabeth Barry, Anne Bracegirdle, and Thomas Betterton] who were as much under fire as Mrs Manley herself'.[30] In Drury Lane's projected intention to stage Marsilia's dramatic 'hodgepodge', *The Female Wits* becomes a satire of the theatre company who choose to produce the play, and the audiences who consumed it. Certainly, Marsilia adopts innovation for its own sake in the play, creating a fantastical and illogical 'Operaish' (p. 44) work that contains little opera and makes no sense to the players who rehearse it. But this reveals her own commercial insight: Marsilia knows that audiences favour innovation over substance, and she gives them what they want. When audiences of *The Female Wits* attended the play, no doubt they laughed at the caricatures on stage, but they were also being asked to laugh at themselves. For the satire implicated the taste of those audiences and readers who had seen or read *The Royal Mischief* and made it into a viable piece of drama.

STAGE REFORM AND FEMALE DRAMATISTS

In the eight years between the performance and publication of *The Female Wits*, the English stage was subjected to an intense scrutiny of its purpose, content, and influence from the movement known as the stage reform debates. The publication that sparked these debates issued from the pen of Jeremy Collier, a theologian and theatre critic. Collier's *A Short View of the Immorality and Profaneness of the English Stage* (1698) bewailed the condition of the modern stage, arguing that it had lost sight of the moral purpose of drama:

> the *Present English Stage* is superlatively Scandalous. It exceeds the Liberties of all Times and Countries: It has not so much as the poor plea of a *Precedent*, to which most other ill Things may claim a pretence. 'Tis mostly meer Discovery and Invention: A new World of Vice found out, and planted with all the Industry imaginable.[31]

Collier's condemnation of contemporary drama as a form that was 'mostly meer Discovery and Invention' resonates with the satire of Manley's *Royal Mischief* in

---

[29] Derek Hughes, *English Drama 1660–1700* (Oxford: Clarendon Press, 1996), 449.

[30] *The Female Wits*, ed. Hook, ix.

[31] Jeremy Collier, *A Short View of the Immorality, and Profaneness of the English Stage* (1698), 54–5.

The Female Wits: the actress Mrs Cross, who is playing the part of Isabella in Marsilia's play, states that 'this is the most incomprehensible Part I ever had in my Life; and when I complain, all the Answer I get is, 'tis New, and 'tis odd; and nothing but new things and odd things will do' (p. 13). Certainly, in its critique of Manley's play, *The Female Wits* voiced many of the same concerns that we hear in the pamphlets that debated the need for reform. As a form, satire was much suited to the purposes of the reformers and their opponents since satirists 'write not merely out of personal indignation, but with a sense of moral vocation and with a concern for the public interest'.[32] In light of this, we might question whether the play's satire is a call for change uttered in the mounting atmosphere of the stage reform movement. If so, its call to condemn the careers of female dramatists was not to gain traction as there are notable differences between the concerns of the play and those of the reformers. Collier nowhere attacks women writers as responsible for the production of immoral stage writings; his playwright targets are all male. This is not because Collier was disinterested in the relationship between the stage and gender. The lengthy first section of *A Short View* is predominantly concerned with a discussion of the negative moral example modern drama presented to women. Collier's attack was one levelled, in large part, at dramatic portrayals of female character; his concern was with *how* gender was staged and its effect upon audiences, not with which gender was staging it.

Collier's silence on the subject of female dramatists may reflect their broader respectability. A number of publications produced at the turn of the eighteenth century provide a useful counter-narrative to the satirical view of contemporary female dramatists as presented in *The Female Wits*. As we will see, these women were responsible in part for publicly promoting their own value, but influential male voices promoted their respectability also. A defence of *The Royal Mischief* was to be forthcoming from the writer and self-proclaimed theatre critic Charles Gildon. An ardent defender both of the Aristotelian poetics of the stage and its morality, Gildon appeared to have no problem with the idea of the female dramatist. We find evidence for this in Gildon's revision of Gerard Langbaine's 1691 work, *An Account of the English Dramatic Poets*, in which he expanded the innovative study (the first of its kind) by updating entries and creating new ones for recent dramatists. In Gildon's hands, Langbaine's six entries for female playwrights increased to nine, now including Manley, Pix, and Trotter. Gildon singled out Manley as one who 'gives us a living Proof of what we might reasonably expect from Womankind, if they had the Benefit of those artificial Improvements of Learning the Men have, when by the meer Force of Nature they so much excel'.[33] His approval of her drama was based upon the same foundation for which he was to critique Rowe in *A New Rehearsal*: Manley adhered to Aristotelian principles in her tragedies whilst Rowe did not.[34] Gildon presents Manley as an instinctive dramatist, one who has naturally imbibed the Aristotelian principles of poetic justice and applied them to *The Royal Mischief*: 'how well the Rules

---

[32] Ruben Quintero, 'Introduction: Understanding Satire', in *Companion to Satire*, 1.
[33] [Charles Gildon], *Lives and Characters of the English Dramatick Poets* ([1699]), 91.
[34] Gildon's critique of Rowe's drama was levelled in the previously cited work, *A New Rehearsal*.

of *Aristotle* are observ'd in this Tragedy, by a Lady who never read him' (p. 91). Whilst Gildon presents Manley's success as an exception to the general rule—as one who has 'distinguish'd her self from the rest of her *Sex*' (p. 90)—*An Account* does not suggest that Manley was the first woman to do so. As noted, the work includes entries for nine female dramatists, the earliest being Elizabeth Cary and Mary Sidney, fostering a gendered sense of lineage. Gildon revises Langbaine's entries to make them more celebratory of female talent: he adds to the number of plays attributed to Aphra Behn, and updates Langbaine in describing her as a dramatist who 'excell'd not only all that went before her of her own Sex, but [a] great part of her Contemporary Poets of the other' (p. 9). Gildon's entries for Pix and Trotter are also complementary: Pix is a 'Lady yet living… [who] has boldly given us an Essay of her Talent' (p. 111); whilst Trotter is 'admirable for two things rarely found together, *Wit* and *Beauty*; and with these a *Penetration* very uncommon in the Sex' (p. 179). *An Account* thus offers a powerful counter-narrative to the satire of the playwrights in *The Female Wits*, and enables us to challenge the authority of the views and characterizations that the play promotes.

Gildon appears to have engaged with further works of theatre criticism in the period between the performance and publication of *The Female Wits*. *A Comparison Between the Two Stages* (1702), published anonymously but attributed to Gildon, is an explicitly satirical work, written in the form of a dialogue between a number of would-be theatre critics. This work was not to treat female dramatists as kindly as *An Account*, with the character of 'Chagrin, a Critick', noting:

> I wonder in my Heart we are so lost to all Sense and Reason: What a Pox have the Women to do with the Muses? I grant you the Poets call the Nine Muses by the Names of Women, but why so? not because the Sex had any thing to do with Poetry, but because in that Sex they're much fitter for prostitution.   (p. 26)

The character of Ramble condemns Chagrin for crossing the polite bounds of criticism— 'Abusive, now you're abusive, Mr. *Critick*' (p. 62)—whilst the character of Sullen goes on to remind them all that "twas a Lady carry'd the Prize of Poetry in *France* t'other Day; and I assure you, if the Account were fairly stated, there have been in *England* some of that Sex who have done admirably' (p. 27). By staging a dialogue between these men *A Comparison* allows for different perspectives: in the work, Chagrin is satirizing women dramatists, yet simultaneously the work's opposing voices attack this critic for his misogynistic views.

The content of *A Comparison* allows us to further contextualize some of the satire at the heart of *The Female Wits*. Gildon reflects on the state of contemporary drama in his preface to the work, suggesting a useful measure of success as the acting of a play for six continuous days:

> *But, indeed, the first temptation I had of spending my Time thus, was, the contemplation of our present Poetry; I believe it never was at so low an Ebb, and yet the Stages were never so delug'd: I am sure you can't name me five Plays that have indur'd six Days acting, for fifty were damn'd in three.*   ('The Preface')

The dialogic voices in *A Comparison* go on to contradict this measure when discussing Manley's *The Royal Mischief*. Sullen notes derisively that the play 'made a shift to live half a dozen Days, and then expir'd' (p. 31). Viewed in light of the preface, Manley's play must be considered a rare success, and Sullen's dismissive tone thereby reveals either his own ignorance or his prejudice against women writers. Whilst its overall discussion of female dramatists is brief, *A Comparison* does draw attention to a number of plays written by contemporary women, chiefly those of Manley and Pix, yet the relative speed with which its speakers are keen to pass over these plays reveals their detrimental views of these works. This reflects most poorly on the speakers themselves. For the disjunction created between what the voices of *A Comparison* say about contemporary drama, and what we have evidence to suggest was the case, suggests that the main satirical target of the work was not the dramatists that it attacked, but the critics themselves whose opinions prove to be so incorrect.

Attention to wider criticism levelled at the stage in the period demonstrates that we should be careful not to read a satire like *The Female Wits* solely through the lens of gender politics, but also through the context of contemporary ideas about theatre and the purpose of drama. Whilst attention to gender reveals a contemporary anxiety about the emergence of professional female playwrights, attention to the wider context of the stage reform debates suggests how minor these anxieties potentially were in comparison to concerns about the way the theatre companies operated, the content of the plays they staged, and their effect on contemporary audiences. In over three hundred pages critiquing the immorality of the modern stage, Collier does not once cite a female dramatist, and whilst *A Comparison* does reference Manley and Pix's plays, Gildon's satire of them reflects most negatively upon the character of Chagrin the critic, as he reveals his own misogynistic and flawed views. If we look more widely across the stage reform literature, we catch only glimpses of attacks on women playwrights. Even the most vituperative of these gendered attacks, such as the satire of Pix in *Animadversions on Mr Congreve's Late Answer* (1698), are minimal compared to the wider attack on male playwrights, and in the latter case the cruel nature of the satire arose from the author's personal grudge against Pix.[35] *The Female Wits* thus belonged to a moment of intense scrutiny of the stage itself, in which we might see the work as a rare example focused on the influence of women dramatists.

---

[35] In *Animadversions on Mr Congreve's Late Answer to Mr Collier* (1698), Pix is satirized as:

> The last that writ, of these presuming two,
>   (For that *Queen Ca—ne* is no Play 'tis true)
> And yet to Spell is more than she can do,
> Told a High Princess, she from Men had torn
> Those *Bays*, which they had long engross'd and worn.

> ([3])

The satire was published anonymously but is now credited to the actor George Powell, who plagiarized a play Pix submitted to him for consideration for the Drury Lane stage. For an account of this episode, and Congreve's public support for Pix, see Melinda C. Finberg, ed., *Eighteenth-Century Women Dramatists* (Oxford: Oxford University Press, 2001), xii.

THE MUSES RESPOND

Milling has noted how, prior to the production of *The Female Wits*, the 'unusual amount' of female-authored plays performed in the 1695–6 season were 'little condemned by satirists of the time'.[36] As we have seen, the play's production in 1696 seems to have had negligible effect in heightening the critique of Manley, Pix, and Trotter in the stage reform debates which followed in its wake. Certainly no evidence survives that any of the three central targets of *The Female Wits* responded directly to the satire. Milling notes that in Manley's case this is extraordinarily uncharacteristic given 'the extent of the vitriol she heaps on those who cross her purposes in her own satiric writing'.[37] What then should we make of this silence: should it be read as the successful misogynistic suppression that Finke argued the play enacted; or should we understand it, conversely, as a refusal to acknowledge any threat posed by the play?

We can trace indirect responses to the play's satirical caricatures of Manley, Pix, and Trotter in their subsequent acts of self-promotion. The year 1700 saw the death of Dryden, the poet laureate and the most prolific dramatist of his generation. Dryden was mourned by women writers as well as their male counterparts. Manley, Pix, and Trotter all contributed to a collection of eulogistic poems printed under the title *The Nine Muses* (1700). Here, the writers embraced the satirical association with Dryden that had been created through *The Female Wits*, and turned it to more serious ends. Anne Kelley sees this innovative volume, the first published collective endeavour by women in England, as representing 'one of the stronger bids by women writers of this period for parity and respect'.[38] Manley's entry is the first in the collection, and she was likely the driving force behind the project.[39] Sincere as the content of the poetic offerings were, the collection served a wider purpose in promoting an association between these writers and Dryden. The volume emulated the male literary establishment, yet simultaneously harboured a challenging feminocentric agenda that asserted the legitimacy of women in this field through the assumption of the personae of the classical muses.[40] Where the *Female Wits* promoted an idea of female rivalry, the *Nine Muses* responded with a display of female collaboration. Indeed, the harshest satire in *The Female Wits* is directed towards women by women, and much of its humour derives from the cruelty bred by this professional female rivalry. Marsilia introduces her fellow female playwrights to one another, describing Calista to Wellfed as:

[T]he vainest, proudest, senseless Thing, she pretends to Grammar, writes in Mood and Figure; she does every thing methodically.—Poor Creature! She shews me her

---

[36] Milling, 'The Female Wits', 119.   [37] Milling, 'The Female Wits', 128.

[38] Anne Kelley, '"What a Pox have the Women to do with the Muses?" *The Nine Muses* (1700): Emulation or Appropriation?', *Women's Writing* 17 (2010), 8–29, at 24.

[39] See the introduction to Delarivier Manley, *The New Atalantis*, ed. Ros Ballaster (London: Pickering, 1991), xii.

[40] See Kelley, '"What a Pox have the Women to do with the Muses?"', 9–11.

Works first; I always commend 'em, with a Design she shou'd expose 'em, and the Town be so kind to laugh her out of her Follies.   (p. 5)

Hypocritically, Marsilia openly proclaims their sisterhood shortly after her attack upon Trotter, labelling them:

[T]he Female Triumvirate; methinks 'twou'd be but civil of the Men to lay down their Pens for one Year, and let us divert the Town; but if we shou'd, they'd certainly be asham'd ever to take 'em up again.   (p. 5)

The Nine Muses thus made tangible the idea of a female literary community which the play had directly satirized, stressing the very values that *The Female Wits* had attempted to tear down.

Whilst we might understand *The Nine Muses* in part as a response to the challenge offered by *The Female Wits*, it is possible that the *Female Wits* was itself a response to earlier writings by Manley, Pix, and Trotter. The most public forum through which women writers engaged with satirical attacks was in the paratextual materials that accompanied their plays. Repeatedly we see that women dramatists did not try to obscure the subject of gender, but embraced it. One of many examples of this is the publication of a young Catharine Trotter's first play, *Agnes de Castro* (1696). The play's prefatory materials, from its title page to the commendatory verses by Manley and Wycherley, to its prologue and epilogue, draw attention to Trotter's gender. Furthermore, in its very adaptation of Aphra Behn's 1688 novella of the same name, the play emphasized a sense of its female-authored creation and lineage. Manley's commendatory verses are positioned before Wycherley's, and have been composed by the printer using a bolder and larger type-face. Her sonnet turns upon this sense of female lineage and Trotter's embodiment of a dramatic talent that will outstrip their male counterparts:

> Orinda, and the Fair Astrea gone,
> Not one was found to fill the Vacant Throne:
> Aspiring Man had quite regain'd the Sway,
> Again had Taught us humbly to Obey;
> Till you (Natures third start, in favour of our Kind)
> With stronger Arms, their Empire have disjoyn'd,
> And snatcht a Lawrel which they thought their Prize,
> Thus Conqu'ror, with your Wit, as with your Eyes.
> Fired by the bold Example, I would try
> To turn our Sexes weaker Destiny.
> O! How I long in the Poetick Race,
> To loose the Reins, and give their Glory Chase;
> For thus Encourag'd, and thus led by you,
> Methinks we might more Crowns than theirs Subdue.[41]

---

[41] Catharine Trotter, *Agnes de Castro* (1696), 'TO THE AUTHOR OF Agnes de Castro'.

Manley's verses employ a proud and militaristic tone, with the apostrophe ushered in by her exclamatory 'O!' in line eleven leading into a defiant refrain that proclaims the worth of female-authored drama. Her poem reads as an assertive celebration of anticipated female victory in the literary battle of the sexes, rather than a defence against discriminatory attacks made upon the female ability to write.

Trotter responded to Manley's show of support by writing commendatory verses for *The Royal Mischief* later that year, modestly claiming that the victory won on behalf of female playwrights had been achieved by Manley:

> For us you've vanquisht, though the toyl was yours,
> You were our Champion, and the Glory ours,
> Well you've maintain'd our equal right in Fame,
> To which vain Man had quite engrost the claim:
> I knew my force too weak, and but assay'd
> The Borders of their Empire to invade,
> I incite a greater genius to my aid:
> The War begun you generously pursu'd,
> With double Arms you every way subdu'd;
> Our Title clear'd, nor can a doubt remain.[42]

Gender stereotypes are actively subverted in Trotter's poem: Manley is promoted as a chivalrous knight who has defended the female right to dramatic writing and triumphed against the vain men who would claim this territory their own. The militaristic language and imagery of the poem is also employed in Pix's commendatory verses to *The Royal Mischief*, which were printed on the page directly underneath Trotter's. This print format projected the formation of a fair triumvirate within the opening pages of the play-text. It was, perhaps, this shared self-avowal of female dramatic ability that the anonymous author of *The Female Wits* set out to ridicule later that year. Indeed, *The Female Wits* could be understood as a response to the triumvirate of women dramatists who had gathered forces in the prefatory materials to *The Royal Mischief*, and who had used Manley's play to proclaim the female victory in drama.

CONCLUSION

As Laura Rosenthal has suggested, it is time to start asking a new set of questions about the relationship between women and writing in the period: 'Feminist scholarship has given us unprecedented access to women writers from the eighteenth century; at the same time, it has framed these writers in particular ways that have inadvertently

---

[42] Delarivier Manley, *The Royal Mischief* (1696), 'To Mrs. *Manley*. By the Author of *Agnes de Castro*', ll. 3–12.

underserved certain aspects of their work.'[43] Certainly, our understanding of the satire embodied in *The Female Wits* is conditioned by the ways in which we choose to read its treatment of gender. As a stand-alone satire, its attack on Manley, Pix, and Trotter may seem relentless, cruel, and highly misogynistic. Yet placed alongside the other rehearsal satires, we may understand the play as belonging to a broader satirical tradition that chiefly took aim at leading male writers, as did the majority of satire written in the period. Viewed through this lens, the satire found in *The Female Wits* starts to appear unique in its choice of targets. If we consider the context of the stage reform debates that played out in the years following the production of the play, we find that women writers were, in the grand scheme of things, of relatively little concern to those moralists and writers who would contest the rightful purposes of drama. Much of the available evidence is suggestive not of the perceived problem of women's newly proximate relationship to drama, but of the success and public appetite for female-authored plays. Manley, Pix, and Trotter succeeded as professional writers despite publicly acknowledging their gender. In fact, their positive avowal of their gender across a shared platform of printed writings between 1696 and 1700 appears more as a strategy to ensure success rather than to impede it. *The Female Wits* may have ridiculed this new female challenge to the male laurels, but in so doing it gestured, conversely, to a new high point in the history of women's fortunes as dramatists.

Despite its initial success, *The Female Wits* did not become a part of the eighteenth-century repertory. It is, perhaps, quite telling that there was no long-term appetite for the play. Buckingham's *Rehearsal* was performed well into the eighteenth century, but the satire of *The Female Wits* belonged to a specific moment. Whilst its content can be read as part of a wider misogynistic silencing of the female pen, its lack of an afterlife points to the failure of its satire to achieve such ends. What then, should we make of Centlivre's claims of the discrimination female dramatists faced? Where can we hear the carping malice of which she complained, if not in printed satires? It might be argued that we hear this malice in the attacks referred to repeatedly in the prologues and epilogues of the period. In his commendatory verses to *Agnes de Castro*, Wycherley anticipated the satirical slurs to which Trotter's play might be exposed, referring to the playwright as one 'Who, but because she'd do you, a good Turn, / Unask'd, unsu'd to, may become your scorn' ('Wycherly *at the Authors request*', ll. 11–12). In the play's epilogue the actress Susanna Verbruggen turned to the men in the audience, stating that if possible she would:

> bid defiance to your Coward Satyr;
> That meanly wou'd a Womans strength oppose.
>
> (Epilogue, ll. 19–20)

Wycherley's appeals to male gallantry and Verbruggen's rallying defence both define 'Satyr' as a predominantly male category. Moreover, they *anticipate* rather than respond to that satire. As with the vast majority of such paratextual materials, their words are

---

[43] Laura J. Rosenthal, 'Introduction: Recovering from Recovery', *The Eighteenth Century* 50 (2009), 1–11, at 5.

entreaties made to pre-empt a reaction, and we have little clear evidence of actual responses to their pleas, satirical or not. If those responses did exist, they were likely overwhelmingly behavioural and oral, as in the case of the male customer in Turner's bookshop who utters a condemnation of Centlivre's work as he throws down a copy of *The Gamester* which he was on the verge of purchasing. If so, have we overestimated the power of satirical writings in curtailing the careers of women playwrights at the turn of the eighteenth century? Printed satires may seem a good means of measuring wider attitudes to female playwrights—and, indeed, to a whole host of subjects—but are the best means perhaps the oral and behavioural ones that are much harder to reconstruct?

Select Bibliography

Finke, Laurie A. 'The Satire of Women Writers in *The Female Wits*', *Restoration* 8 (1984), 64–71.

Hughes, Derek. *English Drama 1660–1700* (Oxford: Clarendon Press, 1996).

Kelley, Anne. '"What a Pox have the Women to do with the Muses?" *The Nine Muses* (1700): Emulation or Appropriation?', *Women's Writing* 17 (2010), 8–29.

Milling, Jane. '*The Female Wits*: Women Writers at Work', in *Theatre and Culture in Early Modern England, 1650–1737: From Leviathan to Licensing Act*, ed. Catie Gill (Farnham: Ashgate, 2010), 119–29.

Morgan, Fidelis. *The Female Wits: Women Playwrights on the London Stage 1660–1720* (London: Virago, 1981).

Rosenthal, Laura J. *Playwrights and Plagiarists in Early Modern England: Gender, Authorship, Literary Property* (Ithaca: Cornell University Press, 1996).

Rosenthal, Laura J. 'Restoration and Eighteenth-Century Drama: New Directions in the Field', *Literature Compass* 5 (2008), 174–94.

Rumbold, Valerie. 'Cut the Caterwauling: Women Writers (Not) in Pope's Dunciads', *RES* 52, no. 208 (2001), 524–39.

CHAPTER 6

···

NATIONAL IDENTITY
AND SATIRE

···

DAVID O'SHAUGHNESSY

Canker: Give us then a national portrait: a Scotchman or an Irishman

Foote: If you mean merely the dialect of the two countries, I can't think it
either a subject of satyr or humour; it is an accidental unhappiness, for
which a man is no more accountable, than the colour of his hair.

Samuel Foote, The Minor (1760)

ANXIETY about immigration and concomitant fears of contagion were an ever present
feature of societal and critical discourse throughout our period. Commentators identified foreign manners, fashions, and fripperies as posing a collective and corrupting
threat to the idealized virtuous English character; they believed that workers were coming over to steal English jobs; and they feared foreign incursions from conquered
imperial geographies. These anxieties stemmed from a variety of sources, but looming
large over the earlier part of the century were the uncomfortable facts that Britain had
invited a Dutchman to take its crown and that it took until 1727 to crown a king who
could actually speak English fluently (albeit still with a distinctly German accent).
Religious concerns had taken precedence when it came to issuing William of Orange an
invitation to take the throne but residual unease with the shakiness of the claim that
James II had abdicated persisted well into the century. The Williamite succession functioned as a proxy for the tensions—albeit often productive tensions—brought about by, as
Howard Weinbrot has argued, the sustained 'broader mingling' of races and nationalities
that occurred in eighteenth-century Britain during the transition from 'the restoration
of the Anglo-Norman French Stuart Charles II to the elevation of the Anglo-German
British Hanoverian George III'.[1]

This chapter has received funding from the European Union's 2020 research and innovation programme
under the Marie Sklowdowska-Curie grant agreement No 745896.

[1] Howard Weinbrot, *Britannia's Issue: The Rise of British Literature from Dryden to Ossian* (Cambridge:
Cambridge University Press, 1993), 2, 479.

Daniel Defoe's feisty satirical riposte to those who saw William's accession as a regressive and polluting event made his literary name. Published in December 1700 or January 1701, *The True-Born Englishman* was a best-seller, enabling Defoe to make the transition from obscure pamphleteer to becoming the leading satirical poet of the day. A virulent anti-Catholic, Defoe was appalled by Whig writer John Tutchin's verse assault on William, *The Foreigners*, which made much play of Dutch 'Vermin' who were 'Boorish, rude, and an inhumane Race' and other associated writings.[2] Defoe's response to this print culture of xenophobia was a playful but caustic exposure of the nonsensical claims of his opponents' racial purity. His explanatory preface sets out his basic premise—'*That those Nations which are most mix'd, are the best, and have least of Barbarism and Brutality among them*' (79)—but this measured view is expressed through railing attacks on Englishmen's degree of self-delusion when the country, conquered and invaded numerous times in its history, is effectively '*Europe's* sink, *the Jakes* where she / Voids all her Offal Out-cast Progeny' (ll. 249–50), home to 'a Mongrel half-bred Race' (l. 340). Defoe's satire smacks more of a breezy jibe rather than an expression of enraged indignation, and all the more forceful for it. Appropriately, he employs a hybrid form with the fashionable heroic couplet amplified by the use of ballad refrain and all its folk resonance. Again and again, Defoe drives home Britain's long history of miscegenation:

> Thus from a Mixture of all Kinds began,
> That Het'rogenous Thing, *An Englishman*:
> In eager Rapes, and furious Lust begot,
> Betwixt a Painted *Britton* and a *Scot*
>
> (ll. 334–7)

Suvir Kaul has discussed how Defoe reverses the image of English colonial expansion by depicting the country as the 'virgin land raped by the violence of competing conquerors', showing us how the poem looks within as well as without Britain's borders.[3] Defoe repeatedly calls attention to the palimpsestic genealogical layering that lies in England's past in his move to expose the hollowness of contemporary xenophobic ingratitude directed towards William. Kaul's observation that Defoe reverses the trope of imperial rapine provides us with a useful way in to thinking about satire and national identity within Britain over the course of this century of imperial expansion. Defoe forcefully reminds his readers that Britain has always been a site of contestation, a reality that cannot be cloaked by any mythologizing about racial coherence. As Joseph Addison would suggest, London's cosmopolitanism was a benign phenomenon that helped confirm Britain's sense of commercial and moral superiority as well as shoring up its Enlightenment credentials:

---

[2] *The True-Born Englishman and other Poems*, ed. W. R. Owens, vol. 1 of *Satire, Fantasy and Writings on the Supernatural by Daniel Defoe*, 8 vols. (London: Pickering & Chatto, 2003), 17–18.

[3] Suvir Kaul, *Poems of Nation, Anthems of Empire: English Verse in the Long Eighteenth Century* (Charlottesville and London: University of Virginia Press, 2000), 88.

There is no Place in the Town which I so much love to frequent as the *Royal-Exchange*. It gives me a secret Satisfaction, and, in some measure, gratifies my Vanity, as I am an *Englishman*, to see so rich an Assembly of Country-men and Foreigners consulting together upon the private Business of Mankind, and making this Metropolis a kind of *Emporium* for the whole Earth.[4]

London's many theatres were also sites where rich assemblies of English and other nationalities would consult together upon the public and private business of mankind. This essay will look primarily at dramatic satire on the London stage as it relates to Irish national identity. In focusing on theatre, it will provide some small redress of the tendency to privilege verse satire over that of plays or novels.[5] Why the particular emphasis on the Irish case? It is certainly true that other national or ethnic identities could prove fruitful. During the 'Second Hundred Years War', British writers were not shy of attacking the French. The Dutch and Germans also featured regularly while anxieties about Jewish residents also emerged in numerous satirical stage depictions, particularly in the 1780s. But it was the Irish theatrical diaspora, of all peoples migrating to Britain in the eighteenth century, that was by far the most populous and successful, and this qualifies it for particular attention. Moreover, while there were certainly satiric dramatizations of the Scots and, to a lesser extent, the Welsh, the 'Stage Irishman' was an integral part of the comic genre.[6] Therefore, the Irish offer a particularly rich opportunity to think about the relationship between satire and national identity: they were regular targets of the mode as well as producing some of its leading proponents.

As the essay works its way through the century, I want to consider London as a site of contestation for this aspirational diasporic grouping for whom satire of national identity was initially a barrier—or representative of a barrier—to acceptance, integration, and social mobility. However, as the century progressed, there was increasing evidence that the practice of satire was understood as a means to demonstrate cultural capital and it became a proxy for increasing tolerance of the Irish and their growing collective confidence. By appropriating and redirecting the invective of satire, the Irish were able to reverse—to some degree at least—long held stereotypes of ignorance and barbarity. Moreover, it might be argued that this movement was enabled through developments in historiography over the period, also a discursive site of much contestation. Aligning satire, drama, and historiography, I want to show how satire here might be understood as a strain of Irish Enlightenment where it was less a means of 'Reformation', as Defoe would have had it, but rather, as Dustin Griffin has laid out, a method of inquiry and provocation,

---

[4] Erin Mackie, ed., *The Commerce of Everyday Life: Selections from* The Tatler *and* The Spectator (Boston: Bedford/St. Martin's Press, 1988), 203.

[5] Ashley Marshall, *The Practice of Satire in England, 1658–1770* (Baltimore: Johns Hopkins University Press, 2013), 11.

[6] G. C. Duggan, *The Stage Irishman* (Dublin: Talbot Press, 1937); J. O. Bartley, *Teague, Shenkin, and Sawney* (Cork: Cork University Press, 1954); Joep Leerssen, *Mere Irish and Fíor Ghael: Studies in the Idea of Irish Nationality, its Development and Literary Expression Prior to the Nineteenth Century* (Cork: Cork University Press and Field Day, 1986); David Hayton, 'From Barbarian to Burlesque: English Images of the Irish c.1660–1750', *Irish Economic and Social History* 15 (1988), 5–31.

and ultimately, a means for the public display of improvement.[7] In a double move, perhaps diminishing its Enlightenment pretensions, satire could expose the failings of the satirized while displaying the sophisticated literary aplomb of the satirist, exposing the cultural gulf between different nations in a contest of public opinion that appears to have been perceived by some as a zero-sum game. Notwithstanding Addison's beaming self-congratulatory sense of London being the natural home of citizens of the world, the cosy camaraderie he describes occludes the competition between these commercial agents, often drawn along national lines, which spread into the realm of culture, particularly for the Irish and Scots. Between these two Celtic tribes, 'almost the same but not quite', 1745 was a date which proved particularly significant, for it allowed the Irish to emerge from the shadow of 1641. For those who chose to migrate to England in our period, the historical accounts of the Ulster rebellion of that year were a significant obstacle.

Swift, History, and the Scots

John Temple's *History of the Irish Rebellion* (1646) was unequivocally vituperative in its assessment of Irish Catholic brutality in the 1641 rebellion: the full title refers to 'the barbarous cruelties and bloody massacres which ensued thereupon' leaving the reader in little doubt as to which way Temple's lurid account was going to play out. Temple's take on the events, as Joep Leerssen has documented, revivified and concretized ideas of Irish savagery which had been extant since Strabo.[8] Other events helped to keep Temple's text in the public consciousness. After Titus Oates's mendacity during the Popish plot of 1678–81, Temple's history was reprinted, as it was again in subsequent times of political stress (for example, 1698, 1716, and 1746). The cumulative effect of these events and the historical writing they provoked had significant cultural repercussions, particularly in terms of the dramatic repertoire. Yet, as noted by David Hayton, satirical depictions of the Stage Irish were often broad-humoured and, after the defeats of James II in 1690 and 1691, the English dread of the 'wild Irish', often along racial grounds, was replaced by more of a contemptuous sneer.[9] The ostensible military prowess of the Irish Catholics— which prompted panic in December 1688 when Irish troops were thought to be rampaging through the south of England—no longer seemed possible in the wake of the battles of the Boyne and Aughrim. Contempt is a far easier emotion to fuse with humour—particularly satire—than fear, and hence we have a proliferation of satires across a variety of genres that poke fun, with varying degrees of hostility, at the Irish.[10]

---

[7] Dustin Griffin, *Satire: A Critical Reintroduction* (Lexington: University of Kentucky Press, 1994).

[8] Leerssen, *Mere Irish and Fíor Ghael*, 58–60.   [9] Hayton, 'From Barbarian to Burlesque'.

[10] See Helen Burke, 'The Irish Joke, Migrant Networks, and the London Irish in the 1680s', *Eighteenth-Century Life* 39 (2015), 41–65.

Thus, it is a given that eighteenth-century print and oral culture frequently saw the Irish and Ireland as an object of satire. The Irish were particularly prone to the 'weak multiculturalism' of eighteenth-century Britain where early fear never quite dissipated entirely, although it did dilute to a disdainful and sniffy tolerance in the mid-century before hardening again after 1798.[11] However, following recent more benign readings of the opportunities identified and exploited by the Irish in eighteenth-century Britain, this essay will look at the Irish who used satire as a means of publicly demonstrating Enlightenment ideas of improvement, politeness, civility, and combative intellectual exchange to a sceptical audience.[12] This satiric practice is linked to historiography and landmark publications of historical texts. It provided satirists, particularly playwrights, with the necessary confidence and ethnographic 'evidence' for the reimagining of the Irish national character. Noelle Gallagher has reminded us of the close links between satire and historical writings, both understood in the early eighteenth century as sharing formal and thematic features. They both had classical antecedents, concerned themselves often with the actions of 'great men', often had didactic objectives, interested themselves in public matters, reached broader audiences than perhaps intended, and were politically engaged.[13] In the competitive space of London, as the Irish and Scots grappled for supremacy, satires were 'frequently and self-consciously mobilized as vehicles for historical representation'.[14] Moreover, significant historical publications influenced the tone of satire produced by key Irish writers: as the Irish proved themselves capable of participating in the Enlightenment discourse of historiography, satire was emboldened and its vitriol diluted. At the same time, the Enlightenment credentials of such works were always under pressure as historiographic and cultural clashes with the Scots occurred regularly: pretensions of Enlightenment could be undermined by sheer rudeness.[15]

Yet before we travel to London, it would seem more than rude to pass over Jonathan Swift in an essay on satire and national identity. Swift's legacy is critical: not only is he generally recognized as one of the most important satirists of the century, his afterlife and influence over subsequent generations of eighteenth-century Irish writers, particularly those of a patriot bent, is substantial.[16] Moreover, he authored two texts which help us establish the case for considering satire of national identity alongside historiography, *The Story of the Injured Lady* (1707) and *A Modest Proposal* (1729).

[11] Helen Burke, '"Integrated as Outsiders": Teague's Blanket and the Irish Immigrant "Problem" in Early Modern Britain', *Éire-Ireland* 46 (2011), 20–42, 25.

[12] See Craig Bailey, *Irish London: Middle-Class Migration in the Global Eighteenth Century* (Liverpool: Liverpool University Press, 2013); *Networks of Aspiration: The London Irish of the Eighteenth Century*, special issue of *Eighteenth-Century Life* 39 (2015), 1–235.

[13] Noelle Gallagher, *Historical Literatures: Writing about the Past in England 1660–1740* (Manchester: Manchester University Press, 2012), 114–16.

[14] Gallagher, *Historical Literatures*, 159.

[15] On the idea of a 'rude' Enlightenment, see Michael Brown, 'The Biter Bitten: Ireland and the Rude Enlightenment', *Eighteenth-Century Studies* 45 (2015), 393–407.

[16] See Robert Mahony, *Jonathan Swift: The Irish Identity* (New Haven and London: Yale University Press, 1995).

In the *Injured Lady*, his early satirical allegory, Swift lays out a litany of Irish complaints related to the union of 1707 before a conclusion which, following on from William Molyneux's *A Case for Ireland* (1699), highlights the problem of corrupted historical memory. England, Swift complains, has torn up the 'old Compact' between England and Ireland in which they agreed to have 'the same Steward' which would allow Ireland to 'regulate [its] Family and Estate by the same Method' as England. The injured lady claims that this agreement was 'writ down in Form' but now 'the Turn he thinketh to give this Compact of ours is very extraordinary' since it is being ridden over roughshod by the lover. Of course, there was no formal constitutional settlement which laid out how England would govern Ireland; the closest document to this was Poynings's Law (1495). The 'compact' alluded to might be this act or might simply be synecdochal of the litany of English legislative measures related to Ireland. Whatever it may be, Swift calls attention to the problems inherent in corrupted historical memory and thus to the importance of correct historical accounts to guide just political behaviour. A true account of the injured lady's character, a history told with 'Modesty and Truth', on the other hand, is a tale of 'Grief and ill Usage'; born to a 'good Estate', the years have brought nothing but oppression and sorrow. In a marvellous twist of one of the standard satirical tropes by which the Irish were represented—one that would persist through the century— Swift reverses the trope of the rakish Irish fortune-hunter and suggests that a true historical account shows just the opposite:

> Some Years ago, this Gentleman, taking a Fancy either to my Person or Fortune, made his addresses to me; which, being then young and foolish, I too readily admitted [...] I was undone by the common Arts practiced upon all easy credulous Virgins, half by Force, and half by Consent, after solemn Vows and Protestations of Marriage.[17]

At the same time, he also redirects the gaze of the English reader, long accustomed to bestial descriptions of Irish physiognomy, to the corporeal and moral degeneracy of his nation's new preferred mistress, Scotland: 'tall and lean, and very ill-shape; she hath bad Features, and a worse Complexion; she hath a stinking Breath, and twenty ill Smells about her besides; which are yet more unsufferable by her natural Sluttishness; for she is always Lousy, and never without the Itch'.[18]

Swift's first Irish pamphlet, written in the slipstream of Anglo-Scottish union and Molyneux's Irish patriot ur-text, is a jolting satirical broadside aimed at correcting the historical record and putting English mismanagement firmly into focus. It does so not only by an acerbic reimagining of the relationship but by appropriating tropes and strategies often used to dismiss the Irish as unworthy of political autonomy on the individual and collective level.

If the *Injured Lady* shows us Swift's capacity for visceral and grotesque imagery to make a political point, his most famous Irish satire, *A Modest Proposal* (1729), written some twenty years later, surpasses it in terms of heightened invective. This bold attack

---

[17] Swift, *PW*, ix. 4.   [18] Swift, *PW*, ix. 3.

on British economic policy towards its Hibernian neighbour is simultaneously appalled by and appalled at the Irish Catholic condition. It outrageously suggests that Irish Catholic children be harvested to feed the country's populace in a breath-taking satire that not only confronts Britain but more generally, undermines Enlightenment trends for improving projects as well as their fetishizing of rationality, measurement, and quantification. Swift also deals with the question of history writing: in *A Modest Proposal* he pokes fun at the claims made about Irish Catholics while perhaps suggesting that historiography, properly conceived, can be an important tool for national self-assertion. He makes a brief but important explicit connection between satire and history:

> But in order to justify my Friend: he confessed, that this Expedient was put into his Head by the famous *Salmanaazor*, a Native of the Island *Formosa*, who came from thence to *London*, above twenty Years ago, and in Conversation told my Friend, that in his Country, when any young person happened to be put to Death, the Executioner sold the Carcase to *Persons of Quality*, as a prime Dainty; and that, in his Time, the Body of a plump Girl of fifteen, who was crucified for an Attempt to poison the Emperor, was sold to his Imperial *Majesty's prime Minister of State*, and other great *Mandarines* of the Court, *in Joints from the Gibbet*, at Four Hundred Crowns.[19]

To unpack the significance of this reference, we must be aware that cannibalism was a habit attributed to the Irish by ancient and medieval historians.[20] Along with incest, bestiality, and a propensity to savage violence, such traits were collective evidence of barbarity and justification for a colonial regime. George Psalmanazar was a notorious impostor whose *An Historical and Geographical Description of Formosa* (1704–5) had been exposed shortly after publication as a fraud. The preface added to the second edition claimed, by way of authenticity, that 'he must be a Man of prodigious parts, who can invent the Description of a Country, contrive a Religion, frame Laws and Customs, make a Language, and Letters &c'.[21] This must have brought a wry smile to the face of the author of *Gulliver's Travels* but it also signalled to the alert reader the connections between historiography and grotesque calumnies on national identity. The satire is polyvalent, a reprimand to the reader who might have been duped at an earlier point in the pamphlet as well as a barb directed at London celebrity publishing fads earlier in the century. The nod to Psalmanazar in *A Modest Proposal* indicates that ideas of national identity as mediated through 'history' need to be carefully scrutinized and that this principle had a particular resonance in the Irish case. Swift was aware of recent historiographical attempts at revisionism with regard to the representation of the Irish. He owned a copy of William Nicolson's *The Irish Historical Library* (1724), a Protestant endorsement of positive Irish representations, and one which debunked what writers such as Strabo had to say as 'imperfect Scraps of Tales, of the barbarous Customs and Manners of the old *Irish*, brought to them from afar; and they drew up the Representation, at full length,

---

[19] Swift, *PW*, xii. 113–14.   [20] Leerssen, *Mere Irish and Fíor Ghael*, 32, 39.

[21] *An Historical and Geographical Description of Formosa*, 2nd edn. (1705), second preface, n.p.

in a more ugly and frightful dress'.[22] Moreover, he was a close friend of Dr Anthony Raymond, noted antiquary, who was engaged in a project to translate Geoffrey Keating's *Foras Feasa ar Éirinn* (c.1634), a strident riposte to centuries of prejudicial accounts of the Irish nation. Keating's indignant preface complains that for centuries British chroniclers of Ireland, 'seem to imitate the Beetle, which … passes over the delightful Fields, neglectful of sweet Blossoms, or fragrant Flowers that are in its way till … it settles itself on some nauseous Excrement'.[23] He continues by listing examples of national traits that have been unfairly transposed onto the Irish character—such as cannibalism, violence, sexual licentiousness—to give the impression of a savage race entirely lacking in culture. Keating's outraged rejection of accounts of Irish cannibalism may have filtered through Swift's mind as he wrote *A Modest Proposal*: Swift was well aware of Raymond's ambitious work and thus it is possible that the reference to Psalmanazar, a scandal by then well over a decade old, may have been connected with Swift's acquaintance with dubious histories through Raymond.

Raymond never published his translation of Keating. Dermod O'Connor assisted for him for a while but eventually—much to Raymond's ire—went to London and published his own translation.[24] *The General History of Ireland* was published by subscription in 1723. The publication of Keating's abrasive narrative in a London translation (perhaps assisted by John Toland) in the wake of the 1720 Declaratory Act signals a more assertive Irish cultural formation in the English capital, one that attracted significant subscribers and readers (subsequent editions were published in 1726, 1732, and 1738). The well-heeled and varied subscriber list, headed by King George and populated by prominent aristocrats, lawyers, soldiers, merchants, archbishops, booksellers, and educators, indicates a growing tolerance for such historical revisionism. Moreover, we also note some names on the list that have particular resonance for Irish patriotism in the eighteenth century—such as Molyneux, Philpot, and O'Conor—that illustrate the links between patriot sentiment and revisionist history.

If historical writings were once the means of impugning the Irish character, later writers understood that harnessing the symbiotic force of history and drama was also the means of redressing it.[25] Keating wrote his history with a specific political purpose of reclaiming Irish history for the Irish and in a way that would unite both the Gaelic Irish with the Old English (i.e. early English Catholic settlers). If history was understood by Keating in the seventeenth century as providing the bedrock for reconciliation and national unity, theatre was a potent cultural forum to build on this groundwork, particularly for writers based in London in the eighteenth century. Such possibilities were

---

[22] William Nicolson, *The Irish Historical Library. Pointing at most of the* Authors *and* Records *in Print or Manuscript, Which may be serviceable to the Compilers Of a General History of Ireland* (Dublin, 1724), 1–2.

[23] Geoffrey Keating, *The General History of Ireland*, trans. Dermod O'Connor (1723), i.

[24] Diarmuid Ó'Catháin, 'Dermot O'Connor, Translator of Keating', *Eighteenth-Century Ireland* 2 (1987), 67–87.

[25] See essays by Bridget Orr and myself in *Ireland, Enlightenment and the English Stage, 1740–1820*, ed. David O'Shaughnessy (Cambridge: Cambridge University Press, 2019).

heightened by the tumultuous effects of the failed 1745 Jacobite rebellion which presented an opportunity that was eagerly grasped by this group.

REBELLION, OPPORTUNITY, AND ENLIGHTENMENT POST-1745

When Scottish troops made it to within 130 miles of London in the autumn of 1745, it was not doom and gloom for all aspects of metropolitan life. 'The Rebellion', as Susannah Cibber wrote to Garrick that September, 'is so far from being a disadvantage to the playhouses that, I assure you, it brings them very good houses'.[26] Cibber was referring to her father-in-law's play *The Non-Juror* (1717), a reworking of Molière's *Tartuffe*, whose depiction of the fiendish Scot Dr Wolf was grist to the mill of contemporary patriotic fervour. Anti-Scottish sentiment was rife, but Scotland's difficulty was also Ireland's opportunity, as Charles Macklin was quick to spot.[27] The rebellion offered Irish writers like Macklin a chance to put the case for Irish civility to English audiences now more perturbed by northern Britons. Charles O'Conor, the major proponent of Irish Catholic Enlightenment of the eighteenth century, is an important enabling figure here. To press the case for civil rights and the repeal of the penal laws, O'Conor understood a shift in the British attitude to Irish culture and history needed to be effected.[28] To that end, he authored *Dissertations on the Ancient History of Ireland* (1748) which acknowledged the influence of Keating while at the same time distancing itself from the fantastical elements of that earlier work. O'Conor was keen to present his book—and by extension, Irish cultural history as a whole—as a model of Enlightenment methodology and civility. Critically, he understood that London was central to the progression of Irish claims for civil rights. In 1757, he wrote to Swift's publisher, George Faulkner, recently returned to Dublin:

> I heartily congratulate with you, dear sir, on your safe arrival in a country to which you have rendered more service than any other public or private writer for several years past. The hints you give and the truths you press are, I think, preferable to essays which fall but into few hands and become profitable in fewer. It was an observation of our patriot Dean (your particular friend) that plans of reformation from <u>without doors</u> were seldom considered <u>within</u>.[29]

---

[26] Cited in *The London Stage 1660–1800: A Calendar of Plays Part III*, ed. Arthur H. Scouten (Carbondale: Southern Illinois Press, 1861), ii. 1187.

[27] David O'Shaughnessy, '"Bit, by some mad whig": Charles Macklin and the Theater of Irish Enlightenment', *Huntington Library Quarterly* 80 (2017), 559–84.

[28] See Luke Gibbons and Kieran O'Conor, eds., *Charles O'Conor of Ballinagare, 1710–91* (Dublin: Four Courts, 2015).

[29] O'Conor to Faulkner, 4 May 1757. *The Letters of Charles O'Conor of Balangare*, 2 vols., ed. Catherine Coogan War and Robert E. Ward (Ann Arbor: Irish American Cultural Institute, 1980), i. 32.

O'Conor's wry wordplay suggests that mixing in London's public sphere had the potential force of parliamentary discussion, at least when compared to trying to effect political change from Ireland. The 'within' of London public opinion was critical to the advance of the Irish Catholic cause. O'Conor used Faulkner to ask Samuel Johnson to write pamphlets for the Irish cause. There is no evidence that Johnson complied but he was certainly sympathetic to O'Conor's aspirations. He wrote to him on 9 April 1757 regarding his recent meeting with Faulkner:

> I have long wished that the Irish Literature were cultivated. Ireland is known by tradition to have been once the seat of piety, and learning; and surely it would be very acceptable to all those who are curious either in the original of nations, or the affinities of Languages, to be further informed of the revolutions of a people so ancient, and once so illustrious.[30]

O'Conor was also motivated by David Hume's graphic depiction of 1641 Irish Catholic violence in his *History of England*, a bugbear he must have thought the Irish had consigned to the bin of history, as he outlined in an open letter to Hume:

> In the picture, for instance, which you give of Ireland, no comely features appear: the deformity of some is exaggerated extremely; others are monstrous, and have nothing like them in the original. Your failure can be easily accounted for: you took your copy from the draughts of others; from men who deemed the suppression of *truth* as necessary to keep their adversaries from rising, as they found the suppression of *justice* necessary to pull them down.[31]

O'Conor's Scottish enmity was compounded by James Macpherson's *Temora* (1763), in which the author laid claim to Scotland being the true 'original' Celtic nation. O'Conor's rebuttal took the form of a revised version of the *Dissertations on the History of Ireland* (1766) which included an extended coda exploding Macpherson's claims. While writing the *Dissertations*, he also made interventions into the London newspapers which were becoming increasingly important to the eighteenth-century public sphere. In one article, echoing the patriot Dean, O'Conor identified the different English treatments of the Irish and the Scots. He also ramped up fears of Scottish violence by reminding his readership of the rebellions of 1708, 1715, and 1745, contrasting those events to the 'quiet and dutiful' behaviour of Irish Catholics, 'perfectly blameless in every respect.'[32] O'Conor was a wily political observer and his scaremongering about Scottish self-interested invaders along with plentiful appeals to English 'liberty' had a particular resonance in

---

[30] *The Letters of Samuel Johnson*, ed. Bruce Redford, 3 vols. (Oxford: Clarendon Press, 1992), i. 152, iii. 23–4.

[31] *The Gentleman's Museum* 1 (April 1763), 56.

[32] *London Chronicle*, 27–30 August 1763. See also O'Conor to John Curry, [15 September 1763]. *Letters of Charles O'Conor*, 157.

1763 and offered Irish activists such as himself an opportunity to align themselves with an indignant English populace.

O'Conor's letter to Hume appeared in the first number of the *Gentleman's Museum*, a short-lived periodical. Nonetheless, the table of contents for this nondescript publication shows the degree to which issues of national identity were to the fore at this moment: there were items relating to *The North Briton* and the new cider tax, both concerns of significant import for the current First Lord of the Treasury, Lord Bute, whose period in office ended in ignominy, also in April 1763, after only eleven months. The Treaty of Paris, which settled the Seven Years War, was finalized in November 1762 and was the death-knell of this Scotsman's political career. Although modern historians hold that the treaty was in fact advantageous to Britain, political opponents were quick to pounce on its perceived shortcomings and link them to Bute's Caledonian roots and his corrupt desire to advance his countrymen's welfare at the expense of the nation. The abuse that Bute received while he was in office and indeed afterwards was scabrous.[33] Chief among those critics were John Wilkes, Charles Churchill, and Charles Macklin.

When Bute took office in May 1762, he initiated a political weekly, *The Briton*, to defend his administration, edited by fellow Scot, Tobias Smollett. One month later, Wilkes established the *North Briton*, an anti-ministerial weekly whose weekly sales were nearly 2000.[34] Horace Walpole commented on its scurrilous tone: 'The *North Briton* proceeded with an acrimony, a spirit, and a licentiousness unheard of before even in this country. The highest names whether of statesmen or magistrates, were printed at length and the insinuations went still higher.'[35] Still, Wilkes escaped prosecution until the infamous Number 45, published 23 April 1763. The story of this seditious libel is well known and need not be rehearsed here. Our interest is in one of the better known associated verse publications written by Wilkes's great friend, Charles Churchill, also a caustic critic of Bute's policies.

The Prophecy of Famine. A Scots Pastoral was published in January 1763 and dedicated to Wilkes. The poem was quickly recognized as one of the most potent and witty attacks on the Bute administration, with a neat conflation of Bute and James II 'STUARTS without end' (115) and a reminder of various Scottish antagonisms on the English, not least of which was the ransoming of Charles I ('Shall we not find, safe in that hallow'd ground, / Such refuge, as the HOLY MARTYR found' [121–2]). Various other examples of Scottish degeneracy can be found including, in an interesting overlap with O'Conor, an attack on Macpherson's *Ossian* poems with the sneering line 'That *old, new Epic Pastoral*, FINGAL' (130). The insinuation being that in Bute's London, Macpherson's hotchpotch of muddled generic miscegenation can 'take, with simple pensions, simple praise' (139). One might also read in these lines an expression of English sympathy to the Irish cultural agenda.

[33] John Brewer, 'The Misfortunes of Lord Bute: A Case-Study in Eighteenth-Century Political Argument and Public Opinion', *Historical Journal* 16 (1973), 3–43.

[34] Peter D. G. Thomas, *John Wilkes: A Friend to Liberty* (Oxford: Oxford University Press, 1996), 20.

[35] Thomas, *Wilkes*, 21.

Around the same time as Churchill was writing, Macklin, an ardent Wilkesite, decided to get in on the act. Perhaps still feeling some vestigial irritation at Smollett's public jeering of him in *Roderick Random* (1748) with regard to the failure of *Henry the VII*, he saw an opportunity to align himself with popular metropolitan English sentiment and he turned to writing satirical comedy.[36] Macklin had already had considerable success with his two-act farce *Love à la Mode* (1759) in which he reworked the suitor scene from *The Merchant of Venice*. In Macklin's version, Charlotte, the wealthy heiress of Sir Theodore Goodchild, is courted by four distinctive types: Mr Mordecai, Squire Groom, Sir Archy Macsarcasm, and Sir Callaghan O'Brallaghan. The Jew, the Englishman, the Scotsman, and the Irishman squabble over the destination of Charlotte's heart (and dowry) with national traits being central to the play's interests. Sir Archy and Sir Callaghan are the principal antagonists with the former determined to ensure the latter reveals himself as a blundering and violent fortune-hunter. Yet it is Sir Archy who reveals himself to be unworthy, his claims of good character undermined by his ignorant sneering at the cosmopolitan richness of London, acclaimed by Defoe and Addison half a century before, in favour of an outdated mind-set:

Why, madam, in Scotland, aw our nobeelity are sprung frai monarchs, warriors, heroes, and glorious achievements; now, here I' the South, ye are aw sprung frai sugar hogshead, rum, puncheons, woolpacks, iron bars, and tar jackets; in short, ye are a composition of Jews, Turks, and refugees, and of aw the commercial vagrants of the land and sea—a sort of amphibious breed ye are.[37]

Moreover, Macklin makes explicit connections to the historiographical dispute between O'Conor and Hume/Macpherson:

Sir Archy: Hut, hut, hut, away, mon, hut awaw, ye mo no say that; what the de'el, consider our fameelies i' th' North: why yee of Ireland, sir, are but a colony frai us, an outcast! a mere outcast, and as such yee remain tull this hoor.

Sir Callaghan: I beg your pardon, Sir Archy, that is the Scotch account, which, you know, never speaks truth, because it is always partial; but the Irish history, which must be the best, because it was written by an Irish poet of my own family, one Shemus Thurlough Shannaghan O'Brallaghan, and, he says, in his chapter of genealogy, that the Scots are all Irishmen's bastards.[38]

On the face of it then, it is unsurprising that Paul Goring reads this play as 'refocusing the gaze' of the audience from the Irish to the Scots. As he documents, local Caledonian reactions to the play were loud and outraged.[39] Nonetheless, this representation of

[36] Tobias Smollett, *The Adventures of Roderick Random*, ed. Paul-Gabriel Boucé (Oxford: Oxford University Press, 1999), 390.

[37] Charles Macklin, *Love à la Mode* (1793), 14–15.   [38] Macklin, *Love à la Mode*, 21.

[39] Paul Goring, '"John Bull, pit, box, and gallery said No!": Charles Macklin and the Limits of Ethnic Resistance on the Eighteenth-Century Stage', *Representations* 79 (2002), 61–81, at 71. See *A Scotsman's Remarks on the Farce of Love a la Mode* (1760).

Macklin as uncritically advocating a 'good Celt/ bad Celt' binary needs further contextualizing as there is no doubt that Macklin was well versed in Enlightenment thought. Equally, even a cursory perusal of his commonplace book indicates that there was a sustained engagement with intellectual ideas of improvement aligned with the composition of his plays. Historical texts formed an important part of his intellectual make-up: we can trace this both in his library and in his brief spell running the 'The British Inquisition' (a salon for sociable public instruction) in the mid-1750s where he lectured on Irish and British history.[40]

Macklin's over-the-top stereotyping, as Michael Ragussis has shown, 'invites the audience to reflect on the very conditions of spectatorship and spectacle that engross it' and thus 'detheatricalizes' the figures.[41] One might then read O'Brallaghan's invocation of his impressively named ancestor (Shemus etc.) as rather tongue-in-cheek on Macklin's part, a gentler satire on the Irish–Scottish debate on national origins and Celtic authenticity and one that speaks of an attitude more open to ideas of improvement than is commonly recognized. O'Brallaghan, after all, does not castigate the Scots throughout, he is equally ready to applaud them when appropriate: 'I dare say [Scottish soldiers at the Battle of Quebec] were not idle, for they are tight fellows. Give me your hand, Sir Archy; I assure you, your countrymen are good soldiers—aye, and so are ours too.'[42]

This paean to Scottish and Irish bravery is an expression of Celtic solidarity that serves to underscore O'Brallaghan's immediately preceding eulogy to the death of General Wolfe. It is a moment in the play that looks to the material and historical truths of the three nations' shared experiences and interests, one that demands that the audience look beyond the highly theatricalized representations of national identity and the hotly-tempered historiographical exchanges. The pressures and tensions of the actual war force their way onto the stage to bring a moment of uneasy sobriety that exposes the shallow artifice of stage stereotypes. This is satire as, in Dustin Griffin's terms, a tool for the public display of improvement; moreover, just as he had done with *Henry the VII*, it was a chance for Macklin to demonstrate publicly his value to the city. Macklin's shift from historical tragedy to satirizing history marks his own intellectual development and increasing assuredness.

History was not only an important strand in the plot of *Love à la Mode*. It also features in Macklin's later play, *The Man of the World*, initially composed around 1762 during the dying throes of the Bute premiership. In this play, the tyrannical and corrupt Pertinax MacSycophant, the Scottish anti-hero, has disinherited his eldest son for daring to prefer English historians over those of Scotland, making clear the narrowness and self-interested nature of his interests. This later play develops many of the ideas of *Love à la Mode*, with Egerton, the eponymous man of the world, representing an idealized political future that rejects the venal parochial politics of his father.

[40] Macklin's history books included O'Conor's *Dissertations on the History of Ireland*, 2nd edn. (1766). See also his lecture notes on 'Hanoverian Kings' in Folger MS. Y.d.515.

[41] Michael Ragussis, 'Jews and Other "Outlandish Englishmen": Ethnic Performance and the Invention of British Identity under the Georges', *Critical Inquiry* 26 (2000), 773–97, at 780.

[42] Macklin, *Love à la Mode*, 19.

Macklin's satire is dualistic in nature: it critiques the local and immediate in order to gesture towards a progressive future. His O'Brallaghan not only demonstrates his own civility by refusing to satisfy traditional expectations of the Stage Irishman (he is brave, honourable, and verbally dexterous) but is also able to move beyond the standard Irish–Scottish enmity and look to the future. Charles Knight has argued that, while satire's mockery of other nations celebrates one's own nation, it simultaneously evaluates the validity of the nationalist claims being made and thus 'calls the project of nationalism into question'.[43] Macklin not only understood this doubleness, he embraced it as part of his Enlightenment self-fashioning. *The Man of the World* is scathing in its critique of the corruption of the Bute administration but the Scottish character of Egerton is a generous gesture by Macklin, one that reaches out to the Celtic other: this is a play written by a very public Irishman with a Scottish hero for an English audience, one that seeks to imagine a political arrangement that accommodates all based on Whiggish ideas of liberty. Macklin's confident deployment of satire enables him to move beyond his 'celebrity' status, built around images and ideas of him as a 'wild Irishman', to become a respectable Enlightened figure in the 1780s and 1790s, the spirit of which is captured in John Opie's portrait of him now held at the National Portrait Gallery.[44]

PARLIAMENT AND THE THEATRE
OF PATRIOT POLITICS AFTER 1782

Macklin's success and general popularity in the 1760s and after was matched, if not eclipsed, by other prominent Irish figures in the British capital's public sphere: Edmund Burke, Oliver Goldsmith, Hugh Kelly, and Arthur Murphy are some of the other figures whose merits were remarked widely. We might also note that fully a third of the original nine members of Johnson's Club, a crucible of English Enlightenment culture founded in 1764, were Irish: Burke, Goldsmith, and Christopher Nugent. Claims of Irish barbarity and incivility became more difficult to sustain in the light of their stature within political and cultural circles. These mid-century figures cleared the way for a new generation of Irish dramatists that shared their predecessors' patriot sentiment but might also be thought of operating with a degree of confidence in the wake of Irish parliamentary independence that demanded new satiric possibilities.

Perhaps the best known indication that a new imagining of the Stage Irishman was expected by London audiences by the 1770s was Sheridan's Sir Lucius O'Trigger in *The Rivals* (1775). The reviewer for the *Morning Chronicle* (18 January 1775) condemned what he saw as the anachronistic satire on the Irish that was 'so far from giving the manners of our brave and worthy neighbours'. Implicit in this critique is the recognition of the new

---

[43] Charles Knight, *The Literature of Satire* (Cambridge: Cambridge University Press, 2004), 59.

[44] On Macklin's dangerous celebrity, see Emily Anderson, 'Celebrity Shylock', *PMLA* 126 (2011), 935–49.

understanding of the importance of the Irish to British military endeavours, soon to be demonstrated again with the American War of Independence. Sir Brallaghan O'Callaghan and other 'reformed' Stage Irishmen, notably Richard Cumberland's Major O'Flaherty (*The West Indian*, 1771), had set the stage for an Irishman who was capable, resourceful, and attuned to the demands of shoring up Britain's commercial, cultural, and political primacy. The concession made by British audiences was a general accept-ance of Irish civility as well as a recognition that loyalty to Britain and Irish patriotism could coexist. Such recognition was important in the wake of the Volunteer movement and the associated agitation on trade rights and political autonomy. These factors coalesced to produce a more confident, more purposeful, and more collectively driven Irish cultural diaspora than had previously been the case. In such an environment, satire softened with the battle for cultural supremacy with the Scots largely won—at least on stage—and the case for Irish civility made.

The 1780s were perhaps the high water mark of Irish theatrical authority in eighteenth-century Britain. Playwrights, patriotic and politicized, were keen to seize the moment and assure their British audiences of the bona fides of their political intentions. Moreover, the advent of the 1782 parliament meant that an environment of confidence pervaded among migrant networks in London, as testified by the foundation of the Benevolent Society of St Patrick in 1783, a key site for Irish patriot networking and frequented by a number of important playwrights such as John O'Keeffe, Leonard MacNally, Dennis O'Bryen, and (probably) Frederick Pilon.[45]

For these playwrights, satire became more diffuse, gentler, and less frantic than the spleen of Swift or the indignation of Macklin. We have in these writers a more concili-atory tone appropriate for Irish patriots who had won considerable concessions, albeit anxious for more as issues relating to Irish trade refused to go away. In O'Keeffe's *The Poor Soldier* (1782), for instance, Pat returns home from the American wars to discover his love Norah is being courted by the English officer Fitzroy. When Fitzroy discovers that Pat saved his life at the Battle of Beattie's Ford (1781), he nobly relinquishes his pur-suit of Norah, in a public demonstration of the complementarity of English and Irish honour, now brothers-in-arms. Leonard MacNally followed his attempt to cast the Volunteer movement in the Whig tradition with theatrical productions that displayed his admiration of cultural artefacts that were unabashedly English in *Robin Hood, or, Sherwood Forest* (1784) and *Richard Coeur de Lion* (1786). Dennis O'Bryen's *A Friend in Need is a Friend Indeed* (1783) explored the nature of friendship and its demands in a new commercial reality in a reworking of Goldsmith's *The Good Natur'd Man* (1768). O'Bryen's play was also instrumental in securing his place alongside Fox in the 1780s and 1790s.[46] Frederick Pilon won a reputation for the rapid production of plays that

---

[45] See Craig Bailey, 'Innovation to Emulation: London's Benevolent Society of St Patrick, 1783–1800', *Eighteenth-Century Ireland* 27 (2012), 162–84 and David O'Shaughnessy, '"rip'ning buds in Freedom's field": Staging Irish Improvement in the 1780s', *Journal of Eighteenth-Century Studies* 38 (2015), 541–54.

[46] David O'Shaughnessy, 'Making a Play for Patronage: Dennis O'Bryen's *A Friend in Need is a Friend Indeed* (1783)', *Eighteenth-Century Life* 39 (2015), 183–211.

functioned as a pointed political critique.[47] In many of these dramatists' productions, satire is still present but it is gentler, less abrasive, and mitigated by the demands of both 'laughing' and sentimental comedy as well as farce.

The close of the century was shaped by the disruptive force of the French Revolution. Questions of national identity had increased force as the English–French binary became more entrenched through conservative propaganda. Ireland's loyalties came under renewed scrutiny as fears of invasion caused England to peer nervously over its shoulder at its other Catholic neighbour. Stage Irishmen from this period continue to appear but, generally speaking, as more docile creatures and with less interesting characterization. Censorship of the theatre had a part to play in this but Irish playwrights seemed to have been muted, certainly relative to the richness of the preceding decade. The 1798 rebellion, the 1803 rising, major disturbances in 1806–16 in Munster and 1819–23 in the south and west of Ireland had a seismic effect on Anglo-Irish relations: one recent account suggests that the early nineteenth century in Ireland might be considered a 'single, gigantic, "theatre of disorder"'.[48] Satire of national identity continues as Maria Edgeworth's *Castle Rackrent* (1800) and Thomas Moore's *Captain Rock* (1824) testify, with these novels specifically linked to the troubles of the early nineteenth century. For the theatre, however, there seems to be a change of tone. The tragedies of Richard Lalor Sheil, Charles Maturin, and James Sheridan Knowles, staged successfully in London, collectively hint that the re-emergence of the tropes relating to Irish national identity of 1641 after 1798 had dampened the satiric spirit considerably and that history was indeed repeating itself as tragedy, not comedy.[49]

SELECT BIBLIOGRAPHY

Bailey, Craig. *Irish London: Middle-Class Migration in the Global Eighteenth Century* (Liverpool: Liverpool University Press, 2013).

Brown, Michael. *The Irish Enlightenment* (Cambridge, MA: Harvard University Press, 2016).

Burke, Helen. 'The Irish Joke, Migrant Networks, and the London Irish in the 1680s', *Eighteenth-Century Life* 39 (2015), 41–65.

Gibbons, Luke and Kieran O'Conor, eds. *Charles O'Conor of Ballinagare, 1710-91* (Dublin: Four Courts, 2015).

Hayton, David. 'From Barbarian to Burlesque: English Images of the Irish c.1660–1750', *Irish Economic and Social History* 15 (1988), 5–31.

Leerssen, Joep. *Mere Irish and Fíor Ghael: Studies in the Idea of Irish Nationality, its Development and Literary Expression Prior to the Nineteenth Century* (Cork: Cork University Press and Field Day, 1986).

---

[47] 'Every writer for the stage, who takes advantage of temporary incidents, and raises a laugh at living folly, deserves commendation and encouragement. No modern dramatist falls under this description more immediately than Mr. Pilon.' *Morning Chronicle and London Advertiser* (24 April 1779).

[48] Thomas Bartlett, *Ireland: A History* (Cambridge: Cambridge University Press, 2010), 246.

[49] See Claire Connolly, 'Theatre and Nation in Irish Romanticism: The Tragic Dramas of Charles Robert Maturin and Richard Lalor Sheil', *Éire-Ireland* 41 (2006), 185–214.

O'Halloran, Clare. *Golden Ages and Barbarous Nations: Antiquarian Debate and Cultural Politics in Ireland, c.1750–1800* (Cork: Cork University Press and Field Day, 2004).

O'Shaughnessy, David, ed. *Ireland, Enlightenment and the English Stage, 1740–1820* (Cambridge: Cambridge University Press, 2019).

Ragussis, Michael. *Theatrical Nation Jews and Other Outlandish Englishmen in Georgian Britain* (Philadelphia: University of Pennsylvania Press, 2010).

CHAPTER 7

···

BANTER, NONSENSE, AND IRONY

Churchill and his Circle

···

ADAM ROUNCE

THE writings of Charles Churchill, his friend Robert Lloyd, and other figures who, in the 1760s, were often referred to as the 'Nonsense Club', occupy a somewhat ambivalent place in the eighteenth-century satirical landscape.[1] These authors were not united by the polemic certainty of railing against established ills and social or political evils, though Churchill became during his brief career (1761–4) a crucial part of the oppositional circle of John Wilkes's *North Briton*, and directed much of his ire against the Bute administration. The other members of the Club—Lloyd, George Colman, Bonnell Thornton, and occasionally William Cowper—often fall into a peculiarly self-conscious satiric mode, with a nonchalant awareness of the writer's ultimate lack of effect. This results in an odd mix of outspoken critique, bracing satiric barbs, and less directly antagonistic writing, including almost affectionate parody, and incidental, ad hoc considerations of the purpose of writing itself.

The 'Nonsense Club' and its relations thus promote a particular sort of satire, in which the dominant register is irreverence—hence repeated uses of pastiche, parody, burlesque, and travesty—and a refusal to take itself too seriously. This has led to a rather complicated place in literary and poetic history for these satirists of the 1760s, where they are noteworthy for coming after the satires of Pope and before later figures (notably Byron), but also marked out early in their reception for not achieving the sort of critical legacy or reputation of their forebears or descendants. Those searching for models for the manner of self-conscious ineffectuality displayed by these writers will find them

---

[1] On membership of the club see Lance Bertelsen, *The Nonsense Club: Literature and Popular Culture, 1749–1764* (Oxford: Clarendon Press, 1986), 3–6; although the name 'refers historically to a group of Old Westminster and London Wits who met regularly every Thursday evening during the late 1750s and early 1760s', the use of it in the present essay is as 'a convenient title for the literary association of Thornton, Colman, Lloyd, Churchill, and Cowper' (2).

contemporaneous with the onset of Shandyism, and the beginnings of Laurence Sterne's pervasive influence on a certain area of British literary culture: Churchill, for example, adopted a Shandean pose in his longest, least cohesive poem, *The Ghost* (1762–3), attracted by the authorial possibility of the claimed impossibility of establishing or defining a subject. An earlier precedent, not for defining Churchill's far more aggressive public persona but in its open avowal of its possible pointlessness, is Colley Cibber's *Apology* (1740), an autobiography that enlightens both writer and reader through its recreation of the history of the self. Cibber's confidence in his material is expressed in an unusual way: 'But why make my Follies publick? Why not? I have pass'd my Time very pleasantly with them, and I don't recollect that they have ever been hurtful to any other Man living. Even admitting they were injudiciously chosen, would it not be Vanity in me to take Shame to myself for not being found a Wise Man?'[2] Cibber defends his more foolish or whimsical tendencies as innocent and harmless, and refuses to take himself seriously, or to pretend to an intellectual capital he neither possesses nor desires. This would be one model (along with Shandyism) for the somewhat studied bohemianism of Churchill and Lloyd. However, the warm and ingenuous aspects of Cibber's autobiography (his admitting that he may be foolish and boring at times but at least he is aware of it) do not filter down to the writers of the other Nonsense Club, who are more likely to point up the folly and tedium of the works of others.

THE NONSENSE CLUB

The productions of the Nonsense Club, broadly defined, begin with Thornton's contributions at Oxford to *The Student* from 1749, proceed through various journals, pamphlets, and poetic appearances, and extend until the deaths of Churchill and Lloyd in 1764. Given such a variety of materials, the present account offers a survey of the Club's *poetic* satire: its attitude towards contemporary poetry, most notable in satires and burlesques; the small but clear originality in the work of Lloyd; and the satire of Churchill, the most immediately consequential poet to emerge from the group.[3]

Thornton's earliest poetic burlesque was his *Ode on St Cecilia's Day*, written in 1749 and revived and performed at Ranelagh House in June 1763. This performance added an aural dimension to its original parodic intent, which was a mainstay of London musical culture: St Cecilia's Day had brought forth odes to the patron saint of music every 22 November from 1683, and Dryden's two most famous examples, *A Song for St Cecilia's Day* (1687) and *Alexander's Feast* (1697), had epitomized the perceived effects of music through poetry. They establish a sort of mimesis that took the abstract qualities of sound

---

[2] Colley Cibber, *An Apology for the Life of Mr Colley Cibber, Comedian, and Late Patentee of the Theatre-Royal* (1740), 2.

[3] As well as *The Connoisseur*, which ran to 140 numbers (1754–6), there is also the long-running *St James Chronicle* (1761–1815), and the shorter spin-off *St James Magazine*, edited by Lloyd from 1762–4. See Bertelsen, *Nonsense Club*, 32–61, 136–40.

and refracted them through the most sophisticated type of versification. Such poems, even apart from their musical settings, utilized the irregular Pindaric ode, where the varied line lengths and stresses were designed to reflect the harmonic relationship between poetry and sound, and to illustrate the action. As Dryden's verse asked in 1687: 'What Passion cannot MUSICK raise and quell!' Even at the most final of judgements, '*The Dead shall live, the living die, / And* MUSICK *shall untune the Sky*.' Given such apostrophes, the role of the poet is suitably paramount; the archetypal poet and musician (such as King David or St Cecilia) does not merely please an audience and enliven a tedious hour, but changes the appearance of reality itself:

> *Orpheus* could lead the savage race;
> And Trees unrooted left their place;
>   Sequacious of the lyre:
> But bright *CECILIA* rais'd the wonder high'r;
>   When to her Organ, vocal Breath was giv'n,
> An Angel heard, and straight appear'd
>   Mistaking Earth for Heaven.[4]

Even the smoothness of the pagan Orphic lyre cannot compete with the devout sounds of the titular saint.

Thornton's performance was intended to produce a very different harmonic range, and his burlesque irreverence extends to his original preface (1749), by one Fustian Sackbut, that claims his poem is 'far superior to the Odes of *Johnny Dryden*, *Jemmy Addison*, *Sawney Pope*, *Nick Rowe*, little *Kit Smart*, &c. &c. &c. or of any that *have* written or *shall* write on SAINT CAECILIA's DAY'. He also makes clear that 'I have strictly adhered to the Rule of making the Sound echo to the Sense', itself a mocking echo of Pope's famous comments on mimesis in *An Essay on Criticism*.[5]

Instead of harps, lyres, organs, or the purity of the human voice, Thornton's subtitle informs the reader that his ode was written for *the Salt-Box, the Jews Harp, the Marrow-Bones and Cleavers, the Hum Strum or Hurdy-Gurdy*, that is, for instruments associated with low rather than high culture. The result is bathos:

> With magic sounds, like these, did Orpheus' lyre
> Motion, sense, and life inspire;
> When, as he play'd, the list'ning flood
> Still'd its loquacious waves, and silent stood;
> The trees swift-bounding danc'd with loosen'd stumps
> And sluggish stones caper'd in active jumps.

Dryden's circumlocution of 'Sequacious' leads to the equally windy but more literal 'loquacious', the trees pull up their stumps for enthusiastic dancing, and the ludicrous

---

[4] John Dryden, *A Song for St Cecilia's Day*, in *The Works of John Dryden*, ed. H. T. Swedenberg, Jr, et al., 20 vols. (Berkeley and Los Angeles: University of California Press, 1956–2000), iii. 201, 203.

[5] Bonnell Thornton, *An Ode on Saint Caecilia's Day, Adapted to the Antient British Musick* (1749), vi.

capering of the stones comes with its own redundancy—what jump is not 'active'? The basic technique is the clashing result of heightened and sublime intentions with earthier materials: 'The croaking frogs / The grunting hogs / All, all conspir'd to raise th' enliv'ning sound'.[6]

What the ode signifies, other than an entertaining travesty of a particular artistic strain, is the limitation of the powers that serious odes proclaim and celebrate. In most Nonsense Club productions, poetry and writing makes nothing happen, and it is the naïve ambitions of those who think otherwise that are most often ridiculed, albeit gently.

In similar vein are the two mock odes to 'Obscurity' and 'Oblivion' of 1760, usually attributed to Robert Lloyd and George Colman. These lampoon the fashionable poetry of sensibility and the sublime, associated with William Mason and Thomas Gray, and epitomized in the latter's two Pindaric odes of 1757, *The Progress of Poesy* and *The Bard* (the particular butts of the ode to 'Oblivion').[7] To their admirers, these were the greatest lyric poems in English, but their detractors saw only a pretentious over-complication of language, and deliberate difficulty to no end—the trappings of a sublime style, but with no substance. As Samuel Johnson would later put it, to the annoyance of generations of Gray's supporters: 'These odes are marked by glittering accumulations of ungraceful ornaments: they strike, rather than please; the images are magnified by affectation; the language is laboured into harshness'.[8] Colman and Lloyd write in more jocular style, but draw a similar conclusion. In the opening of *The Progress of Poesy*, the celebration of the 'Headlong, impetuous' power of sound leads to Mars laying down his arms:

> On Thracia's hills the Lord of War,
> Has curb'd the fury of his car,
> And dropp'd his thirsty lance at thy command.

In 'Ode: to Obscurity', the personage is more contemporary:

> The shallow Fop in antick vest,
> Tir'd of the beaten road,
> Proud to be singularly drest,
> Changes, with every changing moon, the mode.
> Say, shall not then the heav'n-born Muses too
> Variety pursue?
> Shall not applauding Criticks hail the vogue?
> Whether the Muse the stile of Cambria's sons,
> Or the rude gabble of the Huns,

---

[6] Thornton, *Ode on Saint Caecilia's Day*, 10, 11.

[7] The joint authorship was suggested by Southey: 'At those [Nonsense Club] meetings there can be little doubt that the two odes to Obscurity and Oblivion originated, joint compositions of Lloyd and Colman, in ridicule of Gray and Mason.' *The Works of William Cowper*, ed. Robert Southey, 15 vols. (1835–7), i. 50. Gray attributed them to Colman alone (see n. 11).

[8] 'Life of Gray', in *The Lives of the Poets*, ed. Roger Lonsdale, 4 vols. (Oxford: Clarendon Press, 2006), iv. 183.

> Or the broader dialect
> Of Caledonia she affect,
> Or take, Hibernia, thy still ranker brogue?[9]

This is broad-brush satire, mocking the modishness of art that is contemporary for its own sake, and the 'applauding' critical reflex that acclaims it for such novelty, whatever its absurdities or shortcomings; 'variety' here is both linguistic and metrical, and the pursuit of both (such as Gray's seeking inspiration in Welsh, Scottish, Irish, or older German) is presented as artistic tokenism, rather than imaginative or scholarly insight. Gray's exploration of his own poetic efficacy at the poem's end, his self-conscious awareness of his being 'beneath' Milton, Dryden, and Shakespeare, is parodied more directly, albeit a little clumsily:

> Yet shall he mount, and keep his distant way
> Beyond the limits of a vulgar fate,
> Beneath the good how far—but far above the great.
> Yet shall he mount, with classick housings grac'd,
> And, all unheedful of the Critick Mock,
> Drive his light Courser o'er the bounds of Taste.[10]

The mockery in these poems is not particularly acerbic or contemptuous: Gray, the archetypal modern bard, is taken in by fashionable delusions, rather than incompetence; the poet himself, who could be defensive in the extreme about his writing, did not, apparently, mind their satire and seems (wisely) not to have taken such lampoons especially seriously.[11]

The tendency towards satire of other poets, contemporary and otherwise, runs through Robert Lloyd's brief poetic career, and is concomitant with an implicit Popean defence of true taste against modern misjudgements and fashionable mistakes. In 'The Cit's Country Box', the octosyllabics gently mock the pretensions of a nouveau-riche merchant who has moved to what would now be seen as suburban London, in a sort of *Epistle to Burlington* in miniature. His wife wants the house surrounded by Chinese rails, rather than walls and trees, so that passers-by will 'Cry, that's Sir Thrifty's Country Seat'.

> No doubt her arguments prevail,
> For Madam's TASTE can never fail.
> Blest age! when all men may procure,

---

[9] *The Poems of Gray, Collins and Goldsmith*, ed. Roger Lonsdale (London: Longman, 1969), 164. *The Poetical Works of Robert Lloyd*, ed. William Kenrick, 2 vols. (1774), i. 121.

[10] *Poems of Gray*, 177; Lloyd, *Poetical Works*, i. 127.

[11] Thinking the Odes the work of Colman, Gray wrote to Mason in June 1760 that 'he makes very tolerable fun with me, where I understand him (wch is not every where) but seems more angry with you'. A month later, he told his friend Thomas Wharton that 'there was a Satyr printed against me & Mason jointly', but 'I believe his Odes sell no more than mine did, for I saw a heap of them lie in a bookseller's window, who recommended them to me as a very pretty thing.' *The Correspondence of Thomas Gray*, ed. I. P. Toynbee and Leonard Whibley, 3 vols. (Oxford: Clarendon Press, 1935), i. 675, 681.

> The title of a Connoisseur;
> When noble and ignoble herd,
> Are govern'd by a single word.[12]

His wife's wishes are fulfilled, and the result pleases everybody:

> The villa thus completely graced,
> All own, that Thrifty has a Taste;
> And Madam's female friends, and cousins,
> With common-council-men, by dozens,
> Flock ev'ry Sunday to the Seat,
> To stare about them, and to eat.[13]

The elements that make this an early example of metropolitan snobbery should be balanced by the equality of Lloyd's satire—both nobles and commoners are herd-like in their blind adherence to foolish trends. A common thread in his writing is how such obedience to trends and rules produces false taste and inauthentic art. In 'On Rhyme' (1762), a 'progress' poem on the debate between blank verse and rhyme, Milton and Dryden, the pre-eminent examples in each field, are contrasted with less spontaneously gifted or talented authors:

> My Lord, who lives and writes at ease,
> (Sure to be pleas'd, as sure to please)
> And draws from silver-stand his pen,
> To scribble sonnets *now* and *then*;
> Who writes not what he truly feels,
> But rather what he slily steals,
> And patches up, in courtly phrase,
> The manly sense of better days.[14]

Lloyd has an acute sense of the way that such writing was vitiated by its lack of any worthwhile need, and produced merely as if by rote (something a gentleman did); this extends to the choice of sonnet—an archaic form for 1762—and exactly what an artificial, inauthentic poem (a patchwork of other sources and ideas) would use.

Lloyd also extended his satire to more directly political ends, writing, like his friend Churchill, for the anti-government cause of John Wilkes. *The Poetry Professors* (October 1762) was occasionally misattributed to Churchill in the later eighteenth century, and it is easy to see why. It is a vigorous attack upon the fulsome volumes produced by universities in celebration of the birth in April of the Prince of Wales. This ridicule turns into a screed against the ministry of the Earl of Bute and the Scottish cronyism and nepotism that his regime supposedly instigated (the obsession of Wilkes and his friends

---

[12] Lloyd, *Poetical Works*, i. 44.   [13] Lloyd, *Poetical Works*, i. 44, 46.
[14] Lloyd, *Poetical Works*, ii. 106.

and followers). The ostensible target is poetic affectation and the fashion for obscurity, with influences represented as the modern equivalents of Apollo's Pegasus:

> Greek, *Roman*, nay *Arabian* steeds,
> Or those our mother country breeds;
> Some ride ye *in*, and ride ye *out*,
> And to come *home* go round *about*,
> Nor on the green swerd, nor the road,
> And that I think they call an ODE.
> Some take the pleasant country air,
> And smack their whips and drive a pair,
> Each horse with bells which clink and chime,
> And so *they* march—and that is *rhime*.[15]

Lloyd has a facility for describing mediocrity, with the abrupt caesura of the last line making the monotony of most couplets as apparent as the redundant circumlocution of most modern odes, riding in and out to no purpose. It also helps that his own jaunty octosyllabics (his most characteristic poetic mode) evince an informality and irreverence that removes any danger of pretension. His more vitriolic criticism of Scotland seems somewhat incongruous, and has also suffered from comparison with his friend Churchill, whose work was more thoroughly contemptuous. When Lloyd attacks Bute's followers, he takes on Churchill's theme, but lacks his friend's conviction:

> MACPHERSON leads the flaming van,
> LAIRD of the *new* Fingalian clan;
> While JACKY HOME brings up the rear,
> With new-got pension neat and clear
> Three hundred English pounds a year.
> While sister PEG, our ancient *Friend*,
> Sends MAC's and DONLD's without end.
>
> (*Poetical Works*, i. 39)

This mockery of Scottish cultural beneficiaries of the present regime (such as John 'Douglas' Home and James 'Ossian' Macpherson) seems to follow Churchill's more well-known, vitriolic, and successful demolition of Bute and his cultural myrmidons, *The Prophecy of Famine* (January 1763), but it actually predates it by three months.[16] As both satires share phrases and were published in the *North Briton*, it is more profitable to view them as variations on the same satiric ethos than competing writings on the same

---

[15] Lloyd, *Poetical Works*, i. 32.

[16] 'The Poetry Professors' appeared in the first issue of the *St James Magazine* (November 1762), 214–20, and was also printed in two parts in the *North Briton*, 22 (30 October) and 26 (27 November 1762). Macpherson repeatedly flattered Bute as a supporter of Ossian. See Leith Davis, *Acts of Union: Scotland and the Literary Negotiation of the British Nation* (Stanford: Stanford University Press, 1998), 81; for John Home, see Adam Rounce, '"Stuarts without End": Wilkes, Churchill, and Anti-Scottishness', *Eighteenth-Century Life* 29 (2005), 20–43 at 28.

theme, yet with one difference: Lloyd is slightly less sure-footed and convincing when he moves to pure contempt, whereas Churchill's poetry fits quite happily into such a mode.

Lloyd's repeated attacks on false taste and the laboured artifice of modish, superficial writing, and his opposing praise of an aesthetic of spontaneity and directness, also connects him and the Nonsense Club's satiric ethos to the more widely-read satires of his friend, Churchill. The mutual sympathy of the two can be seen in their shared themes: both would write poems influenced by the theatrical world, though Lloyd's *The Actor* (1760) would not prove as successful as Churchill's *Rosciad* (1761). Lloyd offers what is in many ways an acting manual, as well as an engaging survey of what is desirable and what offends in the contemporary theatre, with Garrick (supported by Lloyd and—at least initially—Churchill in the internecine theatrical battles of the decade) as exemplum of 'nature' on stage, but he is not specific in blame: faults (tragedy turning to bathos, over-playing jokes, diction that is monotonous or over-affected) are listed, but not made personal. Churchill, on the other hand, used *The Rosciad* as a trove of individual, often spiteful, theatrical gossip, a subject that attracted and continued to engage all of polite society; this made it in turn easy for him to revise and enlarge it, repeatedly (hence its nine editions to 1765).[17] Not atypical is the following portrait of one John Jackson, an addition to the seventh edition of 1763:

> Next J[]ks[]n came—Observe that settled glare,
> Which better speaks a Puppet than a Play'r;
> List to that voice—did ever DISCORD hear
> Sounds so well fitted to her untun'd ear? [...]
> He sobs and pants to sooth his weeping spouse,
> To sooth his weeping mother, turns and bows.
> Awkward, embarrass'd, stiff, without the skill
> Of moving gracefully, or standing still,
> One leg, as if suspicious of his brother,
> Desirous seems to run away from t'other.[18]

The cumulative effect of these mocking descriptions is of a dislocated and discordant performance, where even Jackson's limbs seem to want to leave him. Jackson would go on to be a theatre manager and tragedian in Edinburgh, and tour the provinces on occasion. An indignant author wrote an interlude for Jackson, specifically to challenge Churchill's 'illiberal and ungenerous, I had almost said inhumane' attempt 'to ruin a young actor, who in the amiableness of a private character, has scarce a superior, and in a public one, has been at least very favourably received'. The interlude's characters discuss how in contemporary irreligious London, 'a parson'

---

[17] For the theatrical wars of the 1760s and the *Rosciad* see Joseph M. Beatty, 'The Battle of the Players and Poets, 1761–1766', *Modern Language Notes* 34 (1919), 449–62, and G. W. Stone and G. M. Kahrl, *David Garrick: A Critical Biography* (Carbondale: Southern Illinois University Press, 1979), 149–55.

[18] Charles Churchill, *The Poetical Works of Charles Churchill*, ed. Douglas Grant (Oxford: Clarendon Press, 1956), 13.

> Will throw off his cassock to talk about plays;
> *And dwell with an air most importantly big,*
> *On the point of a ruffle, or tie of a wig—*

Churchill's appearance is then described, focusing on his 'most monstrous overgrown head' and his face, 'a lion-like knocker screwed on at a door'. There is no reason to be afraid, though, as 'I met him half drunk in the park about three', and he'll now be 'sous'd on the bed'.[19] Such indignance aside, many of Churchill's ungenerous judgements in the *Rosciad* were based on a keen awareness and observation of the theatrical scene. The *Theatrical Review* has this to say about Jackson's debut: 'he was a little deficient in the graceful ease, which, possessed, would render his person the most elegant in the theatre', though he may 'attain this by a due attention to the polite accomplishments'. But 'his voice was so exceedingly weak', that 'we fear it will not a little impede his progress to eminence on the stage'. Moreover, 'now and then his punctuation was tinctured with something of the provincial'. In general, the theatrical audience were used to actors enjoying their celebrity, and some ridicule seemed a small price for them to pay. As Peter Briggs suggested: 'The public rather enjoyed the fun. The actors, for so long a time, had used their privilege of caricaturing prominent people upon the stage, that the whole town was glad to see the tables turned.'[20]

CHURCHILL

It is something of a commonplace to view Churchill as both the most significant British poetic satirist between Pope and Byron, and as an unfulfilled talent, a figure who misdirected his energies. Usually, this qualified achievement is attributed to related factors: Churchill's chaotic bohemian life ended in 1765, when he was only thirty-four, and his creative impetus for the majority of this career—after the enormous success of *The Rosciad* in 1761—was the friendship of Wilkes and the attendant campaign against Bute, making Churchill's poetry a sort of extension of the *North Briton* and a mouthpiece for opposition propaganda. Almost all critical accounts of Churchill before the twentieth century stress this as a narrowing of his talents and an artistic limitation. Writing in the 1830s, Robert Southey represented the views of many when he described how '[n]o English poet had ever enjoyed so excessive and so short-lived a popularity', but 'Popularity which is so easily gained is lost as easily'.[21] The subjects of his poetry were of diminishing interest to future generations and, rather than preserving their fame, Churchill's work became forgotten. For Southey, Churchill wrote and published so quickly that it was inevitable that his poetic reputation would also consume itself.

---

[19] *The Sailor's and Soldier's Return*, in *The Theatrical Review, or Annals of the Drama* (June 1763), 217, 222.
[20] Beatty, 'The Battle', 453.   [21] Southey, *Life and Works of Cowper*, i. 83–4.

Churchill described, repeatedly, how little attention he paid to his composition, and how it would be 'a sin 'gainst Pleasure, to design / A plan, to methodize each thought, each line / Highly to finish'. This is somewhat disingenuous and part of an attractively bohemian persona that, as Bertelsen says, 'had always to write at full speed without a plan' to seem authentic. As he concludes: 'Much of this is humorous exaggeration.'[22] A variant on the modesty topos, Churchill's repeated claims for his relative poetic incompetence, his lack of qualification to be writing down the supposed crimes of Bute, Lord Mansfield and others, are a backhanded way of creating conviction in his readers—we can trust the man without sophistication as he has no designs upon us. Yet these expressions of his lack of skill and craft are obviously crafted, to say the least. A flyting on all things Scottish, *The Prophecy of Famine* forms an opposition between spontaneity and lack of guile, and the affectation of contemporary verse in hock to Bute's patronage:

> *Me*, whom no Muse of heav'nly birth inspires,
> No judgment tempers when rash genius fires,
> Who boast no merit but mere knack of rhime,
> Short gleams of sense, and satire out of time,
> Who cannot follow where *trim* fancy leads
> By *prattling* streams o'er *flow'r-empurpled* meads.[23]

Those who can turn their hands to such poetry are, by implication, either lost within stylistic affectation, or doing it for money. This parody of the poetry of enthusiasm and sensibility is so finely tuned as to make it a source of surprise that the legend of Churchill—the careless, slovenly writer dashing off his verses—acquired such dominance. Yet it was a useful myth, as Churchill's satire works through an unusual sort of indirection, where the level of public falsehood and corruption is almost accidentally discovered by a poetic persona that has no claims upon, or interest in, public or private virtue. This is even true of his most rambling, Shandean poem: *The Ghost.*

The poem purports to be a retelling of the notorious 'Cock Lane Ghost' affair of 1762, which became a nine-day wonder: in brief, it concerned the efforts of one Richard Parsons to attack the character of a bad debtor and ex-lodger of his, William Kent, by the imposture of the ghost of Kent's dead wife, speaking through Parsons's daughter, and claiming that Kent had poisoned her. This ingenious slander was soon revealed for a fake (though doubts lingered on), but not before it had caught the imagination of the public.[24] It was an ideal vehicle for some of the staple invectives of Churchill's satire: attacks on credulous people who should know better, supposedly fine minds being made to look foolish, and a central metaphor, in the insubstantiality of 'the ghost' itself, that he could turn into a larger indictment of contemporary society. The poem's lack of

---

[22] From *Gotham*, Book II, in Churchill, *Poetical Works*, 313; Bertelsen, *Nonsense Club*, 112.

[23] Churchill, *Poetical Works*, 197.

[24] For more details, see Grant's preliminary note to the poem (*Poetical Works*, 483–5), or his *The Cock Lane Ghost* (London: Macmillan, 1965).

cohesion comes from Churchill's over-development of this metaphor. The poem often walks a fine line between deliberate discursiveness and narrative incoherence.

George Gilfillan, one of Churchill's more outspoken nineteenth-century editors, described it as 'a kind of rhymed diary or waste-book, in which he deposited his every-day thoughts and feelings, without any order or plan'. Thomas Lockwood reiterated this complaint: 'One has the feeling at times that the confusion is beautifully calculated. But at other times, less intriguingly, it is obviously the confusion merely of a writer not fully in control of his purposes.'[25] The whimsy of the poem has, at points, a sort of charm that is lacking from much of Churchill's subsequent work. It was published over eighteen months and written in tetrameters—a form Churchill only used twice—where the shorter line suits the conversational address, as Churchill admits that, other than the titular fraud as linking symbol, he has little idea what he is doing:

> But to return—this Book—the GHOST—
> A mere amusement at the most,
> A trifle, fit to wear away
> The horrors of a rainy day;
> A slight shot silk, for summer wear,
> Just as our modern Statesmen are...

Even here, where it is explicitly denied entry, satire creeps in, inevitably:

> Yet in this Book, where Ease should join
> With Mirth to *sugar* ev'ry line,
> Where it should all be mere *Chit Chat*,
> Lively, Good-humour'd, and *all that*,
> Where honest SATIRE, in disgrace,
> Should not so much as shew her face,
> The shrew, o'erleaping all due bounds,
> Breaks into Laughter's sacred grounds,
> And, in contempt, plays o'er her tricks
> In *Science*, *Trade*, and *Politics*.[26]

Satire enters in because public figures deserve chastisement for their absurdities, so that even so laid-back and indifferent a narrator as Churchill has to notice them. He is full of mock-surprise at his satiric effectiveness, in spite of his best efforts to do nothing: he will simply 'The names of Scoundrels minute down / And Libel more than half the TOWN' (*Poetical Works*, 160).

---

[25] *The Poetical Works of Charles Churchill, with Memoir, Critical Dissertation, and Explanatory Notes*, ed. George Gilfillan (Edinburgh: James Nichol, 1855), x. Thomas Lockwood, *Post Augustan Satire: Charles Churchill and Satirical Poetry, 1750–1800* (Seattle and London: University of Washington Press, 1979), 51.

[26] *The Ghost*, Book IV, in Churchill, *Poetical Works*, 163.

Within this pretence of hardly caring about people's iniquities, but being forced to list them anyway, so overt have they become, Churchill's irreverence towards authority means that he especially enjoys being rude about the famous, seeing them as the epitome of an establishment he distrusted for its solemnity and prurience. When reporting on the somewhat preposterous commission to investigate the supposed Cock-Lane Ghost, which included such luminaries as Sir John Douglas, exposer of the fraud of William Lauder, and Samuel Johnson, Churchill relishes the chance to attack the latter:

> Horrid, *unwieldy, without Form*,
> *Savage*, as OCEAN in a Storm,
> Of *size prodigious*, in the rear,
> *That Post of Honour*, should appear
> POMPOSO; *Fame* around should tell
> How he a slave to int'rest fell;
> How, for *Integrity* renown'd,
> Which Booksellers have often found,
> He for *Subscribers* baits his hook,
> And takes their cash—but where's the Book?

Thomas Tyers claimed that 'This writer has heard Churchill declare, "that he thought the poems of London, and The Vanity of Human Wishes, full of admirable verses, and that all his compositions were diamonds of the first water." But he wanted a subject for pen and for raillery, and so introduced Pomposo in his descriptions: For, with other wise folks, he sat up with the ghost.'[27] The presence of such a supposed epitome of rationality as Johnson at Cock-Lane does most of Churchill's work for him, but his further method of attack is to point out that, for a supposed model of authorial and intellectual integrity, Johnson's behaviour had been less than spotless: he had issued the proposal for his edition of Shakespeare in 1756 when it was promised for completion by the end of 1757. It was not published until 1765. His principles with regard to the establishment are equally elastic: 'He damns the *Pension* which he takes, / And loves the STUART he forsakes.'[28] Johnson's accepting a pension of £300 from George III in 1762 made him seem—to a pen like Churchill's—a party hireling, often reminded, as here, of his previous definition in the *Dictionary* of 'Pension' as 'generally understood as pay given to a state hireling for treason to his country'.

Authority always comes out badly in Churchill's satires, and volleys such as the 'Pomposo' passage leave little room for nuance or qualification. This lack of discrimination often appears in the metaphors used to describe Churchill in contemporary

---

[27] Thomas Tyers, *A Biographical Sketch of Dr Samuel Johnson* (1785), repr. in *The Early Biographies of Samuel Johnson*, ed. O. M. Brack, Jr and Robert E. Kelley (Iowa City: University of Iowa Press, 1974), 73–4.

[28] Churchill, *Poetical Works*, 126. Johnson claimed that Churchill's poetry 'had a temporary currency, only from its audacity of abuse, and being filled with living names, and that it would sink into oblivion'. Moreover, '[h]e did not attack me violently till he found I did not like his poetry'. James Boswell, *The Life of Samuel Johnson, LL.D.*, ed. G. B. Hill, rev. L. F. Powell, 6 vols. (Oxford: Clarendon Press, 1934–64), i. 418–20.

writing: Garrick (whose relationship with Churchill had soured by later in 1761), presents in the *Fribbleriad* a figure who sounds for all the world like a modern rock star:

> My name is *Churchill!*—Thus he spoke,
> And thrice he wav'd his knotted oak:
> That done, he paus'd—prepar'd the blow,
> Impartial bard! for friend and foe.[29]

Churchill, it is implied, may not have deliberately set out to undermine both, but the ferocity of his satire has had that effect. Percy Fitzgerald referred to this side of Churchill as a possible consequence of his integrity: he was 'enemy to all shams, tearing away all masks, and with the masks tearing away the skin'.[30]

Churchill was not interested in concessions or qualifications. Those who crossed him or Wilkes were scoundrels and placemen: this was the only conclusion that he would draw, at least in print. This is related to his need to distance his satire from the establishment, with its perverse worldly value system, where corruptions are covered up through politeness. In his poem, *Night*, addressed to Lloyd, Churchill offers a defence of their bohemianism against their moralistic critics, who hide their own sins beneath what Churchill calls, in a nod to Fielding, prudence:

> PRUDENCE, of old a sacred term, imply'd
> Virtue with godlike wisdom for her guide,
> But now in gen'ral use is known to mean
> The stalking-horse of vice, and folly's screen.
> The sense perverted, we retain the name;
> Hypocrisy and Prudence are the same.[31]

The final line is a parody of Pope's *Essay on Man*, where God and nature '[b]ade Self-love and Social be the same'. Churchill imagines a modern sage instructing his pupils:

> be what men *prudent* call;
> PRUDENCE, almighty PRUDENCE, gives thee all.
> Keep up appearances; there lies the test,
> The world will give thee credit for the rest.[32]

Prudence is a synonym for self-interest, and the latter is not a social virtue, no matter how tortuously argued. Compared to this Machiavellianism, Churchill's apparently

---

[29]   David Garrick, *The Fribbleriad* (1761), 4. Thomas Davies did not know whether Garrick 'was induced to look cold upon his panegyrist, or had dropped some expressions' of distaste. In the *Apology* (May 1761) Churchill criticized Garrick as the 'Vain Tyrant' of the theatre (*Poetical Works*, 44), whereupon Garrick supposedly wrote a conciliatory letter, but was advised by a friend against sending it. *Memoirs of the life of David Garrick, Esq.*, 2 vols. (1780), i. 317–20.

[30]   Percy Fitzgerald, *A Famous Forgery: being the Story of 'The Unfortunate' Dr Dodd* (1865), 73.

[31]   Churchill, *Poetical Works*, 58–9.

[32]   Churchill, *Poetical Works*, 59. *An Essay on Man*, III. 318; *The Poetry of Alexander Pope*, ed. John Butt (London: Methuen, 1963), 535.

cynical satiric vision of the world may be more idealistic. Its attraction to readers repelled by such complacencies should not be underestimated, especially when, as here, his ideas are not yoked to the cause of Wilkes and Liberty.

Churchill's rejection of selfishness would become linked in other poems to the folly of opposing his own best interests by his support of the vilified and prosecuted Wilkes. A repeated iteration of Churchill's peculiar form of satiric self-consciousness is that, because he rejects most worldly things, his opinions and values cannot be bought by the usual bribes or flatteries. Instead, his incidental business is to reveal the moral failings of those who have sacrificed their morals for craven earthly reward. His masterpiece in this regard is a late work, the unfinished 'Dedication' to a volume of sermons that he addressed to Wilkes's enemy, William Warburton.

In the 'Dedication to the Sermons', Churchill forms a masterly irony by extending the idea of his own lack of sophistication. The speaker criticizes the *realpolitik* of the world, but repeatedly exonerates Warburton from such charges, only to simultaneously insinuate that he is actually the embodiment of them. He explains his supposed attraction to his opponent:

> State is a farce; Names are but empty Things,
> Degrees are bought; and, by mistaken kings,
> Titles are oft misplac'd; Mitres, which shine
> So bright in other eyes, are dull in mine,
> Unless set off by Virtue; who deceives
> Under the sacred sanction of *Lawn-Sleeves*,
> Enhances guilt, commits a double sin;
> So fair without, and yet so foul within.[33]

Given his aversion to public life and its empty rewards, he needs a role model who does not use his public position for his own gain and whose devotion, scholarship, humility, and selfless contribution to public life would act as a proper example. It soon becomes clear that Warburton is emphatically not the man, despite the speaker's apparent praise:

> He, by his great example, might impart
> A better something, and baptize it Art;
> He, all the feelings of my youth forgot,
> Might shew me what is Taste, by what is not;
> By him supported, with a proper pride,
> I might hold all mankind as fools beside;
> He (should a World, perverse and peevish grown,
> Explode his maxims and assert their own)
> Might teach me, like himself, to be content,
> And let their folly be their punishment;
> Might, like himself, teach his adopted Son,
> 'Gainst all the World, to quote a WARBURTON.[34]

---

[33] Churchill, *Poetical Works*, 432.   [34] Churchill, *Poetical Works*, 433–4.

The inordinately proud, vain, self-serving, and bullying Warburton perpetually attacks the folly of his political, ecclesiastical, and literary enemies. But he is revealed, through the ingenuous speaker, to be the worst possible example to imitate in modern public life, and the surface praise and flattery of the speaker is actually a double-edged series of insults.

Yvor Winters praised the poem as a 'devastating indictment of moral ugliness'; yet Churchill's attack is not an incidental discovery of Warburton's glaring faults, nor was it high-minded in its intent.[35] He turned his guns against Warburton because the latter had denounced Wilkes (and the obscene parodies of his annotations of Pope in the unpublished 'Essay on Woman') in the House of Lords in November 1763. The brilliance of the poem cannot conceal that, like much of Churchill's supposedly disinterested satire, it was motivated to some degree by the spirit of party.

A consequence of Churchill's writing so much for Wilkes's cause was that his satire remained narrowly topical, and his reputation entwined with the arguments and feuds of the 1760s. This was not absolutely the case, as readers such as the young Byron would find him an attractive role model (though also one notable for the brevity of his fame). Given Churchill's early demise, it is impossible to predict what future direction his writing would have taken: despite his poetic advances in terms of satiric and technical sophistication during his brief career, his writing is also reactive and oppositional by nature—even *The Rosciad* is based upon the fundamental follies, absurdities, and excesses of the theatre industry—and Churchill seems contented with such opposition as a satiric reflex, and an accurate reflection of his public relationship with the world.

Churchill's world-weariness and cynicism, however affected, support the suggestion that his poetry was made successful—but also circumscribed—by his times; what cannot be known is whether he would have pursued any alternatives, given the chance. It is telling that his other unfinished and posthumous poem stresses solitude, alienation, and an apparent indifference towards the very subjects in which he had previously taken an interest. In *The Journey*, he tells readers wanting entertainment to find it elsewhere, and follows with a roll-call of satiric targets:

> Let them, tho' modest, GRAY more modest wooe;
> Let them with MASON bleat, and bray, and coo;
> Let them with FRANKLIN, proud of some small Greek,
> Make Sophocles, disguis'd, in English speak;
> Let them with GLOVER o'er Medea doze;
> Let them with DODSLEY wail Cleone's woes,
> Whilst he, fine feeling creature, all in tears,
> Melts as they melt, and weeps with weeping Peers.[36]

Even in this supposedly dismissive passage, there is detail behind the ridicule. After expressing contempt for the affected sensibility of Gray and Mason, Churchill focuses

---

[35] Yvor Winters, *Forms of Discovery* (Denver: Alan Swallow, 1967), 145, where he also offers the solitary and somewhat eccentric judgement that it is 'the greatest English poem of the century'.

[36] Churchill, *Poetical Works*, 441.

on classical learning: Thomas Francklin (1721–84) was well-known as translator of Sophocles (1759) and former Regius Professor of Greek at Cambridge, who had left his post in 1759. According to the *Biographica Dramatica* (1782), he was 'possessed of no inconsiderable share of learning and poetical abilities', but 'contrived to render himself obnoxious to most of his contemporaries'.[37] Churchill attacked his pride and egotism more than once; Francklin's having contributed to Smollett's *Critical Review* would make him a target for the Wilkesite cause, as well. Richard Glover (1712–85) was more famous for his poem *Leonidas* (1737) than for his version of *Medea* (1761). He is mentioned here, in part, because he was one of the beneficiaries of a huge public loan approved by Bute's ministry; he is one of those listed as profiting from it, in an indignant report in the *North Briton*.[38] *Cleone* was a tragedy by Robert Dodsley of 1758, produced in competition with Garrick's production of *The Busy Body* at Drury Lane, giving Dodsley anxieties over its reception. Johnson recorded how '[t]he play was very well received. Doddy, after the danger was over, went every night to the stage-side, and cried at the distress of poor Cleone.'[39]

This quantity of innuendo and contextual knowledge, even in an apparently throw-away series of insults, shows how rich Churchill's satire could be. It is followed by the poem's four-line refrain, which is dismissive in a different sense:

> Thus, or in any better way They please,
> With these great Men, or with great Men like these,
> Let Them their appetite for laughter feed;
> I on my Journey all Alone proceed.[40]

The rejection of worldly interests is so final as to seem almost existential; the poem spends a lot of its narrative claiming not to care about anything, but the refrain has a note of finality (albeit imposed by the poem's posthumous and possibly unfinished status). It may be that Churchill, the disaffected bohemian, was sincere in his dismissal of and indifference to all worldliness.

The very nature of Churchill's satiric persona—its principle of being called to duty because of the wretchedness of public life, rather than through its own merit or suitability—is useful in showing something of a sideways movement in eighteenth-century satire: away from the search for the moral high ground, and towards a hinterland where the weaknesses of the speaker augment their authenticity. This could be argued to be a relatively narrow ground, and Churchill's immediate followers amounted to little (Chatterton's late satires, and many immediate minor imitators). This does not mitigate Churchill's importance or effect—his influence on Byron, in the distant future, was more

[37] David Baker and Isaac Reed, *Biographia Dramatica; or, a Companion to the Playhouse* (1782), 73.

[38] For the public loan see *North Briton* 43 (19 March 1763), in *The North Briton*, 4 vols. (1772), ii. 194–6.

[39] See Boswell, *Life of Johnson*, i. 326. For the background to the play and the quarrel with Garrick, see Harry M. Solomon, *The Rise of Robert Dodsley: Creating the New Age of Print* (Carbondale: Southern Illinois University Press, 1996), 195–215.

[40] Churchill, *Poetical Works*, 443.

obviously consequential—but, like the rest of the Nonsense Club, his self-conscious satires were highly popular within their immediate era, yet fell away as soon as their frame of reference had ceased to be of relevance to future generations not schooled in the intricacies of Butean patronage or the extremes of sensibility. Besides, if Churchill and the Nonsense Club have a real but somewhat ill-defined place in British satiric history, this is not inappropriate, given their consistent rejection of the establishment in most of its forms.

SELECT BIBLIOGRAPHY

Baker, David and Isaac Reed. *Biographia Dramatica; or, a Companion to the Playhouse* (London, 1782).

Beatty, Joseph M. 'The Battle of the Players and Poets, 1761–1766', *Modern Language Notes* 34 (1919), 449–62.

Bertelsen, Lance. *The Nonsense Club: Literature and Popular Culture, 1749–1764* (Oxford: Clarendon Press, 1986).

Briggs, Peter M. '"The brain, too finely wrought": Mind Unminded in Churchill's Satires', *Modern Language Studies* 14 (1984), 39–53.

Davies, Thomas. *Memoirs of the life of David Garrick, Esq.*, 2 vols. (London, 1780).

Davis, Leith. *Acts of Union: Scotland and the Literary Negotiation of the British Nation* (Stanford: Stanford University Press, 1998).

Fitzgerald, Percy. *A Famous Forgery: being the Story of 'The Unfortunate' Dr Dodd* (London: Chapman and Hall, 1865).

Grant, Douglas. *The Cock Lane Ghost* (London: Macmillan, 1965).

Lockwood, Thomas. *Post Augustan Satire: Charles Churchill and Satirical Poetry, 1750–1800* (Seattle and London: University of Washington Press, 1979).

Rounce, Adam. '"Stuarts without End": Wilkes, Churchill, and Anti-Scottishness', *Eighteenth-Century Life* 29 (2005), 20–43.

Solomon, Harry H. *The Rise of Robert Dodsley: Creating the New Age of Print* (Carbondale: Southern Illinois University Press, 1996).

Winters, Yvor. *Forms of Discovery* (Denver: Alan Swallow, 1967).

CHAPTER 8

....

FOXITE SATIRE

Politics, Print, and Celebrity

....

ROBERT W. JONES

In his engaging study, *The Whig World*, Leslie Mitchell paints a vivid picture of the social and political community created by Charles James Fox, the Dukes and Duchesses of Bedford, Portland, and Devonshire, together with their many friends and relations. Parties and gatherings at Chatsworth, Holland House, and Holkham Hall loom large, alongside race meetings and private theatricals; but London was the centre of their operations—the location for political and all other forms of pleasurable intrigue. Political convictions—indefatigably that of parliamentary opposition, paying only lip service to democracy—provided both a bond and a motive, but more than political allegiance held the Whigs together. There was something more than blood too, though that was critical as the Whigs were an intimate and closely-related bunch. Cultural attitudes were held in common: fashionable literary forms were not reckoned much, while Pope was admired greatly; in an equally classical gesture, history from ancient times was read retroactively as a vindication of their own embattled present; meanwhile marriage vows were lightly cast aside, lovers taken, and preposterous bets placed. It was a world at once committed, vivacious, and static. Some of this permanence derived, unhappily enough, from the Whigs' almost total exclusion from power after George III's accession in 1760. Only twice were they in government, in 1765–6 and 1782. Yet the Whigs remained confident despite, and because of, their exclusion from power; comfortable with a sense that even without office they were morally ascendant. With such certainties—and so many cousins—easily to hand, the world of the Whigs is not a little like P. G. Wodehouse's *Life at Blandings*, though with a better reading list and rather more sex. It was certainly a foreclosed world, elite in its composition and narrow in its views.

These habits and associations made the Whigs a curious political phenomenon, and not one obviously geared to action. Whig grandees did not like to involve themselves greatly in matters of party organization or press management, so had others achieve it for them. Mitchell is not blind to this smallness and self-regard, and regrets the ambiguous and exploited position of the 'men of talent' recruited to the Whig cause and thereafter included, somewhat grudgingly, in their social activities.[1] It is, however, from such men that party structure and party literature emerged. Their work would prove crucial in the 1780s. George III's unrelenting hostility, especially towards Fox, placed the Whigs in a weak position. Their efforts were further resisted by the well-organized and well-funded government of William Pitt, which possessed the resources and willingness to control the press and, consequently, the news. The opposition were attacked by government writers such as James Macpherson, who doubted their policies and mocked their principles.[2] To have any chance of success, it became necessary for the Whigs to seek to command the press themselves, and to mobilize writers willing to commit to the Whig cause. Macpherson could then be lampooned—as Mac Ossian amongst other things—freely thereafter.[3] After the party's catastrophic defeat in the 1784 election, Whig leaders were even prepared to commit money to this project, founding the Esto Perpetua Club, located off the Strand, which brought together their best writers and most clubbable toffs. Party organization was delegated to men adept at organizing elections and managing funds.[4] Newspapers were bought or energetically subvened while efforts, not always successful, were made to control their contents.[5]

The responsibility for recruiting and marshalling writers and editors fell to Richard Brinsley Sheridan. The author of several plays and some verse satires by the mid-1770s, Sheridan possessed considerable celebrity in his own right, but had been drawn to the Foxite wing of the Whig party as an associate of Lord John Townshend and General Richard Fitzpatrick. He became an MP (for Stafford) on a Foxite ticket in 1780. Sheridan's role in the Foxite operations is critical, as is the work undertaken by his friends, Joseph Richardson and French Laurence. Mitchell places Sheridan and his comrades on the margins of the exclusive 'Whig World' and he makes a good case for why this was so. However, his sympathetic appraisal overlooks the ways in which Whig writers made their own literary and political culture and did so in ways that went beyond the complacencies of their employers. This world was perhaps just as inter-married and interconnected; Sheridan seems to have worked closely with his brother-in-law, Richard Tickell. Tickell's house often served as a meeting point for members of the group, including Richardson, Laurence, and Sheridan, much to the vexation of his wife, Mary.[6] Their group was equally metropolitan, but centred on the newspapers and booksellers of the capital: print culture in a dynamic and meaningful sense. It was at this vibrant intersection

[1] Leslie Mitchell, *The Whig World: 1760–1837* (London: Hambledon Continuum, 2005), 17, 33–4, 48–9.

[2] James Macpherson, *A Short History of the Opposition during the Last Session of Parliament* (1779).

[3] [Richard Tickell, George Ellis, French Laurence, and Joseph Richardson], *Political Miscellanies: Part the First* (1787), 76–8, 87–8. Subsequent references appear in the text.

[4] See Sir A. W. Ward and A. R. Walker eds., *The Cambridge History of English Literature*, 15 vols. (Cambridge: Cambridge University Press, 1907–27), xi. 35–6; and Donald E. Ginter, 'The Financing of the Whig Party Organization, 1783–1793', *American Historical Review* 71 (1966), 421–40.

[5] See Hannah Barker, *Newspapers, Politics, and Public Opinion in Late Eighteenth-Century England* (Oxford: Clarendon Press, 1998); and Lucyle Thomas Werkmeister, *The London Daily Press, 1772–1792* (Lincoln: University of Nebraska Press, 1963).

[6] Mary Tickell to Elizabeth Sheridan, 'Saturday [March 1785]', Letters from Mary Tickell to Her Sister Elizabeth Ann Sheridan, ca. 1785–1787, Folger MS Y.d.35, f. 15, Folger Shakespeare Library, Washington, DC.

of print and politics that an alternative Whig world was fashioned, not least when it interacted with a still more radical culture of protest. Elite Whigs were wary of closer involvement with the 'people' and especially their more radical leaders, but Sheridan and others were more willing to form connections or offer employment.[7]

This essay engages with the print and politics of Whig culture, specifically focused on Sheridan, his companions, and their brand of self-conscious and print-aware satire. Given the cultural, social, and familial coherence of the group, it makes sense to label their works 'Foxite Satire'. Although it is necessary to acknowledge that Fox himself was not the progenitor of any of their productions, their work shares key themes of his political career, notably the need to oppose the excessive claims of the Crown, the reform of libel legislation and the freedom of the press. India was important, both as point of principle and as source of grievance.[8] Their work therefore constitutes an extension of some of Fox's most pressing concerns. It is also distinctive in its literary assumptions: Milton was greatly admired but perhaps not much enjoyed, while Pope remained an inspiration and model (*Political Miscellanies*, vii). Most dynamically, Foxite satire constitutes an important intervention in the paper wars of the late century: politics by swipe and smear. Sheridan was crucial to these endeavours, but his presence is underestimated often in favour of wealthier members of the group, such as Townshend or Fitzpatrick.[9] Sheridan acted as the meeting point between poets, pamphleteers, journalists, and their elite paymasters. Later in the century, William Godwin noted that Sheridan was always 'putting arrows in [Robert] Merry's hat'; meaning planting newspaper stories.[10] Sheridan's energies, however, do not define what could be a reckless and ebullient group activity. There was perhaps rather too much truth in this satire of one of their gatherings:

> The zealous Whigs, obedient to command,
> Drink till they stare, and call again for more:
> Nor does the Bottle quit their ready hand,
> Till *Whigs* with *Whigs* lie Tumbling on the floor.[11]

The Foxites' failings, and indeed their strengths, are similar to those John Brewer attributes to the Wilkesite culture of the 1760s insofar as it was rough, ready, and indisputably masculine society. The Wilkesites had been adept at mobilizing popular culture, broadening their appeal by engaging in a wide variety of print media.[12] This precedent could be built upon. The Foxites could draw upon a more clearly established 'celebrity' culture, which at once promoted politicians into the public eye (notably Fox and Sheridan) and

---

[7] See Jon Mee, *Print, Publicity, and Popular Romanticism: The Laurel of Liberty* (Cambridge: Cambridge University Press, 2016).

[8] Charles James Fox, *The Speeches of the Right Honourable Charles James Fox, in the House of Commons*, 6 vols. (1815), i. 101, 196–283; ii. 387–96; and iii. 1–13.

[9] See also Christopher Clayton, 'The Political Career of Richard Brinsley Sheridan', Oxford DPhil thesis, 1992.

[10] Mee, *Print, Publicity*, 116–17.   [11] *A Speech at the Whig Club* (London: J. Ridgway, 1792), 10.

[12] John Brewer, *Party Ideology and Popular Politics at the Accession of George III* (Cambridge: Cambridge University Press, 1976), 163–200.

which animated the press. Politics, press, and the stage all combined and comingled by the late century making a heady mix of characters and careers.[13] Gossip, scandal, and scurrility defined Foxite satire in many respects, while the foibles of government and private lives of public men were constant reference points. This emphasis, combined with the Whigs' well-established fear of the press, meant that Foxite satire was distanced from politeness; equally from any enlightened faith in the ability of print to act as a beneficial mode of communication. Print may reveal scandal; but it sheds no light, but rather darkness publishable.

SHERIDAN'S SCHOOL FOR SCANDALS

This apprehension seems particularly and peculiarly Sheridan's. His best known works, *The Rivals* and *The School for Scandal*, are not political satires in the party-orientated sense that concerns this essay. However, they share Foxite concerns about the capacity of newspapers to act as the creators and not merely the disseminators of scandal. Lydia Languish, for example, is delighted by the possibility of entering the world of print, even fantasizing about her reappearance in 'such paragraphs in the newspapers'. The matter appears more darkly in *The School for Scandal* when Snake confirms that he has 'inserted' Lady Sneerwell's malicious paragraphs in the papers. Aware of their machinations, Sir Peter Teazle fears that the gossip magazines will ensure his translation into a public fool.[14] Frank Donoghue has suggested that Sheridan's plays exhibit a fear of print culture, an anxiety rooted in his horror at the mobile and unknowable audience created by it. The argument is sound but underestimates the extent of contemporary fascination with scandal, an interest to which the play enthusiastically responds, even as it registers a distinctly Foxite fear of the press.[15] Newspapers receive more acute treatment in *The Critic* via the character of Mr Puff. Puff is a newspaper man, a writer for hire. He does not care much for whom he writes, or what about. Puff provides a list of his outstanding work:

> Here is 'a conscientious baker, on the subject of the army bread', and 'a detester of visible brickwork, in favour of the new-invented stucco', both in the style of Junius, and promised for to-morrow. The Thames navigation too is at a stand. Misomud or Anti-shoal must go to work directly. Here too are some political memorandums I see. Ay. 'To take Paul Jones, and get the Indiamen out of the Shannon, reinforce Byron, compel the Dutch to—' So! I must do that in the evening papers, or reserve

---

[13] See Tom Mole, ed., *Romanticism and Celebrity Culture, 1750–1850* (Cambridge: Cambridge University Press, 2009); and Felicity Nussbaum, *Rival Queens: Actresses, Performance, and the Eighteenth-Century British Theater* (Philadelphia: University of Pennsylvania Press, 2010).

[14] Richard Brinsley Sheridan, *The School for Scandal and Other Plays*, ed. Michael Cordner (Oxford: Oxford University Press, 1998), 72, 210, 220.

[15] Frank Donoghue, 'Avoiding the "Cooler Tribunal of the Study": Richard Brinsley Sheridan's Writer's Block and Late Eighteenth-Century Print Culture', *ELH* 68, no. 4 (2001), 831–56; see Anna Clark, *Scandal: The Sexual Politics of the British Constitution* (Princeton: Princeton University Press, 2004).

it for *The Morning Herald*, for I know that I have undertaken tomorrow, besides to establish the unanimity of the fleet in *The Public Advertiser*, and to shoot Charles Fox in *The Morning Post*. So, egad, I ha'n't a moment to lose![16]

Puff's to-do list reveals not only his willingness to support any cause, from architectural fancies to river traffic, but also his readiness to do so in print. He is a notable supporter of government causes too, using newspapers to help make the world conform to government spin: the American raider, John Paul Jones, will be reported as captured; the navy unified (though it was riven by the Keppel–Palliser affair); and Admiral Byron's fleet safely (if belatedly) launched into action. Puff's performative paragraphs recreate the world, challenging the claims of the opposition as they do so. Puff can make everything seem better; the art of puffing, he explains 'has a wonderful memory for parliamentary debates, and will often give the whole speech of a favoured member with the most flattering accuracy' or 'with the carelessness of a casual paragraph suggest officers into commands, to which they have no pretention but their wishes': printed words lead where policy is yet to go.[17]

Although in performance this might appear to be merely a short-lived comic effusion, in print it looked more serious. Puff's promise to 'shoot' Fox in the *Morning Post* first appeared, as an additional quip, a month after the play had first opened at Drury Lane. Fox had indeed been shot by fellow MP William Adam on 29 November 1779 after an altercation in the Commons. Fox had claimed that Adam's loyalty to the Crown derived from his characteristically Scottish attention to his own advantage. The duel became the occasion for verse satires and newspaper paragraphs which mocked Fox, who, it was reported, was only saved by a mixture of poorly-prepared weaponry and protective rolls of fat.[18] Newspapers later suggested that he was never so bold in the Commons again, for fear of a worse result.[19] From the perspective of his followers, a response was needed if Fox was not to look a fool. More pressingly it was necessary for Fox's friends to challenge the extent to which the satiric agenda was set by government hacks. Sheridan was attempting this kind of defence in *The Critic*, but others intervened too. The poem *Paradise Regain'd; or the Battle of Adam and the Fox*, mocked the duel in a jovial mock-Miltonic style. The poem relates how Adam is seduced by the devil into challenging Fox.

> Now as in former days of chivalry,
> When right knew no chancery but combat
> Dreadful, when man and beast were pitted in
> Challenge brutal, as in the case of Toleman
> And the greyhound in Gallic annals told,
> Sport royal to behold by kings and queens,
> So was Adam and the fierce Fox engaged;

[16] Sheridan, *School for Scandal and Other Plays*, 311–12.
[17] Sheridan, *School for Scandal and Other Plays*, 311.
[18] *The Morning Post* (30 November 1779).
[19] *Public Advertiser* (1 and 4 December 1779) and *Morning Post* (3 April 1780).

> When quick as flashes from a distemper'd sky,
> O'er charg'd with exhalation nitrous,
> Flex from their pistols the ball, under eye's
> Steady direction; Adam's hit upon
> The Fox's paunch, depo o' former luxuries,
> The bleating lamb, the rice-fed chicken, the
> Tender duckling, and the plump wheat pheasant.[20]

These lines make the whole affair appear somewhat silly, a mighty contest springing from a trivial thing; a Whig *Rape of the Lock*, albeit with guns. The poem certainly laughed them together, as Adam became a significant Whig party organizer. This was a bonus that came later; the immediate point was to praise senior Whigs—Shelburne, Rockingham, and Saville—stressing their great respectability, allowing Fox to rise with them as a clumsy kind of martyr.[21] The poem also sought to execrate government misinformation. The point is made in the mock-dedication to the prime minister. Lord North is praised for his 'great abilities in fact and faction' and for his ability to create 'fib and fable'.[22] The idea of North as a master spin doctor was widely accepted amongst a broad range of oppositional satirists, some of whom took Sheridan's mockery of Puff as their starting point.[23] *Paradise Regain'd* reveals a number of distinctly Foxite features. It is self-reflective and self-consciously literary. Literary parody is central; not least of Milton. The poem is precise in its political allusions, requiring detailed knowledge if its swipes are to be fully understood. It is embedded in the vibrant and knowing print culture of the late century yet remains covert and rather inward looking.[24] It is the work of a small, undoubtedly clever group, a new kind of elite emerging from the shadows of the grandees, but preserving their appetite for distinction. This is perhaps the contradiction of Foxites and their literary offerings: alive to the machinations of the press, fearful of its power in many ways, but never embracing the potential of print without hoping first to impose their own governance upon it.

A Question of *Anticipation*

Puff's speech disclosed the malicious use of the press, a point that early reviewers understood perfectly. The *Public Advertiser* thought Sheridan's attack on newspapers was 'the properest Theme for the Author of The School for Scandal'.[25] The *London Evening Post*

---

[20] *Paradise Regain'd; or the Battle of Adam and the Fox: A Heroick Poem* (1780), 35.
[21] *Paradise Regain'd*, 20–4.   [22] *Paradise Regain'd*, Dedication.
[23] Israel Pottinger, *The Critic; or a Tragedy Rehearsed: a New Dramatic Piece in Three Acts; as it is performed by His Majesty's Servants* (1780). See also David Francis Taylor, '"The Fate of Empires": The American War, Political Parody, and Sheridan's Comedies', *Eighteenth-Century Studies* 42 (2009), 379–95.
[24] Christina Lupton, *Knowing Books: The Consciousness of Mediation in Eighteenth-Century Britain* (Philadelphia: University of Pennsylvania Press, 2012).
[25] *Public Advertiser* (1 November 1779).

commented that Puff's speech contained some 'very good Imitations of *Anticipation*'.[26] The allusion is to Tickell's *Anticipation*, which had been published a year earlier when it had been the defining satirical text of both the parliamentary and London season. Tickell had previously collaborated with Sheridan, providing the spiky prologue to *The Camp* a year earlier. There he had attacked the army camps on the south coast and the government's reliance on contractors.[27] *Anticipation* was an altogether bolder venture. The pretext for Tickell's satire was the opening of parliament, a day on which the ministry offered its account of the nation and its plans for the coming session. During wartime it was also an opportunity for the government to place its confidence in the armed forces and to express its assurance, however implausibly, in the eventual success of their efforts. Parliamentary reporting was severely restricted (to the annoyance of the Whigs) but Tickell avoided these limitations by inventing or rather anticipating debates; dating his text to 23 November, three days ahead of the actual event.[28] The device allowed him to satirize the prolix procedures of the Commons and to lampoon individual speakers. Tickell was equally keen to emphasize press corruption and has a number of his speakers, not least of which is Fox, raise the issue of the press and its relationship to government (*Anticipation*, 37, 49–50).

Although he mocked the Opposition's lugubrious oratory (including Edmund Burke's), Tickell focused his criticism on North and his allies amongst the country gentleman. The mock session begins, following protocol, with the king's speech delivered to the Lords after all the usual fuss between Black Rod and the Speaker. The speech provides another form of flummery. Tickell wisely maintains the decorousness of the occasion, but George III still sounds a fool and his assessment of the state of the nation is as wrong-headed as any of Puff's panegyrics: '[He] concluded with relying on the wisdom and unanimity of Parliament; on the good conduct of Generals and Admirals; on the valor of his Fleets and Armies; and on the zeal and spirit of all his faithful subjects' (*Anticipation*, 4). As Tickell's readers would have understood, this was an optimistic assessment of the situation in November 1778. By this stage in the war, Burgoyne had been defeated and Saratoga and Sir Henry Clinton forced to retreat; the Channel Fleet was divided between warring factions, while in the West Indies the Crown had just lost Dominica to the French now allied with the American rebels.[29] Even so, government supporters follow one another to praise the efforts of the Ministry, the Army, and Navy. Their sycophancy and credulity are equally obvious; and when the opposition begins to make its complaints, loyalists leave for their dinner, or the opera (*Anticipation*, 6–8, 11). The sense that

---

[26] *London Evening Post* (30 October–2 November 1779).

[27] See Robert W. Jones, 'Notes on *The Camp*: Women, Effeminacy and the Military in Late Eighteenth-Century Literature', *Textual Practice* 11 (1997), 463–77.

[28] Richard Tickell, *Anticipation: Containing the Substance of His M———'s Most Gracious Speech to both H———-s of P———-l———t, on the opening of the approaching session, together with a full and authentic account of the debate which will take place in the H———e of C———s* (1778). Subsequent references appear in the text.

[29] See Stephen Conway, *The British Isles and the War of American Independence* (Oxford: Oxford University Press, 2000); Robert W. Jones, *Literature, Gender and Politics in Britain during the War for America, 1770–1785* (Cambridge: Cambridge University Press, 2011).

truth is being either quashed or manipulated runs throughout the text. In this vein, Burke regrets that:

> Though we may censure our Officers, our Ministers at least shew some generalship; if they cannot deceive the enemy, they are prompt enough to mislead their country-men; though they discover but little skill in the arrangement of armies, they have admirable talents in marshalling Gazettes. They have given celebrity to sheep-stealing, and blazoned, in all the pompous prolixity of ostentatious phraseology, the import-ant depredations at—*Martha*'s Island.   (37)

There are longer jokes and many other interventions of just this kind. Lord North's ram-bling speech, for example, is full of disingenuous explanation, but also cliché about honour and confidence (*Anticipation*, 52–63). Tickell was keen to tease individual speakers: Alexander Wedderburn, the Solicitor-General, is mocked for his Scottish accent; General Conway's false modesty is exposed; while John Sawbridge merely throws out alarming phrases (*Anticipation*, 42–3, 69–70, 71). As the mockery of Sawbridge indicates, it is not only the government and its supporters that prove lamentable. Amongst the Opposition, the Hull MP, David Hartley, appears distinctly dreary, Temple Luttrell is obsessed with pointless historical lessons, and Colonel Barré is overcome by his own emotions (*Anticipation*, 11–14, 27–34, 63–7). Burke is treated in what may be a more sophisticated way, perhaps because while not a Foxite, he is an ally of a kind. Like Hartley, his style is lampooned, his dismal prognostications parodied in full—but he is not quite burlesqued. His points still register, even if his style is deprecated (*Anticipation*, 35–41).

The text changes tack and tone, without much effort to be subtle, when Fox finally intervenes. *Anticipation*'s loyalties are abundantly clear at this point. Fox speaks power-fully, denouncing the government for its incompetence and duplicity. As an oration it is a thing of wonder, such that to do justice to his talents is 'totally beyond the utmost efforts of the editor'. Tickell has his hero reason powerfully on the nation's losses and the govern-ment's perfidy in hiding them (*Anticipation*, 44–50). Nor is he easily deflected from his task. Resuming after a rather pointless government intervention, Fox explains that:

> With such Ministers, such principles, such plans, such internal resources, such prospects of alliance; Gentlemen were now called on to echo the Speech, to panegyr-ize an Administration too despicable for satire, to plunge this devoted country in aggravated ruin, and, with remorseless despair, to *desolate* what they had found impossible to *subdue*.   (*Anticipation*, 52)

Despite Fox's torrential eloquence, the parliamentary division at the end of the debate secures a government victory, though with a decent opposition showing (261 votes for, against 148). Undeterred by another predictable defeat, the text closes with the editor's partly-ironic reflections on *Anticipation*, which, he prophesies, will soon be prohibited, members of the Commons having become aghast at its prediction of their weaknesses. The text is adept at exposing the inequities and general decrepitude of political debate at this moment of crisis. There are equal parts of mockery and self-confidence on display, not least because Tickell was sure of his audience, its habits and assumptions. *Anticipation* is consequently best understood as a Foxite closet-drama, to be chuckled over in Whig coffee-houses and at tea-tables.

ESTO PERPETUA: *THE ROLLIAD, PROBATIONARY ODES, AND POLITICAL MISCELLANIES*

The objections and mockeries contained in *Anticipation* were shared with the Foxite journal, *The Englishman*, which was probably edited by Sheridan, and the short-lived *Whig Magazine*. Journalism gave the Foxites a means to assail opponents like North and cabinet ministers such as Lords Sandwich and Germain as well as hate-figures like Admiral Palliser.[30] However, it was in verse and parodies of versification that the Foxites often succeeded best. They were at their most inventive and most successful in the mid-1780s, with 1784 the decisive year. Fox's India bill had been defeated and the unlikely coalition government, which had seen Fox share power with North, had been broken up. George III was widely understood to have acted unconstitutionally to bring these events about. Depressed by his defeat, Fox was never quite the same again.[31] Foxite writers, however, were hugely energized and produced their best works, fashioning their dark materials into three brilliant collective works: *The Rolliad*, *Probationary Odes*, and *Political Miscellanies*. *The Rolliad* is the best known of these works and set a precedent for what followed. Like other Foxite works, it is deeply immersed in print. The printed word and the dangerous profusion of the press serve as both challenge and opportunity throughout.

The Rolliad first appeared in the *Morning Herald* in late 1784 and continued for several numbers before re-emerging as a separate publication. Properly styled *Criticisms on the Rolliad, A Poem*, it was the work of the whole gang and would be reprinted well into the nineteenth century.[32] The satire takes the form of a piece of mock literary criticism on an invented epic poem called *The Rolliad*. Critical terms and comparisons to the classics duly appear; quotations from the text are plentiful and the commentary, on the surface at least, equally fulsome. The central conceit of the epic poem is to have Merlin conduct the Devonian MP John Rolle (renamed Rollo) on a tour of Britain. He appears both egregious and hapless, wandering about, bustling and bumbling. Rolle was not the most

---

[30] See *The Englishman* (1779), and *The Whig Magazine, or, Patriot Miscellany* (1779).

[31] See John Cannon, *The Fox–North Coalition: Crisis of the Constitution 1782–84* (Cambridge: Cambridge University Press, 1969); and L. G. Mitchell, *Charles James Fox* (Oxford: Oxford University Press, 1992).

[32] Sheridan denied any role in the composition in the Commons on 20 April 1785; see Richard Brinsley Sheridan, *Speeches of the Late Right Honourable Richard Brinsley Sheridan: Several Corrected by Himself and Edited by a Constitutional Friend*, 5 vols. (London: Patrick Martin, 1816), i. 151.

obvious target for Foxite abuse. Though he had opposed Fox's demand to recall Admiral Rodney in 1782, he was moderate, even liberal in his views, not least on the slave trade. Yet he supported Pitt on every issue of note and had recently 'coughed down' a speech by Burke. This alone justified his selection as the central figure in a work eager to attack Pitt and Henry Dundas, Pitt's ablest adherent, especially on Indian affairs. The attack on Pitt is relentless. He is dubbed the '*Immaculate Young Minister*' on the title page, inaugurating a steady assault on his masculinity.[33] 'The most beautiful effort of our author's genius', the editors boast, 'is contained in the description of Mr. *Pitt*':

> Pert without fire, without experience sage,
> Young with more art than *Sh—ne* glean'd from age,
> Too proud from pilfer'd greatness to descend,
> Too humble not to call *Dundas* his friend,
> In silent dignity and sullen state,
> This new *Octavius* rises to debate!
> Mild and more mild he sees each placid row
> Of *Country Gentlemen* with rapture glow;
> He sees, convuls'd with sympathetic throbs,
> *Apprentice Peers* and *deputy – Nabobs*!
>
> (*Rolliad*, 5–6)

Simultaneously sophisticated and crass, these lines present Pitt as an effeminate youth, successful only insofar as he appealed to the already fanatical ranks of country gentlemen, the rusticated bastions of the king's arbitrary power. The depiction of Pitt as less than manly is a constant throughout *The Rolliad*, underwritten, inevitably, by the notion that the poem—were it to be seen entire—is an epic. This mode reaches its disagreeable apotheosis in a sketch of Pitt, lauded as a 'beautiful exclamation':

> Shall Chatham's offspring basely beg support,
> Now from India, now St. James's court;
> With pow'r admiring Senates to bewitch,
> Now kiss a Monarch's—now a Merchant's breach,
> And prove a pupil of St Omer's school,
> If either *kinson*, *At.* or *Jen.* the tool?
>
> (*Rolliad*, 23)

Pitt appears as a slave to Charles Jenkinson (a onetime supporter of Bute, later a Pittite and said to possess undue influence) and Richard Atkinson (merchant, and a Director of the East India Company). His effeminacy consequently assumes a more significant degree of nastiness but also political import. His unmanly nature, his pale imitation of his father's appeal to political and commercial elites, compromises everything. Marvelling

---

[33] [Richard Tickell, Richard Fitzpatrick, Joseph Richardson, George Ellis and French Laurence], *Criticisms on the Rolliad, A Poem, being a more faithful Portraiture of the Present Immaculate Young Minister and his Friends than any Extant* (1784), 2–3. Subsequent references appear in the text.

at their own creation, the writers of *The Rolliad* note that although 'cold and cautious criticism may perhaps stare at the boldness of the concluding line, we will venture to pronounce it the most masterful stroke of the sublime' (*Rolliad*, 24). Poor poetry, rotten criticism, and worse politics are the inevitable result. The point is repeated when Rollo is taken on a tour of Westminster, including St Stephen's Hall and the toilets (the Foxites rarely miss a peek into a water closet if they can help it). The government benches are a focus of particular interest as their plushness evokes the luxury of the East while revealing the delicacy of Pitt's bottom (*Rolliad*, 34, 37).

Although the *Rolliad* is arguably the Foxites' best work, the *Probationary Odes* and *Political Miscellanies* were effective in their use of parody to produce complex multi-layered textual forms. The *Probationary Odes*, first published in 1785, is a fine example of this satiric approach. Purportedly the creation of Sir John Hawkins, musicologist and biographer of Samuel Johnson, it was in fact the work of Tickell and Richardson. The text exploits the appointment of Thomas Warton as poet laureate, using it to raise concerns about the recent Westminster election; the so-called Irish Propositions concerning trade with Ireland, then before the Commons; and various other matters, not least of which is the appalling nature of odes, seen as a rather hectic form of verse. The satire rests on the claim that although the egregiously loyal Warton has been appointed by the Lord Chamberlain, Lord Salisbury, his election has been challenged by Sir Cecil Wray, who demands 'scrutiny' of the result.[34] Wray had been narrowly defeated by Fox at the Westminster election in 1784 and had demanded an inquiry, or scrutiny, in response. The matter would occupy Fox, Fitzpatrick, and Sheridan in the Commons for several months. Although they successfully defended Fox's election, Wray became a ready target.[35] In *Probationary Odes* Wray's objection leads to the publication of all the poems published by those aspiring to the laureateship; Wray's own effort appears first, and is, of course, dreadful. The poem's over-blown praise of George III and all-too obvious desire for self-promotion, combined with a decidedly irregular verse, make for a sickly profusion:

> It is because great CÆAR, you are clever –
> Therefore we'd sing of you for ever!
> Sing – sing – sing – sing
> God save the King!
> Smile then CÆAR, smile on *Wray*!
> Crown at last his poll with bay!
> Come, oh! Bay, and with thee bring
> Salary, illustrious thing!—
>
> (*Probationary Odes*, 13)

The point is easily grasped. Wray is presumptive, talentless, and a fool. More, much more, in the same vein soon follows. Poems are offered from such dignified pens as

---

[34] [Richard Tickell and Joseph Richardson], *Probationary Odes for the Laureatship with a Preliminary Discourse by Sir John Hawkins* (1785), 11. Subsequent references appear in the text.

[35] Fox, *Speeches*, i. 437–50; ii. 26–44; and Sheridan, *Speeches*, i. 131–2, 138–41.

those of Edward Thurlow, the Lord Chancellor, Nathanial Wraxhall, William Markham, the Archbishop of York, and, inevitably, Macpherson. The satire is sometimes specific to the individual, such as the mockery of Ossianics or Thurlow's splenetic, vengeful outpourings (*Probationary Odes*, 24–9, 68–72). At other times the aim is simply to run down ode writing as a bad species of poetry. In this respect, the Foxites, progressive in some of their political views, had much in common with an arch Tory like Dr Johnson when it came to their opinion of new and irregular verse forms.[36]

There is a wider impetus behind the project. The laureateship, unlike Fox's hard-won Westminster seat, was a court position. The occupant was obliged to produce verse devoted to the king. By the time *Probationary Odes* appeared, Warton had already committed himself to this cause, praising George III's 'sublime renown' and superlative taste.[37] Warton is mocked mercilessly; rubbished as poet, scholar, and, less honourably, as a man. A key feature of *Probationary Odes*, shared with almost all other Foxite material, is its exuberant deployment of layers of apparatus and front matter. The most spectacular of these, offered as a preface to the competition proper, is 'A Full and True Account of the Rev. Thomas Warton's Ascension in the Christ-Church Meadow'. In this squib, Warton rises above Oxford in a balloon provided by the university's pastry cook. He takes a phenomenal amount of food with him: 'a loaf of Sandwiches, three bottles of old ale, a pint of brandy, a sallad ready mixed, a roll of collar'd eel, a cold goose, six damson tartlets, a few China oranges, and a roasted pig of the Chinese breed': it is the picnic of a gourmand; voracious yet fashionable tastes revealing much about his personality. As if this was not enough, the balloon's ballast is provided by Warton's own scholarly and poetic works, which he is soon required to tip over the side. Warton is incredibly pleased with himself, however, writing that: 'my ascension was majestic' (*Probationary Odes*, xxxix–xlii). He later crash-lands and has to rely on his brother, the scampering 'Dr Joseph', to lend him a fresh wig. Again, Warton's prissiness and concern for appearances marks his political and poetic dubiousness (*Probationary Odes*, xliv). Such foolishness frames the inclusion of his Birth-Day Ode for 1785. Coming after the balloon trip and the excesses of other poets, the poem appears even more wretched than it does normally, its references to George III's 'sacred pattern' of kingship more than usually wooden (*Probationary Odes*, 113–14). Such servility effects a greater diminution, the art of poetry becoming little more than the art of panegyric: making Warton another Puff. The implication confirms the claim made elsewhere in *Probationary Odes*: that poets laureate are little more than 'court dancers', paid to perform for sorry causes and wayward kings (*Probationary Odes*, ix–xi). The worst of Warton's efforts would come in his Odes for 1786 and 1787. His New Year and Birthday Odes laud the king for his resolution in war, kindness in peace, and, in a neat turn of phrase, as a 'patron king'. Warton was a fine poet but his heralding of George III as a successor to Richard the Lionheart was

---

[36] James Boswell, *The Life of Johnson*, ed. Pat Rogers (Oxford: Oxford University Press, 1991), 1074.

[37] See Thomas Warton, *The Poetical Works of the Late Thomas Warton* (Oxford: Oxford University Press, 1802), 86–8.

beneath him. Given these later mistakes, Tickell and Richardson had, to use their own term, *anticipated* Warton, an achievement that they were not shy of celebrating.[38]

The Foxites' next effort, *Political Miscellanies*, began confidently, noting the 'very favourable reception given to the ROLLIAD, and PROBATIONARY ODES, had induced the Editor to conceive, that a collection of political *Jeus d'Esprits*, by the authors of those celebrated performances, would prove equally acceptable' (*Political Miscellanies*, v). The material is genuinely various. Odes, purportedly by William Mason, occur alongside epigrams and eclogues (*Political Miscellanies*, 2–5, 10–15, 21–3); alongside poetry comes 'Lord Graham's Diary', a *faux* naïve account of the opening week of parliament (*Political Miscellanies*, 34–6); a 'Political Receipt Book' containing tips on how to prepare a Chancellor: 'Take a man of great attributes, with a heart as black as his countenance' (*Political Miscellanies*, 49); and an 'Advertisement Extraordinary' requesting information on the missing parents and grandparents of newly created peers (*Political Miscellanies*, 87–8). The variety and ebullience in some measure masks familiar Foxite themes: Warren Hastings and India; the Westminster election and Sir Cecil Wray; fears of secret influence and the work of Jenkinson. Pitt is once more installed as the primary target. In the 'Anecdotes of Mr. Pitt', the prime minister's day is sketched out from rising at nine, through the fastidiousness of his toilette, romping with a friendly dog, before at '*four* he sleeps. —Mr. PITT eats very heartily, drinks one bottle of port, and two when he *speaks*; so that we may hope that Great Britain will long be blessed with the superintendence of this virtuous and able Minster!!!' (*Political Miscellanies*, 40–1). Pitt's perceived delicacy is again the target:

> 'Tis true, indeed, we oft abuse him,
> Because he bends to no man;
> But slander's self dares not to accuse him
> Of stiffness to a woman

Pitt indeed 'dislikes the fair', probably because he can only offer women 'half-measures'. This is nasty stuff. The tone is not lifted by the jovial acclaim given to the suggestion that 'INCAUTIOUS Fox will oft repose / in fair-one's bosom thoughts of worth' (*Political Miscellanies*, 21–2). To claim that the portrayal of Pitt is homophobic is to risk anachronism; but not to mention its wearisome assault on effeminacy (with its misogynistic assumptions) is to be evasive at best.[39] The Foxites were unrelenting in this respect, as they were in their suspicions of anything and everyone remotely connected with Scotland. It is rarely very palatable (*Political Miscellanies*, 11, 76–8; *Probationary Odes*, 54–9).

---

[38] Warton, *Poetical Works*, 98–115; [Richard Tickell and Joseph Richardson] to Thomas Warton, August 1785, *The Correspondence of Thomas Warton*, ed. David Fairer (Athens: University of Georgia Press, 1995), 543–4.

[39] See Randolph Trumbach, *Sex and the Gender Revolution, Volume One: Heterosexuality and the Third Gender in Enlightenment London* (Chicago: University of Chicago Press, 1998).

FOXITE AND ANTI-FOXITE SATIRE

It is worth reflecting, at the close of this essay, on the strength of the satires written against the Foxites. Fox was the target of ridicule even before he entered parliament. Samuel Foote's *The Cozeners* mocked his self-indulgence as early as 1774.[40] Once he had become prominent in politics he featured regularly in print and graphic satires. He was often presented as 'Reynard', terribly hirsute and sometimes boasting a bushy tail.[41] Sheridan attracted his share of satires too, some reflecting on his theatrical involvements, such as *The Critick Anticipated; or, The Humours of Green Room* or *An Epistle from Joseph Surface*, others on his political ambitions.[42] James Gillray, a career satirist of the Foxites, played them a back-handed compliment in 1787 with the publication of his *Anticipation, or the Approaching Fate of the French Commercial Treaty*.[43] The Foxites appear as dogs (as do the government), each intent on ripping the bill to shreds (Figure 8.1). The bill was important to Sheridan and to others; but they would have been struck by Gillray's assumption of their key satiric term. One satire, however, appears to respond directly to Sheridan's prominent place within the Foxite literary scene: *The Beauties of the Brinsleiad*. The text, like *The Rolliad*, claims to be a candid critical examination of a poem which appears only in selected 'extracts'.[44] To this degree the *Brinsleiad* offers a compliment to the Foxites: the *Brinsleiad* is *The Rolliad* imitated. Sheridan is made to look rather simpering, just as Pitt had been in *The Rolliad*. His connections to the theatre and to politics are laid out with skilful malice:

> Skill'd to delight the public or distract,
> With tickling fiction, and with tortured fact,
> To please or point the judgment of the town,
> Write himself up, or write his rivals down.
>
> (*Brinsleiad*, 9)

Sheridan thus appears at the head of the writers and theatre makers clustered around Drury Lane and Fox, to whom he must always play second fiddle (*Brinsleiad*, 31–2). There are some well-taken jibes at the Whigs' use of the daily press not least to the speech-improving memory of William Woodfall, whose *Morning Chronicle* 'remembers what no other hears' (*Brinsleiad*, 33). What the *Brinsleiad* reveals most acutely is how important the clash between Sheridan and Pitt was within the satirical milieu of the

---

[40] Samuel Foote, *The Cozeners. A Comedy* (1776).

[41] See Diana Donald, *The Age of Caricature: Satirical Prints in the Reign of George III* (New Haven: Yale University Press, 1996), 39, 61, 167–72.

[42] See 'R.B.S, Esq.', *The Critick Anticipated; or, The Humours of Green Room* (1779); and *An Epistle from Joseph Surface, Esq. to Richard Brinsley Sheridan, Esq. of Great Queen Street; Chairman of the Sub-Committee for Westminster* (1780).

[43] James Gillray, *Anticipation, or the Approaching Fate of the French Commercial Treaty* (1787).

[44] *The Beauties of the Brinsleiad: or, a Sketch of the Opposition* (1785), iii. Subsequent references appear in the text.

FIGURE 8.1 James Gillray, *Anticipation* (1787) http://hdl.handle.net/10079/digcoll/550795
Courtesy of The Lewis Walpole Library, Yale University

1780s. Fox is immensely important, of course, but Sheridan is singled out rather more than might be expected. The reason may lie in the spat between Sheridan and Pitt during the Commons debate on the 'Preliminary Articles of Peace, between Great Britain and France and Spain', the treaty that concluded the American War of Independence. Although Sheridan had made a significant contribution to the debate, he spoke a second time after Pitt had alluded to his earlier work for the stage. In response, Sheridan compared Pitt to the 'Angry Boy in the Alchymist'; a line repeated in Foxite texts (*Political Miscellanies*, 15).[45]

The anti-Foxite satires that circulated in the 1780s reveal the uncomfortable truth that the Foxite Whigs could be assailed and lampooned from a number of perspectives. They could be attacked, most obviously, as self-indulgent and insular, but also, and with equal force, from radical as well as conservative positions. They did not always convince as reformers, or even as opponents of government, seeming merely to score points. Their satires shared ideas, images, and assumptions as much as they differed from their opponents. Most obviously, it was important for Foxites that their heroes were manly and that effeminacy was despised. This narrow and narrowing perspective reveals the role that political satire played in creating the increasingly fixed regime of identity described by Dror Wahrman. To this degree, they inhabit the same masculine satirical

---

[45] Sheridan, *Speeches*, i. 47.

world as the prints commended by Vic Gatrell.[46] The Foxites were at their best when they replicated print culture, especially the meeting point between high and low forms. There is real glee in *The Rolliad* when new editions of the poem arrive or are anticipated. Further publication means more rubbish ensuring more fun (*Rolliad*, 11, 16, 25). Print culture's darker aspect appears conspicuously in relation to newspapers. The press does not provide only profusion and proliferation: comic plenty is subsumed beneath obfuscation, deception, and the deployment of government power. Although the Foxites manipulated the press themselves, they remained concerned, indeed almost paranoid, that the press was unrelentingly distorting and damaging public culture and debate. They saw this as connected to the rise of gossip, scandal, and libel; much of which they produced themselves. The Foxite vision is of a world of spin and sleaze much like our own.

The satire, it is true, is not especially stern, nor as politically trenchant as that of Charles Churchill, or of Pope, whom the Foxites admired (*Rolliad*, 21, 24). *Anticipation*, *The Rolliad*, and *Probationary Odes* lampoon government ministers but never exclusively, and there is a sense in which they are mocked because they are government minsters, enjoying the privileges and accepting the compromises of their office rather than for reasons that might be defined as ideological. There is no alternative programme suggested, only broad swipes at corruption and undue influence. India was the exception, as in some senses it always was for the Foxites.[47] When *The Rolliad* turns its attention to the government of India, more concrete targets in the form of Warren Hastings appear (*Rolliad*, 37–40). Hastings's conduct brought forward fundamental issues of polity, commerce, and empire. These concerns would form into prosecution by 1787. Corruption and cruelty are then not so much cited or lamented, as *anticipated* in the fullest sense: understood, regretted, and traduced. Exposure of flawed character is the abiding concern. In Foxite satire, character is fixed, even if it is defined as essentially mutable. Personality is not, as it was becoming for novelists, a shifting pattern of desires and opportunities.[48] The true character, most obviously of a government minister, might require some satiric excavation (or a peep in the closet) but it is essentially there all the time, waiting to be revealed. Pope conceived of character in much the same way; and what Pope wrote about women, might be said of what the Foxites thought about Pitt: 'no character at all', save for a formless appetite for 'sway'.[49] Foxite satire, consequently, appears somewhat familiar, rooted in the traditions of English satire. It is rich in the habits and assumptions of Pope, Arbuthnot, and Churchill (so at least they hoped). However, by uniting the talents of Sheridan, Tickell, Laurence, Ellis, and Richardson,

---

[46] Dror Wahrman, *The Making of the Modern Self: Identity and Culture in Eighteenth-Century England* (New Haven: Yale University Press, 2004); Vic Gatrell, *City of Laughter: Sex and Satire in Eighteenth-Century London* (London: Atlantic Books, 2006).

[47] See Jeremy Osborn, 'India and the Company in the Public Sphere', in *The Worlds of the East India Company*, ed. H. V. Bowen, Margarette Lincoln, and Nigel Rigby (London: Boydell, 2002), 215–18; and David Wilkinson, *The Duke of Portland: Politics and Party in the Age of George III* (Basingstoke: Palgrave Macmillan, 2003), 54–8.

[48] See Deidre Shauna Lynch, *The Economy of Character: Novels, Market Culture, and the Business of Inner Meaning* (Chicago: University of Chicago Press, 1998).

[49] Pope, *Poems* (Twickenham), iii.2. 46.

Foxite satire animated the Whigs, providing a canny literary response to George III's ministers. It would stretch plausibility too far to claim that they represented a new cultural formation. But as a group of mostly professional writers, working together, they stand out from the elite Whigs who patronized them. Blue cuff rather more than blue collar, they used pen and print to challenge government, resumption, and sinecures, and did so effectively.

SELECT BIBLIOGRAPHY

Barker, Hannah. *Newspapers, Politics, and Public Opinion in Late Eighteenth-Century England* (Oxford: Clarendon Press, 1998).

Cannon, John. *The Fox–North Coalition: Crisis of the Constitution 1782–84* (Cambridge: Cambridge University Press, 1969).

Donald, Diana. *The Age of Caricature: Satirical Prints in the Reign of George III* (New Haven: Yale University Press, 1996).

Gatrell, Vic. *City of Laughter: Sex and Satire in Eighteenth-Century London* (London: Atlantic Books, 2006).

Mee, Jon. *Print, Publicity, and Popular Radicalism in the 1790s: The Laurel of Liberty* (Cambridge: Cambridge University Press, 2016).

Mitchell, Leslie. *The Whig World: 1760–1837* (London: Hambledon Continuum, 2005).

Trumbach, Randolph. *Sex and the Gender Revolution, Volume One: Heterosexuality and the Third Gender in Enlightenment London* (Chicago: University of Chicago Press, 1998).

PART II

SATIRICAL INHERITANCES

CHAPTER 9

....

THE DOUBLE
PERSONALITY OF
LUCIANIC SATIRE
FROM DRYDEN
TO FIELDING

....

NICHOLAS McDOWELL

THE ENGLISH LUCIAN

....

HENRY Fielding (1707–54) devoted the issue of *The Covent-Garden Journal* on 30 June 1752 to an account of the style and ethics of Lucian of Samosata (*c*.120–180), dwelling in particular upon the inadequacy of all attempts hitherto to render Lucian's Greek into English. Fielding declared Lucian to be inimitable 'in the exquisite Pleasantry of his Humour, in the Neatness of his Wit, and in the Poignancy of his Satire'. Among writers in English, only Jonathan Swift (1667–1745) came close: 'To say Truth, I can find no better Way of giving the English Reader an Idea of the Greek Author, than by telling him, that to translate Lucian well into English, is to give us another Swift in our own Language.' In comparing Swift with Lucian, Fielding was rehashing a scene in his recent novel *Amelia* (1751), in which Captain Booth, 'a pretty good Master of the Classics', and at times an avatar of Fielding himself, opines at length upon his conviction that Swift— who 'hath been generally allowed by the Critics in this Kingdom, to be the greatest Master of Humour that ever wrote'—derived his satirical method from Lucian 'above all others'. Yet Booth is quick to add that he regards not even Swift to be Lucian's equal, proceeding to bemoan the failure to produce a translation from the Greek, whether in English or in French, which is both accurate and true to the character of Lucianic satire. In *The Covent-Garden Journal*, Fielding specifically criticized a translation 'which hath Mr. [John] Dryden's Name to the Preface (for indeed he translated but little himself)', as offering 'the Reader no more Idea of the Spirit of Lucian, than the vilest Imitation by a Sign-post Painter can convey the Spirit of the excellent Hogarth'.[1]

The translation in question, *The Works of Lucian, Translated from the Greek, by several Eminent Hands*, had appeared in four volumes in 1710–11, over a decade after John Dryden's death: Dryden (1631–1700) was in fact responsible only for the 'Life' of Lucian prefixed to the first volume, which he apparently composed around 1696.[2] The essay on Lucian in *The Covent-Garden Journal* was a puff for Fielding's own proposed translation, to be completed in partnership with his friend William Young, who had the superior Greek and with whom Fielding had earlier collaborated on a rendering of Aristophanes' *Plutus* (1742). The previous issue of the journal (27 June 1752) had advertised Fielding and Young's 'Proposals for Printing by Subscription a New Translation into English, of the Works of Lucian, from the Original Greek; with Notes Historical, Critical, and Explanatory'. Declaring himself (in the third person) ideally suited to translating Lucian, Fielding even went so far as to make the claim that he, as much as Swift, was the modern heir of the Greek satirist: 'no Man seems so likely to translate an Author well, as he who hath formed his Stile upon that very Author'.[3] In the event, the translation was not only never completed, but apparently never begun.

The commercial motivation for Fielding's lofty claims for Lucianic satire in *The Covent-Garden Journal* encourages some wariness about taking at face value the assertion that he modelled his own style upon Lucian. Despite the fact that the catalogue of Fielding's library lists nine copies of Lucian, including two French translations and one in English, it has been argued that the influence must have been minimal because Fielding never actually quotes Lucian at any point in his writings. Indeed the apparent failure of Fielding and Young to attract enough subscribers to pursue their proposed translation has been taken as proof that 'Lucian was not widely read in the eighteenth century'.[4] Yet the English Lucian was essentially a phenomenon of the later seventeenth and early eighteenth centuries: the first substantial English translation did not appear until 1634, but was then followed in 1663 by a further large volume of previously untranslated writings and in 1684–5 by a complete works derived via an earlier French version, while the 1710–11 *Works* bemoaned by Fielding was the first complete translation that claimed to be done directly from the Greek.

Moreover, the evidence of Fielding's debt to Lucian should not be measured simply in terms of direct imitation, although that can be found in several of the plays, such as *Tumble-Down Dick* (1736), with its comic quarrelling between pagan gods, and

[1] *The Covent-Garden Journal*, 52 (30 June 1752), in Henry Fielding, *The Covent-Garden Journal and A Plan of the Universal Register-Office*, ed. Bertrand A. Goldgar (Oxford: Oxford University Press, 1988), 286, 288; Henry Fielding, *Amelia*, ed. Martin C. Battestin (Oxford: Oxford University Press, 1984), 324–5.

[2] For the dating of Dryden's 'Life', see the 'Epistle Dedicatory' by the publisher Samuel Briscoe, in *The Works of Lucian, Translated from the Greek*, 4 vols. (London, 1710–11), i, sig. A3r.

[3] Goldgar (ed.), *Covent-Garden Journal*, 289.

[4] Fredrick G. Ribble and Anne G. Ribble, *Fielding's Library: An Annotated Catalogue* (Charlottesville: Bibliographical Society of the University of Virginia, 1996), 26–34; Nancy A. Mace, *Henry Fielding's Novels and the Classical Tradition* (Newark: University of Delaware Press, 1996), 54–7 (55).

The Author's Farce (1732) and *Eurydice, A Farce* (1737), with their underworld settings; or in the Lucianic form of several of the prose satires and dialogues collected in *Miscellanies* (1743), including *A Journey from this World to the Next*, 'Interlude between Jupiter, Juno, Apollo, and Mercury', and 'Dialogue between Alexander the Great and Diogenes the Cynic'. A more expansive conception of 'source' and 'influence' is required to recognize how, in the words of Ronald Paulson:

> [Fielding's] persona of the 1730s derives from the Lucianic protagonist (a Menippus, Cyniscus, Damis, Diogenes, or Lucian himself) who asks questions, probing appearance, idealization, myth, and custom. This questioner begins on earth with pseudo-oracles and prophets, charlatans, and sophistical philosophers, then travels up to Olympus or down to Hades. He questions the gods themselves and throws them into confusion, revealing their shoddy pretensions to omniscience.[5]

In this respect, Fielding, or at least the early Fielding, might be considered a more Lucianic writer than many of those who more ostentatiously took the form of Lucian's works as their model. The most popular of these in early modern Europe were the *Dialogues of the Dead*—tales of encounters with the shades of poets, philosophers, and statesmen that were widely imitated and adapted in comic writing of the late seventeenth and early eighteenth centuries, both in France and England—and the *True History*, the fantastic travel narrative which exerted influence on European prose fiction from Thomas More's *Utopia* (1516) onwards.[6]

Fielding's career as a playwright came to an end with the 1737 Licensing Act, which in effect suppressed his plays: these had been widely attacked in *The Grub-Street Journal* and other periodicals as impious and subversive of Christian order. The anonymous author of *A Discourse on Ridicule* (1716), though a defender of the moral uses of laughter, is representative of one strand of opinion about Lucianic satire in the early eighteenth century in his or her anxiety concerning 'Christian writers, who, in imitation of *Lucian*...have drawn a sportive Picture of the other World, of Hell and Judgment, in order to make smart Satyrs upon the Follies and Vices of Mankind'. Such authors 'appear highly blameable for mingling light Wit, and ludicrous Satyr, with the Mention, and Description of Hell, and Judgment, which a good Christian cannot think of without Awe upon his soul' (19). This chapter considers the importance of Lucianic satire as a model for Dryden, Swift, Fielding, and other writers between 1650 and 1760 in the light of what has been called Lucian's 'double personality' in early modern Europe: for some he was an erudite, witty, and moral satirist of hypocrisy; for others, a dangerously irreligious

---

[5] Ronald Paulson, 'Henry Fielding and the Problem of Deism', in *The Margins of Orthodoxy: Heterodox Writing and Cultural Response, 1660–1750*, ed. Roger D. Lund (Cambridge: Cambridge University Press, 1995), 240–70 (245). See also Ronald Paulson, *Satire and the Novel* (New Haven: Yale University Press, 1967), ch. 4, 'The Lucianic Satirist'.

[6] For a general overview, see Christopher Robinson, *Lucian and His Influence in Europe* (London: Duckworth, 1979).

scoffer and sceptic who brought Christian morality into doubt.[7] By the later seventeenth century, he was more usually regarded as both these things—as well as an exemplary prose stylist—and his scepticism was no small part of his appeal as a satirist. However, the rise of deism at the end of the seventeenth century and its association with subversive religious satire encouraged a perception of Lucianic wit as a weapon of the deists, and this association was not merely impressionistic: the English Lucian of 1710–11 included among its contributors, as we shall see, several of the most prominent deists of the late Restoration.

The 'Lucianic protagonist' identified by Paulson in Fielding's plays was a part given by Lucian most memorably to the Cynic philosopher Menippus, who mocks gods and religions of every stripe and professes no ethical commitment other than to the fearless exposure of falsehood. The figure that this protagonist most resembled in eighteenth-century Britain was the deist freethinker, charged by hostile commentators with employing wit, irony, and ridicule to undermine Christian morality and destabilize the conventional structures of Church and State.[8] The association between Lucianic satire and deism was ambiguously encouraged by Dryden in his preface to the 1710–11 translation, but it created problems of reception and reputation for satirical writers such as Swift and Fielding in the first half of the eighteenth century. By the time Fielding directly named the Greek satirist as a model for his own style in 1752, however, English deism was in decline and any controversial energy carried by the name of Lucian in England had largely dissipated: the process of enervation can be traced in Fielding's own treatment of Lucianic modes.

LUCIAN AND THE 'MEN OF WIT AND SATYR'

Lucian had been placed at the heart of Northern European humanism through the enthusiasm of Erasmus and Thomas More for what the ancient Greeks called *spoudogeloion*, or what was known in Latin as *joco-serium*, or *serio-ludere*: serious playfulness. During a visit to England in 1505–6, Erasmus collaborated with More on translating Lucian into Latin and a collection of their translations was issued in Paris in 1506: it went through eight editions by 1534, with a first printed edition in England in 1528. Lucian's savage satirical treatment of philosophers was justified, Erasmus maintained in the dedication of his Latin translation of Lucian's *The Dream, or the Cock*, because

---

[7] Brenda M. Hostington, '"Compluria opuscula longe festivissima": Translations of Lucian in Renaissance England', in *Syntagmatia: Essays on Neo-Latin Literature*, ed. Dirk Sacre and Jan Papy (Leuven: Leuven University Press, 2009), 187–206 (188). See further Douglas Duncan, *Ben Jonson and the Lucianic Tradition* (Cambridge: Cambridge University Press, 1979), 77–96.

[8] Paulson, 'Henry Fielding and the Problem of Deism', 245. On the deist use of wit and irony, see, most recently, Roger D. Lund, *Ridicule, Religion and the Politics of Wit in Augustan England* (Aldershot: Ashgate, 2012).

there is nothing more hateful, nothing we should less endure, than vice masquerading under a show of virtue. But that is of course how [Lucian] got the name of "blasphemer", which means slanderer, and got it (of course) from those whom he had touched on the raw. He takes the same freedom in merrily carving up the gods, whence his second name of "atheist"—actually rather a complimentary title, considering the superstitious paganism of the religion in question.

Erasmus praised Lucian for his way of 'mixing gravity with his nonsense and nonsense with his gravity, of laughing and telling the truth at one and the same time'.[9] Erasmus's *Moriae Encomium* (1511; 'In Praise of Folly') and More's *Utopia* were both products of the delight the two shared in experimenting with *spoudogeloion*.

The humanist interest in Lucian was wrapped up with the qualities of his Greek prose: the dialogues were considered ideal for the teaching of stylish, idiomatic Greek, and to offer the bonus of combining pleasure with pedagogical profit. Selected dialogues of Lucian thus became a staple in the curricula of English grammar schools from the early sixteenth century onwards, studied in Latin in the lower forms, in Greek in the upper. The Lucianic dialogue also provided the model for Erasmus's *Colloquies*, which became a key component of Latin language learning in English grammar schools. This Lucianic heritage is recalled by the prolific 'Grub Street' satirist Tom Brown (1663–1704) in his 1699 translation of seven of the *Colloquies*, in which he equates Lucian and Erasmus as 'Men of Wit and Satyr, [who] employ'd it as Righteously as the old Heroes did their Arms, in beating down the crying Grievances of their Times'. Just as Lucian mercilessly exposed philosophers who sought 'to dupe and amuse the poor People, by the Fantastick Singularity of their Habits, the Unintelligible Jargon of their Schools, and their Pretensions to a severe and mortified Life', so Erasmus lashed those who went 'by the Name of *Monks* and *Friars*, differing from the former in Religion, Garb, and a few other Circumstances, but in the main the same individual Impostors; the same everlasting Cobwebspinners, as to their nonsensical Controversies, the same abandon'd Rakehells as to their Morals'. Brown admitted to regarding Lucian, 'whose Language is easie and negligent but pure', as his model of satirical style, and indeed Brown was responsible for nine translations in the 1710–11 *Works of Lucian*, including the *True History*.[10] Brown adapted the satirical Lucianic underworld to the gossipy sphere of late Restoration London in his contributions to *Letters from the Dead to the Living* (London, 1702), which includes such items as a 'Letter of News from Joseph Haines of Merry Memory, to his Friends at Will's Coffee-House in Covent-Garden'. The well-known actor and rake Haines, who died in 1701, writes from hell, where he takes on the Menippean role and reports on his encounters with, among others, 'that ancient Quaker *Diogenes*, and these modern Cynicks *Fox* and *Naylor*'—the infamous early Quaker leaders, George Fox and James Naylor (15).

Brown's dig at sectarian enthusiasm hints at one of the probable reasons why Lucian had finally begun to appear in English in the mid-seventeenth century. The translation

---

[9] This translation of the Latin is given in Duncan, *Ben Jonson and the Lucianic Tradition*, 28–9.
[10] *Seven New Colloquies Translated Out of Erasmus*, trans. Tom Brown (London, 1699), sigs. B6r–7v.

of Lucian into English was almost non-existent before the 1630s, seemingly due to moral and religious qualms: the influential English humanist Thomas Elyot may have been responsible for *A Dialogue between Lucian and Diogenes of the Life Hard and Sharpe* (1532?), one of only two extant Tudor translations of Lucian into the vernacular, but Elyot himself made clear his conviction 'it were better that a child should never read any part of Lucian, than all Lucian'.[11] The religious condemnation of Lucian became louder as Europe became increasingly fraught with religious division, and this disapproval was impressively ecumenical. When Luther attacked Erasmus, he leapt on his love of Lucianic satire, accusing him of 'foster[ing] in your heart a Lucian, or some other pig from Epicurus' sty, who, having no belief in God himself, secretly ridicule all who have a belief'; while Calvin thought the popes had learned their impiety 'in the school of Lucian'. On the other side, the *opera omnia* of Lucian was placed on the Papal Index in 1590, two individual dialogues attributed to him, 'Peregrinus' and 'Philopatris', having been prohibited since 1559.[12]

As with Machiavelli (in Edward Dacre's version of *The Prince* in 1640) and Rabelais (in Thomas Urquhart's rendering of the first two books of *Gargantua and Pantagruel* in 1653), Lucian's notoriety apparently meant that he had to wait to enter the vernacular until the grip of ecclesiastical censorship began to loosen in the mid-seventeenth century. Indeed Rabelais, who offered one of the most memorable imitations of the Lucianic trip to the underworld in his giant Epistemon's descent to hell in the second book of *Gargantua and Pantagruel* (five books, 1532–64), was often labelled the 'French Lucian' in England.[13] That said, the first substantial English version of Lucian looks innocuous enough, and it emerged from the pedagogical context in which Lucian had long been used without great concern: *Certain Select Dialogues of Lucian, together with his True History*, was the work of one Francis Hickes, a schoolmaster, and was published posthumously in Oxford in 1634 with a commentary and extensive life of Lucian by his son, Thomas. In this influential apology, which was relied upon by later writers, including Dryden, Thomas Hickes sought to have Lucian 'in some sort vindicated from certaine grosse Aspersions, heretofore cast upon him', forcefully denying there to be any evidence for the claim that Lucian was an apostate from Christianity, and that his apostasy explained his alleged hostility to the religion: there was in fact more virtue to be found in Lucian than in Tacitus.[14]

A more significant translation in terms of its cultural politics for the Restoration reception of Lucian was Jasper Mayne's *Part of Lucian made English, in the yeare 1638*, first published in Oxford in 1663. Mayne (1604–72), a member of the Christ Church wits

---

[11] Thomas Elyot, *The Book Named the Governor*, ed. S. E. Lehmberg (London: Dent, 1962), 30.

[12] *Luther and Erasmus: Free Will and Salvation*, ed. E. G. Rupp and P. S. Watson (Philadelphia: Westminster Press, 1969), 109; William J. Bouwsma, *Calvin: A Sixteenth-Century Portrait* (Oxford: Oxford University Press, 1988), 14, 240 n. 24.

[13] Ann Lake Prescott, *Imagining Rabelais in Renaissance England* (New Haven: Yale University Press, 1978), 9–11, 82–4.

[14] *Certain Select Dialogues of Lucian, together with his True History*, trans. Francis Hickes (Oxford, 1634), sig. B3v.

in Caroline Oxford and a fervent royalist during the Civil Wars, dedicated his substantial translation of fifty of Lucian's works to his patron, the former royalist commander William Cavendish, Marquess of Newcastle. Mayne's preface is distinguished by the political appropriation of Lucianic satire for royalism and anti-Puritanism. He imagines Lucian's reaction at beholding 'a self-conceited Preacher goe up *buskined* to the Pulpit...stuffed with Bombast [and] such *bubbles* of expression'; he would 'doubtless send such *Gargantuan, tumid* Orators to the *Doctor* who cured *Lexiphanes* [subject of a dialogue by Lucian translated by Mayne] of his *Fustian* disease, who upon the taking of a purge was deliver'd of a *Tympany*, and made to vomit all his *tuffe*, affected words'. Lucian's 'easie and negligent' style, as Tom Brown ambiguously called it, offers an antidote both to puffed-up, buttoned-up Puritan preaching and to the republican discourse of 'seditious, Rump *Grammarians*', whose '*Rhetorick* was as *rude*, and *mechanick* as their persons', and who '*defile* the English Tongue with their *Republick* words, which are most *immusical* to the Eare, and scarce *significant* to a *Monarchicall* understanding'.[15] In Mayne's translation, the sharp, sophisticated scepticism of Lucian is celebrated for its capacity to skewer the false claims and bloated rhetoric of self-proclaimed prophets. Lucian's religious scepticism was evidently now seen by those of a royalist and anti-Puritan persuasion as speaking to the mad times through which they had lived.

Mayne recalled first attempting the translations for William Cavendish's 'private *Entertainment*', raising the possibility that reading and discussing Lucian was a commonplace activity in the Cavendish household in the 1630s. This was a period when Thomas Hobbes (1588–1679) was a member of the intellectual circle which gathered around Cavendish and his brother Charles. Hobbes would become notorious, of course, for his allegedly atheistic philosophy, and he was specifically connected with Lucian by early opponents such as John Wallis, who compared the 'impure mouth'—*os impurum*, a particularly scornful Roman insult—and atheism of Lucian to Hobbes's satirical abuse of all claims to exclusive spiritual authority, clerical or otherwise.[16] Hobbes himself described Lucian in the appendix to the 1668 Latin version of *Leviathan* (1651) as 'indeed a blasphemer, but a good writer of the Greek language' ('homo quidem Blasphemus, sed bonus author linguae Graecae'): the second quality was seemingly of more importance to Hobbes than the first.[17] Some modern scholars have agreed with Hobbes's contemporary opponents that his philosophy has a 'clear Lucianic dimension' in its persistent ridicule of philosophical falsehood and religious imposture.[18] Direct debts to Lucianic ridicule of false religious belief occasionally bubble up in *Leviathan*. In the chapter 'Of Religion', Hobbes's scorn for pagan deification of 'a Bird, Crocodile, a Calf, a Dogge, a Snake, an Onion, a Leeke' echoes the mockery of the Epicurean philosopher Damis of human beliefs about the gods in Lucian's dialogue 'Zeus the Tragedian':

---

[15] *Part of Lucian made English, in the yeare 1638*, trans. Jasper Mayne (Oxford, 1663), sigs. A3v, A4r.

[16] John Wallis, *Elenchus geometriae Hobbianae* (London, 1655), 89.

[17] Thomas Hobbes, *Leviathan*, ed. Noel Malcolm, 3 vols. (Oxford: Oxford University Press, 2012), iii. 1190–1.

[18] See Conal Condren, *Hobbes, the Scriblerians, and the History of Philosophy* (London: Pickering & Chatto, 2012), 34 and *passim*.

'For you may clearly perceive how the Report, that passeth up and down in the World, concerning the Gods hath no certainty, or stability in it...the *Memphians*, particularly worship an Ox for their God; and the *Pelusians*, worship an Onion; others, a Stork, or Crocodile, or a Cat, or a Monkey...Are not these things worthy to be laughed at?'[19] For satirical resources for his derision of the history of religious ritual, Hobbes turned to a dialogue that has been described as 'probably the most religiously controversial work of Lucian'.[20]

DRYDEN AND A 'NATURALLY SCEPTIC AGE'

The publisher Samuel Briscoe probably had Erasmus and More in mind, rather than Hobbes, when he observed in the dedication of the first volume of the 1710–11 *Works of Lucian* that '*Lucian* has long been the Darling Pleasure of Men of Sense in every Nation'. In his 'Life' of Lucian which follows Briscoe's dedication, Dryden defended Lucian against the claim that he 'was either a steady Atheist, or a Deist'; rather, Dryden maintained, he was 'but a Doubter, a *Sceptic*...he doubted of everything; weigh'd all Opinions, and adhere'd to none of them'.[21] The distinction between Dryden's characterization of Lucian as a doubter of everything and the polemical character of a deist would have been hard for some readers to discern. As the author of *A Satyr against Atheistical Deism with the Genuine Character of a Deist* (1696) put it in the same year that Dryden likely composed his 'Life': '[a Deist is] a Sceptick of the first Magnitude, and the chiefest of that size too; for discourse him upon never so clear and evident Truths, you must of necessity run in *Infinitum* to prove 'em; since he acknowledges no Principles, further than they serve his turn' (7). The deist is characterized by his scoffing as well as his scepticism:

> Yet such are they, who Scoffingly deride
> Those sacred Mistries, which we ought to dread[;]
> Such *Giants*, with Loud-laughters empty Phrase
> Our Rationall and Holy Faith debase[.]   (12)

Dryden ends his 'Life' of Lucian by making the rather unconvincing claim, for which his earlier discussion has not really laid the foundation, that, since 'the fine Raillery and *Attique* Salt of Lucian' were directed against the pagan gods, 'I know not to whose Writings we owe more our *Christianity*...whether to the grave confutation of *Clemens Alexandrinus, Arnobius, Justin Martyr, St. Augustin, Lactantius* &c. or the facetious Wit of *Lucian*'. 'Our Author's chief Design', declares Dryden in a striking turn of phrase that echoes the Erasmian defence of Lucianic method, 'was to disnest Heaven of so many

---

[19] Hobbes, *Leviathan*, ii. 172 (Malcolm cites Juvenal, *Satires*, 15, ll. 1–10, as the source here, but the presence of the onion in Hobbes's list suggests Lucian); *Works of Lucian* (1710–11), i. 233–4.
[20] Tim Whitmarsh, *Beyond the Second Sophistic: Adventures in Greek Postclassicism* (Berkeley: University of California Press, 2013), 177.
[21] *Works of Lucian*, i, sig. A4r, 26, 28.

immoral and debauch'd Deities'; and, in doing so, he provided Christians with a satirical rhetoric that they could adopt and turn against pagan religion.[22]

Following Mayne's example, Dryden more specifically claimed Lucian's satirical scepticism for anti-Puritanism and anti-sectarianism: arguing against the evidence for Lucian's particular animus against Christianity, any more than pagan polytheism, Dryden nonetheless insisted that Lucian's representation of 'the first *Christians*, with their cropt hair, their whining Voices, melancholy Faces, mournful Discourses, nasty Habits, are described with a greater air of *Calvinists* or *Quakers*, than of *Roman Catholicks*, or *Church of England-Men*'.[23] By 1696, when Dryden supposedly composed his 'Life' of Lucian, he had been a convert to Roman Catholicism for over a decade, so his partisanship here is perhaps unsurprising; more unexpected (and oddly undiscussed in scholarship on Dryden), is how his meditation on the nature of Lucianic satire develops into an apology for religious toleration, on the grounds of the unknowability of religious truth. The universality of Lucian's scepticism is healthy because it precludes the blinkered certitude that is a precondition of religious persecution:

> We have indeed the highest Probabilities for our reveal'd Religion; Arguments which will preponderate with a reasonable Man, upon a long and careful Disquisition; but I have always been of Opinion, that we can demonstrate nothing, because the Subject-matter is not capable of a Demonstration. 'Tis the particular Grace of God, that any Man believes the Mysteries of our Faith; which I think a conclusive argument against the Doctrine of Persecution in any Church ... Those reasons which are cogent to me, may not prevail with others, who bear the denomination of *Christians*; and those which are prevalent with all *Christians*, in regard of their Birth and Education, may find no force when they are used against Mahometans or Heathens. To instruct is a charitable Duty; to compel, by Threatenings and Punishment, is the Office of Hangman, and the Principle of a Tyrant.[24]

Dryden's relativistic argument against religious persecution is not merely a self-interested plea for the indulgence of Roman Catholicism, for he is careful to add that while he is convinced of 'all Truths necessary to Salvation in the *Roman* Church', he 'cannot but detest our Inquisition as it is practis'd in some foreign parts'. Indeed he presents the tolerant England of the 1690s as the ideal society to receive Lucian's sceptical satires on religious authority: 'all knowing Ages being naturally *Sceptic*, and not at all bigotted; which, if I am not much decieve'd, is the proper Character of our own'.[25]

Dryden thus argued in his 'Life of Lucian' for religious toleration on the grounds that the fundamental truths of Christian revelation are incapable of certain demonstration without new miracles, and their acceptance is rather dependent on the probability and reasonableness of the arguments, which may make sense to some types of Christian but not to others, and not to Muslims or pagans. The distinction between this position and the deists' characteristic insistence that diverse religions and sects 'make equal

---

[22] *Works of Lucian*, i. 39, 43.   [23] 'Mr *Dryden's* Life of Lucian', in *Works of Lucian*, i. 20.
[24] *Works of Lucian*, i. 17–18.   [25] *Works of Lucian*, i. 18, 28.

(and equally dubious) claims to moral authority' is far from obvious.[26] As the deist tutor Square observes in a debate with Parson Thwackum about the nature of virtue in Fielding's *Tom Jones* (1749): 'I will maintain it [virtue] may exist independent of any Religion whatsoever. Nay, (added he) you yourself will allow it may exist independent of all but one; so will a *Mahometan*, a *Jew*, and all the Maintainers of all the different Sects in the World.'[27]

It was after 1689 that the arguments for and against deism which were to shape religious controversy in the first half of the eighteenth century first became a matter of urgent polemical debate.[28] As early as 1682, however, and before his conversion to Rome, Dryden had defended Anglican doctrine against Roman Catholic beliefs on the one side, and deist arguments on the other, in his poem *Religio Laici*. The poem was received with anger and derision by Dryden's many enemies precisely because of his reputation as a Lucianic figure, as 'a mocker of religion, an inveterate anti-clerical, and a cynical professional writer'. As Martin Clifford, for example, exclaimed at the notion of Dryden writing on behalf of either Anglicanism or Roman Catholicism: 'How ridiculously doth he appear in Print for any Religion, who hath made it his business to laugh at all!'[29] This reputation stemmed from Dryden's earlier satirical attacks on what the deists liked scornfully to label 'priestcraft', most obviously in *Absalom and Achitophel* (1681), with its opening anticlerical punch—'In pious times, 'ere priestcraft did begin' (line 1).[30] *Absalom and Achitophel*, for all its anti-Whig purpose, makes little firm distinction between clerical orders, nonconformist preachers, and sectarian enthusiasts in its portrayal of a time and place: 'Where Sanhedrin and priest enslaved the nation / And justified their spoils by inspiration' (lines 523–4). There seems little ambiguity in the assertion: 'For priests of all religions are the same / Of whatsoe'er descent their godhead be' (lines 99–100).

It is not necessary to go as far as William Empson, who maintained in the 1970s that *Religio Laici* was really a deist work disguised as a defence of orthodoxy, to see why Dryden was sometimes charged in his later career, much to his vexation, with being one of the deistical mockers of religion.[31] Indeed soon after Dryden wrote his 'Life of Lucian', he characterized Chaucer in the preface to *Fables Ancient and Modern* (1700) in terms similar to his depiction of Lucian, observing that '[a] satirical poet is the check of the laymen on bad Priests...I shall think hereafter to describe another sort of Priests, such as are more easily to be found than [Chaucer's] good Parson; such as have been the last blow to Christianity in this age'.[32] If, as John Spurr has nicely put it, 'Dryden's cast of

[26] Roger D. Lund, 'Introduction', in *Margins of Orthodoxy*, 1–29 (1).

[27] Henry Fielding, *Tom Jones*, ed. Sheridan Baker (New York: Norton, 1995), 83 (III. iii).

[28] The best guide to the rise of deism remains Justin Champion, *The Pillars of Priestcraft Shaken: The Church of England and its Enemies, 1660–1730* (Cambridge: Cambridge University Press, 1992).

[29] John Spurr, 'The Piety of John Dryden', in *The Cambridge Companion to John Dryden*, ed. Steven N. Zwicker (Cambridge: Cambridge University Press, 2004), 237–58 (253); Martin Clifford, *Notes Upon Mr Dryden's Poems* (London, 1687), 34.

[30] Although see the note on 'priestcraft' in Dryden, *Poems* (Longman), i. 454, which offers the possibility that Dryden's use of the term is ironic.

[31] William Empson, 'A Deist Tract by Dryden', *Essays in Criticism* 25, no. 1 (1975), 74–100.

[32] Dryden, *Poems* (Longman), v. 73.

mind was sceptical [and] his imagination was suited to dialogues and debates', then Dryden must have recognized in Lucian both a mode of writing and a sceptical wit with which he felt some sympathy.[33] He surely also identified his own experience of being attacked as a mocker of religion with what he regarded as the misrepresentation of Lucian, whom he defended as a writer who had rather sought to 'check' religious corruption through satire.

'PROFANE AND DEBAUCHED DEISTS'—AND SWIFT

Dryden's reputation was not helped when the leading deist and self-declared Hobbist Charles Blount (1654–93) replied to *Religio Laici* in 1683, claiming in the prefatory address to Dryden that 'I designed this Treatise of mine to be onely an *Addition*, or rather the *Consequence* of yours; encouraging Men to Live up to the *Vertue* of that *Doctrine* you teach'. The irony may seem thick, but Blount skilfully manages to 'imply solidarity with a Dryden who merits the charge of impiety'.[34] Dryden returned the ironic compliment in his 'Life of Lucian' by drawing attention to the responsibility of Blount—whose 'wit, and other Performances' have 'made too much noise in the world, to need a Herald'—for six of the translations of Lucian in the first volume of the 1710–11 edition, including 'Zeus the Tragedian' (rendered as 'Jupiter Tragædus').[35] Indeed Blount was joined among the translators in the 1710–11 English Lucian by several other well-known deists and republicans: Walter Moyle (1672–1721), who proposed in works that circulated in manuscript a minimalist civil religion based on the ancient Roman model to replace the clerical institution of the Church of England; Charles Gildon (1665–1724), who collaborated with Blount on *The Oracles of Reason* (1693) and edited some of Blount's deist writings after he died in 1693; James Tyrrell (1642–1718), radical Whig, brother-in-law of Blount, and close friend of John Locke; and Joseph Washington, a prominent radical Whig lawyer, who in 1692 translated Milton's Latin apology for the regicide, the *Defensio* (1651), complete with 'deist emphases'.[36] As Hardin Craig observed nearly a century ago: 'The cause of the Lucian revival, if we may judge by the group of translators [Dryden] mentions and their friends, was interest in Lucian as a satirist and as a possible deist.'[37]

---

[33] Spurr, 'Piety of John Dryden', 238.

[34] Charles Blount, *Religio laici written in a letter to John Dryden, Esq.* (London, 1683), sigs. A7r, a12r; Michael B. Prince, '*Religio Laici* vs. *Religio Laici*: Dryden, Blount and the Origin of English Deism', *Modern Language Quarterly* 74 no. 1 (2013), 29–66 (37).

[35] *Works of Lucian*, i. 50.

[36] On Blount and Moyles, see Champion, *Pillars of Priestcraft Shaken*, 142–50, 186–91; on Tyrrell and Washington, see Nicholas Von Maltzahn, 'The Whig Milton, 1667–1700', in *Milton and Republicanism*, ed. David Armitage, Armand Himy, and Quentin Skinner (Cambridge: Cambridge University Press, 1995), 229–53 (248).

[37] Hardin Craig, 'Dryden's Lucian', *Classical Philology* 16, no. 2 (1921), 141–63 (154).

Dryden's Lucian, in other words, confirms the attraction of Lucian to the early English deists and suggests that there were good grounds for the hostile association of Lucianic satire with deist polemical techniques. Walter Moyle's prefatory argument to his rendering of Lucian's 'Of Sacrifices' immediately announces this English Lucian as above all a satirist of priestcraft. We are told that Lucian's main target in 'Of Sacrifices'—a treatise which mercilessly ridicules how men pray and petition in their erroneous belief that the gods take any notice of what they do—is the 'Design and Knavery of Priests'. Moyle's ironic comparison with the English clergy is hardly subtle: 'I am glad, for the Honour of my Religion, that the Pagan Priests are the Reverse of ours, and that a satyr upon them is a Panegyrick upon the Clergy of our Church, whose unshaken Firmness to their Principles, Zeal for the Religion and Liberty of their Country, and a thousand other great Qualities, may justly secure them from all the groundless Cavils of our modern Sceptics'. Moyle, of course, was prime among those 'modern Sceptics'. The first volume of the 1710–11 Lucian follows Dryden's 'Life' with four translations by Moyle and six by Blount, several of which are among Lucian's most ferocious satires on the 'Poetical Fictions', as Moyle puts it in one of his prefaces, that men foolishly elevate to embodiments of divinity. Blount translated not only 'Zeus the Tragedian', in which he transmitted into the vernacular the Epicurean philosopher Damis' outright denial of the existence of providence ('all Things . . . come to pass by Chance, and without the Providence of the Gods') but also 'Alexander, or, The False Prophet' and 'Philopseudes, or, The Lyar', both of which ridicule tales of miracles, prophecies, and apparitions as fictions employed by cunning men for their own profit.[38]

The implication of such works for Blount and his fellow deists was that the Christian narrative may similarly be a fiction elaborated for the benefit of particular groups. One of Blount's most notorious publications, later condemned to public burning, was his 1680 translation of Philostratus's third-century life of Apollonius of Tyana, a Pythagorean philosopher and contemporary of Jesus said to have similarly performed miracles but whose teachings had been discredited, while those of Jesus had been developed into the institutionalized doctrine of Christianity—an outcome due, Blount observes in copious marginal annotations to his translation, to the self-interested machinations of those who sought to impose a clerical order upon the people. In Lucian, the religious impostor Alexander is a student from the school of Apollonius; in his preface to *The Oracles of Reason*, Charles Gildon makes explicit the deist connection between Philostratus's Apollonius, Lucian's Alexander, and the behaviour of the contemporary Christian clergy, whom Gildon accused of imitating

> the ancient Founders of Paganism, for having recourse to Stratagems, to reduce Mens Reason to particular Opinions . . . they perceiv'd the Generality of Mankind would easily submit their Reason to every appearance of a Wonder, to fish for their Profit and Glory, with so easie a Bait. *Alexander* the false Prophet, mentioned by *Lucian*, found it turn to his Advantage, in gaining him so great an Interest in the People. And from this Topic *Philostrates* magnifies *Apollonius*.

---

[38] *Works of Lucian*, i. 14, 228. Blount's translations must evidently have been completed before his death in 1693; Moyle dates his translations to 1693.

In his *Two First Books of Philostratus*, Blount cites Lucian on thirteen occasions, including 'Of Sacrifices', to illustrate how the ancient poets invented the absurdly anthropomorphic behaviour of the pagan gods, and he also uses the alleged exemplary demise of Lucian to make the typical deist point that the historical record is not objective truth, but often written out of subjective self-interest: 'If you believe the Monks...*Lucian* was torn in pieces by Dogs which scandal they rais'd upon him for being an enemy to their Religion; notwithstanding other Historians tell us he died in much honour, being Procurator of *Egypt*.'[39]

The 1710–11 English Lucian was thus substantially the work of leading deists and radical Whigs of the 1690s, which might help explain why Fielding condemned the translation as the 'vilest Imitation'. It remained unchallenged as the English translation of the works—despite Fielding's advertised ambitions in 1752—until Thomas Francklin's *Works of Lucian, From the Greek*, appeared in 1780. In his marginal notes on his translation, Francklin offered a commentary on Lucianic influence on more recent literature, observing of the *True History* that 'the reader will easily perceive that *Bergerac*, *Swift* and other writers have read this Work of *Lucian's*, and are much indebted to it'. On the description in the *True History* of a ship suspended in mid-air, Francklin points out that this is 'in the same manner as Gulliver's island of Laputa—From this passage it is not improbable but that Swift borrowed the idea'.[40] Swift's contemporary readers evidently recognized the debt owed by *Gulliver's Travels* (1726) to the *True History*, in terms both of its satirical form—an episodic, eyewitness description of a fantastic voyage—and the content of some specific episodes, such as Laputa. There is, though, a crucial difference: Lucian makes it very clear in the preface to his tale that it is nothing more than a satire on such purported histories and travel narratives, with their ridiculous lies ('such swinging Rappers', as Tom Brown nicely has it in his translation). The success of such ludicrous works shows how lucrative the 'Trade of lying' can be: 'the only true Word in the following History is, that 'tis wholly made up of Lyes'.[41] If, as Fielding claimed, Swift learned from Lucian 'above all others', then he probably learned less from the generic example of the *True History*, which makes its intentions very clear, than from the more indirect and elusive techniques of Lucianic dialogue, which make the reader work hard to discriminate between *jocus* and *serium*. Many of Lucian's dialogues are 'fragments of "overhead" conversation in which the satiric point has to be deduced by the reader from the unconscious self-revelation of the speakers'.[42] This technique of testing the reader to identify the ridicule of abuses through the progressive self-implication of a speaker—whose 'character' is at the same time not consistent but a function of the satiric point being made at a particular moment—shapes both *Gulliver's Travels* and, in more intense and dizzying style, *A Tale of a Tub* (1704) and its companion pieces.

[39] Charles Blount, *The Oracles of Reason* (London, 1693), sig. B4v; Charles Blount, *The Two First Books of Philostratus, concerning the life of Apollonius Tyaneus* (London, 1680), 6.

[40] *Works of Lucian, From the Greek*, trans. Thomas Francklin, 2 vols. (London, 1780), i. 413, 416 n.

[41] *Works of Lucian*, iii. 124–5. Cf. Ashley Marshall, *Swift and History: Politics and the English Past* (Cambridge: Cambridge University Press, 2015), 115–16.

[42] Duncan, *Ben Jonson and the Lucianic Tradition*, 14.

Despite its ridicule of Epicureanism, Hobbesian materialism, and other philosophies associated with the deists, the satirical treatment of religious controversy in *A Tale of a Tub*, which appeared anonymously, was widely received as the work of one of those 'Profane and debauched Deists', who 'pretend commonly in their Discourse and Writings to expose the Abuses and Corruptions of Religion; but (as it is too manifest in some of their modern Books, as well as in their Talk,) they aim really against all Virtue in general'.[43] It was claimed that the 3rd Earl of Shaftesbury, Anthony Ashley Cooper (1671–1713), regarded by his critics as the socially acceptable face of deist anticlericalism, must be the real author, while William Wotton accused the author of having based his satirical style upon that of the infamous Irish deist John Toland (1670–1722), author of *Christianity Not Mysterious, or, A Treatise shewing that there is Nothing in the Gospel Contrary to Reason* (1696), 'who always raises a laugh at the Word *Mystery*, the Word and Thing whereof he is known to believe to be no more than *A Tale of a Tub*'.[44] Swift added a typically tricksy apology to the fifth edition of the *Tale* in 1710 in response to this reception, but the apology did not entirely stop the charge of impiety: in 1711, Matthew Tindal—himself a notorious freethinker—insisted Swift had done far worse than those who were more usually charged with deism and infidelity (such as Tindal himself) in his satirical treatment of religion in the *Tale*. Swift, as an ordained cleric, had 'infinitely outdone that Heathen scoffer [Lucian] in ridiculing the Gospel and treating Christianity with so much Scorn and Contempt'.[45] In the light of the deists' interest in Lucian as a resource and model for their attacks on priestcraft, we can better see why Swift's adaptation in the *Tale* of techniques associated with Lucianic satire provoked quite such a reaction.

FIELDING'S 'TRUE WIT AND HUMOUR'

Dryden's assertion that Lucian's satirical purpose was 'to disnest Heaven of so many immoral and debauch'd Deities' must have caught Fielding's eye, for he quoted it in his apology for Lucian in *The Covent-Garden Journal*.[46] Fielding evidently still felt as late as 1752 that he had to justify the moral and religious basis of plans to render Lucian's '*Attique* Salt' into English, despite evidence that Lucianic satire had lost much of its atheistic reputation by the second half of the eighteenth century. Howard Weinbrot has argued that French imitations of the underworld dialogue, such as Bernard le Bovier de Fontenelle's *Nouveaux Dialogues des Morts* (1683)—quickly translated into English by 'J. D' the following year and again by John Hughes in 1708—and François

[43] Samuel Clarke, *Discourse Concerning the Unchangeable Obligations of Natural Religion* (London, 1706), 20, 29.
[44] William Wotton, *Defense of the Reflections upon Ancient and Modern Learning* (London, 1705), 53; see further Lund, *Ridicule, Religion and the Politics of Wit*, 170–2.
[45] Matthew Tindal, *The Nation Vindicated, from the aspersions Cast on it* (London, 1711), 37.
[46] Goldgar (ed.), *Covent-Garden Journal*, 286.

Fénelon's *Dialogue des Morts* (1712) 'cleansed Lucian's underworld, sentimentalized and Christianized it while adding benign norms'. They did so in part by getting rid of the 'Lucianic protagonist'—the Menippean figure prominent in Fielding's drama. The same 'religious and sentimental softening' of the Lucianic-Menippean tradition has been observed by Weinbrot in English imitations of the later eighteenth century, such as the popular *Dialogues of the Dead* by George, Lord Lyttelton (1760).[47] The moral perspective of Lyttelton—Fielding's classmate at Eton and sometime patron during the 1740s—on Lucianic satire is exemplified by his dialogue between the ghosts of Rabelais and Lucian himself. The two satirists initially congratulate themselves on being such 'audacious Freethinkers' but end up lamenting their failure to exert 'the sharpness of our wit to combat the flippancy and pertness of those who argue only by jests against reason and evidence in points of the highest and most serious concern'.[48]

Fielding had himself been part of this process of 'softening', having moved away from the rude scepticism of the Menippean voices of his plays to the moral certainties of an orthodox Christian framework in his later Lucianic prose. In *A Journey from this World to the Next*, however, composed around five years after the Licensing Act ended his theatrical career, Fielding rewrote Lucian's best-known dialogue of the dead, Menippus's visit to the underworld, to align it with more orthodox, typically Anglican values. Menippus sees all men, whether rich or poor, kings or slaves, sentenced to terrible tortures by Minos, judge of the underworld. In Lucian, characteristically, those who were rich and beautiful in life are indistinguishable from the poor and wretched in death: as the 1710–11 translation has it, 'their Bones were all alike, indiscriminate, nameless and unknown'. This 'spectacle' provokes Menippus to regard 'the Life of Men like some tedious Procession, manag'd and Marshalled by Fortune'. In Fielding's version, Menippus is absent and Minos allows various types through the gate to Elysium for their acts of charity, from a criminal who has cared for his family, to the Lord Mayor of London, to the speaker himself, on account of his 'general Philanthropy'. The focus is on Christian redemption and eternal reward through a balance-sheet of good works in life rather than an authentically Lucianic dissolution of earthly hierarchy before the indiscriminate punishments of the afterlife.[49]

Fielding's turn away from the Lucianic scepticism of his plays towards a reaffirmation of something like Anglican orthodoxy coincided with the decline of deist argument in English public life but also his personal rejection of the deist arguments to which he had apparently been attracted in his twenties.[50] Fielding replayed in his fiction his own experience of early attraction to deism, followed by disenchantment with its implications for Christian morality: significantly, the problem is concentrated in debate on the

---

[47] Howard D. Weinbrot, *Menippean Satire Reconsidered: From Antiquity to the 18th Century* (Baltimore: Johns Hopkins University Press, 2005), 62–85 (69, 84).

[48] George, Lord Lyttelton, *Dialogues of the Dead* (1760), 240.

[49] 'Menippus; or, The Necromancer', in *Works of Lucian*, iv. 208; Henry Fielding, *Miscellanies*, ed. Bertrand Goldgar and Hugh Amory (Oxford: Oxford University Press, 1993), 36. Cf. Regina M. James, 'Fielding Reinvents the Afterlife', *Eighteenth-Century Fiction* 23, no. 3 (2011), 495–518.

[50] See Martin C. Battestin, *Henry Fielding: A Life* (London: Routledge, 1989), 152–7.

ethics of religious ridicule. In *Amelia*, a step in Booth's conversion to Christianity is his conversations with Dr Harrison, who maintains that, while '[n]o Man is fonder of true Wit and Humour than myself... to profane sacred Things with Jest and Scoffing is a sure Sign of a weak and wicked Mind'. Harrison's position echoes a recent attack by John Brown, in his *Essays on the Characteristics* (1751), on the Earl of Shaftesbury's infamous apology for the moral and religious efficacy of ridicule, *An Essay on the Freedom of Wit and Humour* (1709). In *Tom Jones*, Square lives his life devoted to the philosophy of Shaftesbury only to convert to Christianity on his deathbed. In one of his final works, *A Fragment of a Comment on L. Bolingbrooke's Essays*, included in *Journal of the Voyage to Lisbon* (1755), Fielding quotes (roughly and from memory) Shaftesbury's *Essay*— 'ridicule is one of those principal lights or natural mediums by which things are to be viewed, in order to a thorough recognition: for that truth, it is supposed, may bear all lights'—but admits there may be some truth in the censure Shaftesbury has received, 'as truth may by such a trial be subjected to misrepresentation, and become a more easy prey to the malice of its enemies'.[51] Fielding's experience with the Licensing Act in 1737 had made him aware of the dangers of writing scoffing satire without a consistent moral perspective, in the manner for which Lucian was notorious and that was regarded as a defining characteristic of deism. Yet he did not disown Lucian, as he did Rabelais, who was included in the pantheon of satirists invoked as exemplars in *Tom Jones*, alongside Lucian, yet in *The Covent-Garden Journal* three years later was condemned as one of those authors whose design was 'to ridicule all Sobriety, Modesty, Decency, Virtue and Religion, out of the World'.[52] Fielding was keen to advertise, and indeed exaggerate, his debt to Lucian in 1752; and by the time Sterne had Tristram swear 'by the tomb stone of *Lucian*—if it is in being,—if not, why then, by his ashes!', in the third volume of *Tristram Shandy* in 1761, the name of the Greek satirist had lost much of its atheistic charge.[53]

SELECT BIBLIOGRAPHY

Duncan, Douglas. *Ben Jonson and the Lucianic Tradition* (Cambridge: Cambridge University Press, 1979).

Lund, Roger D., ed. *The Margins of Orthodoxy: Heterodox Writing and Cultural Response, 1660–1750* (Cambridge: Cambridge University Press, 1995).

Lund, Roger D. *Ridicule, Religion and the Politics of Wit in Augustan England* (Aldershot: Ashgate, 2012).

Robinson, Christopher. *Lucian and His Influence in Europe* (London: Duckworth, 1979).

Weinbrot, Howard D. *Menippean Satire Reconsidered: From Antiquity to the 18th Century* (Baltimore: Johns Hopkins University Press, 2005).

---

[51] Battestin (ed.), *Amelia*, 425 and note; *Journal of a Voyage to Lisbon, Shamela, and Occasional Writings*, ed. Martin C. Battestin (Oxford: Oxford University Press, 2008), 74. See [Shaftesbury], *Sensus Communis: An Essay on the Freedom of Wit and Humour* (London, 1709), 3.

[52] *Covent-Garden Journal*, No. 10 (4 February 1752), in Goldgar (ed.), *Covent-Garden Journal*, 674; Baker (ed.), *Tom Jones*, 444 (XIII. i).

[53] Laurence Sterne, *Tristram Shandy*, ed. Howard Anderson (New York: Norton, 1980), 139.

CHAPTER 10

··

THE INVENTION OF
DRYDEN AS SATIRIST

··

MATTHEW C. AUGUSTINE

DRYDEN didn't live to see much of the eighteenth century (d. 1700). Though he seems to welcome the dawning of a new era in *The Secular Masque* (1700), that lyric's elegiac tone suggests a body coming to rest, not a charge into the future: "*Tis well an Old Age is out, / And time to begin a New*" (ll. 96–7).[1] Dryden would be surprised to say the least to find that he had become a poet—indeed *the* poet—of the eighteenth century. Perhaps, then, we do better to speak of Dryden as an 'Augustan', as the father of Augustan verse satire. After all, Dryden wrote brilliantly in heroic couplets, the calling card of English Augustanism, and he invoked cultural and political parallels to classical Rome long before Alexander Pope. As Ronald Paulson has pointed out, however, Dryden in fact wrote only three poems that can be classed unproblematically as verse satires, and he was twenty years into a career that spanned more than four decades before he acquired a reputation as a satirist.[2]

One aim of this chapter, then, is to question the inevitability of Dryden's emergence and influence as satirist—both in his own time and in the century that followed. From the middle 1660s and throughout the 1670s, Dryden was the leading poet and playwright in Restoration London. The awkward, ambitious Dryden was also in these years the Town's foremost object of ridicule and abuse, often at the hands of his social superiors—Buckingham, Rochester, even his brother-in-law Sir Robert Howard—but including as well a crowd of hacks and rivals. Though we associate Dryden as satirist most strongly with the disinterested coolness of *Absalom and Achitophel* (1681), such mastery and control was gained through numerous literary skirmishes over the previous two decades. As the poet remarked in his late *Discourse concerning the Original and Progress of Satire* (1693), 'More Libels have been written against me, than almost any Man now living' (4:59).

---

[1] Dryden, *Works*, xvi. 273.
[2] Ronald Paulson, 'Dryden and the Energies of Satire', in *The Cambridge Companion to John Dryden*, ed. Steven N. Zwicker (Cambridge: Cambridge University Press, 2004), 37–58.

Before we can understand Dryden as satire's master, we must understand him first as its victim.

We should also ask how, or even if, Dryden matters to literary history more than three centuries after his death. He has, of course, long been central to accounts of eighteenth-century satire, and more than that, he has held a major place in genealogies of English literature. But if Dryden has not exactly been dislodged from the canon, neither can we say that his critical fortunes look altogether bright at present—arguably Dryden enjoys a less prominent place in English studies today than at any time since the eighteenth century. He is, of course, not alone in this regard, since the very idea of the canon came under fire in the culture wars of the 1980s as exclusionary and oppressive. But this is not enough to explain Dryden's current neglect when measured against other canonical figures like Shakespeare and Milton, a disparity which likely has more to do with the apparent complicity of Dryden's art with the compromises of party and patronage: a consummate marketplace actor, Dryden short-circuits the myth of the Romantic author, who creates 'autonomously like nature...not by an outside motion like a pendulum', in A. W. Schlegel's phrase.[3] Surely, though, Dryden's achievement is thus not the less but rather the more compelling in a neo-liberal age: for while his writing was shaped as a matter of course by considerations of profit and self-advancement, it is Dryden who reminds us, and whose legacy as a satirist confirms, that '*if a* Poem *have a* Genius, *it will force its own reception in the World*' (2:3).

Unlikely Beginnings

Dryden's poetic career began late, especially in an age when writing poetry was often associated with the passions and diversions of youth. By the time he composed his first major poem, an heroic elegy on the death of Oliver Cromwell (1659), Dryden was approaching thirty. For comparison, consider that Abraham Cowley, a poet whom Dryden admired, first appeared as an author at the age of sixteen, when his *Poetical Blossomes* was published in 1633 with an engraving of the boy wonder adorning its frontispiece. Though Milton was in his late thirties when he brought out his first collection of verse, the *Poems of Mr John Milton* (1645), he took great care to provide dates and headnotes that emphasized the precocity of his compositions. Dryden's relative slowness to mature as a poet thus bears remarking insofar as it reminds us that Dryden's art was acquired through a process of labour and learning, and has about it a touch of self-consciousness that would later develop into a highly refined sense of irony. There may also be something compensatory in Dryden's deliberate cultivation of poetic eloquence, for, as he wrote of himself in *A Defence of an Essay of Dramatique Poesie* (1668), 'My Conversation is slow and dull, my humour Saturnine and reserv'd' (9:8),

---

[3] In M. H. Abrams, *The Mirror and the Lamp: Romantic Theory and the Critical Tradition* (Oxford: Oxford University Press, 1953), 212.

attributes, as Dryden well knew, for which he was jeered throughout his career. But in this 'confession' we can also discern those other great satirical gifts of Dryden's: the power of ventriloquism, and a disarming capacity for self-irony.

Indeed, mimicry and impersonation were at the centre of Dryden's first notable satiric exchange, a controversy with his brother-in-law Sir Robert Howard over dramatic form and fashion, but especially the propriety of rhyme. In his early masterpiece, the *Essay of Dramatick Poesie* (1668), Dryden had represented Howard as Crites to his Neander, a piece of casting that played mischievously on Howard's reputation for spikiness and self-regard. Notwithstanding Dryden's deprecation of the *Essay* as a bit of 'rude and indigested' writing which 'serv'd as an amusement to me in the Country, when the violence of the last Plague had driven me from the Town' (17:3), Howard would soon hit back in a preface to his new play *The Great Favourite, Or, the Duke of Lerma* (1668). Evidently composed in a rush, Howard's reply is less interesting for its literary arguments than for its flourishes of personal satire, which we might regard as establishing the baseline for future attacks on Dryden. One of Howard's strategies is to ridicule the impertinence of Dryden's discourse, his habit of speaking beside the point, but there are intimations as well of social indecorum, of the parvenu's failure to observe his place. Thus Howard wonders that Dryden should 'trouble himself twice' about a question, the force of which he mistakes anyway, and 'with such an absolute triumph declared by his own imagination. But I have heard that a gentleman in parliament, going to speak twice, and being interrupted by another member, as against the orders of the House, he was excused by a third, assuring the House he had not yet spoken to the question.'[4] This barb also anticipates the further charge put to Dryden of being deluded by and about his creative gifts: the light of reason is said to shine only obliquely in the author of the *Essay*, rendering 'the shadow larger than the substance', and giving 'the deceived person a wrong measure of his own proportion', a reproof that reads like the *dramatis persona* of 'poet Bayes'.[5]

The dispute between Howard and Dryden would have its conclusion in Dryden's *Defence of an Essay of Dramatique Poesie*, which was published shortly after the appearance of Howard's playbook. In terms of Dryden's development as a satirist, the *Defence of an Essay* is important for a few reasons: for if it sees Dryden combining literary controversy with personal abuse more boldly than he had previously, it also underlined for the recently elevated poet laureate the dangers of satire, precipitating a falling out with his brother-in-law that would not be repaired for nearly thirty years, and exposing Dryden to new levels of mockery and animadversion. Often, Dryden does little more than raise an eyebrow over careless or self-important passages in Howard's text, leaving them 'to be consider'd by the Critiques' (9:4). But when he is not underlining the fatuous pronouncements of his 'noble adversary', Dryden scorches Howard with mock praise: 'As for the Play of the Duke of *Lerma*', he sneers, 'having so much alter'd and beautifi'd it, as he has done, it can justly belong to none but him' (9:4). In the same spirit, Dryden quotes

---

[4] 'Howard's Preface to *The Duke of Lerma*', in *Dryden & Howard, 1664–1668*, ed. D. D. Arundell (Cambridge: Cambridge University Press, 1929), 96.
[5] 'Howard's Preface', 98.

Sir Robert's overblown couplet, '*Repulse upon repulse like waves thrown back, / That slide to hang upon obdurate rocks*', deadpanning, 'After this let detraction do its worst; for if this be not his, it deserves to be' (9:4). Such observations culminate in Dryden's 'emulous' testimony to Howard's style, 'that it is extream poetical, even in Oratory; his Thoughts elevated, sometimes above common apprehension; his Notions politick and grave, and tending to the instruction of Princes, and reformation of States; that they are abundantly interlac'd with variety of Fancies, Tropes, and Figures, which the Criticks have enviously branded with the name of obscurity and false Grammar' (9:10). Answering condescension with contempt, Dryden thus sacrifices his brother-in-law and sometime patron and collaborator to the cankered muse.

It is surely a sign of the laureate's growing stature in Restoration literary culture that the appearance of a new preface by Dryden should have so energized the marketplace of abuse. If Howard was chafed by the *Essay*, he was now apparently brought to the point of challenging Dryden to a duel, at least if we are to believe second-hand reports. In *A Session of the Poets* (1668), a versified compendium of literary gossip, Dryden's humiliation of Howard is cheerfully retailed, but so too is Dryden brought to the bar on charges of theft, ingratitude, and servility. Rather more deliberately, Dryden was also harshly lampooned in a satirical pamphlet entitled *A Letter from a Gentleman to the Honourable Ed. Howard Esq; Occasioned by a Civilized Epistle of Mr Dryden's, Before his Second Edition of his Indian Emperour* (1668), written by one 'R. F.', probably Richard Flecknoe, whom Dryden had maligned in the *Essay of Dramatick Poesie*. As Judith and Steven Zwicker observe of this buzzing cloud of voices, 'The summer of 1668 seems to have been a perfect storm of controversy: over aesthetics and literary practice, perhaps over political association and alliance, and surely over persons and personalities, slights and resentments. Literary vindication was in play, so too were the more dissonant notes of reprisal, and together they provided the certain lure of literary gossip and personal scandal.'[6] Perhaps acting under a more politic impulse, Dryden withdrew the *Defence* 'and did not suffer it to be reprinted'.[7] Obviously, however, sufficient intact copies of the 1668 *Indian Emperour* were in circulation to give the attack currency; and, notwithstanding the awkwardness of the circumstance, Dryden had shown himself capable of mastering satire, though not without a taste as well of its bitter fruits.

Poet Laureate and 'Poet Bayes'

The late 1660s and early 1670s were an exceptionally fertile period for Dryden, giving rise to a string of nearly unbroken successes and establishing him as the foremost poet and dramatist of his age, certain indications of which we have seen above. His *Annus*

---

[6] Judith Zwicker and Steven N. Zwicker, ' "Wanting" and "Very Rare": Dryden's *Defence of an Essay of Dramatique Poesie*', in preparation.

[7] Montague Summers, ed., *Dryden's Dramatic Works*, 6 vols. (London: Nonesuch Press, 1931), 1:liii.

Mirabilis, published in January 1667, sought to ameliorate the previous year's disasters of war, pestilence, and fire—no mean feat—and likely led to Dryden's appointment as poet laureate in April 1668. In the same spring, Dryden became a shareholder in the King's Company—one of the two licensed theatrical companies in Restoration England—in exchange for a promised three plays per year. The prose comedy, *An Evening's Love*, debuted in June 1668 and ran for nine consecutive nights. Another comedy of this period, *Marriage A-la-Mode* (?1671), seems to have been a hit for Dryden as well, though *The Assignation, or Love in a Nunnery* (1672–3) fell flat with audiences. In his own words, however, Dryden was not 'fitted by Nature to write Comedy', and it was only on account of his desire 'to delight the Age in which I live' that he 'forced' his 'Genius' into this vein (9:7–8). His main dramatic energies were devoted to serious plays, and in the early years of his laureateship especially to heroic drama, a genre Dryden proclaimed 'an imitation, in little of an Heroick Poem', with Love and Valour as its subjects (11:10).

It is fair to say that Dryden's heroic plays have not worn well. They have rarely been revived, and they have long been derided for their high-flown language and schematic 'love and honour' plots. Indeed, even in his own day, it was Dryden's identification with the writing and championing of heroic drama that underpinned the Duke of Buckingham's satirical caricature of the poet as the buffoon playwright 'Mr Bayes', a figure that would shadow Dryden for the rest of his career. Both Dryden and his audience, however, were well aware of heroic drama's artificial and exaggerated qualities, and they were equally capable of relishing the genre's melodrama as well as its subversion. Thus, in *The Conquest of Granada* (1670–1), Dryden's heroic masterpiece, the protagonist Almanzor and his rival Zulema petition their prince for the right to woo the beautiful and virtuous princess, Almahide. After an extended give and take, in which Almanzor asserts his noble passion with increasing force, Zulema concedes his challenger's right thusly: 'If you will free your part of her you may; / But, Sir, I love not your Romantique way. / Dream on; enjoy her Soul; and set that free; / I'me pleas'd her person should be left for me' (I.1.3.487–90). When Rochester comes to rewrite Prince Abdalla's line 'Her tears, her smiles, her every look's a Net' (*Conquest*, I.1.3.71) as 'Her hand, her foot, her very look's a Cunt' (l. 18) in *The Imperfect Enjoyment*, he is merely amplifying an earthy scepticism already present in Dryden's text.

'To suppose that enjoyment of parody—even of travesty—is necessarily inimical to enjoyment of the original', as Robert D. Hume and Harold Love write, thus seems 'critically simple-minded'.[8] But with *The Rehearsal* (1671), Buckingham and his friends nevertheless succeeded brilliantly in aping the poet laureate and the kind of plays then popular, among other satiric targets and purposes. A delightfully clever piece of dramatic burlesque, the comedy looks in, as its title suggests, on the dress rehearsal for a new play by 'Mr Bayes' from the perspective of 'Smith' and 'Johnson', two witty men of pleasure. The play-within-the-play structure generates much of the piece's camp energy, and the

---

[8] Robert D. Hume and Harold Love, eds., *Plays, Poems, and Miscellaneous Writings associated with George Villiers, Second Duke of Buckingham* (Oxford: Oxford University Press, 2007), 348. I am broadly indebted to Hume and Love throughout my discussion of *The Rehearsal*.

send-up of Bayes and his ludicrous production works at the level of broad farce as well as the level of specific reference and allusion—the plot, characters, and dialogue of Bayes's play are a veritable hash of Restoration drama from the previous decade.

The qualities satirized in Bayes are familiar in outline from the jibes of Robert Howard, the author of *The Session of the Poets*, and 'R. F.', with the difference that they are here injected with far greater imaginative life and potency. At once obsequious and puffed up with self-importance, mindlessly derivative and incomprehensibly fanciful, the character of Bayes is a jumble of contradictions but with enough of Dryden and of current literary gossip about him for it not to matter. Thus Bayes's rules of dramatic composition, as he relates them to Smith and Johnson, include several different means for appropriating the wit of others: the 'Rule of Transversion', that is, the turning of prose into verse, or verse into prose, 'so alter'd that no man can know it' (1.1.87–102); the 'Rule of Record', whereby 'I come into a Coffee-house, or some other place where wittie men resort, I make as if I minded nothing; (do ye mark?) but as soon as any one speaks, pop I slap it down, and make that, too, my own' (1.1.102–8); and the 'Rule of Invention', according to which the poet does 'but presently turn o'er this Book [of Drama Common-places], and there I have, at one view, all that *Perseus, Montaigne, Seneca's Tragedies, Horace, Juvenal, Claudian, Pliny, Plutarch's lives*, and the rest, have ever thought, upon this subject: and so, in a trice, by leaving out a few words, or putting in others of my own, the business is done' (1.1.113–24).

This is all very funny, of course, and chimes with R. F.'s portrait of Dryden as an 'Ingrossing Plagiary'[9] while also mocking Dryden's pedantic fussing over rules and precedents in his various critical prefaces, the *Essay of Dramatick Poesie*, and its *Defence*. But the character of Bayes is also represented—comically, ridiculously so, yes—as relentlessly experimental and innovative. Explaining in Act Three why every act of his ends with a dance, Bayes insists, 'Sir, all my fancies are [new]. I tread upon no man's heels, but make my flight upon my own wings' (3.1.6–7); in the following act, he instructs Smith and Johnson, 'the last Act beginning with a witty Scene of mirth, I make this to begin with a Funeral', for he 'would not have any two things alike in this Play' (4.1.1–3); and in the final act, Bayes declares his aim to outgo Shakespeare's *Henry VIII* by bringing in four cardinals instead of two bishops, in what will be 'the greatest Scene that *England* saw: I mean not for words, for those I do not value; but for state, shew, and magnificence' (5.1.1–6).

By such devices, Bayes is made sententiously to explicate his nonsense play, and no doubt we are thus meant to apprehend and to laugh at Dryden's special pleading for his own art, his vanity and self-regard, his upstart impertinence. Seen from another angle, though, might we not also appreciate Mr Bayes as a kind of irreverent homage to Dryden's learning, his prolific output, his pushing of generic boundaries and conventions? This is not to say that Dryden relished the portrayal, or that the Duke and his circle wrote entirely in good fun, but it makes little sense to imagine that Buckingham's play was meant to explode Dryden's reputation or to drive heroic drama from the stage.

---

[9] R. F. [?Richard Flecknoe], *A Letter from a Gentleman* (1668), 3.

After all, *The Rehearsal* was produced by Dryden's own company, the King's Men, and there was little to gain by tanking their most reliable hit-maker. We know too that the character of Bayes was a composite of several different figures which evolved over a number of years, and while *The Conquest of Granada* is the most obvious target of *The Rehearsal*'s parodic wit, 'parallels can be adduced to a great many plays'.[10] The fact that this burlesque remained a staple of the comic repertory throughout the eighteenth century, long past the currency of its original victims, suggests that it did not depend for its effectiveness on the recognition of highly topical or personal satire, though such satire was clearly available to those in the know.

Needless to say, in an age of faction and partisanship, literary and political culture were so intimate that satire was inevitably an instrument of polemical warfare, and it is important to recognize some of the political functions of *The Rehearsal* if we hope to appreciate fully the illocutionary force of Dryden's own formal satires. Perhaps the best point of entry to this element of the play is the final scene of Act Two, which sees Bayes demonstrating to his soldiers how to fall dead, in the course of which he breaks his nose on the floor. At the start of the next act, a stage direction indicates, 'Bayes *with a papyr on his Nose, and the two Gentlemen*'. As George McFadden was to argue in 1974, recovering an early eighteenth-century tradition of commentary, the introduction of this physical detail complicates the characterization of Bayes, and indeed seems to pick out a particular individual, Henry Bennett, Earl of Arlington, for abuse.[11] Arlington was known to wear a black patch on his nose, 'to cover a pretended wound he had received at the time of the rebellion',[12] and he was moreover Buckingham's chief enemy at court, and as Secretary of State, the minister in charge of the Crown's absolutist policies, as they seemed to the Duke's 'Country' faction.

The idea that Bayes's bogus dramaturgy is meant in part to blast Arlington's administration of the state allows us to make sense of Dryden's claim, much later in life, that he 'answer'd not *The Rehearsall*, because I knew...that my Betters were more concern'd than I was in that Satire' (4:8). As the most recent editors of *The Rehearsal* contend, however, the detection of a political agenda in the play need not detract from the literary satire or reduce it to a mere cover for more dangerous political commentary.[13] For Dryden was not only poet laureate but also closely aligned with the Yorkist faction at court—it is no coincidence that *The Conquest of Granada* was rather floridly dedicated 'To His ROYAL HIGHNESS The DUKE'. And it was part of the ideological work of heroic plays to burnish Stuart authority and to exalt the station of courtiers. The play's scoffing at Dryden, its parody of the conventions of heroic theatre, its targeting of Arlington, its quasi-allegorical fable of Stuart kingship, are thus all of a piece, reminding us of the layered, multi-dimensional character of satire in this age.

---

[10] Hume and Love, *Plays*, 347.
[11] George McFadden, 'Political Satire in *The Rehearsal*', *Yearbook of English Studies* 4 (1974), 120–8.
[12] Thomas Bruce, Second Earl of Ailesbury, *Memoirs*, ed. W. E. Buckley, 2 vols. (London, 1890), 1:14.
[13] See Hume and Love, *Plays*, 353–4.

If we have lingered over Buckingham's rendition of Dryden as 'Mr Bayes', it is because Dryden only became a satirist by having first been the star of satire written by others: that great mimic, the Duke of Buckingham, and we should add, too, the Earl of Rochester, whose *An Allusion to Horace* ('Well Sir 'tis granted, I said Dryden's Rhymes, / Were stollen, unequal, nay dull many times…', ll. 1–2) circulated in manuscript amongst the court wits during the winter of 1675–6.[14] For not only was Dryden stung into writing *Mac Flecknoe* in part by the insults he suffered at the hands of these writers, he also retooled much of the arsenal which had been aimed at him for the purposes of his own literary offensive. It is, of course, Thomas Shadwell whose reputation Dryden elegantly savages in *Mac Flecknoe*, one of the earliest examples of mock-heroic in English, and the two had been quarrelling in print for a number of years over some of the same questions Dryden had debated with Sir Robert Howard.[15] Critics have thus usually understood *Mac Flecknoe* as personal satire; however, the satirical energies of the poem go far beyond anything in Dryden and Shadwell's previous exchanges. Why should Dryden so drastically raise the stakes of the game now, after some eight years of low-level sparring?[16] The likely explanation is that in attacking Shadwell, Dryden was also attacking by proxy his antagonist's more socially exalted patrons, Buckingham and Rochester.[17] Dryden's use of scribal networks to publish the poem—an exception to his usual practice of print publication—further suggests that he was going after the court wits, and with their own weapon of choice, the manuscript lampoon.

Though the term 'Augustan' has fallen out of fashion of late, Dryden's reputation as a satirist is too bound up with that critical idea to omit mentioning it. For Pat Rogers,

> The great discovery of Augustan satire was a kind of oblique accuracy. Between about 1675 and 1750 a vocabulary was evolved, both in literary and graphic terms, to express a skewed and damaging truth. The violence of lampoon was joined to the finesse of portraiture. In the work of the great practitioners, abuse is made art; a hyperbole of insult is wedded to a malicious realism.[18]

In *Mac Flecknoe*, Dryden thus deploys a high Virgilian style and richly allusive verse in praise of dullness, conjuring an imaginative scene in which the reigning monarch of 'all the realms of *Non-sense*' (Flecknoe) prophecies the coronation of his true son and heir (Shadwell), a vision realized in the poem's comic conclusion. Shadwell had long fashioned

---

[14] On the latter rivalry, see Matthew C. Augustine, 'Trading Places: Lord Rochester, the Laureate, and the Making of Literary Reputation', in *Lord Rochester in the Restoration World*, ed. Matthew C. Augustine and Steven N. Zwicker (Cambridge: Cambridge University Press, 2015), 58–78.

[15] See R. Jack Smith, 'Shadwell's Impact Upon Dryden', *Review of English Studies* 20, no. 77 (1944), 29–44.

[16] For the dating of *Mac Flecknoe* to July–August 1676, see David Vieth, 'The Discovery of the Date of *Mac Flecknoe*', in *Evidence in Literary Scholarship*, ed. René Wellek and Alvaro Ribeiro (Oxford: Clarendon Press, 1979), 63–87.

[17] See Harold Love, 'Shadwell, Rochester, and the Crisis of Amateurism', *Restoration: Studies in English Literary Culture, 1660–1700* 20, no. 2 (1996), 119–34.

[18] Pat Rogers, *The Augustan Vision* (London: Methuen, 1978), 171.

himself as the age's leading 'Son of Ben', a moralist and a classicist, pretensions Dryden lacerates by celebrating Shadwell's claim to an altogether different poetic kingdom: 'Thou art my blood,' Flecknoe declaims, 'where *Johnson* has no part',

> What share have we in Nature or in Art?
> Where did his wit on learning fix a brand,
> And rail at Arts he did not understand?
> Where made he love in Prince *Nicander*'s vein,
> Or swept the dust in *Psyche*'s humble strain?
> Where sold he Bargains, Whip-stitch, kiss my Arse,
> Promis'd a Play and dwindled to a Farce?
> Where did his Muse from *Fletcher* scenes purloin,
> As thou whole *Eth'ridg* dost transfuse to thine?
> But so transfus'd as Oyl on Waters flow,
> His always floats above, thine sinks below.
>
> (ll. 175–86)

Dryden's mastery of the heroic couplet asserts itself here to devastating effect, as he 'poises and wields and flourishes it like a quarterstaff with shifting load inside it.'[19] Perhaps taking hints from Buckingham's compositional practice in *The Rehearsal*, Dryden stitches bits of language from Shadwell's plays and prologues into Flecknoe's peroration (cf. *The Virtuoso*, 'Prethee, Longvil, hold thy peace, with a whip-stitch, your nose in my breech'), insinuating the hollowness of Shadwell's moralism and hoisting him with his own petard. We cannot miss either Dryden's ironic deflection of the familiar charge of plagiarism onto his rival, with the metaphor of borrowing as transfusion further insisting on Shadwell's colossal inertness.

Indeed, as David Hopkins has argued, it is from the 'Absoluteness of Shadwell's dullness'[20] that the poem derives much of its comic grandeur and imaginative power: thus while 'Some Beams of Wit on other souls may fall', Shadwell's 'genuine night admits no ray' (ll. 21, 23); '*Heywood* and *Shirley* were but Types of thee', and 'Even I, a dunce of more renown than they, / Was sent before but to prepare thy way' (ll. 29–32). Flecknoe is John the Baptist to Shadwell's messiah of 'thoughtless Majesty' (l. 26). By celebrating Shadwell's qualities in this way, Dryden would seem to position himself as the arbiter of true wit, the standard-bearer of taste and decorum, a view that corresponds to the conventional notion that 'A work of satire is designed to attack vice or folly. To this end it uses wit or ridicule. Like polemical rhetoric, it seeks to persuade an audience that something or someone is reprehensible or ridiculous; unlike pure rhetoric, it engages in exaggeration and some sort of fiction.'[21] This is a fair digest of commentary on *Mac Flecknoe*—but we may wonder if such understandings are adequate to the poem's high-wire daring. Literary history remembers Shadwell as a 'minor dramatist' who was the

---

[19] A. W. Ward, 'Dryden', in *The Cambridge History of English and American Literature*, ed. A. W. Ward et al., 18 vols. (Cambridge: Cambridge University Press, 1907–21), vol. 8.

[20] David Hopkins, *John Dryden* (Cambridge: Cambridge University Press, 1986), 71.

[21] Dustin Griffin, *Satire: A Critical Reintroduction* (Lexington: University of Kentucky Press, 1994), 1.

victim of Dryden's famous satire, but this does not accurately reflect the standing of these writers in the summer of 1676 when Dryden was composing his poem. Shadwell had been producing roughly a play a year for the Duke's Men since 1668, with more hits than misses, 'and his operatic adaptation of Dryden and Davenant's *Tempest* [1674]', as Don Kunz writes, 'was more profitable than any other opera during the century'.[22] Despite enjoying the office of laureate, Dryden had flopped with two plays after the twin successes of *The Conquest of Granada* and *Marriage A-la-Mode* and was mired in 'the most barren period of his long career'.[23] Shadwell also had powerful friends, as we have seen, and they had been active across several media in disparaging Dryden: *The Rehearsal* was republished in a second edition of 1672 and a third of 1675, and was likely revived on the stage at these times, while Rochester sought to influence fashionable opinion by satirizing Dryden in a scribal lampoon.

Shadwell was thus no fly to be killed for sport, and Dryden needed a brilliant strategy of attack if he wanted to reverse the tide. We have already heard one of Dryden's rationalizations for ignoring *The Rehearsal*, that it concerned his betters more than it concerned him. But he also offers this wonderfully suggestive observation, that he knew 'the Author sate to himself when he drew the Picture, and was the very *Bays* of his own Farce' (4:8). However disingenuous this comment regarding the Duke, might we not apply it to *Mac Flecknoe*? For not only does Dryden enlarge virtually every stock accusation against him in caricaturing Shadwell, he is also prepared to turn the heroic mode on its head, to make a comic feast of its idioms and arguments, a tactic that seems inspired by the very ridicule to which his heroic plays had been exposed. 'Why, I did never, before this, see any thing in Nature, and all that, (as Mr. *Bayes* says) so foolish, but I could give some ghess at what moved the Fop to do it', Smith marvels to Johnson, 'but this, I confess, does go beyond my reach' (2.1.73–5). The same idea—the surpassing quality of Mac Flecknoe's dullness—is at the heart of Dryden's poem, introduced with all the pomp and fanfare of an Almanzor or an Aureng-Zebe (or indeed a Stuart monarch):

> All humane things are subject to decay,
> And, when Fate summons, Monarchs must obey:
> This *Fleckno* found, who, like *Augustus*, young
> Was call'd to Empire, and had govern'd long:
> In Prose and Verse, was own'd, without dispute
> Through all the Realms of *Non-sense*, absolute.
> This aged Prince now flourishing in Peace,
> And blest with issue of a large increase,
> Worn out with business, did at length debate
> To settle the Succession of the State:
> And pond'ring which of all his Sons was fit

[22] Don Kunz, 'Shadwell and His Critics: The Misuse of Dryden's *Mac Flecknoe*', *Restoration and Eighteenth-Century Theatre Research* 12, no. 1 (1973), 15.
[23] George R. Noyes, ed., *The Poetical Works of John Dryden* (Boston: Houghton Mifflin, 1950), xxxv.

> To Reign, and wage Immortal War with Wit:
> Cry'd, 'tis resolv'd; for Nature pleads that He
> Should onely rule, who most resembles me...
>
> (ll. 1–14)

It is a commonplace—a false one—that Buckingham's farce put an end to Dryden's writing of heroic drama, though by the time he wrote *Aureng-Zebe* (1675) Dryden professed to have 'now another taste of Wit', having grown 'weary of his long-lov'd Mistris, Rhyme' (Prologue, ll. 6–8). But after the unbearable lightness of *Mac Flecknoe*, and the self-irony which such lightness cost him, surely there was little left for Dryden to do with the rhymed heroic play.

To see *Mac Flecknoe* as a complex act of exaggerated mirroring and self-projection rather than a univocal exercise in ridicule is, of course, to complicate the poem's meanings, to unsettle its certainties, and so to ready ourselves for the perplexities of *Absalom and Achitophel*, Dryden's most accomplished satire. On its face, this is a very different poem from Dryden's earlier mock-heroic lampoon, casting the events of the Exclusion Crisis in a scriptural dress meant to flatter the king and his followers and to discredit the opposition. The controversy of Exclusion centred on the Duke of York, an open Catholic, whose right to succeed his brother was challenged by the Earl of Shaftesbury (the Achitophel of the poem) and his Whig allies in the name of settling the state on a Protestant heir. The Whigs' leading candidate was James Scott, Duke of Monmouth, the popular but illegitimate son of the king by his mistress Lucy Walter. In 2 Samuel 15, with the story of Absalom's rebellion, Dryden seemed to have the perfect vehicle for his cautionary tale. 'Indeed,' as Godfrey Davies remarked long ago, 'the analogy between the indulgent David and his rebellious son and Charles and Monmouth was so apparent as to suggest that not the idea but permission or encouragement to use it was what Dryden needed', thus countenancing the tradition that Charles himself 'suggested to Dryden the object as well as the framework of his satire'.[24]

But what might the king have made of the portrait with which Dryden opens his poem:

> In pious times, e'r Priest-craft did begin,
> Before *Polygamy* was made a sin;
> When man, on many, multiply'd his kind,
> E'r one to one was, cursedly, confined;
> When Nature prompted, and no law deny'd,
> Promiscuous use of Concubine and Bride;
> Then *Israel*'s Monarch, after Heaven's own heart,
> His vigorous warmth did, variously, impart
> To Wives and Slaves; And, wide as his Command,
> Scatter'd his Maker's Image through the Land.
> *Michal*, of Royal blood, the Crown did wear,

---

[24] Godfrey Davies, 'The Conclusion of Absalom and Achitophel', *Huntington Library Quarterly* 10, no. 1 (1946), 70.

> A Soyl ungratefull to the Tiller's care:
> Not so the rest; for several Mothers bore
> To godlike *David* several Sons before.
> But since like slaves his bed they did ascend,
> No True Succession could their seed attend.
>
> (ll. 1–16)

With astonishing dexterity, Dryden here seems to transverse or rewrite the oppositional image of Charles, of whom it was said, 'There is none that loves him but drunk whores and whoremongers', into an argument not only for the king's warmth and beneficence but indeed his respect for the laws of property and succession.[25] For all of his David-like fecundity, Charles makes no scruple over the principle of constitutional legitimacy, an implicit rebuke to the Exclusionists, who 'Now, wondred why, so long, they had obey'd / An Idoll Monarch which their hands had made; / Thought they might ruine him they could create; / Or melt him to that Golden Calf, a State' (ll. 63–6). Such ironies go some way towards defusing a ready critique of the Crown's profligacy, but Dryden's wit raises a number of other ideas that seem less fit for purpose in the polemical context of the poem: how seriously, for instance, are we meant to take the suggestion that Charles's promiscuity enjoys divine sanction, that his fathering of bastards is analogous to God's creation of Adam, or that polygamy is most suited to man's nature and monogamy a curse? It is not clear, as Jeremy Collier maintained, whether 'This is down right Defiance of the Living God',[26] or whether Dryden, as we say in the age of social media, is merely trolling the opposition, or whether he is here an ironist responsible above all to his own art. But we should be chary of assuming that the poem's imaginative texture may be reduced at all points to Stuart propaganda.

The narrative of the poem follows 2 Samuel 15 as it shadows English politics with Absalom's pretensions to the crown of Israel, his conspiracy with David's counsellor Achitophel, and the disaffection of the Israelites from their anointed king ('And there came a messenger to David, saying, The hearts of the men of Israel are after Absalom', Samuel 2:14). It concludes with a speech by King David (Charles II) expressing his willingness 'to forgive th' Offending Age' (l. 941) lest he should have to draw 'the Sword of Justice' (l. 1002), thus conspicuously pre-empting the biblical David's slaughter of 20,000 Israelites and the gruesome end of Achitophel and his rebellion. The events of Scripture thus become a kind of prophetic lens onto the politics of Exclusion, and few could have missed the meaning of Dryden's application.

In many ways, though, the narrative is secondary to the string of miniature portraits Dryden suspends from it, and for those reading *Absalom and Achitophel* in November of 1681, much of the poem's pleasure surely lay in decoding its grid of biblicized politicians

---

[25] From the prosecution of one Margaret Dixon for 'seditious words', 13 May 1660, *Depositions from the Castle of York: Relating to Offenses in the Seventeenth Century* (1861), 83.

[26] Jeremy Collier, from *A Short View of the Immorality and Profaneness of the English Stage* (1698), in *Dryden: The Critical Heritage*, ed. James Kinsley and Helen Kinsley (London: Routledge & Kegan Paul, 1971), 236.

and grandees. The most famous of these is perhaps Dryden's character of Zimri, 'which', according to its author, 'is, in my Opinion, worth the whole Poem: 'tis not bloody, but 'tis ridiculous enough. And he for whom it was intended was too witty to resent it as an injury' (4:71). He for whom it was intended was of course the Duke of Buckingham, a return of the satiric boomerang ten years in the making:

> In the first Rank of these did *Zimri* stand:
> A man so various, that he seem'd to be
> Not one, but all Mankinds Epitome.
> Stiff in Opinions, always in the wrong;
> Was every thing by starts, and nothing long:
> But, in the course of one revolving Moon,
> Was Chymist, Fidler, States-Man, and Buffoon:
> Then all for Women, Painting, Rhiming, Drinking;
> Besides ten thousand freaks that dy'd in thinking.
> Blest Madman, who could every hour employ,
> With something New to wish, or to enjoy!
> Rayling and praising were his usual Theams;
> And both (to shew his Judgment) in Extreams: [...]
> He laught himself from Court, then sought Releif
> By forming Parties, but coud ne're be Chief:
> For, spight of him, the weight of Business fell
> On *Absalom* and wise *Achitophel*:
> Thus, wicked but in will, of means bereft,
> He left not Faction, but of that was left.
>
> (ll. 544–68)

It is easy enough to determine the polemical upshot of this caricature: Zimri's mercurial insubstantiality is at once a sign of moral lassitude and a condition of political instability, mirrored in Dryden's description of the Jews as 'a Headstrong, Moody, Murmuring race' (l. 45). But the dazzle and interest of this passage far exceed its topical force. On the one hand there is Dryden's turn at playing Voltairean sage, transforming his satire into a philosophy of man. On the other, we can just discern a virtuosic intertextual exchange being made with both Buckingham and Rochester, a restoration of the satiric 'bays' to its givers.[27] But perhaps above all, far from hate—supposed to be the generic currency of satire—there is a kind of glee in Dryden's pursuit of his object, and ultimately a dance between the shape-shifting Zimri, 'every thing by starts, and nothing long', and Dryden's vertiginous verse.

---

[27] In the *Allusion to Horace*, Rochester had assumed the role of Horace to Dryden's Lucilius, whom Horace censures in his Tenth Satire. Dryden's rendition of Buckingham mirrors and reverses this situation, with Dryden here playing Juvenal to the unctuous Greek of Juvenal's Third Satire (as translated by Dryden in 1693), 'A Cook, A Conjurer, a Rhetorician, / A Painter, a Pedant, a Geometrician...' (*Works*, 4:121). There are of course elements too of Buckingham's Bayes.

APOTHEOSIS

In his 'Life' of Dryden, Samuel Johnson observes that:

> In 1681 Dryden became yet more conspicuous by uniting politicks with poetry, in the memorable satire called *Absalom and Achitophel*, written against the faction which, by lord Shaftesbury's incitement, set the duke of Monmouth at its head. Of this poem, in which personal satire was applied to the support of publick principles, and in which therefore every mind was interested, the reception was eager, and the sale so large, that my father, an old bookseller, told me he had [but rarely] known it equalled.[28]

And with the print publication of *Mac Flecknoe* in 1682, together with *The Medall. A Satyre against Sedition*, and some passages Dryden contributed to *The Second Part of Absalom and Achitophel*, it might seem that the laureate's identity and reputation as a satirist was thus secure. After the 'annus satyricus' of 1682, however, Dryden would compose no more original works of satire, though he would continue to be its object: having converted to Roman Catholicism under James II for what appeared to be reasons of expedience and preferment, it was open season on Dryden following the revolution of 1688 and the loss of his public offices. He did in the 1690s publish translations of Juvenal and Persius, which he prefaced with a long *Discourse concerning the Original and Progress of Satire*; his versions of these poets deserve to be better known, and may even, as Emrys Jones has argued, rank 'among his finest poems,'[29] but they have usually been overshadowed by Dryden's *Virgil* (1697), the crowning achievement of his last decade.

Upon his death in 1700, a flood of verse was published to commemorate the great figure's passing, much of it generic and undistinguished, but nevertheless a useful index of contemporary esteem.[30] Here we do find some scattered appreciation for Dryden's poison pen. Charles Brome, for instance, marshals these heroic couplets in praise of Dryden the satirist:

> When juster Indignation rows'd his Hate,
> Insipid Rymes to lash, or Knaves of State;
> Each Line's a Sting, and ev'ry Sting a Death,
> As if their Fate depended on his breath.
>
> (*To the Memory of Mr. Dryden*)

---

[28] Samuel Johnson, *The Lives of the Poets*, ed. Roger Lonsdale, 4 vols. (Oxford: Oxford University Press, 2006), 2:101.

[29] Emrys Jones, 'Dryden's Persius', in *John Dryden (1631–1700): His Politics, His Plays, and His Poets*, ed. Claude Rawson and Aaron Santesso (Newark: University of Delaware Press, 2004), 123.

[30] See Ruth Salvaggio, 'Verses on the Death of Mr. Dryden', *Journal of Popular Culture* 21, no. 1 (1987), 75–91.

But for better or for worse, Dryden's critics and panegyrists, and in turn his eighteenth-century commentators, tended not to focus on his particular brilliance within a given mode or genre but rather on the breadth and variety—not to say unevenness—of his oeuvre, and on the poet's terrific energy and boundless fancy—not to say prodigality (and certainly not 'dullness'). Brome's salute to Dryden's stinging verse is not quite the last thing in *To the Memory of Mr. Dryden*, but far from the first: the hero's shining periods and 'Majestic numbers', his 'Characters', his choice 'Flow'rs of *Greece* and *Rome*', his 'Poetic Rage' when 'In lofty buskins...he rul'd the Stage', all receive higher billing. In *A New Session of the Poets, Occasion'd by the Death of Mr Dryden* (1700), a crowd of poets and poetasters vie for the laurel vacated by 'Wit's mighty Monarch': Tom D'Urfey first endeavours at the bays, 'With twice five hundred Songs, and twenty plays', followed by a 'Brace of Criticks', including Rymer and Dennis, then the 'late-bruis'd' Tom Brown and 'many a Bold, unlicens'd Interloper', then witty Farquhar, Crowne, Blackmore with his 'sad Romantick Stuff', 'elab'rate' Congreve, 'All-pleasing *Garth*', next '*Southern*.../ With haughty *Oroonoko* by his side', and finally the hapless Nahum Tate. While the poem's respect for Dryden is highly ironized, it nevertheless emphasizes the void left by his departure from the literary scene; not even this army of writers, it seems, can replace him.

What may surprise us about these various judgements is how far praise and blame for Dryden resemble each other—the poet laureate and 'poet Bayes' were wires which touched and sparked. We can see this clearly in Johnson's own opinion of Dryden, set down decades later: 'Next to argument, his delight was in wild and daring sallies of sentiment, in the irregular and excentrick violence of wit. He delighted to tread upon the brink of meaning, where light and darkness begin to mingle; to approach the precipice of absurdity, and hover over the abyss of unideal vacancy.' This inclination, says Dr Johnson, produced in Dryden 'nonsense' and 'absurdities', but equally 'the grand and the new', the 'just' and the 'splendid', and he knew Dryden to be a great poet.[31] Thus while the critical balance could be adjusted—Lord Macaulay, for instance, compared Dryden's writings to 'the sluttish magnificence of a Russian noble, all vermin and diamonds, dirty linen and inestimable sables'[32]—in the century and a half after his death, it was possible to censure, even to abhor Dryden, but it scarcely seemed possible to ignore him.

There is then no little irony in the fact that the invention of Dryden as satirist—as he is now mainly remembered, when he is remembered at all—has corresponded to a shrinking not only of Dryden's reputation but of the age in which he wrote. It was, of course, Matthew Arnold in 'The Study of Poetry' who instructed us to regard 'Dryden as the puissant and glorious founder, Pope as the splendid high priest, of our age of prose and reason, of our excellent and indispensable eighteenth century'.[33] But in the rewriting of literary history effected by the moderns, it was the eighteenth century that was

---

[31] Johnson, *Lives*, 2:149–50.
[32] *Critical and Miscellaneous Essays of T. Babington Macaulay*, 2 vols. (Boston, 1840), 1:173.
[33] *The Complete Prose Works of Matthew Arnold*, 10 vols. (Ann Arbor: University of Michigan Press, 1960–78), 9:180.

consigned to the rubbish heap as ground zero in the rise of 'the dissociation of sensibility' and what Leavis called 'the technologico-Benthamite society'.[34] So powerful were these views in the heyday of Eliot's and Leavis's critical authority, they became as it were the lingua franca of the emergent profession of 'Eng. Lit.' In this climate, there must have seemed little hope of making writers of the eighteenth century seem fashionable, but at least they could be made respectable, their learning celebrated, their wit and taste admired, their couplets poised and parsed. Dryden and Pope, Swift, Addison, and Gay were thus made over in the image of Horace, the great Roman satirist, they became 'neo-classical', they became 'Augustan'—and they became boring.

Modern criticism has gone out of its way to exorcize the ghost of 'Mr Bayes' from Dryden's legacy, to honour the laurel he long wore. But in so doing, it has obscured much of what made Dryden great in the first place—his energy, his daring, his complex ironies, his willingness to risk failure and humiliation for the sake of art. For better or for worse, 'Mr Bayes' is essential to Dryden's achievement—as satirist and otherwise.

SELECT BIBLIOGRAPHY

Elkin, P. K. *The Augustan Defence of Satire* (Oxford: Clarendon Press, 1973).

Jack, Ian. *Augustan Satire: Intention and Idiom in English Poetry, 1660–1750* (Oxford: Clarendon Press, 1952).

Hammond, Paul. *John Dryden: A Literary Life* (Basingstoke: Macmillan, 1991).

Hammond, Paul. *The Making of Restoration Poetry* (Cambridge: D. S. Brewer, 2006).

Harth, Philip. *Pen for a Party: Dryden's Tory Propaganda in Its Contexts* (Princeton: Princeton University Press, 1993).

Hopkins, David. *John Dryden* (Tavistock: Northcote House, 2004).

Paulson, Ronald. *The Fictions of Satire* (Baltimore: Johns Hopkins University Press, 1967).

Rawson, Claude. *English Satire and the Satiric Tradition* (Oxford: Blackwell, 1984).

Seidel, Michael. *The Satiric Inheritance: Rabelais to Sterne* (Princeton: Princeton University Press, 1979).

Sutherland, James. *English Satire* (Cambridge: Cambridge University Press, 1958).

Winn, James A. *John Dryden and His World* (New Haven: Yale University Press, 1987).

Zwicker, Steven N. *Politics and Language in Dryden's Poetry: The Arts of Disguise* (Princeton: Princeton University Press, 1984).

Zwicker, Steven N. 'Why Are They Saying These Terrible Things about John Dryden? The Uses of Gossip and Scandal', *Essays in Criticism* 64 (2014), 158–79.

[34] See Eliot's landmark 'The Metaphysical Poets' (1921), in *The Selected Prose of T. S. Eliot*, ed. Frank Kermode (London: Faber and Faber, 1975); also F. R. Leavis, *Mass Civilization and Minority Culture* (Cambridge: Minority Press, 1930), and *Revaluation* (London: Chatto & Windus, 1936).

CHAPTER 11

ALEXANDER POPE AND THE PHILOSOPHICAL HORACE

KRISTINE LOUISE HAUGEN

POPE's satirical poems are hard to like today if we read them as what they can easily appear to be: simple and single-minded hectoring that accosts the reader with a startling presumption of personal authority. Overlong and devoted to painfully obvious morals, they interrupt their exhortations only for blasts of topical satire that are too often unfunny. One might say Pope takes all the defects of Horace's original satires and epistles and makes them worse. But this style became more or less Pope's speciality late in his career, as he published seven imitations of Horace's satires and epistles between 1733 and 1738. For convenience, we call all of this poetry Pope's satirical verse.

A traditional approach to the difficulty has been to take the wide view, placing Pope at the head of a history of British satire intertwined with the history of classical translation. In Harold Brooks's classic argument about the craft of English poetic imitation, early moves towards free translation progressed through a stage of bold modernization and ultimately to Pope's brand of 'greater liberty'. At the same time, Brooks stressed that Pope's audience was meant to evaluate not only his departures from Horace but also his deep involvement, inviting us to explore what Horace's own words could mean in the early eighteenth century.[1]

As moral readings of the satires have languished, critics have prized the parts of Pope's satires that depart decisively from Horace's originals. This has led to brilliant discussion of Pope's politics, personal identity, and, more recently, the field of classical receptions. Meanwhile we have shifted our understanding of Pope as a person and a poet. As critics became disenchanted with a morality in the satires that they viewed as simple or cloying, they also turned away from the middle twentieth century's broad vision of Pope as a

---

[1] Harold F. Brooks, 'The "Imitation" in English Poetry, Especially in Formal Satire, before the Age of Pope', *Review of English Studies* 125 (1949), 124–40, esp. 139–40.

pleasing, gracious personality. That discussion stressed his friendships, his putative kindness, and his sensitivity to art, arguing also that Pope was transparently honest and an orthodox Christian.[2]

In fact, the Horatian imitations can let us recover one vital part of Pope's career that the twentieth-century rehabilitation also discarded: his overweening intellectual ambition and his drive to import knowledge from the continent of Europe for his English audience. These lifelong aspirations of Pope's were often pressed on readers by his nineteenth-century editors Whitwell Elwin and W. J. Courthope.[3] We will see that Pope was serious about humanistic study, deeply concerned to be seen as intellectually expert, and relatively competent in philosophy; he was also given to dissimulation and the habit of writing in code for the informed few. These discoveries should likely shape our approach to his other philosophical poetry. They are also a kind of erudite corollary to Margaret Anne Doody's pioneering argument that Augustan poetry was a world of energy, appetite, and parody.[4]

READING FOR PHILOSOPHY

Pope believed that Horace's satires and epistles were philosophical poems, and in this chapter I want to show how Pope dealt openly and covertly with that philosophy. In the nineteenth century, Leslie Stephen was unimpressed with the results: where Stephen saw in the original of Horace's Epistle 1.1 'a connexion of ideas' in 'Stoical and Epicurean morals', he thought Pope had reduced these to a mere 'string of commonplaces'.[5] Pope certainly did transform and also obscure what he found in Horace, but his methods reached back into the seventeenth century and the Renaissance, both in England and on the continent of Europe.

His educated readers would likely have recognized Pope's approach as that of the Latin humanist commentators through which both they and he approached Horace. They would also have noticed that in all of his satirical poetry except for his two poems on satire, Satire 2.1 and the Epistle to Augustus, Pope chose to imitate poems that engaged ancient Roman philosophy. Pope read the traditionally difficult passages in Horace with precision and erudition, then vied to outdo his predecessors in managing and translating Horace's ideas for his English audience. Such an exact and thoughtful procedure, which Pope often cloaked in the blandest language, was entirely at home in

---

[2] The great scholar Maynard Mack was the protagonist; see for example his *Alexander Pope: A Life* (New York: Norton, 1985) and his edition of the *Essay on Man* (Pope, *Poems* (Twickenham), iii. 1).

[3] See *The Works of Alexander Pope*, ed. Whitwell Elwin and William John Courthope, 10 vols. (London, 1871–89). Courthope's biography, in vol. 5, is more polite and laudatory than the remarks in the individual volumes.

[4] Margaret Anne Doody, *The Daring Muse: Augustan Poetry Reconsidered* (Cambridge: Cambridge University Press, 1985).

[5] Leslie Stephen, *Alexander Pope* (London: Macmillan, 1883), 185.

the genre of satire. As J. Paul Hunter has stressed, satire could accommodate serious argument precisely because Augustan conversation did too.[6]

The philosophy that Pope engaged in Horace's satires was also provocative, even dangerous. This is because Pope repeatedly chose to take up what commentators had pointed to as an especially inflammatory element of Horace's philosophy, namely Epicurus's ancient philosophy of pleasure. This has many elements but centres on the conviction that pleasure is the highest end of human life, when we define pleasure as a contented body and a tranquil mind. Commentators on Horace had often addressed this philosophy through silence, discreet signals, or saying what they did not mean. As we will see from his imitation of Epistle 1.6, which raises the philosophy of pleasure in particularly blatant form, Pope's imitations too offer another and far more sophisticated face if we read them like Renaissance poetry: erudite, elusive, and designed for a wide audience of the innocent alongside a smaller audience of highly attentive and knowledgeable readers.

Pope was bolder than two distinct groups of predecessors. The continental humanists of the sixteenth and seventeenth centuries had explained Horace's philosophy to readers of Latin, including Pope, and shown them dexterous ways of representing controversial ideas. Pope resembled but also outdid them when he buried Horace's Epicureanism in silence, carried Epicureanism over into his imitations in deflated and toothless form, and amplified and adorned it with new explanation. But Pope was not the first English poet to encounter and transform Horace's hedonism; he was only the most extensive and audacious in his interventions and the most independent from earlier humanists' remarks on the same passages. We will see that the theme of pleasure was also a central concern for English translators of Horace since the early seventeenth century, and that two complicated changes elapsed over the century before Pope. Horace's satirical verse replaced his lyrics as the fashionable poetry to translate, and pleasure was increasingly treated not simply as an image or experience but as a logic, a technical ancient philosophy.

It seems Pope wished to be seen as a philosophical and classical expert at least as much as a poetic translator, as an original contributor to the long European conversation over what Horace meant. The Earl of Shaftesbury, an industrious reader of commentaries, depicted himself as such an expert when he explained that Horace's poetry required deciphering and decoding because of Horace's conscious dissembling. In fact, 'the chief Beauty' of Horace's satires and epistles arose from his rigorous logic combined with evasion. Any reader who was an adult and not a schoolboy, Shaftesbury thought, could see how Horace worked to '[Conceal]' an 'Order and Method', to write with 'Artifice' and just as surely 'destroy every such Token or Appearance'.[7] In this conception of authorship, we should read for clues or 'tokens'; we have the option to explain the author in full or discreetly; and philosophical poetry may be read by many but not understood by all.

---

[6] J. Paul Hunter, 'Couplets and Conversation', in *The Cambridge Companion to Eighteenth-Century Poetry*, ed. John Sitter (Cambridge: Cambridge University Press, 2001), 11–35.

[7] Anthony Ashley Cooper, Third Earl of Shaftesbury, *Characteristicks of Men, Manners, Opinions, Times*, ed. Philip Ayres, 2 vols. (Oxford: Clarendon Press, 1999), ii. 139 (Miscellany I, ch. 3). On Shaftesbury's career and erudition, see Karen Collis, 'Shaftesbury and Learned Culture', Oxford DPhil thesis, 2013.

John Dryden proceeded on a similar model when he compared the literary translator to the most audacious of commentators. Dryden warned with apparent pride that he had 'both added and omitted' and, as if incorporating editorial footnotes into his text, 'very boldly made such expositions of my Authors, as no *Dutch* Commentator will forgive me'. Aesthetics and logic were intermingled as Dryden cut only what was not 'beautiful' in English, while his additions, like the truths buried in Shaftesbury's Horace, 'are secretly in the Poet, or may be fairly deduc'd from him'.[8] One very concrete deduction about Horace was displayed pugnaciously in Dryden's preface: 'let his *Dutch* commentatours say what they will, his Philosophy was Epicurean'.[9] In fact, few on the continent would have been surprised. In Dryden's Horace translations, however, he suggested Horace's Epicureanism through silent signals and juxtapositions, never engaging the satires and epistles that are the epicentre of Horace's philosophy of pleasure.

This model of reading and translation recalls the Renaissance, with its love for emblems and deciphering, more than it does our conception of the eighteenth-century imitation, in which we have often argued from fairly straightforward readings of the language that Pope added to Horace. To discover Pope's transformations of the Epicurean Horace, we must read him as we would a philosopher like Machiavelli, Hobbes, or Spinoza, examining silences, contradictions, and seemingly innocuous meanings. How did Horace, the satirical imitation, philosophy, and Pope's elevated view of himself come together to inspire this surprising project late in his career?

WHAT WAS HORACE?

Pope apparently embraced the philosophical Horace in the late 1720s, when a mass of old and new impulses animated his poetry. He had just decided to declare himself as an English philosophical authority through an enormous series of philosophical poems that we conventionally view as beginning with his *Epistle to Burlington* (1731) and culminating in the *Essay on Man* (1733–4), just as he had become an expert literary critic in his *Essay on Criticism*, an expert on classical antiquity in his translations of Homer (1715–20, 1726), and an expert on England's national literature in his edition of Shakespeare (1725). The Epicurean philosophy of pleasure seems to have fascinated Pope, and he wove it into wider ethical and cosmic concerns in the *Essay on Man*, as David Morris and Tom Jones have beautifully shown.[10]

---

[8] John Dryden, ed., *Sylvae* (1685), sig. A2ᵛ–A3ʳ. The passage is discussed, in the context of free translation, in David Hopkins, 'Theories of Translation: Dryden and His Contemporaries', in *The Oxford History of Literary Translation in English*, vol. 3: *1660–1790*, ed. Stuart Gillespie and David Hopkins (Oxford: Oxford University Press, 2005), 61–2.

[9] Dryden, *Sylvae*, sig. A6ʳ.

[10] David B. Morris, 'Pope and the Arts of Pleasure', in *The Enduring Legacy: Alexander Pope Tercentenary Essays*, ed. G. S. Rousseau and Pat Rogers (Cambridge: Cambridge University Press, 1988), 95–117, and Alexander Pope, *An Essay on Man*, ed. Tom Jones (Princeton: Princeton University Press, 2016), xxx–xxxiii, xxxvii–xxxviii.

The fashionable form of the classical imitation let Pope make at least two poetic experiments. First, Horace's long, argumentative poems gave Pope great latitude to explore and transform the philosophy of pleasure, treating it far more coherently and vividly than he had in his *Essay on Man*. Conversely, the imitation form gave plausible deniability to the potential scandal of the philosophy of pleasure: when he published his English imitations side by side with Horace's original Latin, Pope figured as something a little less than an author. As he translated, he served as a reasoning voice who might regulate, deflate, even indignantly reject what Horace had written. These were the arts both of the humanists and of the earlier English translators who had learnt from them to read Horace with inference, suspicion, and self-preservation.

By the late 1720s, too, Pope evidently saw Horace as a systematic writer capable of large, carefully reasoned works. In 1728, he ventilated the startling view that the rambling *Ars poetica* we read today was the product of a rigorously logical mind interrupted or distracted when the work had barely begun: the extant poem, Pope thought, 'was probably only fragments of what he [Horace] designed', and if the *Ars poetica* had been fully executed according to this 'plan', it would display more 'regularity'.[11] In fact, this argument about the *Ars poetica* came directly from André Dacier's French commentary and paraphrase on Horace, first published between 1681 and 1689 and reaching its fourth edition in 1727; Pope praised it to the Duke of Buckingham in 1718.[12] Dacier was deeply committed to the philosophical Horace, and for his new French audience, he was far more explicit than his Latin predecessors about the philosophical dangers Horace presented and the simple morals he thought we should take away.

In this light, the stories that Pope carefully spread about the casual origin and rapid composition of his imitations look very much like the Horatian self-fashioning of ease and spontaneity that Shaftesbury described.[13] Pope's personal letters, too, he claimed had been tossed off effortlessly, even as he carefully reworked them and scrambled to retrieve and recall those that he really had written in haste.[14] The most plausible of all Pope's claims about the imitations may be that Bolingbroke, his philosophical mentor, in some way suggested them. So the satires represent a double Pope: one nonchalant, genteel, and easy, the other triumphantly sharing the ingenious discoveries and insights he drew from his exact studies.

A philosophical Pope could expect a ready audience in England because educated readers were familiar with the idea that Horace was Epicurean, notwithstanding Dryden's posturing. Most modern classicists agree that Horace does often refer to the formal philosophy of his time, above all Stoic and Epicurean ideas, and that at a given

---

[11] Joseph Spence, *Observations, Anecdotes, and Characters of Books and Men*, ed. James M. Osborn, 2 vols. (Oxford: Clarendon Press, 1966), i. 227 (§538).

[12] André Dacier, ed., *Oeuvres d'Horace en latin et en françois, avec des remarques critiques et historiques*, 4th edn., 10 vols. (Amsterdam, 1727), ix. 246; Pope, *Corr.* (Sherburn), i. 492.

[13] Pope, *Corr.* (Sherburn), iii. 348, 350, 353, 358; Spence, *Observations*, i. 143 (§321a).

[14] Pope, *Works*, ed. Elwin and Courthope, vi. xxix–xxx.

moment he may be endorsing, reframing, or slighting the buzzwords that he drops.[15] For continental humanists since the early sixteenth century, the challenge, or the opportunity, to address Horace's dangerous philosophy was all the more compelling because they might address standing debates in relatively open or cleverly elliptical ways.[16] But even in school texts like those of John Bond (1606) and Louis Desprez (1691), explanations of Horace's ideas could be surprisingly frank.[17] Humanists likely perceived Horace's philosophy of pleasure as even more controversial because of Epicurus's manifestly subversive ideas about science and religion: the soul is material and dies with us; the world is made of atoms; the traditional gods do not exist.

What would it mean for an English translation of Horace to resemble a humanist commentary, beyond Dryden's confidence that in both cases an astute reader could discover a hidden sense? The answer lies in shared postures and approaches to both Horace and the reader. The humanists saw themselves as independent guides, sometimes transmitting what they believed Horace meant or even stressing it, but sometimes excusing him, transforming him, or treating him as unmentionable—in a word, saving Horace from himself. Often they aimed not to disclose their author's intention but to explain what he should have said. But because of Horace's enormous prestige, they rarely opposed him outright, although we will see an extreme case where both Pope and Dacier did just this.

The resemblance becomes even clearer for those English translators who took the technical, philosophical approach. The humanists assumed that Horace promoted pleasure only as the starting point for an Epicurean ethical guide to life: they might discuss a vast array of other passages about virtue, false judgement, the mind and body, and more, in a way that might or might not alert uninitiated readers.[18] Because Epicurus advocated virtue and moderation as routes to pleasure, the humanists might also believe some part of Horace was both Epicurean and innocuous, but they conveyed this too through discretion or even contradiction. Erudition was invaluable here, as a humanist might announce that a poem was morally sound but then eagerly discuss its dangerous lines; or, as we will see, he might calmly supply ancient information that made Horace's philosophy easier to understand or even excuse. In the light of these broad orientations

---

[15] On philosophy in Horace, see Marcia L. Colish, *The Stoic Tradition from Antiquity to the Early Middle Ages*, 2 vols. (Leiden: Brill, 1985), i. 161–8, and Roland Mayer, 'Sleeping with the Enemy: Satire and Philosophy', in *The Cambridge Companion to Roman Satire*, ed. Kirk Freudenburg (Cambridge: Cambridge University Press, 2005), 146–59, esp. 153–5, both with references to other literature.

[16] On humanist readings of Horace's Epicurean philosophy down to Denis Lambin's edition of 1561 (2nd edn., 1567), see Anja Stadeler, *Horazrezeption in der Renaissance: Strategien der Horazkommentierung bei Cristoforo Landino und Denis Lambin* (Berlin: De Gruyter, 2015), 181–272 and Michael Roberts, 'Interpreting Hedonism: Renaissance Commentaries on Horace's Epicurean Odes', *Arethusa* 28 (1995), 289–307.

[17] There are also significant philosophical discussions in the Horace editions by Denis Lambin (2nd edn., 1567), Jacob Cruquius (1597), Eilhard Lubin (1599), Adrian Turnèbe (1604), Laevinus Torrentius (1608), Daniel Heinsius (1629), Cornelis Schrevelius (1663), and André Dacier (1681–9).

[18] Modern classicists are not inclined to read poems as philosophically unified wholes or to seek a textual parallel for each line of a poem. Here I am not endorsing the humanists' arguments but exploring them with their literary consequences.

towards classical poetry, the rise of 'free translation' in England looks in part like the adoption of a humanist ethical and intellectual stance, and the rise of the imitation itself, traditionally centring on the culture and distinctive political events of the Restoration, also becomes an international story. The classical imitation connects England with Europe, poets with scholars, and close textual study with independence.

FROM LYRIC TO SATIRE

The English Horace radically changed in genre and sensibility over the seventeenth century.[19] In the early century, almost exclusively his lyrics were translated, often in volumes of selected poems that allowed translators to underscore definite themes; the fifth lyric collection appeared in 1653.[20] But the Restoration saw a fashion for the longer, more argumentative satires and epistles and for the *Art of Poetry*, which tells us that a poem should be pleasing as well as useful (333–4).[21] Over the same time, though not always in the same poet, the vision of Horace's hedonism became increasingly sophisticated, humanist, expert. Whether a translation depicted pleasure as an immediate personal experience or as a more erudite philosophy, these poems also resonated with timely and local meanings: hedonism as personal independence, as morally objectionable, as defiance against Commonwealth jailers, or as the legacy of an eccentric biographical Epicurus. Once we have examined the most satirical, the most philosophical, and the most conspiratorial of his predecessors, we may conclude that Pope's philosophical imitations differed from theirs mainly in degree, not in kind.

The first collected volume of Horace's odes, by John Ashmore (1621), included a small group of poems devoted to Horace's hedonism—love, friendship, drinking, and poetry. This representation of pleasure is undiluted and immediate. But Ashmore's selection is also stark for what it leaves out—not only the odes with Stoic themes but all but one of the poems of patronage to Maecenas and Caesar.[22] Ashmore turned the entire corpus of odes into a retreat from politics into private pleasure: another favourite Horatian and

---

[19] Hedonism has been surprisingly little discussed since the pioneering studies of Maren-Sofie Røstvig, *The Happy Man: Studies in the Metamorphoses of a Classical Ideal*, 2nd edn., 2 vols. (Oslo: Norwegian Universities Press, 1962), i. 233–310 and T. F. Mayo, *Epicurus in England (1650–1725)* (Dallas, TX: Southwest Press, 1934) . More recently, see Joshua Scodel, *Excess and the Mean in Early Modern English Literature* (Princeton: Princeton University Press, 2002), esp. 199–252, and Catherine Wilson, *Epicureanism at the Origins of Modernity* (Oxford: Oxford University Press, 2008), 207–15, 260–4, 268–77.

[20] Joshua Scodel, 'Lyric', in *The Oxford History of Literary Translation in English*, vol. 2: *1550–1660*, ed. Gordon Braden, Robert Cummings, and Stuart Gillespie (Oxford: Oxford University Press, 2010), 212–47, esp. 213–20, and Valerie Edden, ' "The Best of Lyrick Poets" ', in *Horace*, ed. C. D. N. Costa (London: Routledge & Kegan Paul, 1973), 135–59.

[21] See David Hopkins, 'Roman Satire and Epigram', in *The Oxford History of Literary Translation in English*, vol. 3, 218–40, esp. 220–1. For translations of Horace's satires and epistles in the first half of the seventeenth century, Glyn Pursglove, 'Moral Kinds', in *The Oxford History of Literary Translation in English*, vol. 2, 201–11, esp. 203–5.

[22] [John Ashmore], trans., *Certain Selected Odes of Horace, Englished* (1621).

Epicurean theme and a reminder that Jacobean literary culture did not always thematize power and submission.

Thomas Hawkins released a diametrically opposite selection of odes in 1625, reading Horace as a Stoic poet of contempt of riches, calming the passions, deploring the present age, and consolation. Conversely, Hawkins included Epicureanism only to show its defeat or transform it ingeniously into Stoicism. So Hawkins printed Ode 1.34, in which Horace regrets that he has failed to worship the gods, with an accusatory prose summary specifying that Horace's impiety was Epicurean: the summary was translated directly from John Bond's school edition.[23] Hawkins also included two drinking songs of the lugubrious variety, on death, old age, and sorrow, barely mentioning pleasure.[24] Their context in Hawkins's volume turned these into Stoic poems of mental tranquillity and relinquishing cares, with pleasure as a means and not the end. Joshua Scodel has shown how Ben Jonson's drinking songs revalued the ancient Anacreontic and Horatian lyric in a similar way, stressing moderation and depicting conviviality as an instrument of civilization.[25]

Sir Richard Fanshawe began a series of Horace translations by the 1630s, but he printed his distinctly philosophical selection only in 1652 while a royalist prisoner.[26] It is easy to see the collection's hedonism as a rebuke to Fanshawe's republican jailers—he had been forbidden to publish openly political works.[27] Fanshawe published all of the odes, and his renderings make the case that pleasure is compatible with morality, religion, and political duty; Joshua Scodel has shown how Fanshawe removed a homosexual passage, inserted a royalist theme, and added biblical references, including in the ode where Horace recants his Epicurean impiety.[28] But on the plane of personal experience, Fanshawe also amplified Horace's hedonist themes, adding new descriptions of convivial and rural pleasures to Epicurean poems like Ode 1.31, Epode 2, and Satire 2.6. Meanwhile, the seven satires and epistles that Fanshawe translated, with interconnected themes of pleasure and virtue, deployed a combination of experience and technical philosophy: the indispensability of virtue (Epistles 1.1, 1.2), the folly of distracting pursuits (Epistle 1.1, Satires 1.6, 2.6), rural retreat (Satires 1.6, 2.6, Epistle 1.10), and drinking as superior to riches (Epistle 1.5).

Fanshawe also acted strikingly like a humanist when he inserted a large marginal note on Ode 4.7, the melancholy drinking song called *Diffugere nives*, that explained in Epicurus's own words why the principle of pleasure demanded a reasonable and moderate life and forbade gluttony or indiscriminate sex. While Fanshawe's note initially called the principle of pleasure a 'heresie', he noted later that Horace remained an Epicurean in the favourable sense of moderation and reason all his life. In fact, Fanshawe eventually

---

[23] John Bond, ed., *Quinti Horatii Flacci poemata* (1606), 36.

[24] T[homas] H[awkins], trans., *Odes of Horace* (1625), sig. A1ᵛ ('wanton and looser'), 11 (Ode 1.34), 19–20, 66–67 (Ode 2.11, Epode 13).

[25] Scodel, *Excess and the Mean*, esp. 201–13; cf. also 215–18.

[26] *The Poems and Translations of Sir Richard Fanshawe*, ed. Peter Davidson, 2 vols. (Oxford: Clarendon Press, 1997–9), i. 149–235; for the chronology, i. xvii–xix, xxi–xxiii, xxxvii–xxxviii, 370–1.

[27] Restrictions on publishing: Fanshawe, *Poems and Translations*, i. xiii.

[28] Scodel, 'Lyric', 217–18.

revealed, this Epicureanism formed 'the sounder part of his Book which is almost the whole'.[29] As we will see Pope also did, Fanshawe had learnt from the continental human-ists that a potentially alarming passage in Horace could be defused with calm and exact teaching rather than blanket suppression or implausible reinterpretations.[30]

Abraham Cowley and John Dryden advance the story in complementary ways, with Cowley translating Horatian satires in a mode of immediate hedonist experience and Dryden confining his Epicurean philosophical interests to Horace's lyrics. Cowley, one of the century's greatest lyric poets, included scattered translations of Horace's odes as well as three of the satires and epistles in his *Essays* of 1668, with themes of rural retreat, the rejection of wealth, and simple, peaceful pleasure.[31] As David Hopkins has convincingly argued, Cowley knew of Epicurus's philosophy of pleasure and used Horace's tale of the country mouse and city mouse in Satire 2.6 to stage a serious debate over how to apply that philosophy to our lives.[32] However, in the *Essays* in general, Cowley applied a perverse erudition not to reconstructing Epicurus's philosophy in logical terms but to excavating the putative ancient sayings of Epicurus himself, to which Cowley reacted with alternating approval and dismay. As any humanist could have told him, no ancient source could have been less credible than the collections of sayings that circulated under famous people's names. But it is impossible to miss Cowley's assumption that ethics concerns real questions in the lives of real people. We might say Cowley translated satires but treated them as lyrics, that he viewed all of Horace's poems as instalments in the *Essays'* wider theme of the personal experience of pleasure.[33]

By contrast, Dryden studied Epicurean philosophy carefully. But it remained contro-versial at this time, and in his 1685 translations of four of Horace's odes Dryden knew how to deploy silence and intertextuality to suggest meanings that were not visible on Horace's page.[34] Most striking was Horace's relationship with the five excerpts from Lucretius that Dryden translated in the same volume, seemingly chosen to sound like lyrics and satires with themes of passion, advice, and the nature of life. All but one of Dryden's Horatian odes promoted rural retreat or Anacreontic conviviality, and Dryden inserted in them and amplified Horatian-sounding arguments that we should enjoy the present day. While these ideas were indeed compatible with Epicurus's philosophy, by

[29] Fanshawe, *Poems and Translations*, i. 203.

[30] Fanshawe's quotation of Epicurus came from Diogenes Laertius 10.131–2.

[31] Abraham Cowley, *The Works of Mr Abraham Cowley* (1668), with *Several Discourses by way of Essays, in Verse and Prose* as the last pagination; Satire 2.6.79–117 at 109–11, Epistle 1.10 at 111–12, Satire 1.1.1–79 at 128–30.

[32] David Hopkins, 'Cowley's Horatian Mice', in *Horace Made New: Horatian Influences on British Writing from the Renaissance to the Twentieth Century*, ed. Charles Martindale and David Hopkins (Cambridge: Cambridge University Press, 1993), 103–26.

[33] Further on Cowley and personal experience in these poems, see Paul Davis, *Translation and the Poet's Life: The Ethics of Translating in English Culture, 1646–1726* (Oxford: Oxford University Press, 2008), esp. 77–126.

[34] Dryden, *Sylvae*, 52–99 (Lucretius), 124–59 (Horace). On Dryden's studies, Paul Hammond, 'The Integrity of Dryden's Lucretius', *Modern Language Review* 78 (1983), 1–23; on controversies, Paul Davis, 'Dryden and the Consolations of Philosophy', *The Seventeenth Century* 15 (2000), 217–43.

this time they belonged securely to the realm of English poetic *topoi*. But Dryden also provided an arresting philosophical backdrop in the form of a twenty-page translation from Lucretius. This impassioned piece of argument provided a serious and profoundly unorthodox reason why we should enjoy life today: death is final because the soul is mortal. The reader who remembered Dryden's earlier announcement about the Epicurean Horace might grasp that Dryden was allowing his audience to read Lucretius as an enormous and sobering footnote to the hedonist odes. But no one was compelled to make the connection, and more to the point, no one could prove that such a philosophy of pleasure was in Dryden's mind.[35]

On the other hand, Dryden's version of Ode 1.3, a Stoic poem that castigates atheism, makes a crucial change. In Dryden's poem, the Epicureans' attack on heaven seems to arise from a spirit of courage and adventure innate to humanity, and where in Horace Jupiter punishes challenges with 'angry' (*iracunda*) thunderbolts (40), in Dryden a compassionate Christian God punishes but understands that the affront cannot be helped: 'we pull' his 'unwilling thunder down'.[36] Like Fanshawe's, Dryden's choices here announced that he could endorse pleasure without embracing atheism; but Dryden may have thought that case too tricky for the overtly philosophical satires and epistles. Yet like so many contemporaries, Dryden was attracted to the Roman satire in itself, translating and annotating Juvenal and Persius in 1693.[37] The difference was that these poets were safely Stoic moralists who promoted virtue and a creator God.

In the decades before Pope's imitations, the English Horace acquired a final element: conspicuous erudition and expertise. Thomas Creech's Oxford translation of Horace in 1684, coming two years after his 1682 translation of Lucretius, showed the English reader Horace's logical argumentation in the satires and epistles by supplying a summary of each poem, often with numbered points that reappeared throughout the English text. Creech typically translated Horace closely, but when he encountered an Epicurean passage, whether atheist or hedonist, he often acted as a commentator instead, repressing it, softening it, leaving it prominently in place, or even seeming to justify and explain it. We will see a striking example in Epistle 1.6. Meanwhile, the translation of the satires and epistles by Samuel Dunster (1709) and the translation of the lyrics organized by William Oldisworth (1712–13) appeared with Horace's Latin on the facing page. The device was likely encouraged by the popularity of Dacier's edition, although Richard Fanshawe had done the same. Dunster, faced with the philosophy of the hexameter poems, often rendered literally some extremely heterodox passages; yet even he could sometimes shield them from full view in time-honoured ways.

So we would speak far too broadly if we simply contrasted a freely imitating Pope with dully literal predecessors. In each case the translator decided sometimes to convey Horace fairly transparently and sometimes to adapt him for modern reasons, emphasizing

---

[35] Translation of Lucretius 3.830–1094, Dryden, *Sylvae*, 60–79. On his Horatian adaptations, Røstvig, *The Happy Man*, i. 242.

[36] Dryden, *Sylvae*, 124–7.

[37] *The Satires of Decimus Junius Juvenalis Translated into English Verse by Mr Dryden and Several Other Eminent Hands; together with the Satires of Aulus Persius Flaccus, Made English by Mr Dryden* (1693).

favoured themes or repressing or deflating what should not be divulged. These are the methods equally of poetry and of scholarly humanism. The level of argumentative intervention in English translations of Horace's philosophical satires before Pope was in fact extremely similar to the kinds of treatment Horace had received on the continent. But we will see how greatly Pope magnified their tactics in one of his last imitations, also one of the most blatantly philosophical and the most potentially embarrassing to modern moral assumptions.

POPE AND EPISTLE 1.6: DISCRETION AND INDISCRETION

Pope had engaged Horace's philosophy of pleasure before, for example in the first two imitations following his initial imitation on the satirical genre (Satire 2.1; 1733). Satire 2.2 (1734) was read with alarm by many humanists as an Epicurean argument about the pleasures we should choose, even if its advice was bland: luxurious dishes are a false pleasure; moderate living is best. Satire 1.2, *Sober Advice from Horace* (1734), even more obviously concerned an Epicurean choice of pleasures: Horace takes up various classes of women you might sleep with and cautions that all of them are dangerous. By 1738, Pope had turned to imitating Horace's more argumentative epistles, and Epistle 1.6 offered a double challenge to conventional morality. Not only did Horace appear to attack virtue; Pope evidently believed that Horace did so from an Epicurean standpoint. To explain this, excuse it, make it morally acceptable, and even rephrase Horace's stance on virtue in the terms of his own *Essay on Man*, all while writing an apparently simple and easy poem: this was the philosophical feat we will see Pope attempt.

Epistle 1.6 is a catalogue of vain ambitions, or things that people believe will make them happy, like money, art collecting, political power, and parties. Little here is different from Horace's Satire 2.3, Pope's *Epistle to Cobham*, or the *Essay on Man* 4.135–308. But Epistle 1.6 adds the governing advice that we should 'wonder at nothing' (*nil admirari*, 1): the reason is that pointless pursuits raise hope or fear that perturb our mental tranquillity. Laevinus Torrentius in 1608 traced this idea to Epicurus's predecessor Democritus, and for an Epicurean the point of wondering at nothing is hedonist.[38] Anything that disturbs our tranquillity is not a true pleasure but an enemy of pleasure, so that Epistle 1.6 is also ultimately a poem that reasons about the choice of pleasures. As a final incrimination, which a few humanists signalled by citing individual lines, Horace's epistle seemed to be modelled on the opening of Lucretius's *De rerum natura* book 2, another list of vain pursuits that distract us from the life of reason (2.1–54).[39]

---

[38] Laevinus Torrentius, ed., *Q. Horatius Flaccus* (Antwerp, 1608), 648, 649.
[39] Parallels to Lucretius: Adrian Turnèbe, *Animadversionum libri xxx* (Aureliopolis [Geneva], 1604), 29 (book 2, ch. 12); Dacier, *Oeuvres d'Horace* (1727), viii. 224.

Pope took three philosophical approaches as he crafted a poem that could seem effortless to those who read only the English but also impress and surprise those who could retrace his manoeuvres. His successive relations to Horace were enormously divergent: enthusiastic amplification, stark censorship, and bold reinterpretation based on ancient Epicureanism. But such divergence was also common among the humanists, who at moments of stress were apt to respond in energetic and variable ways. Pope's first tactic, learnt from André Dacier's paraphrase and commentary, was a deafening repetition of philosophical key words, which in this poem, unlike some of his other imitations, he actually took from Horace's text. The first half of Pope's Epistle 1.6 centred on the terms 'admire', 'amaze', 'surpriz'd', and 'struck', followed by and overlapping with 'happy' and 'blest'. If you do not preoccupy yourself with pointless distractions, you may achieve happiness: a pedestrian moral that elided the question of virtue and Pope's most vital philosophical interventions.

What the poem seems to be attacking is the Stoic doctrine that virtue is the highest human good and constitutes happiness in itself. Many a humanist declared that Horace was simply wrong when he wrote that 'the wise man will be counted a fool, the just unjust, if he pursues virtue past its proper limits' (15–16). But Pope gave his real attention to a shadowy passage telling us that *if* virtue alone leads to the good life (*recte vivere*), *then* we should abandon pleasures (*deliciis*) and pursue virtue (29–31). Reversing Horace's tone of pronounced doubt, Pope turned his imitation into a full-throated defence of virtue by dealing ruthlessly with the *if*, daringly and ingeniously with the *then*.

First, undoing Horace's attack and establishing a whole new logic for the poem, Pope simply removed the 'If' (*Si*) from the passage about virtue. Obviously, this eradicated the question about virtue itself. It also sharply separated virtue from the many other immoderate pursuits in the poem that Horace prefaced with 'If', as in 'If, after all, we must with Wilmot own, / The Cordial Drop of Life is Love alone' (126–7). With the most radical danger removed, the last line of Pope's passage delivered the edifying message, made thunderous as the last line of a triplet: 'Be Virtuous, and be happy for your pains' (62). This, of course, sounds precisely like the Stoic teaching that virtue in itself is human happiness. From this line alone, then, it might seem that Pope is simply censoring and contradicting Horace; or, to put Pope on a level with the humanists, it would seem he is telling us what Horace should have said. In fact, we should be reminded of the humanists who first announced an easy moral for a Horatian poem, then entered more dangerous ground line by line.

In fact, when Pope completed the thought, rendering Horace's 'Then' about giving up pleasures, he turned from contradiction to a kind of self-interested mind-reading. Slashing through the rhetorical question and implied negations of the original, Pope presented the passage in a way that, he evidently thought, reflected Horace's underlying Epicurean beliefs about pleasure and virtue. Yet Pope also treated the Epicurean position on pleasure and virtue as scandalous, burying it so deeply in ambiguity and insinuation that no one could have detected it in Pope's version without understanding it already.

As Pope's earlier imitations had preached at length, for Epicureans not every pleasure is a true pleasure which leads to happiness. Therefore, to choose the right pleasures, we need judgement and moderation. To Epicureans, virtue is precisely this good judgement and moderation that let us choose the right pleasures. It follows that happiness is impossible without virtue, but only in the sense that virtue is an instrument for achieving pleasure, which remains the highest good.[40]

Pope introduces the idea of choosing pleasures, which is to say the idea of legitimate pleasures, when he tells us to 'despise low Joys, low Gains' (60) and 'Disdain' what a famously incorruptible man 'disdains' (61). Choosing the right pleasures leads directly to being 'blest' (60)—Pope's synonym in this poem for the philosophical idea of happiness, or the best state of human life.

> Would ye be blest? despise low Joys, low Gains;
> Disdain whatever Cornbury disdains,
> Be Virtuous, and be happy for your pains.
>
> (60–2)

In this light, the exhortation in line 62 to 'Be Virtuous' means something very different from what it would in isolation. To 'Be Virtuous' is to exercise moderation and discretion, that is, to choose the right pleasures, which is what really makes us happy. Masquerading as an irreproachable Stoic idea, line 62 is in fact the logical culmination of an Epicurean argument. Pope made many similar reversals and detours in Epistle 1.6, two of which were noticed by Pope's nineteenth-century editor W. J. Courthope.[41] Perhaps we should also be reminded of the dozens of passages in the *Essay on Man* that have been accused of incoherence or philosophical misunderstanding.

But what was the point? Why would Pope work so ingeniously to insert the argument that virtue leads to pleasure, and on the other hand, why did he labour so effectively to conceal it? Conceivably he simply acted as Horace's advocate, using leaps of logic to produce an English passage that could appear intellectually honest to well-informed readers, irreproachable to others. It is likely, though, that Pope's treatment of Epistle 1.6 should strengthen our impression that in his *Essay on Man* he understood and meant what he said about pleasure as the aim of human life.

On the one hand, the Pope of the *Essay* explained that seeking pleasure and avoiding pain are the animating principles of our nature (2.87–92); Epicurus had said that pleasure and pain should be the standards that guide our ethical choices.[42] Pope also spoke of pleasure as the highest good in human life, sometimes adding that we need virtue in order to realize it (4.1–2, 4.79–82). At the same time, Pope seemed to know that these ideas were inflammatory, for as the *Essay* progressed, he wrote with complete ambiguity about whether virtue led to pleasure or vice versa (3.232–4). By the time the *Essay* neared its end, he cloaked pleasure in silence and sang encomiums only about virtue: 'Virtue alone is Happiness below' (4.310), and the grand summation of the entire *Essay*, 'VIRTUE only makes our Bliss below' (4.397; cf. also 4.167–9, 4.349–50). This gradual suppression

---

[40] Diogenes Laertius 10.132.   [41] *Works*, ed. Elwin and Courthope, iii. 319, 326.
[42] For Epicurus on pleasure and pain as the standard of choice, Diogenes Laertius 10.128–30.

of pleasure was noticed by Pope's critic Jean-Pierre de Crousaz, who remarked that 'Virtue has made very rapid and very great advances' between the first epistle of the *Essay* and the fourth.[43] Because many readers might not have felt certain which idea was the more fundamental without understanding Epicurus's ethics in advance, or indeed remembered that there was any relationship at all, this was a strategy of philosophy for the few and persiflage for the many. Meanwhile, where the dangerous passage in Epistle 1.6 is concerned, the evanescing philosophy of the *Essay on Man* meant that Pope's intervention had an intertextual authority a humanist commentator could never have claimed: his own.

It is time to include the Horatian imitations in Pope's philosophical poetry. Reuben Brower did this when he interpreted all of Pope's philosophical poems, including the *Essay on Man*, as a series of Horatian epistles. Brower also pointed out that Pope simultaneously composed the *Essay on Man*, the *Moral Epistles*, and the Horatian imitations, and that his manuscript working materials were interconnected.[44] What is more, Pope's earliest written plan for his great scheme of moral poetry includes subject headings that describe nearly all of his Horatian imitations: poems on the use of pleasure (Satire 1.2), happiness or pleasure (Satire 2.2, Epistle 1.7), 'wrong pursuits of Power, Pleasure, and false Happiness' (Epistle 1.1, Epistle 1.6), and 'Passions, Virtues &c.' (Epistle 1.1). Pope's Epistle 2.2 comes closer to an entry in a 1734 Index, treating the use of riches like the *Epistle to Bathurst*. It looks as if in the Horatian imitations Pope created a dialogic poetry that ventriloquized, expanded, and dramatized the same philosophical questions he had asked elsewhere. He enjoyed this greater freedom in part because he could pretend the satirical poems were witty trifles, but also because, having represented them for his audience like a humanist commentator, Pope was not altogether their author.

Both Pope's attraction to ancient philosophy and his fascination with concealment were deeply traditional. He had predecessors both on the continent and in England for the way he transformed the passage in Epistle 1.6: he innovated in that his revisions were more elaborate, verbose, and systematic. Two earlier English translators had also made Horace speak of abandoning only some pleasures, assuming that he spoke as an Epicurean. So Thomas Creech wrote that we should 'leave' our 'false delights', while Alexander Brome in 1666 spoke of 'vanities'.[45] But in a complementary manoeuvre, both Creech and Brome deleted Horace's hypothetical 'If' as Pope later would, making Horace openly claim that 'Virtue only this can give' (Creech) or '*Virtue is / the onely way to gain true happiness*' (Brome). From one viewpoint, the result was a forbidden Horace joined with a permitted Horace, Epicurean (or perhaps just commonsensical) on pleasure and Stoic on virtue. From another viewpoint, this Horace was entirely Epicurean and spoke of virtue as an indispensable instrument, just as this passage would in Pope. The small scale and caution of these renditions lets them resist decisive decoding, like

---

[43] Jean-Pierre de Crousaz, *Examen de l'essay de M. Pope sur l'homme* (Lausanne, 1737), 200.

[44] Reuben A. Brower, *Alexander Pope: The Poetry of Allusion* (1959; repr. Oxford: Oxford University Press, 1986), 241–2.

[45] Thomas Creech, trans., *The Odes, Satyrs, and Epistles of Horace* (Oxford, 1684), 488; Alexander Brome, ed., *The Poems of Horace* (1666), 316.

many humanist comments on Horace. Pope's bolder adaptations apparently responded to evolving poetic conventions, a climate of comparatively greater freedom of thought, and also, very likely, his perception of his own philosophical stature.

Pope's treatment of Horace also combined and escalated humanist models of distancing and rapprochement. Dacier openly acknowledged that Epistle 1.6 was Epicurean, then announced the useful goal of contradicting it outright: he would show how the idea of wondering at nothing could be 'used' in a better way, 'corrected by the light of truth and reason'.[46] This proved to be an argument that in fact virtue was the highest good, although Dacier never claimed this was Horace's secret meaning.[47] On the other hand, Laevinus Torrentius chose the way of erudite explanation, giving a decisively Epicurean reading of the central passage on 'virtue alone' but immediately offering a context that seemed designed to rescue Horace in his readers' eyes. His explanation stressed that virtue was indispensable for the philosophy of pleasure, while it also initiated his audience into a dangerous subject.[48] Manifestly, both Torrentius and Dacier assumed that modern values fundamentally shape how we understand the past. Their example also shows why Pope could believe it was a task for discernment and expertise, not a diverting and arbitrary pastime, to represent Horace's philosophy to the English-speaking world.

So it means something more important than we thought, and more complicated, to read Pope's imitations as moral and didactic. At the least, we might rethink our received picture of a single, broad reading public in the early eighteenth century fostering ever more open conversation and debate. Of course, the model of two audiences or two ways of reading for Pope's satirical verse likely involved some slippage. Even well-informed readers were required to detect and untangle what Whitwell Elwin called Pope's 'wilful ambiguity', 'equivocations', and 'enigmas'.[49] On the other hand, a less informed reader comparing Horace's Latin and Pope's English might have been inspired to move between audiences, to become more attentive as a reader and more knowledgeable about formal ethics, just as she might have learnt from humanist commentaries about dangerous philosophies and elusive methods of argument. But on the whole, it seems probable that Pope's imitations usually left his audiences as he found them, with experts grasping some or all of his bold manoeuvres but many readers never perceiving that the toothless ideas he pressed on them had been forcibly extorted from crucially different ancient philosophical poems.

Finally, once the moral-didactic satires are understood as philosophical, Pope's personal image and his career leap into a realm of ambition and expertise as defined and understood in the intellectual world of his time. The intertextual form of the imitation positioned Pope as an expert who could burnish an ancient poet's lustre and mediate his ideas for eighteenth-century England, while it also removed Pope a vital step from responsibility for his own words. By engaging Horace's words with the rigour of a scholar but adapting them with the freedom of a poet, Pope could select and transform Horace's

---

[46] Dacier, *Oeuvres d'Horace* (1727), viii. 208–9.   [47] Dacier, *Oeuvres d'Horace* (1727), viii. 224–5.
[48] Torrentius, *Q. Horatius Flaccus* (1608), 651.
[49] *Works*, ed. Elwin and Courthope, i. xix–xx; cf. on the *Essay on Man* ii. 283–93.

dangerous philosophy, hide it in plain sight, and present the whole in a style that to many must have seemed divorced from any formal philosophy at all. And precisely because this satirical style appeared so different from his other philosophical poetry—so unassuming, so Horatian—Pope's imitations worked as an ongoing experiment to expand his programme of philosophical poetry by far more flexible means.

SELECT BIBLIOGRAPHY

Brower, Reuben A. *Alexander Pope: The Poetry of Allusion* (1959; repr. Oxford: Oxford University Press, 1986).

Hunter, J. Paul. 'Couplets and Conversation', in *The Cambridge Companion to Eighteenth-Century Poetry*, ed. John Sitter (Cambridge: Cambridge University Press, 2001), 11–35.

Roberts, Michael. 'Interpreting Hedonism: Renaissance Commentaries on Horace's Epicurean Odes', *Arethusa* 28 (1995), 289–307.

Rogers, Pat. 'Sequences of Reading: Pope's Moral Essays and Imitations of Horace', in *Presenting Poetry: Composition, Publication, Reception: Essays in Honour of Ian Jack*, ed. Howard Erskine-Hill and Richard A. McCabe (Cambridge: Cambridge University Press, 1995), 75–94.

Røstvig, Maren-Sofie. *The Happy Man: Studies in the Metamorphoses of a Classical Ideal*, 2nd edn., 2 vols. (Oslo: Norwegian Universities Press, 1962), esp. vol. 1.

Stack, Frank. *Pope and Horace: Studies in Imitation* (Cambridge: Cambridge University Press, 1985).

CHAPTER 12

···

SWIFT, GULLIVER, AND
TRAVEL SATIRE

···

DANIEL CAREY

GULLIVER'S *Travels* stands as Jonathan Swift's greatest achievement—it constitutes his longest piece of writing, with the widest range of satirical targets, the work that maintains his place on the university curriculum and his reputation in the wider public imagination. The strength of conception in plot and situation makes it, along with *Robinson Crusoe*, one of the two most durable narratives of a century distinguished for its contributions to fictional form. Amid the book's vast accumulation of objects of satire, from politics to warfare, science, gender relations, contemporary philosophy, and human nature, we cannot lose sight of its construction as a work of travel. Travel and the travel book are both essential, constitutive elements of the story, serving as vehicle as well as subject matter for satirical treatment.[1] Recapturing the traditions and preoccupations that informed Swift's handling of travel poses a considerable challenge, given the proliferation of texts in the sixteenth and seventeenth centuries that laid the groundwork for his commentary on travel itself. He arguably represents a decisive culmination in thinking about these traditions, before the transition to a sentimental and Romantic take on the potentiality of the practice and its literary expression.

Two major contexts for thinking about *Gulliver's Travels* provide the basis for this chapter. The first is the usage of travel as a satirical means, that is, as a way of enabling a certain kind of satirical attention to take place. The second, to which I will devote more consideration, is satire on travellers themselves. Here we can identify a couple of significant areas of reflection that shape Swift's account—the issue of the traveller's identity and how it becomes dislocated in travel; and the accusation of lying often levelled against travellers, which relates closely to the dilemma of engaging belief. The conclusions drawn by Swift on identity and mendacity are not in themselves particularly original—they derive from long-standing and well-recognized commentary on the behaviour of

---

[1] For an extensive but somewhat unfocused study, see Dirk Friedrich Passmann, *Full of Improbable Lies: Gulliver's Travels und die Reiseliteratur vor 1726* (Frankfurt: Peter Lang, 1987).

returned travellers and their penchant for fabricating stories of adventure. His genius lies in taking this critique to a new extreme, and by structuring the story in a way that makes the form of travel writing collapse in on itself. In this he was incomparable.

TRAVEL AS A SATIRICAL OCCASION

The first major literary intervention opening out the possibility of travel as a vehicle of satire in the early modern period was Thomas More's *Utopia* (1516), itself inspired in part by Lucian of Samosata's second century AD *True History*. More recognized the potential of grounding the story in particularities belonging to actual history and geography, thereby placing the discussion within the realm of the possible, while enabling byplay over the credulity of the reader and enhancing the status of the inner circle of initiates (paralleled in the Scriblerians' engagement with the Gulliver plot).[2] More also placed an ambiguous figure at the centre of the text—a purveyor of a travel account (Raphael Hythlodaeus), whose story engages his auditors without their being able to determine their precise relationship to the narrative. Raphael is not exactly a 'character', although he does have 'characteristics', and his enthusiasm for the distant territory he describes is never in doubt. Above all, More seizes on the reflexive possibilities afforded by travel narrative: the process of translating between an exotic location and home creates a space of critique. The fact that Raphael has already established himself in Book One—set in Antwerp and organized as a conversation between 'Morus', Peter Giles, and Raphael—as an acerbic critic of European courtiers, kings, military conflicts, international relations, practices of enclosure, and other matters, strengthens the opportunity for reflexive commentary. When Raphael turns in Book Two to his positive narrative of Utopia itself, numerous occasions arise for presenting a favourable contrast with European practices, including the Utopians' disdain for gold and silver which leads them to laugh at the pretension of the visiting Anemolian ambassadors, bedecked in gold cloth and jewellery, who fail to realize that in Utopia precious metals are consigned to the fashioning of chamber pots, stools, and chains for slaves.[3] The problem with Raphael is that he loses sight, as his story progresses, of the ways in which Utopians emulate a number of aspects of European political, diplomatic, and military engagement that he had vociferously condemned in his opening discourse stating why he would refuse to serve as a counsellor to a European prince. These contradictions (unremarked by the narrator, Morus) recall potential reservations about the sunburnt traveller, Raphael, encountered at the outset, who, although he is treated with utmost respect, is clearly consumed by an *idée fixe*. Swift picks up on these possibilities by placing us in the hands of an unstable narrator, Gulliver, who always maintains his plausibility and remains convinced of his ideas, even

---

[2] *The Memoirs of the Extraordinary Life, Works, and Discoveries of Martinus Scriblerus*, ed. Charles Kerby-Miller (New York: Oxford University Press, 1988), 164–5 (ch. XVI).

[3] Sir Thomas More, *Utopia*, trans. Robert M. Adams, 2nd edn. (New York: W. W. Norton, 1992), 47–8.

as he contradicts himself within and between his different voyages. Nor is he a 'character' as such, but rather a medium who bears the weight of shifting satirical priorities. The key point about Raphael is that he disaffiliates from his original identity, attaching himself resolutely to the Utopians and remaining eager to return there as soon as a chance presents itself. We see this scenario played out in *Gulliver's Travels*, but Swift manages something new and more troubling in Part Four, a point to which I will return in the final section.

In the succession of those who exploited the travel form for satirical purposes in their fictions, François Rabelais stands out, especially in the *Quart Livre* of *Gargantua and Pantagruel* (1548; rev. 1552). Swift's attachment to Rabelais is well-known,[4] and we can certainly see connections with Swift's grasp of the comedy of scale in Parts 1 and 2 of *Gulliver's Travels*, as well as the explicit presentation of bodily functions in the context of travel. Although there are salient contrasts between the two, what Frank Lestringant observes of Rabelais holds equally for Swift, namely Rabelais's capacity to develop 'La réversibilité entre le familier et l'exotique, l'ici et ailleurs, l'Ancien Monde et le Nouveau'.[5] In Rabelais's treatment of travel as a satirical occasion, there is no pretence of verisimilitude; rather, he constructs the narrative around a series of 'contes' or stories/tales, episodic in organization, accommodating parable and mock-heroic interludes, as the band of travellers make their way to various islands during their sea voyage seeking knowledge. Rabelais's exuberance, the free rein given to the appetites, his play with language, textuality and orality, his debt to humanism while working with Erasmian adages and classical inheritances, and his delight, above all, in farce, set the text apart. But travel is nonetheless crucial to the story. Here too we can find examples of travel as a vehicle for satire, sometimes briefly indicated, as in the reference to the *Concile de Chésil* (council of fools) commenting on the Council of Trent,[6] at other times more extended, as in the storyline devoted to the conflict between the Papefigues who disparage the pope—not giving a fig—and the Papimanes, who embrace him and his decretals.[7] The peoples of these neighbouring islands have even entered armed conflict, with the Papimanes attacking the Papefigues after one of the latter indulged an inclination to *faire la figue* upon seeing a portrait of the pope on the island of Papimania. They avenged the insult by taking up arms, 'and without warning surprised, sacked and laid waste to the entire island' of their foes.[8] The structural and thematic similarity with Swift's narrative of the conflict between the island of Lilliput and the island of Blefuscu is noteworthy. The original dispute there, based on controversy over the correct end of the egg to crack, resulted in many rebellions and deaths, together with hundreds of volumes on the matter, in a satirical parallel with Catholic and Reformation causes. Rabelais makes his sympathy with

---

[4] Irvin Erhenpreis, *Swift: The Man, His Works, and the Age*, 3 vols. (Cambridge, MA: Harvard University Press, 1983), i. 110; iii. 328.

[5] Frank Lestringant, *Le Livre des îsles: atlas et récits insulaires de la genèse à Jules Verne* (Geneva: Droz, 2002), 261.

[6] François Rabelais, *Gargantua and Pantagruel*, trans. M. A. Screech (London: Penguin, 2006), 718–19 (ch. 18); 768 (ch. 35). See also 798 (ch. 46).

[7] Rabelais, *Gargantua and Pantagruel*, chs. 45–54.   [8] Rabelais, *Gargantua and Pantagruel*, 794.

the anti-papist faction more clear, rather than focusing as Swift does on the triviality and puniness of the antagonists.[9]

Elsewhere Rabelais describes a visit to an island populated by the Chicanous (lawyers given to chicanery), a 'hairy tribe' with a 'strange way of life'. The Chicanous thrive by serving writs on noblemen (prompted by monks or usurers), doling out insults and abuses to encourage their aristocratic adversaries to deliver a savage beating to them. They crave this treatment in order to turn things around and sue for damages, providing them with a living for months on end.[10] The reader's task, complicated by linguistic challenges but otherwise straightforward in this particular case, is to engage in a process of translation between contexts, bringing distant and near into relationship. The pattern is the same in modes of writing related to satire that depend on doubling, whether irony, analogy, or allegory—as we see in the Papefigues/Papimanes scenario or the significant set of episodes surrounding the Island of Tapinois, ruled by Quarêprenant, a figure standing for Lent, and the narrative of the Isle Farouche and its resident Chidlings or sausages, allied with Mardi Gras.[11] Travel has the advantage, by virtue of its dependence on geographical separation and difference, of encouraging such translation between contexts. Furthermore, in the Chicanous instance as in other contexts, Rabelais adopts a deliberate naïvety on the part of the narrator (who has something in common with Gulliver, at times, in this respect), placing the obligation to effect the transfer of meaning onto the reader.

Among later contributions, Joseph Hall's *Mundus alter et idem* (1605?) adopts the travel premise in its satirical portrait of various exotic lands, some given to excessive indulgence, others to rule by women, and others still to moronic and unaccountable customs. Hall draws to an extent on precedents provided by More and Rabelais. The work begins with a prefatory dialogue between friends concerning the merits of travel, as the first-person narrator, a Cambridge graduate, explains his determination to embark on a voyage to the unknown southern land. The use of maps adds to the circumstantial effect, but the satirical description of the journey itself is fanciful in the manner of Rabelais, reporting lands peopled by nations given to extravagant practices, with social, legal, and religious systems to support their proclivities. The large investment in linguistic jokes is also reminiscent of Rabelais, managed by Hall through the humanist apparatus of marginal annotation and a lengthy glossary. The major contrast is Hall's sensibility as a moralist; although he presents the episodes for amusement, the aberrations he relates are subject to implied correction, rather than being embraced in the

---

[9] The Emperor of Blefuscu, in a parallel with France, foments civil conflict in Lilliput between the Big-Endians (Catholics) and Small-Endians (Anglicans), and has welcomed Big-Endian exiles. Regarding the controversy itself, Gulliver states his 'humble Opinion' that the matter should be left to 'every Man's Conscience, or at least in the Power of the chief Magistrate to determine'. Swift, *Works* (Cambridge), xvi. 72.

[10] Rabelais, *Gargantua and Pantagruel*, 698–9.

[11] For the Tapinois, see Rabelais, *Gargantua and Pantagruel*, chs. 29–32; for the Isle Farouche, chs. 36–42. In the prologue to *Gargantua* (1535), Rabelais amusingly rejects the allegories 'caulked' on Homer's *Iliad* and *Odyssey* by Plutarch and others (207).

manner of Rabelais at times. Occasional references to issues of credibility and dilemmas of engaging the reader's belief are suggestive of Swift's later strategy, but at no time is the protagonist drawn to the prospect of integrating into the societies he observes, much less remaining there in perpetuity. For all of the peculiarity of what the story chronicles, the book's title introduces a reflexive possibility, revealing that these alien scenes are at once different and yet the same as in the mother country.

Swift exploited the potential for travel as a vehicle of satirical commentary on a grand scale, sometimes by paralleling English practices in the ways of other countries (such as the extended narrative of deluded naturalists and projectors in Part Three). More often he does so by realizing the satirical potential of Gulliver's obligation to recount his country's customs to various foreign interlocutors in ways that expose these practices to ridicule. He approaches the responsibility innocently for the most part (except for Part Three when he becomes acerbic), but this has the effect of deepening the critique of English politics, social system, and moral depravity, and ultimately human nature itself.

THE ART OF TRAVEL

In order to set the scene for Swift more fully, we can turn to satires directed at travellers themselves, in which a rich field of material emerged in the sixteenth and seventeenth centuries. During this period the redefinition of the purpose of travel around secular goals led a vast array of young men to embark on journeys across the continent in search of enhanced civility, knowledge of languages (above all Italian and French), and lessons in 'policy' gleaned from the observation of European courts and countries, enabling them to shed their rusticity and an unbecoming prejudice in favour of their own customs. The objective of the exercise, aside from the acquisition of particular skills, was to incorporate good customs maintained abroad and to achieve a cosmopolitan refinement. In other words, the emphasis was not only on witnessing but on imitation and emulation. A range of European commentators, including such eminent figures as Justus Lipsius and Francis Bacon, set out a series of norms governing the activity as part of what has become known as the *ars apodemica* tradition or the art of travel.[12] In doing so, they addressed a number of risks posed by travel, one of which remained a particular preoccupation, namely the tendency of returned travellers to disparage their own country, indulging in undue fondness for foreign manners and mores, and imitating them with irritating affectation.

The chance to skewer this behaviour did not long escape the notice of satirists. As early as 1512–13, Sir Thomas More devoted a Latin epigram to the subject of 'An Englishman who Affected to Speak French'. The poem lampoons an exaggerated figure

---

[12] Daniel Carey, 'Advice on the Art of Travel', in *The Cambridge History of Travel Writing*, ed. Nandini Das and Tim Youngs (Cambridge: Cambridge University Press, 2019), 392–407.

'scornful of all things English', who gives himself over to French dress from head to toe and adopts a French servant whom he abuses in the French manner. But the joke is on 'Lalus'[13] whose pretension fails to mask the fact that 'he is as familiar with the French language in general as a parrot is with Latin'. Where his foreign vocabulary fails him, he compensates by pronouncing English words with a French accent and lisping effeminately. In fact, he adopts the same accent for every language he knows, with the exception of French itself, 'the one language he speaks with an English accent'. More concluded by rebuking travellers for their ape-like feigning, and invoked an emasculating punishment: 'Therefore, since he is trying to change from an Englishman to Frenchman, order him, ye gods, to change from cock to capon.'[14]

As the century progressed, the satiric invitation represented by those given to such excesses became well established. In one of the early English contributions to the *ars apodemica* form, Sir Philip Sidney composed a letter of advice to his younger brother Robert on the occasion of the latter's continental tour, which began in 1579. Censuring those whose expeditions left them 'full of disguismentes', whether in apparel or countenance, he warned that they would soon find themselves 'made the sporte of Comedies'.[15] His remark proved prophetic. In *The Merchant of Venice* (c.1596–8), Portia remarks on her English suitor, Baron Falconbridge: 'How oddly he is suited! I think he bought his doublet in Italy, his round hose in France, his bonnet in Germany, and his behaviour everywhere.'[16] In a similar vein, Shakespeare's *As You Like It* (c.1599) features an exchange between Rosalind (as Ganymede) and the melancholy courtier Jaques in which she salutes him as 'Monsieur Traveller' before commenting: 'Look you lisp, and wear strange suits; disable all the benefits of your own country; be out of love with your nativity; and almost chide God for making you that countenance you are, or I will scarce think you have swam in a gondola.'[17]

Ben Jonson entered this satirical territory in 1600 in *Cynthia's Revels*, but the pinnacle of his work in this context came in *Volpone* (1606) with the ludicrous figure of Sir Politic Would-Be, an English knight who seeks to insinuate himself in the affairs of Venice. He enters in Act 2, Scene 1, announcing his profile as a cosmopolitan for whom 'all the world's his soil', unbounded by Italy, France, or even Europe. Peregrine, who offers a running satirical commentary on Sir Politic, notes in an ironic aside that he 'would be a

---

[13] From the Greek λαλλος: talkative or babbling.

[14] 'Ergo ex Britanno ut Gallus esse nititur, / Sic dij iubete, fiat ex gallo capus'. *The Complete Works of St. Thomas More*, vol. 3, pt. 2, ed. Clarence H. Miller et al. (New Haven: Yale University Press, 1984), 152–5. The dating of the epigram to late 1512 or early 1513 places it during a period in which England was at war with France.

[15] Letter to Robert Sidney, tentatively dated to February 1579. *The Correspondence of Sir Philip Sidney*, ed. Roger Kuin, 2 vols. (Oxford: Oxford University Press, 2012), 879. For a wide-ranging review of some of these critical responses, see Sara Warneke, *Images of the Educational Traveller* (Leiden: E. J. Brill, 1995), ch. 9.

[16] William Shakespeare, *The Merchant of Venice*, in *The Complete Works: Modern Critical Edition*, ed. Gary Taylor, John Jowett, Terri Bourus, and Gabriel Egan (Oxford: Oxford University Press, 2016), 1.2.54–6 (1217).

[17] William Shakespeare, *As You Like It*, in *Complete Works*, 4.1.25–8 (1737).

precious thing / To fit our English stage'.[18] Part of the comic effect of Sir Politic is precisely his mangling of standard advice to travellers on their deportment and morals, indicating that he has heard these familiar tenets but assimilated them imperfectly. His self-flattering claims to Peregrine include the fact that although he has lived in Venice for fourteen months, he was taken for a citizen within a week, based on his mastery of local custom. Among his keen insights into Italian ways is 'When you must eat your melons and your figs'. Peregrine asks whether this too is an affair of state to which Sir Politic replies, sagely:

> Here it is:
> For your Venetian, if he see a man
> Preposterous in the least, he has him straight;
> He has: he strips him.[19]

Jonson's satire participates in the 'whipping of abuses' tradition, with exposure of vice and idiocy as the goal, accompanied by some form of recognition and repentance (Sir Politic slopes off in ignominy in Act 5, Scene 2).[20] We have no doubts about how to regard him, given the cues from Peregrine. In *Gulliver's Travels*, we have a different relationship to Swift's protagonist since Gulliver is our guide to the exotic, and a normalizing narrator of his own story. Swift's satire is often structured as irony, requiring the reader to supply an alternative understanding or critique of what Gulliver says (even if at times the invitation is obvious enough). Nor does Gulliver have a moment of recognition in the end, which leaves us in a troubled relationship with him.

The 'character genre', revitalized in the early seventeenth century, provided another locus for satirical attacks on travellers. Jonson explicitly engaged with the tradition in his presentation of the traveller Amorphus in *Cynthia's Revels*, his generically complex satirical comedy. Mercury describes Amorphus as 'one so made out of the mixture and shreds of forms that [he] himself is truly deformed', walking with a clove or toothpick in his mouth, an endless talker and self-promoter, accompanied by a 'zany' or companion (Asotus) who loves to imitate him, not least by eating anchovies and caviar (the 1616 folio version adds macaroni, bavoli, and fagioli to the list).[21] Jonson continued in this vein with attention to a real traveller, Thomas Coryate, in a 'character' included in *Coryats Crudities* (1611).[22] Coryate, the ludic exponent of travel, offered himself up for satirical ribbing from a coterie of wits. Not long after Jonson's portrait appeared, the

---

[18] Ben Jonson, *Volpone or, The Fox*, ed. Richard Dutton, in *The Cambridge Edition of the Works of Ben Jonson*, ed. David Bevington, Martin Butler, and Ian Donaldson, 7 vols. (Cambridge: Cambridge University Press, 2012), iii. 73, 76 (2.1.1; 2.1.57–8).

[19] Jonson, *Volpone*, 3:130–1 (4.1.32–5).

[20] For the parallel moment with Amorphus, see Ben Jonson, *Cynthia's Revels*, ed. Eric Rasmussen and Matthew Steggle, in *The Cambridge Edition of the Works of Ben Jonson*, i. 542–3 (5.5.216–25).

[21] Jonson, *Cynthia's Revels*, i. 479–80 (2.3.66–81).

[22] *The Cambridge Edition of the Works of Ben Jonson*, iv. 189–91. For further discussion of the use of the satirical character in relation to Coryate and others, see Daniel Carey, 'Edward Terry's *A Voyage to East-India* (1655): A Chaplain's Narrative of the Mughal World', *Études anglaises* 70 (2017), 187–208.

Characters collection associated with Sir Thomas Overbury, often reprinted across the century, included a discussion of 'An Affected Traveller' from its second edition onwards (1614). This short piece again emphasizes the ridiculous nature of the traveller seeking attention through his outlandish attire (fashion is his 'religion') and his manner of walking, which shouts 'behold me'. The author of the piece likewise notes the tendency to speak 'his own language with shame and lisping', together with the contempt for (English) beer and cultivation of the toothpick as a particular sign of exotic experience.[23] Richard Brathwaite made his contribution to the genre in 1631, noting the traveller's aspirations to have the 'leane scraps' of his journey published in folio, but the undigested collection and elaborate style make them unattractive to the publisher.[24] Samuel Butler continued the tradition in his character of the 'Traveller' (unpublished until 1759) in an even more acerbic vein. He condemned his target as a 'Native of all Countries, and an Alien at Home', ready to 'quack and blow up himself with Admiration of foreign Parts' in order to generate admiration and to get his auditors to deplore their native land. The entire premise of travel—to acquire political wisdom—depended on diminishing the mother country. The reality was that all this political intelligence came from talking with people he didn't understand, observing statesmen in the streets and imagining he could thereby 'unriddle' their councils, and otherwise achieving insight by bumping along on a mule, in a wagon or a 'felucca' (a sailing vessel used in the Red Sea and Mediterranean), and by visiting inns and hostelries.[25] The whole thing appeared laughable.

As the seventeenth century progressed, the figure of the traveller as a type became well established as an object of satirical attack in a range of genres. Butler employed the verse form in his 'Satyr upon Our Ridiculous Imitation of the French', rounding on a range of abuses, including the devotion to French fashion above all, which had reached 'epidemic' proportions during the Restoration, as the court of Charles II embraced customs and dress witnessed in France during the preceding period of exile. The inclination of those Butler critiqued to 'smatter' French and either pretend to forget their native tongue or to speak it incorrectly added to the offence, making them '*Foreigners* at home'.[26]

The finest exploration of this theme occurred again on stage in George Etherege's *The Man of Mode* (1676), with its supporting character Sir Fopling Flutter, a devotee of French fashion (from the tying of his ribbons to long gloves and a curled periwig)—he declares that 'my clothes are my creatures'—whose speech is littered with French expressions.[27] Sir Fopling's arrival is deferred until Act 3, Scene 2, but we have already been prepared to receive him as a source of amusement for his foolishness, courtesy of various

[23] Sir Thomas Overbury (and others), *Characters*, ed. Donald Beecher (Ottawa: Dovehouse Editions, 2003), 208–9.

[24] Richard Brathwaite, *Whimzies: Or, a New Cast of Characters* (1631), 156–7.

[25] Samuel Butler, *Characters*, ed. Charles W. Daves (Cleveland: Press of Case Western Reserve University, 1970), 102–3.

[26] Samuel Butler, *The Genuine Remains in Verse and Prose*, ed. R. Thyer, 2 vols. (1759), i. 100.

[27] George Etherege, *The Man of Mode*, ed. John Barnard (London: Ernest Benn, 1979), 4.1.285. Presumably Etherege was aware of James Howard's *The English Mounsieur*, performed c.1663 and printed 1674. The play features Mr Frenchlove as the central character, newly returned from his travels, who early on complains that '*England* should be my Country, *I* cannot think my self the least a kin to it, since *I* have

remarks by the central character, the louche and witty Dorimant, and his companion Medley. Sir Fopling appears with a retinue of French servants who form his dancing troupe. He regrets having to take on one Englishman, the 'barbarously' named John Trott. Lamenting Trott's 'English motions', he urges him to follow the pattern before him and adopt the 'French air'. 'Imitation', he claims, 'may in time bring him to something'.[28] Sir Fopling is largely presented as a self-deluded figure of fun rather than being victimized as a form of retribution. Dorimant's French name and the fact that he has been in Paris himself suggests that modishness per se is not rejected, but instead the failure to follow codes with the right appreciation and 'measure', the mark of wit being predicated on comparison. Sir Fopling, by contrast (as a remark from Harriet, Dorimant's love interest and equal in wit, makes clear), is 'a man made up of forms and commonplaces, sucked out of the remaining lees of the last age'.[29] In his defence of the play in 1722, John Dennis stated that it was regarded as the most entertaining work of comedy over the last fifty years. The merited ridicule of Sir Fopling by the other characters for his foolish aping of foreign customs served as an ongoing lesson to travelling youth who would equally find themselves 'the Jest and the Scorn of their countrymen' if they espoused foreign customs and disparaged Great Britain in favour of France or Italy on their return.[30]

The focal point in this tradition of critique concentrated on a series of related issues—imitation, ridiculousness, affection or apishness, and the more encompassing problem of disaffiliation, registered by taking on new customs and fashions, disdaining one's native language, and loudly preferring another country's ways. The wellspring of the critique arguably came from the *ars apodemica* literature which provided guidance not only on what to observe but also on moral dangers associated with travel, among which the threat to identity remained paramount. In 1606, Sir Thomas Palmer condemned the 'fowle and irregular tricke of common Trauailers' which led them to 'innouate new fangles of fashions in their Countrey'.[31] The witty author James Howell, in his *Instructions for Forreine Travell* (1642), took aim at those who advertised their experience abroad with elaborate but absurd sign systems: 'their *gate* and *strouting*, their *bending* in the *hammes*, and *shoulders*, and *looking upon their legs*, with *frisking* and *singing* do speake them *Travellers*'.[32] Others, he continued, employed 'a phantastique kind of *ribanding*' and other outlandish clothing to make themselves known for having 'breathed forraine ayre'.[33] He closed by quoting the Latin epigram by Thomas More, disparaging 'Lalus', with which I began this section.

been in *France*, 'twould vex me plaguly were *I* not a Frenchman in my second nature (that is) in my fashion, discourse and cloathes' (Act 1, Scene 1), p. 4.

[28] Etherege, *Man of Mode*, 3.3.240–50 (barbarous name); 4.1.287–92 (dance).

[29] Etherege, *Man of Mode*, 4.1.302–3. On Dormant in Paris, 4.1.203.

[30] [John Dennis], *A Defence of Sir Fopling Flutter* (1722), 6, 23. Dennis wrote in reply to *Spectator* no. 65 (15 May 1711) which questioned the merits of the play.

[31] Sir Thomas Palmer, *An Essay of the Meanes How to Make our Trauailes, into Forraine Countries, the More Profitable and Honourable* (1606), 107.

[32] One of Frenchlove's attributes, emphasized in stage directions of *The English Mounsieur*, is the making of 'ridiculous legs' (Act 1, Scene 1, pp. 5, 6).

[33] James Howell, *Instructions for Forreine Travell* (1642), 181–2.

The importance for *Gulliver's Travels* of the *ars apodemica* tradition, in which Palmer and Howell participated, lies not just in pointed remarks on the habits of returned travellers, as a warning against losing one's identity, but the fact that contributors to this discussion continued to defend travel as a practice despite evidence of abuses. *Gulliver's Travels* would be much less interesting if Gulliver were merely absurd (there is a reason why Amorphus, Sir Politic, and Sir Fopling are minor characters). The key to Gulliver is that he likewise remains an exponent of travel, committed to *ars apodemica* protocols of observation and reportage, and the assessment of foreign countries, and not simply a buffoon exploited for comic effect. His earnestness is part of the portrait, even as he ends up in confusion. Swift's mockery takes a different and in some ways more harrowing form than the stage appropriation of the fool, belittled in asides.

LYING TRAVELLERS

This cluster of concerns was complemented by a second major area of criticism levelled against travellers, namely their penchant for lying, an association that had become proverbial by the sixteenth century.[34] The problem derived on the one hand from the fact that the distant scene of travellers' experience gave them room to fabricate tales without fear of being immediately contradicted. On the other, a credulous audience awaited them on their return, all too ready to accept extravagant stories as true. Once again, *ars apodemica* commentators intervened to draw attention to the problem. In his essay 'Of Travel', Francis Bacon cautioned against being 'forwards to tell Stories'.[35] The ever-acerbic Joseph Hall gave his opinion in *Quo vadis? A Just Censure of Travel* (1617), reproving those who regarded the great felicity of travel as the fact that it allowed them 'to tell wonders to a ring of admiring ignorants'.[36] Howell similarly attacked the 'hyperbolizing' of travellers, although with less asperity and more good humour than Hall. He noted the tendency of some, whom he compared to Sir John Mandeville, to relate stories by way of '*multiplying glasses*' that caused things to appear greater than they were:

> Such a *Traveller was* he, that reported the *Indian Fly*, to be as big as a *Fox*; *China* birds, to be as big as some *Horses*, and their *Mice* to be as big as *Monkeys*; but they have the wit to fetch this far enough off, because the Hearer may rather *believe it*, than make a voyage so far to *disprove it*.[37]

[34] Morris Palmer Tilley, *Dictionary of the Proverbs of England in the Sixteenth and Seventeenth Century* (Ann Arbor: University of Michigan Press, 1950), T47.
[35] Francis Bacon, *The Essayes or Counsels, Civill and Morall*, ed. Michael Kiernan (Oxford: Clarendon Press, 1985), 58.
[36] Joseph Hall, *Quo vadis? A Just Censure of Travel* (1617), 37.
[37] Howell, *Instructions*, 176–7. He continued with an amusing addition: 'Every one knowes the Tale of him, *who reported hee had seen a Cabbage under whose leafes a Regiment of Souldiers were sheltred from a shower of raine*: Another who was no *Traveller* (yet the wiser man) said, *hee had passed by a place where there were 400 brasiers making of a Cauldron, 200 within, and 200 without, beating the nayles in*; the *Traveller asking for what use that huge Cauldron was?* he told him, *Sir it was to boyle your Cabbage*' (177–8).

The strategy of Part Two of *Gulliver's Travels*, the Voyage to Brobdingnag, becomes clear in this remark.

Literary treatment of these issues took a range of forms. An intriguing early example occurs in William Bullein's *Dialogue... against the Fever Pestilence* (1564), featuring twelve participants, including the impoverished traveller, 'Mendax', who appears late on in the discussion. He makes quite an impression with his outfit of yellow hose, a green Kendal coat, a russet hat, and 'a greate plume of straunge Feathers', befitting the fact that he arrives with news of Terra Florida.[38] In recounting his journey, he commences with a stopover in Tenerife where a deadly battle took place between a dragon and a unicorn, whose horn he managed to secure (and still parcels out in sales as a curative). From there, a continued series of wonders evidently occurred throughout the voyage, apparently encompassing the globe, from witnessing mermaids and satyrs to blemmyes and men who take shade under their one large foot, to parrots playing chess and others philosophizing in Greek, and an accumulation of an abundance of precious stones and metals. Sadly he has none of the latter to show in evidence, due to various mischances. One of his notable tales recalls a 'fletying Island' in the New World—less sinister than Swift's Laputa—possibly a shard of the coasts of paradise, 'swimming aboue the sea, by what meanes I knowe not, whether occasioned by corcke, Wolle. &c. it would by the wind shift fro[m] place to place'. The host 'Ciuis' (the citizen) generously concludes: 'you haue trauailed farre, and maie speake by aucthoritee'.[39]

When he receives the invitation to dine, Mendax sharpens his knife on a whetstone, appropriately enough given the custom of punishing liars by hanging a whetstone around their necks (the whetstone forms part of the Mendax family crest, we learn).[40] In a similar vein, the traveller Amorphus in *Cynthia's Revels* is accompanied by a page named Cos. As Criticus remarks in an aside: 'How happily hath Fortune furnished him with a whetstone!', providing the English translation of the Latin word.[41]

Reflections on the concerns did not take place in an exclusively satirical vein. Shakespeare drew on the embedded association between travel and lying with deeper seriousness in *The Tempest* and *Othello*. Othello's travel tales served to woo Desdemona, recounting his adventures in vast deserts where he met cannibals and men with heads in their chests (blemmyes). But the action of the play makes clear that Othello is in fact the character most vulnerable to taking false stories for true, whether the handkerchief with its predictive power, or, above all, Iago's insinuations about his wife's uncertain fidelity. *The Tempest*, as a travel play, is bound up with these questions. In Act 3, Scene 3 of *The Tempest*, Prospero leads 'strange Shapes' who display a banquet before the distracted survivors of the wreck and perform a gentle dance for them. The cynical Sebastian calls

---

[38] William Bullein, *A Dialogue... against the Fever Pestilence* (1564), fol. 67r.

[39] Bullein, *Dialogue*, fol. 72v, 73v. In the 1564 edition, Mendax departs after the wife of Ciuis disparages him as a ruffian, thief, and keeper of bad company. The later editions of 1573 and 1578 omit her intervention and Mendax continues at length with more stories of Ethiopia and other locations. The servant, Roger, censures him boldly in the end as a liar and knave who has never seen such lands, although Ciuis reassures Mendax that he credits his tale.

[40] Bullein, *Dialogue*, fol. 68r. On the association with liars, see *OED*, n.2b.

[41] Jonson, *Cynthia's Revels*, 1.5.6–7.

this display a 'living drollery' and declares that he will henceforth believe stories of the unicorn and the phoenix reigning in Arabia. His confederate Antonio replies:

> I'll believe both;
> And what does else want credit, come to me,
> And I'll be sworn 'tis true. Travellers ne'er did lie,
> Though fools at home condemn 'em.[42]

However, the play's equation between Prospero, his magic, and the dramatist's creative power suggests an accepting view of this capacity for invention.

Richard Brome's play *The Antipodes* (1640) turned travel fantasy into a comic malady. The deluded Peregrine, a devotee of travel stories who accepts Mandevillian lore as true, receives care from a physician whose remedy entails drugging him and then inventing an ostensible imaginary journey to the Antipodes, assisted by a troop of actors. The scenario may be modelled on the treatment of Christopher Sly in *The Taming of the Shrew* or the prank played on Sancho Panza when he assumes governorship of an imaginary island in *Don Quixote*.

Travel writers responded defensively to these standing accusations, developing a range of rhetorical strategies to repair their reputations—for example, by claiming superior insight to their predecessors based on their own eyewitnessing; enlisting authorities to endorse their work with testimonials; and pointing beyond the text to proofs of various kinds. Another useful strategy was to point out the limited knowledge of home-bred critics, bound to their own place and therefore incapable of appreciating the world's wonders.[43] But perhaps the most straightforward response was to reference the proverb about their status as liars and thereby establish credibility given their willingness to acknowledge the problem. Numerous examples of this approach can be cited,[44] but the same self-authenticating avenue was open to writers interested in presenting hoaxes, like Henry Neville in *The Isle of Pines* (1668). His tale of an Elizabethan shipwreck near Madagascar, and the ensuing population of a deserted island on a grand scale by one Englishman (George Pine) and four women, included a paratextual insistence on the truth of the story by the purveyor of the news. The Dutch navigator who made the report objected to 'Nullifidians' who choose to 'believe nothing but what they see, applying that Proverb unto us, *That Travelors may lye by authority*'. He reminded his (ostensible) correspondent that he deserved 'Credence', 'you knowing my disposition so hateful to divulge Falsities'.[45]

---

[42] William Shakespeare, *The Tempest*, in *Complete Works*, 3.324–7 (3111).

[43] Howell, *Instructions*, 13–14, dismissed such opponents as 'slow and sluggish spirits', comparing them to snails or tortoises crawling only within their own homes or to the tub-bound cynic, Diogenes.

[44] See Daniel Carey, 'The Problem of Credibility in Early Modern Travel', forthcoming in *Renaissance Studies*.

[45] [Henry Neville], *The Isle of Pines* [3rd edn.] (1668), 30. For further discussion, see Daniel Carey, 'Henry Neville's *The Isle of Pines* (1668): Travel, Forgery and the Problem of Genre', *Angelaki* 1, no. 2 (Winter 1993/4), 23–40.

The controversy over accepting the truthfulness of travel accounts entered the realm of philosophy, with John Locke attracting criticism for citing such narratives in order to disprove innateness in the *Essay concerning Human Understanding* (1690) from a range of forceful antagonists, including Bishop Stillingfleet, Henry Lee, and the 3rd Earl of Shaftesbury.[46] Shaftesbury sarcastically rebuked the 'credulous Mr. Locke with his *Indian*, Barbarian Stories of Wild Nations' supposedly demonstrating their lack of innate ideas or principles, 'as Travellers, learned Authors! and men of Truth! and great Philosophers! have inform'd him'.[47] The letter making these remarks appeared in print in 1716. Shaftesbury avoided naming Locke in his *Characteristicks* (1711), but nonetheless he took aim in the same fashion at authors who competed to outdo one another in their description of monstrous brutes and men, while comparing those who imbibed their stories uncritically to Desdemona, beguiled by Othello's extravagant tales.[48] Swift was no friend of the freethinking Whig nobleman Shaftesbury, but they shared a perspective on the embarrassing consequences of investing too much faith in 'Modern *Wonder-Writers*'.[49]

GULLIVER'S TRAVELS

Set against this background, *Gulliver's Travels* can be seen as culminating a tradition of satirical reflection on travel which takes the critique to a new level of extremity. In relation to the alteration of identity caused by travel, commentators recommended somehow fixing it in advance in order to remain inoculated against the disturbing inclination to overthrow one's native customs in favour of the ways of other nations. Howell, for example, espoused the view that if the young men he addressed had 'sucked the pure milke of true Religion, and Orthodoxall truth' they would remain free from this complaint.[50] The issue is handled in a complex fashion over the course of *Gulliver's Travels*. Gulliver typically maintains the posture of someone who is fully committed to his national identity, in spite of the degree of turbulence caused by mounting satirical commentary that accompanies his journeys (whether it comes through direct remarks by his interlocutors, allegorical implication, or in his own summary of dubious English and European practices). His use of observational strategies associated with travel advice, enhanced by new protocols of scientific description, makes him far more than a simple exponent of a prejudiced viewpoint—in this he seems intent on fulfilling his declared ambition of benefiting the public in his relation of exotic experience.[51] At the same time,

---

[46] See Daniel Carey, *Locke, Shaftesbury, and Hutcheson: Contesting Diversity in the Enlightenment and Beyond* (Cambridge: Cambridge University Press, 2006).

[47] Anthony Ashley Cooper, 3rd Earl of Shaftesbury, *Several Letters Written by a Noble Lord to a Young Man at the University* (1716), 39–40.

[48] Anthony Ashley Cooper, 3rd Earl of Shaftesbury, *Characteristics of Men, Manners, Opinions, Times*, ed. Lawrence E. Klein (Cambridge: Cambridge University Press, 1999), 154–5.

[49] Shaftesbury, *Several Letters*, 40.   [50] Howell, *Instructions*, 16.

[51] Swift, *Works* (Cambridge), xvi. 133–4.

Gulliver exhibits a notable tendency to identify himself with his hosts over the course of his voyages (the third voyage, which holds out no such temptation, is in many ways anomalous). During his time in Lilliput, he seems not to grasp the insignificance of the country, whose imperial status he records without comment, along with the titles and magnificence of the emperor, styled the 'Delight and Terror of the Universe', commanding a territory of five thousand 'Blustrugs' or twelve miles in circumference.[52] Gulliver's elevation to the status of *Nardac*—the highest title of honour, conferred after his capture of the Blefuscu fleet—appears to confirm his immersion in the social and political system, whose codes he nonetheless fails to master, signally in the case of urinating on the queen's apartments to extinguish a dangerous fire.

The pattern is made more explicit in the voyage to Brobdingnag. After his discovery in a field by a gigantic farmer, Gulliver makes his way across the country as an object of display and curiosity before finding himself at court. The king's interrogation of Gulliver about matters of religion, law, and government in Europe leads the sovereign, according to Gulliver, to display 'the Prejudices of his Education' in his burst of laughter provoked by asking whether Gulliver is a Whig or Tory. Gulliver shows his national attachment by recording his indignation over the king's contempt for Britain's standing as 'the Mistress of Arts and Arms, the Scourge of *France*, the Arbitress of *Europe* ... the pride and Envy of the World'.[53] Gulliver falls into a trap set for him by his first journey by missing the connection with Lilliputian pettiness. But in the very next paragraph, Gulliver acknowledges that after several months among the Brobdingnagians, growing accustomed to their size and conversation, he lost the horror that first struck him, acknowledging 'that if I had then beheld a Company of *English* Lords and Ladies in their Finery and Birth-day Cloaths, acting their several Parts in the most courtly Manner of Strutting, and Bowing and Prating ... I should have been strongly tempted to laugh as much at them as this King and his Grandees did at me'.[54] The satirical point about travellers becomes acute after Gulliver's recovery at sea following this journey. He speaks in an unaccountably loud volume (better suited to discoursing with his former hosts) and remarks that when he boarded the ship he regarded the sailors crowding around him as 'so many Pigmies', 'the most little contemptible Creatures I had ever beheld'. In fact he had avoided looking at himself in the mirror in Brobdingnag because the comparison gave him so 'despicable a Conceit of my self'. He cannot restrain his laughter at the insignificant objects around him, having adjusted his view to the Brobdingnagian scale. The same trouble continues on his return to England, whether on the street or at home, where, for example, he is unable to see his bowing daughter, since he was 'so long used to stand with my Head and Eyes erect to above Sixty Foot'.[55]

The crucial case is obviously the fourth voyage. Gulliver's lack of identity is in some ways literalized in his rejection of the Yahoo species (although a fulsome embrace at one point by a lascivious she-Yahoo provides an unhappy reminder of the connection).[56]

---

[52] Swift, *Works* (Cambridge), xvi. 63.   [53] Swift, *Works* (Cambridge), xvi. 150.
[54] Swift, *Works* (Cambridge), xvi. 151.   [55] Swift, *Works* (Cambridge), xvi. 208, 212, 214.
[56] Swift, *Works* (Cambridge), xvi. 400–1.

Instead he aligns himself with the rational horses in Houyhnhnmland, despite their effective enslavement of the Yahoos and readiness to contemplate their extermination. As Part Four progresses, Gulliver's disaffiliation becomes complete. After a year in the country, his love and veneration of the Houyhnhnms leads him to vow to spend the rest of his life there in the practice of virtue. Swift deepens the irony by placing this announcement in a chapter whose title begins by affirming 'The Author's great Love of his Native Country', something demonstrated, presumably, by the fact that he ostensibly extenuated the faults of his peers when narrating the odious particulars of English life.[57] The transfer of identification comes about partly as a result of Gulliver's loathing of himself as a Yahoo (again he cannot bear to see his reflection) and partly due to the Houyhnhnms' flattering condescension in distinguishing him from the rest of the breed.[58] Gulliver's departure from Houyhnhnmland only takes place under duress when his master receives an exhortation to cease treating his charge so favourably and either to subjugate or expel him. Gulliver's own detachment from any identification with his kind becomes apparent in his use of Yahoo skins to cover the makeshift canoe he builds to escape and the use of Yahoo tallow to make it sound.[59]

According to *ars apodemica* commentators, the purpose of travel was to adopt worthy customs observed abroad. In this respect, Gulliver's journey is a success as he vows to make himself useful 'by celebrating the Praises of the renowned *Houyhnhnms*, and proposing their Virtues to the Imitation of Mankind'.[60] But he fails in the other key objective, that of resuming his original identity (a whole list of ways to demonstrate it was provided by commentators). Gulliver cannot reintegrate, and famously prefers to spend his time not with his wife and children but in his stables in conversation with two stallions, sadly degenerate and unable to emulate the Houyhnhnms but nevertheless superior to human company. Thus he succumbs to the fault of Raphael in More's *Utopia*, disaffected and unable to see that his setting up of the Houyhnhnms as paragons depends on overlooking their limitations and contradictions (such as the offence they take over his report of the treatment of horses in England despite emulating it their handling of the Yahoos).[61]

After his traumatic expulsion, Gulliver (yet again) receives care from a passing ship, on this occasion a Portuguese vessel. The mariners, he tells us, 'fell a laughing at my strange Tone in speaking, which resembled the Neighing of a Horse'.[62] His clothing is equally curious. He has already told us of his penchant among the Houyhnhnms for imitating their 'Gait and Gesture' which became so habitual that on his return his friends remarked on his trotting like a horse.[63] Swift has found a new way to make the same satirical point about the 'ridiculous imitation' of other nations, to the amusement, if not annoyance, of anyone exposed to antics of this kind. He captures the attitude to

[57] Swift, *Works* (Cambridge), xvi. 388.
[58] Swift, *Works* (Cambridge), xvi. 420.
[59] Swift, *Works* (Cambridge), xvi. 424.
[60] Swift, *Works* (Cambridge), xvi. 423.
[61] Swift, *Works* (Cambridge), xvi. 356–7.
[62] Swift, *Works* (Cambridge), xvi. 429.
[63] Swift, *Works* (Cambridge), xvi. 420.

language[64]—the lisping and affectation attributed to those venturing back from the continent—the change of apparel that signalled an exotic sojourn, and the peculiar manner of walking (Howell's bending at the hams and 'frisking') well-established in the semiotics of travel satire.

If we turn to the question of travel writing as a source of truth, Swift systematically covers the strategies employed by travel writers to authenticate their voyages, addressing the mixture of internal and external schemes for achieving this aim. Gulliver's journeys to the 'remote nations of the world' place him in the unique and privileged position of being the only witness to the exotic destinations he describes. Thus we have only his word. On the one hand this deprives him of one of the stock techniques for elevating the truth value of an account by disparaging predecessors and their errors, but on the other it means that, literally, no one can contradict him. Gulliver's authorly circumspection— the care he takes to frame his narrative within the compass of what he has witnessed, his measurements and comparisons—enhances his credibility on internal grounds. He complements this with an acknowledgement of existing doubts about the honesty of accounts when he relates the massive scale of the king's kitchens in Brobdingnag, remarking: 'perhaps I should be hardly believed; at least a severe Critick would be apt to think I enlarged a little, as Travellers are often suspected to do'.[65] In an ironic passage, Gulliver declines the invitation of the sea captain who rescues him after his Brobdingnag voyage to publish an account of his adventure, observing not only the over-stock of travel books but their focus solely on the extraordinary, in which 'some Authors less consulted Truth than their own Vanity or Interest, or the Diversion of Ignorant Readers'.[66]

The whole issue of truth-telling is of course thematized in the book itself, above all in the fourth part in the encounter with the Houyhnhnms who have no word for falsehood and must approximate it with the phrase that a liar says *the thing which was not*.[67] Gulliver discusses the matter at length with his master, attempting to find some way to register the concept of '*Lying*, and *false Representation*' (endemic among politicians and lawyers at home, he elsewhere relates).[68] The fine example of his hosts leads him to an 'utter Detestation of all Falsehood or Disguise', making truth appear 'so amiable to me, that I determined upon sacrificing every thing to it'.[69] Gulliver nonetheless recognizes that if he told the story of his experience back home his countrymen would accuse him of inventing it and saying the thing which was not.[70]

In the absence of corroborating witnesses, Gulliver has recourse to an alternative form of 'proof' external to the text. He gestures ostensively to physical evidence of his

---

[64] Gulliver complains of the difficulty of translating the Houyhnhnm tongue into 'our barbarous *English*', *Works* (Cambridge), xvi. 362.

[65] Swift, *Works* (Cambridge), xvi. 161.   [66] Swift, *Works* (Cambridge), xvi. 211.

[67] Swift, *Works* (Cambridge), xvi. 349.   [68] Swift, *Works* (Cambridge), xvi. 354.

[69] Swift, *Works* (Cambridge), xvi. 388.

[70] Swift, *Works* (Cambridge), xvi. 353. For further reflections on truth-telling in *Gulliver's Travels*, see Michael McKeon, *The Origins of the English Novel 1600–1740* (London: Radius, 1988), 351; and Michael Seidel, '*Gulliver's Travels* and the Contracts of Fiction', in *The Cambridge Companion to the Eighteenth-Century Novel*, ed. John Richetti (Cambridge: Cambridge University Press, 1996), 81–2. Seidel points out that 'Gulliver's is not the imposter's lie but rather the lunatic's lie' (82).

remarkable adventures, provided by the miniature cattle and sheep nibbling away on Bowling Green in Greenwich, garnered during his time in Lilliput, and the stingers of the wasps severed with his cutlass in Brobdingnag and now on display, he reports, in the repository of Gresham College. The satire on the display of rarities conjoins with the critique of exotica as signs of truth furnished by dubious travellers. When an English merchant vessel redeems Gulliver after his escape from Lilliput/Blefuscu, the captain (named as John Biddel of Deptford to give him particularity) thinks Gulliver is raving, but Gulliver tells us he 'convinced him of my Veracity' by producing the cattle and sheep from his pocket.[71] Part of Swift's point of course is that these validations are only ever internal to the text despite being offered as external proofs.

The matter of style offered a further method to inspire confidence in the reader, with travel writers commonly citing their lack of ornament and humbleness of expression as a virtue that established their unwillingness to deceive. Swift addresses this point in the preface of the publisher to the reader where 'Richard Sympson' notes that

> The Style is very plain and simple; and the only Fault I find is, that the Author, after the Manner of Travellers, is a little too circumstantial. There is an Air of Truth apparent through the whole; and indeed the Author was so distinguished for his Veracity, that it became a Sort of Proverb among his Neighbours at *Redriff*, when any one affirmed a Thing, to say, it was as true as if Mr. *Gulliver* had spoke it.[72]

Sympson also promises interested parties an opportunity to view the original manuscript, complete with material excised from the printed version on the grounds that it contained excessive amounts of nautical information—not a total validation in itself but an indication of openness to scrutiny on his part and a reassurance that the texts contains what others cited as an indication of truth, namely 'particularity'. Of course the Letter from Captain Gulliver in the 1735 edition tells us that this manuscript has been destroyed.[73]

The heavy irony of Sympson's address becomes clear at the end of the work. The decision in the 1735 edition published by Faulkner to include an engraving of Captain Gulliver with a new motto, 'Splendide mendax' (from Horace), arguably declares the scenario too readily. The original frontispiece portrait of Gulliver in the 1726 Motte edition simply indicated Gulliver's name, status, ostensible age (58), and Redriff residence. A second state of this portrait did include a verse from Persius, but it does not give away the joke.[74]

---

[71] Swift, *Works* (Cambridge), xvi. 111. See also his way of convincing the captain who gathers him up after his Brobdingnag adventure, whom Gulliver persuades by displaying his cabinet of (often grotesque) rarities, including stumps of the king's beard, a paring of the queen's thumbnail, and a corn severed from the foot of a maid of honour (210–11).

[72] Swift, *Works* (Cambridge), xvi. 15–16.   [73] Swift, *Works* (Cambridge), xvi. 12.

[74] The 1735 edition constitutes volume 3 of Faulkner's four-volume edition of Swift's *Works*, placing Gulliver's authorial position in another frame and complicating the question of how we respond to the reliability of his voice. For discussion of these portraits, see Janine Barchas, *Graphic Design, Print Culture, and the Eighteenth-Century Novel* (Cambridge: Cambridge University Press, 2003), 28–34; see also the

The real stroke of genius in Swift's organization of the text is to use the final chapter of the book to provide the kind of reassurances that ordinarily came in prefaces to travel accounts, specifically, as the summary has it, 'The Author's Veracity. His Design in publishing this Work. His Censure of those Travellers who swerve from the Truth.' The first paragraph of this chapter is a straight imitation of the promises and reassurances routinely given at the outset of travel books:

> Thus, Gentle Reader, I have given thee a faithful History of my Travels for Sixteen Years, and above Seven Months; wherein I have not been so studious of Ornament as of Truth. I could perhaps like others have astonished thee with strange improbable Tales; but I rather chose to relate plain Matter of Fact in the simplest Manner and Style; because my principal Design was to inform, and not to amuse thee.[75]

He continues in this vein, disparaging previous travellers for their faults which are known to him by virtue of his vast experience, and he intones the solemn wish that a law would be enacted to obligate travellers to swear an oath before the Lord High Chancellor promising their truthfulness before embarking on publication of their writings.

The point is that these reassurances come after Gulliver has demonstrated that he is unhinged and incapable of securing our belief. Swift succeeds precisely by hollowing out genres, making them untenable not from the start but after an induction process in which the narrator has served as an adequate guide. The best example is no doubt *A Modest Proposal* (1729). In *Gulliver's Travels* the same technique is deployed over a longer narrative form. The 1735 prefatory letter builds on this but only through a retrospective reading, since the innocent reader, unfamiliar with him and his work, cannot assimilate the vituperations and the arcane language.

The tradition of travel satire that Swift responded to had in many ways exhausted its potential when he intervened. He both fulfilled its possibilities and moved beyond them with the audacity of his invention, scale of his satirical attacks, and systematic disassembly of the truth claims associated with travel accounts. He transformed existing satirical representations of returned travellers by attaching them to a radically disaffected figure, whose inability to reintegrate himself results not merely from a disdain for his native country but for his species as a whole. Swift's corroding of the genre from the inside marks a moment of transition as the form took on new priorities associated with the sentimental and Romantic over the course of the eighteenth century.

Womersley edition of *Gulliver's Travels*, Appendix A (567–72). The Persius verse reads: 'Compositum jus, fasque animi, sanctosque recessus / Mentis, & inoctum generoso pectus honesto' (In spirit, to be reconciled to what is holy and to what is just; to be thoroughly pure in mind; and to have a heart infused with nobleness and honour' (567n)). The commendatory verses (assembled and probably composed by Alexander Pope) added to the second edition of 1727 had already heightened the fanciful, joking element. The verses are reproduced in Appendix B (573–88).

[75] Swift, *Works* (Cambridge), xvi. 436.

SELECT BIBLIOGRAPHY

Passmann, Dirk Friedrich. *Full of Improbable Lies: Gulliver's Travels und die Reiseliteratur vor 1726* (Frankfurt: Peter Lang, 1987).

Rodino, R. H. ' "Splendide mendax": Authors, Characters and Readers in *Gulliver's Travels*', in *Reading Swift: Papers from the Second Münster Symposium on Jonathan Swift*, ed. R. H. Rodino and Hermann J. Real (Munich: Wilhelm Fink Verlag, 1993), 167–84.

Rogers, Shef. 'The Bibliographical Limits of *Gulliver's Travels*', in *Jonathan Swift and the Eighteenth-Century Book*, ed. Paddy Bullard and James McLaverty (Cambridge: Cambridge University Press, 2013), 135–53.

Seidel, Michael. '*Gulliver's Travels* and the Contracts of Fiction', in *The Cambridge Companion to the Eighteenth-Century Novel*, ed. John Richetti (Cambridge: Cambridge University Press, 1996), 72–89.

Sherbo, Arthur. 'Swift and Travel Literature'. *Modern Language Studies* 9 (1979), 114–27.

Smith, Frederik N. , ed. *The Genres of Gulliver's Travels* (Newark: University of Delaware Press/ London: Associated University Presses, 1990).

CHAPTER 13

....

BELIEVING AND UNBELIEVING IN *THE DUNCIAD*

....

SOPHIE GEE

THE Dunciad was Alexander Pope's longest and most elaborate poem, which he rewrote at least four times over a period of nearly twenty years. Each new version was deliberately more complicated and hard-to-follow than the last. Pope aimed his satire at the literary and intellectual world of eighteenth-century London, and he directed especially bitter attacks against the scholars, editors, and publishers he disdained. The mock-hero of the first two versions (1728–9) was the Shakespeare scholar Lewis Theobald, and when he was replaced in the final lifetime edition, *The Dunciad in Four Books* (1743), it was by the theatrical manager Colley Cibber. *The Dunciad* is a Juvenalian satire on contemporary publishing: the epic complaint of a successful, chronically ill poet about everything that seemed to him most unfair and wrong about his profession. Pope's satire in *The Dunciad* doesn't stop at the literary world, however. He lampoons the corrupt Prime Minister Robert Walpole, Williamite and Hanoverian court culture, other contemporary art forms including music, the new science, and various fads in religious belief. Anyone who reads *The Dunciad* will be struck by the poem's vitriol, and by Pope's fury at virtually all public figures who happen not to share his worldview. But there is another layer to the satire, which this chapter explores by shifting focus from Pope's cultural polemic to his sallies against contemporary developments in philosophy and theology. I argue that Pope attacks fashionable ideas about the nature of God and the material world in *The Dunciad* as a way to explore his own ideas about the complex, often-paradoxical nature of imaginative fiction. Pope's inquiry into the complexities of imaginative writing forms a crucial part of the poem, one that makes *The Dunciad* important and enduring for modern readers. It is also an aspect of the poem that deepens our sense of what Pope's 'worldview' actually was, revealing him to be a more flexible and adventurous thinker than his irritable, obscure satire at first suggests.

POPE'S FICTIONS

The Dunciad is most often read as an example of the topicality and the combative, self-referential nature of eighteenth-century satire. Its very topicality obscures the fact that it is also, paradoxically, one of the greatest imaginative fictions of the first half of the century, written at a moment when imaginative fiction was changing radically, and forever, with the rise of the realist novel. Pope alludes to Homer, Virgil, Spenser, Milton, Dryden, Defoe, and a host of his own contemporaries to fabricate a cosmological drama set in modern London and... the universe. The poem is immersed in fictions while purporting to eschew the fictional; the intricate notes, prefaces, and details are the very elements with which Pope constructs an imaginative *tour de force* of a global apocalypse wrought by the power of bad ideas—an Anthropocene fable in which shoddy thinking, rather than wrongful actions, brings about global disaster. The poem's setting is a hybrid geography, identified as the City of London, but radically altered to become a dystopian arena in which a new breed of pseudo-writers compete fruitlessly for meaningless victory.

Our tendency to overlook *The Dunciad*'s status as a proto-fiction is due partly to the way Pope designed the poem, encasing it in an elaborate architecture of annotations, scholarly apparatus, and topical references, all of which would have felt obscure and over-complicated even to contemporary readers. They have the effect of making *The Dunciad* into an angry, impenetrable polemic directed against a cultural coterie known only to a few. The imaginative achievement of the poem, however, is almost the opposite— Pope constructs a fictional topography that would persuade generations of readers that his account of literary London was the true one. In creating the imaginative ecology of *The Dunciad*, Pope draws on language and imagery belonging to philosophical arguments about God, the nature of material substance, and of spirit. These references provide Pope's lines with a dense, scholarly quality that, again, masks his real work of imaginative novelty in inventing a modern London whose atmosphere is literally, comically, stupefying. The notoriously torpid air of the real city is transformed into a mentally stultifying fog that envelops the Dunces and renders them unable to think. The passage from Book 1 quoted below is rather hard to understand because of the allusions to other texts, but if we pay close attention we see that Pope's deepest commitment as a satirist is to inventing an imaginative fiction, not to restoring fact:

> Dulness o'er all possess'd her ancient right,
> Daughter of Chaos and eternal Night:
> Fate in their dotage this fair Ideot gave,
> Gross as her sire, and as her mother grave,
> Laborious, heavy, busy, bold and blind,
> She rul'd, in native Anarchy, the mind.
> Still her old Empire to restore she tries,
> For, born a Goddess, Dulness never dies.[1]

---

[1] Pope, *Poems* (Twickenham), v. 269–70.

The passage presents a mock-genealogy for the Goddess Dulness. The description alludes to the classical writers Hesiod and Lucretius and the epic poet John Milton, as well as miscellaneous works from Pope's own day, including Samuel Garth's mock-epic *The Dispensary*. Pope's point here is that Dulness's stolid being is a good match for the intellectual culture of mid-century England, where the Hanoverian court of George II is cursed by the same idiocy and compromised legitimacy (monarchical language such as 'possess'd' and 'rul'd' invites us to connect Dulness with the real monarchy). The passage conveys moreover a sense of the inadequacy of the human mind, its propensity to be overwhelmed by false logic and slow, dense reasoning. In certain respects, Pope's satire here is conventional, saying what we would expect any Tory opponent of Walpole and the Georgian monarchy to say: that the regime is slow-witted. This commonplace of Tory satire was intended to rebuke the claim made by Whig intellectuals like John Locke and Joseph Addison that humans are by nature disposed to liberty and virtue, achieved through the exercise of reason.[2] But the interesting thing about these lines is that Pope's language overlaps markedly with old-school republican Whig polemic: scorn for 'ancient right', and the representation of the royal family as deficient, even deformed. Pope's satirical point here is that the Whig revolution of 1688, with its promise to eliminate absolutism and monarchical abuses, has paradoxically produced the very state of affairs it attempted to avert.

Dulness is a more banal version of Satan, the anti-hero of *Paradise Lost*, Milton's republican epic that shaped radical religion and Whig ideology in the eighteenth century. Pope's Dulness is, indeed, the daughter of two minor allegorical characters from *Paradise Lost*, Chaos and Night. As a dysfunctional family triad, Dulness, Chaos, and Night mimic Milton's evil family trio Satan, Sin, and Death, but one of Pope's jokes in *The Dunciad* is that the dull mock-editor Scriblerus doesn't notice the *Paradise Lost* reference, citing Hesiod instead in his note to the passage. The presence of a three-person family in *The Dunciad* would moreover have told Pope's contemporaries that this was also a reference to debates about the Holy Trinity. A controversy raged throughout the late seventeenth and eighteenth centuries about whether the Trinity was true and whether Christ was divine. Conservative Anglicans considered it a matter of unshakable orthodoxy that the Son was equal to God in divinity, whereas more radical Christians insisted it was at best ambiguous, and more likely impossible, that the Son and Father should be substantially identical and equal. The consequence of demoting the Son's importance (a feature of many strains of progressive Christian thought, including Milton's Arianism and all versions of freethinking) was to undermine the authority of formal religious rituals and institutions that bolstered state authority. By embedding *The Dunciad* in a cosmology involving Chaos and Night, Pope indicates that he is making use of the same debates about religious authority and the status of matter or substance

---

[2] See Lawrence Klein, 'Joseph Addison's Whiggism', in *Cultures of Whiggism: New Essays on English Literature and Culture in the Long Eighteenth Century*, ed. David Womersley (Newark: University of Delaware Press, 2005), 108–26; Abigail Williams, *Poetry and the Creation of a Whig Literary Culture 1681–1714* (Oxford: Oxford University Press, 2005), 1–21; Steve Pincus, 'Addison's Empire: Conceptions of Empire in the Early Eighteenth Century', *Parliamentary History* 31, no. 1 (2012), 99–117.

that preoccupied Milton and the republican tradition he drew upon (including classical antecedents like Lucretius). Even though Chaos and Night are figured satirically in *The Dunciad*, the cosmos of Pope's poem paradoxically occupies the imaginative and intellectual landscape of Milton's Chaos.

What about Chaos and Night might have interested Pope from a creative point of view? In *Paradise Lost*, Chaos and Night are allegorical characters formed from, and also embodying, prime matter before creation, thereby challenging the ideas that substance was without its own volition and that creative authority might ever be complete. Imaginatively speaking, this radical view of matter and creation challenged the idea of literary creativity as either authoritarian or mechanical, seeing it instead as dynamic, partially uncontrolled, and incompletely subject to a writer's will. In Milton, Chaos is warring, indeterminate matter that the Son circumscribes to make the 'just circumference' of the world. Uncreated matter is independent and autonomous: it has the capacity to be threatening and unstable even though it has originated in God. In turn, the Son makes use of the wilful nature of Chaos: it animates creation and guarantees independence to created life.[3] Chaos and Night, and the Son himself, belong to an Arian—i.e. a non-Trinitarian, imaginatively unorthodox—universe: they are made from God's substance, and they are also distinct, subordinate, and free-willed. Confused matter, in other words, is a creative resource for Milton, and will become one for Pope: 'in striking contrast to the often harsh disapproval of Chaos in Renaissance theology, science and literary culture, Milton in *Christian Doctrine* describes the confused, disordered matter as good in itself and the necessary basis of a good creation.'[4] Pope's Dulness, then, is born of disorderly, but generative parents. She is substantially distinct from them, since she is a goddess born of non-divine beings (satirically reversing the classical trope of gods with non-divine children); this is the condition which allows her such confused or conflicting personality traits. Divinity gives her the capacity for change (in Pope's satire, instability and caprice), but her non-divine inheritance reproduces the monotonous sameness, the changeless drear, of her parents.

The presence of Milton in the 1743 *Dunciad* is especially interesting given the starring role also played by Richard Bentley, whose 1732 edition of *Paradise Lost* was notorious, and denigrated by Pope in particular. Bentley's edition of *Paradise Lost* went awry because he 'improved' Milton's original text in an attempt to remove ambiguity and paradox. He made especially aggressive changes to passages depicting the universe as being made from uncertain, negotiable substance (passages in Milton that Pope would adapt

---

[3] For scholarship on materialism and Milton see N. K. Sugimura, *'Matter of Glorious Trial': Spiritual and Material Substance in Paradise Lost* (New Haven: Yale University Press, 2009). See also John Henry, 'Occult Qualities and the Experimental Philosophy: Active Principles in Pre-Newtonian Matter Theory', *History of Science* 24, no. 4 (1986), 335–81; John Rogers, *The Matter of Revolution: Science, Poetry, and Politics in the Age of Milton* (Ithaca: Cornell University Press, 1996); John Rumrich, 'Milton's God and the Matter of Chaos', *PMLA* 110, no. 5 (1995), 1035–46; John Leonard, 'Milton, Lucretius and the "Void Profound of Unessential Night"', in *Living Texts: Interpreting Milton*, ed. Kristin A. Pruitt and Charles W. Durham (Selinsgrove: Susquehanna University Press, 2000), 198–217.

[4] Rumrich, 'Milton's God', 1037.

for his satire). Bentley edited with a view to asserting a rational, orderly cosmology, obedient to empirical laws and amenable to human governance. One of Bentley's best-known corrections was to Milton's use of the phrase 'embryon atoms' (*Paradise Lost*, 2.900), renaming them 'infant' atoms in objection to the (literally) chaotic, unrestrained idea of subatomic particles.[5] Milton's embryon atoms were imperceptible and ontologically uncertain, affronting Bentley's model of Milton as an orderly, progressive Whig thinker.[6] But Pope was drawn to precisely this difficulty and material ambiguity in Milton when he constructed the cosmology of the *Dunciad*:

> Here she beholds the Chaos dark and deep,
> Where nameless Somethings in their causes sleep,
> 'Till genial Jacob, or a warm Third day,
> Call forth each mass, a Poem, or a Play:
> How hints, like spawn, scarce quick in embryo lie,
> How new-born nonsense first is taught to cry,
> Maggots half-form'd in rhyme exactly meet,
> And learn to crawl upon poetic feet.[7]

When Warburton added a note to this passage he overlooked Milton and referred again to Garth's more conventional satire *The Dispensary*. Pope not only alludes to *Paradise Lost* here but also preserves the specific Miltonic sense of 'embryonic' as subatomic or pre-formed. His hints are 'scarce quick' (not yet quickened, or animate): developmentally antecedent to the 'new-born nonsense' and 'Maggots half-form'd in rhyme' in the following lines. Pope, in other words, sets Dulness's 'empire' in a landscape that is distinctly unorthodox, featuring wildly autonomous substances and creative energies, undisciplined by stable creative authority and control. The point I want to make here is that Warburton seeks to restrain and discipline the presence of Milton's unorthodox philosophy but Pope does not. Dulness's genealogy is consistent with Pope's satire in the sense that her destructive force is characterized by an absence of authority, discipline, or control. Crucially, though, Pope's animations of the condition of being dull *are* the imaginative achievement of *The Dunciad*; the leaden dystopian London Dulness creates is the essence of the fiction (like T. S. Eliot's *Waste Land*, to which *The Dunciad* has frequently been compared). Collapse and disintegration provide the imaginative register of Pope's poem, setting it apart from the more conventional contemporary writing he disparages.

Through allusions to Milton, and the larger religious debates that informed Milton's writing, Pope encourages readers to link theological anxieties about the individual's relationship to unseen truth with conceptual uncertainties about the power of literary fictions; to see that fiction, like religion, mediated between unknowable human interiority and the visible external world, and thus occupied an ambiguous, unstable position in

---

[5] See Sugimura, *Matter of Glorious Trial*, 231–79.

[6] See Jonathan Williams, 'Happy Violence: Bentley, Lucretius, and the Prehistory of Freethinking', *Restoration: Studies in English Literary Culture, 1660–1700* 38, no. 1 (2014), 61–80.

[7] Pope, *Poems* (Twickenham), v. 274.

relation to empirical phenomena. When we compare this with Pope's earlier verse in which he addresses the nature of the universe, a more conservative view is evident. In *Windsor Forest* (completed around 1713) and the *Essay on Man*, (pub. 1733–4), for example, Pope adopts the classical *concordia discors* position of the cosmos as balanced among four warring elements (a discordant harmony), beyond the control of human reason or volition. In the Miltonic landscape of the *Dunciad*, however, Pope displaces the previous emphasis on a regulated natural order, and instead explores the vicissitudes of undisciplined, unregulated, chaotic will, private interiority and unstable personal conscience. The surreal landscapes of *The Dunciad* are more fascinating than the artfully composed scenes of *Windsor Forest*, and the view of human nature as chaotic, idiotic, and yet vibrant, is more compelling than in the *Essay on Man*.[8]

RELIGION AND FICTION

To his final version of the poem, *The Dunciad in Four Books*, Pope added a section (4.453–528) that satirized contemporary developments in religion, and in particular a controversial phenomenon known as freethinking, or deism. Freethinking was an avant-garde species of Christianity that became notorious in early eighteenth-century England, branded by its opponents as atheistic, dangerous, and often outright nonsensical. Given its volatile mix of ardent belief and unverifiable truth claims, religion was a subject of perennial appeal to freethinking satirists. All varieties of religious belief could be exposed as false or superstitious, and all believers revealed to be naïve or idiotic. The controversy about freethinking focused on the issue of whether people needed visible religious institutions and hierarchies (national churches, bishops) to communicate with God. It was a problem Pope was interested in, and indeed he was accused of promoting freethinking in the *Essay on Man*. This was a potentially damaging accusation, since deists were concerned with undermining the authority of the Church and even the State. If we look closely at Pope's satire on religion in *The Dunciad*, we can see that he was continuing to think seriously about the complex and contentious phenomenon of belief in unseen or immanent truths. Here, the satire on freethinking does double-duty as a way of investigating the new commercial culture of literary realism.

Freethinkers aspired to lay bare the 'reality' underlying the 'fictions' of Christian religion. The better known exponents were Charles Blount, Matthew Tindal, Anthony Collins, John Toland, 3rd Earl of Shaftesbury, and Lord Bolingbroke. These men ranged widely from radicals to reactionaries, with beliefs that varied, in the words of the intellectual historian J. G. A Pocock, from 'actual unbelief to resistance to institutionalized religion and the deferral of revelation to the afterlife'.[9] The unifying thread in their

[8] See James McLaverty, 'Warburton's False Comma: Reason and Virtue in Pope's *Essay on Man*', *Modern Philology* 99, no. 3 (2002), 379–92.

[9] J. G. A. Pocock, *Barbarism and Religion, Volume 1: The Enlightenments of Edward Gibbon, 1737–1764* (Cambridge: Cambridge University Press, 1999), 22.

thinking was that the Anglican Church and its doctrines (especially those regarding salvation and the future life) were instruments of state power, not spiritual truths. They hoped to restore Christianity to its 'natural' state by arguing that authentic belief did not require organized institutions, clergy, or rituals to sustain itself (God was self-evident in the munificence of nature, for example). In brief, freethinkers accused mainstream Anglican religion of elaborate fictions to bolster the authority of the Church, whereas defenders of organized religion accused freethinkers of imaginative delusion and illusory, false beliefs.[10] In both versions, religion and fiction are seen to go hand in hand. Hardly surprising, then, that a satire on religion would show up in *The Dunciad*, where Pope denounces writers and readers who are unable to distinguish true literature from false fiction, as judged by the standards of his own classical education.

The crisis of religious and literary belief that Pope satirizes in *The Dunciad* coincided with the 'rise of the novel', the emergence of newly realistic, probable stories about recognizable people doing recognizable things. The fictional narratives emerging in the early part of the century posed a profound challenge to existing systems of literary representation, including the classical epic form that Pope used as the basis of *The Dunciad*. Across religion, literature, and politics, the assumptions about belief that the freethinkers set out to challenge posed deep epistemological challenges: did systems of faith involving truths that could not be seen still require visible, authoritative, controlling public institutions to make them real?[11] While theories of fiction and reader response were relatively unknown in the early eighteenth century, virtually everyone, from ordinary people to eminent philosophers, had thought about what it meant to have faith in religious truths that could not be verified. Protestantism's great challenge, after all, conceptually and practically, was to connect the realm of temporal experience with the invisible world of divine revelation. It became the conundrum that presented itself with the 'rise of fictionality' also: the attempt to reinterpret quotidian experience in relation to its representation in the new realist fictions.

Religious controversies, especially those surrounding freethinking, preoccupied several of Pope's friends, chief among them the Anglican clergyman William Warburton, the man who was arguably Pope's closest intellectual associate in the last years of his life. In addition to collaborating with Warburton in *The Dunciad* and satirizing the scholar/clergyman Richard Bentley, Pope tosses off numerous references to men who were notorious in the religious debates of the day. (They include Isaac Barrow, Francis Atterbury, Gilbert Burnet and his protégé John Craig, John Wilkins, Samuel Clarke, John Gilbert, Benjamin Hoadly, John Locke, Ralph Cudworth, Henry More, the 3rd Earl of Shaftesbury, Matthew Tindal, Thomas Gordon, and John Toland.) By bringing religious

---

[10] For accounts of the deist controversy see Isabel Rivers, *Reason, Grace and Sentiment: A Study of the Language of Religion and Ethics in England, 1660–1780*, vol. 2 (Cambridge: Cambridge University Press, 2005), 7–84, and Sarah Ellenzweig, *The Fringes of Belief: English Literature, Ancient Heresy, and the Politics of Freethinking, 1660–1760* (Stanford: Stanford University Press, 2008), 1–30.

[11] See Brent Sirota, 'The Occasional Conformity Controversy, Moderation, and the Anglican Critique of Modernity, 1700–1714', *The Historical Journal* 57, no. 1 (2014), 81–105 and Steve Pincus, *1688: The First Modern Revolution* (New Haven: Yale University Press, 2009), 400–36.

controversy into *The Dunciad* so fully, Pope's satire invites readers to notice the interconnections between the dilemmas facing religious and literary belief-systems alike. If the national Church collapsed, might not literary communities also collapse into a diaspora of disparate opinions and reactions? Would literary value no longer be managed by common standards of taste, nor presided over by avatars and guardians of cultural standards? Might the visible institutions of literature, the commonly agreed upon genres, established forms and modes, the canon of authoritative texts and the hierarchies of authors, also be revealed as unnecessary, even illegitimate?

While Pope was finishing the final version of *The Dunciad*, he was mediating—and very likely provoking—a dispute between William Warburton and the Tory politician and philosopher Henry St John, Viscount Bolingbroke.[12] Bolingbroke was a Jacobite and a deist (deism was a version of freethought, though Bolingbroke's views were not fully understood until after his death). His most influential and controversial work was his tract *The Idea of a Patriot King*, composed in 1738, during a trip to England from his political exile in France. In that work Bolingbroke argued for a strong monarch who could revive English constitutional ideals, promote national strength by rejecting partisanship, and pursue international prominence through trade.[13] Pope was Bolingbroke's disciple earlier in his life, and transferred his admiration to William Warburton belatedly. Warburton was a moderate Whig clergyman, an autodidact of modest social origins. The antagonism between Bolingbroke and Warburton was in part a struggle over who 'owned' Pope, England's foremost poet and literary controversialist. It was also a clash between two very different, but equally important, influences on Pope's satirical sensibility, one aristocratic, reactionary, and exceptionalist (Bolingbroke); the other attempting to reconcile a highly idiosyncratic body of thought with mainstream consensus politics (Warburton).

It was Pope himself who fuelled the dispute, first by encouraging Warburton to criticize Bolingbroke's *Letters on the Study and Use of History* (1735), in which Bolingbroke appeared to question the authenticity of the Old Testament. Later, Pope would print 1,500 copies of *The Idea of a Patriot King* when Bolingbroke had licensed only a handful for private circulation. When Bolingbroke learned of the betrayal after Pope's death, he attacked his former friend, and Warburton went on the counter-attack. The crucial point here is that while the *Dunciad* satirizes the impacted, insular quality of Whig intellectual life, Pope and his friends were themselves among the most self-regarding and quarrelsome writers in eighteenth-century England. When encountering the *Dunciad*, it is vital to remember this. Intellectual and cultural energy was generated, not destroyed, by acrimony between charismatic public figures, and the rivalries depicted in Pope's poetry are as much a fiction designed to provoke creative rivalry and literary invention as they are a literal account of commercial publishing in the early eighteenth century.

---

[12] See Brean S. Hammond, *Pope and Bolingbroke: A Study of Friendship and Influence* (Columbia: University of Missouri Press, 1984), 102–19, 158–60.

[13] See David Armitage, 'A Patriot for Whom? The Afterlives of Bolingbroke's *Patriot King*', *Journal of British Studies* 36 (1997), 397–418.

In other words, the imagined apocalypse of the fourth book of *The Dunciad* should be seen as generative as well as destructive, enabling Pope's imaginative fictions to contest with and supplant those of the writers he both admires and deprecates.

Pope had been involved in religious controversy earlier in his career because of his poem *Essay on Man* (1733–4), which imperilled his pre-eminence in the mainstream literary establishment.[14] In the *Essay*, influenced by Bolingbroke, Pope expounded a view of human nature and understanding that appeared (to many) to diminish the role of divine providence and Christian salvation in its account of human virtue and reason, thereby laying the work open to the charge of deism. Warburton came to Pope's rescue against those who tried to use the *Essay* to discredit him, with an essay entitled 'A Vindication of Mr. Pope's Essay On Man: From the Misrepresentations of Mr. de Crousaz, by the Author of The Divine Legation of Moses Demonstrated' (1738). Crousaz was a Swiss reformed theologian in Lausanne whose critique of Pope's essay began the controversy. Warburton's defence was reworked in 1742 (the year Pope finished the last *Dunciad*) as *A Critical and Philosophical Commentary on Mr Pope's 'Essay on Man'*, with a foreword by Ralph Allen, a prominent Whig industrialist with philosophical and literary interests (his niece, and heir, married Warburton in 1745). It remains difficult to determine Pope's precise relationship to deism in the *Essay*. He assured Warburton that there was nothing calculated in his actions: 'I never in my life read a Line of Leibnitz, nor understood there was such a Term of Pre-established Harmony, till I found it in Mons. Crousaz's book.' But then he told Bolingbroke that he'd only printed ten copies of *Patriot King*. The point of rehearsing these details here is to show that Pope was extremely adept at playing one set of ideas off another—he reacted to the lurking presence of deism and Bolingbroke in the *Essay* by attacking freethinking and collaborating with Warburton in the last version of the *Dunciad*.

To think about literature through the lens of religion and religious politics was as entirely routine in Pope's period as it might seem irregular now.[15] Even though Pope was not a theologian, like Milton, nor a clergyman like his great friend Jonathan Swift, he paid more scrupulous, coherent attention to religious and doctrinal debates than Swift, whose parodies (in *A Tale of A Tub* and countless occasional satires) tend to collapse into confusion and incoherence, disarming or merely baffling his readers. In reading Milton, Pope paid careful attention to the implications of Milton's heterodoxy as well as to the poetry itself. This interest in theology is important for what it tells us about Pope's understanding of the relationship between people's invisible imaginative lives and their

---

[14] On the controversy over Pope's possible deism, see B. W. Young, *Religion and Enlightenment in Eighteenth-Century England: Theological Debate from Locke to Burke* (Oxford: Clarendon Press, 1998), 168–212; Howard Erskine-Hill, 'Alexander Pope: The Political Poet in his Time', *Eighteenth-Century Studies* 15 (1981–2), 123–48; McLaverty, 'Warburton's False Comma'.

[15] See Rivers, *Reason, Grace and Sentiment*; Philip Connell, *Secular Chains: Poetry and the Politics of Religion from Milton to Pope* (Oxford: Oxford University Press, 2016); Ronald Paulson, *Hogarth's Harlot: Sacred Parody in Enlightenment England* (Baltimore: Johns Hopkins University Press, 2003); Kristine Haugen, *Richard Bentley: Poetry and Enlightenment* (Cambridge, MA: Harvard University Press, 2011).

visible lives in the world. Pope embedded contemporary religious controversy in the *Dunciad* in part to reflect on the nature of poetic creativity.

WARBURTON AND POPE

Warburton's chief credential before he met Pope was as a defender of Anglican orthodoxy and the established national Church. He was the author of the two-volume *Divine Legation of Moses Demonstrated, on the Principles of a Religious Deist* (1738–41), published shortly before the final version of *The Dunciad*.[16] *The Divine Legation*, though now all but forgotten, was among the most influential and controversial eighteenth-century defences of Anglican orthodoxy. In its own way it is as singular as *The Dunciad*: a deeply counter-intuitive, idiosyncratic investigation of Christianity with a view to refuting the central claims of deism. It is surely the case that Pope decided to collaborate with Warburton to reaffirm his status as a national poet acceptable to the mainstream consensus of court Whigs and moderate Tories, after his problems with the *Essay on Man*. But their shared attraction to unexpected arguments and counter-cultural claims must also have made the collaboration appealing to both men.

In *The Divine Legation*, Warburton set out to refute deism and atheism 'on their own terms', as he put it on the title page. While Warburton was not especially successful in his stated aim (the tract was widely attacked, often convincingly), he did provide a fascinating and rigorous analysis of early eighteenth-century orthodox belief. Warburton's assertions about individual and collective faith in divine mysteries supply us with a crucial background for understanding the collaboration with Pope, showing that both men shared a keen interest in the threats posed by narratives or arguments that might absorb and potentially mislead their readers. The argument Warburton lays out is that Old Testament (i.e. pre-Christian) society managed the relationship between God and humans by way of the law (in the Old Testament world, the civil law and divine law were continuous). Since Anglicanism was deeply connected to Mosaic society (continuing it through the apostolic succession of bishops), Warburton argued that the English state had a mandate to support religion by maintaining a national Church tied to the civil law. He argued, moreover, that religion must be primarily concerned with providence, or the 'doctrine of a future state', since futurity was beyond the authority of the civil law. Warburton's focus on the future state meant that he was invested in 'revealed religion', the truths about God and providence that could only be known, or revealed, after death. At the time Warburton was writing, theologians were divided over whether these revelations or mysteries were the most important part of Christianity, requiring explanation

---

[16] See Ellenzweig, *Fringes of Belief*, 148–53; Ruth Mack, *Literary Historicity: Literature and Historical Experience in Eighteenth-Century Britain* (Stanford: Stanford University Press, 2009), 137–67; J. G. A. Pocock, *Barbarism and Religion, Volume 5: The First Triumph* (Cambridge: Cambridge University Press, 2010), 215–43.

and mediation by the Church, or whether the very fact that they were unknowable made it impossible for human institutions to play any role in their discovery. Warburton took the former view, against John Locke and other well-known thinkers, arguing that religion and the state coexisted in balance, each offering a form of authority that the other could not supply. In this respect Warburton was atypical of other Whig philosophers and intellectuals, who focused on human reason and free conscience rather than divine mystery. The reason for pausing on the details of Warburton's arguments is that they show him thinking seriously (and assimilating the thought of others) about the nature of private conscience, and the degree to which personal belief needed to (or could) be managed and mediated by visible, external institutions, rituals, and laws.

In the *Dunciad* passage quoted above in which Pope constructs Dulness's genealogy along Miltonic lines, we saw that Milton's conception of autonomous reasoning and unfixed matter presented a powerfully independent, authoritative model of human creativity, in which intellectual volition was liberated from constraining human or mechanical laws. For Milton, mental and physical freedom was the only viable solution to the central paradox of Christianity: God has removed himself from the visible world because of human sin, and only sinful humans, thinking freely, can restore divine law to civil institutions. This relationship works because human conscience provides the point of connection between God and man. (Milton viewed conscience as God's 'umpire' located in the human mind—human reason was not separate from divinity but conjoined with it.) The Miltonic, republican model offers a very different picture of interiority from the one Warburton defends against the threat of deism, in which God is removed from earth leaving the visible, apostolic Church in his place. For Warburton, human reason is sufficient to govern the civil state but not religion; religion in turn must lend its mysterious authority to civil government.

The effects Pope creates by incorporating both orthodox and heterodox thought into *The Dunciad* are apparent from this passage from Book 4 in which he mocks the flawed logic of Neo-Platonist philosophers:

> Let others creep by timid steps, and slow,
> On plain Experience lay foundations low,
> By common sense to common knowledge bred,
> And last, to Nature's Cause thro' Nature led.
> All-seeing in thy mists, we want no guide,
> Mother of Arrogance, and Source of Pride!
> We nobly take the high Priori Road,
> And reason downward, till we doubt of God.[17]

If we read these verses for their argument or their narrative content only, we come to the same conclusion Warburton did in the note he added in his 1751 edition of Pope's *Works*: when humans attribute excessive authority to their own reason, they arrive at

---

[17] Pope, *Poems* (Twickenham), v. 386–7.

nonsensical ideas which smack of infidelity. But if we construct our reading of the passage from the effects, allusions, and resonances of the language, we get a different sense of Pope's thinking. The phrase 'timid steps, and slow' is a playful reference to the final lines of *Paradise Lost*, when Adam and Eve with 'wandering steps and slow / Through Eden took their solitary way'.[18] It's an allusion, in other words, to the paradigmatic moment of human alienation from God, when the assurance of divine protection ceases to be empirically available. For Milton, alienation from visible divine presence is caused by disobedience, not flawed reason; reason is both free and independent. Pope's slow stepping philosophers 'creep': another important Miltonic word because of its association with Satan's departure from Hell (ii. 950), with Satan-as-serpent (ix. 180), and with Sin's teeming progeny who creep and 'kennel' in her womb (ii. 656).[19] Pope's reuse of the word is interesting because it ties the state of mental confusion or incomplete knowledge to sin, and also implies that methodical reason actually *can* restore the gap between human and divine that sin has created, since slow and timid steps lead to 'Nature's Cause', i.e. God. There is a strong suggestion that visible action and moral reasoning are, by necessity, aligned, not divided or potentially alienated from each other.

Pope thus implies connection, not disconnection, between thinking and being, abstraction and substance. While the word 'creep' in *Paradise Lost* describes Satan's approach to the serpent it also denotes the footsteps of diminutive animals occupying their proper place in the divine order, 'Cattle, and creeping things, and beast of the Earth, / Each in their kind'.[20] The creepiness of creeping is determined by the conscience of the agent; it is not intrinsic to the action. In Pope's lines, 'common sense' and 'common knowledge' insist on symmetry or identity between the mental and the physical. Pope's ironic freethinking speaker uses 'common' to mean low-born, but in the Miltonic context it means 'belonging to all', an account of sense and knowledge that makes free will and reason equitably available, and capable of restoring Eden (since Eden is the original common, destroyed by sin). The line 'All-seeing in thy mists we want no guide' reiterates Miltonic logic at the level of its language. Those who can see in mist would indeed want no guide; because they would see that it was misty, and would not mind being on the wrong road (Priori Road rather than Posteriori). That Pope invites us to picture a literal misty road is reinforced by his implied pun here—the road not taken, the Posteriori Road puns on 'Post Road', the faster and more direct route in eighteenth-century road systems. The slow steps of the a posteriori philosophers are thereby shown to be a misperception on the part of a priori reasoners, themselves walking unknowingly on a misty byway. To add an additional turn to this reading, Milton has Satan approach the serpent 'like a black mist low-creeping' (9.180), which John Leonard points out alludes to Lucretius's description of a spreading plague, a reminder that the Lucretian universe of undifferentiated atoms, without necessary moral status imputed to them by a divine will, is a crucial aspect of the Miltonic cosmology to which Pope makes such detailed reference.

[18] John Milton, *Paradise Lost*, ed. Alastair Fowler, 2nd edn. (Harlow: Pearson Longman, 1997), 678.
[19] Milton, *Paradise Lost*, 157, 480, 143.   [20] Milton, *Paradise Lost*, 417.

The implication of Warburton's defence of an orthodox national Church was that citizens could be held in a protective embrace between coercive institution (the state) and unregulated interiority (the conscience). As the passage above shows, a heterodox account of the relation between mind and matter reveals that no such mediating visible institution is necessary to support a robust interior life. A crucial point of intersection between Pope's account of literary creativity in *The Dunciad* and Warburton's account of revealed religion in *The Divine Legation* lies in their shared belief that only ancient learning, history, orthodoxy, and institution can protect individuals from the destabilizing effects of private experience or interiority. But we also see that Pope is less orthodox or stable a writer than we might at first expect, and his verse often complicates Warburton's commentary, notes, and editorial suggestions with a pervasive strain of heterodox imagery and philosophical allusion. The Warburton of *The Divine Legation* was himself unconventional and experimental in his arguments and reasoning, and Pope's resistance to convention (while superficially maintaining it) reminds us that these men shared a deep attraction to intellectual eccentricity.

In Book 4 of *The Dunciad*, Pope traces the collapse of civilized culture into Dulness's empire of Chaos and Night. The book begins by reconstructing an episode from conjectured human history that had excited enormous controversy in theology and philosophy: man's change from a natural to a civil state. In *The Dunciad* the change is reversed as Pope's universe shifts from society to a state of nature and then to something that precedes even creation, 'universal darkness'. But the point holds that Pope's setting makes use of a cosmos that was largely the domain of theological and philosophical speculation rather than literary representation. The opening invocation to Book 4 is poised between chaotic nature and orderly civilization, anticipating apocalypse and attempting to forestall it:

> Yet, yet a moment, one dim Ray of Light
> Indulge, dread Chaos, and eternal Night!
> Of darkness visible, so much be lent,
> As half to show, half veil the deep Intent.
> Ye Pow'rs! Whose Mysteries restor'd I sing,
> To whom Time bears me on his rapid wing,
> Suspend a while your Force inertly strong,
> Then take at once the Poet and the Song.[21]

The speaker, we realize, is still anticipating the threatened return to the empire of Chaos and Night prophesied in Book 1. Pope's joke, then, is that in real time nothing has happened since the poem began. The *vis inertia* prevails over the material entity of the poem as much as over the imagined empire of Dulness, and we find ourselves lingering in the dying hours of the created world before returning to an undifferentiated mass of prime matter in both its substantial (Chaos) and substanceless (Night) forms.

---

[21] Pope, *Poems* (Twickenham), v. 339–40.

The imperceptible time-lapse between Books 1 and 4 calls our attention to the fact that *The Dunciad* occupies a particular state of epistemological and ontological anxiety: simultaneous anticipation of and uncertainty regarding the afterlife (since apocalypse and Judgement are nigh). The model Warburton lays out in *The Divine Legation* of an even balancing-act between State and Church was designed in no small part to assuage or manage the very condition that Pope permits to overwhelm the four books of his epic—anxiety regarding a future state. Pope has seized on the target of freethinkers' criticisms, that concern for the afterlife is a fabrication constructed to support priestcraft and institutional religion, and rendered it literally as the psychological and epistemological landscape of *The Dunciad*. Readers and participants cling to the last remnants of the created world, yet rush towards its undoing as a relief from the poem's abiding strain of nervous, grasping uncertainty. When it comes, Dulness's apocalypse is a respite, as Pope figures death as sleep: 'More had she spoke, but yawn'd—All Nature nods: / What Mortal can resist the Yawn of Gods?' (4.605–6).

The invocation to Book 4 just quoted, along with the notes accompanying it, parodied arguments put forward by Platonists, Newtonians, and Lockeans regarding the relation of matter to spirit. The Cambridge Platonists explained the nature of substance in order to refute the Hobbesian insistence on a mechanical, amoral state of nature devoid of essential values and beneficent human reason. They attempted to prove, instead, the existence of an ideal natural order endowed from the first with virtue and reason. Their justification for using a priori logic was to avoid the oppressions of arbitrary authority, arguing that a natural order in the universe preceded human law.[22] But Pope's Chaos, as we might expect, is primarily Miltonic, a connection he emphasizes by way of the phrases 'darkness visible' (*Paradise Lost*); 'Time bears me on his rapid wing' (Sonnet VII, on Time); and the phrase at line 13, 'Seed of Chaos, and of Night' (*Paradise Lost*, again). With the reference to the Epicurean theory of the 'new world' in the note to line 15, Pope acknowledges Milton's own reference to the Lucretian idea that the prime matter of the universe was not divine. Epicurean cosmology admitted the possibility of God's absence or withdrawal from the cosmos, a position which in turn threatened orthodox theology by admitting the existence of substance beyond the reach of providence, matter that could not be brought under orthodox governance. Pope reconstructs the indeterminacy of Miltonic prime matter, neither entirely substance nor spirit, neither entirely orderly nor disorderly, neither formless nor formed. 'Deficient ontology [in chaos] indicates instead a material potency that is the precondition of creation', writes John Rumrich. Even in creation, the disagreeable darkness of Chaos persists, and can be reclaimed, a feature of Milton's universe that Pope shapes his poem around: 'in Milton's allegory Chaos thus represents an indeterminate material principle whose complex disorder persists dynamically in any order'.[23] N. K. Sugimura also pays attention to the philosophically conflicted or incompatible figuration of Chaos in *Paradise Lost*. In pairing Chaos and Night, 'the depiction of the abyss as straightforwardly material increasingly encounters difficulties ... the Lucretian

---

[22] See Sugimura, *Matter of Glorious Trial*, 1–39.   [23] Rumrich, 'Milton's God', 1041.

particulate is revealed to be flooded with the unknown immateriality of Night'. She argues that 'ideas about occult powers and imaginary space with which Milton's allegorical figurations of Chaos and Night engage would be considered philosophical embarrassments to a monist reading of the epic.... Chaos is an active realm of contrariety...It is not, as it would be in a simple Aristotelian framework, pure potentiality.'[24] The indeterminacy which in Milton signals his imaginative hybridization of competing, irreconcilable models of substance, in Pope provides the imagery for his representation of providential instability. In both cases, unease, suspense, and anxiety are created through the poet's seeming theological inconsistency or indecision, an opening out from heterodox debate into literary representation.

Pope repeats the Miltonic 'darkness visible' in the Warburtonian 'Mysteries restor'd', since in the note Pope glosses mystery as 'obscurity'. Dulness's apocalypse reveals the Christian mysteries (an orthodox suggestion) but the joke is that in Dulness's version revelation takes the form of mere darkness (Dulness is mysterious by virtue of being dim or mist-like). Pope gestures towards distinguishing Miltonic 'darkness visible' from orthodox 'mystery restored', but on closer inspection he turns out to be repeating himself, as the Duces might do. He offers another paradox in line 7, 'suspend a while your force inertly strong', the note to which alerts us to Pope's joke here. He pleads with Dulness to suspend her *vis inertia*, a principle in classical mechanics explored by Newton, but since *vis inertia* is the tendency of matter to remain in its present state, it cannot be suspended; it already describes a force that does nothing. The very principle of *vis inertia* itself contained heterodox implications, as Sarah Ellenzweig observes: 'However unintended, the principle of persistence has as its most revolutionary consequence the possibility of a fundamentally self-sufficient, physically autonomous mechanics of motion.... Motion and its persistence could appear to have no need for a divine prime mover, no need for any force or cause other than the moving body itself.'[25] This persistence of destruction in order, of uncreation in creation, is the very condition that guarantees both divine and human freedom in Milton's theology. God cannot reform substance without sacrificing free will. The implications of Miltonic Chaos are clear for his heterodox theology: 'how else could Milton's materialist, monist deity make distinct creatures, volitionally independent of him, who are nevertheless continually dependent on him for the substance and sustenance of their being?'[26] The instability of matter and spirit in Milton is a more radical solution to the dilemma of providence than that presented by Warburton. As already noted, the gap between human volition and divine authority is, for Milton, precisely the condition which makes people free, gives them autonomy and, ultimately, creative power. Uncertainty over the individual's future state is itself the guaranteeing condition of human liberty. For Warburton, the opposite is the case. Providential uncertainty makes necessary a tightly regulated orthodoxy

---

[24] Sugimura, *Matter of Glorious Trial*, 232–3.

[25] Sarah Ellenzweig, '*Paradise Lost* and the Secret of Lucretian Sufficiency', *Modern Language Quarterly* 75 (2014), 389.

[26] Rumrich, 'Milton's God', 1044.

whose doctrines are underwritten by the authority of the civil government. One thinker regards the uncertain relationship between human and divine as an opportunity for human freedom, the other regards the uncertainty as a demand for human control. The implications for fiction are important here: the indeterminate, interpretable gaps opened up by literary texts present readers with new oppositions, new negotiations between interpretive security and pervasive instability.

The Dunciad reflects a marked departure from Pope's representation of religion in the *Essay on Man* and from the satire of his other works. Whether or not the *Essay* is 'deist', it undoubtedly advocated a version of belief that was inclusive, non-partisan, and disengaged from struggles over temporal power and political authority. In this sense it reflected Pope's Roman Catholicism, by imagining a version of faith that transcended denominational and even national divisions, and which paid no particular attention to the status of Christ as Messiah, all distinctive features of reformed Protestant literature in one way or another. The satire of the *Dunciad*, by contrast, depends for its effects on division and debate. These are the very mechanisms driving the poem, including the instability of Pope's own poetic and philosophical commitments. To shape the imaginative landscape of his fiction in *The Dunciad* he oscillates between a 'Warburtonian' view of religion and government and a much more radical, indeterminate account of free will and its relation to the cosmos. Phillip Connell has put this well: while in the *Essay* Pope is nominally professing 'peaceable ecumenism and universal faith', these commitments contrast ironically with his 'abiding sense of the inescapable nature of confessional division as, in some sense, an enabling condition of his poetic voice'.[27] Warburton's decision to defend the orthodoxy of Pope's most ecumenical, idealistically 'Catholic' poem produced the most divisive, partisan, and overtly political satire of his entire career, which was also his greatest act of imaginative creation: *The Dunciad in Four Books*.

SELECT BIBLIOGRAPHY

Connell, Philip. *Secular Chains: Poetry and the Politics of Religion from Milton to Pope* (Oxford: Oxford University Press, 2016).

Ellenzweig, Sarah. *The Fringes of Belief: English Literature, Ancient Heresy, and the Politics of Freethinking, 1660–1760* (Stanford: Stanford University Press, 2008).

Ingrassia, Catherine and Claudia N. Thomas. *More Solid Learning: New Perspectives on Alexander Pope's Dunciad* (Lewisburg: Bucknell University Press, 2000).

McLaverty, James. *Pope, Print and Meaning* (Oxford: Oxford University Press, 2001).

Pope, Alexander and Valerie Rumbold. *The Dunciad: In Four Books*, rev. edn. (Harlow: Pearson Longman, 2009).

Rivers, Isabel. *Reason, Grace and Sentiment: A Study of the Language of Religion and Ethics in England, 1660–1780*, vol. 2 (Cambridge: Cambridge University Press, 2005).

[27] Connell, *Secular Chains*, 214–16.

CHAPTER 14

AUGUSTAN ROMANTICS

MATTHEW SCOTT

THE HORATIAN CONTEXT

THE abduction in April 1944 of General Kreipe, Nazi commander of Crete, by Patrick Leigh Fermor and his ragtag partisans, did little to change the war but in the retelling it must remind us of the shrunken reputation of Horace, once a touchstone of Western canonical authority and a central figure in the poetics of the Augustans. Sequestered by night in a cave near the snow-covered heights of Mount Ida, the general emerged one morning to utter the opening of Horace's ode to Thaliarchus (I. 9): 'vides ut alte stet nive candidum / Soracte' (Do you see how Mount Soracte stands there shining with its blanket of deep snow?).[1] Instantly apprehending that a comparison was being drawn between the two mountains, Leigh Fermor took up the poem and continued in Latin:

> The General's blue eyes swivelled away from the mountain-top to mine—and when I'd finished, after a long silence, he said 'Ach so, Herr Major!' It was very strange. 'Ja, Herr General.' As though, for a long moment, the war had ceased to exist. We had both drunk at the same fountains long before; and things were different between us for the rest of our time together.[2]

The anecdote has an air of gilded improbability but its spirit serves this chapter well: Horace spoke then across a divide of war as an idea of the common culture, and he functions similarly as a means to draw together connections between two traditions in English literary history that appear superficially to be at odds: the Romantic and the Augustan.

These are difficult terms, fraught with both complex and vague associations. In his historical landmark study, Ian Jack used the term 'Augustan' to designate the period from

---

[1] Horace, *Odes and Epodes*, ed. Niall Rudd (Cambridge, MA: Harvard University Press, 2004), 40–1.
[2] Artemis Cooper, *Patrick Leigh Fermor: An Adventure* (London: John Murray, 2012), 184.

1660 to 1750 without any apparent anxiety but he also noted that 'all generalizations [...] about Augustan poetry [...] are likely to be invalid', and called it instead 'a temper of writing, unsusceptible of any but a very wide definition'.[3] The problematic implications here are that the term may be usefully employed even while begging the question of what it truly encompasses. In the field of Romantic studies such double-mindedness remains common. Although the writing of the period is far more diverse in nature than many of the classic accounts of 'Romanticism' implied, we would not wish to dispense with the term altogether. Rather than hoping to trace the influence of the writers of the Augustan upon those of the Romantic period, my aim is to explore ways of linking the two slippery ideas of Romanticism and Augustanism to see how they intersect as literary and cultural traditions.

Howard Erskine-Hill observed a quarter of a century ago, thinking especially of Alexander Pope, that the Augustan idea in English literature is 'especially salient' if seen through the lens of Horace as a literary model.[4] He noted too that Augustanism should not to be seen as a single 'frame of mind' covering the whole of a defined cultural period in the late seventeenth and early eighteenth centuries. Rather, it must be viewed as 'a particular tradition of thought and literary practice' (xii) that runs from 'the last years of Elizabeth' (xi) through to Romanticism and even beyond (350–9), but which is nevertheless most prominent in the period that saw the careers of Dryden, Swift, Pope, and their contemporaries. Erskine-Hill was well aware that the easy notion of the 'Augustan Age', which covers the heyday of eighteenth-century satire, was a lazy one and he was eager instead to trace out a longer tradition of literary thought, the terms of which are operative throughout this chapter. He offered a neat way of uncovering it: the Augustan idea in English literature 'is an awareness of the practicable interdependence of private and public, the public not consuming the private, the private not blocking the public from view' (xvi). This is an idea that seems superficially to be at variance with the conventional view of Romanticism, both in its apparent focus upon the 'Self' and its rejection of what comes before in eighteenth-century poetic practice. Nevertheless, there is much of profit to investigate, not least in the idea of a subtle interplay between the public and private spheres that exists rather conspicuously in the earlier satirical tradition, but which is also present in much of the poetry of the later Romantic period.

Horace is not an immediately obvious Romantic forebear but his legacy in the period is fascinating. At times he can sound almost quintessentially Romantic in mood, as in his famous statement about poetic immortality (from ode III. 30): 'non omnis moriar, multaque pars mei / vitabit Libitinam: usque ego postera / crescam laude recens, dum Capitolium / scandet cum tacita virgine pontifex' (I shall not wholly die, and a large part of me will elude the Goddess of Death. I shall continue to grow, fresh with the praise of posterity, as long as the priest climbs the Capitol with the silent virgins) (216–17). This has relevance to the widespread Romantic notion of the 'Self' as a work of art that

---

[3] Ian Jack, *Augustan Satire: Intention and Idiom in English Poetry, 1660–1750* (Oxford: Clarendon Press, 1952), 146–7.

[4] Howard Erskine-Hill, *The Augustan Idea in English Literature* (London: Edward Arnold, 1983), xvi.

is retained through literary posterity. Vladimir Nabokov translated an imitation of Horace's ode by Alexander Pushkin, the most significant Russian Romantic:

> Not all of me is dust. Within my song,
> safe from the worm, my spirit will survive,
> and my sublunar fame will dwell as long
>   as there is one last bard alive. [...]
> And to the people long shall I be dear
> because kind feelings did my lyre extoll,
> invoking freedom in an age of fear
> and mercy for the broken soul.[5]

Instinct in these lines are ideas that might be found in Keats's letters or Shelley's *Defence of Poetry*, where a sense of the poet's absolute need to speak for humanity in general unites with the idea that poets of all ages contribute, in Harold Bloom's memorable phrase, 'to one Great Poem perpetually in progress'.[6] Horace is central to our understanding of the legacy in Romanticism of the literary ideas of the Augustan tradition and in this chapter I will approach the subject by way of an initial discussion of his general influence upon the Romantics, before considering more specifically the wider matter of where to locate a tradition of Romantic Augustanism that emerges out of eighteenth-century satire.

HORACE AND THE ROMANTIC CRITIQUE OF EMPIRE

Stephen Harrison has remarked that although the most conventionally educated Romantics—Wordsworth, Coleridge, Byron, and Shelley—were schooled in a curriculum that included Horace prominently, they tended to revolt against his influence.[7] He has especially in mind Byron's lines on seeing Soracte during his tour of Italy in *Childe Harold* IV, where he too draws a comparison with Mount Ida as he recalls Horace's ode:

> I've look'd on Ida with a Trojan's eye;
> Athos, Olympus, Aetna, Atlas, made
> These hills seem things of lesser dignity,
> All, save the lone Soracte's heights display'd
> Not now in snow, which asks the lyric Roman's aid.

---

[5] *Horace in English*, ed. D. S. Carne Ross and Kenneth Haynes (Harmondsworth: Penguin, 1996), 224.

[6] Harold Bloom, *The Anxiety of Influence: A Theory of Poetry* (New York: Oxford University Press, 1973), 19.

[7] *The Cambridge Companion to Horace*, ed. Stephen Harrison (Cambridge: Cambridge University Press, 2007), 334.

For our remembrance, and from out the plain
Heaves like a long-swept wave about to break,
And on the curl hangs pausing: not in vain
May he, who will, his recollections rake
And quote in classic raptures, and awake
The hills with Latian echoes; I abhorr'd
Too much, to conquer for the poet's sake,
The drill'd dull lesson, forced down word by word
In my repugnant youth, with pleasure to record

Aught that recalls the daily drug which turn'd
My sickening memory; and, though time hath taught
My mind to meditate what then it learn'd,
Yet such the fix'd inveteracy wrought
By the impatience of my early thought,
That, with the freshness wearing out before
My mind could relish what it might have sought,
If free to choose, I cannot now restore
Its health; but what it then detested, still abhor.

Then farewell, Horace; whom I hated so,
Not for thy faults, but mine; it is a curse
To understand, not feel thy lyric flow.
To comprehend, but never love thy verse,
Although no deeper Moralist rehearse
Our little life, nor Bard prescribe his art,
Nor livelier Satirist the conscience pierce,
Awakening without wounding the touch'd heart,
Yet fare thee well—upon Soracte's ridge we part.

(ll. 662–93)[8]

Byron's apparent rejection of the 'Horace; whom [he] hated so' as a boy is a *topos* of a kind: he is reminding his readers, in a sweep of Romantic rhetoric, that he has changed greatly from the callow youth of schoolboy revolt into a poet of private introspection, and that he has done so largely as a public figure. Horace could hardly be more clearly celebrated—unrivalled as a philosopher, artist, and satirist (poignant and humane rather than brutal)—but he still remains unloved by the mature Byron. The fault lies, however, not with Horace himself but with the system of teaching that denied any feeling for the lyric voice as it forced upon pupils the curse of literal understanding. These lines imply that while for the Augustans it was the gently clear-sighted order of Horace's genius that made him an example of excellence in a world of encroaching dullness, it was this that militated against him for the Romantics. On the whole, Horace comprehended the private from within the space of the public sphere, and the same might be said of Pope; for the Romantic poet, things tend to begin within the confessional and move out from there.

[8] Lord Byron, *The Major Works*, ed. Jerome J. McGann (Oxford: Oxford University Press, 1986), 169–70.

Byron is, however, a poet who lived by ambivalence and a great Romantic exactly because of his confusions. How else could he write both *Don Juan*, the nearest thing to a comical epic in English, and also *Childe Harold* III, which is a deliberately Wordsworthian poem (and a product of Shelley's browbeating advocacy of the older poet)? He had a widely divided consciousness and this plays out in his response to Horace. As a teenager, he translated ode III. 3—a celebration of the steadfast values of the modern Roman against their origins in distant Troy—and he was to return to the 'hated' poet again in his early maturity with *Hints from Horace*, a loose version of the *Ars Poetica*. The early translation is pretty stolid but Byron uses it to hone the idea of a single-minded, aut-arkic, and autonomous masculinity, obedient only to the Self, which will later undergird the Byronic hero:

> The man of firm, and noble soul,
> No factious clamours can controul;
> No threat'ning tyrant's darkling brow
>   Can swerve him from his just intent;
> Gales the warring waves which plow,
>   By Auster on the billows spent,
> To curb the Adriatic main,
> Would awe this fix'd determined mind in vain.[9]

A few years later, when he had set out for the very lands that were encompassed meto-nymically by 'Ilium' in that ode—the place including the Islamic world of the Ottoman Empire and Albania—his companion, John Cam Hobhouse, wrote an imitation of another ode of Horace (II. 6), which anticipates his own death in a foreign land. The original lines that Hobhouse reworks are these: 'ille te mecum locus et beatae / postulant arces: ibi tu calentem / debita sparges lacrima favillam / vatis amici' (That place with its happy stronghold beckons to you and me; there you will duly drop a tear on the warm ashes of your poetic friend) (Horace, *Odes*, 108–9). In free translation, they become:

> Thou too, my B—n, shalt be near
>   To sooth my life, my death attend;
> And weep, for thou canst weep, one tear,
>   To mourn the poet and the friend.[10]

Earlier on, the poem anticipates travels in lands that the two were never to reach, includ-ing Palmyra in Syria, and it is a public statement of aristocratic ambition for the sublime ending, with a certain degree of bathos, in a moment of private grief over a death that never happened. Hobhouse, unlike his companion, lived on to become an eminent Victorian.

---

[9] *The Poetical Works of Lord Byron* (1846), 380.
[10] J. C. Hobhouse, *Imitations and Translations* (1809), 168.

Byron himself, in quasi-Augustan mode, blends the public and private frequently in his early writing, such as when he uses a denunciation of his fellow poets in *English Bards and Scotch Reviewers* to announce his own literary ambitions:

> For me, who, thus unask'd, have dared to tell
> My country what her sons should know too well,
> Zeal for her honour bade me here engage
> The host of idiots that infest her age;
> No just applause her honour'd name shall lose,
> As first in freedom, dearest to the muse.
> Oh! would thy bards but emulate thy fame,
> And rise more worthy, Albion, of thy name!
> What Athens was in science, Rome in power,
> What Tyre appear'd in her meridian hour,
> 'Tis thine at once, fair Albion! to have been —
> Earth's chief dictatress, ocean's lovely queen:
> But Rome decay'd, and Athens strew'd the plain,
> And Tyre's proud piers lie shattered in the main;
> Like these, thy strength may sink, in ruin hurl'd,
> And Britain fall, the bulwark of the world.
> But let me cease, and dread Cassandra's fate,
> With warning ever scoff'd at, till too late;
> To themes less lofty still my lay confine
> And urge thy bards to gain a name like thine.[11]
>
> (ll. 334–53)

The literary models here are obvious: the Dryden of *MacFlecknoe* and the Pope of *The Dunciad* are both latent presences in the poem as Byron seeks satirically to undermine the culture of his own time through reference to past empires (Tyre, Rome, and Athens), but there is another element that will remain key to the poetry of his maturity. This is the explicit critique of current British imperial ambition (and indeed of empire more generally).

The most famous expression of this critique comes in Shelley's *Ozymandias*, which was inspired by the excavation of a statue of Rameses II by the Italian ex-strongman and adventurer, Giovanni Belzoni, in 1817. The sonnet, first published in Leigh Hunt's *Examiner*, vied for attention alongside an unsubtle companion poem by Horace Smith, now best known for his parodies of poetic contemporaries, *Rejected Addresses*, co-authored with his brother. That poem explicitly foresees the death of London as an imperial city. It is a heterodox vision of the British Empire consistent with Byron's own later deliberations on empire in poems such as *The Curse of Minerva* and *Childe Harold* II and IV. In the lines that follow, Byron refers to the folly of Elgin's project to remove the marbles from the Parthenon (a topic that will come to obsess him). The light but stinging satirical voice of Byron's late masterpieces, *Beppo* and *Don Juan*, might rightly be thought to

---

[11] Byron, *Major Works*, 11.

be the key to understanding his debt to the eighteenth-century satiric tradition but in these earlier, politically-engaged works, there is also a blending of public and private selves—the one leaning upon the other in a way that is reminiscent of Erskine-Hill's definition—only in being directly critical of imperial ambition, Byron creates an openly complex form of Augustanism.

Byron and his contemporaries would have been embarrassed by the connections to imperial power that Horace enjoyed but, as James Sambrook has noted, ambivalence about Horace on the grounds of his politics was already occasionally present among eighteenth-century satirists who were concerned to distance themselves from a poet who championed an authoritarian emperor.[12] The Romantics were therefore inheriting a tradition of scepticism about a literary precursor that they nevertheless found rather useful in creative terms. Pope employed his *Imitations of Horace* to satirize the Walpole administration and the reuse of Horace as a political instrument represents a clear line of influence between the Romantics and the English Augustans. Leigh Hunt translated Horace's important ode to Maecenas (ode II. 12) for publication in *The Examiner* in 1812 and it contains a reference to the power of the monarchy (one of his central themes) in its closing stanza. Meanwhile, Byron's friend, the Irish poet Thomas Moore, reworked ode I. 22 to impersonate the voice of Lord Eldon, the Tory Lord Chancellor, sarcastically imagining an unblemished life as one of heartless oppression of the Irish:

> [...] an Irish papist darted
> Across my path, gaunt, grim, and big –
> I did but frown, and off he started,
> Scar'd at me, even without my wig.[13]

The poem betrays a debt of sorts to Swift but is an unsubtle satire.

Rather more interesting is the gentle parody of the ode to Thaliarchus from Horace and James Smith's droll collection, *Horace in London* (1813). The poem begins with a form of the anti-sublime that does not quite achieve bathos: 'Richmond [in winter] is clad in a mantle of snow', which encourages the speaker towards 'two or three bottles of generous wine', but quickly the retreat has less to do with private distance from society than it has with a gentle send-up of that social world:

> The park and the playhouse *my* presence shall greet,
> The opera yield to its delight;
> Catalani may charm me, but ten times more sweet,
> The musical voice of Laurette when we meet
> In tête-à-tête concert at night.
> False looks of denial in vain would she fling,
> In vain to some corner be gone;

---

[12] James Sambrook, *The Eighteenth Century: The Intellectual and Cultural Context of English Literature 1700–1789* (London: Longman, 1986), 197.

[13] James Smith, *Horace in London: Consisting of Imitations of the First Two Books of the Odes of Horace* (1813), 75.

> And if in our kisses I snatch off her ring,
> It is, to my fancy, a much better thing
> Than a kiss after putting one on![14]

The poem takes us a long way from Horace's original ode and instead into the life of Regency high society, whose love of the opera William Hazlitt ridiculed as frivolous escapism in an essay in *The Yellow Dwarf* (1818). The end of the poem in this imitation is broadly true to the spirit of the original because both close with the suggestion of erotic fulfilment but here the context has been shifted to London's *beau monde*. It would be stretching things to describe this as acute satire but, when taken in the context of Horace Smith's own *Ozymandias*, we do get a sense of how Horace himself remains in the period as an inherited vehicle for mocking the public sphere, even within the scope of such an ostensibly private poem as ode I. 9, with which I began.

RURAL EFFUSIONS

The most radical writer of the first generation of Romantics, Samuel Taylor Coleridge, an ostensibly unlikely Horatian and Augustan, is especially interesting for the way in which he blends the public and private, and the pastoral and the political. His famous criticism of *Gulliver's Travels*—most 'complain of the Yahoos, I complain of the Houyhnhnms'—revealed him to be a more acute reader of Swift than his contemporaries but the importance of the earlier satirical tradition, and of Horatian satire in particular, to the shaping of his early poetry and indeed to his most important poetic innovation, the Conversation Poem, is easy to overlook.[15] These are poems of interiority that are also in dialogue with imagined interlocutors and that display, in more or less overt terms, a determined political purpose, which blurs the boundary between the public and private spheres. The epithet conversational might easily be applied to the urbane tone that runs through much of eighteenth-century satirical poetry and J. Douglas Kneale has argued that Coleridge engaged closely with this tradition, and most pointedly with the work of Charles Churchill as he came to create his own conversational form, which he called, on its first publication, the effusion.[16]

This innovative genre—at once an expression of early Romantic inspiration and also a kind of Augustan form reworked—presents its readers, as Kneale has suggested, with a lightly worn, conversational style that belies its actual formality. It is Horatian in being a thing 'in between', as is implied by the original subtitle to one poem in particular, 'Reflections on Having Left a Place of Retirement': 'A Poem which affects not

---

[14] Smith, *Horace in London*, 41.

[15] René Wellek, *A History of Modern Criticism, 1750–1950*, 2 vols. (Cambridge: Cambridge University Press, 1981), ii. 184.

[16] J. Douglas Kneale, *Romantic Aversions: Aftermaths of Classicism in Wordsworth and Coleridge* (Liverpool: Liverpool University Press, 1999), 31.

to be Poetry'—a hesitancy that forces us to ask just what he is about. The poem begins apparently inconsequentially in casual, rather unpoetic description of a rural home— 'Low was our pretty Cot; our tallest Rose / Peep'd at the chamber-window'—but builds to a celebration of the landscape beyond—'God, methought, / Had built him there a Temple'—as though to remind us of the ease with which the domestic comforts of the ordinary can cause us to forget the majesty of a whole of which we all are part.[17] The poem as a whole acts then as a corrective both to its immediate interlocutor and also to readers, as is implied in the later subtitle, which is a foxing tag derived from Horace, 'Sermoni Propria', that underpins its satirical purpose. Behind it lie the difficult political circumstances of the time of writing, when Britain stood on the brink of war with France, and Coleridge blends two kinds of Horatian influence—the *Sermones* and the *Epistulae*—to give us a poem that bridges the two modes. One of the ways in which this is especially manifest in the poems is through the delicate blending of public and private modes of address. These are poems that appear superficially to be topographical pastorals but that are intensely plugged into the historical and political moment, catching very clearly the Augustan idea as Erskine-Hill defined it.

The ode to Thaliarchus, which has clear connections to the mode of writing that Coleridge is attempting, has a long and fascinating history in English translation. John Dryden's important early version of 1685 has a stately, calming, and ordered measure that is quite out of step with the Latin. Peter Levi describes the way in which the poem begins 'with the stiff white snowy peak of Soracte' visible from Rome as an image of a becalmed nature, iced over.[18] From there, things dissolve as wine is brought out and a very different world is imagined, one of dance in the market square with a laughing girl and a love token snatched: 'Everything has altered from the word "dissolve" in line 5: the weather is springlike, life is open air, the cypress and the mountain ash are still and stiff but the young (l. 16) are dancing, there are whispers and laughs, and the girl's finger not quite resisting transforms the mountain' (94). Where Levi sees a transformation to the music of dance in the middle of the poem, Dryden finds a settled peace that is almost statesmanlike:

> With well heap'd Logs dissolve the cold,
> And feed the genial hearth with fires;
> Produce the Wine, that makes us bold,
> And sprightly Wit and Love inspires:
> For what hereafter shall betide,
> God, if 'tis worth his care, provide,
> Let him alone with what he made,
> To toss and turn the World below;
> At his command the storms invade;
> The winds by his Commission blow

---

[17] Samuel Taylor Coleridge, *The Complete Poems*, ed. William Keach (Harmondsworth: Penguin, 1997), 92.

[18] Peter Levi, *Horace: A Life* (London: Duckworth, 1997), 94.

Till with a Nod he bids 'em cease,
And then the Calm returns, and all is peace.[19]

Dryden captures a quality of control that might well be thought exemplary of
Augustanism in a poem that belies it in its original form. Levi's speculations may be a
little wild but he gets at a racy element that is missing in the early translation: 'It is
a remarkable poem [...] and could very well be Horace's first attempt at the alcaeic, a
strong horse that pulls in directions of its own. [...] Horace is not in Rome I think, but he
imagines himself there, only the trees and rivers are really those of the Sabine hills, the
sea where the winds are fighting it out, a queer enough conception but Homeric for a
storm, is surely off Canosa, and there is something about the girls and the dances and the
thieving lovers that suggests somewhere far to the south, Naples or Tarentum' (Levi, 95).
All this is to say, really, that the original poem contains thoughts that are Romantic
rather than Augustan, or rather that it is a good key to unlocking the connections
between the two precisely because it shows how insistent Horace's influence might
remain in the later period.

The movement that Levi suggests, by which Horace begins within the comfort of the
public sphere—making an ordinary observation of the mountains from Rome (the
centre of political life)—but then moves out into the private, sexy world of the rural
retreat where a form of different meaning is found, feels very Romantic exactly because
it speaks of finding true power in the private. This is one way of paraphrasing the end of
Tennyson's version of the same poem, which he produced in tetrameters towards the
end of the Romantic period, when he was still a schoolboy. Here, there is a real feeling of
the poet that Tennyson would become, both remotely orotund and warmly enticing,
and in the cadence of his rhetoric that we can sense the poet of 'Ulysses' and 'Tithonus',
who is at once intimate and distant; those qualities being surely the most obvious vestige
in the modern period of the curious blending of the public and the private that Erskine-
Hill found to be the quintessence of earlier Augustanism:

Leave to the Gods the rest – whose force
Can stay the whirlwind's wasting course;
When they have soothed the maddening jar
Of mingled elemental war,
Nor those tall ash-trees dread the storm
Nor cypress bows his shadowy form.
Why should we fear tomorrow's woe?
    Whatever day the Powers above
Have given, rejoice: nor, while the flow
    Of joy and golden youth delight
    Thy soul – while age avoids thee – slight
The mazy dance – the power of love.[20]

---

[19] Dryden, *Works*, iii. 79–80.   [20] *Horace in English*, 228.

The rival versions by the youthful Tennyson and the mature Dryden lend a sense of a movement between the two periods, and this speaks too of how that particular poem is used and reused in changing ways. A third version by William Cowper is much more condensed and any sense of the sexy end of Horace's original is obviated. Martin Priestman has argued that Horace was a major influence on *The Task*, both by way of Pope's *Imitations* and also through a more general poetry of 'ease' and 'self-deprecation'.[21] In terms of his translation of that ode, what is significant is that Cowper invokes both the poetry of nature and that of the private realm:

> See'st thou yon Mountain laden with deep Snow,
> The groves beneath their fleecy Burthen bow,
> The streams congeal'd forget to flow,
> Come, thaw the Cold, and lay a cheerful Pile
>   Of Fuel on the Hearth,
> Broach the best Cask, and make old Winter smile
> With seasonable Mirth.[22]

When compared to the original, this is a rather superficially smiling scene that conjures thoughts of Christmas cheer; all of which is to say that Cowper gives us a rural, English Horace.

HORATIAN WORDSWORTH

Cowper encourages us to think about the influence of Augustanism upon the central poetic development of the early Romantic period, which is the creation of a new form of the poetry of landscape instilled with the language of introspection. Erskine-Hill noted that the supposed decline of Augustanism over the course of the eighteenth century was in fact moderated by an increasing interest in the Georgic, which fed eventually into the great transformation in topographical poetry that is constituted by Wordsworth's most important poems (354). Kevis Goodman has given the definitive account of this trajectory by showing how the tradition builds from Thomson's *Seasons* to Cowper's *Task* before arriving at Wordsworth's *Excursion*.[23] That Virgilian inheritance is important to the larger narrative that I am tracing here, and it intersects with an ongoing (but not completed) project of Wordsworth's maturity, which was the translation of the *Aeneid*

---

[21] Martin Priestman, *Cowper's Task: Structure and Style* (Cambridge: Cambridge University Press, 1983), 7.

[22] William Cowper, *Poems*, ed. John D. Baird and Charles Ryskamp, 3 vols. (Oxford: Clarendon Press, 1980), ii. 3.

[23] Kevis Goodman, *Georgic Modernity and British Romanticism: Poetry and the Mediation of History* (Cambridge: Cambridge University Press, 2004).

that Bruce E. Graver has carefully reconstructed.[24] Less obvious is the debt that Wordsworth felt to Horace. Cowper comes nowhere near Wordsworth in terms of the intoxicating blend of elements from the external and internal worlds but he hints at their interconnectedness in his translation of ode I. 9. Even if his translation falls a little flat, it does raise the issue of the importance of Horace to Wordsworth, a topic that has been inadequately explored.

Wordsworth was sufficiently drawn to the Horatian pastoral to produce an early translation of ode III. 13 in 1794, which celebrates the spring of Bandusia as a source of inspiration:

> Thy tempting gloom a cool repose
> To many a vagrant herd bestows,
> And to faint oxen weary of the share;
> Thou too 'mid famous fountains shalt display
> Thy glory while I sing the oak
> That hangs above the hollow rock
> Whence thy loquacious waters leap away.[25]

A few years later, as he was working towards the 1799 *Prelude*, he imagined similarly 'loquacious waters' in the form of his own native river Derwent, which 'loved / To blend his murmurs with my Nurse's song' (ll. 2–3).[26] This poem is infinitely more sophisticated than anything in the earlier translation but it contains some of the same essential elements, transformed into a more powerful natural mythology whose focus is the spring from which emanates the song of the poet:

> The noise of wood and water, and the mist
> Which on the line of each of those two roads
> Advanced in such indisputable shapes,
> All these were spectacles and sounds to which
> I often would repair, and thence would drink
> As at a fountain, and I do not doubt
> That in this later time when storm and rain
> Beat on my roof at midnight, or by day
> When I am in the woods, unknown to me
> The workings of my spirit thence are brought.[27]
>
> (I. 368–77)

The trope of the fountain as a figure for the imagination remained with Wordsworth and that of Bandusia specifically appears a number of times in his later poetry. In 'Liberty'

[24] William Wordsworth, *Translations of Chaucer and Virgil*, ed. Bruce Graver (Ithaca: Cornell University Press, 1998).

[25] *Horace in English*, 214.

[26] William Wordsworth, *The Prelude: The Four Texts*, ed. Jonathan Wordsworth (Harmondsworth: Penguin, 1995), 8.

[27] Wordsworth, *Prelude*, 18.

(1835), he considers an opposition between the public and private that is self-consciously Augustan, the one depending upon the other in symbiosis. It is a poem that worries the matter of public displays of privilege against the obscure notion of private liberty. Inevitably, the former come off badly. The bird in the gilded cage may be adored and revered by its mistress but it lives in compromise when compared to the freedom that is offered in Nature; the same, Wordsworth suggests, is true even of the Sovereign. The public life of even the most apparently free is in poor contrast when compared to truly private freedom. We might well expect this to be epitomized for Wordsworth in a portrait of the life of the poet but we might also be surprised to discover that his exemplary case is that of Horace:

> That life – the flowery path that winds by stealth –
> Which Horace needed for his spirit's health;
> Sighed for, in heart and genius, overcome
> By noise and strife, and questions wearisome,
> And the vain splendours of Imperial Rome? –
> Let easy mirth his social hours inspire,
> And fiction animate his sportive lyre,
> Attuned to verse that, crowning light Distress
> With garlands, cheats her into happiness;
> Give 'me' the humblest note of those sad strains
> Drawn forth by pressure of his gilded chains,
> As a chance-sunbeam from his memory fell
> Upon the Sabine farm he loved so well;
> Or when the prattle of Blandusia's [sic] spring
> Haunted his ear – he only listening –
> He, proud to please, above all rivals, fit
> To win the palm of gaiety and wit;
> He, doubt not, with involuntary dread,
> Shrinking from each new favour to be shed,
> By the world's Ruler, on his honoured head![28]

Wordsworth is here directly celebrating Horace on his 'Sabine farm' in a way that contrasts the private life of the poet with the public role that he also played. At this point in his life, Wordsworth must have been thinking about his own gradually emerging public position but Horace clearly also spoke to him in terms of a tension between private poetic inspiration and the social role of the poet more widely, and this is a concern that lies at the heart of his writing from the start.

In both the very early poem, *An Evening Walk* (ll. 72–7) and also in the late 'Musings near Aquapendente' (l. 257), there are further passing references to the ode but the Bandusian spring appears to more striking effect at the start of the river Duddon sonnets (1820), where we learn about 'that crystal Spring / Bandusia, prattling as when

---

[28] William Wordsworth, *Poems*, ed. John O. Hayden, 2 vols. (Harmondsworth: Penguin, 1977), ii. 687–8.

long ago / The Sabine Bard was moved her praise to sing'.[29] Wordsworth then goes on to invoke Epistle 1. 10, celebrating the 'immunities of rural life', and thereby draws a distinction between Horace as a public and private poet. In this poem, it is clearly the latter that he holds up as a conscious forebear and, with this in mind, it is also significant that both here and in the poem just mentioned, the word associated with the spring is 'prattle'. It is a word that both Wordsworth and Coleridge use to call to mind childhood. We might think, for example, of the lines from the latter's little-loved poem, 'The Blossoming of the Solitary Date-Tree: A Lament', which are among the most moving that he wrote:

> But should disease or chance the darling take,
> What then avail those songs, which sweet of yore
> Were only sweet for their sweet echo's sake?
> Dear maid! no prattler at a mother's knee
> Was e'er so dearly prized as I prize thee:
> Why was I made for Love and Love denied to me?[30]

The connection between the two poems is entirely coincidental but it does tell us something interesting. Horace, who is not so completely a poet of childhood (and never a father), was clearly associated somehow in Wordsworth's mind with the origins of his poetic life. This ought not to surprise us in some ways, given the centrality of the Latin poets to his early education, but since Horace is so closely connected with Pope, to whom Wordsworth had an avowed objection, it is nevertheless worthy of remark. That key word suggests that for Wordsworth the origins of their close connection came in youth, when his poetic muse was itself prattling from a fountain of early inspiration.

More than any other writer in the English language, Wordsworth was concerned to reflect upon the ways in which early experiences first form the apparatus of the imagination and then persist as elements within it. My contention is that for him the early experience of Horace formed just such an ongoing link into later life. David Ferry has gone further to speculate that it was the ode on the fountain of Bandusia specifically that Wordsworth had in mind when he wrote in 'To M. H.' (the final poem of his fascinating sequence of Poems on the Naming of Places) of a 'track which brought us to a slip of lawn / And a small bed of water in the woods' and a 'secluded spot, where herds of cattle might shelter'.[31] If we are to believe Ferry, then it suggests that both that specific ode and Horace more generally were very deeply embedded in Wordsworth's poetic consciousness. Robert J. Griffen has argued still more boldly that in Wordsworth's address to his sister at the end of 'Tintern Abbey', the 'pivotal' lines, 'in thy voice I catch / The language

---

[29] William Wordsworth, *Sonnet Series and Itinerary Poems, 1820–1845*, ed. Geoffrey Jackson (Ithaca: Cornell University Press, 2004), 57.

[30] Coleridge, *Complete Poems*, 344.

[31] D. S. Carne-Ross, *Classics and Translation* (Lewisburg: Bucknell University Press, 2010), 316.

of my former heart', derive from Pope's Horatian 'Imitation, To Augustus'.[32] In that poem, Pope, in lukewarm praise of a poetic forefather, asks:

> Who now reads Cowley? if he pleases yet,
> His moral pleases, not his pointed wit;
> Forget his Epic, nay Pindaric Art,
> But still I love the language of his Heart.[33]
>
> (ll. 75–8)

Griffen's is a lavish claim, though one that feels somewhat less so when we consider that Pope himself reused the phrase to recall his father in *An Epistle to Dr Arbuthnot*: 'Un-learn'd he knew no Schoolman's subtle Art, / No language, but the Language of the Heart' (ll. 398–9, Pope 349). That poem, in which Pope delicately blends vulnerable private confession and public satire into a profound form of moral reflection is at once quintessentially Augustan, in Erskine-Hill's terms, and also proto-Romantic.

BYRON'S AUGUSTAN ROMANTICISM

A plausible path can certainly be found from Wordsworth back to the most obvious Augustans by way of Horace but it does not obviate the fact that he was at times highly critical of eighteenth-century poetic diction; and whether or not he learnt somehow, as Griffen suggests, to look for his own poetic consciousness by setting himself against those earlier poets, it cannot be denied that he felt himself to have moved beyond them. We need only think, for an example of this, of his thoughts on the opening of Samuel Johnson's *Vanity of Human Wishes*, given here by William Hazlitt:

> [T]he same idea is repeated three times under the disguise of a different phraseology. It comes to this: 'let observation with extensive observation observe mankind'; or take away the first line, and the second, 'Survey Mankind from China to Peru', literally conveys the whole.[34]

This is, Hazlitt admits, a highly amusing way of exposing 'the unmeaning verbiage' of a certain kind of poetry, but it is also a rather unfair and opportunistic flogging of this particular poem. After all, as William Harmon has pointed out, Johnson had produced an imitation of a Juvenalian original that itself 'mocks pompous diction'.[35] It would be silly to deny the significance of Wordsworth's role in placing a distance between the Romantics and the Augustans but also wrong to see it as the complete picture,

---

[32] Robert Griffen, *Wordsworth's Pope: A Study in Literary Historiography* (Cambridge: Cambridge University Press, 1995), 97–8.

[33] Pope, *Poems* (Twickenham), iv. 201.

[34] William Hazlitt, *The Spirit of the Age: or Contemporary Portraits* (1825), 246.

[35] *Classic Writings on Poetry*, ed. William Harmon (New York: Columbia University Press, 2003), xii.

even (and perhaps especially) in his own case. Long ago, Ian Jack pointed out wisely that, for the most part, Wordsworth's criticism of the poetic diction of the eighteenth century was directed not at the earlier Augustan satirists but at the loco-descriptive poetry of the immediately foregoing generation (Jack, 148). In ignorance of this, the debt to the Romantics of the tradition that underpinned eighteenth-century satire was long underplayed. Satire, as Steven Jones and others have shown over the past two decades, certainly persisted in the Romantic period as a very significant mode of writing about and engaging with the politics of the time.[36] Earlier, I mentioned Horace and James Smith's *Rejected Addresses*; this is only the most noted example of the rich tradition of literary parody in the Regency press, which Graeme Stones and John Strachan have done much to uncover.[37] Meanwhile, the most obvious examples of satire in the period—Shelley's *Peter Bell the Third* (a send-up of Wordsworth) and *The Mask of Anarchy* (inspired by Peterloo in 1819) or Peacock's various works (especially *Nightmare Abbey*)—obviously betray a debt of sorts to the earlier tradition but they are very wedded to their own moment and it would be wrong to think of them as somehow anachronistic imitations of earlier satiric writing.

It is, ultimately, to Byron (and his wider circle) that we must look for the truest inheritance that we might describe as Augustan Romanticism. For a number of years after 1819, Byron was deeply embroiled (on the side of Pope) in a pamphlet war over the earlier poet's legacy (The Pope/Bowles controversy), which now seems like a rather remote and arcane footnote in literary history. At this time, however, while, as Jane Stabler notes, he 'stressed the role of art, the "exquisitely artificial" and the "superartificial"', Byron had returned to his earlier collection, *Hints from Horace*, and he did so, via Pope, in contemplation of the legacy of the Latin poet upon his own period.[38] In the fifth canto of *Don Juan*, he recalls Horace's statement in his epistle I.6 about equanimity, or *ataraxia*, 'a texture of thought and feeling that presupposes detachment from dogmatic thought or conviction of any kind'.[39] The epistle begins: 'Nil admirari propre res est una, Numici, / solaque quae possit facere et servare beatum' ('Marvel at nothing'—that is perhaps the only thing, / Numicius, that can make a man happy and keep him so).[40] These lines, made famous by Pope, are, Christopher Yu goes on to say, 'a motto for the English Augustans' and they are adopted by the mature Byron as a means for understanding his own relationship with his public:

> 'Not to admire is all the art I know
> (Plain truth, dear Murray, needs few flowers of speech)

---

[36] Steven E. Jones, *Satire and Romanticism* (Basingstoke: Palgrave Macmillan, 2000).

[37] *Parodies of the Romantic Age*, ed. Graeme Stones and John Strachen (London: Pickering & Chatto, 1998).

[38] Jane Stabler, *Byron, Poetics and History* (Cambridge: Cambridge University Press, 2002), 103.

[39] Christopher Yu, *Nothing to Admire: The Politics of Poetic Satire from Dryden to Merrill* (New York: Oxford University Press, 2003), 19.

[40] Horace, *Satires, Epistles, The Art of Poetry*, ed. H. Rushton Fairclough (London: Heinemann, 1926), 286–7.

> To make men happy, or to keep them so';
>   (So take it in the very words of Creech).
> Thus Horace wrote we all know long ago;
>   And thus Pope quotes the precept to re-teach
> From his translation; but had *none admired*,
> Would Pope have sung, or Horace been inspired?[41]

Stabler has neatly observed that this stanza, packed as it is with literary reference, enacts a curious completion of Horace by way of Pope: Byron 'hijacks the "*Nil admirari*" dictat and antithetically completes it' (Stabler, 100). The satirical impulse, Byron suggests, begins with the conviction that we ought never to be too wholly enthusiastic about a subject but, paradoxically, as soon as it gets going the very drive to be sceptical is itself immediately undercut by a rival impulse that ultimately overwhelms it. This latter is harder to name than the initial public ambition to be critical or to censure the impulse to 'admire', but it is close to a privately-driven desire to create an object of aesthetic value that is to be valued by the audience on its own terms. Taken like this, Byron censures one form of admiration—a kind of blind enthusiasm that celebrates the products of the public sphere, as voices received by a readership high on the rich diet of contemporary publishing (such indeed as he himself might once have been)—but he also valorizes another. This is a feeling richly committed to the life of art and to a deeply found enthusiasm that emerges from the poetic text. It is an admiration that he himself found in Pope; a wonder and excitement in the fact of the word that continues to speak across the gap of centuries, and it is this that he felt looking at Soracte, even as he knew that the forced understanding of the schooled Horace never quite brought it.

Byron was a writer conditioned by double-mindedness and a profound Romantic as a consequence of it. Productive confusion is often the most interesting state of the Romantic mind, and his appreciation of Horace—whom he evidently 'hated' and loved in equal measure—is a good example of this. He was a poet of double-mindedness; he thought of his readers with double-mindedness; and indeed his readers thought of him with a double-mindedness that confused the public poet of the heroic Romantic sublime with that of privately sinking smuttiness. The public sphere is the place in which moral debates must be had, and Byron was never in any doubt about that (as any reader of *Don Juan* knows), but he understood too that private passions must be held unconditionally as articles of faith in the Self. In this regard, he took Augustanism forward to a later time and he presages a later Romantic, Friedrich Nietzsche, who also saw a complex negotiation of the *nil admirari* as a hallmark of ethical authenticity. Nietzsche's recent biographer, Julian Young, has written:

> What creates complacency, Nietzsche says, is 'historical consciousness'. Such consciousness kills enthusiasm. When everything is historically grasped, we enter a spirit of 'nihil admirari'. So, for example, to become aware of our own moral values as

---

[41] Byron, *Major Works*, 573.

just one item on a vast historical menu of alternative sets of values destroys our commitment to our own values, since we can find no ground for preferring them to any of the alternatives on display. [...] Action, commitment, passion, Nietzsche is suggesting, require a certain chauvinism, a sense of one's own values as the only *possible* values.[42]

Nietzsche's contention is that values must be held in the here and now as though there could be none other. Doubt will surely inhere but it must come accompanied by enthusiastic conviction. This all sounds very un-Horatian but when combined with Byron's qualification we can see that to get to it, one requires the Horatian precept. If we do not acknowledge the capacity in us to become lost in wonder, then we cannot begin to appreciate what might be won by leaving that kind of consciousness at the door. Put another way, Byron's contention is that Horace would not have written of the perils of wonder, had he not felt and dwelt in their inducements. Nietzsche's statement feels like Romanticism run riot, a faith in the Self that is without any checks, and even Byron could not go so far. But Byron did, by embracing the mood of the Augustans in *Don Juan*, write the great poem that embraced his own many enthusiasms, even as they are often coupled with ambivalences, doubts, and moments of self-critique. It is from this kind of equivocation that the digressive mode emerges, and, late in his poem, Byron tells us that *Don Juan* is his 'poetical T[ristram] Shandy' (x, 150); indeed *Don Juan* is surely the most digressive work of literature in English apart from *Tristram Shandy*. An early French critic called that novel 'Horace's monster' on account of the digressions (Stabler, 73). *Tristram Shandy* gains life from its antagonistic relation to Horace from the very start, however, and that critic had failed to acknowledge that without Horace's egg, the chicken to which he objected would not have existed. Similarly, Byron, in refusing the essential diktat of the Romantic ideology to be singular in his subject by writing a poetry of the Self, fused the manner of Augustanism with the thought of his own time so as to create a poem that appears at once to stand outside Romanticism and also to be essential to it.

SELECT BIBLIOGRAPHY

Carne-Ross, D. S. *Classics and Translation* (Lewisburg: Bucknell University Press, 2010).

Erskine-Hill, Howard. *The Augustan Idea in English Literature* (London: Edward Arnold, 1983).

Goodman, Kevis. *Georgic Modernity and British Romanticism: Poetry and the Mediation of History* (Cambridge: Cambridge University Press, 2004).

Griffen, Robert. *Wordsworth's Pope: A Study in Literary Historiography* (Cambridge: Cambridge University Press, 1995).

Jones, Steven E. *Satire and Romanticism* (Basingstoke: Palgrave Macmillan, 2000).

Kneale, J. Douglas. *Romantic Aversions: Aftermaths of Classicism in Wordsworth and Coleridge* (Liverpool: Liverpool University Press, 1999).

---

[42] Julian Young, *Friedrich Nietzsche: A Philosophical Biography* (Cambridge: Cambridge University Press, 2010), 161–2.

Martindale, Charles and David Hopkins. *Horace Made New: Horatian Influences on British Writing from the Renaissance to the Twentieth Century* (Cambridge: Cambridge University Press, 1993).

Stabler, Jane. *Byron, Poetics and History* (Cambridge: Cambridge University Press, 2002).

Yu, Christopher. *Nothing to Admire: The Politics of Poetic Satire from Dryden to Merrill* (New York: Oxford University Press, 2003).

PART III

SATIRICAL MODES

CHAPTER 15

....

MIXING IT

Satire in the Miscellanies, 1680–1732

....

PAUL BAINES

NEAR the centre-point of *Miscellaneous Poems and Translations*, published by Bernard Lintot in 1712, stand two poems about the book in which they appear. Pope's 'Verses design'd to be prefix'd to Mr. *Lintott*'s Miscellany' is a cheerfully disrespectful assault on the publisher's standing in book history. The other, Gay's 'On a Miscellany of Poems. To *Bernard Lintott*' contains mock-georgic instructions for the venture:

> Wouldst thou for Miscellanies raise thy Fame;
> And bravely rival *Jacob*'s mighty Name,
> Let all the Muses in the Piece conspire...
>
> (169)

Gay does not prescribe a hierarchy of 'Muses' so much as the necessity to keep shifting the attention and mood of the reader: the 'Lyric Bard' may sound, but 'Heroick Strains must here and there be found'; 'Nervous Sense' must be offset by the 'melodious Woe' of elegy. Moreover:

> Let not your am'rous Songs too num'rous prove,
> Nor glut thy Reader with abundant Love;
> Satyr must interfere, whose pointed Rage
> May lash the Madness of a vicious Age;
> Satyr, the Muse that never fails to hit,
> For if there's Scandal, to be sure there's Wit.

The diet of erotic lyric to which *Miscellany* readers were subjected will cloy: satire must 'interfere' and, as ever, lash the vices of the age—or rather, it will 'never fail to hit' so long as it gives us something scandalous, a switch from the moral to the titillating which might itself be regarded as satiric. Similarly 'Pindarick Lays' will exhaust our patience unless diverted by 'short-breath'd Epigram' which 'strike at Follies in a single Line' (ll. 22–5). Satire is less an independent contribution to moral reform than a contextual antidote to literary surfeit.

Gay then shifts to a list of authors who must be recruited to the volume, confirming (with some irony) the links between canon-formation, rhetorically-organized publishing showcases, and a new educable readership which are the focus of much recent study of the *Miscellany* ethos.[1] This chapter will address rather the specific presence—or absence—of satire in miscellanies, both collective and single-author, from the 1680s to the Pope–Swift *Miscellanies* of 1727–32, and examine the effects of the format in presenting satire's acerbic pleasures amongst other literary offerings.

THE DRYDEN–TONSON *MISCELLANIES* (1684–1709)

According to a certain philology, there ought to be a natural consonance between satire and miscellany. The prose 'Essay upon Satyr' by the French critic André Dacier, itself printed in Gildon's *Miscellany* (1692), traced the etymology back to the Latin adjective 'satur': 'copious', or, 'to which there was nothing wanting for its Perfection', and particularly to the 'satura lanx', 'a Bason fill'd with all sorts of Fruit, which they offer'd every Year to *Ceres*, and *Bacchus*, as the First Fruits of all they had gathered'. 'Satura' then came to be used to describe miscellaneous works of the mind.[2] Dryden's expanded discussion, in his 'Discourse Concerning the Original and Progress of Satire', imagines a 'Charger, or large Platter...yearly fill'd with all sorts of Fruits'; like Dacier, he asserts that the word was 'afterwards apply'd to many other sorts of Mixtures', including the 'hotch-potch, made of several sorts of Meats'.[3] Johnson, who accepted this etymology in his *Dictionary* (1755) against the rival derivation from the Greek 'Satyr', which had lent the form a certain shaggy aggression, also derives 'Miscellany' from 'miscellenea', or mixed meats; Juvenal (the satirist's satirist) indicates that it meant low-grade food for gladiators (*Satires*, XI. 20). Juvenal's definition of his own project, highlighted by Dryden on the title page of his translation and in the 'Discourse', continues the mixed-diet analogy:

> quidquid agunt homines, votum timor ira voluptas
> gaudia discursus nostri farrago libelli est.

'Whatever people do – vow, fear, anger, luxury, joy, running about – is the hotch-potch of our little book'.[4] 'Farrago' was mixed fodder for cattle; Richard Flecknoe, himself a

---

[1] See especially the works by Benedict, Barnard, and Bullard in the Select Bibliography, below.

[2] *Miscellany Poems upon Several Occasions...And...Translations from Horace, Persius, Petronius Arbiter, &c. With an essay upon satyr, by the famous M. Dacier* (1692), A8v.

[3] The 'Discourse' was a dedicatory letter, 'To the Right Honourable Charles, Earl of Dorset and Middlesex', in *The Satires of Decimus Junius*, trans. John Dryden (1693), xxii.

[4] Juvenal, *Satires*, i. 85–6; Dryden, 'Discourse', xlvii, where 'farrago' is 'a word of the same signification with *Satura*'. For the satire–miscellany equivalence, see also Paddy Bullard, 'Digital Editing and the Eighteenth-Century Text: Works, Archives, and Miscellanies', *Eighteenth-Century Life* 36 (2012), 57–80 (69).

satire-magnet, compiled *A Farrago of Several Pieces* in 1666. The quotation was deftly picked up by Steele's *The Tatler* as its motto—significantly omitting, as Dryden had done, Juvenal's next line, 'et quando uberior vitiorum copia', 'and when did we have a more copious supply of vices', in the interests of a less confrontational outlook.

What more natural then that *Miscellanies* should be full of *Satires*, since the words meant the same thing, and format and genre were equally ascendant? Actually, the alignment is far from simple. Satire was certainly miscellaneous enough, as a recent comprehensive taxonomy reminds us.[5] Dryden's 'Discourse' was less a formal treatise than an unfettered ramble through mixed materials (panegyric, complaint, anecdote, philology), and even in its closest focus, balancing Horace against Juvenal, satire appeared dazzlingly various, moralistic yet full of non-moral pleasures, a matter finally of cognitive identification ('taste') rather than generic coding. 'Satura' was an adjective (feminine, at that), describing attributes, rather than a substantive; it attached itself to different, often formally hybridized objects. But the fact of having to detach it, philologically, from the roughness of 'Satyr' indicates that its connection to the food-miscellany was already archaeological rather than live. Indeed, satire's profile is surprisingly low in the *Miscellanies* that Dryden was responsible for, and if 'miscellenea' was originally a lower-grade mixture than the sanctified first-fruits of the 'satura lanx', there seems to have been a shift in their relative standings.

The Dryden–Tonson series began in 1684 with *Miscellany Poems* and concluded in 1709 with *Poetical Miscellanies. The Sixth Part*. The volumes now stand as canonical examples of the type, though they came out at irregular intervals, under titles themselves miscellaneous, with no set pattern of contents.[6] Poems shifted from one volume to another during reprinting and in the six-volume set with which 'great *Jacob*' Tonson closed the venture in 1716. One consistent feature within this variability, however, was that they did not hand the reader a menu of literary fruits from which satire could be confidently selected. None has 'satire' on its title page; devotees must work to locate satire within a cornucopia of modes. This proposition may sound odd when we pick up the first volume itself.[7] The title page foregrounds translations from Virgil's *Eclogues*, Ovid's 'Love Elegies', and Horace's *Odes*, alongside 'several Original Poems'; but the first three items in the book are *Mac Flecknoe*, *Absalom and Achitophel*, and *The Medall*, the three works on which Dryden's reputation as a satirist was founded.

The three poems had represented satire at work in real time, through appropriately different material witnesses. *Mac Flecknoe* circulated in manuscript from 1678 and had not long since (October 1682) appeared in quarto as 'A Satyr upon the true-blew-Protestant poet, T.S.', a code dropped from *Miscellany Poems*. Shadwell, the target, is identified as an ineffectual satirist, endowed with gall but 'inoffensive', unable to 'bite',

---

[5] Ashley Marshall, *The Practice of Satire in England, 1658–1770* (Baltimore: Johns Hopkins University Press, 2013).

[6] See Stuart Gillespie and David Hopkins, 'Introduction', in *The Dryden–Tonson Miscellanies, 1684–1709*, ed. Gillespie and Hopkins, 6 vols. (London: Routledge, 2008), I. xv–lxix.

[7] *Miscellany Poems* (1684).

unlike (implicitly) the poem itself.[8] *Absalom and Achitophel* had been officially published by Tonson in mid-November 1681, as 'A Poem', while the legal process against the Earl of Shaftesbury was still *sub judice*. In *Miscellany Poems* it appeared with the original address 'To the Reader', where Dryden claimed to have 'rebated' the poem's satiric instincts in the interests of moral, rather than political, efficacy ('The true end of *Satyr*, is the amendment of Vices by correction'). Tate's commendatory poem mentioned the brilliant efficiency of 'your keen Satyr' but saw the poem as a generic polymorph, fusing other genres by implication higher than satire.[9] *The Medall*, issued in March 1682 by Tonson as a bitter invective in the wake of Shaftesbury's release, was, however, labelled 'A Satyre Against Sedition', because (a commendatory poem explains) the situation now demanded the 'satyre' which had previously been reined in.[10] The subtitle is retained in *Miscellany Poems* (including in the running titles). Each of the three has a separate title page and edition statement, but the pagination is continuous; so readers have both modes, the datable historical sequence of 'satiric' poems, interjected into a timeless enchiridion of polite taste, as if detached from circumstance and (with Shaftesbury dead in exile the year before) presented to merely aesthetic scrutiny, lessons in the subgenres of satire (mock-heroic; lampoon; invective). They became meta-satires, extracted from engagement and reconstituted as elements of the mixed diet of a gentleman's literary pleasure.[11]

But if the first 104 pages constitute a block of unmixed (if inconsistently labelled) satire, we then encounter very different things: Ovid's 'Elegies', ironic in their compromised libertinage; sober segments of Virgil's *Georgics*; love and sex across epistle, elegy, and pastoral; a several-hands version of Virgil's *Eclogues*. The reader might, prompted by the sensitizing salt of the book's opening, find satire elsewhere: in Dryden's Prologues, perhaps, or among the versions of Horace, since amidst praise of love and wine we find a translation of III. 6 (by the Earl of Roscommon) under the Juvenalian subtitle 'Of the Corruption of the Times'. It may say 'Ode', but it can be 'Satire' nonetheless; on the other hand, the 'Corruption of the Times' would constitute only a distanced, classical pre-echo of *Absalom and Achitophel*.

Sylvae (literally, 'woods' or 'copious supply') was still more classical than its predecessor.[12] Dryden's preface mentions satire, but almost reluctantly: in an essay on translation, Dryden discusses Horace as 'a Critick, a Satyrist, and a Writer of Odes'. Finding himself tempted towards the satires in a parenthesis—they are 'incomparably beyond *Juvenals*, if to laugh and rally, is to be preferr'd to railing and declaiming'—he remembers this aspect is 'no part of my present undertaking'.[13] Nevertheless, amid showcase versions of Virgil, Lucretius, Theocritus, Tibullus, Catullus, and Ovid, it is still possible to locate some satiric spirit: Dryden's version of Horace's second *Epode* retains the adroitly ironic

---

[8] *Miscellany Poems* (1684), 10.   [9] *Miscellany Poems* (1684), 17–18, 24, italicization reversed.

[10] *Miscellany Poems* (1684), 84.

[11] A tentative explanation of Tonson's contingent reasons for the structure is given in Gillespie and Hopkins, 'Introduction', xl–xli.

[12] *Sylvae; or, the Second Part of Poetical Miscellanies* (1685).

[13] *Sylvae*, sig. a6v, italicization reversed.

final twist (the speaker of the 'beatus ille' fantasy turns out to be a usurer); Edmund Poley's translation of Horace's *Epistles*, I. 18 offers a substantial series of wry observations, just next to a formal imitation of 'The 2d. Satyr of the First Book of *Horace*'— though this proves to be more of an estranged supernatural fantasy than satire as normally understood. These moments only partially fulfil Gay's prescription. Dryden's 'Prologue Intended for the *Duke* and no *Duke*' constitutes an argument about the current literary situation, but its inclusion of a brief mention of 'blunted Satyr' reflexively identifies its relative absence from the book.

One contingent reason for the occlusion of classical verse satire was that *The Odes, Satyrs, and Epistles of Horace* had been 'done into English' by Thomas Creech and published by Tonson with a dedication to Dryden in 1684, while Dryden was gathering his own several-hands version of satire into the Juvenal translation, again for Tonson, of 1693. (Separate translations of Boileau's satires, the other main formal model, appeared in 1679 and 1696.) These monuments diminished the scope for translators, and Tonson's third volume accordingly once again makes satire-hunters work hard.[14] Addison and Bevil Higgons commend the Juvenal venture but their real focus is the ethics of translation, not satire. A large opening selection from Ovid's *Metamorphoses* is balanced by Tate's *Syphilis* (a translation from the Latin of Giralomo Fracastoro, already issued separately by Tonson in 1686) but the book is generally small-scale in its choice of forms. Translations from Catullus offer faintly satirical edge amongst Pindarics and Pastorals. But in 'On Mr. Hobs', Mulgrave proposes that Satires have pleased so much because of the ill-nature of readers: 'And, as the sharp Infection spreads about, / The Reader's Malice helps the Writer out'. Panegyric is preferred, as it is in the conclusion of Dryden's 1681 'Prologue to the University of *Oxford*', where the poet whose 'Loyal Rage' has 'never spar'd the Vices of the Age' finds nothing to raise his 'Spleen' and must therefore 'turn his Satire into Praise'. Sir William Soame's 'To the Author of Sardanapalus' finds that Oldham's 'rude Satires' need some Horatian polish before they can pass for wit.[15] It appears that some aesthetic concern, not simply a lack of classical models to mine, is keeping satire at the margin.

Between Ode and Panegyric, nonetheless, we happen upon a close knot of short poems (159–67) attacking Edward Howard, a writer who did not die until 1712, but who had stopped publishing in 1689, apparently silenced by widespread ridicule. He was also Dryden's brother-in-law, making the inclusion of these funny, easily confident poems, satiric without formal gravity, the more surprising. They are, however, also slightly dated: Waller, whose 'To a Person of Honour: Upon his Incomparable, Incomprehensible Poem' leads the section, had died in 1687, as had the Duke of Buckingham, another contributor; a third, Martin Clifford, had died in 1677. Others were still alive, but this

---

[14] *Examen Poeticum: Being the Third Part of Miscellany Poems* (1693).

[15] *Examen Poeticum*, 99–103, 299–301, 328. Oldham's *Satires upon the Jesuits* (1681) was reprinted extensively after his death in 1683; his *Poems and Translations* (1683) contained original 'satires' and three translated from Horace, Juvenal, and Boileau.

cluster has the look of a cordoned-off exhibit of a literary squabble from a different generation, as if satire was a thing writers used to do to each other.

The next instalment displayed a frontispiece with a central cornucopia of fruit, reminding readers of the potential analogy between 'satura' and 'miscellanea'; but again, the poems themselves discuss satire rather than embody it.[16] In 'To Sir Godfrey Kneller', Dryden writes (of a pun on 'paint', aligning Eve's make-up with Kneller's art): 'Forgive th' allusion; 'twas not meant to bite; / But Satire will have room, where e're I write'; but it does not occupy much room here.[17] Francis Knapp's 'Epistle to Mr. *B—*' is perhaps the only actual satire in the book, and its pose is *against* satire, Mr. B— being dissuaded from engagement against the garret poets of Grub Street: 'why should you spend your time / In Heath'nish Satyr, 'cause a Fool will Rhime?'.[18] Despite this disavowal, the poem could be read as a lampoon against many of the same targets Mr B— might have savaged (only Dryden comes across as the object of literary envy). Sandwiched together between a New Year's Day Ode and a Chorus from Seneca comes a further set of satiric tilts at Howard, two by the Earl of Dorset, another by Edward Ashton (these were also printed in the third edition of *Examen Poeticum*, as if it were hard to position this reclaimed archaeology of wit). The volume closes with Addison's 'An Account of the Greatest English Poets', almost but not quite culminating in Dryden because of his Muse's ability to write in a number of genres, including (in its place) satire: 'If *Satire* or *Heroick Strains* she writes, / Her *Heroe* pleases, and her *Satire* Bites'.[19] This picks up Dryden's own rhyme, just observed, and positions satire not as a moral outburst but as one literary skill counterpoised against another.

The internal balance of the series changes direction after Dryden's death in 1700. *The Fifth Part* was dominated by translations from Ovid's *Metamorphoses*, with a great persistence of amorous elegy and lyric.[20] None of the 132 poems has consistent satiric content. Dorset's 'To the Honourable Mr. E. H. On His Poems' reappears, now on its own, like an apology for absence, except insofar as it introduces newer witty poems by the still-living author. Mulgrave's 'The Rapture' explains that 'Love turns my Satyr into softest Thoughts', a theme repeated in Granville's 'To Myra': instructed by Apollo to rage against women, the poet attempts to 'dip my Pens in Gall', announcing 'Satyr's thy Theam', but fails, betrayed by fondness for women.[21] Walsh's pastoral elegy 'Delia' makes the same point about '*Glycon*, whose Satyr kept the World in Aw', who changed his outlook and output on seeing the lady.[22] Even Granville's 'Cleora', a horrifying tale of a high-grade marriage destroyed by abuse and disease, ends with kinder wishes to the poet's own mistress, as if setting aside satiric vision to pursue amorous ideals. Perhaps Gay's sense that literary *coitus* needs to be *interruptus* by satire was derived from this

---

[16] *The Annual Miscellany: For the Year 1694. Being the Fourth Part of Miscellany Poems* (1694).
[17] *The Annual Miscellany: For the Year 1694*, 93.
[18] *The Annual Miscellany: For the Year 1694*, 266.
[19] *The Annual Miscellany: For the Year 1694*, 325.
[20] *Poetical Miscellanies: The Fifth Part* (1704).
[21] *Poetical Miscellanies: The Fifth Part* (1704), 85, 262.
[22] *Poetical Miscellanies: The Fifth Part* (1704), 614.

explicit softening of a genre normally so antipathetic to women. It continued in *The Sixth Part*, the book that launched the career of the eighteenth century's most famous poetical satirist, Pope.[23] This was (fruitfully for satire elsewhere) bracketed by the rival pastoral sets of Pope and Ambrose Philips, with other contributions interspersed through the text. Pope's Homeric imitation 'The Episode of Sarpedon' counterpoints his Chaucerian comic tale, 'January and May', situated somewhat shockingly after Trapp's paraphrase of Psalm CIV. Pope's fable, while showing hints towards his *Epistle to a Lady* (1735), seems too amused by female sexual misbehaviour to be considered a satire; the same could be said of 'Woman', an anonymous comic tale of sexual infidelity. Anne Finch's 'Adam Pos'd' might constitute an epigrammatic satire on female costume, and a world-weary 'Imitation of the First Satyr of the First Book of *Horace*', by a 'Young Gentleman at *Cambridge*', features between pieces of anaesthetically light social verse. There are no other satires at all: the process that opened with *Absalom and Achitophel* has all but blended satire into a faint spice in the dish.

ALTERNATIVE *MISCELLANIES* (1685–1708)

The Dryden–Tonson series, for all it now appears to exert a powerful canonical force, at once prompted rivals, with similar components and constitution. In her 1685 *Miscellany*, Aphra Behn follows a plangent version of Priam's appeal to Achilles, from the *Iliad*, with 'A Letter from one in the University to his Friend in the Country', a Horatian epistle of dissatisfaction with women.[24] Behn's 'Letter to Mr *Creech* at *Oxford*', a chatty narrative of social observation in a Horatian mode of wry, self-deprecatory, shared comedy that would become very popular in the next century, interrupts (in Gay's terms) a sequence of amorous songs. 'Old England: or New Advice to a Painter', in topical mode, ends another lyric section. Another thin lyric sandwich filling brings us to a riotous 'Description of *Holland*' by Mr. Nevell, and after a similar interval, to Horace, *Odes* III. vi, 'Of the Corrupt, and Degenerate Manners of this Age' (a variant on the Roscommon translation in Dryden's *Miscellany Poems*). Likewise, an 'Oxford' miscellany partly follows Gay's injunction to counterbalance amorous lyric with two updated *Epigrams* of Martial (III. 33 and III. 54), satirizing attempts to live honestly in town, and the narcissism of male fashion, respectively.[25] Versions from Ovid's *Amores* yield to 'Prologue to Perseu's [*sic*] Satyrs Imitated', which appears obliquely to introduce another Martial epigram, VIII. 3, a farewell to writing which concludes with the injunction: 'Do thou with gentile poignant Satyr write, / Such as may please, and heal, as well as bite...'.[26] The invitation is not taken up in the volume itself. Nahum Tate's collection briefly celebrates the satiric

---

[23] *Poetical Miscellanies: The Sixth Part* (1709).
[24] *Miscellany, Being a Collection of Poems by Several Hands* (1685), 41.
[25] *Miscellany Poems and Translation by Oxford Hands* (1685).
[26] *Miscellany Poems and Translation by Oxford Hands* (1685), 161.

vein of 'Wicherly' in Evelyn's 'The Immortality of Poesie' (from Ovid's *Amores*), prompting a version of a Martial epigram and a short literary diatribe, 'To Mr. &c'; but we are soon headed back into familiar amorous territory.[27] A poem on the Exclusion Bill is not a satire but perhaps helps prime us for what comes soon after, 'On the Romantick Office of Credit', a poem on finance presaging major satiric work by Swift and Pope. The 'Miscellany' section of Behn's *Lycidus: or the Lover in Fashion* (1688) opens with 'To a Fair Lady, sent with a Miscellany of Poems', which highlights generic diversity including 'The grinning Satyr, and the smiling Love, / And sure there's something that you may approve' (1). But readers might struggle to find, let alone approve, any 'grinning Satyr' in the actual book; Behn's 'On the Honourable Sir Francis Fane' briefly discusses writing satire well, but in someone else's verse.

These were sizeable books, yielding thin pickings for satire aficionados. In 1692 Charles Gildon struggled to fill a much shorter *Miscellany*, having expected 'several Satyrs for this Collection more than I met with'.[28] Dacier's philological essay was a substitute for activity that did not materialize. (Confusingly, Gildon's own 'Epistle Dedicatory' objected to the supposed misanthropy of Satire, preferring Panegyrics on virtue.) The lead poem, an octosyllabic epistle from Prior to Fleetwood Sheppard, is a catalogue of possible satiric topics which did not have satires attached to them. Gildon did acquire 'The Beginning of the First Satyr of *Persius*' in an updated version of the kind which Dryden's translation was about to render otiose. An imitation of a French satire on women by Tom Brown and 'The Repenting Husband: Or a Satyr upon Marriage', by 'S. W.', together with some crude exchanges about wine and women between Henry and Thomas Cromwell, suggest the effortful maintenance of a fading vein of satiric misogyny.

Some sign, meanwhile, that 'satire' might be worth drawing attention to comes in Lintot's 1702 attempt to camp on Tonson's turf, since its stuffed platter of a title page advertises an actual section of 'Satires and Fables'.[29] These were by a sole unidentified author, and consisted of items such as 'Satire. The Dignity of the Old Poetry, the Degeneracy of the Moderns, for Satire against Lampoon and Flattery'. This meta-Juvenalian rant about the prophetic power of ancient civic satire compared with the 'Lust of Scandal' of the modern lampoon confirms a statement of intent already identified in the previous poem, 'The Introduction', as 'publick Care' and 'Patriot Song'.[30] But the satire section is followed by a tract of Anacreontics and a prairie of inoffensive prose maxims. Lintot hardly followed his own example; his next venture admitted no satire on its title page, though it does contain James Gardiner's 'The Wreck. A Satyr', a gloomy meditation on the shipwrecks of life, and 'A Letter to a Friend...being the Character of a Town Life', ostensibly prompted by satiric feeling.[31]

---

[27] *Poems by Several Hands, and on Several Occasions* (1685), 90–9.
[28] *Miscellany Poems upon Several Occasions* (1692), A7r.
[29] *Examen Miscellaneum. Consisting of Verse and Prose...* (1702), 22–66.
[30] *Examen Miscellaneum. Consisting of Verse and Prose...* (1702), 32, 28.
[31] *Oxford and Cambridge Miscellany Poems* (1708), 309.

POEMS ON SEVERAL OCCASIONS
(1680–1732)

Case's standard bibliography of *Miscellanies* does not yield a great cache of satire-heavy titles.[32] The *Eighteenth Century Short-Title Catalogue* lists well over 1,100 publications with some version of 'miscellaneous' or 'miscellany' in the title between 1680 and 1732; only about forty (roughly one in twenty-eight) of these carry any indication of satirical content. The same period had a cognate formula, *Poems on Several Occasions*, a *Miscellany*-type format for single-authored outputs; an elegant variation on the old posthumous *Works* tradition, it showcased the variety of a writer's talents—their inner several-handedness—not some laborious *respice finem* monument. *ESTC* finds at least 264 items using variants of this between 1680 and 1732 (veiling several *de facto* miscellanies, fruits of considerable hybridization—or miscegenation—between formulae). Only ten of these contain 'satire' as an element of title-page advertising. The 'occasions' that lay behind title pages were 'several' indeed. One writer, the scandalous (and dead) Earl of Rochester, set an unreachable bar for satiric content: his monument was heavily front-loaded with satires showcasing various modes of his opposition to the world.[33] About half the fifty-four poems were in some satiric vein and five of them had the word in the title. Poems of sexual disaster and lyrics intermit, though many of these could be apprehended as satirical too: this was almost *Satires on Several Occasions*.[34] But this was rare: Tonson's edition of 1691 used the same title and retained a few of the satires, but grouped more centrally and in more salubrious, less oppositional company.

Andrew Marvell's posthumous collection (1681) contained in most (censored) copies about 45 poems, none of them labelled 'satire'.[35] It opened with love poems and religious lyrics; then, following 'The Picture of Little *T.C.* in a Prospect of Flowers', comes the lampoon 'Tom May's Death'. The 'Mower' sequence follows with other pastorals, before '*Fleckno*, an English Priest at *Rome*' reopens the satiric vein between Latin epigrams. 'Upon Appleton House' begins a patch of 'state' poems, including 'The Character of *Holland*', a national-interest satire, which however immediately follows a pastoral dialogue. Perhaps, during the Exclusion Crisis which turned Dryden into the state satirist, such items had to be carefully folded into a mix of floral innocence; 'The Loyal Scot', and the 'Instructions to a Painter' series did not appear at all.

Behn's own personal collection of 1684 likewise contained no named satires, though it did feature among the songs and odes 'A Letter to a Brother of the Pen in Tribulation' (a heartless snigger at the expense of Edward Ravenscroft), yet another ironic address

---

[32] Arthur E. Case, *A Bibliography of English Poetical Miscellanies, 1521–1750* (Oxford: Oxford Bibliographical Society, 1935).

[33] *Poems on Several Occasions* (1680).

[34] A book of this title, by 'Porcupinus Pelagius', did actually appear in 1760.

[35] *Miscellaneous Poems* (1681).

'To the Honourable *Edward Howard*', and even the more political 'The Cabal at *Nickey Nackeys*'.[36] It is sometimes assumed that women were excluded from the writing of a genre which demonized them, but Behn and others found ways to pursue it, openly and otherwise: Sarah Fyge, having published *The Female Advocate* (1686) as an 'Answer to a Late Satyr', published one formal 'Satyr against the Muses' alongside other poems of opposition, and Lady Mary Chudleigh, who had responded to an offensive bridal sermon with *The Ladies Advocate* (1701), likewise published a collection angry enough to permit Elizabeth Thomas, in her own satire-inclined volume of 1726, to list 'Satyr' among Chudleigh's talents.[37] It is rather that the *Miscellany* and *Poems on Several Occasions* formulae often quarantined or severely rationed satire, irrespective of gender.

This is not to say that satire was never foregrounded as part of a 'mixed' output, especially amongst older writers. The *Miscellaneous Works* of Charles Sedley, who died in 1701, contained 'Satyrs, Epigrams, Court-Characters, Translations, Essays, and Speeches in Parliament'.[38] Wycherley, alive but rather a relic, published a volume which showcased *Satyrs* first of all.[39] The label was also commonly associated with topical writers outside the Tonson–Dryden fold, such as Edward Ward, 'the satyrical reformer' of *The London Terrae-Filius* (1706). Benjamin Bragge issued *Reflections Moral, Comical, Satyrical, &c, on the Vices and Follies of the Age*, a periodical (1707–8) which advertised for verse contributions. The first three items of Defoe's opportunistic *Collection* of 1703 were poems already published as 'Satyrs'.[40] The *Miscellanies* most occupied by satire were not Tonson's or Lintot's, but those collectively known as *Poems on Affairs of State*, which from 1689 to 1716 reprinted the work of Restoration writers in a certain civic version of 'satire'. Even these rarely put 'satire' on the title page, though outliers to the tradition did.[41]

One publisher who exploited this cultural ambivalence was Edmund Curll, who used *Miscellanies* and the cognate formulae of Tonsonian respectability freely. His title pages were a model of the stuffed platter, though the volumes themselves were often literally stitched together from offprints. Curll understood that 'satire' might be a selling-point *because* it was no longer part of Tonson's genteel collections. His premium classical output was an edition of Petronius's *Satyricon*, repeatedly advertised as 'The SATIRE of T. Petronius Arbiter' (e.g. in his *A Collection of Original Poems*, 1714). His ostensibly Tonsonian editions of Rochester and Roscommon highlighted satiric elements in the

---

[36] *Poems upon Several Occasions; with a Voyage to the Island of Love* (1684).

[37] Fyge Egerton, *Poems on Several Occasions, together with a Pastoral* (London: sold by John Nutt, 1703); Mary Chudleigh, *Poems on Several Occasions* (1703); Elizabeth Thomas, *Poems on Several Occasions* (1726), p. 279.

[38] *Miscellaneous Works of the Honourable Sir Charles Sedley, Bart* (1702).

[39] William Wycherley, *Miscellany Poems: as Satyrs, Epistles, Love-Verses, Songs, Sonnets, &c.* (1704). Pope's early friendship with Wycherley was much occupied with the revisal of the contents of this volume.

[40] *A Collection of the Writings of the Author of the True-Born-English-Man* (1703).

[41] See Matthew Taubman, *Loyal Poems and Satyrs upon the Times* (1685), and Thomas Rogers, *The Loyal and Impartial Satyrist* 'containing eight miscellany poems' (1694). See further Paul Hammond, 'The Restoration Poetic and Dramatic Canon', in *The Cambridge History of the Book in Britain, Volume 4: 1557–1695*, ed. John Barnard and D. F. Mackenzie (Cambridge: Cambridge University Press, 2002), 388–409, and Gillespie and Hammond, 'Introduction', xviii–xix. The Digital Miscellanies Index, http://dmi.bodleian.ox.ac.uk/, provides easy access to 'satire' in Miscellanies from 1680 to 1800.

Restoration canon: twelve of the poems listed in the 1707 contents page have 'satire' in the title, and in the 1709 edition, nine of the first eleven are called satires, with more behind.[42] His first foray into copyright infringement, a collection of Prior, promised 'Odes, Satyrs and Epistles'; it opened with 'A Satyr on the Modern Translators of Ovid's Epistles' and a version of Juvenal subtitled 'A Satyr on the Poets'.[43] Tonson's official edition of 1709 reduced the title to *Poems on Several Occasions*, and declined to identify satire anywhere.

Curll issued *Miscellanies* by many authors, known (Rowe), unknown (Richardson Pack), and fictional ('Joseph Gay'). Some of these, such as Nicholas Amhurst's *Poems on Several Occasions* (1720), were glutted with 'satire' from title page onwards. Latterly, however, the satiric element was less a matter of explicit content than of print-culture orientation, the offensiveness of bookseller against producer, particularly in the case of Swift and Pope. Since 1711 Curll had been somehow acquiring and publishing otherwise hidden work by both in collections like *Letters, Poems and Tales: Amorous, Satyrical, and Gallant* (1718), later incorporated within *A Second Collection of Miscellanies* (1720), with Swift's authorship blazoned on the title page. Pope featured in *Court Poems* (1716), provoking the famous emetic, *State Poems* (1716) and *Pope's Miscellany* (1717), mocking his efforts to retain control. Matters escalated in the late 1720s; prison notwithstanding, Curll issued *The Altar of Love* (1727) in an absurd variety of cobbled-together manifestations, with the 'Atticus' portrait (Pope's character-demolition of Addison, later incorporated as a satiric hotspot in the *Epistle to Dr Arbuthnot*) among its offensive contents, together with a protest against Pope's vindictiveness.[44] Curll also began a series of *Miscellanea* (1727, dated 1726), the first of which led with Pope's occasionally embarrassing letters to Henry Cromwell, and the 'Atticus' portrait, now labelled 'Satire'. (The second volume included Pope's 'Verses' on Lintot, for Curll an easy satiric dig at a rival.) These items were marketable items of Pope's skill in satiric portrait, witnesses to his personal spite, and signs of the publisher's power over authors. One answer to this multivalent offence was satire: *The Dunciad* came out a year later; the other answer was the Pope–Swift *Miscellanies*.

POPE AND SWIFT IN THE *MISCELLANIES* (1709–1732)

Though thirteen of Pope's first twenty-two published poems appeared in *Miscellanies*, Pope was always disrespectful of the form, elaborately comparing his entry into publication to an obituary in the 'Ordinary of Newgate's Miscellanies' (the chaplain's report on

[42] *The Works of the Right Honourable the late Earls of Rochester and Roscommon*, 2nd edn. (London: for Edmund Curll, 1707); 3rd edn., 2 vols. (1709).

[43] *Poems on Several Occasions: Consisting of Odes, Satyrs and Epistles* (1707).

[44] *Altar of Love* (1727), 90–4; Barbara M. Benedict, *Making the Modern Reader: Cultural Mediation in Early Modern Literary Anthologies* (Princeton: Princeton University Press, 1996), 123–4.

executed criminals).[45] Pope also asserted that *Miscellanies* were outlets for those who write 'for diversion only... *Versifiers* and *witty Men*, rather than... *Poets*'.[46] Wycherley, echoing this scepticism, assured Pope that 'the Salt of your Wit has been enough to give a relish to the whole insipid Hotch-Potch' (i.e. Tonson's 1709 *Poetical Miscellanies*), returning metaphor to the original dietary focus.[47] The poems addressed to Lintot by Gay and Pope in *Miscellaneous Poems and Translations* (1712) constituted, similarly, a necessary satiric twist, a sceptical inflection, in an otherwise too-polite assemblage.[48] Pope's contributions move from epic ('The First Book of Statius his Thebais') to mock-epic ('The Rape of the Locke') via the proto-satiric 'On Silence', an attack on Eusden, and the 'Lintot' verses, suggesting a satire-inclined trajectory within the book.[49] Work by Pope was included, less happily, in Steele's *Poetical Miscellanies*, published by Tonson in late 1713 (dated 1714), an uncomfortable attempt to extend the Tonson–Dryden series which more or less eschewed verse satire completely.[50] Steele's 'Dedication' to Congreve prioritizes polite wit above 'sallies' of imagination; in identifying Congreve's comic fable 'Doris' as the proper mode of 'Satyr', Steele gives one of the few instances of the word in the volume, and then includes nothing that matches it. Eusden's 'To the Author of the Tatlers' (251) sees Steele's periodical (under its Juvenalian motto) as having adapted satire for a modern society, and the sequence of polite addresses to women, laments over amorous failure, and occasional stern injunctions from Lucan (not Horace or Juvenal), suggests a deliberate evasion of something; a number of smart epigrams perhaps recall satire in miniature. Pope's own contributions move from 'The Wife of Bath her Prologue, from Chaucer', which might, like 'January and May', be considered satiric were it less tolerant in tone, and a multi-handed spoof Prologue on the butt of the wits, Tom D'Urfey, to completely sober translations from the *Odyssey*, reversing the sequence of 1712.

Lintot published Pope's monumentalist *Works* in 1717; following Congreve's *Works* (published by Tonson in 1710), it ends with a section of 'Miscellanies', but these display little satiric instinct. An edited collection published covertly (by Lintot) in the same year, as *Poems on Several Occasions*, has much comic fable, familiar epistle, and smart epigram, in the approved proportions, but nothing unmistakably satiric, Broome's 'Poverty and Poetry' perhaps coming closest.[51] Writing to Broome on 25 May 1725, Pope disparages again the company one keeps in a multi-author *Miscellany*, offering to help

---

[45] Pope to Cromwell, 1 November 1708, and cf. to Cromwell, 7 May 1709; to Wycherley, 20 May 1709; Pope, *Correspondence* (Sherburn), i. 51–2, 56, 60.

[46] To Cromwell, 17 December 1710; Pope, *Correspondence* (Sherburn), i. 110.

[47] Wycherley to Pope, 26 May 1709; Pope, *Correspondence* (Sherburn), i. 62.

[48] For the genesis of the poems see Pope to Cromwell, 12 November and 21 December 1711; Pope, *Correspondence* (Sherburn), i. 136 and 138.

[49] See James McLaverty, *Pope, Print and Meaning* (Oxford: Oxford University Press, 2001), 12–21; Benedict, *Making the Modern Reader*, 129–37.

[50] For a fuller reading see Benedict, *Making the Modern Reader*, 119–23.

[51] See *Pope's Own Miscellany*, ed. Norman Ault (London: Nonesuch, 1935).

him compile a single-author version.[52] By the time Curll had given him and Swift sufficient provocation, he had developed that idea into a collaborative entity. In a well-known letter to Swift of *c.* 17 February 1727 he declares himself:

> prodigiously pleas'd with this joint-volume, in which methinks we look like friends, side by side, serious and merry by turns, conversing interchangeably…not in the stiff forms of learned Authors, flattering each other, and setting the rest of mankind at nought: but in a free, un-important, natural, easy manner; diverting others just as we diverted ourselves.

Despite scepticism ('There's no end of making Books, Solomon said, and above all of making Miscellanies, which all men can make') Pope maintains that in their case, the 'character in every piece, like the mark of the Elect' preserves their efforts as individual yet connected, an elite contrapuntal duet for the reader to savour.[53]

A model privileging mutually sympathetic authors rather than the agenda of book-sellers no doubt had attractions for Swift. Their title probably recalled William King's, which consisted largely of previously published satires on Whig worthies, and a mock-heroic, *The Furmetary*. Swift had also authorized a covert *Miscellanies*, against Curll's, in 1711.[54] An unauthorized version of the formula coupling Swift with Addison had then appeared in Dublin, so they were once more reclaiming it for authorized use.[55] They put their names only to a 'Preface' of worked-up outrage (quite different from Pope's sunny letter to Swift) against the incursions of Curll into their property and lives.[56] A kind of monumentality incorporates the rough and tumble of literary life. In a high-octane ful-mination of the old excuse, they find themselves obliged to provide texts of these pieces against the crimes of booksellers, even though some represent regrettable 'Sallies of Levity'. Additionally, they apologize 'for the Satire interspersed in some of these Pieces, upon a few People, from whom the highest Provocations have been received'.[57] Publication of these aggressive items is defended in terms prefiguring the elaborations of *The Dunciad Variorum*—while also prompting readers to seek out the pleasures of 'Satire interspersed'.

---

[52] Pope, *Correspondence* (Sherburn), ii. 295.

[53] Pope, *Correspondence* (Sherburn), ii. 426. See Alexander Pettit, 'Introduction', in *Miscellanies in Prose and Verse by Pope, Swift and Gay*, 4 vols. (London: Pickering & Chatto, 2002), I. ix–xviii, for a reading of this letter, and the planning of the volumes; for the sequencing, see Benedict, *Making the Modern Reader*, 139–52, and Bullard, 'Digital Editing', 71–4; Marshall, *Practice of Satire*, 215–17, argues against the 'Scriblerian' coherence of the project.

[54] William King, *Miscellanies in Prose and Verse* (1709); Jonathan Swift, *Miscellanies in Prose and Verse* (1711).

[55] *Miscellanies in Prose and Verse* (1721).

[56] *Miscellanies in Prose and Verse: The First Volume* (1727), 3–16. Motte was very much a subordinate agent.

[57] *Miscellanies in Prose and Verse: The First Volume* (1727), 7, 10.

Against the backdrop of a large-scale sequence that was to run from *Gulliver's Travels* to *The Dunciad* and *The Beggar's Opera*, what is the mix of satiric elements in these *Miscellanies*? The first consists of prose by Swift, opening with sober texts on politics and church government. The *Argument against Abolishing Christianity* which follows is a satire, in Swift's complex-persona, paradox mode; it gives place to *A Project for the Advancement of Religion*, which sounds similar but which, having promised to avoid 'Exaggeration or Satyr' proceeds to propose social regulation in a straightforward way.[58] *A Letter on the Sacramental Test* follows in like mode; then, with no change of beat, comes 'A Tritical Essay up on the Faculties of the Mind', and a raft of Bickerstaff papers from 1708–9, recalling one of Swift's best-known satiric hoaxes. *A Proposal for Correcting the English Tongue* is not the mock-projector fantasy a new reader might suppose but another regulatory effort from 1712, with the grouchily reformative 'Letter to a Young Gentleman' of 1720 behind it. The volume closes with a nosegay of 'Thoughts on Various Subjects', including one detached observation on Satire and Wit in 'very bad Times'.[59] The result of these juxtapositions might be to reposition Swift the bitter satirist of 1726 as Swift the serious reformer who had been creatively vexing the world since 1708: satire is not some viral infection of public discourse, still less simple misanthropy, but the witty end of a full spectrum of public interest, above the generic limitations that 'satire' imposes.

The second volume, in contrast, interweaves political satires of various authorship from the Utrecht period with recent items.[60] Arbuthnot's *Law is a Bottomless Pit* (1712), a Tory view of the politics of the War of Spanish Succession, occupies the first 218 pages (of 358). 'Satire' is not mentioned; rather, Pope obliquely bolts on to it his own double-bluff squib of 1715, *A Key to the Lock*, written in the persona of a zealous Whig, on the lookout for Jacobite allegory. 'Esdras Barnivelt' immediately identifies Pope's *Rape of the Lock* as a satire—not on social frippery or female foibles but on the Barrier Treaty, the subject of an obsessively misread 'key' of the sort which Curll had published to Arbuthnot's obviously political text. Barnivelt uses the word 'satire' at least nine times, in an increasingly complex game, the point of which is that victims *find* satire, and in so doing satirize themselves. Three further squibs of Swift from the pre-Utrecht period are then inserted, including 'A Meditation on a Broomstick', one of the parodies in Curll's *Miscellanies by Dr Swift* (1711). Abruptly, the mode switches to recent work such as 'Memoirs of P.P.' and 'Stradling v. Stiles' before Arbuthnot's *Art of Political Lying* takes us back to 1712 and the projected hack of that period. In the run-up to his own great satiric offence, *The Dunciad*, it was perhaps useful to remind readers of the continuities of wit between two epochs.

In March 1728, another disparate volume emerged in time to stir things up for *The Dunciad*.[61] It opens with *Peri Bathous*, a satiric miscellany in itself, inverting the regulatory

---

[58] *Miscellanies in Prose and Verse: The First Volume* (1727), 173.

[59] *Miscellanies in Prose and Verse: The First Volume* (1727), 398–9.

[60] *Miscellanies. The Second Volume* (1727).

[61] *Miscellanies. The Last Volume* (1727 [1728]). *The Dunciad*, originally planned for the *Last* volume, came out *c.* 18 May.

grammar of Whiggish *artes poeticae* through an anthology of self-satirizing howlers by several hands—the Dunces to be. (It also includes a section on how to do satire for those instinctively unsure.) Some seventy-four poems follow in groups alternately by Swift, Pope, and latterly Gay; having passed the 'bathos' test, they display wit on several occasions. *Cadenus and Vanessa* is a gravitational centre for Swift's poems about witty (and non-witty) women. Pope answers with some anti-lyrics, and fragments of what would become the *Epistle to a Lady*; he allows himself a smutty lampoon against Lady Mary's lampoons. 'Horace *Lib.* 2 *Sat.* 6 Part of it Imitated' (33–41), is the closest to a formal satire in the volume: a wry take on troubles in his days of service to Harley, Swift had said in 1714 the poem would 'serve in some scurvy Miscellany', but this higher-level manifestation was its first.[62] The most obviously satirical section (105–41) is Pope's, pointedly introduced by his 'Verses' to Lintot, now finally in his own author-centred *Miscellany*. 'Macer' attacks Ambrose Philips for soliciting contributions to a miscellany; 'Umbra' mocks Addison's cousin Eustace Budgell; 'Fragment of a Satire' reclaims the 'Atticus' portrait from Curll. After this any principle of selection gives way to witty abundance: epigrams on musical squabbles, the fate of Europe, women who wet themselves at Addison's *Cato*, verses against William Wood, ballads on the South Sea, pseudo-Ovidian epistles from Glumdalclitch and Gulliver's wife, which though plaintive, remind readers of the presence of *Gulliver's Travels* while leavening the tone. There is no settled ethos to this ludic exuberance: the poems contain strokes of satire as they contain strokes of art, but satire is everywhere and nowhere, implicitly one of their talents but too limiting a category to adopt. Almost the only direct mention of satire comes in the last but one poem, Swift's 'To Stella, who Collected and Transcribed his Poems' (290): having dispatched the kind of women (like Elizabeth Thomas) who constitute 'the Goddesses enroll'd / In *Curll*'s Collections, new and old', Swift reminds her that 'True Poets' are 'Lords of Infamy and Praise': 'They are not scurrilous in Satire, / Nor will in Panegyrick flatter'. The adopted position of superiority is ironized by the comic rhyme on 'satire', an absurdly reductive but typical category subversion.

The *Miscellanies* generated their own controversy even before *The Dunciad*.[63] The final volume, in the aftermath, came in 1732.[64] This contained nearly twenty prose pieces, with a separate block of poems which could be transplanted into 'Volume the Last', with *Peri Bathous* extracted thence and bound in to this 'prose' volume—a sort of dignified customization of Curll's stitching frenzies for those who liked their *Miscellanies* less miscellaneous. Pope retrieves his Grub Street reports against Dennis (1713) and Curll (1716) alongside contemporary Scriblerian fantasy-learning spoofs ('Annus Mirabilis', 'The Origine of Sciences'). Nothing prepares readers for the arrival of *A Modest Proposal*, though the short essays that follow are more sober than what precedes. The prose concludes with 'A True and Faithful Narrative . . .', a gibe at both Whiston's scientific lectures and a public whose moral alarm at the effects of a threatened comet fade rapidly away once the danger has passed, rather in the manner of the salutary effects of satire.

---

[62] Swift to Charles Ford, 3 August 1714; Swift, *Correspondence* (Woolley), ii. 45.
[63] *The Twickenham Hotch-Potch* (1728).   [64] *Miscellanies. The Third Volume* (1732).

The poem section opens with Swift's 'The Journal of a Modern Lady', which rhymes 'Satyre' with 'Woman-Hater' to ironize his reputation in that mode. The last, Swift's 'To Doctor D-l—y on the Libels Writ against him', recalls Gay's ironic association of satire with scandal:

> Would Men of Genius cease to write,
> The Rogues must die for Want of Spight,
> Must die for Want of Food and Rayment,
> If Scandal did not find them Payment.
> How cheerfully the Hawkers cry
> A Satyr, and the Gentry buy!
>
> (95)

Satire, so far as it can be expressly countenanced, is for Rogues, not Men of Genius. Almost the concluding words of the enterprise are Swift's own offhand dismissal of generic effect: 'On me, when Dunces are satyrick, / I take it for a Panegyrick' (100).

Such deadpan rhetoric, coming from the author of *A Modest Proposal*, has a twistedly ironic or meta-satiric relation to Swift's overall output, of course, and yet reminds us that he and Pope hardly ever used the formal generic labels of satire. If Tonson's *Miscellanies* had immunized readers against satire, and Curll's had cheapened the currency of both the format and the genre, the author-collective *Miscellanies* of Pope and Swift constituted, across their own formal diversity, a richer, multi-modal feast; perhaps the nearest thing to a *lanx* in which the mix could be *satura* in the old sense, but too restlessly witty to be only that in the modern, except insofar as productive variety was a rebuke to those several hands offensively catalogued in *The Dunciad*.

SELECT BIBLIOGRAPHY

Barnard, John. 'Creating an English Literary Canon, 1679–1720: Jacob Tonson, Dryden and Congreve', in *Literary Cultures and the Material Book*, ed. Simon Eliot, Andrew Nash, and Ian Willison (London: British Library, 2007), 307–21.

Benedict, Barbara M. *Making the Modern Reader: Cultural Mediation in Early Modern Literary Anthologies* (Princeton: Princeton University Press, 1996).

Benedict, Barbara M. 'The Eighteenth-Century Anthology and the Construction of the Expert Reader', *Poetics* 28 (2001), 377–97.

Bullard, Paddy. 'Digital Editing and the Eighteenth-Century Text: Works, Archives, and Miscellanies', *Eighteenth-Century Life* 36 (2012), 57–80.

Case, A. E. *A Bibliography of English Poetical Miscellanies, 1521–1750* (Oxford: Oxford Bibliographical Society, 1935).

deForest Lord, George, et al., eds. *Poems on Affairs of State: Augustan Satirical Verse, 1660–1714*, 7 vols. (New Haven: Yale University Press, 1963–75).

Gillespie, Stuart and David Hopkins. 'Introduction', in *The Dryden–Tonson Miscellanies, 1684–1709: With a New Introduction, Biographical Directory, and Reader's Guides*, ed. Gillespie and Hopkins, 6 vols. (London: Routledge, 2008), I. xv–lxix.

Hammond, Paul. 'The Restoration Poetic and Dramatic Canon', in *The Cambridge History of the Book in Britain, Volume 4: 1557–1695*, ed. John Barnard and D. F. Mackenzie (Cambridge: Cambridge University Press, 2002), 388–409.

McLaverty, James. *Pope, Print and Meaning* (Oxford: Oxford University Press, 2001).

Marshall, Ashley. *The Practice of Satire in England, 1658–1770* (Baltimore: Johns Hopkins University Press, 2013).

Pettit, Alexander. 'Introduction', in *Miscellanies in Prose and Verse by Pope, Swift and Gay*, ed. Pettit, 4 vols. (London: Pickering & Chatto, 2002), I. ix–xviii.

CHAPTER 16

FABLE AND ALLEGORY

GILLIAN WRIGHT

> Weary, at last, of the Pindarick way,
> Thro' which advent'rously the Muse wou'd stray;
> To Fable I descend with soft Delight,
> Pleas'd to Translate, or easily Endite:
> Anne Finch, 'The Critick and the Writer of Fables'[1]

AT the heart of Anne Finch's 'The Critick and the Writer of Fables', published in 1713, is a generic disagreement. For Finch's speaker, the Fable-writer, fable is a modest but quietly satisfying poetic genre. Though the 'aery Fictions' (5) of fable may lack the prestige of 'Pindarick', they are pleasantly accessible for the poet, while also, through their didactic use of 'Birds and Beasts' (7), fulfilling the traditional humanist imperative that poetry should both 'Teach' and 'Divert' (8). To the Fable-writer's interlocutor, the 'Critick', however, fables are merely 'childish Tales', which, despite their current popularity, will never enable their author to 'purchase Fame' (13). Rather than wasting her time with such a trifling genre, the Critick advises, the Fable-writer should instead try her hand at a more worthwhile and efficacious form, satire:

> But urge thy Pen, if thou wou'd'st move our Thoughts,
> To shew us private, or the publick Faults.
> Display the Times, High-Church or Low provoke;
> We'll praise the Weapon, as we like the Stroke,
> And warmly sympathizing with the Spite
> Apply to Thousands, what of One you write.
> 'The Critick and the Writer of Fables', lines 45–50

I am grateful to Tom Lockwood and Kathleen Taylor for advice on earlier drafts of this essay. I am also indebted to Jennie Challinor for discussions about Aphra Behn and to Valerie Rumbold for advice about Gay and Swift.

[1] Anne Finch, *Miscellany Poems* (1713), 162. Italic and block capitals have been normalized to roman in this and other quotations from early modern texts in this essay.

The 'harmless Fable-writer' (52), however, rejects this advice as narrow and ungenerous. Not only, in her view, is the 'single Stream' (51) of satire insufficient to satisfy either readers or writers, but the literary tastes to which it appeals are mean-spirited and grudging; contemporary critics, she notes, are sparing in their praise even for satirists (56–8). While Finch's Fable-writer does not repudiate satire out of hand, its place within her own more liberal conception of literature is evidently both limited and marginal. To be a fable-writer, for Finch, is to distance oneself from satire.

Finch's hostility to satire in 'The Critick and the Writer of Fables' is consonant with her professed literary values elsewhere in her writing. In the preface to an early manuscript, drafted in the mid-1690s, she had denounced 'Lampoons, and all sorts of abusive Verses' for their 'underhand dealing, and uncharitablenesse', insisting that 'I never suffer'd my small talent, to be that way employ'd'.[2] Yet the opposition between fable and satire implied in 'The Critick and the Writer of Fables' is disingenuous, given that fable itself can be satirical; indeed, 'The Critick and the Writer of Fables' is itself both a fable (in the sense of a 'short story devised to convey some useful lesson') and a satire (on contemporary literary fashions).[3] In practice, what seems to have attracted Finch to fable—her favoured poetic form—was not its divergence from satire, but rather the kind(s) of satire which it facilitated. The allegorical mode of fable enabled Finch to denounce both 'private' and 'publick Faults', while steering clear of the personal vindictiveness she detested. Her fables, while lacking overt 'Spite' against named individuals, are unrelenting in their condemnation of human failings and political error.

Finch is one of several satirical English fable-writers who emerged in the late 1680s and early 1690s. The year 1687 saw the publication of two important fabular publications: Francis Barlow's Æsop's Fables, incorporating English poetry by Aphra Behn, and John Dryden's pro-Catholic apologia, The Hind and the Panther. Finch's own earliest fable survives in a manuscript begun around 1690, while Roger L'Estrange's Fables of Æsop, which includes 500 fables, was published in 1692; an enlarged edition, including 260 further fables, appeared in 1699.[4] Early eighteenth-century fable-writers included Bernard Mandeville, Samuel Croxall, and John Gay, as well as Finch.[5] Such late seventeenth- and early eighteenth-century fables differed greatly in matters as important as form, originality, length, number, and literary source. What many had in common, however, was a distinctly satirical focus. A high proportion of these satirical fables, furthermore, deployed the resources of the genre for overtly royalist, pro-Stuart ends.

By the seventeenth century, fable was already well-established as a didactic mode deemed suitable for children (hence the Critick's 'childish Tales'). Any account of late seventeenth- and early eighteenth-century fables needs to consider both why fable emerged as an important satirical genre in this period and also why it appealed so much to pro-Stuart, later Jacobite, writers. In Fables of Power, Annabel Patterson argues that

---

[2] Anne Finch, Folger MS N.b.3, fols. 8v–9r.   [3] OED, 'fable'.
[4] Roger L'Estrange, Fables of Æsop and other Eminent Mythologists (1692); 2 vols. (1699).
[5] Bernard Mandeville, The Grumbling Hive (1705), later incorporated into The Fable of the Bees (1714); Samuel Croxall, Fables of Æsop and Others (1722); John Gay, Fables (1727) and Fables. By the late Mr Gay. Volume the Second (1738).

fables' typical concern with unequal power relations renders them generically amenable to political appropriation, but also notes that this does not necessarily predetermine the ideology of the genre. As she points out, while political fables were far from new in the 1680s, earlier fables were as likely to question as they were to endorse traditional authorities.[6] (Spenser's *Mother Hubberds Tale*, which queries the authority of the sleeping lion, is a case in point.) Even John Ogilby's *The Fables of Æsop*, first published in 1651 and often regarded as a royalist work, includes some less than flattering comments about kings: his fable 75, 'Of the Cat and the Mice', warns against jealous monarchs who renege on their promises 'for small cause', while fable 23, 'Of the Lyon grown old', blames civil conflict on weak kings who allow their 'active Subjects' too much power.[7] One reason for the popularity of fable in the late seventeenth century may in fact be the availability of generic models in the 1680s. Ogilby's *Fables*, reissued in 1665, 1668, 1675, and 1683, and supplemented by his *Æsopics* in 1668, 1673, 1675, and 1684, kept the genre in the public domain; so too did the reprinting of *Mother Hubberds Tale* in the Spenser folio of 1679 and the publication of Jean de la Fontaine's *Fables* in France between 1668 and 1694.[8] Fables would thus have appealed both to writers with an interest in English literary history and those attracted by the modishness of La Fontaine's French—as well as, of course, to those who looked back still further to the genre's classical roots. Assessing why fables held such particular attraction for English Jacobites in this period is one of the key objectives of this essay.

My discussion of the late seventeenth- and early eighteenth-century fable focuses on three of the most innovative and diverse practitioners of the genre: Aphra Behn, John Dryden, and Anne Finch. While Behn, Dryden, and Finch have much in common, including their shared loyalty to James II and opposition to the 1688 Revolution, their fables, collectively, encompass a wide variety of forms, sources, and circulation contexts; they also respond to different political moments (and/or differently to the same political moment). Behn's 110 fables, for instance, adhere to a strict six-line format and are based on predetermined, mainly Aesopian models, while Dryden's highly original and intricately structured *The Hind and the Panther* runs to some 2,600 lines and draws on a wide range of literary and theological sources. Finch falls between Behn and Dryden in respect of length and number: nearly 40 of her poems, ranging from 19 to 103 lines in length ('The Battle Between the Rats and the Weazles'; 'A Tale of the Miser and the Poet'), can be classified as fables, and many others include fabular elements. She also differs from both Behn and Dryden in the length of her engagement with fable, which lasted from the late 1680s or early 1690s until at least 1717. Fable, for Finch, proved both powerful and flexible enough to accommodate events from the immediate aftermath of the Revolution through to the early Hanoverian era.

---

[6] Annabel Patterson, *Fables of Power: Aesopian Writing and Political History* (Durham, NC: Duke University Press, 1991), 15, 52, 75.

[7] John Ogilby, *The Fables of Æsop Paraphras'd in Verse* (1651), sigs. Gggg1r, B1v. On Ogilby's royalism, see Patterson, *Fables of Power*, 86–7.

[8] On La Fontaine, see Jayne Elizabeth Lewis, *The English Fable: Aesop and Literary Culture, 1651–1740* (Cambridge: Cambridge University Press, 1996), 135–8.

Further questions raised by the popularity of fables include whether fable-writers saw the form as a corrective or merely a diagnostic genre, and why—in an age when relatively few women wrote satire—fable seems to have been especially accessible to female writers.[9] To begin answering these questions, I turn first to one of the first satirical fable-writers of the period, Aphra Behn.

APHRA BEHN, *ÆSOP'S FABLES* (1687)

Aphra Behn is unusual among late seventeenth-century fable-writers in several respects. Unlike most fable-writers, including both Dryden and Finch, Behn seems to have had no role in determining such key matters as the topics, length, and structure of her fables. This lack of choice is a direct consequence of the complex history of the volume in which her work first appeared, *Æsop's Fables with his Life: in English, French and Latin*.[10] A first edition of this collection, designed and illustrated by the painter Francis Barlow, had been published in 1666. As its title suggests, *Æsop's Fables* is a polyglot edition: including, for each fable, French and Latin texts by Robert Codrington as well as an English poem by Thomas Philipot and an illustration by Barlow.[11] Each fable fits on to a single opening and follows a near-identical format, with the French on the left (the verso) and the remaining elements on the right (the recto). By far the smallest of these elements is the English poem which is squeezed into two columns between Barlow's illustration and Codrington's Latin. Ranging in length from six to sixteen lines, Philipot's poems are each structurally divided into a main text and a moral.

Barlow's revised edition of 1687 retains much of the format of 1666, while incorporating several new and revised elements. The former include a new prefatory letter addressed to William Cavendish, Earl of Devonshire; the latter include revised versions of the French and Latin texts. Barlow's illustrations to the fables, with a few minor exceptions, remain as before, as does the elaborate *mise-en-page*. The English texts supplied by Behn, replacing Philipot's, fall variously on the spectrum between new and revised material. Some, such as fable XXI ('The Cat and Mice'), XXXVI ('Jupiter and the Frogs'), and XXXVIII ('The Lion and Bear') reuse wording from Philipot, albeit with variations. Others, such as fable XX ('The Fox and Cat') and XXVIII ('The Ape and Fox') have been almost completely altered in Behn's version. Convergence is most common in the concluding moral, which generally comprises two lines in both versions. In the main texts, where Behn frequently had to recast some 10–14 of Philipot's lines into just four, differences tend to be greater. The consistent 4-plus-2 line structure of Behn's fables probably

---

[9] On women and satire, see Ashley Marshall, *The Practice of Satire in England, 1658–1770* (Baltimore: Johns Hopkins University Press, 2013), 28.

[10] On *Æsop's Fables*, see further Edward Hodnett, *Francis Barlow: First Master of English Book Illustration* (London: Scolar Press, 1978), 167–96, 206–20, and Janet Todd, ed., *The Works of Aphra Behn*, vol. 1: *Poetry* (London: Pickering & Chatto, 1992), 427–9 (hereafter cited as 'Todd').

[11] Hodnett, *Francis Barlow*, 167; *ODNB*, 'Thomas Philipot'.

formed part of her commission from Barlow, and was no doubt designed to fill a restricted space more uniformly than had Philipot in 1666.

The 1687 edition of *Æsop's Fables* has mixed political affiliations. Cavendish, Barlow's dedicatee, was a Whig who had supported Exclusion in the early 1680s, while Barlow himself had produced Whig propaganda during the Popish plot of 1679.[12] Behn, by contrast, was a confirmed Tory, who had published a pindaric celebrating James II's coronation in 1685.[13] Quite how Behn became involved in *Æsop's Fables* is not known: Edward Hodnett's suggestion that the crispness of her verse may have recommended her to Barlow is plausible, but does not account for the two collaborators' marked political differences.[14] Behn's choice to work with Barlow is easier to explain: the 1680s were a financially difficult time for her, and the chance of paid work was probably not to be declined.[15] She may also have relished the opportunity to infiltrate Tory ideas into an otherwise Whig-identified volume.

By no means all Behn's fabular contributions to Barlow's *Aesop* are explicitly political. Many of her fables confine themselves to issues of morality and human nature, often to only mildly satirical effect. Thus, for instance, the moral of her opening fable compares the Cock, who prefers a barley corn to a jewel because the latter is inedible, to a 'noysy fopling' who cares only for 'Gay nonsense' rather than 'the noblest Arts and Sciences'.[16] Others revise Philipot's conventional morality in a manner reminiscent of Behn's own comedies, favouring young rather than aged lovers and attractive women over their would-be seducers (Fable XXIX and Fable XCIII). Her version of Fable XCVI, 'The Man and his Goose', retains Philipot's warning against greed but changes his gloss on the goose's eggs as 'golden excrement' to 'golden ore' and omits his concluding advice to 'retrench' one's desires.[17] Satire against the greedy may have been unavoidable in 'The Man and his Goose', but the puritanical overtones of Philipot's morals were not.

Interspersed among Behn's fables, however, are many with unmistakably political applications. Several of these, for instance, favour the wisdom of the elite few over the folly of the many. In 'The Swallow and other Birds', though the percipient Swallow realizes the danger posed by the 'pernicious Hempseed' sown by the Clown, her fellow-birds are too slow and neglectful to prevent its growth (Fable XVIII). In other fables, Behn's revisions to Philipot mock the seditious tendencies of the common people. The moral of 'The Bear and Bee-hives', in Philipot directed against 'pettier Princes', is reapplied by Behn to 'petty tumults by the Rout', while a generalized moral about ingratitude in Philipot's version of 'The Wood and Clown' is given a more explicitly political focus in Behn's condemnation of 'Ungratfull People' who 'given some liberties rebell for all' (Fable LXXXVI and Fable XCVIII). Similarly, 'The Horse and Hart', also subject to a general moral application in Philipot, becomes more explicitly political in Behn:

---

[12] *ODNB*, 'William Cavendish, First Duke of Devonshire' and 'Francis Barlow'.
[13] Aphra Behn, *A Pindarick Poem on the Happy Coronation of His most Sacred Majesty James II* (1685).
[14] Hodnett, *Francis Barlow*, 208.   [15] Todd, xx–xxi.
[16] Behn, 'Fable I', in Barlow, ed. and illustr., *Æsop's Fables* (1687). Behn's fables are hereafter, where possible, cited parenthetically in the main text.
[17] Fable numbers for Philipot's poems are identical to Behn's and are not cited separately.

'He who by th'Rables power a Crowne does weare / May be a King, but is a Slave to feare' (Fable XCIV). The 'Rable', by implication, are not just rebellious, they are also danger-ously inconstant.

As 'The Horse and Hart' indicates, Behn's political satire in *Æsop's Fables* applies not just to groups but also to individuals. In some cases, though probably not 'The Horse and Hart', the target of her derision seems likely to be the Duke of Monmouth, whose rebellion in 1685 would still have been a comparatively recent memory two years later. Janet Todd detects references to Monmouth in the morals of 'The Kite, Frog, and Mouse' ('The fond aspiring youth who empire sought / By dire ambition was to ruine brought'), 'The Sick Lion' ('Twas fair pretences rais'd the western warr'), and 'The Dog and Piece of Flesh' ('So fancy'd Crownes led the young warriour on').[18] She also suspects an allu-sion to Monmouth's erstwhile ally, the Earl of Shaftesbury, in Behn's moral to 'The Ass in a Lion's Skin': 'A hott braind Statesman once sett up for wise, / But knave, and foole was plaine thro the disguise'.[19] Though several of Behn's earlier poems, such as the song 'When Jemmy first began to Love' (1672), hint at a fascination with Monmouth, her response to his rebellion—and to rebels more generally—is sternly punitive. Her moral to 'The Countryman and Snake' warns that 'Mercy extended to ungratfull men / Does but impower em to rebell agen', while 'The Young Man and his Cat' concludes, 'Ill prin-ciples no mercy can reclaime, / And once a Rebell still will be the same' (Fable L and Fable LXXI). Fellow-travellers and protagonists are held equally culpable: the moral to 'The Stork and Geese' declares categorically that 'He that adheres but to a villainie, / (As well as he that acts) deserves to dye' (Fable LVI). Philipot's moral to the same fable advises the reader merely to 'Shun Impious men lest thee som fate inwrap / And mix wth them in ye same dire mishap'.

Behn's tough-minded approach to her fabular commission is perhaps most obvious in her adaptation of Fable XXXIV, 'The Wind and the Sun', and in her two consecutive versions of 'The Lyon and Mouse' (Fables XXIII and XXIV). Her rendering of 'The Wind and the Sun', unusually, is less political than Philipot's. Whereas his moral recom-mends securing political stability through gentle measures ('Empires by mildness still have longer stood / Then by ye rough support of force & blood'), Behn restricts hers to the individual: 'In every passion moderation chuse, / For all extreames doe bad effects produce'. Forced by the fixed structure of *Æsop's Fables* to produce a version of 'The Wind and the Sun' but evidently eschewing Philipot's advocacy of governmental 'mild-ness', Behn responds by depoliticizing the fable. More characteristically, her two versions of 'The Lyon and Mouse' are more overtly political than Philipot's: the fabular animals, merely a 'Lion' and a 'kinde Mouse' in Philipot, become in Behn's Fable XXIII a 'Royall Beast' and a 'kind humble Mouse', while the latter's rescue of the Lion from a snare is likened to the Oak that saved Charles II after the Battle of Worcester. Tellingly, however, Behn's Mouse, a model subject in Fable XXIII, suffers a swift reversal of fortune in Fable XXIV: 'fild with pride' on account of his 'late service', he demands to marry the Lion's daughter, but quickly suffers his comeuppance when she accidentally kills him.

---

[18] Fable XXXV, Fable LI, and Fable LXXX; Todd, 430–1.   [19] Fable LXXII; Todd, 431.

Even model subjects, in Behn's view, are liable to succumb to hubris, and need to remember to know their place.

Behn's contributions to *Æsop's Fables* represent a canny response to what must have been a challenging commission. Unlike Roger L'Estrange, whose 'reflexions' in his *Fables of Aesop* press the Jacobite case so frequently as to risk wearying the reader, Behn wisely rang the changes, mixing political with non-political morals and including moments of sex and humour. While she cannot have hoped to conceal her political agenda from Barlow, it may have been to her advantage that the topical references in her fables were so clearly backward-looking, condemning a rebellion—Monmouth's—that had already been defeated and punished. That fables could look forwards as well as backwards was to be amply, and controversially, demonstrated by another fabular publication of 1687, John Dryden's *The Hind and the Panther*.

John Dryden, *The Hind and the Panther* (1687)

> The nation is in too high a ferment for me to expect either fair war, or even so much as fair quarter, from a reader of the opposite party.
>
> Dryden, 'To the Reader'[20]

The unnamed speaker who addresses the reader at the outset of *The Hind and the Panther* clearly anticipates trouble. Published anonymously in May 1687, *The Hind and the Panther* (hereafter *HP*) dramatizes theological divisions, principally between the Catholic Church (the Hind) and the Church of England (the Panther), that had been rendered acutely topical by the accession of the Catholic James II two years earlier. In his prefatory letter, Dryden claims to have begun the poem in the winter of 1686–7 and to have finished it shortly after the publication of James's *Declaration for Liberty of Conscience* in April 1687 ('To the Reader', 74–8). Openly contentious, *HP* attracted still more hostility on account of Dryden's authorship which, though unacknowledged, seems always to have been an open secret. Just five years earlier, in *Religio Laici* (1682), Dryden had publicly defended the Church of England against Catholicism and dissent. In *HP*, his first major poetic publication following his conversion to Catholicism, he drew on the resources of fable to defend the Church of Rome against its enemies.

Why did Dryden choose to frame his defence of Catholicism as a fable? Unlike Aphra Behn, he was not working to commission; he also had a well-established and mutually respectful relationship with his publisher, Jacob Tonson. The choice of genre for this important religio-political intervention seems likely to have been his alone. Steven Zwicker, noting fable's 'long and distinguished' history as a means of political commentary,

---

[20] John Dryden, *The Hind and the Panther*, in Dryden, *Poems* (Longman), iii. 39.

speculates that the genre may have appealed to Dryden as 'a way of achieving distance and protection, of invoking the tradition of veiled meaning, of putting at arm's length the uncomfortable facts of 1687'.[21] One problem with this explanation, however, is that the 'distance' conferred by the fabular mode of *HP* is much too slight to have afforded Dryden any significant degree of 'protection'. The paper-thin allegory of the Hind and the Panther would have deceived no one, and is in any case all but decoded in the prefatory epistle to the reader. Had Dryden really wanted to protect himself from the consequences of his own satire, other genres—or a less transparent use of *this* genre—would have been better placed to achieve his objective.

The most plausible explanation for the fabular mode of *HP* may lie in a combination of contemporary models, Dryden's track record as a satirist, and his own claims about the poem. As Paul Hammond has shown, precedents for Dryden's application of beast fable to contemporary politics were available in such Exclusion Crisis pamphlets as *The Fanaticks Dream*, *Grimalkin, or, the Rebel-Cat*, or *The Phanatick in his Colours*.[22] Hammond further points out that Dryden had a history, in poems such as *Mac Flecknoe*, *Absalom and Achitophel*, and *The Medal*, of appropriating current cultural motifs and redeploying them for his own purposes. But Dryden's experience as a satirical poet may bear on his choice of *HP*'s genre in other ways too. Although he had not previously used fable as the model for an entire poem, he had deployed fabular references for local effect in works such as *Absalom and Achitophel* (1681) and *The Medal* (1682). His comparison of the 'presbyter, puffed up with spiritual pride' to the 'devouring crane' from Aesop's 'The Frogs and their King' may have directly inspired his depiction of the dissenters as wild beasts in *HP*: a depiction which, as Zwicker observes, contributed crucially to Dryden's construction of dissent as dangerous.[23]

More broadly, Dryden's satirical methods in both *Mac Flecknoe* and *Absalom and Achitophel* may help to explain his choice of fable for *HP*. Both poems are, in effect, character assassinations which employ satire to destroy their antagonists' reputations rather than to correct their behaviour. Dryden would not, probably, have expected Shadwell to become any less dull, or Monmouth and Shaftesbury any less misguided, as a result of his poems; his objective was rather to ridicule their pretensions and sway influential opinion against them. To do this, he co-opted the cultural authority of two highly prestigious textual traditions: classical epic and the Bible. The success of *Mac Flecknoe* and *Absalom and Achitophel* was contingent on Dryden's displaying his mastery of these two traditions, reinventing them into well-informed and internally coherent mock versions of themselves. *HP* resembles *Mac Flecknoe* and *Absalom and Achitophel* in that its effects depend, in part, on the cultural authority of its foundational genre: in this case, fable. It differs from them, however, in that, although satirical, it is not a mock form: though the conventions of fable are strained and exaggerated, they are always

[21] Steven N. Zwicker, *Politics and Language in Dryden's Poetry: The Arts of Disguise* (Princeton: Princeton University Press, 1984), 124.

[22] Paul Hammond, 'A Source for *The Hind and the Panther* in a Beast Fable from the Exclusion Crisis', *Notes and Queries* 29, no. 1 (1982), 55–7.

[23] Dryden, *Poems* (Longman), ii. 31; Zwicker, *Politics and Language*, 130.

taken seriously. What then, were Dryden's aims for *HP*, and why did fable seem to offer the best means of achieving them?

Dryden himself claimed that his original intentions in composing *HP* had been overtaken by events: namely, the *Declaration for Liberty of Conscience*, 'which, if I had so soon expected, I might have spared myself the labour of writing'.[24] While this claim should not necessarily be taken at face value, its implications do make sense of some of the anomalies within *HP*: most obviously, its changing, and increasingly negative, representation of the Panther. Between 1686 and 1687, while Dryden was working on the poem, James's religious policy altered from one of seeking to conciliate the Church of England to one of extending toleration to all forms of Christian worship, in defiance of the Anglican Church. While Dryden's characterization of the Panther in part I as 'sure the noblest, next the Hind, / And fairest creature of the spotted kind' (I.327–8) is consistent with James's more conciliatory approach to the Church of England in 1686, in the course of parts II and III, Dryden's allegory becomes more aggressive, portraying the (by now out of favour) Anglicans as 'at every point compromised by self-interest', opportunism, and greed.[25] Yet, despite these similarities, there are several important respects in which the later sections of *HP* do not precisely map on to James's religious policy and practice. These include Dryden's persistently hostile references to the Wolf (the Presbyterians), whom he continues to portray as the chief threat to the Panther's personal integrity and loyalty to the king (III.120, 166, 895). They also include his equally negative portrayal of the Martin (III.461–638), a figure for James's Jesuit adviser, Father Petre. Although the attribution of the Petre critique to the Panther distances it from Dryden, its validity is never directly disavowed within *HP*. Instead, the conventions of fable enable the poet to sketch out the likely consequences of the Martin's wrong-headed advice for the Hind's 'slandered sons' (III.645), while formally ascribing responsibility for this anti-Jesuit critique to the 'malice' (III.642) of the Panther.[26]

Ideologically, the fabular form of *HP* offered Dryden other advantages. Chief among these was his use of the Hind to represent the Catholic Church. While deer of various kinds are traditional fabular protagonists, they are most usually associated with qualities such as vanity (on account of their antlers) and speed.[27] By contrast, Dryden's construction of his Hind emphasizes her purity and, despite her many enemies, her invulnerability:

> A milk-white Hind, immortal and unchanged,
> Fed on the lawns, and in the forest ranged;
> Without unspotted, innocent within,
> She feared no danger, for she knew no sin.
> Yet had she oft been chased with horns and hounds,
> And Scythian shafts...
>
> *The Hind and the Panther*, I., lines 1–6

---

[24] Dryden, *Poems* (Longman), iii. 42.   [25] Zwicker, *Politics and Language*, 134.
[26] Zwicker, *Politics and Language*, 151.
[27] Thus, for instance, Ogilby's Fable 28 and Philipot's/Behn's Fable XCIV.

By depicting the Hind as innocent and suffering, Dryden creates a version of Catholicism focused entirely on recent English experience. Her milk-white coat and conspicuously harmless habits implicitly preclude any possibility that she too might have 'chased' (persecuted) her enemies, either in pre-Reformation England or in contemporary continental Europe. (The recent persecution of French Huguenots, though elsewhere acknowledged, is attributed firmly to the secular power of Louis XIV.)[28] Her necessary femininity—given that the true Church is the bride of Christ—also enables Dryden to portray her as a caring mother who grieves for the woes of her virtuous young (I.9–22). In this, she contrasts with the Panther, whose relationship with her offspring is poor or non-existent (III.144–59), who is incapable of breeding beyond her own shores (II.265–7), and whose chastity, the Hind fears, has been compromised by the Wolf (III.165–8).

Dryden's use of fable in *HP* has often been perceived as problematic. The sheer length of the poem, as well as the attribution of complex theological arguments—including two embedded fables—to wild beasts has sometimes been thought to push the credibility of the genre beyond its limits.[29] One approach to resolving these generic difficulties, however, is to consider who Dryden's ideal reader, or readers, may have been. As with *Mac Flecknoe* and *Absalom and Achitophel*, it seems unlikely that Dryden, in this controversial poem, was writing for his enemies. Neither Anglicans nor Puritans would have been likely to be much impressed by his account of their beliefs and history, and their response to the poem was indeed predictably hostile.[30] Instead, Dryden's ideal readers are likely to have been fellow-Catholics, who might take heart from his positive representation of the Hind, and James II, who might be flattered by the images of himself as a protective lion (I.304–6) and a 'plain, good man' (III.906). James might, furthermore, learn wisdom from the two embedded fables, and take steps to displace the Martin and head off the Buzzard. He might also learn not to emulate the sectarian intolerance of either the Panther or Louis XIV.

A key issue within *The Hind and the Panther*—the crux of the disagreement between its two protagonists—is that of authority: authority to interpret the Scriptures and to know God's will. But authority is also, inevitably, an issue for the writer of a didactic poem such as *The Hind and the Panther*. Dryden's newly Catholic understanding of true authority, which rejected individual interpretation in favour of the consensus of 'pope and general councils' (II.81), risked undermining his own authority to pronounce on theological and political conundrums, as his narrative in *HP* obliged him to do. Fable, with its appeal to folk wisdom—to a shared culture anterior to Christian doctrine and division—offered him a means of sidestepping such issues and grounding his analysis in trans-denominationally accepted truths. It also, on the model of Spenser's *Mother Hubberds Tale*, allowed scope for him to move beyond analysis into prophecy, though in practice this too proved problematic. The Panther's tale of the Swallows and the Martin,

---

[28] 'To the Reader', Dryden, *Poems* (Longman), iii. 40, 151.
[29] Lewis, *The English Fable*, 99–100.
[30] Zwicker, *Politics and Language*, 147; Dryden, *Poems* (Longman), iii. 379.

which involved just one step into the future—the death of the Swallows and the execution of the Martin—is plausible enough. By comparison, however, the later stages of the Hind's tale of the Pigeons and the Buzzard are rather more tenuous: in large part because Dryden simply could not know whether religious propaganda or practical politics was to prove a greater threat to English Catholicism. The mixed derivation of the Buzzard from both Gilbert Burnet and William of Orange suggests that he was hedging his bets.

HP differs from most fables in being open-ended. The poem closes with both the Hind and the Panther retiring for the night: still at odds, but still, apparently, on speaking terms. Although in 1687, when *HP* was published, much must have seemed possible, the events of 1688 were to close off many of these possibilities, at least for a generation. Dryden was to return to fable once more, in 'The Cock and the Fox' (1700), but the undoubted satire in this adaptation of Chaucer is largely confined to mocking Puritans and religious pretension.[31] The value of fable as a post-revolutionary Jacobite form was to be more fully explored in the poetry of Anne Finch.

ANNE FINCH: A LIFE IN FABLES

Finch's early poetry gives little indication of the importance fable would later assume within her oeuvre, but that little is telling. Her first manuscript collection of her verse, now Northamptonshire MS 283, comprises some fifty poems but includes just one fable, 'The Miller, his Son and the Asse'. Adapted from La Fontaine, 'The Miller' speaks of the young Finch's interest not in fable but in translation: it keeps company in the Northamptonshire MS with translations from Montaigne, Tasso, Petrarch, and Brébeuf as well as adaptations from the Bible. It does, however, include two elements that were to be of continuing importance in Finch's later fables: humour, and a deep scepticism about popular opinion. Its narrative comically describes the several methods used by the Miller and his Son to bring their Ass to market. Trying to keep the Ass fresh and saleable, the Miller and his Son initially carry the animal but are jeered at for their folly by their neighbours. Every configuration they attempt—the Miller, the Son, both, or neither riding the Ass—is greeted with equal derision, till at last the Miller decides to ignore other people's 'reproof, or praise' and follow his own judgement, apparently with success ('This he resolv'd, and did it, and did well').[32] The moral of the fable—that whatever one's choices in life, one may expect censure—reflects Finch's early preoccupation with adverse criticism, but also foreshadows her later insistence on the poor judgement of the people at large.

Since the Northamptonshire manuscript includes poems composed over a period of some years, it is difficult to tell whether 'The Miller, his Son and the Asse' pre- or post-dates the 1688 Revolution. Post-1688 composition, however, is all but certain in the case

---

[31] 'The Cock and the Fox', notes to 479–85, 499, 601, 628.
[32] Northamptonshire MS FH 283, 120, 121, lines 94, 97.

of Finch's next fables, extant in Folger MS N.b.3 and all apparently composed in the late 1690s. Still based, though increasingly loosely, on prior originals, this handful of fables includes two ('There's no To-morrow' and 'For the Better') derived from the staunchly Jacobite Roger L'Estrange, as well as five others ('The Goute and Spider', 'Love, Death and Reputation', 'The King and the Shepheard', 'Jupiter and the Farmer', and 'The Jester, and the little Fishes') drawn from La Fontaine. Collectively, these fables show clear continuities with 'The Miller, his Son and the Asse', while also becoming noticeably darker and more political. Non-political preoccupations are still to be found—a brief meditation on the 'merry Bagpipe' in 'The King and the Shepheard' invokes the power of art;[33] 'Love, Death and Reputation' focuses on issues of human experience—while the comedy of 'The Miller' finds counterparts in 'The Goute and Spider', 'The Jester, and the little Fishes', and 'For the Better'. 'The Goute and Spider' also includes an affectionate address to Finch's husband, whose 'first Fitt of that Distemper' (276) is said to have occasioned the poem (and may also have provided impetus for Finch's satire against doctors in 'For the Better' and 'Love, Death and Reputation'). But neither the humour nor the affection of 'The Goute and Spider' can completely mask its severely traditionalist moral: namely, that everyone—including both the gout and the spider—should 'his propper Station learn to know' (p. 277, line 50). Similarly austere morals emerge from both 'The King and the Shepheard' and 'Jupiter and the Farmer'. In the former, the Shepheard, raised by the King to govern his country, is clearly a good ruler who does not deserve the people's slander, but is just as clearly right to reject ambition and return to his country life. In the latter, the Clown who hopes to make his farm prosper by controlling the weather instead finds himself beset by famine while his neighbours thrive. The Clown, it appears, should either not have tried his hand at farming at all, or been content to accept whatever weather Jupiter thought best.

The post-revolutionary circumstances of the 1690s placed the nonjuror Finch in an ambivalent position. Though she might urge that everyone should know his (or her) 'propper Station', she inhabited a world where, in her terms, proper stations no longer applied. Something of the unease this must have engendered can be seen in 'Jupiter and the Farmer' where, in a change from La Fontaine, the lease for the Clown's farm is administered by Mercury, who 'So rack'd the rent that all who made resort / Unsatisfy'd return'd' (285, lines 7–8). A cancelled reference to 'that Bank'—presumably the Bank of England, established in 1694 to finance the Williamite wars—confirms the contemporary reference. But although Mercury's regime, a figure for William's, is evidently unjust, there is apparently no scope in Finch's quietistic worldview for it to be challenged, much less overturned. Instead the only fitting response, as modelled by the Clown, is to submit to the will of Jupiter: 'Let me but live to reap do thou appoint the way' (286, line 30). There is no remedy except endurance.

Finch's late-1690s fables show her working out not only an appropriate political response to the events of 1688 but also an appropriate public mode of literary engagement.

---

[33] Folger MS N. b. 3, 283, lines 65–6. Further quotations from the Folger manuscript are included parenthetically in the main text.

When she published her *Miscellany Poems* in 1713, it is significant that the only two of her 1690s fables omitted from the volume were 'The Goute and Spider' and 'The Jester, and the little Fishes'. The former, with its intimate references to Heneage and their marriage, was presumably too personal for public display; the latter, which refers unmistakably to the Darien adventure of 1698–9, appears to have been too topical and specific. (The cancelled reference to 'that Bank' in 'Jupiter and the Farmer' is also omitted from the printed edition.)[34] Finch seems to have viewed her mature fables—some, though not all, now of her own invention—as offering a middle way between the equally unattractive extremes of undue self-revelation and the 'Lampoons...and abusive verses' she so much loathed. Through fable, she was able to discuss her own poetry in a humorous and safely distanced manner: witness the creation of the 'harmless Fable-writer' in 'The Critick and the Writer of Fables' or the clash of the Elephant and the Boar in her 'prefatory fable', 'Mercury and the Elephant'. While avoiding personal abuse, she was also able to present a deeply satirical view of the modern world.

Finch's new fables in *Miscellany Poems*, like those of the late 1690s, see her developing themes already apparent in her earlier work, albeit to increasingly pessimistic effect. While humour still forms an important strand within Finch's fables in *Miscellany Poems*— new examples include 'The Prevalence of Custom' and 'The Miser and the Poet'—its implications are now invariably bleak. Though the husband's fixation with alcohol in 'The Prevalence of Custom' is comically presented, he is clearly an incurable drunkard, while the wit of 'The Miser and the Poet' merely accentuates the contrast between the Poet (and gifted fellow-writers such as Prior, Vanbrugh, and Singer) and the philistinism of contemporaries like the Miser. Long-standing themes such as self-delusion and folly ('The Atheist and the Acorn'; 'Man's Injustice against Providence'), the poor judgement of the general population ('The House of Socrates'; 'Democritus and his Neighbours'), and the importance of knowing one's place ('The Brass-Pot and Stone Jugg'; 'The Eagle, the Sow, and the Cat') continue to appear, but with an increasing emphasis on the negative and destructive consequences of mistaken behaviour. The Atheist who questions God's disposition of the world is struck in the eye, while the Stone Jug who foolishly listens to the Brass Pot is smashed to pieces. The discerning few who see through the errors of the world (the Poet, Socrates, Democritus) can do nothing to change public opinion but can only wonder and disengage.

Finch's longest new poem in *Miscellany Poems*, 'Upon the Hurricane', strongly suggests that, although profoundly despairing about the post-revolutionary political settlement, she could see no feasible means of alleviating it.[35] The politics of the new fables in *Miscellany Poems*, which postdate the death of James II in 1701, differ from those of the 1690s only in their still greater disenchantment with, and alienation from, the contemporary world. Instead of looking forward to the restoration of James's line, as so many of

---

[34] Finch, *Miscellany Poems*, 49–50. Further quotations from this volume are included parenthetically in the main text.

[35] Gillian Wright, 'Manuscript, Print, and Politics in Anne Finch's "Upon the Hurricane"', *Studies in Philology* 111, no. 3 (2014), 571–90.

her fellow-Jacobites were doing, the Finch of 1713 continues to look back, reflecting ever more despondently on the events of 1688. Even when, as in 'The Man Bitten by Fleas', she comes close to admitting that there were genuine problems with James II's rule (the Man *was* bitten by the Fleas), she cannot endorse the drastic methods ('Club and Bolts', 226, line 49) resorted to by the nation. 'Passive Obedience' (225, line 29) —the watchword of Anglicans like Finch during James's reign—seems to be still the only acceptable response, in the 1710s as in the 1680s.

In 'The Man Bitten by Fleas', Finch warns that neither 'You, nor your succeeding Heir / Nor yet a long Descent / Shall find out Methods to repair' the ravages of the Fleas (226, lines 45–7). Her apparent conviction that no political solution to the errors of 1688 was now possible may explain why, satirically, there is little difference between her fables in *Miscellany Poems* and those published in *Poems on Several Occasions* (1717) after the Hanoverian accession. If a change of emphasis can be detected in these later fables, it is in 'The Mastif and Curs', where the Mastiff, like so many of Finch's approved protagonists, faces unjust attack from the lesser animals around him. Asked why he declines to revenge himself on his assailants, the Mastiff proudly replies that the enmity, and even the existence, of such 'carping vermin' demonstrates his own innate nobility through force of contrast: 'I were no masty if there were no curs'.[36] Fable could not resolve the intractable wrongs of Finch's world, but it could help her assert an ever more beleaguered Jacobite identity.

FABLE AND SATIRE

The popularity of fables, especially satirical fables, in the late seventeenth and early eighteenth centuries may in part have been due to fashion. There is, nonetheless, good reason why the form may have held particular appeal for English Jacobites during this period. Though the politics of fable are not predetermined, the genre does have inherently conservative tendencies, in that it typically invests its participants with fixed qualities and depends on a received sense of natural order. Given that, in the late seventeenth and early eighteenth centuries, many Jacobites saw natural order as, first, under threat, and subsequently, overturned, their relish for the satirical potential of fable is unsurprising. Similarity of political outlook may also explain the shared attraction to the genre of both Aphra Behn and Anne Finch: an attraction which, given their many obvious differences, cannot easily be explained on grounds of sex. Both women may, however, have appreciated the accessibility of fable, which, unlike some other satirical genres, did not require familiarity with classical literature. For the more cautious Finch, fable also offered a means of writing satire without obviously writing satire.

After Finch, who died in 1720, fable began to decline as a satirical form. The last eighteenth-century English satirist to make extensive use of fables, John Gay, died in

---

[36] Alexander Pope, ed., *Poems on Several Occasions* (1717), 181, line 54.

1732, though the second volume of his fables appeared posthumously in 1738. Gay, like Bernard Mandeville and Jonathan Swift (who used fable in *A Tale of a Tub* and the 'Spider and Bee' episode of *The Battel of the Books*, as well as in the final book of *Gulliver's Travels*) belonged to that generation whose worldview had been formed during, or immediately after, the revolutionary upheavals of the late 1680s.[37] His 1738 *Fables* makes devastating use of fabular conventions to attack ministerial corruption in general and Walpole in particular.[38] It does not, however, attack the king, George II, who figures in Gay's fables as 'a benign and patriotic monarch, dedicated to the common good of the whole nation', in contrast with the grasping, self-interested Walpole.[39] Gay may have learnt the satirical power of fables from earlier poets such as Behn, Dryden, and Finch whose political lives were dedicated to opposing the dispensation that George represented. By the late 1730s, however, the Hanoverian dynasty had become so entrenched that, to all but a few, its existence no longer felt like a breach of natural order. The revolutionary settlement thus normalized, the counter-revolutionary potential of fable fell away. In subsequent decades, fable was to prosper as a didactic mode, expanding beyond its traditional child-focused remit to take on a new role as conduct literature for women.[40] But its obsolescence as political satire was now firmly assured.

SELECT BIBLIOGRAPHY

Hammond, Paul. 'A Source for *The Hind and the Panther* in a Beast Fable from the Exclusion Crisis', *Notes and Queries* 29, no. 1 (1982), 55–7.

Hodnett, Edward. *Francis Barlow: First Master of English Book Illustration* (London: Scolar Press, 1978).

Lewis, Jayne Elizabeth. *The English Fable: Aesop and Literary Culture, 1651–1740* (Cambridge: Cambridge University Press, 1996).

Nokes, David. *John Gay: A Profession of Friendship* (Oxford: Oxford University Press, 1995).

Patterson, Annabel. *Fables of Power: Aesopian Writing and Political History* (Durham, NC: Duke University Press, 1991).

Wright, Gillian. 'Manuscript, Print, and Politics in Anne Finch's "Upon the Hurricane"', *Studies in Philology* 111, no. 3 (2014), 571–90.

Zwicker, Steven N. *Politics and Language in Dryden's Poetry: The Arts of Disguise* (Princeton: Princeton University Press, 1984).

---

[37] On Swift and fable, see Lewis, *The English Fable*, 45–7, 58–60.

[38] David Nokes, *John Gay: A Profession of Friendship* (Oxford: Oxford University Press, 1995), 503–11.

[39] Nokes, *John Gay*, 506.

[40] Examples include Edward Moore and Henry Brooke, *Fables for the Female Sex* (1744) and *Fables and Tales for the Ladies* (1750).

CHAPTER 17

··

BURLESQUE
AND TRAVESTY
Pope's Early Satires

··

BONNIE LATIMER

[W]hen rational beings are represented above their real character, it becomes ridiculous in Art, because it is vicious in Morality.[1]

'What an ignorant thing is vanity!'[2]

THE story of Alexander Pope and Robert Norris is familiar to any student of Pope's work. *The Narrative of Dr Robert Norris, Concerning the Strange and Deplorable Frenzy of Mr John Denn—*(1713) justified the conduct of a doctor who, having attempted to cure a manic patient, found his character traduced. Robert Norris did exist: he was, in Maynard Mack's felicitous phrase, a 'genuine quack', specializing in 'Lunaticks'.[3] Equally real was the critic John Dennis. The pamphlet itself, however, was less straightforward: it was a satiric invention of Pope's.

This chapter begins with a brief reading of *The Narrative*, suggesting that this minor work encapsulates satiric methodologies visible throughout Pope's oeuvre. It then considers three satiric genres: the mock-essay, the dramatic satire, and the mock-heroic poem, from *Guardian* 40 (1713) to *Peri Bathous* (1727), published the year before his first mature satire, *The Dunciad* (1728). Across this period, Pope's satires unite in their use of burlesque and in attacking vain pretenders to knowledge.

---

[1] Alexander Pope, 'Postscript' to *The Odyssey*, 5 vols. (1725–6), v. 299–300.
[2] [Alexander Pope, John Gay, and John Arbuthnot], *Three Hours after Marriage* (1717), 64.
[3] Maynard Mack, *Alexander Pope: A Life* (New Haven: Yale University Press, 1985), 223.

POPE'S SATIRIC METHODOLOGY:
THE NARRATIVE OF DR ROBERT NORRIS

The Narrative begins with 'Robert Norris' justifying its production: he 'should be wanting in my Duty...to him who hath endu'd me with Talents for the benefit of my Fellow-Creatures', if he permitted any misconceptions about himself. He explains that he was approached by Dennis's servant, 'an old Woman with Tears in her Eyes', who reported that Dennis raved about '*Cator*...or some such thing', which she believes to be the name of a witch. This is, of course, a hit at Dennis's virulent criticism of Joseph Addison's play, *Cato* (1713). When Norris visits Dennis, the quack's ignorance means that he mistakes Dennis's marked-up texts as symptoms of mania, not scholarship: 'A Criticism! that's a Distemper I never read of in Galen'. Deciding that Dennis is mad, he '[binds] our Lunatick Hand and Foot down to the Bedsted', before Dennis breaks free, and Norris is obliged to an ignominious retreat. Later, Norris learns that Dennis's mania was caused by reading Pope's own *Essay on Criticism* (1711).[4]

For a clued-up reader in the 1710s, *The Narrative of Dr Robert Norris* formed part of a web of satiric texts. The title's description of Dennis's frenzy as 'deplorable' is a hint of the pamphlet's intentions: Pat Rogers identifies this as a 'give-away word' linking it to a body of Scriblerian satire, 'commonly centred on a delusive figure whose monomania leads to a total breakdown'.[5] The account of Dennis's lunacy and his physical humiliation connect the text to Jonathan Swift's 1708 Partridge papers, in which Swift falsely reported the death of the astrologer, John Partridge, and to the various 'corrections' of the bookseller, Edmund Curll, depicted by the Scriblerians in mocking pamphlets.[6] As well as this Grub Street heritage, Pope's *Narrative* recalls a dramatic tradition of the figurative chastisement of the worthless poetaster.[7]

Such satires work by typologizing their targets as symptomatic of greater foibles, that is, by portraying the victims as instances of wider cultural problems. This was a practice to which Pope would return time and again. Pope's Norris displays his own self-serving vanity, but his characterization also takes aim at the scientific writing of the time. *The Narrative* is, like Pope's pamphlet attacks on Curll, a spoof news report, but also a parody of contemporary medical papers, such as those produced by the Royal Society; these documented real cases, but were in various ways potentially ridiculous. Their empiricist

---

[4] Alexander Pope, *The Narrative of Dr Robert Norris, Concerning the Strange and Deplorable Frenzy of Mr John Denn—*, in Pope, *Prose*, i. 153–68: 155–6, 160, 165–6.

[5] Pat Rogers, '*God's Judgment upon Hereticks*: A "Lost" Satire on Thomas Woolston and Edmund Gibson', *RES* 65 (2014), 78–98: 83.

[6] Shaun Regan, '"Pranks, unfit for naming": Pope, Curll, and the "Satirical Grotesque"', *The Eighteenth Century* 46 (2005), 37–57: 45. Cf. Samuel Wesley, *Neck or Nothing: A Consolatory Letter from Mr D-nt-n to Mr C—rll Upon his being Tost in a Blanket &c.* (1716), and Pope's Curll pamphlets.

[7] Paul Baines and Pat Rogers, 'Pope's First Horatian Imitation? Ben Jonson's Crispinus and the Poisoning of Edmund Curll', *RES* 60 (2008), 78–95.

epistemology meant that they included a wealth of detail, which could be construed as intrusive. A Society paper from the 1720s, for instance, described the autopsy of 130-year-old John Bayle, solemnly noting that 'about half a year before he dyed he longed for some Venison Pasty, but had it not'. Another paper records a foetus crying *in utero*, corroborated with detailed witness statements.[8] Norris's pseudo-medical narrative is comparably crowded with minutiae about his own raiment, the colour of Dennis's eyebrows, and Dennis's clothes, 'begrim'd with Sweat and Dirt'; it draws on fictional testimony from Bernard Lintot, Dennis's (and Pope's) bookseller.[9] The use of circumstantial reportage to give credibility to what is either comically irrelevant or clearly untrue suggests that *The Narrative* works as an exposure not just of Robert Norris, but of scientific writing more widely. Pope's enemies attacked him for making 'Pers'nal Reflections' rather than generic satires, but this underestimated how the pillorying of an individual made general points.[10] As Allen Wood points out, this freighting of individuals with symbolic significance derives from Horatian satire; it serves, in Shaun Regan's words, to 'mythologize...contingent reality' 'into a moral truth'.[11] This investing of individual targets with greater imaginative and cultural resonance informs all of Pope's early satires.

The final point raised by *The Narrative of Dr Robert Norris* is its creation of a sophisticated interplay between texts which works to rescript their original meanings; another key Popean satiric practice. Norris is informed that the mania began when Dennis entered a bookseller's, and

> finding on the... Counter a Book called an *Essay on Criticism*, just then publish'd, he read a Page or two with much Frowning... till coming to these two Lines;
> *Some have at first for Wits, then Poets past,*
> *Turn'd Criticks next, and prov'd plain Fools at last.*
> He flung down the Book in a terrible Fury, and cried out, *by G-d he means Me.*[12]

Now, this is mischievous. Pope's *Essay on Criticism* did slight Dennis: lines 585–7 refer to 'Appius', an allusion to Dennis's play *Appius and Virginia* (1709); also, as J. V. Guerinot notes, the portrait resembled other anti-Dennis satires.[13] So Dennis was not wrong to see the *Essay* as glancing at him. The lines cited above, however, which stigmatize the wit/poet/critic as a 'plain Fool', are much less obviously directed at him. Whether or not Pope had Dennis in mind when he wrote them, they do not inevitably point to the

[8] James Keill, 'Death and Dissection of *John Bayles*', in Benjamin Motte (ed.), *Philosophical Transactions*, 2 vols. (1721–2), vol. 1, Part II, p. 152; [William?] Derham, 'A Child crying in the Womb', in the same volume, 121–2.

[9] Pope, *The Narrative*, 158.

[10] Ned Ward cited in J. V. Guerinot, *Pamphlet Attacks on Alexander Pope, 1711–1744* (London: Methuen, 1969), lvi.

[11] Allen Wood, *Literary Satire and Theory: A Study of Horace, Boileau, and Pope* (New York: Garland, 1985), 16–24; Regan, '"Pranks"', 49.

[12] Pope, *The Narrative*, 166. Cf. *Essay on Criticism* (1711), ll. 36–7, Pope, *Poems*, i. 243.

[13] Guerinot, *Pamphlet Attacks*, lxvi.

critic: until, that is, *The Narrative* makes Dennis self-apply them. Suddenly, the earlier *Essay* becomes an intertext of *The Narrative*, its meanings now revised by the later squib.

The Narrative typifies Pope's use of satiric intertexts; in 1715, Pope would compose an ironic 'key' to his own *Rape of the Lock* (1714), retrospectively endowing it with tongue-in-cheek politics. These pieces serve to inflect the meanings of the earlier text, but also to ironize the pretensions of those who believe that they see further or read more correctly than others, whether that be Dennis's addiction to his own vehement judgements or the extra-diegetic reader who imagines that 'keys' grant them special insight into a text's true, occult meaning. Contemplating such intertexts reminds us, too, how even Pope's 'high culture' works, such as the *Essay on Criticism*, have an inextricable relationship with a Grub Street milieu of satiric ephemera. Guerinot observes that pamphlet satire shaped Pope's career; the poet's pamphlet attacks were concentrated in the period 1711–18, and these provide a backdrop for all his pre-*Dunciad* works, from *The Rape* to his Homeric translations.[14] The extent to which Pope's writing is imbricated in Grub Street and its scurrilous satire has been recognized repeatedly by critics, from Peter Stallybrass and Allon White's insight that 'Pope's own features' could be discerned in 'Grub Street', to the excellent textual scholarship of Paul Baines and Pat Rogers.[15] Reading *The Narrative of Dr Robert Norris* closely, a number of themes emerge which are crucial to his satiric practice more generally: it is both morally corrective and gleefully scurrilous, featuring (to borrow Émile Audra's phrase) *badinage gracieux* and slapstick, equally implicated in high culture neoclassicism and gross travesty.[16] Taken as a body, Pope's early satires use the comic force of burlesque to mount an attack on false pride in knowledge—before proceeding further, however, it is worth pausing on that term, *burlesque*.

BURLESQUE, PARODY, AND TRAVESTY IN THE EARLY EIGHTEENTH CENTURY

At the turn of the eighteenth century, the burlesque gripped the popular satiric imagination—although its meanings were various. A key text is Samuel Butler's influential mock-heroic *Hudibras* (1663–78). To take a representative snippet, the 'Argument' to the first canto outlines

> Sir HUDIBRAS his passing worth,
> The Manner how he sally'd forth;
> His arms and equipage are shown;

---

[14] Guerinot, *Pamphlet Attacks*, xlvi, xlix.

[15] Peter Stallybrass and Allon White, *The Politics and Poetics of Transgression* (London: Methuen, 1986), 116. See Paul Baines and Pat Rogers, *Edmund Curll, Bookseller* (Oxford: Oxford University Press, 2007) and Regan, '"Pranks"'.

[16] Émile Audra, *L'influence française dans l'œuvre de Pope* (Paris: Librairie Ancienne Honoré Champion, 1931), 320.

His horse's virtues and his own.
Th'adventure of the *Bear* and *Fiddle*
Is sung, but breaks off in the middle.[17]

The poem amusingly undermines its hero by prioritizing his horse's virtues; Sir Hudibras's adventures are sung, as in oral epic, but ridiculously interrupted, and consisting anyhow of low matter. The burlesque works by conflating low and high, but its most recognizable feature for late seventeenth-century writers was its distinctive form of an octosyllabic or four-foot line, creating a jaunty rhythm, as above. Richmond Bond demonstrates how, in the 1690s, critics from Dryden to Dennis defined the burlesque in terms of this poetic form.[18]

As the period progressed, though, burlesque was seen not only as a form, but as a cross-generic *mode* whose many manifestations made it difficult to pin down. The burlesque poem *Pendragon* (1698) begins with an 'Advertisement' on the burlesque, acknowledging its verse origins but also framing it as a wide-ranging practice whose 'Liberties and Privileges are unbounded':

> Its Nature is to Ridicule, Flatter, Huff, and Banter, by turns; to Scratch and Claw, and anon to Grin and Bite like a *Satyr*...Endless it would indeed be to recount its various Qualifications and Wild Vagaries...[19]

Here, the burlesque is amorphous in form, defined instead by a slippery mixture of mockery and ironic praise. Other writers theorized this complexity more fully by seeing the burlesque as constituting a wry replication of what should be serious. Richmond Bond sums this up by defining the burlesque in this period as an umbrella term referring to 'the use or imitation of serious matter or manner, made amusing by the creation of an incongruity between style and subject'.[20] The French critic Charles Perrault comparably saw it as 'une espece [*sic*] de ridicule consiste dans la discovenance de l'idée qu'on donne d'une chose avec son idée veritable [*sic*]', or 'a type of mockery which relies on the gap between how a thing is portrayed and its true nature'.[21] The idea of incongruity, *discovenance* (gap, disagreement), or 'disproportion' between subject matter and its treatment is key.[22]

Such a gap can be opened up in one of two ways: things which are normally taken to be 'low' can be treated in a 'high' style, or vice versa. The elevation of low matter is termed *magnifying*, *ascending*, or *ascensional* burlesque; for our purposes, in this period *parody* can be seen as a species of magnifying burlesque, since, in Bond's words, it 'mimics the manner of an individual author or poem by substituting [a] less worthy subject'.[23]

---

[17] [Samuel Butler], *Hudibras* (1663), A2[r].

[18] Richmond Bond, *English Burlesque Poetry, 1700–1750* (Cambridge, MA: Harvard University Press, 1932), 23–31. The following discussion is indebted to Bond.

[19] *Pendragon* (1698), [A3r]–[A4r].   [20] Bond, *English Burlesque Poetry*, 3.

[21] Charles Perrault, *Parallèle des anciens et des modernes en ce qui regarde la poesie* (Paris, 1692), 295.

[22] Michael Edwards, 'A Meaning for Mock-Heroic', *Yearbook of English Studies* 15 (1985), 48–63: 51.

[23] Bond, *English Burlesque Poetry*, 4. As a term, *parody* is less well-used in this period than *travesty* or, particularly, *burlesque*.

Contrastingly, the burlesque degradation of the high is labelled *descending* or *diminishing*; *travesty* is a form of descending burlesque, treating with indignity an inherently worthy subject. Generally, any clash between matter and style risked creating a ridiculous effect, as Pope explained: in poetry, he argues that

> The diction is to follow the images, and to take its colour from the complexion of the thoughts... There is a real beauty in an easy, pure, perspicuous description even of a *low action*... the representations of common... things, in clear, plain, and natural words, are frequently found to make the liveliest impression on the reader [but] the use of the grand style on little subjects, is not only ludicrous, but a sort of transgression against the rules of proportion... 'Tis using a vast force to lift a *feather*.[24]

The deliberate creation of disproportion between a '*low*' action or thing, and a 'grand style' (or its converse) is the foundation of the burlesque. Because of this incorporation of high and low, grand and mundane, the burlesque can be seen as double-voiced; Richard Terry reads burlesque as a mode which allows Pope and his culture to simultaneously say and not-say things, at once to represent and undermine.[25] This is evident in *The Narrative*, in which Norris's aspirations to prove 'of benefit' to 'my fellow creatures' and Dennis's serious literary criticism culminate disastrously in an undignified fistfight.

Burlesque has a broad tonal range: it may be obscene, as in Pope's burlesque of the first psalm.[26] It may also be, in Francis Hutcheson's words, sufficiently mild to 'move Laughter in those who may have the highest Veneration' for the target, with the extraordinary delicacy of *The Rape of the Lock*.[27] Ultimately, like other forms of satire in the period, it has corrective intentions, amending taste or morals. In short, the eighteenth-century burlesque exploits for comic effect the disjuncture between what the culture sees as low and high to draw attention to sins and follies. Pope's early satires use ascensional and diminishing burlesque to satirize false pretensions to learning: nowhere is this more visible than in his mock-essays.

Mock-Essays: *Guardian* 40 and *Peri Bathous*

Generally, the burlesque pervades Pope's 'Grub Street' satires, from his attacks on Curll to his mock-ballads such as *God's Judgment upon Hereticks* (1729). His prose satires of this period include mock-essays, which burlesque not only individual writers, but the whole enterprise of literary criticism; they also characteristically position Pope's own

---

[24] Pope, 'Postscript' *Odyssey*, v. 298.
[25] Richard Terry, '"Tis a sort of... tickling": Pope's Rape and the Mock-Heroics of Gallantry', *Eighteenth-Century Life* 18 (1994), 59–74.
[26] See Norman Ault, 'New Light on Pope', *RES* 18 (1942), 441–7.
[27] Francis Hutcheson, *Reflections upon Laughter* (Glasgow, 1750), 7–8.

work as uniquely conforming to classical critical imperatives. To see this, we can consider two mock-essays from either end of Pope's early period: his satiric review of pastoral poetry in *Guardian* 40 (1713) and his mock-treatise, *Peri Bathous* (1727).

The most succinct account of the events behind *Guardian* 40 remains Edward Heuston's.[28] Pope, along with Ambrose Philips, had published pastoral verses in a 1709 miscellany. Philips's poems were 'puffed' by Joseph Addison's Whig circle—some of them tacitly boosting Philips at Pope's expense. Pope's relationship with Addison's coterie was tetchy at this stage, and the pointed reviews added fuel. In 1713, a series of such essays, penned by Thomas Tickell, appeared in the *Guardian*. Pope responded with his own *Guardian* essay, ironically over-praising Philips's pastorals. *Peri Bathous: Or... the Art of Sinking in Poetry* is 'an inverse manual of rhetoric in which the Longinian sublime is converted into the Popean profound'.[29] It takes the classical sublime—the soaring heights to which poetry can rise—and satirically imagines an attempt to achieve the exact opposite in writing, a senseless torpidity. As with all Pope's satires, there are multiple targets: *Peri Bathous* winks at modern engagements with Longinus (such as Boileau's translation of the Greek author in 1674); again at Dennis, a critic of the Longinian sublime; and at Pope's perennial enemy, Richard Blackmore, whose *A Satyr against Wit* (1700) claims the quality of 'gravity'.[30]

Both mock-essays produce a witty burlesque through quotation. Literary criticism at this period was often polemical, typically picking apart extensive quotations from the work under consideration. To take two examples close to Pope, Dennis's *Reflections Critical and Satyrical* (1711), which savage the *Essay on Criticism*, work through Pope's poem, abusing it almost line-by-line:

> *There are whom Heav'n hath bless'd with store of Wit,*
> *Yet want as much again to manage it.*

By the way what rare Numbers are here? Would not one swear that this Youngster had espous'd some antiquated Muse, who had sued out a Divorce upon the account of Impotence from some superannuated Sinner; and who having been pox'd by her former Spouse...hobble[s] most damnably...[31]

Similarly, Charles Gildon's truly terrible play, *A New Rehearsal* (1714), quotes and then animadverts upon various authors, mostly the tragedian Nicholas Rowe, but also Pope. It positions itself as a piece of literary criticism, 'Containing an Examen of *The Ambitious Step-mother, Tamerlane, The Biter*', and other works, including *The Rape*. *A New Rehearsal* and the *Reflections* are heavy-handed, fulminating against their targets, and employing

---

[28] Edward Heuston, 'Windsor Forest and Guardian 40', *RES* 29 (1978), 160–8.

[29] Brean Hammond, 'Scriblerian Self-Fashioning', *Yearbook of English Studies* 18 (1988), 108–24: 116.

[30] Regan, '"Pranks"', 40.

[31] John Dennis, *Reflections Critical and Satyrical, Upon a Late Rhapsody, Call'd, An Essay upon Criticism* (1711), 11.

standard charges of Augustan literary criticism, such as plagiarism, bawdiness, writing for money, and unmeaning verbiage.

Parodying the form of such criticism, *Guardian* 40 and *Peri Bathous* use burlesque-through-quotation in two ways, both to discredit individual writers and to attack literary criticism as practised by Dennis and Addison's cronies. *Guardian* 40 begins by outlining the criteria for writing 'true' pastoral, according to which, both Virgil and Theocritus 'must be rejected' in large part. Using strategies of ironic praise, the essay points out Philips's embarrassingly rustic character-names ('*Hobbinol, Lobbin, Cuddy*'), his incon-sistencies ('*Philips* hath with great Judgment described *Wolves* in *England*'), and his derivativeness bordering on plagiarism (his 'whole third Pastoral is an Instance how well he hath studied the fifth of *Virgil*'). The burlesque comes into play when Pope begins to quote chunks of Philips's poetry in direct comparison with his own, inviting the reader to observe the contrast between lines such as 'Come, *Rosalind*, O come: my brinded Kine, / My snowy Sheep, my Farm, and all is thine' (Philips) with Pope's own 'In Spring the Fields, in Autumn Hills I love, / At Morn the Plains, at Noon the shady Grove, / But *Delia* always…'. With an ear attuned to 'elegance' as a criterion of successful poetry, the Augustan reader is invited to smirk at Philips's low 'brinded Kine' and 'Farm', in contrast to Pope's 'deviat[ion] into downright Poetry'.[32] In an inversion of how Dennis is retro-spectively branded as the *Essay*'s 'plain Fool', here, Pope's pastorals are reinscribed as the standard of taste.

Guardian 40 seizes on the double-meaning word 'Simplicity', earnestly applying it to Philips's work; in the period's argot, of course, 'simple' could refer to a desirable straight-forwardness or to low intelligence. The repetition of the word allows it to accrue a highly ironic valence. Similarly, *Peri Bathous*, a richly satiric counterpoint to the *artes poeticae* of Horace, Boileau, and indeed Pope himself, puns on the dual senses of words like 'pro-fundity' and 'gravity', brilliantly exploiting the idea of weight, with its simultaneous associations of intellectual depth and sinking. Pope's satiric persona, Martin Scriblerus, begins by outlining his central critical concept of *bathos*, translated by Pope as 'profound' but generally taken to mean a fall from the sublime to the low or ridiculous. Instantly, a satiric rubric is established whereby all authors grouped under the banner of the bath-etic are implicated as low and as lacking in '*common sense*', compared to the tacit standard of the literary sublime, which is equated with 'nature': '[A poet's] eyes should be like unto the wrong end of a perspective glass, by which all the objects of nature are lessened.' The treatise then quotes generously from modern poetry, with each quotation always already disbarred from any pretensions to high culture, and immediately legible as vulgar and ridiculous:

> The Physician, by the study and inspection of urine and ordure, approves himself in the science; and in like sort should our author accustom and exercise his imagination upon the dregs of nature.

---

[32] Pope, *Guardian* 40 in *Prose*, i. 98–101. Heuston argues that Pope is burlesquing Addison here, too ('*Windsor Forest* and *Guardian* 40', 167–8).

This will render his thoughts truly and fundamentally low [...] 'tis the *thought* alone that strikes [...] For instance [...] the following, which is Profundity itself,
  None but Himself can be his Parallel.
Unless it may seem borrowed from the Thought of that Master of a Show in Smithfield, who writ in large letters, over the picture of his elephant,
  This is the greatest Elephant in the world, except Himself.[33]

The 'innocent' suggestion that Lewis Theobald, to whom the first quotation is attributed, nicked a line for his pseudo-Shakespearean tragedy *The Double Falsehood* from a Smithfield hawker clearly burlesques Theobald's high-culture pretensions as stemming from London lowlife. This gleefully perverse conflation is also a hit at the wider practice of literary reviewing, which subjects genuinely high culture texts (such, implicitly, as Pope's own) to ignorant misreading. *Guardian* 40 is 'written in the free Spirit of Criticism': which 'criticism' turns out, of course, to be highly partial, misleading, and ironizing, flouting the Horatian imperative of *scribendi recte*, as opposed to *plus scribere* (writing correctly versus thoughtlessly churning out material).[34]

Satiric Drama: *Three Hours after Marriage*

If burlesque is a mainstay of Pope's satiric prose, it is also a strongly dramatic mode, and Pope's conception of the burlesque includes a theatrical dimension. As James Jackson demonstrates, *The Rape of the Lock* has a quasi-theatrical structure; *The Narrative of Dr Robert Norris* was, equally, born from a stage quarrel.[35] Pope influenced later theatrical squibs: notably, Henry Fielding's *Tom Thumb* (1730) and *Tragedy of Tragedies* (1731) adopt ideas from *Peri Bathous*. In theatrical terms, the burlesque could be a form in its own right: used as after-pieces to tragedies, dramatic burlesques flippantly revised the original piece. Alternatively, the burlesque might occur during a full-length play, in local instances or as a governing mode; this was a tradition inherited from the Restoration.

In the *Epistle to Arbuthnot* (1734), Pope imagined 'a stranger' beseeching his advice for a 'virgin tragedy': he was steeped in the theatre, and it was a means by which his Grub Street enemies attacked him.[36] He was caricatured onstage as Sawny Dapper in *A New Rehearsal*, discussed above, and in 1711, Dennis mocked him as 'Mr Bayes', referring to

---

[33] Pope, *Peri Bathous* (1727), *Prose*, ii. 198–9. The 'Theobald' quotation is a misquotation and misattribution; *The Double Distress* (1701) is by Mary Pix, whereas Theobald's *Double Falshood; Or, the Distrest Lovers* (London, 1728) contains the line 'None but Itself can be its Parallel' (25).

[34] Pope, *Guardian* 40, 97.

[35] James L. Jackson, 'Pope's *The Rape of the Lock* Considered as a Five-Act Epic', *PMLA* 65 (1950), 1283–7; Malcolm Goldstein, *Pope and the Augustan Stage* (Stanford: Stanford University Press, 1958), 13. Goldstein's monograph remains an essential account.

[36] *Epistle to Arbuthnot* (1734), in Pope, *Poems* (Twickenham), iv. 100.

the ridiculous author in the Duke of Buckingham's play, *The Rehearsal* (1672).[37] He would also be a target of John Breval's *The Confederates* (1717). It was from this world of rival theatrical cabals that Pope's collaborative play, *Three Hours after Marriage* (1717), was born, co-authored with fellow Scriblerians Gay and Arbuthnot. *Three Hours* is sometimes described as a farce, and sometimes as a parody of the intrigue comedies of the 1710s.[38] As a play, it was moderately successful, although controversial.[39] Its farcically overdetermined plot concerns the 'virtuoso' and doctor, Fossile, who, as the play opens, brings home his bride, Townley. Fossile wishes for an heir, and so desires a chaste wife: in the best tradition of intrigue comedy, Townley is a determined would-be adulteress, sought by both Plotwell and Underplot, who disguise themselves as a crocodile and a mummy, exhibits in Fossile's collection. The action winds up when Townley is revealed to be already married to someone else, and Fossile is left as guardian of her bastard child—ironically fulfilling his wish.

Like *The Narrative*, *Guardian 40*, and *Peri Bathous*, *Three Hours* attacks self-sufficient pretenders to knowledge and culture—this time through a theatrical burlesque stemming from Restoration stage traditions. There are two legacies to isolate: the rehearsal play and the satiric stage virtuoso. Buckingham's meta-theatrical *Rehearsal* attacks Dryden as 'Bayes', who spends the play supervising a rehearsal, intervening with tasteless suggestions. *The Rehearsal* sparked many imitations.[40] Some reproduced Buckingham's spoofs of heroic diction, such as Fielding's *Tom Thumb*, and some reused the rehearsal-play format, either for their whole structure, as in *The Female Wits* (1697), or as inspiration for a scene. *Three Hours* does both. Like *The Rape*, it skewers 'high' tragic rants, but it does so in composition and rehearsal scenes, and through gross innuendo. The tragedy composed by Fossile's niece Phoebe Clinket is riddled with accidental sexual meanings:

> *Enter Clinket…writing…*
> *Clink.* Hold. I conceive…
> *The raging Seas o'er the tall Woods have broke,*
> *Now perch, thou Whale, upon the sturdy Oak.*
> Sturdy oak? no; steady, strong, strapping, stiff…[41]

Clinket's 'sublime' heroic couplets are undermined by the 'low' meaning generated by the juxtaposition of the 'strapping, stiff' oak and her 'conception'. In this, she resembles Buckingham's Bayes, who is bumptiously venal. The burlesque intensifies in the rehearsal scene, in which Sir Tremendous (Dennis, again) dismisses Shakespeare, Jonson, Otway, Etherege, and Dryden, before trading unwitting double entendres with Clinket:

---

[37] Dennis, *Reflections Critical*, 11, 14.

[38] See, e.g., Peter Lewis, 'Dramatic Burlesque in *Three Hours after Marriage*', *Durham University Journal* 64 (1971–2), 232–9.

[39] George Sherburn, 'The Fortunes and Misfortunes of *Three Hours after Marriage*', *Modern Philology* 24 (1926), 91–109; Guerinot, *Pamphlet Attacks*, xxii–xxiii.

[40] Matthew Augustine addresses the Bayes character and its use by Scriblerians ('"A Mastery in Fooling": Marvell, the Mock-Book, and the Surprising Life of "Mr. Bayes"', *Studies in Philology* 112 (2015), 353–78).

[41] [Pope et al.], *Three Hours*, 5.

CLINK.   I am so much charm'd with your manly Penetration!
SIR TREM.   I with your profound Capacity!
CLINK.   That I am not able—
SIR TREM.   That it is impossible—
CLINK.   To conceive—
SIR TREM.   To express—
CLINK.   With what Delight I embrace—
SIR TREM.   With what Pleasure I enter into—
CLINK.   Your Ideas, most learned Sir *Tremendous*!
SIR TREM.   Your Sentiments, most divine Mrs *Clinket*.[42]

Just as Fielding uses Princess Huncamunca's unbecoming forwardness in *Tom Thumb* to travesty heroic tragedy, or Pope hints at Belinda's concupiscence in *The Rape*, so Clinket's high-minded literary discussions have an ineluctable twin meaning, a burlesque double voice. Here, the appetites for pure knowledge and earthy sex are satirically conflated, just as Ambrose Philips's studied plainness slides disastrously into poetic idiocy.

The coincidence of lust and learning connects *Three Hours* to another Restoration burlesque tradition: the satiric virtuoso. Thomas Shadwell's *The Virtuoso* (1676) pilloried the 'scientists' of the Royal Society, particularly Robert Boyle and Robert Hooke. As well as aiming at specific targets, Shadwell was concretizing an existing stage type: the comic virtuoso, found in plays from the 1660s onwards, such as John Wilson's *The Cheats* (1664), Thomas St Serfe's *Tarugo's Wiles* (1668), and Edward Howard's *The Six Days Adventure* (1671). The stage-virtuoso lived on after Shadwell, as in Aphra Behn's *The Emperor of the Moon* (1687). This stock character is a vain man, sexually dysfunctional or priapic, and self-deluded as to the value of his own esoteric learning. Often, he is unable to distinguish between valuable knowledge and discredited 'wonders'; stage virtuosi cling to outmoded beliefs such as the Paracelsian weapon salve, or anticipate improbable effects from a blood transfusion.[43]

Austin Warren long ago pointed out that Pope frequently conceived of 'scholarship' as ridiculous, and Fossile does represent a Popean distaste for 'formal' learning.[44] He also, however, fits within a burlesque stage tradition where hits at Gresham College (where the Royal Society met) or hermeticism are commonplace. Fossile, like previous stage-virtuosi, arrogates to himself rarefied knowledge: he believes himself master of 'profound Policy', '*Arcana*', and is willing to be flattered as 'de illustrious Doctor'. Tellingly, however, he does not have Latin, and rejects 'Zoology, Minerology, [and] Hydraulicks' in favour of 'Hermaphrodites, monstrous Twins, [and] Antidiluvian Shells'.[45] Most damningly, his 'philosophy' is bent towards discovering whether his bride is a virgin or not. Fossile ends emasculated, holding his erstwhile wife's bastard. His learning cannot disguise—and

---

[42] [Pope et al.], *Three Hours*, 20.
[43] See, e.g. Behn's *Emperor of the Moon: A Farce* (1687), 3; *Tarugo's Wiles: Or, the Coffee-House. A Comedy* (1668), Act III, *passim*.
[44] Austin Warren, 'Pope's Index to Beaumont and Fletcher', *Modern Language Notes* 46 (1931), 515–17.
[45] [Pope et al.], *Three Hours*, 34, 39, 41.

perhaps spawns—a childish curiosity and vanity, and an inability to attain to true manliness. The burlesque is produced in *Three Hours* through the discrepancy between the high pretensions of 'philosophy' and the abject, failed scholar who must admit that, sexually and intellectually, he is 'no Thunderer'.[46]

MOCK-HEROIC: *THE RAPE OF THE LOCK*

Three Hours' mockery of heroic diction and learning connects it, finally, to Pope's greatest early satiric achievement: *The Rape of the Lock*. Scholarship on *The Rape* represents a vast field, but in terms of the burlesque, the poem is best understood through its engagement with two French predecessors, Nicolas Boileau-Despreaux and Vincent Voiture. Boileau and Voiture are associated with two modes, the mock-heroic and *galanterie*, each crucial to the shimmering burlesque of *The Rape*.

Pope's culture, apparently reverent of the epic, in fact engaged with it in awkward ways. Following Milton's death, Claude Rawson argues, the 'heroic standard' associated with epic was 'loosening its grip on English sensibilities'.[47] This was manifest in various ways. One was that it was difficult to write 'straight' epic: we need only think of Richard Blackmore's would-be weighty *Eliza. An Epick Poem* (1705), where the pseudo-Miltonic devils spend pages debating the politics of Renaissance northern Europe. Rather than original epics, translations abound, including Pope's. As Rawson notes, authors such as Abraham Cowley and William Davenant left their serious epics unfinished.[48] The same was true of Pope, who died with his *Brutus* uncompleted, cut off, as Maynard Mack believes, by 'a fine dry sense of what he could not do and what he could'.[49] Fielding's Drawcansir, his parody-hero, feels more typical of the period than Blackmore's Prince Arthur, whose military prowess unhappily inspires 'Confusion...and a chilling Damp'.[50] Epic was subject to irony: William Frost establishes that even in Pope's Homeric translations, there is parody and self-parody.[51]

The mock-heroic predominates over the heroic in Pope's culture. One of its most important theorists and practitioners was Boileau, known for his *Art poétique* (1674) and his mock-heroic *Le lutrin* (1683). His reputation in Britain was mixed: perceived as a major critic and poet, he was also, in the febrile climate of Anglo-French relations of the day, seen as a hired pen of the French government.[52] As a verse-essayist, Horatian

---

[46] [Pope et al.], *Three Hours*, 3.

[47] Claude Rawson, 'War and the Epic Mania in England and France: Milton, Boileau, Prior, and English Mock-Heroic', *RES* 64 (2013), 433–53: 451.

[48] Claude Rawson, 'Mock-Heroic and English Poetry', in *The Cambridge Companion to the Epic*, ed. Catherine Bates (Cambridge: Cambridge University Press, 2010), 167–91: 175.

[49] Mack, *Alexander Pope*, 774.

[50] *Prince Arthur. An Heroick Poem. In Ten Books*, 2nd edn. (1695), 217.

[51] William Frost, 'The *Rape of the Lock* and Pope's Homer', *Modern Language Quarterly* 8 (1947), 342–54: 347–52.

[52] Howard Weinbrot, *Menippean Satire Reconsidered: From Antiquity to the Eighteenth Century* (Baltimore: Johns Hopkins University Press, 2005), 208.

satirist, and Catholic, Boileau is often paralleled with Pope, who has even been dubbed 'the English Boileau'.[53] Most important for our purposes is Boileau's engagement with the mock-heroic. *Le lutrin*'s subject is a pulpit (or reading-desk) and the determination of a 'prélat terrible' to 'exer[cer] son grand coeur, / [Faire] placer à la fin [ce] lutrin dans le choeur'.[54] It features a book-battle and allegorical figures such as La Discorde (a fore-runner of *The Dunciad*'s Dulness). *Le lutrin* is one of a line of parody-epics: as well as *Hudibras*, important antecedents are Alessandro Tassoni's *La secchia rapita* (c.1630) and Paul Scarron's *Virgile travestie* (1648–53), both known in English.[55] The last years of the seventeenth century saw the mock-heroic gain popularity: examples include Dryden's *Mac Flecknoe* (1682) and *The Dispensary* (1699) by Pope's friend Samuel Garth. The mock-heroic generally is a form of ascensional burlesque in which small matter or a low subject is expressed through an improbably high diction. Boileau's theorization saw it as a comic periphrasis around a triviality. He remarked of his own *Lutrin* that although he had 'si peu de matiere pour un Poëme Heroïque, j'entreprendois d'en faire un, sur un Démeslé aussi peu chargé d'incidens que celui de cette Eglise [dans *Le lutrin*]'.[56] The underwhelming *lack* of 'incidens' at the centre of the poem is crucial to a burlesque which does not rely, as some do, on a gross travesty of high matter, but rather on the comedic tension between sublime rhetoric and ephemeral content. Mock-heroic gripped Pope's imagination: useful to note are its themes of learned battles and its tendency towards anti-female sentiments, as femininity debased epic.

A second French influence upon Pope was Vincent Voiture, known in English culture for his delicately flirtatious letters. Voiture was formative for Pope's style; Émile Audra sees Pope as having a decided 'période d'influence voiturienne'.[57] Voiture's legacy was not, however, straightforward: Roger Lathuillère remarks on 'son penchant pour le burlesque'.[58] Louise Curran, too, notes Voiture's employment of a distancing irony in the voices of the gallant lovers he constructs.[59] Equally important is the fact that, as Audra argues, English appropriations of Voiture took on a grosser aspect than the original.[60] An example is John Oldham's loose translation of Voiture's 'Stances sur une Dame dont la juppe [sic] fut retroussée en versant dans un carrosse'; Oldham has the lady's 'coats behind flung up, and what was under shewn to the View of the Company', making his

[53] G. F. Parker, 'Pope and Alceste', *Cambridge Quarterly* 19 (1990), 336–59: 350; Audra, *L'influence française*, 8.

[54] *Le lutrin* (1683) in *Satires. Le lutrin* (Paris, 1884), I: 1–4. My trans: 'A dread priest…whose sublime spirit dared to install a pulpit in the choir'.

[55] E.g., John Ozell's *The Rape of the Bucket* (1715) and Charles Cotton's *Scarronides* (1664).

[56] Ozell (trans.), *Rape*, 13; Boileau cited in H. A. Mason, 'Boileau's *Lutrin*', *Cambridge Quarterly* 4 (1969), 362–80: 365. My trans: although he had 'such a paucity of subject matter for a heroic poem, he essayed one anyway, using a petty quarrel such as that which took place in this church'.

[57] Audra, *L'influence française*, 338.

[58] Roger Lathuillère, 'Voiture et le "bon usage" à l'Hôtel de Rambouillet', *Cahiers de l'Association internationale des études françaises* 14 (1962), 63–78: 64.

[59] Louise Curran, 'Gallantry and *The Rape of the Lock* Reconsidered', in *Anniversary Essays on Alexander Pope's The Rape of the Lock*, ed. Don Nichol (Toronto: University of Toronto Press, 2016), 31–52: 44, 50.

[60] Audra, *L'influence française*, 335–7.

version considerably more explicit.[61] Pope's Voiture period is marked by a quasi-libertine sensibility, displayed in letters such as that sent to the Blount sisters, wittily imagining their resurrection at the Last Judgement exposing 'those white Bums...I dye to see'.[62] Voiturean *galanterie* as construed by Pope's culture included a sexualized, even misogynous edge: indeed, Richard Terry sees it as a burlesque, double-voiced idiom, as inherently anti-female as mock-heroic could be.[63]

Mockery of learning and anti-female satire, gallantry and scurrility, epic and parody all coalesce, finally, in *The Rape of the Lock*. This essay cannot hope to survey the breadth of criticism on the poem, nor to explicate the differences between the truncated two-canto version of 1712, the extended 1714 text incorporating the sylphs, and *The Rape* as found in Pope's monumental 1717 *Works*—nor can it recapitulate the celebrated toilette and ombre scenes or draw out the parodies of epic. Instead, this analysis picks out continuities between Pope's early satire and *The Rape*. Like Pope's other burlesques, *The Rape of the Lock* relies on satiric typologization and innuendo to deflate its target's self-delusions.

The first thing to emphasize when discussing *The Rape* as burlesque is its tonal distance from other such poems: this is not 'The Monster of Ragusa', with its 'Crabs' and 'privy member', or even the 'First Psalm' with its indelicate hints.[64] William Hazlitt described it as 'the most exquisite specimen of filigree work', and its fine, glancing allusiveness and sparkle are essential to appreciating the poem's satiric functions.[65] That said, commonalities between *The Rape* and Pope's other work emerge. For example, Belinda's stellification represents a major interpretative crux. M. E. Grenander has read Pope against Virgil, concluding that Belinda's elevation is 'a pretty conceit', immortalizing both heroine and poet.[66] This can be read differently, however. Turning back to Pope's Robert Norris, John Dennis, or Fossile, we recall that these satiric creations cherish a belief in their own unique insights. Similarly, Belinda is singled out by the sylph Ariel, 'too fine for mortal Sight', who reveals a 'Truth' to which ordinary 'Mortals' are 'blind'.[67] In the other satires, Pope in fact frames his targets as indexical to wider cultural foibles, deluded in their pretensions; like the later dunces, they are handed down to posterity as emblems of quackery and intellectual vanity. Comparably, as a young woman of fashion, Belinda is really

---

[61]   John Oldham, 'Upon a Lady' (1674?) in John Oldham, *The Poems*, ed. Harold F. Brooks and Raman Selden (Oxford: Clarendon Press, 1987), 204–7; Vincent Voiture, 'Stances sur une Dame', in *Poésies*, ed. Henri Lafay (Paris: Librairie Marcel Didier, 1971), 52–6.

[62]   Quoted in James Grantham Turner, 'Pope's Libertine Self-Fashioning', *The Eighteenth Century* 29 (1988), 123–44: 129.

[63]   Terry, '"Tis a sort of...Tickling"'.

[64]   Pat Rogers, '"The Monster of Ragusa": Pope, Addison, and Button's wits', *Review of English Studies* 67 (2017), 496–522, at 517.

[65]   William Hazlitt, *Lectures on the English Poets*, in *Collected Works*, ed. A. R. Waller and Arnold Glover, 12 vols. (London: J. M. Dent, 1902–6), v. 72.

[66]   M. E. Grenander, 'Pope, Virgil, and Belinda's Star-Spangled Lock', *Modern Language Studies* 10 (1979–80), 26–31: 30.

[67]   Pope, *Poems* (Twickenham), ii. 163, 153.

possessed of a 'vacant Brain', and as the 'Subject' of the poem, she is 'Slight'.[68] If Belinda is a proxy for both the historical Arabella Fermor and for women's 'Vanities', then her 'inscri[ption] 'midst the Stars' by Pope is not a benign process, but a permanent equation of her with a set of anti-female commonplaces that derive from the dual-meaning *galanterie* with which she is addressed, and her automatically ironized position as the hero*ine* of a *mock*-epic.[69] As I have shown elsewhere, when Pope addresses Arabella Fermor in the dedicatory epistle, his Voiturean apologia for 'mak[ing] use of hard Words before a Lady' is disingenuous.[70] In the poem itself, the insistent sexualization of the verse, shot through with terms such as ' "trembling", "melting", "soften'd" ', places Arabella/Belinda in the same invidious position as Phoebe Clinket: in each case, whether she is producing or produced by the language, the collision of heroic diction with erotic undertone invites a knowing sneer from the audience.[71] Contemporaries such as Gildon recognized that, as delicate as *The Rape* is, it burlesques its protagonist by subjecting her not only to the expository process involved in expressing her trivialities through 'epic' periphrasis, but also by making that very rhetoric double-tongued: when Belinda 'Burns to encounter two adventrous Knights', such lines work as high diction but also as near-smut.[72]

Such earthiness connects *The Rape* back to the carnality and even scatology of Pope's early satires: his Curll 'beshit[s]' his books and, in *Peri Bathous*, poetry is pathologized as an 'evacuation'.[73] The literary is travestied as the cloacal. Similarly, beneath *The Rape*'s glittering verse, broad physical meanings lurk: Ariel's 'soft Transition' may be read as putrefaction, and most famously, of course, post-1712 versions have Belinda wish that the Baron had seized *any* of her hairs rather than those on her head.[74] Ultimately, all of those other burlesques spoof the intellectual vanity of their targets. *The Rape* is no exception. Donna Scarboro connects *The Rape* to satires on learning when she remarks that Belinda is 'visionary' in the same way that 'philosophers' are popularly represented; also, generally, there is an equation in Scriblerian works, and indeed in the period, between appetites for sex and knowledge.[75] Seen this way, Belinda's matutinal revelation from Ariel is a sexual as much as an intellectual awakening, a 'luscious Hint to the Ladies'; the poem's paralleling of her with philosophical 'sages' due to her communing with the sylphs subjects her to the same bathetic reading as Fossile, lacking Latin and seeking sex.[76]

---

[68] Pope, *Poems* (Twickenham), ii. 151, 143.   [69] Pope, *Poems* (Twickenham), ii. 149, 212.

[70] Bonnie Latimer, 'Alchemies of Satire: A History of the Sylphs in *The Rape of the Lock*', *RES* 57 (2006), 682–700.

[71] Cf. Robin Grove, 'Uniting Airy Substance' in *The Art of Alexander Pope*, ed. H. Erskine-Hill and A. Smith (New York: Barnes and Noble, 1979), 52–87: 68.

[72] Pope, *Poems* (Twickenham), ii. 171. Compare Gildon's description of Belinda's language as 'Bawdy': Charles Gildon, *New Rehearsal* (London, 1714), 43.

[73] *A Further Account of the Most Deplorable Condition of Mr Edmund Curll* (1716), in *Prose Works*, ed. Ault, 284; *Peri Bathous*, 199.

[74] Pope, *Poems* (Twickenham), ii. 149, 198.

[75] Donna Scarboro, ' "Thy Own Importance Know": The Influence of *Le Comte de Gabalis* on *The Rape of the Lock*', *Studies in Eighteenth-Century Culture* 14 (1985), 231–41.

[76] Gildon, *New Rehearsal*, 44.

The Popean burlesque is not merely, however, a witty juxtaposition of bombast with abject reality. At times, it can seem so: Pope's Robert Norris announces ominously that

> if learning be mixed with a brain that is not of a contexture fit to receive it, the brain ferments till it be totally exhausted. We must eradicate these undigested ideas out of the *Perecranium*, and reduce the Patient to a competent knowledge of himself.[77]

This 'reduction' appears a po-facedly punitive project, but encouraging common sense and an acknowledgement of one's limitations is a moral imperative which runs throughout Pope's work. The 'Preface' to the 1717 *Works* imagines that a budding author can be reformed from 'persisting' in writing ill.[78] In his 'Postscript' to the *Odyssey*, Pope makes a statement which should surely inform our reading of his mock-heroics: 'when rational beings are represented above their real character, it becomes ridiculous in Art, *because it is vicious in Morality*'.[79] It is this insistence on perspective and self-knowledge which, I conclude, motivates all his early satires, including *The Rape*: when we are told that 'Steel cou'd the Works of Mortal Pride confound', we should take the sentiment, at least, at face value.[80]

It is a critical commonplace that, in G. Thomas Fairclough's words, for Pope 'bad writing is the outward and visible sign of inward evil'.[81] The correction of such evil is the aim of his satiric project: Allen Wood compares how Horatian and Popean satire brands (*notare*) the *malus* (evil).[82] Seen this way, Pope's satiric subjects are all 'branded'—their 'contingent realities', to re-invoke an earlier formulation, fixed immutably in the form of greater moral truths. This applies to Norris, Dennis, Philips, Blackmore, and Theobald—but also to Belinda, who typifies female 'Levity'.[83] Her asterism does not prevent a genuine asperity. This allows us to read one of the most controversial satiric gestures made by *The Rape*: the inclusion of Clarissa's speech, first inserted in 1717 and encouraging 'good Humour' and 'Sense' in the face of the shearing.[84] It is, as William Frost has shown, a parody of Sarpedon's speech in the *Iliad*, but this does not stop its having serious meaning.[85] It has been read by critics variously as 'poisonous' or as 'straightforward' moralizing.[86] I suggest that Clarissa's speech is best understood as a Menippean incursion, an interpolation of an extra-diegetic discourse of stoic common sense in the face of adversity. The former beauty mourning her charms was a topic addressed elsewhere in the culture (for example, Mary Wortley Montagu's *Saturday. The Smallpox* in *Town Eclogues* (1747)), but Pope's treatment of the subject acknowledges societal constraints whilst advocating their transcendence: 'Good humour only teaches charms to last', he

---

[77] Pope, 'The Narrative', *Prose*, i. 195.   [78] 'Preface' (1717), in Pope, *Prose*, i. 290.
[79] Pope, 'Postscript' to *Odyssey*, v. 299–300. My italics.   [80] Pope, *Poems* (Twickenham), ii. 182.
[81] G. Thomas Fairclough, 'Pope and Boileau: A Supplementary Note', *Neuphilologische Mitteilungen* 64 (1963), 232–43: 241.
[82] Wood, *Literary Theory and Satire*, 33, 37.   [83] Pope, *Poems* (Twickenham), ii. 153.
[84] Pope, *Poems* (Twickenham), ii. 201, 200.
[85] Frost, '*The Rape of the Lock* and Pope's Homer', 343–5.
[86] Andrew Varney, 'A "Tender Correspondence": Pope and *The Spectator*', *Critical Survey* 14 (2002), 42–50: 48; J. P. Hunter, 'Introduction', in *Anniversary Essays*, ed. Nichol, 3–9: 6.

tells Teresa Blount in 1710, in an echo of Clarissa's 'Charms strike the Sight, but Merit wins the Soul'.[87] Unsurprisingly, commentators have seen Pope as using such moments to frame his own experience, quietly equating his disability and marginalized religion with the limitations imposed on 'ladies'.[88] Seen this way, Clarissa's rebuttal of Belinda's fruitless wailing is not a mock-epic set-piece but a real rebuke of vanity, a miniature reprise of Sarpedon's exhortation to 'give to Fame what we to Nature owe'.[89] At this moment, instead of the mock-heroic parasitizing the epic for its own sniggering purposes, the epic casts a shadow over its parody, lending a noble weight to Clarissa's admonitions.

Later in life, Pope imposed a dividing line on his previous works: 'not in Fancy's Maze [I] wander'd long, / But stoop'd to Truth, and moraliz'd [my] song'.[90] This separation of the fanciful and the moral does not hold, however, in reading the early satires, which form part of a dense intertextual web incorporating not only *The Rape*, but disowned works such as the dubious ballads and psalms, and barely-anonymous squibs such as *The Narrative* and the Curll pamphlets, and, indeed, the *Essay* and the Homeric translations. Disparate as they are, the satires vibrate with a shared corrective moral purpose and methodology, the burlesque reduction of their targets to a competent knowledge of themselves—doing so, however, with a verve, a joyous wit, an appealingly sophomoric hilarity, which, after the 1728 *Dunciad*, Pope's work would never quite recover.

SELECT BIBLIOGRAPHY

Deutsch, Helen. *Resemblance and Disgrace: Alexander Pope and the Deformation of Culture* (Boston, MA: Harvard University Press, 1996).

Erickson, Robert A. 'Pope and Rapture', *Eighteenth-Century Life* 40 (2016), 1–31.

Fairer, David. *Pope's Imagination* (Manchester: Manchester University Press, 1984).

Ferraro, Julian. 'Crowds and Power and Pope', *RES* 63, no. 262 (2012), 779–96.

Hammond, Brean. 'Scriblerian Self-Fashioning', *Yearbook of English Studies* 18 (1988), 108–24.

Hone, Joseph. 'Pope and the Politics of Panegyric', *RES* 66, no. 273 (2014), 106–23.

Mell, Donald C., ed. *Pope, Swift, and Women Writers* (London: Associated University Presses, 1996).

Pollak, Ellen. *The Poetics of Sexual Myth* (Chicago: University of Chicago Press, 1985).

Rumbold, Valerie. *Women's Place in Pope's World* (Cambridge: Cambridge University Press, 1989).

Terry, Richard. '"Tis a sort of…tickling": Pope's *Rape* and the Mock-Heroics of Gallantry', *Eighteenth-Century Life* 18 (1994), 59–74.

Turner, James Grantham. 'Pope's Libertine Self-Fashioning', *The Eighteenth Century* 29 (1988), 123–44.

Williams, Carolyn D. *Pope, Homer, and Manliness: Some Aspects of Eighteenth-Century Classical Learning* (New York: Routledge, 1993).

---

[87] 'Epistle to Miss Blount', Pope, *Poems* (Twickenham), vi. 64. Cf. v. 201, at line 34.

[88] Valerie Rumbold, *Women's Place in Pope's World* (Cambridge: Cambridge University Press, 1989), 1–23.

[89] *The Iliad of Homer*, 6 vols. (1717), iii. 241.   [90] Pope, *Poems*, iv. 120.

CHAPTER 18

....

GRAPHIC SATIRE
Hogarth and Gillray

....

JESSE MOLESWORTH

MODERN scholarship has long sought to trace the influence of the Scriblerians, especially Jonathan Swift, Alexander Pope, and John Gay, within the literary realm, whether seen in Henry Fielding's adaptation of the generic traits of the epic to the modern novel, or in Laurence Sterne's adaptation of Scriblerian concepts of virtue to a parlour scale. This essay, by contrast, seeks to understand the extent of the Scriblerian inheritance in the practice of visual satire within eighteenth-century Britain, specifically viewed in the graphic works of William Hogarth and James Gillray.

With respect to Hogarth, this connection is not difficult to establish. Hogarth would suggest it himself, in fact, in his well-known self-portrait *Gulielmus Hogarth* (Figure 18.1). Here in the foreground, next to his dog, Trump, one finds various tools related to his craft, especially his painter's palette and his engraver's chisel. But the portrait itself rests on three books, identified in the original painting as volumes by Shakespeare, Milton, and Swift. The image therefore stages numerous lines of influence and inheritance. The facial resemblance between artist and dog suggests an emotional, almost familial, connection. The 'Line of Beauty' resting on the palette suggests various formal debts to painters and engravers whose style he admired, especially Michelangelo, Leonardo da Vinci, and Albrecht Dürer.[1] Meanwhile, the books suggest a three-pronged literary debt: to Shakespeare's realism of character, to Milton's manipulation of Christian and mythological allegory, and to Swift's characteristically pessimistic brand of satire.

However, Hogarth would do more than simply emulate Swift. This seems implied by his frontispiece to Swift's *Gulliver's Travels* (1726), which appeared scarcely two months after the book's initial publication. Rather than faithfully adapting an actual scene within

---

[1] Hogarth would later clarify the formal and aesthetic features of the Line of Beauty, as well as his debts to Michelangelo, Leonardo, and Dürer in his extended essay, *The Analysis of Beauty*. See William Hogarth, *The Analysis of Beauty*, ed. Ronald Paulson (New Haven: Yale University Press, 1997), esp. 1–14.

FIGURE 18.1 William Hogarth, *Gulielmus Hogarth*, (1748/9)

Gulliver's Travels, Hogarth's engraving, known commonly as *The Punishment Inflicted on Lemuel Gulliver* (Figure 18.2), imagines a continuation of Gulliver's misfortunes at the hands of the Lilliputians. As punishment for urinating on the Royal Palace of Mildendo, the bare-bottomed Gulliver here submits to an enema. Overseeing the operation is the first minister, carried in a thimble on the lower right, and a clergyman, who hovers over the gigantic pump (a 'Lilypucian Fire Engine') in a chamber pot, which he employs as his pulpit. Completely preoccupied with the punishment, the majority of the Lilliputians fail to notice a rat devouring a small child, on the top of the crumbling arch.

Hogarth therefore accepts Swift's criticism of the pettiness and viciousness of the Lilliputians, which implicitly suggests the pettiness and viciousness of the Walpole ministry (Swift's primary targets). But, more importantly, he extends and alters this criticism. Here, the real target is Gulliver himself, who wilfully submits to the punishment, instead of fleeing (as he does in Swift's satire) or overpowering the tyrannical but pint-sized Lilliputians. If Swift's Gulliver is a man of low capability, Hogarth's Gulliver is, by contrast,

FIGURE 18.2 William Hogarth, *The Punishment Inflicted on Lemuel Gulliver* (1726)

a man of no capability. As such, he is a fit emblem for passiveness and submissiveness in the face of the power-hungry Walpole ministry.[2]

Rather than merely adopting Swift's excremental vision, Hogarth transforms and intensifies it. Nowhere in Swift is the idea of an enema suggested (Gulliver is instead threatened with blinding). Nowhere in Swift does a Lilliputian urinate on Gulliver's hat, as Hogarth depicts at the centre of the image (thereby intensifying the hypocrisy of a people who would punish Gulliver for urinating). Nowhere in Swift do the Lilliputians worship with the cult of Priapus, as they seem to in the background of the image. Appropriately, the tone of the caption is playful rather than reverential, mockingly proclaiming that the engraving was 'intended as a frontispiece for the first Volume but Omitted'. Swift may well have suggested the image to Hogarth, as many have speculated.[3] Nevertheless, Hogarth here seems to out-Swift even Swift himself, inscribing the print to 'Nahtanoi Tfiws', bringing him into the fold as a satirical target, and even ventriloquizing him as an imagined competitor—much in the manner that Swift himself might have done.

[2] For these reasons, Paulson describes Hogarth's engraving as the 'first mature "political cartoon"'. See Ronald Paulson, *Hogarth: The 'Modern Moral Subject,' 1697–1732* (New Brunswick: Rutgers University Press, 1991), 167. For a more extended comparison with Swift's text, see David A. Brewer, *The Afterlife of Character, 1726–1825* (Philadelphia: University of Pennsylvania Press), 34.

[3] See Horace Walpole, *Anecdotes of Painting in England*, 3 vols., ed. Ralph R. Wornum (1888), iii. 21.

TWO VISIONS OF APOCALYPSE:
HOGARTH AND POPE

I wish to take this notion of out-Swifting Swift, and by extension the other Scriblerians, into a reading of Hogarth's progress, *The Four Times of the Day* (painted 1736, engraved 1738), especially its dazzling final image, *Night*. The basic connection between these two—Hogarth and Scriblerians—will again appear unsurprising. As Ronald Paulson has most forcefully demonstrated, Hogarth's mock-pastoral vision owes much to Swift's mock-pastoral poems, especially 'A Description of the Morning' (1709) and 'A Description of a City Shower' (1710), as well as to John Gay's poem, *Trivia, or the Art of Walking the Streets of London* (1716). Much like Swift's London, Hogarth's London oozes with filth and waste: spilling chamber pots, overflowing sewers, and undigested scraps of food. Verbal images from Scriblerian poetry appear at times to find direct visual counterparts within *The Four Times of the Day*. The second image, *Noon*, for example, features a dead cat lying in the city sewer, seemingly recalling the well-known closing triplet of 'A Description of a City Shower':

> Sweepings from Butchers Stalls, Dung, Guts, and Blood,
> Drown'd Puppies, stinking Sprats, all drench'd in Mud,
> Dead Cats, and Turnip-Tops, come tumbling down the Flood.
>
> (ll. 61–3)

Meanwhile, the overturned carriage in *Night* (see Figure 18.3) seems to appropriate a similar image drawn from Gay's *Trivia*:

> Ere Night has half roll'd round her Eben Throne;
> In the wide gulph the shatter'd coach o'ethrown;
> Sinks with the snorting steeds; the reins are broke,
> And from the crackling Axle flies the spoke.
>
> (III. ll. 341–4)

Borrowings like this one lead Paulson to describe Hogarth's work as a 'visual re-creation of *Trivia*'—as though to suggest that little distance exists between the two aesthetic endeavours.[4]

But, as with Hogarth's image of Gulliver, I find much more in *Night* than a simple translation of the verbal into the visual. In the same way that it appropriates and reimagines concepts drawn from Christian theology, Greek mythology, and Renaissance iconography, so too it appropriates and reimagines concepts drawn from the more immediate Scriblerian world. This re-mediation is, moreover, more extensive, more

---

[4] Ronald Paulson, *Hogarth: High Art and Low, 1732–1750* (New Brunswick: Rutgers University Press, 1992), 143.

FIGURE 18.3 William Hogarth, *Night* (1738)

omnivorous, than hitherto acknowledged. As much as it owes to Swift and Gay, it owes perhaps more to Pope, whose apocalyptic poem, *The Dunciad*, had been published recently in its variorum edition (1732). *Night*, in short, reimagines not one but several competing visions of apocalypse: Christian, Greek, and Scriblerian.

Let me start by qualifying the term I use above, 'progress', since for various reasons *The Four Times of the Day* has more often been understood by another term, 'cycle'.[5] Unlike earlier works like *The Harlot's Progress* (painted 1731, engraved 1732) and *The Rake's Progress* (painted 1732–3, engraved 1735), or later works like *Marriage à la Mode* (painted 1743–5, engraved 1745) and *Industry and Idleness* (engraved 1747), *The Four Times of the Day* does not follow the unfolding fortunes of one character, or a cast of recurring characters. In addition, the movement of the day, as suggested by the individual titles of the images, *Morning*, *Noon*, *Evening*, and *Night*, might be understood as more cyclical than progressive in its conception, as might the corresponding movement of the seasons, from winter to spring to summer to autumn. (Note the oak leaves worn by the drunken Freemason in *Night*, specifying that the date is 3 September, celebrating Charles II's hiding in a hollow oak tree after the battle of Worcester on 3 September 1651.)[6]

Rather, progress unfolds differently here, through the gradual intensification of Hogarth's social criticism from smaller, localized instances of vice to larger instances of genuine cruelty and violence. *Morning* and *Noon*, for example, begin the sequence by showcasing relatively mild offences related to the twin vices of vanity and hypocrisy. In *Morning*, the focus falls mostly on one individual: a fashionably dressed spinster at the centre of the image, who walks to church without noticing the suffering of her shivering page or the pleas of those huddled around a makeshift campfire. In *Noon*, vanity and hypocrisy have expanded their reach to virtually every character in the image. As a group of ostentatiously dressed French Huguenots file out of church, indulging their own sartorial appetites, a more slovenly group of English face them from the other side, indulging appetites more carnal and gastronomical. *Evening* and *Night*, by contrast, turn from instances of negligence to wilful acts of cruelty. In *Evening*, the focus is again tighter, falling squarely on the crumbling marriage of a dyer and his pregnant wife, who has apparently cuckolded him (such is suggested by a pair of horns hovering over his head). The presence of their two children behind them sharpens rather than distributes this focus: as the children bicker over a gingerbread man, they seem to enact the bitter struggle for custody soon to befall their parents.

In *Night*, though, Hogarth's criticism is both intense and all-consuming. Virtually every character in the image suffers at the hands of another. The drunken freemason in

---

[5] Even the most thorough discussion of Hogarth's work describes it as a 'cycle'. Here, for example, is the book description of Sean Shesgreen's otherwise rich monograph *Hogarth and the Times-Of-the-Day Tradition* (Ithaca: Cornell University Press, 1983): 'William Hogarth's series of paintings and engravings known as *The Four Times of the Day* is a masterpiece of satire, an iconoclastic portrait of everyday life in eighteenth-century London. Now Sean Shesgreen places this cycle, and the works related to it, in their art-historical context.'

[6] Most sources hold that the events of *Night* occur on 29 May, Oak Apple Day, which celebrated the restoration of the Stuart monarchy. I rather accept Shesgreen's rationale for the 3 September dating, which preserves the seasonal progression that Hogarth undoubtedly envisioned. See Shesgreen, *Times-of-the-Day*, 121.

foreground, often identified as the magistrate Sir Thomas De Veil, suffers at the hands of an unidentified person above him, who empties a chamber pot onto the street. De Veil's companion, sometimes identified as Brother Montgomerie, the Grand Tyler of De Veil's lodge, suffers at the hands of De Veil, who appears to have lost his composure and needs to be restrained.[7] So too does the gin merchant behind this central group, who would have been made De Veil's enemy by the Gin Act of 1736 (De Veil was especially known for his harsh sentences). The customer seen in the window suffers at the hands of a barber-surgeon, who delivers a reckless shave, draining him of blood. Those trapped in the overturned carriage suffer at the hands of the bystanding children, who do little to help them escape. And so on. Progress therefore unfolds in *The Four Times of the Day* conceptually rather than narratively, through degrees of cruelty and even violence. Rather than tracing one character, it envisions London and its inhabitants as the central character. Just as destruction is the natural and logical conclusion of *A Harlot's Progress* or *A Rake's Progress*, so too the destruction of *Night* is the natural conclusion of the various behaviours and deeds witnessed throughout the rest of the progress.

Hogarth's apocalyptic vision has typically been understood as a blend of Christian and classical mythological imagery, a mixture of Hell and Hades. Paulson, for example, writes of Justice De Veil as 'a modern Pluto' ruling over the London underworld and its motley cast of Saturnalian revellers. For Paulson and for others, this is no ordinary carriage. Rather, it is 'Proserpina's chariot overturned', transporting its bewildered occupants deep into the bowels of Hades.[8] Likewise the apocalypse of *Night* has been linked to a familiar Old Testament scene of destruction. So, for example, writes Sean Shesgreen:

> If London is a modern form of the underworld, it is even more obviously a contemporary Sodom and Gomorrah. Like those regions, it too is a place of proverbial corruption and wickedness, a city of drunkenness, lust, and idleness where not a single innocent person can be found, to say nothing of ten righteous men. Like those cities, it too is about to be destroyed for its depravity.[9]

One might add here that the connection to the New Testament Babylon seems, if anything, equally strong. Indeed, if the smoke and flames of *Night* channel biblical hellfire and brimstone, then the equestrian statue of Charles II in Charing Cross, seen here ascending over the scene of drunken revelry, seems also to channel a familiar vision of Death:

> And I looked, and beheld a pale horse: and his name that sat on him was Death, and Hell followed with him. And power was given unto them over the fourth part of the earth, to kill with a sword, and with hunger, and with death, and with the beasts of the earth.   (Revelation 6:8)

---

[7] See George W. Speth, 'Hogarth's Picture "Night"', *Ars Quator Coronatorum* 2 (1886), 116–17.

[8] Paulson, *Hogarth: High Art and Low*, 140. Jenny Uglow writes similarly, 'In the city lanes of *Night*, Proserpina becomes a gawping woman tumbled from her chariot, and Pluto a drunken Freemason, a tyrannical magistrate who holds the London underworld in thrall.' See Uglow, *Hogarth: A Life and a World* (London: Faber and Faber, 1997), 303.

[9] Shesgreen, *Times-of-the-Day*, 131.

FIGURE 18.4 William Hogarth, *The Distressed Poet* (1733–5), Birmingham Museums and Art Gallery

But so, too, *Night* reimagines the Scriblerian apocalypse depicted within *The Dunciad*. My reasons for drawing this connection are several, not the least of which is that Hogarth was actively thinking about Pope's poem during the period between 1735 and 1736, when he produced both the paintings of *Night* and *The Distressed Poet* (Figure 18.4), a work usually seen as inspired by *The Dunciad*. Pope's poem, of course, savagely lampoons the Grub Street culture of the hack writer, especially its King of the Dunces, Tibbald (modelled on Pope's would-be rival, Lewis Theobald). Hogarth's painting, *The Distressed Poet*, similarly depicts a Grub Street poet sitting at his desk in a dingy attic, as a milkmaid arrives demanding payment of debts. Might one see Hogarth's poet as an image of Theobald himself? Critics have often assumed so, especially given that many versions of the engraved image feature the following inscription, drawn from *The Dunciad*:

> Studious he sate, with all his books around,
> Sinking from thought to thought, a vast profound:
> Plung'd for his sense, but found no bottom there;
> Then writ, and flounder'd on, in mere despair.[10]

[10] For more on the Theobald attribution, see M. Dorothy George, *Hogarth to Cruikshank: Social Change in Graphic Satire* (New York: Walker and Company, 1967), 30.

Pope even makes an appearance in the painting, in the form of the yellowing image tacked to the wall above the poet, an apparent source of mock inspiration.

Still, I find it difficult to read *The Distressed Poet* as a 'literal illustration' of *The Dunciad*, in the way it is sometimes seen.[11] Pope's poem is grand and cosmic; Hogarth's image is smaller in scale and more familiar in its subject matter. Pope focuses mostly on the reasons for Tibbald's dunce-hood; Hogarth, by contrast, focuses mostly on its material consequences. In fact, the central figure within Hogarth's image is not even the poet. Rather, it is a character not mentioned by Pope: the poet's equally distressed wife, who sits uncomfortably close to the poet's desk, faithfully darning some clothes. It is she who receives the milkmaid and, likely, she who will have to deal with the consequences of her visit. Because of these factors, Hogarth's painting might even be described as pitiable. (No one, I think it is safe to say, would ever apply this adjective to any of the characters encountered in *The Dunciad*.) *The Distressed Poet*, therefore, follows *The Dunciad* without mimicking it, accepting its subject matter but reshaping its criticisms. More strongly, it even seems to warn very explicitly about the dangers of mimicry. Why does the poet suffer from a lack of inspiration? Perhaps because he is talentless; or perhaps because he is attempting to do little more than copy his idol Pope, who features as a source of quasi-divine inspiration (in the image on the wall, Pope wears a papal tiara and is labelled 'His Holiness'). Following Pope too closely—aping Pope—has produced little but nonsense and hackwork. The poet's writing disfigures Pope's corpus, much as the image of Pope worshipped by the poet disfigures the actual body of Pope into that of an ape.

The Four Times of the Day similarly follows *The Dunciad* without aping its central concerns. Geographically, the two works share much, with both mapping a tour through various well-known destinations in London (Covent Garden, St Giles-in-the-Fields, Sadler's Wells, and Charing Cross in *The Four Times of the Day*; The Strand, Bridewell Prison, Fleet Ditch, and Ludgate in *The Dunciad*). Temporally, the two works share even more, with both tracing the events of one day (*The Dunciad* begins on the night after Lord Mayor's Day and concludes on the succeeding night). More to the point, each work concludes with an apocalyptic image of night. We have already seen Hogarth's image of *Night*; compare it now to Pope's description of Night, the goddess whose return is foreseen along with her daughter, Dulness:

> Signs following signs lead on the Mighty Year;
> See! the dull stars roll round and re-appear.
> She comes! the Cloud-compelling Pow'r, behold!
> With Night Primæval, and with Chaos old.
> Lo! the great Anarch's ancient reign restor'd,

---

[11] Ronald Paulson, 'Emulative Consumption and Literacy: The Harlot, Moll Flanders, and Mrs. Slipslop', in *The Consumption of Culture, 1600–1800: Image, Object, Text*, ed. Ann Bermingham and John Brewer (New York and London: Routledge, 1997), 383–400, at 392. Another of Hogarth's major canvases from this period, *Strolling Actresses Dressing in a Barn*, bears the strong influence of Swift and Pope's poetry. On this topic, see especially, Christina Kiaer, 'Professional Femininity in Hogarth's *Strolling Actresses Dressing in a Barn*', in *The Other Hogarth: Aesthetics of Difference*, ed. Bernadette Fort and Angela Rosenthal (Princeton and Oxford: Princeton University Press, 2001), 76–101.

Light dies before her uncreating word:
As one by one, at dread Medaea's strain,
The sick'ning Stars fade off th' aethereal plain;
As Argus' eyes, by Hermes' wand opprest,
Clos'd one by one to everlasting rest:
Thus at her felt approach, and secret might,
Art after Art goes out, and all is Night.

(III. ll. 335–46)[12]

Night appears here and elsewhere throughout the poem as perhaps the most ancient force in the universe: anterior to the written word, anterior to wisdom, anterior even to Dulness herself:

In eldest time, e'er mortals writ or read
E'er Pallas issued from the Thund'rer's head,
Dulness o'er all possess'd her antient right,
Daughter of Chaos and eternal Night

(I. ll. 7–10)[13]

Within Pope's mythology, Night possesses little power to inspire or even to enchant. Rather, as the mother of Dulness, she is responsible for most of the latter's worst characteristics. Dulness is described as 'Gross as her sire, and as her mother grave, / Laborious, heavy, busy, bold, and blind' (I. 12–13).

Hogarth, then, accepts Pope's mythology but pushes it a step further, imagining not Dulness as Britain's chief nemesis but, even more cataclysmically, Chaos and Night. The apocalypse imagined by *The Dunciad* is one in which basic distinctions—primarily aesthetic and epistemological—have become impossible. This is the force of its conclusion:

See sculking Truth in her old cavern lye,
Secur'd by mountains of heap'd casuistry:
Philosophy, that touch'd the Heavens before,
Shrinks to her hidden cause, and is no more:
See Physic beg the Stagyrite's defence!
See Metaphysic call for aid on Sence!
See Mystery to Mathematicks fly!
In vain! they gaze, turn giddy, rave, and die.
Thy hand great Dulness! lets the curtain fall,
And universal Darkness covers all.

(III. ll. 347–56)[14]

The apocalypse imagined by *Night*, by contrast, is one in which basic moral distinctions have become impossible. What should be a festive celebration of the Crown, and by

---

[12] Pope, *Poems* (Twickenham), v. 191–3.   [13] Pope, *Poems* (Twickenham), v. 61.
[14] Pope, *Poems* (Twickenham), v. 193.

extension Britain itself, has taken a dark turn, threatening to consume the British capital in its chaos. Rather than instilling national pride, bonfires and firecrackers have instead become a public menace, causing horses to bolt and carriages to overturn. Rather than illuminating the darkened streets, the torch carried by the linkboy on the left threatens to ignite a shelter and burn everything to cinders. Rather than healing the diseased, the barber-surgeon seems only to prolong and intensify the pain suffered by his customer.

Justice De Veil stands in the middle of this infernal scene as Hogarth's Tibbald, wearing not a crown but the soiled oak leaves of a soiled Britain, whose responsibility to care and provide for its citizens has been long forgotten. In *The Dunciad*, Dulness selects Tibbald as her champion primarily because he, among all of the Dunces, embodies the erasure of aesthetic distinction, so loathed by Pope:

> In each she marks her image full exprest,
> But chief, in Tibbald's monster-breeding breast;
> Sees Gods with Daemons in strange league ingage,
> And earth, and heav'n, and hell her battles wage.
>
> (I. ll. 105–8)[15]

Night has here selected De Veil as her champion primarily because he, among the numerous minions depicted, embodies the erasure of moral distinction so loathed by Hogarth. Known equally for his harsh sentences on gin merchants and for his public drunkenness, on full display here, he is simultaneously chief enforcer and chief subverter of the law.[16] As gods and demons find themselves undifferentiated within Tibbald's art, so justice and villainy find themselves strangely entangled within De Veil's 'monster-breeding breast'. Art cannot exist in a world populated by Tibbald and his minions; but law cannot exist in a world populated by De Veil and his minions.

In this sense, Hogarthian progress reconfigures Popean prophecy. Tibbald's arrival and coronation, of course, hardly come as a surprise within the mythology of *The Dunciad*. Rather these events have been long awaited and even foretold:

> This, this is He, foretold by ancient rhymes,
> Th' Augustus born to bring Saturnian times:
> Beneath his reign, shall Eusden wear the bays,
> Cibber preside Lord-Chancellor of Plays,
> B * * sole Judge of Architecture sit,
> And Namby Pamby be prefer'd for Wit!
>
> (III. ll. 317–22)[17]

De Veil's arrival in *Night* has similarly been predicted and foretold by the gradual intensification of the various acts of vanity, hypocrisy, cruelty, and ultimately violence witnessed

---

[15] Pope, *Poems* (Twickenham), v. 75–6.

[16] For more on De Veil's reputation and unpopularity, see especially Paulson, *Hogarth: High Art and Low*, 140.

[17] Swift, *Poems* (Twickenham), v. 186–8.

throughout *The Four Times of the Day*. His hypocrisy towards the law—deliberate, cynical, and sinister—represents the apotheosis of the milder hypocrisy of the spinster in *Morning*, the supercilious vanity of the French churchgoers in *Noon*, and the familial cruelty of *Evening*. From him, as from Tibbald, flow the various monsters of *Night* (and Night).

Night was not Hogarth's last attempt to reimagine the apocalypse of Dunce-hood described and foreseen by Pope. Nor was it even his bleakest. At the end of his career (and his life), Hogarth produced *Tail Piece: The Bathos* (1764), the image intended to come last when his collected engravings came to be bound together (Figure 18.5). But whereas *Night* subtly manipulates the imagery of apocalypse into a metaphor, translating the idea of the end of time into the end of moral sense, Hogarth here literalizes the idea of the end of time. At the centre of the image, Time reclines peacefully, his scythe and his pipe broken in two, having breathed his last sigh, 'Finis'. Virtually every object within the image echoes this theme: the hourglass by Time's side is broken, the clock

FIGURE 18.5 William Hogarth, *Tail Piece: The Bathos* (1764)

on the crumbling church features no hands, Apollo appears to have died in his chariot, preventing the Sun from completing its cycle, while a crumpled print of Hogarth's own engraving of *The Times, Plate I*, will soon catch fire (thus literalizing the fire illustrated in the image itself).

Because the title of the image deliberately echoes the title of Pope's mock-aesthetic treatise *Peri Bathous, Or the Art of Sinking in Poetry* (the full title of Hogarth's image is *The Bathos, or Manner of Sinking in Sublime Paintings, inscribed to the Dealers in Dark Pictures*), modern scholarship has naturally assumed a direct correspondence between the two works, and between *Tail Piece* and *The Dunciad*. One critic writes, for example, 'The Tailpiece is a visual recreation of Pope's apocalyptic destruction of art at the conclusion of the *Dunciad*, again manifested through the idea of art becoming merely random assemblages of standard images and ideas.'[18] In truth, however, Hogarth's image is darker than either *Peri Bathous* or *The Dunciad*. *Peri Bathous* might be read as hopeful, in the sense that the apocalypse of Dunce-hood has yet to occur. Indeed, as of the time of the writing, the Dunces seem to be leaderless and unorganized:

> Wherefore considering with no small grief, how many promising geniuses of this age are wandering (as I may say) in the dark without a guide, I have undertaken this arduous but necessary task, to lead them as it were by the hand, and step by step, the gentle downhill way to the Bathos; the bottom, the end, the central point, the *non plus ultra* of true modern poesy![19]

The Dunciad, by contrast, completes this apocalyptic vision, granting the Dunces both a king (Tibbald) and a deity (Dulness). Yet it does so in a poem whose rhetoric preserves the aesthetic distinctions undone by the Dunces, thereby salvaging some shred of hope.[20]

Tail Piece, though, demolishes even this shred of hope by describing the apocalypse of Dunce-hood precisely according to the mock aesthetic principles of the Dunces. Consider, for example, Pope's description of amplification in *Peri Bathous*, a device favoured by the Dunces:

> We may define *amplification* to be making the most of a *thought*; it is the spinning wheel of the *Bathos*, which draws out and spreads it in the thoughts over a whole folio; but for which, the tale of many a vast romance, and the substance of many a fair volume might be reduced into the size of a *primer*.

[18] Aaron Santesso, 'Aesthetic Chaos in the Age of Reason', in *Disrupted Patterns: On Chaos and Order in the Enlightenment*, ed. Theodore E. D. Braun and John A. McCarthy (Amsterdam: Rodopi, 2000), 37–50, at 45.

[19] Pope, *Prose*, ii. 186.

[20] Virtually every commanding reading of *The Dunciad*, from the formalist reading offered by Fredric V. Bogel to the cultural reading offered by Peter Stallybrass and Allon White, has rested on distinguishing Pope's own voice from that the Dunces. See especially Fredric V. Bogel, 'Dulness Unbound: Rhetoric and Pope's *Dunciad*', *PMLA* 97 (1982), 844–55; Peter Stallybrass and Allon White, *The Politics and Poetics of Transgression* (Ithaca: Cornell University Press, 1986).

In the Book of *Job*, are these words, '*Hast thou commanded the morning, and caused the day spring to know his place?*' How is this extended by the most celebrated amplifier of our age?

> *Canst thou set forth th' ethereal mines* on high,
> *Which the refulgent ore of light supply?*
> *Is the celestial* furnace *to thee known,*
> *In which I* melt *the golden* metal *down?*
> *Treasures, as from whence I* deal *out light as fast,*
> *As all my stars are* lavish *suns can* waste.[21]

Tail Piece similarly churns out images precisely within Pope's 'spinning wheel of the *Bathos*', translating the overblown rhetoric of amplification into its visual equivalent. Every detail in the image reverberates with the related concepts of death and ends, without seeking to advance these concepts substantially. The pub sign for The World's End literalizes this idea without adding to it. Littered below it are 'ends' of various sorts: the butt end of a rifle, the tattered end of a broom, a candle burning down to its end, and so forth. Strewn nearby are 'lasts' of various sorts: Time's last will and testament (appointing Chaos as his executor), the last page of a play ('Exeunt omnes'), and a cobbler's device known as a 'last' (below Time's will).

The *Dunciad* is bathetic in subject matter but sublime in effect; *Tail Piece*, by contrast, is bathetic in both subject matter and effect. Despite the incursions of the Dunces, Beauty survives in *The Dunciad*, if only within Pope's own rhetoric. In *Tail Piece*, however, Hogarth's favoured visual device, the snaking Line of Beauty, seems conspicuously absent. Where it should appear, it does not, as in the bow at the bottom, which has been broken off, or on the palette, which is cracked and unusable. Hogarth's final image is one, therefore, in which he figures himself, despairingly, as Dunce.

TWO MORE VISIONS OF APOCALYPSE:
GILLRAY AND SHERIDAN

Satirical images therefore existed along a visual/verbal continuum in eighteenth-century Britain, which enabled a fluid circulation within a variety of different media. As Mark Hallett has thoroughly shown, verbal images—Gulliver bestriding Lilliput, for example—were swiftly translated into visual images. Likewise, visual images—Gulliver receiving an enema at the hands of the Lilliputians, for example—were just as swiftly translated into verbal images, and then back into visual images.[22] This circulation made few

---

[21] Pope, *Prose*, ii. 202.
[22] For more on these two examples, see Mark Hallett, *The Spectacle of Difference: Graphic Satire in the Age of Hogarth* (New Haven: Yale University Press, 1999), esp. 131–68.

hierarchical distinctions. As images travelled with relative freedom from one medium to another—newspapers, broadsides, paintings, folio-bound poems, engravings, plays, novels, and so forth—so they travelled, with relative freedom again, from one intended audience to another.

Such is certainly the case for the satirical image described in the previous section: the image of an apocalypse, characterized by a holocaust of Dunces. Later in the century, during the reign of George III, the image would be invoked again, this time by the political caricaturist, James Gillray (1757–1815), the major figure in what has come to known as the 'Age of Caricature'.[23] Rather than configuring apocalypse as the end of rhetorical distinction, as with *The Dunciad*, or the end of moral distinction, as with *Night*, Gillray merges these configurations into one. The image *Presages of the Millennium* (1795), for example, lampoons the various figures responsible for bringing Britain into war with France (Figure 18.6). At the centre of the image is the Prime Minister, William Pitt, a vision of Death on a pale horse, wielding a flaming sword and wearing a band around his head with the word 'Destruction'. Seated behind him, kissing his bare buttocks, is the imp-like George, Prince of Wales (who would become George IV in 1820). Carried along behind in his fiery train are Henry Dundas, the secretary of war (carrying a pitchfork), and the snake-like figure of Edmund Burke, who supported the war despite his opposition to Pitt. The caption underscores the connection to the Book of Revelation: 'And e'er the Last Days began, I looked & beheld a White Horse, & his name was Death, & Hell followed after him ... And I saw under him the souls of the Multitude, those who were destroy'd for maintaining the word of Truth, & for the Testimony.'

The image therefore concentrates equally on Pitt and his allies as it does on such 'souls of the multitude', who appear here in the form of the trampled Whig opposition. Led by the rotund figure of Charles James Fox, who clings to a scroll emblazoned with the word 'Peace', their faces are recognizable: the radical politician John Horne Took, Charles Stanhope, Lord Grafton, William Wilberforce, and, struggling to regain his feet, Richard Brinsley Sheridan. But clustered together as they are in a fleshy blob of limbs and faces, they appear confused and disorganized—closer in kind to the horde of dead swine littering the ground beneath Pitt's charging steed than to a functional political party comprising individual politicians motivated by individual interests and consciences.

As Pope found his King Dunce in Theobald (and later Cibber) and Hogarth found his King Dunce in De Veil, so Gillray, here and elsewhere, figures Fox as King Dunce. 'Peace' may well be the 'word of Truth' mentioned in the caption; but it appears little more than an empty political slogan in the hands of the quaking Fox, completely evacuated of meaning and on the verge of catching fire and going up in smoke. Though nominally opposed to the apocalypse represented by Pitt, Fox's forces are nevertheless one of the 'presages of the millennium' mentioned in the title—made so by their Dunce-like lack of

[23] See Diana Donald, *The Age of Caricature: Satirical Prints in the Reign of George III* (New Haven: Yale University Press, 1996). See also Vincent Carretta, *George III and the Satirists from Hogarth to Byron* (Athens: University of Georgia Press, 2008); Todd Porterfield, ed., *The Efflorescence of Caricature, 1759–1838* (Farnham: Ashgate, 2011); Ian Haywood, *Romanticism and Caricature* (Cambridge: Cambridge University Press, 2013).

Presages of the MILLENIUM; — with — The Destruction of the Faithful, — as Revealed to R. Brothers, the Prophet, &c. attested by M.B. Hallhead.Esq.
And see the Last Days began, I looked, & behold, a White Horse, & his Name who sat upon it was Death; & Hell followed after him; & Power was given unto him, to kill with the
Sword, & with Famine, & with Death; And I saw under him the Souls of the Multitude, those who were destroy'd for maintaining the word of Truth; & for the Testimony —

FIGURE 18.6 James Gillray, *Presages of the Millennium* (1795)

distinction and, therefore, conviction. Elsewhere, Gillray would make this even clearer, as in the well-known *Doublures of Characters, or Striking Resemblances in Physiognomy* (1798), which depicts the Whig Opposition in double: as they pretend to be and as they actually are (Figure 18.7). Sheridan (top row, centre) pretends to be 'A Friend to his Country', for example, but he doubles as 'Judas selling his Master' (note the bag of silver). The Duke of Norfolk (top right) pretends to be a 'Character of High Birth', but he doubles as 'Silenus debauching'. And Fox (top left) pretends to be 'The Patron of Liberty', but closer scrutiny of his physiognomy reveals him to be no less than 'The Arch-Fiend' himself, whose numerous deceptions might be said to have originated the very idea of hypocrisy.[24]

Thus, at the end of the century, Gillray reimagines Dunce-hood as ideological in character and political in medium. This was, as critics have noticed, something relatively

---

[24] For more on this image, see Victor S. Navasky, *The Art of Controversy: Political Cartoons and Their Enduring Power* (New York: Alfred A. Knopf, 2013), 61–2. Gillray would connect Fox to Satan on several other occasions. See especially *The Table's Turn'd* (1797) and *The Tree of Liberty, with the Devil Tempting John Bull* (1798).

FIGURE 18.7 James Gillray, *Doublures of Characters, or Striking Resemblances in Physiognomy* (1798)

new: an 'era of conviction politics, when personal loyalty to an ideology could, for the first time, become an issue'.[25] What was lost was not the distinction between good and bad poetry, as Pope imagined, or between moral and immoral actions, as Hogarth imagined. Rather, what seems to have been sacrificed in the era of ideological allegiance is the distinction between one voice and another. One spoke not for one's own self but, instead, on behalf of the party, or the faction. In print after print, Gillray would employ an array of visual metaphors illustrating the concomitant meaninglessness of words and rhetoric. In *The Bubbles of Opposition* (1788), for example, Fox literally blows his political allies into existence: Burke appears (wearing glasses), as does Sheridan (facing Burke, with blotchy skin) and the Prince of Wales (facing the viewer, recognizable for the slogan 'Ich Dien', or 'I serve', above him) (Figure 18.8). Such bubbles are made from 'Devonshire Sope', suggesting the support of the Duke and Duchess of Devonshire. Perhaps more significantly, they come from the 'Coalition Washing Tub', which rests on a slab of 'Portland Stone', thereby remembering an act perceived as the height of political hypocrisy: when

---

[25] Donald, *Age of Caricature*, 42. See also Christopher Reid, *Imprison'd Wranglers: The Rhetorical Culture of the House of Commons, 1760–1800* (Oxford: Oxford University Press, 2012); and David Francis Taylor, *Theatres of Opposition: Empire, Revolution, & Richard Brinsley Sheridan* (Oxford: Oxford University Press, 2012).

FIGURE 18.8 James Gillray, *The Bubbles of Opposition* (1788)

Fox joined his enemy Lord North in April 1783 to form a coalition opposition (the Fox–North Coalition was nominally headed by the Duke of Portland).[26]

A Smoking Club (1793), published twelve days after France declared war on Britain, similarly employs smoke as a metaphor for hollow political rhetoric. Cleverly, each figure possesses a different manner of smoking (Figure 18.9). The bloated Fox sends a cloud of smoke directly into the face of Pitt, who returns the volley with a long train of smoke that sails over Fox's head. Lord Chancellor Loughborough, to the left, exhales out of each side of his mouth, suggesting both equanimity and duplicity. Meanwhile, the Irishman Sheridan and the Scot Dundas, to the right, stare menacingly at one another through two clouds of smoke; whether or not they can actually see each other, though, is unclear.[27]

Sheridan's increasing role in Gillray's satires of the Whig opposition is worthy of notice. Indeed, if Fox might be seen as Gillray's King Dunce, known principally for his

[26] For more on this image, see James Gillray, *The Satirical Etchings of James Gillray*, ed. Draper Hill (New York: Dover Publications, 1976), 100–1.

[27] For more on this image, see Thomas Wright (ed.), *The Works of James Gillray, the Caricaturist: With the History of His Life* (1873), 166.

FIGURE 18.9 James Gillray, *A Smoking Club* (1793)

hypocrisy, then Fox's long-time ally, Sheridan, might be seen as his Dunce Laureate, uniquely skilled in the art of hollow rhetoric. Gillray's image *Richard Brinsley Sheridan (Pizarro Contemplating over the product of his new Peruvian mine)* (1799), for example, shows the playwright politician glorying in the popular success of his operatic drama *Pizarro*, whose language of anti-colonialism borrowed heavily from his own political speeches.[28] Within Gillray's image, though, Sheridan himself has become colonial exploiter, selling once cherished principles for gold (Figure 18.10). Habited as Pizarro and clutching gold coins spilling from his conquistador's helmet, Sheridan soliloquizes, 'Honour? Reputation? A mere Bubble! Will the praise of posterity charm my bones in the Grave? Psha! My present purpose is all! Gold! Gold! For thee I would sell my native Spain, as freely as I would plunder Peru'. Meanwhile, behind the figure of Sheridan,

---

[28] See Julie A. Carlson, 'Trying Sheridan's *Pizarro*', *Texas Studies in Literature and Language* 38, no. 3/4 (Fall/Winter 1996), 359–78. Numerous other images caricatured Sheridan as Pizarro, such as Cruikshank's *The Return from Pizarro* (1799), *Pizarro Returning from the Gold Mines on Peru!* (1799), and *Returning from Pizarro!* (1799), as well as Gillray's *Pizarro* (1799). See Heather McPherson, 'Caricature, Cultural Politics, and the Stage: The Case of *Pizarro*', *Huntington Library Quarterly* 70 (2007), 607–31; Taylor, *Theatres of Opposition*, 230–2; and Jack De Rochi and Daniel Ennis, *Richard Brinsley Sheridan: The Impresario in Political and Cultural Context* (Lewisburg: Bucknell University Press, 2012), 259–84.

FIGURE 18.10 James Gillray, *Richard Brinsley Sheridan (Pizarro Contemplating over the product of his new Peruvian mine)* (1799)

spirals of cupids hold placards with titles like 'Oracle Puff', 'Morning Chronicle Puff Puff Puff', and 'Morning Herald Puff', suggesting that the performance has been 'puffed', or advertised heavily in local media.

Gillray thus accomplishes several things in the image. First, he imagines Sheridan as another of his own dramatic creations: in addition to Pizarro, he is Puff, the hack playwright from his earlier comedic drama, *The Critic* (1779). Second, he connects Sheridan and, by implication, the entire Fox circle to another relatively new form of discourse: puffery, the hollow rhetoric of modern advertising. If Sheridan is adept at manipulating puffery, both political and commercial, it is precisely because he had exposed it so incisively in his career as playwright. In *The Critic*, for instance, the character Puff, the self-styled 'Professor of the Art of Puffing', proudly claims to have ghost-written a great majority of commercial advertisements, including those for his own plays. He has, in addition, mentored a new breed of commercial auctioneers, instructing them in various rhetorical ploys. One of these, for example, is the art of mixing metaphors: 'Yes sir, by me they were instructed to clothe ideal walls with gratuitous fruits—to insinuate obsequious rivulets into visionary groves—to teach courteous shrubs to nod their approbation of the grateful soil!'[29] As Puff Laureate, he has even codified the practice of modern puffery, much in the manner of the hack author of *Peri Bathous*:

> Yes sir,—PUFFING is of various sorts—the principal are, The PUFF DIRECT—the PUFF PRELIMINARY—the PUFF COLLATERAL—the PUFF COLLUSIVE, and the PUFF OBLIQUE, or PUFF by IMPLICATION.—These all assume, as circumstances require, the various forms of LETTER TO THE EDITOR—OCCASIONAL ANECDOTE—IMPARTIAL CRITIQUE—OBSERVATION from CORRESPONDENT,—or ADVERTISEMENT FROM THE PARTY.[30]

Sheridan, then, connects the hollow rhetoric of modern commercial advertisement with that of the hack playwright. Gillray, by turn, connects these forms of hollow rhetoric with that of the modern politician, especially as employed by the Foxite Whigs. As Gillray would put it in the caption to his most famous image of Sheridan, *Uncorking Old Sherry* (1805), 'he does not very often address the House, yet when he does, he always thinks proper to pay off all arrears, & like a bottle just uncork'd bursts all at once into an explosion of Froth & Air'. Such 'Froth & Air' consists, in Gillray's image, of a torrent of 'Stale Jokes', 'Dramatic Ravings', 'Stolen Jests', and 'Fibs, Fibs, Fibs!' All of these forms of hollow rhetoric—the frothy ravings of politicians, the florid effusions of commercial advertisements, the senseless contrivances of hack playwrights—express themselves, by turn, as modern versions of braying, Pope's master trope for sound without meaning:

> Now thousand tongues are heard in one loud din:
> The Monkey-mimicks rush discordant in.
> 'Twas chatt'ring, grinning, mouthing, jabb'ring all,
> And Noise, and Norton, Brangling, and Breval,
> Dennis and Dissonance; and captious Art,
> And Snip-snap short, and Interruption smart.
> Hold (cry'd the Queen) A Catcall each shall win,
> Equal your merits! equal is your din!
> But that this well-disputed game may end,
> Sound forth, my Brayers, and the welkin rend.[31]

One might therefore sketch the following genealogy of Dunce-hood in eighteenth-century Britain, as it manifested itself across various media, visual, verbal, and dramatic: Tibbald/Bayes (Pope), De Veil (Hogarth), Puff (Sheridan), and Fox/Sheridan (Gillray). This genealogy is undoubtedly incomplete: the twin concepts of Dunce-hood (theme) and apocalypse (image) share a richer history than can be sketched in one essay, or even several. Swift, for example, already seems to have arrived at this connection in the

---

[29] *The Critic*, Act I, scene ii. See Richard Sheridan, *The School for Scandal and Other Plays*, ed. Eric S. Rump (Harmondsworth: Penguin Books, 1988), 148. Gillray would later return to the idea of Sheridan as Puff in *The Theatrical Bubble: being a new specimen of the astonishing Powers of the great Politico-Punchinello, in the Art of Dramatic Puffing* (1805).

[30] Sheridan, *School*, 150.   [31] Pope, *Poems* (Twickenham), v. 128–9.

apocalyptic ending of *Gulliver's Travels*, in which his own Dunce, Lemuel Gulliver, loses grasp of basic distinctions between human and animal. So, too, William Blake would draw a similar connection in *The Book of Urizen* (1794), in which apocalyptic imagery accompanies not the end of time but its beginning, and reason is seen not as an antidote to Dunce-hood but its very source. No doubt other similar genealogies might be sketched. The Scriblerians left their mark on many fields; the practice of graphic satire simply offers one of the most vibrant and suggestive examples.

Select Bibliography

Carretta, Vincent. *George III and the Satirists from Hogarth to Byron* (Athens: University of Georgia Press, 2008).

Donald, Diana. *The Age of Caricature: Satirical Prints in the Reign of George III* (New Haven: Yale University Press, 1996).

Fort, Bernadette and Angela Rosenthal, eds. *The Other Hogarth: Aesthetics of Difference* (Princeton and Oxford: Princeton University Press, 2001).

George, M. Dorothy. *Hogarth to Cruikshank: Social Change in Graphic Satire* (New York: Walker and Company, 1967).

Hallett, Mark. *The Spectacle of Difference: Graphic Satire in the Age of Hogarth* (New Haven: Yale University Press, 1999).

Haywood, Ian. *Romanticism and Caricature* (Cambridge: Cambridge University Press, 2013).

Paulson, Ronald. *Hogarth: The 'Modern Moral Subject,' 1697–1732* (New Brunswick: Rutgers University Press, 1991).

Paulson, Ronald. *Hogarth: High Art and Low, 1732–1750* (New Brunswick: Rutgers University Press, 1992).

Paulson, Ronald. *Hogarth: Art and Politics, 1750–1764* (New Brunswick: Rutgers University Press, 1993).

Porterfield, Todd, ed. *The Efflorescence of Caricature, 1759–1838* (Farnham: Ashgate, 2011).

Shesgreen, Sean. *Hogarth and the Times-Of-the-Day Tradition* (Ithaca: Cornell University Press, 1983).

CHAPTER 19

....

ROMANCE, SATIRE, AND THE EXPLOITATION OF DISORDER

....

JONATHAN LAMB

THREE genres that find a lot in common during the two hundred years separating the publication of Cervantes's *Don Quixote* from Jane Austen's *Northanger Abbey* are satire, romance, and the novel. While these days it is usual to discover a mutual dependence between romance and the novel, and a growing division between the novel and satire, it was generally assumed in the eighteenth century that Cervantes had produced a satire of chivalric and pastoral romance that revealed the potential of realist fiction explored variously by Charlotte Lennox, Henry Fielding, Laurence Sterne, and Jane Austen, among others. I want to begin with a brief characterization of the oldest of these three genres, satire, and then proceed to the other two, with the intention of suggesting an alliance between satire and romance that fuelled the satiric novels of, for instance, Fielding and Sterne.

THE CONFIDENT DISORDER OF ROMANCE

Whether urbane or savage, Roman satire was produced and consumed as a chastisement of the decay of public and private morality. It aimed to correct the vices fostered by the enormous wealth of imperial Rome: luxury, corruption, and lewdness. It was understood, however, that the ground of the satirist was never entirely stable—he had a patron because patronage was an attractive addition to other ostentations of riches, and he had something to write about because corruption was endlessly inventive. If Juvenal's satire of excess is as it were vomited out as fragments of food, at least he had a feast to go to and a vomitorium to puke in.[1] The urbanity of Horace's verse, like the elegant circumstances of his life, participates (even at a distance) in the behaviour he reproaches. The picture of Addison holding court in the *Epistle to Arbuthnot*, teaching his disciples to indulge the faults he pretends to deprecate, is a prevarication Pope laments, although not altogether guiltless of it himself. Among the many contradictions that the energy and wit of satire reconciles, an idea of the best is always adjacent to an experience of the worst. When that elliptical tension is lost, vomiting gives way to what John Henderson calls the Juvenalian frenzy, 'when his transparent efforts to talk sense come apart at the seams'.[2]

In the late seventeenth and eighteenth centuries Roman satiric techniques and even whole satires were imitated by British poets. Possibly imitation was responsible for subjects and modes of attack being too familiar. At any rate Swift tirelessly complains of the public's readiness to accept chastisement vicariously, always understood as applying to other people. You can report that honesty is fled with Astraea and everyone will return thanks for the delivery of a useful and precious truth.[3] As Colin Burrow has pointed out, 'new satirists need new customs and new forms of corruption to give authority to their new poems'.[4] Perhaps it is novelty that is responsible for Juvenalian frenzy, such as the fury of a witty libertine out-libertined by a witless rival in Rochester's *A Walk in St James's Park*. Irony is the method of neutralizing this indignity while still apparently inhabiting it, masking satire as lunatic panegyric or advancing an argument *against* abolishing Christianity. How many hours, one wonders, did Swift spend listening to the inanities of Dublin drawing rooms, or discovering the multifarious rogueries of footmen and maidservants, before he could write *A Complete Collection of Genteel and Ingenious Conversation* or *Directions to Servants*?

Johnson tells this story of Swift's reply to an arrogant lawyer who challenged him to identify himself as the author a satire against him. 'Mr Bettesworth, I was in my youth acquainted with great lawyers, who knowing my disposition to satire, advised me, that if any scoundrel or blockhead whom I had lampooned should ask, "Are you the author of this paper?" I should tell him that I was not the author; and therefore I tell you Mr Bettesworth, that I am not the author of those lines.'[5] So Swift secured himself behind impersonations of the vice or frenzy he aimed to expose, a penetrable disguise that challenged the reader to understand what was meant by what was not being said. Thus the author of the *Tale* elects to praise the whole world, and the author of *Gulliver's Travels* is as particular as the men of Gresham College in delivering the thing alleged as that which

---

[1] Victoria Rimell, 'The Poor Man's Feast', in *The Cambridge Companion to Roman Satire*, ed. Kirk Freudenberg (Cambridge: Cambridge University Press, 2005), 84.

[2] John Henderson, 'The Turnaround: A Volume Retrospect on Roman Satires', in *The Cambridge Companion to Roman Satire*, 314–15.

[3] Swift, *Works* (Cambridge), i. 31–2.

[4] Colin Burrow, 'Roman Satire in the Sixteenth Century', in *The Cambridge Companion to Roman Satire*, 259.

[5] Samuel Johnson, *The Lives of the Most Eminent English Poets*, 4 vols. (1791), iii. 404.

only is, but isn't. But the very reader expected to appreciate this subtlety is part of the multitude ridiculed for its stupidity.

Irony flourishes, provided the reader can see the difference between what is being said and not said. An obtuse public can force the ironist to avow his irony and to confess what he meant when he wrote it, as Swift did in the 1710 'Author's Apology' prefixed to the *Tale*: 'Some of those passages in this discourse which appear most liable to objection, are what they call parodies, where the author personates the style and manner of other writers, whom he has a mind to expose.' If the trick is to expose others by hiding oneself, it is fatal to suddenly appear with a *me voici*, sounding exactly like his own personation and slipping into invective when he assures the reader he is unmoved 'by the ill-placed Cavils of the Sour, the Envious, the Stupid and the Tastless, which he mentions with disdain.'[6] Empson called it 'comic primness' in Gay's satires when he makes it a little too plain that what he despises in others, such as toadying to the great and powerful, is what he has been doing himself. Swift's satiric imagination sets the stakes much higher, for it is not corruption but madness that he has been impersonating in his major satires, and to take off the mask of frenzy is to leave oneself singularly naked, coming apart at the seams as Henderson puts it. In his *Anatomy of Melancholy* Robert Burton finds himself in this predicament every time he tries to set a bound to satire and madness. After asking his reader carefully to study the difference between acting the madman and being mad in earnest, he loses all restraint and then has to plead forgiveness from the readers he has been abusing, 'I have had a raving fit, a phantastical fit... offended others, wronged myself; and now being recovered... cry with Orlando, *Solvite me*.'[7]

Northrop Frye points out that irony is entirely absent from romance; at the same time it is replete with moral and political anarchy that would alarm the censors of civil society.[8] As we shall find, even the device of the double author Swift exploits so well provides no room for reflective judgement in romance, where even if everything is not as it ought to be, it is as it is and no one is about to change it. All of this is very plausibly explored by Henry James in his *Art of the Novel* when he says of romance, 'The only *general* attribute of projected romance... that fits all its cases, is the fact of the kind of experience with which it deals—experience liberated, so to speak; experience disengaged, disembroiled, disencumbered, exempt from the conditions that we usually know to attach to it [and] operating in a medium which relieves it of the inconvenience of a related, a measurable state, a state subject to all our vulgar communities.'[9] Romance has no investment in propriety and consensus, nor any in historical accuracy, and none at all in the moral law of consequences. James goes on, 'The real represents... the things we cannot possibly *not* know, sooner or later, in one way or another.... The romantic stands, on the other hand, for the things that... we never *can* directly know; the things that can reach us only through the beautiful circuit and subterfuge of our

---

[6] Swift, *Works* (Cambridge), i. 7, 6 (italics reversed).

[7] Robert Burton, *The Anatomy of Melancholy*, 2 vols. (London: Dent, 1961), i. 122.

[8] Northrop Frye, 'The Mythos of Summer: Romance' and 'The Mythos of Winter: Satire', in *Anatomy of Criticism*, ed. Robert D. Denham (Toronto: University of Toronto Press, 2006), 182.

[9] Henry James, *The Art of the Novel*, ed. R. P. Blackmur (New York: Charles Scribner, 1947), 33.

thought and our desire.'[10] If the purpose of the novel is social utility measured against the passage of time, romance deals with actions and events taking place in an unfolding present, each enveloped in the energy of its own moment, answerable solely to the criteria of imagination and passion. The elaborate gestes of war and love, sources of all that is valuable in this world—glory, worship, and passionate servitude—are not constitutive fictions, like those of the novel, but repetitions of the unchanging belief in the necessity of violence, the irresistible force of erotic love, and the transfiguring truth of fancy. There is much to feel of anger, desire, humiliation, and grief, but nothing to learn from the experience of excess save that everything is exceptional, even though it happens again and again.[11] Hobbes thought romance stuttering and innumerate nonsense, unable to calculate or account for anything: 'A natural foole that could never learn by heart the order of numerall words, as *one*, *two*, and *three*, may observe every stroak of the Clock, and nod to it, or say one, one, one; but can never know what houre it strikes.'[12]

The words repeated most frequently in this world of confident disorder are 'questionless' and 'doubtless'. They underwrite a conviction of absolute exceptionality that is summed up in the exclamation of Mme de Lafayette's heroine in *The Princess of Cleves*: 'In the whole world there is not another case like mine.'[13] It is not an embarrassment but a triumph to be so peculiar, rising well above all aspiring parallels and ambitious analogies, for the truth is there is nothing like it, therefore no ready means of communicating its glory. As the young Eliza Haywood avers in the narrative of *Love in Excess*, 'There is no greater proof of a vast and elegant passion, than the being incapable of expressing it.'[14] As for the shame attaching to fornication, adultery, incest, and illegitimacy, it is absent from romance. Illegitimacy is perhaps the most dramatic illustration of an unconcern about consequences that invades not only the action but also the structure and temporality of romance. Doubts about origin and posterity are scarcely ever raised, for it is almost as if birth out of wedlock provides a non-dynastic title to positions of greatest power and esteem, a custom honoured in the accession of bastards to principal vacancies that are especially numerous after whole fellowships such as Arthur's and Charlemagne's are obliterated. Galahad, the bastard issue of Lancelot's enchanted encounter with Elaine le Blank, succeeds in the quest for the Sangraal; Arthur, the leader of the Round Table, is the bastard son of Igraine, begotten on her by the besotted Uther Pendragon. Isaie le Triste, the illegitimate son of Iseult and Tristan, restores the chivalry of Britain after the deaths of Arthur and Lancelot.[15] There is a corresponding aristocratic community of adultery. Tristan and Iseult, the wife of King Mark, elope to Joyous Garde where Lancelot is their host, vindicator of the innocence that Guinevere long ago lost to him.

---

[10] James, *Art of the Novel*, 31.
[11] C. S. Lewis, *The Allegory of Love* (New York: Oxford University Press, 1958), 2–3.
[12] Thomas Hobbes, *Leviathan*, ed. Richard Tuck (Cambridge: Cambridge University Press, 2004), 27.
[13] Marie-Madeleine de Lafayette, *The Princess of Cleves*, ed. John D. Lyons (New York: Norton, 1994), 77.
[14] Eliza Haywood, *Love in Excess*, ed. David Oakleaf (Peterborough: Broadview Press, 2000), 101.
[15] John Dunlop, *The History of Fiction*, 3 vols., 2nd edn. (Edinburgh, 1816), i. 276.

It is not possible to satirize romance because it shares none of the shame or rage associated with the satirist's fallen world. Instead of a table of commandments, it acknowledges certain protocols and ceremonies that render violence and adultery consonant with what passes for good order as long as the forms are observed; even malice is worn on the sleeve, perfectly legible. This inversion is performed by Charlotte Lennox's Arabella when she explains the lengths to which constancy in true love is obliged to go, for it is sometimes proof of the most exalted passion to embrace the cause of one's enemy, or one's rival in love, to prove its absolute singularity: 'It is in that peculiarity... that generosity consists, for certainly there is nothing extraordinary in fighting for one's father and one's country; but when a man has arrived to such pitch of greatness of soul as to neglect those mean and selfish considerations, and, loving virtue in the persons of his enemies, can prefer their glory before his own particular interest, he is then a perfect hero indeed.'[16] When they find their daughter's becoming 'particular' ('Can love be controlled by advice?') Mr and Mrs Peachum put it down to her reading romances.

So it is impossible to do anything within the fellowship of chivalry and the cult of amour courtois that is not extraordinary, certain, and decisive, even if it isn't true or right—sex, bravery, and villainy are all exorbitant to the standards an early modern reader might want to apply. 'Clearly we have to do here with the attempt to specify something which contrasts with normality,' says Niklas Luhmann, 'i.e. an unusual situation which makes unusual behavior appear understandable and acceptable.'[17] 'Love then was not as love is nowadays,' says Malory as Lancelot disappears into a bedroom with Guinevere; a remark which is value-free given his other glosses on eros and mutability ('the old love was not so'—i.e. unfaithful) and on Guinevere herself, 'that while she lived she was a true lover.'[18] We can assume that no conflict is taking place in Lancelot's mind when he declares to King Arthur, 'I shall ever make large answer, and prove it upon any knight that beareth the life... that my lady, Queen Guenever, is a true lady unto your lord as any as is living.'[19] And the king, more than once witness to his wife's imminent execution for treachery to his bed, is quite willing to take the declaration in good faith. Nothing stops this from being the madness of a coterie cult except the elaborate ritual of its excesses, the prescribed inevitability of the gestures leading towards adultery and violence: 'The code's unity was set at a level above all codes of behaviour.'[20] The scandal of the princess in *La Princesse de Cleves* is to rupture the code with a domestic punctilio that precipitates the sheer anarchy that ritual excess (like irony in satire) had kept under control.

---

[16] Charlotte Lennox, *The Female Quixote; or, The Adventures of Arabella*, ed. Margaret Dalziel (Oxford: Oxford University Press, 1989), 229.

[17] Niklas Luhmann, *Love as Passion: The Codification of Intimacy*, trans. Jeremy Gaines and Doris L. Jones (Cambridge, MA: Harvard University Press, 1986), 65.

[18] Sir Thomas Malory, *Le Morte d'Arthur*, ed. Janet Cowen, 2 vols. (Harmondsworth: Penguin, 1969), ii. 2.

[19] Malory, *Morte*, 477.   [20] Luhmann, *Love as Passion*, 69.

REALISM AND SATIRE

Cervantes was the first to bring immeasurable romance inside vulgar communities to see how common sense and the subterfuges of desire would get on together. He did this, it was thought, to expose the improbability of romance's claims to worship and glory while licensing every outrageous paradox that passion suggests. Echoing Johnson's fourth *Rambler* paper, Clara Reeve pointed out that the novel does not concern itself with fabulous persons and things, but is instead 'a picture of real life and manners, and of the times in which it was written', and that it owed its genesis to 'the Satire of Cervantes [which] drove these books off the stage'.[21] By introducing young people to the calculable events likely to be encountered as they float down the stream of custom, the novel fulfilled a task on their behalf Johnson had described as teaching an art of probable conjecture. Modern fiction engages readers as yet unfamiliar with the world in 'mock encounters in the art of necessary defence... increas[ing] prudence without impairing virtue'.[22] The liberty that romance gave to imagination and action is supplanted by preparation for experience consistent with the preservation of innocence, an exercise in which imagination, like the novel itself, will be harnessed to the standard of likelihood.

Whether satire is seen as an instrument of equal or auxiliary importance in enforcing the distinction between what really exists in the world and what doesn't, it served ostensibly under the same realist standard as the novel, refining techniques designed to reveal things as they actually are and to make judgements about them. In verse satires such as John Gay's *Trivia: or, The Art of Walking the Streets of London*, portions of Pope's *Dunciad*, and Jonathan Swift's *A City Shower* the experience of urban scenery—transport, drainage, trade, street festivals—bears comparison in its lavish accumulation of the particulars of dirt and excess with Juvenal's third satire. They are contemporary with the first of many variations played on *The London Spy* by Tom Brown and Ned Ward, with many imitators throughout the eighteenth century and the next. The genre derived from continental exponents of social espionage such as *The Turkish Spy* (1683), *Persian Letters* (1721), *The Jewish Spy* (1738), and *The Golden Spy* (1709), all to some degree crossing the line between satire and social anthropology. Charles Gildon's *The Golden Spy* inaugurated an offshoot of spy literature now known generally as the it-narrative in which things—coins, coaches, watches, animals—observe human customs and follies, sometimes in a vein of satire so very sharp one of Gildon's coins has to be restrained for fear of damaging faith in civil society.

In novels such as Fielding's *Joseph Andrews*, Smollett's *Roderick Random*, and Sterne's *Tristram Shandy* the alliance between realism and satire is close, except that the typical definition of Cervantes's satire has been rearranged. Instead of the improbabilities of romance, the social ills of vanity, lust, hypocrisy, mendacity, ambition, and greed are in

[21] Clara Reeve, *The Progress of Romance*, 2 vols. (New York: Garland, 1970), i. 111, 58.
[22] Samuel Johnson, *The Rambler*, ed. W. J. Bate and Albrecht B. Stauss, 3 vols. (New Haven: Yale University Press, 1969), i. 22–3 (no. 4, 31 March 1750).

the spotlight, variously aligned in conspiracies against innocence so unworldly it is obviously inspired by the visionary folly of Don Quixote himself. The vulnerable ignorance Johnson assigned to the female reader of the novel was transposed to the plot of the fiction, an idea that female novelists such as Charlotte Lennox and Jane Austen cleverly exploited. But in all of these experiments the difficulty was exactly as Johnson had defined it: how to endow Quixotic characters with sufficient prudence to cope with the hazards of the world without their being tainted or altered by what they learn. Fielding often complains that the truly virtuous person would easily be a match for a vicious one if he or she could bear to incur the guilt of the contest; so generally it is not prudence but a set of happy coincidences that wins the day for innocence. When Henry Tilney, the embodiment of the narrative voice of *Northanger Abbey*, confronts the moral force of Catherine Morland's naïvety he is faced with a paradox only irony can deal with: 'Your mind is warped,' he tells her, 'by an innate principle of general integrity, and therefore not accessible to the cool reasonings of family partiality, or a desire of revenge.'[23] Sometimes this innocence is so extreme it seems eccentric or fatuous and has to be protected from the reader as well as the world: 'How, in the name of wonder! could your uncle Toby, who, it seems was a military man, and whom you have represented as no fool,—be at the same time such a confused, pudding-headed, muddle-headed fellow?'[24] Certainly such characters are not imitable, as Smollett's favourite designation for this degree of comic unworldliness —'original'—suggests.

The satirical novelist makes two discoveries, then: the first is that the world is too perilous for inexperienced and virtuous characters, who by their simple nature are incapable of mock encounters and probable conjectures; the second is that Don Quixote provides the model for this ingenuous and vulnerable simplicity, his madness being exhibited as an amiable faith in gallantry and active altruism that arms him not against cunning but (often mistakenly and usually violently) against molesters of helpless virtue. It is in effect a projected or performed mode of self-defence: the protection of his own kind who, like him, place no faith in the institutions of civil society such as the law or in common sense. That this involves him in serious misrecognitions of the real, in fact something like a systematic inversion of the real and the imagined, makes no difference to the ardour of his desire to bring about the return of the golden age.

When this degree of idealism is imported into the novel with a character such as Parson Adams, a readjustment of the triad of innocence, the real, and imagination is required. Instead of imagination being used as a training exercise for entry into life, it fashions an alternative to the quotidian that confirms the isolation of the innocent person from social norms, an alienation often aided and confirmed by books. 'Master of mine,' boasts Adams to a former mariner, 'perhaps I have travelled a great deal farther than you without the assistance of a ship. Do you imagine sailing by different cities or countries is travelling?'[25] Such a withdrawal from experience is justified from the

---

[23] Jane Austen, *Northanger Abbey*, ed. Marilyn Butler (London: Penguin, 1995), 205.

[24] Laurence Sterne, *The Life and Opinions of Tristram Shandy, Gentleman*, ed. James A. Work (New York: Odyssey Press, 1940), II.ii.85.

[25] Henry Fielding, *Joseph Andrews*, ed. Paul A. Scanlon (Peterborough: Broadview Press, 2001), 232.

narrative point of view in a series of satirical examples confirming the vulnerability of innocence as a measure of the depravity of the world; from the point of view of the ingenuous character of course it is not understood as a disengagement from the world at all, but a principle of noble action that Sandra Macpherson has shrewdly analysed under the rubric of sentimental realism.[26] This provides the narrative with the values that satire chooses to defend, defined not by probable conjecture but by erecting three levels of mimetic faith in the rescue of the innocent: the hero's in regard of his duty to go to the immediate relief of the distressed; the author's in regard of the Christian value (but not the moral efficacy) of such unreflective altruism; and the reader's in regard of both. Irony arises from the questionable basis of the normative in view of its inaccessibility and hostility to innocence, and from the equally questionable relation of innocence to the ahistorical circuits and repetitions of romance, so generically inappropriate to the novel. So the fantastic world of imagination or vainglory, as Hobbes would call it, is called on to corroborate the place of innocence in the fallen world of the real.

The genre closest to this kind of fiction is the spy-novel and the it-narrative, for in all three the hero and heroine are effectually strangers in an exotic world whose secrets they are deliberately or accidentally disclosing. The price paid for these eccentricities is an agitation that takes a toll on their presence of mind, such as Adams convulsively flinging his precious Aeschylus into the fire, or Walter Shandy reaching his right hand into his left coat-pocket. Tristram Shandy assigns all the wry turns and unpredictabilities of his life to a large uneven thread in the fabric of his brain, an incurable plight that sensitizes him to scenes of mild insanity—mad Maria of Moulins appears twice—a susceptibility shared by the first-person narrators of the sentimental novel, such as the distracted lady Mackenzie's Harley meets in Bedlam and the mad uncle so carefully nursed by Sir George Ellison, eponymous hero of Sarah Scott's novel. Locke was concerned about the wide tolerance he observed for loose minds: 'He ought to look a little farther who would trace this sort of Madness to the root it springs from...a Taint which so universally affects Mankind, the greater care should be taken to lay it open under its due Name.'[27] By the end of the century medical men such as Thomas Trotter and Thomas Beddoes blamed the huge rise in nervous disorders on novel-reading.

THE POSITIVE CONJECTURE OF FICTION

In his decisive intervention into this branch of literary history Michael McKeon has pointed out that while the marriage of satire and the novel was thriving, romance itself was developing its own dialectic relation to changes in other modes of knowledge, such as the rapid advance of empirical science, the widespread interest in Epicurean materialism,

[26] Sandra Macpherson, *Harm's Way: Tragic Responsibility and the Novel Form* (Baltimore: Johns Hopkins University Press, 2010), 110.
[27] John Locke, *An Essay Concerning Human Understanding*, ed. Peter Nidditch (Oxford: Clarendon, 1979), II.xxxiii.3, 395.

and new ideas about what constitutes history and historical writing. He says, 'The key to this dialectic—to the double reversal of romance idealism by naïve empiricism and of both by extreme skepticism—is the dynamic energy of the historicist revolution.'[28] My sense of this double reversal and its sudden access of energy is that romance and scepticism found they had a common interest in the use of imagination, while the 'naïve empiricism' of the New Science and the novel relied on experimental and consensual production of knowledge subject to a standard of probability that neither romance nor scepticism would endorse. All parties in this debate resorted to imagined cases and working fictions in order that the larger purposes of fiction be achieved, but these purposes were very different and scepticism was not the unchallenged arbiter of outcomes.

The positive conjecture of science and the novel was as follows: 'What if what I don't know, I did?' It was fundamental not only to scientific experiments, differential calculus, commercial transactions including marriage, insurance and historical inductions, but also to the structure and reading of novels. We have already seen Johnson explaining how naïve readers were to find the benefit of fiction in the form of a set of hypotheses, 'mock encounters in the art of necessary defence'. Recently Catherine Gallagher has expanded the conjectural basis of this exercise as one requiring the reader 'to make suppositional predictions...to speculate upon the action', for 'the reality of the story itself [is] a kind of suppositional speculation'.[29] The purpose of the positive conjecture is to supply the place of experience until experience comes along to bear it out, and to temper it.

The negative conjecture ran like this: 'What if what I do know, I didn't?' and it was deployed by Descartes in the first of his *Meditations on the First Philosophy* when he annihilates the world perceived by the senses in a single plenary supposition: 'I shall then suppose...some evil genius not less powerful than deceitful, has employed his whole energies in deceiving me; I shall consider that the heavens, the earth, colours, figures, sound, and all other external things are nought but the illusions and dreams of which this genius has availed himself in order to lay traps for my credulity.'[30] In good faith Don Quixote makes the same supposition throughout his career as knight-errant, convinced that the transformation of a giant into a windmill, enemies into wineskins, a whole army into a flock of sheep, and Mambrino's helmet into a barber's basin is owing to the malice of enchanters bent on sullying his achievements. Everywhere he greets the empirical world of material fact as a total fiction. For Descartes the supposition of enchantment was the first step in a radically sceptical enterprise in which all empirical evidence was supposed dubious in order that a residue of pure ontological certainty (the famous *cogito*) might be acquired. Don Quixote's explanation for the sordid quotidian intrusions into the perfection of his adventures procures the same authority for his

[28] Michael McKeon, *The Origins of the English Novel, 1600–1740* (Baltimore: Johns Hopkins University Press, 1987), 64.

[29] Catherine Gallagher, 'The Rise of Fictionality', in *The Novel*, ed. Franco Moretti, vol. 1 (Princeton: Princeton University Press, 2006), 346.

[30] René Descartes, *Discourse on Method and Meditations on the First Philosophy*, ed. David Weissman (New Haven: Yale University Press, 1996), 62.

imagination (and for Dulcinea, its greatest achievement) that Descartes gains for his 'thinking thing', the soul. It establishes a very firm division between physical knowledge and transcendental truth that secures an intuition of singular order and being from the taint of all common associations with the perceivable world of colour, taste, smell, sound, and touch.

From the perspective of empirical observation, of course, this is nothing but madness. Descartes effects a reconciliation between the soul and the experience of sensations and passions, but very much on the soul's terms. Not until just before his death does Don Quixote make this sort of concession, and in the first part of his adventures in the Sierra Morena he believes knights-errant should defeat the trammels of probability by running mad for love. So madness and romance have in common the absoluteness of their rejection of empirical knowledge and the moral law of consequences, and so does satire in scrutinizing a material disorder that it aims to vex further by means of imagination. But the authors or narrators of romances and satires are aware that their mimetic implication in the conduct of extreme innocence and its various travesties leaves them without a handle on the bulk of what Swift calls lazy, impatient, and grunting readers, so whatever impression they are likely to make on their audience depends on a series of oscillations between annihilation and amplification: the demolition and reconstruction of what is solid, sapid, visible, and palpable; the transfiguring charm of refracted angles, varnish and tinsel and their exposure as delusion.[31]

While it is clear that these rival methods of approaching truth—by a meditative, martial, or satiric discipline animated by sudden intuitions of an original and self-evident truth erasing all that came before, or by empirical inquiry focused on an accumulation of suppositions of what the future might hold—have very little in common, it is equally clear that they both rely on fiction to obtain what is desired.[32] And to the extent that each fiction is lodged (as far as Cervantes and the novel are concerned at least) in a larger fiction, then what is represented is modified by the mode of representation. Fielding for instance is careful not to cultivate in his reader the easy credulity of his hero, otherwise the oscillation necessary for irony would be at an end. Richardson on the other hand, having no interest in any but tragic irony (in *Clarissa*) and little in satire aside from the pert exchanges of Pamela and Mr B, is keen to foster what he calls 'historical faith', proximate with Lord Kames's 'ideal presence', by means of innovations in the art of epistolary writing aimed at bringing the reader into the closest possible alignment with the innocence of his heroines. Fielding was bound to read *Pamela* as a first-person exercise in hypocrisy because it abolished the distance needed to appreciate how unnegotiable are the differences between innocence and the forces bent upon its destruction. How could a reconciliation ever take place between Pamela and Mr B that was not the result of a hidden motive or an unexamined contradiction kept secret from the reader?

---

[31] Swift, *Works* (Cambridge), i. 131.
[32] Bernard Williams, *Descartes: The Project of Pure Enquiry* (Brighton: Harvester Press, 1978), 35.

INNOCENCE IN SATIRIC FICTION

In the light of how the interests of satire are confederate with the totality of romantic excess, I want to examine now a satire based on *Don Quixote* that exploits this relation. Samuel Butler's *Hudibras* (1662–77) uses the loose structure of romance but solely, it seems, to pillory its punctilios as shabby deceits. The hero is a Puritan hypocrite whose commitment to war and love extends no further than to interrupting rural pastimes such as bear-baiting and parades of rough music, and to securing the hand of a rich widow, whose fortune he means to embezzle. His squire is a hair-splitting zealot whose conversations with his master mostly refine the doctrinal differences dividing various sects. So there is no guileless hero to act as a catalyst for satire. Butler has struck many of his critics as merely uniting an exploded genre with a depraved character. Romance serves merely to heighten the burlesque disparity between Hudibras's pretensions to glory and love and his lust for power and pelf; and although very funnily delivered, it is a joke that wears thin. Johnson identifies in the poem the same want of focus that enervates the episodes of Altisidora and the Duke and the Duchess in the second part of *Don Quixote*: 'His work must have had ... the defect which Dryden imputes to Spenser; the action could not have been one; there could only have been a succession of incidents, each of which might have happened without the rest, and which could not co-operate to any single conclusion.'[33]

If we are looking for the kind of catalyst Don Quixote supplies for Cervantes's irony, then we would have to say it is provided by the widow, whose formidable defence of her liberty is foreshadowed in Trulla's Amazonian defeat of Hudibras in the first part. Responding to the inflated protestations of her wooer, the widow launches a satire on marriage animated by her digressions on the nature of sexual love, the passion that her lover merely professes but upon whose ecumenical energy every species depends, 'And therefore, though 'tis ere so fond, / Takes strangely to the Vagabond.'[34] Her endorsement of this vagabondage restores the vitality of romance leached from it by the knight's bleak attachment to self, for whom sex is associated only with the fantastic pornographic excitements aroused by Sidrophel's aphrodisiac, 'feeble *Speculative Lust*: / Procurer to th'Extravagancy, / And crazy Ribaldry of Fancy'.[35] The widow frankly approves of adultery and fornication where the appetence of the partners is at least unassisted and mutually passionate: possibly too much so, for she can see liberated sex in the same light as Fanny Hill and Immanuel Kant as a sort of hungry and savage sympathy:

> For what do Lovers, when th' are fast
> In one another's Arms embrac't;
> But strive, to plunder; and convey

---

[33] Johnson, *Lives*, i. 286.
[34] Samuel Butler, *Hudibras*, ed. John Wilders (Oxford: Clarendon Press, 1967), 208.
[35] Butler, *Hudibras*, 201.

> Each other, *like a Prize*, away?
> To change the property of selves,
> As suckling Children are, by *Elves*?[36]

For the widow vagabondage is the solution to fondness carried too far, moving on when love looks like turning to pillage. Nevertheless, her dialogues with Hudibras sharpen her sense of how satisfying it could be if vagabondage without plunder were possible, such as the reconciliation of Oriana and Amadis where there is no predation in 'the loving embraces and the sweet kisses, the tears which, with mouth pressed to mouth, were blended there together'.[37] Her sense of such an alternative explains the air of scornful erotic majesty with which the widow demands of her gloomy Dis if his puissance runs as far as sorcery, 'T'ingage the Devil on your side, / And steal (like *Proserpine*) your Bride'.[38]

In emphasizing the kind of love of which Hudibras is not capable, the widow skirts the issue of self-loss first canvassed by Trulla after beating Hudibras in the battle over the Skimmington, when she offers to lend him back his self, so he can go on fighting for a while on tick. For her it means to be stolen away either by witchcraft or frenzy, to be carried off like Proserpine or 'To change the property of selves'. But the possibility that alienation of the self is the fate awaiting the virtuous woman who marries in a civil state, or that rape or madness is the destiny reserved for lovers who love too entirely, is buoyant in her imagination. It sets the social and political chaos of the Civil War alongside a different but equally extensive disorder in romance, and makes anarchy and loss of reason a risk in both, with this qualification: that romance exhibits the risk and the contradictions that make it so, but not so the vulgar community of Hudibras, busily exploiting the opportunities provided for the theft of selves by the stream of custom.

At this point I want to specify a little further the catalyst for irony that I have been calling innocence in satiric fiction. It is clear that romance and its characters practise outlawry, free and disembroiled as James says, constrained only by the mannerism of excess. They must not indulge the rage of Ciamara in *Love in Excess* who 'raged, stamped, tore her hair' and then, like one of the infamous examples of Hilaire Belloc's *Cautionary Tales*, poisons herself out of sheer exasperation.[39] The curious equipoise of irresistible passion and *bienseance* is maintained in the same novel by young Frankville, who has 'too great a share of good sense not to know that…passion is not to be circumscribed…it would be mere madness…to say a person was blame-worthy for what was unavoidable'.[40] The contradiction Hobbes identifies in that sort of solipsism is the vulnerability of anyone exposed to it who is undefended by the administration of justice; and it is resolved by the guaranteed possession of what is one's own. The contradiction identified by writers of

---

[36] Butler, *Hudibras*, 216. See John Cleland, *Fanny Hill; or, Memoirs of a Woman of Pleasure*, ed. Peter Wagner (London: Penguin, 1985), 219–20; and Immanuel Kant, *The Metaphysics of Morals*, ed. Mary Gregor (Cambridge: Cambridge University Press, 2012), 61–3.

[37] Anonymous, *Amadis de Gaul*, trans. Edwin B. Place and Herbert C. Behm (Lexington: University Press of Kentucky, 1974), 545.

[38] Butler, *Hudibras*, 202.

[39] Eliza Haywood, *Love in Excess*, ed. David Oakleaf (Peterborough: Broadview Press, 2000), 211, 244.

[40] Haywood, *Love in Excess*, 211, 185.

romance as the hardest to make consonant with its formal approach to excess is madness: frenzy and the entire loss of presence of mind; it is resolved by the restoration of wits and ironic distance.

Sergio Zatti sees in *Orlando Furioso* how friction between volition and accident in the action is mirrored in the narrative, where the same crepitation is evident between (as he calls it) *entrelacement*—breaking off, deferring, alluding to other poems—and getting on with telling a story already bulging with a confusion of contrary wills and fortunes. Ariosto's irony balances 'the genre's generous capacity for incorporating other literary forms against the negative weight of its undisciplined exuberance'.[41] This important function Ariosto assigns to what is called wit, or wits, in Sir John Harington's translation. There is an *entrelacement* of unfathomable subtlety in the Sierra Morena where Quixote, ambitious to imitate his models in an original way, resolves to be insane by choice, carefully selecting the most eligible extravagances from the stories of Orlando and Amadis before running mad 'without the least Constraint or Necessity'.[42] Cervantes invites the reader to observe the difference between Orlando's maniacal activity, and Beltenebros's relatively self-possessed retreat to the Poor Cliff where he can indulge a fixed melancholy. In between those alternatives he situates his hero, whose determination to be mad is presented both as the composure of someone bent merely on performing distraction, and as the madness beyond artifice needed to perpetrate such a pretence: 'the skyline beyond skyline of irony' that William Empson praised so eloquently in Cervantes.[43]

There is no character in Butler's poem so thoroughly lost to sense as Orlando who hurls himself towards an unknown destination bereft of language, clothes, and self, destroying everything that comes in his path and menacing such cohesion as the poem possesses. The widow's defence of love and the amoral candour of Trulla is as close as Butler gets to disorder but he's neither disturbed by it nor especially eager to reconcile its contradictions. In *Orlando Furioso* these are much more extreme and infectious. After Orlando retreats to the fatal grove where he reads on the trees a lyric celebration of the mutual love of Medoro and Angelica, he at first tries resist the meaning of their messages, then takes farewell of himself ('I am not I') and begins the dismantling of his personality, casting off armour, sword, horse, and finally his clothes in a comprehensive annihilation of the memorials of any kind of armed fellowship or self-possession. Then he tears up the trees with their awful messages of satisfied desire, bellowing like a beast. As he descends into this frantic state he supposes that it isn't tears pouring out of his eyes in such floods but his vital humour, leaving a vacuum for madness to occupy. For their part Ariosto and 'mine author' construe the vital humour as his wits, now lost and gone to dwell in the moon, where all alienated things repose.

In between their recovery by Astolfo and what seems like the imminent wreck of the Christian Europe Ariosto inserts stories of constancy (Zerbino and Isabella), resolution in battle (Renaldo), and self-possession (Marfisa telling Mandricardo, 'I am mine owne

---

[41] Sergio Zatti, *The Quest for Epic: From Ariosto to Tasso* (Toronto: University of Toronto Press, 2006), 14.

[42] Miguel de Cervantes Saavedra, *Don Quixote*, trans. Peter Motteux (New York: Everyman, 1991), 221.

[43] William Empson, *Some Versions of Pastoral* (London: Chatto & Windus, 1935), 198.

own, mine owner is within me, / He that will have me, from my self must win me') in an effort to stabilize the fluxing elements of war, love, and sanity.[44] But whenever the poet comes close to the subject of Orlando's madness he feels the infection himself, and has to edit his tale: 'And what strange feats his furie brought to pass, / You might perchance beleeue that I were mad, / If none of his of mad pranks I ouerpasse.'[45] In telling the amazing story of how Orlando dug himself into sand until nothing but his head was showing, only to find Medoro and Angelica riding by in amorous colloquy, the narrator breaks into tirade against women in general and Angelica in particular; then he apologizes for this outrage: 'Although I somewhat swarue from reasons scope, / And rash words flow from vnaduised minde: [...] That I did speake was partly of compassion, / With simpathy mou'd of *Orlandos* passion.'[46]

SWIFT AND MADNESS

Between them Ariosto and Butler provide Swift with the instruments of his satire. Madness was for him a lifelong preoccupation and his heroes, notably Lemuel Gulliver and the Author of *A Tale of a Tub*, either start out mad or end up that way. Once it had insanity as its stalking horse there was nothing satiric wit could not do or say. Butler's burlesque he found convenient for his satiric verse where the lunatic extravagance of love or poetic ambition is confronted with the base material origin of its flights: sperm and snot respectively. Pastoral romance is made to carry a ballast of sententious reminders of this fact: Chloe pisses and Celia shits. As for chivalric romance its adventures are given laconic notice—the three brothers of the *Tale* 'travelled through several countries, encountered a reasonable quantity of giants, and slew certain dragons'—but when brother Jack runs mad the Author, formerly an inhabitant in Bedlam, spares no detail of the outrages.[47] Jack is the Author's Orlando whose lost wits extend the dominion of Babel and Chaos and multiply the risks run by a chronicler who previously mislaid his own.[48] Here Swift relies on Cervantes as well as Ariosto by mounting madness upon madness, a pleonasm sporting with alternative possibilities of a crafty derangement ('Jack...calculated the first Revolution of his Brain...prudently') and the entire loss of one's wits.[49]

The *Tale* follows for the most part the model of narrative *entrelacement* that Zatti sees as so central to Ariosto's irony, with the allegory of three brothers punctuated by digressions on a variety of subjects ('And so leaving these broken ends, I carefully gather up the chief thread of my story and proceed').[50] It corresponds to the action of the story of a religious quest for a reconciliation between the lies of Peter and the delusions of Jack that Martin is intended to represent but which is never consummated,

---

[44] Lodovico Ariosto, *Orlando Furioso in English Heroical Verse*, trans. Sir John Harrington (1607), 21
[45] Ariosto, *Orlando Furioso*, 238.   [46] Ariosto, *Orlando Furioso*, 241.
[47] Swift, *Works* (Cambridge), i. 48.   [48] Swift, *Works* (Cambridge), i. 126.
[49] Swift, *Works* (Cambridge), i. 123.   [50] Swift, *Works* (Cambridge), i. 51.

dribbling away into disjointed memoranda for something more like history than an allegory. It corresponds also to the characterization of the reader, whose oscillations between idleness and impatience, carelessness and diligence, superficiality and candour, appetence and frustration or repletion and fastidiosity, follow the same arc as the Author's between amplification and annihilation: 'I am confident to have included and exhausted all that human imagination can rise or fall to.'[51] But at the end of his treatise his commonplace book is empty, and so is his head, and we leave him trying an experiment of writing upon nothing.

The *Tale* resembles *Orlando Furioso* in nothing so much as its focus on madness, especially the physiological symptoms of it, a topic examined through various lenses in its companion pieces where the brain distils a fluid—sperm, ink, mucus—that troubles the projects of empire, letters, and religion. As we have seen, Orlando believes his tears are so copious it must be something more important than salt water coming out of his eyes.[52] When Astolfo finds the jar labelled 'Orlando's Wits' the effluvium is properly identified, and then described: 'It seemd to be a body moyst and soft, / And apt to mount by eu'ry exhalation.'[53] It is indeed by inhalation that it is restored to his brain. Astolfo stuffs the hero's mouth with herbs and holds the jar to his nose: 'This miracle was wrought, / The Iarre was void, and empty'd eu'rie whit, / And he restord unto his perfect wit.'[54] The loss and reincorporation of the material form of knowledge in the form of a balsamic liquid or vapour is deployed by Swift's Author as an alchemical recipe for wisdom, where books refined in a bain-marie are inhaled as an elixir, 'snuffing it strongly up your nose' where 'it will dilate in the brain (where there is any) in fourteen minutes'.[55] But the virtuoso elucidation of the effluvial theory of madness is given in the digression 'Concerning the Original, the Use, and Improvement of Madness in a Commonwealth', where there are two explanations for it. When the body is unable to excrete what is necessary for peace of mind, the residue then rises and dematerializes, invading the brain as a vaporous frenzy, either forming disturbing dreams of power, knowledge, and revelation; or, like a poltergeist, emptying the brain of all its contents: 'By which are mystically display'd the two principal Branches of *Madness*, and which some Philosophers not considering so well as I, have mistook to be different in their Causes, over-hastily assigning the first to Deficiency, and the other to Redundance.'[56] It may be redundancy of vapour is the first symptom, but the brain is left deficient, damaged, or empty. However if madness is to accommodate itself to irony it needs to appear as both something less and something more than frenzy—a fistula *and* a very bright idea.

This is what *entrelacement* requires otherwise excess cannot refer to its code of self-regulation, either of wit or ritual, and the author will merge with his hero or the author with the Author. In the *Tale* there are three moments when this double aspect of excess is blurred or lost and satire threatens to come apart at the seams. The first occurs in the 'Digression on Madness' when the list of big ideas and their squalid counterparts briefly

[51] Swift, *Works* (Cambridge), i. 84. [52] Ariosto, *Orlando Furioso*, 184.
[53] Ariosto, *Orlando Furioso*, 287. [54] Ariosto, *Orlando Furioso*, 330.
[55] Swift, *Works* (Cambridge), i. 126. [56] Swift, *Works* (Cambridge), i. 112.

cease to be ironic, when wit is compared to the bird of paradise that at the end of its flight will fall to the ground, a victim of time and gravity but nonetheless still beautiful, its pathos intact. This is a case of reverse irony, where the expected indignity does not intrude and Swift might be retailing one of his very own ideas. The next comes when the Author experiments with writing upon nothing, exploring the emptiness of his own brain in a kind of staged aposiopesis, defined in *The Art of Sinking in Poetry* as 'an excellent Figure for the Ignorant, as [...] "I can no more," when one really can no more'.[57] Apart from its being truly the case that the Author's brain and its prosthesis, his commonplace book, are both empty and that he is moving rapidly towards an inconclusive terminus and a literalization of the figure, he now loses his grip on the lazy grunting reader, since there is nothing more to be curious about. Irony and the ability to manipulate the reader are two sides of the same coin, and with nothing but nothing left, there is little to distinguish the Author from the author. The third moment occurs in 1710 with the real 'Author's Apology', explaining that he was writing irony all the time to a select audience of men of wit and taste, from which the swinish reader is naturally excluded, having had to be told this explicitly.

It is clear then that the excess of romance and satire offered Swift a huge burst of energy, but fully to exploit it he needed to personate a madman who would not end up saying just nothing. Gulliver's approach to the duality of annihilation and amplification is, in the spirit of Gresham College, to confront speech of the thing which is not with testimony to the thing which is, leading him into interminable catalogues of the former as he defines the latter. But at least his *entrelacement* is never in danger of inane excess, for he can always say the thing which is not not; and thus he concludes, 'I dwell the longer upon this Subject from the Desire I have to make the Society of an *English Yahoo* by any Means not insupportable.'[58] Swift left this device as a legacy for Sterne, whose digressive-progressive method of writing is its next incarnation.

SELECT BIBLIOGRAPHY

Frye, Northrop. 'The Mythos of Summer: Romance' and 'The Mythos of Winter: Satire', in *Anatomy of Criticism, Works*, vol. 22, ed. Robert D. Denham (Toronto: University of Toronto Press, 2006).

Gallagher, Catherine. 'The Rise of Fictionality', in *The Novel*, ed. Franco Moretti, vol. 1 (Princeton: Princeton University Press, 2006), 336–63.

Luhmann, Niklas. *Love as Passion: The Codification of Intimacy*, trans. Jeremy Gaines and Doris L. Jones (Cambridge, MA: Harvard University Press, 1986).

McKeon, Michael. *The Origins of the English Novel, 1600–1740* (Baltimore: Johns Hopkins University Press, 1987).

Macpherson, Sandra. *Harm's Way: Tragic Responsibility and the Novel Form* (Baltimore: Johns Hopkins University Press, 2010).

Williams, Bernard. *Descartes: The Project of Pure Enquiry* (Brighton: Harvester Press, 1978).

Zatti, Sergio. *The Quest for Epic: From Ariosto to Tasso* (Toronto: University of Toronto Press, 2006).

---

[57] Pope, *Prose*, ii. 207.   [58] Swift, *Works* (Cambridge), xvi. 444.

CHAPTER 20

DRAMATIC SATIRE

ROS BALLASTER

FROM 1737, the British stage was subject to the strictest censorship under law of all literary genres. And the introduction of the Licensing Act in that year was defended by a convenient fiction: that the ministry was only taking action that followed classical precedent and with the same ambition to contain licentiousness and libel. Between the fifth and third century BC in ancient Greece there was a transition from Old to New comedy. Metonymy (the individual vice of an identifiable figure stands for systemic corruption) gave way to metaphor (general vice is represented through allegorical embodiment of types):

> Comedy flourished...because it abused the greatest Men in the State by Name; this outrageous Licentiousness, was the Essence of the Old Comedy...By Degrees, however the ill Effects and dangerous Consequences of this kind of Entertainments, appeared in so glaring a Light, that a Law was made, forbidding Poets to abuse People by Name. Hence arose the middle Comedy, somewhat, tho' not much inferior to the old Comedy in ill Language. It was now the Poet's Business to represent, under a feign'd Name, the Person he intended to abuse, in so strong a Light, and with such distinguishing Circumstances, as could leave an *Athenian* Audience no room for Mistake. In process of Time it grew apparent, that this Regulation could not preserve the publick Peace, and therefore others were made, whereby Poets were restrained from representing real Actions, and their Imaginations were so bridled by Law, that they were forced to do that Good which they always pretended to do, viz. To shew the Folly of Vice, and the Wisdom of Virtue, in general Characters, or in other Words, were obliged to study Nature, and not the Times. After these restrictions came the new Comedy...[1]

Matthew Kinservik describes this ministerial narrative as 'a convenient and misleading history' manufactured to justify 'state intervention' to protect private citizens from

---

[1] *Daily Gazetteer (London Edition)*, Friday, 10 June 1737; Issue 611. *17th–18th Century Burney Collection Newspapers.*

public exposure on stage and playwrights from having to cater to crude popular taste.[2] Despite its artificiality and convenience it has a resilient adaptability, suited to representing both the particular imperatives and opportunities that drove stage production in the period and the likely trajectory of the careers of individual playwrights, managers, and players.

Historians of eighteenth-century satire have paid insufficient attention to its theatrical manifestations. Two factors contribute to this neglect. First, the stage was the exclusive victim of censorship before 'publication'. Printed versions of plays (which were not subject to state censorship) could reinstate all or any satiric content erased by the Licenser or a manager for performance. Second, the commercial success of the drama increasingly distanced it from its literary equivalents in the minority markets of print and manuscript circulation; there was exponential growth in the size of the patent theatres and the proliferation of unlicensed playhouses.[3] This means that topical and partisan meanings must either be blindingly obvious or so obscure as to speak only to a small minority of a large audience without undermining the effect of the work as a whole.

And where we cannot uncover such reference in play-texts there may be satirical meanings that accrued in performance. Audiences may find satirical parallels where they are not intended; plays without a satirical meaning in first performance may acquire them in the context of later political circumstance. Moreover, paratexts and minor genres are richer sources for satire than mainpieces. Much of the debate about satire in the drama is conducted in the new industry of printed theatrical criticism—in the periodical, the pamphlet, the companion, paratextual dedications, prologues and epilogues—of the eighteenth century. There was more opportunity for experimentation and topicality in afterpieces and interludes which were cheaper and easier to revive or transport in different performance contexts.[4] Like other examples of satire, play-texts are under constant revision and development, adapting to local political contingency and changes of office. Plays are not static objects once printed or performed; revivals can strip works of political reference or add it.[5]

Further complications arise in that acting is always already a form of allegorical representation (speaking in public of one thing through another). The actor 'stands for' another figure, whether an historical personage or a fictional embodiment of a known type virtuous or vicious. The actor does not play him or herself. As John O'Brien phrases it, theatre in this period is conceived as 'an embodied medium, one that linked spectator

[2] Matthew Kinservik, *Disciplining Satire: The Censorship of Satiric Comedy on the Eighteenth-Century London Stage* (Lewisburg: Bucknell University Press, 2002), 117.

[3] See Jane Moody, *Illegitimate Theatre in London, 1770–1840* (Cambridge: Cambridge University Press, 2000).

[4] See Robert D. Hume, 'Drama and Theatre in the Mid and Later Eighteenth Century', in *The Cambridge History of English Literature 1660–1780*, ed. John Richetti (Cambridge: Cambridge University Press, 2008), 316.

[5] Matthew J. Kinservik, 'The Role of the Censor in the Regulation of the Eighteenth-Century Stage', in *Eighteenth Century Drama: Censorship, Society and the Stage* (2016), http://www.eighteenthcenturydrama.amdigital.co.uk/Explore/Essays/Kinservik [accessed 12 August 2016].

and spectacle in a kind of spell held together by sensory stimuli.[6] Moreover, the mimesis of drama lacks the diegetic frame available to other forms (except perhaps in those moments when actors step out of character to deliver prologues or epilogues). In print forms of satire, the satirist can ironically frame the target he or she ventriloquizes to prompt the interpretative understanding of the reader. To achieve this kind of meta-understanding, dramatic satire of the period often resorts to the rehearsal or play-within-a-play. The important and immediate precedent here was George Villiers, Duke of Buckingham's burlesque of 1671, in which actors play a playwright and his actors in rehearsal and provide an allegory of a little court replete with ignorant follies, idleness, and self-regard, commented on with wry detachment by other actors who play onstage spectators.

These issues—of censorship, of the indeterminate location of satirical intent, of embodiment in performance—shape dramatic satire through the eighteenth century. This chapter considers three periods of intense flourishing and transformation of the form, despite the limitations of a virtual duopoly (the two patent stages) and the few new plays that reached performance. Nonetheless, satire takes many forms on the eighteenth-century stage and is directed towards a multitude of targets. Those targets are usually aesthetic, political, or social in their nature. This essay seeks to demonstrate that the most significant, characteristic, and inventive vehicle for satire on the English stage of the period is meta-theatre, 'rehearsal' plays or plays-within-plays, a device drawn from Aristophanes' practice of performed parody in *The Frogs* (405 BC) when Euripides and Aeschylus compete in the underworld for the prize of Best Tragic Poet by delivering their own best speeches. The major satirical playwrights of the eighteenth century—Henry Fielding, Samuel Foote—were named or claimed inheritance from Aristophanes, master of the Old Comedy. Name-calling, impersonation, a pose of learned vulgarity, and the parodic representation of rivals and celebrities were all practices associated with Aristophanes. And the satiric technique of Aristophanes' *The Frogs*—in which dominant theatrical styles were subjected to performed parody and paralleled with the bombast and hypocrisy of political or social conduct—was returned to at every stage in the development of dramatic satire through the century, even when plays claimed to depart from the rough-and-tumble of older satirical modes.[7]

Meta-theatre not only satirizes, usually from a conservative position, the decline in the ethics and aesthetics of the stage, but by metonymic analogy it charts the same failures in the 'Houses' of contemporary political power and management. While meta-theatre relies on an analogy between stage management and political management, it also insists on the necessary separation of these two worlds. Playwrights, actors, and actor-managers can serve as appropriate figures for vain, blundering politicians inexpertly managing those whose hard-earned money supports their ventures (the audience/the

---

[6] John O'Brien, *Harlequin Britain: Pantomime and Entertainment, 1690–1760* (Baltimore: Johns Hopkins University Press, 2004), 83.

[7] See Edith Hall, 'The English-Speaking Aristophanes, 1650–1914', in *Aristophanes in Performance, 421 BC–AD 2007: Peace, Birds, and Frogs*, ed. Edith Hall and Andrea Wrigley (Oxford: Modern Humanities Research Association and Maney Publishing Legenda, 2007), 66–88.

people), but autonomy from political interest and a primary commitment only to aesthetic and moral achievement must be presented as the primary driver of theatrical endeavour. The meta-theatrical 'piece', the performance which is rehearsed or played within the play, is always a bad play; it must give away its (fictional) creator's incompetence while demonstrating the astute and impartial craftsmanship of its (real) maker who wins the loyalty of the audience through a savvy fitting up of the satirical target.

Metonymy: 1715–1738

It was a satire of the bombastic narcissism of heroic tragedy which served as the main English precedent through the eighteenth century in George Villiers, 2nd Duke of Buckingham's play *The Rehearsal* (1671). David Garrick produced his own altered version of *The Rehearsal* in 1742 and one of his most celebrated roles was that of the foolish playwright, Bayes.[8] Buckingham was mocking John Dryden in his depiction of Bayes, portraying Dryden as a vainglorious author unconcerned about the incoherence and mis-casting of his tragic play so long as it contains and multiplies the stock elements of heroic drama: apparently unmotivated political conspiracy, rhyming couplets, copious deaths, doomed love affairs suddenly embarked upon. Margarita Stocker builds on George McFadden's identification of Lord Arlington, ascendant rival to Buckingham in Charles II's famous Cabal of ministers as the political analogue of Bayes. According to Buckingham, Dryden, appointed Historiographer Royal in 1670, shapes an aesthetic and a practice in the theatre of arbitrary nonsense equivalent to the absolutist pro-Catholic politics of Arlington.[9]

The satire of heroic drama makes 'high' politics correspond with the behaviour of the low—the stage world is one in which low-born actors play mighty kings and queens. But it also makes a conservative complaint that 'high' culture has fallen from its position of moral and political integrity. Early eighteenth-century playwrights who, like Dryden before them, came from more common stock than the aristocratic Buckingham inclined to suggest that low cultural persons and the genres associated with them (pastoral, farce, burlesque) might have more integrity than the elevated worlds they impersonated. John Gay—bright Devon boy, once apprenticed to a silk mercer, who embarked on a literary career in London in the second decade of the eighteenth century supported by his friendship with the young Alexander Pope—authored two meta-theatrical plays that were to dominate the satirical drama for the rest of the century: *The What D'Ye Call It: A Tragi-Comi-Pastoral Farce* (Theatre Royal, Drury Lane, first performed February 1715) and *The Beggar's Opera* (Lincoln's Inn Fields, first performed January 1728).

---

[8] David Garrick, *The Rehearsal*, in *The Plays of David Garrick, Volume II: Garrick's Alterations of Others, 1742–1750*, ed. Harry William Pedicord and Frederick Louis Bergmann (Carbondale and Edwardsville: Southern Illinois University Press, 1980), 6–55.

[9] See George McFadden, 'Political Satire in *The Rehearsal*', *Yearbook of English Studies* 3 (1974), 120–8; and Margarita Stocker, 'Political Allusion in *The Rehearsal*', *Philological Quarterly* 67 (1988), 11–35.

These were Gay's two most successful plays, the former running for twenty-one successive nights and the latter for sixty-two performances in their first seasons and often revived subsequently. Whether or not Gay intended overt political satire in his *Opera*, once the play's success was established the opposition journal, *The Craftsman* (17 February 1728) was quick to claim it for its own, publishing a letter (ostensibly of outrage) by one 'Phil.Harmonicus' detailing the allusions to the ministry of Robert Walpole and his brother, Horatio, in the figures of the corrupt thief-taker, Peachum, and equally corrupt prison governor, Lockit. In the summer of 1728, Walpole shut down Gay's sequel, *Polly*, through the Lord Chamberlain's office, reluctant to be exposed to further public satirical attention.[10]

Both works are mock-heroic; a cast of lower class figures act as though they were characters in a more elevated mode: *The What D'Ye Call It* concerns the steward of a country Justice named Sir Roger. Sir Roger wants to show off his sophisticated familiarity with the theatre by staging for his friends a work that is tragedy, comedy, pastoral, farce, and a 'spice of your Opera' replete with 'a competence of ghosts';[11] the steward engineers the actual wedding of his daughter made pregnant by the Justice's son as though it were part of the conventional marriage catastrophe of eighteenth-century comedy. Along the way in this one-act play, despite a non-sequential plot meeting the Justice's demands, the rustic characters within the play demonstrate strong bonds of affection between male friends, and well-matched pairs of lovers, and deliver some sideswipes at the heartlessness of the local justice system, particularly with respect to pressing young farmers into military service. A further level of irony is present in that Gay implies that the actors lack the fine feeling demonstrated by the characters they play.

The Beggar's Opera builds on these elements and warns against sentimentalizing and idealizing the virtues and principles of the lower classes in pastoral forms. Like *The What D'Ye Call It*, it includes the unlikely last minute reprieve of a death sentence, a rivalry between two women, and a clever playmaker (here a beggar rather than steward). However, its huge success by comparison may lie partly in its metonymic relation to the world beyond the theatre: the criminal and destitute world of the area around Covent Garden just outside the theatre is brought into the theatre to entertain a paying audience. Gay's play makes explicit reference to the problem of slums, of criminal activity prompted by gin addiction, the cost and corruption of the prison system. It also invokes the contemporary figure of Jonathan Wild, the notorious thief-cum-thief-taker hanged in 1724. Peachum—who runs a criminal gang of thieves and impeaches those who resist his authority or fail to meet his business targets—was easy to recognize as a version of Wild. But he was also a version of another 'great man', the Prime Minister, Robert Walpole, who notoriously screened his own self-interest behind other politicians. The play was also a traditional satire in the tradition of Aristophanes and Buckingham, mocking a

---

[10] Calhoun Winton, *John Gay and the London Stage* (Lexington: University Press of Kentucky, 1993), 103–4.

[11] John Gay, *The What D'Ye Call It*, in *Burlesque Plays of the Eighteenth Century*, ed. Simon Trussler (Oxford: Oxford University Press, 1969), Scene 1, l.45, l.39, 66.

modish form that threatened to oust traditional genres, in this case the Italian opera. The rivalry between the two leading female characters, Polly Peachum and Lucy Lockit, for the affections of the highwayman Macheath, reprised that between the two exorbitantly well-paid Italian sopranos, Francesca Cuzzoni and Faustina Bordoni (the latter arrived in London in 1726). In June 1727, the two women and their partisan supporters came to blows at a performance of Bononcini's *Astyanax*.

The appetite for an honest satire delivered from the position of the underdog was not just expressed in the complex layered effects of the meta-theatrical play. Another relatively low-born author dependent on patronage and commercial success also saw success as a satiric dramatist. Robert Dodsley, son of a Nottingham schoolmaster, became acquainted with Alexander Pope while he was in service as a footman to one of Pope's friends. Pope sent on Dodsley's first play to manager John Rich at Covent Garden who mounted the afterpiece entitled *The Toy-Shop: A Dramatic Satire* there in February 1735. It ran for thirty-four performances and went into seven editions in its first year. In this one-act play, society folk come to visit the toy shop where the tradesman has a reputation for plain speaking. The owner attempts to sell them goods that will improve their moral perspicacity (such as a pair of spectacles that show an old gentleman the folly of youth, a set of scales that weigh the balance between promises and their delivery) and meets varying degrees of respect and outrage. Like the playwrights and managers such as Bayes who direct their plays and rehearsals in meta-theatre, the toy-shop owner controls the meanings generated within the space he controls, but here it is the central character who is the satirist rather than the object of satire. One of the ladies who visit him exclaims:

> Why, sir, you are a new kind of a Satirical Parson, your Shop is your Scripture, and every piece of Goods a different Text, from which you expose the Vices and Follies of Mankind in a very fine allegorical Sermon.[12]

The parabolic folk-wisdom of the sermon served Dodsley well and he went on to produce two more plays in the same vein. This was a kind of satire unlikely to cause political offence in that its focus was on promoting virtuous morals and manners without apparently referring to specific persons. The two later plays concern an honest miller of Mansfield who speaks truth to power. In the first, *The King and the Miller of Mansfield* (1737), a hunting king named Harry is lost in Sherwood Forest and has the good fortune to find refuge with John Cockle's family along with the evidence of his courtier's villainies (poachers both of his deer and of the virtue of country girls); he confers a knighthood on his honest subject in reward. In the sequel, *Sir John Cockle at Court* (1738), Sir John once again defeats court affectation and duplicity with the help of his honest daughter, Kitty. Colley Cibber, who played the king, summed up the inoffensive moralism and loyalism of Dodsley's satire, which nonetheless spoke well to popular taste: '*If plain, untutor'd Sense / Shou'd speak blunt Truths, who here will take Offence*.'[13]

---

[12] Robert Dodsley, *The Toy-Shop: A Dramatic Satire* (1735), 17.
[13] Robert Dodsley, *Sir John Cockle at Court* (Dublin, 1738), prologue.

It was, however, the work of a playwright-manager of much deeper learning and with evident connections to opposition movers and shakers that was to cause the most important change in the fortunes of satirical drama of the mid-1730s. Meta-theatre was a staple of Henry Fielding's playwriting. In the hugely successful rehearsal play of *Pasquin: A Dramatic Satire of the Times* (1736), Fielding sets the allegorical and the topically allusive aspects of dramatic satire alongside each other in a double rehearsal led by the Prompter and viewed by the critic, Sneerwell: a rehearsal of a comedy by Trapwit with its action turning on a local election is followed by that of a tragedy by Fustian, the latter an allegorical account of an attempt to overthrow the wise government of Queen Common-Sense by the conspirators associated with her rival, Queen Ignorance. It is estimated that some 25,000 people saw *Pasquin* in its first season; it ran alone for forty nights.[14] Fielding's targets and those associated with the ministry answered Fielding in kind. John Rich, celebrated for his performances as Harlequin and the enormous success of his pantomimes at Lincoln's Inn Fields and Covent Garden, was likely behind the commissioning of a now lost play written by his protégé, Edward Philips, titled *Marforio* which played one night (10 April) at Covent Garden.[15] Marforio is the rival statue to that of Pasquin in ancient Rome. Fielding was quick to respond by extending Pasquin's joke into an attack on pantomime. The action of *Tumble-Down Dick, or Phaeton in the Suds* (first produced on 28 April 1736 at the Haymarket) begins where *Pasquin* left off: with Fustian's tragedy over, and Mr Machine come to practise his entertainment, a serious pantomime. Sneerwell the critic watches the comical pantomime full of cumbersome and unimpressive illusion (a close parody of William Pritchard's *The Fall of Phaeton*) at a cobbler's stall.

Fielding's targets of political corruption, electoral bribery, and the defence of common sense suggested affiliation with the preoccupations of the Patriot opposition to the Walpole ministry. However, Fielding's play was not explicitly partisan and its satire mainly targeted ignorance and vanity in petty local politics. It was when Fielding turned his attention to Walpole's ministry, accusing it of foolish mismanagement, that the Prime Minister moved to extend government control over the theatres and the plays they produced.

Fielding's *The Historical Register for 1736* opened on 21 March 1736 at the Little Theatre in the Haymarket. It offered a series of topical skits presented in rehearsal by the playwright Medley to Sowrwit and Lord Dapper, the former attentive to the failings on stage and the latter more interested in frequenting the Green Room: five Corsican politicians come together to decide to tax ignorance (since taxing knowledge will bring them no profits); four ladies discuss their desire to bear the wax babies of a castrato singer; an auction of virtues and vices recalls the scenario of Dodsley's *Toy-Shop*; actor-managers Pistol (Theophilus Cibber) and Mr Ground-Ivy (Colley Cibber, his father) rant and

---

[14] Thomas Lockwood, 'Introduction', *Pasquin*, in *Henry Fielding Plays Volume III, 1734–1742*, Wesleyan Edition of the Works of Henry Fielding (Oxford: Clarendon Press, 2011), 233.

[15] Judith Milhous and Robert D. Hume, 'Edward Phillips and the Authorship of *Marforio* (1736)', *English Language Notes* 26, no. 1 (1988), 22–5.

assert their absolute authority over the stage-play world until a mysterious figure, named Quidam (an inconsequential person), buys off the Corsican/Patriot politicians with a bribe. He leads them out with a dance and the money falls through the holes in their pockets. Walpole's despotic but 'weak' ministry is paralleled with the ministries of Fielding's fellow and rival theatre managers, the Cibbers. But he also features in the more sinister role of Quidam, a cynical manipulator of the medley and mayhem who turns it to personal advantage. Quidam might also serve as a version of Fielding himself, a figure of mischief apparently marginal to the action who is nonetheless managing the scene from the wings.

After 12 April, the *Historical Register* was performed with another meta-theatrical piece by Fielding, *Eurydice Hiss'd; or a Word to the Wise* and ran for sixteen consecutive performances to the beginning of May (1737). *Eurydice Hiss'd* pushed further the comical analogy between Fielding and the Prime Minister. Sowrwit and Lord Dapper now attend a rehearsal of Spatter's tragedy. The tragedy is the story of the sudden failure of playwright Pillage's version of *Eurydice* hissed off the stage despite his efforts to bribe its audience—and especially stoutly virtuous Honestus. Fielding's burlesque *Eurydice*, despite the casting of popular Kitty Clive in the lead, had been hissed off the stage on its first (and therefore only) night on 19 February. However, the political allusion was evident: to Walpole's 1733 Excise Bill which was hissed out of the Commons in April. The anniversary was celebrated each year and *Eurydice Hiss'd* was carefully timed to play first on 13 April. 'You see here', announces Spatter, 'the Author of a mighty Farce at the very Top and Pinnacle of Poetical or rather Farcical Greatness'.[16] The metonymic and embodied nature of Fielding's satire reaches here an apotheosis: the satirist's final insult is to claim kinship with his target.

Fielding's meta-theatrical experiments proved a form of literary suicide note. The Licensing Act was passed rapidly within two months of its first reading on 24 March 1737. The bill extended the vagrancy laws of Anne's reign, which stated that every person should be deemed a rogue and a vagabond (and liable to a fine of £50 for each offence) for presenting any play or entertainment for 'Hire, Gain or Reward' in a place where such person had no legal settlement in the shape of a patent from the sovereign or his deputies. This effectively gave the two Patent houses a monopoly over spoken drama. Any new work intended for performance was to be submitted, with an accompanying note from the relevant theatre manager, to the Lord Chamberlain for approval at least two weeks before the intended performance. Failure to comply with this requirement would entail an immediate fine of £50 in every case and the loss of the licence and grant under which the relevant playhouse operated. The Lord Chamberlain's office had the freedom to prohibit any play or part of a play.

The effects of the Licensing Act were wide-ranging: among them, the self-censorship of content in new plays for performance; cautious commissioning and the reliance on old and already licensed plays on the part of managers; a shift towards privileging actors and performance as the primary draw; and, paradoxically, a shift towards conceiving

---

[16] Henry Fielding, *Eurydice Hiss'd*, in *Plays: Volume III, 1734–42*, 448.

of drama in terms of the play-script and its passage through the Licenser rather than performance and production.[17] Fielding did not put on another play until 1742 when David Garrick lured him back to write good-natured and unpartisan comedy for Drury Lane.

MIMICRY: 1739–1770

Matthew Kinservik provides an important evaluation of the effect of the Licensing Act. Four 'supposedly anti-Walpole' plays were banned shortly after the act was passed: Henry Brooke's *Gustavus Vassa* (1738), James Thomson's *Edward and Elvira* (1739), William Paterson's *Arminius* (1740), and John Kelly's *The Levee* (1741). But, after 1742, 'the censor had virtually no political content to worry about'. Managers had no appetite to challenge the censor only days before they mounted a new play; fitting a play to submit to the licenser meant that plays 'became cleaner and much less political'.[18] Sentimental comedy had been popular and successful before the Licensing Act. Now it became the vehicle for a satire of manners, fashion, and celebrity rather than specific political figures and vices. Particular satire does not disappear from the stage but the particularity relates to figures in metropolitan society and culture rather than heads of state. And an actor's mimicry of gestures and speech habits associated with a public figure could add a new layer of satirical meaning not evident to the Censor in the written version.

In this middle period of eighteenth-century dramatic satire, it is then perhaps unsurprising that actors begin to be the most significant figures in choosing and staging plays, especially where—like David Garrick or Samuel Foote—they also managed theatres. The different directions that satire could take building on an actor's talent for mimicry will be illustrated here by considering works by two men who appeared together on the London stage at the Haymarket in 1744, Samuel Foote and Charles Macklin: Foote undertook Othello as his debut role under the tutelage of Macklin as Iago. The friendship did not last. Foote imitated Macklin's pompous lecturing on various subjects at the 'British Inquisition' tavern that Macklin had founded on his retirement in 1753; Foote's devastating mockery of Macklin as 'Sam Smatter' caused the Inquisition to close and, two years later, Macklin was declared bankrupt.

Both men were admirers of the work that Kinservik describes as 'the first successful comedy written after the passage of the Licensing Act'.[19] Samuel Foote described Ben Hoadly's sentimental satire, *The Suspicious Husband* (opened Covent Garden, 12 February 1747), as giving 'the highest Delight, without having recourse to the low usual Arts of Bawdy and Bufoonry' in his prose work, *The Roman and English Comedy*

---

[17] See David Thomas, David Carlton, and Anne Etienne, *Theatre Censorship: From Walpole to Wilson* (Oxford: Oxford University Press, 2007); and David Thomas, 'The 1737 Licensing Act and its Impact', in *The Oxford Handbook of the Georgian Theatre, 1737–1832*, ed. David Francis Taylor and Julia Swindells (Oxford: Oxford University Press, 2014), 91–106.

[18] Kinservik, *Disciplining Satire*, 116.   [19] Kinservik, *Disciplining Satire*, 210.

Consider'd and Compar'd (1747).[20] Macklin provides us with an interesting example of meta-theatrical satire in a never-published play available only as a manuscript submitted to the licenser on 17 May 1747, *The New Play Criticiz'd; or, The Plague of Envy* which defended the success of Hoadly's play from the criticism of its detractors. *The Suspicious Husband*—which ran for eighteen nights in its first season and was only closed because David Garrick, who played the rakish Ranger, fell ill—is an important signpost in the transition in the patent theatres to a more character- and manners-based form of satirical comedy with an ambition to promote reform. Its success lay in finding a way to incorporate satire with sentiment. Vice becomes something protagonists recognize in themselves, for which they are disciplined, and which they seek to correct. Often, audiences are encouraged to forge a sentimental connection with the reforming protagonist.

In Hoadly's play, the tormenting jealousy of a husband, Mr Strictland, is exacerbated by shenanigans at his house, where his wife's cousin, Clarinda, and Strictland's ward, Jacintha, are being pursued by two young gallants, Bellamy and Frankly. By aid of a rope-ladder that Jacintha intends to use as a means of eloping with Bellamy, a drunken rake, Ranger, gains access to Mrs Strictland's bedroom and, although she rejects him, the hat he leaves behind proves a stimulus to her husband's suspicions. The four lovers eventually open Mr Strictland's eyes not only to his errors but also the pain he is causing his wife. Macklin was not only defending Hoadly's new kind of sentimental satire, but also getting on the bandwagon with his *New Play Criticiz'd* performed at the Theatre Royal, Drury Lane on 24 March 1747 as a benefit for the author. Where earlier plays made analogies between political and theatrical worlds, Macklin's 'new' satire on those who traduced a 'new' kind of play superimposed a literary frame on the romance plot. In this play, the playwright Canker is eaten up with jealousy at the success of Hoadly's play and is exposed to ridicule by the woman he courts, Harriet, and the man she truly loves, Heartly.[21] Macklin deploys the unforgiving aggression of the 'Old' comedy of Aristophanes to praise the sentimental values of the 'New' satire.

As Matthew Kinservik has shown, Samuel Foote's association with Aristophanes was commonplace but his acquaintance with and imitation of the playwright's satire was less deep than he and others claimed.[22] Foote's satire was not directed at leading political figures but rather at puncturing what he saw as hypocrisy and exposing those who took themselves too seriously to public ridicule. And as a result he seems to have fared relatively well in his career with regard to the Lord Chamberlain's office despite his flagrant

---

[20] Samuel Foote, *The Roman and English comedy consider'd and compar'd. With remarks on The suspicious husband. And an examen into the merit of the present comic actors* (1747), 27.

[21] Charles Macklin, *The New Play Criticiz'd; or, The Plague of Envy* (*The Suspicious Husband Criticized; or, The Plague of Envy*). Larpent manuscript 64 (Huntington Library). Available through: Adam Matthew, Marlborough, Eighteenth Century Drama: Censorship, Society and the Stage, http://www.eighteenth-centurydrama.amdigital.co.uk/Documents/Details/HL_LA_mssLA64, 8 [accessed 18 August 2016].

[22] Matthew Kinservik, 'The "English Aristophanes": Fielding, Foote, and the Debate over Literary Satire', in *Brill's Companion to the Reception of Aristophanes*, ed. Philip Walsh (Leiden: Brill, 2016), 109–28.

flouting of the law. His method of ridicule of well-known figures was to invent fictional stage characters who burlesqued features of celebrities making them both recognizable and ridiculous. 'Foote's innovation', asserts Jane Moody, 'was to make a theatre of character from the celebrities of metropolitan life'.[23]

Two later works by Macklin and Foote see Macklin imitating Fielding's style of plot-less meta-theatre and Foote further developing his brand of character imitation to embrace new satirical targets. Macklin's afterpiece *Covent Garden Theatre; or, Pasquin turn'd Drawcansir* was performed only once on 8 April 1752 as a benefit for Macklin at Covent Garden.[24] Drawcansir is the strutting indiscriminate fighter of the third act of Buckingham's *Rehearsal* and it was the name Fielding adopted for his satirical persona in *The Covent-Garden Journal*. Macklin probably took the part of Pasquin who stands on stage at his rostrum while his sidekick Marforio ushers in a series of town hypo-crites, liars, and fools who unwittingly fulfil the promise of the advertisement they are all studying:

> a New Dramatic Satire... written on the model of the Comedies of Aristophanes, or like Pasquinades of the Italian Theatre in Paris; with Chorusses of the People after the manner of Greek Drama. The Parts of the Pit, the Boxes, the Galleries, the Stage, and the Town to be performed by themselves for their Diversion.[25]

The characters on stage (such as Eternal Grin, Count Hubble-Bubble, Miss Brilliant, Miss Giggle) fail to recognize themselves in Pasquin's mockery. The satiric temperature is turned up towards the close in a mock 'knighting' of the card sharper, Count Hubble-Bubble, by the hangman, Jack Ketch. The play concludes with a now-characteristic meta-theatrical turn recalling Fielding's self-reference as Pillage when Marforio con-fides that there is one more offender yet to see: 'one Charles Macklin, Comedian, of the Theatre Royal in Covent Garden' who has 'written a strange hotch-potch Farce, and puff'd it upon the Town'.[26] Pasquin/Macklin says they will wait to bring him in person to the next court day.

The presence of the actor on stage and a reference to his own powers of mimicry as a vehicle for town satire is also central to Foote's most celebrated and controversial satire, *The Minor* (first performed in Crow Street, Dublin, in January 1760 and transferred to

---

[23] Jane Moody, 'Stolen Identities: Character, Mimicry and the Invention of Samuel Foote', in *Theatre and Celebrity in Britain, 1660–2000*, ed. Mary Luckhurst and Jane Moody (Basingstoke: Macmillan, 2005), 65–89 (67).

[24] *Macklin's Covent-Garden Theatre, or Pasquin turn'd Drawcansir* (1752), Augustan Reprint Society, introduction by Jean B. Kern, pub. no. 116 (William Andrews Clark Memorial Library, University of California, Los Angeles, 1965). Larpent Manuscript 96. Available through: Adam Matthew, Marlborough, Eighteenth Century Drama: Censorship, Society and the Stage, http://www.eighteenthcenturydrama. amdigital.co.uk/Documents/Details/HL_LA_mssLA96 [accessed 18 August 2016]. See also Esther M. Raushenbush, 'Charles Macklin's Lost Play about Henry Fielding', *Modern Language Notes* 51 (1936), 505–14.

[25] Advertisement, *The General Advertiser* (13 March 1752), 3.

[26] *Macklin's Covent-Garden Theatre*, 63.

the Little Theatre, Haymarket, on 28 June 1760). Foote, now at the height of his powers, took Methodism as his target, especially George Whitefield whose persuasive oratory made preaching a greater theatrical draw than the theatre industry under licensing restriction could offer. Whitefield features as Dr Squintum, the Methodist preacher whose spiritual excitations are easily compatible with the sexual ones trafficked by his follower, the brothel-madam, Mrs Cole. In the main plot of the play, a young man about town, Sir George Wealthy, is brought back to morality through the combined play-acting powers of his father, uncle, and a hired mimic, Shift; George undergoes a moral conversion and leaves off bad company as well as saving from forced prostitution his virtuous cousin, Lucy, whom he takes as his wife. Foote took three parts in the play: the mimic Shift; an actor-turned-preacher named Smirk; and Mrs Cole. Here, his powers of mimicry are displayed to bring a town run mad by Methodism to its senses.[27]

Foote's chameleon-like capacity to inhabit the bodies of his satirical targets is an indication of the new hybrid forms of satire in this middle period of eighteenth-century: character-driven, sentimental, embodied. The satirical meaning lies as much if not more in the performance than it does in the emblematic or allegorical representation of a vice or vices in need of correction. It is a satire in tune with an actor's theatre. It also runs the risk of seeming a politically-anodyne form of self-promotion, an empty trick of imitation. Acting is now the tenor rather than the vehicle of dramatic satire.

Metaphor: 1771–1800

The moral turn of satire in the middle of the century flourishes into a full-blown metaphorical technique during its last few decades. Unsurprisingly, perhaps, meta-theatricality fades from its dominance in the satirical repertoire. There was always a risk involved in comparing an authentic form of performance with the foolish, ignorant, and incompetent forms within and beyond the theatre. Such comparisons could be interpreted as a form of vanity and self-promotion as well as a form of 'office politics' only interesting to an audience gripped by the growing celebrity culture of the London stage; all these were accusations directed towards Garrick, Macklin, and Foote. The satires of the last few decades increasingly turned themselves to those social and indeed global ills that were preoccupying the English nation: the effects of empire and imperial ambition, abuses in the prison system, marital and paternal despotism. In these works, topicality is not incidental but a carefully calibrated set of allusions that constitute the play as a space for imagining new socially responsible liberties. Here, general satire, and character as 'metaphor' of general vice, acquires depth and complexity through

---

[27] See Misty Anderson, 'Actors and Ghosts: Methodism and the Theatre of the Real', ch. 4 of *Imagining Methodism: Enthusiasm, Belief, and the Borders of the Self* (Baltimore: Johns Hopkins University Press, 2012).

an engagement with the politics of nationalism and the challenge to authoritarian regimes at home and abroad.

By the later decades of the eighteenth century, sentimental comedy was under attack and the satiric target of burlesque itself: most famously, in Hugh Kelly's *False Delicacy* and Oliver Goldsmith's *The Good-Natur'd Man* which went head to head at the two patent theatres, Drury Lane and Covent Garden respectively. Both were five-act plays which satirized characters with too much sensibility to bring about a happy resolution through positive action. Perhaps the best-known call to return to an older comedy and the restoration of laughter on the English stage came from Oliver Goldsmith in his 1773 *Essay on the Theatre*, published seven weeks before the debut of his comedy, *She Stoops to Conquer*, at Covent Garden on 15 March.[28] However, Goldsmith's play itself—while it was full of wit, energy, and humour—clearly did rely on attracting the sentimental identification of the audience with its protagonists. Indeed, the one overtly aggressive comment on the false performance of sentiment is delivered by Mrs Hardcastle at the close of the play by which time the audience is familiar with her petty household tyranny and unsympathetic treatment of her niece, Constance Neville. When Constance throws herself on her aunt's mercy having returned from a planned elopement with her lover, Hastings, Mrs Hardcastle exclaims 'Pshaw, pshaw, this is all but the whining end of a modern novel' (in his essay, Goldsmith had complained that stage comedy needed no more skill than that of a hack novelist).[29]

Similarly, Richard Sheridan's successful stage comedy *School for Scandal* (premiered 8 May 1777 at Drury Lane) differentiated between justified outrage at cold-heartedness and vicious scandal that passes itself off as satirical wit. The general vices satirized in this work could still be applied to specific topical context: hence, in the context of the American War of Independence, John Leacock in Philadelphia printed a cast list for a production of *School for Scandal* in 1779 which associated characters with key figures in George III's ministry: Lord Bute as Joseph Surface and 'Mr King' (i.e. George III) as Charles Surface.[30]

It was in a later work, however, that Sheridan showed how meta-theatre could continue to be a viable vehicle for political satire, especially in casting a cynical eye over the sentimental fostering of misguided patriotism in times of crisis (here, fear of French invasion in the course of the American War of Independence). In *The Critic; or, A Tragedy Rehearsed* (1779), the ignorant would-be-theatre-patron, Mr Dangle, and the critic Sneer attend a rehearsal of Mr Puff's *The Spanish Armada*. Mr Puff, like other author-managers before him, has lost control of the performance, giving his actors permission to cut the lines they do not understand or find hard to learn. His script has multiplied heroes and villains, lovers and their rivals, willy-nilly and—as always—meaning is

[28]   Oliver Goldsmith, 'An Essay on the Theatre: or, A Comparison between Laughing and Sentimental Comedy', *Westminster Magazine* (Dec. 1772–Jan. 1773).

[29]   Act 5, scene 5, line 212.

[30]   See Robert Jones, 'Richard Brinsley Sheridan and the Theatre of Patriotism', ch. 5 of *Literature, Gender and Politics in Britain During the War for America, 1770–1785* (Cambridge: Cambridge University Press, 2011), 185.

entirely obscure(d) and genres mixed to comic effect.[31] In the tradition of meta-theatre and the rehearsal play, Sheridan represents government as incompetent, and the theatres as craven promoters of a foolish and failing ministry's interest. However, the treatment of Dangle, Sneer, and Puff offers more complexity and intensity in their hungry pursuit of control over players and audience than the types that preceded them. *The Critic* went into production as its author assumed his place as a Member of Parliament, a Foxite hostile to Prime Minister North's ministry and its counsel of nationalistic pride and fear of French invasion. Once more, the style of the satiric target can look uncomfortably like that of the satirist. Sheridan's persuasive power as an orator in the House of Commons was to be his calling card. When Puff embarks on a display of the different branches of effective puffing in the first act, he proleptically imagines the agency of parliamentary speech-making in which his own creator was (to become) adept. Once again, satiric target and satirist are uncomfortably close even as a differentiation between the virtuous and the vicious forms of the same practice is being asserted:

> As to the PUFF OBLIQUE, or PUFF BY IMPLICATION, it is too various and extensive to be illustrated by an instance... [A]bove all, it is a great dealer in reports and suppositions.—It has the earliest intelligence of intended preferments that will reflect *honour* on the *patrons*; and *embryo promotions* of modest gentlemen—who know nothing of the matter themselves. It can hint a riband for implied services, in the air of a common report; and with the carelessness of a casual paragraph suggest officers into commands to which they have no pretension but their wishes.[32]

That Sheridan's Puff is master of the printed and written word, but can only incompetently realize his visions in personal or embodied performance, alerts us to a new dimension in late eighteenth-century satirical drama. *The Critic* opens with Mr and Mrs Dangle at breakfast, Mr Dangle poring through the newspaper for dramatic intelligence and his wife full of alarm about the intelligence of potential invasion. This is a culture where print threatens to be the dominant medium of political and histrionic personality. Sheridan calls for an embodied performance that can contest the written and printed circulation of interested misinformation. The theatre's heroics should lie in resisting, not complying with, authority. They should expose the fictions disseminated in print to hoodwink an audience and prop up a failing regime.

The most innovative and prolific stage satirist of the last decades of the eighteenth century was a woman. Elizabeth Inchbald, actress and accomplished playwright, a Catholic with radical Jacobin sympathies, sought to represent on stage active virtue with an agential capacity to transform and reform such despotism. Paula Backscheider argues

[31] See David Francis Taylor, *Theatres of Opposition: Empire, Revolution, and Richard Brinsley Sheridan* (Oxford: Oxford University Press, 2012), ch. 2.
[32] Richard Brinsley Sheridan, *The Critic*, ed. David Crane (London: W. W. Norton, 1989), Act 2, scene 1, lines 265–83.

that Inchbald's perspective is that of the actress in an ensemble[33] and, here too, embodied experience may inform the way the playwright structures satire. In her successful career, which saw nineteen plays on the London stage between 1784 and 1805, Inchbald returned repeatedly to the problem of how 'to be justly sovereign...and in command without crossing into tyranny'.[34] While her plays often feature a counterforce to despotism, they also involve characters acting in concert to achieve social reform beyond the amelioration of their own alienated circumstances. Despots often reform by recognizing that, far from protecting themselves, they have inflicted harm to themselves by refusing to hear the sufferings of others.

And Inchbald, like many other playwrights of the period, expanded the settings and references of her satiric drama to a global stage: especially colonial states and newly-independent America.[35] Her first major success on the English stage of 1787, *Such Things Are* (twenty-two nights from 10 February) took a contemporary and topical debate about reforming prisons to the West Indian island of Sumatra. It opened three days after Sheridan had delivered a five-hour speech to the House of Commons detailing charges of tyranny, corruption, and oppression against the disgraced Governor General of India, Warren Hastings. Two new visitors to Sumatra arrive at the home of English expatriates Lord and Lady Tremor: Twineall is an affected, sycophantic young opportunist, Haswell an earnest philanthropist. Both meet Lord Flint, a politically adroit aristocrat close to the despotic Sultan of Sumatra. Flint ignores the torment experienced by those unjustly confined in the Sultan's overcrowded prisons. Twineall seeks to ingratiate himself through compliment but is misdirected by Meanright, long-standing household dependant, to say just the wrong thing to each of its members and visitors. As a result, he finds himself confined to the prison. Meanwhile Haswell visits the prison and prepares a book of cases to present to the Sultan for mercy: a Sumatran revolutionary; the father of a young European settler who has been wrongfully imprisoned; a heroic grief-stricken female Christian. The latter is revealed to be the long-lost wife of the Sultan—his lack of pity and negligence towards his own penal system has kept her locked away unbeknownst to him for fifteen years. Haswell also encounters the imprisoned Twineall and saves him from judgement of execution despite his foolish villainy for which he is duly repentant.

Haswell was recognizable as a rendering of John Howard, who published descriptions of prison conditions in Britain and in Asia. Twineall's manners and behaviour mark him out as a disciple of Lord Chesterfield's cynical code of courtly manners, which Inchbald had come to despise, embracing in its place a plain-speaking and benevolent reforming rationalism. Again, sentiment and satire are reconciled and work together to advocate reform, but its agenda is radical by comparison with the Aristophanic conservatism

---

[33] Paula Backscheider, 'Retrieving Elizabeth Inchbald', in *The Oxford Handbook of the Georgian Theatre*, ed. Taylor and Swindells, 604–5.

[34] Backscheider, 'Retrieving Elizabeth Inchbald', 617.

[35] See Daniel O'Quinn, *Staging Governance. Theatrical Imperialism in London, 1770–1800* (Baltimore: Johns Hopkins University Press, 2005).

which was the hallmark of earlier satiric drama such as Hoadly's *Suspicious Husband*.[36] And Inchbald does not avoid the more difficult politics of her subject: Haswell's generosity and concern persuades a violent revolutionary he encounters in prison to return money he has stolen from Haswell and to abandon plans to kill him. The European Elvirus, whose father languishes in prison, is courting in secret Tremor's ward, Aurelia, and threatens Haswell when the latter recognizes him and seems likely to expose his disguise. Inchbald articulates the Rousseauian principles that oppression and tyranny distort man's natural powers of reason and virtue. Inchbald's five-act play is a traditional comedy of intrigue and reform resulting in a marriage (that of Elvirus and Aurelia) and accommodation between competing interests in the household. Despite Inchbald's relative radicalism, two developments in satirical drama are evident. First, dramatic character has acquired a depth, complexity, and psychological tension that moves beyond metonymic representation of individual vice or virtue. Second, satire's topicality is now harnessed to global politics. Despite the fact that theatres relied on print to puff, publicize, and publish, and that their topical references were often now of characters known to the public through print (John Howard's published accounts of prisons), theatres retain an argument for embodied presence—the allure of the actor on stage in role—as the agent of satirical reform. Haswell's benevolent presence in prison, court, and domestic household brings about change in the relations in each.

Performance remains integral, not incidental, to satirical drama throughout the eighteenth century. Playwright actors such as Macklin, Foote, and Garrick wrote and performed roles that not only mocked contemporary celebrities but also asserted the power of the stage to offer aesthetic and sentimental experiences that rival political, religious, or social institutions (the Houses of Parliament, the Methodist chapel) could only travesty. The Licensing Act did not silence satire but it did contribute to the emergence of less topical, more general, critique. Local political and aesthetic instances of vice were, by the end of the eighteenth century, being played out as matters of global concern, while the traditional conservatism of Aristophanic satire still held sway. Satire calls for a return to lost virtues—whether aesthetic, social, or political. These virtues were increasingly represented as buried within character and to be retrieved through stimulating a sentimental response, rather than as restored through public humiliation or punishment.

SELECT BIBLIOGRAPHY

Anderson, Misty. *Imagining Methodism: Enthusiasm, Belief, and the Borders of the Self* (Baltimore: Johns Hopkins University Press, 2012).
Jones, Robert W. *Literature, Gender and Politics in Britain during the War for America, 1770–1785* (Cambridge: Cambridge University Press, 2011).
Kinservik, Matthew J. *Disciplining Satire: The Censorship of Satiric Comedy on the Eighteenth-Century London Stage* (Lewisburg: Bucknell University Press, 2002).

---

[36] See Bridget Orr, 'Empire, Sentiment, and Theatre', in *The Oxford Handbook of the Georgian Theatre*, ed. Taylor and Swindells, 634–5.

Moody, Jane. *Illegitimate Theatre in London, 1770–1840* (Cambridge: Cambridge University Press, 2000).

O'Brien, John. *Harlequin Britain: Pantomime and Entertainment, 1690–1760* (Baltimore: Johns Hopkins University Press, 2004).

Owen, Susan. *Restoration Theatre and Crisis* (Oxford: Oxford University Press, 1993).

Taylor, David Francis. *Theatres of Opposition: Empire, Revolution, and Richard Brinsley Sheridan* (Oxford: Oxford University Press, 2012).

Thomas, David, David Carlton, and Anne Etienne. *Theatre Censorship: From Walpole to Wilson* (Oxford: Oxford University Press, 2007).

Worrall, David. *Celebrity, Performance, Reception: British Georgian Theatre as Social Assemblage* (Cambridge: Cambridge University Press, 2013).

Worrall, David. *Theatric Revolution: Drama, Censorship, and Romantic Period Subcultures 1773–1832* (Oxford: Oxford University Press, 2006).

CHAPTER 21

··

THE PRACTICE
OF PARODY

··

DAVID FRANCIS TAYLOR

WHO decides that a text is a parody? On what basis can the targets or effects of that parody be identified? In essence, as Linda Hutcheon asks, 'Is parody in the eye of the beholder?'[1] These questions are familiar to us now, of course, but at least in Britain they were properly posed for the first time in December 1817, at the trials of William Hone. At the government's behest, Hone had been indicted for publishing three liturgical parodies earlier the same year—*The Late John Wilkes's Catechism*, *The Political Litany*, and *The Sinecurist's Creed*—and the Crown tried him for each of these texts separately over three consecutive days at the Guildhall. It was an experience that exhausted and nearly over-whelmed Hone (as it was designed to do), but each of the long days, in which Hone defended himself, ended in his acquittal. Across the three trials, Hone consistently argued for an intentionalist understanding of parody. Charged with blasphemous libel, he was in the unusual position of being free to profess that his parodies were 'not written for a religious, but for a political purpose—to produce a laugh against the Ministers'.[2] And this purpose was, in Hone's view, all that really mattered. Early on the first day he told the jury that 'they had every thing to do with the intention of the party, and if they did not find that this political catechism was published with an impious and profane intention, they would give him a verdict of acquittal' (*First Trial*, 13). The law, Hone insisted, enshrined this logic: 'If a man striking a blow with an axe at a tree, caused the head of the axe to fly off, and a man was thereby slain, though the circumstance was to be deplored, yet it was but accidental homicide' (*First Trial*, 36; see also *Second Trial*, 16). Just as this man 'would not be punished', so Hone, having sought to satirize the govern-ment and not to ridicule the liturgy, was ultimately innocent. A few years later, in 1820,

---

[1] Linda Hutcheon, *A Theory of Parody: The Teachings of Twentieth-Century Art Forms* (New York and London: Methuen, 1985), 84.

[2] *The Three Trials of William Hone* (1818), *Third Trial*, 22. In this collected edition, the transcripts of the three trials are paginated separately. Henceforth I will refer to them parenthetically as *First Trial*, *Second Trial*, and *Third Trial*.

Byron would defend *Don Juan* against the charge of irreligion along the very same lines. '[A]ll depends upon the intention of parody', he wrote in a then-unpublished response to a review in *Blackwood's Edinburgh Magazine*: 'If it be meant to throw ridicule on the sacred original, it is a sin; if it be intended to burlesque the profane subject, or to inculcate a moral truth, it is none.'[3]

But this was not how the government saw things and at Hone's trials the Attorney-General, Sir Samuel Shepherd, built the Crown's case on opposing foundations. 'It is not enough for a man to say, that he did it for another purpose', Shepherd asserted: 'that cannot be a point for consideration, when the effect of what he has so published is to scoff at the public service of the Church of England. The question is, Did this parody produce this certain effect?' (*Second Trial*, 7). Where Hone stood for intentionalism, then, Shepherd countered with reader-response theory, and even cited the behaviour of the public gathered at the Guildhall in support of this position. Early on the first day, the obligatory reading of the offending parody, *The Late John Wilkes's Catechism*, was met with laughter in some sections of the gallery, and a similar reaction greeted the reading of *The Political Litany* on the second day, compelling Lord Ellenborough—the notoriously testy Lord Chief Justice, who presided over the second and third trials—to call for the sheriffs. Shepherd seized his opportunity. 'I am not sorry for the faint smile just uttered in Court', he stated: 'It establishes the baneful tendency of the work' (*First Trial*, 6). Yet laughs and smiles make for a dangerous kind of evidence, and for all his confidence, the Attorney-General's attempt to claim such (seemingly) involuntary responses for his own argument nonetheless revealed the precarious complexity of his legal and theoretical stance. Hone certainly recognized this, and maintained that Shepherd had misconstrued the audience's response, which was no more than 'the effect of the ridiculous allusions to his Majesty's ridiculous Ministers' (*Third Trial*, 13). Effects, it was clear, are no easier to interpret than intentions; the meaning of a laugh is no easier to extrapolate than that of the parodic text which elicits it.

Shepherd, that is, gave himself the much harder task, and his legal discourse strained as it grappled with the very matter of intention that his key argument so thoroughly complicated. Most especially, that nebulous word 'tendency', which Shepherd invoked again and again, obscured the very agency it professed to locate. 'If the paper have a tendency to inflame, the law says, the party had an intention to inflame; if to corrupt, that he meant to corrupt', Ellenborough barked at one point, jumping to the defence of his floundering Attorney-General (*Second Trial*, 15). Such a claim gestures to what Hutcheon calls the 'encoded intent' of parody: 'when we call something a parody, we posit...an intent that we, as readers, then *infer* from the text's (covert or overt) inscription of it'.[4] There was, in this way, a potentially sophisticated and discernibly modern theory of parody lurking within the prosecution's rhetoric, but it was not one that either Shepherd or Ellenborough were equipped or willing to pursue, and within the legal

---

[3] George Gordon, Lord Byron, 'Some Observations upon An Article in Blackwood's Magazine, No. XXIX, August, 1819' (1820), in *The Works of Lord Byron*, 17 vols. (1833), xvii. 247.

[4] Hutcheon, *Theory of Parody*, 84.

context of 1817 their insistence that authorial intention could be inferred from the reader's response—or even that the latter rendered the former irrelevant—was unlikely to win out over Hone's categorical statements about his own purpose in publishing (and perhaps writing) the parodies.[5] Parody was *not*, the jury decided, in the eye of the beholder.

I have opened with this detailed vignette of Hone's trials, and of their probing of parodic intention specifically, in order to foreground their unusual theoretical richness— and their significance for a discussion of the theory and practice of parody in the long eighteenth century, such as I propose here.[6] In literary critical terms, parody has long since come in from the cold. Where once it was met with Leavisite disdain, the work of theorists from Mikhail Bakhtin to Fredric Jameson has placed it front and centre in ongoing debates about dialogic form, intertextuality, and postmodernity. It has come to be seen, Joseph Dane tells us, as 'the very condition of literature'.[7] As a consequence, the body of scholarship concerned with parody is now considerable and in this essay I will attempt neither a definition of parody nor a careful survey of its major critical inter- locutors. Such tasks have been adeptly undertaken by the likes of Margaret Rose, Linda Hutcheon, and Simon Dentith, and having read their excellent studies, and others, one might reasonably conclude that parody will never quite support the elaborate theoretical scaffoldings we have repeatedly and lovingly tried to construct around it.[8] Here, then, lies the heuristic value of Hone's trials, for they represent both an especially useful late- period vantage point from which to look back across a century and more of parodic practice and play, and also a prism through which some of the key theoretical questions that pertain to eighteenth-century parody can be addressed and properly historicized.

Hone might well be regarded as the first historian of parody and it was in this guise that he successfully exonerated himself and, in the process, thoroughly embarrassed the Liverpool ministry. Each morning he arrived at the Guildhall armed with a small library—'several parcels of books and papers, which nearly covered the table' (*First Trial*, 3)—and, over the following hours, he invoked and recited examples of scriptural parody by the likes of Martin Luther, John Boys, Edmund Burke, John Reeves, George Canning, and James Gillray. '[T]his sort of writing had never been prosecuted',

---

[5] On the question of Hone's possible authorship of *The Late John Wilkes's Catechism* see Marcus Wood, *Radical Satire and Print Culture, 1790–1822* (Oxford: Clarendon Press, 1994), 114–15.

[6] Surprisingly, Hone's trials have been discussed in terms of the histories of radicalism, print culture, and press freedom, but not as a significant moment in the history of parody. For excellent critical accounts of the trials see Olivia Smith, *The Politics of Language 1791–1819* (Oxford: Clarendon Press, 1984), 154–201, and Wood, *Radical Satire*, 96–154.

[7] Joseph A. Dane, 'Parody', in *The Oxford Encyclopedia of British Literature*, ed. David Scott Kastan (Oxford University Press, 2006), http://www.oxfordreference.com/view/10.1093/acref/9780195169218. 001.0001/acref-9780195169218-e-0361. For a good summary of this critical rehabilitation, see Robert L. Mack, *The Genius of Parody: Imitation and Originality in Seventeenth- and Eighteenth-Century English Literature* (Basingstoke: Palgrave Macmillan, 2007), 15–48.

[8] Margaret A. Rose, *Parody//Metafiction: An Analysis of Parody as a Critical Mirror to the Writing and Reception of Fiction* (London: Croom Helm, 1979) and *Parody: Ancient, Modern, and Post-Modern* (Cambridge: Cambridge University Press, 1993); Hutcheon, *Theory of Parody*; Simon Dentith, *Parody* (London: Routledge, 2000).

Hone maintained, so why was he now singled out (*First Trial*, 19)? The nature of this defence, grounded as it was upon a deep understanding of parody's long history and formal distinctiveness, meant that parody was itself in the dock; not for nothing did the press name them the 'Parody Trials'.[9] In this chapter, then, Hone's trials—and the problems and definitions to which they gave special clarity and urgency—serve as the platform that will launch us back into some of the versions of parody that manifest themselves in the works of earlier decades and so, in turn, illuminate contemporary conceptions of what parody is and does in the long eighteenth century. Each of my two sections attends to a specific issue raised in 1817 that can help us navigate and better understand the culture or cultures of parody in evidence in Britain from the late Restoration onwards. In the second part of this essay, I look at the class politics of parodic practice and suggest the extent to which parody was—and is still—inextricably tied to questions of cultural capital and proprietorship. Before this, though, in my first section, I want to consider how the period understood the imperatives of parody and so, perforce, its relationship to satire.

SPECIES OF PARODY

Central to Hone's argument at the trials was his contention that there were 'two kinds of parodies; one in which a man might convey ludicrous or ridiculous ideas relative to some other subject; the other, where it was meant to ridicule the thing parodied' (*First Trial*, 35). This is a vital distinction, as we shall see, but it is by no means a new one. In fact, and as Hone may well have known, it replays a point made by Alexander Pope (in the guise of Scriblerus) in a note to the four-book *Dunciad* (1743): 'It is a common and foolish mistake,' Pope avers, 'that a ludicrous parody of a grave and celebrated passage is a ridicule of that passage...A ridicule indeed there is in every parody; but when the image is transferred from one subject to another, and the subject is not a *poem burlesqued*...the ridicule falls not on the thing *imitated*, but *imitating*.'[10] Such, of course, is mock-epic, as Pope goes on to claim. I want to explore the nature and implications of this bipartite conception of parody at some length but, in the first instance, what is worth noting here is that for Pope and Hone parody must always to some extent be satirical in its inflection; the question thus is not whether it seeks to satirize but rather *what* it seeks to satirize. For them, as more recently for Simon Dentith, parody is intrinsically 'polemical' in that it must, however judiciously, attack something or someone.[11]

Yet this simply does not hold true for a considerable portion of parodic practice in the eighteenth century, as we are reminded by Johnson's *Dictionary*, wherein parody is defined as: 'A kind of writing, in which the words of an author or his thoughts are taken,

---

[9] See, for instance, *Morning Chronicle*, 3 January 1818.
[10] Alexander Pope, *The Dunciad in Four Books* (1743), 116 (note to II.405).
[11] Dentith, *Parody*, 9. Dentith recognizes that the 'polemical' strain of some parody is 'very slight indeed'.

and by a slight change adapted to some new purpose.'[12] Similar statements can be found both early and late in the period; in 1693, Dryden describes the *silloi*, or philosophical parodies, of ancient Greece as 'Verses patch'd up from great Poets, and turn'd into another Sence than their Author intended them,'[13] while in 1823, Isaac Disraeli, closely echoing Johnson, sees parody as 'a work grafted on another work, but which turn[s] on a different subject by a slight change of the expression.'[14] There is no mention of satire or ridicule in any of these formulations, and indeed for many eighteenth-century writers— as Howard Weinbrot has shown—parody was close to, if not a form of, the *imitatio*.[15] Of Pope's *Imitations of Horace*, for instance, William Warburton writes: 'this sort of Imitations, which are of the nature of *Parodies*, add reflected grace and splendor on original wit.'[16]

Even those commentators who admit the satirical impulse of parody often insist not only that it derides some object other than and extrinsic to its target text—as Hone maintains—but further that parody actively exalts that which it appropriates. To be parodied, Disraeli suggests, is to be paid 'a compliment', a view forcefully espoused by William Hazlitt, who contends that parodies and burlesques 'imply something serious or sacred in the originals. Without this, they would be good for nothing.'[17] This sense of the prestige that parody bestows on its model goes some way to explaining the period's predilection for parallel-text editions in which parody and ur-text are set side by side, a typographic juxtaposition that is conducive to what one anonymous parodist calls the 'double pleasure' that a reader receives 'from the striking beauties of the original, and the ludicrous imitation.'[18] We would do well, in light of such practice, to remember the etymological root of *para*, which meant 'beside' as well as 'against'.[19] And, in this way, there is a highly important (and hitherto unexplored) relationship between parody and the project of canon-making in the period, one that literary historians will continue to neglect so long as we adhere to a rigidly Jamesonian notion of parody as critique. The many loving reworkings of Thomas Gray's *Elegy Written in a Country Churchyard* (discussed later in this chapter) or the countless spoofs of Hamlet's 'To be or not to be' soliloquy published in newspapers and periodicals are neither critical nor, in any meaningful sense, satirical; but this does not make them what Fredric Jameson terms

---

[12] Samuel Johnson, *A Dictionary of the English Language*, 2 vols. (1755–6), entry for 'parody'.

[13] John Dryden, *The Satires of Decimus Junius Juvenalis. Translated into English* (1693), xx.

[14] Isaac Disraeli, *A Second Series of Curiosities of Literature*, 3 vols. (1823), i. 157.

[15] Howard Weinbrot, 'Translation and Parody: Towards the Genealogy of the Augustan Imitation', *ELH* 33, no. 4 (1966), 434–47.

[16] William Warburton (ed.), *The Works of Alexander Pope*, 9 vols. (1751), iv. 36–7.

[17] William Hazlitt, *Lectures on the English Comic Writers* (1819), 41. There was no hard or fast distinction between parody and burlesque in the period, as is made clear by Addison's comments about the latter in *Spectator* 249 (15 December 1711) and Fielding's equation of 'Parodies' and 'Burlesque Imitations' in the preface to *Joseph Andrews*, ed. Thomas Keymer (Oxford: Oxford University Press, 1999), 4. In *A School Dictionary; or, Entick's English Dictionary, Abridged and Adapted to the Use of Schools* (1809), parody is defined as 'a burlesque change of another's words' (149).

[18] *Hoey's Dublin Mercury*, 13–15 June 1771.

[19] See Rose, *Parody: Ancient, Modern, and Post-Modern*, 45–6.

'blank parody'.[20] They *do* have a manifest vocation, for they marshal comic appropriation as a mode of celebration and work incrementally both to embed a particular text or passage within the cultural memory and, therefore, to reinforce the ideological robustness of a 'national' literary culture.[21]

There is surprisingly little criticism in the period that regards parody as a vital instrument of literary quality control, a means of exploding bad writing or of evaluating and problematizing generic innovation.[22] Indeed, many authors and critics seem to have agreed on 'the inefficacy of burlesqueing subjects in themselves mean and ridiculous', as an essay in the *London Chronicle* put it in 1765.[23] This is by no means to suggest that parody was not used to police matters of form and style in the eighteenth century; we know that it was. Rather, it is to recognize, first, that the kind of parody in which, to quote Swift, 'the Author personates the Style and Manner of other Writers, whom he has a mind to expose' was neither the only nor the prevailing parodic practice of the period, and, second, that as scholars and more especially as teachers we have focused overwhelmingly on the second of Hone's two varieties of parody (where the target text is also the primary satirical target) at the expense of the first (where target text and satirical target are distinct).[24] This emphasis is understandable. Works such as *The Rehearsal*, *A Modest Proposal*, *The Beggar's Opera*, *Shamela*, *Joseph Andrews*, *Tristram Shandy*, and *Northanger Abbey* are classroom favourites not only because they are such wonderfully rich texts but also because they serve us so well pedagogically; their expressly literary kind of parody helps to render legible the protocols of discourse and genre (the novel most especially) that are usually less visible in 'straight' texts. And when we do broach the kind of parody that takes up a text to satirize something else, it is invariably mock-epic: *The Rape of the Lock*, *The Dunciad*, or perhaps *Don Juan*.

Yet, well beyond the mock-epic, a great deal of eighteenth-century parody shows that it was widely understood to be, in Hone's words, 'a ready engine to produce a certain impression on the mind, without at all ridiculing the sentiments contained in the original work' (*Third Trial*, 21). In what remains of this section, I want to give particular attention to *political* parody as the most discernible and significant tradition of this species of parody—one in which Hone positioned himself. The definitions of parody given

---

[20] Fredric Jameson, 'Postmodernism, or the Cultural Logic of Late Capitalism', *New Left Review* 146 (1984), 53–92 (65).

[21] For a highly problematic attempt to distinguish parody and satire on a formal basis, see Joseph A. Dane, 'Parody and Satire: A Theoretical Model', *Genre* 13, no. 2 (1980), 145–59. Dane argues that 'satire refers to things; parody refers to word. The target and referent of satire is a system of content (*res*); that of parody is a system of expression (*signa*).' As many of the examples I offer in this chapter show, such a binary understanding of form and content is unsustainable.

[22] Such is the imperative of parody for George Kitchin, who describes 'genuine parody as the reaction of central-minded persons to the vagaries of the modes, chiefly romantic' in *A Survey of Burlesque and Parody in English* (London and Edinburgh: Oliver & Boyd, 1931), x. For a good discussion of parody as the vehicle for 'policing the boundaries of the sayable' see Dentith, *Parody*, 25–7.

[23] 'Review of *The Battle of the Genii*', in *London Chronicle or Universal Evening Post* (28 May 1765), 516.

[24] Jonathan Swift, *A Tale of a Tub*, in *A Tale of a Tub and Other Works*, ed. Marcus Walsh, *The Cambridge Edition of the Works of Jonathan Swift* (Cambridge: Cambridge University Press, 2010), 7.

by Dryden, Johnson, and Disraeli all agree that its chief operation is that of repurposing or 'refunctioning', of making 'slight changes' in order to reorient the concerns of a pre-existing text.[25] As one would-be satirical poet notes in the *Public Advertiser*: 'The Writer of a Parody is a Kind of literary Freebooter, who pulls to Pieces another Man's Structure to rebuild it after his own Whim with the old Materials.'[26] This conception of parody as a form that recycles prior structures, narratives, personae, and motifs—that, to continue the above writer's conceit, consciously plays with the very building blocks of a text—to fashion a satire of something else is one that suggests just how much we as literary critics have to gain from attending more closely to the mechanisms of appropriation and adaptation at work in political parody of the eighteenth century.

Let me offer as an example one of the parodies cited by Hone as evidence at his trials: George Cruikshank's *Boney's Meditations on the Island of St. Helena* of August 1815 (Figure 21.1). Reworking Satan's resentful address to the sun as he makes his way to Eden

FIGURE 21.1 George Cruikshank, after George Humphrey, *Boney's Meditations on the Island of St. Helena—or—The Devil Addressing the Sun. Paradise Lost Book IV* (Hannah Humphrey, August 1815). Anne S. K. Brown Military Collection, Brown University Library. [11]

[25] In Rose's definition, literary parody is 'the critical refunctioning of preformed literary material with comic effect' (*Parody//Metafiction*, 35).
[26] *Public Advertiser*, 11 September 1770.

in *Paradise Lost*, and at the same time knowingly adapting James Gillray's earlier travesty of the same scene, Cruikshank depicts a dishevelled Napoleon stood atop St. Helena; he gazes bitterly towards the sun, which sends out in bright beams the names of the military commanders of Waterloo and which encircles a portrait of the Prince Regent, to whom Napoleon hisses: 'To thee I call but with no friendly voice, & add thy name—G—P—Rt!. to tell thee how I hate thy beams, that bring to my remembrance from what state I fell & c.'[27] Hone rightly states that this print is 'a parody on Milton, not turning the passage from that part into ridicule, but meant to ridicule Bonaparte' (*First Trial*, 39). Cruikshank in fact quotes from *Paradise Lost* with great care; only the name in question—George Prince Regent rather than the sun—has been altered from Satan's soliloquy.[28] Here we see exactly the 'slight change' regarded by Johnson and others as the *modus operandi* of parody. By substituting just a few words Cruikshank transforms the episode of Milton's epic into a rich satire on Napoleon's thwarted ambition. Milton's Satan furnishes the graphic satirist with a readily recognizable figure of exile, isolation, and fallen greatness, while the parallel between the Regent and the sun—described in the poem as 'with surpassing glory crowned' and appearing 'like the God / Of this new world'—allows the caricature to conjoin satire and loyalist panegyric in a single parodic gesture (the printseller George Humphrey, a staunch supporter of the Prince, had a hand in the design).[29]

On the one hand, *Boney's Meditations* reveals the startling economy of parody by illustrating how little needs to be done to a target text to politicize or rather *re*politicize it. On occasions, the alterations made by a parodist are so slight that they put the very definition of parody under pressure. Such is the case with *Buff; or, A Dissertation on Naked: A Parody on Paine's Rights of Man* (1792), which seeks to expose the flimsiness of Paine's thesis by delightedly showing just how easily—by the mere switch of a word here or there (all of which are helpfully italicized)—his radical pamphlet might be recast as an argument in favour of naturism.[30] On the other hand, Cruikshank's caricature suggests the extent to which political parody more often than not seeks to bring to the complex, relentlessly shifting world of party-political or geopolitical struggle a sense of narrative (and moral) structure and coherent character. In appropriating a particular scene—such as Satan's address to the sun—a parodist places the political present within a trajectory that has a beginning and, more crucially, a discernible if yet-to-be-arrived-at end, and uses the prior literary text as a typology through which to fix or diagnose the political personalities of the moment. Political parody *narrativizes* politics.[31] But parodic appropriation of this kind invariably brings with it some degree of ambiguity

---

[27] Cruikshank's print is a tribute to Gillray's *Gloria Mundi, or—The Devil addressing the Sun* (22 July 1782), a satire of Charles James Fox.

[28] John Milton, *Paradise Lost*, ed. Scott Elledge, 2nd edn. (New York and London: Norton, 1993), IV. 35–9.

[29] Milton, *Paradise Lost*, 32–4. The publication line of the print reads: 'G H inv^t G. Cruikshank fec^t'.

[30] *Buff; or, A Dissertation on Naked: A Parody on Paine's Rights of Man* (1792).

[31] On the narrativizing function of political parody in graphic satire see David Francis Taylor, *The Politics of Parody: A Literary History of Caricature, 1760–1830* (New Haven and London: Yale University Press, 2018), 10–23.

or polyvalence—emplotment and characterization are rarely stable, of course—that threatens to disrupt the very interpretative framework it installs. Sometimes this excess of meaning undermines the polemical imperative of the parody, but just as often parodists are alert to, and actively embrace, the ambivalences of a target text as a means of generating an irony that resists the overtures of too straightforward an interpretation of their satire. So, as Ian Haywood notes, the parodic analogy on which *Boney's Meditations* hinges ultimately troubles precisely the confident patriotism it would seem to establish.[32] Cruikshank's Napoleon remains both colossal and defiant, and those readers familiar with Milton's poem must know that, though deposed, the Satan of Book IV will go on to shape human history in the most profound of ways. *Paradise Lost* is a less than secure vehicle for British triumphalism.

In the eighteenth century, political parody along the lines I have just described is remarkably common, not only in textual satire but (as Hone recognized) in visual satire too, where the works of Cruikshank, Gillray, and others travesty literature and art so habitually that we might regard cultural parody almost as a structural imperative. There is, indeed, a particular efflorescence of political parody during and after the years of the American War. For instance, and as I have discussed at length elsewhere, the late 1770s see a flurry of political appropriations of Sheridan's comedies, whereby anti-war polemic is given contemporary dramatic form; in one reworking of *The School for Scandal*, possibly written by the Philadelphian John Leacock, the hypocritical Joseph Surface and his misguided but virtuous brother Charles Surface become Lord Bute and George III respectively, with the latter finally put to rights by the pro-peace counsel of Lord Shelburne in the role of Sir Oliver.[33] Such allegorical parody is also a well-rehearsed strategy of satirical commentary in the period's newspapers. In 1743, Horace Walpole published a verse parody of *Macbeth* in *Old England; or, The Constitutional Journal* that excoriated the Patriot ministers responsible for ousting his father, Robert, from office by depicting them as the three witches.[34] In 1771 the Wilkesite *Middlesex Journal* published the well-known soliloquy from Addison's *Cato*—'It must be so—Plato though reason'st well'—alongside a 'Political Parody *on the above* Speech'. Where Cato ruminates upon the immortality of the soul, inspired by Plato's *Phaedo*, the parody imagines a vacillating George III consulting both Samuel Johnson's pro-ministry pamphlet *False Alarm* (1770) and the oppositional *Letters of Junius*—'bane and antidote'—as he considers how best to deal with John Wilkes and his supporters.[35] And at the end of 1793, across two months and seventeen numbers, the *World* serialized a parody of *The Beggar's Opera* in a satire of

---

[32] Ian Haywood, *Romanticism and Caricature* (Cambridge: Cambridge University Press, 2013), 113.

[33] [John Leacock?], *The School for Scandal, a Comedy* (1779). See David Francis Taylor, '"The Fate of Empires": The American War, Political Parody, and Sheridan's Comedies', *Eighteenth-Century Studies* 42, no. 2 (2009), 379–95.

[34] Horace Walpole, *The Dear Witches: An Interlude; being a Parody on some Scenes of Mackbeth*, published in *Old England; or, The Constitutional Journal*, 18 June 1743. See Catherine M. S. Alexander, '*The Dear Witches*: Horace Walpole's *Macbeth*', *Review of English Studies* 49 (1998), 131–44.

[35] *Middlesex Journal*, 24–26 October 1771. This was the second parody of Addison's tragedy published by the *Middlesex Journal*; see also 8 April 1769.

the Whig club that cast John Horne Tooke as Peachum ('A Jacobin is a horrid employment, so is mine'), Paine as Mrs Peachum, and Charles Grey as Macheath ('Suspect my vanity, my volubility, suspect any thing but my Reform').[36] All of this—and I could offer many more examples—gives the lie to Robert L. Mack's puzzling contention that 'it is demonstrably true that the parodists of the mid and late eighteenth century…come to concern themselves less with the overtly political'.[37] Quite the opposite seems to be the case.

As Hone insisted, political parody inhabits and recalibrates a prior text without subjecting it to satire; rather, more often than not, it harnesses the cultural authority of that text as a means of legitimizing its own sustained attack on key statesmen or a particular party. But, as the examples cited above demonstrate, political parody is nonetheless engaged in a complex and—I would argue—interrogative relationship with its model. Even here (perhaps especially here) parody is, to invoke Linda Hutcheon's definition, 'repetition with critical difference'.[38] So, in redeploying *The School for Scandal* as a critique of the North ministry's efforts not only to suppress the rebellion in America but also to win the media war at home by means of selective reporting and subterfuge, the parodist registers the extent to which Sheridan's play itself is concerned with the politics of print and the mediation of social and political life (William Fraser, editor of the government organ the *London Gazette*, aptly takes the role of Sheridan's paragraph-inserter, Mr Snake). Equally, the *Middlesex Journal's* parody of *Cato* is alert to the tragedy's Whiggishness and openly exploits the tension between reflection and action that striates the protagonist's final soliloquy to negotiate its own political position; in portraying George III as Addison's protagonist, the newspaper at once underlines the king's virtue, and thus its own loyalty to the Crown, and also emphasizes the peril of indecision in the face of crisis. And, at a time when ministerial satirists repeatedly castigated reformist Whigs as plebeian sans-culottes, the *World's* parodist turns to *The Beggar's Opera* for a ready equation of high and low, of the similitude between underclass criminality and certain political ideals and practices. That is, these political parodies are also acts of political exegesis; if they repurpose their target texts then they do so in ways that are surprisingly attentive to the ideological nuances and ambivalences of those texts. Parody becomes a mode of political reading.

Of course, the further one pursues this understanding of political parody the more Hone's two categories of parody can be seen to bleed into one another. Thus, in some instances literary parody scrutinizes and mimics generic conventions in such a way as to disclose the ideological work they covertly perform. Swift's *Modest Proposal*—which undertakes a mordant act of ventriloquism to reveal the violence lurking behind political economy's stylistics of dispassionateness—is one obvious example of this kind of parody; two others are the parodies of Robert Southey's dactylics in the *Anti-Jacobin* (1797–8), which stridently relate the poet's formal experimentation to his radicalism as equivalent and equally unwarranted espousals of innovation, and also Austen's

---

[36] *World*, 26, 29 October; 1, 6, 8, 13, 22, 23, 29, 30 November; 9, 13, 14, 20, 21, 25 December 1793; and 4 January 1794. Quotations from 26 October and 8 November 1793.
[37] Mack, *Genius of Parody*, 232.   [38] Hutcheon, *Theory of Parody*, 6.

Northanger Abbey, which, Claudia L. Johnson argues, 'does not refute, but rather clarifies and reclaims, gothic conventions in a distinctly political way' by 'making the distrust of patriarchy which gothic fiction fosters itself the subject for outright discussion'.[39] Such parodies satirize their models as a means of uncovering a politics of form and, ultimately, of critically engaging an entire cultural regime.

Equally, on occasion, manifestly political parodies approach their target texts with wilful insincerity in order to flag their own acts of literary hijacking as analogous to the corrupt practices of the political status quo. Such is the case in *The Three Conjurers, a Political Interlude* (1763), a parody of *Macbeth* which casts as the witches the triumvirate—George Grenville, the Earl of Egremont, and the Earl of Halifax—who orchestrated Wilkes's imprisonment in April 1763 for his scathing criticism of the ministry and Crown in *North Briton* #45. Wilkes described this trio as 'the *three* wretched tools' through which Bute maintained his 'influence' even after his own resignation,[40] and in unapologetically announcing on the title page that his piece is 'Stolen from Shakespear', the writer of *The Three Conjurers* posits his parody's seizures from the national poet as an ironic replaying of the power that Bute and his allies have unconstitutionally siphoned from parliament and the British public.[41] On this last account, highly self-reflexive parody seeks to diagram the mechanisms of illegitimate political action at the level of its own formal procedures, and to collapse the distinction upon which Hone insisted.

PARODY, COMMUNITY, AND CULTURAL CAPITAL

These sophisticated parodies, which actively problematize the very conceptual coherence of categories such as 'the text' and 'politics', return us to some of the questions with which we began—of who determines parody's effects and targets—and I want now to turn directly to the matter of its audiences, and thereby to a necessary discussion of what Dentith terms the 'cultural politics' of parody.[42] Again, this vexed issue was at the centre of the trials in 1817, where the Attorney-General bluntly acknowledged that Hone's true misdemeanour was not to have engaged in liturgical parody per se but rather to have done so in a cheap format (sold for just two pence) that could be—and was—easily disseminated among the lower classes:

> There may be many writings which sensible men may read in their closets; some of them may be highly improper for general circulation, although some may be prop-

---

[39] Claudia L. Johnson, *Jane Austen: Women, Politics, and the Novel* (Chicago and London: University of Chicago Press, 1988), 35.

[40] *North Briton*, 23 April 1763, 1.

[41] *The Three Conjurers, a Political Interlude. Stolen from Shakespeare* ([1763]).

[42] Dentith, *Parody*, 10.

erly open to a free discussion: but the subject of the present question is not to be looked at in this point of view, for the mode of publication plainly shews what the real object is, and fully proves that it was intended that it should find its way among the ignorant and uninformed, where it was calculated to have a gross effect.

(*Second Trial*, 6)

In this formulation, parody is a gentleman's form that properly belongs in the study or library—within the private spaces of the educated and affluent—and that becomes dangerous only when it is wantonly removed from the enclave communities who possess the cultural competency to understand its subtleties and instead offered within a public forum to the 'uninformed' masses, who are liable to misread complex cultural codes never intended for their consumption.

As Dentith notes, parody can and often does 'draw a circle around initiated readers to exclude ignorant ones', and this sociological function has a long history that one could trace at least as far back as Aristophanes.[43] But the 'in-joke' imperative of parody is an especially significant (and sometimes overlooked) part of its appeal and practice in the eighteenth century, as is clear from Fielding's blithe comment that it was 'not necessary' for the mock-heroic moments that punctuate his *Joseph Andrews* 'to be pointed out to the Classical Reader; for whose Entertainment those Parodies or Burlesque Imitations are chiefly calculated'.[44] Reflecting upon this aspect of parody's mechanics in an essay of 1816, Maria Edgeworth comes closer than anyone in the period to articulating a phenomenology of reading parody. '[T]he pleasure we take in parody', she observes, 'arises from the self-approbation we feel from our own quickness in discovering the resemblances and recollecting the passages alluded to'; but, Edgeworth goes on, should we 'not immediately remember them, or if the resemblance must be pointed out, or the allusion explained, our pleasure is must be diminished' and we feel 'pain' and 'mortification'.[45] Parody, for Fielding and Edgeworth, entices the 'classical reader' because it offers a reaffirmation of her or his self-image as one of the discerning few, as part of a community of what at Hone's trials Sir Samuel Shepherd called 'better cultivated minds' (*First Trial*, 5).

Noel Malcolm has argued that 'parodic literary humour' thrived at the universities and Inns of Court in the sixteenth and early seventeenth centuries precisely because of 'an intensification of self-consciousness within the institution itself: the parodies are in-jokes, playing on the participants' sophisticated knowledge of the relevant formulae and codes'.[46] And Oxbridge remains one of the chief sites for the production of parody throughout the eighteenth century, as is readily shown by the numerous parodies of Thomas Gray's *Elegy Written in a Country Churchyard* (1751), which, prompted by Gray's

---

[43] Dentith, *Parody*, 27. As Joseph Dane writes, Aristophanes' *Frogs*, a comedy about tragedy, sought 'to establish an elite community composed of those who recognized the source of the parody' (Dane, *Parody*, 21).

[44] Fielding, *Joseph Andrews*, 4.

[45] Maria Edgeworth, with Richard Lovell Edgeworth, *Readings on Poetry*, 2nd edn. (1816), 206.

[46] Noel Malcolm, *The Origins of English Nonsense* (London: HarperCollins, 1997), 119.

own ensconcement within the walls of Pembroke College, Cambridge, turn the poem into Horatian satires of varsity culture. John Duncombe wrote *An Evening Contemplation in a College* (1753), a gentle send up of cloistered life—'Far from the giddy town's tumultuous strife, / Their wishes yet have never learn'd to stray'—during his fellowship at Corpus Christi, Cambridge;[47] George Ellis produced 'Elegy Written in a College Library' (1777), which substitutes for Gray's uneducated villagers the many redundant works of scholarship under the weight of which the college bookshelves 'groan', while at Trinity College, Cambridge;[48] and Henry Headley was a student at Trinity College, Oxford when he published 'A Parody of Gray's Elegy…the Author Leaving College' (1786), which tells the tale of an Oxford undergraduate who forsakes his studies for a wife.[49] Nor is this phenomenon restricted to responses to Gray. Thomas Maurice was in his final year at University College, Oxford when he published *The Oxonian. A Poem* (1778), a parody of John Phillips's *The Splendid Shilling* (1701)—itself a burlesque treatment of *Paradise Lost* penned while its author was at Christ Church. Each of these parodies is written from within, and addresses, a clearly defined and unquestionably privileged community for whom parody is almost a parlour game, a means of showcasing one's expertise, urbanity, and cultural dexterity. Not for nothing do titles include credentialing phrases such as 'By another gentleman of Cambridge' or 'Written by a college wag'.[50]

It is crucial to any understanding of the *Anti-Jacobin*, for instance, that it be recognized as a collaboration between men united by a discernible class perspective, a shared sense of cultural inheritance, and an Oxbridge education: George Ellis, who we have just met writing parody while a student at Cambridge, was the son of a sugar-planter and the grandson of the Chief Justice of Jamaica; George Canning, the journal's founder and editor, was educated at Eton and Christ Church, Oxford, and had been early groomed for a career in high office; and John Hookham Frere went to Caius College, Cambridge, and before that Eton, where he met and befriended Canning. The *Anti-Jacobin*'s commitment to parody as an effective tool for resisting the encroachments of revolutionary ideology is thus also a resolute expression of upper-class sociability and cultural capital.

This is not to say that all parody in the period was produced by and for the elite communities I have been describing, but it is to acknowledge just how visible, if not self-consciously dominant, this culture was in the production and consumption of parody in eighteenth-century Britain. Hone, of course, did not belong to this privileged group, and at his trials he repeatedly (and provocatively) cast himself, the lower-middle-class autodidact, as Canning's artisanal alter-ego. Why, Hone asked, was he and not 'the Right Honourable parodist' now prosecuted (*Third Trial*, 36)? Citing the satirical poem 'New Morality' as 'the celebrated parody of Mr. Canning', Hone insisted that the one-time

---

[47] [John Duncombe], *An Evening Contemplation in a College* (1753), 9.

[48] [George Ellis], 'Elegy Written in a College Library', in *The New Paradise of Dainty Devices: Consisting of Original Poems* (1777), 48–54.

[49] Henry Headley, 'A Parody of Gray's Elegy, written in a Country Church-yard, the Author leaving College', in *Poems and Other Pieces* (1786), 26–31.

[50] From Duncombe, *Evening Contemplation* and *Whittington's Feast. A New Parody of Alexander's Feast* ([1776]).

editor of the *Anti-Jacobin* ought to be stood in the dock in his place (*Second Trial*, 32). The purpose of this gesture was to expose the class bias on which the British legal system was predicated, but Hone was also making a cogent point about cultural proprietorship. His crime, he told the court, was to have taken up a mode of parody that had long been practised by and for his social superiors, to have attempted something like the democratization of parody, and thus to have upset the gatekeepers of knowledge. The roll call of earlier parodists he mustered to his defence—from Martin Luther to Robert Harley and from John Boys to Burke, Gillray, and, of course Canning—were all either of high religious or parliamentary standing or in the employ of those who were (Hone was quick to mention Gillray's pension).[51] Hone placed himself within this legitimate tradition. He sought to show the jury that had done no more or less than any of these illustrious antecedents and was guilty only of not belonging to what he called 'the right side' (*First Trial*, 41), membership of which, Hone's examples implied, was as much about social status as it was about political principles. The accused cast himself as the plebeian who played—rather too successfully—a patrician's game.

What Hone finally constructed, then, was a history of parody as an institutionalized form, and it is worth trying to understand the shape of this history in relation to more recent efforts by Robert Phiddian and Robert Mack to chart the emergence of parody as major literary mode in late seventeenth-century Britain. For Phiddian, parody becomes an authorized mode in the Restoration period because 'the desire to return to peace and order' drove the creation of a classically-oriented 'conservative literary culture' that was 'explicitly devoted to the emulative arts',[52] while for Mack, parody came to be seen as a threat to the cultural authorities and the 'privileged status' of the printed word, and writers therefore felt compelled to take up parody and self-parody as a prophylactic measure in what was an 'aggressively appropriative' era of literary history.[53] These theses, and also that offered by Noel Malcolm, fundamentally contest Mikhail Bakhtin's narrative of parody. First, they reject the Bakhtinian conception of parody as an essentially popular, carnivalesque form that, in the medieval and early modern periods, speaks subversively and irreverently outside of and back to official culture and its enshrinement of language as 'absolute dogma'; and second, far from regarding the parody as having 'grown sickly' in modern literature, they understand its cultural institutionalization in the seventeenth and eighteenth centuries as a precondition of its richness, complexity, and political imperative.[54]

On the one hand, not least but also not only for reasons of legal expediency, Hone too recognized and underscored the extent to which parody had long operated within the languages and spaces of official culture; it was a practice in which 'a literary man…a man of taste…a man of words' (*Third Trial*, 24) might engage not only with impunity

---

[51] Hone mentions Gillray's pension (which he received from 1797–1801) in *First Trial*, 40–1.

[52] Robert Phiddian, *Swift's Parody* (Cambridge: Cambridge University Press, 1995), 41.

[53] Mack, *Genius of Parody*, 21.

[54] Mikhail Bakhtin, 'From the Prehistory of Novelistic Discourse', in *The Dialogic Imagination: Four Essays*, trans. Caryl Emerson and Michael Holquist (Austin and London: University of Texas Press, 1981), 61, 71.

but almost as his cultural right as a member of the traditional political classes. On the other hand, however, this argument was born of a need to defend a practice of parody that departed radically from the very tradition it elaborated, and which conformed far more closely to Bakhtin's conception of parody's imperatives. As Olivia Smith, Marcus Wood, and Kyle Grimes maintain, Hone's parodies took up texts—the Bible, the liturgy, the nursery rhyme—that circulated widely in both print and, crucially, oral cultures;[55] parodies that, reproduced rapidly and inexpensively, were read or heard by labourers as well as gentleman (a point Hone makes himself) and that therefore struck in equal measure at the political elite's corruption and its claims to ownership of certain discourses and modes.[56] Indeed, as Wood notes, in performing parody after parody, despite the judges' insistence that such evidence was inadmissible and that such 'profane' writings ought not to be read in court, Hone consciously travestied the decorums and languages of the very legal theatre in which the political establishment sought to punish and humiliate him.[57] Parody as institution, as in-joke, and parody as that which problematizes or erodes the cultural hegemony: these two seemingly mutually exclusive positions were strangely and powerfully consanguineous at Hone's trials; they needed each other. Hone never completed his own, long-planned *History of Parody*, but his testimony at the trials perhaps offers us a means of negotiating between opposing accounts of parody's cultural position and function.[58] Taken together, Hone's sense of parody's institutional history and his own carnivalesque practice suggest that we must speak, in the plural, of the eighteenth century's *cultures* of parody. Mapping this constellation of intersecting and at times dialectically involved domains remains our next major task as parody's critics and historians.

SELECT BIBLIOGRAPHY

Bakhtin, Mikhail. 'From the Prehistory of Novelistic Discourse', in *The Dialogic Imagination: Four Essays*, trans. Caryl Emerson and Michael Holquist (Austin and London: University of Texas Press, 1981), 41–83.

Dentith, Simon. *Parody* (London: Routledge, 2000).

Hutcheon, Linda. *A Theory of Parody: The Teachings of Twentieth-Century Art Forms* (New York and London: Methuen, 1985).

Mack, Robert L. *The Genius of Parody: Imitation and Originality in Seventeenth- and Eighteenth-Century English Literature* (Basingstoke: Palgrave Macmillan, 2007).

[55] Smith, *Politics of Language*, 154–201; Wood, *Radical Satire*, 96–154; Kyle Grimes, 'Spreading the Radical Word: The Circulation of William Hone's 1817 Liturgical Parodies', in *Radicalism and Revolution in Britain, 1775–1848: Essays in Honour of Malcolm I. Thomis*, ed. Michael T. Davis (London: Macmillan, 2000), 143–56.

[56] *Second Trial*, 12.   [57] Wood, *Radical Satire*, 105–6.

[58] In the years that followed his trials Hone undertook considerable research for his *History of Parody*, including many days spent in the reading room at the British Museum, but he would never complete it and lost most of his precious collection of parodies during bankruptcy proceedings in the later 1820s. His notes survive in the British Library, MSS Add. 40109–40118, and in the William Hone Manuscript Collection at Adelphi University, Garden City, New York.

Phiddian, Robert. *Swift's Parody* (Cambridge: Cambridge University Press, 1995).

Rose, Margaret A. *Parody: Ancient, Modern, and Post-Modern* (Cambridge: Cambridge University Press, 1993).

Taylor, David Francis. '"The Fate of Empires": The American War, Political Parody, and Sheridan's Comedies', *Eighteenth-Century Studies* 42 (2009), 379–95.

Taylor, David Francis. *The Politics of Parody: A Literary History of Caricature, 1760–1830* (New Haven and London: Yale University Press, 2018).

Wood, Marcus. *Radical Satire and Print Culture, 1790–1822* (Oxford: Clarendon Press, 1994).

PART IV

························

SATIRICAL
OBJECTS

························

CHAPTER 22

....

SATIRICAL OBJECTS

....

SEAN SILVER

THE objects of satire undergo transformations as sensational as anything spun from Ovid's fertile imagination. Consider a metamorphosis: Apollo spies a beautiful young nymph. Struck by Cupid's arrow, infused with more-than-apollonian desire, he pursues her until her flagging body can carry her no more. In her despair, she calls on her father; he, the river-god Peneus, transforms her flesh into wood. It was an attention she never wanted, and a fate she never deserved; even Apollo can't be said to have wanted this. But what began as an ordinary day ends as the crucial event in her life. More: though she began the day more-or-less alone, she ends as part of something more than herself, the focus of an etiological myth. Wood, *hyle*, the very type of brute matter, becomes infused with causation and form. What lingers, as a memory of Daphne traumatic pursuit, is a mythos and cultural significance for the bay tree. The world is made resonant through moments like these, so much so that in the Mediterranean region where Daphne met her apotheosis, the bay laurel is still called by her name. Yet more: the very bays of the laureate retain a memory of Daphne's transformation; the type and figure of poetry, the bay crown, repeatedly signals Apollo's feverish, not-quite contact with his inspiration and desire: poetry recast as the unexpected yield of a failed assault.

Consider, as a contrary example, a second beautiful young nymph—Jonathan Swift's Corinna, undressing in her bower. Like Daphne, the eyes of a voyeuristic poet pursue her; also like Daphne, she is the victim of a transformation, a metamorphosis into brute material. Swift nevertheless sketches a scene that is clearly the reverse of Ovid's. Corinna, her body deformed by years of sexual labour, disassembles herself under the poet's merciless eye. Indeed the whole of Swift's 'A Beautiful Young Nymph Going to Bed' is essentially an extended description of Corinna taking herself to pieces, not just removing her outerwear, but her hair, her teeth, a false eye, eyebrows, padding, plumpers, poultices, rags, and bolsters. Daphne is planted by her father, transformed to living wood; Corinna (the poet reports) has no 'planter' to court her, no plantation owner to protect her from the sexual marketplace.[1] Instead, the entire poem is, in some ways,

---

[1] Quotations are from Swift, 'A Beautiful Young Nymph Going to Bed' (Dublin, 1734).

an extension of her vulnerability, which she has internalized in her dreams: she is pursued not by Apollo, but by watchmen and agents of a proto-modern police force, a creature fully permeated by an urbanized consumer age.[2] It is hard to imagine a clearer case of abjection; the very idea of a beautiful young nymph, in the commodity regime of sexual labour, is rendered grotesque.

Swift's 'Beautiful Young Nymph' is clearly a satire. Felicity Nussbaum's influential 1983 reading of the poem notes its similarity to Juvenal's 6th Satire, and to a series of strikingly similar satires penned by Swift's immediate predecessors.[3] But working out the burden of the poem—the satire's *object*—is a difficult task. We might think that the satire bears on Corinna herself. Swift's pen is at first merciless in tracing her undignified transformation, not sparing to detail the defects of her flesh that age, disease, and sexual labour have inflicted. But inasmuch as satire operates at the level of ideology, tracing the relationship between strategies of 'objectification' and the point or difference the poem seeks to make has proven to be tricky. For the same over-embodiment that is Corinna's curse and her stock in trade is also productive of a second, puzzling direction in the poem. By lingering on scenes of embodiment, on the body as a site of pleasure and pain, the poem treats her as a vehicle for experiences which are not our own, a conduit rather than end of satire. Just when the satire is at its most particular, it reorients itself, swivelling towards Corinna as a victim vulnerable to a striking range of social forces.[4] Whatever is satirical about 'A Beautiful Young Nymph' would seem no longer to bear on her—but to bear upon a culture that has learned to treat sex as one commodity among others.

It is one of the common features of satire, a way that satire performs its ideological work, that its objects, in the word's grammatical sense, become its objects, in the word's lexical or metaphysical sense. This is the transformation I mean to summarize by this chapter's title: satirical objects. In the first place, then, this essay will examine the formal conditions and rhetorical strategies whereby a target of satire is transformed into a material or quasi-material thing. It will ask how moral agents are transformed into things, and how aesthetic police-work or moral judgement calcifies people into (or embroils them among) waste, excrement, or brute matter. But it is also interested in the routes whereby objects are made to do discursive work—the question (or, formally, the *riddle*) of how brute material is able to occupy an important space in the ethical world of the arts. It asks how satire creates the conditions for objects to flash into the virtual space of discourse, and how those objects are made to perform moral functions. Put differently, as a single question, what difference does it make, when satire positions people with, or even as, objects?

---

[2] See Brean Hammond, 'Corinna's Dream', *The Eighteenth Century* 36 (1995), 99–118.

[3] Felicity Nussbaum, *The Brink of All We Hate* (Lexington: University of Kentucky Press, 1983), 104–10.

[4] See Robert Phiddian, 'The Emotional Contents of Swift's *saeva indignatio*', in *Passions, Sympathy and Print Culture*, ed. Heather Kerr, David Lemmings, and Robert Phiddian (New York: Palgrave Macmillan, 2016), 47–67.

This essay proceeds in three parts. In the first, it discusses satire as a system of differences, as a literary mode that creates distinctions between and within social groups. The satires I examine in the first section create ideological boundaries between in- and out-groups, but they do this by harnessing these community boundaries to a second set of distinctions—fundamental, cognitive sorting-work between persons and things, cleanliness and dirt. In the second section, I observe a generic alignment between satire's particular form of wit, as it was understood in the tradition after John Dryden, and the general form of objectification, which trades a global view of something for an enumeration of its parts. Finally, the third section risks a few remarks about the cognitive work that satire performs. This section looks forward to a reverse vector of objectification, whereby it is not always bad to be treated as an object.

Systems of Difference

Satire repeatedly performs a certain kind of transformation: converting persons into things. Its objects become objects. The notion of a transformation, however, masks as much as it reveals, for satire is not primarily a genre of action. Not much happens in satire— at least in the sense of plot or character development. This was true from the start; John Dryden, quoting the remarks of Heinsius on Horace, defines satire itself as '*a kind of Poetry, without a Series of Action*': this is what separates it from drama, epic, or (later) the novel.[5] And while we might aver that plenty of plot-based performances participate in a satirical mode (*The Beggar's Opera*, as a satire on the Walpole ministry, or *Gulliver's Travels* as a satire on Swift's cultural moment) the force of the satire inheres less in its action than in the way that it paints or portrays one or more aspects of a social system.

In the place of action, so its apologists claim, is the genre's moral function; it is penned as an effort to eliminate vice.[6] Its aim is to instigate reform in its particular targets; 'vicious Men,' Dryden insists, 'ought to be upbraided with their Crimes and follies...for their own amendment, if they are not yet incorrigible'. Or, failing this, it remains the poet's office to provide pictures of vice in order to develop (by contrast) 'Rules of a Happy and Virtuous Life'. Even if it doesn't change people, satire might still paint the punishment of moral error 'for the Terrour of others, to hinder them from falling into those [same] Enormities'. William Hogarth's 'Progress' paintings, satires containing more action than most, would appear to be moral satires of this sort; each assembles, as an ethical object lesson, a narrative of the punishment of a vicious way of living: a harlot's death from disease, a rake's descent to madness, a wilfully cruel adolescent grown into a murderous highwayman (and, thereafter, an anatomy lesson).

[5] Dryden, 'Discourse', 77.
[6] On this point, see P. K. Elkin, *The Augustan Defence of Satire* (Oxford: Clarendon Press, 1973). Ashley Marshall canvases contemporary discussions of the purpose of satire in *The Practice of Satire in England: 1658–1770* (Baltimore: Johns Hopkins University Press, 2013), 40–53.

For all their insistence on the genre's moral function, however, satirists themselves seldom chart out the personal transformations that presumably should ensue.[7] Though Alexander Pope is perfectly comfortable taking aim at figures like Lord Hervey or Colley Cibber or Edmund Curll, he is hardly worried that none of them are reformed by his lash. On the contrary, he delights in returning repeatedly to the *same* people, despite his attacks registering no apparent effect in their targets. Hervey, Cibber, and Curll turn up serially, repeatedly, predictably, in multiple satires from *Peri Bathous* to Pope's satirical epistles to the multiple versions of his *Dunciad*. Nor, finally, does satire seem to worry much about its other stated goal: for readers first to identify and subsequently to reform. While Hogarth shows us a madman (or corpse or cadaver), he doesn't trace out what the showing is ostensibly meant to do: that someone else will see the madman (corpse, cadaver) and mend their vicious ways. Hanging, for instance, behind Hogarth's rake is a well-known warning about the pursuit of pleasure. It is a painting of the *Judgment of Paris*, the selection of Venus in a trial of the goddesses which would kick off the destruction of Troy. Paris's choice, which ought to offer the rake an opportunity for reflection and reform, offers instead a pattern or even an object for emulation. In short, like Pope's satires, Hogarth's art evinces little interest in charting the reformation of moral natures. On the contrary, reformation is the bread-and-butter of different genres altogether: of moral pamphlets, bourgeois drama, sermons, spiritual autobiography, and the novel.

Whatever satirists say of satire, its success in reforming its objects isn't what sustains it as a practice. Perhaps it is better, then, to think of satire as the continual construction of systems of differences, offering a strongly slanted opportunity for readers to choose sides. This is one of the major findings of research on satire in the late twentieth and early twenty-first centuries, which has focused less on satire's formal features than on how it produces and maintains distinctions within a larger public.[8] In its eighteenth-century instances, satire tends to fall into a handful of recognizable genres: the verse epistle, the prose novel, the attack pamphlet. Recent scholarship, however, insists on satire not as the forms themselves but as a variety of communicative act (one frequent example is the *Colbert Report*)—an attitude or stance. By this account, which would appear to be a late turning-up of a rhetorical theory, satire is less a distinct genre with its attendant forms, than a discursive mode that creates the opportunities for divisions in a public whole. The content of satire, this approach argues, is less important than the chance it offers for viewers to identify; in producing a way of viewing the world, satire thereby creates communities of interpretation, aligned according to the sides they choose within a satirical discursive situation.

---

[7] Dustin Griffin, *Satire: A Critical Reintroduction* (Lexington: University of Kentucky Press, 1994), 25; Marshall, *Practice*, 51.

[8] Charles A. Knight, *The Literature of Satire* (Cambridge: Cambridge University Press, 2004); Robert Phiddian, 'Satire and the Limits of Literary Theories', *Critical Quarterly* 55, no. 3 (2013), 44–58; Paul Simpson, *On the Discourse of Satire: Towards a Stylistic Model of Satirical Humor* (Amsterdam: John Benjamins, 2003); Heather L. Lamarre, 'The Irony of Satire', *The International Journal of Press/Politics* 14, no. 2 (2009), 212–31.

Even as Pope's verse satires avoid action, they construct hierarchies of relative values, which is to say, static systems of differences. The *Epistle to Arbuthnot* famously begins with a command to 'John' to 'shut, shut the door', but this is as far as the plot may be said to go; we never know if the door is shut, or whether, if it were, this would mark an important event in the poem. The meaning of the poem, on the contrary, unspools under the arrested utterance of Pope's command, which serves to mark a distinction, closing off an inner community from an outer one. This is the classic structure of satire, which canonical poems like Pope's *Epistle to Arbuthnot* have been so important in conventionalizing. The poet constructs a confederacy with an addressee, which is in this case both the implied reader of the poem and the recipient of the epistle, both ourselves and John Arbuthnot. At the same time, it marks a series of relatively static objects, which are formally excluded from this inner circle. As Paul Simpson puts it, 'satire is configured as a triad embodying three discursive subject positions'—the poet, the reader, and the poem's object. Poet and reader (satirist and satiree, in Simpson's lingo) are 'ratified' by the form and function of the address; the target, on the contrary, is 'ex-colluded and is not normally an "invited participant" in the discourse exchange'. By these means, Simpson notes, satire which is 'successfully "taken up" [draws] closer the satirist and satiree', while a 'failed or "misfired" satire tends to destabilize and reshape relationships in the triad'.[9]

The satire of Pope's moment (and perhaps the binarist worldview it helped encourage[10]) is especially stark in the differences it makes, but its strategy of eschewing action in order, instead, to enforce differences between groups is true for eighteenth-century satire generally. The '"first" satiric gesture', observes Frederic Bogel, 'is not to expose the satiric object in all its alien difference but to *define* it as different, as other: to make a difference by setting up a textual machine or mechanism for producing difference'.[11] Languages like French and English (Bogel notes) are weighted towards the first and second person; their 'I's' and 'you's' (je's and vous's) are drawn into a kind of confederacy, grammatically enclosed in a kind of envelope that excludes its third-person others.[12] The subjects (in the grammatical sense of the word) of an utterance, along with their implied audiences, are naturally set off against its objects—beginning with the grammar of the rhetorical posture.

This primal grammar of differences turns up again, in an equally primal cognitive distinction between creatures capable of moral reflection (subjects) and everything else (objects). It is often the case that the whole object plane of satire is tilted towards its

---

[9] Simpson, *Discourse of Satire*, 8.

[10] See Margaret Anne Doody, *The Daring Muse: Augustan Poetry Reconsidered* (Cambridge: Cambridge University Press, 1985); Helen Deutsch, *Resemblance and Disgrace: Alexander Pope and the Deformation of Culture* (Cambridge, MA: Harvard University Press, 1996); J. Paul Hunter, 'Formalism and History: Binarism and the Anglophone Couplet', *MLQ* 61, no. 1 (2000), 109–29.

[11] Frederic V. Bogel, *The Difference Satire Makes* (Ithaca: Cornell University Press, 2001), 42. On ideology, community, and difference, see also Edward Said (himself a powerful reader of Swift), *The World, The Text, and the Critic* (London: Faber and Faber, 1984), 156.

[12] Bogel, *Difference*, 60.

targets; it is not just that the objects of satire are themselves treated like objects, but that they are buried in a confused landslide of bric-a-brac, of debris and its disorder. This tendency is what Irvin Ehrenpreis calls 'negative particularity': particular things, described and signalled by name, gather gravitically around sites of moral or cultural lowness.[13] Whether it be Joshua Reynolds discussing still life as the lowest species of genre painting, Anne Finch remarking that John *'Gays trivia show'd he was more proper to walk before a chair, than to ride in one'*, Alexander Pope eliminating particulars from his translation of Homer's *Iliad*, or Samuel Johnson insisting in *Rasselas* that the work of the poet is not to number the streaks of the tulips, the very presence of a clutter of material things signals a general condition of low culture.[14] The whole of Alexander Pope's *Peri Bathous*, a satirical attack on Grub Street (itself named after a 'grub' or ditch), may be seen as one long meditation on lowness and clutter, on the 'Lower Parnassus' of hack writers recycling wastepaper borne down from higher regions. The ideological associations are manifest: the shared values of civically responsible Augustan public life are moral concepts like virtue, beauty, and charity, while meaningless clutter is associated with the private vices of vanity, pride, and gross accumulation.

But distinctions between meaningless and meaningful things are not found in the world; they have to be made and maintained. Even garbage does not simply exist; seen as a limit case, waste or garbage is created through acts of division, closely shadowing the sorts of differences made by satire. When dirt or disease turns up in literature, it signals a hidden set of ideological motivations. 'The most insidious instances of waste making,' Sophie Gee argues, 'occur where individuals or groups of people are positioned as abject. Eighteenth-century examples include the edible Irish babies in Swift's "A Modest Proposal" and the hairy, filthy Yahoos of *Gulliver's Travels*, seen as a contaminated sub-species by the compassionless Houyhnhnms.'[15] Each of these texts depends upon the hidden workings of a politics of abjection, transforming moral agents into subhumans, animals, or brute objects.[16] Pope's command in the *Epistle to Arbuthnot*, therefore, is not an invitation to action, or the thing that kicks off a plot. The command itself seems to be the point, for it marks out an initial, primitive difference, which a reader is to experience, both ethically and grammatically, as a difference between us and them. Inside are Pope and Pope's two addressees: the receiver of the epistle, and the reader. Outside are the citizens of Bedlam or lower Parnassus, figures of mental instability and disgust; they

[13] Irvin Ehrenpreis, *Literary Meaning and Augustan Values* (Charlottesville: University of Virginia Press, 1974), 48–50.

[14] Joshua Reynolds, *Discourses on Art*, ed. Robert B. Wark (New Haven: Yale University Press, 1997), 50; Anonymous, *The Key to the New Comedy; Called Three Hours after Marriage* (London, 1717), 213; Steven Shankman, *Pope's 'Iliad': Homer in the Age of Passion* (Princeton: Princeton University Press, 1983), 62–73; Robert Folkenflik, 'The Tulip and Its Streaks: Contexts of Rasselas X', *Ariel* 9, no. 2 (1978), 57–71.

[15] Sophie Gee, *Making Waste: Leftovers and the Eighteenth-Century Imagination* (Princeton: Princeton University Press, 2010), 9. Gee's study of waste, like Bogel's of satire, is inspired by Mary Douglas's *Purity and Danger: An Analysis of the Concepts of Pollution and Taboo* (New York: Routledge, 1966).

[16] See Nick Haslam and Steve Loughnan, 'Dehumanization and Infrahumanization', *Annual Review of Psychology* 65 (2014), 399–423.

'rave, recite, and madden'. On the one hand, the voice of the satirist and his reader, engaged in moral discourse; on the other, the objects of satire, embedded in vice, passion, madness, disease, dirt, disorder, danger.

SATIRE'S OBJECTS

I'd like to return to Sophie Gee's point, about the fourth book of *Gulliver's Travels*— which comes to a crisis when Gulliver finally recognizes himself in the glass that the Yahoos provide. Gulliver is on the island of the Houyhnhnm, a race of rational horses; he has just finished a relatively lengthy natural history of Yahoo behaviour, comparing them to other beasts that swim or crawl. Though he has already admitted that the Yahoos are in many respects like him, he nevertheless pens a description that is less ethnography than ethology. They 'swim from their infancy like frogs', he remarks, 'where they often take fish'; they hunt for herbs, roots, and carrion, sometimes catching weasels or '*luhimuhs* (a kind of wild rat), which they greedily devour'. They lie in kennels scooped from the earth; they sleep alone, except for the 'females', who bed with 'two or three cubs'. Having caught a 'young male', Gulliver pauses to observe the rankness of its flesh (the pronoun is Gulliver's)—a 'stink somewhat between a weasel and a fox'. Carrion, stink, and filth: the appearance of dirt marks Gulliver's ideological labour, a distinction between himself and the Yahoos that is made rather than found. It is a crucial distinction between brutes and creatures of reason, between the writers of natural historical description and the objects of this description—a theme to which Gulliver in the fourth book repeatedly returns. The scene is closed when one of these 'odious vermin', Gulliver concludes, 'voided its filthy excrements of a yellow liquid substance all over my clothes'; he takes to a nearby river to clean himself, thereby hygienically policing the very distinction he is earnestly writing to naturalize.[17]

It is in just such another scene of hygiene, a mere page or two later, that the elaborate distinction Gulliver has established, the distinction between creatures of reason and brutes of appetite, is revealed to have been artificial, all along; he believes that he is writing the natural history of a subspecies, when he is in fact penning a satire which reflects uneasily on himself. The signs are all there. Much of the substance of the fourth book is Gulliver offering a history of his own native culture, which his equine hosts translate (for Gulliver's benefit) into what they have observed of Yahoos: they compare, for instance, the British drive for unlimited accumulation of wealth to the Yahoos' crude squabbles over 'certain shining stones of several colours', which they 'hide ... by heaps in their kennels'. But while the connections are manifestly available for Swift's readers, they are lost on Gulliver in the moment he is on the island. Because of the sorting-work that satire performs, because of the choice that it offers instead of the moral improvement it claims

---

[17] See Bryan Alkemeyer, 'The Natural History of the Houyhnhnms: Noble Horses in *Gulliver's Travels*', *The Eighteenth Century* 57, no. 1 (2016), 23–37.

to effect, Gulliver's satire remains the 'sort of glass', in Swift's words, 'wherein beholders do generally discover everybody's face but their own'; the very grammar or structure of satire seems, by Swift's account (and Gulliver's example), to exempt the reader from its force.[18]

It is not until a 'female Yahoo' reveals herself to be a young woman that Gulliver is called into the out-group or object category that his own ethography-as-satire has tended to enforce. The weather is hot; Gulliver is sticky with his own sweat, and is bathing in a river to cool off. It is then that he is 'frightened' by a girl who has witnessed him bathing, she being (he suspects) 'inflamed with desire'. It is a mechanistic, appetitive response at the level of 'brute' impulse, a question of 'appetite'. He perhaps objects to having been objectified. And though he himself immediately recoils at her 'fulsome...embrace', there is also a dimension of mutual recognition, a rebounding response in his own heart, to what he calls a 'countenance [not] altogether so hideous as the rest of her kind'. The whole episode—the girl's frank desire, and Gulliver's own incipient, half-redacted response—begins the long denouement that a careful reader of the preface to Gulliver's *Travels* would already have suspected. Gulliver describes his own 'mortification'—that is, a killing or putting to death, registering while attempting to shed his own body. It is not that he accepts the girl into fellowship with his own species, but that he recognizes his fellowship with a group that he had already categorized as abject. Gulliver's decision to leave humanity, his choice to become a horse, comes therefore as a solution to the riddle of the identity of the Yahoo; Gulliver realizes what the savvy reader of satire has known all along: that 'Yahoo' is a displaced name for 'human', the name of humanity when it is rendered up as an object.

John Dryden's 'Essay on Satire' offers one way of thinking about Gulliver's puzzling misrecognition—and his mortified recognition. Written in 1693, Dryden's treatise is sometimes called the first full description of satire in the English tradition. And it lays out a rule for the art. The height of satire, Dryden insists, consists of repeating a kind of riddle. At its very best, satire will describe its target with enough detail to make it sufficiently known and known as an object of scorn, without using names or words of censure themselves. 'How easie it is to call Rogue and Villain, and that wittily', Dryden remarks. 'But how hard to make a Man appear a Fool, a Blockhead, or a Knave, without using any of those opprobrious terms.' Dryden has offered satire's wit as a species of periphrasis, a mode of 'talking around' or 'circumlocution' that transforms a common notion or proper noun into a flowery near-equivalent. An expanded periphrastic strategy, satire describes someone sufficiently well to make their identity apparent, and even to create them as objects of censure, while nevertheless leaving enough ambiguity for the play of interpretative pleasure. By identifying parts that point to a whole, James Ralph would later (half-seriously) agree, satire works 'to sharpen the Imagination, imploy idle People, and enhance the Value of any Thing discover'd'. It is similar to a riddle, for, 'to this [same] end, were design'd the Mysteries, Hieroglyphicks, and Aenigmas of

---

[18] Jonathan Swift, 'A Battel between the Antient and Modern Books', in *A Tale of a Tub* (London, 1704), 227.

the Antients'.[19] This, in sum, is the riddle of satire's 'raillery', at least by Dryden's influential account; satire hinges on a tactic of misnaming, the substitution of an oblique address where a direct one might have done.

The simplest form of this raillery is the 'half-blank', transformation of a word or name into a few letters, dashes, spaces, or asterisks. Dryden himself, in his *Mac Flecknoe*, disguises Thomas Shadwell as 'Sh— —', which has a double effect. It at once kicks off a minimal act of interpretation, even while opening possibilities which aren't in the name itself. Dryden leaves room, in the double dash, for an imaginative leap to an excremental alternative, which the poem gleefully pursues. The poet, in Dryden's words, spares Shadwell's name, even while 'do[ing] the thing yet more severely'. It isn't merely that this technique, this gutting of a name sometimes called 'emvoweling', protects an author from charges of libel.[20] Readers were surprisingly quick to fill in the dashes.[21] Rather, by offering a small interpretative puzzle, it appears designed to tighten a pleasurable confederacy between satirist and reader. It thereby guarantees a difference between those who engage in the imaginative play to repopulate the name, and the object of this play. This is the most direct means of 'talking around' the object of an utterance—the basis of the periphrastic turn in rhetoric. That it also converts the proper address of a real-world person into a dis-coordinated set of marks on a page—the simplest version of a transformation from person to object—would seem to be an essential feature of the periphrastic tendency of satire: its continual conversion of persons to objects, the parts of an absent whole.

In approaching a thing obliquely, in selecting fragments that suggest without naming, periphrasis is the minimal form of the riddle. 'Fish' become a 'finny tribe', renamed by being reduced to their most iconic or representative limbs; a shepherd's flock becomes a 'fleecy charge', sheep transformed into the vendible commodity borne on their backs. The whole of the fourth book of *Gulliver's Travels* is predicated on just such a riddle, what I have been calling periphrasis—and which Gulliver himself twice calls by its Latin cognate 'circumlocution': it is the disassembly of the rational creature into facts or features capable of description and cataloguing. But the central formal substitution which is the engine of the fourth book of *Gulliver's Travels*, the slow recognition of the human as the sum of its abject parts, only extends a tendency that will be instantly recognizable to readers of eighteenth-century satire: the transformation, or partial transformation, of satire's targets into stuff, clutter, or excrement—humans into Yahoos, or in short, rational subjects into objects of disgust. Swift was particularly well-known for this strategy, what Norman O. Brown called his 'Excremental Vision'.[22] It is the riddling work of satire to address its objects indirectly, even to transform them into

---

[19] See James Ralph, *The Touch-Stone: Essays on the…Diversions of the Town* (London, 1728), xxx, xxiii.

[20] Andrew Benjamin Bricker, 'Libel and Satire: The Problem with Naming', *ELH* 81, no. 3 (2014), 889–921.

[21] Bogel, *Difference*, 5–14.

[22] Norman O. Brown, *Life Against Death: The Psychoanalytical Meaning of History* (Middletown: Wesleyan University Press, 1955), 179–201.

near-equivalents which are nevertheless not quite the thing itself—or, in many cases, the people themselves.

The part–whole relation of periphrastic substitution, this transformation, is the essence of what we might now call objectification or dehumanization; in the place of the global recognition of an individual is a persistent misnaming.[23] Dryden names Shadwell as something less than fully human. Similarly, when John Dennis transforms 'Alexander Pope' into 'A. P—E' (a species transformation by subtraction), or when the same author later insists on tabbing Pope 'Popa', the Latin for 'an *Excrescence*, or *rising Wart*', he is elaborating variations on a theme: naming a whole by a part or batch of parts.[24] Or, when Alexander Pope (in *Peri Bathous*) compares rival authors to various kinds of animals (comparing them to different beasts that swim and crawl, from 'Flying Fishes' to 'Tortoises', with swallow-, parrot-, and porpoise-poets in between), he is anticipating the ethological turn that will be Gulliver's specialty in book 4 of his *Travels*. No doubt Pope thought he was justified in this species of riddling wit, which meets Dryden's criterion of sparing the name (while doing the job more severely),[25] but Aaron Hill bristled to find his initials posted under the category of flying fish, who 'now and then...fly out of the profound, but [whose] wings are soon dry, and they drop down to the bottom'. George Sewell, Charles Gildon, Ambrose Phillips, and William Broome were little more pleased to discover themselves as solutions to the riddling catalogue of Pope's scorn.[26] The response, indeed, was so explosive that Pope later insisted that he meant no one in particular. His targets were responding to the basic sorting-work of satire: the division of subjects from objects, the people solving the riddles from the people who find themselves the objects of someone else's periphrastic pleasure.

SATIRE AND COGNITION

Gulliver's self-recognition as an object suggests an additional way that objects perform moral police-work in literature. This police-work is performed through the vantage point non-human narrators provide. The so-called 'it-narrative', that popular subgenre of eighteenth-century literature, repeatedly offers a defamiliarized view of cultural

[23] Sarah J. Gervais, Philippe Bernard, Olivier Klein, and Jill Allen, 'Toward a Unified Theory of Objectification and Dehumanization', in *Objectification and (De)Humanization*, ed. Sarah J. Gervais (New York: Springer), 1–24, particularly 7–9, a 'unified conceptualization of objectification'.
[24] See John Dennis, *Daily Journal* (11 May 1728), 1–2; *Daily Journal* (11 June 1728), 1.
[25] James McLaverty, 'Naming and Shaming in the Poetry of Pope and Swift, 1726–1745', in *Swift's Travels: Eighteenth-Century British Satire and Its Legacy*, ed. Nicholas Hudson and Aaron Santesso (Cambridge: Cambridge University Press, 2008), 160–75.
[26] On Hill's response, see Christine Gerrard, *Aaron Hill: The Muses' Projector, 1685–1750* (Oxford: Oxford University Press, 2003), 124–7. On the remainder of the initials, see Rosemary Cowler's edition of *Peri Bathous: or, Martinus Scriblerus, His Treatise of the Art of Sinking in Poetry (1728)*, in *The Prose Works of Alexander Pope* (Oxford: Basil Blackwell, 1986), 196–7.

ethics from the narrative position offered by an object; an object is made to voice its travels, thereby creating a morally superior platform for the contemplation of social vice—or, at any rate, a neutral platform from which to view strange practices the object itself can only partially understand. It may be, as Jonathan Lamb observes, that 'it-narratives such as the fourth book of *Gulliver's Travels* go beyond satire and any real desire of human amendment';[27] Gulliver himself opts out of humanity, instead aligning himself, and his tale, with the narrator and story of any number of it-narratives: the tale of a lap-dog, of a starling, or, (in his case) of a horse. But if *Gulliver's Travels* ultimately transcends the function of satire—or perfects it, since satire seldom aims at amendment anyways—it does so by failing in a way that we might not at first recognize, an aspect of objectification that is commonly disregarded. This is in humanity's 'sympathy for all manner of sensations and perceptions not one's own'.[28] It is precisely as a vehicle for experience that an it-narrator achieves its moral status and polemic force. As vehicles of experience, objects rise to a counter-intuitive humanity. The very rhetorical turn that converts a person into an object also activates this reverse current of affect. Gulliver leaves humanity specifically to offer a moral satire on the species, but something else emerges—the beginnings of a poignancy in his self-loathing, his strange choice to exit from human culture activating a reverse current of sympathy.

In light of Robert Phiddian's recent call to ground accounts of satire in 'a cognitive base', it's worth tracing the links satire suggests between community formation and cognitive processing.[29] There has been historical consensus in the cognitive and neuro-scientific discourse that assigning mental states to other beings is a crucial step in determining moral categories.[30] Likewise, there is an emerging basis in neurobiology, cognitive psychology, and the study of social cognition, for suggesting that the moral status of others is loosely aligned with hierarchies like human–animal, subject–object, and so on.[31] Many of the hierarchies that have been mooted over the last decade or so would not have looked alien to eighteenth-century authors and poets; Mark Brandt and Christine Reyna have for instance refurbished the Great Chain of Being as a modern-day model of the everyday cognitive organization of a moral universe.[32] The convenience of the Great Chain of Being, by this account, is that it stands as an index for coordinating strategies of moral perception, from dehumanization and objectification on one end of the chain, and anthropomorphism, personification, and sanctification, on the other.[33]

---

[27] Jonathan Lamb, *The Things Things Say* (Princeton: Princeton University Press, 2010), 47.

[28] Lamb, *The Things Things Say*, 47.   [29] Phiddian, 'Satire', 55.

[30] One useful summary of the literature on this topic is John T. Cacioppo, Penny S. Visser, and Cynthia L. Pickett, eds., *Social Neuroscience: People Thinking about Thinking People* (Boston: MIT Press, 2006).

[31] For instance, Adam Waytz, Kurt Gray, Nicholas Epley, and Daniel M. Wegner, 'Causes and Consequences of Mind Perception', *Trends in Cognitive Sciences* 14 (2010), 383–8.

[32] Mark J. Brandt and Christine Reyna, 'The Chain of Being: A Hierarchy of Morality', *Perspectives on Psychological Science* 6 (2011), 428–46.

[33] See also Adam Waytz, Nicholas Epley, and John T. Cacioppo, 'Social Cognition Unbound: Insights into Anthropomorphism and Dehumanization', *Current Directions in Psychological Science* 19, no. 1 (2010), 58–62.

This is to position such sorting strategies, which are the very essence of satire, as part of a more general anthropological drive to isolate purity from danger.[34] For the Great Chain of Being, that figure so central to the orthodox eighteenth-century worldview, sorts those who we imagine possess mental states from those who we don't, mind from matter.

Recent evidence suggests, however, that schemes like these only address half of what is at work in satire. Objectification has two axes—one oriented around the emptying out of mental contents, and the other around an emphasis on the body as a receptor of experience. This first axis aligns with what Blakey Vermeule has recently identified, in satire, as 'situational mind blindness'.[35] In most literary acts, we are confronted with strings of words that coalesce, as we read them, into entities that are roughly like us. This is one account of why we care about literary characters; we ascribe mental states, including desires, intentions, beliefs, and fears.[36] How this occurs has been the subject of much recent debate, but a consensus suggests that mind-perception—perceiving another as having mental states like our own—means engaging others as moral agents. The reverse seems to be true as well; emptying a body out of its mental contents, or denying it the capacity for mental activity, is part of a mechanism for casting it from moral concern—so much so that one team of researchers has concluded that mind-perception is the foundation and underlying process of moral judgements generally.[37] The example Vermeule offers is the sort of thing that appears regularly in Jonathan Swift's verse and prose satires; she specifically names Swift's 'Mechanical Operation of the Spirit'. The point of the complex strategy of mind blindness, Vermeule concludes, 'is to deny other people the perspective of rational agency by turning them into animals, machines, or anything without a mind'.[38] This would appear to be a cognitive theory of objectification, especially the too-earnest focus on others as objects rather than thinking, rational beings.[39]

---

[34] See Bogel, *Difference*, 42–6, 68–76.

[35] Blakey Vermeule, *Why Do We Care About Literary Characters?* (Baltimore: Johns Hopkins University Press, 2009), 195.

[36] See also Paula Leverage, Howard Mancing, Richard Schweickert, and Jennifer Marston William, eds., *Theory of Mind and Literature* (West Lafayette: Purdue University Press, 2011).

[37] Kurt Gray, Liane Young, and Adam Waytz, 'Mind Perception Is the Essence of Morality', *Psychological Inquiry* 23, no. 2 (2012), 101–24. See also Liane Young and Adam Wayts, 'Mind Attribution is for Morality', in *Understanding Other Minds: Perspectives from Developmental Social Neuroscience*, ed. Simon Baron-Cohen, Michael Lombardo, and Helen Tager-Flusberg (Oxford: Oxford University Press, 2013), 93–103.

[38] Vermeule, *Literary Characters*, 195.

[39] Among recent studies of this position, see J. Graham, B. A. Nosek, J. Haidt, R. Iyer, S. Koleva, and P. H. Ditto, 'Mapping the Moral Domain', *Journal of Personality and Social Psychology* 101 (2011), 366–85; Leor M. Hackel, Christine E. Looser, and Jay J. Van Bavel, 'Group Membership Alters the Threshold for Mind Perception: The Role of Social Identity, Collective Identification, and Intergroup Threat', *Journal of Experimental Social Psychology* 52 (2014), 15–23; L. T. Harris and S. T. Fiske, 'Dehumaniizing the Lowest of the Low: Neuroimaging Responses to Extreme Out-Groups', *Psychological Science* 17, no. 10 (2006), 847–53. These insights were not lost on eighteenth-century arts and sciences. See, among others, Markman Ellis, 'Suffering Things: Lapdogs, Slaves, and Counter-Sensibility', in *The Secret Life of Things: Animals, Objects, and It-Narratives in Eighteenth-Century England*, ed. Mark Blackwell (Lewisburg: Bucknell University Press, 2007), 92–113; Michael L. Frazer, *The Enlightenment of Sympathy*

Objectification is, however, itself a complex thing and in itself not always a moral evil.[40] For a second, complicating axis has emerged, by which objectification helps us register people as the sites and vehicles of experience.[41] Objectification, of this sort, does not deny mental states, or even, exactly, transform moral agents into machines subject to mechanical law. This kind of objectification does not 'shift…[a] person a few notches down the continuum, away from full-fledged personhood and toward inanimacy as a mere object', with 'less agency, less autonomy, less capacity for subjective experience, and so on'.[42] Instead, it registers a person as a capacity for experience, including sensations of pain and pleasure. In this second axis of objecthood, the very fact of embodiment suggests the immanency of experience, including aesthetic responses rooted in an embodied capacity for pleasure and pain.[43] And far from being subordinate to our capacity for imagining the mental states of others, experiencing others as capable of experience may in fact be more crucial to the construction of social affiliation.[44] For this sort of objectification triggers empathetic responses in others that are largely automatic—accompanied, in the words of one team of researchers, 'by immediate attention and parallel controlled reflective appraisal of the causes' of the other person's embodied experiences.[45]

I'd like to trace out a couple of ways that this axis of objectification cuts across the standard account of the cultural work of satire. Joseph Addison's *Spectator* essay for 29 November 1711 describes a member of a theatrical audience who regularly seats himself in the upper reaches of the playhouse, and, when 'pleased with any Thing that is acted upon the Stage, expresses his Approbation by a loud Knock upon the Benches or the Wainscot'. He is commonly known as the 'Trunk-maker in the upper Gallery'. Knocking is the trunk-maker's form of criticism; he neither smiles nor scowls, but bears a huge cudgel of native English oak, which he smites upon the gallery timbers whenever he 'hears any thing that pleases him'. The trunk-maker is clearly a figure of over-embodiment, of immediate sensory experience linked to a brute response—so much so that his enthusiastic thumping sometimes leaves the wainscot significantly battered. He is not named, but described by his emblems and objects; he is reduced to certain parts or implements that are made to stand for the whole: a cudgel, a wainscot.

(Oxford: Oxford University Press, 2010); Luigi Turco, 'Sympathy and Moral Sense: 1725–1740', *British Journal for the History of Philosophy* 7, no. 1 (1999), 79–80.

[40] Sandra Macpherson, *Harm's Way: Tragic Responsibility and the Novel Form* (Baltimore: Johns Hopkins University Press, 2010).

[41] Adam Waytz and Liane Young, 'Two Motivations for Two Dimensions of Mind', *Journal of Experimental Social Psychology* 55 (2014), 278–83.

[42] Kurt Gray, Joshua Knobe, Mark Sheskin, Paul Bloom, and Lisa Feldman Barrett, 'More Than a Body: Mind Perception and the Nature of Objectification', *Journal of Personality and Social Psychology* 101 (2011), 1–14.

[43] Justin Sytsma and Edouard Machery, 'The Two Sources of Moral Standing', *Review of Philosophy and Psychology* 3 (2012), 303–24.

[44] See Waytz and Young, 'Two Motivations'.

[45] Brock Bastian, Jolanda Jetten, Matthew J. Hornsey, and Siri Leknes, 'The Positive Consequences of Pain: A Biopsychosocial Approach', *Personality and Social Psychology Review* 18 (2014), 256–79 (256).

So, too, his commentary is of the simplest sort—a reflex loop from eye and ear to club—but it is, Addison continues, 'so well timed, that the most judicious Critick could never except against it'. And in singling him out in this way, the Spectator engages in the sorting-work characteristic of satire: a sorting which is, to begin with, a spatial one (the trunk-maker is in the upper gallery), then a class or social one (he is an artisan), and finally a cognitive one (he doesn't offer evidence of mental states).

But the satire, if it works, only works when the riddle is unpuzzled—when in other words, the trunk-maker emerges as a figure for a certain species of behaviour. The trunk-maker does not act alone; he demands a sympathetic response from the audience. If the audience, Addison remarks, 'does not concur with him, he smites a second time'; should the theatre again be behind-hand, a third blow 'never fails to produce the Clap'. That is, the satire does not bear upon the trunk-maker—who in any case doesn't, strictly speaking, exist. It bears upon a certain kind of theatre-going audience, which applauds mechanically; the trunk-maker ends up interpellating an audience which claps through a mechanistic reflex. It's worth noting that Addison's essay leans against a loose family of his work that suggests a neurophysiological theory, and which likewise positions moral action against mechanical habit. Addison cites a similar example of an 'ideot' who, accustomed to chiming along with the church-tower, continued to chime for weeks after the bell-tower had itself been torn down. This is a mechanist neurophysiology made manifest at the level of the organism: clockwork man mimicking clockwork tower. The trunk-maker's behaviour, Addison supposes, is less an expression of aesthetic judgement than a blind reflex, not unlike the hammer-blows of his shop or the village clock-chimer. Applause is drawn into this mechanical chain; 'trunk-maker' emerges as a displaced name for the pit. The audience becomes his objects, their hands the cudgels and wainscot of applause; the targets of Addison's satire, like so much of the satire of the Scriblerians, is what Brean Hammond calls *homo mechanicus*, a 'species' responsible for the arts and aesthetic experience understood as a merely 'mechanical and material act'.[46]

The very sensitivity to the trunk-maker as a vehicle of experience, however, opens up the possibility of a straight reading. Thus, John Trolander and Zeynep Tenger read Addison's essay without a hint of satire, clearly identifying (like the audience) with the essay's object, what they call his 'personality'; they cite the honest trunk-maker as a sign of Addison's capacious understanding of the public sphere, which makes space for the direct aesthetic responses of an earnest artisan.[47] Put differently, the trunk-maker, by his very objectification, appears to offer one route towards the making of a public. The attribution of mental states has no place in this process; objectification likewise offers no obstacle, but rather a precondition of this form of sociality. Any number of examples in eighteenth-century literature might be named for this second axis. From Burney's

---

[46] Brean Hammond, 'Scriblerian Self-Fashioning', *Yearbook of English Studies* 18 (1988), 118.

[47] Paul Trolander and Zeynep Tenger, 'Addison and the Personality of the Critic', in *The Spectator: Emerging Discourses*, ed. Donald J. Newman (Newark: University of Delaware Press, 2005), 191–2.

Evelina: Captain Mervan intends his bodily attacks on Madame Duval as satires against France, but they end up driving Evelina, in sympathy, closer to her instead. From Fielding's *Amelia*: Captain Booth, attending to the satires of several young ladies on Amelia's broken nose, finds himself instead sympathetic to her plight, and, when he meets her again, is overwhelmed with 'a thousand tender ideas' rushing 'all at once' upon his mind. Sympathy governs this transverse axis of satire, which emerges (in these instances) through its strategy of objectification.

Attending to this perpendicular axis provides a way of unriddling the counter-movement in Swift's 'Beautiful Young Nymph Going to Bed', the poem with which this chapter began. When Corinna, with 'pains of love tormented', creeps between two blankets—the precise moment named in the title—the poem reorients itself from a catalogue of Corinna's abjection to a sympathetic register of her experience. Her 'pains of love' facilitate a generic reorientation; the 'love-pains' that we would associate with pastoral verse or unrequited desire give way to the bodily wages of a career at the mercy of a sex-work trade. And these pains, the result of the many deformities which themselves pose such obstacles to accepting Corinna as a member of our own social group, become the vector of sympathy; it is here that the poet gives way to an automatic, brute-level response, the empathetic inhabiting of Corinna's embodied position. She dreams of jail and institutions of social reform—watchmen, procurers, constables, and duns—but experiences them in the idiom of bodily suffering; she has internalized them, and, like the object of satire that she is, she 'feels the Lash, and faintly screams'. After having surprised us into voyeuristic desire, and steered us into a well-known discourse of the satire against women, Swift's poem rebounds along the primal chord of embodied experience. The poem attempts an aesthetic reorientation, a transformation occurring at the brute level of embodied response.

Swift has loaded a wide-ranging indictment of a system, the range of biopolitical instruments of bodily control and deformation, into the most personal of experiential vehicles. Objectification, therefore, is not only a mechanism for policing social boundaries; it is also an opportunity for identification, which is the blending of individuals even across what seemed to be clear social groups. The metamorphosis that has occurred is not in Corinna; it is in the implied voyeur, who becomes (like her) an object of the poem. When Corinna is dressed again, and out in the world, she is returned to the state in which the poem found her; she is once again the 'toast of Drury Lane'. But whereas the poem begins by staging voyeuristic desire (the familiar idiom of treating a woman like an object), it now describes a total reversal in the voyeur, who can recognize the solution to the riddle of abject embodiment as the woman operating under the terms of the sexual marketplace. The poem no longer allows room for sexual or voyeuristic desire; through the very vulnerability that attention to Corinna's embodiment makes possible, the same catalogue that seems, in the moment, so undignified, Corinna becomes the vehicle for our own, immediate response to the world that has produced her. Far from casting her into a social out-group, then, Corinna's metamorphosis renders her more human. Objectification names a species of sympathy.

SELECT BIBLIOGRAPHY

Baron-Cohen, Simon, Helen Tager-Flusberg, and Michael V. Lombardo, eds. *Understanding Other Minds: Perspectives from Developmental Social Neuroscience* (Oxford: Oxford University Press, 2013).

Bogel, Frederic V. *The Difference Satire Makes* (Ithaca: Cornell University Press, 2001).

Cacioppo, John T., Penny S. Visser, and Cynthia L. Pickett, eds. *Social Neuroscience: People Thinking about Thinking People* (Boston: MIT Press, 2006).

Douglas, Mary. *Purity and Danger: An Analysis of the Concepts of Pollution and Taboo* (New York: Routledge, 1966).

Elkin, P. K. *The Augustan Defence of Satire* (Oxford: Clarendon Press, 1973).

Gee, Sophie. *Making Waste: Leftovers and the Eighteenth-Century Imagination* (Princeton: Princeton University Press, 2010).

Lamb, Jonathan. *The Things Things Say* (Princeton: Princeton University Press, 2010).

Macpherson, Sandra. *Harm's Way: Tragic Responsibility and the Novel Form* (Baltimore: Johns Hopkins University Press, 2010).

Vermeule, Blakey. *Why Do We Care About Literary Characters?* (Baltimore: Johns Hopkins University Press, 2009).

CHAPTER 23

....

SCIENCE AND SATIRE

....

GREGORY LYNALL

THE agency of satire in necessitating change beyond the realms of print is sometimes claimed, but more often denied. Yet in *The History of the Royal Society* (1667), Thomas Sprat confessed that the 'New Philosophy' should fear 'the humorous, and the merry' most of all: 'by making it ridiculous, becaus it is *new*, and becaus they themselves are unwilling to take pains about it, may do it more injury than all the Arguments of our…dogmatical *Adversaries*'.[1] For Sprat, 'railleurs' might dismiss the new science without giving it due consideration, and their ignorance could breed a potent satiric brutality. To counter this perceived threat, Sprat therefore sought to acquaint satirists with their kinship: 'The Founder of *Philosophy* is confess'd by all to be *Socrates*; and he also was the famous Author of all *Irony*.' The wits should show 'tender[ness]' to their 'Relations', not only out of courtesy but also because it would be creatively advantageous: 'if they shall decry the promoting of *Experiments*, they will deprive themselves of the most fertil Subject of *Fancy*'. These possibilities were particularly acute for writers in the 'English Tongue [which] contains a greater stock of *Natural* and *Mechanical Discoveries*', and so is 'more inrich'd with beautiful *Conceptions*, and inimitable *Similitudes*…than ever any other *Language* could produce'.[2]

Certainly, the discoveries and new ways of knowing associated with the new sciences—particularly after the work of Sir Isaac Newton—inspired and were celebrated in numerous non-satirical poems written by both lay enthusiasts (such as James Thomson) and members of the scientific community (such as John Theophilus Desaguliers).[3] Yet, as this chapter will argue, both of Sprat's calls were also heeded, if unconsciously, in ways he had not envisaged. Many satirists who engaged with

---

[1] Thomas Sprat, *The History of the Royal-Society of London, For the Improving of Natural Knowledge* (1667), 417.

[2] Sprat, *History*, 417–18. Sprat's reputation for eschewing metaphor has been challenged recently: see Claire Preston, *The Poetics of Scientific Investigation in Seventeenth-Century England* (Oxford: Oxford University Press, 2015), 9–10.

[3] See esp. Marjorie Nicolson, *Newton Demands the Muse: Newton's Opticks and the Eighteenth Century Poets* (Princeton: Princeton University Press, 1946).

developments in experimental philosophy and natural history would 'take pains' to understand them, although there is much variation in knowledge, motivation, and satiric intensity. Indeed, some of the most significant satirists on science *circa* 1660–1750 were themselves involved in scientific inquiries. Margaret Cavendish wrote fourteen treatises on natural philosophical topics, although her vitalistic account of nature and methodology of reason (over observation and experiment) set her greatly at odds with the Royal Society; John Arbuthnot was a physician, mathematician, and member of the medico-scientific establishment (Royal Society and Royal College of Physicians). As well as interrogating its truthfulness, utility, and morality, satirists found in natural knowledge 'a vast Treasure of admirable *Imaginations*...wherewith to express and adorn... thoughts about other matters',[4] often adopting ideas from the sciences as clever conceits and insightful vehicles of satiric defamiliarization in their works of learned wit.

This essay does not, however, seek to overthrow absolutely the conventional view of satire being frequently an enemy of science during the late seventeenth and early eighteenth centuries.[5] Instead, the chapter proposes a more nuanced recognition of satire and science as mutually embedded cultural practices, upon which we can ground our understanding of the ways in which satire interrogated the intellectual, social, and political implications of natural knowledge. In particular, I argue that ironic, satiric, and parodic modes were sometimes deployed by the scientists themselves (and by popularizers and appropriators of science) within their works, as major interventions in contests of legitimacy between rival narratives of nature, to air personal grievances, or to enhance the rhetorical power of their more positive claims. This development does not collapse generic boundaries as such: Cavendish, for example, conceived of her work as existing within 'two Worlds' ('Philosophical Observations' and 'Fancy'), with 'Fancy' as a useful tool of imaginative vision in itself.[6] But acknowledging (what we might call) the 'ludic consciousness' of natural philosophy, and observing the potency of the satirical mode within scientific discourse, disrupts any assumption that there is a binary division between the 'scientists' and the 'satirists'.

The Virtuoso as Victim and Vehicle

In the seventeenth century, the word 'science' (*scientia*) generally referred to any knowledge acquired via study and the use of reason, distinct from knowledge based on perception or intuition (*cognito*), or derived from received authority (*eruditio*). During the Restoration and eighteenth century, the word 'science' began to gain the meaning by which we know it today, so that by the nineteenth century it was being used to refer

---

[4] Sprat, *History*, 416.

[5] See, for instance, William Powell Jones, *The Rhetoric of Science: A Study of Scientific Ideas and Imagery in Eighteenth-Century English Poetry* (London: Routledge & Kegan Paul, 1966), 65–78.

[6] Margaret Cavendish, *The Description of A New Blazing World*, appended to *Observations upon Experimental Philosophy* (1666), 'To the Reader'.

to the physical and experimental sciences, and would eventually encompass all disciplines related to the acquisition of knowledge via observation and experiment.[7] For the sake of convenience, this chapter uses the terms 'science' and 'natural knowledge' interchangeably in relation to the diverse practices associated with the new experimental philosophy and natural history which emerged during the early modern period. However, it is more appropriate to talk of the 'sciences' in plural, acknowledging that in this predisciplinary era there were different kinds of scientific pursuit, and that these often reflected different methodologies, motivations, and objects of study, with corresponding variations in cultural significance. As sociologists and historians of science have shown, determining the boundaries between, and provinces of, these sciences, was an intellectual *and* cultural process.[8] Satire, as a cultural mode, can be seen to have played a part in debates about what the sciences are, who performs them, and how their bodies of knowledge are disseminated and employed in society. Certainly, satire had already contributed to the wider discrediting of alchemy which predated, but was accelerated by, the growth of the new science (although alchemy retained potency as a satirical vehicle).[9] But satire would make further interventions in defining the social meaning of scientific inquiry.

The propriety and utility of natural knowledge were contested areas of debate. A natural historian or natural philosopher might claim that their studies involved the physico-theological decoding of God's Book of Nature in all its many facets; that the knowledge they generated could be applied to the advancement of medicine and the improvement of trades; and that this would contribute to the quality of life, national prosperity, and reparation of prelapsarian knowledge.[10] However, as a satirical resource, the unseemly connotations of scientific study prevailed, bound up particularly with the pervasive character type of the 'virtuoso'.[11] A standard repertoire of jokes against the virtuoso developed over the seventeenth century, as indeed did the word's association with natural philosophical and natural historical studies, rather than connoisseurship. The culmination of this satiric type is probably the character of 'Sir Nicholas Gimcrack' in Thomas Shadwell's play, *The Virtuoso* (1676), although its origins can be traced to Aristophanes' *The Clouds* (fifth century BC).[12]

The satiric censure of the amateur scientist was theorized at least as far back as Shaftesbury, who notes that it is when a virtuoso 'has erected *a Cabinet*...and made it

[7] See Karina Williamson, '"Science" and "Knowledge" in Eighteenth-Century Britain', *Studies in Voltaire and the Eighteenth Century* 303 (1992), 455–8.

[8] See esp. Steven Shapin, *A Social History of Truth: Civility and Science in Seventeenth-Century England* (Chicago: University of Chicago Press, 1994).

[9] Gregory Lynall, 'Swift's "Poetical Chymistry": Alchemy and Allusion in the Verse', *RES*, New Series, 63, no. 261 (2012), 588–607, at 589–90.

[10] See, for instance, William Derham, *Physico-Theology*, 2nd edn. (1714), sig. A4r; [John Arbuthnot], *An Essay on the Usefulness of Mathematical Learning* (Oxford, 1701), 3; and Joseph Glanvill, *Scepsis Scientifica* (1665), 182.

[11] See esp. Walter E. Houghton, 'The English Virtuoso in the Seventeenth Century', *Journal of the History of Ideas* 3 (1942), 51–73, and 3, no. 2 (April 1942), 190–219.

[12] See Aristophanes, *The Clouds. A Comedy*, trans. Lewis Theobald (1715), 11–12.

the real Pattern of his Mind, replete with the same Trash and Trumpery of correspondent empty Notions…he then indeed becomes the Subject of sufficient *Raillery*.[13] Typically, the character of the (invariably male) virtuoso is apparently consumed with gathering knowledge and physical specimens of trivial things or ignoble creatures unworthy of polite attention, to the detriment of all other human endeavours, and of no ostensible use to society; and yet he pompously and potentially fraudulently claims his inconsequential pursuits to be of great value. The disparate collections of the virtuosi act as a metonym for their fragmented selves, and their social relationships are threatened as they prioritize the thing over the human. The virtuoso is reduced intellectually, socially, and morally by his search for specimens in environments unbefitting a gentleman, and takes on the physical or behavioural characteristics of the lowly things he fetishizes.[14] Sometimes the virtuoso's pursuits served as versatile proxies used to satirize other impulses. 'Peter', in Swift's *A Tale of a Tub* (1704), for instance, decided to 'turn Projector and Virtuoso' once free from the shackles of his brothers, and his ambitions bring to mind the utilitarian or 'vulgar' Baconianism pursued by Samuel Hartlib and others in the mid-seventeenth century.[15] Yet Peter's artificial and materialistic 'Discoveries, Projects and Machines' (which include the 'Sovereign Remedy for the *Worms*') principally function to caricature Roman Catholic doctrines and practices (including the Sacrament of Penance).[16]

Whilst popular scientific works such as Bernard Le Bovier de Fontenelle's *Entretiens sur la Pluralité des Mondes* (1686) suggested that it was acceptable for women to be an audience of natural philosophy, the female virtuoso was by some considered to be even more curious than her male counterpart because she engaged in activities far removed from those necessary to the domestic sphere.[17] It would not be until later in the eighteenth century that certain fields of inquiry (particularly botany) would garner social approval as female scientific pursuits. In her play, *The Basset-Table* (1705), however, Susannah Centlivre satirized orthodox concepts of female education, and treated 'Valeria', the virtuosa, with some sympathy and even enthusiasm.[18]

Most satirical works, meanwhile, reflected that science was an almost exclusively male activity and, for comic and sometimes satiric purposes, scientific inquiries were often caricatured as a visual lust. For example, from the outset of the Scriblerians' collaborative *Memoirs of Scriblerus*, Martinus's gendered conception of his activities is

[13] Anthony Ashley Cooper, 3rd Earl of Shaftesbury, *Characteristicks, &c.*, 3 vols. (1711), iii. 156.

[14] See Mary Astell, *An Essay in Defence of the Female Sex* (1696), 96–108, and Richard Steele, *The Tatler*, 216, 221, and 236, in *Tatler*, iii. 132–5, 153–7, 217–20.

[15] See Hugh Trevor-Roper, 'Three Foreigners: The Philosophers of the Puritan Revolution', in *The Crisis of the Seventeenth Century: Religion, Reformation and Social Change* (1967; Indianapolis: Liberty Fund, 1999), 219–71, at 239.

[16] Swift, *Works* (Cambridge), iii. 68, 69.

[17] See Joseph Addison, *The Spectator*, 242 (7 December 1711), in *Spectator*, ii. 442–3, and Gregory Lynall, 'John Gay, Magnetism, and the Spectacle of Natural Philosophy: Scriblerian Pins and Needles', *Journal for Eighteenth-Century Studies* 30, no. 3 (Winter 2007), 389–403, at 398–9.

[18] See Judy A. Hayden, 'Centlivre: Joint-worms and Jointures', in *The New Science and Women's Literary Discourse: Prefiguring Frankenstein*, ed. Judy A. Hayden (Basingstoke: Palgrave Macmillan, 2011), 113–31.

made plain: 'I have found in Dame Nature... a very coy Mistress'.[19] In a parody of this Baconian trope, Martinus sees Nature as a seducer tempting the natural philosopher to witness her intimate secrets. The Scriblerians take this motif to its fullest conclusion, in Martinus's compulsive interest in the female body as an object of science:

> [I]n quest of natural knowledge, I was informed of a Lady who was marked with a Pomegranate upon the inside of her right Thigh, which blossom'd, and, as it were, seem'd to ripen in the due season. Forthwith was I possessed with an insatiable curiosity to view this wonderful Phænomenon. I felt the ardour of my passion encrease as the season advanced, till in the month of July I could no longer contain. I bribed her Duenna, was admitted to the Bath, saw her undress'd, and the wonder display'd.[20]

Irony abounds in this example of 'natural' knowledge, as Martinus transgresses the boundaries of decent, polite, and objective curiosity in his passionate, voyeuristic, potentially masturbatory impulse to observe 'this wonderful Phænomenon'. Whilst the homosocial Scriblerians mock Martinus for prying into the private space of the forbidden boudoir, they themselves are (here, and elsewhere) revelling in the comic (but misogynistic) possibilities suggested by the scientific study of the sexual other.[21] Satirists were therefore perhaps just as guilty as the virtuosi they condemned for fetishizing the transgressive. Indeed, Shaftesbury's description of the virtuoso could fit the satirist just as well: 'their whole Delight is found to consist in selecting and contemplating whatever is most *monstrous*, disagreeing, out of the way'.[22]

As Steven Shapin has shown, debates about the boundaries of scientific activity correlated with wider social discussions of what constituted polite culture. The Newtonian philosophy would be celebrated as a marker of social refinement, and thus a route to self-improvement, in publications such as Joseph Addison's *The Spectator*.[23] In some satires (such as Shadwell's play), the virtuosi's unsociability is reflected in their dissociation from (and unacceptability within) the institutions of science, particularly the Royal Society; in other works (including Ned Ward's *London Spy* and Swift's 'Voyage to Laputa'), they are at the centre of the establishment, but paradoxically this position

[19] *The Memoirs of the Extraordinary Life, Works, and Discoveries of Martinus Scriblerus*, ed. Charles Kerby-Miller (New Haven: Yale University Press, 1950), 92.

[20] *Memoirs of Scriblerus*, 93. For a parallel passage from the *Philosophical Transactions*, see 'The Case of Grace Lowdell, Aged about Sixty Years, Who Had an Extraordinary Tumour on Her Thigh', 41.456 (January–June 1740), 365–7 (365).

[21] See also *Annus Mirabilis*, in *Miscellanies in Prose and Verse by Pope, Swift and Gay* (1727–32), ed. Alexander Pettit, 4 vols. (London: Pickering & Chatto, 2002), IV, 85–97; *An Epistle To the most Learned Doctor W—d—d*, in *The Poetical Works of John Gay*, ed. G. C. Faber (London: Oxford University Press, 1926), 639–42; and Judith Hawley, 'Margins and Monstrosity: Martinus Scriblerus his "Double Mistress"', *Eighteenth-Century Life* 22 (1998), 31–49.

[22] Shaftesbury, *Characteristicks*, iii. 157.

[23] Steven Shapin, 'The Image of the Man of Science', in *The Cambridge History of Science*, eds. David C. Lindberg and Ronald L. Numbers, 8 vols. (Cambridge: Cambridge University Press, 2002–), IV, 159–83 (174); Addison, *The Spectator*, 565 (9 July 1714), in *Spectator*, iv. 529–33.

multiplies rather than tempers their zeal and eccentricities.[24] Hovering between the amateur and emerging professional, the collector-antiquarian and natural philosopher, the charlatan and the expert, conceptions of and prejudices against the virtuoso followed emerging disciplinary boundaries, and revealed lines of significant difference within the apparently heterogeneous scientific community.[25] Joseph Spence reports, for instance, that Newton 'could scarce avoid' speaking ill of 'virtuoso collectors' whose 'pursuits are below nature'.[26] This again serves to demonstrate why we must speak of 'sciences' rather than a monolithic single subject of inquiry, and reminds us that, in some cases, scientists and satirists could be found on the same intellectual side. Yet William Wotton lamented that the satires (and/or their audiences) were not discriminating sufficiently between different kinds of scientific practitioner: 'That every Man whom they call a *Virtuoso*, must needs be a *Sir Nicholas Gim-crack*'.[27] And—fulfilling the fears of Sprat—the agency of these satirical works in influencing attitudes towards scientific endeavour was all too evident. John Evelyn, for instance, was disturbed to hear that his *protégée*, Margaret Godolphin, had been 'pleas'd with what the wretches said' when she watched *The Virtuoso*, since he thought he had convinced her 'that God had created nothing so meane and despicable, but what is worthy our highest Admiration and Praise'.[28]

As the period progresses, the figure of the virtuoso tends to lose the tight referentiality evident in Shadwell's play, becoming less associated with specific scientific theories and more a clichéd type of collector. Thus in Mark Akenside's 'The Virtuoso' (1737), the protagonist seems to be a generalized character, with the poem most interested in the 'human' implications of his material pursuits, as 'All things with vitiated sight he spies: / Neglects his family, forgets his friend'.[29] A notable exception is the Scriblerians' *Three Hours After Marriage* (1717), whose protagonist Fossile has long been identified as in some way caricaturing the physician and natural historian John Woodward FRS, whom Arbuthnot had clashed with intellectually over theories of the deluge and whose obstinate demeanour Arbuthnot had witnessed at first hand at Royal Society meetings.[30] Indeed, rather than seeing the play as an assault upon the scientific project, Arbuthnot's colleagues at the Royal Society (particularly its secretary, Sir Hans Sloane) might have relished the jokes at Woodward's expense. Despite the specific allusions to Woodward's scientific opinions, like Akenside's poem, the play should be seen more as exploiting the virtuoso for farcical comedy than as all-out satire, as we watch the ossified Fossile trying

[24] See Thomas Shadwell, *The Virtuoso*, ed. Marjorie Hope Nicolson and David Stuart Rodes (London: Arnold, 1966), 135 (V.vi.17–18); Edward Ward, *The London-Spy Compleat, in Eighteen Parts*, 4th edn. (1709), 61; and Swift, *Works* (Cambridge), xvi. 228–39, 259–74.

[25] See Michael Hunter, *Science and Society in Restoration England* (Cambridge: Cambridge University Press, 1981), 67–8.

[26] Joseph Spence, *Observations, Anecdotes, and Characters of Books and Men*, ed. James M. Osborn, 2 vols. (Oxford: Clarendon Press, 1966), i. 350.

[27] William Wotton, *Reflections upon Ancient and Modern Learning* (1694), 357.

[28] 'Epistle CCCLXXXII: To Electra etc.' (18 July 1676), in *The Letterbooks of John Evelyn*, ed. Douglas D. C. Chambers and David Galbraith, 2 vols. (Toronto: University of Toronto Press, 2014), I, 575.

[29] Mark Akenside, 'The Virtuoso', *The Gentleman's Magazine* 7 (April 1737), 244–5 (ll. 87–8).

[30] Arbuthnot, *An Examination of Dr Woodward's Account of the Deluge* (1697); Royal Society Council Minutes, II (1682–1727), 169–70 (24 May 1710).

to compensate for his many personal failings through the accumulation of objects for his repository, at one point mistaken for a 'Raree-Show'.[31]

Generally missing from discussions of the virtuoso-satires is a recognition of the way in which such works depict virtuosi as *writers*, and especially how the collecting mentality manifests itself textually.[32] William King's first satire on the *Philosophical Transactions*, *The Transactioneer* (1700), is directed particularly at the journal's editor, Hans Sloane. King's Preface implies that Sloane is a 'Master of only Scraps', assembling accounts indiscriminately of such grandiose subjects as 'A Woman that talk'd Obscenely and offer'd her Cow for a Bag-pipe', in the same way that he augments chaotically his cabinets of physical curiosities.[33] Similarly, Swift's *A Tritical Essay upon the Faculties of the Mind* (1707) is a hotchpotch of clichéd aphorisms (many of which reference natural philosophy), which literalizes the fragmentation of modern knowledge in an incoherent, disordered text with no sense of relative importance between its contents.[34]

The nascent form of the scientific essay also became a fruitful facilitator of religious and political satire, combining sparkling topical wit with the intensive species scrutiny practised by the natural historian, in works such as Swift's *Mechanical Operation of the Spirit* (1704) and Henry Fielding's *Some Papers Proper to be Read before the R—l Society, Concerning the Terrestrial Chrysipus, Golden-Foot or Guinea* (1743). In meticulous detail, Fielding's essay brilliantly imitates Abraham Trembley's account of experiments on freshwater polyp (which had been published only a fortnight earlier) to explain the immoral practices of usurer Peter Walter, who could seemingly produce many guineas from a single coin. The repeatability of experiment, so crucial to the validation of new knowledge, is transformed into a statement of Walter's criminal frequency, with the paper insisting on the 'Truth of the Facts . . . as there is not one of them but what I have seen repeated above twenty times'.[35] Whilst Fielding's attitude to science is perhaps more negative elsewhere, here is negligible satire at Trembley's expense.[36] Instead, Fielding embraces the possibilities of the scientific essay as a vehicle of ridicule. Similarly, in *Remarks upon a Book, intitled, The Rights of the Christian Church* (1708), Swift's narrator notes:

> [S]ome Years ago a Virtuoso writ a small Tract about Worms, proved them to be in more Places than was generally observed, and made some Discoveries by Glasses. This having met with some Reception, presently the poor Man's Head was full of

[31] *Three Hours After Marriage*, III.353, in John Gay, *Dramatic Works*, ed. John Fuller, 2 vols. (Oxford: Clarendon Press, 1983), i. 255.

[32] An exception is Brean Hammond's reading of the Scriblerians' *Essay Concerning the Origine of Sciences* (1732): see 'Scriblerian Self-Fashioning', *Yearbook of English Studies* 18 (1988), 108–22, at 114–15.

[33] [William King], *The Transactioneer* (1700), sig. A2v, A4r.

[34] See Gregory Lynall, *Swift and Science: The Satire, Politics, and Theology of Natural Knowledge, 1690–1730* (Basingstoke: Palgrave Macmillan, 2012), 32–5.

[35] *Some Papers Proper to be Read before the R—l Society, Concerning the Terrestrial Chrysipus, Golden-Foot or Guinea*, in *Miscellanies by Henry Fielding Esq*, Vol. 1, ed. Henry Knight Miller (Oxford: Clarendon Press, 1972), 193 and n.

[36] See also Fielding's parody of theories of the deluge in *The Covent-Garden Journal* 70 (11 November 1752), in *The Covent-Garden Journal; and A Plan of the Universal Register-Office*, ed. Bertrand A. Goldgar (Oxford: Clarendon Press, 1988), 370–3.

nothing but Worms; all we eat and drink, all the whole Consistence of human Bodies, and those of every other Animal, the very air we breathe; in short, all Nature throughout was nothing but Worms: And by that System, he solved all Difficulties, and from thence all Cases in Philosophy.

This virtuoso's universalizing impulse is comparable to the deist Matthew Tindal's 'Affectation of forming general Rules upon false and scanty Premisses', in that he blamed the Anglican Church for many of society's supposed ills.[37] As for this 'Tract', Swift's narrator probably has in mind Antoni van Leeuwenhoek's observations on protozoa, published in the *Philosophical Transactions* in 1677.[38] Taking Leeuwenhoek's discovery to its *reductio ad absurdum*, Swift's caricature revels in the monomaniacal potential which the experimental philosophy and microscopical viewing apparently encourages. But, as a satirically-useful similitude within an occasional satire, the target here is primarily Tindal, whose own head is implicitly worm-eaten too.

Traditionally, Swift and the Scriblerians have been viewed as standing at a distance ideologically from the culture of natural knowledge: as 'ancients' who targeted 'modern' learning.[39] This interpretation has only limited validity if we acknowledge that Pope referred to himself as a member of the 'Virtuoso-Class', exchanged geological specimens with Sloane, and celebrated Newton's achievements in numerous ways, not least in the famous 'Epitaph' (1730).[40] Moreover, Arbuthnot was a Royal Society Fellow (and for a number of years, council member), Newtonian, and antiquarian; and there were many personal links between the other Scriblerians and the scientific establishment.[41] As David E. Shuttleton points out, if the Scriblerians were attacking the 'excesses' of learning, it is difficult to determine what 'precise ideological forces were at work' when they differentiated between 'acceptable' and 'abusive' practices.[42] Swift, at least in his earlier works, fits the model of 'ancient' more easily, although his assault on Thomas Burnet's Cartesian *Theory of the Earth* in *The Battel of the Books* (1704) has much in common ideologically with the Newtonian John Keill's *An Examination of Dr Burnet's Theory of the Earth* (1698). Meanwhile, the third part of *Gulliver's Travels*, the 'Voyage to Laputa', is often claimed to express Swift's vehement disapproval of scientifically-led progress, but Newton's involvement, as Master of the Mint, in the imposition of William Wood's coinage on Ireland was clearly a significant motivation for the Dean's venom in that book.[43]

---

[37] *Remarks upon a Book, intitled, The Rights of the Christian Church*, in Swift, PW, ii. 76, 68.

[38] 'Observations, communicated to the Publisher by Mr. Antony van Leewenhoeck, in a Dutch letter of the 9 Octob. 1676. here English'd: Concerning little Animals by him observed in Rain-Well-Sea- and Snow-water; as also in water wherein Pepper had lain infused', *Philosophical Transactions* 12 (1677), 821–31.

[39] *Memoirs of Scriblerus*, 29–36, and Joseph M. Levine, *Dr Woodward's Shield: History, Science, and Satire in Augustan England* (Berkeley: University of California Press, 1977), esp. 240.

[40] Pope, *Corr.* (Sherburn), ii. 264; iv. 397, 391; ii. 458; 'Epitaph. Intended for Sir Isaac Newton, In Westminster Abbey', in Pope, *Poems* (Twickenham), vi. 317.

[41] See Gregory Lynall, 'Scriblerian Projections of Longitude: Arbuthnot, Swift, and the Agency of Satire in a Culture of Invention', *Journal of Literature and Science* 7 (2014), 1–18, at 1.

[42] David E. Shuttleton, '"A Modest Examination": John Arbuthnot and the Scottish Newtonians', *Journal for Eighteenth-Century Studies* 18 (1995), 47–62, at 47.

[43] See Lynall, *Swift and Science*, 57–68, 94–119.

Newton and his theories were not satirized in the collaborative Scriblerian productions, and in the *Memoirs of Scriblerus* he is placed in direct opposition to Martinus, who sought to 'refute Sir Isaac Newton's Theory of *Gravity*' via a madcap scheme to pierce the nucleus of the Earth.[44] However, Newton's notorious followers Samuel Clarke and (particularly) William Whiston came under intense fire from Pope and his friends.[45]

Marjorie Nicolson and George Rousseau's seminal study showed the extent to which Pope was inspired by the sciences, and particularly the Button's coffee-house talks of Whiston, which combined elementary Newtonian physics with the lecturer's own theories of cometary apocalypse.[46] Whiston was, however, a controversial figure in religious matters: his Arianistic 'wicked Works' fuelled suspicions about the atheistical implications of the Newtonian philosophy, and Newton himself prevented Whiston's Royal Society membership.[47] Whiston's economic opportunism in putting forward a method (and an impractical one at that) for determining longitude at sea also caused some, including Arbuthnot, to scoff.[48] Whiston therefore became a prime satiric target of numerous Scriblerian productions, in which he was lampooned or caricatured as an attention- and patronage-seeking, superstitious fool whose Newtonian system-building is tainted by irrational millenarianism, and whose public lectures have contaminated the fragile mentality of the 'mob'.[49] Yet critics have not appreciated enough that Whiston was not just a target, but also a vehicle, of social satire, because he brought into alignment so many different kinds of misguided 'innovation' in thought and activity. 'Whistonian' mock-catastrophe, often caused (or at least, prognosticated) by celestial phenomena (planetary conjunctions, eclipses, or comets), became a potent motif around which the Scriblerians could cluster explorations of social exclusion, public hysteria, faith, and superstition, amongst other matters.

Our new sense of the satires about science during the period, therefore, must appreciate the diversity of responses across all genres. Some works undoubtedly reflected a deep suspicion of the sciences (often for theological or utilitarian reasons), others exploited their comic (and not necessarily satirical) potential, and some adopted science as a versatile satiric vehicle rather (or at least more) than as a target.

---

[44] *Memoirs of Scriblerus*, 168.

[45] On Samuel Clarke and the Scriblerians, see Christopher Fox, *Locke and the Scriblerians: Identity and Consciousness in Early Eighteenth-Century Britain* (Berkeley: University of California Press, 1988), 101, 107–8, and Lynall, *Swift and Science*, 122–42.

[46] Marjorie Hope Nicolson and G. S. Rousseau, *'This Long Disease, My Life': Alexander Pope and the Sciences* (Princeton: Princeton University Press, 1968), 137–49. See also G. S. Rousseau, 'Wicked Whiston and the Wits', in *Enlightenment Borders: Pre- and Post-Modern Discourses: Medical, Scientific* (Manchester: Manchester University Press, 1991), 325–41.

[47] Pope, *Corr.* (Sherburn), i. 26; James E. Force, *William Whiston: Honest Newtonian* (Cambridge: Cambridge University Press, 1985), 194 n. 23.

[48] See Arbuthnot to Swift (17 July 1714), in *The Correspondence of Dr John Arbuthnot*, ed. Angus Ross (München: Fink, 2006), 191–2, and Lynall, 'Scriblerian Projections of Longitude', 3.

[49] See esp. *God's Revenge Against Punning*, in *Miscellanies*, IV, 53–6; *The Humble Petition of the Colliers*, in *Miscellanies*, IV, 72–8; Swift, *Works* (Cambridge), xvi. 236; *A True and Faithful Narrative of What Passed in London*, in *John Gay: Poetry and Prose*, ed. Vinton A. Dearing and Charles E. Beckwith, 2 vols. (Oxford: Clarendon Press, 1974), ii. 464–73.

THE SATIRIC MODE IN
THE WRITING OF SCIENCE

Despite the atmosphere of collaborative activity described by Sprat and others, the period is known as a time of intense rivalry in the scientific arena (between philosophies and institutions, sometimes along national lines), in search of disciplinary and/or public acceptance at the expense of opposing accounts of nature.[50] Notable individual quarrels are those between Robert Boyle and Thomas Hobbes, Newton and Robert Hooke, and Samuel Clarke and Gottfried Wilhelm Leibniz; whilst the Longitude Act (1714) is perhaps the acutest example of a culture of competition surrounding natural philosophy in this period (and one in which satire was clearly operative).[51] It is less recognized, however, that individual proponents of natural knowledge not only probably approved of satirists' attacks upon their rivals, but also joined in occasionally with the raillery themselves. Natural philosophers embraced both facets of the Socratic background Sprat outlined, incorporating ironic moments for satirical or comical effect within their otherwise 'serious' treatises. Recovering these ludic interventions further confirms to us an eighteenth-century culture of science which was not opposed to literary satire as a form of discourse and, when necessary, utilized the distinctive rhetorical power of satiric modes to legitimize truth claims or trash those of others, seemingly unconcerned about the potential for their ironies to be lost on their readers.

Examples can be found throughout the late seventeenth and eighteenth centuries. Henry Stubbe and Robert Crosse were each known for their invectives against the Royal Society, but in Joseph Glanvill they encountered someone who turned on them in similarly ironic fashion.[52] John Wallis, Savilian Chair of Geometry at Oxford, criticized Hooke's hypothesis concerning the movement of the poles in a letter apparently 'made up partly of misrepresentation, partly of designed Satyr'.[53] John Woodward responded with irony to the idea that archaeological remains had been formed in the earth via natural processes, noting the 'great Elegancy' with which these vessels had come to be known as '*Fossil Pots*' in the works of Bohuslav Balbinus and others. Woodward was also known to mock his rivals publicly at Royal Society meetings, telling Sloane to 'Speak Sense or English and we shall understand you'. Leibniz taunted Clarke that Newtonian

---

[50]   See Simon Schaffer, 'Augustan Realities: Nature's Representatives and Their Cultural Resources in the Early Eighteenth Century', in *Realism and Representation: Essays on the Problem of Realism in Relation to Science, Literature and Culture*, ed. George Levine (Madison: University of Wisconsin Press, 1993), 279–318.

[51]   See Lynall, 'Scriblerian Projections of Longitude'.

[52]   See esp. Joseph Glanvill, *Plus Ultra* (1668), 66–7, and Henry Stubbe, *A Specimen of Some Animadversions upon a Book, Entituled, Plus Ultra* (1670), 10.

[53]   Robert Hooke, 'Ansr to Dr Wallis & Way to find yᵉ Meridian. Read to yᵉ RS Apr. 27. 1687', Royal Society Classified Papers 1660–1741, XX, 75, transcribed in David R. Oldroyd, 'Geological Controversy in the Seventeenth Century: "Hooke *vs* Wallis" and its Aftermath', in *Robert Hooke: New Studies*, ed. Michael Hunter and Simon Schaffer (Woodbridge: Boydell, 1989), 207–33, at 213.

accounts of attraction as a non-mechanical power confirmed 'People are...fond again of the tales of fairies'.[54] James Jurin, physician, and one-time secretary to the Royal Society, defended Newton against George Berkeley in two polemical, often satirical, treatises. In a notable section of *The Minute Mathematician* (1735), Jurin imitates *Paradise Lost* in order to cast a soliloquizing Berkeley as Satan, hating the beams of a solar Newton.[55] The disgruntled Dudley Loftus and John Hill, meanwhile, each turned on their scientific institutions (the Dublin Philosophical Society and Royal Society respectively) in satirical parodies in which they aired their grievances.[56]

Even those scientists (and supporters of science) not inclined to write satirically were clearly avid readers of satire and recognized its potential agency within the culture of natural knowledge. The Astronomer Royal, John Flamsteed, in the notorious dispute over the publication of the *Historia Coelestis*, apparently left a couplet from Richard Blackmore's *A Satyr Against Wit* (1700) ('A Bantring Spirit has our Men possest, / And Wisdom is become a standing Jest') on a piece of paper nestled in a bible in Newton's room, to be read as a 'reasonable caution against his credulity'. Mathematician and lecturer John Harris, when accused of authoring King's anonymous *The Transactioneer* (1700), commented that the *Philosophical Transactions* under Sloane's stewardship contained many things which did 'justly deserve Animadversion & Censure'. John Conduitt, in his notes toward a biography of Newton, consciously invoked Swift's *A Tale of a Tub* (1704) when claiming that 'Fancy never got astride Sir I. N's reason' (although we now know of Newton's interest in alchemy).[57] It was recognized on many occasions within scientific culture, therefore, that there were places which other modes of writing could not reach. Satire offered a unique perspective or rhetorical power amidst personal animosities or significant debates about the legitimacy and utility of different forms of science. Perhaps the scientist who embraced this potential most fervently was Robert Hooke, to whom we shall now turn.

In May and June 1676, Shadwell's *The Virtuoso* was the talk of the town. Hooke was told about the play several times by prominent Society members before he plucked up the courage to go himself. Attending on 2 June, Hooke wrote in his diary: 'Damned Doggs. *Vindica me Deus* [God grant me revenge]. People almost pointed'. Shadwell's character of Gimcrack conflated and exaggerated a number of personalities and pursuits

---

[54] John Woodward, *The Natural History of the Earth, Illustrated, and Inlarged*, trans. Benjamin Holloway (1726), 157; Royal Society Council Minutes, II, 156 (29 March 1710); *The Leibniz–Clarke Correspondence*, ed. H. G. Alexander (Manchester: Manchester University Press, 1956), 93.

[55] James Jurin, *The Minute Mathematician* (1735), 60–1. See also James Jurin, *Geometry No Friend to Infidelity* (1734).

[56] Dudley Loftus, 'Satires' (c.1683–4), in *Papers of the Dublin Philosophical Society 1683–1709*, ed. K. Theodore Hoppen, 2 vols. (Dublin: Irish Manuscripts Commission, 2008), ii. 905–19; John Hill, *A Dissertation on Royal Societies* (1750); and John Hill, *Lucina sine Concubitu. A Letter Humbly address'd to the Royal Society* (1750).

[57] John Flamsteed to John Lowthorp (10 May 1700), in Francis Baily, *An Account of the Revd John Flamsteed, the First Astronomer-Royal* (1835), 175; John Harris to Sir John Hoskins (27 February 1699/1700), BL Sloane MS4026, f.253; John Conduitt, 'Notes on Newton's Character', King's College Library, Cambridge, Keynes MS130.7, f.7ʳ, in *The Newton Project*, http://www.newtonproject.sussex.ac.uk.

connected to the Royal Society (and probably most resembled Boyle),[58] yet the association of this 'virtuoso' with the Curator of Experiments seemed to stick, and was used as ammunition by one of Hooke's rivals, the Society Council member Abraham Hill, who 'Floutingly smiled' at Hooke when he returned from a performance.[59]

Although Hooke was a notable victim of ridicule, he was not averse to employing the satiric mode himself. Whilst historians of science have recently sought to assuage our view of Hooke as 'a man of strange unsociable temper', he was undeniably involved in several quarrels during his long scientific career: with Johannes Hevelius, Christiaan Huygens, Adrien Auzout, John Wallis, and, most notably, Newton (who complained of the 'humour' which 'too much' abounded in Hooke's letters).[60] Hooke was well known for his cutting remarks, and this was exploited by those seeking to create mischief within the networks of knowledge: he was sometimes goaded by the Royal Society's secretary, Henry Oldenburg, to supply 'handsom sting[s]' to his critics.[61] Hooke's ability to wound was particularly evident in his dispute with the Polish astronomer Johannes Hevelius. Hevelius, who in his astronomical observations preferred to use his naked eye (guided by a quadrant), was suspicious of the authority of telescopic aids, and attacked Hooke's fervent advocacy of sense-enhancing instruments. Shrewdly, Hooke responded with ironic pity: 'It did much trouble me, I confess, that I could not prevail with him to make use of Telescopical Sights at least, since with less trouble he would have afforded the World Observations, and a Catalogue of the Stars, ten times more exact.'[62] On other occasions, he could be lighter in intent. In his account of the Earth's motion, Hooke joked that the Copernican cosmology was now only denied by 'illiterate persons [who] suppose the Sun as big as a Sieve, and the Moon as a *Chedder* Cheese, and hardly a mile off' and deny 'there may be Antipodes .... For how can they go with their feet towards ours, and their heads downwards, without making their brains addle.'[63]

Hooke not only meted out crushing asides to his intellectual opponents, but also appropriated satiric form for more playful purposes. His *Micrographia* (1665) made an instant impact within Restoration London, disseminating the wondrous discoveries made of a 'new visible World' through detailed textual descriptions and lavish illustrations.[64] Much of *Micrographia* dealt in sober style with the meticulous observations

[58] See Peter Anstey, 'Literary Responses to Robert Boyle's Natural Philosophy', in *Science, Literature and Rhetoric in Early Modern England*, ed. Juliet Cummins and David Burchell (Aldershot: Ashgate, 2007), 145–62.

[59] *The Diary of Robert Hooke 1672–1680*, ed. Henry W. Robinson and Walter Adams (London: Taylor & Francis, 1935), 235–40.

[60] Newton to Edmund Halley (20 June 1686), in *The Correspondence of Isaac Newton*, ed. A. Rupert Hall and Laura Tilling, 7 vols. (Cambridge: Cambridge University Press for the Royal Society, 1959–77), ii. 439.

[61] See Lisa Jardine, *The Curious Life of Robert Hooke: The Man Who Measured London* (London: HarperCollins, 2003), 200.

[62] Robert Hooke, *Lectiones Cutlerianae, or A Collection of Lectures* (1679), 6.

[63] Robert Hooke, *An Attempt to Prove the Motion of the Earth* (1674), 2.

[64] Robert Hooke, *Micrographia* (1665), sig. A4v.

Hooke had made of specimens (particularly insects) under his lens, but he allowed himself to indulge his ludic impulse when describing the behaviour of the louse:

> [A] Creature…so busie, and so impudent, that it will be intruding it self in every ones company, and so proud and aspiring withall, that it fears not to trample on the best, and affects nothing so much as a Crown; feeds and lives very high, and that makes it so saucy, as to pull any one by the ears that comes in its way, and will never be quiet till it has drawn blood.[65]

Hooke's punning 'observations' resemble the kind of riddling description one would find in a Theophrastan character: a mode revived in the sixteenth century and which had increased in popularity, particularly for satiric purposes, during the seventeenth.[66] As a threat to the 'Crown', the louse becomes a caricature of the regicidal Oliver Cromwell, popularly known as not only 'Major-Generall / Of lice and fleas', but also the cruel subjugator of Ireland who advocated a policy to 'kill the Nitts, that they might not growe Lice'.[67] Perhaps Hooke considered this (in some poor taste) to be light relief for Charles II's benefit, to whom *Micrographia* was dedicated. Whatever the intention, like the microscope itself, Hooke's satirical prose gives us an alternative, doubling way of viewing: simultaneously literal and allegorical; truthful in its description (give or take a few anthropomorphisms), yet offering a witty and insightful similitude.

For some, especially Margaret Cavendish, microscopy was an emblem of the perceived narrow vision and uselessness of the experimental philosophy; with more nuance, Pope's *Essay on Man* (1733–4) asks 'what the use, were finer optics giv'n, / T' inspect a mite, not comprehend the heav'n?'[68] Hooke's mock-heroic treatment of the louse shows that, rather than diverting the scientist squarely into the domain of the minute and obscure, microscopy can sharpen one's sense of the wider world. Hooke himself adopted microscopic vision as a brilliant vehicle of social and political satire through which one could look at the world afresh, diminishing targets down to the scale of insect-life, or giving us a magnified view of humanity's physical and moral flaws; a strategy followed in works including Andrew Marvell's *The Last Instructions to a Painter* (1667), Swift's *Gulliver's Travels* (1726) and 'On Poetry: A Rhapsody' (1733), Stephen Duck's 'On Mites: To a Lady' (1736), and Book Four of Pope's *Dunciad* (1743).[69]

---

[65] Hooke, *Micrographia*, 211.

[66] See Benjamin Boyce, *The Theophrastan Character in England to 1642* (Cambridge, MA: Harvard University Press, 1947), 168–77.

[67] [Anon], *A Citie-Dog In A Saints Doublet* (1648), 5; [William Mercer], *The Moderate Cavalier* ([Cork], 1675), 11.

[68] Cavendish, *Blazing World*, 29–33, and *Observations*, 7–13; Pope, *Poems* (Twickenham), iii.i, 39 (*Essay on Man*, I.195–6).

[69] There is, of course, a parallel tradition of satirical telescopy, in which the technology (often aimed at an inhabited moon) is used primarily as a means of political satire, and includes Aphra Behn, *The Emperor of the Moon* (1687), Daniel Defoe, *The Consolidator* (1705), and William Hogarth, *Royalty, Episcopacy and Law* (c.1724).

Hooke's closest contemporary in characterology was Samuel Butler. It is perhaps not surprising, then, that Butler acknowledged Hooke's louse in 'An Occasional Reflection on Dr Charlton's feeling a Dog's Pulse' (a parody which conflated Boyle's meditative style with accounts of vivisection experiments, in order to ridicule the hyperbole of the Royal Society's utilitarian claims). At the end of his 'Reflection', the Boylean narrator remarks that Hooke 'has most ingeniously and wittily made it appear, that there is no differ-ence…between the most ambitious and aspiring Politician of the World, and of our Times especially, and that most importune and vexatious Insect, commonly called a Louse'.[70] Butler perhaps believed Hooke to be unaware of the satirical similitude he had created: nevertheless, here was recognition of rhetorical kinship.

SATIRIZING THE SCIENTIFIC SELF

On many occasions, therefore, the satiric mode made a unique contribution, as a kind of cultural arbiter, within the social circulation and validation of natural knowledge. Yet science was not only a victim, but also a vehicle, of satiric writing, enabling satirists to view their targets in radically new ways. Moreover, it is apparent that irony, comedy, and satire were employed as rhetorical resources by scientists themselves, and recover-ing this history reshapes some of our sense of the relationship between literature and science during the period. To conclude, we will view the writing of Butler through this new prism.

Although Butler composed a number of works which engaged with the experimen-tal philosophy (including *Hudibras*, 1663), his relationship with science has generally been explored through readings of 'The Elephant in the Moon'. This is a hilarious poem of telescopic viewing which its author seemed to enjoy so much he wrote it twice, in two separate forms (tetrameter and heroic couplets). Critical discussions have focused particularly upon the problems of ocular reliability, scientific fervour, and collective confusion the poem raises, and on identifying the Society members caricatured.[71] Extrapolated from 'Elephant', Butler's attitude to science is now generally seen to be one supportive of Baconian principles, including the experimental method, but critical of individual scientists whose work did not meet these standards of inductive knowledge-making.[72]

---

[70] *The Genuine Remains in Verse and Prose of Mr Samuel Butler*, ed. Robert Thyer, 2 vols. (1759), i. 410.

[71] See esp. Marjorie Hope Nicolson, *Pepys' Diary and the New Science* (Charlottesville: University Press of Virginia, 1965), 139–53; Ken Robinson, 'The Skepticism of Butler's Satire on Science: Optimistic or Pessimistic?', *Restoration: Studies in English Literary Culture, 1660–1700* 7 (1983), 1–7; and J. Ereck Jarvis, 'The Royal Society, Collective Vision and Samuel Butler's "The Elephant in the Moon"', in *Literature in the Age of Celestial Discovery: From Copernicus to Flamsteed*, ed. Judy A. Hayden (Basingstoke: Palgrave Macmillan, 2016), 133–47.

[72] See William C. Horne, 'Curiosity and Ridicule in Samuel Butler's Satire on Science', *Restoration* 7 (1983), 8–18.

Meanwhile, the shorter 'Satyr upon the Royal Society' has been neglected critically, yet it perhaps offers us a more vivid sense of Butler's creative doubts in relation to natural knowledge. This undated fragment was published originally by Butler's eighteenth-century editor Robert Thyer as an appendix to 'Elephant', and was given its title in 1928 by René Lamar.[73] The poem stages a weekly meeting between a 'learned Man' and a group of a 'hundred Virtuoso's [sic]'. Seeming to parody Sprat's egalitarian aspirations for the Society, the assembled virtuosi of 'rich and base' backgrounds are 'cast into a Lump', clubbing together to the detriment of their intellectual ambitions.[74] The remainder of the poem follows this chemical analogy as a structural principle, comprising a relentless stream of indiscriminate, miscellaneous questions from these men to their 'Oracle'. Some topics (such as the cause of magnetism and the composition of the Sun) can be traced to areas of investigation described in the *Philosophical Transactions* and Sprat's *History*; others reveal a group open to curious speculation on the 'meaning' of comets and meteors. In outlining the breath-taking sublimity of man's ambitions 'To measure *Wind*, and weigh the *Air*, / And turn a *Circle* to a *Square*', the final stanza anticipates the more graceful critique of philosophical pride in Pope's *Essay on Man*.[75] Yet Butler's tetrameter renders the barrage of speculation even more frenzied, and the poem works up to a kind of bathetic climax, saving the most ridiculous till last, by applying musicology to natural history in asking: 'If *Mares* neigh *alto*, and a *Cow* / A double *Diapason* low'.

What is crucial about the poem, however, is that it catalogues a number of learned speculations in which Butler himself engaged. Butler's manuscript observations concern an eclectic series of questions in natural knowledge, including the moon's orbit, the tides, the nature of light, microscopic vision, and the Sun's composition.[76] It is unclear what the purpose of Butler's scientific notes was, but the sober way in which they are recorded indicates they were not intended to be a stockpile for future satirical deployment, and instead disclose his own interest in such topics. Their frenzied presentation within the 'Satyr' therefore suggests we should see Butler engaging not only in a critique of the Royal Society, as a curious club with too many sophistical questions and not enough answers, but also in a kind of self-provocation or mockery, ridiculing his own pretensions to knowledge or, at least, his passion for speculation.[77] Indeed, this could lead us to question the appropriateness of the poem's title, since it was not assigned by Butler himself: is it really a 'Satyr' and, even if so, is it directed predominantly at the Royal Society, given that the poem soon loses sight of this unnamed assembly, becoming

---

[73] Thyer, ed., *Genuine Remains*, i. 53–7; *Samuel Butler: Satires and Miscellaneous Poetry and Prose*, ed. René Lamar (Cambridge: Cambridge University Press, 1928), 471. All quotations from 'Satyr' use Thyer's edition.

[74] Cf. Sprat, *History*, 63–7.

[75] See Pope, *Poems* (Twickenham), iii.i. 56–9 (*Essay on Man*, II.19–30).

[76] See *Samuel Butler: Prose Observations*, ed. Hugh de Quehen (Oxford: Clarendon Press, 1979), 84, 87, 89, 92, 94–5, and *Hudibras I and II and Selected Other Writings*, ed. John Wilder and Hugh de Quehen (Oxford: Clarendon Press, 1973), 305.

[77] Similar claims could be made regarding the treatment of Arbuthnot's interests in the *Memoirs of Scriblerus* and, as Pat Rogers suggests, of antiquarianism in *The Dunciad*: see 'Pope and the Antiquarians', in *Essays on Pope* (Cambridge: Cambridge University Press, 1993), 240–60.

just a disembodied cacophony of voices? Butler's poem shows us once again that the divide between 'the satirist' and 'the sciences' is not easily defined, that mockery works across a wide tonal spectrum, and that one might be critical of one's own inability to adhere to Baconian principles when possessing a voracious human desire to know which is vastly outweighed by the experimental tools at one's disposal.

SELECT BIBLIOGRAPHY

Benedict, Barbara M. *Curiosity: A Cultural History of Early Modern Inquiry* (Chicago: University of Chicago Press, 2001).

Chico, Tita. 'Gimcrack's Legacy: Sex, Wealth, and the Theater of Experimental Philosophy', *Comparative Drama* 42 (2008), 29–49.

Coppola, Al. *The Theater of Experiment: Staging Natural Philosophy in Eighteenth-Century Britain* (New York: Oxford University Press, 2016).

Hawley, Judith. 'Margins and Monstrosity: Martinus Scriblerus his Double Mistress', *Eighteenth-Century Life* 22 (1998), 31–49.

Hayden, Judy A. 'Centlivre: Joint-worms and Jointures', in *The New Science and Women's Literary Discourse: Prefiguring Frankenstein*, ed. Judy A. Hayden (Basingstoke: Palgrave Macmillan, 2011), 113–31.

Lynall, Gregory. *Swift and Science: The Satire, Politics, and Theology of Natural Knowledge, 1690–1730* (Basingstoke: Palgrave Macmillan, 2012).

Malcolmson, Cristina. *Studies of Skin Color in the Early Royal Society: Boyle, Cavendish, Swift* (Farnham: Ashgate, 2013).

Sarasohn, Lisa T. *The Natural Philosophy of Margaret Cavendish: Reason and Fancy during the Scientific Revolution* (Baltimore: Johns Hopkins University Press, 2010).

Schaffer, Simon. 'Augustan Realities: Nature's Representatives and Their Cultural Resources in the Early Eighteenth Century', in *Realism and Representation: Essays on the Problem of Realism in Relation to Science, Literature and Culture*, ed. George Levine (Madison: University of Wisconsin Press, 1993), 279–318.

Stewart, Larry. *The Rise of Public Science: Rhetoric, Technology, and Natural Philosophy in Newtonian Britain, 1660–1750* (Cambridge: Cambridge University Press, 1992).

CHAPTER 24

....

AGAINST THE EXPERTS

Swift and Political Satire

....

PADDY BULLARD

EVEN when looking at the third and fourth decades of the eighteenth century, when British satire was at the height of its cultural influence, it is rare to find commentators who had faith in its effectiveness as an instrument of political or social change. The ambition of the age was to produce 'general satire', attacking whole descriptions of men and women, if not the entire human species.[1] One of the chief problems with general satire, however, is that the lack of a specific personal target turns the reader's attention uncomfortably towards the satirist's motives and purposes. John, Baron Hervey, writing in 1730 against the tide of satirical polemic that had risen since the Scriblerian *anni mira-biles* of 1726–8, was confident that 'the Honesty of our Minds may recoil against this Propensity to Satyr, and that what is too general, is not universal [...] People may be more shock'd at the Morals of a Satyrist, than pleased with his Wit.'[2] On the opposite side of the debate Paul Whitehead, meditating on the hazards of the satirist's calling in *Manners: A Satire* (1739), voiced a common sense of abuses outstripping admonitory efforts: 'Pointless all Satir in these iron Times, / Too faint are Colours, and too feeble Rhimes.'[3] These attitudes became commonplace in the second half of the century, and the reforming ambitions of satirists were deprecated routinely, even by self-declared satirists like William Cowper:

> What vice has it subdued? Whose heart reclaim'd
> By rigour, or whom laugh'd into reform?[4]

---

[1] For a survey of arguments for and against general satire see P. K. Elkin, *The Augustan Defence of Satire* (Oxford: Clarendon Press, 1973), 118–45; cf. 73–84, though, for expressions of the 'orthodox view' that satire does fulfil warning and monitory functions successfully.

[2] John, Baron Hervey, *Observation on the Writings of the Craftsman* (1730), 6; see also Hervey's *A Series of Wisdom and Policy* (1735), 6–7; reflections on satire that is 'too general' usually allude to *Gulliver's Travels*.

[3] Paul Whitehead, *Manners: A Satire* (1739), 17.

[4] *The Poems of William Cowper*, ed. John D. Baird and Charles Ryskamp, 3 vols. (Oxford: Clarendon Press, 1995), ii. 147.

The most memorable expressions of this theme come from Jonathan Swift, who explored it in the 'Letter from Capt. Gulliver to his Cousin Sympson' added as a preface to *Gulliver's Travels* (1726) in 1735. Half a year after publishing his travels (the Sympson letter is dated 1727) Gulliver 'cannot learn that my Book hath produced one single Effect according to mine intentions'. Seven months should be more than enough time for judges to become 'learned and upright; Pleaders honest and modest, with some Tincture of common Sense...the Physicians banished; the female *Yahoos* abounding in Virtue, Honour, Truth and good Sense'.[5] It is not immediately clear why Gulliver focuses on the learned professions in this roll-call of the unreformed. Perhaps it is the very busy-ness of the doctors, lawyers, and statesmen—their narrow but instrumental ways of working—that aggravates Gulliver's sense of his own admonitions (and, from our perspective, of Swift's general satire) as pointless.

In the realm of the state, questions about the efficacy of satire are similarly vexed. Modern historians of the genre doubt that satire had much impact on eighteenth-century political realities. The ascendancy of Tory satirists at the press did nothing to avert the collapse of Robert Harley's Tory ministry in 1714, or to dislodge Sir Robert Walpole during the 1720s and 1730s, even though (as Swift claimed) 'all the writers [were] on one side' during the period—that is, his side, the broad anti-Whig opposition—'and all the raillers on the other'.[6] In what remains the standard account of relations between satirists and politicians in the early eighteenth century, Bertrand Goldgar finds no evidence of writers urging statesmen to pursue particular measures, or of their campaigns having any discernible political effects: 'the *notion* of all the wit on one side', he concludes, 'had much more political utility that any of the works of wit themselves'.[7] Satirists adopt shifting *personae*, ironic voices, and marginal perspectives, all of which make them ill-suited to the discipline of party organization. 'If satirists for the most part are not committed to a set of political principles', writes Dustin Griffin, 'neither can their work be said to have had much effect on the world of practical politics, either to support tradition or to subvert it'.[8] Once again it was Swift, whose writings, by Samuel Johnson's estimate, gained him 'such power as...scarcely any man has ever enjoyed without great wealth or higher station', who designed his satires most carefully around their practical limitations. In number 35 of *The Examiner* (22 March 1711) he acknowledged that his attacks on the Whig opposition 'may be call'd Satyr by some unthinking People, as long as that Faction is down'.[9] But as soon as they returned to power, Swift predicted, they would have to acknowledge him, their arch enemy, as their advocate, since all he had done in *The Examiner* was to describe their former measures and predict their future policies. This is at once the essence of Swift's raillery, and the most outrageous of his ironic schemes:

---

[5] Swift, *Works* (Cambridge), xvi. 10.   [6] Swift, *PW*, v. 96.

[7] Bertrand A. Goldgar, *Walpole and the Wits: The Relation of Politics to Literature, 1722–1742* (Lincoln: University of Nebraska Press, 1976), 218.

[8] Dustin Griffin, *Satire: A Critical Reintroduction* (Lexington: University Press of Kentucky, 1994), 152.

[9] *Swift vs. Mainwaring: The Examiner and The Medley*, ed. Frank H. Ellis (Oxford: Clarendon Press, 1985), 325.

to present his satire as the only still and stable truth, and to distort the rest of the world around it.

Critical debates about the political dimension of Swift's writing have tended to dwell on party allegiance and ideological alignment. They usually focus on the social-political structures, in other words, through which a satirist might hope to have an influence on public affairs. Some commentators continue to emphasize the neo-Roman themes of thrift, virtue, and liberty that run through Swift's writings, and to stress his basic alignment with Whig principles—Protestant succession to the Crown, frequent parliamentary elections—or even with a Whiggism of the old 'Commonwealthsman' stamp.[10] But the scholarly consensus has moved away from this view. Swift is now seen usually as a Tory by institutional and professional allegiance, and by personal loyalty to fellow veterans of Robert Harley's ministry in the four last years of Queen Anne—albeit a profoundly disaffected Tory by disposition and by experience.[11] Questions about Swift's political character form the background of this chapter, but they are not its real concern. The focus here is on how Swift positioned himself against political professionals and experts. Although Swift's family and profession entitled him only to a middling rank in society, his cultural style was aristocratic. He wrote and behaved like a wit, a cavalier, an *honnête homme*:

> Humour, and Mirth, had Place in all he writ:
> He reconcil'd Divinity and Wit.
> He Mov'd, and Bow'd, and Talk'd with too much Grace;
> Nor shew'd the Parson in his Gait or Face.[12]

This style—glamorous, unfashionable, and rather absurd in a clergyman—led him into opposition against experts and specialists of all kinds, and put him at odds with what he recognized as a new order of professionals, scientists, bureaucrats, and financiers. As a poet and as a man of affairs Swift aspired to the most general accomplishment, pulled off with the greatest negligence and ease. This cultural self-fashioning is important because it feeds back both into the moral positions he adopted as a satirist, and into the political positions he adopted as a polemicist.

This chapter argues that Swift's concern with expertise in politics was also a widespread, even a dominant one among political writers at the start of the eighteenth century. It shows how Swift and his allies understood expertise in terms of its relation to a broader anti-technical programme of statesmanship, one that also advocated 'common

---

[10] For Swift's Whig affiliations see J. A. Downie, *Swift: Political Writer* (London: Routledge, 1984), and David Oakleaf, *A Political Biography of Jonathan Swift* (London: Pickering & Chatto, 2008), 5; for Old Whig themes see Michael Brown, 'Swift, Satire, and the Problem of Whig Regeneration', *Restoration* 39 (2015), 83–77, at 88–9.

[11] F. P. Lock, *Swift's Tory Politics* (London: Duckworth, 1983); Ian Higgins, *Swift's Tory Politics: A Study in Disaffection* (Cambridge: Cambridge University Press, 1994), and Ian Higgins, 'Jonathan Swift's Political Confession', in *Politics and Literature in the Age of Swift: English and Irish Perspectives*, ed. Claude Rawson (Cambridge: Cambridge University Press, 2010), 3–30.

[12] Swift, *Poems* (Williams), i. 194, 'The Author upon Himself', lines 11–14.

sense' as a positive model for political deliberation and 'wit' as a model for discourse.[13] Satire was a common medium for articulating this programme, often in terms that were themselves doubled and ironized. Swift and many of his associates deplored secrecy and innuendo in political life and, at the same time, appropriated them as modes for oppositional satire. They painted modern instrumental thinking and modern technocratic politics as dull and clumsy, while adopting the discourses of those experts parodically as 'mock-arts'.[14] It was the interrelations between this group of satirical themes and political *topoi* that gave them power and significance at the start of the eighteenth century. Those interrelations now require some reconstruction.

EXPERTS IN EARLY MODERN POLITICAL WRITING

The expert's role in government had been an issue for those concerned with political theory long before Swift. A basic problem for anyone trying to trace the history of that concern is that our modern denominative use of the word 'expert' to indicate a specialist person dates only to the nineteenth century. In earlier periods the word was invariably adjectival, and closer in meaning to the etymological roots that it shares with 'experience'.[15] 'Expert' persons were associated with practice and habituation, and not with theoretical science or university training, as they are in common usage today. The word has performed a small summersault in signification since the seventeenth century. In his essay 'Of Studies' Francis Bacon presents the relation of 'Expert Men' to learned persons as one of opposition, not identification, as we might expect:

> For Expert Men can Execute, and perhaps Iudge of particulars, one by one; But the generall Counsels, and the Plots, and Marshalling of Affaires, come best from those that are *Learned*...Crafty Men Contemne *Studies*; Simple Men Admire them; and Wise Men Use them: For they teach not their owne Use; But that is a Wisdome without them, and aboue them, won by Obseruation.[16]

'Expert Men' and crafty men correspond with one another, says Bacon, but it is only expertise modified by observation that has the potential to transform general studies into practical wisdom. The republican James Harrington changed Bacon's emphasis slightly when he quoted these two sentences (reversing their order as he did so, placing more emphasis on the word 'Crafty') in *The Commonwealth of Oceana* (1656).

---

[13] See Sophia Rosenfeld, *Common Sense: A Political History* (Cambridge, MA: Harvard University Press, 2011), 35–54.

[14] See Paddy Bullard, 'Scriblerian Mock-Arts: Pseudo-Technical Satire in Swift and His Contemporaries', *Studies in Philology* 110 (2013), 611–36.

[15] *OED*.   [16] Francis Bacon, *The Essayes or Counsels, Ciuill and Morall* (1625), 292–3.

Trainee statesmen should certainly drink at the fountains of science, Harrington commented, even if they learn nothing of substance at university: 'But what though the water [i.e. academic knowledge] a man drinks be not nourishment? It is the *vehiculum* without which he cannot be nourished.'[17] This is a creative misreading of Bacon's point, which is that learned sciences provide the contents of wisdom, but happen to 'teach not their own use'. The experience that does teach utility is for Bacon a mere vehicle of political science. Harrington, using the same terms, assumes that only practised observation of state councils can provide substantial knowledge for government.

Something that Bacon and Harrington share, however, is a sense that the broad categories of learning and experience, when focused on the question of political expertise, ought really to be triangulated against a third category of political doing, which they call 'craft'. Swift also shared this sense.[18] Learning sits above experience in Bacon's tricolonic rhetoric, and political craft lies somewhere below it, perhaps providing it with practical foundations, or perhaps subverting it. Harrington's figurative language inclines more often to the former possibility. Introducing a legislative 'model' for Oceana's constitution, for example, he describes its authors approvingly as master craftsmen, as 'workmen that squar'd every stone to this structure in the quarrys of antient prudence'.[19] This is a triangle of categories—the scholar, the expert (or person of experience), the craftsman—by which everything that seems solid and foundational in politics and everything that is most provisional and personal can be gathered together.

During the first half of the eighteenth century something surprising happened to this cluster of political keywords. Arguments about statecraft, expertise, and the professionalization of politics—arguments that were useful but not important to earlier writers—became central to the public discussion of politics. The most conspicuous indication of this trend was the title of *The Craftsman*, the political journal founded by Henry St. John, Viscount Bolingbroke, William Pulteney, and the journalist Nicholas Amhurst, in December 1726, at the start of their determined campaign of opposition to the administration of Sir Robert Walpole, and a few months after the publication of *Gulliver's Travels*. Swift never published in *The Craftsman*, but he identified himself with its cause, and his influence on the journal is pervasive. *The Craftsman* became the longest-running and most famous opposition periodical of the period.[20] In the first number 'Caleb D'Anvers' (the journal's fictional editor) tells how *The Craftsman* was chosen as a general title under which to

> lay open the Frauds, Abuses, and secret Iniquities of all Professions, not excepting my own [i.e. the law]; which is at present notoriously adulterated with pernicious mixtures of *Craft*, and several scandalous Prostitutions.[21]

[17] James Harrington, *The Commonwealth of Oceana*, ed. J. G. A. Pocock (Cambridge: Cambridge University Press, 1992), 199.

[18] See Paddy Bullard, 'Gulliver, Medium, Technique', *ELH* 83 (2016), 517–41.

[19] Harrington, *Oceana*, 72.

[20] See Simon Varey, 'The Publication of the Late *Craftsman*', *The Library* 5th ser., 33 (1978), 230–3.

[21] *Craftsman*, i. 6.

Caleb's 'chief business', however, is 'to unravel the dark Secrets of *Political Craft*, and trace it through all its various Windings and intricate Recesses'. To the first readers of *The Craftsman* this sort of concern with political deceit, and with the corruption it was assumed to conceal, would have been familiar. It had been the common coin of partisan polemic since the Restoration. Relatively new, however, was the idea that abuses of government were best explained by analogy with a wider scene of corruption among expert members of the learned professions. It is not immediately clear why *The Craftsman's* founders thought this comparison would be a powerful one. Similarly curious was their decision to describe corrupt professions (and corrupt statesmanship) in terms of their degeneration into 'craft'. Artisans were objects of denigration in classical and humanist culture because their expertise was perceived to be illiberal, their understanding too narrow for the far-reaching affairs of state. It was on this basis, for example, that Swift himself attacked lawyers as the professionals who 'of all others seem least to understand the Nature of Government in general; like under-workmen, who are expert enough at making a single Wheel in a Clock, but are utterly ignorant how to adjust the several Parts, or regulate the Movement'.[22] Craftsmen were also expected to be crafty, that is, distinguished by a shallow cunning or a tendency to deceit. In politics this sort of cunning corresponds with the 'craft' that Thomas Hobbes (borrowing another phrase from Francis Bacon) called 'crooked wisdom', a wisdom that prefers pusillanimous short-term fixes to the long views taken by more magnanimous statesmen.[23] But why did Bolingbroke and Pulteney choose these involved distinctions as the basis for a campaign of popular satire?

WALPOLE AND *THE CRAFTSMAN*

When satirists wrote during the third and fourth decades of the eighteenth century about craft and expertise in politics invariably they had a particular expert in mind: Sir Robert Walpole, the First Lord of the Treasury from 1715 to 1717 and from 1721 to 1742. Walpole enjoyed the reputation of a supreme political technician. Lord Chesterfield, one of his most effective critics after 1737, stated that 'he was both the best parliament-man, and the ablest manager of parliament, that I believe ever lived...So clear in stating the most intricate matters, especially in the finances, that, whilst he was speaking the most ignorant thought that they understood what they really did not'.[24] This corresponds with J. H. Plumb's summary assessment two centuries later, which emphasizes (without direct reference to Chesterfield) 'the same technical competence, the same clarity,

---

[22] *Sentiments of a Church of England Man* (1711), Swift, *PW*, ii. 23; cf. *Gulliver's Travels*, Swift, *Works* (Cambridge), xvi. 371.

[23] Hobbes, *Leviathan*, 54; quoting Bacon, 'Of Cunning', *Essayes*, 127.

[24] Stanhope, Philip Dormer, fourth Earl of Chesterfield, *Characters of Eminent Personages* (1777), 18–19.

the same simplicity...Walpole's abilities were most clearly recognized in his political *expertise*; in the dexterity with which he managed the House of Commons'.[25] 'Dexterity' is a characteristically Swiftian word for describing political ability, and Plumb could almost be channelling Swift's own character of Walpole, sketched in 'An Account of the Court and Empire of Japan' (1728): Walpole 'was perfectly skilled, by long practice,' wrote Swift, 'in the senatorial forms; and dexterous in the purchasing of votes, from those who could find their accounts better in complying with his measures, than they could probably lose by any tax that might be charged on the kingdom'.[26]

Walpole was a difficult target for literary satirists like Swift because he made no pretence of covering up what those satirists took to be his moral failings. One of Swift's maxims was that 'it is as hard to satirize well a Man of distinguished Vices, as to praise well a Man of distinguished Virtues. It is easy to do either to People of moderate Characters.'[27] A reliance on bribery and corruption was the charge repeated most insistently in the pages of *The Craftsman*, charges that Walpole met with bullish effrontery.[28] Indeed, the first minister's bluff dismissal of the humanistic moral codes rehearsed so noisily by the Patriot opposition often gave a powerful negative energy to his politics. The challenge for his adversaries was to find a way of re-describing as shortcomings what were, in the terms of political realists, substantial strengths. Walpole's authority rested on his understanding of the public finances, and on his effectiveness as a public administrator. So *The Craftsman* set out to present Walpole's technical ability as fraudulent, shallow, corrupt—as an unstable and unpredictable form of expertise.

The satirical strategy indicated by *The Craftsman*'s title took on some of this conceptual instability itself. The metaphors and allegories used by the journal's authors tend to blur the boundaries between straightforward artisanal expertise and despicable Daedalian cunning. In the first number 'Caleb D'Anvers' predicts that he will never run out of material because 'the Mystery of *State-Craft* abounds with such innumerable Frauds, Prostitutions, and Enormities in all Shapes, and under all Disguises, that it is an inexhaustible Fund, and eternal resource for Satire'.[29] It was a resource that *The Craftsman*'s authors drew on fairly regularly. The great difference between '*State Craftsmen*' and common artificers, writes 'Jack Hinter' in *Craftsman* no. 8, is that ordinary workmen expect to be rewarded in proportion to their talents, 'and if they do not excel in their Professions, they do not thrive in them. But the Case is very often not the same amongst Those, who govern the great Affairs of the World.'[30] A more positive model of Renaissance statecraft follows in *Craftsman* no. 9, which contains extracts from a letter of Polonius-style advice written by Francis Bacon to the Duke of Buckingham, concerning the promotion of appropriately talented people to offices of

---

[25] J. H. Plumb, *Sir Robert Walpole: The King's Minister*, 2 vols. (London: The Cresset Press, 1960), ii. 234, 2, Plumb's emphasis.

[26] Swift, 'An Account of the Court of the Empire of Japan', *PW*, v. 101.

[27] Swift, 'Thoughts on Various Subjects', *PW*, iv. 243.

[28] Plumb, *Walpole*, ii. 306–7.   [29] *Craftsman*, i. 6.   [30] *Craftsman*, i. 44.

state. 'The Character of a *great Man* was not to be acquired, in those [Elizabethan] times,' comments *The Craftsman*,

> by understanding the paltry Business of a *Money-Scrivener*, or a *Stock-jobber*; by a Skill in Usury, Brokage, and the Tricks of *Exchange-Alley*; or by colloguing with certain *great Bodies* of Men, in order to defraud, bubble, and beggar the rest of the Nation.[31]

Instead of possessing these Walpolean attainments, a statesman need only prove himself to be 'a Man of great Knowledge, Depth, and Penetration in publick Affairs'. These positive qualities at first seem almost meaningless in their generality, but they are oriented significantly towards comprehensiveness of understanding. They are at odds categorically with the facility of the political technician, who prides himself instead on '*ability*'. 'What are commonly called *great Abilities*, in this Age,' according to *Craftsman* no. 99, 'will appear, upon Enquiry, to be nothing but a little, sordid Genius for *Tricks* and *Cunning*, which founds all its Success on *Corruption, Stock-jobbing*, and *other iniquitous Arts*'.[32] Here the positive qualities associated with good statesmanship take a pastoral turn, in line with the anti-metropolitan tendency that often accompanies attacks on experts: 'if you want a Man to employ in any particular *Manufacture* or *mechanic Art*, you will certainly chuse one, who is expert in that Particular; *but in a* Shepherd *or a* Steward, *you desire nothing more than* Frugality, Labour *and* Vigilance'.[33] Such, on the authority of Cicero, were the qualities that Rome expected in her magistrates, and such are the qualities that the British state now requires of its 'stewards'.[34] Once again, the generic attainments that we are told to demand of politicians are defined by contrast with the 'expert' specificity of the craftsman's mechanic art.

What are the sources of this awkward, persistent analogy between politicians and artisans? Its origins certainly predate the rise of Walpole. The most prominent seventeenth-century elaboration of the '*State Craftsman*' metaphor appears in the very first paragraph of Thomas Hobbes's *Leviathan*, in a rather different form to the one found in *The Craftsman*. Hobbes sets up an elaborate comparison between the artificial life of '*Automata* (Engines that move themselves by springs and wheeles as doth a watch)', and the artificial constitution of 'that great Leviathan called a Commonwealth, or State (in latine Civitas) which is but an Artificiall Man'.[35] Hobbes sets up his metaphor to illustrate a materialistic theory of government, so the work of his state artificers is upon the very fabric (that is, the fundamental human materials) of the republic. When Hobbes's contemporaries took up the figure of the craftsman they tended to shift its focus from political making to political doing. In *The Commonwealth of Oceana* James Harrington transformed the idea of the statesman-as-artisan into a complex image of state machinery

---

[31] *Craftsman*, i. 50.
[32] *Craftsman*, iii. 92.   [33] *Craftsman*, iii. 93.
[34] See Cicero, *Pro Cnaeo Plancio*, 62, used as the epigram for *Craftsman*, no. 99.
[35] Thomas Hobbes, *Leviathan*, ed. Richard Tuck (Cambridge: Cambridge University Press, 1991), 9.

gripping and turning its various parts against one another, always maintaining the 'rotation' that was essential to his vision of the commonwealth:

> The councils of this commonwealth, both in regard of their elections, and, as will be shewn, of their affairs, are uniform with the senat in their revolutions; not as whirl-pits to swallow, but to bite, and with the scrues of their rotation to hold and turn a business (like the vice of a smith) to the hand of the workman. Without engins of which nature it is not possible for the senat, much less for the people, to be perfect artificers in a political capacity.[36]

Harrington's use of the craft metaphor for political expertise shows a common-wealthsman's optimism about the operability of what are to Hobbes always recalcitrant human materials. Different again is Samuel Butler's portrait of the Presbyterian politician Anthony Ashley Cooper (later first Earl of Shaftesbury, and Dryden's Achitophel) in part three (1678) of *Hudibras*. This is a breathless tale of low cunning, side-switching, and luck dressed up as expertise:

> By all these Arts, and many more
> H' had practic'd long and much before,
> Our *State-Artificer* foresaw,
> Which way the World began to draw...
> He therefore wisely cast about,
> All ways he could, t'*insure his Throat*.[37]

The difference here is that Butler's Ashley Cooper is someone who operates from the outside on political institutions built up by other hands, almost at arm's length. This is distinct from the Hobbesian artificer, whose actions seem positively to constitute the commonwealth, and from the Harringtonian workman, who holds his materials with an anxious grip. The craft of Butler's '*State-Artificer*' is an ephemeral cunning, narrowly political and operative mainly on the material of his own career. It is a diversion from the serious business of state, but it has the potential to cause considerable political damage.

SWIFT AND THE MYSTERIES OF LILLIPUT

Swift was the writer who transformed this statesman-as-artisan figure into a grand satirical theme. Hobbesian and Harringtonian metaphors of political workmanship are mixed together at the very start of the 'Preface' to *A Tale of a Tub* (1704), Swift's first

---

[36] Harrington, *Oceana*, 123; for prominent use of the same artisanal figure by a royalist, see Robert Filmer, *Patriarcha and other Writings*, ed. Johann P. Sommerville (Cambridge: Cambridge University Press, 1991), 3–4.

[37] Samuel Butler, *Hudibras*, ed. John Wilders (Oxford: Clarendon Press, 1967), 245.

major satire, and one for which politics are a marginal but significant concern. The empty tub of the title is a decoy thrown out by sailors on the ship of state to divert a restive popular whale:

> The *Whale* was interpreted to be *Hobs's Leviathan*, which tosses and plays with all other Schemes of Religion and Government, whereof a great many are hollow, and dry, and empty, and noisy, and wooden, and given to Rotation. This is the *Leviathan* from whence the terrible Wits of our Age are said to borrow their Weapons [...] And it was decreed, that in order to prevent these *Leviathans* [i.e. the wits] from tossing and sporting with the *Commonwealth*, (which of itself is too apt to *fluctuate*) they should be diverted from that Game by a *Tale of a Tub*.[38]

What Swift finds irresistible is the blend of ordinariness and extravagance in the language that Hobbes and Harrington use to describe political processes. The tenor of that language is witty and rather eccentric, he notices, and yet its vehicle moves irresistibly downwards into a world of artificers and workmen, of mariners and coopers. Of course Swift exaggerates both of these tendencies. He seizes on 'mechanic' images of empty barrels, rotating lathes, and foundering ships, and turns them into a series of divagating rhetorical automata each with their own artificial life. They generate in turn streams of images and interpretations, possessed of an unpredictable logic, which is harnessed self-reflexively by Swift in his own satire. In 'The Introduction' to the *Tale* we are shown three 'Oratorical Machines' for the use of 'Orators who desire to talk much without Interruption', namely the pulpit (or 'tub'), the scaffold ladder, and the fairground stage. It seems the most reliable 'machines' for distracting modern wits away from politics, as the *Tale of a Tub* itself proposes to do, are books, some of which have an animal life of their own in the passage above (as have others in the *Tub*'s first appendix, 'The Battel of the Books').

There is an assumption lying behind Swift's satire here, one that he wants to normalize, and does not think to make explicit: that politics is a vocation for which no expert knowledge (as opposed to general learning) is required, and with which narrow technical training is categorically incompatible. The authors of the Old Whig journal *Cato's Letters* stated the case straightforwardly in 1721: 'Of all the sciences that I know in the world', wrote Thomas Gordon,

> [...]that of government concerns us most, and is the easiest to be known, and yet is the least understood. Most of those who manage it would make the lower world believe that there is I know not what difficulty and mystery in it, far above vulgar understandings; which proceeding of theirs is direct craft and imposture: Every ploughman knows a good government from a bad one, from the effects of it.[39]

---

[38] Swift, *Works* (Cambridge), i. 25.
[39] John Trenchard and Thomas Gordon, *Cato's Letters*, ed. Ronald Hamowy, 2 vols. (Indianapolis: Liberty Fund, 1995), vol. 1, 267 (no. 38, 22 July 1721).

The three components of Gordon's argument—the idea that the knowledge of politics is easy and open, that it contrasts with closed mysteries of the craftsman, and, implicitly, that it corresponds with the georgic knowledge of the farmer—sit together in a way that is familiar from classical and humanist tradition. They are configured similarly, for example, by Xenophon in the *Oeconomicus*: farming prepares men for military and political leadership by making them hardy and generous of spirit, according to Xenophon, where handicrafts make them soft and selfish; husbandry, moreover, is 'easily learn'd, by observing the Workmen now and then, and by consulting those who understand it [...] Artificers, will always keep some Secret of their Business to themselves, but the Husbandmen are open and free in their Discoveries.'[40] The figure of the virtuous farmer-patriot had less impact on the English political imagination than it did on the commonwealthsmen of the American colonies.[41] The negative side of Xenophon's configuration, however—the denigration of closed craft knowledge, the analogy with civic life—resonated widely, and gives a context for Swift's satire on mechanics in the *Tale*.

Where the network of values that constructs statesmanship as easy and open (with husbandry as its analogue, and craftsmanship as its opposite) remains largely implicit in the *Tale*, it is fully articulated in *Gulliver's Travels*. Swift returns to it at several points across Gulliver's four journeys, and we see it elaborated differently in various moral contexts. In each of the journeys there is technical excellence to be wondered at, since he has the utopianist's good fortune to be shipwrecked only in advanced civilizations. Lilliput is remarkable for its (relatively) enormous 'machines fixed on wheels' and its sophisticated systems of civil bureaucracy; Brobdingnag has its (relatively) fine-fingered carpenters, seamstresses, and locksmiths; Laputa, of course, is itself an artificial flying island, although its pilots do not seem to know quite how it works; and the land of the Houyhnhnms has a domestic architecture remarkable in its way for convenience and Stoic simplicity. Moreover, in each of the four journeys the connection between technological regime and political system is made explicit. In Brobdingnag, the wise king is astonished to hear that Europe has produced thousands of technical books 'written upon the *Art of Government*': foolish Gulliver is surprised in turn when the king confines 'Knowledge of governing within very *Narrow Bounds*; to common Sense and Reason, to Justice and Lenity', and when he argues that the farmer who 'could make two ears of corn... grow upon a Spot of Ground where only one grew before; would deserve better of Mankind, and do more essential Service to his Country, than the whole Race of Politicians put together'.[42] In Balnibarbi, the retired statesman Lord Munodi tells Gulliver how expert 'Professors' have imposed 'new Rules and Methods of Agriculture and Building, and new Instruments and Tools for all Trades and Manufactures' on the populace, with famine and impoverishment the consequence of their untried

---

[40] *The Science of Good Husbandry: or, the Oeconomics of Xenophon*, trans. Richard Bradley (1727), 38, 95, translating Xenophon, *Oeconomicus*, 15.10–11, 18.9–10.

[41] See Maurie D. McInnes, 'George Washington: Cincinnatus or Marcus Aurelius?', in *Thomas Jefferson, the Classical World, and Early America*, ed. Peter S. Onuf and Nicholas P. Cole (Charlottesville: University of Virginia Press, 2011), 128–68, at 151–3.

[42] Swift, *Works* (Cambridge), xvi. 194.

technology.[43] The consequences of this specialist meddling are social, but Gulliver also explores their governmental analogue in his account of a similarly disastrous 'School for political Projectors'.[44] In the land of the Houyhnhnms, the central criticism levelled by Gulliver's master at European society—that we have been 'very successful in multiplying our original Wants, and seemed to spend out whole Lives in vain Endeavours to supply them by our own Inventions'—is expressed both in disdain for the material overproduction by modern manufacturers, and contempt for the overproduction of civil discourse that Swift identifies particularly with lawyers.[45] Gulliver's wisest interlocutors each identify social degeneration and political corruption with the need of learned experts to impose themselves on others.

The clearest statement of this idea, delivered in terms similar to those used a few years before by Gordon in *Cato's Letters*, is made when Gulliver describes the foundations of the Lilliputian constitution in Part I of the *Travels*. There is a surprising shift of tone here, from the earlier satirical depiction of the Lilliputians as treacherous petty-Machiavellians, to a utopian discourse on their political ideas. As Gulliver reports:

> In chusing Persons for all Employments, [the Lilliputians] have more Regard to good Morals than to great Abilities; For, since Government is necessary to Mankind, they believe, that the common Size of human Understandings, is fitted to some Station or other; and that Providence never intended to make the Management of publick Affairs a Mystery, to be comprehended only by a few Persons of sublime Genius, of which there seldom are three born in an Age: But, they suppose Truth, Justice, Temperance, and the like, to be in every Man's Power; the Practice of which Virtues, assisted by Experience and a good Intention, would qualify any Man for the Service of his Country.[46]

Indeed, it is positively dangerous to entrust public affairs to people distinguished by 'superior endowments of the Mind', because their abilities are likely to be employed in managing and defending their corruptions. Although Gulliver states the idea clearly—that there is no necessary correlation between sound statesmanship and cognitive capacity—there is still considerable circumstantial ambiguity to the passage. Claude Rawson has argued that its altered tone is part of a typically Swiftian literary strategy to unnerve the reader.[47] Swift is seeking to disconcert political interpretation here as well. It is generally understood that the well-known trials of agility undergone earlier in Part I of *Gulliver* by Flimnap, the Treasurer, and his fellow 'candidates for great Employments', are part of Swift's anti-Walpolean satire against servile, technocratic state-craftsmen. Their dexterity at 'leaping and creeping' is exactly proportioned to their lack of virtue and magnanimity.[48] However, it is significant that Swift had begun voicing his opinion of those who 'make the Management of publick Affairs a Mystery' as early as 1714, at

---

[43] Swift, *Works* (Cambridge), xvi. 256.   [44] Swift, *Works* (Cambridge), xvi. 275–84.
[45] Swift, *Works* (Cambridge), xvi. 371, 376, 389.   [46] Swift, *Works* (Cambridge), xvi. 86.
[47] Claude Rawson, *Swift's Angers* (Cambridge: Cambridge University Press, 2014), 118.
[48] Swift, *Works* (Cambridge), xvi. 57.

the end of his brief period of influence as a special adviser to Robert Harley's Tory administration. Indeed, during the decade before Walpole emerged as first minister Swift had despaired of the secretive statecraft of his own political leaders, Harley and Bolingbroke. 'Mystery' is a word Swift used to describe Harley's notoriously secretiveness, his 'Mysterious and procrastinating Manner'.[49] One explanation for the elusiveness of Swift's satire on statecraft in *Gulliver* is that he may have intended it as much for his erstwhile masters—and for Bolingbroke in particular—as he did for his enemy Walpole.

There is evidence to support this hypothesis in several of the pieces that Swift drafted after the fall of Harley's ministry in 1714. Swift always wrote of Bolingbroke as a person of 'an extraordinary' or 'great Genius', and claimed to have warned him pointedly that 'men of great Parts are often unfortunate in the Management of publick Business; because they are apt to go out of the common Road, by the Quickness of their Imagination'.[50] The possibility that Bolingbroke's extraordinary mental capacity might be a disadvantage to his politics is explored in *Some Free Thoughts Upon the Present State of Affairs*, a pamphlet that Swift tried and failed to publish in June 1714. It opens with a meditation on the ideas that 'Politicks were nothing but common sense', and that statesmen cannot 'have many Opportunities of shewing their Skill in Mystery and Refinement, besides what themselves think fit to create'.[51] This anticipates a passage in Part III when Gulliver, lapsing into the language of mechanical craft, observes that state intrigues and plots 'are usually the Workmanship of those Persons who desire to raise their own Characters of profound Politicians'.[52] Both here and in *Gulliver* Swift adds a providential dimension to the sort of secular maxims found in *Cato's Letters*: 'God has given the Bulk of Mankind a Capacity to understand Reason when it is fairly offered; and by Reason they would easily be governed, if it were left to their Choice'. It is only when severed by statesmen who pretend to great political ingenuity that the thread of natural reason, which should connect citizen with state, is broken. Indeed, their craft lies in the engineering of circumstances in which this rupture can happen. And the great genius whose 'Skill in Mystery and Refinement' Swift means here is Bolingbroke himself, whose political manoeuvres tore apart the Tory ministry in 1714. In July 1714 Swift employed his friend Charles Ford to get *Some Free Thoughts* published anonymously by his own printer, Samuel Barber. When Barber, who did not know Swift was the author, unluckily sought approval for the pamphlet from Bolingbroke, Swift could only laugh: 'how comicall a Thing', he wrote to Ford on 18 July, 'Just as if *the Public Spirit* had been sent to Argyle for his Approbation'.[53] Bolingbroke effectively delayed its publication. Within a fortnight Harley had been dismissed from his posts, the queen was dead, and the political landscape changed utterly.

---

[49] 'An Enquiry into the Behaviour of the Queen's Last Ministry', Swift, *PW*, viii. 152; cf. *PW*, vii. 74, 178–80; 'Some Advice to the October Club', Swift, *Works* (Cambridge), viii. 113; Swift to Charles Mordaunt, Earl of Peterborough, 29 May 1714, *Corr.* (Woolley), i. 601.

[50] Swift, *PW*, vii. 98; viii. 152; iv. 251; cf. viii. 134 on the prodigious 'accomplishments of his Mind'.

[51] Swift, *PW*, v. 291–2.   [52] Swift, *Works* (Cambridge), xvi. 282.

[53] Swift, *Works* (Cambridge), viii. 481.

SWIFT AND POLITICAL SATIRE AFTER 1726

The first edition of *Gulliver's Travels* appeared on 28 October 1726, followed shortly by the launch of *The Craftsman* in the first week of December. There are no direct allusions to Swift's writings in the earliest numbers of the *Craftsman* to support any conjecture we might make about his influence on the title and framing narrative of the periodical, or on its campaign to expose the 'secret Iniquities of all Professions'. But references to *Gulliver* become increasingly common as the journal goes on, and Bolingbroke was certainly talking to Swift by the summer of 1727 about helping the opposition's efforts to 'revive & animate the paper wars' of 1711–14.[54] During Swift's last trip to England in April–August 1727 he gave Bolingbroke drafts that included 'A Letter to the Writer of the Occasional Paper', intended as a contribution to the run of 'occasional' and 'extra-ordinary' pamphlets that appeared in support of *The Craftsman*. He was not encouraged to publish, perhaps because the pamphlet attributes to Bolingbroke's writings a set of equivocal characteristics usually associated with Swift's own satire:

> On the other side, a turbulent writer of Occasional Letters, and other vexatious papers, in conjunction perhaps with one or two friends as bad as himself, is able to disconcert, teaze, and sour us whenever he thinks fit, merely by the strength of genius and truth; and after so dextrous a manner, than, when we are vexed to the soul, and well know the reasons why we are so, we are ashamed to own the first, and cannot tell how to express the other.[55]

Turbulence and dexterity are the sort of qualities that Dryden once associated with Achitophel's 'crooked councils', and it is not surprising that Bolingbroke found their application unhelpful to his cause, however flatteringly they set off the compliment about his 'strength of genius'. The idea that *The Craftsman* was set up for 'vexation', more-over, is self-projection of Swift's part: Bolingbroke knew that Swift laid particular claim to that purpose for his own satire. It seems likely that those in charge of *The Craftsman* wanted to keep Swift and the other old Scriblerians at arm's length from the journal.

We can best see the absorption of Swift's satire into the fabric of *The Craftsman* in the mock-advertisements that appeared frequently in the journal from its early issues. These contribute to the journal's anti-Walpolean polemic against expert politicians by deepening a sense of absurdity around the idea that instrumental imperatives could direct civil society, rather than moral ones. The advertisements typically propose fantastic new technologies or projects, creating a strong satirical connection with *Gulliver*, and especially with the academy of projectors at Lagado. So *Craftsman* no. 10 advertises a 'true *political Perspective*, which increases or diminishes any Object at pleasure', alternately magnifying insignificant dangers and shrinking public debts—a concentrated blend of

---

[54] Swift, *Corr.* (Woolley), iii. 92.   [55] Swift, *PW*, v. 95–6.

the crooked technologies of Lagado and Laputan-Brobdingnagian comedies of scale.[56] Joseph Addison's *Spectator* essay on Cardinal Richelieu's academy of politics—itself based on the opening pages of *A Tale of a Tub*, although Swift borrows it back again in Gulliver's account of Blefuscu's 'School of political Projectors'—is discussed in *Craftsman* no. 170. The author of the number (probably Nicholas Amherst) paints over Addison's ironic proposals with a further layer of irony:

> But I must beg Leave to dissent from that excellent Writer, and cannot help thinking that the Business of *Government* may be much more easily learn'd by Rules and Rudiments, than any other Art, or Science whatsoever [...T]he *political Art*, which consists chiefly in *Forms, Precedents*, and *Knowledge of the World*, is subject to every Man's Understanding, and requires nothing more than Assiduity and Information.[57]

Amherst's wit here is particularly fine: it takes the humanistic *topos* of good government being simple, as rehearsed in *Cato's Letters* and *Gulliver*, and misapplies it strategically to a political system that is being narrowed and mechanized by technocrats. There is nothing to Walpolean statesmanship that cannot be learned out of a manual or ledger. Correspondingly, many of the advertisements are for mock-manuals and pseudo-technical treatises: *Craftsman* no. 18 features '*A New* Method *of* Controversy; *Or, An easy Way of shortning Debates, by allowing only one Side to publish their Thoughts*'; no. 56 advertises 'MATCHIAVEL REDIVIVUS; *Or,* The MODERN POLITICIAN. *In Six Parts. Shewing*,[...] *the Art of managing* a chief Favourite *and of* tripping up his Heels...'; no. 202, to take a slightly later example, offers the abstract for 'the Art of Patching up Broken Administrations'; while no. 211 gives 'some Rules for writing in defence of *bad Measures*'.[58] The influence of John Arbuthnot's fragmentary mock-brochure, *Proposals for printing a very curious discourse, in two volumes in quarto, intitled, Pseudologia Politikē; or, a treatise of the art of political lying* (1712), which was itself an elaboration of the essays Swift wrote on political lying in *The Examiner*, is felt strongly here. Indeed, *Craftsman* no. 39 advertises a new Whig periodical called *The Lye of the Day*, while no. 47 is a 'Persian Letter' about the art and profession of stockjobbers, whose 'commerce is *Lying, political Lying*... They call the chief nominal Commodity in which they deal, SOUTH-SEA-STOCK. This is worth more or less in *Idea only*, and the *Lye of the Day* takes or does not take.'[59] In each of these cases the properly moral business of politics has been technologized, a process through which efficiencies and corruptions become indistinguishable.

On the other hand, Swift's influence on *The Craftsman* was limited by the difficulties that Amherst faced when converting *Gulliver's* redoubling ironies into a dynamic polemical strategy. As we have seen already in the case of 'A Letter to the Writer of the Occasional Paper', the ambiguous terms of Swift's satire seem to have raised doubts

---

[56] *Craftsman*, i. 61 (italics reversed).
[57] *Craftsman*, v. 140–5, at 140; cf. *Spectator*, iii. 96 (no. 305, 19 February 1712).
[58] *Craftsman*, i. 107; ii. 78; vi. 169; vi. 235.   [59] *Craftsman*, i. 182; ii. 12–15.

about their usefulness in Bolingbroke, however much he relished them in private correspondence. Bolingbroke's own polemic practice, if we take the influential 'First Vision of Camilick' (*Craftsman* no.16) as an example, dealt in fairly blunt allegory. Swift's own effort at adopting a similarly straightforward oriental frame in the unpublished 'An Account of the Court and Empire of Japan' (1728), another piece intended for *The Craftsman*, lacks the focus and economy of Bolingbroke's original. Why did Swift fail to engage with the challenge of adapting his own satirical schemes into polemic for the changing political scene? Part of the problem may have been that the conventional commonwealthsman attack on technocratic politics had deep associations with hostility to the Church of England, the clergyman being an especially well-established class of crafty 'expert'. Swift took his duties as defender of the Church and its servants very seriously, and was particularly scathing when deist writers like Matthew Tindal used the 'paltry, traditional cant' of connecting statecraft and 'priestcraft'.[60] In other words, Swift's satire on expert statecraft was subtilized, but also weakened, by his sympathy with the expert classes. As Gulliver admits when professing his curiosity about the mechanical academy at Lagado, 'I had my self been a Sort of Projector in my younger Days'.[61]

Swift is fascinated by solid artisanal workmanship, both in the built world and the political state, even though his own 'trade as a Scholar' is categorically different from that of the maker.[62] *Gulliver* shows how sympathetic Swift is with the work of artisans. But an inherited aristocratic-humanist contempt for the banausic arts is still his primary influence when he writes about them. So when Swift imagines in *A Libel on D– D–* (1730), long after his own retirement from politics, what it would be like for his friend Dr Delany to enter that world, the gulf between scholarship and expert state-craftsmanship becomes a source both of deprecation and of compliment:

> True *Politicians* only Pay
> For solid Work, but not for Play;
> Nor ever choose to Work with Tools
> Forg'd up in *Colleges* and *Schools*,
> Consider how much more is due
> To all their *Journey-Men* than you[...]
> You, as a *Critick*, are so curious
> To find a verse in *Virgil* spurious;
> But they can *smoak* the deep Designs,
> When *Bolingbroke* with *Pult'ney* dines.[63]

The ironic shifts between approval and satire are neatly poised in this poem: as so often with Swift, they seem at once straightforwardly serious and circumstantially ironic. The master artisan here, for one last time, is Walpole, who is so far gone in opprobrium that Swift can even give him some *bürgerlich* solidity, diverting the satire towards his

---

[60] Swift, *PW*, ii. 95.   [61] Swift, *Works* (Cambridge), xvi. 258.
[62] Swift to Pope, 10 January 1721, in Swift, *Corr.* (Woolley), ii. 360.
[63] Swift, *Poems* (Williams), ii. 483.

punctilious 'tools' and their vile work. Walpole's promptness as a paymaster somehow makes their servility more humiliating, as it does again in *On Poetry: A Rapsody* (1733): 'A Pamphlet in Sir *Rob*'s Defence / Will never fail to bring in Pence; / Nor be concern'd about the Sale, / He pays his Workmen on the Nail'.[64] But it also inverts the polite humanist's value system: the scholar's learning becomes ornamental, merely 'curious', while political jobbers are allowed to negotiate the deeps of political intrigue. For the opposition polemicist, this still concedes too much to Walpole, to the experts, and to the slickly pragmatic political order that they have created. It confers on them the virtues of directness, and the benefits of honest pay. Swift, however, is grappling with a different set of problems to those of the polemicist. In *Gulliver* he seeks to restrain satire's tendency towards the grotesque and fantastic, towards allegories that are too exuberant, and towards ironies that cannot be resolved. Gulliver's habit of thinking like an artisan, of looking at the world (and the state) as things that are manipulable and solid to the touch, is crucial to this realist impulse.

SELECT BIBLIOGRAPHY

Bullard, Paddy. 'Scriblerian Mock-Arts: Pseudo-Technical Satire in Swift and His Contemporaries', *Studies in Philology* 110 (2013), 611–36.

Goldgar, Bertand A. *Walpole and the Wits: The Relation of Politics to Literature, 1722–1742* (Lincoln: University of Nebraska Press, 1976).

Higgins, Ian. 'Jonathan Swift's Political Confession', in *Politics and Literature in the Age of Swift: English and Irish Perspectives*, ed. Claude Rawson (Cambridge: Cambridge University Press, 2010), 3–30.

Higgins, Ian. *Swift's Tory Politics: A Study in Disaffection* (Cambridge: Cambridge University Press, 1994).

Lock, F. P. *Swift's Tory Politics* (London: Duckworth, 1983).

Marshall, Ashley, ' "Fuimus Torys": Swift and Regime Change, 1714–18', *Studies in Philology* 112 (2015), 537–74.

Oakleaf, David. *A Political Biography of Jonathan Swift* (London: Pickering & Chatto, 2008).

Richardson, John. 'Still to Seek: Politics, Irony, Swift', *Essays in Criticism* 49 (1999), 300–18.

Rosenfeld, Sophia. *Common Sense: A Political History* (Cambridge, MA: Harvard University Press, 2011).

---

[64] Swift, *Poems* (Williams), ii. 646.

CHAPTER 25

....

THE BODY OF THERSITES

Misanthropy and Violence

....

HELEN DEUTSCH

THIS essay takes as its emblem Western literature's original satirist, the monstrous and mean-spirited Thersites, whose singular embodiment and ungovernable speech render him both abuser and abused at the genre's very inception. But before the insolent anger of Thersites, enabling his diatribe and undermining the epic tradition at its very outset, is the heroic wrath of Achilles. As befits a period whose dominant poetic form was the couplet, eighteenth-century satire puts Achilles and Thersites into the balance as inexorably linked mirror images.[1] Both the monstrous Thersites and the semi-divine Achilles are marked out from the society they defy: neither the abject nor the ideal is quite human.

Here, in Alexander Pope's translation, is Achilles' oath of defiance of Agamemnon's authority, sworn on the royal sceptre:

> Now by this sacred sceptre, hear me swear,
> Which never more shall Leaves or Blossoms bear,
> Which severed from the Trunk (as I from thee)
> On the bare Mountains left its Parent Tree;
> This Sceptre, form'd by temper'd Steel to prove
> An Ensign of the Delegates of *Jove*,
> From whom the Pow'r of Laws and Justice springs.
>
> $(1.309–15)$[2]

Achilles swears on the very emblem of royal power that he desecrates. He hurls the sacred emblem to the ground, but his words do greater damage, exposing the violence

---

[1] Byron meditates upon this tradition in his 1824 play, *The Deformed Transformed*, in which the misshapen hero, Arnold, in a Faustian bargain assumes the body of Achilles.

[2] *The Iliad of Homer. Translated by Alexander Pope*, ed. Steven Shankman (London: Penguin Books, 1996), 34.

of the human art that degraded a living tree into a dead ornament, dismantling the sceptre's symbolic power. Pope's translation, as is characteristic of his couplet mode, expands upon and orders the original, balancing the emblem of human imitation of divine authority with the 'temper'd Steel' that, with more composure and less licence than the 'brazen axe', forms both the hero's sword and the scissors with which in his mock-epic, *The Rape of the Lock* (1712–17), composed while Pope was translating the *Iliad* (1715–20), the Baron violates the long-contended honours of Belinda's head. 'The king who devours his people' in the Fagles translation,[3] a Saturn-like monster fit for Swift's 'Modest Proposal' (1729), in Pope's translation becomes the biblical 'Scourge of thy people, violent and base! / Sent in Jove's anger on a slavish race' (1.305–6): a mere tool of divine authority. In the echo chamber of epic tradition which resonates through both Pope's serious and mock-epic efforts, Virgil's version of the oath, and Dryden's translation thereof remind us that '*comas*', the Latin for leaves, is also a word for hair: the Baron's oath on Belinda's lock plays with the oath's original trope of human art as violation of nature, celebrating the feminine artifice at the heart of all masculine epic. Epic, as *The Rape of the Lock*'s cutting wit makes clear, has been undermined by satire from the start: the conquering force of unresisted steel makes heroes and kings whose power, from the satirist's angry perspective, is based on vain and prideful art.

In striking contrast to the mortal tragedy Achilles' gesture initiates, Book 1 of the *Iliad* ends with a divine comedy at a cripple's expense. Hephaestus, the maimed blacksmith god of fire and manufacture, who will later fashion Achilles' armour upon his re-entry into battle, reconciles his feuding parents, Hera and Zeus. He reminds his mother that he is unable to defend her against the divine father's wrath, pointing to his crippled leg, a memento of Zeus flinging him from Olympus when he last tried to intervene. What reconciles the married couple, however, is not so much Hephaestus' eloquent plea for peace but rather the spectacle of the limping god bustling about the Olympian banquet hall, pouring wine. In Dryden's jovial epithet for Hephaestus, 'the rude skinker',[4] we hear the divine artist brought down to human comic form. This unifying mirth at a body deformed by divine violence reveals the origins of another aspect of eighteenth-century satire, the cruel inevitability of laughter at bodies deemed to be either signs of divine punishment or nature's jests.[5]

Thersites thus enters a stage set for the spectacle of the satirist as monster and his words render the sceptre a weapon. While Achilles' oath defies Agamemnon's power in order to affirm his own, Thersites speaks against all kings indiscriminately, his jarring voice

---

[3] Homer, *The Iliad*, trans. Robert Fagles, introduction and notes by Bernard Knox (New York: Viking Penguin, 1990), 1.270.

[4] John Dryden, *The First Book of Homer's Ilias*, in *Fables Ancient and Modern; Translated into Verse* (1700), line 803, in James Kinsley, ed., *The Poems and Fables of John Dryden* (London: Oxford University Press, 1962), 680.

[5] For more on the eighteenth century as a transitional period in the cultural construction of deformity, see the introduction to *'Defects': Engendering the Modern Body*, ed. Helen Deutsch and Felicity Nussbaum (Ann Arbor: University of Michigan Press, 2000), and especially the essays by Lennard Davis and Stephen Pender. On deformity as nature's jest, see Roger Lund, 'Laughing at Cripples: Ridicule, Deformity, and the Argument from Design', *Eighteenth-Century Studies* 39 (2005), 91–114.

the only sound remaining when Odysseus calms the mutinous troops. We first learn of his abusive speech, and then—in a uniquely lengthy and detailed description—of his repulsive appearance:

> Thersites only clamour'd in the throng,
> Loquacious, loud, and turbulent of tongue:
> Awed by no shame, by no respect controll'd,
> In scandal busy, in reproaches bold:
> With witty malice studious to defame,
> Scorn all his joy, and laughter all his aim:—
> But chief he gloried with licentious style
> To lash the great, and monarchs to revile.
> His figure such as might his soul proclaim;
> One eye was blinking, and one leg was lame:
> His mountain shoulders half his breast o'erspread,
> Thin hairs bestrew'd his long misshapen head.
> Spleen to mankind his envious heart possess'd,
> And much he hated all, but most the best:
> Ulysses or Achilles still his theme;
> But royal scandal his delight supreme,
> Long had he lived the scorn of every Greek,
> Vex'd when he spoke, yet still they heard him speak.
> Sharp was his voice; which in the shrillest tone,
> Thus with injurious taunts attack'd the throne.
>
> (2.255–74)

Achilles' heroic defiance, what Pope calls his 'inexorable resentment',[6] is Thersites' slanderous insubordination, yet the latter's vituperative attack on Agamemnon differs from the former's more in style than in substance. He argues that the troops should follow Achilles' lead, abandoning an unjust war in the service of a tyrant: 'Whate'er our master craves, submit we must, / Plagu'd with his pride, or punish'd for his lust' (2.291–2). While Achilles was born for the battlefield and absents it in order to defend his honour, the irreverent Thersites was made to oppose it and has no honour to defend: his most powerful weapon is his relentless abuse, which Pope knowingly renders as licentious wit. 'No one alive less soldierly than you' (2.288), Odysseus taunts him in Fagles' translation, which Pope renders:

> Have we not known thee, slave! of all our host,
> The man who acts the least, upbraids the most?
>
> (2.310–11)

Defanging Thersites' cutting words, Odysseus goes one step further, beating him with the same sceptre Achilles had flung to the ground, reducing him to a creature

---

[6] *Iliad*, 'Observations on the First Book', in Pope, *Poems* (Twickenham), vii. 57.

'trembling... "and shrunk in abject fears"' (2.330), to the amusement of the mutinous troops. Just as with Hephaestus at the end of Book 1, order and unity are restored by the comic spectacle of a deformed body, and the satirist's truth is forgotten.

Thersites may have been momentarily silenced but he founded a dangerous genre; indeed the earliest practitioners of satire in the Greek and Celtic traditions were thought to be able to kill with their words.[7] His words and image endure far beyond the *Iliad*'s tragic conclusion: eighteenth-century satire embraced its monstrous forebear both in content and form, channelling him in both its fascination with abject spectacle and the violence of its critique.[8] The force of eighteenth-century satire's angry bite disarms the complacency of prideful humanity, forcing the reader to contemplate with both laughter and fear the monster that is 'man'.

FREEDOM FROM THE HUMAN

When John Wilmot, Earl of Rochester, libertine satirist and paragon of courtly masculinity both in love and in war, declares in his satire on King Charles II (ante 1674), in a blasphemous rhetorical play on the political theology of the king's two (divinely representative and humanly flawed) bodies—'His sceptre and his prick are of a length; / And she that plays with one may sway the other' (12–13)—he echoes both Achilles and Thersites.[9] Rochester scathingly condemns the unbridled appetite that renders the king an unnatural and impotent tyrant, reducing him to a pair of 'dull, graceless ballocks' (20) and declaring unequivocally, 'I hate all monarchs and the thrones they sit on, / From the hector of France to the cully of Britain' (15). In that insult 'hector', or bully, Restoration slang cuts the heroes of the *Iliad* down to size. When Rochester's speaker in his 'Satire against Reason and Mankind' (ante 1674) begins by declaring

> Were I (who to my cost already am)
> One of those strange, prodigious creatures, man
> A spirit free to choose for my own share,
> What case of flesh and blood I pleased to wear,
> I'd be a dog, a monkey, or a bear,

[7] For an illuminating trans-historical study on this subject, see Robert C. Elliott, *The Power of Satire: Magic, Ritual, Art* (Princeton: Princeton University Press, 1960).

[8] On eighteenth-century satire's preoccupation with the imagination's role in monstrous births both literal and literary, see Dennis Todd, *Imagining Monsters: Miscreations of the Self in Eighteenth-Century England* (Chicago: University of Chicago Press, 1995).

[9] John Wilmot, Earl of Rochester, 'On King Charles', in *Selected Works*, ed. Frank H. Ellis (London: Penguin, 2004). All Rochester quotations are taken from this edition. For more on the Restoration political context of this pornographic satire, see Rachel Weil, 'Sometimes a Scepter is Only a Scepter: Pornography and Politics in Restoration England', in *The Invention of Pornography: Obscenity and the Origins of Modernity, 1500–1800*, ed. Lynn Hunt (New York: Zone, 1996), 124–53.

Or anything but that vain animal
Who is so proud of being rational.

(1–7)

we hear in that strange ambiguity of the hypothetical 'were I', pushing against the parenthetical fact of 'man', a liberating distance from 'the strange prodigious creature' whom the *Satire* both puzzles over and humbles. Beginning with a cruelly ironic self-removal from the monstrosity of the human, the poem concludes with a paean to an equally unique and anomalous ideal, the honest man whom Diogenes searched for in vain:

If upon earth there dwell such God-like men,
I'll here recant my paradox to them,
Adore those shrines of virtue, homage pay,
And with the rabble world their laws obey.
        If such there are, yet grant me this at least,
        Man differs more from man than man from beast.

(220–5)

The work of the *Satire* is thus suspended between two inhuman extremes: the monster and the hero. The word itself, in its original spelling of 'satyr', plays with the human/animal divide under so much pressure during this period, the great age of both the satiric genre of theriophily—which inverts the biblical hierarchy institutionalized by the Great Chain of Being that made man superior to animals, thus permanently destabilizing an anthropocentric view of the universe—and of exploration, discovery, and classification of new species that put the human place on the Chain into question. The singularity and unattainability of the ideal justifies the poem's inhuman sympathy with beasts, its licentiousness, its unending quarrel with the 'rabble world'. For the speaker to 'recant my paradox' would be to renounce the heresy that is wit, along with the incoherent and decidedly ungodly truth that is the human animal.[10]

That same paradox animates Alexander Pope's great theodicy, the *Essay on Man* (1733–4), rendering both the human and humanism an unsettling problem rather than a complacent monument:

Know then thyself, presume not God to scan;
The proper study of Mankind is Man.

---

[10] For the period's delineation of embodied difference in an age of empire, see Felicity Nussbaum, *The Limits of the Human: Fictions of Anomaly, Race and Gender in the Long Eighteenth Century* (Cambridge: Cambridge University Press, 2003). In his dictionary of *Metaphors of the Mind* (Baltimore: Johns Hopkins University Press, 2015), under the entry 'Animals' (28–49), Brad Pasanek explores the evolution of Aristotle's definition of man as a 'rational animal' into an oxymoron at the heart of this essay's exploration of satire, noting that 'the word "beast", which originally includes man, comes…to distinguish lower animals from man' (33).

> Plac'd on this isthmus of a middle state,
> A being darkly wise, and rudely great:
> With too much knowledge for the Sceptic side,
> With too much weakness for the Stoic's pride,
> He hangs between; in doubt to act, or rest,
> In doubt to deem himself a God, or Beast;
> In doubt his Mind or Body to prefer,
> Born but to die, and reas'ning but to err;
> Alike in ignorance, his reason such,
> Whether he thinks too little, or too much;
> Chaos of Thought and Passion, all confus'd;
> Still by himself abus'd, or disabus'd;
> Created half to rise, and half to fall;
> Great lord of all things, yet a prey to all;
> Sole judge of Truth, in endless Error hurl'd:
> The glory, jest, and riddle of the world!
>
> (2.1–18)[11]

Like Satan in Paradise Lost, '[h]urled headlong flaming from the ethereal sky' in a tragic version of Hephaestus' comic fate in the *Iliad*, man falls into the chaos and 'endless Error' of his own being.[12] To be human is to be perpetually suspended between god and beast, and thus to be one's own abject object. When Helen Vendler calls this passage Pope's most compelling self-portrait, she both underlines and overlooks the way in which these lines render humanism itself a satirical project.[13] Later in the poem, Pope will take the same pitiless view of humanity that distinguished the *Satire against Reason*'s speaker from the spectacle of human folly, and which could have been glimpsed on a London street or in his own study:

> See the blind beggar dance, the cripple sing,
> The sot a hero, lunatic a king;
> The starving chemist in his golden views
> Supremely blest, the poet in his muse.
>
> (2.267–70)[14]

Branded Thersites by his critics and sharing his deformity, Pope thus includes himself in the comic landscape of human error created by the *Essay on Man*'s monstrous hybrid of poetry and philosophy, the space of satire and the human animal. The author of the *Essay*'s argument for nature's divinely authored and perfect design was also aware that

---

[11] *An Essay on Man*, Pope, *Poems* (Twickenham), III.i. 53–4.

[12] John Milton, *Paradise Lost*, in *John Milton. The Major Works*, ed. Stephen Orgel and Jonathan Goldberg (Oxford: Oxford University Press, 2003), 1.45.

[13] Helen Vendler, *Poets Thinking: Pope, Whitman, Dickinson, Yeats* (Cambridge, MA: Harvard University Press, 2004), 28.

[14] Pope, *Poems* (Twickenham), III.i. 87.

Hephaestus, the creator of that beautiful image of natural order, Achilles' shield, was excluded from the perfection he constructed.

In *The Animal That Therefore I Am*, Jacques Derrida, called to philosophize by the shame he feels at being nude in front of his cat, observes that 'thinking concerning the animal, if there is such a thing, derives from poetry.... [It] is what philosophy has, essentially, had to deprive itself of. It is the difference between philosophical knowledge and poetic thinking.'[15] Derrida, who argued so passionately for friendship with the other, had much to learn from Swift, whose satire takes difference to the limit, violating all human pride in likeness. Paul Kelleher makes a related point when he notes that the discourse of deformity in the moral philosophy of Anthony Ashley Cooper, 3rd Earl of Shaftesbury, put most baldly in his *Inquiry Concerning Virtue or Merit* (1711), serves to articulate the negative object against which the beauty of the good defines itself, but can never shape philosophy's form. For Shaftesbury, 'the capacity for becoming "worthy or virtuous" is...reserved for humans only', but not for humans deficient in reason: 'for though we may vulgarly call an ill horse vicious, yet we never say of a good one, nor of any mere beast, idiot, or changeling, though ever so good-natured, that he is worthy or virtuous'. The reader of satire will be especially entertained by Shaftesbury's example of the horse, that epitome of reason and virtue in Book IV of *Gulliver's Travels* (1726). When Kelleher argues that the 'truest monster is what Shaftesbury's moral system cannot fully recognize or flesh out, namely a creature who finds no likeness of himself and still has the audacity to relish life and to flourish', even, perhaps, the ability to 'be concerned about those who are *unlike* him', he might be drawing a picture of the self-exiled Gulliver at the end of Book IV, writing to correct mankind despite his despair at human folly.[16]

Pope's *Iliad* translation makes explicit what the original implies and what the self-exposure of his own poetry would work to refute: Thersites' deformed body might be the image of his soul. The same poet who in the scandalous *Rape of the Lock* would self-mockingly begin by asking, 'in Tasks so bold can Little Men engage?' (1.11), in his translation of the *Iliad* renders Thersites in judgement of the satirist's 'envious' wit and 'spleen to mankind'. In that 'envious', we can also hear an echo of Francis Bacon's influential claim that deformed persons 'are commonly even with nature; for as nature hath done ill by them; so do they by nature; being for the most part, (as the Scripture saith), "void of natural affection"; and so they have their revenge of nature'.[17] Pope's Thersites thus merges with Shakespeare's Richard III, who haunts Bacon's essay, excluded not only from human but from animal kind:

[15] Jacques Derrida, *The Animal That Therefore I Am*, ed. Marie-Louise Mallet, trans. David Wills (New York: Fordham University Press, 2008), 7. For satire as the genre that at once creates and undermines difference, see Fredric V. Bogel, *The Difference Satire Makes: Rhetoric and Reading from Jonson to Byron* (Ithaca: Cornell University Press, 2001).

[16] Paul Kelleher, 'Defections from Nature: The Rhetoric of Deformity in Shaftesbury's *Characteristics*', in *The Idea of Disability in the Eighteenth Century*, ed. Chris Mounsey (Lewisburg: Bucknell University Press, 2014), 79, 75.

[17] Francis Bacon, 'Of Deformity', in *The Essays, or Counsels Civil and Moral*, ed. Brian Vickers (Oxford: Oxford University Press, 1999), 99.

> Cheated of feature by dissembling Nature,
> Deform'd, unfinished, sent before my time
> Into this breathing world scarce half made up,
> And that so lamely and unfashionable
> That dogs bark at me as I halt by them.
>
> (1.1.19–23)[18]

Richard's much-disputed deformity, believed by many to be a political fiction and discovered upon the recent exhumation of the king's bones to be fact, reminds us of the Mobius strip of nature and art around which the couplet pair of the divinely maimed Hephaestus and the naturally deformed Thersites revolve.[19] In his portrayal of himself in his 'Horatian poem without an original' and satiric self-portrait, the *Epistle to Dr Arbuthnot* (1735), as 'Dipt…in Ink' by 'sin to me unknown' (125–6)—like Achilles dipped in the River Styx, nearly immortal but for his mother's grip on his heel—Pope reminds us that Achilles, too, was physically damaged by his connection to humanity, making satiric heroism a death-dealing punishment. Lord John Hervey and Lady Mary Wortley Montagu, policing the limits of the human with a confidence common to many who brutally retaliated against Pope's satiric attacks, transform these paradoxes into stigma, joining the unnatural art of Pope's imitations of Horace with Pope's own divinely authored monstrosity, branding him 'at once Resemblance and Disgrace', and 'Burlesque' of the human species.[20] Their unequivocal disgust, their pride in playing God, their vicious savagery, mirror and far exceed Pope's own.

Pope distinguishes himself from his opponents by his ability to 'abuse and dis-abuse' himself, to deride, accept, and ultimately to transform his own deformity into exemplarity.[21] Satire's cardinal Socratic rule, with which the *Essay on Man* begins, is to know thyself. Montaigne, Horace's heir and powerful progenitor of eighteenth-century satire, takes this one step further when he opines: 'I have seen no more evident monstrosity and miracle in the world than myself'.[22] Eighteenth-century satire thus founds itself upon the very thing that it most hates: human singularity. Responding to Swift's statement that 'When I am told that somebody is my *brother Protestant*, I remember that the rat is a fellow creature', William Butler Yeats wrote, 'that seems to me a joyous

---

[18] William Shakespeare, *King Richard III*, ed. James R. Siemon (Bloomsbury: Arden Shakespeare, 2009).

[19] On the paradoxes of natural art surrounding Pope, see Helen Deutsch, *Resemblance and Disgrace: Alexander Pope and the Deformation of Culture* (Cambridge, MA: Harvard University Press, 1996), ch. 1. The 1729 satirical print, 'His Holiness and his Prime Minister', to give one graphic example, depicts a human/rat hybrid of Pope upon a pedestal beneath which is a reference to Pope's 'character of Thersites'. http://www.britishmuseum.org/research/collection_online/collection_object_details.aspx?objectId= 3072098&partId=1&people=111118&peoA=111118-1-7&page=1

[20] *Verses Address'd to the Imitator of the First Satire of the Second Book of Horace* (1733). See also Deutsch, *Resemblance and Disgrace*, 22–3.

[21] Helen Deutsch, 'Bolingbroke's Laugh: Alexander Pope's "Epistle to Bolingbroke" and the Rhetoric of Embodied Exemplarity', *Studies in the Literary Imagination* 38 (2005), 137–61.

[22] Michel Equem de Montaigne, 'Of Cripples', in *The Complete Essays of Montaigne*, trans. Donald M. Frame (Stanford: Stanford University Press, 1981), 787.

saying.'[23] Such joy in rage, such freedom of fellowship with the abject other, characterizes the liberating potential and visceral power of these inhumanely human texts.

The abjection of Thersites thus becomes the satirist's liberty. Pope becomes an epic hero himself in his *Epilogue to the Satires* (1738) as he draws the 'last Pen for Freedom' (2.248), lashing the guilty as Thersites lashes the great, declaring himself a moral exemplar not despite but because of his deformity in his last Horatian poem, the *Epistle to Bolingbroke* (1738). The savage indignation that famously lacerated Swift's heart in his self-authored epitaph, in its addition of '*saeva*' to Juvenal's '*facit indignatio versum*,' infuses him with an inhuman version of the wrath that animated Achilles on the battlefield. The rage of both the satirist and Homeric hero, as Peter Sloterdijk puts it, gain dignity from a 'higher origin': 'Just as the prophet is a medium in the name of the holy word of protest, the warrior becomes a tool for the force, which gathers in him abruptly in order to break through the world of appearances', a violent force to which nothing approximates better than Swiftian irony, wielded by the satiric defender, to the utmost of his powers, of liberty.[24]

BRUTAL REALISM: SATIRE AND THE NOVEL

Eighteenth-century satirists transform the laughter Thersites provokes into both weapon and mirror. In an important corrective to decades of scholarship depicting an age of polite sociability, Simon Dickie has painstakingly uncovered a cruel eighteenth century when all classes delighted in both laughing at and tormenting dwarves, hunchbacks, and cripples. Montagu and Hervey's brutality, Dickie demonstrates, is more rule than exception for the so-called 'culture of sensibility' that had no shame about proving Henri Bergson's point—'our laughter is always the laughter of a group'—at the expense of the physically disabled.[25] In an important response to Dickie, Roger Lund points out that there is more to such laughter than the universal desire to disavow one's own proximity to physical disease and disability, or a Hobbesian enjoyment of 'sudden glory' at the 'apprehension of some deformed thing in another by comparison of which they suddenly applaud themselves'. For Lund, the unquestioned assumption that deformity ' "naturally" inspires the laughter of those who see [it], seemingly finds its origin in tacit assumptions

---

[23] William Butler Yeats to Dorothy Wellesley, 1936, quoted in Michael Steinman, *Yeats' Heroic Figures: Wilde, Parnell, Swift, Casement* (Albany: State University of New York Press, 1983), 140.

[24] Peter Sloterdijk, *Rage and Time: A Psychopolitical Investigation*, trans. Mario Wenning (New York: Columbia University Press, 2012), 8. For Swift's debt to Juvenal in the epitaph, see Claude Rawson, 'Savage Indignation Revisited: Swift, Yeats, and the "Cry" of Liberty', in *Swift's Angers* (Cambridge: Cambridge University Press, 2014), 239–67.

[25] Henri Bergson, *Laughter: An Essay on the Meaning of the Comic*, trans. Cloudesely Brereton and Fred Rothwell (Rockville: Arc Manor, 2008), 11; Simon Dickie, *Cruelty and Laughter: Forgotten Comic Literature and the Unsentimental Eighteenth Century* (Chicago: University of Chicago Press, 2011), see especially ch. 2.

which admit no interrogation and which are so deeply held as to constitute an ideology'.[26] For an Augustan age murderously invested in the beautiful order of nature, 'the appearance, indeed the very existence of the physically deformed, marked them as violations of the argument from design', nature's errors at worst, jokes at best.[27]

Lund founds his argument on the counter-intuitive example of that most delicately satirical of men of feeling, Laurence Sterne, who in his *Sentimental Journey* (1768) observes of the abundance of dwarves and hunchbacks in Paris that 'there is no end to [Nature's] amusements—the goddess seems almost as merry as she is wise'. While Yorick goes on to express sympathy for 'this poor blighted part of my species, who have neither size nor strength to get on in the world', Sterne undermines Yorick's self-congratulatory virtue by making him the butt of nature's joke as, in the process of helping a small boy cross a gutter, he is surprised to discover that the boy 'was about forty'.[28] Swift performs a more brutal version of this manoeuvre when, in Book II of *Gulliver's Travels*, Gulliver himself becomes a *lusus naturae* who endures the taxing trials of being put on show in Brobdingnag, while fighting off the predations of wasps and the malicious competitiveness of the court dwarf.

Sterne's sentimental picaresque civilizes the popular comic genre of 'ramble novels' that entertained so many mid-century readers with bawdy brutality.[29] This genre proleptically epitomizes Henri Bergson's definition of man as an 'animal which is laughed at':

> [T]he comic does not exist outside the pale of what is strictly *human*. . . . Several have defined man as 'an animal which laughs'. They might equally well have defined him as an animal which is laughed at; for if any other animal, or lifeless object, produces the same effect, it is always because of some resemblance to man, of the stamp he gives it or the use he puts it to.[30]

Bergson's reasoning comes very close to Henry Fielding's rationale in his 'comic epic in prose', *Joseph Andrews* (1742), for preferring the comic to the burlesque:

> Indeed, no two species of writing can differ more widely than the comic and the burlesque; for as the latter is ever the exhibition of what is monstrous and unnatural . . . so in the former, we should ever confine ourselves strictly to nature, from the just imitation of which will flow all the pleasure we can this way convey to a sensible reader.[31]

Satire from the picaresque novelist's perspective is the stuff of realism, so it is therefore no surprise that when Thersites makes an appearance it is in the guise of Miss Snapper,

---

[26] Lund, engaging with Dickie, who is quoting Hobbes, 'Laughing at Cripples', 93.

[27] Lund, 'Laughing at Cripples', 94.

[28] Laurence Sterne, *A Sentimental Journey through France and Italy*, ed. A. Alvarez (London: Penguin, 1986), 82–3.

[29] On ramble novels, see Dickie, *Cruelty and Laughter*, 250–81.   [30] Bergson, *Laughter*, 10.

[31] Henry Fielding, *Joseph Andrews*, ed. Martin C. Battestin (Boston: Houghton Mifflin, 1961), 8. See also Dickie, *Cruelty and Laughter*, ch. 4.

in Smollett's *Roderick Random* (1748), a witty hunchbacked woman with fortune enough to make her attractive to the importunate Roderick.[32] Miss Snapper's comic deformity immediately follows the burlesque monstrosity of Miss Sparkle, the stereotypically unnatural old woman who affects the young coquette. Like Thersites exposing Agamemnon, Miss Snapper's wit savages the cowardly army officer with whom she shares a coach. When the notoriously crude and real-life master of the pump room, Beau Nash, makes a joke at her expense at Bath, Miss Snapper retaliates and makes him the butt of her joke. She may lose Roderick to the beautiful and aptly named Narcissa, but her triumph in the battle of the wits aligns her with Smollett and with the freedom of satire. A similar joke in a more masculine register is played on Mr Lovell in Frances Burney's epistolary female picaresque, *Evelina* (1778), whose unnatural foppishness is targeted by the 'greatest brute in Nature', Captain Mirvan, and who is viciously attacked, at this brute's instigation, by a monkey dressed exactly like himself. (Burney may well be remembering the female fop at the heart of the nest of Chinese boxes that is Rochester's verse epistle, *Artemisa to Chloe*, who pays seemingly serious court to a monkey.) When Lovell opines, in response to the Captain's assertion that he has just met his twin brother (the monkey), 'It would have been a most singular pleasure to me, if I also could have seen him; for, really, I have not the least idea what sort of person I am and I have a prodigious curiosity to know', his ignorance reverses the satirist's knowing paradoxes, and his confrontation with the beast literalizes the genre's violent comeuppance.[33]

SATIRE AT THE LIMIT: SWIFT'S VERTIGINOUS INHUMANITY

Swift's inversions of scale provide some of the most potent examples of how the period's satire disorients a reader eager to be in on the joke and aligned with humankind. When he defines satire as '*a sort of* Glass, *wherein Beholders do generally discover every body's Face but their Own*', in the preface to his 'Battle of the Books' (1704), Swift articulates a uniquely human paradox of universal error and individual delusion that epitomizes the genre's violent attempts to reform by replacing self-love with the painful shock of readerly self-recognition. Fittingly, the figure of Thersites in this mock-heroic battle between the ancients and the moderns is attributed to Swift's enemy, the overzealous guardian of the king's library and professional philologist Richard Bentley, who is described by his opponent in battle Scaliger thus: '*the Malignity of thy Temper perverteth Nature; thy* Learning *makes thee more Barbarous, thy study of* Humanity, *more* Inhuman'.[34] While

---

[32] Tobias Smollett, *The Adventures of Roderick Random*, ed. Paul-Gabriel Bouce (Oxford: Oxford University Press, 1981). For Miss Sparkle's 'monstrous affectation', see 303–6. For the 'saytrical lady', Miss Snapper, see 324–38, especially the riposte to Nash on 335.

[33] Frances Burney, *Evelina*, ed. Kristina Straub (Boston: Bedford Books, 1997), 433, 430.

[34] Swift, *Works* (Cambridge), i. 161.

Swift's satiric energy aligns him more with the vituperative and venomous modern spider than the polite humanist bee spreading sweetness and light, the monstrous Bentley is an apt emblem of his satiric vision. At once prideful and abject, despairing and idealistic, god-like and powerless, the worldly strivers Swift attacks in his own image epitomize the ways in which satire strives to humble human pride by holding up a beastly mirror. The experience of reading Swift forces the abject being he defined—through his ironic mouth-piece Gulliver in another echo of Shakespeare's *Richard III*—as 'a lump of Deformity, and Diseases both in Body and Mind, smitten with *Pride*' (502), and the human reader, into identity. Swift's irony is the most extreme yet representative example of satire's ability to undermine both dominant protocols of representation and standard ethical categories. The reader of Swift's satire is forced to embrace madmen, monsters, and the savage others known as yahoos as herself. To read satire, Swift definitively demonstrates, is to be at once humbled by and freed from the limits of the human.

Swift's 'Modest Proposal' (1729), often the first piece of satire that American students read in high school, is at once exception and case in point; exception because, at the height of his brutalizing irony, the speaker momentarily drops his mask and clearly states his point: extreme measures are necessary because the Irish have rejected all reasonable solutions (suggested in other tracts by Swift himself):

> I desire the Reader will observe, that I calculate my Remedy *for this one individual Kingdom of* IRELAND, *and for no other that ever was, is, or, I think, ever can be seen on Earth.* Therefore let no man talk to me of other Expedients: *Of taxing our Absentees at five Shillings a Pound: Of using neither Clothes, nor Household Furniture, except what is of our own Growth and Manufacture: Of utterly rejecting the Materials and Instruments, that promote foreign Luxury: Of curing the Expensiveness of Pride, Vanity, Idleness, and Gaming in our Women: Of introducing a Vein of Parsimony, Prudence and Temperance: Of learning to love our Country, wherein we differ even from* LAPLANDERS, *and the inhabitants of* TOPINAMBOO.[35]

Ireland itself—a divided chaos of a colony whose 'whole people' existed only as a rhetorical invocation in Swift's *Drapier's Letters* (1724)—becomes the monster in these lines, distinguished by a self-hatred that is at once disease and satirical cure, forced to look itself in the face and rank itself below barbarians, just as the reader is forced to imagine in painstaking detail, in alternating moods of calm rationality and self-congratulatory sentiment, that a child of one of 'our [Catholic] savages', served up to an Anglo-Irish table, 'seasoned with a little Pepper or Salt, will be very good Boiled on the fourth Day, especially in *Winter*' (112), or to consider 'buying the Children alive, and dressing them hot from the Knife, as we do *roasting Pigs*' (113). The energy and excess of these lines cannot be contained by any moral: the cruelty and, if the myriad internet memes based on this text are any indication, pleasure of the *Modest Proposal* rest in the reader's uneasy

---

[35] Swift, *PW*, xii. 116.

embrace of his own savagery. Apocalyptic, unforgiving, and playfully cruel, Swift's irony models for us 'the destruction of thought by the destruction of language'.[36]

Swift's irony leaves no safe haven, especially not one's own body. We see his persistent de-familiarization of the body in *Gulliver's Travels*, most revoltingly in the magnifications of the wens of beggars and breasts of court ladies of Brobdingnag in Book II, and most humblingly in the view from a horse's superior perspective in Book IV. The Houyhnhnm master, comparing Gulliver to the Yahoos, observes that he

> could not walk with any Security; for if either of my hinder Feet slipped, I must inevitably fall. He then began to find fault with other Parts of my Body; the Flatness of my Face, the Prominence of my Nose, my Eyes placed directly in Front, so that I could not look on either Side without turning my Head: That I was not able to feed myself, without lifting one of my Fore-feet to my Mouth: And therefore Nature had placed those Joints to answer that Necessity. He knew not what could be the Use of those several Clefts and Divisions in my Feet behind; that these were too soft to bear the Hardness and Sharpness of Stones without a Covering made from the Skin of some other Brute; that my whole Body wanted a Fence against Heat and Cold, which I was forced to put on and off every Day with Tediousness and Trouble. And lastly, that he observed every Animal in this Country naturally to abhor the *Yahoos*, whom the Weaker avoided and the Stronger drove from them. So that supposing us to have the Gift of Reason, he could not see how it were possible to cure that natural Antipathy which every Creature discovered against us; nor consequently, how we would tame and render them serviceable.[37]

This is man viewed from the chilling perspective of 'equine rationality', from which body determines mind and 'form follows function'.[38] The horses' quadruped hoofed body and expanded vision enable their 'taming and rendering serviceable' of the Yahoos, and render the naked Gulliver, who entered the island supposing himself 'great lord of all things', 'a prey to all'. The signs of civilization that distinguish him from the beastly Yahoos—his clothing, opposable thumbs, hairless body, soft hands and feet, and 'supposed' reason— are from this perspective not just useless but debilities. In the Houyhnhnm master's observation about Gulliver's unstable walk we hear Swift's wit, which from our perspective reads like a reversal of Freud's *Civilization and its Discontents*. Man's ascension to bipedal status might raise him above the stink of his own excrement, but only increases his likelihood of falling. So, we might add, does the vertigo from which Swift suffered throughout his adult life, which made him fear the madness from which Gulliver suffers. Swift's Christian pun on 'falling' implicates us all, but it saves us from Gulliver's fanatical

---

[36] John Traugott, 'Swift our Contemporary', *University Review* 4 (1967), 11–34, at 18.

[37] Swift, *Works* (Cambridge), xvi. 357–8.

[38] Srinivas Aravamudan, *Enlightenment Orientalism: Resisting the Rise of the Novel* (Chicago: University of Chicago Press, 2012), 149. Aravamudan discusses *Gulliver's Travels* in the context of Western theriophily and the Oriental beast fable.

misanthropy, leaving us tenuously attached to our own humanity, giddy with what Swift, in 'The Author upon Himself' (1714, 1735) called the 'Sin of Wit'.[39]

THE FEMALE ANIMAL

Gulliver's disconcerting confrontation with his image in the eyes of a fictional horse is followed by a more traumatic and definitive encounter with a human woman. As he bathes naked in a river, with 'my Protector the Sorrel Nag', 'grazing at some Distance', he is embraced 'after a most fulsome Manner' by a 'young Female Yahoo…inflamed by Desire, as the Nag and I conjectured' (482). This episode is a 'Matter of Diversion' to the Houyhnhnms and 'of mortification' to Gulliver:

> for now I could no longer deny, that I was a real *Yahoo*, in every Limb and Feature, since their Females had a natural Propensity to me as one of their own Species: Neither was the Hair of this Brute of a Red Colour, (which might have been some Excuse for an Appetite a little irregular) but black as a Sloe, and her Countenance did not make an Appearance altogether so hideous as the rest of the Kind; for I think she could not be above eleven years old.   (482)

In Gulliver and the nag's 'conjecturing' over the female Yahoo's motivation, and in his definitive glimpse of himself in a Yahoo mirror, we see how women bridge the gap in the eighteenth-century imagination between human and animal, a demeaning association that Mary Wollestonecraft, at the end of the century, would vehemently protest in the name of reason.[40] Gulliver's prideful boast that his pursuer stood out in her not 'altogether so hideous' appearance, his implication that her attraction, unlike the undiscriminating lust of a redhead, was particular, and his ambiguously vague shift from 'their own Species' to 'the kind' which includes him, hints at his own beastly desire, a desire which he definitively renounces upon his return, rejecting the stench of his wife for the pleasant smell of a stable.

If man is a rational animal, then what is woman? Gulliver recognizing himself in a savage female mirror is one of many examples of Swift's complex play with identity categories, a play that is often gendered. In his note to this episode (482), Claude Rawson observes that Swift alludes here to Ovid's myth of Echo and Narcissus, reminding us that

---

[39] Swift, *Poems* (Williams), i. 193. For Swift's distinguishing himself from Gulliver by his rejection of 'Timon's manner' for a wittier embrace of misanthropy, see Rawson, *Swift's Angers*, ch. 4.

[40] See Laura Brown, *Ends of Empire: Women and Ideology in Eighteenth-Century English Literature* (Ithaca: Cornell University Press, 1993), especially ch. 6. For a decidedly less feminist view of this episode and the intersection of race and gender in *Gulliver's Travels*, see Claude Rawson, *God, Gulliver, and Genocide: Barbarism and the European Imagination, 1492–1945* (Oxford: Oxford University Press, 2001), ch. 2.

the original embodied subject of fascination with his own image was male. While Pope's *Rape of the Lock* celebrates Belinda at her glass as both self-worshipping goddess and epic hero arming for battle, Celia herself is absent from Strephon's exploration of beauty's disgusting 'remains' in *The Lady's Dressing-Room* (1730, 1732), in which the magnifying glass reflects Strephon's own face, and the figure of the fatally curious Pandora, fouling his hands in search of 'hope' in Celia's chamber pot disguised as cabinet, is Strephon himself. In poems such as this one and the repugnantly moving anti-Petrarchan *On a Beautiful Young Nymph Going to Bed* (1731, 1734), Swift uses the figure of the woman to point to even more killing paradoxes of humanity *tout court*, illuminating the vast discrepancy between corrupt embodiment and the ideal of beauty encapsulated brilliantly in the speaker of *The Lady's Dressing-Room*'s witty question: 'Should I the *Queen of Love* refuse, / Because she rose from Stinking Ooze?' (131–2).[41]

When Swift's protégée Mary Barber glimpses herself in a mirror, she sees a different sort of monster:

> Today, as at my glass I stood,
> To set my head-clothes and my hood,
> I saw my grizzled locks with dread,
> And called to mind the Gorgon's head.
> Thought I, whate'er the poets say,
> Medusa's hair was only grey:
> Though Ovid, who the story told,
> Was too well-bred to call her old;
> But, what amounted to the same,
> He made her an immortal dame.
>
> (1–10)[42]

Turning female abjection into divinity, Barber uses the mirror to rewrite a misanthropic satiric tradition that bases itself on misogyny. Unlike Perseus who deploys the mirror of his shield to deflect the Medusa's gaze lest he be turned to stone, Barber looks herself in the face and lives to tell a monitory tale to women who think they will never meet her fate. In a world in which the old lady race in *Evelina* was a reality, for a woman to live, speak, and desire beyond her prime was to be a monstrous prodigy. The ageing Lady Mary Wortley Montagu, in her love lyric to her much younger lover, Francesco Algarotti, 'This once was me' (1736), similarly draws upon an Ovidian poetics of gendered transformation to transcend a youthful understanding of herself as beautiful object whose narcissistic lament for her lost beauty after a bout of smallpox she satirized to tragic effect in 'Satturday' (1716, 1747). In that poem's charged allusion

---

[41] Claude Rawson has frequently pointed out that Swift's misogyny moves inevitably towards general misanthropy; see, for example, *Swift's Angers*, 116.

[42] 'To Mrs. Frances-Arabella Kelly' (1734) in *Eighteenth-Century Women Poets*, ed. Roger Lonsdale (Oxford: Oxford University Press, 1989), 125.

to Pope's Belinda in *The Rape of the Lock*, Montagu both evokes the mock-epic reminder that all of masculine epic revolves around female beauty and the question of female desire, and rewrites Belinda's objectification as painful personal experience. While eighteenth-century male satirists use women as objects against which to define their human subjectivity, these female satirists exemplified how to outlive imputed monstrosity in embodied time and through poetic self-transformation. Rather than be transfixed or unhinged by the mirror's ugly truth, both women turn away from the mirror in order to live to tell the tale; each becomes a hero vanquishing a monster that was herself.[43]

MONSTROUS HEROISM

The passivity of Swift's metaphor of satire as glass belies the ways in which the mirror is a weapon that wreaks havoc with the reader's consciousness. Paddy Bullard has recently and cogently identified Swift's weapon as a razor: its targets may fail to see their reflections in its brilliant surface, but its 'sharpest blows leave some sort of mark on their unconscious subjects', though it cuts most deeply into the lacerated heart of Swift himself.[44]

The late work of Pope and Swift amplifies the paradox of satire's potent futility. Consider the epigraph to the final edition of Pope's *The Dunciad: In Four Books* (1743):

Tandem *Phoebus* adest, morsusque inferred parantem

Congelat, et patulos, ut errant, indurate hiatus. (OVID.)

[But Phoebus comes to his aid, and checks the monster, ready for the devouring grasp; whose expanded jaws, transformed to stone, stand hardened in a ghastly grin.][45]

In this remarkable image evoking both 'satire triumphant and satire disarmed',[46] Pope reflects upon himself in various shapes: as a celebrity whose head circulated throughout London print culture more prolifically than any other figure of his day, as a satirist who portrayed himself as delighting in his own cruelty in the *Epistle to Dr Arbuthnot*, begging his sceptical friend to 'let me flap this Bug with gilded wings' (309), as he launches into a

---

[43] For 'This once was me', see Appendix I of Lady Mary Wortley Montagu, *Essays and Poems and Simplicity, A Comedy*, ed. Robert Halsband and Isobel Grundy (Oxford: Oxford University Press, 1977), 381–2. See also Jill Campbell, 'Lady Mary Wortley Montagu and the "Glass Revers'd" of Female Old Age', in *'Defects'*, ed. Deutsch and Nussbaum, 213–51, and Helen Deutsch, ' "This once was me": Lady Mary Wortley Montagu's Ecstatic Poetics', *The Eighteenth Century* 53, no. 3 (2012), 331–55.

[44] Paddy Bullard, 'Swift's Razor', *Modern Philology* 113, no. 3 (2016), 353–72, at 370.

[45] Pope, *Dunciad Four Books*, 21.

[46] Helen Deutsch, 'Pope, Self, and World', in *The Cambridge Companion to Alexander Pope*, ed. Pat Rogers (Cambridge: Cambridge University Press, 2007), 23.

portrait of Lord John Hervey as Sporus, the monstrously effeminate 'vile Antithesis' (325), who mumbles at the game he dare not bite (208); and as a warrior who uses Hervey as a foil against whom he defines his own vicious incivility and 'manly ways' (337). Pope thus embodies a violent paradox: he is on the one hand, the poet Orpheus, beheaded by the Bacchantes and saved from further indignity by Apollo, the god of poetry; on the other, the monstrous serpent with the power to devour those who threaten him, frozen in a posture that transforms the moment of attack into a rictus grin.

Swift declared in a 1725 letter to Pope that his purpose in *Gulliver's Travels* was to 'vex the world rather than divert it' (676). Eleven years later in *The Legion Club* (1736), an epic journey to hell in the guise of the madhouse of demons that for him was the Irish parliament, he channels in trochaic tetrameter the original Celtic satirists who could rhyme rats and curse humans to death. Swift portrays himself as Aeneas at the gates of Avernus beset by allegorical figures and real monsters, reminded by the Sibyl that he fights empty shades. But this Irish hero is guided by Clio, no prophetess but rather the muse of history, who leaves Swift to 'bravely' confront the real monsters of parliament, far more frightening than the 'Phantoms bodiless and vain' who haunt the building's entrance. *The Legion Club* gains its power from translating the imperial fiction of Virgil's Book VI, with its tragic yet triumphant vision of Rome's history as future, into the stinking reality of Swift's colonial moment for which there is no future worth imagining. When history abandons Swift, he is left to plead for assistance:

> How I want thee, hum'rous Hogarth!
> Thou, I hear, a pleasant rogue art.
> Were but you and I acquainted,
> Ev'ry monster should be painted:
> You should try your graving tools
> On this odious group of fools;
> Draw the beasts as I describe 'em,
> Form their features while I gibe 'em;
> Draw them like; for I assure you,
> You will need no car'catura;
> Draw them so that we may trace
> All the soul in ev'ry face.

(219–30)

Hogarth is needed not for his own powers as a satirist (caricature being the visual equivalent of satire) but rather for his ability to convey a reality so monstrously unspeakable that words cannot do it justice. Dropping his stick and lacking Hogarth's pen, Swift confounds a colloquial curse with priestly blasphemy: '*May their god, the devil, confound 'em!*' (242). Each of these examples, marking the end of a satiric era, render the satirist himself both Achilles and Thersites, at once omnipotent and defenceless, which is to say all too human.

Select Bibliography

Aravamudan, Srinivas. *Enlightenment Orientalism: Resisting the Rise of the Novel* (Chicago: University of Chicago Press, 2012), ch. 3.

Bergson, Henri. *Laughter: An Essay on the Meaning of the Comic*, trans. Cloudesely Brereton and Fred Rothwell (Rockville: Arc Manor, 2008).

Brown, Laura. *Ends of Empire: Women and Ideology in Eighteenth-Century English Literature* (Ithaca: Cornell University Press, 1993).

Bullard, Paddy. 'Swift's Razor', *Modern Philology* 113 (2016), 353–72.

Derrida, Jacques. *The Animal That Therefore I Am*, ed. Marie-Louise Mallet, trans. David Wills (New York: Fordham University Press, 2008).

Deutsch, Helen. 'Bolingbroke's Laugh: Alexander Pope's "Epistle to Bolingbroke" and the Rhetoric of Embodied Exemplarity', *Studies in the Literary Imagination* 38 (2005), 137–61.

Deutsch, Helen. *Resemblance and Disgrace: Alexander Pope and the Deformation of Culture* (Cambridge, MA: Harvard University Press, 1996).

Deutsch, Helen and Felicity Nussbaum, eds. *'Defects': Engendering the Modern Body* (Ann Arbor: University of Michigan Press, 2000).

Dickie, Simon. *Cruelty and Laughter: Forgotten Comic Literature and the Unsentimental Eighteenth Century* (Chicago: University of Chicago Press, 2011).

Kelleher, Paul. 'Defections from Nature: The Rhetoric of Deformity in Shaftesbury's *Characteristics*', in *The Idea of Disability in the Eighteenth Century*, ed. Chris Mounsey (Lewisburg: Bucknell University Press, 2014), ch. 3.

Lund, Roger. 'Laughing at Cripples: Ridicule, Deformity, and the Argument from Design', *Eighteenth-Century Studies* 39 (2005), 91–114.

Rawson, Claude. *Swift's Angers* (Cambridge: Cambridge University Press, 2014).

Todd, Dennis. *Imagining Monsters: Miscreations of the Self in Eighteenth-Century England* (Chicago: University of Chicago Press, 1995).

CHAPTER 26

....

SELF-PORTRAITURE

....

LOUISE CURRAN

In the archives of Chatsworth House in Derbyshire is a drawing of Dorothy Boyle, Countess of Burlington (1699–1758), sitting in front of her easel. Married to Richard Boyle, 3rd Earl of Burlington (1694–1753), the architect and patron of the arts, Dorothy was an amateur painter in her own right who was taught by the artist, designer, and landscape gardener William Kent. Of her art, Horace Walpole wrote that she 'succeeded admirably in likenesses; but working with too much rapidity, did not do justice to her genius. She had an uncommon talent too for caricature.'[1] The drawing of Lady Burlington in the act of composition is by Kent (Figure 26.1). It depicts her painting two female heads onto a canvas: one an unfinished, mostly featureless, outline of a face resting on its hand, another more delineated woman's head seen in profile. In comparison with the middle-aged artist who is portrayed wearing a neat, ruffled cap on her head and absorbed in her art, the portrait that she works upon is distinctly youthful. The triangular relationship of the three female heads is suggestive: the older artist looks at the face of a younger woman whilst in between them sits a head that is yet formless and without character.

Kent's image of female character in formation can be compared with Lady Burlington's own sketch of her friend Alexander Pope playing at cards (Figure 26.2). Pope—a rigorous controller of his public image—is depicted in this informal drawing as short and with a distinctly curved spine. A unique drawing (if comparable to another unauthorized sketch of the author by William Hoare) of the poet off-guard,[2] Pope appears not to have been aware of the representation and it was never reproduced in his lifetime. This (possibly covert) act of observation suggests the intimacy of Lady Burlington and Pope's relations. Maynard Mack, who describes the Countess as 'considerably a romp', gives as an example of her wit the fact that in 1738 she 'amused herself ... by sending Pope the gazetteers' worst attacks on him with epigrammatic retorts by herself masquerading

---

[1] Horace Walpole, *Anecdotes of Painting in England*, ed. James Dallaway and Ralph L. Wornum, 2nd edn. (1862), iii. 776.

[2] William Hoare, *Alexander Pope*, c.1739–43, red chalk, 6 5/8 in × 4 1/2 in (168 mm × 114 mm), National Portrait Gallery, London, NPG 873.

FIGURE 26.1 William Kent, *Lady Burlington at her easel in her Garden Room*, c.1740, pen and wash, 23.1 × 18.1 cm, Trustees of the Chatsworth Settlement

as his'.[3] She also acted as the poet's amanuensis and transcribed some of his satires for the press.[4] When it came to her own caricatures, as Mark De Novellis has noted, the Countess's 'rapidly executed sketches were ephemeral in nature, and were not expected to survive for any great length of time', indeed she would draw them on fragments of paper to hand, including the backs of homemade playing cards and pages taken out of books.[5]

Kent made another drawing of the Countess of Burlington that is, perhaps, even more suggestive about female representation in and through portraiture.[6] It depicts the artist in her familiar ruffled cap petting a large owl who sits upon a tree dangling a mouse in its

[3] Maynard Mack, *Alexander Pope: A Life* (New Haven: Yale University Press, 1985), 753.

[4] Pope makes a joke about detecting the 'Hand writing' of his amanuensis in a letter to the Countess of Burlington, [*c.* 8 September 1738], Pope, *Corr.* (Sherburn), iv. 125.

[5] Mark De Novellis, *Pallas Unveil'd: The Life and Art of Lady Dorothy Savile, Countess of Burlington (1699–1758)* (Twickenham: Orleans House Gallery, 1999), 22.

[6] William Kent, 'Woman with three owls', undated, pen and brown wash over pencil, 22.4 × 19.3 cm, Trustees of the Chatsworth Settlement, Witt, album 26a, image 65, negative number 835/25(35). The image is reproduced in W. K. Wimsatt, *The Portraits of Alexander Pope* (New Haven and London: Yale University Press, 1965), 131, example 6.

FIGURE 26.2 Lady Dorothy Savile, Countess of Burlington, *Profile sketch of Alexander Pope in an armchair holding a hand of cards*, undated, pen over pencil, 18.1 × 16.4 cm, Trustees of the Chatsworth Settlement

talons whilst watched over by two smaller owls, one beside her on another branch and one hovering above. The owl image is symbolic. Lady Burlington's studio, known as her 'Garden Room', 'Summer Parlour', or 'Dressing Room', was adorned with the motif of an owl, a reference to the Savile family crest, thus 'defining it as her individual space' (De Novellis, 9) The owl was also the symbol of Pallas Athene or Minerva. Grotesque, satirical, and ugly, the oddness of this image, and others like it in the Chatsworth archives, led William Kurtz Wimsatt to call it a self-portrait and attribute it to Lady Burlington herself on the basis that its style is 'more grotesque and derisive, than the soft and professionally graceful washes of Kent' and that such pictures 'seem the work of a feminine, if somewhat macabre and cruel imagination'.[7] Whichever way we attribute these images—De Novellis's argument for Kent is more compelling (De Novellis, 18)— the fact remains that the association of women and satirical excess is uncomfortable. Pallas Athene is the goddess of wisdom, science, and war, but in Pope's *Dunciad* her symbol also becomes the Grub-Streetian owls, 'appropriated to Dulness as emblems of pompous and boring stupidity'.[8]

---

[7] Wimsatt, *Portraits of Pope*, 123.   [8] Pope, *Poems* (Longman), iii. 21.

These three examples of informal portraits and caricatures are each, to some degree, concerned with ideas to do with private space and public art: the instability of generic categorization; professional artistry and amateur draughtsmanship; representation and self-regard. This chapter explores the image of women looking at themselves and being observed by others in a significant body of satirical writing by women writers in the 1730s, 1740s, and 1750s. Though Swift famously observed that satire 'is a sort of Glass, wherein Beholders do generally discover every body's Face but their Own', these women did the opposite, often unflinchingly so, producing humane reflections on their personal appearances, and on their selves.[9] Like the images by or of the Countess of Burlington, the voices recorded are wry, perhaps even rueful; fun to the point of extravagance; spontaneous and quick; accomplished yet still experimental about the possibilities of what it means to be a woman author or artist. For Lord Shaftesbury, who linked self-reflection and the philosophical agent, philosophy was a civilizing process: 'To philosophize, in a just signification,' he wrote, 'is but to carry good breeding up a step higher.'[10] Self-knowledge through conversation, either with oneself or with others, is a motif of Shaftesbury's thinking and this kind of introspection is replicated throughout satirical verse, particularly that by women. Conversation takes place through the medium of the interlocutor in verse epistles; as answers to previous poems; through voicing the characters of different people (sometimes ventriloquizing, just as the Countess of Burlington mimicked Pope's voice); as the voice of the poet within the poem; and as translation and imitation.

Strictly speaking, satire is overwhelming a masculine genre in the period. In her overview of the practice of satire between 1658 and 1770 in England, Ashley Marshall concludes that 'only a relatively tiny number of women tried their hands at satire in the eighteenth century' and 'on the whole, sociomoral commentary and personal sparring are more prominent than political polemic.'[11] Charles A. Knight provides a compelling reason for why this is the case when he writes that 'satire is a transgressive genre, based on the socially objectionable element of attack, often personal attack. If it often requires male satirists to take a defensive, apologetic position, it places women, who assume a suspicious position even as writers, in a nearly untenable role.'[12] As Mary Barber puts it in the 'Preface' to her *Poems on Several Occasions* (1734), '*a Woman steps out of her Province whenever she presumes to write for the Press*'. Indeed, her excuse for writing is the domestic one of aiming to form the minds of her children through setting moral precepts in verse.[13] Satire is indeed a masculine genre at this moment in history.

---

[9] Jonathan Swift, 'The Battel of the Books', Swift, *Works* (Cambridge), i. 142.

[10] Anthony Ashley Cooper, 3rd Earl of Shaftesbury, *Characteristics of Men, Manners, Opinions, Times*, ed. Lawrence E. Klein (Cambridge: Cambridge University Press, 1999), 407.

[11] Ashley Marshall, *The Practice of Satire in England 1658–1770* (Baltimore: Johns Hopkins University Press, 2013), 28, 314, n. 43.

[12] Charles A. Knight, *The Literature of Satire* (Cambridge: Cambridge University Press, 2004), 6–7, quoted in Paul Baines, 'Female Satirists of the Eighteenth Century', in *A Companion to British Literature, Volume III: Long Eighteenth-Century Literature 1660–1837*, ed. Robert DeMaria Jr (Chichester: John Wiley, 2014), 95–112, at 96.

[13] Mary Barber, *Poems on Several Occasions* (1734), xvii.

Nevertheless, we can find female writers trying out the satirical voice in the period. We are not dealing with formal translations from the most obvious Latin satirical texts of Juvenal and Horace here but with a more equivocal tone of writing that resists and tests a reigning culture of politeness, using caricature, hyperbole, and outright invective to challenge presiding notions of femininity and the idea of the woman author. The context of misogynistic satire of the period meant that all women writers were to varying degrees conscious of personal ridicule.[14] Women in these poems are often depicted as readers of literature and interpreters of meaning who engage with, play against, and often subtly subvert masculine literary forms of Classical translation, pastoral romance, and Petrarchan sonnet. In short, satire is, as Paula Backscheider has remarked, 'that vexed form that becomes more vexed when women write it'.[15]

THE BASHFUL MUSE: MARY WORTLEY MONTAGU AND ELIZABETH THOMAS

In Swift's 'The Lady's Dressing Room', Strephon, who has stolen into Celia's boudoir, makes an 'Inventory' of her 'Litter'.[16] In the manner of a tabloid journalist who gleefully rakes over a murky inner life whilst professing to be appalled by having to report upon such squalor, Strephon's mode of description is one of insinuation. The first garment for itemization is a 'dirty smock':

> *Strephon*, the Rogue, display'd it wide,
> And turn'd it round on every Side.
> On such a Point few Words are best,
> And *Strephon* bids us guess the rest.
>
> (lines 13–16)

Suggestion, of course, only amplifies the grimy atmosphere. The voice of Swift's poem, however, has no such delusions about the essential grubbiness of satire itself:

> To him that looks behind the Scene,
> *Satira*'s but some pocky Quean.
>
> (lines 133–4)

Modern editions of this poem often update the spelling here of 'queen' and thus lose the original pun: According to Johnson, a '*quean*' is a 'worthless woman, generally a

---

[14] For an overview of 'women in the myth of satire', see Felicity Nussbaum, *The Brink of All We Hate: English Satires on Women, 1660–1750* (Lexington: University Press of Kentucky, 1984), in particular, 18–20.
[15] Paula R. Backscheider, *Eighteenth-Century Women Poets and Their Poetry: Inventing Agency, Inventing Genre* (Baltimore: Johns Hopkins University Press, 2005), xxi.
[16] 'The Lady's Dressing Room', Swift, *Poems* (Williams), ii. 526, lines 10, 8.

strumpet'.[17] Such a conflation is compounded by adjectival confusion, also, as 'pocky' might refer to smallpox or to venereal disease. Satira also recalls Statira, the heroine of Nathaniel Lee's bombastic heroic tragedy *The Rival Queens* (1677). Such confusions of register suit Swift's insinuations of bathos: the figurehead of satire is at once a victim of faded grandeur and a ravaged dissolute. Such satire challenges prevailing notions of politeness but it cannot easily distinguish itself from its filthy surroundings.

Lady Mary Wortley Montagu's satire often works as the echo of an earlier male satirist's voice and she famously responded to Swift's poem with 'The Reasons that Induced Dr S[wift] to write a Poem call'd the Lady's Dressing room'. In it, the curtain that Swift had supposedly drawn back to reveal the vile inner sanctum of Celia's toilette is pulled back even further to imagine a prelude to the original poem's story in which the described filthiness of Celia's closet is male revenge for female sexual resistance:

> I'll be reveng'd you saucy Quean,
> (Replys the disapointed Dean)
> I'll so describe your dressing room
> The very Irish shall not come.
> She answer'd short, I'm glad you'l write,
> You'l furnish paper when I shite.[18]

Montagu invokes Swift's own term of 'Quean' (not to mention the fact that '*Celia* shits')[19] but balances it within the parenthetical reply of the 'disapointed Dean', who in turn is compared with the woman who 'answer'd short'. The incompletion of the word 'shite' in the printed edition of 1734 maintains a certain decorum belied by its own transparency, making Celia's verbal shortness a visual joke about brevity and wit rather than inadequacy.

The discrepancy between the idealized version of femininity and its inverse (queen/quean) that both poets highlight is a feature of Montagu's later poem, 'Satturday The Small Pox', which again provides the viewpoint of a woman, Flavia, who is observed at third hand. She is described as a victim of the effects of smallpox:

> A Glass revers'd in her right hand she bore;
> For now she shunn'd the Face she sought before [...]
> Far from my Sight that killing Picture bear,
> The Face disfigure, or the Canvas tear!
> That Picture, which with Pride I us'd to show,
> The lost ressemblance but upbraids me now [...]
> Ye, Operas, Circles, I no more must view!
> My Toilette, Patches, all the Wo<rl>d Adieu![20]

[17] Samuel Johnson, *A Dictionary of the English Language*, 2 vols. (London: 1755), ii. 'Quean'.

[18] Lady Mary Wortley Montagu, *Essays and Poems and Simplicity: A Comedy*, ed. Robert Halsband and Isobel Grundy (Oxford: Clarendon Press, 2004), 276, lines 84–9.

[19] 'The Lady's Dressing Room', Swift, *Poems* (Williams), ii. 529, line 118.

[20] Montagu, 'Satturday The Small Pox Flavia', *Essays and Poems*, 201–4, lines 3–4, 43–6, 95–6.

Flavia refuses to look in the mirror at her ravaged face, though the pose of reversed mirror in hand dramatizes her rejection of external signs. Her call to destroy her real body or her represented one (face and canvas) makes the real and the represented equivalent in terms of societal worth. Like Wortley Montagu's response to Swift's dressing room poem 'Satturday' dramatizes a particular voice and is most effectively read within its setting as part of a series of 'Eclogues' (as Montagu called them) about different women (Roxana, Dancinda, Cardelia, Smilinda, Lydia) or commentary upon such women (such as the reported conversation of Patch and Silliander at St James's Coffee House).

Horace Walpole printed the 'Eclogues' in 1747.[21] As Paul Baines reminds us: 'Most of what Montagu did publish in satiric vein was unacknowledged...as the work of a woman. She wrote in male mode, complete with irreverence and bad language, but also as an aristocrat who largely avoided the contaminations of print identity' (Baines, 103). The coterie world of her poetry meant that there was often a slippage between Montagu's poetic persona and real-life personality that could be problematic as much as productive. Montagu had contracted smallpox in 1715 and survived. During her absence from court, however, these satiric poems were circulated without her permission and one in particular ('Monday Roxana, or the Drawing-room') was interpreted as an attack on Princess Caroline. A reading, which as Isobel Grundy rightly notices in her *ODNB* entry on Montagu, 'disregards the fact that the "attack" is voiced by a character who is heavily satirized'. This disregard is noticeable because ventriloquism is an inherent part of Montagu's poetry. As critics have noted, *Verses Address'd to the Imitator of the First Satire of the Second Book of Horace*, is to a large extent an experiment in parodying Pope's voice in order to make a wider point about his failure to emulate successfully his satiric forefathers.[22] Though 'Satturday' is often read in the context of Montagu's actual experience of suffering from smallpox, in the 'Eclogues' we overhear soliloquies or conversations that cumulatively discourage one single portrait of what women represent. As Halsband and Grundy note about these poems, they are the product of Wortley Montagu's experimentation 'with "mock" forms for several years' (*Essays and Poems*, 182). Though the voices of some of the characters can be identified with real people they are also about the pastoral relationship between women and nature more generally. A measure of their ironic indirection can be ascertained by the way in which the couplet, 'Has Love no pleasures free from Guilt or Fear? / Pleasures less feirce, more lasting, more sincere?', in 'Wednesday The Tête à Tête' (*Essays and Poems*, 189–93, lines 73–4) can be read in various ways: as a translation of Ovid's *Remedia Amoris*; as part of an argument Delia makes to her lover Strephon (in one version Strephon has to make his way down the back stairs when Delia's husband suddenly returns and in another

---

[21] Though they mostly circulated in manuscript during Montagu's lifetime Edmund Curll illicitly printed three of the six poems in 1716.

[22] See Donna Landry, 'Alexander Pope, Lady Mary Wortley Montagu, and the Literature of Social Comment', in *The Cambridge Companion to English Literature, 1650–1740*, ed. Steven N. Zwicker (Cambridge: Cambridge University Press, 1998), 307–29, at 321.

Delia beds down for the night with her lover); and as echoed elsewhere by Montagu without this sense of dramatic irony (see *Essays and Poems*, 158).

Montagu's contemporary, Elizabeth Thomas, was also interested in satire yet unlike Montagu committed herself (albeit anonymously) to print. Her poetry is therefore often interested in the way that the impermanence of women's actual bodies can be offset by the durability of their artistic corpus. In '*To the most ingenious Mrs. Sarah Hoadley, excellent in Painting*', for example, Thomas's friend is exalted for her artistic talent partly because through this medium she can arrest the ravages of time:

> For when th' Original appears
> Quite alter'd, with the Weight of Years,
> No faint Remains of Beauty seen,
> Your Draughts, will shew, what once they've been.[23]

The poems in Thomas's printed collection of *Miscellany Poems* (1722) are highly aware of literary inheritance (particularly the influence of her friend, Dryden) and of the perils of a woman entering the literary marketplace. The idea of 'obscurity' is therefore continually weighed against the 'Terrours' of engaging with critics.[24] In a poem addressed to Lady Dowager De La Warr, '*On Her saying, I hid my Candle under a Bushel*', Thomas considers the reasons why she writes poetry that aims 'to reform this Age':

> And when we to the Press expose our Lays,
> We reap the *Criticks* Censure, not their Praise.
> By ev'ry wou'd-be-Writer, are we maul'd,
> And once in Print, can never be *recall'd*.
>
> (*Miscellany Poems*, 51)

Thomas's collection includes elegies to lost friends and panegyrics to living ones; translations from poets such as Horace and Anacreon and imitations of, for example, Spenser. In '*To William Atwood Esq; Chief Justice of New York, on some Verses He gave me*', the speaker of Thomas's poem admits (despite her 'blushing') to be 'ambitious now of Fame' which 'prompts' her 'to secure a deathless Name' (*Miscellany Poems*, 64).

For all of its confident self-attention, Thomas's poetry is marked out by what Baines has described as 'a vein of wry self-deprecation' (Baines, 104). The satiric impulse to mend the age and curb individual vanity is apparent in many of Thomas's poems, a small number of which outwardly label themselves as satire. '*The true Effigies of a Certain Squire: Inscribed to Clemena*' is one such poem in which the muse is called to help the poet draw the picture of a '*Rake* and *Clown*' and '*Ape* and *Knave*'. The result is pure caricature; a 'hideous *Medley*' of a human creature is compiled (*Miscellany Poems*, 81). An invocation to the muse contains the impetus of the poem's composition: '*Revenge thy Self*, with Satyr arm thy Quill; / Display the Man, yet own a Justice still' (80). The ridiculous

---

[23] [Elizabeth Thomas], *Miscellany Poems on Several Subjects* (1722), 12–14, 14.
[24] See *Miscellany Poems*, 49, 51, 201, and 259–61.

fop is also given a speech in which he equates a woman's 'Closet stuff'd with Books' with 'silly Toys'. Learned women are called 'but learned Fools' who make themselves 'look old, and ugly' in their 'Prime' (82) and whose defence of reading is interpreted as a disguise for unwomanly defiance:

> Perhaps you'll say, in Books you Virtue learn,
> And by right Reason, *Good* from *Ill* discern:
> Ha ha, believe me, *Virtue's* but Pretence
> To cloak Hypocrisy and Insolence:
> Let Woman mind her *Oeconomick* Care,
> And let the Man what he thinks fit prepare:
> (What he thinks fit, I say, or please to spend,
> For those are Fools, that on their Wives depend.)
> Nor need they musty Books to pass their Time,
> There's twenty Recreations more sublime.
>
> (*Miscellany Poems*, 83)

By mimicking the voice and demeanour of this 'ignoble Wretch, this less than Man' (*Miscellany Poems*, 84), the poet means to make her friend, Clemena, laugh. Her impersonation of absurd masculinity in this poem recalls the moment in Richardson's *Sir Charles Grandison* (1753–4) when Harriet Byron, who has had an argument with the priggish Mr Walden on the subject of female learning, looks at her image in a mirror and attempts to recreate his facial tics:

> I have been making mouths in the glass for several minutes, to try to recover some of Mr. Walden's [features], in order to describe them to you, Lucy; but I cannot for my life so distort my face as to enable me to give you a notion of one of them.[25]

The mirror is not associated with female vanity here but with the representation of male farcicality. Both poem and novel use moments of mimicry to comment upon the absurdities of male condemnation of women's learning. The fact that both writings are framed as jokes shared with an understanding female interlocutor demonstrates how women's satire often addressed itself to a sympathetic circle of interpretation where conversation helps to negotiate public and private worlds. Just as Arbuthnot is the foil to Pope's confessional strain in *An Epistle to Dr Arbuthnot*, the woman writer's female interlocutor represents a private intimacy that grounds the public poet within a sympathetic social and moral milieu. Thomas's verse letter to another female poet, Mary, Lady Chudleigh (1656–1710), laments the lack of support for women from male writers, in whose responses '*Malignant* Humour lurk'd in ev'ry Line'.[26] What saves her from despair and apathy at the challenge of taking on male injustice is the wit and learning of Chudleigh's example.

---

[25] Samuel Richardson, *Sir Charles Grandison*, ed. Jocelyn Harris, 3 vols. (Oxford: Oxford University Press, 1972), i. 46.

[26] 'To the Lady Chudleigh, The Anonymous Author of the Lady's Defence', *Miscellany Poems*, 146.

Thomas was later portrayed by Pope as 'Curl's Corinna' in *The Dunciad* in revenge for her selling Edmund Curll some of his letters.[27] As Valerie Rumbold has noted, Pope's now famous designation of Thomas was hurtful 'because aimed at her conception of herself as a writer' (Dryden gave her the name Corinna).[28] Even before *The Dunciad* slur the *Miscellany Poems* register Thomas's sense of how the woman writer is an object of fascination at best and the subject of attack at worst. In '*On Sir J—S— saying in a sarcastick Manner, My Books would make me Mad. An* ODE' she writes that if a woman 'enquire[s] for a *Book*, / Beyond a *Novel*, or a *Play*':

> *Good Lord!* how soon th' Alarms took
> How soon your Eyes, your Souls betray,
> And with what Spite ye look!
> How nat'rally ye stare and scowl,
> Like wond'ring *Birds* about an *Owl*,
> And with malicious Sneer, these dismal Accents howl.
>
> (*Miscellany Poems*, 184)

The learned female reader is met with both discouraging looks and voices (scowls and howls). Just as Thomas ventriloquized the voice of the fop so here she mimics the voices of a misogynous society that is wary of women's reading and, by implication, female individuality. As Catherine Ingrassia has argued, to a woman like Thomas, who was 'buffeted by illness, economic instability and imprisonment', books offered 'continuity, familiar narratives and a provisionally stable identity within a largely fragmented world'.[29] As both material entity and cultural capital, books are intrinsically part of Thomas's narrated personality: '[Her] attention to the book and the library, like the very act of self-narration, emerges as an attempt to fix identity on something…recognize[d] as stable' (Ingrassia, 314). Like the picture of Lady Burlington surrounded by owls the imagery used here is equivocal and plays on the double meaning of the owlish woman as both intellectually wise and freakishly bookish.

THE AUTOBIOGRAPHICAL IMPULSE: MARY BARBER, ELIZABETH TEFT, AND MARY LEAPOR

In Swift's analogy quoted above, the image of the mirror indicates satire's representative folly (a mirror that reflects society's flaws before the writer's own). In contrast, Pope in

---

[27] Pope, *Poems* (Twickenham), ii. 738, line 70. On the sale of Pope's letters, see Paul Baines and Pat Rogers, *Edmund Curll, Bookseller* (Oxford: Oxford University Press, 2007), 173.

[28] Valerie Rumbold, *Women's Place in Pope's World* (Cambridge: Cambridge University Press, 1989), 164.

[29] Catherine Ingrassia, 'Elizabeth Thomas, Laetitia Pilkington and Competing Currencies of the Book', *Women's Writing* 23 (2016), 312–32, at 313.

his first Horatian imitation writes that the mirror's reflection of his flaws is 'proof of his complete self-disclosure and sentimental transparency':[30]

> In me what Spots (for Spots I have) appear,
> Will prove at least the Medium must be clear
> In this impartial Glass, my Muse intends
> Fair to expose myself, my Foes, my Friends.[31]

Pope's act of self-disclosure uses the mirror as a device of unbiased observance in such a way that connects with philosophical writing of the period. Lawrence E. Klein has written of Shaftesbury, that 'he was original in conceiving the pursuit of self-knowledge as a procedure of inner conversation' and that in his *Characteristics of Men, Manners, Opinions, Times* he 'elaborated extensively on the technique of talking to oneself, but he also used dialogic patterns...to illustrate and underpin his point' (*Characteristics*, viii). In elucidating his philosophy of conversation, Shaftesbury gives the example of Plato's *Dialogues* which he argues 'were either real dialogues or recitals of such personated discourses, where the persons themselves had their characters preserved throughout...by this means they not only taught us to know others, but, what was...of highest virtue... they taught us to know ourselves' (87). He draws an analogy between this work and 'a looking-glass' where we 'discover ourselves and see our minutest features nicely delineated and suited to our own apprehension and cognizance':

> No one who was ever so little a while an inspector could fail of becoming acquainted with his own heart. And – what was of singular note in these magical glasses – it would happen that, by constant and long inspection, the parties accustomed to the practice would acquire a peculiar speculative habit, so as virtually to carry about with them a sort of pocket-mirror, always ready and in use.   (*Characteristics*, 87)

If the function of the mirror in Pope's poem is to expose his moral defects as well as his physical deformity then the parenthetical emphasis of his imperfections ('for Spots I have') somewhat diminishes the quality of this confession. The fact that spots can be meant to mean moral flaws, blemishes of appearance, and fashionable beauty spots further complicates this act of self-disclosure, especially since Pope uses the word in 'Of The Characters of Women' to talk about the 'charms' of women as the result of such visual defectiveness: 'Their happy Spots the nice admirer take, / Fine by defect, and delicately weak.'[32]

The image of the looking glass as used by women poets to express the relationship between self-reflection and self-realization is similarly rarely untroubled. Contemporary

---

[30] Helen Deutsch, 'Pope, Self, and World', in *The Cambridge Companion to Alexander Pope*, ed. Pat Rogers (Cambridge: Cambridge University Press, 2008), 14–24, at 18.

[31] Pope, 'The First Satire of the Second Book of Horace Imitated', in *Poems* (Twickenham), iv. 9–11, lines 55–8.

[32] Pope, 'To a Lady. Of The Characters of Women', in Pope, *Poems* (Twickenham), III.ii, 53, lines 42, 43–4.

images of women looking in mirrors more often than not emblemized the toilette as a site of female sexuality and vanity (indeed Swift's famous mirror analogy alludes to Roger L'Estrange's comment that 'a *Wicked Generation* will no more bear *Truth*, in a *Book*, than an *Ill-favour'd Woman* will bear it, in her *Picture*, or in her *Looking-Glass*').[33] The mirror is a complex metaphor, which often provokes, as is the case with Mary Barber's '*To Mrs*. Frances-Arabella Kelly', dismal thoughts about old age:

> TO Day, as at my Glass I stood,
> To set my Head-cloaths, and my Hood;
> I saw my grizzled Locks with Dread,
> And call'd to mind the *Gorgon*'s Head.[34]

Barber's poem invokes many voices: that of the older poet herself; the 'witty Coxcombs' who deride ageing women—'*Rot that old Witch—she'll never die*' (152); Ovid as originator of one version of the Gorgon myth—though he was too 'well-bred' to call Medusa 'old' (151). Yet most of the poem is taken up with the words of the speaker's younger addressee, Frances-Arabella Kelly whose 'lovely Face' (she imagines her saying to herself) 'Will never suffer such Disgrace' (152). Kelly is presented as rejecting the '*Memento mori*' of her older friend and ascribing it to jealousy:

> Her Envy, now, I plainly see,
> Makes her inscribe those Lines to me.
> These Beldams, who were born before me,
> Are griev'd to see the Men adore me:
> Their snaky Locks freeze up the Blood;
> My Tresses fire the purple Flood.[35]

The image of the 'purple Flood' is flagrantly sexual. Kelly is imagined looking at herself in the mirror but her glance is fleeting and noticeably unreflective in the most obvious sense ('A[nd], as along the Room you pass, / Casting your Eye upon the Glass', 152). The ending of three consecutive lines with 'me' reinforces this self-obsession, which by the end of the poem becomes undisguised despotism: 'Heav'n gave me Charms, and destin'd me / For universal Tyranny' (153). Whereas Pope's Belinda in *The Rape of the Lock* is drawn to look at her image by a magnetic pull of passive admiration—'A heav'nly Image in the Glass appears, / To that she bends, to that her Eyes she rears'[36]—Kelly's gaze at herself and at others is strikingly self-possessed as the emphasis on her pronoun suggests: 'I own, of Conquest I am vain, / Tho' I despise the Slaves I gain' (153).

---

[33] A visual example is John Faber the Younger's mezzotint after Philippe Mercier of a young woman en déshabillé regarding herself in the mirror (1739), British Museum, number 1875,0710.2850, with its not so subtle double entendre on 'two Globes'. Roger L'Estrange, quoted by Marcus Walsh, Swift, *Works* (Cambridge), i. 465, n. 1.

[34] *Poems on Several Occasions*, 151.   [35] *Poems on Several Occasions*, 152–3.

[36] *Rape of the Lock*, in Pope, *Poems* (Twickenham), ii. 155, Canto I, lines 125–6.

In another depiction of self-scrutiny using the mirror motif, Elizabeth Teft's sonnet 'On Orinthia *viewing herself in a* Glass' starts with a series of interrogations that are remarkably honest about the speaker's lack of physical charm:

> WAS Nature angry when she form'd my Clay?
> Or, urg'd by Haste to finish, cou'd not stay?
> Or drest with all her Store some perfect she,
> So lavish there, she'd none to spare for me?[37]

This is a disarmingly frank assessment of her physical appearance. The volta of the poem rests on the conceit of the mirror hearing the speaker's voice articulate the moral of the poem, which is conveyed as a hope rather than an expectation:

> Since here defective, Heav'n, be so kind
> With never-fading Charms to dress my Mind![38]

Just as Lady Burlington's owl-adorned studio functioned in a variety of ways, including as her dressing room, so the dressing of body and mind contrasted by Teft often took place within the same surroundings. Tita Chico writes of how women 'regularly used their dressing rooms for solitary activities such as reading and writing' so that 'the dressing-room-as-study conjoined a signifier for female sexuality with the material circumstances for female knowledge production'.[39] Teft, about whom little is known other than that she was from Lincoln and published *Orinthia's Miscellanies* in 1747, describes the mirror in this poem as 'self-surveyed' (54), a compound that both suggests self-regard's intimate reflexivity and the distance of observation. In another poem in the same collection, 'On Learning. *Desired by a* Gentleman', the speaker of the poem is again aware of a lack, in this case of education rather than beauty. Yet despite envying men for their knowledge of Latin, Greek, and Hebrew, the speaker is content to want learning rather than be 'Martial': 'methinks I wou'd not be a Man / . . . I'd rather be the foolish Thing I am' (*Orinthia's Miscellanies*, 9).

There are hints here of the kind of self-depreciation that a satirical poet such as Mary Leapor would develop with more confidence in her posthumously published *Poems Upon Several Occasions* (1748). 'Dorinda *at her Glass*' is consciously reminiscence of Pope's Belinda and 'Of the Characters of Women', as well as John Gay's eclogue, 'The Toilette'. Dorinda, who was once 'the fairest of the Train', now sees her beauty fade and 'the last Sparkles tremble in her Eye':

> To her lov'd Glass repair'd the weeping Maid,
> And with a Sigh address'd the alter'd Shade.[40]

---

[37] Elizabeth Teft, *Orinthia's Miscellanies: Or, A Compleat Collection of Poems* (1747), 54.
[38] *Orinthia's Miscellanies*, 54.
[39] Tita Chico, *Designing Women: The Dressing Room in Eighteenth-Century English Literature and Culture* (Lewisburg: Bucknell University Press, 2005), 74.
[40] Mary Leapor, *Poems Upon Several Occasions* (1748), 1, 2, 3.

Augusta is called to strip the bright ribbons she continues to wear from her head, and in a beautifully realistic domestic detail, 'Change the lac'd Slipper of delicious Hue / For a warm Stocking, and an easy Shoe' (6). Leapor's own apparently awkward physical appearance became part of her posthumous identity as she was, according to a near-contemporary writer, 'extremely swarthy, and quite emaciated... much resembling, in shape, a bass-viol'.[41] The sense of Leapor's voice as much as her appearance being strikingly individual is a commonly held response to her work. In reviewing Roger Lonsdale's *Eighteenth-Century Women Poets* (1989), which did much to resurrect interest in the poet, Malcolm Rutherford observed that her writing is 'a combative, talkative, witty form of verse... quite as satirical as anything in Jane Austen's novels'.[42] More recently, Valerie Rumbold, in a reading of 'Crumble Hall', has memorably termed Leapor's persona the 'alienated insider'.[43]

A further volume of Leapor's *Poems* was printed in 1751 (by Samuel Richardson) and included the poem 'Mira's *Picture. A Pastoral'*. Mira was Leapor's faux-rustic pseudonym for herself and indeed a note to the end of the poem describes how '*This Description of her Person is a Caracature'*.[44] Rather than self-surveillance, the poem relies on a mock-pastoral encounter between Corydon, 'a harmless Shepherd Swain', and Phillario, 'From the great Mart of Business, and of Fame' (294). Instead of Arcadian nymphs the latter notices, 'With studious Brows, and Night-cap Dishabille' (295), a woman 'That looks a Stranger to the Beams of Day' (296). It transpires that this Mira has literary leanings and poetic ambitions:

> PHILLARIO.
> *She* read!—She'd better milk her brindled Cows:
> I wish the Candle does not singe her Brows,
> So like a dry Furze-faggot; and, beside,
> Not quite so even as a Mouse's Hide.
> CORYDON.
> Come, come; you view her with malicious Eyes:
> Her Shape——
> PHILLARIO.
> —Where Mountains upon Mountains rise!
> And, as they fear'd some Treachery at hand,
> Behind her Ears her list'ning Shoulders stand.[45]

The joke is not just on the discrepancy between Mira's dishevelled appearance and the idealized beauty of conventional pastoral heroines (alluded to in Corydon's abbreviated

[41] *Gentleman's Magazine*, 807, quoted in *ODNB*.

[42] Malcolm Rutherford, 'Light on Female Bards', *Financial Times* (16 December 1989), quoted in *The Works of Mary Leapor*, ed. Richard Greene and Ann Messenger (Oxford: Oxford University Press, 2003), xxix.

[43] Valerie Rumbold, 'The Alienated Insider: Mary Leapor in "Crumble Hall"', *British Journal for Eighteenth-Century Studies* 19 (1996), 63–76.

[44] Mary Leapor, *Poems Upon Several Occasions, The Second and Last Volume* (1751), 298.

[45] Leapor, *Poems* (1751), 297–8.

list of beauties: Daphne, Amynta, Delia, Cynthia, Claudia, Phillada, and Cymene) but also in the bathos of literary reference. The allusion to 'Mouse's Hide' recalls Swift's *A Beautiful Young Nymph Going to Bed*[46] just as the 'Mountains upon Mountains rise' brings to mind Pope's *An Essay on Criticism*, about the struggles of literary aspiration.[47] The conversation of Corydon and Phillario makes a mockery of serious poetry by its insistence on recording the truncations of higher register through everyday speech: "'Tis *Mira*, Daughter to a Friend of mine; / 'Tis she that makes your what-d'ye-call—your Rhyme' (296). Such examples bear out Fairer and Gerrard's assessment that it would be 'misleading to think of [Leapor] as a failed Pope' for it is 'in her discomposure—her unexpected juxtapositions, her ear for lively rhythms, and her off-centre angles of vision—that much of her power lies.'[48]

Leapor's early proponents were anxious about the way in which she and her poetry would be read. The 1751 edition of Leapor's poems includes a memoir written by her friend Bridget Freemantle (the 'Artemisia' of her poems) and several of her letters. An apology for publication to a certain extent, it also reflects the autobiographical packaging of much poetry published by women in the period. Self-satire can be seen in this light as interacting with the biographical impulse more generally at the time. In a 'Postscript' to her prefatory letter, Freemantle inserts a caveat about the inclusion of 'Mira's Picture' on the basis that it might 'give the Reader a worse Idea of her Person than it deserv'd'. 'The Poem', she continues, 'was occasioned by her happening to hear that a Gentleman who had seen some of her Poems, wanted to know what her Person was' (*Poems*, 1751, xxxii). It is an awkward statement about a poem that through its sheer enthusiasm for exaggeration celebrates oddity (a 'girl…something out o' the way') and seems, as Margaret Anne Doody has observed, 'to urge the female reader not to internalise these cultural definitions' concerning female beauty and literary intelligence.[49]

'MYSELF TOO PICTURED IN A MEZZOTINT': MARY JONES (1707–1778)

Mary Jones was a poet well placed to explore the complex nature of female personhood and authorial ambition. Connected to aristocratic circles yet not from a family of rank, she likened herself in 1734 to 'a Traveller or Pilgrim, wandering about from House to House, in order to partake of the Benevolence of…good People'.[50] This sense

---

[46] Swift, 'A Beautiful Young Nymph Going to Bed', in *Poems* (Williams), ii. 581, line 13.

[47] *An Essay on Criticism*, Pope, *Poems* (Twickenham), i. 265, line 232 ('Hills peep o'er Hills, and *Alps* on *Alps* arise!').

[48] *Eighteenth-Century Poetry: An Annotated Anthology*, ed. David Fairer and Christine Gerrard, 2nd edn. (Chichester: John Wiley, 2004), 309.

[49] Margaret Anne Doody, 'Women Poets of the Eighteenth Century', in *Women and Literature in Britain 1700–1800*, ed. Vivien Jones (Cambridge: Cambridge University Press, 2000), 217–37, at 226.

[50] Quoted in *Eighteenth-Century Women Poets: An Oxford Anthology*, ed. Roger Lonsdale (Oxford: Oxford University Press, 1989; repr. 1990), 155.

of inbetweenness lends her verse its unique satiric verve. In 'An Epistle to Lady Bowyer', Mary Jones professes herself to be conscious of the burden of poetic inheritance— 'Whilst lofty Pope erects his laurell'd head, / No lays, like mine, can live beneath his shade' she writes. Yet the itch to write is, she admits, irresistible:

> What's fame to me, who pray, and pay my rent?
> If my friends know me honest, I'm content.
>   Well, but the joy to see my works in print!
> My self too pictur'd in a Mezzo-Tint!
> The Preface done, the Dedication fram'd,
> With lies enough to make a Lord asham'd!
> Thus I step forth; an Auth'ress in some sort.[51]

Pope 'lisp'd in Numbers, for the Numbers came'[52] but Jones's reasons for writing are at once more flagrant ('to see my works in print') and more unstable (she is only authoress 'in some sort'). Jones is scathing in this poem about the world of courts and its obsequious flatterers, the queasy workings of patronage with its greasy dedications to nobles and kings (in a particularly arresting line she is forthrightly dismissive of those who 'smile lies, eat toads, or lick the dust', 7).[53] The voice of the poem is personal and, at least superficially, autobiographical:

> Of honest parents, not of great, I came;
> Not known to fortune, quite unknown to fame.
> Frugal and plain, at no man's cost they eat,
> Nor knew a baker's, or a butcher's debt.
>
>   (6–7)

Despite her lowly origins, by 1730 Jones was connected to members of Queen Caroline's circle through her friendships with Martha Lovelace and Charlotte Clayton, Lady Sundon (the 'Stella' of her verse). A poem addressed to Charlotte's daughter, Molly ('On her desiring the Author to write a Satire upon her'), begins with a resolve 'to rail' about 'female vice' (Miscellanies, 54, 55). The poet is likened to a painter whose 'finish'd draught' bears no resemblance to the 'beauteous frame' of its subject. This leads the poet to compare her young subject to Eve before the Fall:

> In Eden thus, its shades among,
>   Ere vice could fix a stain,
> The serpent roll'd his pointless tongue,
>   And hiss'd and twin'd in vain.
> Again fair virtue loves to dwell

---

[51] Mary Jones, Miscellanies In Prose and Verse (Oxford, 1750), 2–3.
[52] Pope, 'An Epistle to Dr. Arbuthnot', line 128.
[53] Notwithstanding this opinion, Jones's collection of poems includes a fulsome dedication 'To Her Royal Highness The Princess Royal And Of Orange', Miscellanies, iii.

> In your engaging form;
> As pure as *Eve* before she fell,
>   As free from inward storm.
> Keen satire now, with soften'd gaze,
>   Unbends her wrinkled brow;
> And looks serenely gen'rous praise,
>   Who never prais'd till now.[54]

The figure of Eve was a staple of anti-women satire in the period. Felicity Nussbaum writes that women are often depicted in such satires as 'Eve's daughters, dangerous temptresses who seduce men and lead them to irrationality, immortality, and even death' (Nussbaum, 27). Here, though, Jones chooses to focus on the moment before the Fall, before 'vice could fix a stain' and when Eve is still 'free from inward storm'. This picture of innocence allows the satirist to shift from criticism to admiration. The way that Jones can unbend her own poetic voice from satirical attack to feeling praise heightens the generic uncertainties of the poem's form.

In a comparable way, 'After the Small Pox' is a gentle and confident counterpoint to the stronger emotions of Montagu's earlier poem on the same subject. It addresses Charlotte Clayton who (according to the evidence of other poems in the collection) contracted smallpox and was marked by it in various senses.[55] Whereas Montagu's victim shuns her own reflection, the representation of women's exterior and interior selves in Jones's poem is more diffuse as the poem employs a range of voices. In three parts, the first stanza sets up the idea of the signs hung out by various merchants (vintners, haberdashers, shoemakers, and tailors) '[e]xpressive of the goods within' ('grapes', 'thread and tapes', 'boots', 'tatter'd suits') whilst the second stanza compares these advertisements to those of 'the nymph divine':

> For what is Beauty but a Sign?
> A face hung out, thro' which is seen
> The nature of the goods within.[56]

The economics of beauty are starkly portrayed. Jones goes on to enumerate the various different types of women and their individual emblems: the coquet with 'smiles, and forward airs' (79); the prude with her frowns; and, most singularly, 'she alone' whose graces are worn as 'a sample in her face'. The last verse deserves to be quoted in full:

> What tho' some envious folks have said,
> That *Stella* now must hide her head,
> That all her stock of beauty's gone,
> And ev'n the very sign took down:
> Yet grieve not at the fatal blow;
> For if you break a while, we know,
> 'Tis bankrupt like, more rich to grow.

[54] *Miscellanies*, 55–6.   [55] See *Miscellanies*, 114–16.   [56] *Miscellanies*, 79.

> A fairer sign you'll soon hang up,
> And with fresh credit open shop:
> For nature's pencil soon shall trace,
> And once more finish off your face,
> Which all your neighbours shall out-shine,
> And of your Mind remain the Sign.[57]

Jones plays with what it means both financially and personally to be bankrupt: to be unable to pay outstanding debts, 'bereft of a quality that one formerly had', and '[d]rained of mental, emotional, or physical resources' (*OED* definitions 2a and 2b). In '*An* Epistle *to Lady* Bowyer', Jones wrote of how her parents knew neither 'fortune' nor 'fame' nor 'debt'. Here, a series of clichés linked to failed finances[58] makes its own point about the need for reconstructing value, especially the reconfiguration of the economics of female appearance.

Both Jones's poetry and correspondence parody the social condition of having to sit and listen to dominant and domineering voices, usually, though not exclusively, male. In this way her satire functions, much as that of Austen, by exposing the implicit comedy of fashionable converse. She describes herself as 'generally a Hearer in company, rather than a Speaker' and, on another occasion, writes about the sensitivity of her ears and hearing, comparing herself to Swift's Gulliver seeking the 'silent Society of his sorrel Mare'.[59] Such 'creations of the self as dramatic characters' was a technique that, as Paula Backscheider has argued, was 'especially liberating and enjoyable' for women, revealing much 'about gendering forces, and about each decade's dominant structures of feeling' (Backscheider, 19). The distance between the inane, sometimes offensive, polite conversation of her contemporaries, and the intelligence of her female circle, provoked Jones to be satirical. There were many 'Characters in Life' she wrote, 'whose Distresses rather destroy our Compassion, than awaken it'.[60] Her own network of friends made her more hopeful though:

> THE Pleasure, I receive from your Correspondence, is like that we find from some well reflecting Mirrour; which, whilst it points out any little Excellence of Feature, is as faithful in discovering a Pimple, or a Freckle. To such a Glass, who, in this progressive State of Good to Better, would not oft repair? Who, with high Desires, and Aims not short of fair Perfection, would not here adjust the doubtful Sentiment, call out the wrong Idea to the Test, and dress and decorate the Mind anew?[61]

Shaftesbury used the example of the mirror to demonstrate how we stage a conversation within the self in order to achieve social polish and develop subjectivity. This was, as

---

[57] *Miscellanies*, 80.
[58] Compare Joseph Thurston, *The Toilette* (1730), 14: 'Already too compleat is Beauty's Store, / And Bankrupt Nature can afford no more'.
[59] Mary Jones to Miss Lovelace, 30 October 1736 and 8 September 1733, *Miscellanies*, 334, 296.
[60] Mary Jones to Miss Lovelace, 30 October 1736, *Miscellanies*, 336.
[61] Mary Jones to Mrs *******, 7 March 1743, *Miscellanies*, 251–2.

many critics have argued, part of a 'Whig project of sociability'.[62] Jones's mirror points out both beauties and blemishes and as a symbol of letter-writing exchange encourages its participants to civilize each other, in a process of what Shaftesbury would call 'amicable collision' (*Characteristics*, 31). Yet there is also wry humour in perfection being personified as 'fair' and the mind's reformation couched in terms of dress and decoration. Elsewhere in her letters, Jones professed to be more interested in 'learning to undress my self' than making her appearance better for show; she would, she admitted, 'rather have my Apron rumpled, than suffer the least discomposure of Mind'.[63]

Sometime around 1737, Mary Jones wrote to a friend in the hope that she would be dealt with gently by posterity. When 'I'm no more', she wrote, and 'when all that remains of me...shall be bound together in one miscellaneous Volume...cast a favourable Eye upon the doubtful page, and treat my Ashes with respect'.[64] The women writers discussed in this chapter are acutely aware of their public image as authors and their personal appearance as women. Like Lady Dorothy Savile at her easel they are conscious in different ways both of how they are represented as artists and how they represent alternative selves through their artistic corpus. The voice of female satire is one involved in a continual process of forming and reforming the self.

SELECT BIBLIOGRAPHY

Backscheider, Paula R. *Eighteenth-Century Women Poets and Their Poetry: Inventing Agency, Inventing Genre* (Baltimore: Johns Hopkins University Press, 2005).

Chico, Tita. *Designing Women: The Dressing Room in Eighteenth-Century English Literature and Culture* (Lewisburg: Bucknell University Press, 2005).

De Novellis, Mark. *Pallas Unveil'd: The Life and Art of Lady Dorothy Savile, Countess of Burlington (1699–1758)* (Twickenham: Orleans House Gallery, 1999).

Doody, Margaret Anne. 'Women Poets of the Eighteenth Century', in *Women and Literature in Britain 1700–1800*, ed. Vivien Jones (Cambridge: Cambridge University Press, 2000), 217–37.

Ingrassia, Catherine. 'Elizabeth Thomas, Laetitia Pilkington and Competing Currencies of the Book', *Women's Writing* 23 (2016), 312–32.

Landry, Donna. 'Alexander Pope, Lady Mary Wortley Montagu, and the Literature of Social Comment', in *The Cambridge Companion to English Literature, 1650–1740*, ed. Steven N. Zwicker (Cambridge: Cambridge University Press,1998), 307–29.

Mee, Jon. *Conversable Worlds: Literature, Contention, and Community 1762 to 1830* (Oxford: Oxford University Press, 2011).

Nussbaum, Felicity. *The Brink of All We Hate: English Satires on Women, 1660–1750* (Lexington: University Press of Kentucky, 1984).

Rumbold, Valerie. 'The Alienated Insider: Mary Leapor in "Crumble Hall"', *British Journal for Eighteenth-Century Studies* 19 (1996), 63–76.

Rumbold, Valerie. *Women's Place in Pope's World* (Cambridge: Cambridge University Press, 1989).

---

[62] For a discussion of such 'paradigms of conversability', see Jon Mee, *Conversable Worlds: Literature, Contention, and Community 1762 to 1830* (Oxford: Oxford University Press, 2011), 37–90, especially 45–6.

[63] Mary Jones to Miss Lovelace, 27 November 1736, *Miscellanies*, 338, 339.

[64] Mary Jones to Miss Lovelace, [Undated], *Miscellanies*, 366. The letter's approximate year of composition can be inferred from its position within the collection.

CHAPTER 27

'LITTLE SNARLING LAPDOGS'

Satire and Domesticity

MELINDA ALLIKER RABB

'DOMESTIC happiness, thou only bliss / Of Paradise that has survived the Fall', enthused William Cowper in a poem inspired by that epitome of drawing room comfort, the sofa.[1] Jane Austen echoes Cowper when Fanny Price is rewarded with Edmund Bertram in *Mansfield Park*'s Edenic close: 'the happiness of the married cousins must appear as secure as earthly happiness can be. Equally formed for domestic life...their home was the home of affection and comfort.'[2] Yet some irony attends the allusions to *Paradise Lost* in both examples of 'happiness'. Milton's distinctive blank verse 'that with no middle flight intend[ed] to soar' now finds its subject in a piece of bourgeois upholstery.[3] Austen's heroine must first endure 'the evils of home' during her purgatorial stay in Portsmouth. She and cousin Edmund, who resemble the biblical first couple insofar as they share a common gene pool, retreat from disillusionment in a society of failed innocence to the edge of the family estate, rather than having 'the World...all before them'.[4] Domesticity as an ideal is no doubt a project of increasing significance during the eighteenth century. Yet, like all ideals, its disappointing human realities are hard to ignore, inevitably provoking, as failed standards of perfection often do, the frustration and anger of satire.

In some contexts, the excerpts from *The Task* and *Mansfield Park* provide evidence of the separation of public and private spheres—the historical trajectory of the eighteenth century proposed and debated for the past several decades by many critics including

---

[1] William Cowper, *The Task and Selected Other Poems*, ed. James Sambrook (London: Longman, 1994), 113.
[2] Jane Austen, *Mansfield Park*, ed. Claudia L. Johnson (New York and London: Norton & Co, 1998), 321.
[3] John Milton, *Paradise Lost*, ed. Alistair Fowler (Harlow: Longman, 1968), 42.
[4] Milton, *Paradise Lost*, 642.

Michael McKeon in *The Secret History of Domesticity*: 'the coalescence of the category of domesticity is perhaps [the] most visible and resonant expression' of the public/private divide. McKeon argues along Marxist lines that the 'state as family' is transformed to the 'family as state'.[5] The reversal leads to the idealized 'intimate domain of the sphere of the modern conjugal family'. Alternatively, feminist critical paradigms and debates deriving from work on gender such as Nancy Armstrong's *Desire and the Domestic Novel*, deduce a programmatic re-gendering of power through the figure of woman in the roles of wife, daughter, sister, and mother.[6] These studies have had little interest in satire. Traditional literary histories of the long eighteenth century assert satire's decline after 1750 when creative energy shifts away from the public sphere described by Habermas and towards home, family, nature, individual subjectivity, and private feelings. Satiric paragon Gulliver must go home at the end of his voyages, but his nausea at the dining table is iconic of domestic dysfunction: better straw in the stable than the cushions of a Cowper-like easy chair. Lord Chesterfield remarked retrospectively at mid-century, 'An English minister shall have resided seven years at a Court . . . without being intimate or domestic in any one house'.[7]

   Although the satirist—aggressive, masculinized, uncivil—seems at first an intruder in the parlour, new discourses of domesticity do not displace so much as offer new opportunities to satire which insinuates itself into new modes of writing almost as soon as they are formed, and changes the shape they ultimately assume. The apparent shift during the later eighteenth century towards innovative experiments like the sentimental, the Gothic, the marriage-plot novel, and the romantic poem contain inherent and potentially pernicious ironies, especially when 'softer' emotions and 'noble' feelings are predicated on a degree of moral hypocrisy, on underlying economic pressures, on imperial ambition, and on reconfigured inequities of power. At what point then and in what ways does domesticity—the particular kind of domesticity we associate with the eighteenth century—become important to satirists? To what degree should we revise existing analytical binaries and historical assumptions? How do we get from Celia's dressing-room mirror in Swift's scatological poem to Sir Walter Elliot's dressing-room mirrors in Austen's *Persuasion*? Both domestic spaces contain ironic symbols of mortal and moral decay, whether a stinking chest full of excrement or a jar full of Gowland's cream.

   One approach would be to trace a century of satire by women, beginning with highly political scandal narratives by Aphra Behn, Delarivier Manley, and Eliza Haywood, and leading to marriage-plot novelists like Charlotte Lennox, Frances Burney, and Austen, as well as to 'working women' poets like Elizabeth Hands and Elizabeth Moody, for whom courtship, keeping house, and raising children offered opportunities for venting

---

   [5] Michael McKeon, *The Secret History of Domesticity: Public, Private, and the Division of Knowledge* (Baltimore: Johns Hopkins University Press, 2006), xix, 110.

   [6] Nancy Armstrong, *Desire and Domestic Fiction: A Political History of the Novel* (Oxford: Oxford University Press, 1990).

   [7] *Letters Written by the Late Honourable Philip Dormer Stanhope, Earl of Chesterfield to His Son*, 2 vols. (1774), ii. 124 (25 March 1751).

the spleen.[8] However, this chapter takes a broader view, in keeping with Samuel Johnson's definition of family: 'those who live in the same house'. The entire population under the same roof—the same *domus*—includes blood relations, servants, other dependants, and even pets. The emergence of the domestic sphere as a subject for satire in the latter half of the eighteenth century may be documented in writings concerned with this mixed population, especially with the precarious lives of dependants, servants, spinsters, illegitimate offspring, and other persons of socially ambiguous standing. At times, this circle widens to include guests, suitors, or friends—that is, people who temporarily enter the domestic dwelling in a personal relationship to its inhabitants, but have no formal authority there.

This chapter argues that such figures are crucial for understanding the relationship of satire to a changing cultural milieu. It argues further that representations of characters of little or no authority or power—such as Jonathan Swift's footman in *Directions to Servants* (1745), Jane Collier's household help in *The Art of Ingeniously Tormenting* (1753), Jane Austen's disenfranchised women in *Mansfield Park* (1814), Tobias Smollett's maiden-aunt, serving-woman, and illiterate bastard in *Humphry Clinker* (1771), and Frances Burney's 'nobodies' in her *Journals* and *Evelina* (1778) —develop two distinctive kinds of satiric fictions that test and criticize the idealization of domesticity. One of the deepest and most productive ironies about the household is that 'to domesticate' means to tame, to socialize, to make more docile and less 'other'—when in fact the array of individuals living in the same house are shown by satirists to embody cross-purposes, anti-social aggression, and insubordination.

THE EVILS OF HOME

A glance back at the 1720s (the decade of canonical satires by Bernard Mandeville, Swift, Alexander Pope, and John Gay) offers perspective. Mandeville achieved notoriety by twingeing two sensitive nerves of the same cultural organism: the philosophical threat posed by Hobbes and the social threat posed by the servant problem. How should we feel about being human and how should we negotiate the material circumstances of the world?

In the *Fable of the Bees*, the most cynical answers to these questions are not found during travels to remote regions such as Gulliver's or in apocalyptic fantasies like Pope's dunces or in prison cells with Gay's highwaymen and beggars. They are found at home in scenes that astutely analyse the intricacies of personal relationships within a household—often a tangled web of manipulation, rivalry, and collusion. When Mandeville attacks Sir Richard Steele's popular moralizing about the 'Excellency of human nature',

---

[8] See, for example, Melinda Rabb, 'Engendering Satire in the Long Eighteenth Century', in *The Cambridge Companion to Women's Writing in Britain, 1660–1789*, ed. Catherine Ingrassia (Cambridge: Cambridge University Press, 2015), 147–63.

he turns to domestic scenes like that of a little girl attempting her first clumsy bow. The episode implicates many household members and develops into a narrative of deepening cynicism as the adults conspire against the children by cultivating their naïve egotism. Seven little twists complicate the ironic 'plot': [1] 'the nurse falls in an extasie of praise; *There's a delicate curtsy! O fine Miss!* ... [2] *Mama! Miss can make a better curtsy than her sister Molly!* [3] The same is ecchod over by the maids, whilst Mama almost hugs the child to pieces; [4] only Miss Molly, who being four years older, knows how to make a very handsome curtsy ... is ready to cry at the Injustice that is done her, [5] till being whispered in the ear that it is only to please the Baby, and that she is a Woman; she grows proud at being let into the Secret, [6] and rejoicing at the Superiority of her Understanding, repeats what has been said with large Additions, and insults over the weakness of her Sister, [7] whom all this while she fancies to be the only Bubble among them'.[9] 'Tis the same with boys', Mandeville continues, when describing the means of making a gentleman out of a 'wild Brat':

> the Mother, to make him pull [his hat] off, tells him before he is two years old, that he is a Man, and if he repeats that Action when she desires him, he's presently a Captain, a Lord Mayor, a King, or something higher if she can think of it, till egg'd on by the force of praise, the little Urchin endeavors to imitate Man as well as he can, and strains all his Faculties to appear what his shallow noddle imagines he is believ'd to be.[10]

Disturbingly vivid scenes of home punctuate the *Fable* as well as the *Essay on Charity and Charity Schools* (1723). Mandeville exposes the untrustworthy motives that underlie apparent intimacy and affection.

Home also is no safe haven of physical safety. A baby drops into the fire, and when the family sow devours a toddler, Mandeville makes sure we hear the crunching of the bones. A well-known theory of satire, articulated in the work of Robert Elliott, is that it acts out symbolically the primitive impulse to kill an enemy.[11] Thus the vocabulary of slashing, cutting, piercing, and otherwise destroying the body is common among satirists 'armed for virtue', as Pope says. But the mutilation of infant flesh belongs in a class by itself. This chapter will mention several more examples in which the perverse 'dead baby joke' exerts a shock value that pushes the relationship between satire and domesticity to a moral limit. A world of savage indignation stands between Shakespeare's image of divine pity as a 'naked newborn babe striding the blast' and Jonathan Swift's image of Irish one-year-olds chopped up in a stew.

Mandeville is equally animated about another fraught domestic issue: servants, from whom 'all the comfort of life must arise'. More than Parliamentary struggles or wars fought on foreign soil, Mandeville indicts the local battles waged between masters and 'raw ignorant country wenches', 'boobily fellows', 'rogues ... not to be trusted', and 'sots'.

---

[9] Bernard Mandeville, *The Fable of the Bees*, edited with an introduction by Phillip Harth (London and New York: Penguin, 1989), 88–9.

[10] Mandeville, *Fable*, 90.

[11] Robert C. Elliott, *The Power of Satire: Magic, Ritual, Art* (Princeton: Princeton University Press, 1960).

His fulminations expose what proves to be a recurrent issue in satiric representations of the household—namely, that the mixture of conjugal family, dependants, guests, and servants epitomized a tension between the claims of blood, lineage, and family, on one hand, and claims of contract, consent, and partnership, on the other. These tensions over kinship versus contract had been acted out at the highest levels during the preceding century's crises of authority, succession, and transmission of power, and they find their way into the sitting room and scullery.[12]

Mandeville's satire is a vehicle for conservative worries about the precariousness of a shifting social order. The hired 'domestic' embodied the confused interdependencies of hierarchical culture. There were many grounds for anxiety: the boundaries between master and servant are permeable; servants are living parodies of their masters and mistresses; servants are really in charge; servants can pervert the children of the house; servants are careless of household goods; servants know the family's secrets and can betray them; servants, no matter how many chores need doing, can exercise the prerogative to leave. '[E]verything in the house is his perquisite', writes Mandeville, 'and he won't stay with you unless his vails [tips] are sufficient…and tho' you had taken him from the dung-hill, out of an hospital, or a prison, you shall never keep him longer than he can make of his place what in his high estimation of himself he shall think he deserves…servants in general are daily encroaching upon masters and mistresses, and endeavouring to be more level with them'. Thus Mandeville's work represents two aspects of the relationship between satire and domesticity, one is cognitive or psychological and manifests itself through the manipulation of thought, emotion, and personal identity; the other is about things, bodily functions, and the maintenance of the physical environment of daily life.

TORMENTING AND TORMENTED

Swift's *Directions to Servants* (1745) and Jane Collier's *An Essay on the Art of Ingeniously Tormenting* (1753) offer some points of comparison between these two aspects of satire and domesticity.[13] Both authors share the view that self-serving, not charity, begins at home. In the background of both texts is a long list of publications (counterparts to conduct books for the genteel) offering un-ironic instructions to servants, among which Eliza Haywood's *A Present for a Serving-Maid* (1743) is noteworthy. Haywood promotes an idealized version of domestic happiness, as indicated in her full title: 'Or, the Sure

---

[12] See Jeannie Dalporto, ed., *Essential Works for the Study of Early Modern Women, Part III, vol. 5: Women in Service in Early Modern England* (Aldershot: Ashgate, 2008); Tom Meldrum, *Domestic Service and Gender 1660–1750: Life and Work in the London Household* (Harlow: Longman, 2000); R. C. Richardson, *Household Servants in Early Modern England* (Manchester: Manchester University Press, 2010); Bridget Hill, *Servants: English Domestics in the Eighteenth Century* (Oxford: Clarendon Press, 1996); J. Jean Hecht, *The Domestic Servant in Eighteenth-Century England* (London: Routledge & Kegan Paul, 1956, repr. 1980).

[13] Swift, *Works* (Cambridge), ii. 433–524; Jane Collier, *An Essay on the Art of Ingeniously Tormenting*, ed. Katherine A. Craik (Oxford: Oxford University Press, 2006).

Means of gaining Love and Esteem…To which are added, Directions for going to Market: Also, For Dressing any Common Dish,…With some Rules for Washing, &c. The whole calculated for making the Mistress and the Maid happy'. Servants, in short, should embrace their subordination, bask in the pleasure of providing for others, and acquire the practical skills requisite for every domestic chore from judging a snipe by the vein under its wing (55) to washing silk stockings (74).[14] Swift and Collier attack this idealized notion of 'happy' power discrepancy in different ways.[15] The speaker of *Directions* is a former footman who offers advice on sixteen different categories of service, each capable of exploiting an employer. *An Essay*, in contrast, counsels employers on strategies for bringing misery to servants, as well as children, humble companions, other dependants, lovers or spouses, and eventually concluding with 'Rules for plaguing all your acquaintance'.[16] Both texts are full of sardonic humour and excess.[17]

Swift's servants are taught how to secure the best food by blaming its disappearance on family pets, how to skim off household funds when sent on errands, how to abuse valuables by wiping dirty shoes on fine damask or urinating into a silver cup, to annoy the family with loud noises, to embarrass everyone by carrying brimming chamber pots down the main stairs, to leave traces of bodily fluids like urine and spittle all over the house, to pollute substances that the family will ingest—and most importantly to avoid blame for any of these and many more transgressions with a litany of outrageous excuses. Collier counters these directions with strategies of a different sort so that servants are always vulnerable and uneasy. Delicacies really are fed to the household animals. Servants are treated with suspicion, barraged with unjust accusations, and threatened with dismissal. They are kept at a distance from the employer's personal effects and bodily parts. Swift and Collier posit two very different scenarios of the mixed population living under the same roof. In *Directions*, this population offers protection to servants: 'Lay all Faults on a Lap-dog, a favourite Cat, a Monkey, a Parrot, a Magpye, a Child, or on the Servant who was last turned off'.[18] In *Ingeniously Tormenting*, the same population supports the interest of the masters: 'keep as large a quantity of tame animals as you conveniently can. If you have children, a smaller number will do. Show the most extravagant fondness you possibly can for all these animals: and let them be of the most troublesome and mischievous sort, such as cats, monkeys, parrots, squirrels, and little snarling lapdogs'.[19] Ultimately both Swift and Collier satirize the empowered classes whose failures of authority, intelligence, and morality are first and foremost domestic failures. But their contrasting perspectives also help to map two different directions taken by later satirists of domesticity.

---

[14] Eliza Fowler Haywood, *A Present for a Serving-Maid* (1743) in Dalporto, *Women in Service*, 55, 74.

[15] While Collier clearly is building on Swift's work, it is less clear as to whether Haywood is a direct source for either. Dalporto argues that Swift is directly parodying Haywood (Introduction, xxxiii), and several passages do support that relationship in striking ways.

[16] Collier, *Ingeniously Tormenting*, 93.

[17] For a fuller comparison of the relationship between Swift's *Directions* and Collier's *Ingeniously Tormenting*, see Rabb, 'Engendering Satire', 150–5.

[18] Swift, *Works* (Cambridge), ii. 457–8.   [19] Collier, *Ingeniously Tormenting*, 16–17.

The home projected by Swift's footman is profoundly material. It contains scores of things—silver lace, snuff boxes, coffee cups, tooth-pick cases, pin-cushions, pistols, riding jackets, ribbons, and foodstuffs from larks to cabbage—that remind the reader that the eighteenth century was an age of increasing commodification and consumption. Historians point out that commercial growth coincided with 'the servant problem' because an individual's growing number of possessions meant a growing need for help to manage and care for them. Swift's teeming lists in *Directions* have the effect typical of his satire. Instead of conveying an orderly plenitude, listed objects go too far. Abundance becomes excess and defies control. Material domesticity is unpleasant and hard to secure from tarnish, waste, breakage, and rot. Things meant to furnish household comfort in fact threaten the inhabitants' well-being: the master's cane is used to stir the fire; the butler spreads germs by 'blowing strongly' into the necks of open ale bottles, the cook bastes delicately flavoured larks with mutton fat, the chamber maid never washes her hands, and so on.[20] Household expenditures, actually extravagant and irresponsible, are rationalized by ludicrous economic measures like making tea with old water used to boil fish and cabbage. Dregs of various wines and cordials are mixed together and reused for guests because 'by this Method you are certain that nothing is lost'. The Butler is advised to '[w]ash the glasses with your own water, to save your Master salt'.[21] Servants are the knaves whose tricks keep foolish employers from 'trouble and vexation'. The illusion of domestic happiness depends on being duped by the varnish and tinsel supplied by an underclass that will carelessly destroy crystal goblets but wait until all are broken before reporting the loss because 'it is the Office of a good Servant to discompose his Master and his Lady as seldom as he can'.[22] A passive-aggressive energy is always just below the surface of such a subversively peaceful state.

Collier's narrator, in contrast, reverses the power dynamic and effectively discomposes her servants as often as she can. Little advice is offered about controlling and abusing household things, but a great deal of insight is given into controlling or abusing household inhabitants. Encourage a serving-maid with kindness, she advises, and then 'fly all at once into a violent rage' to keep her 'vastly puzzled'. '[T]ease and soothe…alternately' in order to keep staff members on edge, and break the self-confidence of any 'good industrious servant, who has done her very best to please you' by 'mortifying' her publicly.[23] If Swift pushes his inventory of domestic objects to an extreme, he pays scant attention to members of the extended family. The footman mentions in passing 'humble' dependants whom servants can snub: 'If an humble companion…or a dependent cousin happen to be at table, whom you find to be little regarded by the Master and the Company…follow the example of your Betters, by treating him many degrees worse than any of the rest.'[24] Collier, however, extends her cast of domestic characters to include many kinds of dependants and relationships existing under the same roof—'it would be tiresome and almost endless, to enumerate every connection'—that are susceptible to emotional

[20] Swift, *Works* (Cambridge), ii. 463.   [21] Swift, *Works* (Cambridge), ii. 466.
[22] Swift, *Works* (Cambridge), ii. 472.   [23] Collier, *Ingeniously Tormenting*, 18–19, 21.
[24] Swift, *Works* (Cambridge), ii. 462.

'tormenting'. She first instructs 'those, who may be said to have an exterior power from visible authority' but moves on to 'those, who have an interior power, arising from the affection of the person on whom they are to work'.[25] Servants and 'humble companions' thus provide the training ground for becoming skilful in an 'art' that can be used widely on almost anyone who dares to venture into the domestic sphere.

For Collier, this private space is where 'our power' can work the most destruction not on material things or corporeal bodies, but on mental well-being. Governments, public institutions, armies, and rulers have nothing of comparable force: 'With what contempt may we…look down on the tyrants of old! On Nero, Caligula…and all such paltry pretenders.'[26] They stripped away worldly goods and used the lash and sword. But '[t]heir inventions ending in death, freed the sufferer from any further torments; or, if they extended only to broken bones, and bodily wounds, they were such as the skill of the surgeon could rectify, or heal: But where is the hand that can cure the wounds of unkindness, which our ingenious artists inflict?'[27] In the modern household, '[t]he practice of tormenting the body is not now, indeed, much allowed…but let us not…regret the loss of that trifling branch of our power, since we are at full liberty to exercise ourselves in that much higher pleasure, the tormenting of the mind.' Indeed, the narrator condoles ironically, by 'plaguing' the mind 'you will have also more power over the body than you are at first aware of'.[28] Swift's influence on Collier is clear and explicit, but she explores new possibilities for bringing satire home.

Questions of gender differentiate the two modes of domestic satire. Swift's *Directions* is grounded in the male perspective of the footman-persona who traverses private and public spheres with considerable freedom. If you gad about town for eight hours after a simple errand, he advises serving men, simply give your master the excuse that '[y]ou were pressed for the Sea-service, and carried before a Justice of Peace, who kept you three hours before he examined you, and you got off with much ado'.[29] Collier's *Tormenting* projects a more enclosed world. The privacy of the home can seem like incarceration in a torture chamber for those seeking protection within its walls. Most of the inmates are women, and to interiorize further, their scenes of pain are located within the heart and mind. Collier's instructions for tormenting 'young women who have been well-educated; and who, by the misfortune or death of their friends, have been left destitute' efface class categories or 'station' between women.[30] The domestic sphere is feminine in the sense that abused objects—like Swift's lump of soot dropped into the soup, or torn book-pages used to light fires—become the abused and objectified 'humble companions' of the household:

> There is some difficulty in giving rules for tormenting a dependent, that shall differ from those already laid down for plaguing and teasing your servants, as the two stations differ so very little in themselves. The servant, indeed, differs in this; she receives wages, and the humble companion receives none: the servant is most part

---

[25] Collier, *Ingeniously Tormenting*, 13. [26] Collier, *Ingeniously Tormenting*, 7.
[27] Collier, *Ingeniously Tormenting*, 7. [28] Collier, *Ingeniously Tormenting*, 10.
[29] Swift, *Works* (Cambridge), ii. 449. [30] Collier, *Ingeniously Tormenting*, 21.

of the day out of your sight; the humble companion is always ready at hand to receive every cross word that rises in your mind: the servants can be teased only by yourself, your dogs, your cats, your parrots, and your children; the humble companion (besides being the sport of all these) must, if you manage rightly, bear the insults of all your servants themselves.[31]

Single women are easy targets, and Collier indulges in some sardonic irony about the treatment of 'Miss Kitty', 'Miss Lucy', 'Miss Dolly', and 'Miss Fanny'. Like Swift's imagined scenes of manipulative behaviour ('When you are in no humour to drive', the coachman is advised, 'tell your Master the horses have got a cold, that they want shoeing, that Rain does them hurt'), Collier's scenes have a grotesque plausibility. Yet unlike Swift's amusing strategies for avoiding an immediate inconvenience, Collier's exert lasting influence: '[Y]ou may generally insult [a ward] with her beauty, yet be sure, at all times, to say so many mortifying things, as shall make her believe you don't think her in the least handsome... by right management every personal perfection may be turned to her reproach.'[32] Collier's narrator knows just the way to sabotage self-esteem and inflict psychological damage: 'There are several good tricks of mortification, which you may apply properly, by attending to people's characters and dispositions, so as to find out what they most value and pride themselves upon.'[33] 'Attending to people's characters' in an intimate setting fosters not sympathy but knowledge of a dangerous kind.

Collier's satire represents the dystopian domestic family through formal techniques such as dialogue and story, well suited to adaptation by later novelists. Distinctive characters emerge from the *Essay*. Female dependants in need of 'protection' are individualized: Miss Kitty is a 'young creature of beauty'; Miss Fanny, unattractive but intelligent; Miss Dolly, high-spirited; Miss Lucy, anxious to please. For each, the narrator provides plots, strategies for torment, and sample conversations guaranteed to reduce each woman to tears. In the case of plain but perceptive Miss Fanny:

> You must begin with all sorts of mortifying observations on her person; and frequently declare that you hate anything about you that is not agreeable to look at. This, in the beginning, will vex the girl... But in time she will find you out... and, if she have good sense, will get above any concern about what you say of her person. As soon as you perceive this, change your method; and level most of your darts against her understanding.[34]

In the case of eager-to-please Miss Lucy:

> Declare, whether true or false, that you have a great hatred of noise; and whenever Miss Lucy steps more softly than common, in order to please you, tell her you wonder how she can stamp about the floor... as if she had wooden shoes on... [and] if she is uniformly careful never to offend your ears, by any noise that she can possibly

---

[31] Collier, *Ingeniously Tormenting*, 22–3.   [32] Collier, *Ingeniously Tormenting*, 24.
[33] Collier, *Ingeniously Tormenting*, 85.   [34] Collier, *Ingeniously Tormenting*, 28.

avoid, you must never omit saying to her, whenever she goes out of the room, "Let me *entreat* you, child, not to bounce the door after you, enough to shake the house".[35]

Chapters pertaining to spouses, friends, children, and company further develop abusive scenes of cruel unpredictability, sarcasm, and sadistic manipulation. Collier is able to target a broad social spectrum without venturing beyond the private, quotidian, and local: 'The lion and tiger come not often in our way... but it is your gnats and wasps... that are your constant and true tormentors.'[36]

CHILDREN AND CHILDHOOD

Before looking at some later eighteenth-century texts that develop the relationship between satire and domesticity along the two lines identified in this chapter, some attention is owing to the difficult motif mentioned earlier: children and childhood. There is no more essential domestic function than to preserve and propagate the beginning of life. In many respects, the eighteenth century (with its lower infant mortality, educational outreach, companionate marriages, primogeniture, cult of sensibility, and so on) is associated with the celebration of childhood as an especially attractive time of love and innocence. Although satire theoretically attacks and kills, it usually does not attack and kill babies. Mandeville, Swift, and Collier, however, take exception to this tradition. In *The Fable of the Bees*, '[t]here is no merit in saving an innocent babe ready to drop in the fire; the Action is neither good nor bad.'[37] No adult stops the carnage when a 'ravenous brute' devours a 'helpless Infant', and the reader is forced to watch the child

> beat down with greedy haste... the defenseless posture of tender Limbs first trampled on, then tore asunder... the filthy Snout digging in the yet living Entrails suck up the smoking Blood, and now and then to hear the Crackling of the Bones and the cruel Animal with savage Pleasure grunt over the horrid Banquet.[38]

The infamous premise of *A Modest Proposal* that 'a child... at a year old [is] a most delicious, nourishing, and wholesome food whether stewed, roasted, baked, or boiled' coolly extends the slaughter to thousands of 'helpless infants[s]'. Swift takes up the idea again in *Directions to Servants* when the Nurse is counselled to keep up her breast milk for another service 'when the child you nurse dies'. Equally blasé is the further advice: 'If you happen to let the Child fall, and lame it, be sure never to confess it; and, if it dies, all is safe.'[39]

Collier dwells even longer on this theme. Children are both victims of torment and the means of tormenting others:

---

[35] Collier, *Ingeniously Tormenting*, 31.   [36] Collier, *Ingeniously Tormenting*, 98.
[37] Mandeville, *Fable*, 92.   [38] Mandeville, *Fable*, 264.
[39] Swift, *Works* (Cambridge), ii. 522.

[S]uffer them...to make such a racket that you cannot hear one another speak; let them...with their greasy fingers, soil and besmear your visitor's clothes, cut their hoods...with scissors; put their fingers, and dirty noses...into the cream-pot, and drivel over the sugar...thrust some bread and butter down the ladies' backs...be more troublesome and offensive than either squirrels, parrots, or monkeys.[40]

Like Mandeville, Collier's narrator assumes that adults restrain violence to children for selfish reasons. In the *Fable*, the baby is snatched from the flames so that the parent will not bear guilt. Similarly, *Ingeniously Tormenting* reminds parents 'never to strike or whip a child' out of 'the regard you ought to have for your own reputation'. There is a better way 'to make away with the troublesome and expensive brats': '[s]uffer them to climb without contradiction, to heights from whence they may break their necks; let them eat everything they like...to sit up as late as they please at night...should they chance to die of a surfeit...your name will be recorded for a kind and indulgent parent'.[41] Should children survive, they can be controlled mentally and emotionally: 'If your children happen to have but weak understandings, upbraid them with every excellence you see abroad; and lament your own hard fate in being plagued with idiots. But, if you see a rising genius in any child...give that child no assistance nor encouragement'.[42] Swift offers his shocking proposal in the face of English colonial oppression of the Irish economy. Collier remains more focused on domesticity as a scene of abused power in its own right. She urges the realities of dysfunctional families (not of all families, of course) as a real social and moral evil in need of reform:

O ye Parents...who intend to make a proper use of your power, let me remind you, that even in this age you are invested, both by law and custom, with *the strongest outward and visible power I know of in this land*. Purchased slaves are not allowed: your servants if you use them ill may leave you .... Your children have nobody to fly to...their very lives, while infants, are...at your disposal.[43]

Insofar as satire uses figures of no sanctioned authority in order to criticize domesticity as an idealized sanctuary—and insofar as it can vex its readers—the brutal violation of the most dependent members of the household insists that the unthinkable must be contemplated as more than a metaphor.

DOMESTICITY AND MATERIALITY

If we pursue these two strains of domestic satire—the household as either an economy of troublesome tangibles or a network of power relationships—we can step from Mandeville, Swift, and Collier to other writers. In Tobias Smollett's *Humphry Clinker*

---

[40] Collier, *Ingeniously Tormenting*, 84.
[41] Collier, *Ingeniously Tormenting*, 36, 37–8.
[42] Collier, *Ingeniously Tormenting*, 39.
[43] Collier, *Ingeniously Tormenting*, 35, emphasis added.

servants and dependants are enmeshed in material problems linked to domestic issues. Semi-literate maid Win manages to articulate all aspects of the ongoing 'servant problem' that provoked Mandeville and Swift: she parodies her 'betters' with her 'pumpydoor' and 'turtle-water' and her pride in mingling with 'the very squintasense of satiety'.[44] She is aware of the wrongdoing of other servants—'at Bath [they] are devils in garnet'—but she will not cast blame—'I defy the devil to say I am a tail-carrier, or ever brought a poor sarvant into trouble'.[45] She knows the private business of her mistress and how to use it: 'what a power of things might not I reveal, consarning old mistress and young mistress'.[46] Her relationship with her mistress is far from pure obedience: 'Mrs. Tabitha sculded a little...but she knows as I know what's what'.[47] She understands that servants live by contract and learns all about the recurrent topic of 'parquisites' and vails.[48] She does not fear dismissal because 'Thank God, there's no want of places'.[49] She aspires to be 'a parson of de-stinks-on' and is in fact elevated to a 'higher spear'.[50]

Home is full of material objects requiring but resisting care: hats, feathers, barrels of beer, medicinal tinctures, oils, curtains, carpets, beds, velvets, laces, a French commode, an odd green shoe, and so on. 'I think everything runs cross at Brambleton-hall', complains unmarried dependant, Matt's sister Tabitha. She struggles to manage scores of things that constantly elude her control, her age, and her spelling, like her 'rose collard neglejay', 'bloo quilted petticoat', 'green robins', and 'the litel box with my jowls'. Her self-interested economies are stratagems for mock-efficiency. She 'won't lose a cheese paring...take care there is no waste'.[51] Her orders reveal power struggles within the domestic 'family'. She ineffectually suspects the lame excuses meant to cover up neglect: 'you tell me the thunder has soured two barrels of beer in the seller. But how the thunder should get there...I can't comprehend'.[52] She echoes Haywood's ideal of 'happy' service: 'If you are found a good and faithfull sarvant, great will be your reward in haven', but she really means that the domestics at Brambleton-hall can expect little material remuneration in their lifetimes.[53]

Domesticity in *Humphry Clinker* devolves materially. When feather beds and mattresses are freshened, they become 'well haired'.[54] A pious sermon becomes a 'pye-house', robbery becomes 'rubbery', grace becomes 'grease', and marriage becomes 'mattermoney'. Disgusting traces of the body and of food are left throughout the novel: Matt's chronic constipation, Chowder's sensitive bowels, the pun on Clinker's name, the complaints about lying in a bed with 'damp shits' or asking to 'have the gate shit every evening' are constant reminders of encroaching dirt and waste. Abstractions become embodied: Win 'nose what [she] nose'.[55] The subject of failed 'domestic happiness' is assessed explicitly in Matt's letter about his old friend Baynard, whose

[44] Tobias Smollett, *Humphry Clinker*, ed. James L. Thompson (New York: Norton, 1983), 41.
[45] Smollett, *Humphry Clinker*, 66.   [46] Smollett, *Humphry Clinker*, 39, 205.
[47] Smollett, *Humphry Clinker*, 40.   [48] Smollett, *Humphry Clinker*, 7, 66, 241, 282.
[49] Smollett, *Humphry Clinker*, 282.   [50] Smollett, *Humphry Clinker*, 333.
[51] Smollett, *Humphry Clinker*, 6, 41–2.   [52] Smollett, *Humphry Clinker*, 42.
[53] Smollett, *Humphry Clinker*, 148.   [54] Smollett, *Humphry Clinker*, 253.
[55] Smollett, *Humphry Clinker*, 282.

'cold, comfortless, and disgusting' home is filled with 'rattles, baubles, and gewgaws' and 'supernumerary servants'.[56] Two of three children have died in this 'topsy turvy' environment, owing to parental neglect. One 'puny...shambling, blear-eyed boy' survives to torment the guests. Their dinner could have been produced in the kitchen of Swift's *Directions*: 'The pottage was little better than bread soaked in dishwashings...ragouts looked as if they had been eaten once and half digested: the fricassees were involved in a nasty yellow poultice; and the rotis were scorched and stinking...the table-beer was sour, the water foul, and the wine vapid'.[57]

Humphry, letter-less in the epistolary novel that bears his name, embodies the permeable distinction between master and servant, as well as the tension between contractual and blood relations. He appears to be the ideal servant until his parentage is discovered, although he merely is transformed into another form of dependency, 'a poor relation... your carnal kinsman'. Matt Bramble speaks with unwitting irony earlier in the novel when his as yet unrecognized illegitimate son offers to serve without a contract: 'Foregad! thou are a complete fellow...I have a good mind to take thee into my family'.[58] As parent, Matt retains 'both by law and custom...the strongest outward and visible power...in this land'. Aptly, Humphry enters the novel as naked as the day he was born. The promise of domestic happiness that accompanies the triple-marriage ending depends on the continuance of a conservative social order in which the abandoned infant Matthew Lloyd is happy to remain only 'a crab of [unintended] planting'.[59]

In contrast, Frances Burney and Jane Austen seem to have taken a lesson from Collier's *Essay on the Art of Ingeniously Tormenting*. Satire on domestic abuses in their work often focuses on the ways in which household members can make each other miserable. Although they do ridicule domestic dirt and disorganization, such scenes avoid the grotesque and stomach-turning details of Swift and Smollett. Satire on the failed ideal of domestic happiness in Burney's *Evelina* includes a meal at the Brangton's, but we simply learn that 'The dinner was ill-served, ill-cooked, and ill managed'.[60] And while young Brangton sneers at his sisters who spend hours 'at the glass' fussing over dress and ornament, we never know if they wear muslin or brocade, lace or ruffles. In Austen's *Mansfield Park*, food is unappetizing in Fanny's Portsmouth home: 'Rebecca's puddings, and Rebecca's hashes, brought to table...with...half-cleaned plates, and not half-cleaned knives and forks'.[61] Possessions do cause problems, but they are few in number. Siblings quarrel over a silver knife; brother William cannot immediately find his hat; a key is mislaid. Unlike Tabitha's box of 'jowls', Fanny owns a solitary ornament, the amber cross that William had brought her from Sicily—more a symbol of spirituality than a costly bijoux. Although it takes several chapters to find something to hang it on, the focus is on the emotions aroused by, not the value of the necklace. Austen's point seems to be that it does not require a superabundance of things to create domestic chaos; it takes people: 'home...was

---

[56] Smollett, *Humphry Clinker*, 267, 266.   [57] Smollett, *Humphry Clinker*, 272.
[58] Smollett, *Humphry Clinker*, 79.   [59] Smollett, *Humphry Clinker*, 193.
[60] Frances Burney, *Evelina*, ed. Kristina Straub (Boston: Belford Books, 1997), 215.
[61] Austen, *Mansfield Park*, 280.

the abode of noise, disorder, and impropriety. Nobody was in their right place, nothing was done as it ought to be.'[62] Her father 'was dirty and gross'; her mother was 'always busy without getting on... wishing to be an economist, without contrivance or regularity; dissatisfied with her servants, without skill to make them better, and... without power of engaging their respect'.[63] The perceiving mind always trumps the feeling body.

Both Burney and Austen are deeply interested in domestic dependants, especially in gifted but distressed female dependants—nobodies, as Burney puts it, who should be somebodies. Full discussion, even a full list of such characters, is beyond the scope of the present chapter, but a few cases can be mentioned. Collier had pointed out the significance of gender: 'There are many methods for young men, in [straitened] circumstances, to acquire a genteel maintenance; but for a girl, I know not one way of support, that does not, by the custom of the world, throw her below the rank of a gentlewoman.'[64] The more interesting the girl, the more interesting her suffering: to tease 'a servant, you have to look for but diligence and good nature; but in a dependent there are many more requisites'.[65] The novels of Burney and Austen are well populated with such figures, as protagonists and secondary characters.

Perhaps Burney's most memorable satire on domestic dependency in the role of the humble companion comes from the account of being unhappily engaged herself, as Second Keeper to the Robes, in the royal household. Adding a page both to the literature of 'directions to servants' and to the literature of 'ingenious tormenting' is her 'Directions for Coughing, Sneezing, or Moving, before the King and Queen' which begins memorably with the injunction, 'In the first place, you must not cough.'[66] As if responding to Collier's instructions 'to those who take young women into their houses, as new subjects of their power', Burney satirizes the entrapment of women in the private sphere as mental and physical torture that violates the most fundamental requirements of a living creature.[67] In order not to cough, sneeze, or move, one must choke, stop breathing, grind teeth together, break a blood vessel, and finally cannibalize one's own flesh:

> if... the agony is very great, you may, privately, bite the inside of your cheek, or of your lips... taking care, meanwhile, to do it so cautiously as to make no apparent dent outwardly. And, with that precaution, if you even gnaw a piece out, it will not be minded, only be sure either to swallow it, or commit it to a corner of your mouth, for you must not spit.[68]

Austen's satire on domestic abuses also turns inward. Aunt Norris seems to have read Collier's chapter on patronesses (where the character of Miss Fanny appears) and has perfected the art of tormenting a humble companion, finding every possible occasion to remind Fanny, 'wherever you are, you must be the lowest and last'.[69] Aunt Norris's 'admonitions' set the pattern for the rest of the household: 'Her elder cousins mortified

---

[62] Austen, *Mansfield Park*, 264.   [63] Austen, *Mansfield Park*, 265.
[64] Collier, *Ingeniously Tormenting*, 21.   [65] Collier, *Ingeniously Tormenting*, 23.
[66] Burney, *Evelina*, 498.   [67] Collier, *Ingeniously Tormenting*, 22.
[68] Burney, *Evelina*, 498–9.   [69] Austen, *Mansfield Park*, 151–2.

her by reflections on her size, and abashed her by noticing her shyness; Miss Lee wondered at her ignorance, and the maid-servants sneered at her clothes...the despondence that sunk her little heart was severe'.[70] Austen's dialogue echoes Collier's when Aunt Norris grows sarcastic:

> I hope you are aware that there is no real occasion for you going into company...it is what you must not depend upon ever being repeated. Nor must you be fancying that the invitation is meant as any particular compliment to you; the compliment is intended to your uncle and aunt, and me...Oh depend upon it, you aunt can do very well without you, or you would not be allowed to go.[71]

Physically enervated Fanny, as critics have noted, has a complex inner life; she speaks few words but thinks thousands of them in response to the tormenting of her mind.

Austen also is unflinching about infants—abandoned (Willoughby's daughter), displaced and orphaned (Frank Churchill and Jane Fairfax), illegitimate (Harriet Smith), and dead (Fanny's sister)—and attacks sugary idealizations of childhood. In *Sense and Sensibility*, Lady Middleton's 'four noisy children...tore her clothes, and put an end to every kind of discourse except what related to themselves'. Their 'impertinent encroachments and mischievous tricks' afflict guests who have 'sashes untied...hair pulled about their ears...work-bags searched, and...knives and scissors stolen away'. A slight scratch on the neck sends 'Sweet little Annamaria' into a tantrum until she is covered with kisses, bathed in lavender water, and stuffed with sugarplums. The narrator acerbically notes: 'the child was too wise to stop crying. She still screamed and sobbed lustily, kicked her two brothers for offering to touch her' until she is silenced with apricot marmalade. Many other instances from Austen's work continue her attacks on idealized domesticity and her exposure of the social and moral problems connected to the dependants within a household: among them are the humiliation of the Dashwood women, the tormenting conversations between 'friend' Lucy Steele and Elinor; Emma's mistreatment of Miss Bates, Harriet, and Jane Fairfax in *Emma*; and the family abuse of Ann Eliot in *Persuasion*. Other writers and texts worthy of analysis could form a list beginning with Letitia Barbauld's *Washing Day* and Laurence Sterne's *Tristram Shandy*.

THE FAMILY PET

Reaching back to Mandeville for examples explicitly connecting satire and the domestic sphere, and demonstrating two contrasting but connected modes of attack, suggests one further member of the domestic group (blood relations, servants, dependants) assembled under one roof—namely, the family pet. The traditional figure of the satyr—the half-goat creature existing in myth—does not make a direct appearance on Cowper's

---

[70] Austen, *Mansfield Park*, 13.   [71] Austen, *Mansfield Park*, 151.

sofa, or on the one upon which Lady Bertram sits, 'doing some long piece of needlework, of little use and no beauty'. This bestial figure seems to have yielded its place to furry housecats and cuddly lapdogs that commonly epitomize tame, affectionate, domestic relations. As Swift wryly put it in 'On the Collar of Mrs. Dingley's Lapdog': 'Pray steal me not, I'm Mrs. Dingley's / Whose heart on this four-footed thing lies'.[72] But more often these creatures prove far from docile. Collier observes that the cat, which seems 'to all appearance...the sweetest best-humoured animal in the world' is really the model of tormenting: she 'sticks her claws into' a still-living mouse, 'plays' with it, and 'triumphs in her power over her wretched captive' before the kill.[73] Mandeville describes a lapdog that 'used to being caress'd will never tamely bear that Felicity in others...[and] would choak himself with Victuals rather than leave any thing for a Competitor of his own Kind'. To the list of canine troublemakers, we can add Pope's mischievous Shock who wakes Belinda with his tongue, 'naughty Fop' who 'f—ts and p—sses around the room', Tabitha's troublesome constipated Chowder, Lady Bertram's spoiled Pug about whom she cares more than for her children, and, of course, Collier's little snarling lapdogs who help to give satire in the domestic sphere its bite.

SELECT BIBLIOGRAPHY

Dalporto, Jeannie, ed. *Essential Works for the Study of Early Modern Women*, Part III, *vol. 5: Women in Service in Early Modern England* (Aldershot: Ashgate, 2008).

Davidoff, Leonore and Catherine Hall. *Family Fortunes* (London and New York: Routledge & Kegan Paul, 1987, revised edn. 2002).

Elliott, Robert C. *The Power of Satire: Magic, Ritual, Art* (Princeton: Princeton University Press, 1960).

Hecht, J. Jean. *The Domestic Servant in Eighteenth-Century England* (London and Boston: Routledge & Kegan Paul, 1956, repr. 1980).

Hill, Bridget. *English Domestics in the Eighteenth Century* (Oxford: Clarendon Press, 1996).

Johns-Putra, Adeline. 'Satire and Domesticity in Late Eighteenth-Century Women's Poetry: Minding the Gap', *Journal for Eighteenth-Century Studies* 33 (2010), 67–87.

McKeon, Michael. *The Secret History of Domesticity: Public, Private, and the Division of Knowledge* (Baltimore: Johns Hopkins University Press, 2005).

Meldrum, Tim. *Domestic Service and Gender 1660–1750: Life and Work in the London Household* (Harlow: Pearson Education, 2000).

Rabb, Melinda. 'Engendering Satire in the Long Eighteenth Century', in *The Cambridge Companion to Women's Writing in Britain, 1660–1789*, ed. Catherine Ingrassia (Cambridge: Cambridge University Press, 2015), 147–63.

Straub, Kristina. *Domestic Affairs: Intimacy, Eroticism, and Violence between Servants and Masters in Eighteenth-Century Britain* (Baltimore: Johns Hopkins University Press, 2009).

Woodward, Carolyn. 'Jane Collier, Sarah Fielding, and the Motif of Tormenting', *The Age of Johnson* 16 (2001), 259–74.

---

[72] Swift, *Poems* (Williams), ii. 763.   [73] Collier, *Ingeniously Tormenting*, 99.

PART V

SATIRICAL ACTIONS

CHAPTER 28

··

THINKING ABOUT SATIRE

··

ASHLEY MARSHALL

THE period between the return of Charles II to the throne and the deaths of Pope and Swift has long been acclaimed the golden epoch of satire, and satire in the long eighteenth century has received quite a lot of scholarly attention. Contemporary commentary—what the producers and consumers, the victims, the censors and censurers of satire had to say about it—has received less systematic scrutiny. Elsewhere I have offered a relatively exhaustive survey of eighteenth-century commentary on satire, featuring the *obiter dicta* of anonymous critics and minor poets and moralizing preachers alongside the more celebrated examples.[1] My objective there was to challenge the overly tidy divisions of satire theory in this period into 'for' and 'against', and to demonstrate that attitudes towards satire were as heterogeneous as the practice of satire itself. What follows is different in both emphasis and coverage.

The present essay focuses on major authors—particularly Dryden, Pope, Swift, Addison, and Defoe—and has principally to do with the fundamental attitudes towards satire rather than with the debates about the particulars of satiric practice. No single essay can do justice to the varied responses to questions such as these: What were appropriate and inappropriate targets, and effective and ineffective methods? Should satire name names or not? Was general satire preferable to individual? My concern here is with larger arguments about the *nature* of satire, the cases made for it, the anxieties about it and challenges to those who wrote and read it, and the language used to define and discuss it. What questions are raised, implicitly or explicitly? What, in other words, were authors thinking about, when they were thinking about satire?

---

[1] Ashley Marshall, *The Practice of Satire in England, 1658–1770* (Baltimore: Johns Hopkins University Press, 2013), ch. 2.

THE OPPOSITION TO SATIRE

The defences of satire take many forms, but they are all partly a response to critics who presumed satire to be mean-spirited attack. In *Enigmaticall Characters* (1658), Richard Flecknoe construes satire as '*rude Assault*' (30), like many others emphasizing the satirist's tendency towards peevishness and derision. Dictionary entries from the beginning to the end of the period call attention to satire's negative attributes. Lexicographers—including Samuel Johnson—define satire as functionally synonymous with slander and defamation. Josua Poole's *English Parnassus* (1657) offers a colourful catalogue of adjectives for 'Satyre':

> Girding, biting, snarling, scourging, jerking, lashing, smarting, sharp, tart, rough, invective, censorious, currish, snappish, captious, barking, brawling, carping, fanged, sharp-tooth'd, quipping, jeering, flouting, sullen, rigid, impartial, whipping, thorny, pricking, stinging, sharp-fanged, injurious, reproachful, libellous, harsh, rough-hewne, odious, opprobrious, contumelious, defaming, calumnious.   (176)

Such characterizations reflect little conceptual flexibility: satire is abuse, nothing more. The case against satire is often a case against the satirist, whose laughter (see Hobbes) reflects a sense of superiority and contempt. The satirist, as detractors depict him, snarls and scourges. In the late seventeenth century, Walter Charleton described 'malignant' satirical wits as sub-human, 'the ill-natured Disciples of *Momus, Derisores, Scoffers*, such who, like Beetles, seem hatch'd in dung, or Vermine bred out of Ulcers; perpetually feeding upon the frailties and imperfections of Human nature'.[2] Later, Ned Ward would castigate Pope in similarly vivid and judgemental terms: the derisory brute 'squirts down frothy Satyrs with contempt'.[3] What is worse, for some critics, is that these wits clearly revel in their contumelies. In 1694 Sir Thomas Blount concluded of satirists, '*Pleasure* [is] their Principle, and *Interest* their God', and a later commentator complains that modern poets have 'deboched' satire, reprehensibly delighting in the expression of malice and in 'the Joy of Spight'.[4] This scepticism about satiric motives is challenged by defenders of satire, who champion its socio-moral importance and redefine the satirist as civic-minded reformer. Shaftesbury and his fellow travellers defend the reasonableness and utility of humour and ridicule. Shaftesbury emphasized, for example, the importance of 'the liberty of laughter', worrying that if the expression of mirth 'is suppressed...it will find an alternative vent, emerging as buffoonery or worse—perhaps civil disturbance'.[5] Thinking about satire in the eighteenth century meant thinking about

---

[2] Walter Charleton, *A Brief Discourse Concerning the Different Wits of Men* (1669), 119.

[3] Edward Ward, *Durgen. Or, a Plain Satyr upon a Pompous Satyrist* (1729), 17.

[4] Thomas Blount, *De Re Poetica: or, Remarks upon Poetry* (1694), 45; *Miscellanies in Prose & Verse, By the most honorable Marquis of Normanby* (1702), 32.

[5] Ronald Paulson, *Don Quixote in England: The Aesthetics of Laughter* (Baltimore: Johns Hopkins University Press, 1998), 119.

the compatibility of reason and ridicule, about the humane implications of laughter, about whether raillery made men more receptive to truth and moral correction or represented a hazard to sober judgement. Some believers in the value of satire nuance their position, complementing their high-minded assertions with an acknowledgement of the aestheticized violence of satiric judgement.

DRYDEN AND THE ART OF SATIRE

The most important attempt to delineate and shape satiric practice at the beginning of the long eighteenth century is Dryden's 'Discourse concerning the Original and Progress of Satire' (1693), prefatory to his translation of the satires of Juvenal and Persius. The 'Discourse' raises questions about etymology and definition, scope and objective, ethics and aesthetics. Behind Dryden's exhaustive account of satire/*satura* is a desire to make what had become in England a disreputable form of writing—personally vicious, vulgar, ephemeral—into a creditable artistic mode. He does not deny the satirist a disciplinary or even retributive role, but unlike many commentators on satire he eschews the language of 'burning, biting, piercing, and blistering', as well as 'the medical and penal metaphors of cure and punishment'.[6] Following the continental scholars Casaubon and Dacier, he explains satire in terms of classical tradition, emphasizing moral purpose and artistic refinement and insisting that good satire presents positives as well as negatives, virtue as well as vice. The purpose of the 'Discourse' is not to codify past and present practices; instead its author projects an idealized concept, 'not so much what satire was and had been as what Dryden and his followers wanted it to be'—to wit, a form based on the *satura* of Juvenal and his precursor Horace.[7]

Dryden maintains, first, that proper satires exhibit a 'Unity of Design'. Even if *lanx satura* (a mixed platter or ragout) implies the opposite—that variety 'be of absolute necessity'—variety should nevertheless 'arise naturally from one Subject'. As in the works of Horace and Juvenal and Persius, 'The Poet is bound . . . to give his Reader some one Precept of Moral Virtue; and to caution him against some one particular Vice or Folly. Other Virtues . . . may be recommended . . . and other Vices or Follies may be scourg'd . . . But he is chiefly to inculcate one Virtue, and insist on that.'[8] Dryden reminds his readers of Aristotle's instruction that tragedy is the highest genre, the 'most Perfect Work of Poetry', precisely because 'it is the most United'. He moves from the discussion of tragedy and 'Heroique' poetry to the 'Antiquity and Origine of Satire', implying that satire should share key qualities of those superior genres, or, put differently, use these genres to raise itself up.[9]

---

[6] Ronald Paulson, 'Dryden and the Energies of Satire', in *The Cambridge Companion to John Dryden*, ed. Steven N. Zwicker (Cambridge: Cambridge University Press, 2004), 37–58, at 39.

[7] Dustin Griffin, *Satire: A Critical Reintroduction* (Lexington: University Press of Kentucky, 1994), 21.

[8] Dryden, 'Discourse', 80.   [9] Dryden, 'Discourse', 26, 27, 28.

Dryden argues for a mode of satire based on analogy—the analogy between classical Rome and Williamite England, then between the classical epic or tragedy and satire. To make a man seem a rogue without calling him one requires the establishment of damning similitudes, and this is the practice Dryden attributes to Juvenal, with whom he identifies in the 'Discourse'. That satirist was 'proper for his Times', since his 'was an Age that deserv'd a more severe Chastisement', a moment in which 'Vices were more gross and open, more flagitious, more encourag'd by the Example of a Tyrant; and more protected by his Authority'. He pointedly reminds readers that 'wheresoever *Juvenal* mentions *Nero*, he means *Domitian*, whom he dares not attack in his own Person, but Scourges him by Proxy' (69). Dryden encourages his audience to think analogically, and though he does not mention William III—whom he satirizes elsewhere—his exposition implies a judgement of the usurper now on the throne.[10] The praise of Juvenal comes by way of an acknowledgement of the tyranny under which that poet lived and wrote; the insinuation about Dryden's own moment is clear. Juvenal's indictment of imperial Rome under Domitian represents a vehicle with which the author of the 'Discourse' can express his own attitude towards Williamite England. The disaffected Dryden of the 1690s knows how to scourge the king by proxy, and his admiration of the public-minded Juvenal—whose 'Spirit has more of the Commonwealth Genius' (65)—elevates the local and historical particulars to the general and universal.

Dryden's concept of satire privileges indirection: 'How easie it is to call Rogue and Villain, and that wittily! But how hard to make a Man appear a Fool, a Blockhead, or a Knave, without using any of those opprobrious terms!' He commends the author who can 'spare the grossness of the Names' and still 'do the thing *yet more severely*'.[11] This effect is best achieved, the logic of the 'Discourse' makes clear, through analogy. In a memorable passage, Dryden likens the worthy satirist to a skilled executioner:

> there is still a vast difference betwixt the slovenly Butchering of a Man, and the fineness of a stroak that separates the Head from the Body, and leaves it standing in its place. A man may be capable, as *Jack Ketch's* Wife said of his Servant, of a plain piece of Work, a bare Hanging; but to make a Malefactor die sweetly was only belonging to her Husband.[12]

The point is that satire is about more than the job it accomplishes, about more than either reformation or humiliation. In his discussion of this metaphor of execution, David B. Morris rightly concludes that 'Dryden . . . offers simply two versions of dismemberment, two types of hanging. The question at issue wholly concerns the aesthetics of

---

[10] Scholars have identified Jacobite sentiments in *Alexander's Feast* (1697), the translation of Virgil's *Aeneid* (1697), and *Fables Ancient and Modern* (1700), as well as in *Amphitryon* (1690) and *King Arthur* (1691); Marshall, *Practice of Satire*, 122–6.

[11] Dryden, 'Discourse', 70, emphasis added.   [12] Dryden, 'Discourse', 71.

injury.'[13] Dryden is committed to a notion of satire that is both artful and civilized in language and manner.

Dryden invites association of himself with the masterful Jack Ketch. 'I wish I cou'd apply it to my self, if the Reader wou'd be kind enough to think it belongs to me', he reflects, specifically for his creation of the Zimri (Duke of Buckingham) portrait in *Absalom and Achitophel*. After praising the skilled metaphorical decapitator, Dryden misleads us with this claim: 'And thus ... you see I have preferr'd the Manner of *Horace*' to that of Juvenal.[14] The claim is specious, but only partly so: the genial Horace offers Dryden a model of right *manner*, but the satiric aims of Horace are a far cry from those of the skilled executioner with whom Dryden aligns himself. Dryden borrows a Horatian manner, but couples it with (and perhaps uses it to cover) Juvenalian intentions.

The 'Discourse' ultimately favours the strong satire of Juvenal. He depicts the politer Horace as entertaining but inefficacious: he wants 'to make his Reader Laugh; but he is not sure of his Experiment'. Juvenal, by contrast, 'always intends to move your Indignation, and he always brings about his purpose'.[15] For all his consciousness of style, Dryden privileges effect over aesthetics: '*Juvenal* was the greater Poet, I mean in Satire', despite being less polished.[16] Dryden celebrates Horace's 'Urbanity' and 'Good Manners', but adds, crucially, 'his Wit is faint; and his Salt, if I may dare to say so, almost insipid. *Juvenal* is of a more vigorous and Masculine Wit, he gives me as much Pleasure as I can bear.'[17] Like the dexterous Jack Ketch, he appreciates the art of doing considerable damage in an aesthetically satisfying way. For Dryden as for Pope, satiric deterrence has everything to do with the stylization of pain, with achieving the 'Sublimity' of Juvenal without 'the meanness of Words and vulgarity of Expression' that marks cruder forms of satiric discourse.[18]

The case of Dryden nicely illustrates an important conceptual distinction: the satiric act versus the representation of that act. Form can mitigate tone, and tone can mitigate content. Dryden perceived English satire to be disreputable, a canon of invective, scurrility, scourging, raillery—culturally illegitimate, deviating from the practice of the ancients. Sixteenth- and seventeenth-century satire had a bad reputation, and the 'Discourse' is an attempt to rehabilitate the mode. Unlike the angry satirists of the late sixteenth century—Donne and Marston, *inter alia*—the satirist as Dryden understands him can 'cover' his invective by imitating his classical forebears. For Dryden, this is largely a matter of form and genre: the use of classical formal verse, and of burlesque or travesty and mock-heroic, serves to make diatribe respectable, refined, literary, sérieuse. Dryden 'conceals' violent satiric impulses behind a proclaimed and adopted Horatian manner. Among Dryden's great contributions to eighteenth-century satiric practice is

---

[13] David B. Morris, *Alexander Pope: The Genius of Sense* (Cambridge, MA: Harvard University Press, 1984), 228.

[14] Dryden, 'Discourse', 71.   [15] Dryden, 'Discourse', 72.   [16] Dryden, 'Discourse', 65.

[17] Dryden, 'Discourse', 63.   [18] Dryden, 'Discourse', 78.

this element of artfulness, this notion that we must think about satire in terms of both content/judgement and language/form.

POPE'S 'SACRED WEAPON'

The locus for Dryden's thoughts on satire is in the 'Discourse'. Pope wrote no comparable extended formal essay on the subject; we see him thinking about satire most clearly in the prefatory material to *The Dunciad* and, later, in his Horatian satires. In both places, as in other epistolary and literary passages, he is essentially defensive, explaining that he writes satire because he is forced to do so (*difficile saturam non scribere*) and presenting his satires as defences of himself and his friends. Pope's practice of satire, as he explains, is personal: he attacks individuals, not general vices. Though many of the butts of his ridicule would seem to be insignificant—hacks and dunces—he maintains that they are worthwhile targets. They are affected, pretending to such beauty or success that they have not achieved and cannot achieve, and/or they have secured the ear of the Great (e.g. Lord Hervey) and do exert power, despite their paltriness.

As Pope becomes more oppositional, from *The Dunciad* through the end of his career, he also masters the art of the satiric apologia. His satires, in fact, are best styled satiric apologias, that 'traditional form in which the satirist justified himself as a moral agent'— and 'the literary form that Pope . . . made his own'.[19] The form provides the aesthetic—the stylization of pain—as well as the moral basis. It is also a vehicle of self-dramatization. Pope establishes his role as satirist, *vir bonus* and a spokesman of truth against whom the vicious and corrupt are to be measured. The notion of the satirist as upright citizen and teacher—the idea that his motives are essentially pure—becomes in this period, thanks to Pope and other champions, the great fiction of satire. Elizabethan satyr-satirists had cheerfully acknowledged an inglorious motive of revenge; in Dryden and especially Pope, we begin to see this personal motivation complemented by a moralistic promise. The crux, though, is that Pope explains himself as a well-meaning naïf who has been bullied into becoming heroic. His satiric apologias stage the conflict between this *vir bonus* and the adversarius, and his satirical judgements are always as much about the satirist as they are about the satirized.

One dimension of Pope's satiric rationale, as we see in the Horatian imitations and elsewhere, is the need for the gentle teacher to break the Horatian mould and become the Juvenalian satirist. As Dryden had found Horace's mildness inappropriate for a degenerate age, so Pope has little patience for Addisonian civilities, for decorum that precludes meaningful critique. In the *Epistle to Arbuthnot* (pub. 1735), he scorns Joseph Addison (Atticus) for being 'Willing to wound, and yet afraid to strike, / Just hint a fault,

---

[19]   Ronald Paulson, *Breaking and Remaking: Aesthetic Practice in England, 1700–1820* (New Brunswick: Rutgers University Press, 1989), 78.

and hesitate dislike'.[20] Addison, in Pope's telling, has little of the 'Masculine wit' that Dryden extols in Juvenal and more closely resembles the tacitly feminized Horace. Pope admits a certain lack of pity with his targets: 'That disdain and indignation against Vice, is...the only disdain and indignation I have...But sure it is as impossible to have a just abhorrence of Vice, without hating the Vicious, as to bear a true love for Virtue, without loving the Good'.[21]

Pope's mode of satire was public, even where the motivations were suspiciously personal (as in *The Dunciad*). The dissuasion of vice required that the malefactor suffer—and suffer before witnesses who might learn, through fear, to deserve better. To the genial Arbuthnot, he explained himself thus: 'General Satire in Times of General Vice has no force, & is no Punishment: People have ceas'd to be ashamed of it when so many are joind with them; and tis only by hunting One or two from the Herd that any Examples can be made...[I]f some are hung up, or pilloryed, it may prevent others'.[22] Pope satirized people, whether recognizable individuals or more widely applicable portraits. He used particularized cases rather than precepts:

> To reform and not to chastise...is impossible, and...the best Precepts, as well as the best Laws, would prove of small use, if there were no Examples to inforce them. To attack Vices in the abstract, without touching Persons, may be safe fighting indeed, but it is fighting with Shadows. General propositions are obscure, misty, and uncertain, compar'd with plain, full, and home examples: Precepts only apply to our Reason, which in most men is but weak: Examples are pictures, and strike the Senses, nay raise the Passions...The only sign by which I found my writings ever did any good, or had any weight, has been that they rais'd the anger of bad men.[23]

In an earlier letter to Gay, Pope had likewise defended individual satire: 'nothing can be *Just* that is not *Personal*', and 'all such Writings...as touch no Man, will mend no Man'.[24]

Pope's endorsement of personal satire brings him into conflict with his friend and fellow Tory Swift. When Pope shared a draft of *The Dunciad* with Swift, the Dean admonished him thus: 'Take care the bad poets do not outwit you', he cautions, 'as they have served the good ones in every Age, whom they have provoked to transmit their Names to posterity'. The hacks and drudges, he continues, 'will be as well known as you if [their] name[s] gets into your Verses; and as to the difference between good and bad Fame [it] is a perfect Trifle'.[25] Swift grasped that general implications were not necessarily kinder or more humane than personal defamation. He certainly contributed more than his share of lampoonery and individuated abuse, but he also took what opportunities he could to increase the breadth of his satire. In *Verses on the Death of Dr Swift* (published 1739), though his impartial speaker applauds him for having 'lash'd the Vice but spar'd the Name', what follows crucially alters the import: 'No Individual could resent, / Where Thousands equally were meant' (ll. 460–2). To specify a target is to allow those not

[20] Pope, *Poems* (Twickenham), iv. 110.
[22] Pope, *Poems* (Twickenham), iii. 423.
[24] Pope, *Poems* (Twickenham), iii. 255.
[21] Pope, *Corr.* (Sherburn), iii. 419.
[23] Pope, *Poems* (Twickenham), iii. 419.
[25] Swift, *Corr.* (Woolley), ii. 623–4.

named to feel exempt; to leave one's ridicule open-ended is to encourage more self-reflection (perhaps) and (definitely) to provoke more discomfiture.

The language of satire for Pope is defensive and martial: 'arm'd for *Virtue* when I point the Pen / Brand the bold Front of shameless, guilty Men'. Effectual ethical satire requires some public violence, as Pope's association of satiric judgement-rendering with the pillory makes clear. Satire is a 'sacred Weapon', the 'Sole Dread of Folly, Vice, and Insolence!'[26] To Arbuthnot, he conveys his pleasure in finding 'that those who have no shame, and no fear, of any thing else, have appear'd touch'd by my Satires'.[27] In the second *Epilogue to the Satires*, he boasted of his powers, confident of his social indispensability:

> Yes, I am proud; I must be proud to see
> Men not afraid of God, afraid of me.
> Safe from the Bar, the Pulpit, and the Throne,
> Yet touch'd and sham'd by *Ridicule* alone.[28]

Pope represents himself as socio-moral custodian, and bestows something almost like divine right on the satiric role: the satiric muse visits those with 'Heav'n-directed hands', and 'the Gods must guide' those hands. The satirist becomes the ultimate guardian, above all other men; it is his job 'To rowze the Watchmen of the Publick Weal', and to 'goad the Prelate slumb'ring in his Stall'.[29]

This martial language is a vital part of Pope's self-fashioning as fearless apologist for moral satire, and—as in Dryden's 'Discourse'—there is tension between content and form, between the satiric act and its presentation. Dryden uses a reputable classical heritage, and the Horatian voice, to aestheticize satire. Pope likewise recognizes the role of genre: classical form endows satiric judgement, even harsh judgement, with respectability. The *apologia* frees him up to speak directly, as a defiant and provoked and righteously indignant loner—as, in Maynard Mack's phrasing, 'the last surviving representative of a certain body of attitudes and values'.[30] His defences of satire are, unsurprisingly, almost always egocentric: '*my* Satire seems too bold' is a characteristic formulation, and in the *Epistle to Arbuthnot* he famously explains that the muse helped him survive 'this long disease, my life'.[31] In *The First Satire of the Second Book of Horace Imitated* (1733), he represents himself as particularly formidable: 'Hear this, and tremble! you, who 'scape the Laws. / Yes, while I live, no rich or noble knave / Shall walk the World, in credit, to his grave'.[32] The *apologia*, in other words, offers a formal justification for and validation of Pope's trenchant personal satire.

---

[26] Pope, *Poems* (Twickenham), ii. 105–6, 212–13.

[27] Pope, *Poems* (Twickenham), iii. 419.   [28] Pope, *Poems* (Twickenham), iv. 324.

[29] Pope, *Poems* (Twickenham), ii. 214–15, 217, 219.

[30] Maynard Mack, *Alexander Pope: A Life* (New Haven: Yale University Press, 1985), 586.

[31] *The First Satire of the Second Book of Horace Imitated*, l. 2 (emphasis added); in the same poem, he explains that, 'Fools rush into my Head, and so I write' (l. 14). The quotation from the *Arbuthnot* is l. 132.

[32] Pope, *Poems* (Twickenham), iv. 17.

ADDISON'S SOCIABLE WIT

Addison's official position is to be uncomfortable about and sceptical of satire, even more so than his friend and fellow Whig journalist Richard Steele. Though Steele—like other contributors to the *Tatler* and the *Spectator*—often discusses the requirements for 'good' or 'true' satire, Addison is relatively reticent on the point. In *Tatler* no. 92, Steele defends satire from those who associate it with libel: 'the Satyrist and the Libeller differ as much as the Magistrate and the Murderer', since the former 'never falls upon Persons who are not glaringly faulty', and the latter 'on none but who are conspicuously commendable'.[33] In no. 242, he issues the oft-quoted proclamation that 'Good-Nature' is 'an essential Quality in a Satyrist' (iii. 241). Because the 'greatest Evils in human Society are such as no Law can come at', he concludes elsewhere, 'We shall . . . take it for a very moral Action to find a good Appellation for Offenders, and to turn 'em into Ridicule' (i. 421). Steele, more hot-headed and polemical than Addison, is unsurprisingly a good deal more tolerant of the satiric impulse.

Addison encourages cheerfulness and mirth, but frequently reflects his anxiety about 'satire', which seems in his lexicon always to imply humour or wit coupled with something other than fellow feeling. He would likely agree with Giles Jacob: 'A little Wit, and a great deal of Ill-Nature, will qualify a Man for a Satirist.'[34] In *Spectator* no. 47 Addison quotes Hobbes admiringly: 'The Passion of Laughter is nothing else but sudden Glory arising from some sudden Conception of some Eminency in our selves, by Comparison with the Infirmity of others.'[35] Laughter at others signals not merriment but pride, Addison continues, and he laments the increasing prominence with which small-minded banterers practise the 'Art of Wit' (i. 203). The 'Stirrers up of Laughter', moreover, only amuse those of 'a gross Taste' (i. 201). This kind of disparaging merriment is, for Addison, not only unsociable but also distasteful, an aesthetic as well as a social problem. As one scholar has aptly suggested, while humour can be 'tempered by reason (judgment) or morality, laughter cannot, because it seems to be individual (neither universal nor communal) and egoistic.'[36] In *Spectator* no. 35, Addison describes a man of 'FALSE HUMOUR' as one whose 'Ridicule is always Personal' (i. 148): 'a Satyrical Author' is an 'angry Writer' who 'vents his Spleen in Libels and Lampoons' to the detriment of government and society (iv. 86). Implicitly denying the possibility of the benevolent satire advocated by Steele, Addison more often concludes

---

[33] *Tatler*, ii. 74.
[34] Giles Jacob, *The Poetical Register: or, the Lives and Characters of the English Dramatick Poets*, 2 vols. (1719–20), 2:xxiii.
[35] *Spectator*, i. 200.
[36] Endre Szécsényi, 'Freedom and Sentiments: Wit and Humour in the Augustan Age', *The Hungarian Journal of English and American Studies* 1–2 (2007), 79–92, at 85.

that 'Our Satyr is nothing but Ribaldry, and *Billingsgate*'. About the public harm done by satire, he is passionate:

> As this cruel Practice tends to the utter Subversion of all Truth and Humanity among us, it deserves the utmost Detestation and Discouragement of all who have either Love of their Country, or the Honour of their Religion, at Heart. I would therefore earnestly recommend it to the Consideration of those who deal in these pernicious Arts of Writing; and of those who take pleasure in the Reading of them.[37]

Satire is unpatriotic, and readers of it are every bit as guilty as its authors.

Nowhere do we find Addison's ally Steele so negative in his formulations: he prescribes without condemning, while Addison manifestly perceives satire as a social, moral, and political threat. This reflects his rejection of private motives for laughter or ridicule. He does not share Dryden's acknowledgement of defensible retribution or Pope's conviction of the justness of public shaming. For Addison, any positive satire has to be ego-less, but he also conceives of satire as by definition an expression of ego. The best articulation of the problem of personality in satire comes in *Tatler* no. 242, which is likely by Addison but if not certainly correlates with his position:

> In all Terms of Reproof, when the Sentence appears to arise from Personal Hatred or Passion, it is not then made the Cause of Mankind, but a Misunderstanding between Two Persons... There is no Possibility of succeeding in a Satyrical Way of Writing or Speaking, except a Man throws himself quite out of the Question. It is a great Vanity to think any one will attend a Thing because it is your Quarrel. You must make your Satyr the concern of Society in general, if you would have it regarded.[38]

Efficacy depends upon reception, and no one will be receptive to purely subjective reproach.

Addison's criticism of satire, however, serves as its own kind of satire, directed at the Tories. He invokes Hobbes, that is, partly to achieve his own political ends. When he defines satire as implicitly Juvenalian, as expressing superiority and derogation, he is manifestly targeting Tory practitioners. Swift's lampoons on the Earl of Godolphin and other political players typify the kind of abuse of which Addison is so loudly sceptical. In challenging this kind of satire, he is insinuating his own—Whig—superiority, and the superiority of Horatian *sermones* to Juvenalian diatribe. Mr Spectator works throughout his paper to satirize the Tories as 'incompetent, simple-minded old men who have lived beyond their usefulness', all the while sustaining an argument that satire is irredeemably bad. What he is himself practising is not satire—at least satire as defined by ignoble Tory standards. 'By claiming not to write satire', Paulson concludes, Addison creates

---

[37] *Spectator*, iv. 88.
[38] *Spectator*, iii. 244; on the authorship of this issue, see the note on iii. 238.

'as rhetorically effective a satire as can be imagined'.[39] Addison's strategy is to use comedy rather than anger as a vehicle for satiric judgement. Like Dryden's Jack Ketch, Mr Spectator does damage without seeming to do damage.

THE AUDIENCE FOR SATIRE

Dryden and Pope are strong voices for satire, in terms both of its private satisfaction and its public utility, and positions similar to theirs are commonly articulated among their contemporaries. Many shared Pope's sense that deterrence was more realistic than reformation. Defending himself against Jeremy Collier's attack (1698), William Congreve reasons that the satirical presentation of mistakes and misdeeds could have positive effect on two different types of audience members: 'as vicious People are made asham'd of their Follies or Faults, by seeing them expos'd in a ridiculous manner, so are good People at once both warn'd and diverted at their Expence'.[40] Following a similar logic, the author of *A Grammar of the English Tongue* (*c.*1710) likens satirists to doctors: both 'propose themselves to the Health of the Patient', and the satirist's medicine can 'correct the Perverse, and deter others from falling into Folly and Vice' (147). Satire is a better disincentive than incentive; it will discourage potential offenders rather than reform its targets.

If the object of satire is not private self-improvement but more general reform of social mores, then the point of ridicule is not the victim's mortification and alteration. The object is rather the edification of the audience. The loudest eighteenth-century advocate of this kind of satire is Henry Fielding, whose stated preference for instruction via example rather than precept is well known. In the 10 June 1740 issue of *The Champion*, Fielding hails William Hogarth 'as one of the most useful Satyrists any Age hath produced', since in his works 'you see the delusive Scene expos'd with all the Force of Humour, and on casting your Eyes on another Picture, you behold the dreadful and fatal Consequence'. Nothing is more instructive than witnessing a base man achieve greatness only to fall into contempt and misery, ending in a state of 'tottering, shaking, trembling; without Appetite for his Dainties, without Abilities for his Women', without pleasure or satisfaction. The satirist, according to this account, should teach people to be 'sensible of the Contempt a Man justly incurs' by his wrongdoing.[41]

Fielding and Pope would agree, then, that one object of satire is public exposure, though Pope's attitude towards satire is in many respects different from Fielding's, more target-centric and more inclined to injure. Pope was proud of his bold use of the satiric weapon, as were many others who adhered to the 'no pain, no [moral] gain' philosophy

---

[39] Ronald Paulson, *The Fictions of Satire* (Baltimore: Johns Hopkins University Press, 1967), 216, 218.

[40] William Congreve, *Amendments of Mr Collier's False and Imperfect Citations* (1698), 8.

[41] Henry Fielding, *Contributions to The Champion and Related Writings*, ed. W. B. Coley (Oxford: Clarendon Press, 2003), 365–6, 367.

of satiric punishment. In *The Muses Looking-Glass* (1706), Thomas Randolph maintains that punitive exposure of targets can be effective precisely because of its sting. When Randolph has 'Satyre' describe how even the 'greatest Tyrants' fear the lash and its attendant public humiliation, he is relishing the lasting effects of witty castigation. A 1740 poet likewise celebrates satire's capacity to shame its targets, and the papal echo is clear: satire is 'that Rod / Men sometimes fear who fear not God'.[42] Or, as Dryden and Mulgrave acclaimed, satire is 'the boldest way, if not the best, / To tell men freely of their foulest faults'.[43] These poets commend satire precisely for its power to humiliate. Shame is an instrument of socialization, satire a public form of purposive mortification.

Defoe's conception of audience signals a different notion of how satire works. He uses satire to instruct and persuade—but not in the way modern scholars tend to think of satirical instruction and persuasion. 'The End of *Satyr*', Defoe affirms in the preface to *A New Discovery of an Old Intreague* (1691), 'ought to be exposing Falshood'. The preface to his *The True-Born Englishman* (1701) announces a similar mission statement: '*The End of Satyr is Reformation*'.[44] As clichéd sentiments often expressed by satirists, these declarations might sound merely self-righteous, but many of Defoe's satires seem to work towards precisely this stated end. The assumption that all expressed justifications for satire are just defensive apologias is part and parcel with P. K. Elkin's fallacious premise that all 'satire is hostile by nature'.[45] When the latter supposition does not hold—as in the case of Defoe—neither does the former. Despite appearances, Defoe's proclamations of satire's positive capabilities are not simply versions of the standard satiric defence.

Defoe the satirist imagines readers who are receptive to the claims of conscience.[46] In *More Reformation* (1702), his poet explains to personified 'Satyr' that he does not hope to reach those who are unreceptive to moral reproach: satire, he suggests, can only 'work' for the man who sins 'like something of a Christian' (l. 636). Other writers also emphasize the importance of audience to satire, arguing (more broadly than Defoe) that readers and viewers of satire must be capable of feeling its sting. The author of *Vanelia: or, the Amours of the Great* (1732) has one character insist that 'Satire loses its Force where Men have lost all Shame' (vii). Defoe's satire seems designed and carefully constructed to speak to readers capable of remorse and self-judgement. His aims as a satirist have little to do with attacking or exposing those he disapproves of and much to do with educating a specific target audience. The readers he addresses in his satire are Christians—usually dissenters or Low Church Anglicans—who share his values. Defoe has plenty of

---

[42] *Laugh upon Laugh, or Laughter Ridicul'd* (1740), 32.

[43] John Sheffield, Earl of Mulgrave, and John Dryden, *An Essay upon Satire*, in *Anthology of Poems on Affairs of State: Augustan Satirical Verse, 1660–1714*, ed. George deF. Lord (New Haven and London: Yale University Press, 1975), 186.

[44] Both poems (along with *More Reformation*) are printed in *Satire, Fantasy and Writings on the Supernatural by Daniel Defoe*, vol. 1, ed. W. R. Owens (London: Pickering & Chatto, 2003); quotations at 37, 83.

[45] P. K. Elkin, *The Augustan Defence of Satire* (Oxford: Clarendon Press, 1973), 1.

[46] See Ashley Marshall, 'Daniel Defoe as Satirist', *Huntington Library Quarterly* 70 (2007), 553–76.

antagonists, but he frequently writes for his allies. This represents a notion of satire remote from exposure and from reformation-of-target: to mount a soapbox and preach to your socio-moral enemies is one thing; to warn the group with which you identify and sympathize about a mutual threat is quite another. Both are legitimate, if sanguine, conceptions of satire's positive functions, but they are worlds apart in practice and purpose.

THE SUBJECT OF SATIRE

The proper and improper focus of satire is too large a subject for exhaustive coverage here, even in the period at issue, but a few key points deserve highlighting. One aspect of appropriate subject is scale: the restriction of satire to follies (rather than vices) is a commonplace, and many writers of the long eighteenth century at least nominally espouse this position. Greater crimes and transgressions should, from the point of view of some contemporaries, be left to the judgement of the courts and God. As Blackmore argues, 'Where then the Legislature ends, the Comick Genius begins, and presides over the low and ordinary Affairs and Manners of Life.'[47] Beyond the question of scope—crimes or foibles, vices or follies—is that of target corrigibility. The author of *Some Critical and Politick Remarks On... Faction Display'd* (1704) presumes that 'true Satyr' exposes only that in men which 'is their fault, and in their power to mend' (7). Or, as Addison announces decisively, 'A Satyr should expose nothing but what is corrigible.'[48] One of Pope's aggrieved dunces complains of *The Dunciad*, in similar terms, that it failed to meet the classical standards for satire: the ancients did not 'lash... Personal Defect', since they understood that 'it was not in the Power of a Man to make his own Fortune, any more than he could make his own Person'.[49]

This emphasis on correctable faults is linked with an increasingly prominent satiric subject: affectation. Exposure of pretension—pretension to wit, to beauty, to learning, to artistic ability and/or critical acumen—does not wholly explain the work of any of the century's major authors, but it is an integral part of their satiric rationale. In *Verses on the Death of Dr Swift*, the impartial speaker praises the Dean for his judicious satire, which 'points at no defect, / But what all mortals may correct'. Swift 'spar'd a Hump or crooked Nose, / Whose Owners set not up for Beaux' (ll. 463–4, 467–8). Those who acknowledged their ignorance were exempt from punishment; what merits satiric exposure is posturing, proud fakery: 'True genuine dulness mov'd his pity, / Unless it offer'd to be witty'.[50] This is not unlike Pope's response to attacks on the *Dunciad*. When his critics lambast 'King Pope' for his pointless denunciation of undistinguished poets, he anticipates Swift's rationale: 'Deformity becomes the object of ridicule when a man sets up for being

---

[47] Sir Richard Blackmore, 'Upon Wit', in *Essays upon Several Subjects*, 2nd edn. (1716), 10.

[48] *Spectator*, ii. 321.   [49] *Codrus: or, the Dunciad Dissected* (1728), 7–8.

[50] Swift, *Poems* (Williams), 469–70.

handsome: and so must Dulness when he sets up for a Wit.'[51] Fielding would later issue a comparable verdict: in the preface to *Joseph Andrews*, he authoritatively concludes, 'The only Source of the true Ridiculous...is Affectation'. Fielding quotes Congreve— 'None are for being what they are in Fault, / But for not being what they would be thought'—and offers Hogarth's *The Distrest Poet* as a visual illustration of this theme.[52] The impoverishment depicted by Hogarth would move us to pity, but the subject's affectation turns our sympathy to laughter.

Few would disagree that charlatanism and hypocrisy are more defensible satiric targets than physical deformity or other uncorrectable misfortunes. The problem is that in practice Pope and Swift—among others—target more than affectation. They denigrate those who promulgate different cultural and political principles from their own. The language of 'affectation' sometimes, in other words, serves to provide a respectable cover for polemical or personal defamation. That said, the fact that 'affectation' became such a compelling rationale for personal attack in the eighteenth century does make clear something about attitudes in this period. Gratuitously malicious satire was widely practised in the late seventeenth century. By the time of Pope and Swift and Fielding, at least nominal justification for such disparagement was becoming requisite. That some of the sharpest critics of affectation also tended to use mock-heroic forms is not surprising. The form highlights the disparity between high and low, emphasizing the immeasurable distance between the affectation of grandeur and the reality of un-heroism.

THE PUBLIC AND PRIVATE
DIMENSIONS OF SATIRE

When eighteenth-century writers think about satire, they collectively worry about a whole host of issues related to society, morality, religion, and politics. Commentators on satire take a stand on the humanity (or not), reasonableness (or not), and effectiveness (or not) of ridicule; many of them either accuse wits of irreligion or challenge such accusations. One awkwardness concerning satire is that it is both a public and a private mode, and the relationship between its private and public motives is not always terribly clear. In the 'Discourse', Dryden suggests that lampoonery can be perhaps justified either on the basis of personal retribution or of shaming a 'publick Nuisance', but the former—private—aim would make most of satire's critics in this period uneasy. Dryden, like Pope, appreciates that revenge is an inevitable if not necessary honourable reason for writing satire, and both men allow more for the role of the ego than does Addison. Much ink is spilled in this period trying to figure out where the line is between

---

[51] Pope, *Poems* (Twickenham), v. 17.
[52] Henry Fielding, *Joseph Andrews*, ed. Martin C. Battestin (Oxford: Clarendon Press, 1967), 9.

public-minded and more personal satire, and attempting to transcend—or to seem to transcend—the subjective impetus for satiric judgement.

Whatever lip service gets paid to the prospect of effecting individual moral reform, in practice the assessment of satire has much more to do with its effect on the community: Does satire establish and enforce public norms, and thus strengthen society? Or does it damage communal bonds by meanly shaming individuals and threatening serious, thoughtful, moral reasoning? Commentators on satire are often implicitly or explicitly concerned with the problem of reconciling satire's private motives—the psychology of writer, audience, and target—with its public effects. A related issue has to do with the desired outcome: Are satirists trying to elicit emotions (pleasure, pain, anger) or to change behaviour? For Pope and many others, the two are intimately related: only shame can lead to reform. But when Dryden admits the possibility of retribution, he is obviously imagining something more emotionally satisfying than socio-morally enriching.

Writing about satire, we should remember, is as personal and partisan in this period as writing satire. The advocates of satire are also practitioners, and the critics are often targeting individual writers who are hardly fellow travellers, either in party politics or in culture wars. Dryden's motives in the 'Discourse' were both literary and political. He hoped to use his theory to shape practice: the poetics he wished to commend and establish was not based on contemporary writing but on the classical tradition, particularly on the models of Horace, Persius, and Juvenal. Dryden also penned his 'Discourse' soon after volumes of state poems began to appear. The 'Poems on Affairs of State' were mostly politicized satires, often abusively personal, many of them directed at the Stuart monarchs and their courts. Dryden was an apologist for both Charles and James, and his desire to marginalize and denounce that kind of satiric poetry is every bit as politically as it is culturally motivated. At the time of the 'Discourse', moreover, Dryden was embittered and financially stressed. He was a Catholic in a violently (and, as of 1689, officially) anti-Catholic country, and his estimation of William was not high. Much of the 'Discourse' is about weighing the relative merits of Juvenal versus those of Horace, and Dryden's praise of Juvenal is pointed: the implication is that his own moment is, like Juvenal's, one in which a bad king deserves to be scourged by proxy. Both Dryden and Pope seem to understand that different times require different satiric voices: as opposition satirists (Dryden in the 1690s, Pope in the 1730s), both acknowledge the utility and even necessity of 'tragic' rather than 'comic' satire. Writing against the barbarians, both laud the gentler Horace while channelling the pain-inflicting Juvenal. Neither feels that he has the luxury of relying upon mild *sermones* to set his world aright.

Commentary on satire in this period often reflects this tension between outrage and civility, between judgement and politeness, between the *act* of satire and the *language* of satire. For Dryden, the response is largely formal: adopting the manner of Horace, writing in the language of classical satire, renders aggressive satiric judgement palatable and respectable. Pope's response is likewise the use of formal (classical) apologia, in which he emphasizes victim blame, poses as the wounded *vir bonus*, and develops the fiction of the noble satirist. Like his Tory contemporaries, Addison understands the value of mitigation, but he camouflages rather than justifies his satiric critique.

What justification there is remains implicit. Despite Swift's self-praise for having 'spar'd a Hump', he goes to comparatively little trouble to defend his satire. What apologies he makes have much to do with his conviction that his enemies are culturally deficient and politically egregious, but his attitude is rarely defensive (like Pope's) or disguised (like Addison's). The Dean tends to be more interested in the practice of satire than its theory, more eager to 'do' topical political, cultural, and moral satire than to dictate or redefine the satiric role.

Thinking about Satire's Legacy

Focusing on the attitudes expressed by major authors gives a somewhat misleading impression of contemporary thoughts about eighteenth-century satire. The corpus of such commentary is vast, and most of what should count in an assessment of contemporary attitudes is patchy, occasional, and partisan. What surveying it suggests, among other things, is that the readers, authors, politicians, and preachers who voiced their thoughts about satiric practice had no inkling that they were living in what would eventually become known as the great age of satire. The majority of these writers, whatever their disparate positions, would undoubtedly be astonished to learn that we celebrate and study such topical, incoherent, controversial, morally and ethically dubious ephemera.

Satire was an uncertain form that made both its defenders and its critics uncomfortable. They did not know what was or was not satire, whether satire was or was not useful, whether it was or was not dangerous, or when they were or were not being targeted. Even the etymology was ambiguous: does 'satire' derive from the Roman '*lanx satura*' (full or mixed platter) or from the Greek 'satyr' (a malcontent who is half-human, half-beast)? Satire's relationship to other kinds of judgement-rendering discursive modes was likewise uncertain: some distinguished objectionable satire from light raillery.[53] For others raillery was worse because more personal and less reform-oriented.[54] Nomenclatural discrepancies and confusion about etymology signal a broader conceptual impasse. Was satire essentially a positive force, with its moral basis and reformative aims, or was it pernicious, beastly, and anti-social?

Classical, continental, and Renaissance predecessors in the practice of satire notwithstanding, 'satire' was nothing like a settled form in the long eighteenth century. It had both supporters and opponents, but as the supporters have no consistent notion of what the form is supposed to do, the debate started out unfocused and remained that way. The extensive corpus of commentary on satire and related concepts—on raillery, lampoonery, wit, laughter, and ridicule—emerges from a wide range of perspectives. Advocates and sceptics and denouncers of the mode seem to concur in feeling apprehensive about it, but the stakes and the questions and the implications vary considerably from debate

---

[53]   *Enigmaticall Characters... from Severall Persons, Humours, & Dispositions* (1658).
[54]   *Some Critical and Politick Remarks On... Faction Display'd*, 12.

to debate and pamphlet to pamphlet. The philosophy of satire in the long eighteenth century remains a fascinating subject for at least two distinct reasons. One is that our authors crafted so many satiric masterpieces—*Mac Flecknoe, Absalom and Achitophel, Hudibras, The Rape of the Lock, Gulliver's Travels, The Beggar's Opera, The Dunciad,* Swift's *Verses, The Vanity of Human Wishes,* and so on and so on—even as they and their contemporaries tried to come to terms with this problematic, ill-defined, much-contested discursive mode. Another is that the diversity of opinion about what satire is and does, the multiplicity of models for 'thinking about satire', perfectly anticipates and complements the radical diversity in eighteenth-century satiric practice. Whether contemporaries knew it or not, the long eighteenth century *was* the *aetas mirabilis* of English satire, a time of rich discussions about ethics and efficacy and about the aesthetics and humanity of humorous judgement—and a time of satiric production that is, quantitatively and qualitatively, simply astonishing.

SELECT BIBLIOGRAPHY

Connery, Brian A. and Kirk Combe, eds. *Theorizing Satire: Essays in Literary Criticism* (New York: Macmillan, 1995).

Elkin, P. K. *The Augustan Defence of Satire* (Oxford: Clarendon Press, 1973).

Griffin, Dustin. *Satire: A Critical Reintroduction* (Lexington: University Press of Kentucky, 1994).

Kernan, Alvin B. *The Plot of Satire* (New Haven: Yale University Press, 1965).

Marshall, Ashley. *The Practice of Satire in England, 1658–1770* (Baltimore: Johns Hopkins University Press, 2013).

Paulson, Ronald. *Don Quixote in England: The Aesthetics of Laughter* (Baltimore: Johns Hopkins University Press, 1998).

Paulson, Ronald. 'Dryden and the Energies of Satire', in *The Cambridge Companion to John Dryden,* ed. Steven N. Zwicker (Cambridge: Cambridge University Press, 2004), 37–58.

Paulson, Ronald. *The Fictions of Satire* (Baltimore: Johns Hopkins University Press, 1967).

Quintero, Ruben, ed. *A Companion to Satire* (Malden: Blackwell, 2007).

Weinbrot, Howard D. *Menippean Satire Reconsidered: From Antiquity to the Eighteenth Century* (Baltimore: Johns Hopkins University Press, 2005).

CHAPTER 29

....

EPIGRAM AND
SPONTANEOUS WIT

....

KATE LOVEMAN

COMMENTATORS in the late seventeenth and early eighteenth centuries regarded the epigram as a wildly popular form of wit. In 1670, Richard Flecknoe began his collection of epigrams by asserting that epigrammatic wit in prose and verse was near ubiquitous: '*Poets* can't *write*, nor *Orators* declame / But all their *wit* is chiefly *Epigram*', he boasted.[1] Flecknoe is more often remembered as a butt of wit than an authority on it, but celebrated critics, such as William Temple and John Dryden, also remarked on the prevalence of epigrammatic wit and its admirers.[2] For these critics, however, epigram's popularity was often a cause for disquiet rather than celebration. The long-standing suspicion of epigram's appeal arose from two principal concerns. The first was the widespread associ- ation of epigram with libellous satire. This was recognized in law and in literature. In 1616, Ben Jonson began his collection of 'Epigrammes' by alerting readers that his poems would defy the expectations created by their genre: these epigrams would not be 'bold, licentious, full of gall', nor publicly shame individuals, nor use obscenity 'to catch the worlds loose laughter'.[3] Epigram, Jonson alleged, was a genre that conventionally catered to readers' basest desires for ridicule, vitriol, and scandal. The second reason to decry the popularity of epigrams stemmed from the perception that these were usually trifling productions—rapidly composed, rapidly consumed, and thus having little claim to endur- ing worth. The qualities that prompted renowned critics to disparage the epigram were qualities that appealed to large numbers of their contemporaries.[4] As the seventeenth century became the eighteenth and critics decried the disreputableness of the epigram,

---

[1] Richard Flecknoe, *Epigrams of All Sorts* (1669, rev. 1670), 2.

[2] William Temple, *Miscellanea, The Second Part*, 2nd edn. (1690), 325–7; John Dryden, dedication 'To John, Lord Marquess of Normanby', in *The Works of Virgil* (1697), fol. e3v.

[3] 'To My Booke', in *The Workes of Benjamin Jonson* (1616), 769. For the legal association of libel and epigram see Edward Coke, *Quinta pars relationum Edwardi Coke* (1605), fol. 125v.

[4] On these tensions see Roger D. Lund, 'The Ghosts of Epigram, False Wit, and the Augustan Mode', *Eighteenth-Century Life* 27, no. 2 (2003), 67–95.

epigrams were coming into print as never before. As will become clear, part of the problem for critics was that the criteria used to judge witty epigrammatic verse were at odds—sometimes deliberately and perversely so—with more conventional routes to forming judgements on literary merit. Probing the associations between epigram, ridicule, and spontaneous wit in the long eighteenth century offers insights into the ways people of different degrees encountered and participated in satire. The publication of epigrammatic wit was not always via manuscript dissemination or print, so this investigation entails tracing some of the most elusive—yet culturally pervasive—acts of satire. These are contexts which are now little understood by readers, but which, in the long eighteenth century, were widely recognized and influential in the interpretation of satirical verse.

DEFINITION AND APPRECIATION

It was easier to identify the characteristics of epigrammatic wit than to define the epigram form itself. As both early modern and recent writers have noted, 'epigram' was a slippery term.[5] An epigram could be in prose as well as in verse, and epigrams dealt in praise as well as blame. Popular subgenres of epigram included the epitaph (words to be carved on a memorial), as well as the mock epitaph (ridiculing a dead individual, or one who was lamentably still living). 'Epigram', as critics informed readers, meant 'inscription', for an epigram was originally a phrase or verse carved upon a building or set up in a public place in ancient Greece or Rome. Martial and other Roman poets were credited, or occasionally criticized, for strengthening the association of epigram with sharp and witty verse.[6] James Doelman has argued that during the early seventeenth century the 'dual face' of the epigram—its situation between the classical and the vernacular, written and oral forms—contributed to its lively part in political discourse.[7] When commentators in the late seventeenth and early eighteenth centuries sought to express the essential qualities of epigram, vitality and conciseness were seen as key: they identified its *'life and quickness'*, or wrote of its *'Brevity… Force, and Energy'*.[8] It was also expected that a verse epigram would end with 'a point'. As Charles Gildon explained, this meant *'Some unexpected, and some biting Thought, / With poinant [sic] Wit, and sharp Expression fraught'*.[9] In the later seventeenth century, epigram as a form of animated, combative wit came to be linked to 'raillery' and 'repartee', recent imports from French. As in Gildon's example, the language used to celebrate epigrammatic wit in the eighteenth century associated it with sudden

[5] Lawrence Manley, 'Proverbs, Epigrams, and Urbanity in Renaissance London', *English Literary Renaissance* 15, no. 3 (1985), 247–76; James Doelman, 'Circulation of the Late Elizabethan and Early Stuart Epigram', *Renaissance and Reformation* 29 (2005), 59–73; James Doelman, 'Epigrams and Political Satire in Early Stuart England', *Huntington Library Quarterly* 69, no. 1 (2006), 31–45.

[6] For example, Flecknoe, *Epigrams of All Sorts*, fol. A2v; Temple, *Miscellanea*, 326; Charles Gildon, *The Complete Art of Poetry*, vol. 1 (1718), 148–9, 150.

[7] Doelman, 'Epigrams', 31–3.   [8] Flecknoe, *Epigrams*, fol. A2v; Gildon, *Complete Art*, 153.

[9] Gildon, *Complete Art*, 153.

pain or a blow successfully struck: epigrams were advertised to readers as 'stinging', 'nipping', 'biting', 'poignant' (sharp), and 'smart' (brisk and cutting).[10]

The briskness associated with epigrammatic wit posed problems for critics who wanted to understand wit's influence. In 1669, Walter Charleton pondered the elusiveness of extempory wit, apparently with members of the restored court and their satirical 'Hitts' very much in mind. 'Acute reflections' made in a 'suddain and jocular' fashion were, he noted, apt to delight company, especially when delivered by people whose 'comeliness of Person' or high rank gave them great 'Confidence', for 'then is their liberty of jesting as it were authorized in all places'.[11] However:

> if those very concise sayings, and lucky *Repartés* (for the Court hath now naturaliz'd that Word) wherein they are so happy, and which at first hearing were entertained with so much of pleasure and admiration; be written down, and brought to a strict examination of their *Pertinency, Coherence* and *Verity*: how shallow, how frothy, how forced will they be found! how much will they lose of that Applause, which their tickling of the ear, and present flight through the Imagination had gain'd! (61)

Since extempory oral wit was rapidly considered by the audience (making 'present flight through the Imagination'), the audience's judgement was easily misled. Being 'written down', Charleton implied, killed this type of wit, partly because a written account could not replicate the enlivening circumstances of delivery, but often because the jest was weak and deserved to die. Later discussion specifically on verse epigrams likewise stressed that these manifestations of wit did not stand up to mature or prolonged scrutiny. In 1697, John Dryden compared 'the lowest Form' of readers to 'our Upper-Gallery Audience in a Play-House; who like nothing but the Husk and Rhind of Wit; preferr a Quibble, a Conceit, an Epigram, before solid Sense, and Elegant Expression: These are Mobb-Readers'.[12] Epigrams ranked low in the early modern hierarchy of genres.[13] Dryden took the additional step of casting appreciation of epigrams as the mark of low-status readers. The wit of epigrams was characterized as mere wordplay and represented as appealing to the many who lacked judgement, such as schoolboys (alluded to in Dryden's reference to 'the lowest Form') and the crowd in the cheapest seats at the theatre. Epigrams were popular because they appealed to the foolish populace. Addison, writing in *The Spectator* in 1712, seconded Dryden's statements on the popularity and the superficiality of epigrammatic wit. Unfortunately, he wrote, 'Our general Taste in *England* is for Epigram, turns of Wit, and forced Conceits, which have no manner of Influence,

---

[10] See, for example, title pages of *The Merry Companion* (Dublin, 1752); *Jack Smart's Merry Jester*, 2nd edn. ([1755?]); *Tom Brown's Complete Jester*, 2nd edn. ([1760?]).

[11] [Walter Charleton], *Two Discourses* (1669), 58.

[12] Dryden, *Works of Virgil*, fol. e3v. Dryden here elaborates on Jean Regnault de Segrais's divisions of readers in *Traduction de L'Eneïde de Virgile* (Paris, 1668), 2–3.

[13] Alastair Fowler, *Kinds of Literature: An Introduction to the Theory of Genres and Modes* (Oxford: Clarendon Press, 1982, repr. 1997), 216–17.

either for the bettering or enlarging the Mind of him who reads them, and have been carefully avoided by the greatest Writers, both among the Ancients and Moderns.'[14]

CIRCULATION

Addison would have had difficulty sustaining his case that 'the greatest' Moderns had scrupulously avoided the epigram, but his contemporaries were often careful about how they acknowledged and circulated their epigrams. If an epigram was satirical, a judicious concern about inviting prosecution under libel laws or the risk of retaliation might make an author think twice before openly acknowledging it. The celebration of spontaneous wit and the low status of epigrams in the literary canon were additional reasons for caution: one should not be seen to exert labour over this kind of composition. Richard Flecknoe advised readers of his collection that the shortness and quickness of epigrams suited his nature as someone who did not love '*to take pains in any thing, and rather* [to] *affect a* little negligence, *than* too great curiosity'.[15] Negligence or 'sprezzatura' (the ability to conceal the effort that went into a performance) was much prized among wits of the late seventeenth century and was near essential when it came to productions in frivolous, occasional genres such as the epigram. Phil Hartle has argued that, unlike Flecknoe, writers connected with the court were wary of publishing epigram collections because the evident labour required to produce a collection of such trifles was a 'paradoxical act' and inconsistent with ideals of genteel, easy authorship.[16] Epigrammatic wit was a means to seek acclaim, but not if one was seen actively to be seeking it. Sprezzatura in matters of composition might therefore extend to seeming nonchalance over print publication, or a reluctance to acknowledge individual epigrams. Meanwhile, epigrams were in high demand—at least among eighteenth-century publishers. With the rapid growth of the periodical press in the early eighteenth century, epigrams were a means to supply the continual need for short pieces to fill newspapers and journals. They could also be used as material for printed miscellanies and jest-books, which were appearing in considerable numbers. Epigrams were a cheap means to boost sales: a few short poems added to an existing poetry collection transformed it into an enlarged second edition or made a collection of an author's works appear more complete than a rival publisher's version.[17] Epigrams already in manuscript circulation could be recruited to these causes—perhaps with the addition of an attribution to a famous name. The result was large numbers

---

[14] *Spectator*, vi. 77 (1713).   [15] Flecknoe, *Epigrams*, fol. A2v. 'Curiosity' means 'fastidiousness'.

[16] Phil Hartle, '"Quaint *Epigrammatist*": Martial in Late Seventeenth-Century England', *Neophilologus* 79 (1995), 336, 346.

[17] One example among many is *Court Poems in Two Parts Compleat, To which are added I. Verses upon Prudery. II. An Epitaph upon John Hewett and Mary Drew* (1719) announced as 'by Mr. Pope' (Edmund Curll was connected with its publication). This was a reissue of previously published sheets, with two additional epigrams that were attributed to Pope.

of epigrams circulating anonymously or with dubious attributions, being repeatedly republished, and sometimes reworked to suit new audiences.

Print was not, however, likely to be where people first encountered epigrams. George Puttenham, writing in 1589, described how epigrams were routinely composed and published in the early modern period. 'Epigrams', he explained, had originated as writings

> made as it were upon a table, or in a windowe, or upon the wall or mantell of a chimney in some place of common resort, where it was allowed every man might come, or be sitting to chat and prate, as now in our tavernes and common tabling houses, where many merry heades meete, and scrible with ynke with chalke, or with a cole such matters as they would every man should know, & descant upon. Afterward the same came to be put in paper and in bookes, and used as ordinarie missives, some of frendship, some of defiaunce, or as other messages of mirth.[18]

The practice of writing on the walls, doors, and ceilings of private houses and public buildings continued across the seventeenth and eighteenth centuries. Taverns, alehouses, coffee-houses, shop windows, courting spots, and privies were some of the favourite locations for graffiti. Juliet Fleming points out that the act of writing on public buildings did not necessarily carry the transgressive implications that it would today—it was often the content of the writing, rather than the act of writing itself, that violated moral or social boundaries.[19] Puttenham mentions chalk and coal as writing materials, but pencil and candle-smoke were also used. Windows might be etched using a diamond ring or a diamond pencil (a tool for etching glass), so writing on glass was linked with high-status men and women, as well as with ring-brandishing lovers.[20] The location of a verse could add to its meaning and its piquancy. For example, to claim that a libellous epigram had first been displayed in a famous forum, such as the Royal Exchange, implied the author or a scribe felt strongly enough to risk capture in order to ensure maximum publicity. If the epigram was located in a private or elite space, then the impression was of an astutely targeted attack and an insulting violation.

Very little of what appears to have been a wealth of early modern graffiti survives today. However, among the extant sources are print publications that purport to record contemporary graffiti. In the 1730s a series of collections entitled *The Merry-Thought: or, The Glass-Window and Bog-House Miscellany* printed 'Epigrams, Sonnets, and Whims' 'Faithfully Transcribed from the Drinking-Glasses and Windows in the several noted *Taverns, Inns*, and other *Publick Places* in this Nation'. The editor of *The Merry-Thought* joked with readers that they needed to act quickly to send him choice examples, since events such as pre-holiday cleaning or games of football would otherwise erase the

---

[18] [George Puttenham], *The Arte of English Poesie* (1589), 43–4.

[19] Juliet Fleming, *Graffiti and the Writing Arts of Early Modern England* (London: Reaktion Books, 2001), 50–8.

[20] *The Merry-Thought: or, The Glass-Window and Bog-House Miscellany, Parts 2, 3 and 4*, facsimile reprint, intro. Maximillian E. Novak, Augustan Reprint Society 221–22 (Los Angeles: William Andrews Clark Memorial Library, University of California, 1983), Part 4 [1732], title page, 17; Fleming, *Graffiti*, 55–7.

poems forever (football, as today, led to smashed windows).[21] The verses printed were predominantly amusing poems on lust, love, and shitting. They included epigrams headed '*Star-Inn at Coventry, in a Window*', from a wall at '*the Cardinal's-Cap in Windsor*', '*In a Boghouse at Richmond*', and '*In a Barber's Shop*'. Some were described as '*in a Woman's Hand*'.[22] Epigrams in *The Merry-Thought* collections were often followed by verses that they had provoked:

> *Hampton-Court, at the Mitre, 1718.*
> How have I strove to gain the Fair?
> And yet how little does she care?
> But leaves me starving with Despair.
> 'Tis now full Eight, I fear her Spouse
> Has given her a Rendezvous.

> *Those five Lines were crossed out; but then follows:*
> D—mn the first Lines, they are not mine,
> T'abuse a Lady so divine;
> Altho' I waited for her Hours,
> I have enjoy'd her lovely Powers,
> Her Wit, her Beauty, and her Sense,
> Have fully made me Recompence.

> Captain R. T. July 10. 1710 [recte 1718].

> *Underwritten.*
> Friend Captain T,
> If thou can'st C,
> Mind what I have to say to thee,
> Thy Strumpet Wh—re abhominable,
> Which thou didst kiss upon a Table,
> Has made thy manly Parts unable.

> Farewel, &c. Z.B.[23]

The gentlemanly rake, 'Captain R.T.', begins with elevated and conventional poetic diction, only for the closing couplet of the first stanza to reveal, first, the existence of the lady's husband and then R.T.'s fears that this husband has supplanted him in a tryst. At this 'point', the perfect rhyme of the triplet is supplanted by mere eye-rhyme (Spouse/Rendezvous) and falters comically. Distinguishing a poor rhyme from a historical rhyme can be tricky in early modern poetry, but this final couplet was scarcely a smooth match.[24]

---

[21] *The Merry-Thought*, Part 3, 'Preface'.

[22] *The Merry-Thought*, Part 1, 3rd edn. ([1731]), facsimile reprint, intro. George R. Guffey, Augustan Reprint Society 216 (Los Angeles: William Andrews Clark Memorial Library, University of California, 1982), 10, 19, 21, 24, 31.

[23] *The Merry-Thought*, Part 1, 23–4. Given the sequence heading, the year '1710' under the second verse is a misprint for 1718. 'Captain R.T.' signs other poems '1718' (Part 3, 12).

[24] The correct and fashionable pronunciation of 'rendezvouz' was 'rendevoo' according to John Jones's *The Art of Right Spelling and Pronouncing All the Words of the English Tongue* (1721, first published 1701), 85. For suggestions of other possible pronunciations see William Matthews, 'Variant Pronunciations in the Seventeenth Century', *Journal of English and Germanic Philology* 37, no. 2 (1938), esp. 197.

After R.T. retracts in the next verse, the new writer Z.B. intervenes to dismiss his romantic bliss, dramatically lowering the register and tone, and introducing 'abhominable' rhymes. These manoeuvres all serve to satirize R.T.'s abilities in verse and in bed (or, as Z.B. alleges, on the table).

The conventions, methods, and typical locations of epigrammatic graffiti were assumed by editors of printed collections to be well known to their readers. For example, in 1735, Jonathan Swift's collected works included a series of epigrams said to have been composed '*On seeing Verses written upon Windows in Inns*'. Readers were to infer that Swift's verses had been engraved on the same window. In his first poem, Swift complained of the 'Window scrawl'd by ev'ry Rake' and 'bid the D—l take / The Di'mond and the Lover'. That poem was followed by two more satires on the theme of lovers' devilishly bad poetry, including:

> Another.
> By *Satan* taught, all Conj'rers know
> Your Mistress in a Glass to show,
> And, you can do as much:
> In this the Dev'l and you agree;
> None e'er made Verses worse than he,
> And thine I swear are such.[25]

Imagined in the supposed context of the window, this constituted not just an insult but a challenge. Readers of the printed collection were to understand Swift's window verses as an invitation to the original readership (visitors to the inn) to laugh, and as a standing provocation to passing lover-poets to respond. In 1589, Puttenham had depicted epigrams as invitations to engage. To him, these were satirical, sociable writings done to provoke public talk, to cement bonds of friendship, or engage another in verbal combat. Over 140 years later, these understandings held good: while epigrams might appear to want to give a definitive and summative commentary on a topic, they were circulated in contexts that encouraged responses in kind.

VERSE GAMES

The tradition of writing or posting epigrams on buildings offered one set of contexts for interpreting satirical verse in print or manuscript. A related set of understandings for appreciating satire came from practices of competitive verse. Training in epigram composition was part of an extended education and it included a competitive element: grammar schoolboys and university students were required rapidly to compose Latin and Greek verses, sometimes with prizes awarded for the best contributions.

---

[25] [Jonathan Swift], *The Works of J. S, D.D, D.S.P.D. in Four Volumes* (Dublin, 1735), ii. 469, 470.

Hence, presumably, Dryden's gibe at epigrams as 'the lowest Form' of verse, admired by schoolboys. Competitive verse composition easily became an extracurricular pursuit among students.[26]

Beyond grammar school and university students, informal training in extempore verse was gained through pastimes. The best-known of these pursuits was 'crambo'. An early reference to a game called 'crambe' (signifying 'repetition') came in a masque by Jonson written in 1624. Under the name 'Crambo', this pastime became particularly fashionable in the 1660s, and it remained current throughout the eighteenth century.[27] The rules of crambo were regarded by writers as being so obvious that the term very rarely required explanation; however, it was used for several kinds of extempore verse game. In the standard version, one player invented a line of verse, and then each participant had to devise a line that rhymed—the aim being to keep the rhyme going as long as possible. If you repeated a word or failed to come with a rhyme, you lost and might pay a forfeit.[28] Other mentions of 'Crambo' concern a challenge involving the completion of rhyming couplets or refer to the pastime elsewhere called *bouts-rimés*, in which players are given a list of rhyming words and have to invent lines to fit them.[29] Crambo, in its various forms, was suited to mixed company and many types of social gathering. Thus, on 19 May 1660, Samuel Pepys found himself travelling to The Hague and 'playing at Crambo in the waggon'. The players were a group of fellow Englishmen, including George Pinkney (an embroiderer), the twelve-year-old son of Pepys's employer, and a 'very sober' naval chaplain.[30]

Significantly, when crambo is mentioned in printed sources it is often to instance bad verse, or in reference to highly suspect or strained rhymes that were designed to amuse. For example, Henry Bold's collection of *Poems Lyrique, Macaronique, Heroique* (1664) was prefixed by a sarcastic commendatory verse from Norton Bold, his brother and an Oxford scholar:

> *Reading thine unstrained Verse, oh how it rue'th,*
> *That I ne followed Crambo from my youth!*
> *And that I ne're consorted much with Those*
> *Who use what ever's spoke, to clink ith' Close.*[31]

---

[26] Hoyt Hopewell Hudson, *The Epigram in the English Renaissance* (Princeton: Princeton University Press, 1947), ch. 4.

[27] [Jonson], *The Fortunate Isles* [1625], fol. B3v. Crambe means 'cabbage' but came to signify dull or unwarranted repetition from its use in phrases such as 'crambe bis cocta' (cabbage boiled twice). *Early English Books Online* (http://eebo.chadwyck.com) reveals a concentration of references to 'crambo' in plays and light literature starting around 1660.

[28] Edward Phillips and J[ohn] K[ersey], *The New World of Words: or Universal English Dictionary* (1706).

[29] *Ben Johnson's Jests* (1751), 140, cf. *bouts-rimés* as detailed in *Spectator*, i. 339–41 (no. 60, 1712).

[30] *The Diary of Samuel Pepys*, ed. Robert Latham and William Matthews, 11 vols. (1970–83, repr. London: HarperCollins and Berkeley: University of California Press, 2000), i. 149, 107.

[31] Henry Bold, *Poems Lyrique, Macaronique, Heroique, &c* (1664), fol. A5v. Other references to crambo as strained and amusingly bad verse include *Pantagruel's Prognostication* ([1660?]), fol. A6r and *The Visions of Dom Francisco de Quevedo Villegas*, [trans. Roger L'Estrange], (1667), 237.

This verse was artfully bad, with words ostentatiously truncated or elided to fit the metre, some convoluted grammar (Oh how it rue'th), and unusual spelling to encourage a wrenched accent (by splitting 'rueth' with an apostrophe, the poet sets up the rhyme word to be stressed 'you-*th*'). While it was possible to dazzle with brilliant and apt rhymes in crambo, much of the fun seems to have come from contriving—or being forced to contrive—egregious and groan-worthy rhymes.[32] In the late 1660s and 1670s, rhyming couplets and end-rhymes were receiving much critical attention thanks to their prominence in heroic drama and panegyric.[33] The counterpoint to the use of couplets in august genres was a fashion for satires involving suspect rhyme: a fashion that coincided with the height of the crambo craze in the 1660s. Samuel Butler's *Hudibras* (1663), one of the most acclaimed satires of the Restoration, made great play with inventive rhyme, inviting readers' amusement at the more dubious instances. For example, the narrator observed that ancient heroes claimed to be descended from Jupiter in order to disguise that 'they were of doubtful gender, / And that they came in at a Windore'.[34] 'Gender', meaning 'generation', did not rhyme with 'window'. 'Windore' was an accepted, if unusual, spelling, and one favoured by Butler when he wanted emphasize a window's use as an illicit entrance.[35] His variant spelling and imperfect rhyme drew attention to the pun.

If one criterion that influenced verse games was gauging amusingly bad rhyme, another was judging where playfulness ended and sincerity began. Verse games could create a space for licensed insults. *England's Jests Refin'd* (1687) related an episode involving Jonson and his contemporary, Josuah Sylvester. Sylvester had been the subject of a complimentary epigram in Jonson's 1616 collection of epigrams. However, late seventeenth-century jest-books were not interested in Jonson as a studious author of print compliments but in his legendary skills in repartee and improvisation:

> *Ben-Johnson* and *Silvester* being very merry one day at [the Devil] Tavern, began to Rhime upon one another; so *Silvester* began thus:
>
> > *I* Silvester
> > *Lay with your Sister.*
>
> To whom *Ben-Johnson* answer'd:
>
> > *I* Ben. Johnson
> > *Lay with your Wife.*
>
> *That*, says *Silvester, Is no Rhyme; but Faith, 'tis true though*, says *Ben-Johnson*.[36]

---

[32] Comic doggerel verse was associated with a burlesque style and, in the early seventeenth century, had been popularized by several literary clubs. See Timothy Raylor, *Cavaliers, Clubs and Literary Culture: Sir John Mennes, James Smith and the Order of the Fancy* (Newark: University of Delaware Press; London and Toronto: Associated University Presses, 1994), especially ch. 7.

[33] See Tom Lockwood, 'Rochester and Rhyme', in *Lord Rochester in the Restoration World*, ed. Matthew C. Augustine and Steven N. Zwicker (Cambridge: Cambridge University Press, 2015), 277–9.

[34] [Samuel Butler], *Hudibras, The First Part* (1663), Wing B6300, 87.

[35] Cf. Butler, *Hudibras, The First and Second Parts* (1674), Wing B6311, 246. On the pronunciation see *Gazophylacium Anglicanum* (1689), fol. Bb3r.

[36] *England's Jests Refin'd* (1687), 78–9.

This story had been appearing in jest-books since 1660, along with other instances of Jonson's '*Extemporary* Verses'.[37] The joke (such as it was) was that Jonson professed to put perfect truth over perfect rhyme, thereby leaving Sylvester to decide where jest became earnest, and wit became insult—it was a simple move on Jonson's part, but a difficult one to respond to appropriately. A skilful player could use the uncertainty created by the conditions of the game to their own ends. In Defoe's *Moll Flanders* (1721), the antiheroine proves just such an adept gamester. Moll participates in a playful exchange of window verses with one of her suitors, who is under the impression that she is a wealthy gentlewoman rather than an impoverished would-be bigamist. In the course of their rhyming exchange, Moll's admirer writes '*I scorn your Gold, and yet I Love*', leading her to respond '*I'm Poor: Let's see how kind you'll prove*.'[38] To Moll's admirer it appears that her professions of poverty are intended simply to mock trite declarations of unconditional love—including these professions as they appeared in window poetry. He therefore believes that she has simply 'jested' with him about her poverty, and that he has won the exchange by obtaining an invitation to pursue her. However, as Moll explains to her readers, whether her lover was 'in jest or in earnest', she had written only the truth, making it difficult for her prospective husband to reproach her when he discovers that she genuinely has little money.[39] Moll emerges as the true winner and, through her strategic use of language, the better poet. Wits in this kind of game show their skills in quick ingenuity with rhyme, in concise expression, and in their artful exploitation of the boundaries between sincerity and jest to voice unwelcome truths in relative safety.

Yet in a society that prized extempore wit, what were men and women to do who worried about their ability to join in extemporary verse games, even at the basic level of finding a rhyme? Clearly the answer was to practise—to rehearse your impromptu wit. Edward Phillips's *The Mysteries of Love & Eloquence* (1658) therefore offered a number of resources for improving one's responses on 'sudden occasions of Writing or Discourses', including 'a Riming Dictionary, consisting of Monasyllables, for the endings of Verses, applicable for those that are yong Practitioners [*sic*] in the pleasant Sport named *Crambo*'. These were lists of rhyme words to memorize ('Stab, Scab, drab, slab, crab', etc.).[40] As Norton Bold's poem suggests, crambo had a reputation almost from the start of being a training ground for would-be poets. By the 1690s, its very popularity seems to have led to a decline in its social élan: it was mocked as a pursuit of novice poets and, repeatedly, of maidservants.[41] The rhyming wit and wordplay involved in extemporary verse games and hudibrastic satire was also under attack. In 1711, an issue of *The Spectator*, written by Addison, recalled a dream vision in which the narrator visited the temple of Dullness and found 'a Cluster of Men and Women laughing very heartily, and diverting themselves at a Game of *Crambo*. I heard several *double Rhymes* as I passed by them, which

---

[37] *England's Jests Refin'd*, 78–80; *A Choice Banquet of Witty Jests* (1660), 107.

[38] 'Prove/love' was a conventional and unexceptionable rhyme in early eighteenth-century poetry.

[39] [Daniel Defoe], *The Fortunes and Misfortunes of the Famous Moll Flanders* (1721), 92–3.

[40] E[dward] P[hillips], *The Mysteries of Love & Eloquence* (1658), fol. A4v, 193.

[41] For example, William Congreve, *Love for Love* (1695), 3; [Mary Astell], *An Essay in Defence of the Female Sex* (1696), fol. A6r, 120; *A Trip to Ireland* ([London?], 1699), 1.

raised a great deal of Mirth.'[42] A 'double Rhyme' rhymed two syllables, with the first stressed and the second unstressed, as in double/trouble. In crambo, responding with a double rather than single rhyme was an achievement, and 'Mirth' came from cunning or deliberately daft solutions. Double and even triple rhymes in these veins were a characteristic of hudibrastic verse. Canto 2 of *Hudibras* played up to this delight in its opening couplet: 'There was an ancient sage *Philosopher*, / That had read *Alexander Ross* over.' Addison complained that these particular lines were 'more frequently quoted, than the finest Pieces of Wit in the whole Poem'. For Addison, this was 'ignorant' rather than informed appreciation, and his influential writing portrayed crambo and ingenious double rhymes in particular as 'false Wit'.[43] His implication was that participants in such pursuits prized sound over sense and were not knowingly relishing feats of witty rhyming, but responding witlessly.

INTERPRETING COURT SATIRE

There was more wit involved in crambo-playing than Addison was prepared to concede, and these shared games proved a useful resource for authors and their readers. The understandings that underpinned popular verse games and epigrammatic exchanges were among the contexts used to frame court satire for a wide readership. Jest-books were one route by which satires reputed to have originated at the Restoration court reached readers. The characters appearing in seventeenth-century jest-books included court jesters such as Archie Armstrong (Charles I's jester) and John Scoggin (supposedly jester to Edward IV)—these were men famed for mocking the errors of kings and courtiers to their faces. From Charles II's court, Rochester and Killigrew were recruited to this jest-book tradition. Killigrew Thomas must have seemed an obvious candidate since, in the 1660s, his satirical quips to Charles had earned him the official role of court jester.[44] However, it was Rochester and his satirical verses that caught jest-book compilers' imaginations, and he far outpaced Killigrew in jest-book appearances across the eighteenth century. Rochester was appearing in printed jest-books by the mid-1690s. It was by this point safer to expose Charles II's courtiers in print, since Rochester and Killigrew were dead and there had been a major change of political regime as a result of the Revolution of 1688. The jest-book writers' interest in extempore court satire decades after the supposed events is not surprising. Jest-books, while they might promise the latest jokes, frequently offered choice wit from the last few hundred years. This was chiefly because their compilers were given to large-scale recycling of previous collections: the inclusion of a tale in one collection could lead to it reappearing for decades in subsequent jest-books, with the addition of new stories about the subject in a similar vein. Prolific

[42] *Spectator*, i. 361 (no. 63, 12 May 1711).
[43] *Hudibras, The First Part*, 71; *Spectator*, i. 341–2 (no. 60, 9 May 1711).
[44] Pepys, *Diary*, ix. 66–7.

copying and adapting of Rochesterian verses meant that, within a decade or so of Rochester's death, variants of epigrams attributed to him were circulating with different accounts of their genesis.[45] Jest-book compilers joined in, recording stories they had encountered orally, in manuscript, or in print, or else inventing new scenarios. An example is the poem now known as 'Impromptu on Charles II'. This was described in late seventeenth- and early eighteenth-century manuscripts as having been 'Writte on the Glass', while according to Rochester's *Works* (1707), the poem had instead been '*Posted on* White-Hall-Gate' (the main entrance to Whitehall Palace).[46] The version in the *Works* began with deixis suitable to the poem's supposed location:

> Here lives a Great and Mighty Monarch,
> Whose Promise none relies on,
> Who never said a foolish Thing,
> Nor ever did a wise one.

(135 (fol. Ii5r))

In 1727, *A Collection of Epigrams* provided an alternative version, subsequently reprinted in *Rochester's Jests* (1758). This variant claimed that the poem, beginning 'Here lies the mutton-eating king', had been '*Written on the Chamber Door of King* Charles II'. In this inventive combination of mock epitaph with the tradition of illicit posting, the king was very much alive, but too busy enjoying whores (mutton-eating) to act outside of the bed-chamber.[47] Although the supposed posting of a poem in a privileged space at court could add frisson for readers, this was not to cast elite or court wit as a radically distinctive practice from more commonplace satirical graffiti. Instead, editors, collectors, and scribes were busy creating and transmitting stories about famous wits that fitted their understanding of the widespread uses of the epigram—as a form used for mock epitaphs, as public provocation, in windows, and on doors. The proliferation of jest-books, and their compilers' judicious recycling, meant that these works were principal contributors to the growing corpus of Rochesterian stories and verses in the eighteenth century, and they remain important sources for modern editions of Rochester's poems.

Jest-book compilers also used verse games to communicate the nature of Rochester's wit to readers. The four-line satire, usually beginning, 'Here's Monmouth the witty', offers a case in point. This appeared in manuscript miscellanies in the 1670s and was first printed in 1693 in a jest-book.[48] Jest-book compilers did not simply reproduce the verse,

---

[45]   On the circulation of satires see Harold Love, *English Clandestine Satire 1660–1702* (Oxford: Oxford University Press, 2004), ch. 8; Harold Love, *The Culture and Commerce of Texts: Scribal Publication in Seventeenth-Century England* (Amherst: University of Massachusetts Press, 1998), esp. 247–50.

[46]   'First Version', in *The Works of John Wilmot, Earl of Rochester*, ed. Harold Love (Oxford: Oxford University Press, 1999, repr. 2005), 292, cf. 'Ninth Version', 294, which Thomas Hearne recorded in his diary as 'put in one of the windows'. *The Miscellaneous Works of the Right Honourable the Late Earls of Rochester and Roscommon* (1707), 135 (fol. Ii5r).

[47]   *A Collection of Epigrams* (1727), epigram 133, fol. G3v, cf. *Rochester's Jests*, 2nd edn. (1758), 111.

[48]   *Works of Rochester*, ed. Love, 295–8; *England's Merry Jester* (1693), 15–16—this version and early printing is not recorded in Love's edition.

but added explanatory context. *Ornatissimus Joculator* (1703) set the scene for readers: 'The late Earl of *Rochester*, who liv'd in the Reign of K. *Charles* the Second, was very well known to be an ingenious Man, and his Poems sufficiently shew how ready he was at making of Verses.' One day, King Charles 'in a merry Humour' greeted Rochester with 'they say you can make good Verses extempore; prethee let's hear some of 'em now'. Charles then set the subject as the people present. Rochester initially declined 'For fear I should offend your Majesty', but was commanded by the king to speak. He began:

> *Here's* Monmouth *the Witty, and* Lauderdale *the Pretty,*
>   *And* Frasier, *the learned Physitian*;
> *But above all the rest, here's the Duke for a Jest,*
>   *And the King for a great Polititian* [sic].
> O'my Conscience, says the King, he has satyriz'd upon us all! No wonder indeed that you begg'd my Pardon, for you were resolved to stand in need of it.[49]

The set-up stresses that Rochester's 'extempore' speech was covered by an explicit licence—his satire, like a jester's, was countenanced, so this was no example for others to follow. The political content of the satire was also downplayed since the editor provided no gloss on the targets of Rochester's verses, other than to note that Dr Frazier was famously stupid. It went unsaid that the Earl of Lauderdale was hugely obese and the Duke of York unable to take a joke. In *Ornatissimus Joculator*, this jest was followed by a similar episode:

> At another time the King and some of his Lords were at *Crambo*, and the Word happening to be *Lisbon*, there was none cou'd Rhime to it; at last, says the King, Was *Rochester* but here, I'll engage he'd Rhime to it presently.

A gentleman is duly sent off to fetch Rochester. He, on hearing the 'Crambo' problem, proposes to do it 'in a Stanza' (thereby foregoing the standard rule to rhyme in a couplet). With another advance pardon granted,

> *Rochester* taking a Glass of Wine in his hand, begins thus:
>   *Here's a Health to* Kate, *our Soveraign's Mate*
>   *Of the Royal House of* Lisbon;
>   *But the Devil take Hyde, and the Bishop beside,*
>   *That made her Bone of his Bone*
> At which his Majesty frown'd upon him, and bid him be gone.[50]

Once again, there was no gloss offered for the political context: that Edward Hyde, Earl of Clarendon, was suspected of deliberately matching Charles with a barren wife, the

---

[49] *Ornatissimus Joculator* (1703), 15–16. This is an earlier printing of this version of the poem than the 1745 instance identified by Love (*Works of Rochester*, 295–6).

[50] *Ornatissimus Joculator*, 16. This 1703 printing of the poem is earlier than the year of first printing (1738) given in Love's *Works of Rochester*, 290 and *John Wilmot, Earl of Rochester: The Poems and Lucina's Rape*, ed. Keith Walker and Nicholas Fisher (Oxford: Wiley-Blackwell, 2013), 134.

Portuguese princess Catherine, in order to further his own dynastic interests. Significantly, however, the jest-book preamble represents the 'Lisbon' epigram as a game of crambo. This was not, by 1703, considered a game fit for courtiers. In labelling the Lisbon joke a 'crambo', however, the jest-book compiler emphasized to readers that the wit lay not just in the political satire, but in the technical aspect of the verse. Crambo aficionados would recognize that Rochester had achieved a desirable double rhyme for 'Lisbon', thereby displaying ingenuity according to the rules of the game. His solution is what would now be called a mosaic rhyme, involving more than one word. Crambo players would also recognize that the unconventional solution to the rhyming problem was supposed to elicit ironic groans as well as cheers. 'Lisbon' had the alternative form 'Lisbone', so employing this variant pronunciation would lead to a surprising full rhyme with the phrase 'his Bone'.[51] However, the spelling used in *Ornatissimus Joculator* prompted readers to hear the final phrase as an amusingly awkward half-rhyme to accompany the satirical punch line: then, as now, Lisbon/his Bone was a far from perfect solution. This jest-book was not a one-off case of 'crambo' being used to popularize Rochester and transmit Rochesterian verse. The same anecdote was repeated in *England's Witty and Ingenious Jester* (1718), *Ben Johnson's Jests* (1751), and *The Universal Jester* (1754).[52] *Ben Johnson's Jests* also ended with three poems on the theme of women's sexual desire. Two of these, 'The Maiden's Disappointment' and a two-line epigram 'On Women's Denial', were said to be '*by Lord* Rochester'; and the third was headed 'Verses *made at* Crambo', with a layout indicating these were *bouts-rimés* (140).

The poems securely attributed to Rochester often make particularly skilled use of metre and rhyme. For example, Tom Lockwood has drawn attention to the 'formal ingenuity' of Rochester's rhymes and to their allusiveness when seen in terms of Restoration debates about poetic composition.[53] Rochester's informed contemporaries were best situated to appreciate the ways in which his verse critiqued the likes of Dryden. However, for Rochester's less informed contemporaries, and for their successors well into the eighteenth century, poetry linked to Rochester's name was read in relation to graffitied epigrams and popular verse games. The ways of appreciating verse learned from crambo and similar sports were part of the enjoyment of Rochester's poems, and of the poems attributed to him. This was why associating Rochesterian satire with crambo continued make sense to editors at a point when crambo was derided as 'false Wit'. It is unlikely that these interpretative techniques were confined to the short verses explicitly described as extemporary, since many of the satires associated with Rochester employed colloquial terms and elision to give the impression of improvised, casual verse. 'This yould beleive

---

[51] Evidence from the *Early English Books Online* and *Eighteenth Century Collections Online* databases shows 'Lisbon' was the usual form, with 'Lisbone' a common variant, and 'Lisbonne' another alternative. Cf. Matthews, 'Variant Pronunciations', 195–6.

[52] W.W., *England's Witty and Ingenious Jester* (1718), 5–6; *Ben Johnson's Jests*, 58–9; Ferdinando Killigrew, *The Universal Jester* (1754), 35.

[53] Lockwood, 'Rochester and Rhyme', 270. On Rochester's use of metre see Harold Love, 'Rochester's "I' th' Isle of Britain": Decoding a Textual Tradition', in *English Manuscript Studies 1100–1700*, 6, ed. Peter Beal and Jeremy Griffiths (London: British Library, 1997), 202–3.

had I but time to tell yee / The pains it costs the poor laborious Nelly', runs one exemplary couplet from the satire 'In the Isle of Brittain'.[54] The poems circulating under Rochester's name also played games with rhyming couplets and especially with the words used 'to clink ith' Close' (to borrow Norton Bold's phrase). One tactic was to use the first line of a couplet to set up a grand theme, using the second line to undermine the sentiment and register. 'A Ramble in St. James's Park' offers 'But though *St. James* has the honor on't, / 'Tis consecrate to *Prick* and *Cunt*'.[55] Emphasizing obscenities through placing them as rhyme words was another tactic, and a good rhyming pair of this kind, such as 'on't/Cunt', was worth using more than once. 'In the Isle of Brittain', meditating on the king's prick, explains: 'Tho safety, laws, religion, life lay on't / T'would break through all to come to dearest C.'[56] Around the time these poems were written, Flecknoe judged that one of the pleasures of an epigram was the fulfilment of expectation through rhyme:

> What *Airs* in point of *Musick* are, the same,
> In point of *writing* is your *Epigram*,
> Short, quick and sprightly; and both these and those
> When th'Ear expects it, comes unto a close.[57]

Flecknoe implies that readers were listeners and that they keenly experienced the anticipation generated through rhyme. Given the prevalence of epigram composition and rhyming games, he had good reason to believe so. In the 1660s and 1670s with the likes of crambo widely played, Rochester and other satirists had an audience who were primed to appreciate, on the one hand, a surprising choice of word to complete a rhyme and, on the other, less than perfect rhymes in the cause of ironic humour. A reader or listener unaccustomed to Restoration political satire would find 'cunt' to be an unexpected rhyme word, and perhaps more witty for that reason—it not being in their mental crambo dictionary, so to speak. Someone who had encountered a few satires on the court would have a more finely honed sense of the words that lampoons habitually contained—the pleasure would lie seeing the poet fulfil both the expectation of sound (the closing rhyme) and sense (bold obscenity). The early audiences for Restoration lampoons would not only have been listening for the next political target and judging the poet's success at hitting his satirical mark. They would also have been gauging the wit in rhyming—appreciating the 'hit' of an amusing double rhyme, or greeting with special mirth a particularly ingenious way of introducing an obscene rhyme word. Since the settings for epigrams and verse games were often taverns or toasting, and drinking was a common topic of satires linked to Rochester, the implication is that these verses were suited to rowdy, less than sober audiences who might make their views on certain targets and rhymes very audible. The commonalities between Rochesterian satire and verse games may also have stimulated individuals and groups to participate in the verse making. One of the reasons the satires that circulated under Rochester's name exist in many versions

---

[54] *Works of Rochester*, ed. Love, 88.   [55] *Works of Rochester*, ed. Love, 76.
[56] *Works of Rochester*, ed. Love, 88.   [57] *Epigrams of All Sorts*, 1.

is because his contemporaries kept expanding or reworking them. The culture of manuscript satire encouraged this kind of engagement, but Rochesterian satire's links to verse games and epigrammatic exchanges perhaps made it especially attractive for would-be poets: like the verses on tavern walls, it looked like a challenge to join in.

CONCLUSIONS

In 1669, Walter Charleton observed that much extemporary wit did not stand up to considered judgement. A certain unease about the standards for judging epigrammatic wit continues today among editors. Notably, editors of Rochester's works, including David Vieth and Harold Love, have chosen to emphasize spontaneity by titling certain verses (but not others) 'impromptus': 'Impromptu on Charles II' ('Here lives a Great and Mighty Monarch'), 'Impromptu on Queen Catherine' (the Lisbon verse), and so on.[58] These titles have their roots in anecdotes about spontaneity supplied with early records of the verses, but the word 'impromptu', in this context, is a modern addition, for it was very rarely used as a title in English printed verse before the middle of the eighteenth century. By choosing to designate a poem as an 'impromptu' (instead of, for example, 'Epigram on Charles II' or just 'On Charles II'), editors signal their readers to be ready to suspend conventional standards for judging poetry in favour of admiring (perhaps imaginary) improvisational wit. In other words, an editor is tacitly cautioning readers not to necessarily expect profound insight or intricately crafted verse. Lost in these modern references to traditions of extemporary wit, however, is what describing a verse as spontaneously composed could signal to early readers. Spontaneous, epigrammatic satire as practised at court was represented as an outrageous performance in which only a few could participate unscathed. Yet epigram was regarded as 'entry level' poetic composition and the competitive wit associated with the court had parallels in less august verse games. Epigrammatic graffiti and rhyming games were common ways for people from a range of stations to encounter and compose verses. Verse games taught participants and their audiences to recognize the skill in rapidly producing a well-turned rhyme and must have tended to increase their awareness of how rhyme words in poetry were used to set up and surprise expectations. These pastimes therefore fostered appreciation of the adept use of diction and rhyme. They also involved appreciating the inept—or rather the seemingly inept—in satirical verse. A rhyme that was imperfect but inventive, or one that was deliberately strained for comic effect, could provide more enjoyment than an elegant couplet. While the nonchalant production of skilful spontaneous verse was much admired, there was also cachet to be gained from entertaining others with amusingly awkward, jury-rigged lines—although this was not kind of skill

---

[58] For example, *The Complete Poems of John Wilmot, Earl of Rochester*, ed. David M. Vieth (New Haven and London: Yale University Press, 1962, repr. 2002), 21, 134, 135; *Works of Rochester*, ed. Love, 289, 291, 292.

that literary critics wanted to celebrate. Popular games involving epigrammatic and spontaneous wit taught ways of understanding and appreciating poetry that could be applied beyond the epigram genre—which, we should remember, was never one with well-defined formal boundaries. During the late seventeenth and eighteenth centuries these pastimes influenced the reception and appreciation of satires including Rochesterian verses and *Hudibras*. The practices of graffiti and verse games were ephemeral but they have left abiding traces in the literary history of the long eighteenth century.

SELECT BIBLIOGRAPHY

Doelman, James. 'Circulation of the Late Elizabethan and Early Stuart Epigram', *Renaissance and Reformation/Renaissance et Réforme* 29, no. 1 (2005), 59–73.

Doelman, James. 'Epigrams and Political Satire in Early Stuart England', *Huntington Library Quarterly* 69, no. 1 (2006), 31–45.

Fleming, Juliet. *Graffiti and the Writing Arts of Early Modern England* (London: Reaktion Books, 2001).

Guffey, George R. Introduction to *The Merry-Thought: Or, The Glass-Window and Bog-House Miscellany*, Part 1, Augustan Reprint Society 216 (Los Angeles: William Andrews Clark Memorial Library, University of California, 1982).

Hartle, Phil. '"Quaint *Epigrammatist*": Martial in Late Seventeenth-Century England', *Neophilologus* 79, no. 2 (1995), 329–51.

Lockwood, Tom. 'Rochester and Rhyme', in *Lord Rochester in the Restoration World*, ed. Matthew C. Augustine and Steven N. Zwicker (Cambridge: Cambridge University Press, 2015), 270–90.

Love, Harold. *English Clandestine Satire 1660–1702* (Oxford: Oxford University Press, 2004).

Love, Harold. *Scribal Publication in Seventeenth-Century England* (Oxford: Clarendon Press, 1993). Reprinted as *The Culture and Commerce of Texts: Scribal Publication in Seventeenth-Century England* (Amherst: University of Massachusetts Press, 1998).

Lund, Roger D. 'The Ghosts of Epigram, False Wit, and the Augustan Mode', *Eighteenth-Century Life* 27, no. 2 (2003), 67–95.

Matthews, William. 'Variant Pronunciations in the Seventeenth Century', *Journal of English and Germanic Philology* 37, no. 2 (1938), 189–206.

CHAPTER 30

SATIRE AS EVENT

JOHN McTAGUE

THIS chapter focuses on three 'practical satires', all of which attach themselves to particular events, which are of dubious, if not baldly fallacious, historicity. The episodes in question are the alleged impersonation of a mountebank, Alexander Bendo, by John Wilmot, 2nd Earl of Rochester, in the summer of 1676; the prediction of the death of the astrologer John Partridge by Jonathan Swift, and the 'confirmation' of that prediction's fulfilment, in the spring of 1708; and Alexander Pope's surreptitious administration of an emetic draught to the bookseller Edmund Curll on 28 April 1716. These satires are being thought of as 'practical' for two reasons. Firstly, as kinds of practical joke, they appear to involve or invite kinds of extra-textual participation, especially encouraging what Kate Loveman has called 'feigned credulity', a more socially-engaged species of suspended disbelief.[1] Secondly, they reflect an anxiety regarding satire's limited 'practicality' or real-world efficacy, comically overstating the consequences of satire in the world (incredible gullibility, vomiting and stooling, death). Reading these three episodes together, it is hard to ignore their shared interest in mortality and the fragility and permeability of bodies. In these hoaxes and deceptions, mortification lives up to its morbid and bodily etymology. Certainly, they embarrass their victims. Yet that mortification is achieved in ways that relate to the older, more physical and literal senses of the verb: 'to render necrotic'; 'to lose life or vitality, to waste away', 'to destroy or inhabit the vitality, vigour, activity, or potency of'; 'To deprive of life; to kill, put to death', 'to render insensible' (*OED*, 'mortify, v.'). The means by which Swift and his coadjutors 'mortify' Partridge, after all, is by pretending that he is dead, and by so pretending over a period of years. Indeed, the extended limbo in which Partridge is suspended by the hoax brings to mind one final shade of meaning: 'To make (raw meat, game, etc.) tender by hanging, keeping, etc.'

Interested as they are in broadcasting their specific effects on specific people, these practical satires can seem particularly vindictive. Their combination of violence and

---

[1] See Kate Loveman, *Reading Fictions, 1660–1740: Deception in English Literary and Political Culture* (Aldershot: Ashgate, 2008), 66–9.

shaming recalls an old-fashioned honour code of retributive violence.[2] In the *Dunciad Variorum* (1729), Pope responds to the criticism that the 'dunces' he had attacked in *The Dunciad. An Heroic Poem* (1728) 'are too obscure for Satyre', beneath his dignity as a satirist.[3] He figures his satire as a form of extra-legal redress:

> [O]bscurity renders them more dangerous, as less thought of: Law can pronounce judgement only on open Facts, Morality alone can pass censure on Intentions of mischief; so that for secret calumny or the arrow flying in the dark, there is no public punishment, but what a good writer inflicts.[4]

The tendency for the dunces to publish their attacks on Pope anonymously, shooting arrows in the dark, is presented as a kind of cowardly sniping. There is an almost obscured allusion here to Francis Bacon's 1625 essay, 'Of Revenge': 'Some, when they take *Revenge*, are Desirous the party should know, whence it commeth: This is the more Generous.... But Base and Crafty Cowards, are like the Arrow, that flyeth in the Darke.'[5] Bacon is conflating elements from Psalm 91 ('Thou shalt not be afraid for the terror by night; nor for the arrow that flieth by day; Of the pestilence that stalks in darkness, Or of the destruction that lays waste at noon'[6]). He, and perhaps Pope, may also have in mind 'the wicked' who 'shoote in the dark' in Psalm 11:2.[7] Pope adopts the image of the arrow flying in the dark from the Psalms, via Bacon, to suggest that the dunces' anonymity or obscurity is not just a sign but a guarantee of their wickedness, justifying his personal attacks as a means of dragging such 'Base and Crafty Cowards' into the full glare of justice. However, what looks like a forensic tracing of origins might really be a way of taking aim, disguised. In the 1728 *Dunciad*, the dunce's names were obscured by partial blanks (e.g. 'C—l' for 'Curll'), deliberately encouraging speculation.[8] So, whilst the passage above suggests that Pope's particular satire used a kind of ballistic analysis to retrace the parabola of the dunces' arrows, at least a part of Pope's strategy in 1728 was to loose one in the general direction of Grub Street, in order to see who yelped.[9] This difficulty of

---

[2] Shaun Regan notes that Pope's account of the poisoning of Curll in his letter to John Caryll '[draws] upon a gentlemanly model of retribution against rogues' (' "Pranks, Unfit for Naming": Pope, Curll, and the "Satirical Grotesque" ', *The Eighteenth Century* 46 (2005), 37–59, 37).

[3] Pope, *Poems* (Longman), iii. 129.   [4] Pope, *Poems* (Longman), iii. 130.

[5] Francis Bacon, *The Essayes or Counsels, Civill and Morall*, ed. Michael Kiernan (Oxford: Clarendon Press, 1985), 17.

[6] KJV Psalms 91:5–6. Kiernan notes that Bacon makes the same conflation in the 'Charge against Somerset' (188 n. 27–8).

[7] The wicked 'shoote in the dark' in the version familiar to English Catholics (Douay-Rheims (1635, vol. 2), where the Psalm is numbered 10). In the King James Version, they 'privily shoot'.

[8] On the complex games of identification provoked by Scriblerian texts, see Freya Johnston, 'Alexander Pope: Unlocking the Key', *RES* 67 (2016), 897–913.

[9] Thomas Alcock describes Rochester's impersonation as a similarly speculative ('Experimental') attack on the title page of his manuscript account: 'he aim'd at Physicall Practise | and shott his *Experimental Darts* | at the Greedy to be wounded' (Thomas Alcock, *The Famous Pathologist or The Noble Mountebank*, ed. Vivian de Sola Pinto (Nottingham: Sisson and Parker, 1961), 23, my emphasis). Elsewhere, Bacon warns that 'the arrow that flies by night' makes 'men die other men's deaths', because 'it hath no aim and certainty' (*Essayes*, 188 n. 27–8).

determining who started it, to use the language of the playground, is both a problem and an opportunity for practical satire. As attacks masquerading as defences, they purport to identify and punish malefactors, but really engineer circumstance or fabricate history, forcing their targets to confess a 'truth' that would never otherwise pass their lips, thereby justifying their punishment. If one goes back far enough etymologically, to revenge means 'to force to speak'.[10] Bacon tells us that 'a Man that studieth *Revenge*, keepes his owne Wounds greene, which otherwise would heale, and doe well'.[11] The vindictive person's wounds are 'greene' not because they are mortifying or rotting, but 'greene' as in 'recent, fresh, unhealed, raw', a past injury forced to speak to the present.[12] These three practical satires seek to harness and maintain something like the potential energy of the invisible arrow hanging in the air, keeping wounds green, unhealed, and raw.

The Counterfeit's Example

John Wilmot, 2nd Earl of Rochester (1647–80), was a Restoration courtier, poet, and dramatist whose reputation as a rake and mischief-maker has been preserved and expanded by his poetic self-representations, contemporary rumour and lampoon, and posthumous anecdote.[13] According to his early biographer, Gilbert Burnet, the earl 'took pleasure to disguise himself as a porter or as a beggar; sometimes to follow mean amours'. '[A]t other times', Burnet continues, 'merely for diversion, he would go about in odd shapes'.[14] Rochester's alleged impersonation of the Italian mountebank, Alexander Bendo, is the most notorious of these 'odd shapes'. The pamphlet that Rochester's editor Harold Love has given the title of 'Alexander Bendo's Brochure' most probably appeared in the summer of 1676. This 'sympathetic impersonation' of doctors' handbills is the most reliable documentary evidence we have of Rochester actually impersonating the mountebank, but as evidence of a 'real' performance, it is inconclusive at best.[15] It spends much of its time engaged in broad political satire, playing with the non-distinction between the 'real' and the counterfeit, offering miraculous but unaccountable cures to the public (particularly women), before closing by inviting readers to visit Bendo at the sign of the Black Swan in Tower Street. Bendo opens by inveighing against a 'company'

---

[10] The verb 'revenge' deriving from Latin 'vindicare', formed through the following combination: '*vim*, accusative singular of *vīs* force + *dic-*, stem of *dīcĕre* to say' (*OED*, vindicate *v.*, etymology).

[11] Bacon, *Essayes*, 17.   [12] *OED* green, *adj.* 7. B.

[13] Many of these anecdotes are collected in John Adlard, ed., *The Debt to Pleasure* (New York: Routledge, 2002). For a briefer summary, see Anne Righter, 'John Wilmot, Earl of Rochester', *Proceedings of the British Academy* 53 (1967), 47–69, 50–5.

[14] Adlard, *The Debt to Pleasure*, 52.

[15] 'Sympathetic impersonation' is Love's phrase (*The Works of John Wilmot, Earl of Rochester* (Oxford: Oxford University Press, 1999), 437).

who have 'impose[d] upon the people ... in Physick, *Chymical* and *Galenic*, in *Astrology*, *Physiognomy*, *Palmistry*, *Mathematicks*, *Alchimy* and even Government it self; the last of which I will not purpose to discours of, or meddle at all in'.[16] It would not take a particularly sophisticated reader to notice that the mountebank was protesting too much, especially as 'Government' comes at the end of a list featuring some dubious sciences, rubbing shoulders with alchemy.[17] Rochester is setting up a situation in which distinctions are eroded or discernment fails: apparently legitimate disciplines (Mathematicks) are mixed indifferently with quackery (Palmistry). This is elaborated on in a passage no critic of this pamphlet has allowed to pass unremarked:

> [I]f I appear to any one like a Counterfeit, even for the sake of that ought I to be construed a true man, who is the Counterfeits example, his original, and that which he imploys his industry and pains to copy; is it therefore my fault if the Cheat by his Wits and Endeavours makes himself so like me, that consequently I cannot avoid of resembling him.[18]

Here indifference bleeds into a kind of mimetic infection, as the counterfeit does not just ape but contaminates the real. Anne Righter notes that, in this passage, Rochester 'overthrows ... the basic conviction of antithesis'.[19] Bendo is not simply suggesting that the true can sometimes be mistaken for the false, but that in a certain sense, or 'in a world like this', they are *effectively* identical.[20] That said, it is possible to overstate Bendo's relativism. He is interested in essential distinctions, but insists that they can only be perceived by way of various kinds of mortifying experience.

Bendo gives four examples of apparently opposed characters—brave men and cowards, bankrupts and rich men, politicians and fools, true and false physicians—and draws attention to the identity of their behaviours. However, while 'the difference betwixt all these' is 'nice in all appearance', it remains 'infinite in effect'.[21] If Bendo comically undervalues the 'real' distinctions between these figures (courage, for instance, is 'only one point of honour'), he remains unwilling to discard them, emphasizing the process by which such differences are found out. That process resembles the playing out of a hoax. It is 'real Cash' which makes the difference between the bankrupt and the solvent merchant, 'a great defect indeed, and yet but one, and that the last found out, and still then the least perceived'. The bankrupt is full of potential only for as long as he is able to defer discovery. Whilst such a discovery may be inevitable, there is no guarantee it will be made quickly; that his 'defect' is the last found out (when he is unable to pay his debts) suggests that 'true' knowledge comes with a price tag. The discoveries of the coward and the false doctor are even more mortifying. 'Courage' is a point of honour which 'only

---

[16] Rochester, *Works*, 112.
[17] Don Bourne reads the pamphlet as one of Rochester's 'sharpest criticisms of Charles II' in ' "If I Appear to Any One Like a Counterfeit": Liminality in Rochester's *Alexander Bendo's Brochure*', *Restoration: Studies in English Literary Culture, 1660–1700* 32 (2008), 3–17, 3.
[18] Rochester, *Works*, 113.   [19] Righter, 'John Wilmot, Earl of Rochester', 49.
[20] Rochester, *Works*, 113.   [21] Rochester, *Works*, 114.

one trial can discover' (i.e. 'trial' by combat).[22] The exposure of the coward may be embarrassing; it may also involve their death, or that of those they are supposed to protect. Finally, and with the most understated comedy, Bendo declares that when it comes to impostor quacks and true physicians, "tis only your experience must distinguish betwixt them".[23] This revelation comes by way of an experience that is doubly mortifying. Firstly, one way of being sure that a doctor is not a 'true' one is to be killed by them. Secondly, Rochester implies that the only way of determining whether Bendo is a real doctor or not would be to turn up at his premises, leading to mortification of a different kind.

Kirke Combe points out that Bendo names no essential difference between the politician and the fool. He is being straightforwardly satirical, but also hinting that politicians are especially difficult to 'find out'.[24] This is developed in a comparison of the mountebank and politicians, whose unifying quality is their ability to defer revelation. Like Swift's Bickerstaff, Rochester openly courts the possibility of exposure.[25] 'I'le only say something to the honour of the Mountebanck', he continues, 'in case you discover me to be one':

> [H]e draws great companies to him by undertaking strange things which can never be effected. The Politician (by his example no doubt) finding how the people are taken with specious, miraculous, impossibilities, plays the same game, protests, declares, promises I know not what things, which he's sure can ne're be brought about; the people believe, are deluded and pleased, the expectation of a future good which shall never befal them draws their eyes off a present evil: Thus are they kept and establish'd in Subjection, Peace, and Obedience; he in Greatness, Wealth, and Power.[26]

The hoaxer and the politician are able to keep their subjects in tow for as long as they are able to keep them in suspense. As befits an advertisement, Rochester's pamphlet stimulates a desire that can only be maintained by people who are willing to forgo experience, to uphold the fiction that Alexander Bendo is 'real' (either really a true doctor or really a false doctor, it matters little), in the face of the clear knowledge that he is not. To the attentive reader, the advertisement effectively promises disappointment

---

[22] Courage and cowardice may have been playing on Rochester's mind, having fled the scene of a fatal brawl in Epsom on 18 June 1676. See James William Johnson, *A Profane Wit: The Life of John Wilmot, Earl of Rochester* (Rochester: University of Rochester Press, 2004), 245–61, esp. 250–1.

[23] Rochester, *Works*, 114.

[24] Kirke Combe, *A Martyr for Sin: Rochester's Critique of Polity, Sexuality, and Society* (Newark: University of Delaware Press, 1995), 127.

[25] 'Besides', writes Bendo, 'I hope you will not think I could be so imprudent, that if I had intended any such foul play my self, I would have given you so fair warning by my severe observations upon others' (*Works*, 113). In *A Vindication of Isaac Bickerstaff*, Bickerstaff asks if it would 'be probable I could have been so indiscreet, to begin my Predictions with the only Falshood that ever was pretended to be in them', Swift, *Works* (Cambridge), ii. 72.

[26] Rochester, *Works*, 114.

by way of mortifying experience; it also challenges them to subject themselves to the fiction regardless.

One such reader was Rochester's former servant, Thomas Alcock, who sent a transcription of Bendo's brochure to the earl's daughter Ann Baynton and her husband Henry on New Year's Day 1688. Alcock prefaced the transcription with a supposedly eyewitness account of Rochester's 'practice' as Bendo. This account has generally been too readily accepted as authentic. Loveman's take on it is instructive. She warns, '[e]arly modern readers... were particularly fond of recounting the credulity of other readers'. 'The performance aspect of this hoax', she continues, 'either never happened, or was subject to exaggeration from the first report'.[27] Indeed, Alcock describes a production that would not have looked out of place at Drury Lane Theatre: supported by a cast of characters pretending to make mysterious medicines (and dressed like the witches in *Macbeth*), Rochester is costumed 'in an old overgrown Green Gown... lyned through with exotick furrs of diverse colours, an antique Cap, a great Reverend Beard', and 'a Magnificent false Medal... wch the King of Cyprus (you must know) had given him for doing a signal Cure upon his darling Daughter the Princess Aloephangina, who was painted in a banner'.[28] This is more than reportage. Bendo's medallion is made, according to Alcock, of 'Prince's mettle', a cheap alloy that imitates brass or gold. Alcock is offering the perspectives of an audience member or victim and perpetrator by turns, bolstering his claims to first-hand knowledge. The King of Cyprus and his bawdily-named daughter are supposedly a part of the fictional world Alcock wants us to believe that Bendo had constructed. The revelation that the medallion was made of a 'false' alloy, on the other hand, is a sort of backstage knowledge. However, these are not production notes, but a kind of meta-commentary. 'Aloephangina' is a purging medicine, the name of which has the ring of 'vagina'.[29] It enables Alcock to impute that the 'signal cure' Bendo administered to the King of Cyprus's daughter was sexual, a move in line with bawdy jokes elsewhere.[30] 'Prince's mettle' is also functioning allegorically in ways that it could not in a 'performance' intended to trick people.[31] Alcock enters into the spirit of Rochester's pamphlet, certainly, but his descriptions are full of entertaining excursions intended to test the Bayntons' credulity, or their willingness to feign it. As with the 'lying games' Loveman describes, Alcock mixes obscure 'factual' detail with invention.[32] Bendo's acquaintance with the 'King of Cyprus' shores up his claim to an Italian background. The reference is to Charles Immanuel II (1634–75), the recently deceased Duke of Savoy, whose ancestors adopted the title 'King of Cyprus' in 1396, and who lived

---

[27] Loveman, *Reading Fictions*, 13–15.   [28] Alcock, *Famous Pathologist*, 28–9.

[29] On the uses of aloephangina pills, see J. Pechey, *A Plain Introduction to the Art of Physick* (1697), 331.

[30] See the description of Rochester's cross-dressing seduction of female clients (Alcock, *Famous Pathologist*, 26–7).

[31] If Bendo told the audience his medallion was made of 'prince's mettle', he would alert them to the fakery of his practice; if he did not say such a thing to the audience, they would assume it was brass (or, indeed, gold). Alcock may be picking up on the original pamphlet's reference to 'false Metal', which can only be discovered 'by trial' (*Famous Pathologist*, 113).

[32] Loveman, *Reading Fictions*, 66–9.

in Turin. Although the Duke of Savoy had 'a vigorous sexual life' resulting in five illegitimate children by three mistresses, none of them were named 'Aloephangina'.[33]

Yet, since Vivian de Sola Pinto's discovery and publication of the Alcock manuscript, critics have generally taken this extension of Rochester's hoax at face value, and in doing so, revealed some of the ways in which practical satire operates. For instance, at the end of his account, Alcock writes, 'It was some time rumour'd that they were an Inchanted Crew, raised and laid by Necromancie' (30). He is exaggerating readerly credulity for Ann Baynton's entertainment. Rochester's biographer Johnson, however, reports the joke as fact.[34] To intimate that there really were 'customers' who thought such a thing is not to analyse but to perpetuate Alcock's shamming. Similarly, Combe writes, '[w]e as in-the-know readers enjoy the [hand]bill *because* we know other, less informed readers are fooled by it'.[35] However, though we, like contemporaries, might like to imagine credulous victims—and while the hoax might *require* us to imagine such victims—to say that we 'know' the hoax has succeeded is to take as read practical satire's representation of its own successes.[36] Such interpretations are driven by an assumption that a practical satire requires real victims suffering in the world. However, victims are less necessary than participants—people like Alcock—who can furnish representations of dupes. Practical satire appeals to a persistent and powerful desire to report the credulity of others, but participation is a felicity from which we need to absent ourselves to properly understand these episodes, and to avoid mortifications of our own.

As Dead as Dr Partridge

In December 1687, while Alcock was busy writing his account, there appeared a pamphlet called *Mene Tekel*.[37] In it, the radical Whig astrologer John Partridge predicted the death of the king, James II, or at least did so by implication. The following year, James II was dethroned, but, of course, did not die. Undeterred, Partridge reissued his prediction, with the brazen qualification that the king had suffered 'a civil death', which he insists was 'worse than *Death*'.[38] That is, Partridge represents the success of his own prediction, flying in the face of mortifying experience. Jonathan Swift arrived in England in January 1689. Whether or not he saw Partridge's *Mene Tekel* and its sequel at that time,

[33] Robert Oresko, 'Maria Giovanna Battista of Savoy-Nemours (1644–1724): Daughter, Consort, and Regent of Savoy', in *Queenship in Europe 1660–1815: The Role of the Consort*, ed. Clarissa Campbell Orr (Cambridge: Cambridge University Press, 2004), 16–55, 24.

[34] 'Dr. Bendo's sudden disappearance was reported by his baffled clients to be the effect of necromancy' (Johnson, *A Profane Wit*, 257).

[35] Rochester, *Works*, 125.

[36] Loveman's reading of the tales of people 'duped' by *Gulliver's Travels* as 'a Scriblerian game' demonstrates a more sensible approach to such accounts (*Reading Fictions*, 166–7).

[37] Alcock dates his transcription 13 December 1687 (*Famous Pathologist*, 38).

[38] John Partridge, *Mene Mene, Tekel Upharsin* (1689), sigs. A3–A3ᵛ. Italics inverted.

he was familiar enough with them by the spring of 1708 to parodically commemorate Partridge's activities.[39] In *Predictions for the Year 1708*, probably published in February, Swift poses as Isaac Bickerstaff, a gentleman minded to reform the science of astrology.[40] Having stated this intention, he gets straight down to business: John Partridge, he says, will 'infallibly dye upon the 29th of *March* next'.[41] Naturally, Partridge did not die. Just as naturally, Swift insisted that he did, in a mock-elegy and epitaph, and *The Accomplishment of the First of Mr Bickerstaff's Predictions*, in which an 'impartial' observer attends Partridge's deathbed.[42] In his almanac for 1709, Partridge reassured his readers that he was still breathing. Swift was unable to resist this invitation, and in *A Vindication of Isaac Bickerstaff* refuted that fact with a serious of brilliantly absurd arguments. As well as Bickerstaff being adopted by Steele and Addison as the voice of their influential periodical, *The Tatler*, in April 1709, a number of continuations and rejoinders emerged in ensuing years.[43]

One reason for the Bickerstaff hoax's success is the sheer comic joy attendant on addressing a living person as though they were dead. Against this kind of appeal Partridge could do little, and (with one exception) his responses served as more grist to the satirist's mill.[44] In 1709's *Vindication of Isaac Bickerstaff*, for instance, Bickerstaff gleefully reports the response of 'Above a Thousand Gentlemen' to Partridge's insistence that he was yet living: '*They were sure*', he writes '*no Man alive ever writ such damned Stuff as this*. Neither did I ever hear that Opinion disputed: So that Mr. *Partridge* lies under a *Dilemma*, either of disowning his Almanack, or allowing himself to be, *No Man alive*.'[45] Bickerstaff recasts Partridge's continued existence as an unaccountably impolite obstinacy:

> [I]f an *uninformed* Carcass walks still about, and is pleased to call it self *Partridge*, Mr. *Bickerstaff* does not think himself any way answerable for that. Neither had the said Carcass any Right to beat the poor Boy, who happen'd to pass by it in the Street, crying, *A full and true Account of Dr.* Partridge's *Death*, &c.[46]

---

[39] On *Mene Tekel* and Swift's knowledge thereof, see N. F. Lowe, 'Why Swift Killed Partridge', *Swift Studies* 6 (1991), 70–82. For details of Partridge's career as a radical Whig propagandist, see *ODNB*; John McTague, '"There is no such man as Isaack Bickerstaff": Partridge, Pittis, and Jonathan Swift', *ECL* 35, no. 1 (2011), 83–101; John McTague, 'A Letter from John Partridge To Isaac Manley, 24 April 1708: Provenance and Authenticity', *Notes and Queries* 59, no. 3 (2012), 197–202, 198; and Valerie Rumbold's Headnote to *Predictions*, in Swift, *Works* (Cambridge), ii. 36–40.

[40] On dating, see Swift, *Works* (Cambridge), ii. 642–3, and G. P. Mayhew, 'Swift's Bickerstaff Hoax as April Fools' Joke', *Modern Philology* 61 (1964), 270–80.

[41] Rochester, *Works*, 49.

[42] See Mayhew, 'Swift's Bickerstaff Hoax' and Valerie Rumbold, 'Burying the Fanatic Partridge: Swift's Holy Week Hoax', in *Politics and Literature in the Age of Swift: English and Irish Perspectives*, ed. Claude Rawson (Cambridge: Cambridge University Press, 2010), 81–115.

[43] For an account of some of these responses see Swift, *Works* (Cambridge), ii. 645–7.

[44] The exception is the preface to Partridge's *Merlinus Redivivus* for 1714, which engages wittily with the comic potential of death and resurrection (see John Partridge, *Merlinus Redivivus* (1714), sig. A1ᵛ, and Rumbold, 'Burying', 101–2).

[45] Swift, *Works* (Cambridge), ii. 71.   [46] Swift, *Works* (Cambridge), ii. 72.

'Partridge's' response to this doubly mortifying experience is understandable enough, but only the first layer of the joke. Valerie Rumbold sees in '*uninformed*' an allusion to Aristotelian form or soul, that which gives shape and purpose to matter.[47] Losing his temper, Partridge is barely able to hold himself together; he is also said to be disintegrating in more fundamental ways. Indeed, to be 'as Dead as Dr. Partridge' came to mean something quite specific: to suffer a kind of 'civil death', or a slaying of reputation.[48] At the end of the *Vindication*, Bickerstaff complains that he has been 'employed, like the General, who was forced to kill his Enemies twice over, whom a *Necromancer* had raised to Life'.[49] In 1710, Defoe wrote that Partridge, having suffered 'a Death without a Grave', 'was mercifully admitted to walk about after he was dead'.[50] Defoe recognizes that, despite Bickerstaff's complaints, the transformation of John Partridge into an undead punch-bag is precisely the point.

Keeping the punch-bag suspended and swinging became more important as the hoax progressed. In the first pamphlet, Bickerstaff is explicit in his request for a fair hearing: 'A little time will determine, whether I have deceiv'd others, or my self; and I think it no very unreasonable Request, that Men would please to suspend their Judgements till then.'[51] This seems to set the parameters of the hoax, or the space in which it will operate: from publication until 29 March. Like Bendo, Bickerstaff submits to the prospect of being 'hoot[ed]...for a cheat and an impostor' by '*Partridge*, and the rest of his clan' should his predictions fail. In the *Vindication*, po-faced, he reports, 'several of my Friends had the Assurance to ask me, Whether I were in Jest? To which I only answered coldly, *That the Event would shew*'.[52] Swift is mocking astrology's supposed reliance on this kind of confirmation, but the success of this practical satire was never really dependent on a real 'event'. In the midst of the hoax, Swift realizes the importance of suspension and participation, developing into what Rumbold identifies as his 'impressive blend of fertility and detachment in relation to the Bickerstaff project'.[53] The first sign of this is his decision to pull one of his punches: *An Answer to Bickerstaff*, originally intended to follow on the heels of *Predictions*, did not emerge until after his death. Rumbold contends that Swift refrained because publication 'would have brought the hoax to what would in the event have been a premature end'.[54] This pamphlet is written in the voice of a sceptical 'Person of Quality', who sees through the *Predictions* for the

---

[47] Swift, *Works* (Cambridge), ii. 72 n. 26.

[48] The phrase is used of Richard Steele by William Wagstaffe, and refers to the damage done to Steele's reputation by the furore surrounding 1713's *The Importance of Dunkirk Consider'd*: 'Our Author has given his reputation such a Stab, that I can scarcely think but he is in some Measure guilty of self Murder, and as dead as Dr. *Partridge*, or any other Person he *killed* formerly' (*Miscellaneous Works of Dr William Wagstaffe* (London, 1726 [1725]), 135).

[49] Swift, *Works* (Cambridge), ii. 74.

[50] Daniel Defoe, *A Condoling Letter to the Tatler* ([1710]), 7.

[51] Swift, *Works* (Cambridge), ii. 57.   [52] Swift, *Works* (Cambridge), ii. 74.

[53] Swift, *Works* (Cambridge), ii. xxxvi.

[54] Swift, *Works* (Cambridge), ii. 645. For Loveman, Swift's withholding of this 'explanation of the bite...shows that there was a widespread understanding of how shams worked and were to be enjoyed' (*Reading Fictions*, 161).

hoax it is: 'it is a *bite*: he has fully had his jest, and may be satisfied'.[55] This is quite final: crying 'a bite' marked the end of a sham.[56] *An Answer* also suggests that Bickerstaff's prognostications might be more coercive than predictive:

> [I]f [Partridge] . . . has any faith in his own art, the prophesy may punctually come to pass by very natural means. As a gentleman of my acquaintance, who was ill-used by a mercer in town, writ him a letter in an unknown hand, to give him notice that care had been taken to convey a slow poison into his drink, which would infallibly kill him in a month; after which the man began in earnest to languish and decay, by the mere strength of imagination, and would certainly have died, if care had not been taken to undeceive him before the jest went too far.[57]

Swift encountered this reading of prophecy as scaremongering in Pierre Bayle's 1705 account of the predictions Partridge made in 1688.[58] *An Answer* rather bluntly explains what its replacement, *The Accomplishment*, dramatizes: the former precludes the feigning of credulity before the jest has gone not 'too far', but not far enough. Abandoning closure and explication in favour of continuation and performance, Swift decides to show rather than tell. In *The Accomplishment*, the impartial observer asks an ailing Partridge 'whether the Predictions Mr. *Bickerstaff* had published relating to his Death, had not too much affected and worked on his Imagination':

> He confess'd he had often had it in his Head, but never with much Apprehension, till about a Fortnight before; since which Time it had the perpetual Possession of his Mind and Thoughts, and he did verily believe was the true Natural Cause of his present Distemper.[59]

Satire is operating here less like medicine than like a placebo, as Bickerstaff's Partridge confesses the 'real' (i.e. psychosomatic) efficacy of prediction as coercion.[60] By choosing *Accomplishment* over *An Answer*, Swift does not just keep Partridge in limbo for a little longer, but inaugurates the 'Possession' of Partridge's voice that is the key to furnishing him with a death without a grave.

The riotous *Squire Bickerstaff Detected*, a pamphlet which has proved difficult to attribute, but which is certainly not by Swift, is driven by the kind of wish fulfilment that motivates Alcock's account, exaggerating not just the severity but the duration of Bickerstaff's effect on Partridge, whose voice the pamphlet appropriates.[61] 'Partridge' complains of a succession of his neighbours invading his house or haranguing him on

---

[55] Swift, *Works* (Cambridge), ii. 574.   [56] See Loveman, *Reading Fictions*, 154–5.
[57] Swift, *Works* (Cambridge), ii. 574.   [58] See Lowe, 'Why Swift Killed Partridge'.
[59] Swift, *Works* (Cambridge), ii. 62.
[60] On the metaphorical connections between satire and medicine, see Noelle Gallagher, 'Satire as Medicine in the Restoration and Early Eighteenth Century: The History of a Metaphor', *Literature and Medicine* 31 (2013), 17–39.
[61] On attribution, see Swift, *Works* (Cambridge), ii. 565–6.

the street, united in their insistence upon his being dead. Although the pamphlet helps to give Partridge a death without a grave, 'Ned, the Sexton' tries hard to give him a grave without a death. He asks the astrologer, 'whether his Grave is to be plain or brick'd?' Partridge, having answered his door ably enough, denies his decease ('you know I am not dead'). With indignation, Ned retaliates, 'Alack-a-day, Sir . . . why, 'tis in Print, and the whole Town knows you are dead.'[62] For Ned, the public signs of death (an announcement in print, church bells) trump the flesh-and-blood man with whom he converses. Ned is modelling the kind of participation that practical satire requires. He is not simply a gull. Nor, for that matter, is Partridge. Practical satire works not by 'tricking' unsuspecting 'victims', but by persisting belligerently in spite of everyone's consciousness of its fakery. 'Partridge' describes the effects of this obstinacy not just on his business, but his health: 'In short, what with Undertakers, Embalmers, Joiners, Sextons, and your damn'd Elegy-Hawkers . . . I got not one Wink of Sleep that Night, nor scarce a Moment's Rest ever since.'[63] The imagined effect here is one of suspended agitation, a state in which Partridge is maintained for a long time. The assumption has generally been that *Squire Bickerstaff Detected* followed quickly on the heels of *Predictions* in 1708.[64] However, we can say with some confidence that it appeared on 19 August 1710, when an advertisement in the newspaper *The Post Boy* says it was published 'this day'. The advertisement is not for a second or later edition, but the first appearance. A bantering notice written by Joseph Addison in *The Tatler* no. 216 (for 26–29 August) warns that 'an ignorant Upstart in Astrology has publicly endeavoured to persuade the World that he is the late John Partridge, who died the 29th of March, 1708'. 'Beware of Counterfeits', it continues, 'for such are abroad.'[65] Addison is picking up on 'Partridge's' reluctant cry of protest in *Squire Bickerstaff Detected*: 'The famous Dr. *Partridge!* No Counterfeit, but all alive!'[66] In a letter to Thomas Wharton on 24 August, Addison writes: 'Among the prints which I send you by this Post, the "Essay upon Credit" is said to be written by Mr. Harley, and that of "Bickerstaff detected", by Mr. Congreve.'[67] The attributions are gossip—the 'Essay on Credit' is Defoe's—but the fact that said *Essay* is advertised in *The Post Boy* for 15 August 1710 confirms that Addison is passing on new publications to Wharton, strongly suggesting in turn that this is the first appearance of 'Bickerstaff detected'. Finally, Defoe's *Condoling Letter to the Tatler* (discussed above) was published around 20 September 1710, and latches on to the Bickerstaff persona in ways that suggest a recent reading of

---

[62] Swift, *Works* (Cambridge), ii. 569.   [63] Swift, *Works* (Cambridge), ii. 570.

[64] Herbert Davis dates the piece to April 1708, without saying why: Swift, *PW*, ii. xiv. In her edition, Rumbold says it appears 'presumably during 1708' (Swift, *Works* (Cambridge), ii. 565), though she notes the 1710 advertisement discussed below in 'Burying', 109. W. A. Eddy gives '1709 [?]' in 'The Wits vs. Partridge the Astrologer', *Studies in Philology* 29 (1932), 29–40, 39. More recently Claude Rawson suggested 'ca. 1710', following D. F. McKenzie, whose Congreve edition dates the piece from the Addison letter also discussed below ('Congreve and Swift', in *Representation, Heterodoxy, and Aesthetics: Essays in Honor of Ronald Paulson*, ed. Ashley Marshall (Lanham: Rowman & Littlefield, 2014), 21; *The Works of William Congreve*, ed. D. F. McKenzie, 3 vols. (Oxford: Oxford University Press, 2011), III.269).

[65] *Tatler*, iii. 135.   [66] Swift, *Works* (Cambridge), ii. 571.

[67] *The Letters of Joseph Addison*, ed. Walter Graham (Oxford: Clarendon Press, 1941), 232.

Squire Bickerstaff Detected.[68] So, rather than quick-wittedly contributing to a barrage of harassment in April and May 1708, *Squire Bickerstaff Detected* encourages readers to imagine a John Partridge who has had 'scarce a Moment's Rest' for the past two and a half years.[69]

QUIV'RING THERE

Five and a half years later, Pope disturbed the repose of the bookseller, Edmund Curll, by tricking him into drinking an emetic draught, a '*Revenge by Poison*' that was suited to Curll's crimes.[70] On 26 March, Curll released *Court Poems*, a slim volume containing three poems by Pope's friends, John Gay and Lady Mary Wortley Montagu, which were published without their knowledge.[71] A preface insinuated authorship of the whole by these two poets in turn, before finally reporting the opinion of 'a distinguished Gentleman' that the author was Pope. He responded to this malicious misattribution by forcing Curll to speak publicly what he never did in private (in accordance with the etymology of 'vindicate'). Summoning Curll to a meeting through the offices of his publisher Lintot on 28 March, the poet questioned him about *Court Poems*, and appearing to accept an explanation, drank the bookseller's health. Curll duly drank Pope's, unwittingly consuming the poison dissolved in his wine. Pope's pamphlet, *A Full and True Account*, then picks up the narration from inside Curll's home, where he is taken violently ill, summons some of his business associates, and proceeds to make 'a verbal Will'.[72] This is really a catalogue of his ill deeds, which in its limp apologetics reflects the kind of moral apathy Pope constantly associates with the commodification of literary endeavour. As the market debases literature into so much paper, so Curll's 'purging' begins as a confession and ends as so much effluent. At first, Curll manages to speak 'between the Intervals of his Yawnings and Reachings', but as the account progresses, the difference between involuntary retching and speaking collapses.[73] When '*Mr.* Pemberton' objects to an item in Curll's will, we are told, '*some Dispute might have arisen, unbecoming a dying Person, if* Mr. Lintott *had not interposed, and Mr.* Curll *vomited*'. That indifferent 'and'

---

[68] Note particularly their shared interest in graves. For date see Paula R. Backscheider, *Daniel Defoe: His Life* (Baltimore: Johns Hopkins University Press, 1989), 329.

[69] The unrest is imaginary: on the appeal and fallaciousness of the idea that John Partridge's almanac was 'stopped' by Swift's hoax and that the hoax affected his personal and political life permanently see Richmond P. Bond, 'John Partridge and the Company of Stationers', *Studies in Bibliography* 76 (1963), 61–80, and McTague, 'A Letter from John Partridge To Isaac Manley', 201–2.

[70] The act is so labelled in the title: *A Full and True Account of a Horrid and Barbarous Revenge by Poison on the Body of Mr Edmund Curll, Bookseller* (1716).

[71] Of the three episodes examined in this chapter, this is the one most likely to have taken place in something like the manner described. See Paul Baines and Pat Rogers, *Edmund Curll, Bookseller* (Oxford: Oxford University Press, 2007), 82, and Curll's own matter-of-fact report of the incident in *The Curliad* (1729), 20–1. Baines and Rogers give a detailed account of the affair (63–110).

[72] *Full and True Account*, 3.   [73] *Full and True Account*, 3.

between Lintott's interposition and Curll's vomit mischievously suggests equivalence, leaving it comically unclear which intervention is the more effective. Later, the 'Confusion and Imperfection' of the *Account* is attributed to Curll's being 'perpetually interrupted by Vomitings'; Pope's pamphlet mimics Curll's 'dissolution' as the famous lines in his 1711 poem, *An Essay on Criticism*, perform the metrical effects they describe (as when we hear that 'ten low Words oft creep in one dull Line').[74] Curll's voice shifts in tandem with his bowels, too: '*In this last Paragraph* Mr. Curll's *Voice grew more free, for his Vomitings abated upon his Dejections* [i.e. excrements]'.[75] That strange sense of location—the idea that Curll's voice grew more free '*in this last Paragraph*'—indicates Pope's reduction of Curll to print: his body is subsumed into text. Hilariously, Pope implies that in reported speech such as 'I have vilify'd his Grace the Duke of M——gh', Curll is *speaking* in the partial blanks his publications used as a means of evading prosecution. The interruption of these names may represent the effect (and precise timing) of Curll's 'Vomitings', cementing the impression that he has become identical with the tricks of his own publications.

According to E. V. Chandler, Pope published his two accounts of the poisoning 'to make sure that his trick was publicly immortalized'.[76] That Curll's private condition was rendered public is vital, but Chandler has the events in the wrong order. Rather, Pope poisoned Curll so that he could 'publicly immortalize' the trick: the event is subordinate to the satire. Pope takes the decision to poison Curll not, as has been suggested, because his disability left him unable to give the bookseller a drubbing, but because of the particular metaphorical opportunities that a vomiting and defecating bookseller afforded.[77] For Regan, Pope's '*inscription* of bodily debasements was a productive process which actively constituted its target, rather than one which described the already available facts of his victim's carcase'.[78] Like Swift and Rochester, Pope is not interested in finishing Curll off. The poisoning gives him the opportunity to appropriate Curll's person. In its last paragraph, *A Full and True Account* leaves Curll suspended, stinking, on the brink of death:

> The poor Man continued for some Hours with all his disconsolate Family about him in Tears, expecting his final dissolution; when of a sudden he was surprizingly relieved by a plentiful foetid Stool, which obliged them all to retire out of the Room. Notwithstanding, it is judged by Sir *Richard Bl[ackmor]e*, that the Poyson is still Latent in his Body, and will infallibly destroy him by slow Degrees, in less than a Month. It is to be hoped the other Enemies of this wretched Stationer, will not further pursue their Revenge...[79]

---

[74] *Full and True Account*, 5, 6; Pope, *Poems* (Twickenham), i. 276–83 (ll. 337–73).

[75] *Full and True Account*, 3.

[76] E. V. Chandler, 'Pope's Emetic: Bodies, Books, and Filth', *Genre* 27 (1994), 351–76, 362.

[77] Maynard Mack suggests the revenge takes this form because of Pope's being 'incapable of giving Curll the caning he deserved' (*Alexander Pope: A Life* (New Haven: Yale University Press, 1985), 296). See also Chandler, 'Pope's Emetic', 353.

[78] Regan, '"Pranks, Unfit for Naming"', 38.

[79] *Full and True Account*, 6. On the 'latency' of the poison in Curll's body, see Regan, '"Pranks, Unfit for Naming"', 49.

Recalling both the *Predictions* and *An Answer to Bickerstaff*, this conclusion marks out an interval of time, at the end of which its victim will 'infallibly' die. The hope that Curll's enemies 'will not further pursue their revenge' is to be read ironically as an invitation. When *A Further Account of the Condition of Edmund Curll* appeared in August 1716, its title page said that it was 'To be published weekly'. This was less a genuine ambition than an encouragement to collaborators.[80] Suspended sentences like these give readers space in which they can maintain their feigned credulity.

In the loosest sense, Pope found some collaborators in the shape of the boys of Westminster School, though it took longer than a month. In retaliation for Curll's surreptitious and error-ridden publication of a funeral oration given by their head boy, they summoned him on 2 August, and, amongst other humiliations, tossed him in a blanket.[81] Samuel Wesley junior, a staff member at the school, then published *Neck or Nothing*, a poem in the voice of the eccentric bookseller John Dunton, mockingly commiserating with Curll and describing his punishments, which are illustrated in an engraved frontispiece.[82] According to Regan, Wesley sought in his verse to 'maintain [Curll] in the impolite postures of physical abjection and social humiliation depicted in the illustration'. Like Pope's pamphlets, he argues, *Neck or Nothing* is compensating for 'the truncation, or temporally delimited nature, of Curll's punishment'.[83] In a collision of narrative and plastic art that anticipates, oddly enough, moments in Keats's 'Ode on a Grecian Urn', Wesley's Curll is agitated yet still, hung, 'quiv'ring there', like a mortifying piece of meat ('For ever warm, and still to be enjoyed'?).[84] These lines ekphrastically anticipate the frontispiece engraving:

> . . . aerial thou
> Aloft shall thy Proportion show;
> For ever carv'd on Wooden Plate,
> Shalt hang I'th'Air like Mahomet.
> Whatever thine Effigy might do,
> Thy Person could not hover so.[85]

That Curll's 'Effigy' can hover in ways his 'Person' could not is the key to the allure of suspension, for Wesley, and the other practical satirists examined here. The problem with Curll's 'person' is its dull dependence on gravity, from which his effigy releases him. *Neck or Nothing*, *A Full and True Account*, Alexander Bendo's brochure, and *A Vindication of Isaac Bickerstaff* are successful practical satires because they chastise their targets

---

[80]   See also the puzzling 'Part I.' on the first page of *Squire Bickerstaff Detected*.

[81]   See Baines and Rogers, *Edmund Curll, Bookseller*, 94–7. Pope has Curll refer to being 'toss'd in a Blanket' in *A Further Account of the most Deplorable Condition of Edmund Curll* (1716), 14.

[82]   Reproduced in Baines and Rogers, *Edmund Curll, Bookseller*, 96.

[83]   Samuel Wesley, *Neck or Nothing: A Consolatory Letter from Mr D-nt-n to Mr C-rll upon his being tost in a Blanket* (1716), 47.

[84]   Wesley, *Neck or Nothing*, 9; John Keats, 'Ode on a Grecian Urn', in *The Complete Poems* ed. John Barnard (Oxford: Oxford University Press, 2006), 345.

[85]   Wesley, *Neck or Nothing*, 10.

whilst managing, with their readers' collusion, to keep the mortifying experience of coming back down to earth forever in prospect.

Pope was also quite capable of collaborating with himself, and he does so nowhere more fully than in *The Dunciad* (major versions in 1728, 1729, 1742, and 1743). Serving as it does, in part, as an updatable catalogue of injuries suffered and inflicted by Pope, it is unsurprising to find the Curll poisoning enshrined in Book II. During a series of scatological games, Curll emerges both victorious and 'Obscene with filth' from a running race.[86] Having teased him with a number of phantom poets, the goddess Dulness eventually gives him a prize more tangible: a tapestry depicting the practical punishments endured by authors such as Defoe, Tutchin, Ridpath, and Roper. Amongst them, suspended in the air, is Curll:

> Himself among the storied Chiefs he spies,
> As from the blanket high in air he flies,
> And oh! (he cry'd) what street, what lane, but knows
> Our purgings, pumpings, blanketings and blows?
> In ev'ry loom our labours shall be seen,
> And the fresh vomit run for ever green![87]

The tableau depicted in the frontispiece to *Neck or Nothing* forms the basis of Pope's 'emblem' for Curll. Folding his own chastisement of the bookseller into Wesley's, he commemorates a particular detail from *A Full and True Account*, where the 'contents' of Curll's vomit are said to be 'as Green as Grass'.[88] In 1716, the greenness served to indicate Curll's choleric disposition.[89] In these lines, however, like the 'green' wounds of the vindictive man, the vomit is 'forever green', fresh and raw, the past forced to speak to, and in, the present. In his landmark study of the *Dunciads*, Aubrey Williams defended Pope's exaggerated caricaturing of the dunc99 as 'a necessary part of the "distancing" of the ephemeral in art, of getting the bee into the amber'.[90] Granted, the suspension of Curll here, and in *Neck or Nothing*, feels more like a pinioning than an embalming. Nevertheless, as Wesley's Curll is 'forever carv'd in Wood', so here his vomit remains 'for ever green', held in a suspended agitation maintained by print's fundamental iterability.

One of the *Dunciad*'s triumphs is the way it makes historical events and persons seem as if they exist only in order to be included in its verse and paratexts, pressing event into the service of satire. Indeed, as the 'publisher' of the first version of the poem explains: 'the *Poem was not made for these Authors, but these authors for the poem*'.[91] The identity of the 'real' dunces, Pope pretends, matters little, for he has a supply as constant as fresh greenery to decorate his fireplace: 'I should judge', says the 'publisher', 'that they were

---

[86] Pope, *Poems* (Longman), iii. 219.   [87] Pope, *Poems* (Longman), iii. 231.
[88] *Full and True Account*, 3.
[89] In humoral medicine, choler causes an excess of irritability, and is identified with or found in (green) bile (*OED* choler, *n.*).
[90] Aubrey Williams, *Pope's Dunciad: A Study of its Meaning* (London: Methuen, 1955), 62.
[91] Pope, *Poems* (Longman), iii. 15.

clapp'd in as they rose, fresh and fresh, and chang'd from day to day, in like manner as when the old boughs wither, we thrust new ones into a chimney'.[92] This 1728 version, we might recall, is the one populated by those indeterminate blanks that yawn for a name, as a fireplace does for a bough. At the outset of the *Dunciad*'s long life, and throughout it, Pope stresses the importance of maintenance, creating space for satirical activity, and policing it. In its refusal of closure, its appropriation of its targets' voices, and its deployment of the trappings of historicity to obscure the liberties it takes with 'events', the *Dunciad* resembles, and may have learned from, the practical satires discussed here. Pope, continually tinkering with his most expansive satire, is reluctant to put the dunces down. While they are often falling about, they are also figured by the poem as a swarm, 'conglob'd' around their goddess, 'quiv'ring there' in pointless orbit.[93] Retaliating against the arrows flying in the dark for which he held them responsible, Pope turns the precipitate dunces into projectiles that will—that can—never land.

Select Bibliography

Baines, Paul and Pat Rogers. *Edmund Curll, Bookseller* (Oxford: Oxford University Press, 2007).

Bourne, Don. '"If I Appear to Any One Like a Counterfeit": Liminality in Rochester's *Alexander Bendo's Brochure*', *Restoration: Studies in English Literary Culture, 1660–1700* 32 (2008), 3–17.

Loveman, Kate. *Reading Fictions, 1660–1740: Deception in English Literary and Political Culture* (Aldershot: Ashgate, 2008).

Lowe, N. F. 'Why Swift Killed Partridge', *Swift Studies* 6 (1991), 70–82.

Regan, Shaun. '"Pranks, Unfit for Naming": Pope, Curll, and the "Satirical Grotesque"', *The Eighteenth Century* 46 (2005), 37–59.

Rumbold, Valerie. 'Burying the Fanatic Partridge: Swift's Holy Week Hoax', in *Politics and Literature in the Age of Swift: English and Irish Perspectives*, ed. Claude Rawson (Cambridge: Cambridge University Press, 2010), 81–115.

---

[92] Pope, *Poems* (Longman), iii. 15–16.   [93] Pope, *Dunciad in Four Books*, 285.

CHAPTER 31

....

LEGAL CONSTRAINTS, LIBELLOUS EVASIONS

....

JOSEPH HONE

THE relationship between satire and the law during the eighteenth century was an uneasy one. Satirists faced numerous legal constraints, most notably the laws against treason and seditious libel. What was the impact of those laws on satirical writing during the eighteenth century? This chapter investigates the numerous and increasingly experimental strategies that satirists used to evade prosecution by the English authorities. A second, related aim is to examine how legislators adapted old laws and developed new ones to combat the threat of politically dangerous satire. This conflict between satirists and lawmakers generated a period of literary and legal innovation, with numerous important legal precedents established in the first decade of the eighteenth century. Naturally, the first half of this chapter is largely focused on that period. Legal precedents established in the first decade endured throughout the century, affecting not only the satirical milieu but also canonical masterpieces by authors such as Jonathan Swift, Alexander Pope, Henry Fielding, John Wilkes, and others.

Laurence Hanson identified the significance of press legislation for students of satire more than eighty years ago.[1] And yet, despite some important revisionist work by scholars such as Thomas Keymer and Andrew Benjamin Bricker, most literary critics still assume that there was such thing in the eighteenth century as 'a recipe for legally safe satire'.[2] My aim in this chapter is to convey the scale of the legal challenge facing satirists and to demonstrate that writing satire was frequently more risky than many

---

[1] Laurence Hanson, *Government and the Press, 1695–1763* (Oxford: Oxford University Press, 1936).

[2] Vincent Carretta, *The Snarling Muse: Verbal and Visual Political Satire from Pope to Churchill* (Philadelphia: University of Pennsylvania Press, 1983), 40. For examples of the revisionist scholarship, see Thomas Keymer, *Poetics of the Pillory: English Literature and Seditious Libel, 1660–1820* (Oxford: Oxford University Press, forthcoming); Andrew Benjamin Bricker, 'Libel and Satire: The Problem with Naming', *English Literary History* 81 (2014), 889–921; Ian Higgins, 'Censorship, Libel and Self-Censorship', in *Jonathan Swift and the Eighteenth-Century Book*, ed. Paddy Bullard and James McLaverty (Cambridge: Cambridge University Press, 2013), 179–98.

scholars have presumed. Outspoken satirists risked imprisonment, the pillory, and worse. It is important that we distinguish between satires that were publicly acknowledged by their authors and satires that were published anonymously. Satires belonging to the first of those categories needed to be ambiguous enough to provide their authors with plausible deniability. Satires from the second group were usually blunt lampoons or 'libels' and therefore had to be published in an anonymous format that the authorities could not trace back to the printer or author. Different options were available to satirists who pursued either of those strategies, although both routes entailed distinct risks. The whole subgenre of verse libel actually owed its definition to the law. Views about the subversive potential of libellous satire transformed during the century in response to shifting political circumstances and literary trends. The purpose of this chapter is not to provide an overarching narrative about the evolution of English satire: such narratives are usually simplistic at best and plain wrong at worst. Rather, satirical authors found specific local solutions to specific local problems. Tracing the messy histories of satire and press legislation in tandem suggests new ways of mapping the genre from the last decade of the seventeenth century through the eighteenth century.

SATIRE AND THE LAW

What laws affected satirists in the eighteenth century? The censorship regime facing eighteenth-century satirists emerged from that of the seventeenth century. For most of the seventeenth century, the press was regulated by pre-publication licensing.[3] Before 1695, the law stipulated that texts needed to be licensed before they were printed or published. Usually this was a straightforward matter of registering a title with the Stationers' Company, paying a small fee, and having the text approved by the Surveyor of the Press, who acted as chief government censor. Obtaining licences for satires, however, could prove tricky, particularly if the government or individual ministers were being lampooned. Yet because topical satires sold well—and because they were usually short and cheap to produce—lots of printers and publishers simply bypassed the licensing process and issued the texts anonymously. Equally importantly, the process of obtaining a licence could be quite time consuming. Most satires needed to be issued promptly in order to retain their topical relevance, so registering for a licence was not always an expedient business decision for publishers. As one partial commentator observed in 1693, it 'appears the Law is far insufficient to the end which it intends. Do we not see, not once or oftner, but weekly, nay daily, that continued *Jacobite Libels* against our present happy Establishment, are printed and dispersed amongst us; for all that *Licensing* can

---

[3] There were temporary lapses in licensing in 1641 and 1679. See Mark Knights, *Representation and Misrepresentation: Partisanship and Political Culture* (Oxford: Oxford University Press, 2005), 16; T. Crist, 'Government Control of the Press after the Expiration of the Licensing Act in 1679', *Publishing History* 5 (1979), 49–97.

do?'[4] In short, licensing did little to quell the flood of printed satires in the 1690s and nothing about satires that circulated in manuscript only. In 1695, the government refused to prolong the Licensing Act. New measures were needed to restrain the most egregious offences of the press.

After the lapse of the Licensing Act, the government's three main instruments of censorship became the common law of libel (including seditious libel, blasphemous libel, and criminal libel), the 'Act for the more Effectual Suppressing of Blasphemy and Prophaneness' (9 Will. III, c. 35), and various treason statutes (mostly based on 25 Edward III) which prohibited imagining or writing about the monarch's death, declaring war against the monarch, or aiding his or her enemies. As both John Barrell and Murray Pittock have demonstrated, those last three categories of treason proved immensely flexible during the eighteenth century.[5] Jacobite authors and printers in particular could be impeached for imagining or inciting the monarch's death.[6] Because Jacobite satires were a particular nuisance in the late seventeenth and early eighteenth centuries, treason statutes were enforced quite vigorously then. The execution of the Jacobite printer William Anderton in 1693 demonstrated that printing or publishing of 'malicious, scandalous, and traitorous libels' could be interpreted in the courts as an 'overt act' of treason punishable by death.[7] Under Anne, new treason laws (6 Anne c. 7) were introduced that applied specifically to the book trade. As a direct consequence of those new laws, the young printer John Matthews was found guilty of treason for his role in printing and publishing the scandalous Jacobite pamphlet *Vox Populi, Vox Dei* in 1719 and was subsequently hanged.[8]

Seditious libel laws were effective against both the 'making' and the publication of libels.[9] During the seventeenth century, both categories needed to be proved in court to secure a conviction. Lampoons were not deemed to be libels until they were 'published', which included sharing or circulating texts in manuscript form.[10] By the start of the

---

[4] *Reasons Humbly Offered for the Liberty of Unlicensed Printing* (1693), 5.

[5] John Barrell, *Imagining the King's Death: Figurative Treason, Fantasies of Regicide, 1793–1796* (Oxford: Clarendon Press, 2000); Murray Pittock, *Material Culture and Sedition, 1688–1760: Treacherous Objects, Secret Places* (Basingstoke: Palgrave Macmillan, 2013).

[6] On the government persecution of Jacobite publications, see Paul Monod, 'The Jacobite Press and English Censorship', in *The Stuart Court in Exile and the Jacobites*, ed. Eveline Cruickshanks and Edward Corp (London: Hambledon Press, 1995), 125–42; Pat Rogers, 'Nathaniel Mist, Daniel Defoe, and the Perils of Publishing', *The Library*, 7th ser. 10 (2009), 298–313.

[7] William Cobbett, ed., *A Complete Collection of State Trials and Proceedings for High Treason*, 34 vols. (London: Bagshaw, 1809–28), xii. 1245.

[8] See R. J. Goulden, '*Vox Populi, Vox Dei*: Charles Delafaye's Paperchase', *The Book Collector* 28 (1979), 368–90.

[9] My account of the development of seditious libel laws draws on Philip Hamburger's seminal article on 'The Development of the Law of Seditious Libel and the Control of the Press', *Stanford Law Review* 37 (1985), 661–765.

[10] On the manuscript circulation of libels in the seventeenth century, see Andrew McRae, *Literature, Satire, and the Early Stuart State* (Cambridge: Cambridge University Press, 2004); Harold Love, *Scribal Publication in Seventeenth-Century England* (Oxford: Clarendon Press, 1993); and Harold Love, *English Clandestine Satire* (Oxford: Oxford University Press, 2004).

eighteenth century, the distinction between making and publishing collapsed, firstly in the trial of Henry Neville Payne in 1696 for a lampoon on the death of Queen Mary (87 Eng. Rep. 584–7). Despite the prosecution having no conclusive evidence that Payne intended to circulate this libel, the presiding judge ruled that the actual act of 'reducing' a libel 'into writing' was the 'making' of a libel and 'making a libel is an offense, though never published'. Put simply, scribbling a lampoon down on paper—and not necessarily composing it—was now seditious libel. A second trial in 1699 (91 Eng. Rep. 363–5) found another man guilty of 'writing and collecting' satires, both of which were now deemed to be acts of 'making' libels and thus sufficient grounds for sentencing. Although neither of these cases involved the prosecution of a satirist per se, we need to understand the broader significance of the rulings. During the seventeenth century, a court had needed to prove intent to publish to prosecute under seditious libel laws. By the start of the eighteenth century, legal emphasis had shifted from the circulation of libels to the act of writing them down. Culpability now lay more firmly than before with the satirist.

Seditious libel laws absorbed many of the functions previously associated with *scandalum magnatum*. Under this law (2 Rich. 2 Stat. I *c*. 5) peers and government ministers could file against satirists for defamation. However, this procedure required the plaintiff to prove in court that all defamatory statements made were demonstrably false. Moreover, if the court found the defendant not guilty then those defamatory statements were, by implication, true. Hence, very few charges were filed under *scandalum magnatum* laws during the century.[11] Developments to libel laws after the trial of the radical Whig hack and satirist John Tutchin (87 Eng. Rep. 1014–28) for defaming the government made seditious libel prosecutions even easier. Following traditional laws of defamation, Tutchin's counsel had argued that 'nothing is a libel but what reflects upon some particular person', and Tutchin's papers, they insisted, reflected on the government as a whole.[12] The judge rejected this argument and declared that seditious libel could now encompass reflection on the government as a whole as well as reflection on individual ministers. Whereas seventeenth-century seditious libel laws had been defined quite specifically and were consequently difficult to administer, at the start of the eighteenth century, judges began to interpret those laws in increasingly generalized ways. Those interpretations established key precedents that endured throughout the century. As late as 1764, one anonymous lawyer was able to assert that libel suits were 'not confined or limited by any thing besides the discretion of the Attorney-General himself'.[13] The broadening of libel laws in the first decade of the eighteenth century effectively made it much easier for the government to detain and successfully prosecute satirists.

[11] John C. Lassiter, 'Defamation of Peers: The Rise and Decline of the Action for *Scandalum Magnatum*, 1497–1773', *The American Journal of Legal History* 22 (1978), 216–36.

[12] 90 Eng. Rep. 1133.

[13] *An Enquiry into the Doctrine Lately Propagated Concerning Libels, Warrants, and the Seizure of Papers* (1764), 8.

CLANDESTINE SATIRE

How did satirists navigate those new legal constraints and avoid prosecution? The simplest and most effective option was maintaining anonymity. Put simply, if the government could not discover who wrote a satire, then they could not prosecute. But maintaining anonymity was more difficult in practice than in theory. The authorities had numerous means of discovering the identities of libellous authors and used all their resources to bring those authors to justice, including, but not limited to, professional espionage, bounty hunting, employing freelance informants, and, as last resorts, intimidation, arbitrary detention, and interrogation. Frequently all of those methods were used in conjunction.

Satirists who circulated works in manuscript only were less likely to be discovered than satirists who published in print. The reason for this was simple. Manuscript satires were easier than printed books to keep secret and did not require collaboration with printers or booksellers. Moreover, the nebulous authorship of manuscript lampoons made the format intrinsically deniable. For instance, contemporary readers attributed the High Church lampoon *Faction Display'd* (1704) to various plausible Tory authors, including Thomas D'Urfey, Francis Atterbury, William Pittis, and Matthew Prior— although those attributions were based solely on guesswork and hearsay. Despite the lack of proof, Prior became seriously embarrassed by his association with the libel and swore 'before God, Angels, and Men I neither did write that Book, or any Line in it, nor do I directly or indirectly know who wrote the whole or any part of it'.[14] Some years later, Pittis alleged that Bertram Stote, a Tory MP for Northumberland, was the author, and that he had nothing to do with it.[15] Conversely, both Alexander Pope and Giles Jacob believed that William Shippen wrote the libel.[16] When *Faction Display'd* was finally printed, two prefatory verses were appended praising 'the Unknown AUTHOR' and 'The Concealed AUTHOR of this Excellent POEM' as a 'Matchless Genius!'[17] We still do not know who wrote *Faction Display'd*. The poem's unstable authorship, originally a ploy to avoid litigation, has led to its exclusion from traditional literary histories.[18]

Forensic graphology or the analysis of handwriting became an important tool for tracking down and prosecuting libellous satirists. One case worth considering is that of

---

[14] *The Literary Works of Matthew Prior*, ed. H. Bunker Wright and Monroe K. Spears, 2 vols. (Oxford: Clarendon Press, 1959), ii. 797.

[15] William Pittis, *The Proceedings of Both Houses of Parliament in the Years 1702, 1703, 1704 upon the Bill to Prevent Occasional Conformity* (1710), 56.

[16] British Library, C.28.e.15; Giles Jacob, *An Historical Account of the Lives and Writings of Our Most Considerable English Poets* (1720), 306.

[17] *Some Critical and Politick Remarks on a Late Virulent Lampoon Call'd Faction Display'd* (1704), 3; *Faction Display'd* (1704), sigs A2^r–A3^r.

[18] The poem is edited alongside other libels and lampoons from the period in *Poems on Affairs of State: Augustan Satirical Verse, 1660–1714*, ed. George de Forest Lord et al., 7 vols. (New Haven: Yale University Press, 1963–75), vi. 648–73. Hereafter *POAS*.

Samuel Johnson's future mentor, Richard Savage. While gathering evidence against Savage in 1717, Robert Girling (undoubtedly a government spy) concentrated on Savage's handwriting. Having obtained manuscript copies of Jacobite lampoons by Savage from the bookseller Robert Tooke, including *An Ironical Panagerick on His Pretended Majesty George* (1715), *The Pretender* (1715), and *Britannia's Miseries* (1716), Girling informed the secretary of state that Tooke had taken his copies 'from the Origanal Maniscript's of Mr. Richard Savage's own Wrighting, and some of these Coppy's I have seen my Selfe, of Mr Savage's own hand Wrighting, which I Know p'ticulerly well'.[19] Savage's modern editor Clarence Tracy writes that 'there is no apparent reason why Tooke's copies were not used' in the lawsuit.[20] But Girling's desire to identify Savage's 'own hand Wrighting' makes sense once we remember the verdict of the Payne case in 1696, when the original act of writing out the libel was deemed the 'making' of it. Likewise, the spy's explanation that he knew Savage's handwriting 'p'ticulerly well' provides a somewhat menacing insight into the extent of his espionage. Only a timely parliamentary amnesty covering all acts of sedition performed in the 'late un-natural Rebellion' saved Savage from the pillory or worse.

Savage was caught out by a combination of government surveillance and secret informants within the book trade. Girling could not have assembled his cache of evidence without the aid of the bookseller, Robert Tooke. Whistle-blowing was an entrenched part of the government surveillance programme, which relied on the complicity of various members of the book trade. Reasons for informing on the clandestine press were many. Some informants simply worked for a fee. Tooke was well known among booksellers for his mercenary attitude and may well have sought financial remuneration for his intelligence. Other printers and authors were coerced into informing on their colleagues. Savage himself had escaped an earlier charge of 'having a treasonable Pamphlet in his possession' only by informing on a Jacobite printer.[21] Disaffected and destitute printers, such as Robert Clare, often made excellent spies. Having been forced out of his business by hostile colleagues, Clare found employment providing the government with the names of the authors, printers, and publishers of controversial tracts and libels, including Ned Ward's *Hob Turn'd Courtier* (1703) and *Hudibras Redivivus* (1705), for which Ward was subsequently fined and pilloried.[22] Clare likewise discovered Daniel Defoe's authorship of the controversial *The Dyet of Poland* (1705), which had been issued with a misleading Polish imprint. In the cutthroat world of the early eighteenth-century book trade, spies and informants posed very real threats to the security of satirists and other libellous authors.

Jonathan Swift was among the most adept satirists of the eighteenth century insofar as he always covered his tracks superbly. His personal copy of the treason statutes

[19] National Archives, SP 35/7/78.

[20] *The Poetical Works of Richard Savage*, ed. Clarence Tracy (Cambridge: Cambridge University Press, 1962), 15.

[21] *The Weekly Packet*, 175 (12 November 1715).

[22] Henry L. Snyder, 'The Reports of a Press Spy for Robert Harley: New Bibliographical Data for the Reign of Queen Anne', *The Library*, 5th ser. 22 (1967), 326–45 (343).

which he kept in his library would have been, in Ian Higgins's words, 'a cautionary reference book for a writer of seditious libels'.[23] Stephen Karian's pioneering work has recently illuminated how Swift strategically limited the manuscript circulation of his verse lampoons—poems such as 'A Wicked Treasonable Libel' (1718)—to closed groups of political allies.[24] Swift's printed satires were always published anonymously or pseudonymously and usually with the assistance of a trade publisher who, for a small fee, allowed his or her imprint to be used as a means of disguising Swift's and his printer's involvement.[25] Swift habitually fled London immediately after his most explosive satires were printed and sometimes before. He left London for Ireland after the publication of *A Tale of a Tub* (1704), for instance, which many commentators believed to be a blasphemous and heretical text.

The conditions surrounding the publication of *Gulliver's Travels* in 1726 were even more circumspect and deserve some attention here. Swift arranged the publication pseudonymously under the alias of Gulliver's imaginary cousin, 'Richard Sympson'. Swift prepared two manuscripts: the first in his own hand and the second in the hand of an unidentified scribe. The first manuscript was kept safe by Swift while the transcript was delivered to the bookseller, Benjamin Motte, presumably so that Swift's handwriting could not be identified. Motte received the transcript in mysterious circumstances: according to Pope, Motte 'knew not from whence, nor from whom' the copy was 'dropp'd at his house in the dark, from a Hackney-coach'. By 'computing the time', Pope told Swift, 'I found it was after you left England'.[26] Even the most industrious press spy would have found it difficult to link the absentee Swift to the printed text of *Gulliver's Travels* because Motte himself was ignorant of Swift's involvement. As Swift himself later explained: 'I have writ some things that would make people angry. I always sent them by unknown hands, the Printer might guess [that Swift was the author], but he could not accuse me.'[27] Swift handled the press in a way that guaranteed authorial anonymity in the predictable event of litigation.

Although Swift was protected by his anonymity, like most booksellers, Motte attached his name to the book and was therefore liable to prosecution. Writing in the guise of 'Richard Sympson', Swift had assured Motte that the *Travels* 'may be thought in one or two places to be a little Satyrical, yet it is agreed they will give no Offence'.[28] Yet Motte was evidently unconvinced and, like Swift, took precautions to shield himself from

---

[23] Ian Higgins, *Swift's Politics: A Study in Disaffection* (Cambridge: Cambridge University Press, 1994), 13.

[24] Stephen Karian, *Jonathan Swift in Print and Manuscript* (Cambridge: Cambridge University Press, 2010); and Stephen Karian, 'Swift as a Manuscript Poet', in *Jonathan Swift and the Eighteenth-Century Book*, ed. Paddy Bullard and James McLaverty (Cambridge: Cambridge University Press, 2013), 31–50.

[25] On trade publishers, see Michael Treadwell, 'London Trade-Publishers 1675–1750', *The Library*, 6th ser. 4 (1982), 99–134; John Horden, '"In the Savoy": John Nutt and His Family', *Publishing History* 24 (1988), 5–26; John D. Gordon III, 'John Nutt: Trade Publisher and Printer "In the Savoy"', *The Library*, 7th ser. 15 (2014), 243–60.

[26] Swift, *Corr.* (Woolley), iii. 52. See David Womersley's textual introduction in Swift, *Works* (Cambridge), xvi. 627–40.

[27] Swift, *Corr.* (Woolley), iii. 556.   [28] Swift, *Works* (Cambridge), xvi. 595.

litigation. He did this by censoring Swift's text.[29] Motte's desire to avoid seditious libel is clear from a key censored passage discussing the reign of Queen Anne and her Tory ministers. In Swift's original, this passage from the episode with the Yahoos and Houyhnhnms included a satiric barb at King George and his first minister, Robert Walpole. But in Motte's rendition the passage is just very general, as well as historically and geographically distanced from contemporary Britain: 'in some former Reigns here, and in many other Courts of Europe now, where the Prince grew indolent and careless of their own Affairs through a constant Love and Pursuit of Pleasure, they made use of such an Administrator.'[30] This sort of broad stroke was legally safe whereas the specificity of the Swiftian original more readily lent itself to applications with contemporary Britain. Soon after publication, Pope reported to his friend that he found 'no considerable man very angry at the book: some indeed think it rather too bold, and too general a Satire.'[31] Swift complained bitterly that Motte had 'mangled, and abused, and added to, and blotted out' parts of his text, but nonetheless appears to have recognized that the friendly reception of the first edition of *Gulliver's Travels* as a 'general' satire may have stemmed from Motte's edits and not his own caution.[32]

IRONY, INNUENDO, AMBIGUITY

Anonymity was not an option for ambitious satirists who wished to claim credit for their work. Those satirists needed to exercise a degree of self-censorship through the creative use of indirection, irony, innuendo, and, to use Annabel Patterson's influential phrase, 'functional ambiguity'.[33] Shaftesbury summed up the link between irony and equivocation concisely at the start of the century: 'If men are forbid to speak their Minds seriously, on certain Subjects, they will do it ironically.'[34] Following Shaftesbury, most literary scholars have assumed that there was a loophole in the law that made it impossible to litigate against ironic satire. Contemporary trials paint a different picture. Returning to the legal records reveals that irony was no defence against charges of seditious libel.

Irony became litigable with the trial of Dr Joseph Browne (88 Eng. Rep. 911–12) for his reputed authorship of the lampoon *The Country Parson's Honest Advice to My Lord Keeper* (1706), which circulated widely in manuscript before Browne supplied a printer

---

[29] The now standard account of these revisions is James McLaverty, 'The Revision of the First Edition of *Gulliver's Travels*: Book-Trade Context, Interleaving, Two Cancels, and a Failure to Catch', *The Papers of the Bibliographical Society of America* 106 (2012), 5–35.

[30] Swift, *Works* (Cambridge), xvi. 710–11.   [31] Swift, *Corr.* (Woolley), iii. 52.

[32] Swift, *Corr.* (Woolley), iii. 57.

[33] Annabel Patterson, *Censorship and Interpretation: The Conditions of Writing and Reading in Early Modern England* (Madison: University of Wisconsin Press, 1984); see too, Debora Shuger, *Censorship and Cultural Sensibility: The Regulation of Language in Tudor-Stuart England* (Philadelphia: University of Pennsylvania Press, 2006).

[34] Anthony Ashley Cooper, Earl of Shaftesbury, *Characteristics of Men, Manners, Opinions, Times*, ed. Lawrence E. Klein (Cambridge: Cambridge University Press, 1999), 34.

with the copy.[35] This trial established an important legal precedent. Browne's satire was an exercise in total irony and thus, according to traditional accounts of seditious libel, should have been legally safe. The opening lines read:

> Be Wise as *Somerset*, as *Somers* Brave,
> As *Pembroke* Airy, and as *Richmond* Grave;
> Humble as *Orford* be; and *Wharton*'s Zeal
> For Church and Loyalty wou'd fit thee well;
> Like *Sarum* I would have thee love the Church;
> He scorns to leave his Mother in the Lurch.[36]

Browne's deadpan irony is deceptively simple. He relied on his readers to recognize the disjunction between noun and adjective without actually signalling this in the poem: that Somerset was *not* wise and nor was Somers brave. Browne knew that he was safe against charges of *scandalum magnatum* because that procedure could potentially establish in court Somerset's stupidity and Somers's cowardice, which the peers were naturally keen to avoid. Browne should theoretically have been protected from seditious libel by the rule of *mitior sensus*, which stipulated that potentially defamatory language should be interpreted by jurors in its most innocuous sense only. After all, he had framed his satire as 'Honest Advice'. Consequently Browne's counsel pleaded that the words 'did not import a scandal, but, in their natural signification, carry a credit'. But the judge replied that 'information will lie for speaking *ironically*' before allowing the jury to decide whether the poem was ironic. Importantly the jury's responsibility did not extend to whether the poem constituted a seditious libel, only to decide the *intent* of the author. They deemed the poem 'to be wrote *ironice*' and Browne was sentenced to the pillory. This ruling became a landmark precedent. In 1729, the courts upheld that jurors should interpret libels 'such as the generality of readers must take it in, according to the obvious and natural sense of it' (94 Eng. Rep. 207). This new common-sense approach effectively ensured that irony was no defence against charges of seditious libel. The ruling was upheld in 1713, when Daniel Defoe was imprisoned for a series of ironic pamphlets on the Protestant succession—including *Reasons Against the Succession of the House of Hanover* (1713) and *An Answer to a Question That Nobody Thinks Of: Viz, But What If the Queen Should Die?* (1713)—despite, as Defoe himself noted, the blatant intent of those

---

[35] Although Browne admitted handing the manuscript to the printer, he denied that he 'was the Author, or desired the Publication': Joseph Browne, *A Letter to the Right Honourable Mr Secretary Harley* (London, 1706), 5. While this may simply have been a prudent statement under the circumstances, on this occasion there is also good reason to believe Browne. In the spring Harley interviewed one Anne Watkins, a spinster who admitted that Browne had actually copied the text from her personal collection of manuscript poems, which she had left 'lying upon a Chest of drawers' one day when he visited. She claimed to have transcribed the lampoon from a copy belonging to her friend Patrick Robarts, who had picked it up earlier that same day (British Library, Add. MS 70023, fols. 172–3; cf. fols. 56–7, 167). On Browne, see J. A. Downie, 'What If Delarivier Manley Did *Not* Write *The Secret History of Queen Zarah*?', *The Library*, 7th ser. 5 (2004), 247–64.

[36] *POAS*, vii. 156–7.

pamphlets: 'Nor is this Irony concealed, *as has been suggested formerly*; but it is express'd plainly, and explicitly.'[37]

Gutted names were another hugely common feature of purportedly 'legally safe' satire. For instance, the reference to '*Seymour*'s Daughter' in the first printed edition of Browne's *Humble Advice* reads only '*S—y—r*'s Daughter'.[38] Take the following passage from the first edition of Alexander Pope's *The Dunciad* (1728):

> Ear-less on high, stood pillory'd *D—*
> And *T—* flagrant from the lash, below:
> There kick'd and cudgel'd *R—* might ye view,
> The very worstead still look'd black and blue.

> (ii. 127–30)

Everybody who was anybody knew that Pope meant Daniel Defoe, John Tutchin, and George Ridpath here—three notorious libellers—but the ambiguity of this typographical trick theoretically made it difficult to press charges.[39] Hence Joseph Addison complained about authors who, 'when they would be more Satyrical than ordinary, omit the Vowels of a great Man's Name, and fall most unmercifully upon all the Consonants. This way of writing', Addison continued, 'was first of all introduced by *T—m Br—wn*, of facetious Memory, who, after having gutted a Proper Name of all its intermediate Vowels, used to plant it in his Work, and make as free with it as he pleased, without any danger of the Statute'.[40] Swift likewise claimed, while sneering at Richard Steele, that 'we are careful never to print a Man's Name out at length; but as I do that of Mr. *St—le*: So that although every Body alive knows whom I mean, the Plaintiff can have no Redress in any Court of Justice'.[41] In *A Tale of a Tub*, he also warned that satirists who did not 'emvowel' proper nouns 'must expect to be imprisoned for *Scandalum Magnatum*: to have *Challenges* sent him; to be sued for *Defamation*; and to be *brought before the Bar of the House*'.[42]

Most scholars have taken such claims of legal safety at face value. And yet, as Andrew Benjamin Bricker's recent work demonstrates, evasive naming practices usually provided satirists with 'little or, in most instances, no legal protection'.[43] Indeed, Swift's frequent insistence on authorial anonymity suggests he understood the limitations of gutted names and might, in Bricker's words, have been 'cheekily parodying a common piece of Grub Street logic'.[44] The landmark ruling came in 1713, with the prosecution of William Hurt for printing *The British Embassadress's Speech to the French King* (1713)— in Swift's words 'the cursedest Libel in Verse come out, that ever was seen'.[45] Hurt was caught after an anonymous tip-off that this 'scandalous and treasonable paper' was

---

[37] *Defoe's Review*, ed. John McVeagh, 9 vols. (London: Pickering & Chatto, 2003–11).

[38] *POAS*, vii. 643.

[39] See Thomas Keymer, 'Defoe's Ears: *The Dunciad*, the Pillory, and Seditious Libel', *The Eighteenth-Century Novel* 6–7 (2009), 159–96.

[40] *Spectator*, iv. 537.   [41] Swift, *Works* (Cambridge), viii. 229.

[42] Swift, *Works* (Cambridge), i. 32.   [43] Bricker, 'Libel and Satire', 890.

[44] Bricker, 'Libel and Satire', 898.   [45] Swift, *Works* (Cambridge), ix. 517.

'being dispersed by one Robins a shoe-maker', who the secretary of state then used to track down the printer.[46] Although Hurt gutted most of the names that appeared in the libel, the judge nonetheless ruled that 'Defamatory Writing expressing only one or two Letters of a Name, in such a Manner, that from what goes before and follows after, it must needs be understood to signify such a particular Person, in the plain, obvious, and natural Construction of the Whole'. Put simply, a gutted name 'is as properly a Libel, as if it had expressed the whole Name at large'.[47] Nor were allegorical names or sobriquets defensible after 1728, when, in a case brought against the notorious Jacobite paper *Mist's Weekly Journal* (94 Eng. Rep. 207), the attorney-general successfully ruled that 'it lies upon the counsel for the King only to shew, that this construction, which they've put upon paper, is such, as the generality of readers must take it in according to the obvious and natural sense of it; and if upon hearing of the paper read the jury are of that opinion, they are bound in their consciences to find the defendant guilty'. The judge in that case cited the precedent of Joseph Browne's case in which 'even irony was held to be a libel'. As with trials for irony, the jury could now decide on the 'obvious and natural' meaning of a satire without being bound to the literal sense of the words on the page.

There were, though, some options still available to eighteenth-century satirists. Genuine ambiguity of message was not litigable because in such cases no court could establish guilt beyond reasonable doubt. Hence we rarely see suits filed against authors who used ambiguity in the way that others used innuendo and irony. Vagueness and generality were likewise useful tools for the satirist—and for the publisher too, as Motte's interference in *Gulliver's Travels* demonstrates. Classical satirists established precedents for other strategies of misdirection, most notably historical application. As Dryden observed of Juvenal in his *Discourse Concerning Satire* (1693), 'wheresoever *Juvenal* mentions *Nero*, he means *Domitian*, who he dares not attack in his own Person, but Scourges him by Proxy'.[48] Swift deployed this strategy to particular effect in *The Fable of Midas* (1712), a smear-job against his political enemy the Duke of Marlborough, as did Pope in his Horatian imitations of the 1730s and Paul Whitehead in *The State of Rome Under Nero and Domitian* (1739). The cleverness of this approach was that it required readers to make an imaginative leap. Some readers would find sedition where others would not. Jurors could not find satirists employing this technique guilty, although there was, as ever, a very fine line between scourging by proxy and litigable innuendo.

Censorship and the English Stage

In the face of rampant press censorship, some satirists turned to the stage. Seditious libel laws did not technically apply to the theatres. Most comedies from the early part of the century were not strictly satirical—or, if they were satirical, the butt of the joke was

[46] *The Manuscripts of the Earl of Dartmouth*, Historical Manuscripts Commission (London: HMSO, 1924), 315.
[47] William Hawkins, *A Treatise of Pleas of the Crown*, 2 vols. (1716–21), i. 194.
[48] Dryden, *Works*, iv. 69.

seldom the government, but rather general social mores, as with Pope, John Gay, and John Arbuthnot's flop *Three Hours After Marriage* (1717). Some burlesques simply parodied operatic bombast, as in Henry Fielding's *The Author's Farce* (1730) or Henry Carey's very silly *The Tragedy of Chrononhotonthologos* (1734). There was nothing to censor here. But other dramatists in the late 1720s began to lampoon the government, as in Gay's landmark satire, *The Beggar's Opera* (1728), where a story of beggars, thieves, and prisoners highlighted similarities between the worlds of crime and prostitution and of corrupt Walpolean governance. Fielding followed Gay in a series of anti-Walpole productions including *Pasquin* (1736), *The Historical Register* (1737), and *Eurydice Hiss'd* (1737), and there were also controversial anonymous plays such as *The Fall of Mortimer* (1731) which found an analogue for contemporary misrule in medieval British history.[49]

New theatrical patents granted in 1715 by George I had extended the purview of the theatre companies. Colley Cibber and the other managers argued that the new patents 'made us sole Judges of what Plays might be proper for the Stage' and would henceforth submit no scripts for royal approval before performance.[50] Despite those new liberties, as an officer of the Crown the Lord Chamberlain still held considerable powers over 'the Decency and Good Manners of the Stage', and could, in Dryden's words, 'restrain the licentious insolence of Poets and their Actors, in all things that shock the Publick Quiet, or the Reputation of Private Persons, under the notion of *Humour*'.[51] Hence, in 1729, the Lord Chamberlain was able to stop rehearsals for Gay's new play *Polly*, a much nastier sequel to *The Beggar's Opera*. It was never performed in Gay's lifetime. Likewise, the Little Haymarket Theatre was raided under the Lord Chamberlain's orders after the company staged *The Fall of Mortimer* in 1731. The precise authority of the Lord Chamberlain's actions in either case is unclear.[52] Nonetheless, the theatre managers thought it prudent not to dispute the matter further.

In 1737, the powers of the Lord Chamberlain were codified with the new Licensing Act (10 Geo. II *c*. 28). Fielding's increasingly hostile plays were the principal stimulus behind the legislation and a particular bugbear of Walpole, who had tried and failed to impose new legislative controls over the theatres in 1735. In March 1737, the opposition journal, *Common Sense*, published a naughty allegorical satire entitled *The Vision of the Golden Rump*—possibly by the Jacobite principal of St. Mary Hall, Oxford, William King—which attacked George II and Walpole in lurid detail. Instead of prosecuting the journal's editors for seditious libel (which, under the circumstances, would have been quite easy), Walpole exploited the opportunity to pass new censorship legislation. Details are murky, but contemporary rumours suggest Walpole fabricated a dramatized version of

<hr />

[49] On this first phase of Fielding's career, see Robert D. Hume, *Henry Fielding and the London Theatre, 1728–1737* (Oxford: Clarendon Press, 1988).

[50] Colley Cibber, *An Apology for the Life of Mr Colley Cibber*, ed. Robert W. Lowe, 2 vols. (1889), i. 276–9.

[51] Dryden, *Works*, iv. 10.

[52] Judith Milhous, 'Theatre Companies and Regulation', in *The Cambridge History of British Theatre*, ed. Joseph Donohue et al., 3 vols. (Cambridge: Cambridge University Press, 2004), iii. 108–25 (120–1).

The Golden Rump which he then used as evidence for the necessity of stage licensing.[53] The stipulations of the new bill were many, including financial penalties against unlicensed theatres and strict controls on the construction of new playhouses. Most importantly, though, all new plays now needed to be submitted for the Lord Chamberlain's approval at least a fortnight before performance. There was no process of appeal against the Lord Chamberlain's rulings and the censor was not obliged to explain his decisions. In practice, this resulted in total political control of the theatres and effectively expunged political satire from the British stage overnight.

How did eighteenth-century dramatists negotiate those new restrictions? Some playwrights continued unabashed. Theophilus Cibber observed in 1756 that while '*the Laws now in being are sufficient for punishing those Players, who shall venture to bring any seditious Libel upon the Stage*', lots of licentious plays were still being staged '*not for want of Law*', but for *want of Prosecution*'.[54] Most commercially astute and risk-averse dramatists changed tack, though, and began writing more generalized social satires that obtained licences without difficulty. Dramatic satire after 1737 had considerably less bite. But while edgier plays could no longer be staged, they could sometimes still be printed. When *Polly* was prohibited from the stage by the Lord Chamberlain in 1729, Gay commissioned an expensive subscription edition from which he kept most of the profits. Henry Brooke likewise organized a subscription edition when his *Gustavus Vasa* was refused a licence in 1739. Such arrangements guaranteed a sizeable financial return in lieu of performance. Fielding, on the other hand, saw the introduction of licensing as an opportunity to quit the stage and seek a new career as a lawyer and, later, novelist.

WILKES, CHURCHILL, AND THE 1790S

From the 1750s onwards, verse satire became decreasingly political and, in Ashley Marshall's recent judgement, increasingly literary. 'The relative political stability of the 1750s and 1760s, along with Pope's posthumous influence on poetry, seem powerfully to affect the practice of verse satire. With few exceptions, what we find in this material is much less heat and urgency than we have seen before, and a great deal more obvious concern with poetic craft.'[55] Social and political changes resulted in shifting literary sensibilities and the gradual mellowing of political satire. By 1760, few satirists were still writing hard-hitting lampoons in the manner of Joseph Browne, John Tutchin, or William King. Prosecutions of satirists for libel nonetheless continued unabated, although, as we shall see, legal action was usually only pursued against individuals whom the authorities had additional reasons to want punished.

[53] For a judicious assessment of the case, see Thomas Lockwood, 'Fielding and the Licensing Act', *Huntington Library Quarterly* 50 (1987), 379–93.
[54] Theophilus Cibber, *Two Dissertations on the Theatres*, 3 vols. (1756), iii. 85–7.
[55] Ashley Marshall, *The Practice of Satire in England, 1658–1770* (Baltimore: Johns Hopkins University Press, 2013), 288.

The most explosive libel trials of that later period were of John Wilkes in 1763 (98 Eng. Rep. 327–55), both for his contributions to the anti-ministerial *The North Briton* and for his blasphemous lampoon, *An Essay on Woman* (1762). Originally conceived by Thomas Potter as an obscene (and fairly bad) parody of Pope's *An Essay on Man* (1734), Wilkes had inherited the unfinished manuscript on Potter's death in 1759 and modified and completed the poem soon after. His printers were ordered to produce thirteen copies only, one for each of the twelve members of Wilkes's club and one other for his library.[56] The print run was kept secret. As Wilkes interpreted them, libel laws only guarded against published works. Wilkes was certain that printing a dozen copies for himself and friends was a private act and not a publication. Evidently he had not studied the Payne trial in 1696, when the simple act of writing out a libel was deemed legally equivalent to publication. This would prove a costly mistake.

After the publication of the controversial issue forty-five of *The North Briton* in the spring of 1763, the government were actively seeking reasons to impeach Wilkes. The *Essay* provided them with all the evidence they needed. By unhappy accident, one of the proof sheets for the *Essay* had been used as scrap paper and picked up by another printer, who in turn handed it to the relevant authorities. The government attorney, Philip Carteret Webb, then bullied Wilkes's printer to give up the other sheets and falsified more blasphemous lines.[57] Because the proofs were corrected in Wilkes's own hand, he, like Payne and Savage before him, could not dispute having 'made' the libel. Unlike those earlier trials, though, the charges brought against Wilkes for *An Essay on Woman* were concocted merely as leverage. The government did not really care about this private lampoon, but simply wanted to ensure Wilkes's good behaviour after the more serious case of his anti-ministerial journalism in *The North Briton*. The Secretary of State offered to drop the charges over the *Essay* on the condition that Wilkes would desist from his ongoing civil rights litigation against the government.[58] Wilkes resisted these attempts at blackmail. His defence argued that he 'never entertained the remotest Idea of publishing' the poem.[59] This appeal did not work. For *An Essay on Woman* alone Wilkes was fined £500, sentenced to twelve months in prison, and bound to good behaviour for a further seven years. He fled to France before the sentence could be enforced.

Yet Wilkes was an exceptional case. His colleague and collaborator Charles Churchill never faced a libel suit despite the political aspects of his verse satires. Major poems such as *The Prophecy of Famine* (1763), *An Epistle to William Hogarth* (1763), and *The Candidate* (1764) excoriated the government in savage terms yet received no real legal attention. Churchill was not considered an enemy of the state to the same extent as Wilkes, whose additional careers as an MP and journalist made him a far greater threat. Soon after, Evan Lloyd was imprisoned for insulting the High Sheriff of Wales in *The Methodist* (1766), but that resulted from private action for defamation rather than

---

[56] See Arthur H. Cash, *John Wilkes: The Scandalous Father of Civil Liberty* (New Haven: Yale University Press, 2006), 130.

[57] Cash, *Wilkes*, 148–9.   [58] Cash, *Wilkes*, 143–4.

[59] British Library, Add. MS 30885, fol. 155.

seditious libel. The period of crisis surrounding the American War of Independence elicited a great deal of satire, very little of which seems to have provoked the ire of the authorities. John Wolcott, who wrote under the sobriquet Peter Pindar, faced no charges of libel for his lampoon on the excesses of George III in *The Lousiad* (1786), despite that text's errant popularity. The government continued to impeach opposition journalists and pamphleteers such as Henry Woodfall, William Davies Shipley, and Thomas Paine, although the total number of prosecutions fell through to 1789.[60]

After the start of the French Revolution and throughout the 1790s, though, press prosecutions increased rapidly. More than two hundred convictions for seditious libel were made between 1790 and 1832, which marked a substantial increase over preceding years.[61] Not all of those prosecutions were for literary satires—most were for journalism or cartoons. Yet as Gary Dyer and Vic Gattrell both acknowledge, libel laws continued to be effective against satire and were increasingly enforced.[62] Why the sudden increase in censorship? Political factors were important. The emergence of radical Jacobinism in Britain had already prompted Prime Minister William Pitt to suspend *habeas corpus* and increase government surveillance. New libel prosecutions resulted from the same impulse to crack down on political undesirables.

However, the heavy-handed use of libel prosecutions also proved deeply unpopular with the public and actually provoked rather discouraged satirists. Spurred into action by Whig opposition leader Charles James Fox, who introduced the bill into parliament, the government recognized an opportunity to placate the opposition by reforming libel laws. Under existing legislation, the role of the jury in libel cases was to determine points of fact only. Judges ruled whether a text constituted or did not constitute libel. Jurors simply decided whether the defendant was the author or publisher of the particular work in question. In some cases jurors were able to decide on the 'obvious and natural' meaning of ironic satires. But determining whether that meaning was libellous remained the prerogative of the judge. The Libel Act of 1792 gave jurors the right to determine not only the facts of authorship and publication but whether or not the text was libellous.

The highly publicized passing of Fox's Libel Act was an attempt to convince the public that government repression of the press was over, while actually retaining most of the powers needed to prosecute radicals. Ultimately, the impact of this legislation on satire was negligible. Legal definitions of libel remained vague. Libels were, in practice, whatever the government chose to prosecute. Attorneys merely needed to persuade a jury that the content of a publication was seditious. Because the government still retained the capacity to pack juries, convincing jurors was seldom difficult.

---

[60] For the statistics, see Michael Lobban, 'From Seditious Libel to Unlawful Assembly: Peterloo and the Changing Face of Political Crime c.1770–1820', *Oxford Journal of Legal Studies* 10 (1990), 307–52 (309).

[61] Philip Harling, 'The Law of Libel and the Limits of Repression, 1790–1832', *Historical Journal* 44 (2001), 107–34.

[62] Gary Dyer, *British Satire and the Politics of Style 1789–1832* (Cambridge: Cambridge University Press, 1997), 71–4; Vic Gatrell, *City of Laughter: Sex and Satire in Eighteenth-Century London* (London: Atlantic, 2006), 483–546.

The number of prosecutions for seditious libel continued to rise after 1792. Fox's Libel Act paid nothing more than lip-service to freedom of expression.

CONCLUSION

At the start of the eighteenth century, the government perceived oppositional satire as a serious political threat and took numerous legal steps to constrain what satirists could and could not legally write and what printers and booksellers could print and sell. Lawyers adapted old legislation and developed new laws that made it increasingly difficult to avoid conviction. Grounds for prosecution shifted from acts of disseminating satires to processes of inscribing them. Harsh penalties faced satirists who were convicted of breaking the law. The authorities devoted numerous resources to catching and convicting satirists and their printers. Equally, though, many satirists and printers developed clandestine strategies to overcome these risks—retaining anonymity, circulating texts in manuscript, and making satire more ambiguous. But those techniques were not a panacea. If the government decided that a satire was truly objectionable or dangerous they could usually discover the likely author and assemble enough evidence to secure a prosecution, even if that required packing juries.

Although legislation became no less oppressive, shifting generic norms resulted in fewer prosecutions of satirists for libel throughout the century. By the end of the century, journalism and cartoons occupied the ground where satire had stood at the start of the century. Literary tastes shifted over the course of the century and satire consequently developed as a genre away from the clandestine lampoonery of authors such as Jonathan Swift, Joseph Browne, and Richard Savage. By the end of the century most political poetry was not strictly speaking satirical. Government enforcement of libel laws now focused for the most part on journalism and not satire, although the laws of seditious libel remained effective over satire. Despite the reform of libel laws in 1790s, censorship of the satirical press continued virtually unchecked into the nineteenth century. Satire changed but libel laws did not.

SELECT BIBLIOGRAPHY

Black, Jeremy. *The English Press in the Eighteenth Century* (Philadelphia: University of Pennsylvania Press, 1987).

Bricker, Andrew Benjamin. 'Libel and Satire: The Problem with Naming', *English Literary History* 81 (2014), 889–921.

Hamburger, Philip. 'The Development of the Law of Seditious Libel and the Control of the Press', *Stanford Law Review* 37 (1985), 661–765.

Hanson, Laurence. *Government and the Press, 1695–1763* (Oxford: Oxford University Press, 1936).

Higgins, Ian. 'Censorship, Libel and Self-Censorship', in *Jonathan Swift and the Eighteenth-Century Book*, ed. Paddy Bullard and James McLaverty (Cambridge: Cambridge University Press, 2013), 179–98.

Keymer, Thomas. 'Defoe's Ears: *The Dunciad*, the Pillory, and Seditious Libel', *The Eighteenth-Century Novel* 6–7 (2009), 159–96.

Keymer, Thomas. *Poetics of the Pillory: English Literature and Seditious Libel, 1660–1820* (Oxford: Oxford University Press, forthcoming).

Kinservik, Matthew J. *Disciplining Satire: The Censorship of Satiric Comedy on the Eighteenth-Century London Stage* (Lewisburg: Bucknell University Press, 2002).

Kropf, C. R. 'Libel and Satire in the Eighteenth Century', *Eighteenth-Century Studies* 8 (1975), 153–68.

Love, Harold. *English Clandestine Satire* (Oxford: Oxford University Press, 2004).

Patterson, Annabel. *Censorship and Interpretation: The Conditions of Writing and Reading in Early Modern England* (Madison: University of Wisconsin Press, 1984).

CHAPTER 32

···

QUARRELLING

···

ALEXIS TADIÉ

At the 1799 Salon, the French painter Anne-Louis Girodet exhibited a portrait of the celebrated actress Mlle Lange. Unfortunately, the sitter did not find the portrait to her liking and asked for it to be withdrawn from exhibition while refusing to pay what she owed him. Incensed by this breach of contract, the painter sent it back to the sitter in pieces and produced in response a portrait of Mlle Lange as the Greek princess Danae, whom Zeus impregnated in the form of a shower of gold. She appears naked, dutifully showered with gold pieces, which in the present instance she proceeds to gather, being helped by Eros. Facing her, in place of the more mythologically accurate eagle, a turkey wears a wedding ring, symbolizing her marriage to a wealthy man, while a dove wearing a 'fidelitas' neck-band lies slain by a gold piece, and another, wearing the sign of 'constantia', is flying away from the scene. The satirical uses of mythology were obvious for all to see—Girodet referred to a classical episode to enact his vengeance and to destroy Mlle Lange's career on stage and in salons. This basic quarrel—a sitter refuses to pay the painter for the portrait which she has ordered— gives birth to a satirical production which, in turn, resolves the quarrel, defeating one of the protagonists.

This episode illustrates some of the links between satire and quarrels, where the mean- ingful historical context of the work is given by the quarrel between painter and sitter, while the artistic and cultural resources at the artist's disposal are ironically called upon both to attack the opponent in the quarrel and to produce a work of art whose humorous efficiency lies in the indirectness of parody. Not all satires offer such direct responses to quarrels, or indeed direct interventions in quarrels, but the connections between the two modes require examination. Satire, in this instance, enables the painter to trans- form the private nature of the quarrel into a public—and publicized—event. And indeed quarrels of the early modern period often became public events in which further partici- pants could intervene, and the public be made a judge of events. Quarrels sometimes proceed from private disagreements which become fully-fledged controversies. This is why quarrels can initially be found in correspondences in all their forms—a private correspondence can develop into a controversy, such as was Leibniz's practice; conversely, public letters contribute to quarrels, open letters being a common way of indulging in a quarrel. They have a long history, and occasionally relied on publications, bearing titles such as *Letter to…concerning…* The structure of letter/reply/further letter seems canonical in controversies, pointing both to the obvious dialogical nature of polemics, and to the circumstantial nature of the texts involved. Other related titles include memoir, critique, discourse, observation, essay, history, etc. This does not of course mean that all these forms are involved in a quarrel, but rather that quarrels often resort to generic forms which are brief and easily published, so as to retain the dialogical pattern and a relevant temporality. This movement between the private and the public is also one that characterizes satire; there are many instances of satirical 'letters' which ignite and foster quarrels at the same time as they rely on the satirical mood to project differences—one thinks of instances such as Edmund Burke's *Letter to a Noble Lord* which echoes, in many ways, Alexander Pope's *Epistle to Dr Arbuthnot*. The inscription of certain satires in contexts of developing quarrels enabled in particular the articulation of the private and the public spheres. The emergence of the public, and of public opinion, can be linked to the context of quarrels—not only because the public came to be the ultimate judge of disputes but also because of the fundamental public characteristics of disputes. This suggests in turn both a space where satires can resonate and a movement back towards texts which engaged in defining ways with an audience. Satires vary from the acerbic, which concentrate on specific targets, to the entertaining, which aim to make the reader laugh. The former, indeed, were condemned by some writers in the eighteenth century: 'Lampoons and Satyrs, that are written with Wit and Spirit', writes Addison, 'are like poison'd Darts, which not only inflict a Wound, but make it incurable.'[1] And while some forms of satires such as libels or lampoons are directly related to the development of controversies, it is mainly in Menippean satires, in the tradition of Lucian's *Dialogues*, that quarrelling, conceived as an activity which shapes literary form, comes to occupy centre stage.

While quarrels may appear more focused than satire, because they are first and foremost (acrimonious) exchanges between two parties, satires also rely on quarrelling as an energizing presence, sometimes hoping, as in the case of Girodet, to deal a definitive blow to the opponent. While not all quarrels resort to the satirical mood, to see all satires in terms of quarrels would run conversely the risk of reducing the satirical genre to one where targets and norms take precedence over irony, indirectness, 'display and play'.[2] Hence, this chapter examines the ways in which the practice of quarrelling may inhabit and give form to satires, hoping to provide an analysis of these complex relationships from a few, remarkable instances of satirical practice in quarrelling.

---

[1] *Spectator*, i. 97.
[2] Dustin Griffin, *Satire: A Critical Reintroduction* (Lexington: University Press of Kentucky, 1994), ch. 3.

'Violently Tending to
a Decisive Battel'

The story of the quarrel between Ancients and Moderns has often been told.[3] While the French quarrel developed in the later seventeenth century with the public reading by Perrault of his poem 'Le siècle de Louis le Grand'—a long way from being a satirical text—further interventions in the quarrel occasionally involved satires or pamphlets. Boileau's tenth satire, on women, is connected to the ongoing debate. On the English side, satirical texts also materialized the positioning of some of the protagonists.

Before Swift published his 'Battel of the Books', a title which is sometimes used to refer to the whole controversy, Defoe had made use of the conceit of the battle in his poem 'The Pacificator'—itself partly proceeding from a French inspiration. In his *Nouvelle allégorique*, Antoine Furetière had pitted against each other two sides, one led by Princess Rhetoric, who rules over the kingdom of Eloquence with the help of her chief minister, Good-Sense, the other by Prince Bombast, who governs the country of Pedantry, in order to address the hierarchy between the *doctes* (the learned who use obscure jargon) and the *mondains* (who favour *salons* and modern genres), coming out in favour of the latter.[4] The vocabulary used in quarrels is predictably more often agonistic than irenic, favouring opponents, fights or weapons, reminding us that physical encounters are sometimes a temptation, sometimes the outcome, often the matrix, and that at certain periods of history they were dominant in certain circles.

The war described in 'The Pacificator' opposes the 'Men of Sense' and the 'Men of Wit'. The beginning of the poem recalls conflicts with France but voices above all fears of civil feuds at home. In a variation on the classical locus of the pen and the sword, the fight is clearly started by writings: 'The Pen's the certain Herald of a War', suggesting a continuity between words and physical fights.[5] While it may be argued that pamphlet and lampoon wars stand for physical engagement, Defoe sees in words the prelude to more direct confrontations: 'Men Quarrel first, and Skirmish with ill Words, / And when they're heated then they draw their Swords.'[6] The poem is of course topical, the fight being led on one side (the men of sense) by the physician Richard Blackmore (Nokor in the poem), whose epic poem, *Prince Arthur* (1695), like the subsequent *King Arthur* (1697), was prefaced by a diatribe against the theatre, and who consequently 'threw *Drammatick Wit* upon its Back'.[7] Nokor is then attacked by '*Light Dragoons*' and the rhyming '*Forty thousand Arm'd Lampoons*', suggesting the revenge of the defenders of

---

[3] Subheading from Swift, *Battel of the Books*, in *Works* (Cambridge), i. 153.

[4] Translated into English as *The Rebellion: or, an Account of the Late Civil-Wars, in the Kingdom of Eloquence* (1704). Antoine Furetière, *Nouvelle allégorique ou Histoire des derniers troubles survenus au Royaume d'Eloquence* (Paris, 1658); see Alain Viala, 'Querelle de la nouvelle allégorique', http://base-agon.paris-sorbonne.fr/querelles/querellede-la-nouvelle-allegorique, accessed 25 April 2016.

[5] Daniel Defoe, *The Pacificator. A Poem* (1700), 2.   [6] Defoe, *Pacificator*, 2. Cf. Griffin, *Satire*, 93.

[7] Defoe, *Pacificator*, 3.

the stage, as well as the attacks by the likes of John Dennis in his *Remarks on a Book Entitled Prince Arthur* (1696). He is then followed by Jeremy Collier, whose diatribes against the morality of the stage were central to the quarrel of the theatres. His initial skirmishes bring him some success before being, in turn, slain by ten thousand wounds. Further attacks by other characters are inconclusive, leading the wits to proclaim their victory. But Blackmore rides again to the rescue and attacks the wits.[8] The fight then develops between Blackmore, for the men of Sense, and Samuel Garth, for the Wits, not over the morality of the stage but over the respective prerogatives of physicians and of apothecaries. While the immediate context is that of the medical quarrel, the opposition between Garth and Blackmore also concerns the (in)ability of the moderns to write epic poems, thus suggesting complex connections between quarrels.[9] Blackmore was indeed attacked from several parts for his two epic poems on Arthur. One assailant was John Dryden, who had objected to Blackmore's criticisms in his *Satyr Against Wit*, and had subsequently described him as '*Pedant, Canting Preacher, and a Quack*'.[10]

The battle that ensues is fierce, led for the wits by such authors as Dryden, Congreve, etc. They are all defeated by the triumphant Blackmore/Nokor, who is celebrated in the mock-epic: 'The Troops of Wit, Disorder'd, and O'r-run, / Are Slain, Disperc'd, Disgrac'd, and Overthrown; / The Shouts of Triumph reach the distant Sky, / And *Nokor* lies Encamp'd in the Field of *Victory*'.[11] The different waves in the attack clearly evoke episodes in the various quarrels. Rumour has it that the Wits are rearming, which indeed suggests further tracts in the ongoing dispute, but the poem concludes rather on the necessity of peace, on the hope for an alliance between sense and wit.[12] 'Wit is a King without a Parliament, / And *Sense* a Democratick Government', writes Defoe, suggesting both the necessity of an alliance between wit and sense ('*United: Wit* and *Sense*, makes Science thrive'), and bringing at the same time to the fore the political dimension of such quarrels, within the context, in particular, of the Exclusion Crisis.[13] And when at the end of the poem Defoe confines all authors to the genre at which they excel, he includes himself as the master of the lampoon.

More generally Defoe's poem is concerned with the possible weakening of England brought about by quarrels, and with possible remedies to the situation. Although the poem appears to be animated by an initial concern with the advance of the French armies, it focuses on the quarrels at home, moving from the quarrel about the stage, to the quarrel between Blackmore and Garth over medical practice, while evincing more than an echo of the Ancients and Moderns controversy—the Christ Church

---

[8] An allusion to his *A Satyr Against Wit* published in 1700.

[9] On this quarrel, see Véronique Gély, 'La "dispute sur l'emploi de la fable": la fiction en cause', forthcoming.

[10] John Dryden, Prologue to *The Pilgrim* (1700). The turn of phrase is perhaps remembered by Swift, in his concluding Epitaph to 'An Elegy on Mr. Partridge': 'Here Five Foot deep lyes on his Back, / A *Cobler, Starmonger*, and *Quack*', in Swift, *Poems* (Williams), i. 101.

[11] Defoe, *Pacificator*, 10.

[12] On the forthcoming attack, as well as on the whole context of *The Pacificator*, see Albert Rosenberg 'Defoe's *Pacificator* Reconsidered', *Philological Quarterly* 37 (1958), 433–9.

[13] Defoe, *Pacificator*, 8, 13.

Wits were in particular supporters of Boyle while the men of Sense would have upheld Bentley—and of ongoing debates about the writing of modern epics, both in France and in England. Defoe's satirical poem brings to the fore the deep connections between the various issues at stake in these quarrels. While quarrels may appear to oppose individuals over specific issues, in fact they involve groups of various natures (armies), and possibly a wider public. Further, quarrels are not circumscribed, but are connected as 'The Pacificator' makes clear. The quarrel over the immorality of the stage implied political and religious stances also relevant to a structuring of the disputes. More generally, the Ancients and Moderns controversy proceeded from complex networks that reflect the political positioning of the protagonists, the nature of the medium in which the argument was conveyed, and perhaps also other disputes that were not obviously connected—such as the quarrel over apothecaries or the quarrel about the morality of the stage. While it attempts to resolve the crisis by defending an alliance between wit and sense, Defoe's satirical intervention in 'The Pacificator' articulates these issues and offers an analysis of these quarrels at the same time as it distances itself from them.

Swift's interventions in the quarrel between Ancients and Moderns take at least two forms, brought together in the same volume: *A Tale of a Tub* and *The Battel of the Books*. They address the ongoing debate between on the one side William Temple and the Christ Church Wits who asserted the authenticity of the *Epistles of Phalaris*, and on the other William Wotton and Charles Bentley, who undermined that authenticity. The publication of a number of texts during the 1690s structures the quarrel. *A Tale of a Tub* was composed around 1697, the allegory on religion having probably been written about a year earlier.[14] The *Battel of the Books* was composed between 1697 and 1698, and the first edition, which also contained *A Discourse Concerning the Mechanical Operation of the Spirit*, was published in 1704. The complex structure of the whole volume, the learned apparatus of the *Tale* and the mock-heroic model of the *Battel* satirize the controversy and its false knowledge, provided, not so much a further contribution to the debate or a direct engagement with the arguments, as a possible fatal blow to one of the sides. Through the complex learned apparatus and juxtaposition of texts in different modes, Swift ventriloquizes and annihilates all the different voices in the quarrel.

Both a defence of his former protector, Sir William Temple, and an attack on natural philosophy and the new science, Swift's publication is at once an intervention in the local context of the *Phalaris* controversy in England and a reaction to the wider European context of the quarrel. The *Battel* in particular drew on Boileau's *Le lutrin* (1674) where a skirmish inside a bookseller's shop finds participants using books as powerful projectiles.[15] It also referred back to two French texts which had told the history of the quarrel in the language of war: Gabriel Guéret, *La Guerre des auteurs anciens et modernes* (1671), and François de Callières, *Histoire poétique de la guerre nouvellement déclarée entre les anciens et les modernes* (1688). While the *Tale* stages in the scholarly apparatus of the text some of the different voices involved in the quarrel, the *Battel*

---

[14] For details see Marcus Walsh's commentary, Swift, *Works* (Cambridge), i. xxxvi–xxxix.
[15] Boileau's satirical poem was also an influence on Garth's *The Dispensary* (1699).

transfers the anxiety of the threat posed by the Moderns to the Ancients' intellectual life, to the violence of the encounter between the different volumes. Critics have argued about the degree of hostility in Swift's attack on the Moderns. He clearly represents in both texts the complexities of the quarrel, the anxieties generated by these wars. He is at the same time taking sides and causing the controversy, through the satirical tone, to come to an end.

In Swift's text, the battle itself is prefaced by a dispute between the spider and the bee, which reworks the Renaissance conceit to be found in Montaigne and Bacon among others. In the same way that Swift uses in the *Tale* the apparatus of erudition to satirize the debate, he recalls the metaphor better to attack the very nature of the quarrel—the episode ends with the industrious bee flying away to a bed of roses leaving the spider 'like an Orator, *collected* in himself, and just prepared to burst out'.[16] The satirical structure of the text, and the depiction of the controversy between Ancients and Moderns 'violently tending to a decisive Battel', enable Swift not only to attack the Moderns or to defend the Ancients, but to articulate the dynamics of the confrontation.[17] And while the genre of the mock-heroic draws on Homer at every turn, some episodes provide occasions for lighter dismissal of the protagonists. The Homeric tone is clearly apparent for instance in the final episode where Boyle, defending Temple, General of the Ancients, attacks Wotton and Bentley and, helped by Pallas Athena, kills them both with his spear. In the same conceit which he would use in his later argument with Partridge, Swift here stages the death of both Bentley and Wotton in the heroic victory of Boyle over them. He supplements the Homeric overtones of the contest with a bathetic description of their sad demise: 'As, when a skilful Cook has truss'd a Brace of *Woodcocks*, He, with Iron Skewer, pierces the tender Sides of both, their Legs and Wings close pinion'd to their Ribs'.[18]

Satire, in particular in its Menippean form, uses quarrels in complex ways. It can constitute an intervention in an ongoing dispute, taking sides, opposing the overall force and varied nature of its rhetorical modes to local arguments. It can also stage within the form the quarrel itself, integrating the to and fro movement of the controversy into a pseudo-scholarly apparatus, giving greater public resonance to such skirmishes, or transforming the verbal exchanges into an outright war—reminding ourselves in the process of the close links between quarrels and their possible physical resolution. Indeed, the imagined death of the protagonists enacted in the satirical text echoes the archetypal resolution of quarrels through duels. While Defoe uses this form to dismiss the quarrel and aspire to a union between Sense and Wit, Swift's satirical tone enables him to launch a violent attack on the Moderns, to send them to a fictional death, and to suggest, within the whole volume, the complexities of the dispute. Satire brings to the fore the connections between more localized quarrels, the European dimension of the argument, the variegated nature of the controversy in all its religious, political, scientific, and literary aspects, and the occasional violence of the oppositions,

---

[16] Swift, *Works* (Cambridge), i. 151.   [17] Swift, *Works* (Cambridge), i. 153.
[18] Swift, *Works* (Cambridge), i. 164.

while affording the satirist a certain distance from the scene of the confrontation between these paper warriors.

Glad of a Quarrel

In 1708 Jonathan Swift dealt an apparently fatal blow to the astrologer John Partridge.[19] Using the rhetoric of the astrologer, he foretold his death, which he confirmed in spite of Partridge's protests. In so doing he waded into an ongoing controversy, writing satirical pamphlets from which Partridge never really recovered. Recent critical engagement with the episode has shown that the famous hoax was articulated to the challenge posed by his almanacs to the relation between Church and State.[20] Partridge, who held radical Whig views, had been undermining the principles held by more conservative defenders of the Church, voicing religious and political comments in his almanacs. Using the persona of Bickerstaff, Swift parodied the form of the prediction, both to attack Partridge and to dismiss the practice of almanacs. At the beginning of the paper, Bickerstaff mocks both Partridge and his rival Gadbury for indulging in predictions as well as for peddling drinks and pills. And he later boasts previous accurate predictions of his own before indulging in a series of important prophecies relating to the death of the enemies of the Allies, and to the demise of the house of Bourbon, but without directly engaging with Partridge's politics. Instead, he prefaces these considerations with the mention of 'a Trifle', the impending death of Partridge on 29 March 1708. The following pamphlet 'The Accomplishment of the First of Mr. Bickerstaff's Predictions' published in the same year, was later followed by the 'Elegy on Mr Partridge' (1708) and 'A Vindication of Isaac Bickerstaff Esq' (1709). In predicting and confirming the death of Partridge, Swift performed more than a hoax on the astrologer. He intervened in a long-standing controversy and scored a political point. In spite of Partridge's attempts at refuting both the prediction and the political argument, accusing Bickerstaff of being disloyal to Protestant England, the astrologer appears in the devalued form of a controversialist who has lost the fight.

What satire achieves, through the parodic use of the form of the prediction, which was one of the central elements of Partridge's rhetorical strategy in his almanacs, is the kind of victory from which Partridge, in spite of later attempts, had trouble extricating himself.[21] More particularly satire plays a central role in the quarrel, being the means by which Swift's attacks against Partridge are enacted, finding the astrologer's more earnest replies ineffectual (in his 1709 almanac in particular, as well as in 'Mr. Partridge's Answer

[19] Subheading from Pope, 'To Arburthnot', *Poems* (Twickenham), iv. 100, line 67.
[20] See Valerie Rumbold, 'Burying the Fanatic Partridge: Swift's Holy Week Hoax', in *Politics and Literature in the Age of Swift*, ed. Claude Rawson (Cambridge: Cambridge University Press, 2010), 81–115.
[21] Although his ensuing silence is not directly linked to Swift's attacks, but to contractual difficulties which prevented him from publishing an almanac until late in the year 1713. Rumbold, 'Burying the Fanatic Partridge', 101.

to Esquire Bickerstaff's Strange and Wonderful Predictions for the Year 1708', which may or may not have been written by him). Posing as an astrologer, Swift stoops to the level of Partridge, because one only quarrels with one's equals, at the same time as he retains the necessary distance and aloofness not to be implicated in Partridge's inadequate knowledge. The masquerade, the satirical reliance on *personæ* of various kinds, sometimes within the same piece, enables both the staging of the quarrel and the retreat from the conflict. Further, the structure of the quarrel, which rests on a dialogue made public through the use of the potentialities afforded by instant publications, is compounded by its articulation of wide-ranging debates over popery, support for William III, and the denunciation, by Partridge, of alleged corruption in the Church of England. In spite of the satirist's affected distance, also reminiscent of the concluding remarks of *A Modest Proposal*, the structure of quarrels is directly relevant to the parodic movement of prediction and confirmation of the death of Partridge, at the same time as the satirical mode ensures the victory of Bickerstaff over Partridge.[22]

Similar exchanges and practice may be found in other celebrated quarrels between writers of the eighteenth century. The dispute between Pope and Colley Cibber performs the same tasks. While the Bickerstaff–Partridge exchange was focused in time, quarrelling between Pope and Cibber lasted a few decades, only to be interrupted by Pope's death. Their opposition is often said to have started in 1717 with a hoax played on Cibber by Gay, who had Cibber play a part in his play *Three Hours After Marriage*, only for Cibber to realize later that it was in fact a caricature of himself. It was pursued with Cibber parodying Gay's play in a performance of Buckingham's *The Rehearsal*. Pope threatened Cibber with caning if he persisted, and the following night Gay and Cibber fought, after the performance of *The Rehearsal*.[23] While this was the first skirmish, reminding us that not all literary quarrels are exclusively verbal, in the same year Cibber staged performances of his play, *The Non-juror*, which attacked and mocked many Jacobites and non-jurors—to which Pope replied with the anonymous *A Clue to the Comedy of the Non-Juror* (1718). But the quarrel had possibly started a couple of years earlier, when Cibber and two other friends enticed Pope to a house of pleasure in order to make fun of him—and indeed Cibber recounts the story in his 1742 *Letter from Mr Cibber to Mr Pope*.[24] Numerous pamphlets and engravings were published following Cibber's revelations, giving even more publicity to the event. While Cibber was probably not directly responsible for these productions, he thought this proved his victory over Pope. As Norman Ault has argued, it is both the event of late 1714 or early 1715, and the later recounting of the story, which led to Cibber's promotion to the throne of the Dunces.[25]

[22] See Jonathan Swift, 'Predictions for the Year 1708', *Works* (Cambridge), ii. 57.

[23] See Maynard Mack, *Alexander Pope: A Life* (New Haven: Yale University Press, 1985), 775; and Norman Ault, *New Light on Pope: With Some Additions to his Poetry Hitherto Unknown* (London: Methuen, 1949), 300.

[24] See Colley Cibber, *A Letter from Mr Cibber* (London, 1742), 47–9.

[25] Ault, *New Light*, 304.

With the appointment of Cibber as poet laureate in 1730 the quarrel develops—the public figure of the official poet offering ample opportunities for efficient caricatures. It is of course not impossible that Pope would have desired to be poet laureate himself, as his enemies had mentioned on several occasions.[26] The controversy sparked by the appointment led to numerous mocking rhymes and attacks on the recipient, some by Pope. Two months after Cibber's appointment, for instance, Pope published anonymously 'Of the Poet Laureate', a mock-learned treatise in which the author first describes the history of that ancient tradition, then the ceremonial attached to it, suggesting for instance the introduction of ivy, because 'it is emblematical of the three virtues of a court poet in particular; it is *creepy*, *dirty*, and *dangling*'.[27] The next part examines the qualifications of the poet laureate and finds Cibber exceptionally well-suited to the role, although he also considers the relative merits of Dennis and Tibbald.

Throughout Cibber's tenure, his odes were published in the periodicals of the times with ironical annotations.[28] Cibber went so far as to adapt the images of dullness and darkness which Pope had made familiar in the first *Dunciads*: 'long before Pope set out to add a fourth book to the *Dunciad* or to revise the first three books in consistency with the fourth, Cibber had emerged as the *de facto* hero of the *Dunciad* as contemporary satirists adapted, parodied, or alluded to passages from the *Variorum*, replacing Theobald with Cibber as the new king of Dulness'.[29] Further episodes in the quarrel include Cibber's *An Apology for the Life of Colley Cibber* (1739), which attacks Pope and to which he responded with contempt, and *A Letter from Mr Cibber to Mr Pope* (1742). *The Dunciad* in four books comes to celebrate Cibber's position as the king of Dunces, bemoaning the corruption of poetry by politics, and placing the process of selection and of anointment of poet laureates at the heart of his satire. Well may Cibber then have published other open letters, in 1743 and 1744, the coronation of Cibber as king of Dunces had been well and truly celebrated, and the quarrel, once again, resolved in a masterly satirical composition.

Both episodes show how quarrels resonate. In spite of appearing to pit two protagonists against each other, quarrels, in order to develop, rely on the role of other participants, on the involvement of and appeal to the public, on the potential force of publications, and on the availability of an idiom in which to attack the opponent. The satirical mode, in such exchanges as the Pope–Cibber or the Swift–Partridge quarrels, seems to intervene as the culmination of the process rather than as the starting point, as the fatal blow, rather than as the origin of the quarrel. This may be due to the nature of quarrels and to the ways in which they are initiated.

---

[26] See Roger D. Lund, 'The Crown of Dulness: Pope, Cibber, and The Laurel', *The Age of Johnson* 23 (2015), 239–72.

[27] Pope, *Poems* (Twickenham), v. 413.

[28] Cibber talks about 'near twenty Years having been Libell'd by our Daily-paper Scribblers', Cibber, *Letter*, 7.

[29] Lund, 'The Crown of Dulness', 255.

THE WORLD BEING GIVEN TO MAN
FOR A SUBJECT OF DISPUTATION

The ability of satire to play a decisive part in quarrels is best exemplified by the *topos* of satire as a weapon: 'Satire's my Weapon, but I'm too discreet / To run a Muck, and tilt at all I meet; / I only wear it in a Land of Hectors, / Thieves, Supercargoes, Sharpers, and Directors', writes Pope in his 'First Satire of the Second Book of Horace Imitated', adding: 'Its proper Pow'r to hurt, each Creature feels.'[30] Pope's 'Epistle to Dr Arbuthnot' was, according to the 'Advertisement', published as a response to attacks.[31] The satire provides a response to the attack, underlines the source of the quarrel, and calls upon the public to be the judge of the argument. But satire is also the place where quarrels can be acted out, where duncess of various kinds meet and are confronted, before being sent back to oblivion. *The Dunciad* is perhaps the best example of a text irrigated by quarrels.

The early versions of *The Dunciad* were articulated around the opposition between Lewis Theobald and Pope over Shakespeare. Theobald, the author of *Shakespeare Restored* (1726), had attacked Pope's *Shakespeare* (1725) for providing an incorrect edition of Shakespeare, based on insufficient attention to detail. Pope of course held the opposite view, one where the sense of the whole rather than the microscopic focus on detail was crucial.[32] *The Dunciad* provides a satiric intervention in the quarrel, one which, by placing Theobald on the throne of the Dunces, aims at bringing the controversy to an end. Theobald, the hero of the poem, is busy, ready to 'crucify poor *Shakespear* once a week'.[33] A devotee of Dulness, he reclaims the text through his commentaries.[34] Dulness then places Tibbald on the throne. Tibbald, having become the king, reigns over a land of dunces, whose appearances sometimes take the form of a contest, as in the diving competition organized by Dulness to see 'who the most in love of dirt excel'.[35] It is the occasion for a parade of authors to disappear in various ways, such as the first of them, John Dennis, who 'Shot to the black abyss, and plung'd down-right. / The Senior's judment all the crowd admire, / Who but to sink the deeper, rose the higher.'[36] Others who follow endure a similar fate. The urinating contest between Edmund Curll and William Chetwood had earlier enabled Pope to dismiss both in similar fashion: 'Chetwood, thro' perfect modesty o'ercome, / Crown'd with the Jordan, walks contented home.'[37] So that, even in its earlier incarnations, *The Dunciad* is the occasion for Pope

---

[30] Subheading from Pope, *Poems* (Longman), iii. 309, note to line 286; Pope, 'First Satire of the Second Book of Horace', *Poems* (Twickenham), iv. 11, ll. 68–71; 13, l. 85.

[31] Pope, *Poems* (Twickenham), iv. 95.

[32] See Harold Weinbrot, *Menippean Satire Reconsidered: From Antiquity to the Eighteenth Century* (Baltimore: Johns Hopkins University Press, 2005), 236.

[33] Pope, *Poems* (Twickenham), v. 83, l. 164.   [34] Pope, *Poems* (Twickenham), v. 83, ll. 165–8.

[35] Pope, *Poems* (Twickenham), v. 133, l. 265.   [36] Pope, *Poems* (Twickenham), v. 135, ll. 276–8.

[37] Pope, *Poems* (Twickenham), v. 124, ll. 181–2. A jordan is a chamber-pot. In later versions Chetwood is replaced by Samuel Chapman and finally by Thomas Osborne.

of settling accounts, of provoking enmity, of responding to attacks. The satirical mode enables the poet to plunge his enemies into the 'disemboguing streams'[38] of oblivion while addressing the political and poetical corruption of the world.

The formal complexities of the last version, in four books, are well known. The critical apparatus which surrounds the text is longer than the poem itself—what Cibber in his *Letter* calls 'those loads of Prose Rubbish, wherewith you have smothered your *Dunciad*.'[39] The poem is prefaced by different texts, it is even more extensively annotated than the earlier version, and it boasts an appendix comprising several pieces, including the preface to the first 'imperfect' editions of the poem, a list of publications 'in which our Author was abused, before the Publication of the Dunciad', advertisements, a continuation of papers on the Pastoral published in the *Guardian* (itself a quarrel with Philips), as well as the aforementioned 'Of the Poet Laureate'. Like *A Tale of a Tub*, it integrates into the materiality of the text the temporality of its successive editions. Like Swift's intervention into the dispute between Ancients and Moderns, it integrates in the footnotes and commentaries the voices of opponents and critics, the better to ridicule them. Like its predecessor, it makes use of all the potentialities of the written text, of the mock scholarly apparatus, of the tradition of 'learned wit' which characterizes in part satirical practice in the eighteenth century, from Swift to Sterne. Like *A Tale of a Tub*, it constructs the (intellectual) world into a cacophony of quarrels.

The texts which stand at the beginning of the last version of the *Dunciad* are allegedly penned by different authors. Not only do they justify the long title of *The Dunciad in Four Books*, but they place the reading in a context of debate, critical examination, and conflicting perceptions. They suggest that the origin of the satirical poem lies in a reply to attacks, rather than in a malicious will to debase other writers. These writers are on the contrary identified as the 'first Aggressors'.[40] Like quarrelling, satirical practice is therefore seen as a response, a reaction to an individual attack, or to the widespread practice of (anonymous) slander in the press. But apparently unlike a quarrel, the author's response was to avoid the fight: 'He has laughed, and written the DUNCIAD'.[41] At one level the published work is the consequence of the poet's laughter, a particular weapon in the fight against these authors: 'our Author, in his very laughter, is not indulging his own Ill nature, but only punishing that of others'.[42] At another level it connects with the reader, providing the occasion for his or her laughter. Ricardus Aristarchus stresses in particular that the qualities of the 'lesser Epic Hero, should be *Vanity, Impudence,* and *Debauchery,* from which happy assemblage resulteth *heroic Dulness,* the never-dying subject of this our poem'.[43] In turn, these qualities give rise to *buffoonery,* and hence to laughter. And of course through careful editing and quotations from Cibber's *Life* as well as from his *Letter*, precisely identified in the notes to his essay, Ricardus Aristarchus confirms Cibber as a worthy hero of the epic poem. Further, the

---

[38] Pope, *Poems* (Twickenham), v. 133, l. 259.   [39] Cibber, *Letter*, 9.
[40] Pope, *Poems* (Twickenham), v. 12.   [41] Pope, *Poems* (Twickenham), v. 12.
[42] Pope, *Poems* (Twickenham), v. 19.   [43] Pope, *Poems* (Twickenham), v. 256.

prefatory essay by Ricardus Aristarchus establishes the close poetic and political connection between Cibber and Walpole, which runs through the poem, the former comparing himself to the latter for 'good Government while in power.'[44]

While these preliminary pieces orchestrate various perspectives on the mock-epic at the same time as they contribute to its dialogical form, it is of course in the footnotes that the quarrelsome dimension of the text surfaces. The footnotes proliferate from the very first one, devoted to an exegesis of the title and a dialogue between different distinguished sources such as Theobald or Bentley, taking over the page and the text. Belonging to a practice consonant with Menippean satire,[45] the mock annotations enable Pope to orchestrate the dialogical nature of the text, to stage the different arguments, quarrels, and ironical presentations of diverse authors and authorities. The practice of annotation of one's own text, which still surfaces in the twentieth century in such works as Vladimir Nabokov's *Pale Fire* or David Foster Wallace's *Infinite Jest*, is the occasion for lengthy digressions more than precise elucidations, for ironical quotations rather than relevant clarifications.

The footnote to line 106 of book I, for instance, appears to comment on the line: 'And all the mighty mad in Dennis rage.'[46] It is in effect the occasion for a thorough attack on John Dennis, first in the guise of a disclaimer relating to Dennis's madness ('This is by no means to be understood literally, as if Mr Dennis were really mad'), then in the relation of the fury that Dennis feels towards Pope, and finally in ascribing a quotation from Giles Jacob's *Lives of the Poet*, where Dennis is praised, to Dennis himself.[47] Similar tactics are used vis-à-vis Theobald, the original hero of the *Dunciad*, or towards Ozell, whose panegyric by Jacob is supplemented by a long praise of himself: 'As for my *Genius*, let Mr. *Cleland* shew better Verses in all *Pope*'s Works, than *Ozell*'s version of *Boileau*'s *Lutrin*...Let him show better and truer Poetry in the *Rape of the Lock*, than in *Ozell*'s *Rape of the Bucket* (*la Secchia rapita*.) And Mr. *Toland* and Mr. *Gildon* publicly declar'd, *Ozell*'s Translation of *Homer to* be, as it was *prior*, so likewise *superior* to *Pope*'s.'[48] The age has produced uniform mediocrity ('Prose swell'd to verse, verse loit'ring into prose'), and given birth, with 'Small thanks to France, and none to Rome or Greece', to the Moderns: 'a Cibber, Tibbald, or Ozell'.[49] Quarrels require a laying bare of the argument in order for the public to become a judge; the same impulse prompts Pope's satirical move mischievously to reveal to the public the full vacuity and vanity of his opponents. But instead of simply winning the argument or the fight, it is through the reader's laughter thus provoked that he achieves his goal.

The fractious nature of quarrels, and of Pope's perception of the literary world, is materialized in the numerous footnotes, where attacks or defences of Pope are launched,

---

[44] Pope, *Poems* (Twickenham), v. 262.   [45] Weinbrot, *Menippean Satire*, 6.

[46] Pope, *Poems* (Twickenham), v. 277, l. 106. The footnote exists in the earlier version.

[47] See James McLaverty, 'Pope and Giles Jacob's "Lives of the Poets": The "Dunciad" as Alternative Literary History', *Modern Philology* 83, no. 1 (1985), 29.

[48] Pope, *Poems* (Twickenham), v. 198 (Errata).

[49] Pope, *Poems* (Twickenham), v. 290, ll. 274, 283, 286.

where diverse commentators are given the opportunity to vent their opinions: Bentley, Scriblerus, and of course Pope himself. Such fragmentation of the text materializes the quarrels between authors but echoes as well the practice of the Moderns, enjoined by Dulness, to appropriate and to 'mince' everything 'to bits':[50]

> Leave not a foot of verse, a foot of stone,
> A page, a grave, that they can call their own;
> But spread, my sons, your glory thin or thick,
> On passive paper, or on solid brick.[51]

Pope both celebrates and satirizes the noises made by all these quarrels, the pronouncements of various authors and their attempts to speak. In a passage of book II, in particular, the Goddess invites them to learn and indulge in 'the wond'rous pow'r of Noise',[52] yielding a cacophony which defines the literary world and its enduring reliance on the antiquated modes of scholastic syllogism and sterile disputation:

> Now thousand tongues are heard in one loud din:
> The Monkey-mimics rush discordant in;
> 'Twas chatt'ring, grinning, mouthing, jabb'ring all,
> And Noise and Norton, Brangling and Breval,
> Dennis and Dissonance, and captious Art,
> And Snip-snap short, and Interruption smart,
> And Demonstration thin, and Theses thick,
> And Major, Minor, and Conclusion quick.[53]

While myriad quarrels inhabit the text of *The Dunciad*, the main structure of the poem is of course dependent on a central quarrel, that between Cibber and Pope. The coronation of Cibber as king of the Dunces and the triumphant mood of book IV celebrate the victory of Dulness and of Cibber as her cherished hero. Up until the last version of the poem, Cibber had been at the background of various satirical lines and poems by Pope, including in the first versions of *The Dunciad*, but the publication of Cibber's *Letter* led him to reconsider the main intent of his poem and to relegate Theobald to the footnotes. By 1742, Theobald was no longer needed. The authorial 'By Authority' at the beginning of the text replaces the 'Pretender' with Cibber:

> We have ordered the said Pretender, Pseudo-Poet, or Phantom, utterly to vanish, and evaporate out of this work: And do declare the said Throne of Poesy from henceforth to be abdicated and vacant, unless duly and lawfully supplied by the LAUREATE himself.[54]

---

[50] Pope, *Poems* (Twickenham), v. 353, l. 120.
[51] Pope, *Poems* (Twickenham), v. 354, ll. 127–30.
[52] Pope, *Poems* (Twickenham), v. 306, l. 222.
[53] Pope, *Poems* (Twickenham), v. 307. ll. 235–42.
[54] Pope, *Poems* (Twickenham), v. 252.

Apart from Pope's desire to settle, once and for all, the quarrel and to assign Cibber to his just place in history, the replacement of Theobald by Cibber displays a fundamental feature of the kinship between satire and quarrel. The structure of the literary world is such that the throne of the Dunces needs to be filled, or rather comes to be filled only by its most worthy aspiring candidate, the Laureate—a quarrel with Theobald can make way to a quarrel with Cibber. It is the structure of the poem itself which allows for such replacement. Although there are marked differences between the first and the final versions of *The Dunciad*, the nature of the poem is such that the force of the satire can be directed at Theobald, or at Cibber—one worthy hero replaces another worthy hero. This suggests in turn the structural dependence of the poem on quarrelling, placing as it does the conflictual mode at the heart of the satire. The organization of the mock-epic around the hero—his accession to the throne at the end of book I, the public games of book II, the visions of book III, the final triumph of Dulness through the restoration of Night and Chaos at the end of the poem—unites the poetic figures of the epic and the form of the quarrel. By extolling Cibber, by asserting the triumph of Dulness and the demise of truth, philosophy, sciences, religion, or morality, by the (absence of) vision of the final line of the poem, Pope shows that the forces of destruction have conquered the world, and the principles of empty disputation have triumphed. Particular quarrels disappear behind the cacophony and subsequent destruction of all voices.

The Dunciad constructs a world which brings together individual quarrels—such as that which developed between Pope and Dennis or Ozell, and above all between Pope and Cibber—and the larger issues raised by the dispute between Ancients and Moderns, including the relationship between poetry and politics in an age of debased standards, emblematically presided over by Walpole.[55] It articulates these quarrels, and a vision of the literary world, around the central dispute between Cibber and Pope. It does so using the core structural principle of the quarrel, which enables him to move from the 1728 version to the 1743 version, from Theobald to Cibber, from satire to a fully-fledged mock-epic. While *The Dunciad* celebrates the power of the printed book and the force of all its devices (poem, annotations, footnotes, quotations, prefaces, appendix, etc.) in the composition of satire, it also shows the satirical mood's reliance on, and possible kinship with, the forms of quarrels: the reply to an initial affront, the desire to bring the controversy into the public domain, perhaps the better to appeal to the public's judgement, the dialogical form which preserves individual voices while (necessarily) distorting them, the complexities of terminating them—in the case of *The Dunciad*, through the final apocalypse—while retaining at the end a degree of satirical distance. *The Dunciad* thus makes a private quarrel (possibly originating in Cibber's indiscretions), public. The text articulates a literary opposition (Cibber's poor talent, as viewed by Pope) and a political context (Cibber as poet laureate). It examines the state of the Republic of Letters (characterized by quarrels, skirmishes, and fragmentation) and relates it to the political

---

[55] Cf. Weinbrot, *Menippean Satire*, 244; Ronald Paulson, *Breaking and Remaking: Aesthetic Practice in England, 1700–1820* (New Brunswick: Rutgers University Press, 1989), 82.

environment (the corruption of politics under Walpole). And it relies on the structure of quarrels to orchestrate the cacophony and vacuity of the literary world.

CONCLUSION

While not all satires rely on quarrels—Marshall notes that much of the satire in the age of Pope is either 'jolly' or 'pointed and particularized'[56]—some satirical texts use the modes of disputes as part of their strategies. They spring from an alleged answer to an attack, since a quarrel develops with a reply. They adopt the pretence of equality, either through the use of a *persona*, or through the critical appearances of objectivity, because one only fights with one's equals. They bring the matter to the public: a quarrel needs a judge who is called upon to adjudicate. They stage a conversation or a critical encounter between different parties, emphasizing the dialogical nature of disputes. They end through the (real or performed) death of one of the protagonists, or are interrupted because different arguments have developed elsewhere. The structural organization of quarrels shapes the mood and the form of the satirical text.

Satirical texts can further provide powerful weapons in quarrels, aiming to put an end to the controversy and to silence the opposition. Partridge's replies prove ineffectual in the face of Bickerstaff's predictions. Cibber's letters cannot obliterate the force of *The Dunciad*—the first *Letter* seems to have provided Pope with a final reason to promote its author to the throne of the Dunces, rather than with an end to the argument. This is because satire has taken the specific quarrels onto a different plane. Satirical texts, in particular of the Menippean variety, reveal the connections between different disputes, emphasizing the presence of the same protagonists from quarrel to quarrel, suggesting the role of individual quarrels within an overarching controversy, orchestrating their mutual relevance, bringing to light crucial issues at stake behind individual skirmishes—the religious differences reactivated by political events, the complex relationship between literature and politics, the fear of doom which may be seen to inhabit a culture. While satire may be instrumental in specific contexts of quarrels, the Menippean tradition develops their potentialities and constructs a world suffused with disputes where the protagonists battle it out, leaving the author to stage their final demise, and to retreat, having exposed the impostors. Boyle and Bentley disappear at the end of *The Battel of the Books*, 'so closely joyn'd, that *Charon* would mistake them both for one, and waft them over *Styx* for half his Fare',[57] while the end of the text is lost; Chaos is restored at the end of *The Dunciad*, 'And Universal Darkness buries All.'[58]

---

[56] Marshall, *Satire*, 205.   [57] Swift, *Works* (Cambridge), i. 164.

[58] Pope, *Poems* (Twickenham), v. 409, l. 656.

Select Bibliography

Bruyn, Frans de. 'Wit, and Burke, and Pope: The Literary Art of Self-Defence in *An Epistle To Dr Arbuthnot* and *A Letter To A Noble Lord*', *Journal for Eighteenth-Century Studies* 15 (1992), 35–49.

Bullard, Paddy and Alexis Tadié, eds. *Ancients and Moderns in Early Modern Europe: Comparative Perspectives* (Oxford: The Voltaire Foundation, Oxford University Studies in the Enlightenment, 2016).

Fumaroli, Marc. 'Les abeilles et les araignées', in *La Querelle des Anciens et des Modernes (XVIIᵉ–XVIIIᵉ siècles)*, ed. Anne-Marie Lecoq (Paris: Gallimard, 2001), 7–218.

Griffin, Dustin. *Satire: A Critical Reintroduction* (Lexington: University Press of Kentucky, 1994).

Levine, Joseph M. *The Battle of the Books: History and Literature in the Augustan Age* (Ithaca and London: Cornell University Press, 1991).

Mack, Maynard. *Alexander Pope: A Life* (New Haven: Yale University Press, 1985).

Marshall, Ashley. *The Practice of Satire in England 1658–1770* (Baltimore: Johns Hopkins University Press, 2013).

Norman, Larry. *The Shock of the Ancient: Literature & History in Early Modern France* (Chicago: University of Chicago Press, 2011).

Paulson, Ronald. *Breaking and Remaking: Aesthetic Practice in England, 1700–1820* (New Brunswick: Rutgers University Press, 1989).

Rumbold, Valerie. 'Burying the Fanatic Partridge: Swift's Holy Week Hoax', in *Politics and Literature in the Age of Swift*, ed. Claude Rawson (Cambridge: Cambridge University Press, 2010), 81–115.

Weinbrot, Harold. *Menippean Satire Reconsidered: From Antiquity to the Eighteenth Century* (Baltimore: Johns Hopkins University Press, 2005).

CHAPTER 33

SEXING SATIRE

JILL CAMPBELL

SEXUAL appetites and acts are an insistently recurring topic of eighteenth-century satire; they also provide an important register for thinking about the kinds of energies that animate satiric drives and acts themselves. The satiric poems of Alexander Pope contain many instances of both kinds of treatments of sex, which I will draw on for my primary examples in what follows, concentrating particularly on his repeated attacks on two sexually-suspect antagonists, Lady Mary Wortley Montagu and Lord Hervey, and on their replies, with the second half of the essay devoted to an extended reading of *Sober Advice from Horace*. Even within the historic span of Pope's life (1688–1744), however, patterns of association between sexual and satiric acts shift notably in ways that I will also trace, using Samuel Garth's *The Dispensary* and its prefatory materials and Rochester's poems as reference points to gauge these shifts, and to observe the occasional persistence of earlier models within significant change.

Female licentiousness, male debauchery, and same-sex desire are all regularly targeted for satiric attack, and they often appear as pivot points within more general satiric accounts—as when an extended portrait of Hervey as the castrated boy-lover 'Sporus' provides the culmination of Pope's wide-ranging satiric complaint in *Epistle to Arbuthnot*, or when Wortley Montagu appears under the name of the licentious 'Sappho' at key moments in a number of poems. An insinuation of sexual aberration spreads outwards, too, into Pope's satiric treatments of a great range of other follies and vices; aesthetic, political, and moral failings are rendered repellent by a suggestion of sexualized deviance, from the narcissistic exhibitionism and Oedipal regression Pope attributes to the poet laureate Colley Cibber in *The Dunciad* to the ravenous orality, scatological energy, and anal fixation with which Pope characterizes corrupt politicians and shameless aristocrats in *Sober Advice from Horace* and *Epilogue to the Satires*. Sex is not a separable subject of attack within eighteenth-century satire.

In fact, sexuality warrants satiric diagnosis and exposure particularly as it is revealed to colour or contaminate other aspects of identity and experience. This is a common subject for debunking by other eighteenth-century satirists as well as Pope. Authors of 'secret histories', such as Delarivier Manley in *The New Atalantis* (1709), purport to expose the sexual backstories to political actions and dramas. Henry Fielding sends up

Parson Tickletext's confusion between pious transport and sexual arousal in the prefatory materials to *Shamela* (1741) and links Methodist enthusiasm to lesbian seduction in *The Female Husband* (1746), while Jonathan Swift depicts the mistaking of bodily vapours for intellectual elevation in *A Tale of a Tub* (1704). Sexuality frequently appears in eighteenth-century satire as a crux for its approach to the general problem of dualism, or body and mind. In one familiar trope, satire tears away the covering of pretences to spiritual, intellectual, aesthetic, or civic aspiration from the libidinal, bodily motives that masquerade in their guise.

At times satirists extend this exposure to their own undertaking. Often claiming satire as a high calling, eighteenth-century writers also frequently portray it as itself fuelled by libidinal energies, including sadistic aggression, masochism, scopophilia, fetishism, and scatology. Such energies give satire visceral traction and primal force, but they may also discredit its own claims to higher, corrective purpose.[1] By the fourth book in the final version of *The Dunciad*, satire's eyes are riveted upon Mother Dullness's private parts: 'She mounts the Throne: her head a Cloud conceal'd, / In broad Effulgence all below reveal'd.'[2] The satirist himself can neither rise above this perspective from below nor escape the gravitational pull of the profoundly materialist world he condemns.

For some of Pope's immediate predecessors, including some men of the generation that sponsored him when he was young, the proper relation between satire and sexuality is not, however, disengagement. In late seventeenth-century poetry such disengagement or insusceptibility is itself regularly ridiculed as a quintessential form of 'Dullness'. Instead poetry, including satiric poetry, is praised as exerting a powerful erotic allure. For these writers, a free flow among language, 'wit', imagination, and bodily, sensory experience elicits and distinguishes the state of erotic arousal. In Pope's satires, sexual cathexes threaten to corrupt language with bodily urges, and, conversely, to turn bodies into mere text. Pope's treatments of such mergings range, however, from disillusionment and mortal threat to transport and enchanted transformation.

THE TOUCH OF SATIRE

In Pope's poetry satire is often tactile, caught up in a web of a particular kind of 'touching'. In the opening of the first dialogue of *Epilogue to the Satires*, the poet's friend, who laments the difference between Pope's 'lash[ing]' attacks on vice and Horace's 'polite, insinuating stile', notes how delicately Horace 'touch[ed] the failing of the sex'.[3]

---

[1] Focusing on satire's relation to aggression in Horace's *Satires*, Book I, Catherine Schlegel argues that 'the genre of satire flirts with verbal violence and has literary-genetic roots in speech genres of attack and coercion', *Satire and the Threat of Speech: Horace's 'Satires', Book I* (Madison: University of Wisconsin Press, 2005), 4, 7.

[2] Pope, *Poems* (Twickenham), v. 341, 407.

[3] Pope, *Poems* (Twickenham), iv. 298–9, lines 11–20. Subsequent quotations of Pope's Horatian poems will cite poems from this volume by line number.

In the last forty-five lines of the *Epilogue*'s second dialogue, as the poet rises to a fervent defence of his methods, variants of the word 'touch' appear three times to convey the necessity of his own more forceful manner of satiric touching. In the face of his 'Country's Ruin', when men 'not afraid of God' and 'safe from the Bar, the Pulpit, and the Throne' are 'touch'd and sham'd by *Ridicule* alone', the poet must reach to grasp not a 'polite' style but a 'sacred Weapon', avowing, 'Rev'rent I touch thee! but with honest Zeal' (lines 207–19; and see line 233).

In late seventeenth-century verse, satire's figurative touch is often more amorous than either righteous or 'nice'. In one of the commendatory poems to Samuel Garth's *The Dispensary* (1699), Christopher Codrington conflates author and poem to declare, 'I read Thee over with a Lover's Eye.'[4] Writing with unabashed excess in luxuriant triplets (and the occasional Alexandrine), Codrington develops an extended analogy between literary and sexual pleasures:

> I wou'd a Poet, like a Mistress, try
> Not by her Hair, her Hand, her Nose, her Eye;
> But by some Nameless Pow'r to give me Joy.
> The Nymph has G-----n's, C-----l's, C-----l's Charm
> If with resistless Fires my Soul she warms
> With Balm upon her Lips, and Raptures in her Arms.
>
> (lines 10–15)

Notably, the poem that produces such ravishment in the reader is not an erotic lyric but a mock-epic satire on a conflict between London apothecaries and physicians, which would provide an important prototype for *The Dunciad*. Codrington nonetheless urges the reader to abandon himself to the transporting pleasures of the poem rather than strive to exercise his judgement on either its satiric claims or its conformity to poetic rules. In fact, he heaps scorn on those who would set out to do the latter by likening them to men who boast of chastity only because they lack the power to touch, or to taste:

> Critics, and aged Beaux of Fancy chaste,
> Who ne'er had Fire, or else whose Fire is past,
> Must judge by Rules when they want Force to Taste.
>
> (lines 7–9)

Such men are termed 'dull' in the poetry of the Earl of Rochester and his female contemporary Aphra Behn. This flat-sounding, monosyllabic word contains a multitude of meanings in the Restoration, but its usage in that period frequently suggests, in particular, an insufficiency of erotic sensibility or sexual capacity, a semantic emphasis that largely recedes from view by the time 'Dullness' gives its name to the anti-heroine of *The Dunciad*. The words 'dull' and 'dullness' appear repeatedly in Rochester's poems, marking those many moments when he attests to the inferiority or even pointlessness of

---

[4] Christopher Codrington in Samuel Garth, *The Dispensary*, unnumbered prefatory pages. The poem appears in multiple editions; I here cite the 7th edition (1714).

existence bereft of erotic and sexual pleasure: only 'dull Life' persists 'when Love is at an End', for only a 'dull Heart' is without 'Am'rous thought'; anyone invulnerable to the 'wounding Eyes' of the poet's mistress must be 'profoundly Dull'; the once valiant 'Disabled Debauchee' has been forced by age and illness onto 'the Dull Shore of lazy Temperance', but he urges his younger comrades to reject the constraints of 'Dull Morals' and to perform their own reckless, heroic feats.[5] Old age provides some excuse for the dullness of impotence and decay, but young men indifferent to erotic attraction warrant satiric scorn. In his epilogue to *Circe* (1677), Rochester makes the link directly between this pervasive celebration of erotic urges and the proper enjoyment of writing:

> Poets and Women have an Equal Right
> To hate the Dull, who Dead to all Delight
> Feel pain alone, and have no Joy but spite.[6]

In this view, sexual feeling epitomizes a general capacity to feel 'Joy', qualifying one as truly alive rather than essentially 'Dead', and therefore a worthy reader of poetry. To lack such urgings, to be capable only of feeling pain and spite, is to deserve to be hated and cast out from the society of women and poets alike.

While the prefatory materials of *The Dispensary*, saluting its author as both physician and poet, link the quasi-somatic effects of poetry to the healing arts as well as to erotic pleasure, in Pope's poetry, when sex and language are conjoined, their pairing is likely to call up thoughts of poison. This set of associations appears with particular intensity and insistence in Pope's many depictions of Lady Mary Wortley Montagu, the aristocratic wit, poet, and one-time friend and collaborator of Pope whom he would satirize under various epithets at least twenty times after their falling-out in the late 1720s. Intimations of a perverse and pernicious conflation of sexuality and language also characterize many of Pope's attacks on Wortley Montagu's friend Lord Hervey. Courtier, MP, political writer, ally of Prime Minister Walpole, and poet, Hervey is most famously figured in Sporus, the sexually ambiguous 'vile Antithesis' of *Epistle to Arbuthnot*, but he also appears frequently in Pope's poems under the epithet 'Lord Fanny' (British slang for the female genitals). The devastating couplet on Wortley Montagu as 'Sappho' in *First Satire of the Second Book of Horace* (1733)—which, combined with a milder insult to Hervey, would prove the opening sally in a multi-episode satiric exchange—appears in a passage devoted to the varying 'Power[s] to hurt' wielded by different individuals. Unlike the corresponding passage in Horace's poem, which emphasizes the single natural weapon each creature uses to attack, Pope's imitation insists on the twin verbal and physical perils posed by each of his satiric subjects, beginning with slander and poison and culminating in libel and sexually transmitted disease:

> Slander or Poyson, dread from *Delia's* Rage,
> Hard Words or Hanging, if your Judge be *Page*.

---

[5] *Works of John Wilmot, Earl of Rochester*, ed. Harold Love (New York: Oxford University Press, 1999), 4–5, 11, 27–8, 44–5.

[6] Rochester, *Works*, 'Epilogue to *Circe*', 122.

> From furious *Sappho* scarce a milder Fate,
> P-x'd by her Love, or libell'd by her Hate...

(lines 81–4)

The double threats from Delia and from the notoriously severe Judge Page each merit only one line, whereas the dangers posed by Sappho extend into a couplet, as it unfolds a cruel and ironic dilemma: neither her love nor her hate leaves Sappho's intimates unharmed.[7] While 'P-x'd' harkens back, alliteratively, to 'Poysons' three lines before, it redistributes the aggressive threat of Delia's 'Rage' across Sappho's full emotional spectrum; and it locates the danger Sappho poses not in some toxic compound she might acquire and deploy but within her own body, which is both sexual and meaningfully marked—itself at once matter and text. In a disingenuous typographic wink, Pope holds back from spelling 'poxed' out fully, as if thus protecting his satiric target from the full exposure of her bodily disease—while in fact calling graphic attention thereby to the scandalous implications of the word. In itself, 'poxed' is medically ambiguous: Wortley Montagu's own body was indeed lastingly poxed by the nearly fatal case of smallpox she suffered in the years of her friendship with Pope; and, as a pioneering promoter of smallpox inoculation in England, she had also engaged in preventative 'poxing' of her son and friends; but in the context of the lines preceding and as a threatened effect of her 'love', the word seems much likelier to refer to the 'great-pox', or syphilis.[8] Subjecting a common word to the satiric convention of eliding letters in proper names (a technique for avoiding charges of libel), Pope advances 'Pox' d' as a further name for Wortley Montagu/Sappho, one made up of typographic and bodily marks. Or perhaps, more precisely, he intimates darkly that she wields the power thus to rename *you*.

This compact but complexly damning couplet would be recalled several times in the course of Pope's subsequent poems, twice dramatically interrupting the flow of satiric dialogue as a charged memento of the unresolved problem of names. Somehow that problem—central to the project of satire—is associated in these disruptions with the threats of sexuality and contagion that Pope attaches to Lady Mary. In 1733, when challenged about the Sappho couplet through an intermediary, Pope in fact denied that it referred to Wortley Montagu, claiming that the lines could easily be applied to four other 'remarkable poetesses & scribblers' of unsavoury reputation and expressing surprise that Wortley Montagu would 'take them to your Self', as if the responsibility for the application of 'Sappho' to her were her own.[9] Rejecting this demurral, Wortley Montagu and Hervey struck back in a powerful counter-attack, *Verses Address'd to the Imitator of*

---

[7] I consider some of the same features of this passage in the course of a different argument in 'The Scriblerian Project', *The History of British Women Writers, 1690–1750*, vol. 4, ed. Ros Ballaster (Basingstoke: Palgrave Macmillan, 2010), 96–112.

[8] Maynard Mack discusses these layers of reference and resonance in the word, concluding that Wortley Montagu's role in promoting inoculation 'almost enabl[ed] it to function as a compliment while at the same time identifying its victim, and, possibly, if it came to legal prosecution confusing the issue', *Alexander Pope: A Life* (New York: Norton, 1985), 559.

[9] Lord Peterborough to Montagu, n.d., *Letters and Works of Lady Mary Wortley Montagu*, ed. Lord Wharncliffe, 2 vols., 3rd edn. (London: Bohn, 1866), ii. 22.

the First Satire of the Second Book of Horace (1733).[10] In his headnote to *Epistle to Dr Arbuthnot* two years later, Pope justifies his publication of that poem as a self-defence against 'the very extraordinary' attacks upon him by Wortley Montagu and Hervey. He explains that it is at the urging of the physician-friend to whom he dedicates the poem that he has chosen to omit the names of his antagonists, though they have made 'free use' of his. Within the poem itself, it is Pope's mention of the name 'Sapho' that triggers his interlocutor's panicked interjection, 'Hold!...No Names', with an intimation that by using names Pope may put his bodily safety at risk; the poet quickly counters that what he fears more is the madness-inducing 'Slaver' of flattery (101–5). The same configuration of concerns is prompted again by mention of Wortley Montagu in Pope's *Epilogue to the Satires. II* (1738), where the threat of Sappho's corrupt and corrupting body and words lies under the 'X' formed by the poet and his friend's rapid back-and-forth about who may or may not be named (lines 19–23). Throughout this series of poems, Wortley Montagu's imagined sexuality imperils both physical and verbal integrity, as it threatens the boundary between body and language.

In Wortley Montagu's and Hervey's emphatic riposte to Pope's *Satire II.i*, a sexuality defined by aggression and the threat of physical harm is an aberrant one, and one that they attribute to their satiric antagonist rather than to themselves or other members of the social world for which they speak. Striking back at Pope's attacks on them as sexual beings, Hervey and Wortley Montagu dismiss his satire most absolutely by excluding him altogether from that realm of eroticized literary exchange that we saw evoked in Rochester's 'Epilogue to *Circe*' and Codrington's commendatory poem to Garth. Wortley Montagu and Hervey position themselves as inheritors of that realm partly by alluding to their own class standing (despite the anonymity of the poem's publication) and by proceeding with the easy assurance that their social status entails. In contrast, they denigrate Pope as a kind of social and poetic upstart, describing his birth as 'obscure', sneering at the 'Toil' with which he labours at his poems, and asserting that he would not be welcome at the homes of his poems' readers (lines 20, 24, 100). Although Pope may insinuate that Wortley Montagu and Hervey are both sexually suspect, he and his own poetry are simply 'dull' in the sense we found so prominent in Rochester's poems: 'If none do yet return th'intended Blow, / ', they sneer, 'You all your Safety, to your Dullness owe' (lines 89–90). Comparing Pope to a 'fretful' little porcupine who 'impotently' shoots forth 'harmless Quill[s]', they warn him that his rancorous aggression may yet elicit physical punishment from more powerful people (lines 60–78). Throughout, their counterattack proceeds from the assumption that poetic and sexual energies *should* be closely connected; Wortley Montagu and Hervey demonstrate Pope's disqualification as a satirist by insisting on his exclusion from sexual love.

[10] The attribution of this poem is uncertain, but most scholars conclude that it is a joint production of Wortley Montagu and Lord Hervey, with Wortley Montagu taking the lead role. It was published anonymously in March 1733. See the headnote to the poem in *Lady Mary Wortley Montagu: Essays and Poems and Simplicity, a Comedy*, ed. Robert Halsband and Isobel Grundy (New York: Oxford University Press, 1993), 265.

Beginning with derision for the evident failure of Pope's attempts to imitate Horace, they quickly progress to a judgement on his diminutive and disabled body as a similarly failed 'imitation' of the authentic, living human form:

> Thine is just such an Image of *his* [Horace's] Pen,
> As thou thy self art of the Sons of Men:
> Where our own Species in Burlesque we trace,
> A Sign-Post Likeness of the noble Race;
> That is at once Resemblance and Disgrace.
>
> (lines 11–15)

In the triplet that drives their point home, so egregious is Pope's misshapen body that it is not a body at all, but rather a mere sign of one—and a crude sign at that, an inexpert and inadvertently 'Burlesque' representation, like the primitive images on sign-boards outside London shops. Wortley Montagu and Hervey return quickly from this jeering attack on Pope's person to the literary subject of his divergences from Horace: where Horace's satire is 'delicate', 'clear', 'elegant', and 'pure', Pope's is 'coarse', 'dark', 'crabbed', 'rude', and 'mean' (lines 16–24). Yet this account, too, re-converges quickly on the matter of Pope's body, and now particularly of its sexual nature, as that is manifest in his conduct of satire:

> *Satire* shou'd, like a polish'd Razor keen,
> Wound with a Touch, that's scarcely felt or seen,
> Thine is an Oyster-Knife, that hacks and hews;
> The Rage, but not the Talent to Abuse;
> And is in Hate, what Love is in the Stews.
> 'Tis the gross Lust of Hate, that still annoys,
> Without Distinction, as gross Love enjoys
>
> (lines 25–31)

Identifying satire, as Pope does, with a kind of 'Touch', Wortley Montagu and Hervey contend that he is incapable of the particular form of touching that satire should employ. The 'Oyster-Knife' with which he instead 'hacks and hews' extends their association of Pope's poetry with degrading labour, and also recalls the uncouth voice, repetitive cries, and rude demeanour of the London 'Oyster-Wife'. But their consignment of Pope to the street-stalls of Billingsgate, vending oysters, is only on the way to placing him within an imagined inverse corollary to the 'Stews', a place where 'the gross Lust of Hate' might be transacted, 'without Distinction', as a purely physical and commercial act. It is the deviance of Pope's body that first destines him to alienation and exclusion from both sexual and literary communion:

> Not even Youth and Beauty can controul
> The universal Rancour of thy Soul; […]

But how should'st thou by Beauty's Force be mov'd,
No more for loving made, than to be lov'd?

(lines 44–9)

Destined from birth to be among the 'Dull' who, in Rochester's 'Epilogue to *Circe*', feel 'pain alone, and have no Joy but spite', Pope deserves to be hated and cast out by both women and poets, in Wortley Montagu and Hervey's bitter riposte. The poem closes with Pope wandering alone and accursed, like 'the first bold Assassin', 'the Emblem of [his] Crooked Mind, / Mark'd on his Back, like Cain, by God's own Hand' (lines 107–11). Early in the poem, Pope's aberrant body was reduced to a flattened and crude representation, a 'Sign-Post Likeness'. At the poem's end he must inhabit a body that, while 'Mark'd' and functioning as an 'Emblem' and visible sign, also isolates him in permanent exile and suffering.

NAMING, SATIRIC FIXATION, AND DESIRE

The year after his vitriolic exchange with Wortley Montagu and Hervey in *Satire II.i* and their *Verses*, Pope published an imitation of Horace's *Satire I.ii* anonymously under the title of *Sober Advice from Horace, to the Young Gentlemen about Town. As deliver'd in his Second Sermon. Imitated in the Manner of Pope* (1734)—teasingly identifying the poem with his own 'Manner' but not with his own pen. The problem of names in satire that elsewhere clings especially to the sexually threatening figure of 'Sappho' here extends to a coy suppression of the name of the author himself. The content of this early satire by Horace is more exclusively sexual than his later satires, and Pope's imitation of it is decidedly cruder than his other Horatian imitations both in content and in poetic form, including multi-syllabic rhymes, two rhyming triplets, rough and rollicking metre, and an inset monologue by a penis ('that honest Part that rules us all', imagined as 'ris[ing]' to speak, lines 87–92).[11] As James McLaverty suggests, the poem 'responds to the "Pope incapable of loving/Pope sexually inadequate" charge of *Verses to the Imitator of Horace* by attacking the sexual morality of the court and Quality'—but also, I would add, even more fundamentally by dramatizing the poet as himself both sexually knowing and sexually daring, subject to risky appetites of his own.[12] Incongruously, in the apparatus to the poem, Pope combines this relatively single-minded focus on sexual subject matter with a parodic send-up of the editing practices of one of his favourite literary targets, Richard Bentley. He calls attention to the fact that the Latin text he supplies in parallel text is the one prepared by Bentley, and he supplies pedantic scholarly notes purportedly by Bentley, which

[11] The headnote to Horace's *Satire I.ii* in the Loeb edition deprecates it as 'coarse and sensational in tone, and doubtless one of Horace's earliest efforts'. Horace, *Satires, Epistles, Ars Poetica*, trans. H. Rushton Fairclough (Cambridge, MA: Harvard University Press, 1999), 17.

[12] James McLaverty, *Pope, Print, and Meaning* (Oxford: Oxford University Press, 2001), 195.

yoke textual fastidiousness to outrageously explicit sexual subject matter—female genitals, castration, the 'Taste of Antiquity' for pederasty, and the English word 'Fuck'.

In the first of these 'Notae Bentleianae', henceforth signed 'BENT', Pope's fictional Bentley complains that the poet has converted some of the male malefactors of Horace's *Satire I.ii* 'into so many LADIES', and indeed, the first portion of Pope's imitation does bring female sexual appetites to the fore in a way his Horatian original never does. He acknowledges as much when he alters Horace's declaration of his satire's point—'*dum vitant stulti vitia, in contraria currunt* [in avoiding a vice, fools run into its opposite]'— to a statement of his own expanded 'Theme': 'Women and Fools are always in Extreme' (line 28). Of course Wortley Montagu appears early and often among the offending 'Ladies', beginning with passing references to her and to Lord Hervey in the poem's second line. Adapting Horace's opening sketch of all the groups currently caught up in a flurry of mourning, Pope replaces the male singer Tigellius with the actress Anne Oldfield as the celebrity object of the town's public grief:

> The Tribe of Templars, Play'rs, Apothecaries,
> Pimps, Poets, Wits, Lord *Fanny*'s, Lady *Mary*'s,
> And all the Court in Tears, and half the Town,
> Lament dear charming *Oldfield*, dead and gone!
>
> (lines 1–4)

Creating plural forms of their proper names or familiar epithets and whisking them in as the seventh and eighth terms in a rapid catalogue of group identities—even thus managing a rhyme between Lady Mary's grand name and a lowly vocational 'Tribe'—Pope casually reduces his antagonists to types or categories of person rather than individuals. He is not done with either of them, however, in this quick, dismissive gesture; he will return to each repeatedly in what follows to provide more patient and individualized, if fragmentary and incremental, attacks. Surprisingly, however, he will also build in this poem to a different kind of reference to Wortley Montagu: one that expresses wistful longing rather than hatred and disgust, both for his former friend and long-time antagonist herself, and for the erotic charm associated with an earlier view of satire.

Pope's opening comment about Oldfield distinguishes her from the 'generous' male singer of Horace's poem and associates her with the terms of his attack on Sappho in *Satire II.i*, in a glancing parody of the ideal of the Sister Arts' combined force: 'Engaging Oldfield! who, with Grace and Ease, / Could joyn the Arts, to ruin, and to please' (lines 5–6). He follows this questionable tribute with a survey of women, including the actress Teresa Constantia Philips and Wortley Montagu as 'Fufidia', whose notorious appetites for property as well as for sex have ruined men, extending in the latter case to her own son. The two women are reduced to ravening orifices or 'Ends' that devour both property and people:

> 'Treat on, treat on', is her [Philips's] eternal Note,
> And Lands and Tenements go down her Throat. [...]

[Fufidia] starves herself, so little her own Friend,
And thirsts and hungers only at one End.

> (lines 13–14, 17–24)

This imagery recurs in what follows, as women's bodies dwindle, grotesquely, to two hypertrophied 'ends', whether rendered such by the destructive demands of their own appetites ('*Rufa*'s at either end a Common-Shoar [sewer]', line 29) or by men's ravenous fixations ('But diff'rent Taste in diff'rent Men prevails, / And one is fired by Heads, and one by Tails', lines 35–6). It is characteristic of the perverse rapacity of such 'Ends' in women, however, that its elemental force overrides distinctions among kinds of appetite, blending material greed with gustatory hunger (in Philips's case) or with untrammelled sexual drives (in Wortley Montagu's)—as if, finally, these bodies have only one orifice, which threatens to swallow all.

Wortley Montagu's naming here as 'Fufidia' already identifies her as aberrant, or a site of distortion, since (as 'BENT.' points out) Horace's English imitator has adapted her name from the male form, Fufidius, making her a sort of cross-textual transsexual; and her insatiable fixation on material gain in the passage involves her in a variety of masculine financial dealings. Pope begins his portrait of Wortley Montagu as Fufidia with a citation of the word 'P-x' with which he marked her in *Satire II.i*, but he now employs that word ambiguously, in a syntax that leaves it unclear whether it does or does not adhere to her: 'With all a Woman's Virtues but the P-x, / Fufidia thrives in Money, Land, and Stocks...'. He does not relinquish his oft-reiterated charge of Wortley Montagu's licentiousness, but he here suggests that compulsive greed may be even more fundamental to her appetites:

> For Int'rest, ten *per Cent.* her constant Rate is;
> Her Body? Hopeful Heirs may have it *gratis.*
> She turns her very Sister to a job,
> And, in the Happy Minute, picks your Fob...

> (lines 19–22)

Guilty of sexual licence, Wortley Montagu's deepest appetites are paraphilic: there is an irrational libidinal quality to her greed, which distracts and absorbs her even in the midst of the sexual act. Suggestively, Pope's euphemistic phrase for that act, 'the Happy Minute', harks back to Restoration poetry, where 'the Happy Minute', 'Lucky Minute', and 'Tender Minute' are favoured locutions for sexual consummation and sometimes specifically for orgasm. Pope's echo of this signature phrase from the libertine poetry of the preceding generation is bitter and ironic: whatever defiant idealism might cling to the phrase's affirmation of strictly ephemeral physical pleasures is here dispelled by Fufidia's absorption in material gain at the very moment of consummation. This satire unmasks sexuality as itself a cover for other base drives.

A more specific, extended, and pointed echo of the poetry of the previous generation works to quite different effect later in the poem, however, though again in the context of

Pope's obsessive return to the figure of Wortley Montagu. As his imitation moves towards a sustained treatment of Horace's main theme in the poem—the 'sober advice' that sexual appetites may be satisfied as fully, and much more safely, with a common wench or willing whore than with another man's noble wife—Pope alludes twice more in passing to Wortley Montagu's sexual misadventures, touching upon her complicated financial dealings with a French admirer (lines 53–4) and then insinuating her ready willingness to expose her body (lines 124–5). As the poem rises to its culmination in the speaker's impassioned account of his own sexual habits, the name of 'Montagu' makes a more surprising appearance:

> I'm a plain Man, whose Maxim is profest,
> 'The Thing at hand is of all Things the *best.*' [...]
> Give me a willing Nymph! 'tis all I care,
> Extremely clean, and tolerably fair,
> Her Shape her own, whatever Shape she have,
> And just that White and Red which Nature gave.
> Her I transported touch, transported view,
> And call her *Angel! Goddess! Montague!*
>
> (lines 153–4, 161–6)

Beginning his first-person account with a possible intimation of masturbation ('Thing' has previously been used in the poem to refer to female genitals but could also denote a male part reliably 'at hand'), the speaker next adds a 'willing Nymph' to the scenario of the fulfilment of his desires, and then moves beyond his description of that nymph's serviceable, generic body to a simultaneously sexual and poetic 'transport': in rhythmic exclamations, the speaker's imagination transforms the nameless woman to an '*Angel!*' or '*Goddess!*' and, at its greatest height, to the reviled, threatening, and deeply desired figure of '*Montague!*' This act of imaginative calling informs the quality of 'touch', we are told: the speaker's own transport mirrors his transmogrification of a woman ('Her I') through the coinciding of touch, vision, and calling by name. His touch of 'her' is simultaneously physical and virtual or imaginative.

It is also distinctly textual. In attesting to such an experience of touch, Pope recalls a passage of verse from a poem published more than thirty years before, one devoted to the subject of poetic rather than sexual pleasure, invoking the latter only as an extended figure for the former. That passage appears in the commendatory poem by Codrington to Garth's *The Dispensary* that we considered early in this essay as a particularly concentrated instance of the Restoration ethos of eroticized literary pleasure and desire. Having established his tribute's sustained conceit at the poem's opening—'I read Thee over with a Lover's Eye'—Codrington explains that such an eye, whether turned on a poet or a mistress, looks for 'resistless Fires' and 'Raptures' rather than scrutinizing parts or seeking to discover 'Faults' (lines 4–11). In a close parallel with the passage in Pope we are considering, he suggests that erotic 'Magic' both transcends and attracts names. A 'Nymph' with the 'nameless Pow'r to give [him] Joy' also evokes the (respectfully emvowelled) names of celebrated beauties: 'The Nymph has G-----n's, C-----l's, C-----l's Charm / If with resistless Fires my Soul she warms / With Balm upon her Lips, and Raptures in her Arms' (lines 12–15). Pope's inclusion of the fanciful word 'Nymph' in the 'I'm a plain Man' passage of *Sober Advice*, where it stands out against a background of professedly modest and pragmatic concerns, may hark back to this passage in Codrington, as does the general idea of erotic projection and renaming. His lines about sexual transport, however, even more closely recall a further couplet from Codrington's poem, one in which Codrington brings his extended comparison back to the immediate subject at hand, repeating the device of measuring transport by reciting illustrious names but now applying it directly to the pleasures of Garth's poem:

> Lost in our Pleasure, we Enjoy in you
> *Lucretius, Horace, S-----d, M----gue.*
>
> (lines 21–2)

If the allusion to Codrington's lines in some sense mitigates the strangeness of Pope's voicing of the name 'Montague' at the moment of his imagined sexual transport, it also redoubles it: in the context of this echo, the name he exclaims at the height of his transported touch—'*Angel! Goddess! Montague!*'—may not denote his long-time satiric target, Lady Mary Wortley Montagu, after all, but rather Charles Montagu, one of Pope's early literary subscribers and patrons. The two emvowelled names in Codrington's catalogue refer to titled poets and patrons of his time: John Sheffield, Duke of Buckinghamshire, and Charles Montagu, Earl of Halifax. Placing the names of these contemporaries in immediate succession to those of two great poets of the ancient world, Codrington pays a handsome tribute to them as well as to Garth. Pope might recall this couplet with special interest because Sheffield and Montagu had figured in his own literary career; both considerably older (and socially grander) than he, they sponsored and encouraged him in his early years. Pope would recollect Sheffield's support, along with that of Garth and a roll-call of other distinguished friends, in the passage of *Epistle to Arbuthnot* in which he responds to the question of why he chose to publish (lines 135–44). The nature of those tender ties, to which he had also done homage in the dedications and notes to his youthful pastorals, seems far from the ribald subject matter and cynical stance of *Sober Advice*; but the lacing of echoes of Codrington's poem into his Horatian imitation creates some cross-hatching between these seemingly very different realms. Collapsing the relation between tenor (literary transport) and vehicle (sexual transport) in the passage from Codrington that he draws upon as he imitates Horace's unsentimental account of sex, Pope depicts himself as thinking of literary pleasures and of affective ties among male poets and patrons at the very moment of physical enjoyment—as if literary matter and literary cathexes flow up from the deepest wells of his unconscious. He may not, like Fufidia, in the 'Happy Minute' pick 'your Fob'; but that minute finds him stealing, perhaps even unawares, the resonances of someone else's poetic line. It also finds him blending, through allusion, heterosexual drives and deeply-felt homosocial relations among men.

In this complexly layered moment late in *Sober Advice*, Pope conjures a convergence of bodies and words that is transporting rather than toxic, in stark contrast with the poisonous or infectious effects of that mixture elsewhere in his poems. Fleetingly, poetry and sexuality are likened not by the aggression, scopophilia, and relentless appetites that drive them both, but by the power of fantasy, imagination, and words to elevate and to transform. Significantly, this alternate perspective on the link between satire and sexuality enters the poem through an infusion of phrases and ideas from a poem dating from the previous generation. The intertextuality harks back specifically to a commendatory poem that dwells lavishly on the loving and admiring bonds among men both within a living coterie and across time. Codrington's poem, expanding extravagantly on its conceit of male poet as mistress, shows the lack of inhibition about homosocial and even homoerotic ties that is evident in many Restoration poems and letters but that has receded dramatically by the time of Pope's Horatian imitations, with their frequent harping, in particular, on the figure of the effeminate and bisexual Lord Hervey.[13]

LADY OR LORD FANNY

Hervey will be familiar to most readers of Pope's satires as the object of his sustained attack in *Epistle to Arbuthnot*, where his sexual fluidity as Master and Miss, tripping Lady and strutting Lord, is treated as the damning sexual counterpart to his political opportunism and corruption, and where his renaming from Paris to Sporus in *The Works* brands him as a dependant, a play-actor, and a catamite. Within *Sober Advice*, we have glimpsed him at the poem's opening, paired with his friend Wortley Montagu, in a dismissive but momentary reference to the generic categories of 'Lord *Fanny*'s, Lady *Mary*'s' (line 2). Two brief and glancing references to Hervey can be found in what follows: he is implicitly feminized by his appearance alongside his wife within the catalogue of female offenders who illustrate Pope's claim that 'Women and Fools are always in Extreme' (30); and he is cited, again alongside his wife, in the complaint of that 'honest Part that rules us all', when it demands whether, in its moments of urgent need, it ever asked 'for any / Such Nicety, as Lady or Lord *Fanny*?'--- (lines 91–2). Within the whirlwind of imputations and insinuations that make up *Sober Advice* the satiric treatment of Hervey may seem incidental. And yet his presence in the poem—and that of the homosexuality or bisexuality with which he is associated—is diffuse but powerful, adhering most pervasively in the triangulated relations among Pope's Latin original, his English imitation of it, and those pedantic textual footnotes attributed to 'BENT.' that I earlier called 'incongruous' or seemingly unrelated to the poem's main focus on sex. In the

[13] The growing literature on the historical emergence of a minoritized and ostracized category of the 'homosexual' in eighteenth-century England includes Alan Bray, *Homosexuality in Renaissance England* (London: Gay Men's Press, 1982); Randolph Trumbach, *Sex and the Gender Revolution: Heterosexuality and the Third Gender in Enlightenment London* (Chicago: University of Chicago Press, 1998); and Thomas A. King, *The Gendering of Men, 1660–1750*, 2 vols. (Madison: University of Wisconsin Press, 2004–7).

movements across these elements of the text, Hervey is set against the figure of Pope himself in some surprising ways.

Sexualized relations among men appear on the surface of *Sober Advice* at several points (lines 60n, 81–2). Most startlingly, in a passage where Horace quotes Cato's approval of a friend's fornication at a brothel on the grounds that it is better than 'grinding away' with other men's wives, Pope adds a new element to the speaker's citation of those alternatives that would be worse than 'busy[ing]' oneself sexually in a brothel or park:

> 'Proceed (he cry'd) proceed, my Reverend Brother,
> ''Tis *Fornicatio simplex*, and no other:
> 'Better than lust for Boys, with *Pope* and *Turk*,
> 'Or others Spouses, like my Lord of ---
>
> (lines 40–4)

The allusion to an undesirable 'lust for Boys' has no basis in this passage in Horace, which simply touches on the poem's general theme of the dangers of adultery. The explicitness of this reference to boys as an object of sexual desire is unusual in Pope's corpus, though here placed in the mouth of a sexually knowing and cynical speaker. Particularly striking is the speaker's casual assignment of such 'lust' to 'Pope and Turk', as if that scandalous inclination is well known.

The phrase 'Pope and Turk' is in fact formulaic and would be familiar to Pope's readers; his speaker's rapid incorporation of it in Pope's exclamatory line feels that way even to later, uninitiated readers, contributing to the line's distinctive effect. The phrase derives from a widely circulated metrical prayer by Robert Wisdom that appears at the back of Sternhold and Hopkins's Psalter:

> Preserve us, Lord, by thy dear word;
> From Turk and Pope defend us, Lord:
> Both which would thrust out of his throne
> Our Lord Christ Jesus, thy dear Son.[14]

The phrase that Pope echoes from this prayer—a compressed, monosyllabic synecdoche for the paired threats of Catholicism and Islam—was the subject of some ridicule in the seventeenth and eighteenth centuries, featuring as a particularly risible illustration in attacks on the inferior poetry of Sternhold and Hopkins's popular work. Pope himself picked up on this vein of ridicule and complaint both in *Epistle II.1* (lines 235–6) and in a 1725 letter to Swift—adding a punning play on the phrase's special application to his own surname (and his Catholicism): 'My name is as bad a one as yours, and hated by all bad poets, from Sternhold and Hopkins to Gildon and Cibber.'[15]

---

[14] *The Whole Book of Psalms, Collected into English Metre, by Thomas Sternhold, John Hopkins, and Others* (London, 1709), n.p.

[15] Pope, *Corr.* (Sherburn), ii. 334, cited in McLaverty, *Pope, Print*, 200. As McLaverty notes, the *Twickenham* editors point out the pun on Pope's surname in glossing his use of the phrase from Sternhold and Hopkins in *Epistle II.i* but take no notice of it in relation to the stranger line in *Sober Advice* (200).

While the phrase 'Pope and Turk' thus served as shorthand for inferior poetry, rote recitation, and the aesthetic and cultural attitudes of parochial audiences who knew no better, neither Wisdom's prayer itself nor later references to it specifically associate the dangers posed by Pope and Turk with 'lust for Boys', as Pope's use of the phrase in *Sober Advice* might imply. English traditions of imputing homosexuality both to Catholic clergy and to Turks may lay the groundwork for Pope's startling jump of associations there. But why, in his repurposing of Wisdom's phrase in *Sober Advice*, would Pope allow the double reference to the Catholic Pope and his own proper name to associate him, even for a moment, with a charge of pederastic 'lust'? McLaverty proposes that this very peculiar moment in *Sober Advice*—passed over in utter silence by editors and almost all critics—may represent either a bluff, intended to prompt attacks that would justify Pope's own planned attacks on Hervey, or a 'double bluff', an odd moment of 'confession' in plain sight.[16] In either case, this moment of seemingly plain speaking about sex *qua* sex, as a matter of the unruly body alone, is complexly bound up in the drives of literary appetite and textual fixation.

While Pope thus adds an explicit reference to same-sex 'lust' where it does not appear in the original of Horace's *Satire I.ii*, Horace's poem contains two references to homosexuality (one disputed, one clear) that he notably omits in his imitation; and the complex play of suppression and activation that Pope builds around those references suffuses *Sober Advice*, complementing the surprisingly overt but condensed and enigmatic line in which Pope himself is named. The figure of Lord Hervey flits about in this more diffuse but insistent treatment, shadowing Pope's own momentary, ambiguous cameo in the one-liner about 'lust for boys'. Most notably, in a passage from which Pope omits Horace's mention of a 'slave-boy' as a sexual object, he invents a footnote for 'BENT.' that moves back through several passages in the poem to highlight the *'true taste of Antiquity'* for *'delicate Youth'*—illustrating that taste by quoting the poem's earlier reference to 'such Nicety as Lady or Lord F---' (lines 116–19n in the parallel text of Latin). Through the deflection of Horace's overt references to male–male sexuality into the space of parodic scholarly footnotes, the figure of Hervey or 'Lord Fanny' is also closely linked to that of 'Dr. Bentley', and to the obsessive and fetishistic quality of Bentley's avid textual pursuits. Whereas the allusion to Sternhold and Hopkins's Psalter in his line about 'lust for boys' links that topic to literary ignorance and xenophobia, Pope's suspension of Horace's references to homosexual acts across the space of text and footnote poses the question of sexuality's relation to cosmopolitan learning, the love of classical culture, and a fascination with language.

The stuttering and aposiopesis prompted by the thought of Wortley Montagu that we have seen in several of Pope's satires take place on a larger spatial scale in *Sober Advice*, scattering the poem's progress across an open pair of pages, with their parallel columns of Latin and English texts and appended footnotes, and indeed back through previous pages in the poem. In this poem, the problem of the relation between bodies

---

[16] McLaverty, *Pope, Print*, 200.

and names is attached to the poet himself, whose name is suppressed as author of the poem but then appears inside the poem, under cover of a pun within a formulaic phrase, in a loaded allusion to pederasty. That allusion links the dispersal of the poet's body and name to the figure of Hervey, whose expanded satiric epithet as 'Lady *or* Lord *Fanny*' becomes a kind of blinking strobe light, appearing in the poem's text at one point and reappearing at the centre of a wide-ranging footnote later. In its initial context in lines 91–2, where the 'honest Part that rules us all' demands whether it has ever asked 'for any / Such Nicety, as Lady or Lord *Fanny*', the phrase seemed to refer to two people, both celebrated beauties at court, female and male. When it reappears, however, in 'BENT.'s' footnote to the later passage, the phrase refers instead to one person in his two alternating guises, the sometime-Lord, sometime-Lady whom we will meet in *Epistle to Arbuthnot* under the name of Sporus.[17] Whereas the poet's ability to rename a simple 'willing Nymph' as '*Angel! Goddess! Montague!*' bespeaks the power of words to transform and 'transport', the idea that the sex of an individual's body may swing one way or another, determined by merely verbal denomination, is treated as disturbing and abhorrent. The 'matter' of bodily sexuality becomes subject to textual emendation in this view, just as in 'BENT.'s' final footnote to this poem (175n), he gleefully proposes altering 'Luck' in Pope's text to 'Fuck', restoring the bold physicality of Horace's original precisely by diddling with a single letter: to fuck or not to fuck is an epiphenomenon of words.

CONCLUSION

When it takes individual people as its targets, satire frequently 'objectifies' those people, insisting on the distance between them and the satirist's own position as a thinking, feeling, and speaking self. Satire focused on sexual character or behaviour particularly emphasizes the embodiment of its targets, sometimes using a heightened treatment of their bodies to place them below the fully human. Proper names (or recognizable satiric epithets) also appear as a kind of hinge between bodily and verbal entities; the name of a 'real' person connects an embodied individual to a piece of language—it 'refers'. In Pope's poetry, tensions and disputes about satiric method (whether to practise 'particular' or 'general' satire, whether to name names) often erupt in tight conjunction with sexual subject matter, as so often when 'Sappho' enters a poem. The act of naming, or language itself, Pope intimates, may be corrupted by Wortley Montagu's misuse both of her body and of words, and by the confusion she creates between them. While for poets of the Restoration, a somatic, and especially an erotic, experience of language is a measure of its transporting power, Augustan poets regularly warn

---

[17] McLaverty makes this suggestion, without distinguishing between the phrase's appearance in the poem's text and in the later footnote (*Pope, Print*, 199).

against a blurring between bodily sensation and verbal art. At times, however, Pope's satires surprisingly hark back to an earlier ethos of eroticized ties between reader and writer and among writers, placing his own work in the domain of erotically charged words, and even fleetingly linking Pope himself to one or the other of his most hated satiric targets: Lady Mary Wortley Montagu and Lord Hervey. In these moments, Pope suggests satire itself as a kind of sex.

SELECT BIBLIOGRAPHY

Deutsch, Helen. *Resemblance and Disgrace: Alexander Pope and the Deformation of Culture* (Cambridge, MA: Harvard University Press, 1996).

Fuchs, Jacob. *Reading Pope's 'Imitations of Horace'* (Lewisburg: Bucknell University Press, 1989).

Haugen, Kristine. *Richard Bentley: Poetry and Enlightenment* (Cambridge, MA: Harvard University Press, 2011).

Jones, Emrys. 'Pope and Dulness', in *Pope: Recent Essays by Several Hands*, ed. Maynard Mack and James A. Winn (Hamden: Archon, 1980), 612–51.

McLaverty, James. *Pope, Print, and Meaning* (Oxford: Oxford University Press, 2001).

Norton, Rictor. *Mother Clap's Molly House: The Gay Subculture in England, 1700–1830* (London: Gay Men's Press, 1992).

Sedgwick, Eve Kosofsky. *Between Men: English Literature and Male Homosocial Desire* (New York: Columbia University Press, 1985).

Stack, Frank. *Pope and Horace: Studies in Imitation* (Cambridge: Cambridge University Press, 1985).

Trumbach, Randolph. *Sex and the Gender Revolution: Heterosexuality and the Third Gender in Enlightenment London* (Chicago: University of Chicago Press, 1998).

CHAPTER 34

....

RIDICULE AS
A TOOL FOR
DISCOVERING TRUTH

....

LAWRENCE E. KLEIN

RIDICULE as a test of truth was very much an eighteenth-century formulation—a 'celebrated question', according to Lord Kames.[1] The point of origin for the formulation was Anthony Ashley Cooper, the 3rd Earl of Shaftesbury (1671–1713), writing during the reign of Anne. Treatments of ridicule as a test of truth, prompted by Shaftesbury, had a long life, ricocheting among writers across the decades of the eighteenth century and in Ireland and Scotland as well as in England. Indeed, the most extended responses to Shaftesbury's statements about ridicule appeared fifty years after he wrote, in John Brown's *Essays on the Characteristicks* (1751) and Allan Ramsay's *Essay on Ridicule* (1753).

Brown and Ramsay wrote at a moment of transition in discussions of ridicule. Shaftesbury was a philosophical moralist but he was also an ideological writer. In the first half of the century, discussion of ridicule was controversial, inflected initially by the politics of party and for decades by the politics of religion. However, by the middle of the century, partisan dispute had ebbed, and even religion was a good deal less controversial. Brown and Ramsay both provide evidence of a shift in the paradigms in which ridicule was to be situated, from religious controversy to enlightened exploration of the nature of humanity: attention to ridicule shifted in focus from its relation to truth, primarily religious truth, to its relation to taste.

Although the word 'ridiculous' was already commonly used in the sixteenth century, 'ridicule' only began appearing in the later seventeenth. Like the word 'politeness' (with which it was affiliated), it was a borrowing from the French. Ridiculing was, of course, nothing new, and the practice in the eighteenth century has recently been illuminated

[1] Henry Home, Lord Kames, *Elements of Criticism*, 3 vols. (Edinburgh, 1762), ii. 55.

by socio-cultural histories of laughter.[2] However, the starting point of this essay is the fact that ridicule—its nature, power, import, and uses—became a topic of definition and reflection.[3] Contemporaries thought of theirs as an 'Age of Ridicule' in which the foibles and follies of commercial life and fashionable society were mocked along with the hypocrisies and corruptions of politicians and the idiosyncrasies and extravagancies of lovers, collectors, academics, philosophers, and students of nature.[4] At the same time, many were uncomfortable with the conspicuousness of what Shaftesbury called 'the test of ridicule', especially when it targeted religious demeanours and doctrines.[5]

Discussions of ridicule in the eighteenth century could draw on humanistic tradition suggesting that ridicule had moral and cognitive value. Horace was often quoted: *Ridentem dicere verum quid vetat?*, 'what prevents the man of mirth from telling the truth?';[6] *Ridiculum acri fortius et melius magnas plerumque secate res*, 'Mirth, for the most part, cuts through weighty matters with greater firmness and ease than seriousness'.[7] For many then, ridicule functioned within the Horatian ambition to synthesize the *utile* and the *dulce*, the useful and the agreeable, the instructive and the pleasant. Edward Young (1683-1765) appreciated the Horatian approach, writing that Horace 'appears in good humour while he censures; and therefore his censure has the more weight, as supposed to proceed from Judgment, not Passion'.[8] Meanwhile, Anthony Collins (1676–1729) educed Erasmus as 'one of the greatest and best Authorities for the *pleasant* and *ironical* manner of treating *serious* Matters'.[9] The residue of these humanistic tropes appeared in such a demotic example of print as John Dunton's *Athenian Mercury*, a periodical providing short answers to readers' questions. In 1691, the question was posed: 'How far is it consistent with Wisdom to Banter?' With qualifications, the answer was: 'it may be necessary, by way of Satyr, to shame some Persons out of *Ill Actions*, when other Methods fail, and it has been often found effectual'.[10] Thus, there was a long tradition of deeming ridicule useful in serious matters and especially in the pursuit of moral correction.

---

[2] For instance, Kate Davison, 'Occasional Politeness and Gentlemen's Laughter in Eighteenth-Century England', *Historical Journal* 57 (2014), 921–45; Simon Dickie, *Cruelty and Laughter: Forgotten Comic Literature and the Unsentimental Eighteenth Century* (Chicago: University of Chicago Press, 2011); Vic Gatrell, *City of Laughter: Sex and Satire in Eighteenth-Century London* (London: Atlantic, 2006).

[3] Corbyn Morris, *An Essay towards Fixing the True Standards of Wit, Humour, Raillery, Satire, and Ridicule* (1744) was devoted almost entirely to such distinctions.

[4] *The Freethinker*, No. 23, 9 June 1718.

[5] Anthony Ashley Cooper, Third Earl of Shaftesbury, *Characteristics of Men, Manners, Opinions, Times*, ed. Lawrence E. Klein (Cambridge: Cambridge University Press, 1999), 8.

[6] Shaftesbury, *Characteristics*, 4; Anthony Collins, *A Discourse concerning Ridicule and Irony in Writing* (1729), 1.

[7] Shaftesbury, *Characteristics*, 9; Collins, *Discourse concerning Ridicule*, 1; Francis Hutcheson, *Dublin Journal*, No. 12, 19 June 1725, republished in James Arbuckle, *A Collection of Letters and Essays on Several Subjects, Lately Publish'd in the Dublin Journal*, 2 vols. (1729), I, 96; James Beattie, 'An Essay on Laughter and Ludicrous Composition', in *Essays* (Edinburgh, 1776), 324; George Campbell, *The Philosophy of Rhetoric*, 2 vols. (1776), I, 72n.

[8] Edward Young, *Love of Fame, the Universal Passion*, 2nd edn. (1728), A4r–A5v.

[9] Collins, *Discourse concerning Ridicule*, 10–12.

[10] *The Athenian Mercury*, No. 12, 5 September 1691.

Moreover, in that tradition, the moral and cognitive value of ridicule was linked to rhetorical questions: How does the speaker or writer persuade the listener or reader? What was the most effective form of discourse?

These issues were raised in a compact way by Abel Boyer (1667?–1729), the émigré Huguenot journalist, in a characterization of 'modern moralism':

> Some, with a Supercilious Gravity, have magisterially inveigh'd against the Vices of Mankind; whilst others, by the nipping Strokes of a Side-wind Satyr, have endeavour'd to tickle Men out of their Follies. The former have generally been abandon'd to the ill-bred Teachers of Musty Morals in Schools, or to the sowr Pulpit-Orators; whereas the latter have been admitted to the Cabinets of Princes, the Toilets of the Fair Sex, the Conversation of the Polite, and in short, have been Carest and Admir'd by those very People they most abus'd.[11]

Boyer contrasted a grave and magisterial style of discourse with one that was better bred and more suitable for conversation, in short, one that both edified and entertained. Politeness conveyed a style of discourse that combined moral seriousness with lightness and wit, of which ridicule was one instrument. Ridicule was one answer to problems of rhetorical efficacy in a period when publications expanded in quantity and variety, readership widened, and print content was shaped by an urban reference point.

Boyer mapped his rhetorical distinction spatially, contrasting ecclesiastical institutions (the school and the pulpit) with worldly urban settings. Boyer's model was a convenient device of legitimation for writers in the public sphere, whatever their attitude towards the Church. Shaftesbury, among others, did advance polite, gentlemanly, and rhetorically playful discursive modes as a challenge to the dominance of clerical discourse in morals and spiritual welfare. However, the rise of politeness was not necessarily anticlerical. The periodicals of Joseph Addison and Richard Steele were exemplars of the polite approach, articulated in the *Spectator*'s goal of resituating 'Philosophy out of Closets and Libraries, Schools and Colleges, to dwell in Clubs and Assemblies, at Tea-Tables, and in Coffee-Houses'.[12] In their periodicals, Addison and Steele did not challenge the moral authority of clerics, nor did they endorse ridicule unambivalently. Churchmen themselves recognized that changes in the discursive climate were putting pressure on inherited idioms of clerical discourse.

However, the tradition of putting ridicule to use for purposes of moral reform only overlapped in part with the idea that ridicule was a test of truth, the idea ascribed to Shaftesbury. In 1753 Allan Ramsay made an effort to clarify confusion in discussions of ridicule by observing 'that there are two sorts of Ridicule; one of which is employed in discussing propositions, or matters of enquiry; and another, which has manner and actions for its province'.[13] As already suggested, many writers did acknowledge 'the utility

---

[11] Abel Boyer, *The English Theophrastus: or, the Manners of the Age* (1702), A4r.

[12] *The Spectator*, ed. Donald F. Bond, 5 vols. (Oxford: Clarendon Press, 1965), i. 44.

[13] Allan Ramsay, *An Essay on Ridicule* (1753), 6.

of *ridicule* as an instrument of moral culture'.[14] 'Propositions, or matters of enquiry' were a different matter, and Shaftesbury was often taken to have argued that ridicule was a test of truth in this sense. For several decades after Shaftesbury's death, he was assimilated to conflicts between the orthodox and freethinkers. As John Redwood pointed out several decades ago, the main challenge to churchmen in the early eighteenth century was not innovation in philosophy and science but a sceptical and scoffing attitude encapsulated in the term 'ridicule' and embodied, in their view, by freethinkers.[15] Shaftesbury's clerical opponents took him as a freethinker seeking to undermine orthodox doctrines through a rhetoric of ridicule; they responded by insisting on the autonomy of argument. For a number of decades, religion and ridicule constituted a conspicuous controversial binary, though, at the same time, the religious themselves put ridicule to use.

By the middle of the century, the evident security of the Church as well as the passing of the freethinking generations diminished orthodox anxiety about ridicule. However, the interest in ridicule did not disappear. Rather, the topic was transposed from the politics of religion to a new context in which Shaftesbury's influence continued to be felt. It is important to observe that Shaftesbury himself would not have had much time for Ramsay's distinction between 'propositions, or matters of enquiry' and 'manner and actions'. Truth, for Shaftesbury, meant wisdom, which was simultaneously an acknowledgement of certain propositions and an orientation of the self. For Shaftesbury humans were able to achieve wisdom through a mixture of rational, imaginative, affective, and sensory capacities. Such ideas were influential in subsequent thinking about the nature of humans and of their grasp on the world. In the second part of the century, this influence helped to insert ridicule into a discourse about taste and aesthetics, primarily by Scottish writers. Many were churchmen and academics for whom politeness was an adjunct, not an antithesis, to academic inquiry and for whom rhetoric was inseparable from inquiry and understanding.

SHAFTESBURY, RIDICULE AND GRAVITY

While Shaftesbury was the point of departure for this long discussion, his contribution was elusive. Thomas Carlyle confessed in 1829, 'We have oftener than once endeavoured to attach some meaning to that aphorism, vulgarly imputed to Shaftesbury, which however we can find nowhere in his works, that "ridicule is the test of truth" '.[16] By contrast, Benjamin Ibbot, in his 1713–14 Boyle lectures, was certain that Shaftesbury

---

[14] Beattie, 'Essay on Laughter', 425.

[15] John Redwood, *Reason, Ridicule and Religion: The Age of Enlightenment in England 1660–1750* (London: Thames and Hudson, 1976), 12–14.

[16] Thomas Carlyle, review of *Mémoires sur Voltaire*, *Foreign Review* 3 (1829), 419–75, at 431.

'wrote a prophane Book, to prove, that Ridicule is the only infallible test of Truth'.[17] Ibbot cited Shaftesbury's *Sensus Communis* (1709), itself an elaboration of *A Letter concerning Enthusiasm* (1708). In the latter work Shaftesbury did refer to 'the test of ridicule', but neither work simply celebrated ridicule. Both were, rather, compact versions of themes he would continue to elaborate in all the components of *Characteristicks of Men, Manners, Opinions, Times* (1711).

Shaftesbury was a philosophical moralist, with a clear idea of truth. He understood the cosmos as an orderly design which embodied principles of truth, beauty, and goodness. His account of the cosmos was theistic without being specifically Christian. Indeed, since human sociability and moral capacity were built into the cosmos, the fundamental Christian doctrine of future rewards and punishments could be abandoned. This, far more than anything Shaftesbury said about ridicule, was his principal error according to the orthodox.[18] The knowledge of the cosmos was attained, according to Shaftesbury, by a cognitive psychology harnessing reason, imagination, feeling, and sensation. This explains why, for Shaftesbury, the perception of beauty was perhaps the most efficient route to truth: ridicule, meanwhile, sniffed out 'what is deformed' and tested delusion.[19] This also explains why he assigned cognitive value to the categories of 'temper', 'humour', 'sense', and 'taste'. Imagination and affect shaped perception and understanding; delusions arose from distortions of emotion as well as of ideas. For Shaftesbury, 'good humour' was proximate to 'cheerfulness' and extended to such terms as 'wit', 'raillery', and 'ridicule'. His critics found this semantic ranginess tended to evasion.[20]

As a philosophical moralist, Shaftesbury was interested not just in elucidating cosmic truth but also in putting it to work in human life. He identified philosophy with wisdom, the human capacity to live the good life. Since knowledge was both ontological insight and existential orientation, insight was not enough: humans had to be persuaded to lead a life in keeping with the nature of the cosmos. The transformational possibilities of the human self and of society generally could only be realized through the powers of persuasion; thus the tasks of rhetoric overlapped with those of philosophy. Shaftesbury's writings were complex fabrications, moving among genres, deploying dialogic motifs, adopting various voices, and resisting demonstrative closures with irony and jokiness. All this induced puzzlement among critics about his real ambitions and meanings. The most significant response to Shaftesbury was the effort to detach argument itself from all this rhetorical play.

However rhetorically minded, Shaftesbury rejected oratorical models of rhetoric. Like Abel Boyer, he was convinced that authoritative utterance, exhortation, and didacticism were bound to be ineffective: the magisterial style advanced the interests

[17] Benjamin Ibbot, *A Course of Sermons Preach'd for the Lecture Founded by the Honourable Robert Boyle... in the years 1713, and 1714* (1727), 192.

[18] See George Berkeley's critique of Shaftesbury in the third dialogue of *Alciphron* (1732).

[19] Shaftesbury, *Characteristics*, 59.

[20] William Warburton, *The Divine Legation of Moses* (1738), xxxi; Brown, *Essays on the Characteristics*, 7–9, 70.

of the orator at the expense of the listener and failed to encourage the capacity of the individual to exercise judgement and achieve moral autonomy. Wisdom was furthered by conversation, not oratory. The individual needed to engage in inner dialogue, and society had to nourish freedom of exchange. 'Justness of thought and style, refinement in manners, good breeding, and politeness of every kind can come only from the trial and experience of what is best.' Liberty of examination and of exchange, for Shaftesbury, led to an understanding of 'the real temper of things' and were the antidote to human delusions, the figments that individuals imposed on themselves and that authorities imposed on societies. Such liberty included 'the freedom of wit and humour' in the subtitle to *Sensus Communis*, or, as Shaftesbury explained in his *Letter concerning Enthusiasm*, 'wit can never have its liberty where the freedom of raillery is taken away'.[21]

Shaftesbury's commitment to liberty had an obvious political valence since 'liberty' was the watchword of contemporary Whiggism in its arguments against unlimited royal authority and independent ecclesiastical power. He was writing amid fierce partisan controversy, when both Whigs and Tories felt, intensely and correctly, that the future was in the balance. His distinctive contribution to Whiggism was a politics of discourse and culture centring on liberty of exchange.[22] His critique of the orthodox was grounded on an idea of 'priestcraft': the suspicion that the impostures of clerics served a project of material and political arrogation. The orthodox therefore had good reason to see Shaftesbury as an antagonist who found ecclesiastical power dangerous, Christian doctrines delusory, and Christian didacticism ineffective. As against the authority of Monarch and Church, Shaftesbury idealized an enlightened cultural order in which gentlemen, imbued with stoic insight and polite manners, would dominate: he was very much engaged in a 'politics of cultural authority'.[23]

This background helps to explain why Shaftesbury wrote *A Letter concerning Enthusiasm* and not a letter concerning ridicule, Benjamin Ibbot notwithstanding. Shaftesbury was stimulated to write the *Letter* by the appearance in London in 1706 of the French Prophets, Protestant refugees from Louis XIV's campaigns against them in the Cevennes. They brought with them a millennial message that found English followers. The French Prophets generated a huge response, in which critics, Shaftesbury among them, applied long-standing discourses about affective disorders including 'enthusiasm'.[24] Ridicule, for Shaftesbury, was a method for leeching a passion, not contesting a proposition.[25] At the same time, Shaftesbury's cognitive psychology enabled

---

[21] Shaftesbury, *Characteristics*, 12; also *Characteristics*, 31, 33.

[22] Lawrence E. Klein, *Shaftesbury and the Culture of Politeness* (Cambridge: Cambridge University Press, 1994), Part II.

[23] Justin Champion, *Republican Learning: John Toland and the Crisis of Christian Culture, 1696–1722* (Manchester and New York: Manchester University Press, 2003), 12–14.

[24] Hillel Schwartz, *Knaves, Fools, Madmen, and That Subtle Effluvium: A Study of the Opposition to the French Prophets in England, 1706–1714* (Gainesville: University Presses of Florida, 1978), 42; Michael Heyd, *'Be Sober and Reasonable': The Critique of Enthusiasm in the Seventeenth and Early Eighteenth Centuries* (Leiden: E. J. Brill, 1995), 211–40.

[25] Heyd, *'Be Sober and Reasonable'*, 220.

him to build on the complex semantic history of 'enthusiasm', not just as an aspersion for a pathology to which the religious psyche was particularly susceptible but also as an encomium for the capacities that energized the psyche, lifting it towards higher things. Shaftesbury mocked the Prophets (as did some religious writers[26]) but he also embraced proper enthusiasm as a psychic capacity conducing towards cosmic insight. Enthusiasm was a cause of delusion but, as well, a route to truth.

Mary Astell, one of Shaftesbury's first and most percipient critics, had many objections to *A Letter concerning Enthusiasm*, but one of her most salient was what she regarded as a duplicitous attitude towards enthusiasm. To her, the cognitive status assigned by Shaftesbury to imagination and affect constituted an abandonment of reason and argument. She was perhaps the first to identify as an intellectual defect Shaftesbury's conflation of the rhetorical and the philosophical.[27]

For Shaftesbury, undermining errant passions was not the only function of ridicule: it also challenged illegitimate authority. While ridiculing the Prophets, Shaftesbury took advantage of the controversy to attack the religious establishment. Indeed, Shaftesbury was less worried by the French Prophets than he was by the polemical defence of the Anglican Church by its High Church wing, as embodied in figures such as Samuel Parker and Henry Sacheverell (with whom Mary Astell was aligned). Shaftesbury objected to the repressive idiom among some High Church clerics. He argued that persecution was not as effective as ridicule in eliminating pathological enthusiasm: the magistrate could not enforce wisdom, and, if anything, repression was likely to exacerbate enthusiastic passions.[28]

However, Shaftesbury was not just concerned with the persecutorial power of the Church but also with its intimidating cultural style, summed up in the term 'gravity'. As Shaftesbury linked 'ridicule' and 'railery' to 'wit' and 'good humour', he linked 'gravity' to zeal and bad temper, to 'zealot-writers in religious controversy' and their 'provoked rage, ill-will and fury'. Those who claimed that certain 'subjects are too grave' for ridicule sought to limit understanding in two ways. First, gravity was an unappealing form of discourse and, so, was bound for rhetorical failure: 'the world, however it may be taught, will not be tutored'. People were more likely to be drawn towards good judgement if examination was free and pleasant: the instructive had to be rendered agreeably. Indeed, while the 'magisterial' mode of the grave elicited 'reverence and awe', it discouraged active examination: ''Tis of admirable use to keep understandings at a distance and out of reach'.[29]

Second, gravity was potentially a device of delusion and fraud. 'Gravity is of the very essence of imposture' to which 'grimace and tone are mighty helps'. When Shaftesbury invoked ridicule, it was a tool to tease apart the truth of statements from the gravity, or authority, with which they were delivered: ridicule undermined grave imposture.

---

[26]   For instance, Edmund Calamy, *A Caveat against New Prophets* (1708), 38, who noted that 'A Ludicrous Spirit is not likely to be of God'.

[27]   Mary Astell, *Bartl'lemy Fair: Or, an Enquiry after Wit* (1709); David Alvarez, 'Reason and Religious Tolerance: Mary Astell's Critique of Shaftesbury', *Eighteenth-Century Studies* 44 (2011), 475–94.

[28]   Shaftesbury, *Characteristics*, 34–5.   [29]   Shaftesbury, *Characteristics*, 8, 32–5, 68.

Ridiculous ideas fell by the wayside while true ideas withstood the test of ridicule. He saw ridicule not as an abandonment of reason but as its instrument ('For what ridicule can lie against reason?'), capable of sifting out the 'truly serious'. Truth may bear all lights, including 'ridicule itself, or that manner of proof by which we discern whatever is liable to just raillery in any subject'. Thus, Shaftesbury differentiated laughing at everything from finding what is laughable. The truth, including religious truth, was invulnerable: 'provided we treated religion with good manners, we can never use too much good humour, or examine it with too much freedom and familiarity. For, if it be genuine and sincere, it will not only stand the proof, but thrive and gain advantage from hence; it be spurious, or mixed with any imposture, it will be detected and exposed.'[30]

CLERICAL CRITICISMS OF RIDICULE

Shaftesbury's writings belonged to an era of fiercely partisan dispute: he identified Tories as enemies of liberty, and the Church as a Tory institution. He did not live to see the Hanoverian succession and, in consequence, the Whig hegemony. He would have celebrated the post-1714 consolidation of the 1688 Revolution. However, he might have been startled by the success of the effort to bring the Church over to the Whig side. In this context, the discussion of ridicule evolved. It was churchmen, High or Low but largely Whig, and their allies who kept alive the topic of ridicule and a critique of Shaftesbury's claims for it. Edmund Gibson (1669–1748), the bishop of London, was the foremost ecclesiastical agent of the new collaboration of Whiggism and the Church. He also gave thought to the rhetoric of religious persuasion. His *Pastoral Letters*, issued from 1728, were attempts to address ordinary believers with practical divinity rather than sophisticated argument. Here he warned: 'When you meet with any book upon the subject of religion, that is written in a ludicrous or unserious manner, take it for granted that it proceeds from a deprav'd mind, and is written with an irreligious design.' For Gibson, sacred things required a serious cast of mind.[31]

As Brian Young has pointed out, the controversial vitality of the post-1714 period was not fuelled solely by witty freethinkers: clerical culture had not succumbed to somnolence, and clerical writers gave as good as they got.[32] The repressive approach was still endorsed by some clerics.[33] However, by and large, the orthodox supported freedom of debate, drawing on traditions of Protestant thought as well as Revolution Principles. For one, William Warburton (1698–1779) introduced the *Divine Legation of Moses* (1738) with an endorsement of 'Freedom of the Press', asking how 'the generous Advocate of

---

[30] Shaftesbury, *Characteristics*, 8, 17–18, 30, 35, 17–18.
[31] Gibson's initial *Pastoral Letter* (pages 8, 42), quoted in Redwood, *Reason, Ridicule and Religion*, 26.
[32] Brian Young, *Religion and Enlightenment in Eighteenth-Century England: Theological Debate from Locke to Burke* (Oxford: Clarendon Press, 1998), 6.
[33] For instance, by the author of *For God or the Devil, or, Just Chastisement no Persecution* ... (1728).

Religion' could, 'when in earnest convinced of the Strength of Evidence in his Cause, desire an Adversary, whom the Laws had before disarmed; or value a Victory, where the Magistrate must triumph with him?'[34]

Many clerics in the post-1714 period shifted from defending the Church against the Whigs to defending Christian religion against the freethinkers, to whom Shaftesbury was assimilated and assigned a leading role. Freethinkers, such as Matthew Tindal, John Toland, and Anthony Collins, did resort to reason to undermine the persuasiveness of revelation in the name of a fully rational religion. However, they also relied on an array of rhetorical tools, which aggrieved the orthodox. Roger Lund has discussed how the 'philosophic drollery' of Hobbes evolved into a tradition of heterodox wit in which he situates Shaftesbury.[35] Anthony Collins forthrightly associated freethinking with the ridicule of religion: 'the Opinions and Practices of Men in all Matters, and especially in Matters of Religion, are generally so absurd and ridiculous that it is impossible for them not to be the Subjects of Ridicule'.[36] No wonder that the *Independent Whig* (1720), a product of the anticlerical Thomas Gordon (*c*.1691–1750) and a bugbear of the orthodox, devoted a number to 'Priests *afraid of* Ridicule'.[37]

The orthodox were indeed worried about freethinking ridicule, criticized as disrespectful to sacred things, damaging to the prestige and effectiveness of the clergy, and intellectually evasive. As George Berkeley (1685–1753) wrote in the *Guardian*, 'There is not any Instance of Weakness in the *Free-Thinkers* that raises my Indignation more, than their pretending to ridicule Christians, as Men of narrow Understandings, and to pass themselves upon the World for Persons of superior Sense and more enlarged views'.[38] Benjamin Ibbot (1680–1725) was a typical representative of the new alliance of Church and Whig State, and he took on freethinking in defence of orthodoxy in his Boyle lectures of 1713 and 1714. The freethinkers, he said, treat 'the most serious Subjects, in the most light and jocose Manner, in a way of Mirth and Merriment, and represent the gravest things in the most ridiculous dress'. In addition, they attack the clergy, rendering 'the Cause itself of Religion odious and ridiculous' by exposing the defects of its ministers. All of this 'indeed is agreeable to the profess'd Maxims of a great Master and Leader in their own Sect, who affirms, and has wrote a prophane Book, to prove, that Ridicule is the only infallible test of Truth; and that the best way to know what is True, is to try whether it will bear being Ridicul'd'.[39]

Shaftesbury was also very much in the sights of William Warburton, eminent among the orthodox and thoroughly Whig in political orientation. *The Divine Legation of Moses* began with a long dedicatory introduction to 'the Free-Thinkers', with a prominent place given to Shaftesbury. Like Benjamin Ibbot, Warburton criticized the freethinkers'

---

[34] Warburton, *Divine Legation*, I, iii; also, Ibbot, *Course of Sermons*, 179–80, and Brown, *Essays on the Characteristics*, 4.

[35] Lund, *Ridicule, Religion and the Politics of Wit in Augustan England*, 31, 62, 93.

[36] Collins, *Discourse concerning Ridicule*, 19.

[37] Thomas Gordon, *Independent Whig*, 12 October 1720.

[38] *The Guardian*, ed. John Calhoun Stephens (Lexington: University Press of Kentucky, 1982), 263.

[39] Ibbot, *Course of Sermons*, 179–80, 191–2.

anticlericalism: the habit of shifting attention from religion itself to its officiants diverted discussion from 'the Discovery of Truth'. However, for Warburton, the entire pattern of freethinking discourse was averse to truth-seeking. The freethinkers, according to Warburton, offered themselves as 'Petitioners for oppressed and injured Truth', but they did not meet Warburton's norms for this role, which was characterized by 'Seriousness and Gravity', by sincerity and clarity: 'The principal Concern therefore of the Writer, while his Passions are in their natural State, must needs be to deliver and explain his Sentiments and Opinions with all possible Perspicuity'. Indeed, Warburton's critique amounted to the charge that the freethinkers replaced argument with malign forms of rhetoric. Freethinkers chose to ridicule rather than argue: '*Ridicule* is become your favourite Figure of Speech; and your Writers have composed distinct Treatises to vindicate its Use, and manifest its Utility'. Indeed, 'one, in whom your Party most glories, has wrote in Defense of this abusive Way of *Wit and Raillery*, on serious Subjects', namely, Shaftesbury. Irony and buffoonery routinely obscured meaning rather than clarifying it. So did impersonation, another freethinking 'figure of speech'. According to Warburton, such impersonation had no role 'in the Discovery of abstract speculative Truth'. The 'personate Character' 'embroils rather than directs us in the Search of Truth; has a natural Tendency to promote Scepticism; and if not this, yet keeps the Dispute from coming to an Issue'. Of Shaftesbury's assertion that ridicule could not damage truth, Warburton did assent that 'all the Wit in the World can never render it ridiculous'; nonetheless ridicule could distort truth, making it appear to be error, or could disguise it, making it appear to be folly. Thus, the method of ridicule was 'the most Unfair and Pernicious, that a sincere Searcher after Truth can be betrayed into: That its natural Effect is to obscure the Understanding, and to make the Heart dissolute'.[40]

The distinction between argument and rhetoric, deployed by Warburton, figured centrally when John Brown (1715–66) came to treat ridicule in *Essays on the Characteristics* (1751). According to Brown, 'the whole Weight of this Question concerning the Application and Use of *Ridicule*' depended on a rationalist cognitive psychology, alternative to Shaftesbury's, in which feeling and imagination were dependent on 'the superior and leading Faculty of Reason'. These faculties gave rise to the main types of 'literary Composition': poetry, which pleases, was built on imagination; eloquence, which persuades, on passion; and argument, which instructs, on reason. This was not a scheme conducive to the synthesis of instruction and pleasure. Brown assented that ridicule belonged to eloquence; however, 'to Instruction or Inquiry, every Species of Eloquence must for ever be an Enemy'. Shaftesbury's position looked especially vulnerable when he was presented as having argued that ridicule 'may be successfully applied to the *Investigation of unknown Truth*'.[41]

---

[40] Warburton, *Divine Legation*, viii, ix, xi, xviii, xxix–xxxvii. *The Divine Legation* appeared first in 1738, with a second part in 1741 and a fragmentary third part in 1788, posthumously.

[41] Brown, *Essays on the Characteristics*, 15–16, 29, 46, 6.

GENTEEL RIDICULE

Like Shaftesbury, Warburton professed a confidence in liberty of examination but he insisted that serious examination involved argument, directness, and sincerity. Nonetheless, in the introduction to the *Divine Legation*, he educed Francis Hare's *The Difficulties and Discouragements Which Attend the Study of Scripture* (1714) as a specimen of 'beautiful satire' and a 'fine tuned Piece of Raillery', which illustrated 'the Difference between the *Attic* Irony, and Elegance of Wit, and your intemperate Scurrility, and illiberal Banter'.[42] It is a mistake to think that the orthodox simply juxtaposed religion and ridicule: ridicule, it was obvious, could also serve religious ends. One defender of orthodoxy wrote: 'The Opposers of Christianity have not been found the only Masters of Raillery, the Laugh has turn'd against them, and I verily believe, in a little Time, they may come to be the Objects of ridicule, as well as Indignation.'[43] The principal burden of Anthony Collins's *Discourse concerning Ridicule and Irony in Writing* (1729) was precisely to show how frequently orthodox writers had themselves resorted to ridicule:

> Let any Man read the Writings of our most eminent Divines against the *Papists*, *Puritans*, *Dissenters*, and *Hereticks*, and against one another, and particularly the Writings of *Alexander Cook, Hales, Chillingworth, Patrick, Tillotson, Stillingfleet, Burnet, South, Hickes, Sherlock* and *Edwards*, and he will find them to abound with *Banter, Ridicule*, and *Irony*.[44]

The orthodox were themselves caught up in the cultural shift towards politeness, and, while defending the clerical estate, they recognized the utility of the gentlemanly tone. A guide to the way in which polite ridicule and orthodoxy could be reconciled was found in the iconic periodicals of Joseph Addison (1672–1719) and Richard Steele (1672–1729). The essay periodical of the Spectatorial sort was a pillar of polite culture, defining and celebrating a certain normative gentlemanliness. As Boyer suggested, such gentlemanliness assigned an important role to practices of satire and ridicule. After all, the periodicals were built on the Horatian pairing of instruction and delight, as an Addisonian confession suggested: '...were I left to my self, I should rather aim at Instructing than Diverting; but if we will be useful in the World, we must take it as we find it. Authors of professed Severity discourage the looser part of Mankind from having any thing to do with their Writings.'[45] As others also suggested, ridicule might accomplish goals impossible to reach by other discursive means. To that end, Addison claimed to be repurposing ridicule. 'I have new-pointed all the Batteries of Ridicule', he wrote,

---

[42] Warburton, *Divine Legation*, v, vi, x.
[43] 'Richard Hooker', *The Weekly Miscellany*, 2 vols. (1738), i. 377.
[44] Collins, *Discourse concerning Ridicule*, 5.   [45] *Spectator*, ii. 205.

directing it against delusion and vice. 'I have at last shewn how that Weapon may be put to a right use, which has so often fought the Battels of Impiety and Prophaneness.'[46] The periodicals adopted the weapons of wit for the defence of religion and morals.

However, Addison and Steele gave careful consideration to the correct kind and use of ridicule. As distinct from Abel Boyer's view of the sermon and the satire, Addison aimed not to supplant the sermon so much as to supplement it. In the *Guardian*, Addison suggested a division of labour between the clerics and the journalists: 'while they are employed in extirpating Mortal Sins, and Crimes of a higher Nature, I should be glad to rally the World out of Indecencies and Venial Transgressions.'[47] A related distinction was made in the *Tatler*, where Steele pointed out that, while the law targeted real crimes, its capacity to punish moral vice was limited; hence, the periodical took it upon itself 'to find a good Appellation for Offenders, and to turn 'em into Ridicule under feign'd Names.'[48] However, Addison and Steele were cautious in their endorsement of ridicule. Ridicule's efficacy depended on its being linked to good nature and good will.[49] The 'true Art of Raillery' is 'when a Man turns another into Ridicule, and shows at the same time he is in good Humour, and not urg'd on by Malice against the Person he rallies.'[50] However, the periodical writers recognized that ridicule had a propensity to slip into malevolence and contempt. Indeed, one *Spectator* by Addison called ridicule a qualification of 'little ungenerous Tempers',[51] and another, by Steele, suggested that raillery was almost by definition counter to 'good will'.[52]

These periodicals, which embodied the gentlemanly idiom in public discourse, were frequently reprinted and endlessly imitated. In the context of the debate about ridicule, a telling instance was the publication of such a Spectatorial periodical under ecclesiastical auspices. As already indicated, the leading figure, Edmund Gibson, sought to reach ordinary believers through a sincere and accessible rhetoric in his *Pastoral Letters*. He was also at the centre of a network of patronage which positioned him as commissioner for a variety of writings as responses to perceived threats to religion. One of these was *The Weekly Miscellany* produced by William Webster (1689–1758).[53]

Like so many other periodicals, *The Weekly Miscellany* was inspired by the periodicals of Addison and Steele. It shared their goal of purveying literary and ethical knowledge to a general readership while offering a somewhat more explicitly orthodox emphasis. Webster admitted that 'in an Age of so much *Politeness*, and so *improved* a Taste, two such grave Words, as *Religion* and *Morality*, make but an awkward Figure in the Front of a Paper supposed to be written for *Entertainment* as well as *Instruction*'. At the same time, entertainment was not to be abandoned since, as Webster wrote, 'We shall think any Pieces of *inoffensive* Wit and Humour very consistent with our Design ...'.[54]

---

[46] *Spectator*, iv. 65.   [47] *Guardian*, 392.
[48] *The Tatler*, ed. Donald F. Bond, 3 vols. (Oxford: Clarendon Press), i. 421.
[49] *Tatler*, iii. 144–6, 241.   [50] *Tatler*, i. 409.
[51] *Spectator*, ii. 466.   [52] *Spectator*, iii. 582–6.
[53] A recent study of Gibson's publishing operation is Jamie Latham, 'The Clergy and Print in Eighteenth-Century England, c.1714–1750', PhD dissertation, University of Cambridge, 2017.
[54] *Weekly Miscellany*, i. 2–3, 7; see i. 172.

Of course, the handling of wit was a delicate matter: it was a noble faculty that 'requires the strongest Guard of Prudence and Virtue to keep it within it's [*sic*] Bounds, and to it's [*sic*] proper uses'. Thus, the *Weekly Miscellany* took explicit issue with Shaftesbury: 'Ridicule is no test of Truth; and to crack Jokes upon a Thing, can never prove it wants either Beauty or Evidence. The Christian Religion is, and will be, as lovely, certain and beneficial, as if those merry Folks had never wagg'd their Heads, loll'd their Tongues, or shook their Sides at her.' At the same time, the periodical defended ridicule, even against those 'of a settled Persuasion, that *Banter* and *Ridicule* are inconsistent with the *Dignity* of our *Nature*, or the *Gravity of a Serious Design*'. The *Miscellany* endorsed the usefulness of ridicule: 'Some Arguments, though the Subject be grave, are too *absurd* to be expos'd so effectually by a plain Argument, as by *Raillery*. This Way perhaps they may be made ashamed of their Folly, when their Prejudices would be too strong of the clearest *Reasoning* in the strict *argumentative* Form.'[55] Webster assented therefore to the position that argument alone could not answer all arguments: ridicule was more efficient in some cases.

RIDICULE AND THE SCOTTISH ENLIGHTENMENT

In the middle decades of the eighteenth century, the forces that had energized the debate between the orthodox and the freethinkers lost steam. Freethinking tracts and Whig anticlericalism died out, while the Church had become a pillar of the Whig Establishment.[56] Indeed, Shaftesbury and his era now seemed historically distant. While John Brown still thought Shaftesbury worthy of a book-length critique, he conceded that Shaftesbury had operated in a particular and challenging context of 'Bitterness and Rancour' when opponents of 'an unlimited Freedom of the Press, attempted to make a most unnatural and cruel Separation of *Truth* and *Liberty*'. This explained Shaftesburian invective 'against this intolerant Principle'.[57] In a similar vein, Allan Ramsay remarked that, since Shaftesbury's time, religion had become less factionalized and politicized and so ceased to be an eligible target of ridicule: it was no longer 'a tool for the politic and seditious work withal, but a matter entirely of private concern, subject to no jurisdiction, but that of conscience or private opinion...'.[58]

As early as 1743, Mark Akenside implied that the assimilation of ridicule to ideological controversy, notably by divines, was wrong-headed: 'The manner of treating these subjects in the science of human nature should be precisely the same as in natural philosophy; from particular facts to investigate the stated order in which they appear, and then apply the general law, thus discovered, to the explication of other

---

[55] *Weekly Miscellany*, i. 50–1, 210.   [56] Young, *Religion and Enlightenment*, 40–1.
[57] Brown, *Essays on the Characteristics*, 3.   [58] Ramsay, *Essay on Ridicule*, 54–5.

appearances, and the improvement of useful arts.'[59] Thus, the discussion of ridicule gravitated towards an 'enlightened' framework, a science of humanity, especially evident among Scottish writers. In early eighteenth-century England, ridicule had appeared as an aspect of emergent politeness, a worldly idiom that was juxtaposed to the grave and magisterial style of academics. In enlightened Scotland, it was treated in an academic discourse which located ridicule as a feature of human communication, rhetoric, and, more particularly, literary expression.[60] In the universities, the Scots produced a synthesis of the polite and magisterial styles, and they treated ridicule in a discourse, academic and gentlemanly, concerning taste, based on an understanding of the capacities of the human mind. This understanding, though much developed and formalized, still owed a good deal to foundations laid by Shaftesbury and Addison.

An important intermediary in this intellectual development was Francis Hutcheson (1694–1746). When still a teacher in Dublin, Hutcheson had considered ridicule in several essays for the *Dublin Journal*. Though he did not mention ridicule as a test of truth, his reflections on laughter were sympathetic to Shaftesbury's discussion. Hutcheson wrote, for instance, that the true, the good, and the beautiful were impervious to ridicule, and that ridicule was a remedy for enthusiasm and the inflated imagination supporting it. As others had argued, ridicule trumped gravity: lesser vices 'are often more effectually corrected by *Ridicule*, than by grave Admonition. Men have been laughed out of Faults which a Sermon could not reform.'[61]

More significant was Hutcheson's reflection that 'we have a great number of *Perceptions*, which one can scarcely reduce to any of the five Senses, as they are commonly explained; such as the Ideas of *Grandeur, Dignity, Decency, Beauty, Harmony*; on the other hand, of *Meanness, Baseness, Indecency, Deformity...*'.[62] Hutcheson was building on Addison's ideas about the pleasures (and displeasures) of the imagination while also deploying a Shaftesburian notion of internal 'sense' (called here '*Perceptions*'). As indicated earlier, Shaftesbury ascribed cognitive utility to a complex of reason, imagination, feeling, and sensation. He used the word 'sense' to refer to interior dispositions to understand ethical and aesthetic realities. Hutcheson famously took up many of Shaftesbury's ideas, developing and formalizing them over the course of his career in Ireland and then Scotland. In the same year as these essays on laughter and ridicule, he published *An Inquiry into the Original of Our Ideas of Beauty and Virtue* in which he identified the origins of human ethical and aesthetic susceptibilities in internal senses.

When Mark Akenside came to write his own poetic *Pleasures of Imagination*, he developed Addison's ideas, going beyond 'these parts of the subject, which hold chiefly of admiration or naturally warm and interest the mind' to include 'pleasure in observing the tempers and manners of men, even where vicious and absurd' or, in other words, the

---

[59] Mark Akenside, *The Pleasures of Imagination* (1744), 96, n. 75.

[60] Colin Kidd, 'Enlightenment and Ecclesiastical Satire before Burns', in *The Scottish Enlightenment and Literary Culture*, ed. Ronnie Young, Ralph McLean, and Kenneth Simpson (Lewisburg: Bucknell University Press, 2016), 95–114 at 106.

[61] Arbuckle, *Collection of Letters and Essay*, i. 98–105.

[62] Arbuckle, *Collection of Letters and Essay*, i. 88.

pleasure of ridicule.[63] In a Shaftesburian way, Akenside's ridicule was not a merely rational perception of incongruity or dissonance but a passionate response to that perception: 'we have a *natural* sense or feeling of the ridiculous'. Since this sense was given by the Supreme Being, it should hardly have been subject to blanket vilification by the orthodox. In a way that anticipated Ramsay's distinction between the ridicule of propositions and the ridicule of manners, Akenside stated that ridicule 'is not concern'd with meer speculative truth or falshood' but rather with matters suitable for 'approbation or blame'—'actions and passions, good and evil, beauty and deformity'. Thus the question '*whether ridicule be a test of truth*' referred to ridicule's capacity to distinguish false claims on our approbation from the true claims of the just and becoming.[64]

The merging of Shaftesburian 'sense' with Addisonian 'pleasures of imagination' was further developed in Alexander Gerard's *An Essay on Taste* (1759). Gerard (1728–95) explicitly acknowledged a debt to Hutcheson, writing that 'taste consists chiefly in the improvement of those principles, which are commonly called *the powers of the imagination*, and are considered by modern philosophers as *internal* or *reflex senses*...'.[65] Ridicule was among these 'senses' or 'pleasures' along with novelty, sublimity, beauty, imitation, harmony, and virtue. Ridicule, for Gerard, was a sense 'which perceives, and is gratified by the odd, the ridiculous, the humorous, the witty; and whose gratification often produces, and always tends to mirth, laughter, and amusement'. Flushing out 'incongruity', 'inconsistence', and 'dissonance', ridicule was 'useful and agreeable'. The other senses perceived what is truly 'grave and momentous'; ridicule targeted what may present itself as serious but which, because of the presence of some incongruity, is actually ludicrous.[66]

About the time that Gerard's *Essay* appeared, Hugh Blair (1718–1800) began lecturing in Edinburgh on language, rhetoric, and literature, though he did not publish the summative *Lectures on Rhetoric and Belles Lettres* until 1783. The *Lectures* were wide-ranging, but they built on a taxonomy of the pleasures of taste similar to that in Gerard. Gerard had illustrated his discussion of ridicule with examples from Samuel Butler, Joseph Addison, and Jonathan Swift.[67] Blair announced that the 'chief subject' of the *Lectures* was the appreciation of literary eloquence.[68] Ridicule thus appeared as part of 'the province of Comedy', where ridicule targeted 'follies and slighter vices' and other character defects of people, 'which render them troublesome in civil society'. Ridicule was useful 'to polish the manners of men, to promote attention to the proper decorums of social behaviour, and above all, to render vice ridiculous'. Following the old commonplace, Blair wrote: 'Many vices might be more successfully exploded, by employing ridicule against them, than by serious attacks and arguments.' However, Blair, a minister of the Church of Scotland (as was Gerard), was more cautious than Gerard about the reliability of ridicule as a tool: ridicule could range from true wit to mere buffoonery. Moreover,

---

[63] Akenside, *Pleasures*, 4–5, 70.   [64] Akenside, *Pleasures*, 97–101.

[65] Alexander Gerard, *An Essay on Taste* (1759), 2.

[66] Gerard, *Essay*, 66–9.   [67] Gerard, *Essay*, 70–3.

[68] Hugh Blair, *Lectures on Rhetoric and Belles Lettres*, 2 vols. (1783), i. 92–3.

repeating a point made by Warburton, ridicule was liable to mislead: 'For ridicule is far from being, as some have maintained it to be, a proper test of truth. On the contrary, it is apt to mislead, and seduce, by the colours which it throws upon its objects; and it is often more difficult to judge, whether these colours be natural or proper, than it is to distinguish between simple truth and error.'[69]

Henry Home, Lord Kames, was dismissive of the concern, prominent in Warburton and Blair, that ridicule distorted the truth and brought it into disrepute. 'To condemn a talent for ridicule because it may be perverted to wrong purposes, is not a little ridiculous.' Kames stood by the resilience of truth and beauty to ridicule: 'where an object is neither risible nor improper, it lies not open to any quarter to an attack from ridicule'. Thus, he saw no 'harmful consequence' if ridicule was used. His interpretation of the 'celebrated question, Whether ridicule be or be not a test of truth?' was similar to the idea found in Gerard, Akenside, Hutcheson, and Shaftesbury: 'The question stated in accurate terms is, Whether the sense of ridicule be the proper test for distinguishing ridiculous objects from those that are not so?'[70]

CONCLUSION

Allan Ramsay's distinction between ridiculing 'propositions, or matters of enquiry' and ridiculing 'manner and action' did capture a feature of discussions of the relation of ridicule and truth. Though Shaftesbury would not have accepted this distinction, some of his critics certainly did, projecting on him the view that ridicule was a kind of self-subsistent guide to truth. However, in practice, it proved difficult to keep separate the truth of propositions from the truth of manners. Many writers accepted that ridicule had a role in correcting manners, but held that human actions were informed by beliefs: truths of speculation were difficult to segregate from the validity or worthiness of actions. Kames captured this situation when he wrote: 'Were we destitute of this test of truth, I know not what might be the consequences: I see not what rule would be left us to prevent splendid trifles passing for matters of importance, show and form for substance, and superstition or enthusiasm for pure religion.'[71] Ramsay, having begun his essay distinguishing propositions and manners, ended conflating them, in a very Shaftesburian way, by positing 'a more then [sic] accidental connection betwixt the *utile* and the *dulce*': 'in speculative, as well as in active life, *the ways of Wisdom are* really *ways of pleasantness*; and…a true philosopher, that is, a man of candour, sense and knowledge, has a better chance than ordinary of improving the understandings of those with whom he converses, at the very instance that he makes them laugh'.[72]

---

[69] Blair, *Lectures*, ii. 528, 529, 533.   [70] Kames, *Elements*, ii. 55–7.
[71] Kames, *Elements*, ii. 57.   [72] Ramsay, *Essay on Ridicule*, 81–2.

Select Bibliography

Aldridge, Alfred Owen. 'Shaftesbury and the Test of Truth', *PMLA* 60 (1945), 129–56.

Amir, Lydia. *Humor and the Good Life in Modern Philosophy: Shaftesbury, Hamann, Kierkegaard* (Albany: SUNY Press, 2014).

Billig, Michael. *Laughter and Ridicule: Towards a Social Critique of Humour* (London: Sage Publications, 2005).

Carroll, Ross. 'Ridicule, Censorship, and the Regulation of Public Speech: The Case of Shaftesbury', *Modern Intellectual History* 15 (2018), 353–80.

Dickie, Simon. *Cruelty and Laughter: Forgotten Comic Literature and the Unsentimental Eighteenth Century* (Chicago and London: University of Chicago Press, 2011).

Herrick, James A. *The Radical Rhetoric of the English Deists: The Discourse of Skepticism, 1680–1750* (Columbia: University of South Carolina Press, 1997).

Klein, Lawrence E. *Shaftesbury and the Culture of Politeness* (Cambridge: Cambridge University Press, 1994).

Lund, Roger. *Ridicule, Religion and the Politics of Wit in Augustan England* (Farnham and Burlington: Ashgate, 2012).

Pittock, Joan H. 'The Scottish Enlightenment', in *The Cambridge History of Literary Criticism, Volume IV: The Eighteenth Century*, ed. H. B. Nisbet and Claude Rawson (Cambridge: Cambridge University Press, 1997), 546–59.

Redwood, John. *Reason, Ridicule and Religion: The Age of Enlightenment in England 1660–1750* (London: Thames and Hudson, 1976).

Schwartz, Hillel. *Knaves, Fools, Madmen, and That Subtile Effluvium: A Study of the Opposition to the French Prophets in England, 1706–1714* (Gainesville: University Presses of Florida, 1978).

PART VI

SATIRICAL
TRANSITIONS

CHAPTER 35

MORALIZING SATIRE
Cross-Channel Perspectives

JAMES FOWLER

THE popularity of verse satire in Britain during the late seventeenth and early eighteenth centuries is linked with the phenomenon known as 'Augustanism'. During the period 1660–1740, major political upheavals—the Restoration (1660), the Glorious Revolution (1668), indeed the dawn of each new monarch's reign—presented an opportunity for poets to draw flattering (or not-so-flattering) comparisons with the age of Augustus Caesar, conventionally celebrated as one in which 'arms and arts' jointly flourished.[1] But Augustanism was never a narrowly British phenomenon. After all, 'The English of the 1660s, celebrating the coming of their "Augustan age", looked not only to their new Augustus, Charles II, but to a parallel inauguration across the Channel—the personal rule (from 1661) of the Sun King [Louis XIV].'[2] In this context, the returning English court experienced neoclassical French influence 'as a challenge for emulation'.[3] This challenge manifestly continued, for poets, into the latter half of the eighteenth century.

Meanwhile, Augustan-era apologists of verse satire in the tradition of Horace, Juvenal, or Persius revived a range of moral justifications to be found in the texts of Antiquity and the Renaissance. These were, on the whole, couched in terms of the public interest. One familiar, not to say clichéd argument ran along the following lines: if a satirist subjects vice and folly to ridicule, surely this will encourage wise and virtuous conduct in all who read or hear his verse. Such reasoning could be applied in varying ways to Horace, Juvenal, and Persius (and up to a point to Lucilius, who survived only in fragments). But a different, more narrowly focused argument applied to Horace alone. Having fought for

[1] The phrase is used by Dryden in the closing lines of *Astraea Redux* (1660): Dryden, *Poems* (Longman), i. 54.

[2] Jeffrey Barnouw, 'Britain and European Literature and Thought, 1660–1780', in *The Cambridge History of English Literature, 1660–1780*, ed. John Richetti (Cambridge: Cambridge University Press, 2005), 423–44, at 432.

[3] Barnouw, 'Britain and European Literature', 424.

the Republic under Brutus, that poet came to enjoy the long, uninterrupted patronage of Augustus Caesar and his intimate Maecenas. These circumstances suggested the argument: perhaps the general good might be promoted above all by a satirist who succeeds in provoking laughter, not in the many, nor even the few, but in one, supremely powerful man: Caesar himself. For historical reasons, the question did not arise in the case of Persius or Juvenal, writing under Domitian and Nero respectively.

If this argument concerning Horace resonated with seventeenth-century writers, it was doubtless because poets depended, still, on patronage; and the 'happy few' were patronized by kings. Unsurprisingly, the best-known examples (Boileau patronized by Louis, or Dryden by Charles) suggested comparisons with poets writing under Augustus. This having been said, comparisons with Horace were not always flattering. For Horace, evidently, embodied a particular kind of danger as well as a possibility of good. Could a poet 'befriended' by the mighty, and perhaps by a tyrant, be trusted not to make satire serve the ends of panegyric? Would he seek to influence Caesar (or one of his avatars) for the good of all, or for his own, private good? These considerations help to explain why, in the period 1660–1740, French and British satirists used imitation and criticism of Horace to praise or blame, not only the Roman poet but each other. Below, we will trace this phenomenon through three critic-poets (Boileau, Dryden, and Pope). We will then consider aspects of the wider literary and cultural context which informed their writing.

Boileau

Nicolas Boileau-Despréaux is, perhaps, now mainly remembered for his *Art poétique* (1674). But before that poem appeared Boileau was known, above all, for nine satires that had appeared in the 1660s. These poems show the poet self-consciously identifying with Horace as a figure who not only wrote accomplished verse satire, but did so for the good of a nation.[4] As Horace addresses the *princeps* in *Epistle to Augustus*, so Boileau addresses Louis XIV. He does so especially in *Discours au roi*, which he uses to preface his *Satires*.[5] But throughout the collection, Boileau implicitly speaks to the king wherever he engages with policies related to church, aristocracy, and *parlements* as they were constituted under the *ancien régime*.[6] Boileau's identification with Horace, thus

---

[4] Russell Goulbourne considers the influence of Juvenal as well as Horace on Boileau's *Satires*. See his 'Satire in Seventeenth- and Eighteenth-Century France', in *A Companion to Satire Ancient and Modern*, ed. Ruben Quintero (Oxford: Blackwell, 2007), 141–3.

[5] For details of the expanding content of the *Satires* across successive editions, see Nicolas Boileau, *Satires*, ed. Charles-H. Boudhors, 3rd edn. (Paris: Les Belles Lettres, 1966), 173–5. All translations of Boileau's satires (originally written in rhyming Alexandrines) are my own; they will be followed by line-number references based on Boudhors's edition. My translations of other (Alexandrine) verse by Boileau will be based on *Art poétique*, ed. Sylvain Menant (Paris: Flammarion, 1969).

[6] See Gordon Pocock, *Boileau and the Nature of Neo-classicism* (Cambridge: Cambridge University Press, 1980), 39.

understood, emerges most clearly, however, in the prefatory *Discours au roi*, which shows that 'aesthetic judgements are always implicated in relations of power'.[7]

DISCOURS AU ROI

The title *Discours au roi* may predispose readers to expect a panegyric to Louis. Moreover, any such expectation is likely to be reinforced by the first four lines:

> Young valiant hero, whose sublime wisdom
> Is no tardy fruit of slow old age,
> And who alone – with no minister – like the gods
> Carry all unaided, see all with your own eyes.

> (ll. 1–4)

However, readers acquainted with Horace's *Epistle to Augustus* will hear an echo of that poem's opening:

> Cum tot sustineas et tanta negotia solus,
> res Italas armis tuteris, moribus ornes,
> legibus emendes, in publica commoda peccem,
> si longo sermone morer tua tempora, Caesar.

> (ll. 1–4)[8]

By alluding to Horace in this way, Boileau invites his readers to interpret his own poem according to certain conventions associated with satire, understood not only as 'satura' but also as 'sermo'. For in the seventeenth century (as in Antiquity), readers did not sharply distinguish between satires and epistles; indeed, both could be referred to, in Horace's time, by the Latin term 'sermones'. Friedrich Klingner describes the culture of the *sermo* as one of 'complete discretion; a discretion that prefers allusions and playful pretence to direct statements'.[9]

In *Epistle to Augustus*, 'Horace' uses somewhat circular logic to explain that he sees one insuperable impediment to his praising the *princeps*: his Muse is a satiric, not a panegyric one. This being the case, panegyric, from his pen, would blemish rather than enhance Caesar's reputation (ll. 257–9). In *Discours au roi*, Boileau gives a new twist to

---

[7] See Michael Moriarty, 'Satire and Power in Seventeenth-Century France: The Case of Boileau', *Forum for Modern Language Studies* 30 (1994), 293–304 (304).

[8] See *Horace: Satires, Epistles and Ars Poetica*, ed. and trans. H. Rushton Fairclough (Cambridge, MA: Harvard University Press, 2005; originally published 1926), 396. All references to Horace will be to this edition, in which English translations are provided opposite the Latin original.

[9] Friedrich Klingner, 'Horace's Letter to Augustus', in *Horace: Satires and Epistles*, ed. Kirk Freudenburg (Oxford: Oxford University Press, 2009), 335–59 (338).

this argument: like Horace, he offers no praise to his patron in the here and now, but, unlike Horace, he holds out the possibility of praise in the future:

> I, who scarcely know Phœbus and his delights,
> I, but lately weaned on the nine sisters' Hill,
> Whilst waiting for age to mature my muse,
> I exercise and divert her on lesser subjects.
>
> (ll. 63–6)

The *Discours au roi* recalls Horace's *Epistle* in another respect: the poet emphasizes that, by contrast with the panegyrist, the satirist concerns himself with matters so trivial that he and the monarch effectively occupy two separate realms (Parnassus and 'the world'). This is implicit in the lines from Horace, quoted above, where the poet suggests he would be culpable if he distracted Caesar from affairs of state. In Boileau's poem, the satirist wields his pen to 'scold' vice wherever he finds it. By contrast, the king is active in a realm where, Jupiter-like, he wields thunderbolts and dispenses justice through fear:

> Whilst your [mighty] arm, feared by all nations,
> Armed with thunder, restores justice to the world,
> And causes evil men to cower in fear of wrath,
> I, with pen in hand, scold this vice and that.
>
> (ll. 67–70)

But the poet subsequently exposes the 'separate realms' motif as an illusion. The satirist will never be left to his own devices as long as any power remains in the hands of the vicious. For the simple fact that he 'calls a spade a spade' and 'dares to laugh' antagonizes such individuals:

> And here's the rub: my frivolous, rhyming muse
> Calls a spade a spade, and cannot hold her tongue.
> This is what frightens the wits of our day,
> Who, white without, are black as black within. [...]
> All these folk, who panic at the very word 'satire',
> Hasten to pursue whoever dares to laugh.
>
> (ll. 83–90)[10]

Boileau cultivates an ambiguity in the final line of the extract above. For the verb 'faire le procès à' can be taken in either a literal sense ('pursue though the courts'), or a metaphorical one ('attack', 'criticize', perhaps on literary grounds). In this Boileau is doubtless indebted, once again, to Horace, but this time to *Satires* 2.1. In that poem, an ambiguity is introduced by the poet's complaint that, according to his critics, his satires are 'ultra legem'

---

[10] Boileau's contemporaries perhaps heard an echo here of the oft-quoted question: 'quamquam ridentem dicere verum / quid vetat?' (Horace, *Satires* 1.1, ll. 24–5).

('beyond lawful bounds'). But the phrase is ambiguous; it may imply a crime against the laws of Parnassus or those of Rome. As Jeffrey Tatum explains, Horace exploits this double meaning to suggest that 'the spheres and sensibilities of the jurist and the poet' are not in fact clearly distinct.[11] Indeed, the phrase 'ultra legem' points to a conflict which can only be resolved by recourse to a justice (that of Caesar) which transcends the laws of jurists and poets alike.

Boileau uses the ambiguous verb 'faire le procès' to similar effect. Given his tendency to pursue truth through laughter, the satirist is always pursued in turn by 'les esprits de ce temps'; but before what tribunal? Does the world allow Parnassus its own, separate 'court'? The question leads to the *cause célèbre* of Molière:

> Their heart, which knows itself, and [therefore] flees the light,
> Whilst scorning God (Almighty), fears Tartuffe and Molière.
>
> (ll. 101–2)

These lines evoke the king's response to Molière's satirical comedy *Le Tartuffe*. For, having watched a first, three-act version of the play, performed at Versailles in May 1664, Louis declared it could not be performed in public. Contemporary readers were in a position to make the following application: rather than ban *Tartuffe*, the king could have dispensed the kind of higher justice which, in Horace's *Epistle to Augustus*, the poet counts on receiving from Caesar. Then, perhaps, Boileau's Muse could have 'matured' into panegyric (as hinted in ll. 63–6, cited above). But if the poet writes panegyric regardless, he and the prince may fulfil the joint destiny evoked by Horace at the end of *Epistle to Augustus*: brief ridicule, followed by eternal oblivion. After all, according to Horace's poem, bad panegyric, like all inferior writing, will serve at best as wrapping for sundry merchants' wares (ll. 264–70).

Thus in *Discours au roi* Boileau adapts the 'playful and discreet' *sermo* to Louis XIV's France. The conventions of *sermo* are forgiving or flexible enough to allow Boileau to insert the following declaration of poetic independence:

> And however great your sovereign power,
> If my heart did not command my hand as I write these lines,
> Neither hope of gain, nor reason, nor proverbial wisdom
> Could force a praising rhyme from me to you.
>
> (ll. 111–14)

Boileau retreats from this position somewhat in subsequent lines (ll. 115–34). But the (Parnassian) conventions of the *sermo* entail that this poem should not be read as a dialectical argument moving irreversibly 'forwards'; the echoes of the poet's proud independence are audible, still, through the ritual kowtowing and self-mockery. Boileau has learned this art from Horace.

---

[11] See Jeffrey Tatum, '*Ultra Legem*: Law and Literature in Horace, *Satires* 2.1', in *Horace: Satires and Epistles*, ed. Freudenburg, 231–44, at 234.

'Pension'd Boileau'

The 1668 edition of Boileau's *Satires* is prefaced by *Discours au roi* and concluded by *Satires* IX, plus the *Discours sur la Satire* (written in prose). In *Satire* IX, Boileau addresses the question of patronage. In doing so, he imitates Horace, *Satires* 2.1. But whilst Horace had created a dialogue between the poet and a jurist (Trebatius), Boileau has the poet debate satire with his own mind. At one point, this 'mind' advises the abandonment of satire for panegyric, for the sake of profit and self-advancement:

> Thus, finding profit in your flights of fancy,
> You would see your verse bear fruit each year;
> And, moved by the hope of gain, your muse
> Would sell an ounce of smoke for its weight in gold.
>
> (ll. 32–5)[12]

This suggestion is clearly as ludicrous as it is contemptibly mercenary; for what is the 'weight in gold' of an ounce of 'smoke'? (Here, 'smoke', or incense, serves as a metaphor for praise.) The poet's principled riposte serves to warn Louis, as in the *Discours au roi*, that panegyric that is purchased without being earned will end in ridicule:

> An insipid poem that flatters without wit
> Dishonours hero and author alike.
>
> (ll. 49–50)

However, Boileau's material relations to the court and the king changed radically in 1674. In that year he published a new edition of his *Œuvres* containing his existing nine *Satires* and *L'Art poétique*, plus *Le Lutrin* (Cantos I–IV), several verse epistles, and a translation and commentary of Longinus. He also began to receive royal patronage. In *L'Art poétique*, without a trace of irony, the poet presents his new, 'pensioned' status as superior to that of writers who depend on remuneration by bookseller-printers. In the passage below, the poet refers to money received from a patron as 'un tribut légitime' (a legitimate tribute). By contrast, any writer paid by a bookseller (*un libraire*) might as well be forcing Apollo to work for wages:

> Labour for glory, and let sordid profit
> Never be the aim of an illustrious writer.
> I know a noble mind can, without shame or crime,
> Derive a legitimate tribute from his work;
> But I cannot bear those famous authors
> Who, replete with glory but hungry for money,

---

[12] Cf. Horace, *Satires* 2.1, ll. 10–12.

Apprentice their Apollo to the bookseller,
And of a divine art make a mercenary trade.

(IV, ll. 125–33)

From this point on, whilst Boileau still writes poems to Louis in which he blends praise with subtle irony, he also engages in 'straight' panegyric, especially in odes and war poems. One of these in particular may seem to fulfil Horace's warning to Augustus, or his own to Louis, that bad panegyric serves only to ridicule its object. The poem in question is the *Ode sur la prise de Namur* (1693). Whilst in *Discours au roi* the comparison of Louis with Jupiter is compensated by the poem's ambient irony, in *Ode sur la prise de Namur* the line 'C'est Jupiter en personne' ("'Tis Jupiter himself'; l. 49) is unrelieved by humour of any sort. That this *Ode* invited ridicule was not missed by British poets including Matthew Prior, who in 1695 (when Namur had been retaken from the French) published *An English Ballad. On the Taking of Namur, by the King of Great Britain, 1695*. Boileau's original was printed opposite the English parody, to excellent effect.

Yet Boileau's panegyrics and war poems did not suffice to extinguish his reputation in England, supported as it was by poems written in the 1660s and the early 1670s. Indeed, 'Amongst the major figures of the time, only Swift, Defoe and Thomson are virtually silent on Boileau.'[13] To give a fuller impression of Boileau's influence in Britain, it would be necessary to say more concerning *Le Lutrin* and the *Art poétique* in particular. The former, mock-epic poem (whose Golden Age 'source' was Virgil) had great resonance, especially during the religious strife of the Stuart years; we will return to this point below, in our discussion of Dryden.[14] As for Boileau's (Horatian) *Art poétique*, it inspired or provoked many literary responses, including Roscommon's *Essay on Translated Verse* (1681), Mulgrave's *Essay upon Poetry* (1682), and George Granville, Lord Lansdowne's *Essay upon Unnatural Flights in Poetry* (c.1700). The latter is hostile to 'foreign' influence in general; but of course, such emphatic resistance to Boileau and the French also attests to their importance, experienced in 'anxious' mode.[15]

DRYDEN

It would be foolhardy to deny Dryden's seminal *Discourse concerning Satire* (1695) a place in any discussion of Augustan verse satire. It belongs here specifically because it shows Dryden situating his own satires not only in relation to ancient precedents including Horace, but also vis-à-vis modern 'rivals' including Boileau. Dryden was anticipated by the Earl of Orrery in writing a play 'on the French model' to please the newly restored

[13] A. F. B. Clark, *Boileau and the French Classical Critics in England (1660–1830)* (Geneva: Slakine Reprints, 1978; originally published 1925), 36.

[14] Clark, *Boileau and the French Classical Critics*, 13.

[15] See Nicolas Boileau, *Art poétique*, ed. D. Nichol Smith (Cambridge: Cambridge University Press, 1919), xxvi–xxviii.

Charles II.[16] But he soon came to dominate Restoration emulation of the French. As a playwright and critic, he maintained a balanced, heuristic approach to French neoclassicism and, in particular, the Quarrel of the Ancients and Moderns: witness his famous dialogue, *Essay of Dramatic Poesy* (1668). But as a verse satirist, Dryden was (and is) seen as being more straightforwardly indebted to Boileau. *Le Lutrin* is often said to have inspired Dryden's mock-epics (*MacFlecknoe, Absalom and Achitophel*, and *The Medall*), which were printed in the 1680s, under the reign of Charles II. The poet's career, on which, as Steven Zwicker states, 'the forces of patronage, partisanship and print culture' converged, reflects the political upheavals of his age.[17] Towards the end of the 1690s, now in 'inner exile' (no longer laureate, and a Roman Catholic writing under a Protestant king), Dryden re-engaged with the ancients through translations and commentaries. The *Discourse concerning Satire*, though written in prose, is reminiscent of a Horatian *sermo*, in that it uses allusion to draw the reader into a game of displacements and substitutions. Commenting on Dryden's mature style, Zwicker claims that 'no one—not Milton or Marvell, not Browne or Burton, not even Clarendon—could touch the subtlety, the mastery and the ironies of Dryden's prose'.[18] These qualities are exemplified in the *Discourse*, where Dryden uses a range of figures, but especially Boileau and Horace, in order to reflect critically on his own relation to Latin and French satire.

Dryden's *Discourse concerning Satire* performs many functions. It serves as a preface to new translations of Juvenal and Persius; it is a tribute to the Earl of Dorset, Dryden's current patron; it offers a 'description' of satire, with a prescriptive edge; it compares existing scholarship on Horace, Juvenal, and Persius, and proposes a new, comparative account. Woven through the entire text, however, is the key notion that 'satire is of the nature of moral philosophy, as being instructive'.[19] Whether he is describing satire in general or commenting on particular poets, be they ancient or modern, Dryden distinguishes between mastery of verse and the use of satire for the public good. His comparison of Horace and Juvenal is particularly revealing in this connection. As far as verse is concerned, 'the victory is already on the side of Horace'.[20] But Juvenal is the greater poet 'in satire', for the following reasons: 'his thoughts are sharper; his indignation against vice is more vehement; his spirit has more of the commonwealth genius; he treats tyranny, and all the vices attending it, as they deserve, with the utmost rigour'. Juvenal, it seems, writes for the public good. By contrast, Horace is 'a Temporizing Poet, a well-mannered Court Slave, and a Man who is [...] ever decent, because he is naturally servile'.[21] According to this account, the moral failings which tarnish Horace's performance as satirist resemble failings in his patron Augustus. For, the author argues, if the *princeps* revived a law against 'lampoons and satires', it was not for the public good but to prevent mention of the bloody crimes that had marked his ascent to power.[22] Horace availed himself of this same law to kill 'two crows [with] one stone'; for it served him as a pretext

---

[16] See Barnouw, 'Britain and European Literature', 425.

[17] See Steven N. Zwicker, 'Dryden and the Poetic Career', in *The Cambridge History of English Literature, 1660–1780*, ed. Richetti, 132–59, at 132.

[18] Zwicker, 'Dryden and the Poetic Career', 155.   [19] Dryden, 'Discourse', 55.

[20] Dryden, 'Discourse', 58.   [21] Dryden, 'Discourse', 65.   [22] Dryden, 'Discourse', 67.

under which to attack his foe Cassius Severus. As portrayed here, Augustus and Horace do not pursue any common goal, but two convergent sets of (selfish) interests.

It goes without saying that Dryden's discussion of the ancients has ramifications for his discussion of the moderns. His initial mention of Boileau in *A Discourse* precedes his account of Horace and Augustus, and is seemingly complimentary: 'I might find in France a living Horace and a Juvenal, in the person of the admirable Boileau'. Next, Dryden salutes the role played in Boileau's career by Louis XIV, who, as 'the patron of all arts, is not much inferior to that of an Augustus Caesar'.[23] But this Augustan 'compliment' to the French poet and his prince is undercut by two ironies. One can be detected on first reading: in praising Louis, 'Dryden had before him the extreme example of King William [III], who was fixated on military adventures and entirely uninterested in intellectual or artistic pursuits'.[24] The other is no less effective, but is 'retroactive': when the reader reaches the passage examined above, in which the motives of Horace and Augustus are exposed as self-seeking, the joint 'compliment' to Boileau and Louis is revealed to be a mixed blessing, or no blessing at all. Through this game of echoes, Dryden makes a general case against the 'insider satirist'. The question then arises: what are the ramifications for Dryden himself, since he depends on patronage no less than Horace or Boileau?

Dryden provides elements of an answer, but the task of identifying and correlating these falls to the reader. Boileau is mentioned once again towards the end of the *Discourse*, when Dryden dwells on the way in which the moderns have improved on the satire of the ancients. Tassone and Boileau are saluted, the former for inventing and the latter for polishing mock-epic; Boileau's nearest English equivalent is Dorset, unrivalled master of 'fine raillery'.[25] Dorset's satiric technique is famously compared with that of the executioner Jack Ketch, whose wife boasted that he alone could 'make a malefactor die sweetly'. As for himself, Dryden claims only to have achieved the 'Jack Ketch' stroke once in his career, in *Absalom and Achitophel*. In that poem, he had used biblical references to portray the events of the so-called Popish plot in mock-epic vein. Dryden congratulates himself on one passage only: 'The character of Zimri [Buckingham] in my *Absalom* is, in my opinion, worth the whole poem; 'tis not bloody, but 'tis ridiculous enough.'[26] This is surely to suggest that elsewhere in the poem, there may be other portraits that are, in fact, bloody. Dryden's contemporaries would not strain for an example. For the poet depicts the 1st Earl of Shaftesbury as 'Achitophel', manoeuvring against the royal line as though he were (Milton's) Satan himself. Seventeenth-century readers were further able to reflect that this portrait of Shaftesbury might have encouraged the spilling of real blood, for its appearance was timed 'with the express intention of prejudicing Shaftesbury's trial', which it nevertheless failed to do.[27]

These closing pages add a new resonance to Dryden's earlier reflections on poets and their patrons in Rome, France, and England. The allusion to Horace and Augustus raises

---

[23] Dryden, 'Discourse', 12.

[24] James Anderson Winn, *John Dryden and his World* (New Haven: Yale University Press, 1987), 459.

[25] Dryden, 'Discourse', 70.   [26] Dryden, 'Discourse', 71.

[27] See John Dryden, *'Absalom and Achitophel' and Other Poems*, ed. Philip Roberts (London: Collins, 1973), 121.

the question: in 'executing' (his portrait of) Shaftesbury, had Dryden, like Horace long before, slavishly followed the lead of a prince who was 'not altogether so good as he was wise'?[28] The allusion to Louis and Boileau suggests that Dryden could have achieved greater feats in poetry than 'bloodily' attacking this Whig or that poetaster, had Charles resembled Louis. But 'being encouraged only with fair words by King Charles II, my little salary ill paid, and no prospect of a future subsistence, I was then discouraged in the beginning of my attempt [to write an epic poem]; and now old age has overtaken me'.[29] In this haunting piece, Dryden has bequeathed to his successors the most eloquent 'Augustan' account of verse satire in Rome, France, and Britain; but it is shrouded in *fin-de-siècle* (and dusk-of-life) regrets. Augustan verse that depends on patronage cannot be 'of the nature of moral philosophy'; be it panegyrical or satirical, it is corrupted at source.

POPE

The story of Pope's response to Boileau begins early in his writing career. In 1704, Lintot printed J. Ozell's translation of Charles Perrault's 'Les Hommes illustres qui ont paru en France pendant ce siècle' (1697). (Perrault, it will be recalled, was Boileau's antagonist in the *querelle des anciens et des modernes*.) There followed a translation, again by Ozell, of Boileau's *Le Lutrin*; this contained criticism of Boileau, and also of the Restoration poet and dramatist Wycherley.[30] Pope was roused to write *Epigram. Occasion'd by Ozell's Translation of Boileau's Lutrin* (1708; published 1727). For a poet barely twenty years old, indeed any poet, Pope's use of prosody for satirical ends is already impressive. In the extract below, Ozell, reduced to 'he', is barely able to carry the weight of a final stress; moreover, deprived of an end-stop, he becomes the puny syllable from which a heavy enjambment is precariously suspended. This serves to present Pope's target as visibly and audibly unequal to that with which 'he' is made to rhyme: the trisyllabic, safely end-stopped 'Wycherley':

> Reviving *Perault* [*sic*], murdr'ing *Boileau*, he
> Slander'd the Ancients first, then *Wycherley*.[31]

By implication, the *Lutrin* deserved a better translator-commentator than Ozell; by implication, too, Boileau had been right to champion the ancients, and Perrault just as wrong to champion the moderns.

However, in *An Essay on Criticism* (1711), Pope sounds a different note. In the extract below, the poet distances himself from both sides of the *querelle des anciens et des modernes*:

---

[28] Dryden, 'Discourse', 77.   [29] Dryden, 'Discourse', 23.

[30] On the warm friendship between the young Pope and an ageing Wycherley, see Pat Rogers, *The Alexander Pope Encyclopedia* (Westport: Greenwood Press, 2004), 338.

[31] Pope, *Poems* (Twickenham), vi. 37.

> Some *foreign* Writers, some our *own* despise;
> The *Ancients* only, or the *Moderns* prize:
> (Thus *Wit*, like *Faith*, by each Man is apply'd
> To *one small Sect*, and All are *damn'd beside*.)[32]

In these lines, the poet's attack on literary sects (foreign versus British, ancients versus moderns) damns Boileau and Perrault equally. Boileau is subsequently singled out for further criticism:

> But *Critic Learning* flourish'd most in *France*.
> The *Rules*, a Nation born to serve, obeys,
> And *Boileau* still in Right of *Horace* sways.[33]

Here, the association of the French poet with dull 'Critic-Learning' and the rule-bound behaviour of a servile nation is, of course, unflattering. Robin Sowerby finds these lines 'unduly sharp' because of the *Essay*'s debt to Boileau's *Art poétique*.[34] But this is to measure Pope's verse against a gentlemanly ideal of literary attribution which he had no strong reason to embrace. The young English poet's dig at Boileau, made even whilst he borrows from him, reflects the values of the turn-of-the-century Augustan milieu to which he aspired. He had been admitted early to Augustan-poetic circles; William Walsh was a particular mentor (see *An Essay on Criticism*, ll. 729–36). In a letter predating the *Epigram* on Ozell, the younger poet asks Walsh, concerning Virgil especially: 'how far the liberty of *Borrowing* may extend?' His mentor replies, 'the best of the modern Poets in all Languages, are those that have the nearest copied the Ancients'.[35] The tenor of this advice suggests that for Walsh and his peers, 'borrowing' and 'copying' can bring prestige, but are not without danger; and it is safer to copy the ancients than the moderns. In these extracts, Walsh and Pope echo Augustan anxieties related to indebtedness, be it termed 'borrowing', 'copying', or 'imitation'. Samuel Johnson suggests that, in choosing to have references to relatively ancient (Greek) rather than modern (French) scholarship attached to his translations of Homer, Pope failed to resist the principle: 'no man loves to be indebted to his contemporaries'.[36]

This context helps us to understand Pope's shifting attitude to Boileau, as expressed in his verse. For Walsh and his peers, the French poet had long represented a modern standard to be equalled or surpassed by the British. Pope cannot have doubted that the very poems which he would use to announce his 'arrival' on the literary scene—*An Essay on Criticism* (1711) and *The Rape of the Lock* (1712)—would be compared with Boileau's *Art poétique* and *Le Lutrin* respectively. As far as *An Essay on Criticism* was concerned,

---

[32] Pope, *Poems* (Twickenham), i. 285.   [33] Pope, *Poems* (Twickenham), i. 322–3.

[34] Robin Sowerby, 'Pope and Horace', in *Horace Made New: Horatian Influences on British Writing from the Renaissance to the Twentieth Century*, ed. Charles Martindale and David Hopkins (Cambridge: Cambridge University Press, 1993), 159–83, at 161.

[35] Pope, *Corr.* (Sherburn), i. 19, 20.

[36] Samuel Johnson, *Lives of the English Poets*, 3 vols. (Dublin, 1780), ii. 300–1.

the question would inevitably arise: to what extent had Pope drawn on Horace's *Ars poetica*, and to what extent on Boileau's *Art poétique*? Pope's own notes as recorded in the Twickenham text emphasize his debts, above all, to Quintilian among the ancients.[37] Any concerns felt by Pope on that score were soon justified. In a review of *An Essay on Criticism* that appeared in *The Spectator*, Joseph Addison insinuates, even whilst praising Pope, that he was indebted to Boileau: 'And here give me leave to mention what Monsieur Boileau has so very well enlarged upon in the preface to his works, that wit and fine writing do not consist so much in advancing things that are new, as in giving things that are known an agreeable turn.'[38] Addison's 'compliment' to Pope (that he gives an agreeable turn to others' thoughts) is superbly back-handed. This is especially clear for any reader who recalls Pope's couplet: 'True Wit is Nature to advantage dress'd / What oft was thought, but ne'er so well expres'd'.[39] For (prompted by Addison's remark) such a reader might reflect that Pope's wit 'dresses', not what 'oft was thought', but what Boileau, in particular, had thought.

We can observe Pope increasingly taking distance from Boileau in *Imitations of Horace*, written in the 1730s. In 1733, Lady Wortley Montagu and Lord Hervey attacked Pope in a satire entitled *Verses addressed to the Imitator of the First Satire of the Second Book of Horace*. Pope responded defiantly, by writing more *Imitations*. (He had the Latin poems and his own versions printed on facing pages, so that readers could more easily admire his mastery of the form.) The poems by Horace which Pope chose to imitate include *Satires* 2.1 and *Epistles* 2.1. Since we have already examined Boileau's debt to these specific poems, we will focus on Pope's versions of the same 'originals'. This approach will allow us to show how the English poet subtly negotiates his relation to Boileau, as a rival Augustan poet and imitator of Horace.

The First Satire of the Second Book of Horace Imitated

We have already seen that Horace, *Satires* 2.1 assumes the form of a dialogue, in which the poet discusses his satires with Trebatius. In Pope's version, the voice of Trebatius is replaced by that of 'F.', standing for William Fortescue, 'a court insider and confidant of Walpole'.[40] Meanwhile, the poet's voice in the dialogue becomes that of 'Pope' ('P.'). But Horace's *Satires* 2.1 invites further key substitutions, notably for Lucilius, traditionally seen as the founder of Roman verse satire of the more polished kind. In *Satires* 2.1, Horace uses Lucilius to suggest that a satirist with powerful friends (Laelius and Scipio) can attack vice without exposing himself to serious danger (ll. 62–5). When we compare this with the corresponding passage in Pope's *Imitation* (an easy

---

[37] This can be ascertained rapidly by consulting the footnotes marked '[P]' in *The Poems of Alexander Pope*, ed. John Butt.

[38] *Spectator*, ii. 485–6 (no. 253). The original passage is to be found in Boileau's prose preface: see *Satires*, ed. Boudhors, 4.

[39] Pope, *Poems* (Twickenham), i. 272–3.

[40] See Paul Baines, *The Complete Critical Guide to Alexander Pope* (London: Routledge, 2000), 120.

task for the eighteenth-century reader, given the dual-text presentation), we find that Lucilius has been replaced by Boileau and Dryden. Boileau comes first:

> Could pension'd *Boileau* lash in honest Strain
> Flatt'rers and Bigots ev'n in *Louis'* Reign?[41]

In Horace's 'original', there is no hint that Lucilius lacked courage or probity. Pope's version, however, hints that Boileau lacked both. Yet on a first reading we might only hear praise for the French poet. After all, Pope writes that he '[lashes] in honest strain', which suggests probity; and the fact that he did so 'ev'n' in the reign of Louis, an absolute monarch, might be thought to emphasize his courage. But on reflection, we notice that the word 'pension'd' jars with 'honest', suggesting that, precisely because Boileau was 'pension'd', and therefore dependent on, and protected by, the king, he would surely only choose victims to whom Louis was hostile or indifferent. This is scarcely conducive to '[lashing] in honest strain'. The attack on Boileau has ramifications for the question concerning Dryden which fills out the next couplet:

> Could Laureate *Dryden* Pimp and Fry'r engage,
> Yet neither *Charles* nor *James* be in a Rage?

If we have read the question on Boileau ironically, then we are likely to answer: yes, Dryden could engage 'Pimp and Fry'r' without enraging the Stuarts; but this involves neither courage nor probity, since, as 'Laureate Dryden', he surely chose victims to whom his royal masters were (at best) indifferent. The third and final question in this sequence concerns Pope:

> And I not strip the Gilding off a Knave,
> Un-plac'd, un-pension'd, no Man's Heir, or Slave?[42]

This question, at least, seems to elicit an unqualified 'yes'. Here, Pope's contemporaries would catch an allusion to the fact that the poet, ensconced at Twickenham, has earned enough money, from the printing and sales of his Homer translations, to be free from mercenary motives. By implication, he lacks the constraints attached to patronage, and so can indeed 'lash in honest strain'.

Like one of Pope's despised critics preserved 'in amber' (*Epistle to Arbuthnot*, l. 169), 'pension'd Boileau' remains sempiternally on display in the lines quoted above. Across a space of more than fifty years, they smack of a riposte on Pope's part to Boileau's defence of royal patronage in the *Art poétique*. We have already quoted the lines in question; but it is worth repeating them here (this time in the original French), so that we can imagine the reaction of the 'un-placed, un-pension'd' Pope to Boileau's scorn of money gained in the literary marketplace, where renowned authors, he claims, 'Mettent leur Apollon aux

---

[41] Pope, *Poems* (Twickenham), iv. 15.   [42] Pope, *Poems* (Twickenham), iv. 16.

gages d'un libraire, / Et font d'un art divin un métier mercenaire' (*Art poétique*, IV, ll. 125–33). Pope's lifelong scorn for the 'scribblers' of Grub Street, expressed especially in the *Dunciad*, may seem to converge with Boileau's contempt for the book trade; but the English poet insists that *he* represents a new ideal, which transcends both Grub Street 'scribbling' and the 'pension'd' servility of court poets.

To Augustus

Pope resumes his attack on Boileau in the fifth of his *Imitations of Horace*, entitled *To Augustus*. The fact that George II was also named Augustus was a gift to Pope, who wittily juxtaposes passages where Horace praises Caesar with lines that damn George. Hence, for instance, Pope laments that he cannot 'mount on Mæonian wing, / Your Arms, your Actions, your Repose to sing!', where 'repose' suggest that the king's inaction prevents the poet from writing Virgilian panegyric.[43]

Once again, the dual-text presentation allows the reader to admire Pope's ingenuity; and once again, Boileau and French influence are attacked. The anti-French motif is worked into Pope's consideration of poetry as a force capable of working for the good of the state (or the public good). Pope invites George to ponder this topic in the following lines:

> Of little use the Man you may suppose,
> Who says in verse what others say in prose;
> Yet let me show, a Poet's of some weight,
> And (tho' no Soldier) useful to the State.[44]

In the course of his demonstration of this point, Pope contrasts Dryden with Swift to form examples of what can be achieved by the dependent and independent satirist respectively. 'Unhappy Dryden' wrote 'to please a lewd, or un-believing Court', while Swift deserves to have as his epigraph 'The Rights a Court attack'd, a Poet sav'd'.[45]

Dryden's failure to be 'useful to the State' is linked, by Pope, to influences arriving from France. Towards the end of his *Epistle*, Pope (in imitation of Horace's history of Roman satire) gives a fanciful history of British satire. After humble beginnings in rural festivities, it degenerated into invective lampoon, as 'Triumphant Malice rag'd thro' private life'; laws were passed, in response to which most poets 'warped to Flattery's side'. However,

> [...] some, more nice,
> Preserv'd the freedom, and forebore the vice.
> Hence Satire rose, that just the medium hit,
> And heals with Morals what it hurts with Wit.[46]

---

[43] Pope, *Poems* (Twickenham), iv. 229.

[44] Pope, *Poems* (Twickenham), iv. 211.

[45] Pope, *Poems* (Twickenham), iv. 213, 215.

[46] Pope, *Poems* (Twickenham), iv. 217.

This Golden Age was not to last. Where Horace blames the Greeks for a decline in Roman literature, Pope blames the French:

> We conquer'd France, but felt our captive's charms;
> Her Arts victorious triumph'd o'er our Arms;
> Britain to soft refinements less a foe,
> Wit grew polite, and Numbers learn'd to flow.[47]

In this, Pope continues, Waller and Dryden played their role, for both learned correctness from the French, and provided models for other British poets:

> Waller was smooth; but Dryden taught to join
> The varying verse, the full resounding line,
> The long majestic march, and energy divine.

Pope here imitates the French tendency he finds in Dryden, by a telling change in rhythm. Following 'Waller was smooth', which is quite staccato, Pope lists the refinements which 'Dryden taught' across three consecutive rhymes ('join', 'line', 'divine'). This tends to slow the progress (or 'march') of the surrounding lines. And the last line ('The long majestic march [...] energy divine') extends to twelve syllables, effectively intruding an Alexandrine into the otherwise constant flow of heroic couplets. The Alexandrine was, of course, a harbinger of French neoclassicism. Perhaps we should read these lines simply as an exemplification of Pope's skill: as he describes Dryden's debt to the French, he mimics the 'majesty' of his verse. However, we may detect a hint of irony when we notice a resonance between this passage and *An Essay on Criticism*:

> A *needless Alexandrine* ends the Song,
> That like a wounded Snake, drags its slow length along.[48]

In this couplet, as in lines 267–9 of the *Epistle*, Pope imitates what he describes (an Alexandrine). But here, at least, it is clear that he deploys this strategy in order to mock, not only those critics who admire nothing but (neoclassical) 'smoothness', but also any poets who use the twelve-syllable line as a failed 'flourish'. There is danger, it seems, in the 'soft refinements' which Waller, Dryden, and others have learned from the French.

In the last hundred lines of the *Epistle*, Pope returns to the attack on French tradition. He explains to George that most poets render themselves a nuisance to any king because:

> We needs will write Epistles to the King;
> And from the moment we oblige the town,
> Expect a place, or Pension from the Crown [...]
> Be call'd to Court, to plan some work divine,
> As once for LOUIS, Boileau and Racine.[49]

---

[47] Pope, *Poems* (Twickenham), iv. 217.   [48] Pope, *Poems* (Twickenham), i. 280.
[49] Pope, *Poems* (Twickenham), iv. 227.

Here, disdain of Boileau and Racine seems designed to allow Pope to argue for the sincerity of any panegyric which he, Pope, a British 'Horace', might address to the British Augustus, George. Of course, this neatly anti-French, pro-British pose is subject to irony throughout the poem, not least in the closing section: 'But Verse alas! Your Majesty disdains; / And I'm not used to Panegyric strains'. It seems that George will not receive panegyric from Pope both because he has sought none, and because Pope does not write well in that mode. But the poet also insinuates that any panegyric flights on his part would have resulted in ridicule; after all, 'A vile Enconium doubly ridicules', and 'Praise undeserv'd is scandal in disguise'.[50] However, none of this negates the earlier attack on French influence. On the contrary: Pope's satire cuts both ways.

We saw above that Boileau (so decried by Pope) skilfully imitates Horace's *Sermones* 2.1 and *Epistles* 2.1 in such a manner that he can satirically engage with Louis and his court. In the light of this, it is impossible not to suspect multiple debts to Boileau in Pope's *Imitations of Horace*. (I have focused the readings above in such a manner as to allow convergences to emerge.) In rare instances debts can be established beyond reasonable doubt. For instance, the 'Advertisement' that prefaces Pope's *Epistle to Augustus* renews observations on Horace to be found in Boileau's *Discours sur la Satire*. We can also find persuasive evidence within Pope's *Epistle* itself. Consider the following couplet: 'Besides, a fate attends on all I write, / That when I aim at praise, they say I bite'. I am aware of no lines in Horace, *Epistles* 2.1 that provide an 'original'. But in Boileau's 'Satire IX', we find: 'But do you not see that this furious throng / Will find raillery [*raillerie*] in such lines, too?' (ll. 295–6). Speaking more generally, however, we can only state with certainty that, however often Pope has borrowed from Boileau, he presents himself as imitating (only) Horace.

To conclude our comments on Pope: the 'Augustan' milieu prized (inventive) imitation of the ancients over imitation of the French (or British) moderns. Nevertheless, whilst 'lashing' Boileau (and, to a lesser extent, Dryden), Pope remains ambivalent towards Horace. His *Imitations* cannot be read except as a kind of tribute. But, connected with the 'patronage' motif, there is a subjacent criticism of Horace that helps support Pope's claim to a new kind of moral integrity. This helps to explain the passage in the first *Epilogue to the Satires*, where Pope writes of the ancient poet:

> His sly, polite, insinuating stile
> Could please at Court, and make AUGUSTUS smile;
> An artful Manager, that crept between
> His Friend and Shame, and was a kind of *Screen*.[51]

And it also throws light on Pope's intriguing *Epitaph: For One who would not be buried in Westminster-Abbey* (1738):

> HEROES, and KINGS! Your distance keep:
> In peace let one poor Poet sleep,

---

[50] Pope, *Poems* (Twickenham), iv. 229.   [51] Pope, *Poems* (Twickenham), iv. 299.

Who never flatter'd Folks like you:
Let Horace blush, and Virgil too.[52]

Augustan satire with true moral purpose, it seems, arises long after Augustus lived and died, but strictly on condition that the example of a Horace, a Boileau, or a (French-leaning) Dryden is avoided.

CONCLUSION

We have mainly discussed receptions of Horace by three Augustan-era writers drawn from that hotly debated entity, the literary canon. But the way such writers situate themselves in relation to Horace is of course linked to broader cultural phenomena. For instance, there is a great deal more to be said concerning the shift from the model of literary production exemplified by Horace, Boileau, and Dryden, writing under patrons, to the quite different model pioneered by Pope. The context created by war also merits further examination. For roughly two decades around the turn of the seventeenth century, France and Britain were almost continuously in conflict; and this is reflected in British reception of French poets. But since verse satirists dispose of irony, 'The reciprocities of national insult are in fact very complex'.[53] An example is provided by Prior. Above we saw how he mocks Boileau's *Ode sur la prise de Namur*. But in *A Letter to Monsieur Boileau Despréaux, occasion'd by the Victory at Blenheim, 1704*, Prior hints that all war poems should be taken with a generous pinch of (satiric) salt: 'I grant, old Friend, old Foe, (for such We are / Alternate, as the Chance of Peace and War)'.[54]

An immensely influential writer who died towards the end of this turbulent period is Anthony Ashley Cooper, 3rd Earl of Shaftesbury and grandson to the first Earl (Dryden's 'Achitophel'). In his highly influential *Characteristics* (1711; 1714), Shaftesbury makes a case that, across all epochs and nations, fine satire, political freedom, and good conduct rise or fall together. He mentions Boileau as a 'noble satirist' writing under a tyrannical king, but generally turns his gaze towards his beloved ancients—which is to say those ancients, including Horace, who in Shaftesbury's view turn away from all-encompassing relativism to embrace practical or moral philosophy.[55] It should also be noted that, as a verse satirist, Boileau was more enthusiastically imitated in Britain than in France. Examples include a friend of Pope's, Edward Young, who in *Love of Fame* (1728) 'borrowed fairly liberally' from Boileau.[56] Similarly, Walter Harte writes a poem to salute the

[52] Pope, *Poems* (Twickenham), vi. 376. See Howard Weinbrot, 'Pope and the Classics', in *Alexander Pope*, ed. Pat Rogers (Cambridge: Cambridge University Press, 2007), 76–88, at 77–8.

[53] Claude Rawson, 'War and the Epic Mania in England and France: Milton, Boileau, Prior and English Mock-Heroic', *Review of English Studies* 64, no. 265 (2013), 433–53, at 447.

[54] *Literary Works of Matthew Prior*, ed. H. Bunker Wright and Monroe K. Spears, 2 vols. (Oxford: Clarendon Press, 1959), i. 221.

[55] *Characteristics*, ed. Lawrence E. Klein (Cambridge: Cambridge University Press, 1999), 98.

[56] See Clark, *Boileau and the French Classical Critics*, 34–5.

Dunciad that pays tribute to Boileau as well as Pope, and to which is attached an English translation of Boileau's *Discours sur la satire*.[57] On the French side, a commentator of especial relevance is Voltaire. During his sojourn in England (1726–8), the *philosophe-poet* worked on his *Lettres philosophiques* (1734), published in English as *Letters concerning the English Nation* (1733). In those passages he devotes to British authors, Voltaire offers praise to a number of English and (in Swift's case) Irish satirists, but warns French readers that their island-bound (not to say parochial) concerns cause them to suffer in translation. Above such writers, Pope dazzles like the pole star of the moderns: 'His Compositions [...] are vastly clear and perspicuous; besides, most of his Subjects are general, and relative to all Nations.' Still, whilst praising Pope's international 'reach', Voltaire does not spare him the already conventional comparison with his French predecessor, Boileau.[58] In brief, many more than a trio of great names were involved in Augustan-era discussions of ancient versus modern, and French versus British, satire. Few, however, reflected so fascinatingly as Boileau, Dryden, and Pope on how far, and under what conditions, Horatian satire might be justified as uniquely 'useful to the State'—which would make it deceptively important, and deceptively moral.

SELECT BIBLIOGRAPHY

Baines, Paul. *The Complete Critical Guide to Alexander Pope* (London: Routledge, 2000).

Barnouw, Jeffrey. 'Britain and European Literature and Thought, 1660–1780', in *The Cambridge History of English Literature, 1660–1780*, ed. John Richetti (Cambridge: Cambridge University Press, 2008), 423–44.

Clark, A. F. B. *Boileau and the French Classical Critics in England (1660–1830)*, 2nd edn. (Geneva: Slatkine Reprints, 1978).

Klingner, Friedrich. 'Horace's Letter to Augustus', in *Horace: Satires and Epistles*, ed. Kirk Freudenburg (Oxford: Oxford University Press, 2009), ch. 14.

McLaverty, James. 'Pope and the Book Trade', in *The Cambridge Companion to Alexander Pope*, ed. Pat Rogers (Cambridge: Cambridge University Press, 2007), ch. 14.

Moriarty, Michael. 'Satire and Power in Seventeenth-Century France: The Case of Boileau', *Forum for Modern Language Studies* 30 (1994), 293–304.

Pocock, Gordon. *Boileau and the Nature of Neo-classicism* (Cambridge: Cambridge University Press, 1980).

Rawson, Claude. 'War and the Epic Mania in England and France: Milton, Boileau, Prior and English Mock-Heroic', *Review of English Studies* 64, no. 265 (2013), 433–53.

Sowerby, Robin. 'Pope and Horace', in *Horace Made New: Horatian Influences on British Writing from the Renaissance to the Twentieth Century*, ed. Charles Martindale and David Hopkins (Cambridge: Cambridge University Press, 1993), ch. 8.

Tatum, Jeffrey. '*Ultra Legem*: Law and Literature in Horace, *Satires* 2.1', in *Horace: Satires and Epistles*, ed. Kirk Freudenburg (Oxford: Oxford University Press, 2009), ch. 9.

---

[57] *An Essay on Satire; particularly on the Dunciad* (1730).

[58] Voltaire, *Letters concerning the English Nation*, ed. Nicholas Cronk (Oxford: Oxford University Press, 2009; originally published 1994), 110.

CHAPTER 36

....

PAMELA AND THE SATIRISTS

The Case for Eliza Haywood's Anti-Pamela *(1741)*

....

JENNIE BATCHELOR

There were no plays, no operas, no masquerades, no balls, no public shews, except at the little theatre in the Hay-market, then known by the name of F—g's scandal-shop; because he frequently exhibited there certain drolls, or, more properly, invectives against the ministry: in doing which it appears extremely probable, that he had two views; the one to get money, which he very much wanted, from such as delighted in low humour, and could not distinguish true satire from scurrility; and the other, in the hope of having some post given him by those whom he had abused, in order to silence his dramatic talent.[1]

A *Satirist*, whose Aim is to reform, will paint the *Offence* in its strongest Colours, but draw, as much as possible, a Veil over the Face of the *Offender*...[2]

THE range of terms adopted to describe the print and cultural phenomena occasioned by the publication of *Pamela; or, Virtue Rewarded* (1740) does not yet rival the extraordinary number of imitations, parodies, and multi-media spin-offs provoked by Samuel Richardson's novel. But while we continue to debate the degree of analytical purchase that labels such as the *Pamela* 'Phrenzy', 'vogue', 'media event', or 'controversy' afford us, we can at least agree that satire was one of the dominant registers of this 'Grub Street

I would like to thank Chloe Wigston Smith and Kim Simpson for their comments on an earlier draft of this essay.

[1] Eliza Haywood, *The History of Miss Betsy Thoughtless*, ed. Christine Blouch (Peterborough: Broadview, 1998), 66–7.

[2] Eliza Haywood, *The Parrot. With a Compendium of the Times* (1746), no. 8, n.p.

grabfest'.[3] Thomas Keymer and Peter Sabor's definitive biography of the *Pamela* debates illuminates three key areas of contention around which controversy turned: first, the novel's self-declared role in promoting a new mode of prose fiction; second, its exposure of the collusion between the worlds of print and commerce; and third, the text's troubling social and gender politics.[4] The principal satirical emphasis of each of the responses to *Pamela* varies from text to text, image to image, and artefact to artefact. So intimately connected are these areas of concern, however, that they are rarely articulated in isolation, and coalesce in a single image to which *Pamela* satirists, no matter what their avowed aim, obsessively returned: the beautiful, (un)adorned body of a young servant girl.

Sartorial metaphors and detail saturate *Pamela* and the satires it spawned. Even before the novel's publication, its first readers prophetically understood that its reception would rest upon the perceived dis/unity between the heroine's virtuous appearance and inner character.[5] Aaron Hill, for instance, in one of the epistolary puffs so scathingly criticized by Henry Fielding in *Shamela* (1741), urged the swift publication of Richardson's manuscript without further rewriting by linking the humility of Pamela's style with the purity of the novel's moral ambition. Overlaying the 'native Simplicity' of Pamela's language and sentiment with 'Strokes of Oratory' would be like 'too much Drapery in Sculpture and Statuary', he wrote, a 'disguise' that would 'marr the Reflections and unnaturalize the Incidents'. Better to 'have *Pamela* as *Pamela* wrote it; in her own Words, without Amputation, or Addition', presented to readers in 'her neat Country Apparel, such as she appear'd in, on her intended Departure to her Parents; for such best becomes her Innocence and beautiful Simplicity'.[6]

Hill's leveraging of the well-worn rhetorical association of dress and expression, embodied in the innocently seductive figure of Pamela in the homespun clothing, became tantalizingly threadbare in the anti-Pamelist backlash.[7] Hill's erotically charged account of

---

[3] 'Phrenzy' is Parson Oliver's term in Henry Fielding's *Shamela* (1741). *Anti-Pamela, or Feign'd Innocence Detected and Shamela*, ed. Catherine Ingrassia (Peterborough: Broadview Press, 2004), 238. 'Vogue' is one of several phrases used by Alan Dugald McKillop in *Samuel Richardson, Printer and Novelist* (Chapel Hill: University of North Carolina Press, 1936), 45. William B. Warner adopts 'media event' in *Licensing Entertainment: The Elevation of Novel Reading in Britain, 1684–1750* (Berkeley and London: University of California Press, 1998), 176–230. In their introduction to *The Pamela Controversy: Criticisms and Adaptations of Samuel Richardson's Pamela, 1740–1750*, 6 vols. (London: Pickering & Chatto, 2001), Thomas Keymer and Peter Sabor use 'controversy' on the grounds that it 'more clearly registers the extent to which critics have seen writers on *Pamela* as playing, with different degrees of knowingness, for serious ideological stakes' (i. xvii). 'Grub Street grabfest' is also Keymer and Sabor's term (i. xiii).

[4] Thomas Keymer and Peter Sabor, *Pamela in the Marketplace: Literary Controversy and Print Culture in Eighteenth-Century Britain and Ireland* (Cambridge: Cambridge University Press, 2005).

[5] See Jennie Batchelor, *Dress, Distress and Desire: Clothing and the Body in Eighteenth-Century Literature* (Basingstoke: Palgrave Macmillan, 2005), 19–51.

[6] Samuel Richardson, *Pamela; or, Virtue Rewarded*, ed. Thomas Keymer and Alice Wakely (Oxford: Oxford University Press, 2001), 8–9.

[7] These words are taken from a letter prefaced to the swiftly published second edition of *Pamela*, published on 14 February 1741, in which Hill wrote that Richardson had 'reconciled the *Pleasing* to the *Proper*. The *Thought* is every-where exactly *cloath'd* by the *Expression*: And becomes its Dress as roundly, and as close, as *Pamela* her Country-Habit.' Richardson, *Pamela*, 508.

the transparency of Pamela's modest words and homespun appearance—divested of the '*Pride of Ornament*', and displayed 'without a *Covering*' that in 'its Want of *Drapery*' only '*Increase[d]*' her 'Loveliness'—was a gift to *Pamela* satirists who linked the disingenuousness of Richardson's servant and the dubious morality of the novel that bore her name.[8] In Fielding's hands, Pamela famously became Shamela, a character whose name links literary fraud, woman's deceit, social ambition, and the titular heroine's dress: a sham, one of few material possessions bundled up by Shamela and Mrs Jewkes in a parody of the famous scene in Richardson's original, was a 'set of false sleeves to put on over a dirty shirt, or false sleeves with ruffles to put over a plain one'.[9] The art of exposing *Pamela*, for many of her most cynical commentators, was to debunk the heroine's literal and metaphorical dress as disguise. Taking their lead from Pamela's first and most influential critic, Mr B., Fielding and his fellow satirists sought to expose the novel's hypocrisy by endlessly stripping the servant's clothed body to see if there was any substance beneath. To quote the author of *Pamela Censured* (1741): 'No young Gentleman who reads this, but wishes himself in Mrs *Jervis*'s Place to *turn* Pamela *about and examine all her Dress to her under Petticoat*.'[10] Yet whereas Mr B. found under the servant girl's dress compelling evidence of her virtue in the form of the letters she had stitched to her underskirts, anti-Pamelists uncovered only tissues of lies that undermined Pamela's and Richardson's claims to moral authority.

Pamela's failure to foreclose satirical readings has been subject to intense critical scrutiny that has identified a range of internal factors—from Pamela's inappropriately dressed language to Richardson's failure to control the literary tropes he evoked in order to displace—as well as external explanations—most notably ambient social and gender prejudice. Rather than rehearse these arguments, this chapter revisits them through the lens of one of the *Pamela* controversy's most compelling, yet least understood, interventions: Eliza Haywood's *Anti-Pamela* (1741). The only known *Pamela* satire to have been authored by a woman, *Anti-Pamela* remains overlooked and usually enters the critical conversation as little more than a discursive footnote or few paragraphs in accounts of the fallout from the publication of Richardson's novel. *Anti-Pamela* barely features more prominently in studies of Haywood's career, despite its welcome and recent re-evaluation. Described by T. C. Duncan Eaves and Ben D. Kimpel as a cynical effort to 'capitalize on *Pamela*'s popularity', the relationship between *Anti-Pamela* and Richardson's novel is frequently cast as parasitic or, to quote Richard Gooding, 'tenuous'.[11] This essay's starting point is a simple question: Why do we assume that *Anti-Pamela*'s relationship to

---

[8] Fielding quotes these words in Parson Tickletext's opening letter in *An Apology for the Life of Mrs Shamela Andrews*, noting how 'frequently' the novel presents Pamela in this way in 'Images...which the coldest Zealot cannot read without Emotion'. Fielding, *Shamela*, 236.

[9] Fielding, *Shamela*, 262. On the definition of the sham, see Francis Grose, *A Classical Dictionary of the Vulgar Tongue* (1785).

[10] Anon., *Pamela Censured*, reprinted in *The Pamela Controversy*, ii. 50.

[11] T. C. Duncan Eaves and Ben D. Kimpel, *Samuel Richardson: A Biography* (Oxford: Clarendon Press, 1971), 130; Richard Gooding, '*Pamela*, *Shamela*, and the Politics of the *Pamela* Vogue', *Eighteenth-Century Fiction* 7 (1995), 110 n. 2.

Richardson's novel is less meaningful or satirically on point than that of its rival textual interlocutors?[12] After all, *Pamela* satires such as *Joseph Andrews*, which also works as a stand-alone textual production, are not given as short shrift as Haywood's novel. Moreover, *Anti-Pamela* has a good deal in common with its more obviously satirical anti-Pamelist brethren. Like Fielding's Shamela, the deliciously devious Syrena Tricksy is unashamedly ambitious, while the virtuous gestures she performs throughout the novel are repeatedly proved to be empty. Like Fielding and the author of *Pamela Censured*, Haywood also works away in her novel at the sartorial signs and metaphors mobilized by Richardson and Hill as evidence of his heroine's authenticity. Syrena begins the text as an apprentice to a mantua-maker—a literal manufacturer of appearances—and possesses a surname that evokes the critical scene in Richardson's novel in which the heroine 'trick[s]' herself up in the homespun gown and petticoat and which was required to do so much ideological work in the Pamela/Shamela debate.[13] Yet *Anti-Pamela* is driven by so much more than the literal and figurative dressing down of a heroine that is the *modus operandi* of so many anti-Pamelist works. In exposing sexual double standards and the difficulties faced by working women, *Anti-Pamela* is a satirical novel with real-world referents. A self-conscious and complexly intertextual work, it is not simply a parody of a single text, but is a satire of the novel as a form that was complicit in, and further entrenched, sexual double standards and damaging myths of gender.

That we have not seen *Anti-Pamela* as a work of 'true' satire, but as a 'scurrilous' (read: opportunistic) capitalizing on the *Pamela* phenomenon is partly a consequence of a general reluctance to see eighteenth-century women's writing, and particularly the female-authored novel, as satirical.[14] It is also the legacy of a more local problem: the extent to which satirical representations of Haywood, the grotesquely promiscuous author of amatory fiction lampooned in *The Dunciad* (1728), who later turned to writing sentimental literature when it proved financially expedient, has overdetermined how we read her work. Confronting Haywood's fraught position in the history of satire, this chapter argues, permits the nature of *Anti-Pamela*'s contribution to the *Pamela* controversy to come into view. Only then can we see that the satirical target of Haywood's highly self-reflexive novel is not simply, or even complexly, the hypocrisy of a fictional character whose duplicity reveals the hypocrisy of the novel to which she gives her name. On the one hand, on the level of plot, its subject is the difficulties women encounter when they seek to wrest control of their self-representation through their wardrobes, work, and words. On the other hand, the novel's tenuous position in literary scholarship

---

[12] A notable exception is Keymer and Sabor's *Pamela in the Literary Marketplace*, which also aligns *Anti-Pamela* with the spirit of 'true satire' that Haywood evokes in *Betsy Thoughtless*, although its account of the text as a morally black and white novel is very different from my own. *Pamela in the Marketplace* (87–94).

[13] Richardson, *Pamela*, 55.

[14] Exceptions include Ronald Paulson, *Satire and the Novel in Eighteenth-Century England* (New Haven: Yale University Press, 1967); and Frank Palmeri, *History, Novel: Narrative Forms, 1665–1815* (Newark: University of Delaware Press, 2003). See also Claudia Thomas Kairoff, 'Gendering Satire: Behn to Burney', in *A Companion to Satire: Ancient and Modern*, ed. Ruben Quintero (Oxford: Blackwell, 2007), 276–92, which argues for a female satirical novel tradition.

reveals how hard it is for women's satirical wit to be taken seriously. In affording these insights, *Anti-Pamela* exposes the fault line between sentiment and satire that Richardson failed to stabilize in the form of the new species of fiction *Pamela* intended to inaugurate, as well as the troubling implications of his efforts to do so for working women, whether servants or authors.

HAYWOOD AS AN OBJECT OF SATIRE

Few writers' careers have been more thoroughly refracted through the lens of satire than Eliza Haywood's, even if, as Kathryn King has demonstrated, her enemies were 'fewer in number than we had imagined'.[15] Nonetheless, the figures of Fielding's Mrs Novel and Pope's bestial 'Juno.../ With cow-like udders and with ox-like eyes' have cast long shadows over the reception of Haywood's work.[16] Satire has been the dominant structuring principle of the narrative we have spun about Haywood's life and work since at least the publication of *The Progress of Romance* (1785). Clara Reeve's account of Haywood as a writer of novels of scandalous intrigue—sometimes satirical in nature and, in turn, satirized for their indecorous excesses—who reformed and turned to sentimental fiction when Richardson's success made other fictional forms commercially unviable, is enduringly resilient.[17] The 'Story of Eliza Haywood's novels', as Paula Backscheider dubs it, has been multiply retold in the past two decades, but perceptions of her career as one of two halves—the amorous/sometimes satirical and the sentimental—are difficult to dislodge.[18] Susan Staves, for instance, identifies the 'turn' in Haywood's career away from 'romance and scandal' to 'conduct books' and 'more moral novels', such as *The History of Miss Betsy Thoughtless*, as an important staging post in the eighteenth-century literary marketplace more widely. Crucially, the turn is seen to mark the emergence of a 'new kind of popular' women's writing, produced in the wake of *Pamela*, that Staves links to the successful suppression of '[s]atire against women writers' and their newfound 'accept[ance]'.[19] Haywood immunized herself from satire, in other words, by ceasing to practise it herself. Accounts such as Staves's pay particular attention to the publication of *The Female Spectator* (1744–6) and its titular eidolon: a reformed coquette who relinquished a misspent life of 'Vanity' in order to use her 'Experience' and 'Education' to be 'both useful and entertaining to the Publick'.[20] Such characterizations of Haywood's

---

[15] Kathryn R. King, *A Political Biography of Eliza Haywood* (London: Pickering & Chatto, 2012), 6.

[16] On the character of Mrs Novel see King, *A Political Biography*, 65–6; See Pope, *Poems* (Longman), iii. 233.

[17] Clara Reeve, *The Progress of Romance, Through Times, Countries, and Manners*, 2 vols. (1785), i. 121.

[18] Paula R. Backscheider, 'The Story of Eliza Haywood's Novels: Caveats and Questions', in *The Passionate Fictions of Eliza Haywood: Essays on her Life and Work*, ed. Kirsten Saxton and Rebecca P. Bocchicchio (Lexington: University Press of Kentucky, 2000), 19–47.

[19] Susan Staves, *A Literary History of Women's Writing in Britain, 1660–1789* (Cambridge: Cambridge University Press, 2006), 229.

[20] Eliza Haywood, *The Female Spectator*, 4 vols. (1744–6), i. 3.

work seem more than a little wilful in their autobiographical reading of the 'Female Spectator' as a proxy for Haywood herself. It is also more than a little curious that this serial publication, which first appeared some three years after the appearance of *Pamela*, should come to have such a pivotal role in an argument about the development of post-Richardson prose fiction. Haywood, who was notoriously astute at reading and manipulating trends, was never so fashionably late to any other literary party she attended.

The timing of *Anti-Pamela*'s composition, which appeared seven months after *Pamela* on 16 June 1741, might alone urge that it merits scrutiny as a more immediately reactive indicator of Haywood's thinking about the novel's past and possible futures at a critical moment in its history. Ironically, it seems that the transitional status of the novel as a text that harks back to earlier, amatory and scandalous conventions while capitalizing on the fashion for Richardsonian didacticism—Syrena is utterly humiliated by the novel's close— has obscured its significance. Dazzled by the 'brilliance of *Shamela*' and distracted by Haywood's tactic of rewriting *Pamela* and *Shamela* 'without referring to existing frames of representation'—Mr B. becomes not *a* Booby but fragmented into a 'series of much smaller male roles'—it is perhaps unsurprising that Richardson scholars have dismissed *Anti-Pamela*.[21] It is stranger that the novel has failed to command attention in Haywood studies, beyond the small body of scholarship by, most notably, Catherine Ingrassia and Rivka Swenson.[22] Scholarship on Haywood's politics and satirical credentials pays *Anti-Pamela* scant attention. Toni Bowers's study of the political implications of early eighteenth-century seduction stories makes no mention of the novel despite containing important discussions of Haywood's other fiction and the politics of virtuous resistance in *Pamela*.[23] King's indispensable political biography of Haywood makes a passing reference to *Anti-Pamela* in the context of a discussion of her friendship/rivalry with Fielding but the novel does not merit an entry in the biography's index.[24]

The problem the novel presents, as Andrea Austin argues, is partly one of form. Hovering, as *Betsy Thoughtless* does, on the fuzzy boundary between social satire (a genre which has real-world referents) and parody (an intertextual mode), *Anti-Pamela* represents an early, unsatisfying attempt by Haywood to appropriate a masculinized genre, associated with 'metaphors of aggression, sexual potency', and 'oedipal struggle', for 'feminist criticism'.[25] However, unlike the more technically accomplished *Betsy Thoughtless*, *Anti-Pamela* fails to hit its mark, Austin claims. The 'simple comparison'

---

[21] Keymer and Sabor, *Pamela in the Marketplace*, 87.

[22] See Catherine Ingrassia's *Authorship, Commerce, and Gender in Early Eighteenth-Century England: A Culture of Paper Credit* (Cambridge: Cambridge University Press, 2005) and her introduction to her edition of *Anti-Pamela* (7–43) which situates the novel more nearly within the terms of the *Pamela* controversy. See also Rivka Swenson's insightful 'Optics, Gender, and the Eighteenth-Century Gaze: Looking at Eliza Haywood's *Anti-Pamela*', *The Eighteenth Century: Theory and Interpretation* 51 (2010), 27–43.

[23] Toni Bowers, *Force or Fraud: British Seduction Stories and the Problem of Resistance, 1660–1760* (Oxford: Oxford University Press, 2011).

[24] The novel is not discussed, either, in Juliette Merritt's important *Beyond Spectacle: Eliza Haywood's Female Spectators* (Toronto and London: University of Toronto Press, 2004).

[25] Andrea Austin, 'Shooting Blanks: Potency, Parody, and Eliza Haywood's *The History of Miss Betsy Thoughtless*', in *The Passionate Fictions of Eliza Haywood*, ed. Saxton and Bocchicchio, 259.

between Richardson's Pamela and Syrena Tricksy, whom Austin labels a 'prostitute' despite the heroine's rejection of the term, is 'too slight and static a vehicle'. The novel's equation of Richardson's virtuous servant and Haywood's whore pales against the 'thoughtful' and intertextually richer web of references drawn on in the characterization of the female protagonists in *Betsy Thoughtless*, Austin concludes, and 'comprises a failure' on Haywood's part 'to explore the terms she equates [the chaste and the fallen] or to question the categorizations they imply'.[26] To put it another way, Haywood's criticism of Richardson's novel is barely more sophisticated than the pre-reformed Mr B.'s misogynist reading of Pamela's character. Too conservative to be considered of a piece with Haywood's amatory fiction, yet too reliant on amatory tropes to contribute to the respectable women's writing that *Betsy Thoughtless* represents, its satire judged as too diffuse, by some, and too local by others, *Anti-Pamela* is a difficult novel within Haywood's body of work. As the rest of this chapter will argue, close attention to the formal, stylistic, and thematic links, and pointedly satirical disjunctions between *Anti-Pamela* and *Pamela*, reveals that troubling her readers may well have been precisely Haywood's point.

ANTI-PAMELA AS SATIRE

Although as Keymer and Sabor suggest, *Anti-Pamela*'s satire appears diffuse on the level of character and plot, close comparison of its title page with *Pamela*'s suggests several areas of specific satiric critique. (It seems unlikely that Haywood had a hand in the design of the title page, but the content of it, nonetheless, sets the tone of the work it introduces astutely.) Putting aside, momentarily, the most critical difference—the hard to pin down 'Anti' in the title of Haywood's novel—the first key points of departure advertised by *Anti-Pamela*'s title page are moral and formal. If *Pamela* is a story of 'Virtue Rewarded', then *Anti-Pamela* is one in which 'Feign'd Innocence'—although whose is not explicitly defined—is 'DETECTED'. After foregrounding the exposure of hypocrisy, *Anti-Pamela*'s full title notes an important formal difference from Richardson's original. Abandoning the epistolary form so critical to the literal unfolding of *Pamela*'s plot—the 'SERIES of FAMILIAR LETTERS FROM a Beautiful Young DAMSEL', stitched to the heroine's underskirts—*Anti-Pamela* alternatively comprises 'a Series of SYRENA'S ADVENTURES'. That Haywood's novel also contains many letters—indeed, correspondence is at least as important to its narrative arc as it is to *Pamela*'s—is another feigning to which this chapter will return.

Anti-Pamela's title page refuses to acknowledge *Pamela*'s claim to be a work published '[i]n order to cultivate the Principles of VIRTUE and RELIGION in the Minds of the YOUTH of BOTH SEXES' by providing no equivalent wording. Instead, the title page nods to the truth claims asserted by Richardson's novel and ups the ante in the verisimilitude stakes. Unlike *Pamela*, *Anti-Pamela* is a 'Narrative which *has really* its Foundation

---

[26] Austin, 'Shooting Blanks', 263 and 281–2 n. 15.

in Truth and Nature' (emphasis added). *Pamela* advertises itself as a new species of prose writing that has been 'intirely divested of all those Images, which, in too many Pieces calculated for Amusement only, tend to *inflame* the Minds they should *instruct*'. Refusing directly to address, but underscoring by deflection, Richardson's attack on the amatory mode with which Haywood had been so closely associated, *Anti-Pamela* instead rests its claims to public utility on the assertion that Syrena's narrative 'arms against a partial Credulity, by shewing the Mischiefs that frequently arise from a too sudden Admiration'. Again, the question of who is being armed against whom is not entirely clear, although the title page's final claim that the novel has been '[p]ublish'd as a necessary Caution to all Young Gentleman' offers one, albeit ultimately inadequate, way of interpreting the assertion.

The reworking of Richardson's title page signals the distinctiveness and ambition of *Anti-Pamela*'s contribution to the *Pamela* controversy and establishes its satiric aims. Unlike *Shamela*, which proclaimed on its title page an intention to refute 'the many notorious FALSHOODS [*sic*] and MISREPRESENTATIONS of a Book called *PAMELA*' by exposing the 'matchless ARTS of that young Politician', *Anti-Pamela* primarily seeks not to unmask the pretensions of a heroine and her author. From the outset, we understand more explicitly than we do from Fielding's title page that these local grievances matter only because they are tied to much wider questions about the truth claims of the senti-mental novel and the fictions of gender and morality, clothed as 'nature' by Richardson, to which these claims were tenuously yoked. In keeping with other satires of *Pamela*, *Anti-Pamela* foregrounds female virtue as performance, not essence. As Swenson notes, the main satirical thrust of Haywood's work is the 'truism that appearances cannot be trusted'.[27] When Haywood adverts as much, however, this is no misogynist comment on woman's inherent duplicity as it is in texts such as *Pamela Censured*. Instead, Haywood emphasizes how carefully taught women must be to learn to value themselves and their prospects on such performances; how risky such strategies are; and the role that the novel, in Richardsonian guise, plays in naturalizing such self-defeating acts.

If Pamela's agency lies in a virtuous resistance made materially manifest in her modestly adorned body and letters, then Syrena's attempts at self-determination are characterized by acquiescence to sexual pleasure masked by a cultivated corporeal hypocrisy (which is, in turn, threatened by the written word). Critics have characterized Syrena Tricksy as a whore and sexual 'predator',[28] but *Anti-Pamela* asserts that, by nature, its heroine is an innocent, taught before she was 'out of her Bib and Apron' to become 'one the most subtil Mistresses in the Art of Decoying' by her mother, Ann.[29] A quick study, by her 'thirteenth year' Syrena performs virtue like 'the most experienc'd Actresses on the Stage', her body readily adapting to 'imaginary Accidents' created by her parent: 'her Colour would come and go, her Eyes sparkle, grow Languid, or overflow

---

[27] Swenson, 'Optics, Gender, and the Eighteenth-Century Gaze', 33.

[28] Keymer and Sabor assert that the 'primary distinction' between Pamela and Syrena is that the latter is 'predator rather than prey'. *Pamela in the Literary Marketplace*, 7.

[29] Eliza Haywood, *Anti-Pamela*, ed. Ingrassia, 53. Subsequent references will be given in the text.

with Tears, her Bosom heave, her Limbs tremble; she would fall into Faintings, or appear transported' (54). The effect of these gestures is only intensified by the vestiges of 'Innocence' Syrena retains from 'Infancy' even long after the 'boldest and most audacious' of her sexual intrigues (53).

Such comic accounts of Syrena's bodily performances of virtue—pinching her arms and hands until they are 'black', falling into 'a Fit', rolling her eyes and tearing at her 'Hair and Cloaths' (114)—seem superficially to rehearse *Shamela's* most insistent parodic strain: that Pamela's greatest and only virtue is her ability to feign the modesty she lacks. Closer attention to the text's language, plot, and self-conscious intertextual allusions, which point to the unnaturalness and psychic cost of such performances, reveals instead that *Anti-Pamela* is more interested in satirically exposing the sentimental virtue for which Pamela is rewarded as an already debased currency that has no value to working women like Syrena or Pamela herself. These women may perform the protocols of sensibility, but as the anti-Pamelist backlash underlined, could never be in control of their meaning in a society in which women's characters were deemed inherently suspect.[30] As one of Syrena's lovers, Mr L—, remarks more poignantly than he understands: 'The World... is not well agreed about the true Signification of those words, *Virtuous* and *Honourable*— ... But, we'll leave the Definition to the Casuists' (96). Mr L—, of course, like every male character in the novel, has a vested interest in defining these terms according to his own inclinations. However, what signifies virtue and honour is more than a casuistical problem for labouring women like Syrena, whose fate is not only tied to such definitions, but whose ability to wrest control over their interpretation is also persistently undermined by men, from Mr B. and Mr L—to the author of *Pamela Censured*, who are determined to read them as they wish.[31] In making this point—as the novel does repeatedly—*Anti-Pamela* reveals itself to be more than a parody of Richardson's flawed project to elevate the novel form. Haywood's work is also a satirical reflection on the fallout from *Pamela's* publication, which demonstrated that the exemplary morality the novel rewarded in the heroine's marriage to Mr B. could never have had currency in a world predisposed to read women's virtue, and particularly labouring women's virtue, as a contradiction in terms. Syrena and her mother know this to be true,

---

[30] Syrena's work is described in much more detail than Pamela's. As Chloe Wigston Smith argues, *Anti-Pamela* 'engages a vibrant conversation about the problem of female labour and its ties to publicity' as Syrena mobilizes her advanced needlework skills to seduce unwitting men. *Women, Work, and Clothes in the Eighteenth-Century Novel* (Cambridge: Cambridge University Press, 2013), 164–7. Like writing and the corporeal signs of virtue Syrena feigns, however, these performances similarly prove unreliable forms of self-expression. Syrena must learn that her 'sexuality' cannot 'substitute for genuine labour' (167).

[31] Ingrassia makes the point that while *Anti-Pamela* seems to affirm 'the very gendered construction of female domestic virtue' by punishing Syrena for her failure to abide by it, the novel 'more profoundly' demonstrates how these are 'hollow signifiers that can be appropriated and used at will' (*Authorship, Commerce and Gender*, 115). Such an argument might make *Anti-Pamela* seem more like other anti-Pamelist texts which, as already indicated, commonly suggest sentimental virtue is merely a disguise that can be put on or taken off like a suit of clothes. My argument here is *Anti-Pamela* redefines the terms of the debate to make clear that it does not matter what kinds of virtue (feigned or genuine) women enact in the world; they will be read by men howsoever they choose.

but discover that this knowledge is insufficient to ensure the heroine's successful navigation of the society in which she lives and works.

By the time that Syrena's family raises the money for her apprenticeship as a mantua-maker, she has already learned that the 'Business' of her life is, 'by an artful Management' (66), to cultivate appropriate displays of the sexual behaviour that she and her mother hope will rescue her, Pamela-like, from a tedious life of manual labour. The novel is clear that the lesson doesn't come as naturally as the Syrena-as-predator metaphor would suggest, however, as her first sexual encounter with Lieutenant Vardine makes plain. Syrena and Vardine's unsatisfactory affair is structured around a reimagining of the moment in *Pamela* when Mr B. gives his servant a haul of 'fine Things' from his dead mother's 'Closet'. The gift includes 'fine *Flanders* lac'd Headcloths', 'fine Silk Shoes' that delight the 'astonish'd' Pamela, 'Ribbands and Topknots', 'rich Silver Buckles', as well as 'Two Pair of rich Stays'. But it is the gift of 'Four Pair of fine white Cotton Stockens, and Three Pair of Fine ones', and seemingly only these, that makes Pamela 'inwardly asham'd'.[32] Pamela is not in a position, nor anti-Pamelists would suggest seemingly inclined, to reject an object that encodes Mr B.'s will to possess her. In *Anti-Pamela*'s elaborate reworking of this brief scene, Syrena poignantly refuses a similar gift, a move that implies Pamela should and could have made a different decision in the similar scenario with Mr B. Shortly after arriving at her employer's, Syrena is dispatched to a haberdasher's shop to purchase silk. There she is greeted as a neighbour by 'a fine Gentleman with a lac'd Hat and Cockade, looking over some white Stockings' (60). After feigning a blush, as her mother had 'bid' her to when a 'Gentleman had his Eye' upon her (60–1), Vardine proceeds to inform Syrena that he lodges near her and has 'observed' her from 'the first Day' she arrived in town. Syrena gestures to leave, but is prevented when Vardine asks her to help him 'chuse a Pair of Stockings' for a 'young relation in the Country' (61). Syrena feigns offence at the suggestion, whereupon Vardine presses the stockings so aggressively into her hands that her 'Fingers ake[d] for an Hour after'. More attempts to 'force them' onto the resistant mantua-maker follow, but Syrena resolves 'not to take them for all he could do'. Vardine leaves 'very much out of Humour' (62).

Syrena does 'not repent…having refused the Stockings', even though she notes, Pamela-like, that 'they were very pretty' (62). She believes that Vardine loves her, a belief that makes her mother 'angry' that her daughter should be so gullible as to be blind to the 'wide Difference between Love', in which the aim is 'to make the beloved Object happy', and '*Likeing*', which seeks only 'to gratify itself' (65–6). Syrena subsequently loses interest in Vardine when she realizes that 'his fine Cloaths' deceived her—he has 'Wit' but no 'Estate'—and begins to regret that she did not take the 'Stockings', which would 'have been clear Gains' and made the exchange marginally profitable (69). Vardine ultimately out-plots the heroine, however, by arranging to meet her in St James's Park, during which assignation they take refuge in a tavern during a storm, as the great queen Dido 'r[a]n into a Cave with a wandring Solider' (75). Proving herself a much less capable reader than she is an actor, Syrena observes with never a truer word that

---

[32] Richardson, *Pamela*, 19.

'Great Folks may do any thing'. However, Vardine's reference to the *Aeneid*, which signals the inevitability of Syrena's fall, is lost upon her as he proceeds in his attempted seduction by once again forcing the stockings on her (75). When Syrena denies that she has any claim to the stockings, Vardine makes explicit what Mr B. refuses to openly admit: 'they are bought and paid for' and with that payment, he believes, he has secured the right to own the prospective wearer's body as well. Moving into the third-person, the novel's conspicuous narrator proceeds to describe the execution of Vardine's plot. Syrena is made to 'drink...Wine' and is described 'trembl[ing]', 'confused', and 'frightened' until she loses 'all Memory of the Place, or Danger she was in' as she is plied with 'Protestations' of love punctuated, 'by way of Parenthesis', with 'a Kiss'. His 'Attack' is soon complete. After 'the momentary Rapture'—which seems 'wholly his'—is passed, the 'Power of Reflection' returns to Syrena. She regains consciousness as 'an unhappy ruin'd Girl' (75).

The episode warrants detailed consideration as an exemplary illustration of the complexity and force of *Anti-Pamela*'s multi-layered and multi-directional satire. The novel's allusions to Richardson's novel sympathetically underscore the untenability of Pamela's and Syrena's position as working women who, unlike queens, have perilously little agency. Pamela takes the stockings, though ashamed; Syrena refuses to take them. Like Dido, both women fall prey to the machinations of men, although Pamela, uniquely among this unlikely triumvirate, will be dubiously rewarded with marriage to her would-be seducer. Haywood's heroine is not so lucky. If, as Ingrassia suggests, Syrena 'understands the business of pleasure', then Haywood shows that her business is a rather sordid one.[33] The language used to describe her sexual encounter with Vardine closely recalls that of Haywood's *Fantomina* (1725) and repeats the earlier novella's strategic confusion of agencies, tenses, and pronouns in its elliptical description of the 'bold' and 'resolute' Beauplasir's undoing of the 'fearful' and 'confus'd' Fantomina.[34] *Anti-Pamela*, however, is emphatically more brutal and much less unambiguous: Syrena pays dearly for a gift she tried much harder than Richardson's heroine to refuse.

Pamela's incorporation and displacement of 'many of the narrative and thematic elements found in *Fantomina*', particularly masquerade, seduction, and voyeurism, have been analysed at length by William Warner.[35] *Anti-Pamela*'s nods to its author's 1720s novella, however, are rarely registered despite being emphatic, even on the level of plot: seeking 'recompence for what he [Vardine] had robb'd her of', Syrena, in a series of guises, will continue to attempt to seduce credulous men until she is eventually found out, not by pregnancy, but by another woman (77). *Anti-Pamela*'s structural, linguistic, and thematic allusions to *Fantomina*, as evidenced in the aforementioned episode, are more significant still. They serve not to out Pamela as a Fantomina by another name, as we might expect of anti-Pamelist satire: for one thing, as Syrena's naïve response to the example of Dido implies, Haywood is too attuned to the question of how class

---

[33] Ingrassia, *Authorship, Gender and Commerce*, 111.

[34] Eliza Haywood, *Fantomina and Other Works*, ed. Alexander Pettit, Margaret Case Croskery, and Anna C. Patthias (Peterborough: Broadview Press, 2004).

[35] Warner, *Licensing Entertainment*, 194.

circumscribes women's agency to draw so crude a parallel. Instead, and long before twentieth-century scholarship turned its attention to the same subject, what *Anti-Pamela* revealed through its harking back to amatory fiction via its remediation in *Pamela*, is Richardson's reliance upon textual precedents he understood poorly. If as Warner argues, amatory fictions such as *Fantomina* spectrally surface in *Pamela* as a form of 'textual interference' that 'menaces the "truth effect"' of Pamela's letters by threatening to shamelize them from within, in *Anti-Pamela* similar allusions agitate differently.[36] The issue is not only, for Haywood, that Richardson's voyeuristic virtue-in-distress novel was as likely 'to *inflame* the Minds' of its readers as the amatory fictions it claimed to supersede. More particularly, what *Anti-Pamela* reveals through its deft and disturbing rewriting of Fantomina's seduction/rape by Beauplasir, is that the sexual adventuress Fantomina that Richardson attempted to overwrite in the creation of his passively virtuous heroine, never existed in the form he imagined in the first place. The worryingly amorous and agential women of amatory fiction that *Pamela* attempts to displace are, Haywood's novel reveals, fantasies created in the minds of their male readers and not drawn by the pens of their female authors. Neither Syrena nor Fantomina, ultimately, has any more agency than Pamela does. When *Anti-Pamela* reads *Pamela* through *Fantomina*, it does so satirically to condemn the misogynist logic that underpins Richardson's project to reconcile the '*Pleasing*' with the '*Proper*' in the form of his passively virtuous and much-tested heroine. *Pamela*'s self-professed counter-fiction of gender fails to convince, *Anti-Pamela* suggests, in large part because it is based upon a wilful misreading of the 'inflam[matory]' novels, such as *Fantomina*, that it claims to disavow. The argument is only underlined by the irony that Richardson's heroine was subject to the same kinds of misreadings that Haywood's heroines were. The anti-Pamelist backlash proved nothing so well as the insidious role that fiction played in perpetuating myths of femininity that, even when reconstructed, seemed only to confirm women's underlying duplicity.

FALSE FORMS AND TRUE SATIRE

That Haywood's satire is more squarely directed at the project than the plot of *Pamela* is further indicated by *Anti-Pamela*'s self-conscious texuality. Whereas Richardson famously attempted to undergird the alleged truth claims of his novel by presenting it as a real narrative mediated by an editor, the reader of *Anti-Pamela* is never allowed to be in any doubt that they are reading a work of fiction. The novel is replete with puns that draw attention to how perceptions of women's characters are dictated by cultural and, very specifically, textual discourses over which they have no control. Take, for instance, the telling reference made by one of her many lovers to having 'before met with Women of *Syrena*'s stamp' (150). The turn of phrase is a familiar one in Haywood's fiction and is symptomatic of what Deidre Lynch reveals to be a widespread recognition in the period

---

[36] Warner, *Licensing Entertainment*, 199 and 192.

of the 'technological' and 'material supports' of the meaning of character in a 'literate culture'.[37] More specifically, in *Anti-Pamela*, the wordplay underscores one of the novel's principal themes: how women's 'characters' precede them and dictate the terms of their future circulation within that culture. The role that texts, from novels to letters, play in this technology of character is writ large in Haywood's novel and is underscored by the many metafictional elements to which *Anti-Pamela* has recourse, from references to kisses as parentheses to the frequent interpolations of the novel's conspicuous narrator. Arguably, however, it is in the breaking up of the epistolary form of *Pamela* and *Shamela*, and the switches from first- to third-person the novel's occasional use of letters affords, that permits Haywood's best work as satirist to be done.

Third-person narration mediates our reading of Syrena's letters. While her secret correspondence with her mother, the repeated discovery of which precipitates the heroine's descent into disease and 'extreme Poverty' (164), emphasizes her amorous inclinations, the narrator's accounts give a different side to Syrena's story. The narrator's descriptions of Ann Tricksy's ambitious tutelage of her daughter and of Vardine's 'Attack' on Syrena, for example, allow us to see that while Haywood's heroine is more than capable of 'acting the Coquette' and may even, sometimes, enjoy it (125), she is also consistently lied to by men and routinely abused. In the novel's conclusion Syrena will finally be out-plotted, not by one of her lovers, who are mostly too stupid or materially invested to see through or know how to manage her, but by one of her lovers' wives. Mrs E— fabricates three letters to implicate Syrena in an entirely fictional affair with a Mr C—, who has a fiercely jealous wife. Proving again that Syrena is a poorer reader than performer, the 'deceiving' heroine is thoroughly 'deceived' herself by the fraudulent letter (223). Condemned for the one liaison in the novel she never actually entered into, Mrs E—'s epistolary plot culminates in Syrena being 'dragg'd away like the lowest and most common Prostitute... a Fate, indeed, she long since had deserv'd', though as the narrator notes, it ironically fell upon her 'when she gave the least Occasion' for punishment (225). In presenting the letter as a fraudulent medium, Haywood's novel casts doubt upon the textual mode that Pamelists offered up as evidence of the unadorned simplicity of the virtue of Richardson's heroine. But again, Haywood goes beyond mere parody. In revealing how correspondence can never be taken at its word, *Anti-Pamela* underlines one of the key lessons of the *Pamela* controversy: letters, like gestures or clothes, are unreliable vehicles for female self-expression unless they are used to deceive others, as by Mrs E—. Lying is the only thing, it seems, that women can be trusted to do well.

By giving detailed attention to one of Syrena's many adventures, this chapter has sought to capture something of the complexity and density of Haywood's satire to argue that more attention should be given to: the novel as a whole; to its dialogue with *Pamela*; and to its relationship to Haywood's other writings, from which it has been cast adrift.

---

[37] Discussing the etymological roots of character (denoting 'either a "brand" or "stamp"'), Deidre Shauna Lynch notes that Haywood's amatory fictions 'pivot, self-reflexively, on the discovery of characters' in scenes that acknowledge 'the material and replicable elements' of character in a 'culture increasingly dependent on print'. *The Economy of Character: Novels, Market Culture, and the Business of Inner Meaning* (Chicago and London: University of Chicago Press, 1998), 30–1.

Undoubtedly the novel's tricksy tone and plot complicate its satire, a mode that does not have a natural home in fiction. Satire in novels, as Ashley Marshall notes, 'tends to be very different from satire in verse', the plot and demands of characterization diluting the satire so that it is perhaps more appropriate to say that 'fictional works are often satiric but rarely "satires"'.[38] (*Shamela*'s status as a parody puts it in a different, and less awkward, category.) The characterization of Syrena undoubtedly compounds the interpretative problems involved in reading *Anti-Pamela* as a work of satire which, like sentimental fiction, claims an investment in 'improving society'.[39] The heroine's 'headstrong and ungovern'd appetites' are emphatically punished by the novel's close. She is unquestionably a hypocrite and a liar, who at her lowest accuses Mr L— of raping her in a desperate and failed attempt to force a marriage proposal. Yet the novel is clear that most of Syrena's amorous targets are far from innocent and most get what they want from her, some by force. And while Syrena may be 'inconsolable' at the notion of being dispatched to Wales, the narrator hints at more pleasurable prospects she might look forward to in her period of punishment. What 'befel her' there, we are told, 'must be the Subject of future Entertainment' (227). This is, in other words, no straightforward denunciation of an anti-heroine. Rather than condemn her for her yielding to pleasure, the narrator merely points out that 'Had [Syrena] been less leud, her Hypocrisy, in all Probability, had obtain'd its end' (198).

The nature of the narrator's interpolations, coupled with the novel's ambiguous tone and complex web of intertextual allusions, make it difficult to accept the title page's assertion that this is a novel offered as a 'necessary caution to all Young Gentlemen'. The most cautionary tale told in *Anti-Pamela*, and one of the most salutary tales of the *Pamela* controversy as a whole, is surely how little control working women have over how their bodies, actions, and words are read. Whether felt or feigned, women's sentiments, it teaches us, are always liable to be read satirically, whether in books or the world beyond their pages. In making this point, Haywood's novel reveals itself to be not anti-Pamela, but anti-*Pamela*. The text is no mere exposure of the underlying vice of a fictional character. *Anti-Pamela* is a satire of the emerging sentimental novel, a form that, as Haywood's work reveals, is doubly disingenuous: first, in its denial of its indebtedness to the amatory tradition it professes to displace; and second, in its attempt to naturalize fictions of gender that, whether internalized (as by Pamela) or performed (as by Syrena), leave working women subject to the attacks of men from Mr B. and Vardine, to the swarm of anti-Pamelists determined to prove that Richardson's heroine was a whore after all.

Catherine Ingrassia is undoubtedly right that *Anti-Pamela* 'goes beyond a mere response to Richardson's *Pamela*' and as 'a fully developed fiction can stand alone'.[40] Yet to downplay the novel's engagement with Richardson's original and the controversy it spawned is to document only some of its achievements. Certainly, *Anti-Pamela* is a troubling satire and a disturbing novel. If it earns a place in the richly expanded taxonomy

---

[38] Ashley Marshall, *The Practice of Satire in England, 1658–1770* (Baltimore: Johns Hopkins University Press, 2013), 231.

[39] Paulson notes that the difference between the genres is not in aim but in their competing emphasis on the 'activity of evil' or the 'benevolence of the good'. *Satire and the Novel*, 237.

[40] Ingrassia, 'Introduction', in *Anti-Pamela and Shamela*, 11.

of satiric modes established by Marshall, in which it is not mentioned, it must be as a 'provocation': aiming to stimulate 'thought, issue a warning, or unsettle the reader'.[41] The novel's morally ambiguous tone and its failure to stick closely to the plot and characterization of Richardson's original content make the reading experience a disorienting one. *Anti-Pamela* also unsettles in its agitation of our sense of the trajectory of Haywood's career: funnier, yet also much darker, than *Fantomina*, it is no mere belated amatory novel, nor does it subscribe to the sentimental mode that *Pamela* played such an important a role in inaugurating and with which Haywood's later fictions have been aligned. It is precisely the transitional nature of Haywood's text that makes it such a difficult, yet on point, engagement with *Pamela* and the controversy it spawned and such a significant development in Haywood's own career. *Anti-Pamela* encapsulates the spirit of 'true' satire to which Haywood alludes to in *Betsy Thoughtless*. Unlike the 'scurrilous' satire of which Haywood retrospectively accused her fellow interlocutor Fielding, 'true' satire is as complex and unsettling as the world it exposes. It does not deal in moral certainties precisely because it recognizes that such certainties are intricately woven fabrications rather than realities. The work of satire, *Anti-Pamela* implies, is to lay bare those constructions and what motivates them, and to set aside the fantasy that we can strip away the veneer of words, gestures, or literal or metaphorical clothes to some underlying, authentic essence that is not already stamped by prejudice or culturally/textually determined. In performing this work, true satire is presented by *Anti-Pamela* as the best antidote to the cultural fictions of gender promoted by the mid-century novel.

SELECT BIBLIOGRAPHY

Austin, Andrea. 'Shooting Blanks: Potency, Parody, and Eliza Haywood's *The History of Miss Betsy Thoughtless*', in *The Passionate Fictions of Eliza Haywood: Essays on her Life and Work*, ed. Kirsten Saxton and Rebecca P. Bocchicchio (Lexington: University Press of Kentucky, 2000), 259–82.

Ingrassia, Catherine. *Authorship, Commerce, and Gender in Early Eighteenth-Century England: A Culture of Paper Credit* (Cambridge: Cambridge University Press, 2005).

Keymer, Thomas and Peter Sabor. *Pamela in the Marketplace: Literary Controversy and Print Culture in Eighteenth-Century Britain and Ireland* (Cambridge: Cambridge University Press, 2005).

King, Kathryn R. *A Political Biography of Eliza Haywood* (London: Pickering & Chatto, 2012).

Marshall, Ashley. *The Practice of Satire in England, 1658–1770* (Baltimore: Johns Hopkins University Press, 2013).

Paulson, Ronald. *Satire and the Novel in Eighteenth-Century England* (New Haven: Yale University Press, 1967).

Staves, Susan. *A Literary History of Women's Writing in Britain, 1660–1789* (Cambridge: Cambridge University Press, 2006).

Warner, William B. *Licensing Entertainment: The Elevation of Novel Reading in Britain, 1684–1750* (Berkeley and London: University of California Press, 1998).

---

[41] Marshall, *Practice of Satire*, 31.

CHAPTER 37

THE EDGE OF SATIRE

Post-Mortem and Other Effects

PETER ROBINSON

'WELL tried through many a varying year, / See LEVET to the grave descend'.[1] So Dr Johnson wrote in 1783 of his household friend Robert Levet. The writer's condensing intelligence may be calling on an angry passage about poetic fame from the third book of *The Dunciad*:

> On Poets' Tombs see Benson's titles writ!
> Lo! Ambrose Philips is prefer'd for Wit!
> See under Ripley rise a new White-hall,
> While Jones' and Boyle's united labours fall:
> While Wren with sorrow to the grave descends,
> Gay dies unpension'd with a hundred friends.[2]

Levet is 'Officious, innocent, sincere' and also 'Of ev'ry friendless name the friend', so Johnson hears Pope's couplet rhyme too. If William Hogarth's *Marriage à la Mode* points its moral by illustrating the deaths of the couple through a sexually motivated duel in the fifth plate and a suicide by poisoning in the sixth, the sight of the mortally wounded husband and expiring wife can also prompt pity. The edge of satire is then, I argue, the place it most sharply cuts and, simultaneously, where its burlesque points may be blunted because transformed by fatality into effects more resembling elegy and lament. This may be because death as a termination of life will hark back to the conditions that provoked or hastened it, while death as a removal from the world at the same instant removes the coordinates within which a satirical thrust could strike home. Death in a Christian culture is also believed to issue its victims into the presence of judgements far more definitive and unfunny than any lines of poetry, prose, or engraving. It is perhaps in the nature of

---

[1] Samuel Johnson, *Poems*, ed. E. L. McAdam, Jr with George Milne (New Haven: Yale University Press, 1964), 314–15 for all subsequent citations.

[2] Pope, *Poems* (Twickenham), v. 336, lines 325–30.

satire to have an edge, both in that it needs to be sharp, and to be perpetually at risk of tipping into the other-than-satire that surrounds it on all sides.

One long-fermented prompt for these and the following reflections is drawn from a passage in Walter Jackson Bate's *Samuel Johnson*, where he suggests that the author's works can be understood as the product of 'a distinctive literary type, eminently characteristic of him, that we might call "satire *manqué*" or "satire foiled"' which the biographer describes as a 'double action in which a strong satiric blow is about to strike home unerringly when another arm at once reaches out and deflects or rather lifts it'.[3] Johnson, then, offers a focus for attempting to isolate the edge of satire, for Bate's proposal is that we read him as an author whose work is located on or near that edge, at the point where a satirical impulse finds itself missing or foiled. Yet though this is a suggestive observation, I'm neither sure it is quite accurately expressed, nor that it only applies to Johnson. It may even be in the nature of satire to risk missing or being foiled, and that, even when actively present, it is only so because at risk of suffering the conditions, or something like them, that Bate intuits. What's more, if this is the case, then there will be reasons for it that lie in the nature and predicament of satire and satirist.

'Judge Not, that Ye be Not Judged'

Early in his seventy-third year of life, on Thursday 17 January 1782, Samuel Johnson wrote to his physician and friend Thomas Lawrence:

> Our old Friend Mr. Levett, who was last night eminently cheerful, died this morning. The man who lay in the same room hearing an uncommon noise got up; and tried to make him speak, but without effect, he then called Mr. Holder the apothecary, who though, when he came, he thought him dead, opened a vein but could draw no blood. So has ended the long life of a very useful, and very blam[e]less man.[4]

Three days later, Johnson wrote in his journal:

> JANUARY 20, SUNDAY. Robert Levett was buried in the church-yard of Bridewell, between one and two in the afternoon. He died on Thursday 17, about seven in the morning, by an instantaneous death. He was an old and faithful friend; I have known him from about 46. *Commendavi*. May God have had mercy on him. May he have mercy on me.[5]

Johnson in the letter to his doctor refers to Levet as 'a very useful, and very blam[e]less man', while in his memorandum-book he does not presume that his human judgement

---

[3] Walter Jackson Bate, *Samuel Johnson* (London: Chatto & Windus, 1978), 494.

[4] Samuel Johnson, *Letters*, ed. Bruce Redford, 5 vols. (Oxford: Oxford University Press, 1994), iv. 6.

[5] Samuel Johnson, *Diaries, Prayers, and Annals*, ed. E. L. McAdam, Jr with Donald and Mary Hyde (New Haven: Yale University Press, 1958), 311.

will necessarily carry any weight in the higher court: 'May God have had mercy on him'. Thus it is as if the scriptural injunction to 'Judge not, that ye be not judged' were in his mind, and so, reflexively, Johnson adds: 'May he have mercy on me'.[6] This pattern of thought, one in which the descriptive evaluation of others entails implicit self-description and evaluation, is a crucial doubling of implication to be tracked when reading what Boswell calls 'the following pathetick verses' that Johnson then wrote on the death of his old friend. His biographer reports hearing them for the first time at Mrs Thrale's house in Argyll Street on 21 March, noting that Johnson 'repeated to me his verses on Mr. Levet, with an emotion which gave them full effect'.[7]

'On the Death of Mr. Robert Levet' is a self-conscious piece of writing. Its descriptive evaluation of the poem's subject is never forgetful of the fact that our portraits of others are implicit self-portraits, by back projection along the perspectival lines implied by our view. The poem is a double portrait of its subject in a sustained implicit comparison and contrast with its author. In addition, its self-consciousness and self-concern ('have mercy on me') accompany an unusual level of technical awareness in the poet. Neither of these reflexive qualities is value-free either, and there is room for disagreement about whether they benefit the poem. My view is that they do, and this assumption is a part of what makes them so visible to me, and thus makes them figure so prominently in my account of a poem which was first published in *The Gentleman's Magazine* in August 1783:

> Condemn'd to hope's delusive mine,
>   As on we toil from day to day,
> By sudden blasts, or slow decline,
>   Our social comforts drop away.
>
> Well tried through many a varying year,
>   See Levet to the grave descend;
> Officious, innocent, sincere,
>   Of ev'ry friendless name the friend.
>
> Yet still he fills affection's eye,
>   Obscurely wise, and coarsely kind;
> Nor, letter'd arrogance, deny
>   Thy praise to merit unrefin'd.
>
> When fainting nature call'd for aid,
>   And hov'ring death prepar'd the blow,
> His vig'rous remedy display'd
>   The power of art without the show.
>
> In misery's darkest caverns known,
>   His useful care was ever nigh,
> Where hopeless anguish pour'd his groan,
>   And lonely want retir'd to die.

---

[6] Matthew 7:1.
[7] James Boswell, *The Life of Samuel Johnson*, 2 vols. (London: Dent, 1906), ii. 432.

No summons mock'd by chill delay,
    No petty gain disdain'd by pride,
The modest wants of ev'ry day
    The toil of ev'ry day supplied.

His virtues walk'd their narrow round,
    Nor made a pause, nor left a void;
And sure th' Eternal Master found,
    The single talent well employ'd.

The busy day, the peaceful night,
    Unfelt, uncounted, glided by;
His frame was firm, his powers were bright,
    Tho' now his eightieth year was nigh.

Then with no throbbing fiery pain,
    No cold gradation of decay,
Death broke at once the vital chain,
    And freed his soul the nearest way.[8]

The version given in *The Life of Samuel Johnson* has variants of spelling and punctuation, as well as, in verse 5, line 2 'His ready help was ever nigh', and Boswell notes the existence of a *viva voce* earlier version for line 4: 'And Labour steals an hour to die'. This note may be what leads the Yale editor of Johnson's *Poems* to assume that the earlier version is the one first heard by Boswell on 21 March. In addition, verse 7 lines 3–4 are smoother and there is a 'His' for 'The' at the beginning of the last line: 'And sure the eternal Master found / His single talent well employ'd'. Boswell's text also has the plural 'gradations of decay' in its final verse.

Bate's intriguing description of Johnson as a man threatening actively to dislocate his own shoulder, or of another's arm intervening to foil the satirical blow in the moment it is about to strike seems not quite to capture the complexity it identifies. For it isn't as if 'The Vanity of Human Wishes', subtitled *The Tenth Satire of Juvenal Imitated*, doesn't strike blows at humanity as observed under that 'extensive view' and at exemplifying individuals, including a fellow writer:

In life's last scene what prodigies surprise,
Fears of the brave, and follies of the wise?
From Marlb'rough's eyes the streams of dotage flow,
And Swift expires a driv'ler and a show.[9]

Though describing Swift as 'a show' may have been meant to indicate his being shown 'to tourists for a fee', rather than that he drivelled and performed, the edge of the lines implies that 'as he lived so did he die'. Johnson's means here include the heroic couplet as developed for satirical purposes in the later seventeenth century, as, for example in these lines from 'To the Memory of Mr Oldham' (1684) where Dryden, speculating how

---

[8] Johnson, *Poems*, 314–15.   [9] Johnson, *Poems*, 91 and 106, and see note to line 318.

'For sure our souls were near allied', asserts that 'One common note on either lyre did strike, / And knaves and fools we both abhorred alike'.[10]

If verse satire does have an edge it is likely to be at the line endings of its couplets, and especially when the rhyme word closes the pair of lines. The relation of sharpness in satire to its musicality, set off by the punning verb 'strike' that closes in the similarity with 'alike', is at the heart of a poem that speculates how age might have taught Oldham 'the numbers of thy native tongue', yet allows, imitatively, that 'satire needs not those, and wit will shine / Through the harsh cadence of a rugged line'.[11] If Bate is right about Johnson's imitation of Juvenal, then the blow that is being prepared but not delivered would show in the style of the rhyming—having to avoid, as in Dryden's lines on Oldham, a cut at 'strike' and blow delivered with 'alike'. Yet when Johnson addresses 'knaves and fools' himself, in the passage on Archbishop Laud's rise and fall, the formal shape is not dissimilar and the punning sharp: 'Around his tomb let Art and Genius weep, / But hear his death, ye blockheads, hear and sleep'[12]—with fierce cuts at the double caesura comma-ing off those 'blockheads' who thus recall the site of Laud's execution.

Still Swift's expiration as 'a driv'ler and a show' in *The Vanity of Human Wishes*, and a notorious passage from Johnson's 'Life of Swift' in which his late-life decay, illnesses, and madness are detailed, were in Bate's mind as he made his suggestive point:

> Yet Johnson was not and could not be a satirist. He had not only the 'aversion' to it mentioned by Mrs Thrale, but also a hatred and fear of it, which is what led him to be so antagonistic and unfair to Swift. Against this background, Johnson's lifelong struggle for good humor (a 'willingness to be pleased') and his efforts to check or suppress anger suddenly light up. They show that he did not dare to release the strong satiric impulse partly because it was so strong. But something else is involved— charity and justice he is always bringing to 'helpless man'. He could not simply watch. He had to participate; and his own willing participation sets a bar to satire.[13]

Thus Bate gives three reasons for this resistance to satirical writing: (1) the impulse to good humour and 'to be pleased', (2) to be a participant and not simply a watcher, and (3) to be charitable and just. Yet it might be said that these requirements are not ones that satirists can do without either, for the three are general ethical encomia, not only personal traits of Johnson's—ones to which he feared he couldn't always rise.

Satirists need to be pleased by *some* and admirers of their qualities too, so they may articulate ideals embodied in persons, and thus make contrasts with those who are felt not to rise to such standards, as in Dryden's 'An Ode, on the Death of Mr. Henry Purcell', where, at its close, the musician's rivals are rebuked as a means for underlining his loss to the world:

> Ye brethren of the lyre, and tuneful voice,
> Lament his lot; but at your own rejoice;

---

[10] *The Oxford Authors John Dryden*, ed. Keith Walker (Oxford: Oxford University Press, 1987), 245, 246.

[11] Dryden, *Poems* (Longman), ii. 232.   [12] Johnson, *Poems*, 100.

[13] Bate, *Samuel Johnson*, 493.

> Now live secure, and linger out your days:
> The gods are pleased alone with Purcell's lays,
> Nor know to mend their choice.[14]

Yet such a rebuke can appear blunted to the extent that the tacit rivalries it pinpoints have been rendered yet more pointless by the greater man's demise. Here too is a post-mortem effect—for the role death can play is as a satirist of the impulse to satire. And the praised dead, such as the prominent Purcell or the obscure Levet, find themselves keeping company with asides on the not praised. Satirists are inevitably participants too, participating by satirizing, and they underline it even when seeming to exclude themselves by contrast, as when Pope continues the passage from *The Dunciad* with which I began: 'Hibernian politics, O Swift! thy fate; / And Pope's, ten years to comment and translate.'[15] Thus, however excoriating, satire and satirists cannot do without the concept of just and deserved criticism, something that is not incompatible with charity. The impulse to be charitable too might be a quality that is engaged in Horatian satire, at least, even if the more excoriating kinds will not allow it—and in this *The Rape of the Lock* might be understood as a sustained, if doomed, act of indulgent charity, attempting to laugh the protagonists out of their enmity by the gentlest of portrayals designed to mitigate all round.

So in Johnson's *The Vanity of Human Wishes*, too, a satirical edge appears even if its thrust is somehow foiled in the mode that Bate describes:

> What happens, therefore, is that ridicule, anger, satiric protest, are always in the process of turning into something else. It is this process that is important. We have here what amounts to another genre or form of writing, the essence of which is not satire at all but which begins with satiric elements and an extremely alert satiric intelligence (indeed, an imagination that often seems most fertile and concrete when stung by exasperation). But then the writer—still fully aware of the satiric potentialities, still taking them all into account—suddenly starts to walk backwards and then move towards something else.[16]

Yet however much poets might want to be watchers and not implicated in what is being satirized, they are condemned to be participants (if in nothing else than being human and so doomed to die like all the rest of us). Contrasting kinds of death can be used for satirical purposes—it being implied, as noted, that Marlborough and Swift had their ends coming to them. This belief is also evoked in the last stanza of Johnson's elegy for Levet:

> Then with no throbbing fiery pain,
> No cold gradation of decay,
> Death broke at once the vital chain,
> And freed his soul the nearest way.[17]

---

[14] Dryden, *Poems* (Longman), iv. 364.   [15] Pope, *Poems* (Twickenham), v. 336.
[16] Bate, *Samuel Johnson*, 493–4.   [17] Johnson, *Poems*, 314–15.

The implication is that the easeful mode of Levet's death is a reward for his life of simple virtues, and there are implications in play here for others including the author himself.

The rhythm and form of 'On the Death of Mr. Robert Levet' has another level of thematic significance that becomes more evident when compared with a remote ancestor of the poem, both in Johnson's life, and in European poetry. Bate also notes that the elegy 'is in the calm Horatian style he had come to love as a boy at Stourbridge'.[18] Of the poems translated in his schooldays, 'Ehev fugaces, Postume, Postume', no. 14 in book 2 of Horace's *Odes*, is the one that most closely foreshadows the themes Johnson re-evokes.[19] The Loeb Classics edition prefaces its translation with the subtitle 'Death is Inevitable'. Nisbet and Hubbard note in their commentary that the 'first three stanzas constitute a rolling period that seems designed to imitate the flood of time',[20] a flood which is mimetically re-echoed in the wine spilt across the floor by the indifferent heir at the poem's close, who may nevertheless more appropriately enjoy while he can what the poem's addressee has hoarded beyond his own death. When Johnson came to translate the poem in 1726, he used the same ABAB rhymed octosyllabic tetrameter quatrain stanzas that he would deploy over half a century later for his Levet elegy:

> Alass, dear friend, the fleeting years
>   In everlasting circles run;
> In vain you spend your vows and prayers,
>   They roll, and ever will roll on.

Yet the use of rhyme in the translation's quatrains, a formal characteristic not present in the Latin original, introduces a circling motion to the 'rolling...flood' that Horace's commentators underline in his poem's three-quatrain-long, first twelve-line sentence.

The syntactically self-contained quatrains of Johnson's translation, even when he closes them with semi-colons, model time differently from Horace's original. Though demonstrating a less calibrated rhythmic burden than the elegy for Levet, this translation imagines time as returning upon itself, circling down the years, and adds that this circling motion contains within it the wished-for potential to slow down, to ignore, and to transcend, that 'flood of time':

> Your shady groves, your pleasing wife,
>   And fruitfull fields, my dearest friend,
> You'll leave together with your life,
>   Alone the cypress shall attend.
>
> After your death, the lavish heir
>   Will quickly drive away his woe,

---

[18] Bate, *Samuel Johnson*, 563.

[19] Horace, *Odes and Epodes*, Loeb Classics, trans. C. E. Bennett (Cambridge, MA: Harvard University Press, 1914; rev. edn. 1968), 142 and 144.

[20] R. G. M. Nisbet and Margaret Hubbard, *A Commentary on Horace: Odes Book II* (Oxford: Oxford University Press, 1978), 225.

The wine you kept with so much care
Along the marble floor shall flow.[21]

Johnson's quatrains model a pausing and stopped movement contrasting with and working against the 'everlasting circles' that 'run' and which 'ever will flow on' in the first verse. Johnson's translation ends on the word 'flow' but his poem halts at that point both by concluding its period there, and by the echo back to 'woe'. If Horace's poem throws itself syntactically headlong into the flood of time so as to enforce its satirical point about death's inevitability and our helplessness both before and after death, Johnson's translation reproduces that sense in the poem, but formally resists its forward movement, by the rhymed closure of its quatrains. It is granted an overtly Christian purpose in the Levet elegy, something Johnson could not have done in his translation from Horace without anachronistically falsifying its Stoic Epicureanism in the face of inevitable death.

'THE SINGLE TALENT WELL EMPLOYED'

Among works of Johnson's, though, that Bate doesn't attribute to his 'distinctive literary type' is the elegy for Levet, which he later economically evokes and characterizes:

> The situation of man is put at the outset in a short phrase, 'Hope's delusive mine.' We are like slaves condemned to dig in the mines. For we are working in the dark, forced to take our chance on what we may find; and the mine is 'delusive' because it will never really yield what the heart had hoped. The image of the mine or cave has an archetypal richness: the cold, crowded cellars in the London slums into which Levet, with his sturdy trudge of several miles each day, would descend to minister to the sick poor ('In misery's darkest caverns known, / His useful care was ever nigh'); the caverns are the human mind itself, in which hope haunts incentive and from which the sense of duty and responsibility emerges to help us march through life; and, finally, the grave [...][22]

As noted, it's a distinctly self-conscious poem, written in ABAB rhymed octosyllabic iambic tetrameter quatrains. There is only one variation to this accentual syllabic pattern: line 5, 'Well tried through many a varying year', has ten syllables, while the words which produce the two-syllable variations are 'many a' and 'varying'. Further, the relationship between this self-consciousness and the poem's subject is figured in the first two lines of the penultimate stanza: 'The busy day, the peaceful night, / Unfelt, uncounted, glided by'. This suggests that Levet lived in such an active and unreflective way that he didn't count the passage of time, but it also implies, through its careful syllabic repetitions, that Johnson *is* counting, in life and in the poem. As he reports at the time of Levet's death,

[21] Johnson, *Poems*, 13–14.   [22] Bate, *Samuel Johnson*, 563.

'I have known him from about 46' and, in the poem: 'now his eightieth year was nigh'. The line 'Unfelt, uncounted, glided by' also underlines its distinctly counted and not gliding undercurrent with the commas between the second and third, and the fifth and sixth syllables, separating the adjectives from the verb with preposition.

So 'many a varying' performs its sense by varying the metrical pattern with the additional syllables of two anapestic feet in place of iambic ones. By contrast, 'Unfelt, uncounted, glided by' is an instance of the counter-mimetic, because the metrics and punctuation underline what is *felt* and *counted* by slowing the line with commas, counteracting the 'glided' just enough to register an implicit contrast between literal temporal duration and the psychologically elastic time that insomniacs for instance, and Johnson was one, experience. There is an even more striking instance of the counter-mimetic, again activated by the poem's recourse to negative constructions, in the antepenultimate stanza:

> His virtues walk'd their narrow round,
> Nor made a pause, nor left a void;
> And sure th' Eternal Master found,
> The single talent well employ'd.

This verse is concerned with those three issues of evaluation that I noted above in Johnson's letter to his doctor and which Boswell quoted from the memorandum-book: 'a very useful, and very blam[e]less man', 'May God have had mercy on him', and 'May he have mercy on me'. The self-conscious strategy in 'Nor made a pause, nor left a void' serves to express an unusual range of implied thoughts and feelings about an apparently ordinary life and its value. Johnson's poem makes a pause at the caesura, and leaves a void of white paper at the line ending. The line thus tacitly expresses what it overtly denies. Levet was missed (by the writer, at least, and also by his many nameless friends in need) and the great gap made by his absence cannot be filled. This allows for an understanding of individual and personal uniqueness even in a form of modest social conformity—being both privately missed and yet publicly 'invisible', as it were. Such an 'irreplaceable invisibility', and the unique value of seemingly ordinary people, looks forward to Wordsworth's 'A slumber did my spirit seal' and the invisibility of the girl in the Lucy Poems, written some fifteen years after Johnson's death.

Yet the elegy for Levet also contains instances of the writing that Bate so perceptively identifies:

> Yet still he fills affection's eye,
> Obscurely wise, and coarsely kind;
> Nor, letter'd arrogance, deny
> Thy praise to merit unrefin'd.

What may not be quite right about Bate's description of the second arm foiling the first is that, here and elsewhere in Johnson's writing, the blow has actually been struck.

In his Horatian quatrains it is not so much that social follies are gently mocked with an indulgent good humour, as that the piercing, Juvenalian, criticisms are stated within a context that takes the edge off them. It is not that the 'letter'd arrogance' is allowed and understood as a natural human weakness that may be gently upbraided, the idea that the literary are susceptible to contempt for the less educated, and inclined not to see virtue if it is not dressed in their robes, remains in these lines, making its point for as long as the poem is read.

Further self-awareness and self-criticism is implied in Johnson's allusion to the Parable of the Talents. This biblical allusiveness is an aspect of the poem that most who comment on it will pause over, as does one critic, who takes the wish for the deed in its dealings with the 'Eternal Master':

> Johnson strikingly reverses the Parable of the Talents in Matthew 25: 13–30. There the bad servant is eternally punished for burying rather than investing his absent master's gift as a single talent—a sum of money. Here Johnson knows that God will reward his friend who handsomely used God's humble but essential gift[.][23]

Yet the poet's own reflections after Levet's death make it clear that he does not know that 'God will reward his friend', for he notes: 'May God have had mercy on him'. Nor does Johnson presume on an assurance that his friend 'has handsomely used God's humble but essential gift'; though calling him 'a very useful, and very blam[e]less man', he does not do God's judging for him. One way to construe this double-minded judging would be in the supposed 'intrinsic' and 'extrinsic' terms of aesthetic evaluation. Johnson's 'a very useful, and very blam[e]less man' is a human attribution of qualities, while praying for God's mercy upon Levet (or yourself) is a deferring of certainty about definitive evaluation to the all-seeing. The compulsion to defend 'intrinsic' value in aesthetics may then be part of the long-running attempt to sustain an analogous form of religious certainty in the secular cultural management of art's prestige. Yet it is worth noting that in his cultural context Johnson saw it as essential to Christian belief that human evaluation would never presume to encompass the divine—or as he puts it in 'The Vanity of Human Wishes': 'Still raise for good the supplicating voice, / But leave to heav'n the measure and the choice'.[24]

As Bate observes, Johnson keeps the idea of being buried in the ground as a running and, again, self-conscious theme throughout. Not only are we 'Condemned to hope's delusive mine' in the first line, working underground in the Roman lead mines, but in line 6 we 'see Levet to the grave descend', as Johnson had done on 20 January 1782.[25] Then in line 17 we hear how 'In misery's darkest caverns known, / His useful care was ever nigh', and Johnson then touches this burial-in-the-ground theme again in the

---

[23] Howard D. Weinbrot, 'Johnson's Poetry', in *The Cambridge Companion to Samuel Johnson*, ed. Greg Clingham (Cambridge: Cambridge University Press, 1997), 38.

[24] Johnson, *Poems*, 108.

[25] Allusion to 'damnare in metallum' is noted in Samuel Johnson, *The Complete English Poems*, ed. J. D. Fleeman (Harmondsworth: Penguin Books, 1971), 228–9.

'single talent' allusion to the Parable of the Talents. The biblical story is an exercise in how to interpret a metaphor: 'For *the kingdom of heaven is* as a man travelling into a far country, *who* called his own servants, and delivered unto them his goods. And unto one he gave five talents, to another two, and to another one; to every man according to his several ability.' The first two servants 'went and traded with the same', doubling their money, but 'he that had received one went and digged in the earth, and hid his lord's money'. The climax of the parable seems on the face of it shockingly harsh:

> Then he which had received the one talent came and said, Lord, I knew thee that thou art a hard man, reaping where thou hast not sown, and gathering where thou hast not strawed:
> And I was afraid, and went and hid thy talent in the earth: lo, *there* thou hast *that is* thine.
> His lord answered and said unto him, *Thou* wicked and slothful servant, thou knewest that I reap where I sowed not, and gather where I have not strawed:
> Thou oughtest therefore to have put thy money to the exchangers, and *then* at my coming I should have received mine own with usury.
> Take therefore the talent from him, and give *it* unto him which hath ten talents.
> For unto every one that hath shall be given, and he shall have abundance: but from him that hath not shall be taken away even that which he hath.[26]

This parable might seem hardly compatible with the one from which Ruskin took his title *Unto This Last*, in which the workers in the vineyard are all paid 'a penny a day' for different amounts of work, or that it 'is easier for a camel to go through the eye of a needle, than for a rich man to enter into the kingdom of God', or the parable of the rich man and Lazarus.[27] Rather, the Parable of the Talents might go better with the one about not hiding your candle light under a bushel, or the parable immediately preceding that of the talents, that concerning the wise and foolish virgins and their lamps.[28] It is a metaphor, though one in which the detail of the vehicle, the coin burial, the money markets, the lord being one who advocates the compounding of capital, painfully conflict with the tenor, explained in the rest of Matthew 25, that the servants investing and multiplying their talents are 'the righteous', about whom Jesus observes 'I was thirsty, and ye gave me drink: I was a stranger and ye took me in: Naked and ye clothed me: I was sick, and ye visited me: I was in prison, and ye came unto me.'[29] While the interpretation of the parable, including the illustrative instance that 'I was sick, and ye visited me' is appropriate to Johnson's elegy, nevertheless, even given this wholly metaphorical interpretation of a story cast in the terms of usury, the idea that the more you have the more you'll get and the less you have the even less you'll keep all but enforces a reinterpretation on the grounds that Jesus could not have literally meant *that*, could he?

---

[26] Matthew 25:14–29, and see also Luke 19:12–18.
[27] See Matthew 20:1–16, Matthew 19:24, and Luke 16:19–31.
[28] See Luke 11:33–6, and Matthew 25:1–13.   [29] Matthew 25:35–6.

Johnson does reinterpret and revalue the Parable, deploying metaphors of his own, not least by having it that Levet exercised his single talent underground, in 'misery's darkest caverns'. Thus, we might conclude, he invested it by burying it. He didn't put it out to the money markets to have it multiply by usury; he buried it in the ground, like the unworthy servant, but, unlike the reprimanded servant, he set to multiplying it in use in this subterranean form, as, Johnson might be implying, do all of us who work in 'hope's delusive mine'. This is how 'On the Death of Mr. Robert Levet' echoes a key question in 'The Vanity of Human Wishes' when that poem asks, taking the edge off its satire: 'Where then shall Hope and Fear their objects find?'[30] The tact required in understanding that 'sure' in 'And sure th' Eternal Master found, / The single talent well employ'd', far from underlining that 'Johnson knows that God will reward his friend', rather does the opposite, introducing an uncertainty that needs shoring up with its 'sure'.[31] Johnson may have been hearing things in that earlier elegy, including satire, for Dryden had written: 'For sure our souls were near allied', though Oldham being 'too little and too lately known',[32] the senior poet cannot be certain, and hence his use of 'sure'.

Yet this is not the only way that the parable is troubling for Johnson, as it has been for others.[33] Once again, the critic's desire to praise and protect his subject is blanking off an entire aspect of the poem's double portraiture. Here is that same critic on how Levet was rewarded for the value expressed by his life:

> As the allusion to Matthew denotes, the Eternal Master also rewards Levet: 'Death broke at once the vital chain, / And free'd his soul the nearest way'—nearer to God, who welcomes Levet as a good and faithful servant who has entered the far country that is Heaven. Johnson's secular poem spiritually comforts the poet and the poet's readers. As Johnson says in his prologue to Oliver Goldsmith's *The Good Natured Man* (1768), 'social sorrow loses half its pain'.[34]

Yet part of Levet's virtue is in not thinking any such thing, nor thinking that he has been rewarded with good health, rather than that he happens to have it, and so doesn't notice time passing. However, to put it like this, being under the illusion that living a good life means receiving reward for it in knowing that you have done so ought to prompt the thought that the opposite must be equally true: if you are not conscious of having lived well, or harbour feelings of shame and guilt, and you are not enjoying a healthy old age, and you fear that you will die slowly and painfully, and you are feeling the bars of the temporal prison closing around you, then, presumably, that same Eternal Master is punishing you for having failed to invest your many talents properly. But it is really not

---

[30] Johnson, *Poems*, 107.

[31] See Chester F. Chapin, *The Religious Thought of Samuel Johnson* (Ann Arbor: University of Michigan Press, 1968), with a discussion of 'faith' and 'trust' at 74–5.

[32] *John Dryden*, ed. Walker, 245.

[33] See John Ruskin, '*A Joy for Ever*,' being *The Substance (with additions) of the Two Lectures on The Political Economy of Art* (1857, 1880) in *The Library Edition of the Works*, ed. E. T. Cook and Alexander Wedderburn, 39 vols. (London: George Allen, 1903–12), xiv. 98–9.

[34] Weinbrot, 'Johnson's Poetry', 39.

all right, and not Christian, for Johnson as poet and man to identify himself with Levet's virtues. That too is presuming: Johnson will have also known what the story of the two thieves who were crucified beside Jesus has been understood to teach, namely that we should neither presume nor despair. If Johnson were to think of himself and Levet as equivalents of the two thieves, then it is more than appropriate that he should pray God to 'have had mercy on' Levet and to add: 'May he have mercy on me'.

'A SECOND VIEW OF THINGS HASTILY PASSED OVER OR NEGLIGENTLY REGARDED'

The double portraiture in Johnson's poem depends upon the assumption of a contrast between the life he is descriptively valuing and that of the poet writing. This contrast has already been pointed to in the different inflections of the word 'uncounted'. If the days and nights were 'Unfelt, uncounted' for Levet, they are being described as such by someone who is capable of counting them, of someone who suffered from bouts of depressive inertia and sat up late with friends for fear of insomnia. This implicit portraiture of another life lived behind the negatives deployed to evaluate Levet is more painfully present in the troubling implications of the Parable of the Talents for Johnson himself. We literary critics invested in maintaining the prestige of literature may take it as read that Dr Samuel Johnson, poet, dramatist, novelist, biographer, editor, lexicographer, critic, was a man of many talents, and that through a life of labour he employed them all. Yet this is not how it might have seemed *in medias res* when, for instance, confronted with Charles Churchill's gibe, composed by 1762, on the non-appearance of works for which people had paid their subscriptions: 'He for subscribers baits his hook, / And takes their cash – but where's the book?'[35] And, what's more, as noted, it was not part of Johnson's moral and religious philosophy to presume upon the judgement of the Almighty.

This value in not presuming upon the certainty of a human valuation feeds back into the form of conduct that is literary style. A poem that praises in another 'The power of art without the show' has, so as to avoid bad faith, to be underlining standards for its own art as well. There are two types of doctors who are having their presumptions revalued in the poem: doctors of literature and those of medicine. Neither Johnson nor Levet were awarded their title of 'Doctor' as a consequence of having passed examinations, so there is a qualification to make about both their qualifications. Johnson was obliged to leave Pembroke College, Oxford, in 1729 for lack of funds and without a degree. He was only subsequently awarded an honorary doctorate at the same university in 1775.[36] Levet was a 'quack' doctor whose only claim to the title is that he was sometimes

---

[35] See Bate, *Samuel Johnson*, 391.
[36] He received an honorary doctorate from Trinity College, Dublin, in 1765.

referred to in this way. In each case, relevantly, the social status evaluation is based upon an attribution by others of an honorific that has been granted for services performed independently of any professional qualification.

Johnson was, remember, writing to his own doctor when he reported on Levet's death, his addressee a man uniquely in a position to understand any implied contrast between Johnson's medical history and Levet's either in that communication or the subsequent elegy. This descriptive evaluation of behaviour in different kinds of doctor is the aspect of the poem that Bate might have thought of as satire *manqué* or foiled, while in the criticism of that other kind of doctor, the medical kind, Johnson revisits Pope's comment on speed of action and the wants of every day: 'The hungry Judges soon the sentence sign, / And wretches hang that jury-men may dine'. The association of these practices with the solar cycle ('declining from the noon of day, / The sun obliquely shoots his burning ray') also takes the edge off any serious satirical thrust, as if we were in Horatian territory here, because the behaviour of judges and jurymen is, like night following day, simply what people are like.

But Johnson criticizes the arrogance of the literary doctors and the pride of the medical ones by means of the shaped contrast with the object of the poet's elegiac feeling:

> In misery's darkest caverns known,
>   His useful care was ever nigh,
> Where hopeless anguish pour'd his groan,
>   And lonely want retir'd to die.
>
> No summons mock'd by chill delay,
>   No petty gain disdain'd by pride,
> The modest wants of ev'ry day
>   The toil of ev'ry day supplied.

This is again effected by the use of the negatives 'Nor, letter'd arrogance, deny', 'No summons mock'd', and 'No petty gain'. The blow is thus delivered to those to whom it is intended, by means of its being withheld from one who, the poem affirms, deserves to be praised and doesn't deserve to be criticized for neglecting patients whose offered payments it might be humiliating to the proud to accept. The criticism of the arrogantly lettered might also be turned upon himself, self-harming, as it were—since Johnson's poem is his evident means for heading off such a possible, though false, criticism. This poet-critic's view of 'Lycidas' is implicated here too, including its passage of satire against the clergy. Johnson objects to Milton's 'leisure for fiction' and censures the polemical digression on the state of the clergy under Laud.

His poem's praise of Levet is contrastive in that it occasions a rebuke to 'letter'd arrogance', suggesting that the proper way to bring medical aid and to produce poetry, shall we say, is through 'The power of art without the show'. Levet also exemplifies admirable qualities in his relation to payment for work, or talents for talents, in his relation to what Ruskin called 'plain money'.[37] Unlike some of the medical profession (is the poem's

---

[37] Ruskin, 'A Joy for Ever', 99.

implication), Levet is described as ready to attend anyone in need, and he would not stoop to marking his superiority by refusing the small payments that his poor patients pressed upon him: 'No summons mock'd by chill delay, / No petty gain disdain'd by pride'. Again we see how the negatives function in this poem to imply other standards of behaviour that Levet virtuously failed to embody. Yet, again, let it be remembered that however much Johnson wishes not to be associated with 'letter'd arrogance', that, nevertheless, is the danger for him, and that is what he also warns himself against. Once more, it would be a poor satirist who was blind to the possibility that he had himself succumbed to the denigrated qualities pointed out in his verses, and Johnson's poem avoids that obvious pitfall of the genre by tacitly allowing these accusations of arrogance, delay, and pride to echo back upon himself. 'Physician, heal thyself', of course; and that goes for literary critics and poets too.[38]

So Johnson is engaged in an exercise of revaluation, by means of the interaction between his burying and unearthing metaphors: the lead in the mine, the unrefined merit, the obscure working with obscured misery, the burial of Levet, and the single talent, all of which are revalued by the unearthing which happens with the freeing of his soul the nearest way. This process of valuing Levet, devaluing the tardy doctors and arrogant literati, and revaluing the singly talented, explicitly links action in and upon the world with the writer's Christian worldview, a view which is clearly not unthinkingly accepted, for, as I have suggested, the 'sure' in the stanza on the Parable of the Talents is not only not presuming upon divine judgement, but also complexly pondering that biblical passage. Michael Thompson, the founding exponent of Rubbish Theory, a dynamic anthropological study of 'the creation and destruction of value', calls upon Johnson while articulating the relations of worldview to action and vice versa. He cites 'An Allegory of Criticism' from *The Rambler* 27 March 1750:

> The task of an author is, either to teach what is not known, or to recommend known truths by his manner of adorning them; either to let new light in upon the mind, and open new scenes to the prospect, or to vary the dress and situation of common objects, so as to give them fresh grace and more powerful attractions, to spread such flowers over the regions through which the intellect has already made its progress, as may tempt it to return, and take a second view of things hastily passed over or negligently regarded.[39]

Thompson's point in citing 'so noble a view of creativity, expressed with such clarity and force by so great a figure as Samuel Johnson' is to note that its compound process is 'denied' and 'suppressed' because of an understandable fleeing from the idea that we can 'teach what is not known' (the radical interpretation of that idea being: *not known even by the teacher before its discovery through work*) and that we can and will revisit old

---

[38] Luke 4:23.
[39] Cited in Michael Thompson, *Rubbish Theory: The Creation and Destruction of Value* (Oxford: Oxford University Press, 1979), 150.

evaluations to transform our rubbish, those 'things hastily passed over or negligently regarded', into national treasures.

There are a number of verbal echoes of his early translation of Horace in 'On the Death of Mr. Robert Levet': there is the 'friend' echo; there is the constrained circling motion of the years and the stanzas, elaborated and developed in the later poem; there is the 'fatal blow' phrase which is echoed in 'death prepared the blow'; there is the poem's opening word 'Condemn'd' which appears similarly as the initial word in line 20 of the translation. Thomas Woodman notes of the later elegy that the 'sombre repeated pattern of Johnson's quatrains acts out the relentless movement of time—"As on we toil from day to day"'.[40] This is true; but it is also true of the Horace translation, written in the same stanza form: 'They roll, and ever will roll on'. Does the later poem add to the rhythmic significance of its figured inexorability? To my ear, Johnson's late poem not only echoes the 'flow of time' theme in the Horace, and the impossibility of resisting the change and decay that they will bring with them, a part of the Stoic effort to disarm death by facing it and the Epicurean urging to enjoy life while you can. Johnson's early translation already shows how he can adapt the unrhymed stanzas of the Horace original to rhymed tetrameter quatrains. Contrasting this translation with the late elegy shows how the pausing of the latter, its resistance to the glide of time, also coincides with its Christian hope.

In his portrait of Levet, then, Johnson has been able to transform the inexorability of time into a positive for his untroubled friend ('Unfelt, uncounted, glided by'), while for him the pauses and voids model the self-conscious and reflective writer's sense of time as both slower, and more troubling; but also the pausing produces a counter-force, or counter-principle to the inexorability. This too coincides with the Christian hope, because it not only promises a release from the temporal imprisonment, but also invites hope of eternal life in heaven. So the poem models a movement through a counted time to a timeless ending. Nevertheless, it does not presume upon this outcome. Nothing in the poem, *pace* some of its critics, says that Levet has gone to Heaven or that he has got his reward. It simply points towards that embodied belief about the course of a human life within the Christian dispensation.

The contrast between Levet and Johnson also touches on the problem of the examined and the unexamined life. Socrates famously said at his trial that 'The unexamined life is not worth living' (*Apology* 38a), while, I might add, the over-examined life is unbearable. Yet Levet is presented as someone who lived a good, unexamined life, while Johnson's poem implicitly reflects on whether being self-consciously self-reflective (as his poem is) will make for a life more worth living. It is understandable that readers don't necessarily see this aspect of the poem, its tacit self-portraiture side, because it attempts to have, precisely, the power of art without the show. It exemplifies in its confessional reticence how the power (and the truth) of the poem would be dissipated if it were identifying itself with the values it ascribes to Levet—for it would not only be falsely modest about its talents, but falsely self-satisfied about their investment. Just as Johnson cannot and should not presume on God's justice and mercy, so he will not presume upon the

---

[40] Thomas M. Woodman, *A Preface to Samuel Johnson* (London: Longman, 1993), 152.

judgement of readers. He will, however, warn readers by means of his satirical impulse, and himself, about the dangers inherent in assuming that your talents can, because you happen to possess them, free you from the constraints of modesty, industriousness not thwarted by pride, generosity of spirit, or presumption of virtue through the benefits of education: 'Nor letter'd arrogance deny / Thy praise to merit unrefin'd'.

SELECT BIBLIOGRAPHY

Bate, Walter Jackson. *Samuel Johnson* (London: Chatto & Windus, 1978).

Chapin, Chester F. *The Religious Thought of Samuel Johnson* (Ann Arbor: University of Michigan Press, 1968).

Johnston, Freya. 'Samuel Johnson and Robert Levet', *Modern Language Review* 97 (2002), 26–35.

Thompson, Michael. *Rubbish Theory: The Creation and Destruction of Value* (Oxford: Oxford University Press, 1968).

Venturo, David F. 'The Poetics of Samuel Johnson's Epitaphs and Elegies and "On the Death of Dr. Robert Levet"', *Studies in Philology* 85 (1988), 73–91.

Vilmar, Christopher. 'Johnson's Criticism of Satire and the Problem of the Scriblerians', *Cambridge Quarterly* 38 (2009), 1–23.

Weinbrot, Howard D. 'Johnson's Poetry', in *The Cambridge Companion to Samuel Johnson*, ed. Greg Clingham (Cambridge: Cambridge University Press, 1997), 34–50.

Woodman, Thomas M. *A Preface to Samuel Johnson* (London: Longman, 1993).

CHAPTER 38

SATIRE TO SENTIMENT

Mixing Modes in the Later Eighteenth-Century British Novel

LYNN FESTA

IT is something of a critical cliché that the eighteenth century witnesses a transition from the age of satire to an age of sentiment, yet satire persists and commingles with the sentimental in the second half of the century in novels by Henry Fielding, Sarah Fielding, Henry Mackenzie, Oliver Goldsmith, Laurence Sterne, Tobias Smollett, and Frances Burney, among others. This essay addresses both the incursion of satiric strains into the sentimental novel and the sentimentalization of satiric objects, focusing on the capacity of each mode to grapple with broader historical currents (burgeoning commerce, urbanization, imperial expansion, and the blossoming discourses of humanitarianism and human rights). In these novels, precipitous shifts from the satiric to the sentimental suggest the inadequacy of existing literary conventions in the face of seismic historical changes. The use of mixed modes exposes the tensions between the ideals exalted in the texts (both satiric and sentimental) and the material facts that novelistic realism empha-sizes; the movement between satire and sentimentality in texts marks out the difficulty of defining a stable vantage point vis-à-vis these objects. Writers of the period are concerned with the performative dimensions of sentimental and satiric rhetoric: the communities and individual subjectivities called into being by each mode, the models of causality each institutes, and the forms of action each initiates (or fails to incite).

Although satire and the sentimental purport to share a common agenda—to improve society by eliciting powerful moral responses in their readers—they do so by conflicting means. Whereas the sentimental seeks to elicit pity for suffering virtue, satire invites hatred towards vice; whereas the sentimental text fosters sympathetic solidarity with a disempowered other, satire institutes critical communities united over and against the reviled object.[1] The sentimentalist's tears invite protagonist and reader alike to bask in

---

[1] See Ronald Paulson, *Satire and the Novel* (New Haven: Yale University Press, 1967), 219–65.

the self-congratulatory pleasures of humanity, while satiric laughter produces a queasy movement between revulsion and unwilling self-recognition, identification and self-critical displacement. If sentimental texts invite absorption in the affective responses to another's suffering rather than critical scrutiny of its material causes and effects, satire endeavours to sunder such easy identifications in order to produce a critical vision of the world. Yet both modes face a kind of impasse: even as satiric denunciation produces a bleak vision of a world incapable of amelioration, sentimental effusions risk producing tears without emendation. Although both modes appeal to past formations to try to explain the historical present, they both struggle to justify their relation to futurity: to the capacities of the individual—and of the text—to alter the state of things to come.

The conventional narrative about the supplanting of the satiric by the sentimental draws on well-established teleological narratives of the rise of the novel and the growing importance of the middling sort to the culture of eighteenth-century Britain.[2] In this account, the newly prosperous commercial classes disdain the raillery and ridicule of Restoration and Augustan elites, staking their claim to authority through the cultivation of moral sensibility, which assigns value to interior traits and the performance of virtue rather than to birth and rank. Yet satire does not follow Alexander Pope into the grave in 1744, leaving the sentimental to lord it over the literary landscape. To be sure, formal verse satire loses the pre-eminent role it held through the 1730s and the market for sentimental literature grows in the latter part of the century, but, as Ashley Marshall and Simon Dickie have shown, satire endures in novels, popular jest-books, and a variety of less canonical forms, migrating into other genres—not least into the sentimental novel to which satire is usually opposed.[3] There is no clean break between an 'Age of Satire' and an 'Age of Sensibility'.

Indeed, long before the mid-century ascendancy of the sentimental, satire was accommodating itself to strains of moral sense philosophy that drew the two seemingly antithetical modes closer together. Satire had long been understood as a rhetorical form designed to persuade its reader to adhere to a higher standard of morality. In satire, John Dryden claims in his influential 1693 *Discourse concerning the Original and Progress of Satire*, 'all Virtues are every where to be prais'd, and recommended to Practice; and all Vices to be reprehended, and made either Odious or Ridiculous'.[4] The question of whether 'the scourging of Vice' becomes an 'Exhortation to Virtue' drives ongoing debates over the rival merits of Juvenalian invective and milder Horatian satire that anticipate the sentimental interest in moral pedagogy (Dryden, 55). Although Dryden

---

[2] See Andrew Wilkinson, 'The Decline of English Verse Satire in the Middle Years of the Eighteenth Century', *Review of English Studies* 3, no. 11 (1952), 222–33; Thomas Lockwood, *Post-Augustan Satire: Charles Churchill and Satirical Poetry, 1750–1800* (Seattle: University of Washington Press, 1979); Vincent Carretta, *The Snarling Muse: Verbal and Visual Political Satire from Pope to Churchill* (Philadelphia: University of Pennsylvania Press, 1983), 211; Ashley Marshall, *The Practice of Satire in England, 1658–1770* (Baltimore: Johns Hopkins University Press, 2013), 255.

[3] Marshall, *Practice of Satire*; Simon Dickie, *Cruelty and Laughter: Forgotten Comic Literature and the Unsentimental Eighteenth Century* (Chicago: University of Chicago Press, 2011).

[4] Dryden, 'Discourse', 81.

insists that it is 'an Action of Virtue to make Examples of vicious Men' in order to amend those who are 'not yet incorrigible', other writers recognize that the satiric laceration of vice may not produce positive models for imitation.[5]

Over the course of the period, the punitive aspects of satire increasingly fall into disfavour. The preference for the smiling and polite Horace, who 'laughs to shame all Follies, and insinuates Virtue, rather by familiar Examples, than by the severity of Precepts', is connected to a broader shift in the value assigned to laughter, above all, the rejection of Hobbes's account of cruel mirth as '*Sudden Glory*' incited by the revelation of one's superiority to a lesser being.[6] Early Whig writers, such as Joseph Addison and Richard Steele, distinguish themselves from Tory satirists by preferring kinder, gentler forms of admonishing humour and even proto-sentimental scenes of suffering: 'I will break from this satirical vein', Steele announces in *The Tatler*, and 'turn my Thoughts to raising Merit from its Obscurity, celebrating Virtue in its Distress, and attacking Vice by no other Method, but setting Innocence in a proper Light.'[7] In keeping with moral philosophy's characterization of humanity as sociable, polite, and benevolent, early periodicals seek to excite human goodness through sympathy rather than satirically lashing it into being. What Clausewitz remarked of politics and war might be extended to literature: the sentimental is the continuation of the satiric by other means.

Yet the insistence that 'Good-Nature' is 'an essential Quality in a Satyrist'[8] is countered by persistent suspicions about the malevolent impulses behind it: 'Wit, cohabiting with Malice, had a son named Satyr, who followed him, carrying a quiver filled with poisoned arrows', Samuel Johnson writes in 1750, pointing to a satiric appetite for cruelty for its own sake.[9] The sadistic glee of the roaster, the novelist Henry Fielding states, suggests 'a great Depravity of Nature, which delights in the Miseries and Misfortunes of Mankind', although, for Fielding, sentiment tempers cruelty.[10] Although a well-dressed person tumbling in the street excites laughter as 'one of those...spontaneous Motions of the Soul, which...none can prevent', Fielding observes, '[w]hen we come to reflect on the Uneasiness this Person suffers, Laughter, in a good and delicate Mind, will begin to change itself into Compassion.'[11] The satiric and the sentimental exist in a complex play of checks and balances that seeks to reconcile laughter with the period's vision of sociable, sympathetic humanity.

---

[5] Dryden, 'Discourse', 60. On the rehabilitation of Juvenal and its connection to sentimentality, see W. B. Carnochan, 'Satire, Sublimity, and Sentiment: Theory and Practice in Post-Augustan Satire', *PMLA* 85 (1970), 260–7.

[6] Dryden, 'Discourse', 63; Thomas Hobbes, *Leviathan*, ed. Richard Tuck (Cambridge: Cambridge University Press, 1996), 43. See Stuart Tave, *The Amiable Humorist: A Study in the Comic Theory and Criticism of the Eighteenth and Early Nineteenth Centuries* (Chicago: University of Chicago Press, 1960).

[7] *Tatler* 71 (22 September 1709), i. 492.   [8] *Tatler* 242 (26 October 1710), iii. 241.

[9] *The Rambler* 22 (2 June 1750), *The Rambler*, vol. 1, The Yale Edition of the Works of Samuel Johnson, vol. 3. ed. W. J. Bate and Albrecht B. Strauss (New Haven: Yale University Press, 1969), 123–4.

[10] Henry Fielding, *Champion* (13 March 1739–40), in *The Champion*, 2 vols. (1741), 1.357.

[11] Henry Fielding, 'Essay on the Knowledge of the Characters of Men', *Miscellanies, Volume One*, ed. Henry Knight Miller (Oxford: Clarendon Press, 1972), 160.

Whereas satire appeals to objective models of vice and virtue, 'clear-cut patterns of right and wrong... evident to a reasonable, unprejudiced mind',[12] the sentimental sought to bring the two principal senses of the word sentiment—as moral precept and as feeling—into alignment. Sentimental texts persuade by feeling, not logic: we hear the story of suffering, and intuitively feel the truth. Our 'Sense of Right and Wrong', as Shaftesbury put it, is 'as natural to us as natural affection itself'.[13] Moral sense philosophy assumes an intuitive sense of good and evil. Inasmuch as 'vice and virtue are not discoverable merely by reason', but 'by some impression or sentiment they occasion', Hume argues, 'morality... is more properly felt than judg'd of'.[14] Yet inasmuch as vice and virtue cease to be 'qualities in objects' and become 'perceptions in the mind' (Hume, 469), the sentimental appeal to feeling exposes what satire treats as objective norms to a dangerous relativism, even to the point of imperilling the notion of truth as something in which the public has a stake. Sentimental novels both capitalize on this subjective response and, at times, use satire to subject it to critique.

Both formally and thematically, the sentimental novel was, from its inception, ripe for satire. In contrast to the single-mindedness of satiric texts—the argument of satire, Dryden argues, should be 'confin'd to one particular Theme', with 'other Vices... only... transiently lash'd' (79)—the sentimental is often fragmentary, neither coherent nor progressive, and its very incoherence raises questions about its moral efficacy. Indeed, the sentimental novel stylistically incarnates the muddled (lack of) argumentation that earlier in the century was the object of much Scriblerian satire. If, as Dustin Griffin notes, satire 'can through parody invade *any* literary form', the sentimental novel—with its unreliable narrators beset by sighs, swoons, tears, and blushes, its dilation on trivial events narrated in a breathless present-tense, and its (often cloying) tales of persecuted virtue—was easily overrun.[15] The rapidity with which Richardson's 1740 *Pamela* spawned satiric ripostes is undoubtedly a result of its blockbuster success, but it also reveals something about the formal elements that make sentimentality so susceptible to satire: above all, the frequent use of first-person narration or epistolary form, which eliminates the corrective voice of a narrator able to present authoritative objective standards. Thus Fielding's *Shamela* exposes the seeming inwardness of Richardsonian self-description as hypocritical doubleness, transforming Pamela's account of her persecution and near-rape by Mr B. into the self-serving manipulation of the gullible Squire Booby. Fielding's satiric reduction of Pamela's moral qualities to a mere spoken word—'so we sat down and talked about my Vartue till Dinner-time'[16]—converts her insistence on her moral and sexual inviolability into a rhetorical effect, while the repeated effusions of Fielding's Parson Tickletext—'methinks I see Pamela at this instant, with all

[12] Paulson, *Satire and the Novel*, 7.

[13] Shaftesbury, 'An Inquiry Concerning Virtue or Merit', in *Characteristics of Men, Manners, Opinions, Times*, ed. Lawrence Klein (Cambridge: Cambridge University Press, 1999), 179.

[14] David Hume, *A Treatise of Human Nature*, ed. L. A. Selby-Bigge (Oxford: Clarendon Press, 1980), 470.

[15] Dustin Griffin, *Satire: A Critical Reintroduction* (Lexington: University Press of Kentucky, 1994), 3.

[16] Henry Fielding, *Shamela*, in *Joseph Andrews and Shamela*, ed. Martin Battestin (Boston: Houghton Mifflin, 1961), 323.

the pride of ornament cast off'—recasts the novel's interest in virtue in distress as thinly disguised prurience (305).

Notwithstanding protestations about their moral value, both satire and sentiment offer aesthetic and sexual pleasures that are not easily harnessed to the cause of virtue. ('Il y a un peu de testicule,' as Diderot wrote in a 1760 letter, 'au fond de nos sentiments les plus sublimes et de notre tendresse la plus épurée.'[17]) Both sentimentality and satire may lead to self-congratulation rather than moral emendation or right action. If 'SATYR gratifies self-love', as the poet William Shenstone claims in 1764, so too does sentimentality flatter readers' fantasy versions of their own sensibilities.[18] Thus Sterne's Yorick concludes a sentimental rhapsody on the pleasures of charity with a self-reflexive take-down: 'But in saying this—surely I am commending the passion—not myself.'[19] Love of virtue may prove to be love of self. The 'angry satirist's pleasing emotional arousal and satisfied conscience', Dustin Griffin points out, bear comparison to the gratifications offered by the tearful effusions of 'the man of sentiment, and the Richardsonian heroine' (179).

The delight extracted by the sentimental reader from scenes of human misery is not far distant from the pleasure taken in the pain inflicted by satire's punitive lash. If satire satisfies an appetite for outrage by exhaustively anatomizing vice, novels of sensibility serve up an unending diet of scenes of suffering for the rapacious maw of the sentimental epicure. As the French author Marie-Jeanne Riccoboni writes to the actor David Garrick in 1769: 'on feroit volontiers des malheureux pour goûter la douceur de les plaindre.'[20] Efforts to make satire the scapegoat for the cruelties internal to the sentimental are doomed to fail; the infliction of pain is intrinsic to the mode. When Sarah Fielding, without any discernible irony, notes that the bereaved daughters of a dying man show 'such Agonies of Grief and tender Sorrow, as gave our Hero great Pleasure', she points to the perverse delight—even complicity—in the misery of others that lies at the heart of sentimental fiction.[21] It is to the unexpected profits gleaned from sentimental affliction and satiric outrage that we now turn.

SENTIMENTAL LOSSES
AND SATIRIC RETURNS

Sarah Fielding's 1744 'moral romance', *The Adventures of David Simple*, and its sequel, the 1753 *Volume the Last*, portray the titular hero as a sentimental Diogenes, seeking not an honest man but a virtuous 'friend' in an unwelcoming urban landscape. David's quest

[17] Denis Diderot, *Correspondance*, ed. Georges Roth, 16 vols. (Paris: Éditions de Minuit, 1957), iii. 216.

[18] William Shenstone, *The Works in Verse and Prose*, 2 vols. (Dublin: G. Faulkner, 1764), ii. 9.

[19] Laurence Sterne, *A Sentimental Journey* (New York: Penguin, 1978), 57.

[20] David Garrick, *The Private Correspondence of David Garrick with the Most Celebrated Persons of his Time*, 2 vols. (1832), ii. 561.

[21] Sarah Fielding, *The Adventures of David Simple and Volume the Last*, ed. Peter Sabor (Lexington: University Press of Kentucky, 1998), 36.

takes him from the London Exchange to taverns and coffee-houses, from the haunts of the wealthy to the garrets of the poor. Between encounters with an array of selfish, venal, and deceitful types, David experiences great misfortunes himself and weeps over the sad tales of the virtuous few. The narrator lauds David's faith in human goodness, while using the satiric figures he meets—the proud Orgueil, the trash-talking Spatter—to disabuse David of his honourable but naïve beliefs. David's gullibility exposes the inadequacy of sensibility without reason, while the satirical figures point to the inhumanity of a world governed by reason alone. Although the satirist Orgueil, for example, has good principles, his rectitude issues from pride, not benevolence. That he 'looked upon Compassion as a Weakness' is deemed an irredeemable sin by the narrator and David alike: satire without sympathy, both insist, is wrong (*DS*, 57).

Fielding concludes the 1744 novel by rewarding her man of feeling with retirement from the corrupt world with a community of like-feeling souls. She revokes this sentimental dispensation in the bleak 1753 sequel, however, afflicting David with Job-like tribulations—betrayal by trusted associates, financial ruin, the death of his wife, children, and friends, followed by his own demise. Fielding's narrator accompanies the moving portrait of David's decline into poverty with a lucid satirical dissection of the motives and responses of the false friends surrounding him, forestalling the facile rewriting of David's poverty into a romantic vision of decorative indigence. 'By Poverty', she clarifies,

> I mean distressed, not narrow Circumstances…when you pay *Cent. per Cent.* for every Necessary of Life, by being obliged to buy every thing by retail: when, if you endeavour to keep up a fair Out-side, and paint not your Poverty in the most ghastly Shape, your nominal Friends will call you extravagant: whilst, on the other hand, if you set your Poverty in full View, such Friends will generously think you too low for their Regard.   (276)

There is nothing picturesque about David's destitution, and it does not call forth the benevolence of those around him. Although the second-person address interpellates the reader, Fielding excites pity by satirically describing the *failure* of sympathy, excoriating the selfish sentiments lodged in others' hearts.

David dies in a state of Christian fortitude but, tellingly, the sole survivor of his circle of friends is the satiric sentimentalist, Cynthia, who recognizes both the goodness and the evil of her fellows. For Fielding, the cure for the heartlessness of the present world is neither satire nor sentiment, but the one tempered by the other. The novel itself offers an apprenticeship in exactly such a doubled mode of reading: while the focalization through David invites us into his naïve perspective, the allegorical names such as Spatter, Orgueil, and even David Simple, serve as signposts to their true natures. If the sentimental elements of the novel invite us to feel for David, the satire reminds us that we must not read like him.

The sentimental and the satiric likewise exist in dynamic opposition in the work of Laurence Sterne. With its cast of eccentrics, its Scriblerian erudition and its mockery of rigid intellectual systems, its Rabelaisian energies and double entendres, Sterne's *Tristram*

Shandy (1759–67) clearly positions itself in a satiric tradition. Yet Sterne's novel also contains many of the hallmarks that would become standard features in later sentimental works: wordless exchanges, fractured language, myriad scenes of sympathy, sustained attention to the feeling body, and an interest in the affective responses of the individual to the world. The intertwining strands of satire, sentiment, and bawdry baffled, delighted, and offended early readers of Sterne's motley text, and the first volumes were sometimes characterized as unchaste and even immoral—'interlarded with obscenity', the *Monthly Review* reproached.[22] Only gradually did the view of Sterne as an arch-sentimentalist emerge. Immense enthusiasm for the pathetic deaths of Yorick and Le Fever prompted Sterne to amp up the sentimental elements to boost the sales of later volumes, and an eager public embraced the turn. 'One of our critics once remarked, *in print*, Mr. Shandy—that he thought your excellence lay in the PATHETIC', the *Monthly Review* gushes in 1765. 'I think so too.... [A]rouze, transport, refine, improve us. Let morality, let the cultivation of virtue be your aim.'[23]

The vision of Sterne as an inexhaustible mine for sentimental nuggets was reinforced by anthologies like the *Beauties of Sterne*, which went through seven editions within a year of its 1782 publication. 'Selected for the heart of sensibility', the collection isolates sentimental vignettes from the action, excising the bawdy or satiric elements that might disrupt the pleasurable consumption of pure feeling. Thus Tristram's encounter with Maria, the pipe-playing, goat-keeping maiden pathetically deserted by her lover, concludes with Tristram tottering 'with broken and irregular steps . . . to my chaise',[24] rather than with the satiric deflation of the line that immediately follows in the novel, as Tristram shakes off his sentimental posture and briskly canters on: 'What an excellent inn at Moulins!' he exclaims.[25]

Early consumers of these anthologies presumably failed to recognize the canny satiric dissection of sentimental reading that accompanied affecting moments of Shandean *tendresse*. When, in *A Sentimental Journey*, Yorick detours to visit 'poor Maria' as a five-star attraction in his emotional Baedeker, he confesses that ''tis going, like the Knight of the Woeful Countenance, in quest of melancholy adventures—but I know not how it is, but I am never so perfectly conscious of the existence of a soul within me, as when I am tangled in them' (137). The Quixote-like quest is a form of sentimental self-seeking, as the first-person witness uses others' suffering to discover the 'existence of a soul within me' in a kind of affective cogito: *I feel, therefore I am*. Although Yorick declares that he cannot understand what causes this surge of emotion ('I know not how it is'), the artful rhetoric of such set pieces—with their shrewd selection of touching detail and deliberate calibration of distance—unveils the intense labour needed to fabricate sentimental

[22] *Monthly Review*, 26 (January 1762), qtd. Alan B. Howes, ed., *Sterne: The Critical Heritage* (London: Routledge & Kegan Paul, 1974), 141.

[23] *Monthly Review* 32 (February 1765), qtd. Howes, ed., *Sterne: The Critical Heritage*, 167, 168.

[24] *The Beauties of Sterne* (1782), 92.

[25] Laurence Sterne, *Tristram Shandy*, ed. Melvyn New and Joan New (New York: Penguin, 1978), 9.24.530.

feeling; this is not an organic, spontaneous overflowing of instinctive sympathy. Sterne simultaneously invites the reader to dabble in sentimental feeling and satirically dissects its formal operation, tracing the wilful manipulation that displaces sympathy from the suffering object to the moved spectator.

No philanthropic aim justifies this sentimental rubbernecking; Yorick describes what he *would* do to comfort Maria, 'wast thou in my own land', working himself up to a pleasurable lather over the good deeds he might perform in a purely hypothetical scene of his own devising. So moved is he by his own imagined benevolence that 'Nature melted within me, as I uttered this' (139). Yorick's tears do nothing material to relieve Maria's suffering; indeed, it is Maria who is obliged to attend to Yorick, rinsing his tear-soaked handkerchief in a nearby stream and then drying it in her bosom, with typical hints of Sternean bawdry. The feelings available for the readers' sympathetic delectation are not Maria's but Yorick's; we are united in shared feeling towards a common object who is excluded from the circle of tearful witnesses. Maria never recounts her full story; she conveys her feelings through melancholy piping, leaving Yorick with infinite amplitude to fill in the emotional blanks. The feelings with which Yorick sympathizes are all his own. Indeed, so absolute is Yorick's command over the intensity of his vicarious grief that when his sorrowful feelings for Maria overshadow the pleasures of his journey, he deliberately snuffs them out: 'I had got almost to Lyons before I was able to cast a shade across her', he announces (140).

It is unclear how many of Sterne's tearful readers caught the irony of a sentimental reading practice that embraces and discards victims at will. If sentimental feeling misses its ostensible mark (inviting the reader to feel with Yorick, not for Maria), so too may satire go astray. As Swift famously remarked, '*SATYR is a sort of* Glass, *wherein Beholders do generally discover every body's Face but their Own*.'[26] The formal structures of satire and sentiment cannot police readerly identification. The question that sentimental literature poses for its readers—are the feelings I am having really my own?—finds a counterpart in the suspicion raised by satire: do I get the joke, or am I part of the joke? The difficulty of deciding whether sentimental texts are parodic or in earnest is one symptom of this interpretative volatility, and later writers exploit the indeterminacy of these two modes in order to expose the social and political consequences of each form of reading.

SENTIMENTAL VICES, SATIRIC VIRTUES

Mackenzie's 1771 *The Man of Feeling* depicts the individual's sentimental education as a reflection of a moral and political order in decline. Recounted by an older narrator familiar with the titular man of feeling's tale, the main narrative tells the story of Harley, an impoverished gentleman who travels to London in hopes of gaining a lease on lands that are rightfully his. En route, he encounters assorted sharpers and an array of unfortunates:

---

[26] Swift, *Battle of the Books*, in Swift, *PW*, i. 140.

a young woman driven mad by the loss of her beloved, a poor prostitute, and a former acquaintance, 'Old Edwards', returned from service in India to discover his family in ruins. Unsuccessful in his mission, Harley returns home and, unable to confess his love to the neighbouring squire's daughter, dies of a mysterious illness.

Although the ingredients for a just-add-tears-and-stir sentimental novel are present, our ability to read *The Man of Feeling* as such is hampered by a narrative frame that mediates our encounter with the narrator and Harley. In the opening, the unknown editor describes rescuing the manuscript from its use as gun wadding by an unsentimental curate. Although the putative editor notes that he found 'some very trifling passages' affecting and would have wept 'had the name of a Marmontel, or a Richardson, been on the title-page', the absence of a brand-name author has checked his tears: 'One is ashamed to be pleased with the works of one knows not whom.'[27] In reminding us that sensibility is a fashionable commodity, the editor draws attention to the artificial manufacture of purportedly spontaneous emotion for an eager market. Indeed, Mackenzie's novel would itself become so popular that it too would serve as a sentimental litmus test. Lady Louisa Stuart's famous letter to Sir Walter Scott recalls the obligatory performance of emotion at readings of *The Man of Feeling* in the 1770s: 'I had a secret dread I should not cry enough to gain the credit of proper sensibility.' (So dramatically had literary fashions changed by 1826, she adds, that the most pathetic moments have become risible: 'Nobody cried, and at some of the passages, the touches that I used to think so exquisite—Oh Dear! They laughed.'[28])

It is difficult for modern readers to view *The Man of Feeling* without irony. Bathetic touches abound: a beggar asks for charity and 'the dog began to beg too:—it was impossible to resist both' (59), while chapter titles such as 'The Man of Feeling in a Brothel' echo Sternean bawdry. Many episodes satirize what passes for sentimental ethics. The sad history of the fortune-telling vagrant Harley encounters upon first setting out on his journey suggests the beggar is largely to blame for his own woes. Mackenzie places us at a satiric distance from Harley's decision to give charity to this less-than-laudable character: 'Virtue bade him consider on whom he was going to bestow it.—Virtue held back his arm:—but a milder form, a younger sister of virtue's, not so severe as virtue, not so serious as pity, smiled upon him: His fingers lost their compression;—nor did virtue offer to catch the money as it fell' (61). Feeling and judgement—the provinces of sentiment and satire, respectively—do not coalesce; indeed, the disconnect between them is the pointed object of Mackenzie's commentary. Harley is the puppet of personifications: first of the 'Virtue' that acts as a prudential monitor and then of an unnamed trait, milder than virtue and less serious than pity, that disburses largesse in his stead. Harley possesses none of Yorick's self-satirizing canniness about the array of motives, both self-serving and benevolent, that govern seemingly good deeds. Although beatitudinous relief offers a sentimental payoff, Harley does not weigh the consequences of his actions.

[27] Henry Mackenzie, *The Man of Feeling*, ed. Maureen Harkin (Peterborough: Broadview, 2005), 49.
[28] Letter of 4 September 1826, *The Private Letter-Books of Sir Walter Scott*, ed. Wilfred Partington (New York: Frederick Stokes, 1930), 273.

Mackenzie's satiric exhortation—to use effects, not affects, to determine moral ends—is undermined by the episodic form of the sentimental text. The isolated vignettes featured in the sentimental novel snap the narrative conjoining of cause and effect that allows ephemeral emotion to be translated into action. The sentimentalist is always belated, filled with lamentation for an evil that has *already* happened and that cannot be changed. *The Man of Feeling* likewise concludes with virtue vanquished. Harley dies as one who is too good for this world, and the narrator ends up in the disenchanted isolated posture of the Juvenalian satirist: 'I sometimes visit his grave; I sit in the hollow of the tree. It is worth a thousand homilies! ... but it will make you hate the world—No: there is such an air of gentleness around, that I can hate nothing; but, as to the world—I pity the men of it' (139). Satire has lost its sting and subsided into melancholic meditation. Such a turning inward towards privatized feeling proves to be the only refuge from an incurably self-interested commercial order.

Whereas the satirist, as Paulson argues, is concerned with 'the moment of action'[29] and the judgement attached to it, the sentimentalist dwells on suffering, indulging in what Mackenzie would later describe as a 'sickly sort of refinement [that] creates imaginary evils and distresses'. Mackenzie condemns sentimental readers 'who pay in words what they owe in actions; or perhaps, what is fully as dangerous, who open their minds to *impressions* which never have any effect upon their *conduct*, but are considered as something foreign to and distinct from it. This separation of conscience from feeling is a depravity of the most pernicious sort.'[30] The sentimental tribute of a tear does not, Mackenzie insists, satisfy one's moral or political obligations. Worse, sentimentality often buttresses an unjust order, naturalizing the status quo by celebrating the beneficence of the ruling classes and forestalling revolution through palliative acts of local relief. In representing suffering as the result of the isolated deeds of corrupt individuals, the sentimental disguises structural injustice.[31]

Yet we should not juxtapose sentimental mystification with satiric realism as the hard-nosed unveiling of brutal truths. Satire, like sentimentality, often proves ineffectual in amending the world; it too, as the essayist Vicesimus Knox points out, 'has seldom answered its ostensible end of reforming the age'.[32] Indeed, as its proponents argued, sentimentality often served as a crucial impetus for right action, above all, in political movements such as the campaign for the abolition of the slave trade.[33] If the inefficacy of

[29] Paulson, *Satire and the Novel*, 4.

[30] *Lounger* 20 (18 June 1785), in *The Lounger* (Edinburgh: William Creech, 1785–7), 79.

[31] John Mullan, *Sentiment and Sociability: The Language of Feeling in the Eighteenth Century* (Oxford: Oxford University Press, 1988); David Denby, *Sentimental Narrative and the Social Order in France, 1760–1820* (Cambridge: Cambridge University Press, 1996); Robert Markley, 'Sentimentality as Performance: Shaftesbury, Sterne, and the Theatrics of Virtue', in *The New Eighteenth Century: Theory, Politics, English Literature*, ed. Felicity Nussbaum and Laura Brown (London: Methuen, 1987), 210–30.

[32] Vicesimus Knox, *Essays, Moral and Literary*, 2 vols. (1778), 2.147.

[33] Markman Ellis, *The Politics of Sensibility: Race, Gender, and Commerce in the Sentimental Novel* (Cambridge: Cambridge University Press, 2004); Charlotte Sussman, *Consuming Anxieties: Consumer Protest, Gender & British Slavery, 1713–1833* (Stanford: Stanford University Press, 2000); Lynn Festa, *Sentimental Figures of Empire in Eighteenth-Century Britain and France* (Baltimore: Johns Hopkins University Press, 2006).

the sentimental hero makes him a satiric target, sensibility nevertheless provides literary and rhetorical resources that allow the disenfranchised to escape from the confined roles to which satire relegates them. Thus it is not satire but sensibility that drives Parson Primrose's impassioned plea for prison reform in Oliver Goldsmith's 1766 *The Vicar of Wakefield*. Ignoring his fellow prisoners' jeers, Primrose succeeds in 'giving sensibility to wretches divested of every moral feeling', making them 'social and humane' (148). The vicar's argument recapitulates the turn from satire to sentiment on the level of social policy, pleading for changes that would 'direct the law rather to reformation than severity'.[34] Appealing to the common humanity upon which sensibility insists—'as their faces are like ours, their hearts are so too'—Primrose proclaims that the law should not 'punish vice', but should be 'the protector ... of the people', albeit through a model that produces Foucauldian self-disciplining subjects (150).

Although some critics have read Goldsmith's novel as pure satire, it was not read as such by contemporaries.[35] While the restricted viewpoint of his first-person narrative exposes Primrose's foibles and blind spots to narrative and dramatic irony, he is none-theless depicted as a genuinely good man. His benign nature makes him the unwitting engine of the myriad distresses that furnish occasions for sentimental responses in the narrative, and Goldsmith's reservations about sensibility are on full display in the figure of Mr Burchell (the good Sir William Thornhill, roving among his tenants in disguise). Mr Burchell tells the vicar his story in the third person, subjecting Sir William's errors as a 'man of consummate benevolence' to impersonal critique (20). Having lost his 'regard for private interest in universal sympathy', Sir William 'laboured under a sickly sensibil-ity of the miseries of others', a debilitating empathy that led to improvidence: 'though he talked like a man of sense, his actions were those of a fool' (21). Nor does Goldsmith miss the opportunity for dramatic irony: so absorbed is the vicar in Mr Burchell's affecting tale that he fails to notice that his daughter has fallen into the river and is about to drown. His agitation upon perceiving her plight leaves him paralyzed; it is Mr Burchell—now a man of action—who saves her.

Sir William (aka Mr Burchell) is the *deus ex machina* in the broader plot of the novel as well. In the closing chapters of the novel, calamities fall hard and fast upon the vicar: the destruction of his house, his imprisonment for debt, the reported death of one daughter, the kidnapping of the other, and the arrival of his son George in chains. The revelation of Mr Burchell's true identity expedites the systematic reversal of the vicar's misfortunes in a parody of the compressed dispatch with which many sentimental novels conclude. Rather than satirically dismantling the novel's conventions, Goldsmith allows the virtuous vicar his happy ending, tailoring the world to human wishes, however wist-ful or improbable. This contrived sentimental ending, George Haggerty argues, preserves a space for the indulgence of 'those feelings that an intellectual approach to the novel makes unacceptable', even as its forced nature reminds us of the intractable corruption

---

[34] Oliver Goldsmith, *The Vicar of Wakefield*, ed. Arthur Friedman (Oxford: Oxford University Press, 1999), 148.

[35] See Samuel Woods, '*The Vicar of Wakefield* and Recent Goldsmith Scholarship', *Eighteenth-Century Studies* 9 (1976), 429–43.

on which satiric realism insists.[36] Whereas Mackenzie and Goldsmith seek to shelter the sentimental from the corrosive effects of satire, the novelists to whom we now turn will use satire's powers of negation to create and preserve the possibility of sentimental subjectivity.

THE SENTIMENTAL KNOT
IN THE SATIRIC LASH

Sentimental conventions are an easy target in late-century texts. Like Goldsmith, Tobias Smollett crams the endings of his satirical novels with sentimental clichés: he reinstates long-lost relatives, miraculously restores fortunes, abruptly reforms the vicious, and muscles the marriageable parties into couples as if to show that only the clunky machinery of fiction can bring justice and joy to a corrupt world. Privileging satiric outrage over the sentimental litmus test of tears, Smollett uses 'spontaneous indignation instead of spontaneous benevolence as the test of virtue'.[37] He reduces sentimental postures to a caricatural rictus, exploiting the gap between sentiment and deed. Indeed, sentimental effusions often accompany vicious acts. As Paulson points out, Smollett's 'villains tend to weep when confronted by the goodness they are in the process of destroying. Peregrine, when he attempts to ravish Emilia, finds the "tears gushing from his eyes" ' (Paulson, 235). Would-be sentimental victims are systematically converted into satiric instruments. Roderick Random's status as an orphaned outcast, unjustly stripped of his status as a gentleman, does not make him an object of pity; instead, he is proud, violent, and vengeful towards his enemies.

Yet the evil against which Smollett's protagonists are pitted is much greater than the specific types they encounter and cannot be defeated by a blow. The hostile forces arrayed against them are personified as individual villains and soundly thrashed, but the systemic corruption they represent is so all-pervasive as to be undefeatable. So closely knit are the relations locked in place by peculation, patronage, corruption, and faction that resistance seems futile. Smollett writes at a moment in which the expanding scope of commerce in an increasingly global economy strains the tools of both satire and sentimentality to their limits. Smollett's exhaustive satirical catalogues cannot attain the lofty vantage necessary to offer a purchase on the whole. Capitalist abstractions defy concrete instantiation, and Smollett's satirists flail at the ghostly traces of systemic forces that cannot be understood by analogy with individual actors. The clerks, crimps, ministers, and merchants who serve as cogs in the machine of empire are local symptoms of a corrupt system that, in its complexity and abstraction, lies beyond satiric reach; the most telling

---

[36] George Haggerty, 'Satire and Sentiment in *The Vicar of Wakefield*', *The Eighteenth Century: Theory and Interpretation* 32 (1991), 36.

[37] Alan Dugald McKillop, *The Early Masters of English Fiction* (Lawrence: University of Kansas Press, 1956), 152.

signs of its existence are the disabled sailors, destitute women, and orphaned children it spits out at intervals for satiric and occasionally sentimental contemplation.

Nowhere is this more visible than in Smollett's final novel, the epistolary *Humphry Clinker* (1771), which follows a family of eccentrics and their servants on a tour of Britain. The principal satiric letter writer, Matt Bramble, is a valetudinarian man of sensibility, who rails against the contamination of bodies both politic and personal. Bramble's famous diatribes against adulterated foodstuffs and Bath water—that composite of 'sweat, and dirt, and dandruff' washed from the bathers and quaffed by the clients in the pump room—stem from an abiding disquiet about purity and origins that reflects the influx of goods and peoples from the outer reaches of empire in the wake of the Seven Years War.[38] As 'clerks and factors from the East Indies, loaded with the spoil of plundered provinces; planters, negro-drivers, and hucksters' make their way to the metropole, they expose a global system that exceeds the tools available to comprehend—much less control—it (36). Bramble's satiric attacks on external contaminants underwrite his dream of autarchy: withdrawal to his own estate, in the castle of his skin.

In *Humphry Clinker*, the body of satire—scatological, punishable, mechanistic— converges with the body of sensibility. Bramble's acute responsiveness to noise, dirt, and all manner of disorder also makes him susceptible to others' woes. 'His blood rises at every instance of insolence and cruelty', Bramble's nephew Jery notes. 'On the other hand, the recital of a generous, humane, or grateful action, never fails to draw from him tears of approbation' (64–5). Bramble's sensibility makes him both a cantankerous social critic and a secret philanthropist. If sensibility leaves the feeling subject exposed—Bramble, Jery tells us, 'is as tender as a man without a skin, who cannot bear the slightest touch without flinching' (49)—it also undermines the autonomy upon which propertied individualism depends. 'He affects misanthropy', Jery observes, 'in order to conceal the sensibility of a heart, which is tender, even to a degree of weakness' (29). Bramble's irascibility helps reaffirm the thresholds threatened both by a changing economic order and by sympathetic feeling. Satire on these terms is a necessary counterweight to sentimental vulnerability.

In Frances Burney's 1778 *Evelina: or, the History of a Young Lady's Entrance into the World*, satire and sentiment are likewise inextricably intertwined. The sentimental heroine's epistolary account of her entry into London society and her courtship by the paragon Lord Orville is interspersed with the heroine's satirical observations about worldly manners, patriarchal privilege, and the marriage market. Evelina alternates between spirited sketches of the absurd individuals she encounters and tearful accounts of the social solecisms she has committed in her ignorance of the rules. Her role as a sentimental heroine helps provide cover for her satiric critiques of others, as her naïvety becomes the gender-sanctioned instrument through which she penetrates social veneers. If Evelina's outsider status—her unknown parentage and her country upbringing by the good Mr Villars—allow her to satirize the social rituals of the aristocracy and the

---

[38] Tobias Smollett, *The Expedition of Humphry Clinker*, ed. O. M. Brack (Athens: University of Georgia Press, 1990), 45.

pretensions of her vulgar cousins, her lack of fortune, birth, and paternal protection leaves her vulnerable to the predation of men.

Satire cannot defend Evelina against the violence that threatens her at every turn. In the first half of the novel, the heroine is slapped, manhandled, mistaken for a prostitute, almost abducted by Sir Clement Willoughby, and repeatedly accosted by men in public places. Only the noble Lord Orville, 'the most delicate of men', treats Evelina with consistent respect.[39] The power men wield over women is thinly disguised by gallantry in polite society, but the threats that menace Evelina at every turn reveal the pervasive violence that upholds patriarchy. Nor is Evelina the only victim. Evelina's grandmother, Madame Duval, is flung by the boorish prankster Captain Mirvan into a ditch; two frail elderly women are forced to run a ludicrous footrace; and the Captain presents the effeminate Lord Lovel with a monkey dressed *à la mode* who savagely bites him. Although Captain Mirvan, along with the '*masculine*' Mrs Selwyn, is often understood to be assuming Evelina's earlier satiric function in the later parts of the book, these cruel practical jokes seem to be less the transfer of Evelina's verbal satire into a physical register than a continuation of the masculine monopoly on power that renders Evelina prey (307).

By incorporating the satirist as a character, Burney quarantines the objectionably aggressive aspects of satire in the individual figures of Captain Mirvan and Mrs Selwyn. She thus distances herself, as author, from the unfeminine 'propensity to satire' for which Mrs Selwyn is criticized, camouflaging her own satiric transgressions by satirizing her fictional satirist (307).[40] Evelina must likewise renounce satire in order to earn her 'happy ending' (union with Lord Orville), as she internalizes the lessons of domestic womanhood and colludes in the novelistic rescripting of patriarchy as benign paternalism. Yet the torments inflicted upon Evelina show that sympathy, benevolence, and adherence to a domestic ideal do not suffice, as John Zomchick has argued. 'Cruel removals are necessary for the flourishing of domestic ideology', and that labour is outsourced to the satirist, who does the dirty work of expelling undesirable elements from the world of the novel.[41] Relinquishing its claim to reform, satire in Zomchick's account becomes an agent of purgation that thus 'enables the construction of a unified bourgeois subject' (348). The sentimental production of the domestic ideal on these terms is founded upon the negating work of satire.

In Jane Austen's 1811 *Sense and Sensibility*, satire is intertwined with sentiment both thematically and formally. Austen finds much to mock in the emotional theatrics associated with sensibility. Her would-be unconventional heroine, Marianne, embraces the most hackneyed of sentimental clichés with her passion for dead leaves and taste for the picturesque. Austen's satire, however, opens up graver concerns about the perils of giving too much power to sensibility, for Marianne's wilful violation of the conventions that govern the display and concealment of feeling leave her dangerously exposed to

---

[39] Frances Burney, *Evelina*, ed. Kristina Straub (Boston: Bedford, 1997), 340.

[40] See Sara Gadeken, 'Sarah Fielding and the Salic Law of Wit', *SEL* 42, no. 3 (2002), 541–57.

[41] John Zomchick, 'Satire and the Bourgeois Subject in Frances Burney's *Evelina*', in *Cutting Edges: Postmodern Critical Essays on Eighteenth-Century Satire*, ed. James Gill (Knoxville: University of Tennessee Press, 1995), 363.

social censure. In committing herself fully to the notion that her own feelings are a reliable moral compass—'if there had been any real impropriety in what I did', she tells a censorious Elinor, 'I should have been sensible of it at the time, for we always know when we are acting wrong'[42]—Marianne endorses a form of radical individualism that pits her personal appraisal of good against socially-codified morality. For Austen, sensibility on its own is not a reliable barometer: sentimentality's devotion to the truth of inward feeling risks unmooring the shared rules on which both satire and the social order depend.

Austen's free indirect discourse gives form to the tension between subjective feeling and satirical judgement. In free indirect discourse, the narrator's third-person voice delivers the feeling-filled language of a character's mind without resorting to first-person form, tracing the intricacies of subjective sentiments without relinquishing the narrator's satirical prerogatives. When Elinor discovers that her erstwhile suitor, Edward Ferrars, has been secretly engaged to another, the narrative shifts into free indirect discourse to offer both Elinor's sentiments and the narrator's ironizing commentary thereon:

> Her resentment of such behaviour, her indignation at having been its dupe, for a short time made her feel only for herself; but other ideas, other considerations soon arose.... Had he feigned a regard for her he did not feel? Was his engagement to Lucy, an engagement of the heart? No.... He certainly loved her. What a softener of the heart was this persuasion! How much could it not tempt her to forgive! He had been blameable, highly blameable, in remaining at Norland after he first felt her influence over him to be more than it ought to be. In that, he could not be defended; but if he had injured her, how much more had he injured himself; if her case were pitiable, his was hopeless.... She might in time regain tranquillity; but *he*, what had he to look forward to? Could he ever be tolerably happy with Lucy Steele; could he, were his affection for herself out of the question, with his integrity, his delicacy, and well-informed mind, be satisfied with a wife like her—illiterate, artful, and selfish?
>
> (119–20)

Although the passage begins in the voice of the narrator, as the charges against Edward are appraised and reappraised, they become Elinor's attempt to diminish the pain of Edward's betrayal by recasting his motives in a more gratifying light. Elinor moves from baffled injury to comforting reappraisal ('he certainly loved her') to self-congratulatory affirmation ('her influence [had been] more than it ought to be') to veiled schadenfreude ('how much more had he injured himself') and finally to a vicious takedown of her rival ('illiterate, artful, and selfish'). The psychological nuance of Austen's description of Elinor's sensibility commingles with the narrator's ironic insight into what motivates her thinking, as Elinor redefines Edward's choices in ways that flatter herself in order to palliate the narcissistic wound. Because free indirect discourse permits the narrator's asymptotic approach to the character's mind without collapsing the distinction between them, it allows the sentimental and the satiric to subsist in delicate balance. By showing what passes in the mind even as it analyses and judges thoughts, free indirect discourse

---

[42] Jane Austen, *Sense and Sensibility*, ed. James Kinsley (Oxford: Oxford University Press, 1998), 59.

subtly—insidiously—enacts the moral correctives at which both satire and sentiment purportedly aim. It does so, however, neither through the external force of the satiric lash nor through the immediacy of sentimental identification. Rather the intensity of the interpretative demands that free indirect discourse makes on readers produces forms of reflexivity that supersede the seeming impasse between the satiric and the sentimental, while exposing the powers—and the limitations—of each.

Select Bibliography

Carnochan, W. B. 'Satire, Sublimity, and Sentiment: Theory and Practice in Post-Augustan Satire', *PMLA* 85 (1970), 260–7.

Carretta, Vincent. *The Snarling Muse: Verbal and Visual Political Satire from Pope to Churchill* (Philadelphia: University of Pennsylvania Press, 1983).

Denby, David. *Sentimental Narrative and the Social Order in France, 1760–1820* (Cambridge: Cambridge University Press, 1996).

Dickie, Simon. *Cruelty and Laughter: Forgotten Comic Literature and the Unsentimental Eighteenth Century* (Chicago: University of Chicago Press, 2011).

Ellis, Markman. *The Politics of Sensibility: Race, Gender, and Commerce in the Sentimental Novel* (Cambridge: Cambridge University Press, 2004).

Festa, Lynn. *Sentimental Figures of Empire in Eighteenth-Century Britain and France* (Baltimore: Johns Hopkins University Press, 2006).

Gadeken, Sara. 'Sarah Fielding and the Salic Law of Wit', *SEL* 42 (2002), 541–57.

Haggerty, George. 'Satire and Sentiment in the Vicar of Wakefield', *The Eighteenth Century: Theory and Interpretation* 32 (1991), 25–38.

McKillop, Alan Dugald. *The Early Masters of English Fiction* (Lawrence: University of Kansas Press, 1956).

Mullan, John. *Sentiment and Sociability: The Language of Feeling in the Eighteenth Century* (Oxford: Oxford University Press, 1988).

Paulson, Ronald. *Satire and the Novel* (New Haven: Yale University Press, 1967).

Sussman, Charlotte. *Consuming Anxieties: Consumer Protest, Gender and British Slavery, 1713–1833* (Stanford: Stanford University Press, 2000).

Tave, Stuart. *The Amiable Humorist: A Study in the Comic Theory and Criticism of the Eighteenth and Early Nineteenth Centuries* (Chicago: University of Chicago Press, 1960).

Wilkinson, Andrew. 'The Decline of English Verse Satire in the Middle Years of the Eighteenth Century', *Review of English Studies* 3, no. 11 (1952), 222–33.

Zomchick, John. 'Satire and the Bourgeois Subject in Frances Burney's *Evelina*', in *Cutting Edges: Postmodern Critical Essays on Eighteenth-Century Satire*, ed. James Gill (Knoxville: University of Tennessee Press, 1995), 347–66.

CHAPTER 39

···

SATIRE IN THE AGE
OF THE FRENCH
REVOLUTION

···

JON MEE

THE French Revolution debate in Britain produced an upsurge in political satire. Participants quickly turned to the traditional weapons of invective and libel in print and graphic media. For those who regarded the Revolution as the triumph of the spirit of Enlightenment, a manifestation of a disinterested desire for improvement, this print warfare was a source of dismay. The political writer David Williams, himself no mean satirist as it happens, traced the problem to the 1780s and the rise of the newspapers as a political force.[1] He identified a division between 'Philosophical & satirical writers' with Charles James Fox's manipulation of the press in the run-up to the 1784 Westminster election. '*Under proper direction*', he claimed, the latter 'would have submitted to the former'.[2] Now he thought satirists too inclined to personal abuse. In 1791, Williams was to establish the Literary Fund for authors in distress, partly to encourage writers towards a higher calling than the 'rancour' he thought tarnished literary culture. The Fund survived and even flourished, despite infiltration from anti-Jacobin quarters after 1795, but the hopes of Williams for an end to rancour in the public sphere were very far from ever being met.[3]

The chronology provided by Williams is useful, if only to get away from any idea that there was some prior period of purely rational debate in the immediate aftermath of the French Revolution, before the satirists got going. Some of the most brilliant passages of Thomas Paine's *Rights of Man* (1791–2), for instance, have the panache and vigour one

---

[1] See, for instance, David Williams, *Royal Recollections on a Tour to Cheltenham, Gloucester, Worcester and Places Adjacent* (1788).

[2] 'Observations on the Press' [1803?], Pelham Papers, British Library, Add MS 33124, ff. 78–81.

[3] For a discussion of Williams and the Literary Fund in the context of the early 1790s, see Jon Mee, *Print, Publicity, and Popular Radicalism: The Laurel of Liberty* (Cambridge: Cambridge University Press, 2016).

would expect of an author steeped in eighteenth-century satire. Take his description of Burke as a stooge of his patrons, 'employing his talents to corrupt himself':

> He pities the plumage, but forgets the dying bird. Accustomed to kiss the aristocratical hand that hath purloined him from himself, he degenerates into a composition of art, and the genuine soul of nature forsakes him.[4]

In this pointed use of satire, Paine was only responding to Burke in kind. Burke's sentimental defence of the ancient regime was partly founded on representation of radical writers as versions of the unworldly rational projectors of a kind familiar from Jonathan Swift's satires on the Royal Society. Burke had not hesitated to represent the respected dissenting clergyman Richard Price as just such a projector for welcoming the Revolution in his *Discourse on the Love of One's Country* (1790):

> [A] man much connected with literary caballers, and intriguing philosophers; with political theologians, and theological politicians .... I know they set him up as a sort of oracle; because, with the best intentions in the world, he naturally philippizes, and chaunts his prophetic song in exact unison with their designs.[5]

Price died soon after this savaging, but the crowd of Tory satirists that followed in Burke's wake soon allotted his place to William Godwin. Trained as a Dissenting clergyman, Godwin seemed a perfect fit for the idea of the rational projector whose failure to understand things-as-they-are betrays him into utopian enthusiasm, especially when his *Enquiry into Political Justice* (1793) seemed to advance reasons why one might sacrifice one's mother—in favour of the French philosopher Fenelon—on the grounds of universal benevolence. The passage gave the decade's conservative satirists a weapon they never surrendered: the notion that theoretical ideas of philanthropy necessarily eroded actual social obligations.

'WHAT MAKES A LIBEL?'

Radicalism in the 1790s has come to be associated with natural rights theory in a way that does little justice to the comic zest of Paine's writing in *Rights of Man* or, especially, the often personal attacks in his *Letter Addressed to the Addressers* (1792), written in response to the Royal Proclamation against seditious writings of May 1792. The Proclamation called on magistrates to exercise their powers to curtail the flood of publications inspired by *Rights of Man*. Prosecutions for seditious libel in the 1790s soon

---

[4] Thomas Paine, *Rights of Man*, ed. Eric Foner (London: Penguin, 1984), 51.

[5] Edmund Burke, *Reflections on the Revolution in France*, ed. Conor Cruise O'Brien (London: Penguin, 1969), 94.

exceeded the numbers for the whole of the rest of the century.[6] Even on the Opposition side, the financiers of the Whig Party were becoming increasingly anxious that they were funding 'outrageously democratic' opinion in places like the *Morning Post*.[7] The most obvious case was Sampson Perry, who reoriented *The Argus* newspaper towards an explicitly radical position over 1791–2. The paper poured scorn on Pitt's ministry, but also on those members of the Opposition who proposed themselves as natural leaders of reform. Paine himself seems to have anonymously supplied some of the copy that appeared in *The Argus* from 1791, as too did the gentleman radical John Horne Tooke, and the poet Robert Merry. Previously famous as the poet Della Crusca and covertly part of Sheridan's stable of newspaper satirists, Merry wrote for *The Argus* under the name Tom Thorne, with a particularly personal animus towards the Minister:

> When PITT was OUT OF PLACE, He thought
> It wrong that Boroughs should be BOUGHT;
> And SOLEMNLY DECLAR'D, the Nation
> MUST HAVE A FAIR REPRESENTATION.
> BUT now, become a Courtly Minion,
> WE find he alters his opinion;
> And shews, in language rather warm,
> HE LOVES HIS PLACE, and HATES REFORM.
> This proves a difference, no doubt
> 'Twixt being IN, and being OUT.[8]

On 8 May 1792, the same day it printed this squib, *The Argus* carried a paragraph claiming that the Commons was 'not composed of the real representatives of the people'. An *ex officio* information served on Perry deemed the paragraph a libel on the House, but the publisher was already in the King's Bench Prison for previous misdemeanours.

By the final months of 1792, Merry, Paine, and Perry had all left for the new republic in France, where they became active members of the British Club in Paris.[9] Satirists were feeling increasingly constrained by the work of the Association for the Preservation of Liberty and Property against Republicans and Levellers set up at arm's-length from the government by the civil servant John Reeves and his allies. Publishers of *Rights of Man* such as James Ridgway, another former associate of Sheridan's Whig propaganda stable, found themselves harried and eventually imprisoned, but not just for publishing Paine. Ridgeway and his associate H. D. Symonds had been enthusiastically distributing a

---

[6] For a discussion of debates on prosecution numbers in the decade, see Philip Harling, 'The Law of Libel and the Limits of Repression, 1790–1832', *Historical Journal* 44 (2001), 107–34.

[7] The phrase appears in a letter from James Gray to Robert Adam, 22 September 1791, quoted in Donald E. Ginter, 'The Financing of the Whig Party Organization', *American Historical Review* 71 (1966), 436.

[8] *The Argus*, 8 May 1792. On Perry and his association with Merry, Paine, et al. at the newspaper, see Mee, *Print, Publicity, and Popular Radicalism*, 119–21.

[9] For details, see David V. Erdman, *Commerce des Lumières: John Oswald and the British in Paris, 1790–1793* (Columbia: University of Missouri Press, 1986).

scabrous pamphlet called *The Jockey Club*. The Prince of Wales described it to his mother as 'the most infamous & shocking libelous production yt ever disgraced the pen of man'.[10] Brought out anonymously in three parts over the course of 1792, its author was Charles Pigott, a graduate of Eton and Cambridge. Pigott had mixed in the high-rolling circles associated with Foxite satire, although he had been critical of their leader's pose as the man of the people from at least 1784. By the time the third part of *The Jockey Club* came out late in September 1792, Pigott was openly republican. To the astonishment of the *Analytical Review*, Part III began with a deeply unflattering comparison of George III and Louis XVI that implied that the deposition of the latter in August would, and ought, soon to become the fate of the former.

More than its content, what really caught the attention of commentators on *The Jockey Club* was its method. Pigott drew in his readers with lurid gossip about goings on in high life. The *Analytical Review* approved of the political sentiments, but judged much of his satire 'too *personal* for us to attempt to accompany the author in his biographical sketches'.[11] With no sympathy for Pigott's politics, the author of *The British Constitution Invulnerable* (1792) could be blunter: 'gross ideas are concealed under equivocal expressions and indecent subjects amplified'.[12] By the end of 1793, Pigott was in gaol, arrested after a fracas in a London coffee-house. Pigott's drinking companion William Hodgson—probably in his cups—had loudly condemned George III as 'a German hog butcher'. The charges against Pigott were thrown out, although Hodgson remained in gaol for several years.[13] Possibly, the experience pushed Pigott further towards the more popular sections of the London radicalism. Certainly, by February 1794, he was a member of the London Corresponding Society (LCS). Soon after this time, Pigott brought out *The Female Jockey Club* with Daniel Isaac Eaton, one of the LCS's major publishers. Outraged by a passage claiming she had received '*select* visitors in her private apartments', Lady Elizabeth Luttrell sued Eaton for libel. Attacking aristocratic women for displaying themselves at gaming tables was becoming a familiar part of the growing moralism of public culture, but Pigott's version was far from usual. It opposed an enlightenment celebration of natural energies to aristocratic artifice. In *The Female Jockey Club*, lewd punning often shares the page with a critique of 'superficial delicacies and luxuries' opposed to 'those heavenly enjoyments, which *Nature* has indulgently yielded, to make the bitter draught of life go down'.[14]

Pigott died in June 1794, but his biggest contribution to radical satire was the posthumous *Political Dictionary* (1795). There are few better illustrations of John Barrell's claim

---

[10] George, Prince of Wales, to Queen Charlotte, 24 September 1792. *The Correspondence of George Prince of Wales 1770–1812*, vol. II (1789–1794), ed. Arthur Aspinall (London: Cassell, 1963), 285–6.

[11] *Analytical Review*, 12 (1792), 529, reviewing the fourth edition of Part I.

[12] *The British Constitution Invulnerable. Animadversions on a Late Publication, entitled The Jockey club* (1792), 16.

[13] See the accounts of the incident given in Charles Pigott, *Persecution!!! The case of Charles Pigott* (1793) and William Hodgson, *The Case of William Hodgson, now confined in Newgate, for the payment of two hundred pounds, after having suffered two years' imprisonment on a charge of sedition...*(1796).

[14] Charles Pigott, *The Female Jockey Club, or A Sketch of the Manners of the Age*, 6th edn. (1794), 176 and 6. See the lengthy report on the Luttrell trial in *The Times*, 31 July 1794.

that political struggle in the 1790s was often about the meaning of words.[15] In the *Political Dictionary*, the vocabulary of traditional liberties that conditioned most eighteenth-century political discourse is presented as a smoke screen designed to exclude the people from participation. The attachment to constitutional monarchy is vilified as a Whig preference for closed networks of 'influence' over democratic transparency. The Church is pithily dismissed as 'a patent for hypocrisy; the refuge of sloth, ignorance and superstition, the corner-stone of tyranny'.[16] The *Political Dictionary* fitted perfectly in the stable of publications Eaton had been using to discredit the compact of Church and State from the time he launched as a radical publisher late in 1792. The most impressive item in his catalogue became *Politics for the People* (1793-5), initially launched as *Hog's Wash or a Salmagundy for Swine*. Like any number of other radical satires, Eaton was parodying Burke's warning that the ancient regime would be trampled to death under the hooves of 'a swinish multitude'.[17]

The weekly format of *Hog's Wash* allowed for a quick response to events, its reprints of classic political texts leavened by topical squibs and parodies of prayers and fast-day sermons. The result was boisterous and accessible, the whole atmosphere of the journal a challenge to traditional patterns of deference, but *Politics for the People* is suffused with a knowledge of eighteenth-century satirical antecedents. The self-conscious use of precedent had the paradoxical utility of allowing Eaton and other radicals to present themselves as part of a long-standing tradition of English liberty. Much the same was true of the many bracing texts created, gathered, and forged by Thomas Spence in his journal *Pig's Meat* (1793-5). When Spence was first arrested at the end of 1792, the Bow Street Runners discovered extracts from Swift in his pocket (along with chapter 25 of Leviticus).[18]

Spence was acquitted on a technicality when his case came to court. Despite ramping up the number of prosecutions, the government was similarly unsuccessful in a rapid sequence brought against Eaton: the last in February 1794 for publishing John Thelwall's allegory of the decapitation of a royal gamecock 'King Chanticleer' in *Politics for the People*.[19] In court, John Gurney, Eaton's attorney, argued that the government had been so eager to find a libel that it had itself effectively libelled the king by identifying him with the gamecock; more obvious, Gurney argued, to see the gamecock as Louis XVI,

[15] John Barrell, *Imagining the King's Death: Figurative Treason, Fantasies of Regicide, 1793–1796* (Oxford: Oxford University Press, 2000), 1.

[16] Charles Pigott, *A Political Dictionary: Explaining the True Meaning of Words* (1795), 9.

[17] Burke, *Reflections on the Revolution in France*, 173.

[18] See *The Case of Thomas Spence, Bookseller, the Corner of Chancery Lane* (1792), 6. The second extract published in the first volume of *Pig's Meat* uses Swift's sermon on false witness. Later in the same volume, 'An Unpleasant Lesson for the Pig's Betters' is drawn from 'Voyage to Laputa' in *Gulliver's Travels*. See *Pig's Meat*, 3rd edn., 2 vols, (1795), 1: 7 and 87. For a fuller discussion of Spence's satirical method with texts from earlier in the eighteenth century and elsewhere, see John Halliwell, 'Acts of Insincerity? Thomas Spence and Radical Print Culture in the 1790s', in *Romanticism, Sincerity, and Authenticity*, ed. Tim Milnes and Kerry Sinanan (Basingstoke: Palgrave Macmillan, 2010), 201–18.

[19] See 'King Chauntclere; or, The Fate of Tyranny', *Politics for the People*, no. 8, 16 November 16, 1793, 1: 102–7. The article took the allegory from a speech made by Thelwall at the Capel Court debating society on the question of 'the comparative Influence of the Love of Life, of Liberty, and of the fair Sex', 102.

or tyrants in general.[20] The satirical self-consciousness of radicals about strategies of safe printing can be glimpsed in the fact that just three issues before 'King Chaunticlere', Eaton had published a sonnet—'What Makes a Libel?'—drawing attention to the difficulties posed by parodies and other uses of figurative language for attaining prosecutions under the laws of libel. Shortly after the acquittal verdict, Spence, under the title 'examples of safe printing', openly mocked the use of innuendoes in indictments for libel.[21] Innuendoes were a requirement of the legal process that required the prosecution to explain exactly the meaning of figurative or ironic phrases accused of libel. Spence enjoined his readers to learn the lessons of Eaton's trial: 'Let us thus, O ye Britons, shew what we do *not* mean, that the Attorney General may not, in his Indictment, do it for us.'[22]

This flow of satirical self-confidence was halted by the arrest, in May 1794, of key radicals on charges of treason: Spence and Thelwall were among them, but Eaton fled to avoid arrest. When the trials finished, with Thelwall the last of the accused to be acquitted in December, there was an upsurge of satirical bravura. After the six-month hiatus, 1795 witnessed a torrent of radical satire. Perhaps the major source of this flood was Richard 'Citizen' Lee's shop, 'The Tree of Liberty'. Most of Lee's output was made up of anthologies of extracts from Pigott and other writers, for a penny a time. Lee seems to have particularly delighted in issuing satires that imagined the death of the Prime Minister. A series of mock playbills that originally appeared in *The Telegraph* at the end of 1794, probably written by Robert Merry, Joseph Jekyll, and others who had links with Sheridan, mocked Pitt in the guise of an Italian street performer, 'Gulielmo Pittachio'. The first—*Wonderful Exhibition!!!*—promised that Pittachio would end by 'exhibiting his own Person on The TIGHT ROPE'.[23] Lee and others followed up by reissuing expanding versions of a satire on the death and dissection of Pitt—again from an original newspaper satire—that imagined the Prime Minister on his deathbed expiring in the convulsions of 'a violent *diarrhœa*'. Aiming to provide some comfort, the Archbishop of Canterbury mistakenly produces *Essay on Political Lying* instead of the Book of Common Prayer.[24] Lee crossed a line, however, with the short satires, *The Happy Reign of George the Last* and the broadsheet, *King Killing*. When these were freely distributed at LCS mass meetings, the government claimed it had to act, arrested Lee, and brought the Convention Bills or Two Acts before parliament. For Peter Pindar, arguably the greatest satirist of the decade, the protests against the Bills represented 'liberty's last squeak', the end of the Englishman's traditional right to poke fun at government.

[20] See the facsimile of Eaton's trial in *Trials for Treason and Sedition, 1792–1794*, ed. John Barrell and Jon Mee, 8 vols. (London: Pickering & Chatto, 2006–7), Gurney's comments are at 1: 291–2.

[21] The poem was published on the title page of *Politics for the People*, no. v, October 26.

[22] *Pig's Meat*, 2: 14.

[23] The series has been usefully collected in John Barrell, *Exhibition Extraordinary!!: Radical Broadsides of the Mid 1790s* (Nottingham: Trent Editions, 2001).

[24] *A Faithful narrative of the last illness, death, and interment of the Rt. Hon. W. Pitt, late Chancellor of the Exchequer*, 5th edn. (1795), 3 and 8. *Essay on Political Lying* is misattributed to Swift as was often the case in the eighteenth century.

LIBERTY'S LAST SQUEAK?

John Wolcot, or Peter Pindar, was the most popular satirical poet of the last two decades of the eighteenth century. His early targets were varied, ranging from the Royal Academy to James Boswell, but he was particularly harsh on the king. Exploiting gossip passed on from the royal household, the most sustained of his attacks, published in five parts between 1785 and 1795, was *The Lousiad*'s mock-epic skewering of the monarch's pretensions to homely domesticity:

> THE LOUSE I sing, who, from some head unknown,
> Yet born and educated near a throne,
> Dropp'd down—(so will'd the dread decree of Fate,)
> With legs wide sprawling on the Monarch's plate.[25]

Arguably, Pindar's satires only cemented the idea of George III as a father to his people, however ridiculous, as opposed to a tyrant against whom revolt was necessary.[26] For some satirists of the royal family, the advent of the French Revolution brought a cessation of hostilities but, in Peter Pindar's poetry, there was no let up. Paine was a target of some of Peter Pindar's satires, but even in the fraught year of 1795, Wolcot did not pull any punches on the king and his ministers: 'Who, whilst their plunder'd subjects starve / Are mid their hoarded millions seen'.[27]

Wolcot participated in the social world of newspaper satire that included Merry and others, but never directly associated with the popular radical movement. Nevertheless, its members clearly delighted in his attacks on the elite. Spence, for instance, republished Peter Pindar's 'Resignation: An Ode to the Journeymen Shoemakers' and 'Ode to Burke' in his *A Fragment of an Ancient Prophecy* (1796) and lauded him as 'POET OF THE PEOPLE'.[28] Amid the many other fierce assaults on the king and his ministers in the tense atmosphere of 1795, Wolcot had contributed the fifth and final canto of *The Lousiad* and *The Royal Tour and Weymouth Amusements*. After the king's coach was attacked on the way to the opening of parliament in October, the loyalist press turned their attention to Wolcot in earnest, effectively accusing him of the treasonous act of imagining the king's death, and threatening prosecution.[29] Given the difficulties in prosecuting satires under the libel laws, especially when they came from the pen of a

---

[25] *The Works of Peter Pindar*, 3 vols. (1794), 1: 193.

[26] See the development of this argument in Vincent Carretta, *George III and the Satirist from Hogarth to Byron* (Athens and London: University of Georgia Press, 1990), 269–73.

[27] John Wolcot, *The Royal Tour, and Weymouth Amusements* (1795), 38.

[28] Thomas Spence, *A Fragment of an Ancient Prophecy. Relating as some think to the Present Revolutions* (1796), 6–11.

[29] See the account of the episode in John Barrell, *The Spirit of Despotism: Invasions of Privacy in the 1790s* (Oxford: Oxford University Press, 2006), 138–40.

public favourite with no explicit connections to the radical societies, the government took its preferred course of subornment.

Negotiations brokered by another notable newspaper satirist, but with loyalist sympathies—John Taylor—opened the prospect of Wolcot receiving a pension in return for his cooperation, or, at least, silence, but these talks broke down. Pindar returned to the fray in the final months of 1795 with protests against the Two Acts in *The Convention Bills* and *Liberty's Last Squeak*. The title poem of *Liberty's Last Squeak* takes the form of a mock-elegy on the passing of Pindar's favourite mode—attacks on the king and his ministers. The bills before parliament are represented as an unprecedented assault on English liberties:

> FAREWELL, O my PEN and my TONGUE!
> To part with such friends I am loath;
> But, PITT, in majorities strong,
> Voweth horrible vengeance on both.

Peter Pindar made it clear to his readers that his attacks on the king had brought with them the threat of prosecution:

> The meanness no more of high folk
> In the rope of your satire shall swing;
> For, behold, there is death in the joke
> That squinteth at Queen or at King.[30]

Wolcot continued to write satire after *Liberty's Last Squeak*, but with a new sense of restraint under unfamiliar conditions set out in the dialogue *One Thousand Seven Hundred and Ninety-Six* (1797). Whereas the younger writer Tom announces his intention to attack Pitt, Reeves, and others, the figure of the older and wiser Peter counsels caution and laments the passing of 'that rich hour of Liberty gone by!' Literature in general is reduced to a 'barren Field as dangerous as Murder. Let REEVES be the Interpreter, and every line of every pamphlet, verse or prose, shall by this Gentleman's sagacious commentary smell of treason as strongly as the *whisper* of an Anti-*Pittite* proclaims *rebellion*.' This drear landscape opens onto a more general vista of a culture entering a dark age: 'O TASTE, O REASON, to our Isle return!'[31] The outcome is that Peter Pindar endures only as a vestige of a vanished independence. Ironically enough, Wolcot's narrative of incipient cultural decline was one mirrored in loyalist satire after 1795 in its increasing attacks on what it took to be the literary symptoms of a deeper ideological malaise.

Peter Pindar's popularity as a satirical poet was mirrored in James Gillray's heyday as a graphic satirist. 'Socially and politically', Jonathan Bate has suggested, 'caricature was the most influential art of the 1790s and early 1800s'.[32] From quite early on, Reeves and

[30] John Wolcot, *Liberty's Last Squeak* (1795), 1 and 2.

[31] Peter Pindar [John Wolcot], *One Thousand Seven Hundred and Ninety-Six; a satire in four dialogues. Dialogue the first and second* (1797), 32 and 28–9.

[32] Jonathan Bate, 'Shakespearean Allusion in English Caricature in the Age of Gillray', *Journal of the Warburg and Courtauld Institute* 49 (1986), 196–210 (196).

his associates were certainly concerned about the power of caricature to shape the popular imagination.[33] Publishers clearly wished to cash in on the public interest in the political turbulence of the times, but few caricaturists seem to have been sympathetic to the radical cause, with the exceptions of William Holland and Richard Newton. Generally speaking, most of the decade's graphic satires are ambiguous in one way or another, to say the least, even where they purported to be supporting anti-reformist slogans, enjoying the taste for irreverence and the grotesque for which the medium was widely celebrated.

Immediately after *Reflections* was published in 1790, Burke had come in for some rough treatment. Several prints presented him as a fanatic in his hatred of the Revolution, and played on his perceived Catholic past in a way that would appeal to populist Protestant taste.[34] This reflex is present in Gillray's *Smelling Out a Rat; or, The Atheistical Revolutionist disturbed in his Midnight Calculations* (1790), despite ostensibly centring its hostile gaze on Richard Price (Figure 39.1). With its framed picture of the

FIGURE 39.1 James Gillray, *Smelling Out a Rat; or, The Atheistical Revolutionist disturbed in his Midnight Calculations* (1790) http://hdl.handle.net/10079/digcoll/553395 Courtesy of The Lewis Walpole Library, Yale University

[33] See the discussion of the worries about this material shared by Reeves and his correspondents in Diana Donald, *The Age of Caricature: Satirical Prints in the Age of George III* (New Haven and London: Yale University Press, 1996), 142.

[34] Most of these caricatures are usefully gathered in Nicholas K. Robinson, *Edmund Burke: A Life in Caricature* (New Haven and London: Yale University Press, 1996).

execution of Charles I in the background, the print seems designed to perpetuate Burke's idea of the clergyman as an enthusiastic throwback to the levellers of the seventeenth century, but Burke himself—looming over Price as a grotesque nose with glasses—is ridiculed as an inquisitorial bogyman at odds with traditional ideas of English liberty. This kind of double perspective is typical of Gillray's output. Many of his most famous caricatures focus on the savagery of the Revolution in France itself, but also dwell with a kind of disconcerting glee on the scenes they depict. Among the most striking is *Petit souper, a la Parisienne;—or—a family of sans-culotts refreshing, after the fatigues of the day* (1792), a comment on the recent September massacres, where the caricaturist's sense of the comic grotesque jostles uneasily with the horror of the content (Figure 39.2). Perhaps picking up on Burke's many references to the Revolution's cannibalistic tendencies, Gillray's print lacks his moral outrage. Nor do Gillray's many representations of George III seem any more concerned than Peter Pindar's for the welfare of the supposed father of the nation. Correspondents wrote to Reeves demanding action be taken

FIGURE 39.2 *Petit souper, a la Parisienne;—or—a family of sans-culotts refreshing, after the fatigues of the day* (1792) http://hdl.handle.net/10079/digcoll/552244 [7] Courtesy of The Lewis Walpole Library, Yale University

against 'the many shameful and libelous prints upon our Gracious Sovereign and his Family, which are to be seen in the Printshops in Piccadilly, Bond Street, Oxford Road, etc.—that is in the shops of Fores, Mrs Humphrey and Holland'.[35] Holland, who published most of the attacks on the monarchy engraved by Richard Newton, ended up being arrested and sent to prison at the same time as Ridgeway, but not for publishing caricatures.[36] Like Isaac Cruikshank and Thomas Rowlandson, Gillray seems to have been more willing to trade in mockery of Paine. Some formal relationship with Reeves was brokered in 1793, but it seems to have foundered on Gillray's refusal to stay on-message.[37] In 1795, he happily joined in with the general execration of Pitt in the build-up to the Two Acts, perhaps because he felt the general apprehension of a possible curb on his licence to pillory public figures of all stripes.

Like Peter Pindar, Gillray was no radical, but also no respecter of persons. Fox, in particular, was regularly attacked for posing as the Man of the People. His relative sympathy for the Revolution is exposed as a mask for carnal desires, an idea shared by Gillray's *A Democrat,—or Reason & Philosophy* (1793) (Figure 39.3) and Isaac Cruikshank's *A Right Honourable: Alias a Sans Culotte* (1792) (Figure 39.4). A saturnine Fox flogging Pitt is at the centre of one of Gillray's greatest caricatures: *Promis'd Horrors of the French Invasion—or Forcible Reasons for negotiating a Regicide Peace* (1796) (Figure 39.5). The subtitle points to a source in Burke's *Letters on a Regicide Peace* (1796) where the reader is encouraged to imagine some of the scenes shown in the print, but typically for Gillray the energy threatens to overspill the frame; and the caricaturist seems to share Fox's savage delight in administering the scourge. Still, the frame is not exceeded, and the 'imaginative excess', to use Ian Haywood's terms, of 'hyperbolic re-enactment' may form part of the ultimately reassuring pleasure of the print; one of the reasons, perhaps, that people, including George Canning—who is suspended from a lantern in *Promis'd Horrors*—vied to be caricatured by Gillray. Ultimately everything is comprehended and perhaps safely contained by Gillray's satiric eye.[38]

Gillray's carnivalesque energies rarely extended to positive representations of 'the people'. John Bull, supposedly representative of the sturdy independence of the nation, is most often a buffoon, easily duped by Pitt's cries of alarm. Initially sceptical of Reeves and his claims about the threat of Revolution, Gillray had issued *John Bull bother'd—or—Geese Alarming the Capitol* (1792) as a commentary on the ministry's exaggerated claims about the threat of revolution in the build-up to Paine's trial (Figure 39.6). Later, Gillray joined Cruikshank and others in showing John Bull as the dazed victim of Pitt's

---

[35] Quoted in Donald, *Age of Caricature*, 147.

[36] Holland was indicted for publishing Paine's *Letter to the Addressers* on 17 December 1792. See David Alexander, *Richard Newton and English Caricature in the 1790s* (Manchester: Manchester University Press, 1998), 34, and, for the relationship between Holland and Newton, 16–48.

[37] Draper Hill, *Mr Gillray the Caricaturist: A Biography* (London: Phaidon Press, 1965), 43–4.

[38] See Ian Haywood, *Romanticism and Caricature* (Cambridge: Cambridge University Press, 2013), 9, and on Canning's appearance in *Promis'd Horrors*, 60.

FIGURE 39.3 *A Democrat,—or Reason & Philosophy* (1793). http://hdl.handle.net/10079/digcoll/ 550994 [10] Courtesy of The Lewis Walpole Library, Yale University

FIGURE 39.4 Isaac Cruikshank, *A Right Honourable: Alias a Sans Culotte* (1792) http://hdl. handle.net/10079/digcoll/550763 [9] Courtesy of The Lewis Walpole Library, Yale University

wartime taxation policies. These prints lack the popular insubordination of Richard Newton's *Treason!!* (1798), where John Bull farts in the face of the king as Pitt warns: 'That is Treason, Johnny'. Nevertheless, there was a feeling among loyalist opinion that Gillray was too dangerous to be off the leash, and his services—notionally at least—were secured by a pension from 1797 to 1801, when he served on the newly-founded *The Anti-Jacobin* (1797–8) and its successor, *The Anti-Jacobin Review*, over the course of its first six

FIGURE 39.5 *Promis'd Horrors of the French Invasion—or Forcible Reasons for negotiating a Regicide Peace* (1796) http://hdl.handle.net/10079/digcoll/951355 Courtesy of The Lewis Walpole Library, Yale University

volumes (1798–1801).[39] Gillray regularly collaborated with loyalist propagandists, working up sketches provided by the *Anti-Jacobin*'s circle and collaborating to illustrate poems it supplied. His caricatures seem to have gained in political point from being fed by political insiders like Canning, a minister at the Foreign Office. Attacks on the royal family had already ended by this stage, but about this time Gillray's attacks on Pitt stopped as well.[40]

PERSONAL PARTICULARS

The *Anti-Jacobin* coterie that hired Gillray built upon William Gifford's satirical attacks on the poetry of Robert Merry and the Della Cruscans in the *Baviad* (1791) and then the *Maeviad* (1795). Gifford's target was a perceived nexus of literary sensibility and political

---

[39] See the detailed account in Hill, *Mr Gillray*, 56–117.

[40] For further details of the Canning/Gillray relationship, see David Taylor's Chapter 21 in this volume.

FIGURE 39.6 *John Bull bother'd—or—Geese Alarming the Capitol* (1792) http://hdl.handle.
net/10079/digcoll/550415 [8] Courtesy of The Lewis Walpole Library, Yale University

radicalism. However imaginary in many cases, it was also the straw man tilted at by a
slew of anti-Jacobin novels that appeared after 1795, usually with Godwin as their most
obvious target and often accompanied by copious extracts from his *Political Justice* put
into the mouths of characters more or less verbatim. With the popular radical movement
driven underground by the Two Acts, the focus of these novels was less often on the LCS
or other popular radical societies than on a seduction plot, often ending in tragedy for
the gullible young woman who casts off traditional values in the name of 'the new light';
as does the heroine in Mrs Bullock's *Dorothea; or A Ray of the New Light* (1801), only to
find herself betrayed and abandoned by the advocate of the new morality. Apart from
the references to Godwin, thinly disguised versions of the biographies of Mary Hays and
Mary Wollstonecraft were frequently used as proof of the necessary consequences of
casting aside orthodoxy. The details of Wollstonecraft's unhappy love life presented in
Godwin's *Memoirs of Wollstonecraft* (1798) were something of a godsend in this respect,
and it was often cited directly by anti-Jacobin novelists. In Robert Bisset's *The Highlander*
(1800), Mr William Subtlewould—who quotes directly from *Political Justice*—even
gives an account of his wife's pre-nuptial affairs. Sometimes the role of the sentimental
seducer bifurcated into types of Godwin and Thelwall: the unworldly enthusiastic
philosopher and the zealous popular agitator, as, for instance in George Walker's

The Vagabond, where they appear as Stupeo and Citizen Ego respectively. Walker described his novel as 'an attempt to parry the Enemy with their own weapons': the trope hints at his ambivalence in using a medium so frequently identified with cultural decline.[41] What H. J. Pye called '*novellism*' implied that the medium was inherently associated with fashionable laxity in politics and morals.[42]

Much more confident in the cultural authority of their medium were the satirical poets, self-consciously wielding the Juvenalian lash, who took up where Gifford had left off, including the poets of the *Anti-Jacobin*. Their publisher, John Wright, continued to exploit their popularity through various anthologies after the newspaper itself had folded.[43] Beyond this charmed circle and its close connections to government, the most prominent of these verse satirists was T. J. Mathias. His *Pursuits of Literature* was published anonymously and issued in parts across 1794–7, with new editions quickly following. Mathias showed no scruples about the personal nature of his attack on writers who he felt were degrading literary culture. The 'Introductory Letter to a Friend' added to editions from 1798 stoutly defended the method: 'It must come home to the bosoms, and often to the vices of particular men. It never has its full force, if the author of it is known or stands forth; for the…worthiness of any man lessens the strength of his objections.'[44] Mathias added a twist to this traditional defence of personal satire related to his sense of a general cultural decline. If government had waged war against the radical societies in the courtroom, Mathias advocated the need to open up a literary front against a perceived enemy within, sapping the nation's moral defences through 'modish song, or fashionable prose.'[45] From this perspective, satire became an 'instrument' by which the private sphere could be policed. 'Private malignity' was unjustified; except 'to maintain and enforce publick order, morality, religion, literature, and good manners, in those cases, in which the pulpit and the courts of laws can seldom interfere, and rarely with the effect; the community may authorize and approve it'. The problem with this list was that it brought many writers into Mathias's range that were very far from being supporters of 'the illiterate blasphemy of Thomas Paine', or 'the contemptible nonsense of William Godwin'.[46]

Gifford, Mathias, and their collaborators tended to be explicit in referencing their classical antecedents in asserting the authority of traditional culture. Mathias self-consciously presented himself as the successor to Pope in *The Shade of Alexander Pope on the Banks of the Thames* (1798). There, the darkness that descends in *The Dunciad* is replaced by the cult of sensibility pictured as the forerunner of a Europe-wide revolutionary ferment. Particular culprits were named and shamed in lengthy notes that threatened to overwhelm the main text, as they had in *Pursuits of Literature*. Formal verse satire of this kind, Gary Dyer points out, tended to be the reserve of 'Anglicanism,

---

[41] George Walker, *The Vagabond, a novel, in Two Volumes*, 2 vols., 3rd edn. (1799), 1: vi.

[42] H. J. Pye, *The Aristocrat, a novel, in Two Volumes* (1799), 1: 54.

[43] Initially in the octavo *Poetry of the Anti-Jacobin* issued in 1799.

[44] T. J. Mathias, *The Pursuits of Literature. A Satirical Poem in Four Dialogues*, 6th edn. (1798), vii.

[45] Mathias, *Pursuits*, 19.   [46] Mathias, *Pursuits*, 17.

university education, and conservative politics'.[47] Certainly Gifford, Mathias, and Richard Polwhele, author of *Unsex'd Females* (1798), a savage attack on women writers dedicated to Mathias, each held sinecures or ecclesiastical livings, but their form of personal satire was subject to criticism from within their own ranks by those who thought it ranged too widely across the field of literature and descended too often to gossip and 'personalities'. The perceived excesses of *Pursuits of Literature* provoked William Boscawen's *Progress of Satire* (1798). Boscawen's earlier translations of Horace had been sneered at in the final part of *Pursuits* (1797):

> I never shar'd the profits of the gown,
> Nor yet, with Horace and myself at war,
> For rhyme and victuals left the starving Bar.[48]

In his notes, Mathias, as usual, took pleasure in expanding upon the allusion to Boscawen's personal circumstances: he had been found a job at the government victualling office after struggling to make a legal career. Boscawen was certainly not without connections. He was part of a group that included the playwright Richard Cumberland, John Reeves, and James Bland Burges, undersecretary at the Foreign Office until 1795, who gathered at John Wright's shop in Piccadilly. This 'Porcine Club'—as they sometimes chose to call themselves—was actively involved in the anti-Jacobin policing of culture, but carried on Boscawen's vendetta against Mathias.[49] They published a rolling series of 'Mathiasiana' in the Treasury newspaper, *The Star*, over the autumn of 1800. The project seems to have stalled because Reeves started to feel that things were going too far: 'the hacking & hewing at Mathias' was showing too little respect for 'the feelings . . . due to a gentleman, & a scholar'.[50]

Probably nettled by their earlier fracas, Boscawen was still pushing for further publication of the 'Mathiasiana' in January 1801, but his original response to Mathias in 1798 had argued that the scattergun approach to literary gossip in *Pursuits of Literature* was undermining the more general policing operation against a perceived Jacobin cultural conspiracy.[51] *The Progress of Satire* also hints that the genre, especially of a Juvenalian

---

[47] Gary Dyer, *British Satire and the Politics of Style, 1789–1832* (Cambridge: Cambridge University Press, 1997).

[48] *The pursuits of literature: a satirical poem in dialogue. With notes. Part the fourth and last* (1797), 12–13.

[49] Bland Burges's correspondence reveals there was a conscious conspiracy to infiltrate the Literary Fund by this group. On 6 February 1798, Boscawen wrote to Bland Burges about candidates for the presidency of the Fund. He was careful to suggest choices that would avoid 'alarm[ing] the Democrats, who, tho' inferior in number, may be more alert in attendance than us!' See 'General Correspondence of James Bland Burges, 1773–1824', MSS Dep Bland Burges 22, f. 4. Bodleian Library, Oxford. I am grateful to David Fallon for directing me to the Bland Burges correspondence. For more on the anti-Jacobin groups meeting in London bookshops in this period, see David Fallon, 'Piccadilly Booksellers and Conservative Sociability', in *Sociable Places: Locating Culture in Romantic-Period Britain*, ed. Kevin Gilmartin (Cambridge: Cambridge University Press, 2016), 70–94.

[50] Reeves to Bland Burges, 30 November 1800, Dep. Bland Burges 23, ff. 144–5.

[51] Boscawen suggested to Bland Burges that they might publish a revised version in a cheap pamphlet in a letter of 14 January 1801. See Dep. Bland Burges 23, f. 8.

stripe, was becoming increasingly anachronistic within modern literature. When he sent the poem to Bland Burges in 1798, Boscawen described it as 'a sort of Manifesto of Poets agst Criticks, or rather of Poets of a different kind agst Satirists'.[52] *The Progress of Satire* starts by distinguishing between Mathias's scattergun and Pope's moral vision, but then takes a different turn and suggests Pope himself was sometimes too vindictive, especially towards Joseph Addison, 'whose amiable and excellent character, should, at all events, have protected him against a treatment so severe'.[53] Gifford's attack on Della Cruscanism—acknowledged by Mathias as his prototype—was a waste of powers, Boscawen thought, on a passing vogue that certainly didn't need a second iteration.[54] The essay suggests both that satire is in decline, reduced by Mathias to 'a system of *espionage* (into the conversations of literary men)', but at the same time also implies that it is a genre unsuitable for modern tastes (associated by implication with Addisonian sentiment).[55] The internecine conflict over the 'Mathiasiana' suggests something of the difficulty surrounding these issues even among associates. Significantly, perhaps, Boscawen's involvement in the Literary Fund predated the anti-Jacobin infiltration of 1798. He may well have shared the dislike of 'rancour' in the cultural sphere even before Mathias mocked him. Inevitably perhaps, the initial exchange between Boscawen and Mathias was only the opening salvo in a series.[56] Possibly the times were becoming increasingly anxious about the encouragement provided by the Juvenalian lash to what Coleridge feared was becoming an 'age of personality...of literary and political Gossiping', but satirical attack and defence, as the continuing exchanges between Boscawen and Mathias suggest, continued to play as conspicuous a part in early nineteenth-century letters as it had in the 1790s and most of the rest of the previous century.[57]

SELECT BIBLIOGRAPHY

Alexander, David. *Richard Newton and English Caricature in the 1790s* (Manchester: Manchester University Press, 1998).

Baker, James. 'Isaac Cruikshank and the Notion of British Liberty, 1783–1811', PhD thesis, University of Kent, 2010.

Barrell, John. *Imagining the King's Death: Figurative Treason, Fantasies of Regicide, 1793–1796* (Oxford: Oxford University Press, 2000).

Barrell, John. *The Spirit of Despotism: Invasions of Privacy in the 1790s* (Oxford: Oxford University Press, 2006).

---

[52] Boscawen to Bland Burges, 6 February 1798, Dep. Bland Burges 22, f. 4.

[53] William Boscawen, *The Progress of Satire: An Essay in Verse with Notes, containing remarks on The Pursuits of Literature* (1798), 12.

[54] Boscawen, *Progress of Satire*, 17.   [55] Boscawen, *Progress of Satire*, 19.

[56] See, for instance, William Boscawen, *The Progress of Satire, An Essay in Verse with Notes*, 2nd edn. (1798); *Supplement to The progress of satire, containing remarks on the pursuer of literature's defence* (1799); and responses by Mathias in *A translation of the passages from Greek, Latin, Italian, and French writers, quoted in the prefaces and notes to The pursuits of literature* (1798).

[57] Samuel Taylor Coleridge, *The Friend*, ed. Barbara E. Rooke, 2 vols. (Princeton: Princeton University Press, 1969), 2: 138.

Bate, Jonathan. 'Shakespearan Allusion in English Caricature in the Age of Gillray', *Journal of the Warburg and Courtauld Institute* 49 (1986), 196–210.

Bugg, John. *Five Long Winters: The Trials of British Romanticism* (Stanford: Stanford University Press, 2014).

Carretta, Vincent. *George III and the Satirist from Hogarth to Byron* (Athens and London: University of Georgia Press, 1990).

De Montluzin, Emily Lorraine. *The Anti-Jacobins 1798–1800: The Early Contributors to the 'Anti-Jacobin Review'* (Basingstoke: Macmillan, 1988).

Donald, Diana. *The Age of Caricature: Satirical Prints in the Age of George III* (New Haven and London: Yale University Press, 1996).

Dyer, Gary. *British Satire and the Politics of Style, 1789–1832* (Cambridge: Cambridge University Press, 1997).

Erdman, David V. *Commerce des Lumières: John Oswald and the British in Paris, 1790–1793* (Columbia: University of Missouri Press, 1986).

Fallon, David. 'Piccadilly Booksellers and Conservative Sociability', in *Sociable Places: Locating Culture in Romantic-Period Britain*, ed. Kevin Gilmartin (Cambridge: Cambridge University Press, 2016), 70–94.

Ginter, Donald E. 'The Financing of the Whig Party Organization', *American Historical Review* 71 (1966), 433–9.

Halliwell, John. 'Acts of Insincerity? Thomas Spence and Radical Print Culture in the 1790s', in *Romanticism, Sincerity, and Authenticity*, ed. Tim Milnes and Kerry Sinanan (Basingstoke: Palgrave Macmillan, 2010), 201–18.

Harling, Philip. 'The Law of Libel and the Limits of Repression, 1790–1832', *Historical Journal* 44 (2001), 107–34.

Haywood, Ian. *Romanticism and Caricature* (Cambridge: Cambridge University Press, 2013).

Hill, Draper. *Mr Gillray the Caricaturist: A Biography* (London: Phaidon Press, 1965).

Mee, Jon. *Print, Publicity, and Popular Radicalism: The Laurel of Liberty* (Cambridge: Cambridge University Press, 2016).

Robinson, Nicholas K. *Edmund Burke: A Life in Caricature* (New Haven and London: Yale University Press, 1996).

Wood, Marcus. *Radical Satire and Print Culture 1790–1822* (Oxford: Oxford University Press, 1994).

CHAPTER 40

··

OUT OF SOMERSET

Or, Satire in Metropolis and Province

··

CAROLYN STEEDMAN

The term *satire* implies a comparison to higher examples and an instrumental purpose—anything to avoid just being funny.[1]

To soothe thy wearied limbs in slumber, Alderman History tells his tedious tale.[2]

How on earth does a historian write about satire—satire *in, of,* or *about* the city—when all critical roads, and the very programme for writing this chapter, lead to London? She has been tired of London all her life, and has not lived there since she left the city of her birth at the age of eighteen—with no intentions to return. It is the dirt, the smell, the press of people, eight million stories in the naked city (or, in mid-eighteenth-century London, 750,000 narrators, insistently pressing their concerns upon you, all different, all the same). It is the nagging anxiety that, worse come to worst, you could not walk out of it, as you could walk out of Birmingham or Bristol, then or now.[3] People crashing into you with nary a sorry and volatile temper, as observed by John Gay, in *Trivia; or the Art of Walking the Streets of London* (1716), his hyperbolic warning of what will happen if you argue for the right of way, even if the argument is only a glance.[4] Matthew Beaumont reminds us that ' "Be singular!" ' is the metropolitan imperative. 'It dictates that people have constantly to prove that they are someone as opposed to no one', but if you're up from the provinces it is hard to be anything on London's streets.[5] Above all, it is the noise

---

[1] Simon Dickie, *Cruelty and Laughter: Forgotten Comic Literature and the Unsentimental Eighteenth Century* (Chicago: University of Chicago Press, 2011), 44.

[2] Henry Fielding, *The History of Tom Jones*, ed. R. P. C. Mutter (Harmondsworth: Penguin, 1966), 607.

[3] See Matthew Beaumont, *Night Walking: A Nocturnal History of London, Chaucer to Dickens* (London: Verso, 2015), 143.

[4] John Gay, *Trivia: Or, the Art of Walking the Streets of London* (1716), 66–7.

[5] Beaumont, *Night Walking*, 327.

(then and now): the 1606 *Seven Deadly Sins of London* fulminated about the barrage of noise produced by London trades, with 'hammers…beating…Tubs hooping, Pots clinking'.[6] In 1728, Erasmus Jones was apoplectic about the city sounds that harried him: 'NOTHING is so apt to fling me into the Spleen, as harsh Noises and uncouth Sounds; a Sow-gelder's Horn, or a Poet's repeating his own Verses, never misses to set my Spirit and my Teeth on Edge.'[7] Insistently-told stories (no one listening, they fade in and out of aural consciousness) make up the edifice of sound that is the city. The stories are beautiful and touching, but they keep getting told, over and over again, especially when the low, or the working and non-working poor, are made to utter them, as in Ned Ward's 'Merry Observations' (1718), in which he predicts that at Whitsuntide that year 'many [will] loiter about the Fields, without a Penny in their Pockets…Many wrangling Disputes will happen abroad between Man and Wife about, whether two two-penny Cakes are not better than one Goats Cheese-cake; and whether a Pot of Ale for three-half-pence, is not much cheaper than the same quantity for three-pence, put into a Stout Bottle, and ripen'd in the Oven.'[8] Ned Ward's monthly *The London Spy* (1698–1700) entertained readers with the country booby arrived in London, suffering sensory overload. But there's never really a laugh to be had, in any of this *soi-disant* city-satire literature, because it instructs you to sneer at the habits and manners of the low, obviating any fun you—or they—may possibly have (or may have had).

I have never willingly written about London *in historical mode*, it being so atypical: its structure of government and social structure, its population, its economy have never raised compelling, or even interesting, historical questions for me. London exerted its gravitational pull when I encountered the anonymous *Low-life: Or, One Half of the World Knows not how The Other Half Live* (1750?, 1752, 1764). An extraordinary, dream-like survey of what was '*transacted by People of almost all Religions, Nations, Circumstances, and Sizes of Understanding in the Twenty-four Hours, between Saturday-Night and Monday-morning*', one never-happened June day in London, 1750, has, I was surprised to find, been treated as documentary by some historians, and as satire by many more nineteenth-century essayists and novelists.[9] Charles Dickens, the Mayhew brothers, and George de Sala absorbed *Low-life's* time-structure and elaborated its use of *vignette*; but as they did this at a time when the cultural and literary task was to distance the modern, mid-nineteenth-century writer from crude and cruel 'olden times', the sentimentality of their own writing about disabled crossing-sweepers and crippled bird-sellers obscured the sentiment that *Low-life* (and its precursor literature) inscribed in relation to the poor Londoners who throng its pages. The motions of the heart learned from eighteenth-century sentiment, satire, and history (all as textual forms and forms of thinking) was overlaid, slowly and incrementally, in the city written by Pierce Egan (many Toms and

---

[6] Thomas Dekker, *The Seven Deadly Sinnes of London* (1606), 26.

[7] Erasmus Jones, *A Trip through London containing Observations on Men and Things* (1728), 42.

[8] Edward Ward, 'Merry Observations upon Every Month and Every Remarkable Day throughout of the Year', in *T…B…'s Last Letter to his Witty Friends and Companions* (1718), 84–5.

[9] For publication history see Carolyn Steedman, 'Sights Unseen, Cries Unheard: Writing the Eighteenth-Century Metropolis', *Representations* 118 (2012), 28–71.

Jerries, from 1821 onwards), by the Mayhews (in the 1840s and the 1850s), and by George de Sala, in 1859. By the time a traveller in the land of the London poor could devise a title like *Low-Life Deeps: An Account of the Strange Fish to Be Found There* (1875) any connection with the sentiments of eighteenth-century city-satire had been severed.

Any fresh reading of Pierce Egan's *Tom and Jerry* will send me into a rage of mute resentment: at the assumption that London *is life itself*—that there is no life outside London; at its coy and condescending notes of explanation about London cant and London slang 'to the *Provincials*'; its inability to imagine any place at all outside London except Tom Jones's Somerset—and even the road on the way back to town for Tom and Jerry is a *topos* in which 'nothing of importance happens'; its unthinking and condescending division of London's Low inhabitants into those who work, and those who will not work.[10] A new, wearisome reading of *Tom and Jerry* may produce the satisfying insight that Henry Mayhew must have made his own 'Cyclopaedia of the Conditions and Earnings of THOSE THAT *WILL* WORK, THOSE THAT *CANNOT* WORK, AND THOSE THAT *WILL* NOT WORK' in reference to Egan's Boys; and I can have the only laugh available—at my own perspicacity—in realizing for the first time that the major hazard of a costermonger's life must have been to have a young swell drop in on you and engage you in long discourse about something-or-other, detaining you from your lawful and peaceful purposes of selling greenstuff on the street, for hours and hours, and all because 'LIFE, in all its various shapes, he was determined to see; and whether he was animatedly engaged in squeezing the hand of some lovely countess at St. James's; or passing an hour with a poor coster-monger in the back settlements of St. Giles's, Tom was never at fault!'[11] But how historically and politically numb Corinthian Tom actually was. 'In order to prepare your mind for the scene you are about to experience, be not surprised, my dear JERRY', says he, 'in observing the *Beggar* who has been writhing to and fro all the day in the public streets in terrific agony, to excite your charity and torture your feelings, here meet his fellows to laugh at the flats, count over his gains, and sit down to a rich supper'.[12] *Tom and Jerry*'s pretence at ethnography, its displacement of sentiment, always to others, never *actually felt* by the Boys, is disturbing still to readers who have learned their eighteenth-century lessons of social sympathy. Egan does have words with us about the shallowness of his characters:

> distress, to Tom, was like unto a pathetic tale which he had perused; and the mere idea of a hungry man, with no money in his pockets, counting the trees in St. James's Park to beguile the *tedious* hour of dinner-time, to appease an empty stomach... would have made Tom laugh heartily, as a sort of creative good joke, instead of believing that such *bitter* things could possibly have existence in a land of charity and benevolence.[13]

---

[10] Pierce Egan, *Life in London; Or, The Day and Night Scenes of Jerry Hawthorn, Esq. And his elegant Friend Corinthian Tom, accompanied by Bob Logic, The Oxonian in their Rambles and Sprees through the Metropolis* (1821), 11, 109–25, 286–91.

[11] Egan, *Life*, 44.   [12] Egan, *Life*, 343.   [13] Egan, *Life*, 61.

Egan describes the task of the text, which is to explore all the classes making up 1800s London; during its course

> on the one hand, roars of laughter [will be] excited from the ridicule of surrounding circumstances; yet, on the other, traits of the highest sensibility... [will be] discovered, and the "big tear," rich in effect, seen silently stealing down the iron cheek of some debauchee, who had thought himself immoveable upon all appeals to his feelings, yet found to be vulnerable when the secret and irresistible touches of NATURE have suddenly broke in upon his dissipated pursuits.[14]

Is this satire? Is this just a little bit satirical? I do not know; I do not know what satire *is*. As the sweet, elegiac Cruikshank engraving which is the end-stop to Egan's book announces of Jerry, retired to Hawthorn Hall from London and Life Itself, I have always been 'Gone to Roost'.[15] I am not a proper, or even competent, reader of city satire.

Eminent eighteenth-century language philosopher James Beattie devised a theory of funniness, which rested on the political structure of any given society; he believed that a limited constitutional monarchy like England's, 'where persons of all ranks, and those ranks so very different, often meet in society, and the public welfare depends on their living on good terms... each within the sphere of his own prerogative', was the most 'favourable to every species of *comic* writing'. In Britain, as opposed to France, 'the *manners* of individuals, and more outward circumstances of life... supply the materials for wit and humour... [because] more diversified'.[16] He did not remark on the one-way traffic of 'ludicrous composition'; that the high almost invariably satirized the low, and that the costermonger laughing up his sleeve at Tom's assumptions about low-life (if laugh he did) is quite lost to historical view. One purpose of this chapter is to reveal some satirical workers of the later century. Satire *could* be funny, according to Beattie; but he made a typically enlightened distinction between satire and comedy, by keeping them apart conceptually: 'As to Satire, we must observe, that it is of two sorts, the Comic and the Serious; that human foibles are the proper objects of the former, and vices and crimes of the latter; and that it ought to be the aim of the satirist to make those ridiculous, and these detestable. I know not how it comes to pass, that tile Comic Satire should be so much in vogue', he mused.[17]

And there are *mes semblables, mes confrères*, most of them dead and gone historians— to tell me that it really cannot be done by a historian, 'this satire and the city' malarkey. Or rather, that it can only be done with London, as not-at-all dead and gone historian Vic Gatrell says in *City of Laughter*. He asks questions about satire's focus on the capital limiting the appeal of caricatures to provincial audiences. He reminds us that Swift noted of Pope's *Dunciad* that 'twenty miles from London no body understands [its]

---

[14] Egan, *Life*, 39.   [15] Egan, *Life*, 376.

[16] James Beattie, 'On Laughter, and Ludicrous Composition', in *Essays On Poetry and Music, as they affect the Mind. On Laughter, and Ludicrous Composition. On the Utility of Classical Learning* (Edinburgh, 1778), 321–486.

[17] Beattie, *Essays*, 427.

hints'.[18] And, he says, putting London to one side, the provincial town could not produce satire, never mind an understanding of London satire: its sociability was 'too intimate for local satire to be accommodated comfortably', says Gatrell.[19] He notes the pirating of satiric prints, especially in Dublin (which was the second most important locus of the print industry after London), but satiric prints were entirely absent from eighteenth-century Edinburgh inventories, for example. (Probate records are one way a historian has of assessing what goods, including books, paintings and prints, were valuable to people in the past.) Much earlier commentators than Gatrell had noted the intense localism of visual and textual satire, and its uselessness for the sociological or historical understanding of a society. In 1791, Gebhard Wendeborn thought of the immense quantity of English caricatures and satirical prints shipped to his native land, where they commanded high prices. 'Singular and ridiculous', he thought the practice; for 'very few of those who pay dearly for them, know anything of the characters or transactions which occasioned [them]. They laugh at them, and become merry, though they are entirely unacquainted with the persons, the manners and customs which are ridiculed.' The 'wit and satire' of such prints were local to London, and 'entirely lost' upon their German and other European consumers.[20]

There were many eighteenth-century voices to tell that satire is no business of the historian. Had not Edward Gibbon magisterially proclaimed in 1777 that 'Diligence and accuracy are the only merits which an historical writer may ascribe to himself; if any merit, indeed, can be assumed from the performance of an indispensable duty?'[21] I am not allowed to have any doings with satire, according to eighteenth-century historians. In dictating new rules of historical composition in 1783, Hugh Blair said that the historian 'must neither be a Panegyrist nor a Satyrist'. 'Impartiality, Fidelity, and Accuracy, are the fundamental qualities of an Historian'; his office is to

> ...record truth for the instruction of mankind. This is the proper object and end of history, from which may be deduced many of the laws relating to it and if this object were always kept in view, it would prevent many of the errors into which persons are apt to fall, concerning this species of Composition.[22]

It is clear that my eighteenth-century *semblables* were proscribing the writing of history as satire, or satiric history; modern historians are happy to accept literary form as a kind of evidence for what could be thought and expressed in the past, as a route to disinterring

---

[18] Swift, *Corr.* (Woolley), iii. 189.

[19] Vic Gatrell, *City of Laughter: Sex and Satire in Eighteenth-Century London* (London: Atlantic, 2006), 239–40.

[20] Gebhard Friedrich August Wendeborn, *A View of England towards the Close of the eighteenth century. Translated from the original German, by the author himself*, 2 vols. (1791), ii. 213–14.

[21] *The History of the Decline and Fall of the Roman Empire. By Edward Gibbon, Esq.; Volume the First* (1776), 'Advertisement', 588.

[22] Hugh Blair, *Lectures on Rhetoric and Belles Lettres*, 3 vols. (Dublin, 1783), iii. 41–2, cited by Mark Salber Phillips, *Society and Sentiment: Genres of Historical Writing in Britain, 1740–1820* (Princeton: Princeton University Press, 2000), 40–1.

mentalité. But satire is a particularly difficult form to use in this way, what with its tricky rhetorical (and local, particular, and non-philosophical) nature. It also raises hard questions about how it was read, questions that are not raised to the same degree by, say, the novel or the nursery rhyme, where we have good and abundant evidence about appropriation and understanding from a wide variety of readers.

Hayden White may have designated satire one of the four modes of emplotment in nineteenth-century European historical writing; but this was done, as Mark Phillips points out, at the expense of ordinary readers of ordinary texts, who in the eighteenth century were more likely to have read George Buist's *Hume's History of England, abridged, from the invasion of Julius Caesar, to the Revolution in 1688. For the use of schools and young gentlemen* than Hume's own six volumes, published between 1744 and 1761.[23] By the new century James Mackintosh believed that British historians had learned well these eighteenth-century lessons about satire, history, and sentiment: history should not be written in the spirit of satire that was exercised, he believed, by some French authors. It was not the historian's business to 'sneer or laugh at men, or to lower human nature'.[24] A historian should maintain the 'dignity of man, and the import-ance of his pursuits'.[25] In this way, history researched (another thing the French did not do) and written by a serious historian might create 'a fellow-feeling' in the reader, excite his or her passions, and provide the delight of reading and imagining 'the character and actions' of people in the past. Mark Phillips argues that this empathetic reading of history had been long-prepared; that eighteenth-century historians' interest in the 'habits and manners' of people in the past was underpinned by, or shared, a textual and affective origin in trip-through-town literature of the earlier century. Thus Phillips can tie together *A Trip through Town, Containing Observations on the Customs and Manners of the Age* from 1735 and the 1797 *Cries of London*, authored by Timothy Ticklecheek. Ticklecheek's ethnography of London life was designed to instruct small children by the display of 'habits, manners, customs and characters of various people who traverse London streets with articles to sell'. A 'Cries' published by the children's bookseller Elizabeth Newbery the year before (she had been issuing it since 1775, so it was a seller) reminded girls and boys that Pope had declared the proper study of man to be mankind, which was what they were about to undertake. The first of the sixty-two 'elegant cuts' which adorned it would have formed the cover before its being bound, and depicts an oyster-seller (I *think* she is selling oysters; a far cry after Hogarth), whose verse is: 'Let none despise / The merry Cries / Of famous LONDON TOWN'.[26] But if we follow

---

[23] Hayden White, 'Burkhardt: Historical Realism as Satire', in *Metahistory: The Historical Imagination in Nineteenth-Century Europe* (Baltimore: Johns Hopkins University Press, 1975), 230–64; Phillips, *Society and Sentiment*, 9.

[24] James Mackintosh, 'Sismondi's *History of France*', *Edinburgh Review* 35 (1821), 488–509. Discussed by Phillips, *Society and Sentiment*, 215.

[25] Phillips, *Society and Sentiment*, 150.

[26] *The Cries of London, As They are Daily Exhibited in the Streets* (1796); see William Hogarth, 'The Shrimp Seller', sometimes known as 'The Oyster Seller', oil on canvas, 25 in × 20 in, 1740–1745, National Gallery, London.

Phillips's path of history-writing through sentiment and sympathy, then no 1790s child would have known how to despise a poor oyster-seller; indeed, would already know that 'the very meanest, as they are generally termed, of human society, are far from being unworthy of our attention.'[27] Newbery's little book ends darkly, or maybe, in its very last line simply, with a pretty picture for little girls, as if there is simply no more to be said, and with a verse 'Description of London'. These stanzas could not have been read by an eight-year-old without her knowing some of the ways of satire, or at the very least, about sarcastic inversion:

> O LONDON is a dainty place,
> A great and gallant City:
> For all the streets are pav'd with Gold,
> And all the folks are witty.
> And there's your Lords and Ladies
> That ride in Coach and Six;
> That nothing drink but Claret Wine,
> And talk of politics.
> And there's your Beaux, with powder'd cloaths,
> Bedaub'd from head to chin;
> Their pocket-holes adorn'd with gold,
> But not one souse within.
> And there the English Actor goes
> With many an hungry belly;
> While heaps of gold are forc'd, God wot,
> On Signor Farrinelli.
> And there's your dames, of dainty frames,
> With skins as white as milk;
> Dress'd every day in garments gays
> Of satin and of silk.[28]

And to add to all the hesitations about visiting eighteenth-century London as a scene of satire is the very great disability of not really knowing what satire is, or was. I was taught definitions of satire at school and that *B–* was for Bolingbroke; or possibly as an undergraduate, when I believed the task was to look behind Pope's 'hints, and initial letters, [and] town facts' for something that resembled a historical reality, even if that reality was only that someone had written them. Dustin Griffin's proposition that satire is a mode or procedure, a disposition towards social and political reality that can invade any form (the novel, the epic, the street ballad), that can be used by any writer (a stocking maker—for reasons about to become apparent—or a historian) has been of inexpressible consolation to me in this excursion to satire's city.[29] Even so, the shade of Lady Middleton hovers (and one really does not want *to be* Lady Middleton), who fancies Elinor and

---

[27]   *Cries of London*, iv.   [28]   *Cries of London*, 132–3.

[29]   Dustin Griffin, *Satire: A Critical Reintroduction* (Lexington: University Press of Kentucky, 1995), 2–3.

Marianne satirical 'because they were fond of reading...perhaps without exactly knowing what it was to be satirical'.[30]

OUT OF SOMERSET

What does it mean? Where *is* it? In its form, or in its disposition? In the intention of the writer, or in the mind of the reader, who may make satire out of the telephone book, or witty, pretty folk of London Town, if she has a mind to it? Was Pierce Egan being just a little bit satirical when he located Jerry Hawthorne's home in Somerset? Would he have to have apprehended, somehow, the history of eighteenth-century society and sentiment, to be so satirical? For Henry Fielding had contemplated these questions as long ago as 1749. By Chapter 1 of the second book of *Tom Jones*, he has already laid Somersetshire open to our view, or introduced one little corner of the south-western division of the kingdom where lies the Allworthy estate. A whole book on, he announces what it is he is writing ('we have properly enough entitled this our work, a history, and not a life') and his historical method:

> we intend... [rather] to pursue the method of those writers, who profess to disclose the revolutions of countries, than to imitate the painful and voluminous historian, who, to preserve the regularity of his series, thinks himself obliged to fill up as much paper with the detail of months and years in which nothing much remarkable happened, as he employs upon those notable aeras when the greatest scenes have been transacted on the human stage [...][31]

Shewing what Kind of History this is; what it is like, and what it is not like involves telling the reader that 'when any extraordinary scene presents itself... we shall spare no pains nor paper to open it at large... but if whole years should pass without producing anything worthy of notice, we shall not be afraid of a chasm in our history; but shall hasten on to matters of consequence, and leave such periods of time totally unobserved'.[32] Then, *having a good laugh*, he ignores the distinction between the ordinary and the extraordinary for a thousand pages. For what happens in law and love and everyday life in one remote rural village speaks to the polity at large, to parliament, the Inns of Court, and to Westminster Yard where sits Lord Chief Justice. The point about London's dominion over the way the provincial world *is* and how it is *written*, is made at several points throughout the text. Perhaps—this could be argued—the *good laugh* becomes satiric.

Let us take all these questions and pursue them in some country place; some place in the country that isn't London; some city that isn't the Great City of the World. Can satire

---

[30] *The Novels of Jane Austen, Vol. 1: Sense and Sensibility*, ed. R. W. Chapman, 3rd rev. edn. (Oxford: Oxford University Press, 1933), 246.

[31] Fielding, *Tom Jones*, 87.   [32] Fielding, *Tom Jones*, 88.

be produced in provincial places? Are provincial readers competent to understand it, whether it arrives from London by mail coach, or is penned (or sketched) in some town garret two hundred miles from the Metropolis? Could a cottage *ever* produce such a thing, whatever it is?

GONE TO ROOST

Our definition of 'city' must be an elastic one. Nottingham was not a city at the turn of the nineteenth century; city status was bestowed as part of Victoria's Diamond Jubilee celebrations, signified in a letter from the Prime Minister, the Marquess of Salisbury, to the mayor in June 1897. But in 1800 it had a population of about 29,000; it was the county town and administrative centre of the county of Nottinghamshire and, with the surrounding country districts, the epicentre of the nation's stocking manufacture. 'A fashionable, elegant town', says John Beckett at the Nottingham Heritage Gateway.[33] 'The situation is not exceeded by any in England, and in the princi-pal streets are many fine houses...The streets are broad and open and well paved...it even exceeds imagination', said a 1771 visitor, also pointing out that 'the town is a county of itself'; that besides being the seat of county government, it was 'governed by the mayor', and possessed its own magistracy, many JPs being appointed from among its numerous aldermen who were also, often, major merchant-manufacturers in the knit-wear industry.[34] These factors were important in the making of Joseph Woolley the stocking maker's satiric moments.

Joseph Woolley (c.1770–1840) lived in the framework knitting (stocking making) village of Clifton, some three miles south-west of Nottingham. His diaries and account books (six volumes of these survive for the years between 1800 and 1815) detail: the stocking shapes he knitted and what he got from them; his spending on booze in every alehouse in every village between Clifton and Nottingham and often further afield; his father's small-time dairy enterprise (Samuel Woolley was typical in this region south of the River Trent in combining framework knitting with cow-keeping); who was doing what with whom in the fields and closes of Clifton; the turbulent sexual life of his neighbours; the names of his gooseberry bushes, stolen from the garden ground where he supplemented his knitting income with market-gardening in these hard and lean and Luddite years; the new Rector maximizing the profits of his living and treating his servants and other parishioners very badly; punch-ups on the road back from Ruddington, the open village a mile away where his Friendly Society met; a lot of what the local magistrate did, in and out of his justicing room (these were Sir Gervase Clifton's

---

[33] http://www.nottsheritagegateway.org.uk/places/nottingham/nottingham1660to1800.htm, accessed 14 February 2018; Robert Sanders, *The Complete English Traveller; or, A New Description of England and Wales... Together with the Manners and Customs of the Inhabitants &c* (1771), 489–93.

[34] Sanders, *Complete English Traveller*, 493.

estates, Clifton one of 'his' villages and where he lived when not at his London house or pursuing his interests in Bath) in Clifton Hall, adjacent to the parish church. *An Everyday Life of the English Working Class* would not—could not—exist without Woolley's diaries.[35] *All of Life* is here, in a place with a population of about 400 in the first decade of the nineteenth century, but quite large enough for the exercise of Woolley's satiric style. He produced many 'scenes' of life about his neighbours including Sir Gervase Clifton, as when in 1804 the magistrate brought the plebeian woman he took up with after his wife's death down to the village to view recent improvements made to the parish church. The job was finished and the contractors ('undertakers') were treating their workmen to dinner at the Coach and Horses (prop. Thomas Langford Snr); as Woolley said 'they had a Good Job and at the Conclusion they treated their men as hansomly'.[36] During the course of dinner 'Sir Gerveses Lady or other wis his hore . . . went by Langfords' to have a good gawp at the workers at play. Woolley heard of—or over-heard—Sir Gervase telling his companion that she would see a fine spectacle of low-life drunkenness: 'he told hir that they would Git as drunk as blaggers but he was mistaken for there was not one man drunk'.[37] The point for Woolley in telling this tale was perhaps to turn back on itself—reverse the comic traffic—of a century of condescending travel to the Country of the Poor in order for the High to witness the incomprehensible debauch-ery of the Low. When Woolley had no axe to grind, simply told a tale for his own amuse-ment, he can make the reader laugh out loud at the ludicrous picture he flashes before your eyes (it does not really need saying that he was not writing for an audience, and certainly not for me; but as Alderman History, I am obliged to make this remark). One Monday night in October 1803, 'Charles [H]odget wanted to frig thomas hardeys Whife but She would not Let him and so he haunted about the house in his Shirt till about four oclock the next morning with nothing but is shirt and shoes on.'[38] The picture remains throughout the narrative explanation (which Woolley nearly always provided). The everyday swims into focus in the very next line: 'the reason he was so bold is whife staid all night at nottingham Goose fair so he could have is fling but he could not come on for she [Mrs Hardey] went and slept with bradley and his whife'. There are many such scenes recorded throughout the diaries. With Cervantes and Henry Fielding in mind (he bought his own copy of *Tom Jones*), Woolley developed great facility in set-pieces describing fights between men, and women (particularly energizing these), and between sexual partners. But it was the city—the town of Nottingham—that provoked his most modern visual and sexual satire.

He went into Nottingham nearly every Saturday of his diary-writing life, most likely to deliver the stocking shapes he had knitted to a middleman hosier along the way; to get shaved and spruced up, read the papers at the barbers, and for his own Saturday night out. What else he did in Nottingham, I do not know, though his accounts for monies

---

[35] Carolyn Steedman, *An Everyday Life of the English Working Class: Work, Self and Sociability in the Early Nineteenth Century* (Cambridge: Cambridge University Press, 2013); Nottinghamshire Archives (NA), DD 311/1–6, Diaries of Joseph Woolley framework knitter, for 1801, 1803, 1804, 1809, 1813, 1815.

[36] NA, DD 311/3, 24 August 1804.   [37] Steedman, *Everyday Life*, 101–2.

[38] NA, DD 311/2, 3 October 1803.

spent in the town are punctuated with 'spent foolishly...'. He wrote several satirical vignettes of dead-drunk Clifton women vomiting in Nottingham gutters, Clifton husbands and wives having a right set-to on market day. These brief scenes could have been written about Clifton incidents; the city setting makes very little difference to their telling. But it was not a Saturday night that produced his finest satiric set-piece, when Woolley was highly amusing (he certainly amused himself) in describing the stratagems of young men seeking out sex in the city. In August 1805, two of his Clifton friends went to Nottingham Races (as did he). They 'baught a List of the Spoarting Ladies and at night they agreed to Go and See too of them they were to meet at Such a place at such a time'. But Gervase Reckless met up with 'an old Companion from mansfield...and went to Sneiton feast with him in Sted of meeting Thomas Langford' (son of the Clifton Coach and Horses landlord) as arranged. 'Langford staid wating and havering about till verey Late at night and then was forst to come home by him Self Like a fool as he was...daming and Swareing because he was dispointed of is miss and Company too on the rode'.[39] Undeterred, the lads were back the next day with a different strategy. Woolley saw them at the race ground arm in arm, flaunting themselves around 'Just Like Some people of vast Great property and...above Speaking to their betters So I Leve you to Gess if they would Spek to their infearers'. When they had splendoured their way around the race course (without being taken any notice of by anyone, Woolley dryly noted) they rambled off to a public house, where 'fop Like they strutted and splanded about to show themselves till the sober part of the Companey was quiet Sick to see them'. Then the fine 'Jentlemen must Go to the play'. Bustling up to the gallery in fashionable disarray, 'their hats Set in Stile', waistcoats unbuttoned to show the neckerchiefs they 'had stuck in their besoms to make them Look Like a fann tale pidgeon', they appeared to have forgotten the sporting ladies, and even the strategy of attracting some misses by their display. After all, said Woolley they were just a 'Stokenor and Cobbler' and everyone knew it, despite the gloves 'which they wore for fear people Should know their profession and for fear that the Ladies should be frited at their Coars bare hands'. The Boys (and Woolley) knew all about the fashion-clothes of the fop—that is the taken-for-granted of his commentary. More interesting is Woolley's thesis about fashion-consumption, masculinity, and what came to be called 'respectability'. Reckless and Langford performed their pretensions to gentility, or gentlemanliness, by how they dressed and how they behaved; Woolley was highly amused by their failure to convince their audience that they were anything but a stockinger and a shoemaker.

Some theatre-goers may have managed to watch *The School of Reform*, which promotes an elegant strategy for married women seeking ascendancy over their husbands, confound all expectations by *just keeping quiet*.[40] Also playing was 'a Whimsical Description of Town [&] Country by Mr Adcock. To which will be added a new Comic Pantomic Ballet called Hurry Scurry: or the Tailors' Rumpus'. Performance commenced

---

[39] NA, DD 311/3, 6 and 7 August 1805. Section of 1804 notebook covering 1805.

[40] Thomas Morton, *The School of Reform, or, How to Rule a Husband: a Comedy, in five Acts, as perform'd at the Theatre-Royal, Covent-Garden* (1805).

on 6 August—'being the first Race Day'—and lasted the week.[41] *School of Reform* was playwright Thomas Morton's great success, praised twenty years on and in the twenty-first century for its introduction of low-life language and psychology to the stage. A central character is the low-born criminal, Robert Tyke. When William Hazlitt saw an 1820 performance with Tyke played by a specialist in rustic Yorkshiremen, he called the play 'the sublime of tragedy in low life'.[42] (Woolley too, wrote many of his marital tragedies in the comic mode.) 'Hurry Scurry: or the Tailors' Rumpus', also staged that night, may have represented working-class *mores* to a (partly) working-class audience, but we are never likely to find out how, as this kind of mimed comic interlude was designed to evade theatrical censorship and no copy of it (if copy there ever was) has survived.

Woolley wrote about none of this, only implied that *he* was familiar with theatre-going and knew when to laugh and when to applaud. He was watching the show up in the gallery where the lads were once more looking out for the sporting girls: 'I believe that the Ladies atracted... there atention more than the players', said Woolley. Tom and Gervase had new curlicued 'fashonable stick[s] in their hands as full of nobs and in and outs or bended in all the... forms Emagenable which they made use of to nap the Seats with when aney thing they atracted their atention in the play but that was verey seldom for they under stood the play Jast as much as if one of their four footed brothers Long Ears'. When it was all over they were 'so tired with showing their ignorance at the races and at the play that they Cold not Walk home that night'. They slept on a settle in an alehouse 'and Come of from there about seven o clock the next morning without their brackfasts'. Gervase Reckless 'went to bed and Lay till about five oclock in the afternoon and so too fools Spent their money and they was neither Company for themselves nor aney body Else'.

All three of them (Joe, Tom, and Gervase) had cognizance of fop-behaviour and fop-fashion. Pierce Egan's genealogy of the Dandy is just plain wrong, according to Woolley: 'I feel induced now to describe, for the benefit of posterity, the pedigree of a Dandy in 1820. The DANDY was got by Vanity out of Affectation—his dam, *Petit-Maitre or Maccaroni*—his grand-dam, *Fribble*—his great-grand-dam, *Bronze*—his great-great-grand-dam, *Coxcomb* and his earliest ancestor, FOP'.[43] We could say that the Fop was satirically *à la mode* in Nottingham in 1805; but it is neither here nor there that my visual imagination for this scene has been shaped by the Cruikshanks' engravings; that I see the Boys parading around the race course, their coats cut to show their bum, their skinny legs, their huge white gloves, their enormous cravats, their hats tipped just so, as depicted by Thomas Rowlandson, or impossibly, by George Cruikshank (for in 1805 he was but thirteen years old). But I would like to know how Woolley's satiric imagination was formed. A daily mail coach ran between London and Nottingham, even on a Sunday, carrying among many other cultural products, books and pamphlets to stock

---

[41] *Nottingham Journal*, 5 August 1805.
[42] Jim Davis, 'The Sublime of Tragedy in Low Life', *European Romantic Review* 18 (2007), 159–67.
[43] Egan, *Life*, 42, n. 5.

Nottingham's five bookshops.[44] But not one of these booksellers advertised themselves as print-sellers, as was the case in other towns similar in size to Nottingham. Woolley took part in the political 'papers wars' in the lead-up to the 1803 Nottingham election: he spent 2s 2½d on pamphlet material. Some of the election fight was conducted by means of written (but not graphic) satire.[45] Alderman History cannot write that Woolley must have seen fashion plates and illustrations, in the comic press, scandal sheets and visual satires (but he must have).

Textually-speaking we can observe of Woolley's writing that he performed satirically not so much best, as more insistently and self-consciously in the Day at the Races episode than he did back home, three miles away, in Clifton (though I find his 'Knitters' Tuesday Night', fully described in *An Everyday Life*, much funnier).[46] We can observe this: Woolley did not *need* to be in Nottingham (a city) to see with a satiric eye; but the wide expanses of Nottingham Race Course provided a perspective on the fops and fools parading around it. The interior of an eighteenth-century theatre afforded view not only (or not primarily) of the harum-scarum enacted on the stage, but of the audience, its comings-and-goings, a thousand little scenes enacted in the aisles, the pit, the staircase up to the gallery, especially if the gallery was where you were watching, as was Woolley in August 1805. Such sites of sociability were architecturally and topographically arranged to provide perspective on *la passagiata*; and we should say 'perspective', not 'distance', for Tom and Gervase were Woolley's mates, his neighbours, on whom he frequently passed wry, almost-affectionate, satiric comment. But here, now, the wide open spaces of Nottingham, its high pavements and public squares, allowed him to look for longer and tell a more sustained tale; it ended with Reckless's hangover, all the way back in Clifton.

HOMAGE TO ELIZABETH HANDS

Satire was thus—can I say this?—a mode, a perception, exercised between friends, who were all working men and women, friends and neighbours. It could be exercised by the Low against the High, or elite persons, as we have seen Woolley attempt with Sir Gervase Clifton Bart. and 'is hore [and] a very fine Woman'. But for excellent verse satire penned by a working-class woman about her employers, and which appeared in the local press

---

[44] 'The True Britain Coach, White Lion Inn Nottingham to Belle Sauvage Inn, Ludgate Hill... everyday...Cheap Travelling', *Nottingham Journal*, 5 July 1800; Edward Willoughby, *The Nottingham Directory* (Nottingham, 1799).

[45] NA, DD 311/2, 31 January, 2 and 9 April, 21 May 1803; Daniel Parker Coke, *The Paper War, Carried on at the Nottingham Election 1803. Containing the Whole of the Addresses, Songs, Squibs, etc. Circulated by the contending Parties including the Books of Accidents and Chances* (Nottingham: W. & M. Turner, 1803); see Malcolm I. Thomis, 'The Nottingham Election of 1803', *Transactions of the Thoroton Society of Nottinghamshire* 65 (1962 for 1961), 94–103.

[46] NA, DD 311/1, 12 October 1801.

and in an edited volume, I shall eulogize Warwickshire maidservant Elizabeth Hands, but not at great length, for it has been done already.[47] And we move now to the county town of Warwick and the city of Coventry (population 5,500 and 16,000 respectively in 1800) with poetry, including the satiric, produced out in the sticks, in the tiny settlement of Bourton-on-Dunsmore, five or so miles from Rugby (pop. 1,486 in 1800). Hands lived here from about 1785 with her blacksmith husband and their children. I imagine her insubordinate satire to be set in the county town, for two major pieces of Warwickshire literature, Catherine Thomson's *Constance* (1833) and George Eliot's *Middlemarch* (1871–2), forces this reader to a new genealogy of female class-and-county satire. (Argument available on request from the author.)

The immortal phrase 'An Ode on a Dishclout' is Hands' is used in her satire 'A Poem, On the Supposition of an Advertisement appearing in a Morning Paper, of the Publication of a Volume of Poems, by a Servant-Maid', which was published at Coventry in 1789. One of the twittering gentry gathered in the drawing room has a good laugh at the very idea of servant writing poetry: ' "He, he, he," says Miss Flounce: "I suppose we shall see / An ode on a Dishclout—what else can it be?" '

> 'I once had a servant myself,' says Miss Pines
> 'That wrote on a wedding some very good lines.
> Says Mrs Domestic, 'And when they done,
> I can't see for my part what use they were *on*;
> Had she wrote a receipt, to've instructed you how
> To warm a cold breast of veal, like a ragout,
> Or to make cowslip wine, that would pass for Champagne,
> It might have been useful, again and again'.[48]

It is Hands's knowingness and her control of it, for fashioning into a good joke, that astonishes. Modern critics have scarce got the measure of the insubordination—the daring impudence—that the two 'Suppositions' imply (at least to social historians whose understanding of female domestic service in this period is framed by the pathos and melodrama—our knowledge of gender and labour exploitation—taught by the last half century of women's history). There is simply not a way of concluding that these two poems were offensive to none: they are, surely, intentionally offensive, and wonderfully so. Hands appears to have got away with a sustained satire on bourgeois and gentry manners and to have laughed heartily at their provincial pretensions to literary taste as well as at the mean-mindedness of their cuisine. The maidservant watching them knows more than they do. Part of the hilarity (and its edginess) comes from her placing herself within the scene she observes from her place by the wainscot. What I did not understand

---

[47] Elizabeth Hands, *The Death of Amnon: A Poem, with an Appendix: containing Pastorals, and other Poetical Pieces* (Coventry, 1789), 47–9, for the 'Supposition of an Advertisement...', 50–6; for 'A Poem, on the Supposition of the Book Having Been Published and Read'; see Carolyn Steedman, 'Poetical Maids and Cooks Who Wrote', *Eighteenth-Century Studies* 39 (2005), 1–27.

[48] Hands, *Death of Amnon*, 49.

when I first wrote about Elizabeth Hands, what I still do not understand, is why they let her get away with it. Hands received a good deal of encouragement to publish her book, from one of her employer's sons, from many clerical and landowning gentleman of Warwickshire and the wider Midlands, though they were probably after the title-piece, 'The Death of Amnon', which is serious sustained biblical commentary in the heroick style. (The volume which also contained her two 'Suppositions' listed 1,200 subscribers, two of whom lived in Nottingham.) What *were* they up to, the Warwickshire *bon ton*, the Midlands *tout monde*, in letting her get away with it?—the stunning effrontery of her; the verve and brilliance of her satire? Suddenly, you can see the costermonger mask his irritation as Corinthian Tom barges into his one-room dwelling where he sits refurbishing a few cauliflowers for sale, hide his laughter behind his filthy handkerchief as the young swell discourses about the *Truth of a Costermonger's Life*, on *All of Life* in this Great City: '*Wery* true, sir; wery true', he snorts, tucking it up his ragged sleeve. The costermonger knows, as did Pierce Egan, how frightened Tom is of being laughed at himself, but how the rules for obviating the laughter ('he made it an invariable rule never to profess a knowledge of any science or circumstance, from which, upon a more minute inquiry, he might be detected and held up to ridicule for his vain-boasting pretensions') fall away at the street-seller's broken door.

So two workers—a domestic servant and a stocking maker—raise questions about the uses of satire in class analysis; about satire's audiences and satire's users. Joseph Woolley and Elizabeth Hands can bring satire a little way into the city of laughter (the town of laughter), though it resides anywhere the writer wants it to be: village or city or right up your alley. Vic Gatrell gives Beattie a bad write-up as a theorist of laughter and humorous writing ('ludicrous composition'). 'This ponderous essay was saturated in classical citations, and was notable for its inability to tell jokes', he says, 'but it offered the most widely read and ambitious discussion of laughter in the eighteenth century'.[49] Whether or not we expect our cultural and literary theorists to be funsters, the last point is, surely, *the* point—that we need to know better the producers and consumers of satire, and more about their main topic, which was the addled, desperate, and ludicrous encounters of a class society, anywhere they took place.

SELECT BIBLIOGRAPHY

Beaumont, Matthew. *Night Walking: A Nocturnal History of London, Chaucer to Dickens* (London: Verso, 2015).

Borsay, Peter, ed. *The Eighteenth-Century Town: A Reader in English Urban History 1688–1820* (London: Longman, 1990).

Dickie, Simon. *Cruelty and Laughter: Forgotten Comic Literature and the Unsentimental Eighteenth Century* (Chicago: University of Chicago Press, 2011).

Gatrell, Vic. *City of Laughter: Sex and Satire in Eighteenth-Century London* (London: Atlantic, 2006).

---

[49] Gatrell, *City of Laughter*, 169.

Howell, Philip. 'Sex and the City of Bachelors: Sporting Guidebooks and Urban Knowledge in Nineteenth-Century Britain and America', *Ecumene* 8 (2001), 20–50.

Landry, Donna. *The Muses of Resistance: Labouring Class Women's Poetry in Britain, 1739–1796* (Cambridge: Cambridge University Press, 1990).

O'Byrne, Alison. 'The Spectator and the Rise of the Modern Metropole', in *The Cambridge Companion to the City in Literature*, ed. Kevin R. McNamara (Cambridge: Cambridge University Press,2014), 57–68.

Phillips, Mark Salber. *Society and Sentiment: Genres of Historical Writing in Britain, 1740–1820* (Princeton: Princeton University Press, 2000).

Steedman, Carolyn. *An Everyday Life of the English Working Class: Work, Self and Sociability in the Early Nineteenth Century* (Cambridge: Cambridge University Press, 2013).

Steedman, Carolyn. 'Sights Unseen, Cries Unheard: Writing the Eighteenth-Century Metropolis', *Representations* 118 (2012), 28–71.

Vickery, Amanda. *The Gentleman's Daughter: Women's Lives in Georgian England* (New Haven: Yale University Press, 1998).

....

CHAPTER 41

SATIRE, MORALITY, AND CRITICISM, 1930–1965

....

CLARE BUCKNELL

THE eighteenth century was a great age of writing about satire. As a literary art undergoing an extraordinary period of practical development, it was discussed energetically and combatively. The morality of the satiric attack, the differences between wit, ridicule, and raillery, and the relative merits of the ancient Roman satirists were debated at length in *The Tatler* and *The Spectator*.[1] A number of poets, well known and less well known, produced heroic couplet essays on the nature and uses of satire.[2] Some satirists thought of themselves as theorists and historians of the genre as well as practitioners: John Dryden, for instance, prefaced his 1693 translation of the satires of Juvenal and Persius with a critical *Discourse on the Original and Progress of Satire*. In the first half of the century especially, verse satire was considered to be such a public mode of social or political commentary, and its uses so controversial, that to write satire also meant defending one's reasons for doing so or at the very least considering the possible consequences. Published satires typically had critical prefaces setting out the intellectual basis for the poet's engagement with the genre, and the poems themselves often contained self-reflexive lines about the moral or technical features of the task in hand.

SATIRE AND BIOGRAPHICAL CRITICISM

....

Given this flourishing line in criticism during the neoclassical revival, it might seem odd that the history of satire reception over the next hundred and fifty years should have taken the course it did. Serious modern critical work on eighteenth-century satire took a

---

[1] See *Tatler*, ii. 73–8 (no. 92, 10 November 1709); *Spectator*, i. 97–100 (no. 23, 27 March 1711); *The Adventurer*, no. 133 (12 February 1754), 1–6.

[2] Contemporary didactic poems on satire include Harte's *An Essay on Satire* (1730), Whitehead's *An Essay on Ridicule* (1743), and Boscawen's *The Progress of Satire* (1798).

remarkably long time to get off the ground. During the Victorian period, Dryden, Pope, Swift, and others tended to be passed over or dismissed outright by critics, who felt that their verse did not fit the narrow post-Romantic definition of poetry that had prevailed since the beginning of the century. Leslie Stephen, for instance, insisted that 'lofty poetry' could 'only spring from some inner positive enthusiasm', which satire—'by its nature negative'—could not share; and, likewise, Matthew Arnold claimed that Dryden and Pope's verse belonged to 'an age of prose and reason', and could not touch the 'imaginative life of the soul' in the way that true poetry should.[3] 'Though they may write in verse, though they may in a certain sense be masters of the art of versification', Arnold argued in 'The Study of Poetry' (1880), 'Dryden and Pope are not classics of our poetry, they are classics of our prose'.[4] As Stefan Collini has shown in the context of John Morley's 'English Men of Letters' series (1878–92), this judgement about the prosiness of the eighteenth-century satirists was partly a nationalist one: it was a recapitulation of the old prejudice that any verse displaying qualities associated with 'French' rationalism—argumentation, systematic thought, polished versification—must be inherently un-English and unpoetic. 'It was always easier', Collini writes, 'to find the approved qualities in, say, Johnson or Wordsworth than in Dryden or Pope'.[5] Stephen, who provided the volume on Pope (1880) for 'English Men of Letters', was unwilling to grant even that Pope had managed satisfactorily to imitate the French way of doing things. 'Boileau would have been revolted by the brutal images which Pope does not hesitate to introduce', he declared. 'It is a curious phenomenon that the poet who is pre-eminently the representative of a polished society should openly take pleasure in unmixed filth.'[6]

The comment about 'unmixed filth' touches on the other reason why Victorian critics were unwilling to devote sustained attention to eighteenth-century satire. Their approach to the reading of poetry was strongly biographical, founded on a conviction that poets, like other figures from history, were worth writing about to the extent that a knowledge of their lives and works would be likely to have a 'morally elevating effect' on readers.[7] This, it was felt, could never be the case with men like Swift and Pope. Their poems—read with the historical literalism that Victorian critics tended to espouse—seemed full of rank hatred for the world and its people, and their victimization of powerless opponents looked ungenerous and malevolent. For Stephen, a reading of An Epistle to Dr Arbuthnot (1735) or The Dunciad (1743) showed Pope to be a 'cruel little persecutor', a man of 'abnormal character' who took delight in 'coarse abuse', 'concentrated malice', and 'personal venom', and attacked his dunces for complex vengeful motives of his own.[8] 'There is something cruel in Pope's laughter, as in Swift's', Stephen wrote. 'The missiles

---

[3] Leslie Stephen, *English Literature and Society in the Eighteenth Century* (London: Duckworth & Co., 1904), 120.

[4] Matthew Arnold, 'The Study of Poetry', in *Selected Prose*, ed. P. J. Keating (London: Penguin Books, 1970; repr. 1987), 358–9. See also Stephen, *English Literature and Society*, 115–16.

[5] Stefan Collini, *Public Moralists: Political Thought and Intellectual Life in Britain, 1850–1930* (Oxford: Clarendon Press, 1991), 357.

[6] Leslie Stephen, *Alexander Pope* (1880; repr. London: Macmillan, 1902), 118–19.

[7] See Collini, *Public Moralists*, 356.   [8] Stephen, *Alexander Pope*, 120, 130, 118, 119.

are not mere filth but are weighted with hard materials that bruise and mangle.' He admitted to feeling 'half ashamed of confessing to reading *The Dunciad* with pleasure'.[9] Later, when he came to write his more substantial work on the period, *English Literature and Society in the Eighteenth Century* (1904), he claimed more robustly that it was not possible to read *The Dunciad* 'without spasms both of disgust and moral disapproval'.[10] Even George Saintsbury, whose 1916 book *The Peace of the Augustans* aimed to show against the critical tide that Pope, Swift, Gifford, and others were actually poets, could not help attributing the denigration of Grub Street to 'Pope's poisonous and self-torturing spite'.[11]

The pull of biographical criticism continued to be felt strongly during the first decades of the twentieth century, though in a new direction. In a wave of what Terry Castle has dubbed 'Rococophilia'—the revival of eighteenth-century styles and attitudes by British Modernists after the First World War—writers engaged in passionate defences of the eighteenth-century satirists.[12] In his lecture *Pope* (1925), Lytton Strachey asserted that it was 'time to consider the master of the eighteenth century with a more impartial eye' than the Victorians had managed, and recognize that real poetry might just as well be found 'in a game of cards, or a gentleman sneezing at Hampton Court' as in the sorts of lofty scenes that Arnold adumbrated.[13] Strachey's 'impartial eye', though, turned out to be less analytical than it might have been, and his study of Pope's heroic couplet technique returns repeatedly to the personal grudges, 'malignant fury', and 'murderous insolence' that are assumed to stand behind the satire. Pope was 'naturally drawn to the contemplation of human beings', Strachey concludes, 'and the feelings which these contemplations habitually aroused in him were those of scorn and hatred'.[14] Edith Sitwell, meanwhile, met the Victorians head-on with a new biography of Pope (1930), designed explicitly to present the poet 'in his true light as a good and exceedingly loveable man'.[15] Sitwell's account, like Strachey's, avoids directly treating satire as a genre, commenting only on local qualities of the verse and, rather bizarrely, the perceived suitability of the heroic couplet measure, 'with its sustaining rhymes, its outward cage', to 'a poet of Pope's tiny and weak body'. ('It is nearly always possible to judge of the poet's physique from his technique', she writes.) Her biography opens by claiming that it will save the reputation of Pope's satires from the 'general blighting and withering of poetic taste' presided over by Arnold, but proceeds to make only passing reference to *The Dunciad*, the *Imitations of Horace* and their political and social valences.[16] It seems to have been easier to defend Pope's personal character than engage with the qualities of the satires.

---

[9] Stephen, *Alexander Pope*, 120.   [10] Stephen, *English Literature and Society*, 133–4.

[11] George Saintsbury, *The Peace of the Augustans: A Survey of Eighteenth Century Literature as a Place of Rest and Refreshment* (London: G. Bell and Sons, 1916), 92–3.

[12] Terry Castle delivered the 2011 Clarendon Lectures at Oxford University on 'Rococophilia: The Eighteenth Century and British Modernism'.

[13] Lytton Strachey, *Pope: The Leslie Stephen Lecture for 1925* (Cambridge: Cambridge University Press, 1925), 10–13.

[14] Strachey, *Pope*, 29–30, 24–5.

[15] Edith Sitwell, *Alexander Pope* (London: Faber & Faber, 1930), 1.

[16] Sitwell, *Alexander Pope*, 266, 2.

The Satire as a Moral Art

The earliest recognitions that something might be changing in the way critics thought about satire came in the pages of *Scrutiny* in the early 1930s. Sherard Vines's survey of a reissued edition of Dryden's poetry (1932) noted with pleasure that critical interest in Dryden seemed to have taken an upturn in recent years. 'Through our poets, and our more professionally academic critics', Vines wrote, 'his credit is slowly rising'. Extracts from Dryden's verse appeared in I. A. Richards's *Principles of Literary Criticism* (1924); inspired by Dryden and Pope, contemporary poets such as Edgell Rickword were coming back to the heroic couplet; and, most importantly, Dryden's satires no longer had to be carefully packaged to appeal to what Vines calls called 'the pseudo-Wordsworthianism of the early twentieth century'.[17] Led by the growing body of professional critics who produced scholarly editions and commentaries, attitudes to satire seemed gradually to be changing. F. R. Leavis, who devoted the second of his *Scrutiny* 'Revaluations' essays to Pope (1933), was likewise willing to admit that progress had been made on the Dryden front, and indeed with satire in general. 'It may be', he suggested, 'no longer necessary to discuss whether satire can be poetry, and we may have entirely disposed of Matthew Arnold'. Nonetheless, there was some way to go yet in the battle to discredit biographical criticism. 'Elementary things still need saying', Leavis reminded his readers. 'Such terms as "venom", "envy", "malice" and "spite" are, among modern connoisseurs, the staple of appreciation.'[18]

What seemed to be required was a new critical language in which the art of satire, rather than the feelings that might have inspired it, sat at the centre of debate. In his 'Revaluation' Leavis gestures towards this language, noting that *The Dunciad* is 'certainly poetic creation, even by Romantic standards', and that its verse, by virtue of imagery, tone, and mood, 'demonstrates [...] irresistibly that satire can be great poetry'.[19] Geoffrey Walton, reviewing Geoffrey Tillotson's *On the Poetry of Pope* (1938) in *Scrutiny* a few years later, made the same point in relation to Pope's *Moral Essays* (1731–5). 'It seems to me', he suggests, 'that a more disinterested reading of his poetry and a closer study of his use of words and verse rhythms would have enabled Mr. Tillotson to see more clearly the reasons why Pope's satires are great poetry'.[20] This is true, but the problem with it and with Leavis's comment is that neither has anything to say about satire *qua* satire, only about the degree to which lines of verse that happen to be in a satire are good poetry. Elsewhere in his essay, Leavis resituates Pope's poetry in a tradition with which he— under the influence of T. S. Eliot—is more comfortable. 'Pope is as much the last poet of the Seventeenth Century as the first of the Eighteenth', he argues. 'His Wit is Metaphysical

---

[17] Sherard Vines, 'Dryden Redivivus', *Scrutiny* 1 (December 1932), 283–5.
[18] F. R. Leavis, 'Revaluations (II): The Poetry of Pope', *Scrutiny* 2 (December 1933), 268–84 (268–9, 277).
[19] Leavis, 'Revaluations (II)', 282, 284.
[20] Geoffrey Walton, 'The End and the Means', *Scrutiny* 6 (March 1938), 433–4 (434).

as well as Augustan.'[21] It is easier, Leavis seems to be saying, to compare local effects in Pope's poetry to the wit of Donne or Cowley than to make any claims for what eighteenth-century satire might do differently, or especially.

In 1940, the Dryden scholar Louis Bredvold wrote an article that set about programmatically to 'reopen the question of the nature of satire'.[22] 'A Note in Defence of Satire' starts by admitting that its task is an uphill struggle. 'In the current standard treatises', Bredvold writes, 'satire appears as the least attractive and the least defensible of the many manifestations of the comic spirit'. Accordingly, 'the lover of good satire is now put to it to defend his taste'. Bredvold's case for the defence is not concerned with satire's 'publicist function', the political or social uses it may have in the life of a community; these are 'accidental effects' of the genre and have little to say about 'the essential nature of satire'.[23] Instead, what interests him is the moral quality of 'indignation' (Juvenal's *indignatio*) that he perceives at the heart of the satiric attack. For Bredvold, what makes satire defensible is that its indignation at a social or political ill is no mere 'personal feeling of resentment or desire for retaliation', but the expression of a broader public morality, 'an affirmation of some standard which we as good men cannot refuse to sustain'. Satire, he writes, 'is an indictment, and as such appeals to some sort of categorical imperative, to what is right and just'. The judgement it makes 'springs from some over-individual principle within us, not merely from our ego'. Indeed, the 'whole art of satire', Bredvold suggests, 'rests on the assumption of the moral sympathy and agreement of the reader with the writer'.[24]

This is designed explicitly to reject any lingering Victorian arguments about the unpleasantness and unjustifiability of satire, and to correct those who still think that satirists write out of private spite. But it also has larger cultural resonances. For Bredvold, writing in 1940, satiric indignation is urgently needed, more so now than ever, because it confirms the existence of the strong moral positives ('valid universal principles') upon which decent civilizations are founded. 'It is a popular *non sequitur* in our era', he observes, 'to berate the wickedness of the world and then add in bitterness of spirit that there is no good'. The continuing legibility of satire proves positively that in the darkest of times there is still a 'communion of men—few though they may be—for whom things matter', enough good citizens whose moral idealism is 'activated through [their] sympathetic response' to the satirist's anger.[25] In 1943, reviewing James Sutherland's new Twickenham edition of *The Dunciad* for *Scrutiny*, Leavis had similar things to say about the moral certainties and civilized ideals standing behind Pope's satire. *The Dunciad* is not, he argued, like some of Swift's satires an exhibition of 'contempt, disgust, hatred, and the will to spoil and destroy'.[26] Rather, the 'satiric antipathy' it dramatizes is a celebration of positive Augustan values. '"Order" for Pope is no mere word', Leavis writes,

---

[21] Leavis, 'Revaluations (II)', 270.

[22] Louis I. Bredvold, 'A Note in Defence of Satire', *ELH* 7 (1940), 253–64 (253).

[23] Bredvold, 'A Note in Defence of Satire', 253, 255, 257.

[24] Bredvold, 'A Note in Defence of Satire', 259–60, 262.

[25] Bredvold, 'A Note in Defence of Satire', 262–4.

[26] F. R. Leavis, '*The Dunciad*', *Scrutiny* 12 (Winter 1943), 74–80 (75).

'but a rich concept imaginatively realised: ideal Augustan civilisation. [...] It is the comprehensive positive from which the satire works.'[27] Elsewhere, he notes that Pope and his contemporaries were 'in complete accord about fundamentals', about what mattered to their society and what the substance of its moral identity was. 'How firmly he [Pope] realised the substance, and how habitually present to him were the positive bases, one is apt to find most strikingly evidenced in the neighbourhood of his most spirited satiric passages', he wrote of the 'Timon's Villa' episode in the *Epistle to Burlington* (1731).[28] Neither he nor Bredvold were in any doubt that Pope and his fellow satirists really felt the indignation, outrage, or disbelief they described; as Stephen and Strachey had done before them, they held satire to be the expression of personally held convictions, albeit ones that were social and sympathetic enough for all right-thinking readers to share.[29]

In 1940, a Harvard scholar named David Worcester took the critical defence of eighteenth-century satire in a new direction. In his book *The Art of Satire*, Worcester argued that satire was an indirect mode, not a direct one. He agreed with Bredvold, Leavis, and the rest that satires were motivated by powerful personal feelings, but insisted that in persuasive and successful pieces these angry sentiments were disguised or framed by a set of rhetorical conventions. Satire, Worcester wrote, was 'the engine of anger, rather than the direct expression of anger': the satirist must 'simulate coolness and detachment', however strong his initial feelings, interposing a 'rhetorical pattern of astonishing complexity' in between 'his naked sentiment and the reader'.[30] Worcester's approach to satire required, as Bredvold's had done, a recapitulation of the reasons why satire merited literary study; but it also needed some sort of historical discussion of rhetoric, in order to drag rhetorical work out of the scholarly disfavour in which it had been languishing. Worcester approached this difficulty head-on. 'Rhetoric is in disgrace', he argued in his opening chapter. 'Nowadays when we say that a piece of writing is "rhetorical", we usually mean to call attention to its tumid style and trumpery of orna-mentation—its false rhetoric, in other words.'[31] The challenge for the modern scholar of rhetoric was, therefore, to distinguish false rhetoric from the art of persuasion more broadly, and to show that rather than making a piece of writing decorative and over-complicated, rhetorical forms aimed at comprehensibility and universality.

Like Bredvold and Leavis, Worcester was interested in satire as a moral art, and his discussion focuses as theirs does on the reciprocity between satire's moral function and the shared 'fundamental' codes of right and wrong that underpin decent political societies. Where he departs intellectually, however, is in the importance he accords to rhetoric in this narrative. Rhetorical conventions, for Worcester, act as intermediaries between the convictions of the satirist and the shared moral imperatives of the society he belongs to: they transform personal feelings of anger or resentment into social indig-nation, and make something public and high-minded of a private sentiment. 'The true

---

[27] Leavis, '*The Dunciad*', 77.   [28] Leavis, 'Revaluations (II)', 274.
[29] See, e.g., Leavis, '*The Dunciad*', 75.
[30] David Worcester, *The Art of Satire* (Cambridge, MA: Harvard University Press, 1940), 18, 22.
[31] Worcester, *Art of Satire*, 8–9.

function of rhetoric', he argues, 'is to teach the writer how to translate the undefined stirring in his breast into an objective form that speaks to all men'.[32] As an instance of this translation process, Worcester looks at eighteenth-century burlesque and mock-heroic. In his analysis, mock-heroic is a distorted vision of society that neglects to supply the conventional or normative framework from which it departs (it is a kind of 'extended simile' that lacks one of its terms). As such, it relies on the reader to be an active participant in the creation of meaning, supplying the moral ideal that is imaged in negative by the text's rhetorical transformations (Dryden's *Mac Flecknoe* (1682), for instance, is funny and pointed because we can see Aeneas and Ascanius behind Flecknoe and Shadwell). 'It is the reader's part to supply knowledge of the model', Worcester writes. 'So long as the author can depend on his audience for the necessary information, he need not utter a word of reproach or obloquy; his audience will provide the curses.'[33]

This conclusion had historical and political implications. Worcester argued that satire's indirectness, its reliance on a readership capable of 'providing the curses', meant that it flourished in ages (such as the seventeenth and early eighteenth centuries) when a broad understanding of the categories of rhetorical speech flourished alongside a stable notion of the organization and ideals of political society. There was a clear contemporary warning to take from this. In 1940, Worcester felt that satire was suffering from the general fashion for 'everything [...] ironical' that had swept through the public sphere. What satirists needed, he thought, was to achieve a 'purposeful, intellectual communion with the reader', and reclaim some of the 'moral responsibility' they seemed to be shrinking from. There was much at stake: in the decline of the old reciprocal relationship between the satirist and his audience he foresaw the sort of political 'sterility' that could 'give encouragement to the absolute authority of Nazism, Fascism, and Communism'.[34]

THE RHETORIC OF SATIRE

Whether this was an exaggeration or fair warning, the view from after the war looked rather different. In the following decade large-scale moral and political conclusions were sidelined as the least important part of Worcester's work. Instead, the hint that subsequent scholars took from him concerned rhetoric. During the 1950s, Pope, Swift, and others became 'occasional beneficiaries of New Criticism and its close explorations into ambiguity, irony, and innuendo', scrutinized by careful formal analysis that deliberately downplayed the sorts of historical and contextual inquiries that had previously dominated the study of satire.[35] Ian Jack's *Augustan Satire: Intention and Idiom in English*

---

[32] Worcester, *Art of Satire*, 9.   [33] Worcester, *Art of Satire*, 41–2.
[34] Worcester, *Art of Satire*, 166–8.
[35] W. B. Carnochan, 'Swift: the Canon, the Curriculum, and the Marketplace of Scholarship', in *Reading Swift: Papers from the Fourth Münster Symposium on Jonathan Swift*, ed. Hermann J. Real and Helgard Stöver-Leidig (Munich: Wilhelm Fink, 2003), 13–21 (17); see also Dustin Griffin, *Satire: A Critical Reintroduction* (Lexington: University Press of Kentucky, 1994), 28–9.

Poetry (1952) and Martin Price's *Swift's Rhetorical Art: A Study in Structure and Meaning* (1953), for instance, both concentrate on the patterns of rhetorical design at work in individual satires and the broader generic categories to which these patterns belong.[36] Jack's study focuses on neoclassical doctrines of literary decorum and the 'levels of idiom' suited to particular rhetorical occasions, drawing examples from Dryden's *Mac Flecknoe* and Pope's Horatian imitations; Price takes Swift as his subject and considers the rhetorical building blocks—structures of analogy, opposition, and argumentation—that make up the 'internal necessity' of each 'single work'.[37] The most influential treatment of the rhetoric of satire in the early 1950s, however, came from Price's doctoral supervisor at Yale, Maynard Mack. Mack's article 'The Muse of Satire' (1951) begins, as Worcester's book had done a decade earlier, with a discussion of the particular applications of rhetorical analysis in the context of satire scholarship. 'In the case of satire', Mack writes, 'what is desperately needed today is inquiry that deals neither with origins nor effects, but with artifice'.[38] The biographical and historical approaches favoured by old-fashioned scholars, he argues, 'can and should be supplemented [...] by a third kind of inquiry treating the work with some strictness as a rhetorical construction: as a "thing made"'. This sort of treatment has been made possible by New Critical scholars, who as part of a more 'general revival of rhetorical interests and disciplines' have endeavoured to 'recapture some of the older exegetical skills' in textual scholarship.[39]

Mack's article applies this new rhetorical work to Pope's Horatian satires. 'Even in these apparently very personal poems', he argues, 'we overlook what is most essential if we overlook the distinction between the historical Alexander Pope and the dramatic Alexander Pope who speaks them'.[40] Under the influence of 'romantic theories of poetry as the spontaneous overflow of powerful emotions', nineteenth- and twentieth-century readers have grown unaccustomed to thinking about poems as dramatic fictions, and treating poetic speakers as characters in a rhetorical situation rather than direct mouthpieces for the poet. Tricked by the obliquity of the relationship between the historical Alexander Pope and the speaker of the *Imitations of Horace* or *The Dunciad*, they fail to see that Pope himself is as unhelpful a guide to the character of his dramatic *personae* as the historical Jonathan Swift is to the more obviously fictive Modest Proposer.[41] For Mack, the conclusion to be drawn from reading passages of lofty self-aggrandizement in the later Horatian satires is not that Pope himself must have been a vain man, but that given the nature of the rhetorical enterprise he was engaged in, high-flung modes of

---

[36] Other notable rhetorical studies of satire produced during this period include Rebecca Parkin, *The Poetic Workmanship of Alexander Pope* (Minneapolis: University of Minnesota Press, 1955); Ellen Douglass Leyburn, *Satiric Allegory: Mirror of Man* (New Haven: Yale University Press, 1956).

[37] Ian Jack, *Augustan Satire: Intention and Idiom in English Poetry, 1660–1750* (Oxford: Clarendon Press, 1952); Martin Price, *Swift's Rhetorical Art: A Study in Structure and Meaning* (New Haven: Yale University Press, 1953), vii.

[38] Maynard Mack, 'The Muse of Satire', *Yale Review* 41 (1951), 80–92 (82).

[39] Mack, 'The Muse of Satire', 81–2.   [40] Mack, 'The Muse of Satire', 83.

[41] Mack, 'The Muse of Satire', 84.

presentation were suitable ways of 'supporting the *ethos* a satirical poet must have'. He shows that what Pope's satiric speakers say and how they select and characterize their antagonists are functions of the internal logic of the satiric fiction, rather than responses to external realities. The bitter 'Sporus' portrait in the *Epistle to Dr Arbuthnot*, for instance, is 'called for', at just this point, not by the poet's actual feelings about a contemporary, but by the drama of feelings that has been building inside the poem'.[42]

Mack trained and taught at Yale, and was part of a larger group of scholars there during the 1950s and early 1960s who studied satire from a New Critical perspective. Collectively, these scholars—Mack, Price, Alvin Kernan, Robert C. Elliott, Ellen Douglass Leyburn, and others—produced, as Dustin Griffin has suggested, 'a rhetorical theory of satire'. Their scholarship, Griffin writes, tended 'to separate the work from the author who produced it, the world out of which it grew, and the audience towards which it was directed'.[43] It was resolutely anti-biographical. Elliott's *The Power of Satire* (1960), for instance, argued that the trajectory of satire's development from a primitive curse ritual to a literary art had been one of increasing impersonality and indirectness: what interested him was the distance satire posited between the real-life satirist and his dramatic speaker, and the kinds of social mores or legislative constraints that had interposed to encourage this distancing process over time.[44]

Kernan's two major books on satire, *The Cankered Muse* (1959) and *The Plot of Satire* (1965), both began by sketching out the reasons why the old biographical methods had no place in contemporary critical inquiry. Historical literalism, Kernan argued, 'makes of satire a type of propaganda originating in the author's prejudices'; it denied individual texts 'the independence of artistic status', and instead directed the reader's attention 'towards some second object, the personality of the author or the contemporary social scene'.[45] His approach, like Mack's, involved a 'more sympathetic understanding of rhetoric' than was traditionally offered by post-Romantic studies of poetry, and focused on the internal logic of satiric texts and the nature of the fictions or 'master tropes' they constructed.[46] In *The Plot of Satire*, for instance, he reads the catalogue of stylistic faults listed in Pope's *Peri Bathous* (1727) as an index to the major rhetorical figures used by eighteenth-century satirists in their depictions of 'dullness': this allows him to deal with texts as different as John Gay's mock-heroic poem *Trivia* (1716) and Ben Jonson's comedy *Volpone* (1606) in the same argument, on the basis that they delight in opposite and complementary patterns of rhetorical trope.

This is a typically ahistorical way of proceeding. For Kernan, interested in the internal structures of texts rather than the circumstances in which they were produced, satire may be thought about generically as a collection of rhetorical characteristics (certain kinds of image, figure, or dramatic plot) that crop up in texts from all sorts of times and

---

[42] Mack, 'The Muse of Satire', 87–8, 92.   [43] Griffin, *Satire*, 29.

[44] Robert C. Elliott, *The Power of Satire: Magic, Ritual, Art* (Princeton: Princeton University Press, 1960).

[45] Alvin Kernan, *The Plot of Satire* (New Haven: Yale University Press, 1965), 4–5; Alvin Kernan, *The Cankered Muse: Satire of the English Renaissance* (New Haven: Yale University Press, 1959), 2.

[46] Kernan, *The Plot of Satire*, 26.

places. 'The specific forms of dullness change from age to age and satirist to satirist', he writes, 'but the action of dullness and the plots which imitate it remain the same'.[47] Since the applications of satire as a rhetorical occasion are unchanging, there must be commonalties to be traced through its dramatic figures and master images across time. 'It should be possible', Kernan writes, 'to define in very general terms the essential satirist, those traits, attitudes, passions, which every author of satire brings together'.[48] In this he shares some ideas with the Canadian scholar Northrop Frye, whose book *Anatomy of Criticism* (1957) sets out to think about genres atemporally as myths or 'structural principles', enduring intellectual patterns that lend form and meaning to human experience. Satire, as one such structuring myth, is made up in Frye's schema of a set of tropes and images that recur in texts separated by hundreds of years: the theme of anti-intellectual mockery, for instance ('setting ideas and generalisations and theories and dogmas over against the life they are supposed to explain'), is alive in various forms in early modern satires by Erasmus and Rabelais, but also finds its place in Swift, Sterne, and Peacock.[49]

Though the critical focus was now firmly on rhetoric and form, the question of satire's morality did not entirely vanish from the debate. One of the more challenging suggestions raised by rhetorical analysis was that the moral positions a satire held (or that its dramatic speakers were represented as holding) might be dependent on the formal or technical requirements of the genre rather than on any extra-textual moral commitments of the satirist's. The implications of this suggestion for the early moralist defences of eighteenth-century satire were far-reaching: could it be the case that moral feelings were incidental to satire rather than the formative inspiration behind it? Mack's essay of 1951 on Pope made some early hints in this direction, arguing that Pope's self-presentation in the *Imitations of Horace* as a 'fundamentally virtuous and tolerant man' was an element of the satire's persuasive strategy, rather than (necessarily) a reflection of the poet's historical character. It was 'imperative', Mack argued, for a satire to establish an 'authoritative ethos' if it was to get its moral and political teaching across; and to project this 'ethos' successfully the satirist needed a dramatic mouthpiece—in Pope's case, the figure of the *vir bonus*, or 'plain good private citizen'—who would be calculated to appear 'stable, independent, urbane, wise', and win the reader's confidence in his 'moral insight'.[50] More radically, Mack suggested that there was no reason to think of this 'ethos' itself as grounded in any existing moral standard or political position. Instead, the various ethical and political conflicts dramatized in the Horatian satires (everything, he argued, that could be gathered under Pope's line 'the strong Antipathy of Good to Bad') might be nothing more than a 'fictive war' between good and evil: a climactic 'drama of feelings'

---

[47] Kernan, *The Plot of Satire*, 103.

[48] Kernan, *The Cankered Muse*, 16. On the possibility of schematizing satire's rhetorical patterns, see also John M. Aden, 'Towards a Uniform Satiric Terminology', *Satire Newsletter* 2 (1964), 30–2.

[49] Northrop Frye, *Anatomy of Criticism: Four Essays* (Princeton: Princeton University Press, 1957), 310, 230.

[50] Mack, 'The Muse of Satire', 86, 89, 91.

whose clashes and contrasts were designed to satisfy the formal requirements of a bipartite satiric structure.[51] Satire was a dramatic mode and it needed a good plotline.

In *The Satirist* (1963), the American scholar Leonard Feinberg developed some of Mack's suggestions. The satirist's adoption of a moral position, Feinberg argued, was an essentially pragmatic choice. The reason why early modern satire tended to take a moral view on the world was not because (or primarily because) the satirist was interested in moral reform. Instead, a writer who wanted his work to be read would need to 'choose material with which his audience [was] familiar, and an attitude with which it [was] sympathetic', and material that 'involved ethics and morality' would be familiar and attractive in just this way. Because the satirist chose this 'socially acceptable kind of criticism', his satire would be 'likely to appear "moral"'—but, Feinberg emphasized, morality was 'usually incidental to his aesthetic intention, peripheral to it, and motivated to a large extent by purely technical requirements'.[52] What Feinberg had in mind by 'technical requirements' were the particular themes, images, and actions that served satire's essential dynamics of irony and comic incongruity. Chief among these was hypocrisy, 'the single greatest source of satiric material'. Hypocrisy (or vanity, or duplicity, or anything that involved a mismatch between representation and reality) provided 'precisely the kind of incongruity' that was most 'suitable for the satiric method', Feinberg said.[53] So, whilst writing about hypocrisy might be likely to bring moral concerns and moral feelings into the scope of the argument, these were in themselves incidental and only circumstantially interesting: it was the rhetorical shapes and forms that incongruity could take in satire (bathos, irony, travesty, mock-heroic, and the rest) that mattered.

In an article of 1964, Kernan wrote about what he thought of as a major technical difficulty that New Critical scholarship on satire had thrown up. Rhetorical analysis had shown that eighteenth-century satires, like lyric poems, could be read as closed systems, internally consistent networks of intricate formal connections. According to this kind of reading, the logic of satire was purely textual: its functions made sense relative to one another, but their meaning collapsed outside the framework of the individual poem or prose passage. In his article, Kernan argued that the principal rhetorical figures in eighteenth-century satire ('the major actions of dullness—degrading, magnifying, and jumbling') were all 'relative movements': that is, they needed to be 'plotted' against 'certain fixed points' outside the boundaries of the individual work if they were to have any meaning in themselves.[54] If the satirist could not point to some authoritative and commonly held measure of value external to the text, it would be very difficult for him to show *why*—for instance—the presentation of a louse as Ulysses in Peter Pindar's *The Lousiad* (1785–95) was absurd and comic. For his satire to succeed, he must 'contrive in some manner to demonstrate that the mad world he constructs is truly mad, that it is the

---

[51] Mack, 'The Muse of Satire', 85, 92.

[52] Leonard Feinberg, *The Satirist: His Temperament, Motivation, and Influence*, 2nd edn. (New Brunswick: Transaction Publishers, 2006), 40.

[53] Feinberg, *The Satirist*, 38–9.

[54] Alvin Kernan, contribution to 'Norms, Moral or Other, in Satire: A Symposium', *Satire Newsletter* 3 (1964), 2–25 (12).

breech which is up, not the head'—that something must be up if, in the case of *The Lousiad*, a little insect was at the centre of an epic narrative. There were ways, Kernan showed, to demonstrate this plainly, and to establish a set of 'cardinal points on the satiric compass' against which the text's rhetorical transformations could be seen clearly for what they were; but they all relied on professions of lofty moral certainty from the satirist of just the sort that New Critical scholarship had revealed to be generic and dramatic rather than sincere. 'The most direct way of establishing the necessary reference points', Kernan wrote, 'is to provide a spokesman for the truth [...] who breaks into the narrative and tells us what is wrong with the world'. But how was the reader to know that the particular version of the 'truth' issued by the satirist's spokesman was the right one? Why should the satirist be believed if there was only 'his word for it'?[55]

'Truth' might seem an oddly old-fashioned thing to find mentioned in scholarship of this nature, but the kinds of moral or political standards ('cardinal points') that Kernan is talking about here are a long way away from the confident 'categorical imperatives' that critics such as Bredvold and Worcester had in mind in 1940. New Critical analysis of satire had shown that there were still interesting things to say about the moral content of satiric texts as well as their form, and it had demonstrated that knowing more about the rhetorical techniques with which satires were made allowed for more subtle conclusions to be reached about the nature of satiric morality. But the sceptical framework within which critics of the late 1950s and early 1960s approached the question of moral norms had little in common with the positivism of earlier accounts. Frye's *Anatomy of Satire*, for instance, suggested that the moral universe the genre traditionally inhabited was a distinctly unsatisfactory one, 'full of anomalies, injustices, follies, and crimes'. Any norms of behaviour it encoded were 'low' and pragmatic, expressions of 'tried and tested' common-sense wisdom or 'church porch virtue'.[56] In *The Satirist*, Feinberg also dealt with moral norms, but took the argument a step further and argued flatly for the impossibility of a broad consensus over what might count as 'good' and 'evil' in human behaviour. 'Sceptical intellectuals', he wrote, must 'consider the possibility that good and evil are complementary and indispensable components, incapable of absolute identification'.[57] One thing that the study of late seventeenth- and eighteenth-century satire had shown, he argued, was that when satiric speakers claimed to be moralists or offered up moral wisdom, it was very often not the sort of morality that twentieth-century audiences could respond to or recognize. The rakish behaviour presented on the Restoration stage, for instance, might look immoral now, but had it been then? If Wycherley and Congreve were simply 'expressing the morality of the dominant group at King Charles' court', should the social mores they dramatized be measured by contemporary polite standards?[58] Historical as well as rhetorical sensitivity, Feinberg suggested, was required for a sophisticated grasp of the relationship between moral norms and satiric representation.

---

[55] Kernan, contribution to 'Norms, Moral or Other', 12–13.   [56] Frye, *Anatomy of Satire*, 226–7.
[57] Feinberg, *The Satirist*, 28.   [58] Feinberg, *The Satirist*, 28.

SATIRE, HISTORICISM, AND MORALITY

The return to historical thinking in Feinberg's discussion was more than just an academic move: it was also the expression of a wider political consciousness, a way of looking at the world that had its roots in the recent experience of wartime.[59] One of the prompts for thinking about morality—and the morality of satire—somewhat differently in the 1950s and early 1960s was the extraordinary nature of the evils committed under wartime administrations (for transatlantic scholars, the German and Soviet administrations), and the proselytizing justifications composed in their defence by writers and publicists. 'Is the Marxist, or Stalinist, or post-Stalinist reformer, who believes that the end justifies the means, a moralist?' Feinberg asks. 'Was the anti-Christian Nazi who devoutly prac-ticed Hitler's pagan morality, a moralist? Satire has been written in defence of all these positions.'[60] For Bredvold in 1940, it was still possible to assert with confidence that all 'true satirists' were motivated by moral idealism, working together as a kind of 'invisible church [...] of good men' to articulate the 'eternal verities' of decency and righteous indignation.[61] From the post-war vantage point, by contrast, the landscape of moral politics looked very different, and the scope of satire's moral work seemed to shrink in size accordingly. Some scholars remarked that the existence of Hitler created problems for satire, as the evil he embodied was beyond its capacities to take on. 'Some villainies are too awful for us to despise', the American critic Gilbert Highet wrote.[62] The lines that had previously marked the limits of what was conceivable in human action and thought had been crossed. It was clearer than ever before that there was no such thing—in life or in art—as a supra-human moral consensus, whose values and codes could transcend national and social barriers. The war had made all positivist statements and confident diagnoses look naïve; the only thing to be said with certainty was that people held wildly divergent views of what was right, and with sufficient conviction to make them the foundations of institutions and policy.

In late 1964, an academic journal called the *Satire Newsletter* devoted most of its third number to a 'symposium' on moral norms in satire. The *Newsletter* was a relatively new operation: its first issue had appeared a year previously, edited by a board of eminent specialists including Kernan, Frye, Elliott, Mack, and others. It published original short satiric poems and stories, reviews of academic monographs on satire and stand-alone critical readings, and aimed to elevate the genre of satire from its current status as 'the leper of literature' to a legitimate object of scholarly study.[63] Its symposium on satiric morality collected responses to the question of how explicit satiric works of various

---

[59] It has been argued more generally that the experience of war might have been a factor in the sudden upsurge of interest in satire amongst scholars of the 1950s and 1960s: see, e.g., Brian Connery, introduction to Feinberg, *The Satirist*, x.

[60] Feinberg, *The Satirist*, 34.   [61] Bredvold, 'A Note in Defence of Satire', 263–4.

[62] Gilbert Highet, *The Anatomy of Satire* (Princeton: Princeton University Press, 1962), 22–3; see also Leonard Feinberg, *Introduction to Satire* (Ames: Iowa State University Press, 1967), 30.

[63] 'Highet's *Anatomy* and Some Critics', *Satire Newsletter* 2 (1964), 70.

historical periods tended to be about the moral standards they held—or, indeed, whether they were founded on moral standards at all.[64] A small number of contributors contended that successful satires were characterized by their ability to communicate, even if implicitly, a set of fixed norms by which the human conduct they dramatized was being judged. The vast majority of scholars, though, took a more circumspect approach to the problem, adopting the same relativist line as Feinberg on the question of satire's moral life.[65]

'Few if any values are universally held, and many more are not very widely shared', wrote the Swift scholar Edward Rosenheim, arguing that the closest thing contemporary society had to a public morality was a thin 'substratum of common belief', a set of 'tacit, common assumptions about what is right or wrong' whose foundations lay in custom rather than normative principles.[66] Norman Knox, the author of a 1961 book on Renaissance and eighteenth-century understandings of irony, acknowledged likewise that the truth-claims historically thought to be the province of satire were contingent rather than universal. 'Our heads are full of truths', he argued, 'not all moral, not all of great significance, not all logically consistent with each other, and not all unrelated to time, place, context, and so forth'. For Knox, satire could only be sure of winning a broadly sympathetic readership when the 'truths' or normative standards it embodied were so uncontroversial as to be a kind of moral lowest common denominator. The example he gave was Swift's *Modest Proposal* (1729), where, even if the more complex ironies were missed, the point about cannibalism being a poor solution to social ills was unlikely to be disputed.[67]

Maurice Johnson, another Swift scholar, used the symposium to interrogate some of the confident conclusions previous readers had reached about the values of eighteenth-century satires. 'Respected scholars and critics have announced that in terms of Augustan ecclesiastical thought and historical particulars, Swift framed the Houyhnhnms as unequivocal models for imitation', he wrote. 'These scholars and critics seem very sure of themselves.' Properly understood, Johnson argued, there was nothing 'unequivocal' about eighteenth-century satire, or about satire in general; more often than not, a satiric text was liable to leave its reader in a state of moral uncertainty ('unsure of himself, uneasy, suspicious of his accustomed conclusions'), rather than reassured as to the orthodoxy of his beliefs.[68] Feinberg's contribution to the discussion, meanwhile, reiterated some of the arguments made a year previously in his book about moral relativism. '*Whose* moral norm is satire based on?' he asks. 'A universal norm? It is hard to prove that one exists. [...] A democratic norm? But there has been satire on behalf of communism, fascism, and aristocracy.'[69] If a communist writer of satire thought of himself as a

---

[64] See 'Moral Norms and Satire: A Forthcoming Symposium', *Satire Newsletter* 2 (1964), 71.

[65] For an example of the positivist approach, see Various, 'Norms, Moral or Other, in Satire', *Satire Newsletter* 2 (1964), 25.

[66] Various, 'Norms, Moral or Other, in Satire', 22–3.

[67] Various, 'Norms, Moral or Other, in Satire', 15.

[68] Various, 'Norms, Moral or Other, in Satire', 10–11.

[69] Various, 'Norms, Moral or Other, in Satire', 8.

moralist, could it really be the duty of an American critic to tell him that he had got hold of the wrong moral norms? As Rosenheim pointed out, there were—again in the light of the last twenty years of global history—unpleasant political implications to being 'prescriptive' about the sorts of things satire ought to be saying and doing. 'If we feel free to prescribe the satirist's social or moral purpose', he warned, 'there is no reason why we should not similarly define his *province*—the kind of issues or victims which are properly the object of his attention'.[70]

There was not much of a consensus among contributors as to the nature of satiric morality, but one thing a number of them did agree on was that were limits to the intellectual work literary critics were equipped to perform. Scholars could still interest themselves in moral and political questions as they cropped up in an incidental fashion in the course of rhetorical investigation, but the anxieties raised over the subjectivity of moral norms produced a widely held feeling that it was not the province of any cultural commentator—least of all the literary scholar—to try to police the things that other people should value or deplore. Rosenheim, as we have seen, argued that critics had no business prescribing the satirist's 'social or moral purpose' or delineating the political space of the satiric attack. And Feinberg, similarly, insisted that critics had overstepped the mark in thinking of themselves as moralists, claiming the cultural authority to evaluate the moral backbone of satiric texts when the war had shown that there could not possibly be any universal consensus over values. 'In the middle of the twentieth century', he wrote in the *Satire Newsletter*, 'who has the right to set up his own preferences as moral norms?' If 'thousands of intelligent and sophisticated readers' enjoyed ambiguous and inconclusive satires such as Fielding's *Jonathan Wild* (1743) or Book IV of Swift's *Gulliver's Travels* (1726), what critic could possibly be 'eminent enough' to inform them that they were 'all, regrettably, mistaken?'[71]

It seems unlikely to have been a coincidence that the rise of close formal analysis in satire criticism during the 1950s and 1960s took place concurrently with the move away from large-scale moral claims. As Collini has shown in the context of British intellectual history, the post-war years were a period of increasing specialization in literary study. Critics became 'professional explicators of increasingly opaque texts', textual scholars who dedicated themselves to the elucidation of meaning using complex practical tools and techniques. Where the language of literary criticism had—particularly in the inter-war years—been expansive and flexible enough to serve as the 'chief idiom for cultural criticism' in the widest sense, now it was a specialized academic mode that flourished in universities rather than in newspapers or on the radio.[72] Literature was experiencing a kind of disciplinary retrenchment: scholars who found themselves unwilling to encroach on what had become specialist philosophical or historical debates worked all the more industriously to fence off the practices and arguments that would make their subject unique. Academics working on eighteenth-century satire (particularly those employed in American universities where New Criticism had taken off) cultivated

---

[70] Various, 'Norms, Moral or Other, in Satire', 21.
[71] Various, 'Norms, Moral or Other, in Satire', 8.   [72] Collini, *Public Moralists*, 348, 370.

techniques of rhetorical exegesis and practical criticism because they sought to develop a purely formal language in which they could talk about satiric texts, one that was not also steeped to some degree in moral philosophy, history, or biography. For these scholars, taking a closer look at the works of Dryden, Pope, or Swift was an opportunity to develop specialist rhetorical terms and a specialist technical framework—and, beyond these, a textual basis for the evolution of 'English Literature' as a set of replicable academic practices and concepts.[73]

SELECT BIBLIOGRAPHY

Bredvold, Louis I. 'A Note in Defence of Satire', *ELH* 7 (1940), 253–64.

Collini, Stefan. *Public Moralists: Political Thought and Intellectual Life in Britain, 1850–1930* (Oxford: Clarendon Press, 1991).

Douglass Leyburn, Ellen. *Satiric Allegory: Mirror of Man* (New Haven: Yale University Press, 1956).

Elliott, Robert C. *The Power of Satire: Magic, Ritual, Art* (Princeton: Princeton University Press, 1960).

Feinberg, Leonard. *The Satirist: His Temperament, Motivation, and Influence*, 2nd edn. (New Brunswick: Transaction Publishers, 2006).

Frye, Northrop. *Anatomy of Criticism: Four Essays* (Princeton: Princeton University Press, 1957).

Highet, Gilbert. *The Anatomy of Satire* (Princeton: Princeton University Press, 1962).

Jack, Ian. *Augustan Satire: Intention and Idiom in English Poetry, 1660–1750* (Oxford: Clarendon Press, 1952).

Kernan, Alvin. *The Cankered Muse: Satire of the English Renaissance* (New Haven: Yale University Press, 1959).

Kernan, Alvin. *The Plot of Satire* (New Haven: Yale University Press, 1965).

Mack, Maynard. 'The Muse of Satire', *Yale Review* 41 (1951), 80–92.

Parkin, Rebecca. *The Poetic Workmanship of Alexander Pope* (Minneapolis: University of Minnesota Press, 1955).

Price, Martin. *Swift's Rhetorical Art: A Study in Structure and Meaning* (New Haven: Yale University Press, 1953).

Worcester, David. *The Art of Satire* (Cambridge, MA: Harvard University Press, 1940).

---

[73] Dustin Griffin and Ashley Marshall both note how influential the results of this critical moment continue to be in satire scholarship. See Griffin, *Satire*, 1–2; Ashley Marshall, *The Practice of Satire in England, 1658–1770* (Baltimore: Johns Hopkins University Press, 2013), 2.

Index